REFERENCE

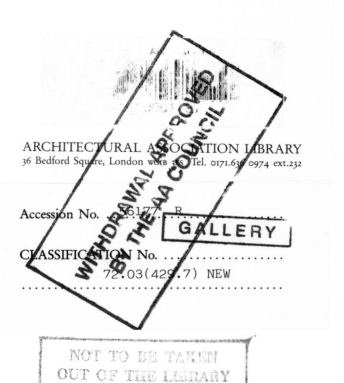

THE BUILDINGS OF WALES

FOUNDING EDITOR: NIKOLAUS PEVSNER
ADVISORY EDITOR: JOHN NEWMAN
EDITOR: BRIDGET CHERRY

GLAMORGAN
(MID GLAMORGAN, SOUTH GLAMORGAN AND WEST GLAMORGAN)

JOHN NEWMAN

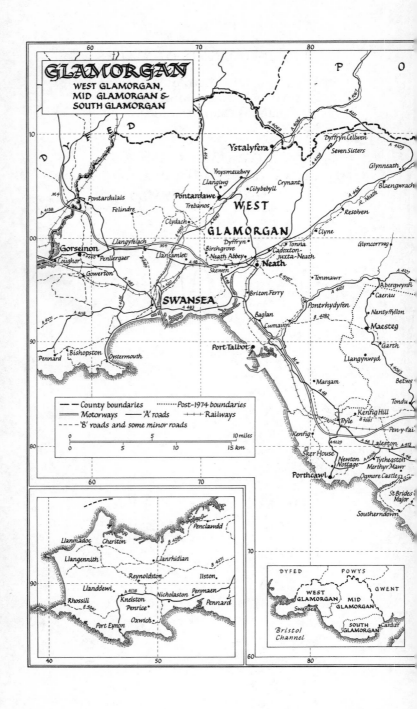

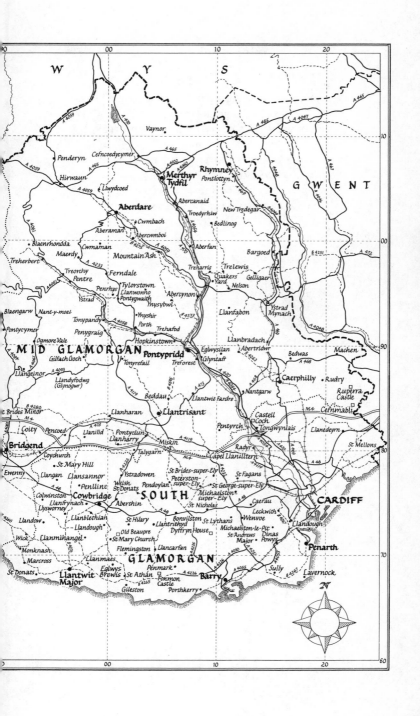

The preparation of this book has been greatly helped
by grants from
THE TRUSTEES OF THE DAVIES CHARITY
from
THE BOARD OF CELTIC STUDIES OF THE
UNIVERSITY OF WALES
and from
CADW (WELSH HISTORIC MONUMENTS)

Glamorgan

(MID GLAMORGAN, SOUTH GLAMORGAN AND
WEST GLAMORGAN)

BY

JOHN NEWMAN

WITH CONTRIBUTIONS BY

STEPHEN HUGHES

AND

ANTHONY WARD

THE BUILDINGS OF WALES

PENGUIN BOOKS
UNIVERSITY OF WALES PRESS

PENGUIN BOOKS
Published by the Penguin Group
Penguin Books Ltd, 27 Wrights Lane, London w8 5tz, England

Viking Penguin, a division of Penguin Books USA Inc.,
375 Hudson Street, New York, New York 10014, USA
Penguin Books Australia Ltd, Ringwood, Victoria, Australia
Penguin Books Canada Ltd, 10 Alcorn Avenue, Toronto, Ontario, Canada m4v 3b2
Penguin Books (NZ) Ltd, 182–190 Wairau Road, Auckland 10, New Zealand

Penguin Books Ltd, Registered Offices: Harmondsworth, Middlesex, England

First published 1995

isbn 0 14 071056 6

Made and printed in Great Britain by
Butler & Tanner Ltd, Frome and London
Set in 9/10 pt Monotype Plantin

TO HELPFUL AND HOSPITABLE SOUTH WALIANS
WHO MADE US 'MORE THAN WELCOME'

CONTENTS

LIST OF TEXT FIGURES AND MAPS

ACKNOWLEDGEMENTS FOR THE PLATES

We are grateful to the following for permission to reproduce photographs:

Cadw: 14, 36
Martin Charles: 2, 3, 7, 10, 12, 27, 33, 34, 37, 58, 59, 67, 82, 84, 94, 98, 103, 106, 108, 111, 114, 115, 120, 121, 124
Conway Library, Courtauld Institute: 6, 13, 22, 23, 24, 47, 48, 50, 51, 52, 53, 65, 68, 81, 90, 92, 95, 100, 107, 110, 117, 119
Terry James: 5
A. F. Kersting: 35, 41, 91
RCAHMW: 4, 8, 15, 16, 17, 18, 19, 20, 21, 25, 26, 28, 29, 30, 31, 32, 38, 39, 40, 42, 43, 44, 45, 46, 49, 54, 55, 56, 57, 60, 61, 62, 63, 64, 66, 69, 70, 71, 72, 73, 74, 75, 76, 77, 78, 79, 80, 83, 85, 86, 87, 88, 89, 93, 96, 97, 101, 102, 104, 105, 113, 118, 122, 123
Edwin Smith: 99, 109, 112
Swansea City Council and Martin Charles: 116
Jean Williamson/Mick Sharp: 1
Christopher Wilson: 9, 11

The plates are indexed in the indexes of artists and places, and references to them are given by numbers in the margins of the text.

MAP REFERENCES

The numbers printed in italic type in the margin against the place names in the gazetteer of the book indicate the position of the place in question on the index map (pp. 2–3), which is divided into sections by the 10-kilometre reference lines of the National Grid. The reference given here omits the two initial letters (formerly numbers) which in a full grid reference refer to the 100-kilometre squares into which the county is divided. The first two numbers indicate the *western* boundary, and the last two the *southern* boundary, of the 10-kilometre square in which the place in question is situated. For example, Aberthin (reference 0070) will be found in the 10-kilometre square bounded by grid lines 00 (on the *west*) and 10, and 70 (on the *south*) and 80; Oystermouth (reference 6080) lies in the square bounded by grid lines 60 (on the *west*) and 70, and 80 (on the *south*) and 90.

FOREWORD

Of the six volumes planned for The Buildings of Wales, *this is the third to be published, and its author is the third to contribute to the series. He is an Englishman with little prior familiarity with the Principality, and his undertaking to write about the buildings of Glamorgan would have been impossibly rash had it not been for several favourable circumstances. First, there has been collaboration with two expert contributors, Dr Anthony Ward, who has written the Introduction and Gazetteer entries on prehistoric and Roman monuments, and Stephen Hughes, who has written those on industrial archaeology. Then, Glamorgan has been given special attention over the past quarter of a century by the Royal Commission on Ancient and Historical Monuments in Wales. The Commission's publications, in particular on domestic architecture, from castles to cottages, have been indispensable. The warmth and enthusiasm of local people in response to visits and enquiries have also been a great encouragement, as is gratefully acknowledged in the Dedication. They have contributed enormously to the enjoyment with which this voyage of discovery has been carried out.*

Funds to cover the research for the series were administered by Dr Alan Kemp while he was Registrar of the University of Wales, and subsequently by Ned Thomas, Director of the University of Wales Press. I am grateful to them both for the interest they have shown in the progress of the Glamorgan volume and for their advice. Welcome extra funding has been provided by Cadw, through the Civic Initiatives (Heritage) Grant Scheme, and I want to acknowledge the efforts of John Carr in arranging this for the present volume and subsequent volumes in the series.

The groundwork for the whole enterprise was laid by Anne Warren, who extracted information from most of the fundamental printed sources, and from that goldmine of unpublished material, the files of the Incorporated Church Building Society at Lambeth Palace Library. Without her notes, the travelling could not have been undertaken. Thomas Lloyd provided leads to many sources which we should not otherwise have known about. Others who kindly supplied her with information, published and unpublished, are Dr Denis Evinson, Olwen Jenkins, Geoffrey Orrin, Dr Simon Unwin and Margaret Walker.

My visiting was facilitated by the ready cooperation of incumbents and churchwardens in opening churches, and of secretaries and caretakers in opening chapels. Several of them subsequently provided important pieces of information from documents in their care. Although it is sadly the case nowadays that churches cannot be left open unattended, and although tradition has not required chapels to be open except at service time, the validity of my request to see inside was never questioned. The compilation by Cadw (Welsh Historic Monuments) of Lists of Buildings of Special Architectural or Historic Interest *is undoubtedly fostering a sense of pride and responsibility for buildings, which are increasingly recognized to be both community assets and of general public interest.*

Visits to a number of important private houses were arranged through the good offices of Dr Alison Maguire. I am most grateful to the owners of these and other buildings not normally open to the public for letting me view the interiors of their properties. I owe it to them to stress that public access is normally possible only if advertised.

Much travelling was done from a base in the Thomases' cottage at Moorshead, but the exploration of Swansea was made particularly agreeable by Olwen Jenkins, who loaned us her house in Killay. Guides to buildings of which they had special knowledge and who showed me what I should otherwise have missed were Donald Buttress (Llandaff Cathedral), John Goodwin (University of Wales, Cardiff), John Roberts (buildings by the Welsh School of Architecture), Martin Snead (chapels in Merthyr Tydfil) and Matthew Williams (Cardiff Castle and Insole Court, Llandaff).

Peter White, Secretary of the Royal Commission on Ancient and Historical Monuments in Wales, and his staff have helped in many ways. In particular, Hilary Malaws advised over the selection of photographs, and Jack Spurgeon generously showed me his files on castles to be included in the Commission's as yet unpublished volume on castles after 1217.

Several local experts generously made the results of their researches available for the benefit of the book: Nevil James (Llandaff), Jeremy Lowe (Llancaeach-fawr), Bernard Morris (Swansea), Philip Riden (Cardiff's urban growth and Cardiff architects), Neil Sumner (workmen's institutes), Diane Walker (churches in Roath) and Elisabeth Whittle (Gnoll Grounds, Neath). Information on Victorian stained glass came from Peter Cormack, Martin Harrison and David Lawrence. John Perkins and Dr Eric Robinson advised on the identification of building stones. Lisbeth David gave access to a copy of R.J. Zaugg's thesis on Llandaff. Dale Owen provided an authoritative list of the works of the Percy Thomas Partnership and information about other C20 buildings. William Clarke allowed me to explore the files of his family firm, the sculptors and church furnishers Clarke of Llandaff. Public librarians have responded helpfully to queries, in particular Adrian Burton at Bridgend and Susan Scott at Treorchy. J. Vivian Hughes at Port Talbot kindly enabled me to sample the computerized index to the Cambrian *newspaper. Information officers of County and Borough Councils, head teachers and others with access to records have also replied to my enquiries, in some cases going to considerable trouble to do so.*

I have been saved from errors and embarrassment by those who have read and commented on sections of the text: Dr Prys Morgan (Swansea and Gower), Dr David Robinson (medieval abbeys), Jack Spurgeon (castles), Peter Webster (Roman Cardiff) and Dr Christopher Wilson (Llandaff Cathedral). Peter Howell read the entire Gazetteer text, suggested many improvements and forced rethinking and even revisit-

ing. Bridget Cherry read everything, and did her best to ensure that the current high standards of The Buildings of England *should be applied also in Wales. In spite of all this help, errors and omissions are sure to remain, so readers are encouraged not to hesitate in writing to the publishers when they can correct mistakes or supply information. I am pleased to be able to express my thanks to everyone mentioned in these paragraphs, and also, for various reasons, to Howard Colvin, Annabelle Harle, Rodney Hubbuck, the late Professor Mike Jarrett, Derrick Kingham, Dr Joanna Martin, Robert Scourfield, Dr Chris Wakeling and Dr Jeffrey West.*

Many new pictures have been taken for the book, by the photographers of the Royal Commission, who in many cases have ranged far outside their normal ambit; by Dr Philip Ward-Jackson of the Conway Library, Courtauld Institute of Art, in the course of his survey of sculpture in Wales; and by Martin Charles, whose camera can achieve the seemingly impossible.

In production the text benefited from the scrupulous copy-editing of Caroline Palmer. Photographs were rounded up by Susan Rose-Smith with her usual panache. The maps were drawn by Reginald and Marjorie Piggott, and the plans by Alan Fagan. Stephany Ungless has coordinated everything with firm efficiency.

A long and complicated undertaking such as this is sweetened by the companionship and support of friends and family. I am especially grateful to two people. Allan Braham occupied the back seat on many journeys with amazing patience and kept me in mind of the European context. My wife, Margaret, was fully involved from start to finish, in Glamorgan at the steering wheel or map in hand, and back home at the computer, where she produced the entire typescript with truly professional speed and accuracy.

INTRODUCTION

Glamorgan is by far the most heavily populated of the historic counties of Wales, including as it does both of the Principality's two cities, and the lion's share of its industrial heartlands. In 1991 its population stood at 1,288,000.

Since 1974 there have been three Glamorgans, South, Mid and West, reflecting, if not exactly matching, the three contrasting parts of the historic county: Vale, uplands and Gower. The Vale of Glamorgan, extending from the River Taff in the E to the Ogmore River in the W, is a quiet, undulating country where the best farmland lies. Inland, the underlying limestone is fractured here and there into sudden shallow escarpments, and at the coast towards the Bristol Channel it forms low, white cliffs which could be quarried for building stone. Further W the cliffs die away, and vast areas of sand dune advance towards the hills, beneath the steelworks of Port Talbot, as far as the mouth of the River Avon (Afan). N of the A48, from Cardiff to Kenfig, extends a tract of higher, less fertile land, the Border Vale, onto which modern light industry has encroached a good deal.

The uplands of the coal measures, rising to the N in a sharply defined escarpment, form the most extensive of the county's three components. They are drained by two river networks. The larger, consisting of the Rhymney, Taff, Cynon and Rhondda, flows SE-wards to enter the Bristol Channel at Cardiff, the smaller, Ogwr, Garw and Llynfi, joins the SW-ward-flowing Ogmore River. Until the C19 the narrow, steep-sided valleys and the moorland ridges between them remained remote and sparsely inhabited. Since then, first iron-working round Merthyr Tydfil and then coal-mining everywhere have filled the valleys from end to end with terraces of workers' cottages. With the decline and death of both these heavy industries, the pits and spoil-heaps which scarred the hillsides have largely disappeared, and the slopes are green again. But now the tops have been made productive, as vast conifer plantations blanket many square miles of moorland.

To the W lies Gower. North Gower is an extension of the uplands, but the Gower Peninsula, extending W-wards into the Bristol Channel, has a character of its own. Here the ancient landscape remains least impaired. The central tract of high ground is largely uncultivated commonland, and the beaches and rocky headlands of the coast, a holiday paradise, show gratifyingly few permanent signs of the tourist hordes.

Glamorgan has its towns, all of them children of industry:

Merthyr Tydfil of iron, Neath of copper, Aberdare, Maesteg, Pontypridd of coal, Penarth and Barry of the coal trade. But the county's glory is its cities.

Swansea has a wonderful site between the bay and the hill. The town grew first as a seaside resort, then as a centre of heavy industry, and finally as a port. This fluctuating identity, and the blitz of 1941 which smashed the town centre, have left Swansea shapeless, but unexpectedly rich in handsome classical buildings.

Cardiff, by contrast, gains no advantage from its flat site. But fortunately its rampant growth in the C19, when it became the premier port in the world for the export of coal, had extraordinary architectural consequences. No other British city can boast a Victorian seigneurial fantasy like Cardiff Castle, or ranks of proud civic buildings like those in Cathays Park. Since 1922, when the city boundaries were extended to take in the 'cathedral village' of Llandaff, Cardiff's architectural diversity has become yet more extreme.

All landscapes and most urban developments reflect the super-imposition of layers of settlement and exploitation. In Glamorgan, viewed as a whole, it is perhaps the awareness of the overlaying of one culture on another which gives the county its special character.

The patterns of prehistoric settlement, still readily traceable in the Gower Peninsula, hover also over the moors of the hill country. Early Christian centres are indicated by remarkable concentrations of carved stone crosses. The new pattern imposed by the Norman incursion into South Wales from the 1080s is obvious in the parish churches of the C11–C13, thickly scattered over the Vale and round the Gower coast, sparse in the hill country. The establishment of a cathedral at Llandaff and the planting of Cistercian monasteries further w, at Margam and Neath, were part of the Norman strategy of control. The numer-ous castles in the s and e, many of them no more than defensible earthworks, relate to this same pattern.

The Act of Union (1536–43), which amalgamated the Norman lordships of Glamorgan and Gower into a single county, marked the start of a new phase, of agricultural prosperity. Non-defensible mansions and new-built farmhouses sprang up where the land 2 could be made fertile. This prosperity survived into the C18 only in diminished form. The Georgian country seat is a rarity in Glamorgan. Land-owning families, too, were turning from agri-culture to industry. They, quite as much as immigrant entre-preneurs, promoted the industrial revolution which changed the face of so much of the county in the C19. The valleys of the hill country had barely been discovered by Picturesque travellers 3 before they were transformed into the Valleys, alive with whirling pit-head machinery, smoking chimneys, and an ever-increasing immigrant population of workers and their families. For them the valley-bottom terraced settlements were built, punctuated with chapels and workmen's institutes.

The c20 has seen a steady ebbing of heavy industry. To some extent that has made it possible to appreciate and enjoy again parts of the county which had seemed to be permanently blighted. On the other hand, many industrial installations were ruthlessly swept away between the 1960s and 1980s, so that the all too few surviving relics of coal-mining, iron- and copper-working and tin-plating have gained a poignancy by their very rarity as much as by the extraordinary history of enterprise, hardship and community solidarity which they recall.

But there are no ghost towns in the Valleys. The development of light industry and greatly improved communications have enabled the Valley settlements to live on, albeit with high levels of unem-ployment, and as yet too little pride in the witnesses of former religion and culture, so that the chapels and institutes continue to dwindle year by year.

As the C20 reaches its close, the pre-eminence of Swansea and Cardiff is further reinforced. The population growth of these cities may have levelled off, but their cultural significance, even in the context of Britain as a whole, steadily increases. The Marina development at Swansea and the huge schemes for revitalizing Cardiff Bay, with their provision for middle-class housing, leisure and culture, and to a lesser extent for light industry, encapsulate the ambitions and priorities of today.

PREHISTORIC AND ROMAN GLAMORGAN:
THE VISIBLE EVIDENCE

BY ANTHONY WARD

The very incomplete record for early human activity in Glamorgan should be viewed in the context of environmental change over the millennia, which has had important consequences for land use and monument construction. The impact of such change has to be considered in terms of two contrasting topographic zones: the coastal plain, including the Vale of Glamorgan and the Gower Peninsula, and the inland hills. There is no visible evidence for the very earliest human activity in the region on account of glacial erosion and changes in sea level. However, CAVE sites on Gower have produced tools of UPPER PALAEOLITHIC form made of both stone and bone, dating to the later stages of the Devensian Glaciation after c. 35,000 B.C. Between c. 22,000 and 12,000 B.C. there was a hiatus of occupation coinciding with the coldest phase of the glaciation, although occasional seasonal forays may have occurred. Goat's Hole Cave, Paviland, Rhossili, is famous on account of the discovery of the partial skeleton of a man dated to c. 26,000 years ago, the earliest burial known in Britain. Mobile bands hunted and gathered seasonal resources across a region including land now under the sea, in an environment ranging through time from cold parkland to arctic or sub-arctic tundra.

Consistent climatic improvement from about the ninth mil-lennium B.C. led to afforestation. By c. 6000 B.C. woodland covered the region, including the high hills up to 2,000 ft (600 metres), except for coastal marshes, dunes and rocky outcrops. These environmental changes coincided with a period of human activity conventionally termed the MESOLITHIC, which is known only through diagnostic stone tools – microliths. Early Mesolithic tools are mostly confined to landscapes at lower altitude, although there is evidence for increased exploitation of the uplands after c. 6000 B.C., probably as part of a seasonal cycle. Hunting, trapping, and gathering both terrestrial and marine resources sustained a population which was expanding at the same time as rising sea levels quite rapidly reduced the available landscape.

By c. 4000 B.C. there is evidence in South Wales for food production in the form of domesticated livestock and cultivated cereals. Pottery, an innovation, and new tool forms, typical of the NEOLITHIC, are found too. The development of food production and emergence of Neolithic cultural traditions are ill understood. Almost certainly, more than a simple colonization by newcomers was involved. Indigenous hunter-gatherers probably contributed to the adoption and dispersal of new ideas and resources during a transitional period of intensified exploitation of the landscape prior to c. 4000 B.C. This eventually developed into subsistence practices in which food production figured prominently. The environmental record indicates a diminution of woodland. This was often localized and short-term, although more permanent in the uplands where it was accompanied by soil degradation. Cultivation and animal husbandry by early farmers will have contributed to this.

Only a fragmentary picture emerges of Neolithic economic and domestic activity in Glamorgan. A sub-oval building, probably a small house, has been found at Mount Pleasant, Newton Nottage, while traces of shelters on Cefn Glas, Blaenrhondda, at the head of the Rhondda Fawr and beneath Great Carn, Cefn Bryn, Llanrhidian, indicate transient settlement. These date from the early to mid third millennium B.C. Accumulations of stone tools elsewhere, including on the hills, also indicate settlement. Many coincide with evidence for later Mesolithic activity, and the seasonality of hunting and gathering cycles was probably perpetuated by early herders through transhumant movements to exploit seasonally available grazing and browsing. Polished stone axes which have been shown to have originated in Pembrokeshire, North Wales and Cornwall place the area within a wide-ranging chain of contact. Axes of flint, a material not occurring locally in suitable form, also indicate distant contacts.

A dozen or so MEGALITHIC CHAMBERED TOMBS are the best evidence for Neolithic communities in Glamorgan. All are located along the coastal belt, apart from a site near Carn Llechart, Clydach, in the western hills, though its identification as a tomb is debatable. Others have certainly been destroyed. They began to be built somewhat after the adoption of food production between 4000 and 3700 B.C. Various designs have been identified. Both tombs at Penmaen, Gower, have transepted chambers within long cairns. Tinkinswood, St Nicholas, and the tomb at St Lythans in the Vale of Glamorgan have a single chamber at the end of a long

1   Capstone
2   Drystone walling revealed by excavation
3   Reconstructed drystone walling
4   Line of inner wall
5   Blocked entrance
6   Cist
7   Upcast

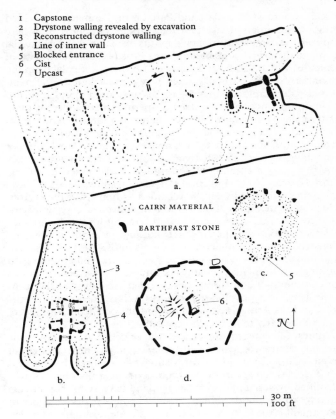

CAIRN MATERIAL

EARTHFAST STONE

N

⌐──────────┬──────────┬──────────┐ 30 m
└──────┴──────┴──────┴──────┴──────┘ 100 ft

Neolithic chambered tombs and Bronze Age cairns
a. St Nicholas, Tinkinswood; b. Penmaen, Parc Cwm; c. Llanrhidian,
ring cairn near Great Carn, Cefn Bryn; d. Clydach, Carn Llechart

mound. Both types are paralleled in western and central southern England in a grouping known as the Cotswold–Severn tombs. The Sweyne's Howes, Rhossili, may be examples of Portal Dolmens, a type of tomb present on both sides of the Irish Sea, but they are too poorly preserved for this to be certain. Alternatively, they may belong to a grouping of tombs within oval or round mounds along the West Wales coast, which are not closely defined in terms of constructional characteristics. Arthur's Stone, Cefn Bryn, Llanrhidian, is an example. In most cases the design allowed access to the chamber after construction of the mound or cairn. The sub-megalithic character of the Nicholaston chamber, to which there was no access after construction of the mound, suggests that it is not of the same tradition as more monumental tombs.

No tomb in Glamorgan has been excavated to a standard which allows detailed consideration of the burial rite. However, both

Tinkinswood, St Nicholas, and Parc Cwm, Penmaen, contained
multiple inhumations. Recent excavations of tombs elsewhere
indicate the complexity of such deposits, in which skeletal material
is often disturbed and incomplete. Possibly only elements of
skeletons which had been defleshed elsewhere were placed in the
chambers, or else parts of bodies were removed after interment.
It is also debatable whether the tombs were used to inter most of
a community over a relatively short period of time, perhaps two
or three generations, or whether there were intermittent burials
over a much longer period, representing only a few of the popu-
lace. Use of the tombs by a family or several related families
probably involved ancestor veneration, and tombs are usually
interpreted as a communal declaration of the longevity of territorial ownership, a sepulchral title deed in stone. Favoured low-
lying sites with tombs can be regarded as home territories from
which some members of the community travelled to exploit seasonal resources. These included both grazing for stock and supplementary food obtained through hunting, gathering and fishing.
Construction and primary use of tombs in the Cotswold–Severn
tradition stopped towards the end of the fourth millennium B.C.,
although monuments probably continued to serve as focal points
for communities and sometimes received secondary burials centuries later. It is possible that the less well defined tombs in the
area, such as Arthur's Stone, Llanrhidian, or Nicholaston, were
built in the early third millennium B.C.

After tomb construction ceased, the evidence of monuments is
less impressive compared with other regions where a range of
ceremonial and ritual structures survive – cursuses, henges and
stone circles. Apart from the crop mark of a possible HENGE
identified by aerial photography at Llanddewi, such monuments
have yet to be found in Glamorgan. The next major category of
monument is the ROUND BARROW or CAIRN, examples of which
are widespread both at lower altitudes and in hill country. Round
barrows and cairns were built for the best part of a thousand years
from the second half of the third millennium B.C. onwards. Their
construction may initially antedate but largely coincides with
the appearance, first, of copper, and later of bronze metallurgy,
heralding what is normally termed the EARLIER BRONZE AGE.
By the early second millennium B.C. Neolithic ceramic traditions
developed into food vessels and cinerary urns. But first they
paralleled an innovative pottery form with distinctive, often fine
decoration, the BEAKER, which is found across much of Europe.
The initial spread of the beaker may indicate a widely adopted
cult, with rites involving the vessel, rather than a movement of
people. In Glamorgan beakers have been found with individual
inhumed burials beneath mounds or cairns. For example, at the
Sutton Barrow, Llandow, in the Vale, the crouched skeleton of
an adult male in a rock-cut grave was accompanied by a beaker,
perhaps dating to the late third millennium B.C. The small covering mound was enlarged early in the second millennium B.C. to
accommodate cremation burials, one associated with a cinerary
urn. A further urn-cremation was later buried in the mound.

Many round barrows and cairns are probably multi-phase structures, built and used over a considerable period.

The diversity of structures is illustrated in the Vale by barrows
variously built of a combination of earth, turf, stone and timber.
Annular settings of stakes, possibly fence supports, and stone
rings have been found within the mound. One of the barrows on
Breach Farm, Llanblethian, comprised a turf and clay mound
which incorporated a circular stone wall 80 ft (24.4 metres) in
diameter. A central pit contained the cremations of three individuals accompanied by two bronze axes, a bronze dagger, a small
pottery vessel, and fine flint arrowheads and scrapers probably
dating towards the middle of the second millennium B.C. Different
designs of cairn, too, can be recognized. For example, the Beacon,
Rhossili, is a conical stone pile retained by a boulder kerb, while
Crug yr Afan, near Abergwynfi, is a stone mound enclosing a clay
core, surrounded by a ditch, and covering a stone cist. The kerb
circles of Carn Llechart, Clydach, and Carn Caca, Clyne, have
as their principal feature a ring of slabs retaining a low cairn
incorporating a cist. Ring cairns, annular banks of stone, such as
those near Great Carn, Cefn Bryn, Llanrhidian, may, given the
absence of burials, have served a ceremonial rather than a sepulchral function. Standing stones, too, represent primarily ritual
sites, broadly contemporary with round barrows and cairns. While
cremated bone was found beneath the Bridgend standing stone,
more extensive excavation elsewhere indicates that the standing
stone is frequently only part of a complex of features, including
stone 'platforms', pits, and post settings.

Barrows and cairns, and also standing stones, seem often to
have been sited with care, sometimes in impressive groups, as on
Garth Hill, Pentyrch, in order to mark communally significant
locations, or to demarcate boundaries and even routes between
grazing grounds. Their widespread distribution indicates a
marked increase of activity in upland landscapes, in which tree
cover was diminishing, leading in places to the creation of open
heathland. Traces of a few annular timber buildings have been
found beneath barrows, while both animal husbandry and cereal
cultivation are known, but evidence for settlement and subsistence continues to be scarce and ephemeral. 'Cooking
mounds', accumulations of burnt stone alongside streams, as on
Cefn Bryn, Llanrhidian, can in some cases be dated to the early
second millennium B.C., although their chronology extends across
hundreds of years. Transhumance, with the implication of a
degree of social mobility, is suggested as the reason for both the
extension of activity in the uplands and to some extent the meagre
settlement evidence. Burial rites are now more focused on the
individual, with displays of status evident in grave goods such as
those accompanying the Breach Farm cremations at Llanblethian.
This indicates individuals whose authority and power could well
have been more widely influential. In other parts of Britain by
this period hierarchical societies are still more evident.

After c. 1500 B.C. evidence for burial and ritual, which has
dominated the region's archaeology for several millennia, wanes.

Mound and cairn construction ceased, but existing monuments continued to receive burials with secondary cremations inserted in and around them. Significant developments in metal-working during the MIDDLE and LATE BRONZE AGE include the replacement of flat and flanged bronze axes by palstaves, of tanged spearheads by socketed types, while dirks developed as more effective stabbing weapons than earlier daggers. Towards the close of the second millennium still more aggressive weaponry in the form of bronze swords appears, while socketed axes began to be manufactured. A well-known hoard of metalwork from Pennard on the S Gower coast dating to around 1000 B.C. includes such objects, which are most likely to have originated in southern England or even France, demonstrating the region's integration into a wider economic sphere. High-quality craftsmanship in flint disappears.

Evidence for settlement continues to be sparse, apart from a few cave sites where conditions favour its survival. Elsewhere in southern and western Britain by this period partitioned landscapes have developed, with houses, fields and grazing ranges datable from rather before 1500 B.C. Nothing similar can be identified with assurance in Glamorgan. Unenclosed house circles in the hills might just have originated at this time, although they are usually considered to be later. The linear boundary, settlement and plot on Rhossili Down could also belong to the later second millennium B.C., although they too may date centuries later. Also the clusters of stone clearance heaps, for example on Cefn Bryn, Llanrhidian, or Rhos Gwawr, Aberdare, could indicate agricultural improvement, but the currency of stone clearance, notoriously difficult to date, is potentially very long.

Around 1200 B.C. a cyclical climatic decline evident from the later third millennium B.C. culminated in a marked deterioration, in which conditions became both colder and wetter. These continued well into the first millennium B.C. Climatic decline, coupled with the cumulative effects of human attrition, produced tracts of degraded landscape, particularly in the uplands, instigating a phase of peat formation. The Glamorgan hills henceforth appear to have sustained much lower levels of activity. The consequences of this are evident from the distribution of first millennium B.C. monuments, generally concentrated on land at lower altitude. These, in contrast to those of the preceding millennia, represent settlements.

Most of the known settlements are defended, in the sense that they are enclosed by banks and ditches. The proliferation of DEFENDED SETTLEMENTS, paralleling the emergence of aggressive weaponry in the later second/early first millennia B.C., testifies to social tensions, which must, at least in part, be the result of economic pressures generated by the impact of climatic deterioration on the productivity of the high hill country. The earliest defended enclosure known in Glamorgan is Coed y Cymdda, Wenvoe, built on a hillslope. The timber-revetted bank and the ditch enclosing an area of 1.23 acres (c. 0.5 hectare) probably date between 900 and 800 B.C., constructed after a period of

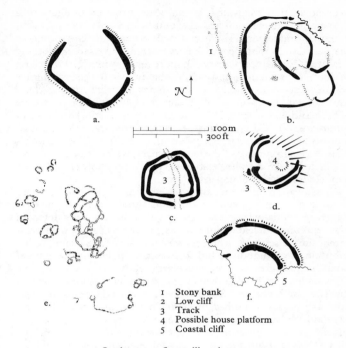

1 Stony bank
2 Low cliff
3 Track
4 Possible house platform
5 Coastal cliff

Settlements, first millennium B.C.
a. Wenvoe, Coed y Cymdda; b. Treorchy, Maendy Camp;
c. Llangynwyd, Caer Blaen-y-cwm; d. Clyne, Melin Court Brook;
e. Blaenrhondda, Garreg Lwyd; f. Rhossili, The Knave

unenclosed settlement indicated by later second millennium B.C. pottery. Increasingly, widespread hilltop settlement and defence can be found elsewhere in Britain at this period.

There is much variation in the scale and defences of enclosures dating broadly to the first millennium B.C., and in the choice of location. This is well illustrated within one relatively restricted area, the Gower Peninsula, where, for example, the hillslope enclosures on Hardings Down, Llangennith, all have contrasting layouts; the large hilltop site of Cilifor, Llanrhidian, is a true hillfort; the Bulwark, Llanmadoc, defined by dykes, banks and ditches, straddles a ridge; and small enclosures such as the Knave and Paviland, Rhossili, utilize the natural defences of coastal promontories. Enclosures can incorporate more than one episode of construction. For example, the Bulwark, Llanmadoc, was built in two or more phases, while the hilltop enclosure of Mynydd y Castell, Margam, appears to have been enlarged.

Enclosures are normally classified according to siting, the size of the area enclosed, the number and form of the banks, ditches and entrances, and, where there is more than one bank, the space between banks. The chronological implications of classification are largely hypothetical since only Coed y Cymdda, Wenvoe, has

been adequately excavated. It can be said that small enclosures
2.5 acres (*c.* 1 hectare) or less in extent, with a single rampart with
a timber framework, such as Coed y Cymdda, are probably
the earliest, continuing to be constructed and used over many
centuries. Enclosures with much more massive multiple ramparts
of dump construction, however, probably date to the last quarter
of the first millennium B.C. Examples of such sites include
the coastal enclosures of Dunraven at St Brides Major
(Southerndown), Nash Point at Marcross, Castle Ditches and
Summerhouse Camp, Llantwit Major, and the larger inland
hillforts such as Caerau, near Cardiff, and Cilifor Top, Llanrhidian. The chronology of these enclosures, which may often have
originated as smaller, less elaborate sites, is probably complicated
with several phases of construction.

Classification in terms of form and location can be more
rewarding when applied to function rather than chronology.
Larger, potentially later, enclosures with more imposing defences
may represent nucleated settlements, which on analogy with excavated sites elsewhere were centres for the storage and redis-
tribution of commodities linked to a local political power base.
Smaller enclosures were probably farmsteads occupied by a single
or extended family. Platforms within some enclosures represent
the sites of buildings. Subsistence at lowland enclosures was
probably based on both cereal-growing and animal husbandry.
Mynydd y Castell, Margam, for example, is well sited to take
advantage of the resources of the coastal plain to the S and the
hills to the N. Both the major coastal enclosures in the Vale of
Glamorgan and the smaller examples along the Gower coast
could have exploited marine resources in addition to a fertile
hinterland. Animal husbandry may have been more important at
smaller enclosures in the southern margins of the hills, such as
Melin Court Brook, Clyne, or Caer Blaen-y-cwm, Llangynwyd.
Some such sites developed into more elaborate complexes with
annexes or corrals created between wide-spaced concentric banks.
Examples include Y Bwlwarcau, Llangynwyd, and Maendy
Camp, Treorchy. The latter is located to allow use of contrasting environments, open high hills behind and the valley slopes
and floor in front, which were probably still partly wooded. Both
sheep and cattle may have been important in the pastoral regime.

Settlements without the protection of bank and ditch undoubtedly complemented the enclosures. The complexes of houses,
plots and annexes at Buarth Maen, Aberdare, and Garreg Lwyd,
Blaenrhondda, are examples of such sites in the uplands which
may date to the later first millennium B.C., although their chronological range is potentially wider. It is not clear whether such
settlements were of lesser status than enclosures of defensive
character, or whether they were occupied only on a seasonal basis
as part of a transhumant cycle. Little is known of unenclosed
settlement at lower altitude, although excavations at Merthyr
Mawr Warren at the mouth of the River Ogmore have indicated
traces of settlements, at one of which metal-working was practised. That this may, however, be an exceptional settlement area

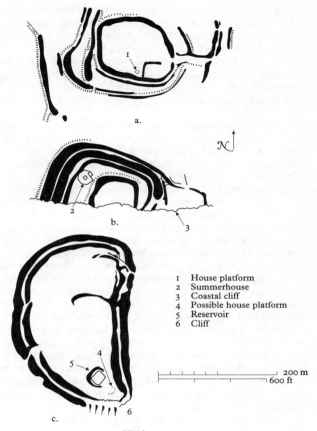

N

1 House platform
2 Summerhouse
3 Coastal cliff
4 Possible house platform
5 Reservoir
6 Cliff

200 m
600 ft

Hillforts
a. Llanmadoc, The Bulwark; b. Llantwit Major, Summerhouse
Camp; c. Margam, Mynydd y Castell

is suggested by the presence of exotic pottery and metal objects datable between the C5 and C2 B.C., which are interpreted as indicating maritime commerce focused on a sheltered landing. Late first millennium B.C. circular timber buildings at Biglis, St Andrews Major, and Moulton, Llancarfan, in the Vale of Glamorgan indicate a more usual form of open settlement, probably in a patchwork of fields, open pasture and managed woodland.

Both bronze and iron metal-working are in evidence at Merthyr Mawr Warren (*see* p. 30). Iron objects, and hence the IRON AGE, appeared in Glamorgan from *c.* 600 B.C. A hoard of metalwork dating to this period was recovered from Llyn Fawr lake, Blaenrhondda, at the foot of the northern escarpment of the hills. It is remarkable because objects of Continental Halstatt C origin, including some of iron manufacture, accompany items of native bronze-working traditions. Later innovatory metal-working traditions of the early La Tène are also present in Glamorgan, for example, brooches from Merthyr Mawr Warren. The Llyn Fawr hoard is best seen as a votive offering, a rite apparently commonly performed at watery locations in Britain in the first millennium B.C., and is a reminder of the significant influence of natural locations on the communal psyche. On the basis of evidence elsewhere in southern Britain, settlements may have contained shrines too.

There is little formal burial known from Glamorgan. An antiquarian account describes the discovery in the early C19 of inhumations on Ogmore Down, St Brides Major, which appear to have been warrior burials dating to the later first millennium B.C. on the basis of the helmets and weapons described.

Society in the region evolved during the first millennium B.C. into a structure which in general terms probably fits descriptions by Roman commentators in the CI B.C./CI A.D. of the Celtic peoples of western Europe. Relations between local kings, chiefs, warriors and farmers were regulated within tribal society by a reciprocal patron/client system based on kinship, economic and military ties. Although there may have been limited settlement in the region by immigrants as a consequence of commerce, technological innovation and political alliance, an essential continuity of indigenous peoples is probable. The numerous defended enclosures, many probably no more than farms, indicate a tradition of raiding in a periodically factious society, although often the scale of the defences may reflect the status of the inhabitants as much as the practicalities of warfare. By the CI A.D. Glamorgan and adjacent areas were occupied by a tribe known to the Romans as the Silures. However, the extent of the political unity which this implies, other than in resistance to external aggressors, is uncertain.

In the century before the ROMAN INVASION in A.D. 43, small enclosures continued to be built in Glamorgan, as indicated by comprehensively excavated sites at Mynydd Bychan, Penlline, and Whitton Lodge, St Lythans, in the Vale. They contained several circular timber buildings and appear to have been farms. However, little is known of the character of occupation at larger hillforts such as Cilifor, Llanrhidian, or Caerau, near Cardiff, at this time. The initial Roman advance stopped at the River Severn with the establishment of a legionary fortress at Gloucester probably in A.D. 49–50. There were Roman forays into Silurian lands, and, on the evidence of the historian Tacitus, a legion was defeated in A.D. 52. In the mid 50s A.D. a legionary fortress was built at Usk, Gwent, to advance the frontier, and a fort placed at Cardiff to establish a forward base still deeper in Silurian territory. During the 60s A.D. the Romans were occupied elsewhere in Britain, but temporary MARCHING CAMPS such as those at Coelbren, Dyffryn Cellwen and Blaen-cwm Bach, Tonna, could have been built during occasional expeditions in Glamorgan.

Towards the mid 70s A.D. a renewed interest was taken in extending control over South Wales, and before A.D. 78 the Silures had been subjugated within a pincer movement along the Glamorgan coast, perhaps using naval support, and inland along the valleys of the Usk, Gwent, and Towy, Dyfed. Again camps such as those at Coelbren and Blaen-cwm Bach would have been used. Consolidation of the conquest is seen with the construction before A.D. 80 of earth and timber FORTS at river crossings such as Loughor (Leucarum) and Neath (Nidum) and along strategic routes in the hinterland at Coelbren, Caerphilly, Gelligaer and Penydarren (Merthyr Tydfil). The site of at least one other fort probably awaits discovery in the Vale of Glamorgan between Cardiff and Neath in order to complete the network. Auxiliary troops garrisoned forts with support from a legionary base which had now moved to Caerleon, Gwent. Forts were connected by a ROAD SYSTEM, along which there were minor posts or signal stations such as that on Hirfynydd, Dyffryn Cellwen, alongside Sarn Helen between Neath and Coelbren. PRACTICE CAMPS, for example on Gelligaer Common, resulted from exercises in the vicinity of forts. By c.A.D. 160 almost all forts in Glamorgan were abandoned, some having undergone modification and reduction in size early in the C2 A.D. Exceptions appear to be Gelligaer where use of a later stone-built fort continued perhaps as late as A.D. 190, and also Cardiff, which may have been occupied until the early C3 A.D. or later. Garrison reductions from the early C2 A.D. onwards reflect relatively rapid Romanization of the Silures, for whom a cantonal capital was built at Caerwent, Gwent, for civil administration. No major town, however, was established in Glamorgan, although *vici* settlements serviced forts such as Cardiff, where extra-mural timber buildings ranging from the late C1 to mid C3 A.D. have been found, and also, possibly, Loughor. A substantial sub-urban civil settlement has been found at Cowbridge. This, too, may have been military in origin, perhaps indicating the location of one of the lost forts.

Rural settlements with varying degrees of Romanization are known, particularly from the Vale of Glamorgan. At Biglis, St Andrews Major, a pre-Roman open settlement lasted until the mid C4 A.D., although Romanization was limited, and timber buildings continued to be constructed there. Major pre-Roman defended enclosures now became sites for farmsteads: at The Bulwarks, Porthkerry, three successive rectangular stone buildings were occupied between the C1 and C4 A.D.; excavation at Cae Summerhouse, Merthyr Mawr, has revealed stock pens, a corn-drier and evidence for occupation from the late C1 to mid C4 A.D.; and similarly dated activity associated with a rectangular building is known from Caer Dynnaf, Cowbridge. While the small enclosure at Mynydd Bychan had gone out of use by c.A.D. 120, occupation of Whitton Lodge, another immediately pre-Roman enclosed farmstead, continued with increasing Romanization until c.A.D. 340. Initially there was a Roman-style granary and then in the mid C2 A.D. rectangular stone buildings replaced circular timber structures. Later remodelling included the installation of hypocaust heating. There seem to have been highly Romanized farms or even villas at Moulton, Llancarfan, and Dan-y-graig, Newton Nottage, though knowledge of these sites is limited. VILLAS are certainly known at Ely, Cardiff, and Llantwit Major, with mosaics, hypocausts and bath suites, and probably at Llandough (near Penarth), although the full plan here has not been established. This, too, had a bath suite. Away from the Vale, fragments of a mosaic pavement from Oystermouth church suggest a high-status Romanized building, while small quantities of Roman pottery at small enclosure sites such as Burry Holms, Llangennith, hint at continued use for an unknown period. Little is known of the activity in the hills. There may have been civilian settlement in *vici* around forts, although this is unlikely to have survived military withdrawal. The unenclosed settlement of Hen Dre'r Gelli, Ystrad, above the Rhondda Valley, produced C2 and C3 pottery.

Sub-urban nucleation, integration with a far-flung trading network, and a fiscal tax regime brought changes to society and economy, including increasing commerce and industrial specialization. A mixed agricultural regime operated above subsistence level in the coastal region, and in the uplands it is assumed that the emphasis was on animal husbandry. Traces of fields have been noted through aerial photography in the Vale, probably complementing the farms and villas, the latter controlling estates. Roman Glamorgan has produced little evidence for religious life. Imperial and military cults were undoubtedly introduced and, as elsewhere, native and imported traditions conflated. There is no material evidence for the appearance of Christianity, although the proximity of early church dedications to Romanized settlement suggests continuity of religious practice. The LATE ROMAN PERIOD is marked by the construction of a major new fort at Cardiff *c.* A.D. 280 to provide a base on the Taff Estuary for naval patrols in response to increased coastal raiding. Refortification at Loughor, a site of strategic importance on an estuary, in the mid to late C3 A.D. is also indicated. The unfinished late C3 A.D. building at Cold Knap, Barry, may also relate to maritime activity. Decline in Romanized rural settlement after the first quarter of the C4 A.D. is symptomatic of the insecurities of the time, and perhaps coincided with a decrease in the demand for agricultural produce. The fort at Cardiff was abandoned, probably some time after 375 A.D., and around 410 A.D. Rome abrogated responsibility for Britannia. The remains of thirty-seven mostly male skeletons, several showing signs of violent death, scattered amongst the still-standing walls of the Llantwit Major villa, could date to the very late or immediate post-Roman period, demonstrating a reversion to more unsettled social conditions.

BUILDING MATERIALS

Glamorgan is a STONE county. From the coastal cliffs between St Brides Major and Penarth to the craggy ridges of the Rhondda and the tops above Merthyr Tydfil, building stone lies exposed. Virtually anywhere in the county it is possible to open up a shallow quarry and find workable stone. That is not to say that Glamorgan has ever been self-sufficient in this respect, for it largely lacks the highly prized 'freestones', which can be cut in any direction to produce a smooth face.

The oldest building stones are the Old Red sandstones of the Devonian series, which occur in the SE of the county, round Cardiff and also on Gower. They contribute to the mixed coloration of the walls of such churches as St Mellons and Rumney, Cardiff. The C16 parts of Cefnmabli and the walls of Ruperra Castle (1626) are built of Old Red sandstone, though the stonework must from the first have been intended to be rendered over.

Far more important are the stones next in age, Carboniferous limestone and Pennant sandstone from the Coal Measures. Islands of Carboniferous limestone outcrop in the Vale, at St Brides Major, and SE of Cowbridge, providing material for the walls of Old Beaupre, for example, in an area where almost all the building stone is Lias (see below). Away on the northern boundary of the county Carboniferous limestone outcrops again as a rim beyond the extremity of the coalfield. The vaulted undercroft, all that remains of Morlais Castle, N of Merthyr Tydfil, constructed on a bare limestone moorland top, best demonstrates its possibilities. The Gower Peninsula is largely of Carboniferous limestone. Here as elsewhere buildings constructed of this material were rendered or limewashed, as neither the rough texture of the stone nor its whitish-grey colour were particularly valued.

In the late C19 certain pink-stained Carboniferous limestones which could be quarried N and W of Cardiff roused renewed interest. The most extraordinary display is the pink, random-laid walling of the Great Western Hotel, Cardiff, which came from the Creigiau quarry at Pentyrch. Swelldon stone, quarried at Ely, is much more subtly coloured, grey tinged with rose. For a brief period in the 1880s and 1890s it appealed to Cardiff churchbuilders. Bodley used it for both his Cardiff churches, as did Bruce Vaughan for St James, Roath, and Kempson for the outer aisles added to the medieval church of St John.

Pennant sandstone, by contrast, is not localized, but the most durable component of the Coal Measures which form the hill country of the northern half of the county. It is extremely weatherresistant but too hard to cut to a smooth surface, and was usually used by C19 builders in a rock-faced, hammer-dressed form. In colour it varies from richly iron-stained brown to greenish-grey and even a silvery grey commonly referred to as 'blue'. The earliest major building constructed of Pennant sandstone is Caerphilly Castle, the dark weathered hue and the shallow coursing of the slabby uncut stones adding much to its air of massive menace. But Pennant sandstone is particularly associated with Glamorgan's industrial prime. Though the structures of the ironworks and the coal mines have largely vanished, the ubiquitous terraced housing in the Valleys is universally constructed of Pennant and other

Carboniferous sandstones, their dour coloration enlivened with dressings of red or yellow pressed brick (see below) – or nowadays with the multicoloured paint which covers so much of the brickwork. Large-scale commercial quarries were developed in the C19 to supply these vast demands, at Pontypridd, at Pwll-y-pant near Caerphilly, owned from 1870 by the Marquess of Bute, and at Newbridge, over the border in Gwent.

The shallow bedding of Pennant sandstone was sometimes exploited to form densely textured walling of stones laid in thin courses, as for instance in the early C16 at Llancaeach-fawr, Gelligaer. In the mid C19 John Prichard was fascinated by this characteristic, and used it to wonderful effect in several of his churches, Llanharan, for example, or finest of all, Baglan.

Among the Triassic stones, the most generally desirable is Quarella sandstone. This is one of only two freestones to be found in the county, and from the mid C16 provided virtually all the indigenous cut stonework used in buildings of any pretension. It was quarried at Bridgend, where it was available in three colours, cream, buff and a greenish grey, this last being the most common and characteristic. By the C19 the quarries appear to have been largely worked out. The same type of stone occurred locally elsewhere, as most memorably at Pyle, from where Thomas Mansel Talbot was able to raise in the mid 1780s dark greenish-brown stone of superlative quality for the Orangery at Margam. The rustication and the exquisitely carved skulls and garlands in the attic of the Orangery have not lost their crispness after two hundred years.

The second Triassic stone is a complete contrast, Radyr stone. This, as its name suggests, is another product of the Cardiff area, and was quarried near Llandaff Bridge from the mid C19 until 1920. Radyr stone is a breccia, or conglomerate, consisting of a red sandstone in which nodules of Carboniferous limestone are embedded. Thus it is rough-textured and difficult to cut. Victorian attempts to use it for decorative shafting have failed, as the surface has broken down; but large, roughly tooled blocks have proved extremely durable, and were much used locally for bridges and walls, as well as for cottages and a few more substantial buildings. If cut to a smooth face and used internally, Radyr stone can look almost like a mottled marble, and its rich colour appears particularly sumptuous, as is demonstrated above all in the interior of Butterfield's St Augustine, Penarth.

The third Triassic stone is a gypsum or alabaster, found in the cliffs near Penarth. This too was not exploited before the C19. Prichard used all these three stones together, Quarella, Radyr and Penarth alabaster, in the wonderfully polychromatic interior of St Margaret, Roath, Cardiff. But normally Penarth alabaster was used as a veneer, by Prichard in the chancel of Baglan church, by his imitators in the church at Pen-y-fai, and to greatest effect by W. D. Caröe on the walls of the principal staircase at the University of Wales, Cardiff.

The two most important limestones in the county belong to the oldest group of Jurassic stones. Lias limestone is the underlying surface stone of almost the whole of the Vale. It was readily quarried from the cliffs at Lavernock, s of Penarth, and at East Aberthaw, Penmark. Inland, the major quarry was at the foot of Leckwith Hill, but most buildings in the Vale will have been constructed of Lias quarried in the immediate locality. The stone occurs in shallow, regular beds, easy to quarry and easy to use in coursed masonry. On the other hand, it will not cut to a smooth face, but has a flaky surface which is its readily recognizable characteristic. So this is another stone which before the C19 was normally rendered over, and certainly required a freestone to be used with it for high-quality dressings. Nevertheless, it was exploited by the Romans, who built their fourth fort at Cardiff of Lias limestone, and by the Normans, who used it for all the walling of their castles in the Vale and for the dressed stone in some of them. Occasionally Lias was intended to remain visible, doubtless because its blue-grey colour was admired. The prime examples of this practice in the county are the two most ambitious late C15 towers, the NW tower of Llandaff Cathedral and the tower of St John, Cardiff. In the C19 Lias limestone came to be used in the s and E of the county almost as freely as Pennant sandstone, as the façades of numerous Gothic chapels and many villas at Barry and Penarth testify.

That leaves Sutton stone, a highly unusual stone, part of the Liassic beds, but containing fragments of Carboniferous limestone. It occurs in only one locality, in the cliffs close to Southerndown, in the parish of St Brides Major. In spite of its composition, Sutton stone is a freestone. In colour it is whitish-grey, almost like Portland stone. It is, however, coarse-grained with a pitted surface. Its hardness and durability were recognized very early, and by the C12 it was prized as by far the best local stone for dressed work. In the early C13 it was transported to the NW by the monks of Margam and Neath for the ashlar parts of their abbeys and conventual buildings, and in the late C13 Gilbert de Clare brought it 20 m. (32 kilometres) to the NE to dress his great castle at Caerphilly. By the later Middle Ages the quarry was running low, leading to much subsequent reuse of cut Sutton stone, most notably at The Van, robbed from Caerphilly Castle under a licence granted in 1583. After that it became virtually unobtainable, although the ashlar façades of the C17 Summer Banqueting House at Margam, and even of Cowbridge Town Hall, 1830, are of Sutton stone.

The finest quality limestone, therefore, had to be imported. There is evidence that even in Roman times a certain amount of Bath stone was in use in Glamorgan. It is a measure of the ambition with which the nave of Llandaff Cathedral was rebuilt in the early C13 that its arcades and w front are constructed of Dundry stone, imported across the Bristol Channel from Somerset. At Old Beaupre the 'tower of the orders', dated 1600, is faced with Bath stone, probably shipped over in ready-cut pieces. Similarly, in the later C18, Thomas Mansel Talbot, having no freestone on his Gower estates, shipped in 400 tons (406 tonnes) of Bath stone to face his new mansion, Penrice Castle.

During the C19, with the development of rail transport, a great variety of stones became available. Bath stone remained far and away the most popular until at the end of the century Portland stone took its place. In Cathays Park, Cardiff, Portland stone facing was *de rigueur* for all buildings, from the City Hall and Law Courts *c.* 1900 to the latest parts of the Welsh Office and the University in the 1970s.

Several high-quality sandstones also came into widespread use. Most important was the sombre greenish-grey Forest of Dean sandstone, which could be cut to a smooth ashlar and was a particularly suitable companion for Pennant sandstone walling. William Burges popularized the use of Forest stone when he made a conspicuous show of it on his great new Clock Tower at Cardiff Castle *c.* 1870, ashlar from base to wall-head.

Red sandstones became popular at the end of the century, not only Forest of Dean red, but also those further afield from Shropshire and Staffordshire. They could be used in combination with Radyr stone walls, or with red pressed brick and terracotta, as most spectacularly at the Pierhead Building in Cardiff Docks.

BRICK was first used internally and invisibly, and by English standards very late. The earliest structure to make use of it is the 'tower of the orders' at Old Beaupre, and its earliest large-scale use comes a quarter of a century later at Ruperra Castle. Not until the late C17 is there any brickwork which was clearly intended to be visible, and that is merely string courses in the range added to Cefnmabli at that time. The first sign of a change of heart is seen in the mid-Georgian red brick stables at Penrice Castle and the late Georgian seaside terraces of Swansea. Brick-making on a large scale developed as a by-product of industrial processes, particularly of coal-mining. Both Archibald Hood at Llwynypia, Tonypandy, and the Powell Duffryn Coal Company at Aberaman established brickworks which by the end of the C19 became extremely productive. The smooth, hard-surfaced, machine-pressed bricks, either yellow or bright red, used in this period for facings and dressings were produced within the county at Morriston, on the northern outskirts of Swansea. For prestige buildings, however, pressed bricks were normally imported, either from Ruabon in North Wales, or, once again, from across the Bristol Channel, where Cattybrook near Almondsbury, SW of Bristol, was the primary source of supply.

During the C20 fashions in bricks have fluctuated. In the years up to 1914 a reaction against pressed brick in favour of hand-made bricks of small dimensions which could be laid in shallow courses affected one or two fashionable architects, notably Glendinning Moxham of Swansea. By contrast, in the 1960s and 1970s grey concrete bricks were popular, as being in keeping with the indigenous limestones and the traditions of rendering and lime-washing. Appropriately, the Welsh Folk Museum at St Fagans makes use of them. During the 1980s Glamorgan fell into line with the rest of the country as it revelled once more in brickwork of many hues. The marinas at Cardiff, Penarth and Swansea all make the point.

ROOFING MATERIALS are easily dealt with. From the medieval period and probably from Roman times, stone slates were used for more substantial buildings, thatch for modest ones. Today stone slates have virtually disappeared, replaced by the thinner, smoother slates from the great quarries of North Wales. Thatch, on the other hand, remains a popular roofing material for farm-houses and cottages in the Vale and Gower. Clay tiles were virtually unknown before the 1930s, when Sir Percy Thomas adopted the then fashionable pantile for exposed roof-slopes, as for example on the Temple of Peace and Health, Cathays Park, Cardiff. The main subsequent contribution made by clay tiles to Glamorgan scenery has been to fragment the uniformity of the slate roofs of Valley terraces.

PRE-NORMAN CHRISTIAN REMAINS

Several important centres of early Christianity in Glamorgan are known, but no traces of early churches have been found. The visible remains of the first six centuries of Christianity in Gla-morgan consist instead of nearly eighty carved stones, grave markers, grave-slabs and standing crosses. Many of the most impressive stones are to be found at sites which are known from documents to have been important early monasteries. From St Illtyd's monastery at Llantwit Major a group with particularly informative inscriptions survives in the parish church there; at Llandough, near Penarth, a monastic site associated with St Dochdwy, is the only cross shaft still *in situ*. At St Dyfrig's, Llandaff, though the dimensions of the small pre-Conquest church are known, nothing visible remains but a fragment of a similar cross shaft, while there is even less to indicate the early importance of St Cadoc's foundation at Llancarfan. On the other hand, Coychurch, Margam and Merthyr Mawr, none of which figure in the early chronicles, all have important stones, those at the first two formerly standing in their respective churchyards. So they too must have been important, even though the documentary evidence is missing. Llangyfelach and Llanmadoc, on the evi-dence of more meagre remains of carved stones, may have been other early ecclesiastical centres. The only pre-Norman ecclesi-astical site to have been excavated is Burry Holms, Llangennith, on an island at the western tip of the Gower Peninsula, where traces have been found of a timber church and other buildings within an enclosure. This must have had more the character of a hermitage than an ecclesiastical power centre.

The earliest stones are grave markers, carved merely with inscriptions, datable between the C5 and early C7. One still stands in its original position, high on a mountain ridge at Gelligaer, but the others have been brought into shelter, at Llanmadoc, Margam, Merthyr Mawr and Capel Llanilltern.

The majority of the later stones, from the C9 onwards, are

decorated with interlace or plaitwork patterns. They form a con-
centration greater than all the surviving stones from the rest of
Wales put together. Only St David's has a comparable group.
Interlace at its crudest can be seen on a C9 slab at Reynoldston.
A group of recumbent grave-slabs of the same period are incised
with encircled cross-heads entirely formed of plaitwork: Baglan,
Llangyfelach, Margam. Much more impressive are the large, slab-
like standing crosses with disc heads and broad, tapering shafts.
On these the crowning encircled cross, with a square panel at
the end of each arm, reminiscent of crosses in Irish decorated
manuscripts, is all spun out of plaitwork, and intricate plaitwork
panels cover the shaft, front, back and even round the edges. The
6 finest and best-preserved of these, the 'Houelt' stone at Llantwit
Major, probably commemorates a Welsh king who died in 886.
Here the plaitwork is highly formalized, extremely close to mid-
C9 Irish carved interlace, and a panel bears an inscription in half-
uncial letters. The 'Enniaun' stone at Margam imitates it quite
closely. Further mutilated or fragmentary stones belonging to the
group are at Llangennith and Llantwit Major, while the 'Conbelin' stone at Margam, although its shaft has been truncated and
the carving is slightly less assured, is the noblest of the whole
group. This retains its base, incised with a crude figure scene,
and on the shaft are figures of St Mary and St John which dissolve
into plaitwork. Figures also occur on a contemporary cross-head
at Llangan and on the somewhat later cross shaft at Llandough,
but they are all feeble and insignificant compared with the figural
sculpture on Northumbrian or Irish crosses.

The stocky, slab-like character of Glamorgan crosses is even
more apparent in the group datable to the C10 and C11, where
the cross looks like a spoked wheel sunk into the head of the slab.
The 'Ilquici' and 'Ilci' stones at Margam best represent this type.

The tall, slender type of cross shaft familiar in other centres of
Christianity was also used in Glamorgan. Best-preserved and
most evocative is that at Llandough, near Penarth, which still
stands upright in the churchyard to its full height, lacking only
the cross head. It consists of four parts: a base, and two shaft
sections with an intervening knop. The shaft sections have angle
rolls and pronounced entasis. Apart from the figure sculpture
already mentioned, the Llandough cross shaft is covered with
plaitwork. It is dated to the decades around 1100. At Llandaff
there is part of a similar cross shaft, and fragments of slender
shafts of different patterns remain at Llantwit Major and
Coychurch, one at the latter retaining its cross head.

MEDIEVAL ECCLESIASTICAL BUILDINGS

The Twelfth Century

The Norman ecclesiastical reorganization of Glamorgan was
thoroughgoing. The monastic community at Llandaff became

the headquarters of a diocese, incorporated into the province of Canterbury. For its benefit the bishop in 1120 undertook to rebuild the small church there as a cathedral. At the western extremity of the lordship of Glamorgan two monastic foundations were sited, Neath, a Savigniac house, in 1130 (Cistercian from 1147) and Cistercian Margam in 1147. To Ewenny, in the Vale, a small Benedictine community was attached in 1141 under the patronage of St Peter's, Gloucester.* The building of parish churches, densely in the Vale, sparsely in the upland areas, also got under way.

The impressive sanctuary arch which survives from Bishop Urban's early C12 cathedral at Llandaff, and parts of two high-level windows, show that it was a richly decorated building, though it cannot have been a large one. Details link it to the school of masons working on Old Sarum Cathedral from c. 1125. Ewenny Priory church survives almost complete, architecturally 7 much influenced by the late C11 work at its mother church of Gloucester, built in a single campaign, apparently not until after 1141. The tunnel-vaulted choir with quadripartite rib-vault over the E bay, a rare and evocative survival, and the nave N arcade with mighty cylindrical columns are equally impressive. At Margam Abbey the six bays which survive of the nave arcades demonstrate powerfully the deliberately austere style of Cistercian architecture in its early decades. Keeled rolls on the W windows, however, hint at a slackening of resolve by the last quarter of the C12.

Almost all C12 PARISH CHURCHES seem to have been simple two-cell buildings, consisting of an aisleless nave and a chancel, which may have been apsidal, as in the excavated examples of St Baruch's Chapel, Barry, and Burry Holms, Llangennith, or square-ended, as at St Peter, Cogan, Penarth, and Monknash. The only known C12 church with an aisled nave, Llantrisant, was unfortunately rebuilt in the C19. It can be deduced that Llantwit Major incorporates a cruciform aisleless building of the C12, designed for a crossing-tower. The church which most fully retains its Norman character is Marcross, where the chancel arch has wild zigzag and the S doorway billet decoration and nook-shafts with foliage caps, suggesting a late C12 date. Other churches with decorated chancel arches are Llandough near Penarth, where the arch is reconstructed and not *in situ*, but suggests a sizeable and lavishly decorated building, and Penmark, where the arch is pointed but decorated with zigzag comparable in style to that at Ewenny Priory church. Plainer C12 arches are at St Brides Major, St Donats, Colwinston and Penrice. The richly decorated, late C12 arch reset as a S doorway at Rhossili may have been made as a chancel arch. St Brides-super-Ely has a medley of brought-in C12 pieces. Also reset are the grandest survivals of later C12 11 decorated architecture in the county, the two doorways in the nave at Llandaff Cathedral.

---

*Monastic cells were also established under the Benedictine rule at St Mary, Cardiff, and at Llangennith in Gower.

Early Gothic

A new era was inaugurated at the turn of the C13 by major campaigns of enlargement at Llandaff Cathedral and Margam Abbey. Neither can be dated except stylistically, and both show the influence of great churches in western England. At Llandaff the early Gothic work consists of a four-bay westward extension of the nave, *c.*1200, which established a new scale and a new height for the church, and a new w front. The finely proportioned arcades have continuous chamfers and triple shafts in the cardinal directions, the shafts carrying excellent stiff-leaf capitals. These components link them closely to Glastonbury Abbey and Wells Cathedral, the central buildings of a 'West Country school' of the late C12 and early C13 identified by Harold Brakspear in a celebrated study. Although Llandaff is less ambitious and lavish than these, the high quality of the design and of the sculpture suggests that leading masons and sculptors of the 'school' worked here. The idiosyncratic clerestory is almost entirely a mid-C19 reconstruction by *John Prichard*, but the alternation of sharply contrasted wide and narrow shafted openings must closely reflect the original design. On the w front the three great lancets are linked together internally by banks of shafts, and externally by steeply pointed blank arches, creating a bold alternating rhythm. A subtlety here is the convex curvature of the walling within the narrow arches, contrasting with the concave framing of the lancets. Further counterpoint comes in the boldly isolated doorway below, which has a semicircular rather than a pointed head. The shaft capitals of this doorway have foliage inhabited by a seated figure and birds, fully worthy of the sculptors of Wells. The figures of a standing bishop in the tympanum and of a seated saint in the gable (now brought into St David's chapel) complete the sculptural programme. What form the C13 w towers took is largely unknown. When the C12 nave was rebuilt later in the C13, the arcade was imitated in a simplified and less substantial form, but continuing the stiff-leaf capitals. In the two-bay sanctuary rebuilt in the early C14 yet further simplification took place. The Lady Chapel added at the E end about the same time is square-ended, simply vaulted, and somewhat lacking in character.

The eastern arm at Margam Abbey was also rebuilt at the beginning of the C13. Of this all too little survives. However, the stump of the SE crossing pier shows that it had banked attached shafts, similar to those on the interior of the w front at Llandaff Cathedral, but in detail indicating a direct connection with Glastonbury Abbey. At Margam, the rebuilding of the chapter house came first, twelve-sided externally, circular within, a combination of forms found a little earlier at Worcester. The carved shaft capitals combine trumpet scallops and embryonic stiff-leaf, and on the capital of the central shaft the foliage is fully developed, if less lush than at Llandaff. Sadly, the chapter house rib-vault collapsed in 1799, leaving only stumps of the ribs in place. The vaulted chapter house vestibule, however, survives, an elegant piece of mature E.E. design, with grouped shafts carrying many-moulded arches, runs of dogtooth but no foliage carving.

At Neath Abbey the earliest evidence is also *c.* 1200, or even a little earlier, in the lay brothers' range. But although more of the monastic plan survives at Neath than at Ewenny or Margam, only one element remains intact, the pure but simply vaulted mid- 9 C13 dormitory undercroft. Even the craggy heights of the abbey church W front retain little of architectural detail, though slight 14 traces remain of a rib-vaulted porch to shelter the W doorway. But documentary evidence combined with the remaining cut stonework makes it clear that the cloister and the rest of the monastic quarters were constructed in the early to mid C13, while the abbey church was rebuilt in a single long campaign from *c.* 1280 to *c.* 1330. At least two changes of design during that half-century can be discerned in the fabric, but no major departure from the plan which had been established at the outset. The early C14 vault boss carved with Christ in Majesty shows tantalizingly 20 what of high quality must have been lost.

Much of the wealth of monasteries in the C13 came from large-scale farming. The physical evidence of this is in the remains of monastic GRANGES. The ruined barn at Monknash, a grange of Neath Abbey, gives the best idea of the scale of these establishments. The similar barn at Llantwit Major, where there was a grange of Tewkesbury Abbey, was unfortunately allowed to fall down during the C19, but a C13 gatehouse and a circular dovecote remain. A similar, but non-monastic, C13 dovecote is at Barry. 38 Two FRIARIES were built at Cardiff. Of the Dominican nothing remains to be seen but the excavated plan laid out in Coopers Fields, NW of the castle. Of the Franciscan nothing but the name of Greyfriars Road indicates its site.

Gothic Parish Churches

Post-Norman parish churches can for convenience be discussed in two sections, one corresponding roughly to the period of monastic building, *c.* 1180–1330, i.e. E.E. and Dec, the other late medieval, or Perp.

The most impressive of the E.E. AND DEC CHURCHES are those with a cruciform plan and a crossing-tower. Cheriton is a 15 virtually unaltered cruciform church of the early C13. The handsome shafted S doorway with its stiff-leaf capitals, and the details of the tower arches, link it to Llandaff Cathedral. Remains of the cruciform church at Llantwit Major, in particular fragments of carved capitals, suggest a different connection, with the chapter house at Margam Abbey, and a date *c.* 1200. The image niche at 21 Llantwit Major, surrounded by an exquisite Jesse Tree with heads in stiff-leaf foliage, also datable stylistically to the early C13, may have been made as a reredos for the now-destroyed chancel. Coychurch is the only aisled cruciform church, datable to the mid 17 to late C13. The arcades consist of octagonal piers with moulded caps and bases still of the water-holding form. There is a clerestory on the S side only, and the W front is a self-conscious composition. Both make use of quatrefoil windows. Coity, where the nave is

distinctly wider than the other arms, requiring squints through
the crossing piers for nave altars, belongs to the early C14, as the
26 beautiful cusped intersecting tracery of the w window shows. St
Athan is of comparable date. At St George-super-Ely an earlier
nave was incorporated into a cruciform building, again probably
in the C14. Michaelston-le-Pit has curiously shallow, lean-to
transepts.

When Cowbridge church was built on a large scale in the late
C13, though only a chapel in Llanblethian parish, it was given a
massive tower between chancel and nave, but later enlargement
has made it unclear whether transepts were intended. Llysworney
is an unenlarged example of the plan, the tower between chancel
and nave, but no transepts.

The only C13 church with a fully aisled nave, other than
Coychurch, is at Llantwit Major, a much-enlarged replacement
of the chancel and transepts of the cruciform church. The nave
16 is of four bays, and there is a long, aisleless chancel, but the
arcades are oddly primitive, just big square piers carrying pointed
but unmoulded arches. The s aisle at Llancarfan has a C13 arcade
of similar character, though here the imposts are crudely carved
with heads and bunches of grapes.

The normal Glamorgan church plan consists of chancel, nave
of slightly greater width and height, and w tower. Very few w
towers can be confidently dated as early as the C13. Cadoxton-
juxta-Neath is one example, where the w doorway of the tower has
two keeled rolls. Others probably include the towers at Bedwas,
Llandow and Llangennith. Whether the simple two-centred
chancel arches and tower arches in many churches, constructed
without cut stone and plastered over, can be dated as early as the
C13 is a moot point. St Fagans is an early C14 church (with traces
of a C12 predecessor) on this plan, but is quite exceptional in the
elegance of its triple-shafted chancel arch, the geometrical tracery
25 of its chancel windows, and its piscina and triple sedilia. Other
contemporary churches include Coity, already mentioned, and
St Nicholas. At Llancarfan the chancel was rebuilt some time
between 1284 and 1307. It has an E window with intersecting
tracery. A little later the s aisle was widened, given two-light
windows with cusped Y-tracery and extended eastwards to form
a chapel. Here the windows have cusped intersecting tracery. The
s transept added to Flemingston church has similar detail. The
remodelling of the s transept at St Athan with large windows
having cusped reticulated tracery must date to shortly after 1351.
St Mellons, which has similar tracery and a chancel arch moulded
with two double waves, must all have been built, chancel, s chapel
and nave, in the mid C14. The s aisle at St Hilary, its arcade
graced with paired continuous hollow chamfers, is another mid-
C14 addition. At Llanblethian the big s transept may be an
addition of the C14.

The other addition which began to be made in the C14 is the
porch, normally on the s side of the nave. Most remarkable are
the N and s porches at Penrice, almost as large as transepts, the
latter with a cruck-like inner door frame. The only two-storey

porch is at Llantwit Major, also a rustic piece. Most porches, if
they are datable, are Perp, of the C15 or early C16.

Late Medieval Churches

New churches of the late medieval period are few, all but one
apparently replacing churches on the S coast of the county overwhelmed by encroaching sand dunes in the C14. On Gower
the rebuilding of Penmaen and Rhossili may have taken place
somewhat earlier, but further SE Tythegston and Pyle are Perp.
Pyle church is substantially built of squared limestone blocks,
perhaps reused from besanded buildings at Kenfig. The date 1471
occurs in the roof. Tythegston is quite humble and lacks a tower.
The one remaining new Perp church, St John, Cardiff, is very 30
different, a swagger town church, testimony to the prosperity of
Cardiff in the late C15. However, it too owes its existence to the
forces of nature, as its mother church, St Mary, was gradually
being undermined by the River Taff. The plan consists of a
clerestoried chancel, reusing a C13 S arcade, with N and S chapels,
and an aisled nave. The arcades are of a typical West Country
form, the piers shafted in the cardinal directions, the shafts with
polygonal caps, and with intermediate hollow chamfers carried
without a break into the two-centred arches. Even more reminiscent of the lavish late medieval churches of Bristol and Somerset is the magnificent W tower, its four stages clasped by diagonal
buttresses and crowned by deep but delicately detailed openwork
battlements and corbelled-out pinnacles. The NW 'Jasper' tower
of Llandaff Cathedral is similarly designed, its (reconstructed)
openwork crown equally elaborate. It takes its name from Jasper
Tudor, Duke of Bedford, who was lord of Glamorgan 1484–95.
The date of both towers is presumably *c.* 1490. The third late
C15 tower of exceptional scale, though neither so large nor so
decorative as the others, is at Llanblethian. The tradition that it
was erected at the expense of Lady Anne Neville in 1477 seems
to have no documentary basis. The standard Glamorgan church
tower is unbuttressed and generally has small belfry windows,
sometimes mere slits. The battlements almost always project on
a corbel table. A score of towers have saddleback roofs, some
combined with battlements, one or two, e.g. Llansannor, gabled
in all four directions. Saddleback towers at Llanmihangel and
Newton Nottage have a defensive character, as does the tower at
St Brides Major. The few tower vaults are constructed without
cut stone, except for that at Llangynwyd. Here the tower arch is
unusually tall, but not as nobly lofty as that at Penmark, or,
indeed, those at St John, Cardiff, and Llanblethian.

Newton Nottage and Laleston towers, together with the chancel
at the former and the S porch at the latter, seem to be the work
of the same, rather fantastical, designer, who used deep hollow
mouldings and sculptural enrichment in a distinctive way.
Hollow-moulded window surrounds are characteristic also of the
Perp enlargement at Cowbridge. The S aisle arcade here is of
West Country type, but crude proportions. But this is as nothing

compared with the crudity of the elephantine two-bay arcade cut
through the s wall of the chancel at St Lythans.

Most, if not all, churches in the late Middle Ages were fitted
up for roods. The entry doorway, mural stair and second, high-
level doorway which gave access to the rood loft, are to be found
normally at the E end of the nave N wall, with a high-level window
in the s wall opposite.

The late medieval timber roofs which survive are of two sorts.
Wagon roofs are found particularly where there is an above-
average width to span, as in the nave at Coity, the w church at
Llantwit Major and both the nave and s aisle at Llancarfan. That
in the nave at Coychurch has angels supporting the principals,
foliage bosses and a celure over the site of the rood; that at Pyle,
as noted above, is dated 1471. The other type of roof is more
unusual, more elaborate, and found in small churches. This has
arch-brace principals resting on short wall-shafts, a moulded
28 collar purlin, and wind-braces. Good examples are at Llansannor,
at St Mary Church and Llanmihangel, both incorporating celures,
and at Flemingston. Such roofs at Betws, Gileston and Llanfrynach are heavily restored. The smallest example is in the porch
at Llandough by Cowbridge.

Church Fittings and Furnishings

Surviving medieval fittings in Glamorgan churches are somewhat
miscellaneous and few are of high artistic quality. Most common
are FONTS. Many of these are simple tubs almost impossible to
date in isolation. However, there is a group of tub-shaped fonts
carved with what is clearly Norman decoration. Those at Kenfig
(Maudlam), Llantwit Major and St Donats have a bold scale
pattern; that at St Lythans is incised with bold zigzag. Fonts of
the C13 are at Bonvilston and Capel Llanilltern, with rhythmic
leaves on a circular bowl, Llanilid, with rows of trefoils in relief,
18 and Oystermouth and Welsh St Donats, both scalloped underneath. Those at Flemingston, a square bowl chamfered down to
a round stem, and Llangan, circular on an octagonal stem, probably also belong to this period. The nine-sided font at Llancarfan,
the underside of the bowl carved with crude leaves, is harder to
date. Eight-sided fonts are normally Perp. Most of these are plain,
but examples at Llanharry and Pyle have chip-carved discs and
childish trees on the faces, while the font at Llantrisant just has
chip-carved discs. Those at Pendoylan and St George-super-Ely
have encircled quatrefoils on alternate faces. Only at St Fagans is
the decoration fully elaborated, with an encircled quatrefoil on
every face and a panelled stem.

Several churches retain medieval HOLY WATER STOUPS, but
27 only at Newton Nottage is the stoup decorated. Also at Newton
Nottage, and far more remarkable, is the C15 stone PULPIT,
carved with a crude but telling Flagellation scene and set under
an arch with flying angels.

The most impressive fitting is the REREDOS, of which three,
perhaps four, examples in stone and one in timber survive. All

are elaborately designed, so that in this respect, if in no other, Glamorgan's medieval ecclesiastical heritage is of national importance. The C13 Jesse niche at Llantwit Major, already men- 21 tioned, may have been designed as a reredos. The late C14 stone reredos at Llantwit Major, extending the full width of the chancel, 29 is on an altogether grander scale, with large canopied niches and rows of small canopied niches on two levels, and richly moulded side doorways. The stone reredos at Llandaff Cathedral, now *ex situ*, is similarly laid out but plainer. That still in place in the Lady Chapel at the cathedral is smaller and heavily overpainted. The timber reredos is at Llancarfan, much mutilated but still crowned by a row of nine vaulted and richly pinnacled canopies.

SCREENS, by contrast, are few and disappointing. The earliest, perhaps of the early C14, is at Ewenny Priory, with close-set mullions supporting a row of stretched quatrefoils. Simple Perp screens are at Llancarfan, Llanmaes, Llantrithyd, Porthkerry and St John, Cardiff, where one section is of perhaps the 1530s, with Renaissance detail. Of the rood lofts which existed in virtually every church until the Reformation nothing remains.

To complete the survey of medieval church fittings, mention can be made of the pews at St Mellons, the heraldic door at Gileston and, a great rarity, the timber Easter Sepulchre at Coity. The medieval timber lectern at St Donats is brought in.

WALL-PAINTINGS are very fragmentary. Llantwit Major has the most extensive, parts of at least three different schemes, including a geometric background to the rood. What is left at Colwinston, Llanfrynach and Llanmaes is slight and hard to decipher. Of medieval STAINED GLASS there is nothing except the imported Netherlandish panels at Aberpergwm, Glynneath.

Monuments

Medieval MONUMENTS survive in some numbers from the early C13 to the early C16, though too many are weathered or otherwise damaged. The outstanding piece for quality and state of pres- ervation is the tomb-slab at Ewenny Priory commemorating the 22 founder, Maurice de Londres. It has fine stiff-leaf and bold, yet exquisitely refined lettering, and can be dated *c*. 1205, con- temporary with two other only slightly less impressive slabs at Ewenny. Among C13 effigies, the group representing bishops at Llandaff Cathedral is the most important, providing an instructive demonstration of the development in figure-carving from *c*. 1220 to *c*. 1290. The late C13 figure at Neath Abbey of an abbot holding a church, though poorly preserved, can be compared with these. Also datable to the C13 is the worn effigy of a warrior at Llan- trisant, identified as a Welsh lord, and the strange coffin lid at Llantwit Major carved to reveal the head of a priest.

The finest individual figures date to the C14. Of these, the early C14 figure of a lady at Flemingston and the late C14 figure of a 23 cross-legged knight at Llansannor are of exceptional quality. The only well-preserved family chapel is that of the de Berkerolles at St Athan, where there are two monuments, both with diminutive

figures against the sides of the tomb-chests, and full-scale effigies
on top of a cross-legged knight and a lady. That commemorating
24 Sir Roger de Berkerolles †1351 has unusually strongly characterized figures and is set under a bold ogee arch with cusped sub-
arches and a small, hovering figure of God. Other, less well
preserved figures of cross-legged knights are at Llangennith,
Ewenny and Margam (a fragment). The splendid incised slab at
St Brides Major, depicting a cross-legged, chain-mailed knight
bearing sword and shield, has been dated c. 1335. The figure of a
knight at Coity is oddly undersized. Effigies of civilians, none
particularly notable, can be found at Llanblethian, St Hilary,
Llantrithyd and St Mary, Swansea (a fragment), and there is one
of a priest at Llantwit Major. At Llandyfodwg is a most unusual
low-relief figure of a pilgrim.

The largest group of c15 and early c16 effigies is again of
military figures. By this time the lively, cross-legged pose had
gone out of fashion. The earliest straight-legged example is at St
Hilary, date of death 1423. Three others are in Llandaff Cathedral,
recumbent knights beside their fashionably dressed ladies, alabaster effigies on high tomb-chests with weepers. The dates of
death range from 1461 to 1528. There is also an isolated mid-c15
alabaster figure of a lady. The latest in the series is at St Brides
Major, the lavish canopied tomb of John Butler †1540, yet here
the knight once again takes up the cross-legged pose.

The late medieval effigies of bishops at Llandaff Cathedral are
worn and rather unimpressive, though for that of Bishop John
Marshall †1496 a painted tester depicting the Assumption of the
Virgin has, most remarkably, survived. To complete the tally
there is a worn figure at Colwinston, a worn cadaver at Llandaff
Cathedral, and two brought-in effigies, perhaps from France, at
Aberpergwm, Glynneath.

BRASSES were not favoured as a form of memorial, probably
because of the distance from the main centre of production,
London. Only two survive in the county, one at Llandough near
Cowbridge commemorating a lady (†1427) and one at St Mary,
Swansea, c. 1500 commemorating a knight.

Outside most medieval churches, normally opposite the porch,
stood a CHURCHYARD CROSS. The bases survive of many such
crosses, of three, four or five quite high steps. In several cases
there is also the cross shaft, while in a very few the cross-head
survives in whole or part. Most complete are the crosses at
31 Llangan and St Donats, where the canopied and pinnacled cross-
heads are intact, the former sheltering Passion scenes and figures
of saints, the latter a Crucifixion. They may be dated c. 1500.

MEDIEVAL SECULAR BUILDINGS

Castles

The imposition of Norman rule in South Wales, inaugurated by
William I's expedition to St David's in 1081, was not achieved

without fierce Welsh opposition. It took the Norman marcher lords of Glamorgan and Gower the best part of two centuries to secure their hold on the northern parts of their lordships. The physical evidence of this struggle remains in an extraordinary concentration of castles. The majority of them are earthworks thrown up in the first confused decades. As Norman power was consolidated during the C12, stone towers and enclosure walls were erected on top of many earthworks. During the C13 Richard de Clare and his son Gilbert built a series of spectacular new castles further N, in the struggle against the great Welsh prince Llywelyn. Castles erected by the Welsh, on the other hand, seem to have been insubstantial, and of them there is little to see.

The Norman EARTHWORKS are of two sorts, mottes and ring-works. The large motte erected at Cardiff within the walls of the Roman fort must have been ordered by William I on his return journey in 1081. Of the ten other surviving mottes, none approaches it in size. Talybont, at Pontardulais, is in North Gower, but the rest belong to an arc of earthwork castles from the W to the NE of Cardiff, erected by Norman families to safe-guard their recently granted lands, at St Nicholas, Ystradowen, Miskin, Pendoylan, Llantwit Fardre, Radyr, Rhiwbina, within the present boundaries of Cardiff, and above Ruperra Castle. The tiny motte at Gelligaer further N in the hill country was probably erected by the Welsh.

Ringworks are more numerous than mottes. They are found in the fertile Vale, where land was more valuable and land grants thus less extensive, and also in the Gower Peninsula. Both areas are near to or beyond the southern extremity of glacial drift, where the soil covering the underlying rock was too thin for the construction of mottes. In all, twenty-one ringworks without subsequent masonry castles upon them have been identified, two-thirds of them with something substantial still to see. But by their nature ringworks are less impressive than mottes, so only Llanilid and St Nicholas Gaer remain visually striking. Excavations at Bishopston and Penmaen have provided evidence for the palisades and other timber structures which reinforced the earthworks.

Among EARLY MASONRY CASTLES, Cardiff again stands out. 32 The polygonal shell keep was constructed on top of the motte there probably between 1136 and 1147. Otherwise, during the C12 the typical masonry castle consisted of a square or rectangular tower, either free-standing or astride an enclosure wall. Kenfig Castle had pilaster buttresses, but there is little evidence of exter-nal embellishment elsewhere. Penlline has herringbone masonry. Coity and Dinas Powys have been reduced to little more than foundations, Oystermouth and Fonmon are embedded in later work. Best preserved, though only recently recognized for what it is, is the Mansel Tower at St Donats Castle, where, as at Coity, a faceted curtain wall was built integrally with the tower. Much the most eloquent of these small C12 keeps is that at Ogmore Castle, where two splayed windows survive from a first-floor hall, and even a fireplace with a fragmentary hood on shafts with scallop capitals. The diminutive rectangular keep at Loughor, datable *c*. 1300, shows that the C12 concept of fortification was long-lasting. The only example which may have been of indigenous Welsh construction is the thin-walled tower at Baglan, of which fragments remain.

33 Newcastle, Bridgend, is in a class of its own. Here the keep tower has disappeared, but the elaborate enclosure wall survives almost intact, with two rectangular towers, one of them protecting the principal entrance. The entrance itself is a showpiece, with its finely cut ashlar and beaded clasps carved round the segment-headed gateway. It has been suggested that it may have been built 1183–9, the years when Henry II took the lordship of Glamorgan into his own hands.

The DE CLARE CASTLES of the mid to late C13 reflect much new thinking about castle design. Their towers are characteristically drum-shaped and the gatehouse becomes an important defensive element in its own right. Richard de Clare, lord of Glamorgan 1230–62, built Llantrisant Castle *c*. 1246–52 with several drum towers, one of which still stands, and he probably built Castell Coch, in two phases. This consists of three massive circular towers closely packed together, and a rectangular hall, but only the lower parts of the C13 walls survive (see below, p. 102).

The castle which Richard's son, Gilbert de Clare, under the threat of the Welsh prince Llywelyn, began in 1268 at Caerphilly far outstripped all that had gone before. Indeed, considered nationally, Caerphilly Castle is of the greatest importance as the immediate forerunner of the great series of eight castles built by Edward I in mid and North Wales between 1277 and 1295, to secure the conquests which brought the Principality permanently under English rule. The royal castles at Harlech and Beaumaris in particular develop Caerphilly's design principles. The first,
35 main phase of construction at Caerphilly, 1268–71, embodies the principle of concentric fortifications. The rectangular inner ward, sheltering the hall and other apartments against its S wall, is defined by a drum tower at each angle, and two residential gate-towers, each with pairs of cylindrical towers in front and cylindrical turrets at the rear angles. The E gatehouse, the larger and grander, was intended as the constable's residence and was independently fortifiable like a keep. All this is surrounded by a narrow middle ward, protected by much lower walls with broad, curving angle bastions, and outer gatehouses to E and W, also with cylindrical frontal towers. The outermost defence is a broad moat developing into a lake on the S side, a form of protection which Gilbert knew had proved its worth at Kenilworth Castle.
36 In the late 1270s the castle was further strengthened when the N lake was formed, restrained by a great dam with polygonal buttressing towers, and three more gate-towers, also with polygonal rather than cylindrical forms.

At Llangynwyd are the scanty traces of a de Clare castle which replicated the E inner gatehouse of Caerphilly. Between 1288 and 1294 Gilbert constructed Morlais Castle, Merthyr Tydfil, on a craggy ridge at the northern extremity of his lordship. Here a regular plan was impossible, so a curtain wall round a lozenge-shaped enclosure was strengthened where most vulnerable by five round towers. Of this piece of defiance all that remains is the rib-vaulted undercroft of one of the towers, miraculously preserved among the rocks.

More puzzling is Castell Morgraig, an only slightly less devastated ruin on the ridge s of Caerphilly. Here a square enclosure had horseshoe-shaped angle towers and a rectangular keep-like tower. Opinions are divided as to whether this is an unusually ambitious attempt by the Welsh at castle-building, or a tentative effort by the de Clares before the valley site for Caerphilly Castle had been chosen.

THE EARLY C14. The influence of Caerphilly Castle can be traced in a number of fortifications put up c. 1300. The fortified gatehouse became popular. Several have the polygonal towers typical of the later gatehouses at Caerphilly, and even such details as bull-nosed mouldings, which suggest that masons from Caerphilly subsequently undertook other jobs in the area. The Bishop's Castle at Llandaff, probably built for Bishop William de Braose before 1287, has a handsome and well-preserved gatehouse of this kind, and so does St Quintin's Castle at Llanblethian, known to have been erected by the younger Gilbert de Clare 1312–14. The gatehouse which forms the main feature in the remarkable defensive walls at Ewenny Priory belongs to the group, and there is further evidence of the activity of these masons in the unfortified early C14 house at Old Beaupre. Two contemporary castles on Gower, Pennard and Oystermouth, have gatehouses with twin drum towers, the latter now lacking the front faces of the drums. The most significant element of the rather meagre and fragmentary castle at Barry is an early C14 gatehouse with bow-fronted turrets. The gatehouse is virtually all that survives of Neath Castle, built after 1321, with three-storeyed drum towers; it stands nearly to full height but robbed of dressed stonework. The gatehouse at St Donats Castle is more severely practical, 34 a plain rectangle in plan, but equipped for a portcullis and drawbridge. On the other hand, it has survived complete. Its trefoil-headed lancet windows and the details of the shafted chimneypiece in the room over the archway date it c. 1300.

The heroic period of castle-building, when military considerations dominated design, was over by the early C14. In the mid 1320s Hugh le Despenser reconstructed the hall at Caerphilly Castle in sumptuous fashion, employing royal craftsmen who introduced lavish ballflower ornament alien to Glamorgan. At Swansea Castle the splendid surviving range contained a state 37 apartment. Its artfully spaced arrow loops suggest an eye to decoration rather than defence, as the fanciful arcaded parapet above confirms. The latter corresponds with work at the palaces built in Pembrokeshire at St David's and Lamphey by Henry de Gower, Bishop of St David's 1328–47. The same spirit ruled about the same time at Oystermouth Castle, when a new chapel was allowed to display large windows with cusped, intersecting tracery high above the mass of the castle. The lightly fortified Weobley Castle, Llanrhidian, gives a particularly clear indication of domestic arrangements in the early C14. Here a well-windowed hall is placed above the kitchen, and a well-windowed chamber above a pair of store rooms.

DOMESTIC IMPROVEMENTS characterize the remodelling of castles in the later C14 and C15. At the Turbervilles' Coity Castle the improvement took place in two phases. The first included the creation of a stone-walled outer ward, and in the inner ward, two vaulted chambers in the C12 keep and a new hall on a vaulted undercroft against the S curtain wall. A vaulted passage beside the hall led to what was intended to be an ambitious chapel. In the second phase a large barn was erected in the outer ward, and a smaller chapel was constructed, later heightened with a showy window overtopping the curtain wall. At the Stradlings' St Donats Castle the C15 was the period of improvement. Here a ground-floor hall with a deep porch and a broad and deep dais bay was built on the E side of the inner ward, with elaborately approached service rooms. A lodging range stands on the W side. At Cardiff Castle Richard Beauchamp, Earl of Warwick (lord of Glamorgan 1423–39), erected a new block, the so-called Western Apartments. Though much altered in the C18 and C19, they are still the handsomest piece of late medieval domestic architecture in Glamorgan. The polygonal W tower is comparable to the late C14 Guy's Tower at Warwick Castle. The E-facing range contained hall and inner chamber, each provided with polygonal stair-turret and elegantly buttressed window bay.

It remains to mention only the weakly fortified Candleston Castle, Merthyr Mawr, where the upper-floor hall has a remarkably splendid chimneypiece.

Unfortified Manor Houses

By the early C14 some landowners were building UNFORTIFIED MANOR HOUSES. The most romantic of these nowadays is the group of ruined structures which constituted East Orchard Manor, St Athan, the seat of the Berkerolles during the C14. Here hall range, kitchen and chapel were all detached from one another. Old Beaupre, as built c. 1300, was more coherent, gatehouse and hall forming a single range, joined at r.-angles to a kitchen range. Another, more irregular range formed the third side of a court-yard. At Pencoed House, Capel Llanilltern, a large and handsome double-wave moulded arch is virtually all that survives of what must have been an important house of the same period.

Glebe Farm, Cheriton, is at least as early as these, though smaller and much mutilated. The Hospital of the Blessed St David (now Cross Keys Inn), Swansea, is datable 1332–4, but its original layout has been completely obscured.

A small group of late medieval hall-houses remains. The only ground-floor hall still open from floor to roof is Cogan Pill, Penarth. The other example of this type, Castellymynach, Pentyrch, has been subdivided horizontally. Of the two first-floor halls, that at Castle Farm, St George-super-Ely, has undergone antiquarian improvement, that at Garnllwyd, Llancarfan, survives only in part. All have arch-braced roofs, similar to those in contemporary churches, though only at Cogan Pill is there a collar purlin; only at Garnllwyd were there wind-braces. Flemingston Court, datable to the early c16, shows a decisive development, for the hall is single-storeyed, set below a great chamber, and flanked by a parlour and a pair of unheated service rooms. The kitchen was at first detached, but a later kitchen was built adjoining the parlour – not the service rooms.

The few remaining late medieval parsonages introduce the fully storeyed house type which was to become the basis of all houses at sub-gentry level from the early c16 onwards. Only Church Farm, Llandow, was certainly built with an open hall. The Old Rectory (now school), Llantwit Major, datable to the early c16, was quite a sumptuous affair, with a two-storey porch and heraldic overmantel, but its interior arrangements have been completely altered. The Old Rectory at St Andrews Major is even less eloquent. The Old Rectory, St Donats, now a ruin, was storeyed from the start. The late c15 Chantry House in the churchyard at Llantwit Major, and Church Farm, Porthkerry, probably of the early c16, in effect one room below and one above, intercommunicating by a mural stair, are the forerunners of hundreds of later Glamorgan farmhouses.

GENTRY HOUSES

Early Sixteenth Century to the Mid Seventeenth Century

The Reformation, followed by the Dissolution of the Monasteries in the 1530s, led in Glamorgan, as elsewhere in Britain, to vast social changes and the rise of new families to local power. In Wales, the Act of Union (1536–43) extended the scope of these changes, enabling leading Welsh families to gain property and influence on an equal footing with those of English extraction. During the ensuing century virtually all the wealthiest and most powerful families rebuilt their houses or built anew. Only the Stradlings at St Donats remained content with their castle. The conventual buildings of the former monasteries were all developed into major mansions, by the Carnes at Ewenny, where nothing but a few mullioned windows remain, by the Mansels at Margam, where nothing at all is left of this period, and by Sir Richard Cromwell, alias Williams, at Neath, now a complicated and tantalizing ruin. The Franciscan friary at Cardiff similarly formed the nucleus of a mansion of the Herberts. A fine range there dated 1582 was demolished as recently as 1967 and will be mentioned further below. The Herberts also took over the major house in Swansea, New Place, which again does not survive. Fragments of it were in 1840 incorporated into the Home Farm at Singleton Abbey, Swansea.

Of the eight surviving major houses, only one, St Fagans Castle, retains its interiors. Five are in ruins: consolidated ruins at Neath Abbey, Old Beaupre and Oxwich Castle, but ruins continuing to decay at Llantrithyd and Ruperra. The Van, Caerphilly, has been reconstructed since 1990 and is habitable again. Cefnmabli, after many years as a hospital, and many more empty, was gutted by fire in 1994. Among the lesser houses, the picture is not so bleak, but here, too, there are unconsolidated ruins, most notably the two houses at Llantwit Major.

Few of these houses can be dated precisely, the earliest firm date being 1582. So stylistic evidence has to be brought into play. Cut stonework provides the best clues, and in particular WINDOWS, so much so that it is worth setting out the main diagnostic features. Arched window lights can be assumed to be earlier than those with straight heads. The hollow-chamfer moulding of mullions is earlier than the sunk chamfer. Window hoodmoulds with square stops normally antedate those with plain returns. Large, multi-mullioned and transomed windows are found with arched lights and hoodmoulds (Oxwich Castle and Llantrithyd). But the grander houses datable to the 1580s onwards have their mullion-and-transom windows with straight-headed lights, and instead of hoodmoulds, continuous string courses running across at the level of the window heads (St Fagans Castle, parts of Neath Abbey). This is clearly connected with a greater sensitivity to overall composition by this time.

DOORWAYS normally have four-centred arched heads. FIRE-PLACES similarly have flattened arches, though at the end of the period square fireplace openings with mantelshelves on classical scroll brackets make their appearance. However, only at Nottage Court, Newton Nottage, after 1608, are such fireplaces part of the original structure. STAIRS of the late medieval type constructed in the thickness of the wall (mural stairs) were by the mid C16 giving way to properly lit stairs rising in short, straight flights round a square pillar (Oxwich Castle, Old Beaupre). The open well variety was of course a C17 development. The only such stair in its original state is at Great House, Aberthin, of before 1658.

Although castles with both the appearance and the reality of defence were by the early C16 a thing of the past, several of the earlier houses of this period retain aspects of defensibility. Most remarkable is Llancaeach-fawr, Gelligaer, an upland house of tall, compact form, its walls riddled with mural stairs, many of its inner doorways equipped for drawbars, and a plan which has been interpreted as allowing the isolation of the owner's personal quarters in case of emergency. Llancaeach-fawr has its hall on the first floor, itself a feature of defensible planning, but the hall is not open to the roof. More impressive first-floor halls with plaster vaults rising into the roof space are at Llanmihangel Place, datable between c. 1528 and 1559, where the dais oriel is part of a polygonal gabled turret, a unique feature, and at Sker House, a medieval house extended, where the vault has collapsed.

Of the major mansions, one undoubtedly had a first-floor hall. This is Oxwich Castle where, excitingly, the first-floor hall is part

of a soaringly lofty range which had a long gallery running the full 40
length of the top storey. A multiplicity of smaller rooms were
clustered at the ends of the main range beside the two pillar stairs,
and in three tower-like projections at the back. Their single-light
windows contrast strongly with the vast windows of hall and
gallery. The window details, arched lights and hollow chamfers
suggest an early date, although probably not before 1559. At Neath
Abbey the medieval dormitory undercroft was incorporated and
its lighting improved with enlarged windows, so that it could serve
as a ground-floor hall. The great chamber was sited above it, with
an impressive long gallery at r.-angles. Both upper rooms were
lit by enormous mullion-and-transom windows, with straight-
headed lights, probably dating to the late C16.

The upper-floor hall, with its overtones of defensibility, is
typical of houses found in border areas elsewhere in Britain. But
ground-floor halls in storeyed houses, normally associated with
the settled parts of Tudor England, also occur regularly. Flemingston Court, which has all the signs of an early C16 date, has
already been mentioned. Sutton, Llandow, is more complex and
much harder to interpret. Cefnmabli had a single-storey ground-
floor hall with deep recesses at the dais end reminiscent of the
C15 hall at St Donats Castle. This was a courtyard house built on a
substantial scale, though drastic later alterations confused things.
Llantrithyd Place was another substantial mid-C16 house, which
had long wings forming a U-plan and a long gallery in the upper
storey of the hall range, but it is now too ruined to be eloquent.
Llansannor Court is the best-preserved house of this class, still
with arched window lights, but showing a new urge towards
symmetry in its main elevation, which may date it to the 1570s or
even later. Treguff, Llancarfan, is also of the later C16. The two
greatly ruined houses at Llantwit Major, Boverton and Old Place,
both a full three storeys high, are known to have been built mainly
in the 1590s. They must have looked monotonous with their many
rather undersized and regularly spaced windows.

A serious regard for symmetry began to dictate house design
only in the 1580s. The demolished Herbert House, Cardiff, dated
1582, showed this in the composition of its central section, three-
storeyed with a pair of boldly projecting, five-sided window bays.
At The Van, Caerphilly, a completely regular four-bay block built
soon after 1583 is oddly tacked on to an irregular earlier range.
Finally, St Fagans Castle, completed before 1596, presents a 41
symmetrical front, symmetrical sides and a regular plan, an
embryonic double pile with a central porch and short, forward-
projecting wings. In its four-light, transomed windows under
continuous string courses and its even-sized gables, it is very
similar to The Van, but the plan suggests the intervention of a
London-based surveyor. Great House, Aberthin, is a reduced
version of it. Nottage Court, Newton Nottage, however, of after
1608, though fully symmetrical, has the porch in the l.-most of
three gabled projections, a local idiosyncrasy also observable at
The Van and Boverton.

By the end of the C16 castle-building seemed so remote that

some of its typical features could be employed without any defensive connotations. This is particularly true of GATEHOUSES and BATTLEMENTING. The gatehouse at Oxwich Castle bearing Sir Rice Mansel's arms is early enough and large enough to be taken seriously. But the little gatehouses at The Van, c. 1583, Old Beaupre, 1586, and Llanvithyn, Llancarfan, 1636, are hardly more than playthings. At Old Beaupre the gatehouse is integrated with a high-level forecourt promenade which was originally protected by battlements. At St Fagans Castle the new house was surrounded by an embattled wall with a similar wall-walk, partly
42 reconstructing the medieval curtain wall. Ruperra Castle, 1626, is a complete new house in castle mode, closely comparable with Lulworth Castle, Dorset, of about twenty years earlier. It is built in four ranges round a light well, with bold drum towers at the angles and idiosyncratic windows with arched lights. The original gables between the towers have been replaced by C19 battlements, so at first it looked less castle-like than it does today. The entrance porch has classical details, shell-headed niches and strapwork.

There remains to mention in this section the single most spectacular surviving feature of any of these houses, the 'TOWER OF
43 THE ORDERS' at Old Beaupre. It is dated 1600, and its ashlar and carved parts are of Bath stone. The character and quality of its columns and strapwork decoration relate it to structures and church monuments in Gloucestershire and Somerset. It must have been imported ready-carved from across the Bristol Channel.
45 The tower-like porch at Ruperra Castle is simpler.

A little more can be said about INTERIORS. The finest surviving room of the period is the hall at Llanmihangel Place. The stone fireplace with an overmantel of heraldic shields and embattled cresting is datable c. 1528/59 and is clearly comparable to a fireplace and overmantel at Old Beaupre. The full-height wall-panelling with decorative frieze and royal arms, and the ribbed plaster ceiling which dominates the room and also embellishes the dais oriels, must be later in the C16. Other architectural chimneypieces include one at The Van, Caerphilly, and an early C17 group with classical scroll brackets: at Llansannor Court carrying a full entablature, at Nottage Court, Newton Nottage, and at Llancaeach-fawr, Gelligaer, carrying a moulded shelf.
48 Of what must have been splendid C17 alabaster overmantels at Llantrithyd, two armorial shields remain in the church.* The best panelling is at Nash Manor, Llysworney, and St Fagans Castle, the latter dated 1624. Both sets have giant pilasters, and both are in combination with timber caryatid and heraldic overmantels, one at St Fagans dated 1635. Similar early C17 carved shields of arms with strapwork are at Castellymynach, Pentyrch. Plainer panelling can be found at Llancaeach-fawr, Llansannor Court and Great House, Aberthin. Plasterwork remains are even more

*Far finer than any chimneypiece surviving *in situ* are the late C16 pair at Dyffryn
47 House, of alabaster, with caryatids and relief overmantels, brought in probably from an unidentified house in England. Also at Dyffryn House are two further chimneypieces made up of magnificent C17 timber figures from the Netherlands or Germany.

tantalizing, especially when it is known that great houses like Ewenny Priory and Llantrithyd had enriched plaster ceilings. Now (apart from Llanmihangel Place – *see* above) one can mention only the grotesquework frieze at Sker, the fragmentary friezes at Fishweir, St Mary Church, and Llansannor Court, and individual relief motifs at Castleton, St Athan, at Treguff and Llanvithyn, Llancarfan, and at Great House, Llanmaes, of *c.* 1700. That leaves one really exciting piece of interior decoration to mention, the wall-paintings at Castellymynach, Pentyrch. The black and white grotesquework dated 1602 is quite conventional, though unique in Glamorgan, but the trompe-l'oeil figures and seascape are hard to parallel anywhere in Britain.

When so little remains of the sumptuous settings with which some gentry families surrounded themselves, the CHURCH MONUMENTS of the period, where the survival rate is so much higher, form a valuable supplement, even though Glamorgan families do not seem to have been especially self-indulgent in erecting them. The only chapel-full is at Margam, where four 50 generations of Mansels are commemorated by tomb-chests bearing recumbent effigies, the first three a set, with small angle obelisks, erected 1611/31, the fourth († 1638) more advanced in style and with emblematic reliefs. The most elaborate, and poly-chromatic, monument, also to Mansels, is at Llantrithyd, dated 49 1597, where recumbent and kneeling figures commemorate three generations in the one monument. Large obelisks and small columns constitute the architectural components. The recumbent figures on a tomb-chest at St John, Cardiff, to Herbert brothers who died in 1609 and 1617, are less assertive, and those without their original setting at Coychurch († 1591) and Llantwit Major are of much poorer quality. At Llanmihangel († 1591) is a recumbent figure, its lower part covered by the cross-incised lid of the tomb-chest, a belated imitation of a medieval conceit.

There are several small wall-monuments with figures between columns kneeling at prayer desks, of the type found throughout Britain in the early C17. That at Cowbridge (to a Carne of Nash Manor, Llysworney) is dated 1616; the two at Margam commemorate Bussy relatives of the Mansels († 1623, 1625). At St Donats members of the Stradling family are commemorated not only by a sculptured monument of the type († 1609) but, much more unusually, by three painted panels with figures for earlier generations (dated 1590). The wall-monument at Wenvoe 51 († 1636) is unique in having allegorical reliefs and small crowning figures of Virtues. It is also of high quality. Finally, there is the much later monument at St Brides Major († 1698) with a pair of 52 touchingly characterized demi-figures, still early Stuart in spirit.

Mid Seventeenth Century to the Mid Eighteenth Century

This is a fallow period for Glamorgan's gentry houses. It seems to be related to the fact that over this century there was only one new entrant into the elite group of gentry families (Jones of Fonmon), while many long-established families either faltered and failed to renew themselves, or moved to what they saw as more favourably placed estates in England.

Among major houses, only two could show important work of this period. Cefnmabli, the seat of the Kemeys family, was modernized and extended in the late C17 with hipped roofs on concave plaster eaves, brick string courses (an unusually early use of brick for show) and windows of timber cross form as well as sash windows. The comparable work at Margam Abbey, datable before 1684, has all been swept away. This is a grievous loss, for by this time the Mansels of Margam had become one of the county's dominant families, and enough is known of the appearance of the C17 house to establish that it was the largest and most impressive house of its period in Glamorgan. Nevertheless, there does survive at Margam the most ambitious piece of classical architecture after Old Beaupre's 'tower of the orders'. This is the 58 façade of the Summer Banqueting House, two-storeyed with Corinthian columns over Ionic, forming a three-bay composition with arches in the centre bay and flanking niches. Some fanciful detailing betrays a provincial hand, but this is a serious piece of architecture, and one wonders what else of comparable quality has disappeared without trace.

The formal, two-storey, hipped-roof type of house, with vertically proportioned windows and reticent classical detail, pioneered in England by Inigo Jones and his followers from the 1630s, does not occur in Glamorgan before 1700, and even then only on a modest scale. Gwaun-y-bara, Rudry, of c.1690 has end gables and windows of squat proportions. Great House, Llanmaes, 1699/1733, is sashed but of three storeys and gabled. The façade of Great House, Llanblethian, dated 1703, has naive pedimental gables. Gileston Manor, however, is a perfect five-bay example of the type. Unfortunately it cannot be closely dated. Tyn-yr-heol, Tonna, is another, less impressive, example. Cadoxton Lodge and Ynysgerwyn, Cadoxton-juxta-Neath, were two more, both unfortunately pulled down in the 1960s. Llandaff Court (now Cathedral School), built 1744–6, is large enough, of nine bays and three storeys, and represents the early C18 development of the type by such provincial architects as Francis Smith of Warwick, with its roof behind a parapet (altered to a hipped roof in the C20). Llanharan House as first built was similar in spirit and not much later. The tradition continued to c.1770, date of the remodelling of Pwll-y-wrach, Colwinston, by the same master mason as No. 3 High Street, Cowbridge, and West Farm, Llantwit Major. As for internal features, mention can be made of the staircases at Gileston Manor, with twisted balusters, and at Llandaff Court, with turned balusters, both with carved tread-ends.

POST-MEDIEVAL FARMHOUSES

The agricultural prosperity of Glamorgan in the C16 and C17 is reflected in the surviving farmhouses datable to this period. Many, even among the smallest, have good-quality detail of cut stone in windows, doorways and fireplaces, and substantial, decoratively chamfered timber ceiling joists. Walls are universally of stone, for the tradition of timber-framing so strong in mid Wales, which extended into Monmouthshire, failed entirely to penetrate Glamorgan. Roofs were covered with thatch or slates. In materials, as in many aspects of planning, the links with Somerset and Devon, across the Bristol Channel, are stronger than those with much of the rest of Wales.

In the Vale houses may cluster in loosely textured villages, of which Merthyr Mawr and Tythegston are the best surviving examples. By far the biggest concentration is at Llantwit Major. Or they may stand in independent farmsteads. In Gower the village cluster is less characteristic, and in the uplands unknown. Here the farmhouses, many of them with dwelling house and accommodation for cattle in a single range, stood completely isolated on the mountain slopes. Even today, many of those that survive can be reached only by mile-long unmade tracks. Upland houses normally made do with a minimum of stone for dressings, and with timber for window mullions, internal door frames and fireplace lintels.

Storeyed construction was universal, so that the provision of stairs was essential, even in upland longhouses, which were normally single-storeyed below a habitable roof-space. Roofs are universally constructed with principal rafter trusses, normally with collars, and in many cases curved feet to the principals, a feature which the Royal Commission interprets as a relic of cruck construction, otherwise virtually unknown in the county. Particularly typical is the single-unit house, consisting of a hall below, a chamber above and a habitable roof-space. Even where this type was extended to a second unit, heated or unheated, the vertical connection predominates. Stairs were constructed of stone, in the thickness of the wall. Either they spiral up in one angle of the building, or they ascend in a straight flight within a thickened wall, exactly like late medieval rood-loft stairs in churches.

A second principal of farmhouse planning was that the hall fireplace should be set in a gable-end wall, not in a side wall, a position which seems to have been associated with the gentry-level house and the tradition of the hall open to the roof. Among the few examples of lateral-chimney farmhouses, mention may be made of the quite exceptional, three-and-a-half-storey Newbridge Farm, Merthyr Mawr, of *c.* 1600, and Tophill Farm, Gelligaer, dated 1583, in effect a small gentry house, with a two-storey porch and an unusually spacious stair. In the largest farmhouses, where the hall unit is set between two further units, the hall fireplace is set in a central cross-wall. The subsequent lengthways extension of many small early houses has also created this arrangement. In both cases the typical combination is found of a cross-wall with a wide fireplace, on one side of it the door to a mural stair, and on the other a door to a secondary room. Good examples readily visible, as the houses are now inns, are the Blue Anchor, Penmark, and the Carne Arms, Llysworney. This line-up of openings relates to the two primary plan-forms of Glamorgan farmhouses, as

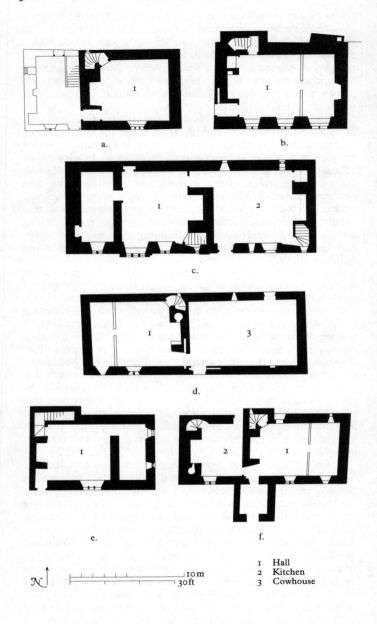

Rural house plan types
a. Single-unit, end-entry, later extended; b. Two-unit, end-entry;
c. Three-unit, hearth-passage; d. Longhouse; e. Two-unit, lobby-entry;
f. Three-unit, lobby-entry

defined by the position of the entrance doorway. These are described by the Royal Commission as 'end-entry' and 'hearth-passage'. In the 'end-entry' type one of the doors beside the hearth in the gable end is the entrance door. Such houses might consist merely of a hall below and a chamber above, or they might have an inner room, heated or unheated, at the far end away from the entrance. Almost always such houses have been extended at the entrance end, so that the original doorway has become internal, as, for example, at the Old White Hart, Llantwit Major. One such unextended house is Diana Cottage, Merthyr Mawr, datable quite late, *c.* 1700. The most eloquent c16 example is Tŷ- 55 mawr, Byeastwood, Coity, where the inner ground-floor room has a fireplace, and the chamber above is even provided with a garderobe. The latter balances the mural stair projection in the windowless N wall. The windows all face S, mullioned, but of two types, those in the hall and the unheated room above with arched lights, those in the private rooms, parlour below and chamber above, with square heads to the lights. Such sophistication on a small scale is worth pondering.

Houses built with a second unit on the hearth-ward side of the hall unit, and the entrance doorway opening into this second unit, form the 'hearth-passage' group. This is quite different from the gentry-level screens-passage arrangement, where the screens passage is in the space of the hall. The hearth passage is normally part of the service area, and in many cases the entrance doorway was not matched by another doorway at the far end, so a through passage was not an essential feature. Hospice, Bridgend, is a handsome mid-c16 example, the entrance doorway within a two-storey porch, the passage giving access to two service rooms on one side and to the hall on the other. The inns mentioned above belong to this type, and so does the exceptionally complete Old Swan Inn, Llantwit Major. Gelynis Farm, Radyr, is a finely 56 detailed c16 example which has the three-light windows for the hall and chamber above in a projecting bay, and the arched lights of these windows subtly differentiated from the arched lights of the other, smaller windows. Tŷ-maen, St Brides Major, has windows with square-headed lights and must be of the early c17. Tynewydd House, Treherbert, at the N end of the Rhondda Fawr, is dated, apparently, 1652. Its plan is as elaborate as its internal timberwork, so that it is altogether uniquely ambitious for the northern uplands. Another uniquely developed example of this type is Great House, Llantwit Major, where the plan is an irregular Greek cross. It seems to have been built all of a piece in the late c16.

Where the hearth passage gives entrance not to service rooms but to a cowhouse built in range with the hall unit, a 'longhouse' is formed. Glamorgan longhouses are, as has been said, single-storeyed with lofts, but the characteristic line-up of inner entrance doorway, hall fireplace and door to a mural stair is found in them too. Most longhouses occur in the pastoral uplands, so dressed stonework is not to be expected. A c17 date is deduced by the Royal Commission for most of them, and the much-altered

Gelli-wrgan, Llanwonno, actually has a datestone of 1616. Inevitably, very few remain unaffected by distorting alterations, both rendering the cowhouse habitable for humans, and adding an extra storey. Nant-y-fedw, Glyncorrwg, which has been wholly relegated to use as a store, gives an unusually good idea of what this type of farmhouse originally looked like. Hafod-tanglwys-isaf, Aberfan, is a well-preserved example of the longhouse derivative, where a barn takes the place of the cowhouse. Longhouses were built as far s as the border country between the uplands and the Vale. Thus Hill Farm, Lisvane (Cardiff), originated as a longhouse. In the Vale itself, however, they are extremely rare. To-hesg, Llantwit Major, standing within the developed area of the C17 town, must always have been wholly exceptional.

The lobby-entry plan, found only from *c.* 1600, may in part have developed from the end-entry plan. Here the entrance doorway, instead of being in the gable-end wall alongside the hall fireplace, is round the corner in the front wall, placed so that a small lobby is created between the doorway and the side of the hall chimneybreast. Where the hall is accompanied only by an inner room, this creates an extremely lopsided front elevation, as can be seen, for example, at Batslays, St Athan. At Laleston Inn, Laleston, the arrangement is still clearly discernible, in spite of later extension beyond the entrance doorway. This was a two-unit house, as the two-storey window bay proclaims, with a pair of two-light windows, one for the hall and one for the parlour. Later additions to other houses of this type largely obliterated the asymmetry, a particularly successful example being the gentrification of Bryn-chwith, Llandyfodwg, where a single-unit lobby-entry house was greatly extended beyond the gable-end wall, and a two-storey porch added off-centre to the door in an attempt to achieve a symmetrical elevation.

A second type of lobby-entry house is quite different. Here there are two units, a hall unit and a unit including normally a kitchen but sometimes a parlour, behind the hall chimney. Here the doorway can be in the centre of the entrance front, though not aligned with the hall chimneystack. If the hall also has an inner room, the symmetry is thrown out, as at Maendy, St Brides Minor, dated 1607, where a two-storey porch covers the entrance doorway. Tyle-coch, Betws, which has lost its porch, has fine ashlar detail and a parlour in a rear wing. Its details suggest that it may date from before 1600.

All these houses have the fireplace of the outer room in a gable-end wall. In order to create a completely symmetrical lobby-entry plan it was necessary to place the hearths of the two units back-to-back. The most successful and best-preserved realization of
54 this concept is Llanmihangel, Pyle, datable *c.* 1600. This has a spacious kitchen in a rear wing. Kenfig Farm, Kenfig, is smaller, with a centrally arranged double mural stair at the back. At Tŷ-maen, Colwinston, early in the C17, and Downs Farm, Dinas Powys, late in the C17, the entry lobby is enlarged and the centrality of the entrance stressed by bringing it forward slightly from the main wall-plane.

Inevitably, certain houses do not fit into any of these patterns. At one or two the entrance into the hall is in the front wall, unrelated to the fireplace gable end. Fishweir, St Mary Church, 57 is a large and well-preserved early example. Here hall and kitchen have their fireplaces back-to-back, the latter exceedingly wide; the four-light upper windows and the plaster frieze in the principal upper chamber show the gentility of its owners. The arched window lights suggest a mid-C16 date. A characteristic C17 example is Breach, Llanblethian, where there is a heated outer room and upper rooms lit by gabled dormers. It shows how a coherent appearance could be created from such a plan. An exceptionally well-preserved upland example, though now disused, is Blaengwrach Farm at Blaengwrach, another is Llanfair-fach, Capel Llanilltern. Cae'rwigau-isaf, Pendoylan, datable to the late C16, is the best-preserved representative of a rare type, in which the hall is entered in the gable wall opposite the fireplace.

Pre-C18 TOWN HOUSES hardly form a discernible type in Glamorgan, since nothing so early survives at either Cardiff or Swansea, although the medieval burgage plots at Cardiff, in High Street and St Mary Street, are still discernible in the pattern of Victorian rebuilding. Cowbridge was laid out with burgage plots in the C13, but the only early houses built there in truly urban fashion, gable end on to the street, are the much-altered Nos. 32–34 High Street. Otherwise, the early houses of Cowbridge can be categorized with the rural buildings of the rest of the county.

FARM BUILDINGS never again approached the giant size of the barns of the monastic granges. A few gentry houses in the Vale are accompanied by impressive BARNS. The barn at Old Beaupre, though only of five bays, so not particularly large, is the oldest, datable c. 1500. The finest group is at Llanmihangel Place, where the mid-C16 seven-bay barn was extended c. 1600 by a matching stable. Largest of all is the lofty, eight-bay barn at Fishweir, St Mary Church.

The other early type of building concerned with animal husbandry is the DOVECOTE. Dovecotes were normally circular and domed. Excellently preserved medieval examples are at Llantwit Major, the most evocative survivor from the monastic grange there, and at Cadoxton Court, Barry. There are ruined C16 examples at Oxwich Castle and The Van, Caerphilly. But the most extraordinary dovecote in Glamorgan is Culver Hole, Port-Eynon, a four-storey construction in a cleft in the cliffs, which may well date back to the late medieval period.

The same constructional tradition survived into the C18, for circular, corbel-topped PIGSTIES. About twenty survive, an easy one to glimpse being at Church Cottage, St Hilary.

The MODEL FARM is a great rarity in Glamorgan. Home Farm, Penrice, arranged round a rectangular yard, is an C18 example. But the most memorable farm building there is the square granary, built in 1807 of red brick. In the mid C19 the Windsor Estate built Pentrebane Farm, St Fagans, with an elaborate barn. Otherwise there is nothing to mention, other than the early C19 farm buildings at Cog Farm, Sully, which have cast iron roof trusses.

MID EIGHTEENTH TO
EARLY NINETEENTH CENTURIES

Mansions and Villas

The near hiatus in country house-building during the first half of the C18 is filled by one other example not yet mentioned. This is the enlargement of Hensol Castle, Pendoylan, in 1735, by the addition of wings with pointed-headed windows and battlements. Unfortunately, the date and character of the house to which these wings were added are unknown, so it is not clear whether or not this Gothicism, rare and remarkable at such a date, was prompted by a desire to relate to what was there already. But Hensol introduces the *leitmotif* of Glamorgan country houses and their parks during the second half of the C18: the interplay between Gothic and classical, or perhaps, to put it a better way, between medievalism and modernism.

The most straightforward juxtaposition is between a castellated exterior and classical interiors. Fonmon Castle, remodelled from 1762 by *Thomas Paty* of Bristol, shows the minimum of medievalism. The rambling house, which had developed from a C12 defensive tower, was given battlements overall, but the windows are rectangular and sashed. Inside, the talented plasterer *Thomas Stocking* was allowed to have his head in Rococo embellishment, in the hall ceiling and more particularly in the decoration of the
61 splendid tripartite library. Kilvrough Manor, Pennard, probably built by 1774, has a similar combination of battlements and sash windows, but forms a regular, though unconventional composition, a five-bay entrance front and a longer garden front at r.-angles, with three-sided, full-height end projections. Here the interiors are Adamesque. Penllyn Castle, Penlline, built between 1789 and 1804, is also castellated, but otherwise amateurishly classical and has mid-C19 interiors.

The Adam style, with a slightly provincial inflection, had reached Glamorgan at Tythegston Court by 1769–71. Here a medieval tower house was completely absorbed in a two-stage enlargement, of *c.* 1769 and the mid 1790s, so the whole house is Neoclassical, though the two phases are not well integrated externally. The interior is the most complex and charming of its
62 period. The Doric hall and the staircase with turned balusters are typical mid-C18 work, but the plasterwork clearly shows knowledge of Adam's neo-antique style, though combined in the stairwell with naturalistic swags and flowers and even a Gothic touch in the cornice. The plasterer here was *John Elson*. Another quite early Neoclassical house was Coytrahen, Tondu, *c.* 1775–6, but of this only an ignominious fragment survives.

Robert Adam himself designed one major house in the county, Wenvoe Castle, built in 1776–7 for Peter Birt. This was castellated, though lacking in the 'movement' which he imparted to most of his late castle-style houses. Today only a four-bay fragment of Wenvoe survives, so the best piece by *Adam* in the county is now the single-storey Doric portico imported from Bowood, Wiltshire, and re-erected in 1956 at Roath Court, Roath, Cardiff. At Wenvoe the impressive stable court, Neoclassical rather than castellated, is attributed to *Henry Holland*. 65

Holland was working in Glamorgan in the late 1770s, when he gained the commission to remodel the Western Apartments of Cardiff Castle for the first Marquess of Bute, after a scheme submitted by Robert Adam in 1777 had been rejected as over-ambitious. Holland's addition of three-bay rectangular wings and insertion of sash windows throughout produced the largest castellated mansion in the county, the only one developed from a conspicuous medieval core, but one lacking in evocative power, to judge from early views, for Holland's work was later almost totally submerged (*see* p. 101). Holland's interiors were, once again, Neoclassical, and the most exciting feature of Holland's Cardiff Castle must have been the circular staircase in the Beauchamp Tower. What must be an echo of this is found in the beautiful, if austere, circular top-lit staircase added to Llanharan House by an unknown architect after 1806. 64

Gnoll, at Neath, was one further castellated mansion of exactly this period, built 1776–8 for the Mackworths, the leading family of industrial entrepreneurs, to the design of *John Johnson* of Leicester. The house was pulled down in 1956, but the castellated seats in the grounds and the octagonal, castellated Ivy Tower on the hillside at Tonna nearby survive as features in the elaborate pleasure grounds, with fishponds and cascades, which accompanied the house. Garden buildings elsewhere were Gothic. Most remarkable is the stone-vaulted, octagonal summerhouse at Sketty, Swansea, built in the early C19 in the grounds of Sketty Park House for another industrialist family, the Morrises of Morriston. The only other Gothic garden building to note is Batty Langley style, and datable before 1776, in the grounds of Rookwood Hospital, Llandaff, Cardiff.

The finest and most complete architectural achievement of the late C18 in the county is not that of a celebrated London architect, but of *Anthony Keck* of King's Stanley, Gloucestershire, working for Thomas Mansel Talbot of Penrice and Margam. At Penrice between 1773 and 1794 Keck and Talbot created a fascinating marriage between Gothic and classical, and between art and nature, a beautiful concept exquisitely realized which survives virtually unchanged. On a steep hillside below the ruins of the C14 castle, which was converted into an aviary, Keck built a tall, compact villa, reminiscent of the villas of Sir Robert Taylor of the 1750s and 1760s, with a bold, full-height bow on its seaward front. 60 The ground falling away below the house was landscaped by *William Emes*. The park gates are trimly classical, but the lodges which flank the main gates are embodied in a mock ruin, making the ambivalence of the whole creation apparent at the outset. At his other estate, Margam, Talbot treated the past with greater ruthlessness, sweeping away the great rambling house which had developed from the monastic quarters, and laying out gardens rather than building a new residence. Here, from 1787 to 1790,

Keck had the chance to erect a masterpiece, the enormous
59 Orangery, 327 ft (99.67 metres) long including the end pavilions,
which housed a library and sculpture collection and made it the
longest orangery in Britain. It is the outstanding Neoclassical
building in the county, the counterpoint between smooth ashlar,
vermiculated rustication and sparing carved decoration brilliantly
managed.

The interior decoration at Penrice and in the library pavilion
of the Margam Orangery uses an Adamesque vocabulary, but
with restraint, so that the two chimneypieces imported from Italy
in 1772 and installed at Penrice appear as the exotics they are.

The influence of Penrice is obvious at Stouthall, Reynoldston,
nearby, built 1787–90 by the Swansea architect *William Jernegan*.
It is the best surviving house by Jernegan, who seems to have
been much employed in and around Swansea. His octagonal
villa, Marino, Swansea, of 1784, later became the centrepiece of
Singleton Abbey. His Sketty Hall, Swansea, of 1792, has been
greatly extended. Bryn-y-môr, Swansea, of *c.* 1820, has also been
much enlarged, but can still just be recognized for the neat villa
it originally was.

Penrice's villa character and its reticence, particularly in interior
decoration, seem to have established a fashion among local land-
owning families, and are found in a group of early C19 rebuilt
country seats, Merthyr Mawr House of 1806–8 by *Henry Wood* of
Bristol, Ewenny Priory of 1803–5, and the exquisite Castellau,
Llantrisant, probably datable before 1807. Castellau has bowed
ends and a delightful semicircular staircase rising in a bowed
projection at the back.

John Nash, at Rheola, Resolven, *c.* 1812, introduced important
new components to villa design. Rheola has two fronts at r.-angles
to one another, each with a canted projection at one end, so there
is no symmetry, even though the style is classical. The verandas
and deep, bracketed eaves are also innovations, which establish
Rheola as a descendant of Nash's pioneering Cronkhill, Shropshire, of 1802, where Picturesque principles were first applied to
an Italianate idiom. The veranda and Rheola-like eaves at Castellau suggest that it may have been remodelled *c.* 1820. Another
house influenced by Nash's Picturesque Italianate is Coed-
66 arhydyglyn, St George-super-Ely, completed in 1820, which is
made imposing outside by a Greek Doric entrance loggia, and
63 inside by a magnificent staircase reminiscent of James Wyatt, but
which in its details supports the attribution of the house to *Edward
Haycock*. The Cottage, St Hilary, is a close imitation of Rheola
on a modest scale, but is undated. Llansannor Court carries the
type into the 1840s.

Meanwhile, castellation remained as seductive as ever. By far
the most dramatic castle-style mansion in Glamorgan is Hensol
67 Castle, Pendoylan, as enlarged between *c.* 1790 and 1815. The
entrance front was heightened and an entrance tower with
cylindrical angle turrets applied to it, fully in the spirit of Robert
Adam's late castles. Unfortunately, it is not known who designed
this heroic piece. Clyne Castle, Oystermouth, polygonal in plan,

seems to have been castellated in 1800, but subsequent extensions and remodellings have compromised its character. The latest and the historically most significant of the group is Cyfarthfa Castle, Merthyr Tydfil, built in 1824–5 by *Robert Lugar* for William Crawshay, the great ironmaster, to overlook his Cyfarthfa Iron-works. Lugar was an exponent of Picturesque architecture as expounded by Humphry Repton and demonstrated by Nash, so Cyfarthfa is built on an L-plan punctuated by towers varied in size and form, but neither the architect nor his client seems to have had his heart in the project. The interiors combine a simple Gothic in the entrance hall with simple classicism in the reception rooms.

In the early C19 mansions which evoked abbeys were becoming as fashionable as those in castle style. As the ironmaster went to a prominent London architect for his mock castle, so the head of the principal copper-smelting family, J. H. Vivian, commissioned a London architect, *P. F. Robinson*, to fashion for him a mock abbey. Singleton Abbey, Swansea, grew from the nucleus of Jernegan's villa, Marino, acquired by Vivian in 1816. From *c.* 1818 until 1837 Robinson enlarged and transformed it into a full-scale Tudor-style mansion with many bay windows and an array of pinnacles, each front a different composition, and, rising from one corner, a tall thin tower, now unfortunately demolished. Inside, the Tudor style was carried on in ceilings with moulded beams and timber panelling and chimneypieces, combined with brought-in Continental pieces. In the park at Singleton Abbey *Robinson* constructed several cottages ornés, to serve as gate lodges and to accompany the home farm. Two survive, together with a Swiss chalet also to *Robinson*'s design. At Clyne Castle, Oystermouth, *Robinson* built a group of cottages ornés, now mostly altered and hard to recognize.

Not only industrialists wanted to evoke the past in their houses. The greatest Glamorgan land-owner of the period, Christopher Rice Mansel Talbot, son of Thomas Mansel Talbot, when he decided to re-establish Margam as the family seat, employed *Thomas Hopper* to design a vast neo-Tudor house, designated 68 Margam Abbey, but drawing on the forms and conventions of Tudor secular architecture. Its most memorable feature, the two-storey belvedere tower, is an elaborated quotation from the genuine Tudor tower at the family seat of Talbot's mother, Melbury House, Dorset. Margam Abbey, built 1830–5, was gutted internally in 1977, by fire which spared only the entrance vestibule and the soaring, vaulted staircase, Fonthill Gothic rather than neo-Tudor.

To conclude this section, the Round Houses at Glyntaff may 72 be mentioned. They are a pair of cylindrical tower houses with pointed windows, all that remains of the eccentric Dr William Price's 'Druidic museum', built *c.* 1838.

Urbanism

Before the end of the C18 Glamorgan's towns, however long their history, had failed to expand much beyond their medieval size.

In 1801 the population of Swansea was under 7,000 and that of Cardiff still remained under 2,000. Industrialization would soon change that. Morriston, Swansea, has the earliest formal street pattern, laid out soon after 1768 for John Morris's copper-workers by *William Edwards*, stonemason and dissenting minister. The grid pattern was typical of the period. Wide, straight Woodfield Street, with a church on axis at the s end, is recognizable as the spine of the original layout. The sole survivor of Morris's buildings for his workers is the fragment of the extraordinary Morris Castle, built *c*. 1775 as a block of flats and intended as an eye-catcher.

Mention of *William Edwards* makes this the appropriate place for a short excursus on his most celebrated achievement, the single-span stone bridge which he constructed over the River Taff p. at Pontypridd in 1756. When built, it had the widest span, 140 ft 525 (42.7 metres), of any arched bridge in Britain, and it was not surpassed in that respect for a further forty years. Constructionally the bridge was of the traditional Welsh mountain type, with a steeply curved profile and a crown barely twice the depth of the arch voussoirs. What made it revolutionary was the piercing of the spandrels with circular voids to equilibrate the counter-thrusts, a solution which Edwards reached only after three other attempts at building the bridge during the previous decade had failed. Of the other, smaller bridges in the county by or attributed to *Edwards*, only the altered and undated bridge at Pontardawe survives.

The development of the iron industry soon made Merthyr Tydfil by far the largest town in the county, but its growth was notoriously unplanned. Nothing remains of its early housing except a terrace datable to the 1820s in the suburb of Georgetown, and another of similar date put up by the Crawshays at Williamstown.* At Dowlais no iron-workers' housing remains, only the monumental stable block erected in the 1820s for the Dowlais Company's horses. The only formally composed workers' housing is the well-preserved set of three terraces which com- 71 prise Butetown, Rhymney, all that was built of a new town for the employees of the Union Iron Company, in the first decade of the c19.

These, then, are the meagre and scattered remains of early industrial housing, and something of a frontier character clings to them. Meanwhile, Swansea was developing the more genteel ambition of becoming a seaside resort. By 1791 substantial terraces had been built on The Burrows, s of the town centre and close to the shore. The surviving terraces are of the early c19, Prospect Place and Cambrian Place faced with red brick, the slightly later Gloucester Place stuccoed. Cambrian Place is a highly eccentric design, with giant relieving arches into which metal verandas are fitted over the first-floor windows, and may have been designed by *William Jernegan*, whose Assembly Rooms stand alongside.

*But see the reconstructed terrace of 1800 from Merthyr Tydfil at the Welsh Folk Museum, St Fagans.

Cardiff can show nothing like this. It has just two fragments of Neoclassical street architecture, the incomplete façade of what was presumably an inn in Castle Street, a composition worthy of Henry Holland, and No. 5 High Street, with attached columns and a pediment, built as a bank in 1835.

By *c.*1820 civic pride was beginning to find architectural expression, so that it is possible to point to a small group of EARLY C19 PUBLIC BUILDINGS. The Assembly Rooms at Swansea, 1810–21, have already been mentioned. *William Jernegan* cannot be said to have found a particularly appropriate civic expression, with his fussy Soanian façade. *Thomas Bowen* of Swansea at Neath Town Hall in 1820 employed free-standing Doric columns, though they are uncharacteristically slender for that date. His Swansea Guildhall of 1825–9 boasted a loggia with Greek Doric columns, but this was completely absorbed in the great enlargement of 1848 (*see* below). At Cowbridge Town Hall, 1830 by *Isaiah Verity*, quite a monumental effect is created by nothing more than three full-height relieving arches. The first town in Glamorgan to gain a really grand civic building was Bridgend in 1843, when *David Vaughan* erected the mighty Greek Doric Town Hall there. Sadly, this was pulled down in 1971. Its Greek Ionic counterpart, the Royal Institution of South Wales at Swansea, however, has been recently restored and serves as Swansea Museum. This pure and scholarly building was erected 1839–41 to the design of *Frederick Long* of Liverpool. A climax and conclusion was reached 1848–52 when Swansea Guildhall was enlarged by *Thomas Taylor*, a virtually unknown London architect, into a Corinthian palazzo with free-standing and attached upper columns deployed with a sophistication and bravura almost worthy of such an Italian Baroque architect as Juvarra.

Churches

CHURCHES have been held back to the end of this section because there is so little to mention. The chapel (now a ruin) built in the late C17 at Talygarn by Sir Leoline Jenkins, and the minimal classical enlargement of St Thomas, Neath, in 1730, are isolated survivals. Admittedly, the situation would have looked somewhat different had not *John Wood* of Bath's temple-like construction within the dilapidated Llandaff Cathedral, 1736–52, been eliminated a century later. MONUMENTS are almost as rare, if one discounts the rustic tablets erected in the decades around 1700 and dominating the interiors of churches such as Laleston and St Mary Hill. Otherwise only a few individual monuments are worth seeking out. From the early C18 there are the large, plain monument like a reredos erected at Margam after 1711, and at Ewenny, far superior, an exquisite cartouche of the best London workmanship (†1713). Good tablets are at Llantrithyd (†1700), Wenvoe (†1704) and Llanmihangel (after 1722, worthily commemorating a Lord Mayor of London). The tablet at Penrice of 1726 has pretty floral carving, and also at Penrice is the touching memorial to a baby (†1746), the inscription carved on a napkin held by a putto. A tablet at Cowbridge borrows its design from James Gibbs's *Book of Architecture* (1728), and a number of others pallidly reflect the same source. The best example of the fashion for coloured marbles in mid-century is the wall-monument at Penmark of *c*.1756. The best example of Adamesque Neoclassicism is the large tablet at Wenvoe, commemorating Peter Birt †1791, who had commissioned Adam to build him his house fifteen years earlier. Compared with that, the outsize wall-monument at St Thomas, Neath (†1794), looks very old-fashioned, with a sarcophagus of almost Rococo outline. It is signed by the mysterious *Jones Dunn Drew*.

INDUSTRIAL STRUCTURES

BY STEPHEN HUGHES

Industrial South Wales has been called the 'Crucible of the Industrial Revolution'. Glamorgan, the county at the centre of the main coalfield, was the world centre for no fewer than three metallurgical industries in the late C18 and C19, firmly based on the rich underlying resources of the 'Great Mineral Basin of South Wales'. This contains rich seams of coal interleaved in the lower measures with iron ore and also with the greenish-brown Pennant Sandstone that became the universal building material of the area. The underlying limestone layers surface around the edges of the coalfield and were exploited as a flux for the great ironworks, as well as being used in kilns in order to make lime to improve the surrounding agricultural land. In between the coal measures and the limestone are areas of millstone grit, amongst which, in areas of geological disturbance, could be found deposits of silica sand used to mould the reverberatory bricks necessary for the lining of furnaces.

However, despite these great mineral riches, only the coastal areas could be developed for heavy industry until cheap bulk transport for heavy industrial goods became available. The valley CANALS, built in the canal-mania years of the 1790s, facilitated large-scale industrial expansion on the shallow mineral deposits available in the Heads of the Valleys region to the N of the county. The resultant need for more intensive systems of upland transport gave rise to the world's largest system of EXPERIMENTAL RAILWAYS, constructed in the first three decades of the C19 – pioneering features on large overland railways that were to give the world the modern public locomotive railway.

Much else in this process of industrial development was to be of world significance. The south-western edge of the coalfield was accessible by coastal transport and formed the nearest source for the huge quantities of coal needed for the SMELTING of the COPPER reserves of Devon and Cornwall. The Swansea area became the world centre of this industry in the late C18 and C19.

In this period some 90 per cent of Britain's copper-smelting capacity was located within 20 m. (32 kilometres) of Swansea, along with many allied non-ferrous smelters producing brass, lead, nickel, silver, yellow-metal and arsenic.

Coal, iron ore and limestone deposits in near proximity to one another produced vast IRON-SMELTING AND -WORKING complexes around Merthyr Tydfil which gave it the largest iron-works in the world in the first half of the C19. South Wales was the greatest producer of iron in Great Britain, the world's first industrial nation, from 1796 until 1847.

The availability of iron and steel, of tin from Cornwall and of a reserve of metallurgical skill, allied with the insatiable market for TINPLATE in the USA made the Swansea Valley into the world centre of this trade as well. Tinplate – iron or steel bar rolled into sheets and coated with a wash of tin – had first been manufactured in Britain at Pontypool (Gwent) in the C17. By 1913 four out of five tinplate workers in Britain lived within 20 m. (32 kilometres) of Swansea, and many local towns were dependent on the industry.

In the late C18 and early C19 the COAL INDUSTRY was widely perceived as being subservient to the main consumers in the iron and copper industries. However, by the mid C19 the great steam coal trade was developing. Coal exported principally from Cardiff and later from Barry fuelled the huge steamship fleets of the world, and the Cardiff Coal Exchange determined the world price for such coal. Production in the South Wales coalfield peaked in 1913, and it was the largest coalfield in Britain from then until 1925.

Overall, then, Glamorgan had four industries arguably of international importance, served by an early railway system that pioneered the modern railway system of the globe. Very few subsidiary industries were developed alongside these, and what there were tended to be highly localized and of limited significance. The following introduction will largely examine the varying extent of survival of the buildings, structures and other works of the principal industries.

The Copper Industry

The record of survival for the remains of the earliest of the large industries, that of COPPER-SMELTING AND -WORKING, is not good. The Lower Swansea Valley Plan of 1967, for the clearance 'of the largest area of dereliction in Europe', made no provision for the retention of significant historic copper-smelting plant. Indeed, the best furnace remains from the industry are now to be found in Bristol, and the most significant copper 'battery' mills are to be found in the Greenfield Valley at Holywell (Clwyd), around Bristol and at Walthamstow, Greater London.

The first, Elizabethan, copper-smelter at Aberdulais, Tonna (1584–98), in the Vale of Neath has left no traces visible on the National Trust's museum site at Aberdulais, which instead has visible foundations and ruins of a C19 tinplate works. Traces of

the early works may instead be incorporated in the water-power
site opposite, S of the Aberdulais Falls, on or near where the C17
Dulais Rock public house still stands. In the second decade of
the C18 two copperworks were built at what became the world
centre of the copper industry in Swansea, but neither has left
visible traces. Illustrations survive of the Llangyfelach or Landore
Copper- (Lead- and Silver-) works, Swansea (1717–48), and
reveal it to have been a structure of some distinction. A monumental masonry aqueduct led water at a high level into the main
furnace house, or hall, of the works, which had a prominent clock-
turret on the roof. The flanking tall and slender chimneystacks
of the reverberatory furnaces were characteristic architectural
features of all the non-ferrous smelters.

Some fragments of the Great Workhouse of the White Rock
Copper- (and Brass-) works (1737–1871) survive, built into a
hillside at the White Rock Industrial Archaeology Park, Swansea.
These remains are of a very long, rectangularly planned reverberatory furnace house built of local Pennant Sandstone rubble
with brick dressings.

The building of the Fforest Copper- (and Brass-) works (1748–
1851) at Morriston, Swansea, introduced the idea of a more
formalized and conscious symmetrical layout, with architectural
trimmings to the factory buildings. The works consisted of a very
elegant series of Georgian buildings. Circular furnace houses
stood at the four corners of the site, with reverberatory furnaces
arranged against the walls and conical roofs pierced by four to
eight furnace flues. A parallel for the architectural form of this
arrangement can be seen in the surviving octagonal building of
the Bersham Ironworks near Wrexham (Clwyd), where air furnaces were similarly arranged against the enclosing walls. Circular
wall-openings, ventilation from the intense heat, were a prominent characteristic of these and many other buildings of the
Glamorgan metals industries; the Crawshay ironworks were
especially noteworthy for this feature. At the centre of the works
stood an octagonal refinery with a roof-top cupola, also with
reverberatory furnaces against its outer walls. The talented Glamorgan architect-engineer *William Edwards* was employed to
build furnaces and other masonry structures at Morriston,
Swansea, by Morris, Lockwood & Company. For example, the
three-arched masonry bridge, the Beaufort Bridge (demolished
in 1969), over the River Tawe connecting the Fforest Copperworks with the adjacent copper-rolling mills, has been attributed to him. He may also have been responsible for the design
of the smelting works. A public road ran over the bridge and into
the works through a pedimented gate with a clock in the gable
surmounted by a works cupola and bell. On its N side, flanking
the gate, stood a two-storey works laboratory, resplendent with
central Venetian windows on each storey. Unfortunately, the only
remains traceable today are a nondescript shed from the later use
of the site as a zinc works (until 1923) and the filled-in water-
feeder pond.

Pictorial evidence of the form of most of the large non-ferrous works is sadly incomplete. By the 1790s the main design consideration was the need to house the multiple ranks of reverberatory furnaces which are required for the successive roastings of ore involved in what was called the Welsh method of smelting. The ideal method of housing them was in large sheds similar to the (re-roofed) examples which survive on the Upper Bank Copperworks site at Swansea from the early C19. Design drawings for such a works by *William Jernegan* survive in the National Library of Wales. These were probably for the main smelting house of Morris, Lockwood & Company at their now demolished Landore Copperworks of *c.* 1790. Little of the exuberance of their earlier Fforest Copperworks is shown in this simple structure. Most noteworthy are the split levels dictated by the steep slopes down to the navigable River Tawe. The growing number of smelters on each side of the river had small navigable canals (sometimes penetrating underground) near their eaves levels. These supplied coal from the adjacent hillsides, while river quays and docks at their lower ground level brought non-ferrous ores from Devon and Cornwall and shipped out ingots and simple finished products.

A number of material innovations were pioneered in the structures built by the copper magnates. Herbert Mackworth's mansion and park buildings at Gnoll in Neath had copper glazing bars, as does the Whiteford Point Lighthouse, Llanmadoc, which lights the approaches to the copper smeltery ports of Penclawdd and Llanelli. This lighthouse also had, until recently, copper roofing sheets of a type that was earlier used on the buildings of the Swansea copperworks. The large quantities of iron-rich slag from the copper-smelting process were also cast into both building and coping stones of various designs. Nothing survives built of this material as grandiose as the castle folly at Clifton, Bristol. However, Morris Castle, Morriston, Swansea, has battlements, string courses and quoins made from slag. A huge retaining wall at the Hafod works (*see* below) is also built of this material, and the nearby workers' housing has garden walls capped by copper slag blocks. The gable walls of the Crown Copperworks at Skewen, near Neath, are also constructed of this material, as were parts of the Middle Bank Works at Swansea, complete with lunette windows. By far the largest non-ferrous (copper, silver and gold) works of the early C19 was the Vivians' Hafod works at Swansea, founded in 1810. Here for the first time a non-ferrous works employed thousands rather than hundreds, and approached the scale of the huge industrial enterprises centred on the ironworks of Merthyr Tydfil. The Hafod works remained in use for copper-rolling until 1980, and some of the specialist buildings of this, and the eventually linked Morfa Copperworks, survive. On the former Morfa works site stands an aisled, late C19 former electrical generating hall, with arcades of cast iron arches and a clock-turret on its roof. Inside the former main gate of the Morfa works is a mid-C19 stone-built office block, and outside is a large, brick-built early C20 replacement in classical style with stone dressings to its openings. Outside the former gate of the

Hafod works is a range of late C19 white-rendered buildings that were also offices.

The water-powered copper battery mills were not as numerous as the smelteries. One small building, adjacent to a wheelpit, remains at the site of Ynys-y-gerwyn Works, Aberdulais (*see* Tonna), in the Vale of Neath, and a similar stone building stood until the 1980s at the Fforest-uchaf forge site at Morriston, Swansea. The large rubble-stone building housing the present Swansea Museum stores on the Morfa works site was probably first built in 1828 as the steam-powered rolling mills for the Rose Copperworks company. The two tall, stone-built engine houses on the Hafod works site housed successive steam engines powering copper-rolling mills, which were operative in an adjacent lightly framed building (now demolished). The uniflow engine of 1910 in the second housing remains in place with its adjacent copper rolls.

Canals

Small canals served the metals works in the later C18 and penetrated deep underground to working coal faces. The first, the Clyn-du Level, at the Fforest Copperworks in Morriston, is thought to date to the building of the works in 1748, which would mean that it predates Gilbert and Brindley's more famous underground canals at Worsley, Lancashire, by some twelve years. Some of these local canals were later absorbed into the arterial valley canals, largely engineered by the families of *Thomas Dadford* (who had worked with James Brindley) and *Thomas Sheasby* in the 1790s. The main engineering features were the large number of locks provided and some quite impressive aqueducts, of which the three-arched Ystalyfera Aqueduct, the lofty single-arched Abercynon Aqueduct (now entirely a road-bridge) and the ten-arched Aberdulais Aqueduct, Tonna (constructed by the local engineer *William Kirkhouse* in 1823), are the main survivals. Technologically, these canals were remarkable for their provision of water to power a large number of important canal-side works. The Swansea Canal also demonstrates the early use in a British canal of hydraulic mortar (made from hydraulic limestone quarried from the site of Port Talbot docks); this was used as a waterproofing medium for locks and aqueducts instead of the hitherto more usual puddling clay. The first iron girder bridge to be built since those constructed by the ancient Chinese was probably the one built over the Glamorganshire Canal at Rhyd-y-car, Merthyr Tydfil, in the 1790s. The local engineering prodigy *Watkin George* was involved with the engineering of the canal. In the 1830s three cast iron aqueducts, ornamented with Tuscan columns, were cast at Neath Abbey Ironworks and erected over the Neath Canal in order to carry mountain streams.

Ironworks

The valley canals allowed the growth of large ironworks in the Heads of the Valleys region, although the western valleys of

Glamorgan could not easily share in this development until the application of Nielsen's hot blast process allowed the use of local anthracite coal in blast furnaces from 1837 onwards.

MASONRY BLAST FURNACES are very substantial structures, and there are more remains of these enduring monuments than of the comparatively delicate headstocks and engine houses of later collieries. Welsh blast furnaces and limekilns were almost universally built into the surrounding hillsides to facilitate the charging of furnaces with raw materials. In flatter areas expensive lifts had to be constructed to achieve this. The availability of coke as a fuel allowed the construction of the first multi-blast-furnace ironworks at Blaenafon (Gwent) in the 1780s. At the great Cyfarthfa Ironworks in Merthyr Tydfil, largest of such works in the world in the first and second decades of the C19, six of the seven blast furnaces survive. Also in Merthyr Tydfil are the lower parts of two other multi-furnace banks at the former Penydarren and Ynysfach works. The remains of the fourteen furnaces of the mighty Dowlais Ironworks at Merthyr Tydfil (largest ironworks in the world in the third and fourth decades of the C19) are now invisible underground. The site of the single row of eleven furnaces at the Ystalyfera Ironworks in the Swansea Valley is now only marked by the massive charging wall that remains in the valley-side. Other substantial multi-furnace remains survive from the ironworks at Hirwaun, at Gadlys, Aberdare, and at Banwen, Dyffryn Cellwen. Earlier charcoal-fuelled furnaces remain, un-recognizably, at Angelton, near Bridgend, and more impressively by Melincwrt Waterfall, Resolven, in the Vale of Neath. The introduction of a less crushable fuel, coke, allowed furnaces to assume the monumental proportions shown by the twin Neath Abbey Ironworks furnaces (arguably one of the most important industrial archaeology sites in Wales). The great steel-clad blast furnaces, visible from the M4, at the gigantic Port Talbot works show what resulted from the evolution of the circular metal-clad furnace in the later C19 and C20.

Furnaces in the later C18 and early C19 had their air-blast provided by massive WATER WHEELS, up to 50 ft (15.24 metres) in diameter, since it was water rather than coal which drove the early Industrial Revolution in upland Wales, as also in Scotland. This sometimes led to the construction of monumental AQUE-DUCTS, in order to provide enough water at the right elevation to power these wheels. The massive Bont Fawr (1824–7) at 77 Pontrhydyfen, with its four lofty masonry arches, followed in the tradition of the earlier copperworks aqueducts formerly at Llangyfelach and Taibach (Port Talbot).

From 1793 to 1796 the works water-feeders at Cyfarthfa, Merthyr Tydfil, were built in a composite wooden and iron aque-duct, '80 feet above the bed of the river . . . and . . . 606 feet in length', by the local engineers *Watkin George* and *William Aubrey*. It was an innovation of international technological significance. The surviving lower (iron) aqueduct named Pontycafnau (the 74 'bridge of troughs') once formed the substructure for the main high-level wooden river crossing and was itself the first iron aqueduct. It can be shown to have influenced the subsequent design of Telford's celebrated iron-built canal aqueducts at Longdon-upon-Tern (Shropshire) and Pontcysyllte (Clwyd).

Ironworks usually required WATER RESERVOIRS to feed their needs. Many, such as the Park Lake at Cyfarthfa Castle, were enclosed by low earth dams, but Neath Abbey Ironworks has a high masonry dam with cast iron outlet and overflow pipes.

As furnace banks were enlarged, and new ones constructed in the C19, it was usual to add long, comparatively narrow and high, stone-built ENGINE HOUSES, which totally enclosed steam engines pumping blasts of air into the adjacent furnaces. The most impressive is the now re-roofed blast-engine house at Ynysfach, Merthyr Tydfil. Its three storeys of semicircular arched openings framed in white limestone ashlar masonry piercing a shell of Pennant sandstone, are monumental hallmarks of the Crawshay
76 ironmasters. The Maesteg Ironworks blast-engine house forms the lobby to a new sports centre and that at the Gadlys Ironworks, Aberdare, has been refurbished as offices. All are ashlar, hipped-roof, monumental structures with semicircular arched openings. Other examples survive at Banwen (Dyffryn Cellwen), Tondu, Tonna and Venallt, Blaengwrach. The brick engine hall at Dowlais, Merthyr Tydfil, was a far larger structure, built to house several engines powering the mightiest of the furnace banks. The recently demolished brick blast-engine house at Landore Siemens Steelworks, Swansea (the fourth-biggest in the world when built c. 1865) had terracotta fittings and a roof-top tank.

At the charging bank, or top level of the blast furnaces, were serried ranks of KILNS for calcining the iron ore, as survive at Gadlys Ironworks, Aberdare, and rows of coking kilns, as in the bank surviving at Cefn Cwsg, Kenfig Hill.

At the foot of the furnaces were fairly simple gabled sheds, or CAST-HOUSES, with one gable end abutted against the furnace drawing-arch so that the molten iron could be discharged into furrows excavated within them. The best survivals of these structures in Glamorgan are at Cefn Cribbwr, Kenfig Hill (c. 1771).

FORGES were required to turn the cast iron 'pigs', or ingots, produced in these cast-houses into wrought iron. The masonry dam and substructures of anvils and hammers can be seen at the forge at Clydach (1784), which serviced Ynysgedwyn Ironworks (see Ynysmeudwy). The forges of Cyfarthfa Ironworks were massive structures with huge, curved cast iron trusses, with spacing circles in the apex of the roof above curved tie-pieces. A smaller cast iron roof can still be seen on the Neath Abbey Ironworks forge. Other domestic buildings built by the iron-masters were given similar roofs – such as the barn at Cog Farm, Sully. Forges built in the third and fourth decades of the C19 were given more sophisticated roofs with wrought iron tension and cast iron compression members. Examples of this were at the Pentrebach Forges, Merthyr Tydfil, and survive in the former ranges of the Crawshays' Treforest Tinplate Works. The intense heat of the forges was alleviated by open sides to the buildings. The Crawshays' forges at lower Cyfarthfa, Merthyr Tydfil, and

Hirwaun Ironworks had wall-plates supported with cast iron trusses. An upper wall-plate beam was supported by characteristic compressive rings of varying diameter, in turn supported by an arched lower member. The only visible surviving example of this arrangement is in the smithy of the Crawshays' Treforest Tinplate Works. 75

The use of iron sheeting for roofs (a local precursor of corrugated iron) is recorded, and local ironworks produced PRE-FABRICATED CAST IRON CONSTRUCTIONAL KITS of interlocking cast iron beams. A mid-C19 example of this has been moved from the Brown Lenox Chainworks at Pontypridd to the Ynysfach Engine House, Merthyr Tydfil. The Neath Abbey Ironworks produced many integral steam engine and flooring units for colliery engine houses, of which an example can still be seen at Glyn Pits, Pontypool (Gwent).

A problem of the C19 South Welsh economy was the lack of development in specialized metal goods manufacturing, such as took place in the locality of consumer markets in the English Midlands. Cornish influence resulted in the establishment of a Trevithick ENGINE MANUFACTORY at Abernant Ironworks, Aberdare, and of the engine and general manufactory at Neath Abbey Ironworks. The building for the latter survives among the pre-eminently important remaining structures of the Neath Abbey Ironworks, but is lacking its original cast iron roof. Other specialist manufacturing ironworks developed by the mid C19 were the Ivor Ironworks in Merthyr Tydfil and the Millbrook Ironworks in Swansea.

Early Railway Structures

The metals works of South Wales necessitated the construction of a huge network of HORSE-WORKED RAILWAYS – perhaps some 1,800 m. (c. 2,900 kilometres) in total length – in order to connect these works, with their attendant mines and quarries to the canals and coastal docks. A large number of internationally significant early railway structures survive in Glamorgan, in a density not equalled elsewhere in the world. By the 1690s wooden surface railways were being constructed in Glamorgan, and by 1760 the first recorded intermediate tunnel on a surface railway had been built at Landore, Swansea. In 1779 the first all-iron rail seems to have been ordered from Coalbrookdale by the Swansea copper manufacturer John Morris. It was perhaps inevitable that the largest ironworks should produce the first iron railway bridges.

Pontycafnau, Merthyr Tydfil, was authorized in 1793, and this 74 A-frame structure, with a span equal to that of the Cyfarthfa Ironworks forges (formerly standing alongside), bears a striking resemblance to a roof truss. The works engineer *Watkin George* had trained as a carpenter, and the main members of the bridge are held together by dovetail and mortice-and-tenon joints. The rail deck runs on a cast iron leat housing, and the central strut originally extended upwards to support a second aqueduct at a high level. The abutments of a second bridge of similar pattern remain in front of the Cyfarthfa furnaces. The first railway bridge with a date cast-in is the arched girder span of 1811 at Robertstown, Aberdare. It should be noted that these, and other such structures, predate George Stephenson's iron Gaunless Bridge, built in 1825 on the Stockton and Darlington Railway, County Durham.

A wrought iron lattice-girder bridge carried the Penydarren Tramroad over the Morlais Brook in Merthyr Tydfil, but this undated structure collapsed in the 1970s.

Many fine masonry arches and viaducts remain from the early railway system in South Wales. Timber trestle bridges were widely used on the extensive 'public railways', sanctioned under the terms of the 1790s Canal Acts, but were often replaced by stone structures. Very impressive large railway arches include that at Quakers Yard on the Penydarren Tramroad. Multi-arched viaducts include examples at Bridgend, Port Talbot and Cwmavon.

Before the development of steam excavators and of joint stock companies with large capital resources, the construction of major earthworks on these early lines was not feasible, and instead high causeways were used to cross declivities. These early C19 civil engineering works consisted of a core of earth or rubble sandwiched between parallel stone walls. They were generally constructed of local Pennant Sandstone rubble with stepped offsets reducing the thickness of retaining walls as they rose. By far the most impressive surviving example is that adjacent to the Hirwaun Ironworks, crossing high above the Afon Cynon on a substantial segmental arch.

The world's first recorded run by a steam locomotive took place on the Penydarren Tramroad in 1804 between Merthyr and Abercynon. Among the many remains of its course is the tunnel through the charging bank of the Plymouth Ironworks in Merthyr Tydfil. The county saw many other early locomotive experiments, and indeed the early regular use of steam locomotives.

The world's first railway passenger service ran on the Oystermouth Railway from Swansea by 1807, and the station, or stopping-place, at The Mount in Swansea (in front of the present Swansea Museum) must have been the world's first station, though it is unclear whether the early coach was stationed alongside any huts or other buildings marking the point of embarkation.

A remarkable collection of early railway WAREHOUSES in Wales from the second to the fourth decades of the C19 includes that at Porthcawl Docks.

The Coal Industry

The navigable rivers of south-western Glamorgan and the various canals and feeder railways gradually facilitated the expansion of an export trade in coal. Together with the coal-hungry metals works, they helped the Glamorgan-centred South Wales coalfield to become the largest in the United Kingdom, and the world centre of steam coal supplies for the mighty steamship fleets of the world.

Architecturally, the main remains of the COAL INDUSTRY are the engine houses for the winding and pumping engines which served the thousands of shafts driven into the Glamorgan soil. The rate of reuse for these handsome structures is not good, and from the five hundred or more pits operating in South Wales in the peak year of the industry in 1913, only a handful are destined to remain.

The earliest active coalfield in Glamorgan lay where the coal measures touched the coast around Swansea and Neath. Recorded activity began in the C14, and by the C18 deep mining had started, with substantial water leats being constructed to drive large winding and pumping water-engines. The intensity of activity was such that local artisans could gain the experience necessary to become skilled engineers. John Morris, of Morriston, the copper and coal magnate, employed a Mr Powell, who had been a blacksmith and who, Morris said, 'only had to perceive in order to comprehend and from comprehending, to execute.' He worked for Morris from 1763, until he was scalded to death while repairing one of his steam engines in 1783. In that time he had applied his steam engines to rotary motion, and hence to a coal-winding capability (in addition to their previous pumping ability), years before James Watt was to do so. The architectural evidence for this achievement survives in the adjoining part of the Swansea coalfield area at Gwernllwynchwith, Llansamlet, where a small engine house of the long, narrow and high dimensions indicative of a rotary-engine housing survives on the site of a coal pit in use before 1784. In a neighbouring field in Llansamlet, on the N side of the M4, survives an early C19 pumping-engine house at the former Scott's Pit (1817–19). This tall, Pennant Sandstone structure is typical of such features, in which masonry and steam engine formed a composite machine, the thick beam-bob wall of the engine house supporting the pivot of the engine beam. The beam of the engine extended through a large opening in the beam-bob wall to drive pumping rods which extended downwards into the shaft of the colliery adjacent to the housing.

Other similar engine houses survive substantially intact at Felindre and at Crimea Colliery, Ystalyfera (c. 1854), in the area in and around the Swansea Valley. The Bryngwyn engine house (1868), Bedwas, in the Rhymney Valley, housed an unusual inverted Cornish engine.

The development of a large steam coal industry, independent of the previously dominant ironworks, was achieved despite the fragmented pattern of ownership within the coalfield. Local entrepreneurs played a large part in developing localized concerns based on existing technology, housed in fairly traditionally designed structures. When William Thomas Lewis sank the Bertie and Trefor shafts at Trehafod in the Rhondda, in the period 1878–90, he housed the compound steam engines which powered the colliery in long, two-storey engine houses of rusticated stone with characteristic chapel-like semicircular-headed windows.

They now form the centrepiece of the Rhondda Heritage Park, Trehafod. Large open ranges of boilers had tall chimneystacks alongside, but the surviving engines in their houses at Lewis Merthyr, Trehafod, at Tŷmawr, Hopkinstown, and Elliot East Colliery, New Tredegar, also have small cast iron pipe exhausts extending up their rusticated stone walls to terminate above the line of their roofs.

79   The fact that the neighbouring Hetty Shaft (Tŷmawr) at Hopkinstown, alongside Lewis Merthyr Colliery, belonged not to W.T. Lewis but to the Great Western (Railway) Colliery Company indicates the extent of the fragmentation of ownership in the coalfield. This fragmentation in turn limited the capital available for widespread mechanization, or for sustained efforts to establish a technological lead over rival mid-European coalfields. In the decade to 1913, the Powell Duffryn Steam Coal Company, the largest on the coalfield, laid out pits on more modern lines. There was one large, central engine house for the two shafts at each colliery, with large winding engines, pumps, compressors and generators, and a second large building for colliery workshops. The interiors of these buildings were neatly tiled, with Art Nouveau decoration between the great arcades of semicircular arched openings (themselves supporting overhead crane tracks) along the flanking walls. The buildings of Penallta

80 Pit, Gelligaer (1906–9), housed one of the last steam-driven sets of machinery (electrified in 1962–3). The larger, but recently demolished Britannia Pit (1910–14), near Bargoed, was similar in form, but a more restricted site resulted in its being the first in the world to be powered totally by electricity (generated at adjacent steam-powered collieries). The similar Taff Merthyr, Trelewis, 1928, has been demolished, but Tower, Hirwaun, 1944, remains, with large parts of its original electrical equipment.

Perhaps the most evocative symbol of the industry is the COLLIERY HEADGEAR. Pre-C18 pits, and others built in that century, had simple hand-winding winches built over them, similar to those still seen on village water-drawing wells. More elaborate wooden frameworks with a low pulley over the shaft accompanied the introduction of horse-drawn winding engines (gins) from the end of the C18. Low cast iron frames accompanied the use of water-balanced winding tubs in the early C19. Large high-level winding pulleys on wooden supports came in with the introduction of big engine houses, and steam-winding and pumping arrangements, at the shaft-tops, which were required for the raising of railway 'tubs' or 'drams' from the depths below.

Technical development and the increasing depth of shafts resulted in the gradual replacement of pitch pine support towers by lattice-girder towers. The design of these depended on the house style of the colliery company concerned. Merthyr Vale Colliery (1869) at Aberfan, built by Nixon's Navigation Company, had a tower built of sections of bull-head rail, which were bound together at intervals by wrought iron bands riveted to the rail flanges. Originally the tower was braced by cables rather than the more orthodox diagonal struts. The recently demolished headgear of Harris's Navigation Pits at Deep Navigation Colliery, Treharris (1872), were supremely elegant structures, with shallow, long bracing struts from the great beam-engine houses, themselves braced by arched trusses extending down towards the base of the pit towers. The surviving twin headgear (1878–90) at the Lewis Merthyr Navigation Collieries Ltd pit at Trehafod is similarly designed, but lacks some of the finesse of the elegant arch-braced structure formerly to be seen at Deep Navigation Colliery. Two late steel lattice-girder headframes survive at Cefn Coed Colliery, Crynant (1926–7).

By the end of the C19 wrought iron and steel joists were already beginning to replace lattice-girder towers. The earliest remaining one accompanies the Hetty Shaft winding-engine house built at 79 the Great Western Colliery at Trehafod in 1875. The extremely restrictive, long, narrow site meant that the diagonal struts for this headframe rose at a very steep angle, because of the limited space available between engine house and headframe. Twin headframes of rolled steel in more conventional form also survive at Penallta (1906–8). Other specialized colliery features, such as the 80 distinctive fan-houses, are mentioned in the Gazetteer.

The Tinplate Industry

The rise of an additional metals-centred industry paralleled that of the coal industry in the mid and later C19. This was the TINPLATE INDUSTRY, from which a remarkable range of buildings, built 1834–5 by the great Crawshay dynasty of Cyfarthfa Ironworks, survives at Treforest. This has the best surviving 75 ranges of tinning bays in Glamorgan and a set of early wrought and cast iron roofs. This great range of buildings is the most complete of any works associated with the huge iron-making concerns of Glamorgan.

The American demand for tin-plated utensils stimulated a trade based on the lower Swansea Valley, where parts of works survive at the Beaufort Tinplate Works, Llansamlet, and at Pontardawe and Briton Ferry. As with colliery and ironworks housing, the dominant architectural theme was great austere masonry sheds with semicircular-headed windows and doors, structures that had a powerful looming presence among the terraces and chapels of the workers.

Harbours and Docks

Metal ore imports and refined metal and coal exports resulted in the construction of a great series of HARBOURS along the coast. The first enclosed dock was probably that built by Sir Humphrey Mackworth on the E side of the Neath Estuary (begun 1695–7), which could take craft of up to 100 tons (101.6 tonnes). A much larger dock was that built, 1796–8, at the seaward end of the Glamorganshire Canal, S of Cardiff, where a mile-long basin could accommodate one hundred ships of up to 200 tons (203.2 tonnes). The first Bute Dock at Cardiff (1839) accommodated

300 larger ships. Dock schemes were also started in the C19 at Penclawdd, Swansea, Neath, Briton Ferry, Port Talbot, Porthcawl, Penarth and Barry. These ports, with their monumental masonry quays and piers, much of which survive, were built largely to deal in bulk raw materials and so did not require the large ranges of warehouses that were necessary to house the high-value imports taken to the docks at London, Liverpool or Bristol. Architecturally most distinctive were the engine houses required to pressurize the hydraulic power pipes leading to the great lock gates and equipment of each of the ports. A constant reserve of power was maintained by the steam engines raising heavy weights to the top of pressurized water columns in towers adjacent to the engine houses, as at Swansea South Dock.

Imposing Docks Offices survive at Cardiff, Penarth, Barry and Swansea, whilst several warehouses survive at Porthcawl, Swansea and Cardiff.

Some structures of great significance were connected with the ports and their associated traffic. Large amounts of imported grain came into the growing population centres of Cardiff and Swansea. Weaver's Mill and silos, Swansea (1900–2), recently demolished, formed the first multi-storey concrete-framed building in Britain.

William Jernegan's cast iron lighthouse (1804) on the w pier of the tidal Swansea Harbour was one of the first architectural uses 73 of that material. His Mumbles Lighthouse, Oystermouth, *c.* 1793, is probably the best preserved of all the originally coal-fired lighthouses in Britain. The slender tower of the Flat Holm Light, Barry, is a remarkably tall light, again originally coal-fired.

Passenger Railways

The existence of the intensively developed heavy transport system, centred on canals and early horse-drawn railways, meant that PUBLIC LOCOMOTIVE RAILWAYS were built relatively late in Glamorgan. The restrictive terrain also meant that *Isambard Kingdom Brunel* built his Taff Vale Railway, 1836–41, to a standard gauge. One particularly fine Brunel viaduct with chamfered arches and capitals survives at Quakers Yard. His only timbered viaduct to remain in use survives on the South Wales Railway (1845–52) mainline at Loughor. Other buildings and structures by him remain at Swansea, Bridgend and Briton Ferry. Much 78 later is the impressive swing-bridge over the river at Neath, 1892–4.

NONCONFORMIST CHAPELS

The chapel is the building type people most readily associate with Glamorgan. As workers and their families poured into the county, and in particular into the Valleys, to find employment first in the metalworks and then in the coal mines, the chapels they built became not only places of worship but, with their Sunday schools, the centres of social life and culture. Now, when the physical evidence of Victorian industry has almost entirely disappeared, many of the chapels remain, eloquent evidence of aspirations that reached beyond everyday life. Dwindling congregations and lack of statutory protection, which means that there is little incentive to convert chapels to other uses, have led to the destruction of all too many, but former industrial settlements with a chapel on every other corner can still be found. Good examples are Skewen, Cefncoedycymer, and, most remarkable, Trecynon at Aberdare. By the last third of the C19 chapel-going had become fashionable among the middle classes of burgeoning Swansea and Cardiff, as is demonstrated most vividly by the stately Nonconformist temples of the early 1870s at Swansea and Morriston, and the lofty Gothic towers and spires of Nonconformity in the suburbs of Cardiff, and in Penarth and Barry at the turn of the century.

The proliferation of places of worship was also the result of the multiplicity of denominations. The first Baptist congregation had been established as early as the 1650s by John Myles at Ilston on Gower, where something of its place of worship can still be seen. The Baptists later became the most prolific chapel-builders of all, creating by reaction a late C19 fashion for immersion fonts in Established churches (*see* especially Gelligaer). The first Method-ist place of worship in the whole of Wales was built in 1742 at Groeswen, on a hilltop above Caerphilly. Howell Harris of Tre-vecca in Breconshire, who inspired this initiative, was one of the founders of Calvinistic Methodism, the exclusively Welsh form of Methodism which even today remains separate from the Wesleyan mainstream. John Wesley preached in Glamorgan, and Wesleyan Methodist chapels, though less numerous than those of the Calvinistic Methodists, are found throughout the county. The Calvinistic Methodists are also known as Presbyterians, not to be confused with the Scottish Presbyterians, for whom an expensive chapel was built in the 1860s in both Swansea and Cardiff. The Independents, counterpart of the Congregationalists in England, also built numerous chapels. Chapels for Unitarians and Quakers are much rarer, reflecting the limited impact of these traditions in the county. Neither, furthermore, experienced the further split-ting factor which has done so much to multiply chapels: the establishment of complementary, or rival, Welsh-speaking and English-speaking congregations by the Baptists, the Inde-pendents, the Calvinistic Methodists and Wesleyan Methodists.

The Baptists of Ilston made use of an abandoned medieval chapel. So the first time a new building was used to focus the identity of a new denomination was in 1742, when Howell Harris's Methodists built their 'New House' at Groeswen, Caerphilly, to be both place of worship and school. It consists of little more than a room above a semi-basement, overshadowed by the adjoining later C19 chapel. Groeswen is very unusual, in that the original building was retained when a new one was built. Normally con-gregations which outgrew their chapels showed no sentimentality, but rebuilt on the same site, in many cases more than once. So

the surviving chapels, almost as numerous for the period 1890–
1914 as for the entire period up to that date, are in relatively few
cases the original ones. A spur to rebuilding in the early C20 was
given by the 'Revival' of 1904–5, which generated great religious
fervour. But its effects seem to have worn off quite quickly, as
chapel-building was slowing down by 1914, and in the post-war
period came virtually to a standstill.

For the purposes of architectural analysis, it is the exteriors of
chapels which count. But it may be helpful to start with some
generalizations about their interiors.

All denominations conformed to certain principles of interior
layout. The pulpit raised at one end is invariably the focal point,
with below it the 'big seat', a broad enclosure with seating for the
deacons or elders of the congregation. Wesleyan Methodists,
however, have a communion rail instead of a 'big seat'. Baptists,
once they had come to terms with the idea of baptizing within the
chapel, raised the pulpit above a baptismal tank, boxed in except
when a baptism was to take place. Permanently visible immersion
fonts can be found in a few chapels (Tredegarville, Roath, Cardiff,
and Hope, Bridgend).

Seating for the congregation was designed to provide for the
largest possible numbers – seating for 1,000 is not uncommon –
so pews cover the maximum floor area, leaving two fairly narrow
access aisles, and frequently extending to the far wall on either
side of the pulpit. Until at least the 1860s low box pews were the
norm. Galleries were (with the rarest exceptions) intended, and
almost always provided, on three sides, or in the grander chapels
on all four sides, resting on thin cast iron supports. Around the
turn of the century some Gothic chapels were laid out on Anglican
lines, the galleries set back inconspicuously in transepts.

A large organ, above and behind the pulpit, a characteristic
feature of many chapels, seems not to have become normal until
the last quarter of the C19, and many organs are later insertions.

Decoration, spurned in early chapels, is generally confined to
an arched feature on the wall behind the pulpit, gallery fronts
enriched with joinery or pierced metalwork, and the embellishment of the ceiling with plaster roses, some of which distract
attention from the ventilation louvres made necessary by gas
lighting. At the turn of the century many chapels had their
windows filled with bold abstract stained glass in designs reminiscent of C. R. Mackintosh or Art Nouveau, and occasionally
stained glass with figure subjects can be found.

Early Chapels

Chapels before the 1850s were simple, utilitarian buildings with
rendered walls and no dressed stonework. The internal layout of
pulpit and galleries dictated the pattern of windows and doors.
Since so many congregations in the C18 had worshipped in converted cottages, it is not perhaps surprising that early purpose-
built chapels were arranged cottage-wise, with a long wall, not a
gable end, facing the road.

The early Calvinistic Methodist chapel at Aberthin, of 1780 (now altered), was, unusually, distinguished by having pointed heads to the windows. The Quaker meeting house at Neath, built c. 1799, is more domestic-looking, with two storeys of sash windows. The chapel at Llangynwyd, dated 1795, has segment-headed windows. The earliest surviving example of the typical early C19 long-wall formula is at the former Unitarian chapel at Bridgend, dated 1795. This has two tall, round-headed windows in the centre of the façade and two storeys of windows in the outer bays, which makes for a curious, syncopated appearance. It relates to an internal layout where the pulpit stood backing on to the front wall between and below the central windows, while the outer windows let in light above and below galleries. At Bridgend the entrance is not in this façade but at one of the short ends. Here, furthermore, the interior has been modernized. The Unitarian chapel at Clydach, isolated on a high-lying moor, is another exceptionally early example (1801) of this layout. A mature version of the arrangement is the Calvinistic Methodist chapel at Llantrisant of 1826, in spite of refurbishment in 1886. Here two 83 doorways in the long wall, flanking the centre pair of windows, give access to the interior of the chapel between the pulpit and the ends of the galleries. The stone-faced Cymmer chapel at Porth, 1834, is another well-preserved example, though it is due to be dismantled for re-erection in the nearby Rhondda Heritage Park, Trehafod. At St Fagans a chapel of this type, dated 1837, with its pair of entrance doorways sheltered by a later porch, stands abandoned. The large Baptist chapel at Rhymney, built in 1839, and surviving little altered inside, has the pulpit backing on to an internal lobby and a theatrical arrangement of pews, angled towards the preacher. The Baptist chapels at Peterston-super-Ely dated 1843, and at Cefncoedycymer, dated 1844, have also survived well, and so have the Independent chapel built in 1850 for the copper-workers at Cwmavon and the charming square-plan chapel at Godre'rhos, Crynant, of 1855, which concludes the series.

The square-plan chapel crowned by a pyramid roof was normally laid out with the pulpit and minister's seat at the far end from the entrance, and galleries on the other three sides. Entrance might be through a central doorway, flanked by long windows, continued down across the line of the galleries, as at the well-preserved Independent chapel at Cowbridge, 1828; or there might 81, 82 be two widely spaced doorways, with windows above them, and in the centre windows above and below, making a regular two-storey façade, as at the well-preserved Welsh Baptist chapel at Hengoed, Ystrad Mynach, 1829. Here in embryo are the two formulations of classical chapel façade which will last beyond the end of the C19, the one a unified, full-height composition, the other with two storeys of openings.

Other square-plan chapels with two-storey façades are at Merthyr Tydfil, 1829, Llantwit Major, 1830, Swansea, 1830, and Aberdare, 1841. The Cowbridge type is used in a number of early rectangularly planned chapels where the entrance is in the gable end, as at Lisvane, Cardiff, 1856, Tondu, 1859, and Rhymney, 1862. The gable-end chapel at Pentyrch of 1862 is unusual in having its pulpit backing on to the entrance wall. The much earlier gable-end chapel at Parkmill, Ilston, dated 1822, is quite exceptional, having pedimented side porches. It was paid for by Lady Diana Barham, like half-a-dozen other smaller and simpler chapels on the Gower Peninsula.

The only other early plan for chapels is octagonal, and of this there is a single representative, the chapel in Lombardic style built at Margam in 1838 under the eye of C.R.M. Talbot of Margam Abbey, clearly a special case. It was rebuilt in 1976 on a new site at Port Talbot.

All the chapels mentioned so far, with the exception of the last, accept the tradition launched by Wren's City churches that round-headed windows are all that is needed to establish an ecclesiastical character. It would be going too far to call them classical. But from the 1840s the inherent classicism in the tradition was made more and more explicit.

Classical Chapels c. 1840–1914

The earliest chapels with façades which demonstrate a serious grasp of classical design are both of 1841. They are, not surprisingly, at the iron boom town of Merthyr Tydfil. Both, it appears, were designed by *T. H. Wyatt*, who had in 1838 built the Market Hall there, now demolished. Both of Wyatt's chapels are two-storeyed, of three broad bays, both with the centre bay brought forward slightly under a pediment. At both, the columned central doorway is of Serliana derivation. The town-centre High Street Baptist chapel, though stuccoed, makes quite a powerful architectural statement from these ingredients, while the less prominently placed Zion Baptist chapel depends on good proportions and sophisticated stone-cutting for its effect. For a London-based architect to be involved in chapel design was highly unusual, and for a further quarter of a century local masons, surveyors, and in particular ministers, remained responsible for it.

Neither of Wyatt's chapels has retained its original interior. But two others in this area give a fine impression of the large scale and theatrical character achieved by this date. Zoar (now Zoar-Ynysgau Welsh Congregational) chapel, Merthyr Tydfil, 1841–2, by the Rev. *B. Owen*, is externally crude compared with Wyatt's contemporary chapels, but it has a spectacular interior, the deep gallery round three sides angled in seven cants to face the pulpit at the far end. Steeply raked seating up here complements the box pews below. Originally there were upper-level windows on all four sides. The almost equally large Welsh Baptist chapel at Rhymney of 1839, though somewhat remodelled in 1859, has already been mentioned for its seating angled towards the pulpit, and also has high-level lighting all round. The earliest firmly dated chapel with a gable in the form of a full-width pediment is the Welsh Baptist chapel at Aberdare of 1851. The earliest use of pilasters to carry a pediment comes a year later, also at Aberdare, at the Welsh Baptist chapel at Trecynon, by *T. Joseph*. The English Wesleyan chapel at Aberdare of 1859 provides the first proper temple front, with full-height pilaster strips carrying the pediment. But all three are modest, and hardly acceptable as the self-conscious harbingers of a new concept.

The 1860s show a new maturity both in design and structure, for from now on it becomes normal for chapel fronts to be faced with rubble-stone with cut stone dressings. The full temple concept, with proper Tuscan pilasters carrying a pediment, arrives in the 1860s in a group of Welsh Baptist chapels in West Glamorgan, the later two certainly designed by the Rev. *H. Thomas*. They are at Neath, 1862–3, where there is a central Venetian window, at Clydach, 1868, and Morriston, Swansea, 1869–70. Long, thin windows between the pilasters inevitably detract from their templar character, and at the Morriston chapel, which is free-standing and has a splendid galleried interior, give a misleading impression of unimpeded internal space. Far more ambitious temple-chapels were soon erected in the area. At Morriston itself in 1872–3 there rose the mightiest of them all, the Tabernacl 85, 86 Welsh Congregational chapel, designed by *John Humphrey*.[*] This has coupled Corinthian columns on the entrance front and pilasters down the flanks, where two storeys of windows make clear that the interior is galleried, as indeed it is on all four sides. But the exterior is much more than a temple. Projections at the sides of the entrance façade acknowledge the gallery stairs; an arcade imposes itself between columns and pediment; and there is even an elaborate steeple. At the same time, in the centre of Swansea, the Argyle Welsh Presbyterian chapel, 1873 by *Alfred Bucknall*, displayed a temple front with four recessed Composite columns, but Doric pilasters down the flank, and *George Morgan* of Carmarthen, widely employed by Baptists, put up the Mount Pleasant chapel, 1874–6, fronted by the only proper free-standing portico to survive on any chapel in the county. Here too the façade extends either side of the portico to accommodate the gallery stairs, and there are five entrance doorways, one in each bay. Inside, the gallery arrangements are unexceptional, but the organ at the far end is set within a giant Serliana opening. The end of this short-lived phase is marked by the Siloh Congregational chapel at Landore, Swansea, dated 1876–7, by *T. Freeman* and *Thomas Thomas*. Capel Eglwys Bach at Pontypridd, of 1899, with its pediment over the centre bay carried on pairs of giant Corinthian half-columns, is a belated throw-back to a formula otherwise completely outmoded at the end of the century.

The name of the Rev. *Thomas Thomas* of Landore is associated with a variant of the pedimented chapel. This is where a giant relieving arch breaks up into the underside of the pediment, in order to make way for a tripartite window above the door. This may be an echo of the way Wren treated the transept ends at St

---

[*]This is how he signed his name, not 'Humphreys', the form found in printed sources.

Paul's Cathedral, or it may be derived from a Palladian motif popularized by Lord Burlington (York Assembly Rooms). The idea doubtless came from engravings of such buildings. Thomas's adaptation required long, narrow side windows to light the gallery stairs. Pilasters may or may not be introduced to carry the pediment. The most characteristic examples of Thomas's work are Ebenezer Independent chapel, Swansea, 1862–3, and the Independent chapel at Nantyffyllon and Tabor chapel, Maes-
84 ycwmmer, Ystrad Mynach, both dated 1876, both the latter with pilasters. The chapel at Resolven of the previous year is less ambitious and has been reconstructed. The Calvinistic Methodist chapel at Cwmavon, dated 1873, may also be by Thomas.The motif of the giant relieving arch was picked up elsewhere in the early 1860s. The Welsh Presbyterian chapel at Bridgend by *Robert Roberts*, 1862, is a fine example, with Ionic pilasters. By far the most satisfying rendition, scholarly and well proportioned, is *John Humphrey*'s Mynyddbach Congregational chapel, Treboeth, Swansea, of 1865–6. Its interior, galleried all round under a coved plaster ceiling, anticipates his Tabernacl chapel, Morriston. The giant relieving arch also turns up on chapel façades at Neath (1864–6), Aberdare (*E. Griffiths*, 1867), Skewen (1868), and again in the 1890s over a wider area, at Coity (1890), Cwmaman (1891), Pontycymer (1892).

Some temple-like chapels are in a Romanesque or Lombardic style, with corbelled gables rather than pediments. The Welsh Wesleyan chapel of 1853 at Merthyr Tydfil, attributed to *I. K. Brunel*, and now a mere shell, is the earliest example. The most ambitious essay in this style is *Habershon & Pite*'s Methodist chapel at Canton, Cardiff, of 1869. The same firm built the Methodist church in central Swansea in similar style in 1872. *George Morgan* of Carmarthen, whose natural vocabulary was classical, built Lombardic Baptist chapels in Swansea (Dinas Noddfa, Plas-marl), 1884, and in Merthyr Tydfil, 1896–8.

The two-storey type of façade also found a full-blooded classical statement in the 1860s. *E. Roberts*'s Tabernacl chapel at Pontypridd, 1861, gives the pedimental form of the gable a new emphasis, the cornice mouldings strongly projecting on moulded brackets. But this was not the way forward. Much more thoughtful and impressive is *J. Hartland & Son*'s Tabernacl Welsh Baptist chapel of 1865 in the centre of Cardiff. Here a clear demarcation is made between the recessed centre, with a row of four arched doorways below and a row of four windows in an arcade above, and the flanking stair-turrets. The roof is invisible behind a solid parapet. The interior too is exceptional, its flat ceiling coffered, and the galleries extended round all four sides. *Hartland & Son* had already in 1863 built the Methodist Free chapel, also in central Cardiff, but nothing more is heard of them after the mid 1860s as designers of chapels, the younger Hartland dying in 1869. Façades with flanking stair-turrets, however, enjoyed a modest popularity. The sub-classical Independent chapel at Tonypandy, 1867–8, is a good example; the Romanesque Methodist chapel at Oystermouth, 1877–8 by *A. Totten*, is another, where full-height towers were intended. At the Welsh Calvinistic Methodist chapel at Pentre, 1881 by the Rev. *William Jones*, the centre is pedimented but the side turrets do not project. Jones's design was elaborated a quarter of a century later in the majestic Welsh Independent chapel, also at Pentre, designed by his son-in-law, *W. D. Morgan*, 1906–7.

By the end of the century classical chapels were rarer than Gothic ones, but unhackneyed examples round the turn of the century are to be found, for example *Seward & Thomas*'s Welsh Congregational chapel of 1893–4 at Barry, and *Jones & Thornley*'s Baptist chapel at Penarth, 1895, with an upper arcade and even a clerestory. One architect in the Valleys upheld the classical flag to the end. He was *R. S. Griffiths* of Tonypandy, whose plain but grand Welsh Baptist chapel at Penygraig of 1902 was designed in collaboration with *D. Pugh Jones* (for whom *see* below, p. 110). Griffiths's major work is the Calvinistic Methodist chapel at Tonypandy, begun 1908, with its subtly decorated interior, but in the same year he remodelled the Welsh Baptist chapel at Treorchy, and in 1909–10 built the Calvinistic Methodist chapel at Ynyshir. A contemporary chapel practitioner was *W. Beddoe Rees* of Cardiff. In his book *Chapel Building* of 1903 he argued the case for classicism as the appropriate style for chapels, but in practice he had to bend to the wind of fashion, and only a minority of his surviving chapels are in a classical style. His Welsh Independent chapel at Glyncorrwg of 1904 was an early work and is now spoilt. Half a decade later he put up three chapels, all variants of a single design, which reinterpret traditional ideas in an Edwardian Beaux-Arts idiom, two at Maesteg, for Welsh Presbyterians in 1907 (now disused) and for Welsh Baptists the following year, and one at Penclawdd in 1910 for Independents. Their interiors, with segmental ceilings carried on upper arches and columns which spring from the pierced-metal gallery fronts, and their coordinated furnishings, are rare ensembles of real architectural quality.

That leaves one or two oddities to mention: the small but galumphing Unitarian chapel of 1886 in Cardiff by *E. H. Bruton*, the Arts-and-Crafts-influenced Calvinistic Methodist chapel at Roath, Cardiff, by *J. H. Phillips*, 1899, and its echo at Resolven, 1904, for English Baptists, the Jacobean Baptist chapel at Bargoed, 1906–7 by *James & Morgan*, and the Netherlandish Welsh Baptist chapel by *Morgan & Elford* of 1900–1 at Mountain Ash. Finally, the Calvinistic Methodist Forward Movement was a law unto itself, to judge by its surviving halls, at Canton, Cardiff, of 1893, an essay in Jacobean Gothic; at Barry of 1903 by *George Thomas*, with a circular entrance turret; and at Cathays, Cardiff, of 1906 by *Veall & Sant*, a massive twin-towered, sub-Gothic affair.

It is clear that many chapels were thoroughly refitted instead of being rebuilt, but much remains to be done in order to document such changes. One spectacular example is the lavish refitting in 1902 of Ebenezer Welsh Independent chapel at Trecynon, Aberdare, by *Owen Morris Roberts & Son* of Portmadoc. The

splendid interior of the Welsh Independent chapel at Tonypandy
must be the result of a refitting, perhaps by the same firm.
Similarly, the chapel built beside the bridge at Pontypridd in 1861
was gorgeously refitted in 1910 by the local firm of *A. O. Evans,
Williams & Evans*, as can be readily appreciated, since the building
is now a Historical Centre open to the public.

Gothic Chapels

Gothic chapels, although beginning to appear as early as the
1850s, are a phenomenon of the period from *c.*1890 to 1914.
The popularity of Gothic among Glamorgan's Nonconformists
developed in Cardiff and was always greater in the E of the county
than in the W. An example of this contrast is already provided in
the 1850s, in the design of CEMETERY CHAPELS. At Dan-y-
graig Cemetery, St Thomas, Swansea, of 1856 the chapels by
W. Richards are differentiated from one another, that for Anglicans being Gothic but that for Dissenters in a round-arched
style. At Cathays Cemetery, Cardiff, by contrast, *R. G. Thomas*'s
chapels, built 1859, are both Gothic.

   R. G. Thomas of Newport was the architect of Cardiff's earliest
Gothic chapel, the Congregational (now Ebeneser) chapel in
Charles Street, of 1854–5. This is a richly Dec aisleless building
with steep-pitched roof and buttresses, fully abreast of develop-
ments among Anglicans. Inside, the same can be said of the
elaborate timber roof and lack of side galleries. It is imitated by
W. G. Habershon in his Tredegarville Baptist chapel at Roath,
Cardiff, 1861–3, though he uses geometrical and plate tracery.
Here the plan develops a transept. A transeptal plan was used in
1865–6 by *F. T. Pilkington* of Edinburgh in his central Cardiff
chapel for Scottish Presbyterians (now City United Reformed
Church), together with his own, here very alien, brand of Gothic,
with spiky forms and much sculpture. The other Scottish Pres-
87 byterian chapel in the county, St Andrew's, Swansea, is nearly
contemporary, 1862–4, and likewise a demonstration of tri-
umphalist Gothic, by the obscure *J. Dickson*. Lofty, octagonal
towers crown the entrance front. Asymmetrical towers with
stumpy spires are (or were) a feature of the Gothic chapels, at
Tondu, 1867 by *Wilson & Willcox* of Bath for Wesleyan Methodists, and Aberdare, 1878–9 by *W. D. Blessley* of Cardiff for Presbyterians. The local architect who made Gothic chapel design his
own was the short-lived *H. C. Harris* of Cardiff. He seems to have
designed the Calvinistic Methodist chapel at St Mellons, in 1869,
when he was only eighteen. His Capel Pembroke Terrace, Cardiff,
of 1877, also for Calvinistic Methodists, roused comment in the
national press. Tall and compact, it has a handsome, symmetrical
façade with large traceried windows high up, in the early French
style recently introduced to Cardiff by William Burges, flanked by
bow-ended entrance turrets, which lead to the galleried interior.
Inside, Harris revived the early type of plan which sites the pulpit
against the entrance wall with galleries on the other three sides,
but combined it with Butterfieldian brick patterning of the walls.

His much larger, aisled chapel in Roath, Cardiff, influenced by James Brooks rather than Burges, but with galleries inserted into the arcades, has unfortunately been pulled down. The Presbyterian chapel at Pontypridd which Harris designed in 1883, the year before his death, is more conventional in its arrangement of galleries, though the prominent stair-turrets, timber-framed at the top, again show the influence of Burges. The composition towards the road includes the cant-ended hall, the first of many examples in which hall and Sunday school are composed with Gothic chapels to form a unified complex. Another good early example of this grouping is also at Pontypridd, the English Congregational chapel by *Potts, Sulman & Hemmings* of 1888. And in 1895 the local architect *A. O. Evans* built a showy Gothic chapel and school for Wesleyans at the other end of the same street in Pontypridd.

The twenty years up to the beginning of the First World War saw Gothic become decisively the favourite style for chapels. Large, urban chapels of this period normally had arcades, clerestoreys and transepts. All that prevented such chapels from being full-blown copies of late medieval churches was the omission of anything like a chancel arch, in the interest of unimpeded internal visibility, and the introduction of galleries in the transepts. The Welsh Presbyterian chapel in Barry, 1894 by *T. G. Williams* of Liverpool, introduces the new idiom. The Methodist chapel at Roath, Cardiff, of 1896–7 by *Ingall & Sons* of Birmingham, with its chapel-like hall alongside, is an exceptionally ambitious early example. The local firm which embraced this approach was *Jones, Richards & Budgen*, with *Henry Budgen* its design partner. The façade of their English Wesleyan chapel at Barry of 1897–8 echoes St George's Chapel, Windsor, but its interior was intended for galleries. Their Methodist chapel at Roath, Cardiff, of 1897–8 is cruciform with strong East Anglian overtones and has a tower. At Penarth *Richards & Budgen* in 1899 used the same approach in their Trinity Methodist chapel, and *Budgen* in 1906, still working for Methodists in Penarth, built another landmark tower. The interior of this chapel has been completely altered. *W. E. Knapman*'s chapel (now United Reformed church) at Barry of 1904 is a close relative. But the most extraordinary departure is St Andrew's chapel, Roath, Cardiff, of 1899–1901, where *Habershon, Fawckner & Groves* introduced features copied from Tintern and Melrose Abbeys and erected a steeple worthy of Pearson himself.

Among smaller Gothic chapels an Arts and Crafts freedom from convention is found at *E. A. Johnson*'s Unitarian chapel at Merthyr Tydfil, 1901–3, and *E. G. C. Down*'s Presbyterian chapel at Canton, Cardiff, 1903, its serried row of battered buttresses a memorable feature of Cathedral Road. *George Morgan & Son* of Carmarthen even essayed Gothic in their Baptist chapel at Barry of 1902–3. Its gawky exterior conceals a splendidly resolved interior with upper arcades carrying an elaborate timber roof. But the last word must be given to *W. Beddoe Rees*, whose pretty but formulaic Gothic chapels occur all over the county. Their interiors are designed for galleries, which are approached by stairs in projecting polygonal turrets, one of them normally carried up as a small tower, flanking a handsome traceried window over the central entrance. Beddoe Rees had crystallized the formula by 1901, in the Plasnewydd Presbyterian chapel at Roath, Cardiff. He repeated it in 1903 at Caerphilly, in 1904 for English Baptists at St Thomas, Swansea, with two towers, for Independents at Maesteg in 1911, and twice in 1913, at Rhyddings, in central Swansea, for Congregationalists, and at Whitchurch, on the edge of Cardiff, for English Baptists. The Whitchurch chapel is particularly charming, sited in a walled burial ground on a green. Internally, his chapels are normally galleried on three sides, the gallery fronts of pierced metal, the standard pattern having repeated palmettes, as he used in his classical chapels.

NINETEENTH-CENTURY CHURCHES

Early Nineteenth-Century Churches

The building of new churches and the rebuilding and remodelling of old began to be viewed with rekindled interest in the years after 1800, but at first little of architectural value resulted. Thomas Mansel Talbot's reckless neo-Norman remodelling of the exterior of the C12 abbey church nave at Margam *c.*1805–10 forcefully marks the new departure. More sympathetic, and significantly later, was John Montgomery Traherne's restoration of the church of St George-super-Ely in 1838, with reconstructed crossing arches and plaster rib-vault. William Williams's enlargement of Aberpergwm church, Glynneath, 1840–1, with enriched plaster vaults, and brought-in stained glass and monuments, is a thorough-going effort in this vein.

The earliest new classical churches, of 1820–1 at Merthyr Tydfil, and 1823–4 at Swansea by *William Jernegan*, are now both unrecognizable after subsequent remodelling. *Edward Haycock*'s cruciform Holy Cross, Port Talbot, of 1827, though refitted, retains its minimal Gothic character. St John the Baptist, Clydach, of 1845–7, is similar, a T in plan. The only surviving classical church is *Philip Hardwick*'s for the Rhymney Iron Company's employees at Rhymney, 1840–3, substantial but plain. The contemporary neo-Norman St Mary, Butetown, Cardiff, 1840–5, is much more significant. It was built at the expense of the second Marquess of Bute, to the design of *Thomas Foster* of Bristol, and has a remarkable plan, an aisled nave, an E apse not expressed externally, and E of it, facing the road, a mighty twin-towered façade. By comparison, *T. H. Wyatt*'s Commissioners' church of 1836–7 at Glyntaff, also neo-Norman and quite large, is unimpressive.

Before 1850 new Gothic churches were, therefore, few in number, and the lancet-style churches built in 1850 at Penclawdd and Resolven and by *W. Richards* in 1850–1 at Pontardulais are simple aisleless affairs. The first attempt to respond to Pugin's call for aspiring Gothic ecclesiastical architecture is St David, Merthyr Tydfil, 1846–7, by the chameleon-like *T. H. Wyatt* of *Wyatt & Brandon*, though its style is severe E.E. and the whole building overstretched for the money available. On a smaller scale, the church at Skewen, designed by *R. C. Saunders* in 1848, is equally forward-looking.

The Work of John Prichard

By the mid 1840s *John Prichard* was poised to establish himself as the leading church architect in south-east Wales. Prichard was born in 1818, the son of a vicar choral of Llandaff Cathedral. He trained under Thomas Walker, who had attended the private architectural academy of A. C. Pugin and was able to bring the young man into contact with Benjamin Ferrey and, not least, into the orbit of A.W.N. Pugin himself. Prichard absorbed the Puginian lesson that Gothic could and should be the C19 architectural *lingua franca*, suitable for secular buildings as much as for ecclesiastical, and capable of responding, in the hands of a scholarly and resourceful architect, to all the challenges of the Victorian age. So it is unfair to him to separate his churches from his secular work, and his whole achievement in the county will be surveyed here together.

Prichard's architectural career began at Llandaff Cathedral, where the restoration of the Lady Chapel had started under *T. H. Wyatt* in 1841. Prichard's design for the Lady Chapel E window, an ambitious Geometrical composition, was carried out in 1843, and by 1845 he was in charge of the entire restoration, even though Wyatt remained as 'honorary architect' until 1853. Wyatt's master plan was set aside even though that involved remodelling Wyatt's new Lady Chapel gable. Meanwhile he began to receive church commissions. His first, the rebuilding of the medieval upland church of Llanfabon in 1847, he carried out, surprisingly, in neo-Norman. The rebuilt nave of St Illtyd, Bridgend, 1849–50, is Geometrical Gothic, but lacks personality. His collaboration with *Benjamin Ferrey*, also in 1849–51, in building a new church at Merthyr Mawr marked an important stage 89 towards his architectural maturity. By this time Prichard was architect to the diocese of Llandaff. The next year he built at Troedyrhiw a church which self-consciously develops some of the ideas found at Merthyr Mawr, particularly the composition of the bellcote-crowned w end. By contrast his rebuilding of the body of St Michael and All Angels, Cwmavon, also in 1850–1, is oddly rough and ready.

In 1852 Prichard took into partnership the young London architect *J. P. Seddon*, whose Gothic hotel built in that year at Southerndown shows that the two saw eye to eye about the suitability of Gothic for secular buildings. The partnership was primarily intended to enable Prichard to embark on the restoration of the choir and nave of Llandaff Cathedral while developing a general practice, but the two men seem to have stimulated each other's imagination, and Seddon, furthermore, gave the practice access to Pre-Raphaelite artists in London. The partnership of *Prichard & Seddon*, between 1852 and 1863, built some of the most imaginative neo-Gothic works of the period and was admired far beyond the confines of south-east Wales. Their preferred style was Geometrical and early Dec of the end of the C13. Unfortunately, their major work in Glamorgan, the reconstruction of the body of Llandaff Cathedral, was severely damaged by a landmine in 1941. In particular, only fragments survive of the rich choir fittings carved by *Edward Clarke* of Llandaff, and a single figure from the pulpit by the Pre-Raphaelite sculptor *Thomas Woolner*. *D. G. Rossetti*'s altarpiece 'The Seed of David' was saved, but no longer acts as reredos for the high altar, the role for which it was designed. In his reconstruction of the upper parts of the sanctuary, choir and nave Prichard strove to reinstate the medieval design. The octagonal superstructure of the chapter house, by contrast, was his own invention.

Among *Prichard & Seddon*'s churches, Pentyrch, of 1853–7, best demonstrates their youthful verve, now that All Saints, Cwmavon, 1853–5, has been demolished. Their two Cardiff churches were both unfortunately compromised by subsequent changes of design. At the cruciform St John, Canton, built in stages from 1854, their original conception can still be appreciated; but St Andrew (now Eglwys Dewi Sant), a highly original design of 1859, introducing passage aisles even before G. E. Street in 1864 incorporated them in his All Saints, Clifton, Bristol, proved largely unattainable for lack of funds and was completed to a much less daring design by *Alexander Roos*. Only the resourceful handling of the stonework of the w front demonstrates the original architects' fresh approach, even in small matters. Llanharan church, 1856–7, though quite small and inexpensive, shows a similar attention to detail. St Margaret, Mountain Ash, 1861–2, is harder to judge after the enlargement of its chancel. In church restorations they were happy to invent, increasing the interest of humdrum medieval buildings. Whereas *Prichard* alone at Cowbridge, 1850–2, did not obtrude his personality, *Prichard & Seddon* at St Nicholas (1859–60), St Mary Church (1862) and Bonvilston (1863–4) are unmistakable. Only their extensive reconstruction of St Mary, Aberavon, Port Talbot, 1858–9, fails to sparkle.

Once *Prichard* was on his own again (with Seddon practising independently in London), he extended the series of strongly characterized churches. Ystradowen, 1865–8, is one of the most charming, the tower with saddleback roof clearly intended as an idealization of a medieval Glamorgan type. Here the internal polychromy has been painted out, but a fine set of fittings and stained glass survives. St Clement, Briton Ferry, 1864–6, is remarkable for its timber arcade, a feature which Prichard repeated towards the end of his life at St Catherine, Canton, Cardiff, 1883–6. His aisleless, cruciform church at Tondu of 1868 is the best surviving example of his use of internal polychromatic brickwork, but this is as nothing compared with the extraordinary polychromy in stone and brick which overwhelms the interior of St Margaret, Roath, Cardiff, another aisleless cruciform building, erected 1869–70. This was paid for by the third Marquess of Bute and has fine fittings, though the reredos is now at St Anne, Roath. A third church on the same plan, but the only one to be fully completed structurally and given a full set of fittings, is St Catherine, Baglan, 1875–82, where funds were unstinted and where Prichard demonstrates both his sure sense of form and proportion, and his loving handling of local materials. Here there is a crossing tower with spire and a vaulted chancel. The Bute mausoleum, added to St Margaret, Roath, Cardiff, 1881–6, is also vaulted, 94 and its lavish carving contrasts strangely with the smooth granite slabs of the tomb-chests it houses. Prichard's last church, St Mary, Nolton, Bridgend, 1885–7, its steeple completed after his death, has a late Victorian air, with a spacious, clerestoried interior hardly interrupted by the high, wide chancel arch or the slender arcades. His other churches, St David, Ely, Cardiff, 1870–1 and 1882, Tongwynlais, begun 1875, Ogmore Vale, begun 1876, the incomplete Bargoed, begun 1877, and the rebuilding of Whitchurch, Cardiff, 1882–4, are all minor works. The restorations carried out in the later part of his career show less zest than when he was working with Seddon and require no further comment. (For Prichard's church fittings *see* below, p. 97.)

That leaves Prichard's magnum opus, his new S W tower and spire at Llandaff Cathedral, foundations laid 1860, built 1867–9. 91 This brilliantly provides coherence and authority to the whole building, its great height counteracting the cathedral's low-lying site, its taut outline complementing the reserve of the medieval work. The figure sculpture on the tower is by *H. H. Armstead*, Prichard's preferred sculptor from the mid 1860s.

Prichard's secular practice was, until late in his career, confined to an offshoot of his ecclesiastical one, schools, rectories and diocesan buildings. He rebuilt Cowbridge School, 1849–52, in conventional Tudor, as also the diminutive school at Gelligaer, 1850–1. *Prichard & Seddon* forged a characteristic style, combining Geometrical and Dec details with distinctly French late Gothic silhouettes. St Fagans Old Rectory, 1858–9, is the prime example, 97 the strongly polychromatic parsonage at Peterston-super-Ely of *c.* 1857 anticipating it on a somewhat smaller scale. The Probate Registry, Llandaff, Cardiff, of 1860–3 is a purer extrapolation of late C13 style. The little parish schools at Llandough near Cowbridge, 1859, and at Ewenny, 1866, illustrate just as well the architects' resource and loving touch in detailing.

Prichard's later houses show equal liveliness, but perhaps less discretion. His own house at Llandaff, begun *c.* 1863, was designed with, perhaps, excessive elaboration, but only the office part was brought to completion. Other houses at Llandaff, Ely Rise, of unknown date, and No. 63 Cardiff Road, 1870, develop some of his early parsonage themes. The additions to Rookwood, also at Llandaff, of 1881, are positively reckless. Nazareth House, an almshouse and school built at Cathays, Cardiff, for the third Marquess of Bute from 1875, has been much enlarged, but perhaps always looked somewhat institutional. Prichard also received commissions which took him out into the wider secular world. The miners' convalescent home, The Rest, Porthcawl, 1874–8, has the vastly overhanging eaves of a Swiss chalet, supported on weird black brick buttresses. This new idiom had been tried out on a small scale at Llanmadoc Old Rectory, c. 1872. The Police Station at Porthcawl, 1877, falls back on a Tudor style, but at the Magistrates' Court, Bridgend, 1880–1, Prichard made a serious effort to develop his school style of c. 1860 on a large scale.

Churches c. 1850–1914

No other architect active before the 1880s can be seen in the round in Glamorgan. Most of the outstanding churches are by London architects, who worked under the patronage of one or other of the principal land-owning families. They came and went from the county like comets. First was the little-known *Andrew Mosely*, whose Puginian church at Aberdare of 1851–2, complete with soaring spire, still dominates the centre of the town. Hard on its heels comes St Fagan, Aberdare, largely paid for by the Baroness Windsor 1852–4 and again in 1856 after a fire. Here the architect was a pupil of Pugin, *T. Talbot Bury*, but the building is unimpressive. *Henry Woodyer*, by contrast, built St Paul, Sketty, Swansea, as early as 1849–50 for J. H. Vivian, the copper magnate, as an idealized version of an English parish church of c. 1300, with a family burial chapel attached. Later additions have unfortunately over-regularized it. Much later, in 1878, Vivian's son called Woodyer back to put up a church for the family's copperworkers, St John, Hafod, Swansea, in a highly regular, Perp style, not at all what one expects from Woodyer. The showy and expensive church at Pontardawe built 1858–60 must be mentioned here. The architect was a Swansea man, *J. H. Baylis*, working for the tinplate entrepreneur W. M. Parsons, and attempting to emulate Sir Gilbert Scott. *Scott* himself appears only as a restorer of churches, St Mellons, 1858–9, and St Hilary, 1861–2, the latter a drastic but well-considered and well-funded scheme.

   John Norton of London and Bristol introduced a more advanced, more muscular style at Ystrad Mynach, 1855–7, for the Rev. George Thomas, member of a long-established land-owning family in the Rhymney Valley. Norton went on to become the favoured architect of Howel Gwyn, the power behind the mid-Victorian development of Neath. At Neath itself *Norton*'s St David's, 1864–6, is a dominant Streetian town church, with a brilliantly polychromatic interior. In 1871 *Norton* built Gwyn a church on his estate at Dyffryn, a quieter affair. His St Catherine, Pontypridd, 1866–70, is another urban focal point. *G. E. Street* himself built only the little country church of Capel Llanilltern, 1862–3, though his restoration of the medieval church at St Fagans is a distinguished and characteristic piece of work. At both he worked for the Windsor family. But to rebuild the medieval church at Penarth, overlooking the family's new dock and what was to become a fashionable new town, the Baroness Windsor chose not Street but *Butterfield*. The new St Augustine, Penarth,

1865–6, is one of Butterfield's finest churches, big-boned and austere outside, highly charged in the polychromatic patterning of its interior. The rebuilding of Llandough church, just N of Penarth, by *S. C. Fripp* of Bristol, is exactly contemporary, similar in concept, but smaller and artistically inferior.

The church which matches Butterfield's in quality is *Bodley & Garner*'s St German, Roath, Cardiff, 1881–4. This ushers in the 92 late Victorian style, tall, spacious and elegant, flowingly Dec rather than Geometrical. Alone among churches by London architects, it exerted widespread influence locally. It is also unusual in being accompanied by a school and a clergy house by the same architects. *Bodley & Garner*'s slightly later St Saviour, Splott, Cardiff, 1887–8, is far less authoritative.

The last of the celebrated London architects to design churches in the county was *J. L. Pearson*. His remodelling of St Tydfil, Merthyr Tydfil, 1894–1901, is an ingenious and convincing essay in Burgundian Romanesque; his church at Treharris of 1895–6 is E.E. but unmemorable. He is most truly himself at the stately, if rather mournful, St Theodore, Port Talbot, erected 1895–7 as a family memorial by Miss Emily Talbot.

The Talbot sisters of Margam Abbey and Griffith Llewellyn of Baglan Hall, the county's most generous church-builders in the later C19, otherwise patronized local architects. Prichard received his best church commission, at Baglan, from Llewellyn, as did the heir to Prichard's practice, *F. R. Kempson*, at Pentre. Kempson's church, of 1887–90, is no match imaginatively, though its great size and relentless internal polychromy give it a certain grandeur. The Talbots' favourite architect was *G. E. Halliday*, and at Nicho- 96 laston in 1894 he got his chance to show what could be done, even on a tiny scale, with lavish funds and highly skilled craftsmen. Kempson, Halliday and *E. M. Bruce Vaughan* between the later 1880s and 1914 dominated the church-building scene. *Kempson*, in partnership with *C. B. Fowler*, enlarged St John, Cardiff, 1889–91, and built new churches in Barry and Penarth in 1893–4. Later, working on his own, he was responsible for two others just worth mentioning, St Martin, Roath, Cardiff, 1899–1901, which had a richly painted interior, now lost, and St Agnes, Port Talbot, 1909–10, which attempts to recapture the polychromy of Pentre. *Kempson*'s most important work is St Michael's Theological College, Llandaff, Cardiff, 1905–7, a conventional essay in collegiate Gothic.

Bruce Vaughan was the most prolific of these architects, constantly busy from 1881 until the outbreak of war. Church-building formed the core of his practice, and he was responsible for thirty-five surviving churches in the county, many being cheap and simple buildings for Valleys communities. Good examples are the two at Porth, St Paul, 1886–8, on a steep slope, and St John, Cymmer, 1888–9, ingeniously economical with a timber arcade. His major church, St James, Roath, Cardiff, 1892–3, owes a good deal to Bodley's St German, but in addition has a finely composed tower and spire. In his later years *Bruce Vaughan* had several more opportunities to build ambitiously, at Oystermouth, 1901–3,

Landore, Swansea, 1902–3, Clydach, 1903–5, Miskin, 1906–7, and Barry, 1907–15, but none achieves a stylistic advance or a really memorable personal statement.

Halliday was more forward-looking than the others, regularly designing in the Perp style, and occasionally suggesting awareness of Arts and Crafts fashions. His use of half-timbering, at Garth in 1891, and in combination with red brick at Llwydcoed, 1895, makes them unique among churches in the county. His most ambitious essay in this genre is not a church, but the Llewellyn Almshouses of 1897 at Neath, which look as if they have strayed from Surrey. Nicholaston church of 1894, already mentioned, is a showcase for the crafts, but in its historicist dependence on c13 precedents cannot be called Arts and Crafts. The Perp church of 1895–6 at Cwmparc, Treorchy, is a better indication of Halliday's awareness of contemporary currents. His attempts to build the big, light-filled and proudly towered Perp church of his dreams proved hard to carry through. In the mid 1890s, at Maesteg, he was forced into drastically reworking his design in the face of a sharply reduced budget, and at Cathays, Cardiff, it proved impossible to build the tower. His church at Barry, 1903–5, with excitingly expansive windows towards the street, stands sadly incomplete. Two late churches, however, at Radyr, 1903–4 and 1910, and at Porthcawl, 1912–14, do achieve a successful outcome, the one dark and solemn outside, the other airy and ashlar-faced within.

Only one more architectural practice needs to be mentioned in this context. In 1889 *J. P. Seddon* reappeared in the county, setting up in partnership with the imaginative young *J. Coates Carter*. In that year they began two ambitious town churches, tall and elegant, with unbroken internal spaces, modelled on Bodley's St Augustine, Pendlebury, Manchester, of twenty years earlier, but with the idiosyncrasy of cross-gabled bays to the aisles. All Saints, Penarth, does not survive in its original form, but St Paul, Grange-town, Cardiff, completed in 1902 with a modified e end and without the upper stages of its mighty tower, is the finest late Victorian church in the county after Bodley's at Roath. *Carter*'s earlier church at Neath, 1888–91, already suggests his ambition. The other churches of *Seddon & Carter*, however, at New Tre-degar of 1892–3 and Adamsdown, Roath, Cardiff, of 1902–3, are cheap and simple. Only the slabby forms of their bellcotes reveal their independent-minded designers.

Whereas the Established church benefited from the generosity of industrialists and land-owners, not excluding the third Mar-quess of Bute, who on coming of age converted to Catholicism, Roman Catholics themselves could rarely hope for such favours. On the other hand, Catholic immigrant workers tended to be concentrated in the large towns, so a few capacious churches, imposing but simple, were all that was required. The Catholic churches built in Glamorgan between the mid c19 and 1914 number less than a dozen, including four in Cardiff, two in Swansea and one each in Merthyr Tydfil, Maesteg and Mountain Ash. Well-known London firms supplied routine E.E. designs:

Hansom at Swansea in 1847, at Roath, Cardiff, in 1861 and at Merthyr Tydfil in 1893, *Pugin & Pugin* for St David's Cathedral, Cardiff, in 1884, and for the equally large St Joseph, Landore, Swansea, in 1886. The small church of 1906 at Maesteg is also theirs. At the end of the period, however, the straitjacket could be discarded. *F. A. Walters* built at Canton, Cardiff, in 1907 in a sub-Byzantine style, while at Splott, Cardiff, *F. R. Bates* of Newport in 1911, making the first of what would be many appearances in the county by his firm, chose a freely handled Perp.

Fittings and Monuments

No Victorian church was complete without architect-designed FITTINGS. *John Prichard*'s are strongly personal and worth seeking out, in the churches he restored as well as in his new ones. Particularly characteristic are his cylindrical stone pulpits, judiciously trimmed with stiff-leaf foliage. His fonts are less personal. Strongly pegged and dowelled timberwork, probably designed at first by his partner, *J. P. Seddon*, is also a feature of many churches (and of Llandaff Cathedral, where the sanctuary s and nave w doors are fine pieces). The most complete ensembles of fittings are at Baglan and Ystradowen. Further pairs of pulpit and font can be found at Pentyrch and Llanharan (both by *Prichard & Seddon*), at St Margaret, Roath, Cardiff, at Tondu and Tongwynlais. A fine pulpit is part of the restoration of St Mary Church. The sumptuous pulpit at Merthyr Mawr is clearly by *Prichard*, but must be considerably later than the church. Reredoses are less numerous. Apart from the remains of the reredos at Llandaff Cathedral, examples are at St Anne, Roath, Cardiff (made for St Margaret, Roath), and Baglan, with figures by *Armstead*.

Butterfield's St Augustine, Penarth, has a font and dominant reredos, typical of the architect in their stark geometry, in strong contrast to Prichard's contemporary pieces. Of the other major churches by London architects, *Pearson*'s St Theodore, Port Talbot, has an understated pulpit and font, *Bodley & Garner*'s St German, Roath, a flamboyant organ case and plainly handsome font.

Among the younger generation of native architects, *G. E. Halliday* at Nicholaston in 1894 had the richest opportunity to incorporate a lavish set of fittings. Here they are indeed hard to distinguish from the richly carved details of the building, all exhibiting the consummate craftsmanship of *William Clarke* of Llandaff. *Clarke* was also heavily involved with the Prichard-pastiche church at Pen-y-fai, 1900–3, where the reredos has figures carved by *Goscombe John*, the outstanding local sculptor, whose work will be noted further below. The marble and alabaster REREDOS with a row of figures under canopies, a type popularized by Sir Gilbert Scott back in the 1860s, became the fashionable costly fitting. Besides the examples already mentioned, *Kempson* installed such reredoses at Pentre and at St Mary, Aberavon, Port Talbot, both in 1890, the latter with figures by *Armstead*. In 1891 he erected a small but particularly fine one in St John, Cardiff, the figures being one of the earliest important pieces by *Goscombe John*. Later examples can be found in churches by *Halliday*, at Cwmparc, Treorchy, and Porthcawl (based on the medieval reredos at Llantwit Major), and also by *Bruce Vaughan*, as the focal point of his new chancel at St Margaret, Mountain Ash, 1904, and at his new church at Clydach, as late as 1921. By that time a different sort of reredos had come into fashion, the German or Netherlandish type favoured by Bodley, of wood with gilt or polychrome figures and large shutters. Examples can be found at St German, Roath, Cardiff, 1921–2 by *Cecil Hare*, and by *Coates Carter* at St Mary, Nolton, Bridgend, 1921, and SS Andrew and Teilo, Cathays, Cardiff, 1924.

Only four further items need to be mentioned, the large gesso relief at SS Dyfrig and Samson, Grangetown, Cardiff, by *Henry Wilson*; the bronze adaptation by *N.H.J. Westlake* of Fra Angelico's Transfiguration, at St Peter, Cogan, Penarth, 1896; the charming Art Nouveau font, its stem formed as a rooted tree, carved by *William Clarke* to *Halliday*'s design for St Elvan, Aberdare, in 1903; and the highly imaginative font cover of 1909 by *Arthur Grove* at Cadoxton-juxta-Neath.

STAINED GLASS was as important as architect-designed fittings. It could exclude the outside world, and instruct and uplift worshippers. Some architects took considerable interest in stained glass design. Grisaille glass can achieve exclusion while preserving architectural purity, as *Prichard* demonstrates at Ystradowen, where a ruby disc in each window was intended to continue the polychromy of the walls. He used a quieter scheme at Tondu, where *Clayton & Bell* made the glass. At St Margaret, Roath, Cardiff, the original grisaille glass by *Saunders & Co.* has largely been superseded by figural windows. *Halliday* sometimes followed the same method, as his little early church at Garth shows particularly well.

Architects and donors, however, both maintained an overwhelming preference for narrative scenes and figures. The earliest scheme is by *Wailes* in the chancel at Merthyr Mawr, *c.* 1850. Also by *Wailes* is the splendid E window at Prichard's Troedyrhiw, but produced a dozen years after the church. Later, Prichard favoured *Morris & Co.* The window of 1863 at Coity and sequence of five windows at Llandaff Cathedral, 1866–74, demonstrate this, and so, most impressively, does the contribution made at Baglan in 1880 by windows to *Burne-Jones*'s design. The single window of 1873 at Llantrisant by *Morris & Co.* was Prichard's personal gift – and makes an interesting comparison with the Pre-Raphaelite-inspired window beside it of 1872 by *G. H. Cook*. *Morris* glass not connected with Prichard can be found at Margam, 1873, Newton Nottage, 1877, and, a particularly fine window of 1869, at St John, Cardiff.

The glass by *Hardman* in several windows at St Fagans is associated with *G. E. Street*'s restoration of 1859–60. *Clayton & Bell* supplied the E window at Gelligaer in 1867, at the conclusion of *Buckeridge*'s restoration, and their E window at St Hilary was inserted in 1872 under *Scott*'s direction. The most characteristic example of collaboration between architect and stained-glass-maker is at St Augustine, Penarth, where *Butterfield c.* 1866 employed his protégé, *Alexander Gibbs*, to supply windows, principally the majestic E window, the focus of the glowingly coloured chancel.

High Victorian architects liked their stained glass brilliant and strongly coloured. At the end of the century more subdued coloration and less emphatic design were preferred. This approach can be seen in the great E window supplied by *Burlison & Grylls* for *Bodley & Garner*'s St German, Roath, Cardiff, 1900. *Bodley* also designed at least some of the series of windows, beginning in 1890, with which *Burlison & Grylls* replaced Prichard's grisaille at St Margaret, Roath, Cardiff. *Clayton & Bell* were *Pearson*'s favoured firm, but at his St Theodore, Port Talbot, only the beginnings of a scheme by them was carried out before the architect's death. One other linkage between architect and stained-glass-maker can be mentioned. At *F. R. Kempson*'s magnum opus, St Peter, Pentre, 1887–90, the E window is a typical flamboyant piece by *W. F. Dixon*. A similar window by *Dixon*, also of 1890, is over *Kempson*'s reredos at St Mary, Aberavon, Port Talbot. The fact that *Kempson* completed Prichard's St Mary, Nolton, Bridgend, must explain the presence of another E window by *Dixon* there, too unrestrained to be wholly compatible with Prichard's architecture. *Dixon*'s earliest windows, of 1882 at Llanmaes, and 1884 at Pendoylan, have a distinctive charm that is lost in his more hectic later works.

Most stained glass, in Glamorgan as elsewhere, was inserted by individual donors without an architect's involvement. It is possible only to pick out the most impressive. Artistically most interesting are the two examples of *Henry Holiday*'s classicizing style of the late 1880s, at Penderyn, 1886, and at Ystrad Mynach, 1888, both made by *Powell*'s. Also by *Powell*'s is the Burne-Jones-like vision of Heaven in the E window at Margam, of 1905. For sheer craftsmanship it would be difficult to beat the finest windows by *Lavers & Westlake*, as at Wenvoe, 1896, and Reynoldston, 1905.

Inevitably, certain firms came to be widely employed, and equally inevitably produced much hack-work. Two deserve to be mentioned. A West Country firm which from the 1860s supplied a very passable substitute for the work of Hardman or Clayton & Bell was *Joseph Bell* of Bristol. Characteristic examples are at Llanharry, 1868, Resolven, 1869, Peterston-super-Ely, *c.* 1870, and, particularly effective, Ynyshir, 1885. There must be many more windows by Bell at present unrecognized. From the mid 1890s, however, the busiest practitioner in South Wales was *R. J. Newbery*. Stylistically, Newbery's windows employ the richly detailed, Netherlandish or Germanic idiom of other contemporary firms, such as Ward & Hughes and the later Burlison & Grylls. Signed or documented windows by him are in at least twenty-four Glamorgan churches. A list of the most ambitious starts with the early windows celebrating captains of industry, at

Dowlais, Merthyr Tydfil, 1896, St Tydfil, Merthyr Tydfil, 1896, and St Margaret, Mountain Ash, 1900. Major E windows by *Newbery* are at Penmark, 1898, Pentyrch, 1906, St Peter, Pontardawe, *c.*1907, and St John, Radyr, 1915. The W window at Ynyshir, 1905, is equally grand.

Stained glass, so much of it memorializing in purpose, naturally leads on to VICTORIAN MONUMENTS. In the early C19 artistically noteworthy monuments were, if possible, even rarer than they had been during the preceding century. *Sebastian Gahagan*'s deathbed relief at St Brides Major (†1814) is altogether exceptional. A coherent series is at last encountered in the 1830s, with the early works of *John Evan Thomas* of Brecon, who trained in London under Chantrey and went on to be widely patronized in South Wales. Early tablets by Thomas are at St Nicholas (†1835) and Cowbridge (†1837), and there is a fine medallion portrait at St Hilary (†1841). The mourning female on his monument at Llanishen, Cardiff (†1850), has a weightiness and naturalism worthy of Chantrey himself. Thomas, somewhat surprisingly, supplied the allegorical figures for the Gothic wall-monument of 1856 in Llandaff Cathedral, Cardiff, the latest in a group of nine Gothic monuments, extending over twenty years. They are at Cadoxton-juxta-Neath (†1833), Penmark (†1834), St Thomas's church, Neath (after 1837) signed *Bedford*, St George-super-Ely (1838), Cowbridge (†1841), St Thomas, Neath, again (†1844), Clydach (†1855), and Flemingston (1855), suitably commemorating the celebrated antiquary Iolo Morganwg.

These, however, are minor works compared with the three mid-Victorian Gothic shrines created for leading county families. The earliest is the burial chapel at *Woodyer*'s St Paul, Sketty, Swansea, where a life-size marble angel by *P. Tenerani* commemorates the death of J.H. Vivian's wife in 1848, and canopied Dec recesses are provided for further members of the family. In Cardiff Castle the third Marquess of Bute had *Burges*, 1873–6, incorporate a tiny vaulted chapel on the spot where the father he never knew had died in 1848. *J.E. Thomas*'s bust of the second Marquess faces a gilt bronze altar representing the Empty Tomb. The last Talbot heir is commemorated at Margam by a poignant marble effigy by *Armstead*, 1881, lying under an E.E. canopy on slender shafts with stiff-leaf caps, an ensemble of considerable nobility. Its designer is at present unknown.

The other site for ambitious monuments is the restored Llandaff Cathedral. Two bishops are spectacularly treated, Ollivant (†1882) by *Armstead*'s grandiose recumbent effigy, and Lewis by *Goscombe John*'s dramatic preaching figure of 1909. What must be *Armstead*'s earliest work in the county is also at Llandaff Cathedral, a tomb-recess designed by *Prichard* with sculptured reliefs, date of death 1863. *Goscombe John*'s effigy of Dean Vaughan, 1899–1900, is in close imitation of Ollivant's. To complete the tally, the large brass at Gelligaer (†1879) by an unknown maker deserves to be mentioned.

VICTORIAN AND EDWARDIAN
SECULAR BUILDINGS

High Victorian Gothic Houses

Prichard & Seddon's important contribution to Gothic domestic design has already been discussed. They had been anticipated only by *Woodyer*'s remarkable, but now sadly distorted, enlargement of Parc Wern, Swansea, of 1851–3. The romantic gate-lodge to Singleton Abbey, Swansea, however, which must also be by Woodyer, suggests what Parc Wern may have been like. A more sober expression of Gothic, as approved by the Ecclesiologists, can be found at Llandaff, Cardiff, the Deanery, 1861–3 by *Ewan Christian*, and his three other houses there. Hendrefoelan, Sketty, Swansea, of about the same date, by the little-known *W. B. Colling*, is Pugin Tudorized. *John Norton*'s villa at Oystermouth, of the mid 1860s, in its strident polychromy outdoes anything of the same period by Prichard & Seddon, but was later unsympathetically enlarged by the architect. *Charles Buckeridge*'s enlargement of the rectory at Gelligaer, 1863, is another example of High Victorian Gothic.

All this pales before the spectacular transformation of Cardiff 98 Castle wrought by *William Burges* for the young third Marquess of Bute beginning in 1868. Henry Holland's regularization of the C15 range was undone, and a series of towers raised behind and beside it, stunning in their multifarious variety and linked on the townward side to a convincingly defensible enclosure wall. Burges's ambition, brilliantly realized in large part by the time of his death in 1881, was to give physical substance to a dream of what medieval castles might have looked like, based on the evidence of late medieval French and Burgundian illuminated manuscripts and the recently published archaeological deductions of Viollet-le-Duc. The Clock Tower at the SW corner, the first component to be constructed, 1869–73, was conceived as a public statement, providing a beacon for the great expansion of Cardiff which would soon give the town an entirely new scale. Otherwise, the castle was a private world, the rooms in the Clock Tower designed for the third Marquess in his bachelordom, the rest of the interiors for him and his wife. Only through the many illustrations which appeared in the architectural press could the public gain an inkling of the exotic splendours within. The statues on the Clock Tower and the later animals perched on the enclosure wall towards Castle Street hint at the role of the figurative arts inside the castle. Burges conceived each room thematically, with complex, idiosyncratic iconographies, which called for the combined efforts of sculptor, painter, joiner, metal-worker and stained-glass artist. His principal sculptural designer and modeller was *Thomas Nicholls*, though the Italian *C. Fucigna* was used for several important individual figures; his principal figure-painter *Frederick Weekes*, succeeded by *H. W. Lonsdale*; his decorative painters were *Campbell & Smith*; his favoured metal-worker

Barkentin & Krall, and the stained-glass-maker who best interpreted his designs, *Saunders & Co.*, succeeded in 1880 by
Worrall & Co. All these were London-based, and worked in the
county almost exclusively for Burges, but according to the Cardiff
sculptor Goscombe John, the castle works provided a training
ground which greatly enhanced local craft skills. His own father,
Thomas John, was chief carver at Cardiff Castle, working under
Nicholls in the 1870s. The finest rooms at Cardiff Castle include
the two major bachelor rooms in the Clock Tower, the now
somewhat overpainted Winter Smoking Room, expounding the
theme of love, and, at the top of the tower, the astrological
99 Summer Smoking Room, where the arts interpenetrate mar-
vellously. In the main body of the castle the most impressive
100 ensembles are the dining room, in which hospitality is epitomized
by Old Testament stories of Abraham, Lord Bute's extraordinarily
personalized bedroom, the Arab Room, incomplete at Burges's
death and inscribed by Bute to memorialize their collaboration,
the Chaucer Room, Lady Bute's tower-top bower and, most
exotic of all, the Moorish roof garden. The larger rooms, library
and banqueting hall, have less power, the latter also largely carried
out and in part designed by Burges's successor *William Frame*.
The great stair, which must have been one of the castle's most
amazing spaces, has unfortunately been swept away. After Burges's death in 1881 a good deal remained to be done to complete
the interiors of the castle. Where he had left no designs they were
supplied by *William Frame*, his former assistant.

When work was well under way on Cardiff Castle, in the early
1870s, Bute and Burges diverted some of their attention to the
101 ruined de Clare castle, Castell Coch. An archaeological analysis
of the ruins by Burges and by the brilliant historian of military
architecture G. T. Clark of Talygarn formed the basis of a total
reconstruction which is both faithful to the late c13 design and
aesthetically impressive, an essay in juxtaposed cylinders. The
courtyard, with its timber balconies, is strongly indebted to
Chillon on Lake Geneva. The interior at Castell Coch, which was
intended to become an occasional summer retreat for the Butes
and their children, consists of four principal rooms. They are in
a similar spirit to those at Cardiff Castle. But only the drawing
room and Lady Bute's bedroom are to *Burges*'s own design, and
virtually nothing was executed under his supervision, so there is
not the same highly charged atmosphere here as in so many of
the interior spaces in Cardiff Castle.

Burges's other building in the county was much smaller and
more accessible: the sturdy, early French Gothic house he built
in Park Place, Cardiff, 1871–5 for the chief engineer of the Bute
docks, James McConnochie. Its expansive, heavily mullioned
windows, its steep roofs and dormers, its dominating chimneystacks, all made an authoritative statement in a Gothic language which had already been employed by Prichard for a decade
and a half without apparently creating any following at all.

W. D. Blessley was the local architect who first showed signs of
having learnt a lesson from Burges. His impressive row of lofty

Gothic villas, also in Park Place, Cardiff, of 1875–6, represents him best. His Pascoe House, Butetown, Cardiff, also of 1875, suggests how Burges's spirit could be modified for the commercial world. His contemporary Great Western Hotel, St Mary Street, Cardiff, shows that on a larger scale his imagination soon ran out. The strongly Burges-style villas at the foot of Cathedral Road, Canton, Cardiff, are unattributed. *H. C. Harris*'s early French Gothic chapel in Cardiff, of 1877, has already been mentioned. It is perhaps the single most convincing example of the impact Burges made on local architects. *Harris*'s house in Park Street, Bridgend, of 1875, shows the same influence.

The last and by far the loudest echo of Burges is *William Frame*'s Pierhead Building, 1896–7, which trumpets the Bute 103 achievement alongside the great series of Bute-financed docks on which the wealth and expansion of Cardiff had been founded. Its red terracotta outside and lavish faience within, however, suggest a second influence, that of Alfred Waterhouse.

Two full-blown country houses close to Cardiff show the most earnest efforts to ape Burges, particularly in their interiors. Insole Court, Llandaff, has a complex history, but additions of 1873–5, including a tower, and interior remodelling by *Edwin Seward* of *James, Seward & Thomas*, 1875–80, were heavily Burgesian. There is even a painted frieze by *Weekes* in imitation of his frieze in the Winter Smoking Room in Cardiff Castle. Tŷ-to-maen, St Mellons, 1885, by *E. M. Bruce Vaughan*, is all of a piece, Tudor Gothic, the Burgesisms inside, mighty hooded chimneypieces in two rooms, and stained glass by *Campbell & Smith*. The carved stonework is by the local carver *W. Clarke*. *G. T. Clark*, however, building to his own design a substantial country house at Talygarn over a thirty-year period from 1865, showed no sign of specific Burges influence. Externally, Talygarn is in a subdued Scottish baronial style. But inside are many spectacularly decorated rooms, carried out by Italian firms which specialized in early Renaissance-style ensembles and Venetian Cinquecento-style ceiling paintings. Talygarn is unique in the county. So was its owner, for Clark, industrialist and architectural historian, was also Glamorgan's only Victorian amateur architect. Besides his house, he designed a substantial church at Talygarn in 1887, but it is not memorable.

Mid-Victorian Public Buildings

Outside Cardiff these form a small but varied collection. The Guest Memorial Reading Room, Dowlais, Merthyr Tydfil, built 70 in 1863 to the design of *Sir Charles Barry* (who had died in 1860), is, with its raised Tuscan portico, highly unusual for its date. The Custom House at Penarth of 1865, by the young Cardiff architect *G. E. Robinson*, is the only classical essay of the 1860s to carry equal conviction. Then there is a gap until the 1880s. *H. C. Harris*'s ambitious Town Hall at Maesteg, 1881, has the tall proportions and steep roof of a civic building of the Netherlandish Renaissance, but not the lavish detail. *John Norton*'s Gwyn Hall at Neath of 1887 remains faithful to Dec Gothic, but without much enthusiasm. At Swansea there is surprisingly little to report, only *Henry Holtom*'s Central Library and College of Art, 1886–7, with its French pavilion roof.

Cardiff from c. 1870 to 1914

From the 1870s to beyond the end of the century the GROWTH OF CARDIFF attracted architects like moths to a flame. E.M. Bruce Vaughan was a rare example of a Cardiff architect born and bred. In spite of the impact exerted by William Burges's buildings, the growth of what came to be dubbed the 'Chicago of Wales' exhibited a bewildering eclecticism. The two Venetian Quattrocento palazzi of 1878 can set the scene, the Prince of Wales Theatre, St Mary Street, by *Blessley & Waring*, and, particularly unnerving in its authenticity, 24–26 Queen Street, by *C.E. Bernard*. *Edwin Seward*, however, captured the most glittering commissions, so that in the mid 1890s it was noted that Seward was to Cardiff as Waterhouse was to Manchester. He trained in Yeovil and came to Cardiff as principal assistant to G.E. Robinson. From 1875 he was in practice with W.P. James, and his major commissions of the early 1880s were carried out under the name *James, Seward & Thomas*. The first of these, the Free Library in The Hayes, begun in 1880, is Elizabethan, with a mullion-and-transom oriel worthy of Burghley. The Royal Infirmary, Newport Road, Roath, first phase 1882–3, is Tudor Gothic, but made imposing by a central tower unmistakably influenced by Waterhouse. The huge Coal and Shipping Exchange, of 1884–8, which fills Mount Stuart Square, Butetown, is disappointingly ill-defined, Mixed Renaissance, as it would have been called at the time. The Free Library extension of 1894–6 can be similarly labelled, but is much tauter and more convincing, and indeed is Seward's most impressive work. It attractively introduces emblematic sculpture. The little Turner House Gallery, Penarth, 1887–8, is also memorable for its sculpture, Ruskinian Lamps of Truth flanking the entrance. Modern alterations have obscured its Queen Anne character. Finally in 1902 *Seward* took Swansea by storm, when he won the competition for the Harbour Trust Offices with a design in the newly fashionable Arts and Crafts Baroque style. This too incorporated sculpture and was clearly influenced by the new Cardiff Town Hall and Law Courts then rising in Cathays Park (*see* below).

Others who made a significant mark on Cardiff were the architects who worked for the major estates. *Alexander Roos* of London, the Bute Estate's architect from 1851 to 1868, must have been responsible for the original semi-Palladian houses in Mount Stuart Square, Butetown, of the mid 1850s, of which a few survive, and the Jacobean Dock Chambers there of *c.* 1860, as also for Windsor Place on Bute land near the town centre. His successor, *E.W.M. Corbett*, is better documented. His large additions to *Prichard*'s Nazareth House, 1887 etc., maintain the Gothic style. But the former County Club, Westgate Street, of *c.* 1890 hovers between Jacobean and Queen Anne. He defined this style more firmly at the South Wales Institute of Engineers in Park Place, 1893, and used it with gusto at the Royal Hamadryad Hospital, Butetown, 1902–3, and in the extension of 1907 to the Institute of Engineers. At all three red brick and red stone unite with red terracotta. *Corbett*'s hand is to be seen in the extensive housing development on the Bute Estate, most notably in Ninian Road, Roath, and Cathedral Road, Canton, completed in 1900, where the still Gothic character of the houses demonstrates the enduring strength of the tradition established by Burges, though there is no longer any recognizable trace of his personal style.

The Tredegar Estate, which developed middle-class Tredegarville from 1857 and artisan Splott from 1881, gave extensive employment to their architects, first *W. G. & E. Habershon* and later *Habershon & Fawckner*, of London and Newport.

The Windsor Estate also retained an architect at the end of the C19, *Harry Snell*. He had little to do with the Windsor artisan housing in Grangetown, Cardiff, and all his significant buildings are to be seen at Penarth. The exotic Public Baths there, 1883–5, were designed by him in collaboration with *H. C. Harris*. The Jacobean Public Library, 1904–6, is his best work. Again, the handsome houses, in a quiet but substantial Jacobean style, which line the residential streets of Penarth, presumably owe much to *Snell*.

The finest late Victorian and Edwardian COMMERCIAL ARCHITECTURE is concentrated in and around Mount Stuart Square, Butetown, where the coal companies had their headquarters cheek by jowl with one another on all four sides of Seward's Exchange Building. Most of Cardiff's leading practices are represented, from *W. D. Blessley*, whose semi-Gothic Pascoe House of 1875 has already been mentioned, to *Henry Budgen*, whose Cambrian and Cymric Buildings, 1907–10, 1911, are in a Dix-huitième style with Rococo touches. *William Frame*'s Pierhead Building of 1896–7, already mentioned (p. 103), must be acknowledged again here, a celebration of commercial achievement promoted by aristocratic initiative, festooned as it is with Bute heraldry.

This cosy scene, in which Cardiff's architects shared commissions between them without any outside interference, was rudely shattered in 1897, with the announcement of the winner of the competition for the first of the public buildings in Cathays Park. These were the Town Hall (City Hall from 1905) and Law Courts, and the competition for their design, assessed by Alfred Waterhouse, was won by the newly emerging London firm of *Lanchester, Stewart & Rickards*. The second and third premiated designs were also by London firms, and Seward was unplaced. The winning design was classical, of great ebullience and resource, planned to create impressive, logically interlinked internal spaces in the Beaux-Arts tradition, and grouped externally with a fascinating interplay between dome, tower, portico and mirror-image façades, all enriched by abundant sculpture. Nothing like this had been seen in Wales before, and by the time the buildings were opened in 1905 it was clear that they had set a new standard

109, 110

for civic architecture throughout the British Isles. Two other buildings in Cathays Park emulate the classicism, as also the scale and impressiveness, of the City Hall and Law Courts, but in contrasting styles. Neither attempts to repeat their rich Franco-Austrian brew, though both laboured under the requirement that their cornice lines should respect that of the City Hall and Law Courts. The earlier of the two is the University College of South Wales, designed in 1903 by *W. D. Caröe*. This has a long, elaborately subdivided frontage facing the central gardens of Cathays Park, and a heroically scaled central library, both complete by 1909. Caröe's intention was to exploit the fresh, even naive, classicism, still touched by the Gothic spirit, of mid-C17 architecture at the ancient English universities. However, such an idiom is too frail to sustain the scale of Caröe's commission, and for all its incidental delights, the University College must be judged a failure. The courtyard to the E was completed in stages up to 1954 by *Caröe* and his son *Alban Caroe*, on a progressively simplified plan.

Caröe's training as a Gothicist had made him suspicious of the constraints which the classical style by its nature imposes. The architects of the third major building, *Smith & Brewer*, who won the competition to design the National Museum of Wales in 1910, had made their name with works in the Arts and Crafts spirit. For a large-scale public work, however, they abandoned their previous allegiance in favour of an American Beaux-Arts idiom worthy of McKim, Mead & White. Their competition-winning plan had extraordinary panache, but was seriously curtailed in construction, partly due to the interruption of the First World War.
112 Only the restrained S front and the enormous entrance hall, a remarkable three-dimensional adventure, were realized as originally conceived. The main phase of construction lasted from 1913 to 1927, and the building, continued in stages, finally reached completion, to a modified design by the *Alex Gordon Partnership*, as recently as 1993.

One more building in Cathays Park deserves to be mentioned in the same breath as these three, the compact but stately Glamorgan (now Mid Glamorgan) County Hall by *Vincent Harris & T.A. Moodie*, 1908–12. The colonnaded front elevation, the palazzo-like rear and the semicircular Council Chamber are all equally distinguished and architecturally related to one another with satisfying logic.

Of the other early buildings in Cathays Park, one, the charming, *trianon*-like University Registry of 1903–4, is by a Glamorgan architect, *H. W. Wills*, here in the partnership of *Wills & Anderson*. *Wills* had, 1893–5, put up the first significant building to overlook Cathays Park, Aberdare Hall, a hostel for women students of the recently founded University College. In its red brick and terracotta and its Jacobean style, it was utterly different from what was so soon to occupy the Park.

Cathays Park is an excellent place to study EDWARDIAN ARCHITECTURAL SCULPTURE. The attics of the City Hall and Law Courts are inhabited by symbolic groups in the spirited

Baroque of the New Sculpture, executed from 1903 by *Henry Poole, Paul Montford* and *F. W. Pomeroy*. The figure groups in the corresponding positions on the National Museum of Wales are appropriately tighter and held more firmly within their architectural frame. They date from 1914–15, and the sculptors are *T. J. Clapperton, Gilbert Bayes* and *L. R. Garbe*. At the Glamorgan County Hall the sculptural groups, by *Albert Hodge*, are considerably more arresting, as they are at ground level, and in a magnificent neo-Greek style. There is one important internal sculptural ensemble, in the City Hall, the crowd of white marble statues of great figures of Welsh history in the upper-level reception hall. The scheme, carried out 1913–16, was masterminded by *J. Havard Thomas*, but pride of place is given to a figure of St David by Cardiff's most distinguished sculptor, *Goscombe John*. Several bronze statues by *John* stand in Cathays Park, but undoubtedly the finest and most original work of sculpture there is *Albert Toft*'s South African War Memorial of *c.*1909, crowned 111 by a winged figure of Peace brandishing an uprooted olive tree.

The Late Victorian and Edwardian Period outside Cardiff

Contemporary PUBLIC ARCHITECTURE elsewhere in Glamorgan is almost equally interesting, if not so consistently impressive. Now was the time for major dock offices. The equally wholehearted Wren-style Docks Office at Barry, 1897–1900, was much more in tune with the times than Frame's Burgesian Gothic at the Cardiff Pierhead Building, though its inexperienced architect, *A. E. Bell*, lacked the imagination to capitalize fully on this major commission. At Swansea, as has been noted, *Edwin Seward* in 1902–3 built the Harbour Trust Offices in a quite convincing Baroque.

Then there is a group of municipal buildings. First comes *E. A. Johnson*'s somewhat overheated Town Hall at Merthyr Tydfil, 1896–7, its lavish early Renaissance detail executed in orange terracotta. In 1902–3 three town councils held competitions which produced contrasting results. Architecturally most satisfying are the District Council Offices at Pontypridd by the distinguished 113 London architect *H. T. Hare*. His is a beautifully judged building, like a late Stuart market hall, but purer and just a little grander. Barry's fast-burgeoning pretensions are well expressed by the vigorous but disjointedly Baroque Municipal Buildings by *C. E. Hutchinson & E. Harding Payne* of London. At Mountain Ash, *J. H. Phillips* of Cardiff for his Town Hall looked to the same sort of precedents as Hare, and handled them with a provincial naiveté.

It is in the centre of Swansea that Edwardian Baroque finds its richest expression in the county, culminating in a series of important buildings by leading local architects in the half-decade before 1914. *Glendinning Moxham*'s Glynn Vivian Art Gallery, 1909–11, 114 is the most impressive, small but monumental. The Central Police Station, 1912–13 by *Ernest Morgan*, the newly appointed Borough Architect, is similar in style, but much larger and less tautly organized. *C. T. Ruthen* (later Sir Charles Ruthen, Director-General of Housing to the Ministry of Health) was responsible for three buildings in an idiosyncratic, picturesque version of the style: the Mond Buildings, 1911, and the Exchange Buildings and Carlton Cinema, both begun in 1913.

Banks

Several further types of building deserve a brief review across the whole of this period. Most consistent over the longest time-span are BANKS, Barryesque, Palladian, Baroque, and finally neo-Grecian, but exceptional in being unswervingly classical from the 1850s onwards. Two fine early examples by specialist bank architects are in St Mary Street, Cardiff, 1857 by *Thomas Lysaght*, and in Aberdare, 1857–8 by *William Gingell*, both using the Barry palazzo style. There is nothing more to report until the 1890s. *E. W. M. Corbett*'s bank in Butetown, Cardiff, 1891, is quietly Palladian, *J. A. Chatwin*'s in High Street, Cardiff, 1892, is similar, but has pilasters, suited to its prominent site. Rivalry between banking companies and the taste for stronger classical effects around the turn of the century produced remarkable competitive groups of banks in Windsor Road, Neath, where *Glendinning Moxham* designed two (1894 and 1908–9), and Wind Street, Swansea, where he designed one (1915). Strong meat too is *P. J. Thomas*'s Genoese-style bank of 1901–2 at Merthyr Tydfil. The climax of this tradition was not reached until the late 1920s, in the noble and scholarly National Provincial (now National Westminster) banks by *F. C. R. Palmer & W. F. C. Holden*. Examples are in the groups at Neath and Swansea, but the magnum opus of this partnership in the county is the neo-Grecian bank at Butetown, Cardiff, 1926–7.

Educational Buildings and Libraries

To turn from commerce to education is to leave the world of *laissez-faire* and to enter an ideological environment. The provision of educational facilities had for long been an offshoot of religious commitment, so inevitably the design of schools was caught up in the architectural debates of the 1840s which centred on the revival of a medieval ecclesiastical style. *John Prichard*'s village schools of *c.* 1860 in the Pugin–Butterfield idiom have already been mentioned. An even earlier example is *Woodyer*'s former school at Sketty, Swansea, of 1853, built for J. H. Vivian in association with the church Woodyer had just completed for him. *Prichard*'s rebuilding of Cowbridge Grammar School, a C17 foundation, is Tudor, not yet touched by the precepts of the Ecclesiologists, and the same can be said of his little school at Gelligaer, 1850–1. Howell's School for Girls, Llandaff, Cardiff, built in 1858–9 to the design of *Herbert Williams* after the dismissal of *Decimus Burton*, hovers between Tudor and Dec, and is notable for its size and for its towered and turreted skyline. *Thomas Taylor*'s Tudor Swansea Grammar School of 1851–3 has largely been pulled down, but the powerful early Gothic range added in 1869 survives, though not in use. It is by *Benjamin Bucknall*, the disciple of Viollet-le-Duc. One other Gothic school is at Neath, 1857 by *Egbert Moxham*. The schools built by *Sir Charles Barry* at the expense of Lady Charlotte Guest at Dowlais, Merthyr Tydfil, 1853–5, in a style reminiscent of Tintern Abbey have, sadly, been pulled down.

The Elementary Education Act of 1870, which ushered in the modern era of universal education for children, led to a revolution in school buildings. Many local school boards, established by the Act, faced with providing enough school places for the rapidly expanding towns, had to construct schools on an entirely new scale, many of them intended for over 1,000 pupils. Girls normally occupied the ground floor of a board school, boys the upper floor, with infants in a separate building. In Glamorgan board schools classrooms were grouped normally along a broad central corridor (a 'marching corridor' as it was called), or in a few cases separated by glass partitions from a central hall, from which the head teacher could survey the less experienced teachers and their charges in the classrooms. The ideas of E.R. Robson, architect to the London School Board, reached Wales by means of his book *School Architecture* (1874). In particular Robson's self-conscious break with Gothic for schools and his substitution of 'Queen Anne' were influential in Glamorgan. The first instance of the new style is a freak, the National (i.e. church) school (now St German's Court) at Roath, Cardiff, 1874 by *G. F. Bodley*, architect of the London School Board offices, opened the same year.

The earliest board schools to survive in the county are three fairly small ones by *H. C. Harris*, at Penarth, 1875–6, Bridgend, 1875, and Pencoed, 1881, the latter two drawing on Norman Shaw rather than Robson. The Cardiff School Board distributed commissions among leading local architects, but too many of the first wave are demolished, or in the case of *J. P. Jones*'s school at Canton, 1881–2, spoilt. *E. M. Bruce Vaughan*'s at Grangetown, 1883, and Canton, *c.* 1887, stay faithful to the pointed arch. The earliest large, typical board schools are two at Barry, both by *Seward & Thomas*, 1887–95 and 1890–2, one dramatically sited and picturesquely incoherent, the other a highly regular, town-centre group. More successful than either is *Jones, Richards & Budgen*'s Hannah Street school at Barry of 1899. It displays in a 102 particularly lively way the enormous, simplified Venetian windows which were the most popular form to illuminate the classrooms, as well as the symmetry of plan and main façade which characterize all the large schools. Cardiff's later board schools belong to the late 1890s onwards. The largest and also the most enjoyable is *Veall & Sant*'s of 1896–8 at Canton, with wittily placed sculpture and inscriptions. *E. W. M. Corbett*'s of 1894–5 at Roath Park is a textbook essay. *J. H. Phillips*, who was something of a specialist in school design, was responsible for the austere board school at Penarth of 1897–8. Swansea from the mid 1890s had its own educational architect, *G. E. T. Laurence*, who had trained in Robson's office and practised from London. Laurence experimented with three-storeyed arrangements, a vogue in London board schools of the period, placing the infants on the ground storey, below the girls and boys. At his school at St Thomas, 1897, the steeply sloping site justified this arrangement. But he repeated it in 1900 at Manselton, in what was the most expensive of all the board schools in the county, where turrets and decorative enrichments produce an effect that calls to mind nothing so much as an Elizabethan prodigy house.

Under the Welsh Intermediate Education Act of 1889 a small number of 'Higher Grade' schools, built to a higher specification for smaller numbers of older and more advanced pupils, were put up. By far the most expensive was *George Thomas*'s of 1897 in The Parade, Roath, Cardiff (now Coleg Glan Hafren), in a charming and well-handled early French Renaissance style, later extended in the same style. The other sizeable intermediate schools are at Aberdare, 1892–6 by *J. H. Phillips*, and Penarth, 1894–7 by *Harry Snell*.

When the responsibility for school-building was in 1902 taken over by county councils, two county education architects were appointed, *D. Pugh Jones* for the eastern half of the county, *W. James Nash* for the western. Between them they were responsible for scores of schools, most of them of no special merit. *Nash*'s schools are neatly designed and prettily detailed with the minimum of stylistic affectation. Good examples, both single-storeyed with central pavilions, are at Port Talbot, 1911, and Pontardawe, 1914. *Pugh Jones*'s schools were at first more routine, that of 1911–13 at Caerphilly being a rare example with some individuality. In the inter-war period he designed several large, formal schools in a Neo-Georgian style, e.g. Caerphilly, 1922, Tonyrefail, 1933. Nevertheless, there was still scope for individual commissions to go to local architects, as in the memorable instance of the Higher Standard School in Aberdare, designed by *Thomas Roderick* and built 1905–7. Here is the swansong of the central hall plan, but here too is an architectural show, of flamboyant shaped gables and neo-Jacobean tower, to emphasize the local pride that publicly funded school building could engender in the early C20. The only other special case requiring mention is *J. Coates Carter*'s additions to Harris's board school in Penarth, for their heraldic and figural friezes, c. 1905–10.

FURTHER EDUCATION BUILDINGS have already been partly discussed. *H. W. Wills*, who has been encountered working in Jacobean and Dix-huitième guises for the University College in Cathays Park, Cardiff, built the neo-Tudor Technical College on Mount Pleasant, Swansea, in 1897–8, with quite a powerful tower. A sensational tower was the centrepiece of the late Perp Medical School built for the University College of South Wales, Cardiff, in Newport Road by *E. M. Bruce Vaughan*, 1911–21. Also in 1911 *G. E. T. Laurence* built the Elizabethan Teacher Training College at Townhill, Swansea, spectacularly sited, but only in plan taking advantage of its site. By contrast, *Teather & Wilson*'s Teacher Training College at Barry, 1913–14, also on a fine, high-lying site, is a self-confident neo-Wren essay.

PUBLIC LIBRARIES are a characteristic production of the first decade of the C20, thanks to the generosity of the philanthropist Andrew Carnegie. Several of the leading local practices gained attractive commissions thereby. There was no agreement as to style, though the need for high and well-lit reading rooms encouraged the Gothicists. Thus *Bruce Vaughan* in his two public libraries in Cardiff suburbs, 1900–1 at Grangetown and 1906 at Canton, could keep to his preferred style. The best of the Gothic examples is a third one at Cardiff, the Cathays Library of 1906 by *Speir &* 108 *Beavan*. This charming and lucid demonstration of the then fashionable butterfly plan is architecturally in a class of its own. *E. A. Johnson*'s Arts and Crafts Tudor library at Dowlais, Merthyr Tydfil, of 1903–6, is pretty too, exploiting a sloping site. Jacobean examples are at Roath, Cardiff, 1900–1 by *Teather & Wilson*, at Whitchurch, Cardiff, 1904 by *R. & S. Williams*, and, more substantial, *Harry Snell*'s major work in Penarth, 1904–6. Only at the end of the decade did a memorable classical library appear, *W. Dowdeswell*'s amusing Baroque miniature of 1909 at Treharris.

One further type of educational – and also recreational – building remains to be mentioned, the WORKMEN'S INSTITUTE. This was a speciality of the South Wales coalfields, where many of the mining communities between *c.*1890 and 1914 succeeded in building huge, cubic institutes, which provided libraries and reading rooms as well as gymnasia and even, in some cases, basement swimming pools. They were normally paid for by voluntary deductions from miners' pay packets, but this did not prevent architectural display, at least externally, on the most ambitious of them. Always the detail is classical, of board-school or Arts and Crafts Baroque derivation. Most workmen's institutes were designed by architects practising in the Valleys, *Jacob Rees* of Pentre, for example, at Blaengarw, 1893–4, and Treorchy, 1895, and *Thomas Roderick* of Aberdare, whose institute at Aberaman, 1907–9, is one of the architecturally most convincing. The showiest of all, encrusted in many-coloured terracotta, Nixon's Institute at Mountain Ash, 1898–9, is by *Dan Lloyd* of Aberbeeg, over the border in Gwent. On the rare occasions when Cardiff architects were called in, as *W. Beddoe Rees* at Pontardulais in 1905–6 and *E. M. Bruce Vaughan* at Llanbradach, 1912, they conformed to local conventions. The architects of two of the most dominating institutes are so far unknown, Abercynon, 1904, and the mighty addition at Treorchy, 1913.

Domestic Architecture

The account of building activity in the county during the quarter century before 1914 would be seriously incomplete without some further discussion of domestic architecture, from the country mansions of coal magnates to miners' housing in the Valleys. The coal magnate who built on a uniquely grand scale was John Cory, whose Dyffryn House, near St Nicholas, of 1893–4, was designed by *E. A. Lansdowne* of Newport. The result is a squat and old-fashioned essay in Barryesque Italianate, though the house abounds inside with splendid brought-in chimneypieces of various periods from the early C17 to the mid C19. The celebrated gardens at Dyffryn were laid out for Cory's son *c.* 1906 by the fashionable garden designer *Thomas H. Mawson.* A smaller, later and far more sophisticated residence for a coal entrepreneur, where house and garden are designed as one, is Craig-y-parc, Pentyrch, by *C. E. Mallows*, 1914–18. Here the source of influence is much more nearly contemporary, Lutyens of the turn of the century. But Mallows imposed his own logic on the ensemble, so that exterior and interior work together in a highly satisfying way.

C.F.A. Voysey is the most famous name among the architects commissioned to design houses in the county at this period. Tŷ
107 Bronna, Fairwater, Cardiff, built 1903–6, is immediately recognizable as his, contained and austere under its overall hipped roof. Only the arcaded ground storey, made possible by the hillside site, and the entrance at the short end, are exceptional. Voysey's handling of materials, stone and roughcast externally, timber and ironwork within, place him in the mainstream of the Arts and Crafts movement. The local architect who aligned himself enthusiastically with the movement was *J. Coates Carter.* All his most interesting work is to be seen at Penarth. His school additions have already been mentioned. The earlier of his church halls, Woodland Hall, designed in 1896, is an up-to-date Arts and Crafts essay. His group of houses in Victoria Road, 1892 and *c.* 1902–3, includes two built for himself. In the later one Arts and Crafts bravura is tinged with whimsy. Whimsical too are his two
104 nearby buildings of 1906, All Saints Parish Hall, where inspiration from H. H. Richardson is unmistakable, and the startlingly rectilinear Paget Rooms.

Penarth is a good place to study the best middle-class housing of the period. Several spacious streets were laid out by the Windsor Estate from the mid 1880s, presumably using their estate architect, *Harry Snell.* The contemporary developments in Cardiff promoted by the Bute and Tredegar Estates have already been mentioned (pp. 104–5).

Miners' housing in the Valleys is an entirely different story. Here standardization reigned. An important bench-mark was set by the Artisans' and Labourers' Dwellings Improvement Act of 1875. The only significant survivals of pre-1875 housing are the terraces at Llwynypia, Tonypandy, built by Archibald Hood for his miners. This is an unusually regular development, the terraces banked in rows up the hillside, and accessible only by footpaths. The only mining community which shows any sign of having been built to a predetermined plan is Treherbert, developed from the late 1850s, where the ground landlord was the Marquess of Bute. Generally, whether landlords, colliery companies or miners' building clubs were acting as developers, the mining communities grew haphazardly, with long terraces conforming to the exigencies of the narrow valleys. Pennant Sandstone walls were relieved by red or yellow machine-pressed brick dressings. Only the tinplate workers of Pontardawe were housed in semi-detached pairs rather than in terraces. The period of greatest building activity was

the 1890s and 1900s. Rarely can any particular development be
precisely dated, so Stanleytown, Tylorstown, known to have been 105
built in 1895 by *T. R. Phillips* of Pontypridd, is an exception.

The Garden City movement left quite a mark on the county,
both in Cardiff and in Swansea, in response to the need for slum
clearance, and in the Valleys, to provide workers' housing to an
improved standard. Swansea Corporation in 1910 mounted a
Cottage Exhibition, whereby prototype cottages were built in a
layout directly influenced by *Raymond Unwin*. This was the start
of the Mayhill development on the Town Hill, and cottages were
built to designs by London architects such as *P. Morley Horder*
and *Pepler & Allen*, but also by the local architect *C. T. Ruthen*,
who was soon to become a housing expert on the national scene.
The Garden City type layout of the rest of Townhill, Swansea,
followed from 1920, with the Borough Architect, *Ernest Morgan*,
in control. At Cockett, Swansea, a second scheme, Fforestfach
Miners' Village, was begun in 1912, the architects being *Pepler &
Allen*, but only the first eight houses were built to their design.

Much more was achieved in the suburbs of Cardiff, where
Rhiwbina Garden Village was laid out to a plan by *Raymond* 106
Unwin in 1912. The houses, designed by *A. H. Mottram*, in the
first phase, 1912–13, survive largely unaltered, set behind hedges
in tree-lined streets and square-ended culs-de-sac. *Unwin* was
also involved in the equally large but less well preserved Garden
Suburb at Barry from 1915, where the architect was *T. Alwyn
Lloyd*.

Even earlier than these were the beginnings of Wyndham Park,
Peterston-super-Ely, promoted by the Cory family, and laid out
in 1909 to be part of a huge amphitheatrical scheme by *Thomas
Adams* and the garden designer *T. H. Mawson*. A terrace of
remarkable flat-roofed houses turns up in the middle of the
development. Otherwise, here as elsewhere, the simplified Arts
and Crafts style of Parker & Unwin is in evidence. In the Valleys
the earliest development on Garden Village lines is at Gilfach
Goch, begun in 1910; the smallest but architecturally most distinguished is Scales Houses, Llwydcoed, 1912–14, by *E. G. Allen*
of *Pepler & Allen*; and the largest scheme is *W. Beddoe Rees*'s
Fernhill Garden Village at Abercwmboi, 1913–16.

BETWEEN THE WARS

This was a difficult time for Glamorgan. The decline in the
demand for steam coal, just beginning to become apparent by
1914, had by *c.* 1924 become catastrophic, so that the nationwide
depression of the late 1920s was particularly severe in Glamorgan.
Crisis levels of unemployment were reached in the 1930s, most
notoriously in Merthyr Tydfil, where the iron industry had completely collapsed and there was nothing yet to take its place.

But pride, whether national or local, is very hard to kill. Among

the most notable products of the inter-war years are monuments
of one kind or another. First come WAR MEMORIALS. The
115 Welsh National War Memorial in Cathays Park, Cardiff, is an
exceptionally beautiful composition of Corinthian columns
encircling bronze statues, of 1924–8 by *Sir Ninian Comper* and
the sculptor *Bertram Pegram*. Only its iconography is hackneyed.
In this latter respect the two most ambitious purely sculptural
war memorials are of some interest. That at Llandaff, Cardiff, of
1924 by *Goscombe John*, has a central personification of Llandaff,
that at Merthyr Tydfil, by *L. S. Merrifield*, 1931, is centred on a
figure of Fate. The cenotaph at Penarth, 1924, has a Victory
figure by *John*. War memorial stained glass windows can be found
in numerous churches, but none is of special merit. The one
outstanding example of inter-war STAINED GLASS is the intensely
coloured vision of the Heavenly Jerusalem by *Karl Parsons*, of
1927–8, at All Saints, Porthcawl.

   The most extraordinary reflection of local pride is the new
Guildhall erected at Swansea 1932–4 to the design of *Sir Percy
Thomas*. Thomas was the single most successful architect Glamorgan has ever produced, twice President of the Royal Institute
of British Architects and in 1939 awarded its Gold Medal, so it is
worth putting the Swansea Guildhall in the context of his career.
In 1909 he became design partner in a partnership with *Ivor Jones*,
the first fruit of which was the hot red and yellow Y.M.C.A.
Building at Merthyr Tydfil, in the emphatically detailed Baroque
popular at that moment. In 1911 *Ivor Jones & Percy Thomas* won
the competition for the Technical Institute in Cathays Park,
Cardiff. This, now the Bute Building, constructed 1913–16, for all
its size and prestigious location, is disappointingly conventional.
Nevertheless, it gives a foretaste of the restraint and preference
for sheer, unmodelled surfaces which is such a notable feature of
Thomas's major buildings of the 1930s. After the war the practice
was, not surprisingly, largely inactive until the mid 1920s. Empire
House, Butetown, Cardiff, 1926, is a piece of Lutyenesque com-
mercialism. However, the commercial commission of two years
later, the extension to Howell's drapery shop, St Mary Street,
Cardiff, inspired a really distinguished piece of American Beaux-
Arts classicism, too high-flying perhaps for its purpose, but the
building with the most powerful presence in Cardiff's premier
street.

   The Swansea Guildhall commission came next. *Ivor Jones &
Percy Thomas* won the competition in 1930, with a lucid plan
and porticoed elevations in three directions. Cost limitations
proscribed the porticoes, for which were substituted giant coffered
arches. This enabled the entire exterior to be treated as a series
of white ashlar boxes with minimal detail, above which sails a tall,
slender tower. *Thomas* seemed to have assimilated Modernist
imagery without abandoning classical principles of design. Internally, the classicism comes back with a vengeance, in a series of
neo-antique vaulted and columnar spaces unmatched in Britain
at this period. There is indeed a timeless quality about these
rooms, in particular the columned Council Chamber, like the

interior of an antique temple, and its vaulted ante-hall. The
Brangwyn Hall, a concert hall with ebullient Art Deco details and 116
fittings, houses the remarkable series of mural paintings by *Frank
Brangwyn*, celebrating the British Empire through a vision of
brilliantly coloured jungle scenes.

Thomas's large extension to Glamorgan County Hall, Cardiff,
1932, did not offer a second opportunity for splendour, so he
settled for a quiet, Neo-Georgian idiom which successfully
reduces the apparent bulk of what is in effect an office block. A
stone's throw further N in Cathays Park *Thomas* (no longer in
partnership with Jones) erected in 1937–8 a smaller essay in his
Swansea Guildhall manner, the Temple of Peace and Health.
Once more, this was a war memorial, and it consists of two office
wings, one for workers for peace, the other for workers for health,
with in the centre a minimalist temple portico leading to a gleam-
ing black, green and gold templar space with no obvious function.

Meanwhile *Thomas* designed a number of private houses, some
Voyseyesque (Fairwater, Cardiff, 1921, 1927, Lisvane, Cardiff,
and St Nicholas, both 1939–40), some Neo-Georgian (Radyr
c. 1927, Michaelston-le-Pit, 1939–40).

Thomas's buildings reflect the ambivalence and perhaps dis-
quiet of an architect still working in the traditions which had been
established at the turn of the century, but aware of the entirely
different idiom and values of the newly emergent Modernism.
During the 1930s Modernism itself hardly showed its face in
Glamorgan. Among religious buildings there is only the brave
little Expressionist church at Beddau, 1936, by a so-far unidentified architect. Among domestic ones there is only the white-
walled, flat-roofed house at Penarth by *Gordon Griffiths*, 1939.
Among schools, neo-Wren and Neo-Georgian continued, often
with pleasing results. There is one exception, the refreshingly
direct D-plan Mayhill Junior School at Townhill, Swansea, by
Ernest Morgan, taking advantage of a panoramic view. On the
industrial front there are the pithead baths of 1938 at Penallta
Colliery at Gelligaer. Only among hospitals is there a major
Modern building, *W. A. Pite, Son & Fairweather*'s Sully Hospital
for tubercular patients of 1932–6. Here medical theory went hand-
in-hand with the new aesthetic, for the requirement for maximum
curative light and air encouraged steel-framed construction,
making possible large windows angled towards the sunlight, and
white-painted wall surfaces. The architects eliminated the pitched
roofs of their first design, once they had grasped the implications
of this novel vocabulary. By contrast, at the other two large
hospitals of the 1930s, Llandough Hospital by *Willmott & Smith*,
completed 1934, and the East Glamorgan General Hospital, Llantwit Fardre, 1938–9 by *Bradshaw, Gass & Hope*, an unhappy
struggle takes place between the new medical ideas and the old
architectural style.

ARCHITECTURE SINCE THE SECOND
WORLD WAR

The post-war period extends for half a century. As far as Glamorgan is concerned, it can be divided into two halves, which may
be termed Modernist and, rather than Post-Modernist, Pluralist.
    For thirty years, from 1945 to the mid 1970s, a Modernist idiom
established itself as the *lingua franca*. This came about through
the intervention of a small number of English architects, most
notably *G. G. Pace* of York, and through the conversion to Modernism of local authority architects' departments and the leading
private practices. Here the outstanding names are the Cardiff
City Architects Department, under *John Dryburgh*, 1957–74, and
two practices, that of Sir Percy Thomas (continued first under
his son *Norman Thomas* as *Sir Percy Thomas & Son*, then from
1964 as *Sir Percy Thomas & Partners*, and finally from 1971 as the
Percy Thomas Partnership) and that of T. Alwyn Lloyd (first as
T. Alwyn Lloyd & Gordon, and then as the *Alex Gordon
Partnership*). Before considering the work of these practices, the
achievements of the outsiders can be encompassed through a
survey first of religious buildings, then of educational.

Religious Buildings

George Pace's parabolic reinforced-concrete arch spanning the
nave of Llandaff Cathedral is the single most eloquent statement
of the Modernist ideal in the county. It uses a material characteristic of the C20 in a way which dramatizes the scale and
spatial character of the medieval building without making any
concessions to medieval forms. The concrete cylinder which it
supports has both the practical function of housing the pipes of
the positive organ, and the emblematic purpose of displaying
117 *Epstein*'s hieratic figure of Christ in Majesty, and a heavenly host
of angels reused from the wrecked Victorian organ and choir
118 stalls. *Pace* also built two chapels at Llandaff, St David's Chapel,
1953–6, added to the N side of the nave of the Cathedral, and the
free-standing chapel at St Michael's Theological College, 1957–9.
Both have white plastered walls and vaults imaginatively illuminated, inspired in equal measure by simple medieval North
Country churches and Le Corbusier's chapel at Ronchamp. *Pace*'s
only other significant building in the county, St Teilo, Cockett,
Swansea, 1961–3, is outside brutally uncommunicative, but shows
an exhilarating internal management of space. Here the major
structural component is a series of asymmetrical laminated timber
arches.
    It is interesting to compare St Teilo with *Seely & Paget*'s slightly
later St Mark, Gabalfa, Cardiff, of 1967–8. Here too the interior
is spanned by laminated timber arches, but the octagonal plan,
the even lighting and the openwork concrete tower sited axially
over the entrance all make this a less radical, more soothing

statement. The most prolific firm designing churches in the 1960s was *F. R. Bates, Son & Price* of Newport. Nearly a dozen are to be found in the county dating between 1960 and 1969, mostly for Roman Catholics. They make a show of reinforced concrete structure, unified interior space and unexpected light sources, but none approaches the power of Pace's chapels.

CREMATORIA form the other architecturally interesting type of religious building. The crematorium at Margam, 1969 by *F. D. Williamson & Associates*, is straightforwardly Modernist. The crematorium at Llwydcoed, 1970–1 by *H.M.R. Burgess & Partners*, is more arresting, a composition of monopitch roofs to top-light the chapels. The Mid Glamorgan Crematorium at Coychurch, 1969–70 by *Fry, Drew, Knight, Creamer*, is quite exceptional, a remarkable illustration of *Maxwell Fry*'s ideas about making crematoria more sympathetic and numinous. This is much in the idiom of late Le Corbusier, contrasting low, undulating walls of reused Pennant sandstone boulders for the memorial cloister with a concrete-walled chapel of unmistakably Ronchamp-like outline. The cloister and free-standing chapel of remembrance are enhanced by richly coloured abstract stained glass by *Timothy Lewis* and students of Swansea College of Art.

STAINED GLASS has remained a lively and much-patronized art form, and deserves a further paragraph at this point. Artists of national repute were sometimes called in. *Hugh Easton*'s figure of Christ, 1955, at St Martin, Roath, Cardiff, is unforgettable. Emotionally charged abstract windows by *Piper* and *Reyntiens* are at Llandaff Cathedral, Cardiff, 1959, and at St Mary, Swansea, 1965–6. The huge panel of painted glass at St David's Hall, Cardiff, 1984–5, designed by *Hans Gottfried von Stockhausen* of Stuttgart, should also be mentioned.

But it is successive initiatives derived from Swansea College of Art that make stained glass in the county since the late 1940s exceptional. In 1947 *Howard Martin* the designer and *Hubert Thomas* the glass-painter, who had both trained at the College, set up *Celtic Studios*. Their work is stylistically conservative. The window which enabled them to set up in practice is at St Michael and All Angels, Manselton, Swansea. Windows by *Celtic Studios* dating over the ensuing thirty years can be seen in scores of Glamorgan churches, even if a coherent scheme such as that at Crynant, 1951–66, is an exception.

From the 1960s *Timothy Lewis* has masterminded much more varied production, his own and that by others connected with Swansea College of Art. His moving abstract window at Llangyfelach, 1963, is strongly influenced by Graham Sutherland. The glass at Coychurch crematorium, by *Lewis* and others, was executed throughout the 1970s up to 1983. The other showplace for teachers at the College and its former students is St Mary, Swansea, where there are experimental windows in a wide variety of idioms by *Kuni Kajiwara*, 1981, *Catrin Jones*, 1982, and *Rodney Bender*, 1985. The latest windows, however, show disappointing loss of nerve, as can be observed most clearly at St Luke, Aberdare, where *Timothy Lewis*'s fascinatingly unconventional window of 1966–8 faces his much less adventurous one of 1990.

Public Buildings

EDUCATIONAL ARCHITECTURE of this period, it has to be admitted, is considerably less memorable. Reinforced-concrete-framed multi-storey slabs with more or less curtain walling are the characteristic components. The earliest examples, by London firms, which popularized the idiom in the county, all include Corbusian mannerisms. Earliest of all is the College of Further Education at Merthyr Tydfil, 1950–2 by *Yorke, Rosenberg & Mardall*, with a main range five and six storeys high. The Colleges of Further Education at Aberdare and Gorseinon by *Gollins, Melvin, Ward & Partners*, c.1954–5, are both two-storeyed. All three remain incomplete. The largest and most assured essay in this idiom is *Denis Clarke Hall*'s school at Kenfig Hill, also of the mid 1950s. During the 1960s the curtain-wall slab became the staple component of school design, as for example in the schools built for Cardiff City Council by their Architects Department under *John Dryburgh*. Cantonian High School, Fairwater, was built by the department 1961–3, and Fitzalan High School, Canton, in two phases, 1962–3 and 1966–8. The *Percy Thomas Partnership* designed an elegant variant in the Girls' Comprehensive School at Barry, 1969–73.

Both the constituent parts of the University of Wales in Glamorgan, when faced in the late 1950s with the need to expand, turned to *Sir Percy Thomas & Son*, as did the Welsh College of Advanced Technology. The Redwood Building, Cathays Park, Cardiff, for the latter, of 1960–1, is Modern without much spirit. The first phase of University College, Cardiff, on the other side of Cathays Park, now the Law Faculty, 1958–62, can be similarly characterized. Only for University College, Swansea, was there a spacious campus, in the park of Singleton Abbey. The master plan drawn up by *Verner O. Rees* in 1934, of which only the library was completed, in 1937, was set aside, and a much more expansive layout planned. This was fundamentally axial, and Fulton House, 1958–62, at the head of the axis, with a great glass-fronted block between projecting brown brick wings, retained in its symmetry a residuum of classicism. In the 1960s pressure to increase student numbers led to a distortion of the overall plan at University College, Swansea, and at University College, Cardiff, its abandonment in favour of a much higher-density scheme. The best building on the Swansea campus is the library extension of 1963–4, the externally exposed steel structure making possible a freely planned double-height space inside. At Cardiff the *Percy Thomas Partnership* was forced to put up a twelve-storey tower (completed 1967) fronted towards Cathays Park by a group of lower slabs, of seven storeys and of four, 1968–70. Cleanly detailed though they may be, and faced with Portland stone between the window bands, their alien nature in this classical paradise is impossible to ignore. The contributions made by *Alex Gordon &*

Partners to University College, Cardiff, are smaller, cubic, faced with dark brown or red brick: the Music Department of 1970, backdrop to a fine bronze by *Barbara Hepworth*, the Sherman Theatre, 1970–1, and the Students' Union, completed in 1973. Mention should also be made of the Arts and Social Sciences Library of 1972–6 by *Williamson, Faulkner Brown & Partners*, with its exposed concrete frame.

The University Hospital of Wales, Cathays, Cardiff, where teaching and patient care were combined in a single huge complex, proceeded throughout the 1960s, to the design of *S. W. Milburn & Partners*. It is dominated by long, parallel slabs, one eight-storeyed, the other five-storeyed. At the Prince Charles Hospital, Merthyr Tydfil, built 1965–75, the *Percy Thomas Partnership* adopted a similar idiom.

The most successful post-war building in Cathays Park, Cardiff, is *John Dryburgh*'s Central Police Station, 1966–8. The *Percy Thomas Partnership* is best represented elsewhere, by B.B.C. Broadcasting House, Llandaff, Cardiff, 1963–7, in which the various contrasted functions of the different parts are expressed by contrasts in size, fenestration and facing materials, and by the Welsh Folk Museum, St Fagans, 1968–74. This shows a somewhat forbidding Modernist face to the outside world, but inside develops an attractively informal courtyard, using its structure 121 ingeniously to facilitate display. A little later there is the Welsh Maritime Museum, Butetown, Cardiff, 1975–7 by *H.M.R. Burgess & Partners*, a simple red brick box, capped by a spaceframe roof and lit at eaves level. The mid 1970s also saw the first schemes by the *Welsh School of Architecture*, all small-scale, but all with the freshness and vigour radiated by students participating in the making of real, permanent buildings. The library and health centre at Cowbridge, 1973–4, is the earliest and best-preserved. 120 The primary school at Bridgend, 1974–5, has been enlarged, and that at Penarth, 1975–6, is likely to be so.

Domestic Building

HOUSING during this quarter-century which is deserving of mention here divides sharply into large-scale local authority schemes and small-scale private ones. The relentless northward expansion of Cardiff gave great opportunities to the City Architects Department under *John Dryburgh*. In the Valleys *F. D. Williamson & Associates* built Lewistown at Llangeinor *c.* 1967, wisely sited in the traditional valley-bottom position, but the much larger development at Penrhys, 1966–9 by *Alex Robertson, Peter Francis & Partners*, occupies an exposed hilltop site. Both partake of 'hill village' imagery, laid out in short, stepped terraces, with roughcast walls and monopitch roofs. The attractive staff housing built by *Alex Gordon & Partners* for Atlantic College, St Donats Castle, in the mid 1960s uses flat roofs and black brick, in combination with black weatherboarding. The one-off houses, all in sheltered locations, remain into the 1970s faithful to the flat roof. Earliest is a group of concrete-framed houses, of 1968 by *T. G. Jones &*

J. R. Evans at Dinas Powys. Also at Dinas Powys are the two most substantial groups of houses by *Hird & Brooks*, of the early to mid 1970s. Other examples of the satisfyingly undemonstrative, if introspective, work of this firm are at Llansannor and, a piquantly sited singleton, at Llandaff, Cardiff.

Industrial Buildings

After the Second World War the steel and tinplating industries were drastically rationalized and concentrated by the Steel Company of Wales. The massive Abbey Steelworks at Port Talbot were constructed 1948–52, and the tinplate works at Velindre, Llangyfelach, 1952–6 (one of a pair, the other being at Trostre, near Llanelli, over the border in Dyfed). The far-extending ranks of steel-clad rolling mills give these works a memorable image. The architects involved were *Sir Percy Thomas & Son*. The same firm, the *Percy Thomas Partnership*, has been responsible 1974–87 for the most inventively designed factory of the era succeeding that of heavy industry in South Wales: Amersham International Radiochemical factory, Whitchurch, Cardiff. Its bulk, clad in glass-reinforced-plastic, is shaped and coloured so that it settles inconspicuously into the landscape, in contrast to its predecessors' dramatic march across the countryside.

Light industry, which has replaced so much of the county's traditional heavy manufacturing over the past half-century, has produced virtually no memorable factory buildings. *Wallis, Gilbert & Partners*' Hoover Factory at Abercanaid of 1946–8 has the interest only of priority. Otherwise the American factory idiom of sheer, enigmatic cubes is represented most conspicuously at the Sony Factory at Pencoed, and on a particularly large scale by the Bosch Factory, 1989–90 by *A.D. Shepherd & Partners*, at Miskin.

THE LATE TWENTIETH CENTURY

The PLURALIST phase of Glamorgan's C20 architecture begins in the late 1970s and looks set to continue beyond the millennium. The first major post-war public building to accommodate itself to its setting and its neighbours, rather than asserting its difference from them, is St David's Hall, Cardiff, 1978–82 by the *J. Seymour Harris Partnership*. Its broken and complex form enables it to become absorbed into the central city fabric (though the gawky roof does not help), while the reinforced concrete framing and internal cantilevering make for a variety of unexpected internal spaces, in particular the capacious yet intimate concert hall itself. The *Peter Moro Partnership*'s Taliesin Theatre at University College, Swansea, completed in 1984, though free-standing and brick-clad, is conceived in a similar spirit and is architecturally better resolved.

The two new county halls built after Glamorgan was in 1974 split into three make a fascinating contrast. The West Glamorgan County Hall, Swansea, 1979–84 by the *West Glamorgan County Architects Department*, takes self-indulgent advantage of a spacious seaside site, with arms reaching out in all directions. Yet it retains the Modernist image, of white walls and windows in long bands. The South Glamorgan County Hall, 1986–7 by *J.R.C. Bethell*, 122 the County Architect, stood when first built in even more splendid isolation, inaugurating the redevelopment of Cardiff Bay. But here, while the plan is rigorously contained in four ranges round a courtyard, rising at their highest to five storeys, overhanging roof-slopes and a sloping brick plinth pull the building ground-wards and deny its formality. What links the two buildings, then, is the way they avoid the easily graspable overall form. Two further examples of this ethos can be noted. The Princess of Wales Hospital, Bridgend, 1981–5 by the *Alex Gordon Partnership*, anticipates Bethell's strategy at Cardiff Bay. *Wyn Thomas & Partners*, in their large extensions to the Engineering Department for University College, Cardiff, in particular the Trevithick Building, 1987–9, use a more mannered idiom, making play with porthole windows, but they too have learnt how to diminish apparent bulk in order to settle a building into its surroundings.

Yet formalism was by no means dead in the 1980s, and rears its head in unexpected places. Even unadulterated classicism can be found, most notably in the wings added by *McColl Associates* to the Grand Theatre, Swansea, 1985–8, and, appropriately, in the long-awaited final phase of the National Museum of Wales, Cardiff, by the *Alex Gordon Partnership*, completed in 1993.

Formalism more or less dependent on classical assumptions can be found in other guises. Commercial architecture has acknowledged once again the value of the resonances it can arouse, as can be seen at *Moxley Jenner*'s shopping centre of c. 1990–1 at Neath, a parody of a primitive temple, and the stately parade of industrial units on the St Mellons Business Park, c. 1990 by *The Wigley Fox Partnership*. The most successful recent deploy-ment of strict symmetry to give a small building presence is at the Crown Court, Swansea, 1985–8 by the *Alex Gordon Partnership*. 123 Without a single classical moulding, its well-proportioned sym-metry enables it to confront effectively the Guildhall opposite. A completely different type of formalism is the exaggeration of one component of a building to give character to the whole. This is done to alarming effect in Crickhowell House, the first office block in the Cardiff Bay Development, Butetown, Cardiff, by *Holder Mathias Alcock*, completed in 1993. Here the staircase is set at one angle, glazed full-height and carried up into a sort of beak, which gives the whole building a predatory air.

The *Welsh School of Architecture* during the 1980s maintained its role as miniature architectural barometer. Its Branch Library, Ely, Cardiff, 1985–6, is neo-Primitivist, mixing Soane and John Outram in equal measure. Its surgery at Church Village, Llantwit Fardre, 1986–7, has strong overtones of the neo-Victorian. Its sheltered housing at Canton, Cardiff, also 1986–7, is a charming

fantasia of decorative brickwork. In fact, care and resourcefulness
in the use of brick is one of the most notable features of all these
buildings. Recently, however, the School has struck out in a new
direction, as is shown by its Day Centre at Tonyrefail, 1992–3,
employing a visible lightweight metal structure to equally charming effect. A similar idiom on a larger scale was used *c.* 1991–2 by
Powell, Alport & Partners for the medical centre at the University
Hospital of Wales, Cathays and Heath, Cardiff, and by *Ahrends,
Burton & Koralek* 1993–5 for the Science Exhibition Centre,
Butetown, Cardiff, a telling waterside building.

The most notable architectural development during the 1980s
has been on an altogether more extensive scale than any other
post-war schemes, the redevelopment of the disused dock areas
of Cardiff, Swansea and Penarth. The docks have been cleared
of ex-industrial impedimenta, their waters recolonized as marinas,
and extensive housing built to appeal to middle-class boating
enthusiasts. At all three, the temptation to evoke the imagery of
Victorian dockside warehouses has been too powerful to resist.
Brick is the preferred material, and the vertical linkage of windows
under eaves-level gablets, echoing warehouse hoists, is a constantly recurring theme.

Portway Marina Village, Penarth, built from 1984 as one of the
last works of the celebrated London firm of *Chamberlin, Powell,
Bon & Woods*, is the smallest and least demonstrative of these
schemes, achieving both coherence and variety in the close-knit
terraces and courtyards round the former dock basin. At Swansea
a much bigger and more varied redevelopment took place, a
Maritime Quarter, where several architectural practices were
employed. Two dominate. The *Burgess Partnership* built four
interlocked squares, the Maritime Village, 1984–7, using the
idiom fairly soberly, red and blue metal balconies the only indul-
124 gence. The *Halliday Meecham Partnership*, at work 1985–8, were
much more unrestrained, and in the intricate spaces between
their dockside housing and their terraces overlooking Swansea
Bay created a miniature Post-Modernist world, full of architectural jokes and whimsy. In this they were abetted by *Robin
Campbell*, the Swansea City Council special projects officer, who
introduced sculpture, automata and inscriptions to amuse and
puzzle, and even, by the shore, an observatory, 1989, dressed up
as the Tower of the Ecliptic.

The redevelopment of the vast, desolate area round the Bute
East Dock at Cardiff has provided the biggest challenge, and since
1987 has become part of the even more ambitious Cardiff Bay
Development Scheme. As well as the South Glamorgan County
Hall and Crickhowell House, already mentioned, both at the s
end of the dock, a concentration of housing and small-scale offices
has gone up to the N and W of it. Although a single architectural
practice, *Holder Mathias Alcock*, has been responsible for most of
these, Cardiff's marina is the least well integrated of the three.
The massive terraces on the dockside itself are crude in detail.

Much more is due to be built in the Cardiff Bay development
area. The Cardiff Bay Opera House was the subject of an inter-

national competition in 1994, won by the Iraqi-born architect *Zaha Hadid*. If her design becomes a reality, Cardiff will be able to boast a building of greater architectural significance than anything built in the county over the past fifty years.

FURTHER READING

Glamorgan is fortunate in having a comprehensive history of its social, economic and institutional developments to underpin the study of its architecture. This is the *Glamorgan County History* (general editor Glanmor Williams). The most relevant volumes in the present context are Volume II, *Early Glamorgan* (1984), Volume III, *The Middle Ages* (1971), *Early Modern Glamorgan* (1974) and *Industrial Glamorgan from 1700 to 1970* (1980).

An even more exhaustive survey of the county's monuments and buildings up to *c.*1800, omitting churches, by the Royal Commission on Ancient and Historical Monuments in Wales, is well on its way to completion (*see* below for individual volumes).

Earlier surveys containing comments on buildings begin with the Elizabethan pioneer Rice Merrick's *Morganiae Archae-ographia: A Book of the Antiquities of Glamorganshire*, edited in 1887 and again, by B. Ll. James, in 1983. T. Dineley's *The Account of the Official Progress of the First Duke of Beaufort through Wales, 1684* (ed. R. W. Banks, 1888) is illustrated with Dineley's pen vignettes of buildings. Among the travellers who wrote just before the onset of industrialization, the most observant and opinionated is B. H. Malkin: *The Scenery, Antiquities and Biography of South Wales* (1804, reprinted 1970). The tradition of these writers has been carried on into the present century by C. J. O. Evans, in *Glamorgan: Its History and Topography* (2nd ed. 1943), and by P. Howell and E. Beazley, in *The Companion Guide to South Wales* (1977), which is particularly eye-opening for those interested in buildings. Short but authoritative accounts of a number of major buildings can be found in the Proceedings of the Summer Meeting of the Royal Archaeological Institute, 1993, published as a supplement to the *Archaeological Journal*, vol. 150. Periodicals which regularly include articles of architectural interest are *Archaeologia Cambrensis* (covering the whole of Wales), *Morgannwg* (the journal of the Glamorgan History Society), *Gower* (the Gower Society), and *The Glamorgan Historian* (ed. Stewart Williams), eleven volumes, 1963–79. The lists of statutorily protected buildings issued by Cadw (Welsh Historic Monuments) are a great deal more than planning tools, and incorporate much primary research. Most towns in the three Glamorgans have been re-surveyed over the past decade, but rural areas, and in particular the Valleys, still await survey to a high standard.

The archaeology of Glamorgan to the end of the Roman

occupation is fully discussed in *Glamorgan County History*, vol. II (1984), ed. H. N. Savory. Supplementary information can be found in the National Museum of Wales guide catalogues by H. N. Savory, *Bronze Age Collections* (1980) and *Early Iron Age Collections* (1976), and in S. Green and E. Walker, *Ice Age Hunters: Neanderthals and Early Modern Hunters in Wales* (1991). The Annual Reports of the Glamorgan–Gwent Archaeological Trust, *Archaeology in Wales* (Council for British Archaeology (Wales)), and *Morgannwg* all provide information on recent work and discoveries in the county. A useful field guide containing short descriptions of sites is E. Whittle, *The Cadw Guide to Ancient and Historic Wales: Glamorgan and Gwent* (1992). This can be supplemented by reference to the RCAHMW *Inventory of the Ancient Monuments in Glamorgan*, vol. I, parts 1 and 2 (1976).

The county's Celtic crosses are exhaustively described in the RCAHMW *Inventory*, vol. I, part 3, *The Early Christian Period* (1976). The Welsh, and indeed Irish, context for them is indicated in V. E. Nash-Williams, *The Early Christian Monuments of Wales* (1950).

An overview of medieval ecclesiastical architecture in the county is given by L. A. S. Butler in *Glamorgan County History*, vol. III, chapter viii. For Llandaff Cathedral there is no modern study, so J. H. James, *History and Survey of Llandaff Cathedral* (1898, revised 1929), remains valuable. However, F. J. North, *The Stones of Llandaff Cathedral* (1957), is a classic, and generally illuminating about the building stones of the county. The relation of the C13 work at Llandaff to other West Country great churches is discussed in H. Brakspear, 'A West Country School of Masons', *Archaeologia*, vol. 31 (1931). The controversial interpretation, and in particular dating, of Ewenny Priory church have been discussed by W. St Clair Baddeley in *Archaeologia Cambrensis*, 6th series, vol. 13, part 1 (1913), by C. A. R. Radford in the Ministry of Works guide (6th ed. 1976), and most recently by M. Thurlby in the *Journal of the Society of Architectural Historians*, vol. 47 (1988). The two Cistercian abbeys are fully documented in W. de Gray Birch's two monographs, *A History of Margam Abbey* (1897) and *A History of Neath Abbey* (1902). Neath also has the benefit of a full Ministry of Works guidebook, by L. A. S. Butler (1967). For Margam there is as yet nothing similar. Three-quarters of the eighty-odd surviving medieval churches in the county are covered by G. Orrin's two volumes, *The Gower Churches* (1979) and *Medieval Churches of the Vale of Glamorgan* (1988). They are packed with information, though ecclesiological rather than architectural in bias.

Medieval castles were the subject of a major publication by Glamorgan's most distinguished Victorian antiquary and historian, G. T. Clark, whose *Medieval Military Architecture in England* (two volumes), which covers Welsh castles, came out in 1884. The significance of Caerphilly Castle in the history of castle-building is also brought out in R. Allen Brown, *English Castles* (1954). The first part of the RCAHMW's exhaustive survey of Glamorgan castles, *Inventory*, vol. III, part 1a, *The Early Castles*,

From the Norman Conquest to 1217, was published in 1991, and the second part is far advanced. Meanwhile, for later castles reference must still be made to Ministry of Works/Department of the Environment guides. C. N. Johns, *Caerphilly Castle* (1978) is a tour-de-force. Others are P. Floud, *Castell Coch* (1954), and W. G. Thomas, *Weobley Castle* (1971). An important reinterpretation of St Donats Castle is in *Archaeological Journal*, vol. 150 (1993). Unfortified medieval monuments have their volume in the RCAHMW's *Inventory*, vol. III, part 2, *Medieval Non-defensive Secular Monuments* (1982). E. Whittle's *A Guide to Ancient and Historic Wales: Glamorgan and Gwent* (1992), mentioned above, covers medieval sites.

Post-medieval houses have been covered by the two parts of Volume IV of the RCAHMW's *Inventory: The Greater Houses* (1981) and *Farmhouses and Cottages* (1988). In order to understand the place of Glamorgan's vernacular architecture in Wales as a whole, P. Smith's *Houses of the Welsh Countryside* (1975), a further product of the RCAHMW, is essential reading. For the most important lost country house, Margam, there is P. Moore's 'Two paintings of Margam House' in *Archaeologia Cambrensis*, vol. 123 (1974), and the same author has published a monographic booklet on Margam Orangery (1986). Demolished country houses in general, including some, such as Adam's Wenvoe Castle, of which significant fragments remain, are the subject of T. Lloyd's *The Lost Houses of Wales* (2nd ed. 1989). Several surviving early C19 houses have been treated in monographic booklets, H. M. Thomas, *Merthyr Mawr House* (1976), and R. A. Griffiths, *Clyne Castle, Swansea* (1977) and *Singleton Abbey, Swansea* (1988). To these may be added J. Cornforth's articles in *Country Life*, on Penrice Castle (19 and 25 September 1975) and Tythegston (13 October 1977), and R. Haslam's on Merthyr Mawr House (1 November 1984) and on the early C19 house at Ewenny Priory (23 October 1986). Glamorgan's landscape gardens find their place in E. Whittle, *The Historic Gardens of Wales* (1992).

There is no comprehensive survey of C19 industrial remains, so the best introduction can be found in J. B. Hilling, *Cardiff and the Valleys* (1973). For the W of the county a brief history and a guide to sites is given in S. Hughes and P. Reynolds, *A Guide to the Industrial Archaeology of the Swansea Region* (1988, revised 1989). For coal-mining, covering much more than has survived on the ground, W. G. Thomas, *Welsh Coal Mines* (National Museum of Wales, 1986) can be consulted, together with the comprehensive survey of recorded structures by the RCAHMW, *Collieries of Wales* (1994). Successive forms of transport are dealt with by C. Hadfield, *The Canals of South Wales and the Border* (1960), and D. S. M. Barrie, *South Wales* (1980), Volume XII of *A Regional History of the Railways of Great Britain*. The most significant bridges are dealt with by T. Ruddock, *Arch Bridges and their Builders* (1979), part I, chapter v, for Pontypridd, and W. L. Davies, *Bridges of Merthyr Tydfil* (1992). D. B. Hague, *The Lighthouses of Wales* (1993), concludes this section.

The growth of towns is an important topic in Glamorgan. An

overview for Cardiff is given in W. Rees, *Cardiff, A History of the City* (1962, 2nd ed. 1969), strongest before *c*. 1800 and not entirely reliable on architectural matters. For the history of Cardiff's explosive growth in the C19 there are two fascinating studies, M. J. Daunton, *Coal Metropolis, Cardiff 1870–1914* (1977), and J. Davies, *Cardiff and the Marquesses of Bute* (1981). For Swansea there is the attractive *Swansea, an Illustrated History*, ed. G. Williams, 1990, of which chapter vii, on 'Art and Architecture', by P. Morgan is especially relevant. *Barry, The Centenary Book*, ed. D. Moore (1984, revised 1985), is exceptionally informative about buildings. For the history of industrialization in the Valleys, E. D. Lewis, *The Rhondda Valleys* (1959), is illuminating.

The author who has done most to draw attention to Glamorgan's C19 architecture and to get it taken seriously is J. B. Hilling. His articles in the *Glamorgan Historian*, on the buildings of Cardiff and Llandaff (1969, 1971) and on those of Merthyr Tydfil (1972), formed the basis of his book *Cardiff and the Valleys* (1973). His *Plans and Prospects* (1975) is the catalogue of the first general exhibition of architectural drawings for Glamorgan buildings. Recently the documentation of Cardiff's architecture has been put on a new footing by two unpublished studies, the 'Survey of Cardiff', prepared in 1989 for Cardiff Bay Development Corporation, and P. Riden's 'Cardiff, The Making of a City Centre', 1993. R. J. Zaugg's unpublished Ph.D. thesis is valuable in laying to rest some myths about buildings in Llandaff.

Among Victorian architects of national celebrity who worked in the county there are monographs for Butterfield (by P. Thompson, 1971), for Pearson (by A. Quiney, 1979) and, most relevant of all, for Burges (by J. Mordaunt Crook, 1981). See also for Burges's major works, M. Girouard in *Country Life*, 6, 13, 20 April 1961 (Cardiff Castle) and 10, 17 May 1962 (Castell Coch). Local architects, even Prichard, have still not been fully assessed in print, though for Prichard's partner Seddon there is M. Darby's *Catalogue* of architectural drawings in the Victoria and Albert Museum (1983). For buildings by Edwin Seward there are two valuable short monographs, A. S. Aldis, *Cardiff Royal Infirmary, 1883–1983* (1984), and J. M. Gibbs, *James Pyke Thompson: The Turner House, Penarth, 1888–1988* (1990). The London architects who descended on Glamorgan in the Edwardian period are well covered in A. S. Gray, *Edwardian Architecture: a Biographical Dictionary* (1985). For the sculptor Goscombe John there is F. Pearson's exhibition catalogue, National Museum of Wales, 1979. For other Edwardian sculpture see S. Beattie, *The New Sculpture* (1983).

Housing in the C19 and early C20 has been extensively investigated. J. B. Lowe and D. N. Anderson, *Iron Industry Housing Papers*, 1–3 (1972), were extended by J. B. Lowe, *Welsh Industrial Workers' Housing 1775–1875* (1977). For terraced housing in general, S. Muthesius, *The English Terraced House* (1982), provides the context. H. Long, *The Edwardian House* (1993), includes a section on housing in Roath, Cardiff. For Garden Villages there are W. Davies, *Rhiwbina Garden Village* (*c.* 1985), and

N.A. Robins, *Homes for Heroes* (1992), on the development of Townhill, Swansea.

The only building type with an authoritative book to itself is the school, excellently covered in M. Seaborne, *Schools in Wales 1500–1900, A Social and Architectural History* (1992). A. Jones, *Welsh Chapels* (1984), gives a short overview. Denominational histories and guides to individual chapels are rich sources which remain to be systematically tapped. Eight of the most memorable Victorian churches (and two chapels) are evaluated in the *Faber Guide to Victorian Churches*, ed. P. Howell and I. Sutton (1989). A pioneering article is D. Walker, 'The Bute Mausoleum at St Margaret's Church, Roath', *Archaeological Journal*, vol. 150 (1993). Prichard's church restorations are the subject of O. Jenkins's unpublished Architectural Association thesis, 1985.

Otherwise it is necessary to go back to the contemporary periodicals which document building activity so copiously up to 1914. The *Builder* (from 1843) is the most comprehensive, the *Building News* (from 1855) tended to be favoured by the avant-garde, but for some reason Burges had his work published exclusively in the *Architect* (founded 1869). For Victorian churches the unpublished papers of the Incorporated Church Building Society in Lambeth Palace Library are of fundamental importance.

Architecture since 1919 continued to be recorded in the building periodicals, but less systematically, and with a notable slackening of interest in what was happening w of the River Severn. Sir Percy Thomas, *Pupil to President – Memoirs of an Architect* (1963), is the brief and chatty, but none the less valuable autobiography of Glamorgan's premier c 20 architect. G. G. Pace has been the subject of an authoritative and splendidly illustrated monograph by his son, Peter Pace (1990).

GLAMORGAN

ABERAMAN

The settlement developed in relation to the Llettyshenkin Collieries Upper and Lower, sunk before 1850, across the Cynon River to the N E.

ST MARGARET OF ANTIOCH. Built in 1883 at the expense of Sir George Elliot, for his employees in the Powell Duffryn mines. An unexceptionable cruciform church with an E apse, badly in need of a vertical feature. Lancets, and geometrical tracery. *E. H. Lingen Barker* was the architect. – STAINED GLASS. In the five E lancets Nativity to Ascension, by *Mayer & Co.* of Munich. – W window Faith, Hope and Charity, by *Jones & Willis*, 1899.

PUBLIC HALL AND INSTITUTE. 1907–9 by *Thomas Roderick & Son*, at a cost of *c.*£7,500. One of the towering workmen's institutes which mark the Cynon Valley, of red brick with stone dressings. The façade is quite a sophisticated five-bay composition. Pedimented doorways in the three wide bays, those at the side leading to the hall, the central one to the library and institute. Polygonal full-height shafts frame the two narrow bays. Large central mullioned window in two parts, rectangular below, semicircular above. Broad shaped gable to crown all.

ABERCANAID/ABERCANNAID
1 m. s of Merthyr Tydfil

Abercanaid grew up to house workers at the Plymouth Ironworks, the 'compact establishment' which produced the best quality bar iron in the 1840s. The celebrated TRIANGLE, mid-C19 terraces for its employees, on a triangular layout, was demolished in the 1970s. From the late 1940s the Hoover Factory became the principal influence on development.

ST PETER AND ST PAUL. The original church, now in use as a hall, stands close to the road. Nave and lower chancel, with crudely laid walling and plate tracery. (By *G. E. Robinson*? Compare his churches at Vaynor and Cefncoedycymer, qq.v.) In 1911 *T. Edmund Rees* of Merthyr Tydfil built a new church further back. This is also of little interest, a nave and chancel in one, built of rubble sandstone with dressings of red brick. Stone intersecting tracery in the W window, and a truncated W bellcote. – STAINED GLASS. Nave sw, St Peter and St Paul, 1965, designed by *Wippell & Co.*

GRAIG CHAPEL. 1905. Round-arched, under a pedimental gable. Rock-faced sandstone.

SEION INDEPENDENT CHAPEL. 1908. Classical. Cement-rendered. The rusticated lower storey supports arcaded upper windows linked by areas of channelled walling. Overall pediment.

PENTREBACH HOUSE, ¼ m. NE, by the roundabout. An interesting contrast with the Crawshays' Cyfarthfa Castle, Merthyr Tydfil (*see* p. 441), for this was built for Anthony Hill, owner of the Plymouth Ironworks. Here is no romantic castle, just a seven-bay, two-storey mansion, rendered white and with the minimum of classical trappings, quoins and a pediment over the doorcase. Recent glazed veranda.

HOOVER FACTORY, N of the Pentrebach roundabout. 1946–8 by *Wallis, Gilbert & Partners*. Two long two-storey ranges at r.-angles to one another. The entrance on the chamfered corner. Brown brick. Windows in continuous bands. Inevitably at that date a sober performance by the firm whose factory at Perivale in West London had famously linked the name of Hoover with Art Deco. Large later additions to the N.

PENYDARREN TRAMROAD. Much of the route of the first recorded journey of a railway steam locomotive (built by Richard Trevithick) in 1804 is traceable S of Merthyr Tydfil. The well-known early railway and mining engineer *George Overton*, also responsible for the first survey of the Stockton and Darlington Railway, constructed the line 1799–1802. It ran 9 m. (15.3 kilometres) from the Glamorganshire Canal to a junction with the Dowlais tramroads. Some sections of the tramroad have been totally remade by the insertion of the trunk sewer from Merthyr to Cardiff, but other sections survive as a well-preserved terrace in the wooded Taff Gorge. Many lengths of stone sleeper-blocks are visible, and others must be buried. The very heavy traffic which developed from the then iron-making capital of the world resulted in the construction of multiple passing-loops, the remains of which can also be seen. The section of line running N-wards from the viaduct near the Dyffryn Taff Hostel, Edwardsville, to the Black Lion signalbox near Merthyr Vale includes one road overbridge at Pontygwaith and two large masonry arches over the Taff at Quakers Yard (*see* p. 536). The PLYMOUTH IRONWORKS TUNNEL lies just E of the roundabout on the A470, under the former charging bank of the Plymouth Ironworks. The first tunnel used by a railway locomotive, it is 10 ft 9 in. (3 metres) wide at its base, 13 ft 1 in. (4 metres) wide at springing level and 12 ft 5 in. (3.8 metres) high. In the recent 'restoration' a new wall has been built around a few of the original arch stones, and the tunnel gated and blocked with a mosaic panel. Mosaic also covers the floor of the tunnel.

ABERCWMBOI

0000

An unusually long, unbroken street of terraces runs along the valley bottom.

BETHESDA WELSH BAPTIST CHAPEL, John Street. 1864, set on a bank above the street and presenting a handsome classical façade, rusticated below, divided above into three bays by pairs of short Corinthian pilasters which carry the pediment. Rendered and painted. Simple unaltered interior with box pews and shallow galleries on three sides. Panelled ceiling in two squares with decorative plaster borders and coloured central roses.

WORKMEN'S HALL AND INSTITUTE, John Street. 1913, classical too, but more moderate than most workmen's halls in the Cynon Valley. Only two-storeyed, the façade to the road of rock-faced sandstone, the ashlar dressings now painted over. Central pedimental gable on scrolls and a big Venetian window between round ones, above the twin entrance doorways.

FERNHILL GARDEN VILLAGE, on the hillside to the s. Designed by *W. Beddoe Rees*, more familiar as an architect of chapels, for the Aberaman Housing Society, an arm of Welsh Garden Cities Ltd. Planned in 1913 to have 200 houses. By 1916 190 had been built. Quite a spacious layout, terraces not long, frontages broken with gablets and bracketed porch-hoods. The original materials, pebbledash above red brick, are barely appreciable now, as almost every house has been remodelled.

ABERCYNON

0090

At the confluence of the Cynon and the Taff, at first a hamlet called Navigation. The colliery development, a grid of streets above the w bank of the rivers, came in the 1880s and 1890s.

ST DONAT, Aberdare Road. By *G. E. Halliday*, 1897–8. On a sloping site above the village, a complicated group, with saddleback-roofed porch tower to the sw, and cross-gabled s aisle. Simple vocabulary of lancets. Rock-faced sandstone walls. Doulting stone for the e and w windows, harsh red Cattybrook brick to n and s. The red brick interior now painted out. – STAINED GLASS. Christ between SS Teilo and Donat. 1947 by *A. L. Wilkinson*.

WORKMEN'S HALL AND INSTITUTE, Mountain Ash Road. Dated 1904. The building dominates the whole settlement from its steeply sloping site, four-storeyed in front, but only two-storeyed to Edward Street at the back. Polychromy of blue Pennant sandstone, red brick and white Portland stone. Finialed gable ends.

AQUEDUCT. A single arch, built *c.*1791 to carry the Glamorganshire Canal and a road over the Taff. Now only the road uses it. Stonework rendered over.

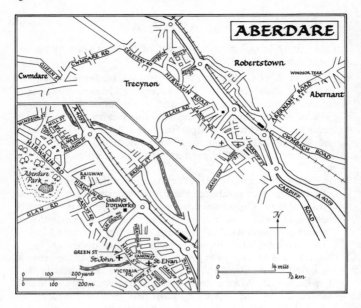

ABERDARE/ABERDÂR

Aberdare was one of the county's ancient upland parishes (strictly, a chapelry of Llantrisant), as humble medieval St John's church indicates. Industrial growth began early in the C19, the Gadlys Ironworks opening in 1827, the first steam-coal mine a decade later. During the middle decades of the century, the Cynon Valley, with Aberdare at its head, became the most prolific centre of steam-coal production. By 1856 Aberdare's output of coal exceeded 1 million tons. The population in 1851 was 15,000, by 1861 it had reached 32,000. Yet by 1894 it had risen only to 40,000. Even today, the 1850s is the period which gives the town its special flavour. Its principal space, Victoria Square, its principal church, St Elvan's, half-a-dozen chapels, and its market buildings, all date from the 1850s. Mid-C19 terrace housing still dominates the town's several residential centres, round Canon Street, laid out in 1854, up the hillside s of Cardiff Street, and at Trecynon, to the NW of the Gadlys Ironworks site. Industry on the other hand has retreated, leaving Aberdare with the air of a market town, bypassed by the new A4059 from end to end. Only between the two churches, along High Street and Green Street, has mid-C20 redevelopment opened up the texture of the town.

St John, Green Street. The medieval church of Aberdare. Low-lying and inconspicuous, it must always have been a humble building. Nave with truncated w bellcote, lower chancel. The nave walls of local Pennant sandstone are of the original build, and so, more eloquently, is the s doorway, pointed with a continuous triple roll, datable *c.* 1300. Chancel rebuilt in 1777 and enlarged 1871–6. The windows, grouped ogee-headed lancets, are of the latter date. Inside, the nave has an arch-braced roof, perhaps partly late medieval, now boarded. – FONT. Medieval. Octagonal, with a roll at top and bottom. – STAINED GLASS. E window and four others of 1876. Nothing special, the figures in the E window now deprived of their background. – W lancet, *c.* 1984 by *John Petts*. – MONUMENT. Thomas Edwards †1803. Signed by *Lancaster* of Bristol. With a large relief of a kneeling woman mourning over an urn, an early example in the county of this overworked theme.

St ELVAN, Victoria Square. Built as a chapel of ease to St John, but eclipsing it in strategic siting, lofty form and landmark steeple, the product of a long-standing campaign by the second Marquess of Bute and the dynamism of a new incumbent, the Rev. John Griffith. 1851–2, by the little-known London architect *Andrew Mosely*. Rock-faced local Pennant sandstone from Dyffryn dressed with Bath stone. Dec style. Four-stage W tower and spire set back behind a pierced parapet. Aisled nave with N porch and transept towards the principal approach from Market Street. Lower chancel, given a N chapel in 1884. Outer S aisle and S chapel added by *Halliday* in 1910–11. Architecturally, all this is of no special merit, though as first built the church was perfectly up-to-date.

The interior is a revelation. The nave and aisles, extremely lofty and spacious, are divided by slender piers, alternating round and octagonal, all with octagonal caps. But more than that, everything has been whitened, so that one feels momentarily as if one has stepped into a C17 Dutch painting of a church interior by Saenredam or van der Heyden. The chancel and its N chapel are, by contrast, polychromatic, decorated in 1961 by *Stephen Dykes Bower* in his characteristic green, red and white. The painted boarded ceilings are especially effective. – SCREEN. 1890 by *William Tate*. Lofty, Perp. Painted by *Dykes Bower* and surmounted by his loft and rood. – FONT. An interesting Art Nouveau piece. Red sandstone bowl on a drum-shaped green marble shaft surrounded by shaft-like sandstone trees rooted in the base. 1903, designed by *Halliday*, carved by *W. Clarke* of Llandaff. – PULPIT. Timber. Perp. Said to have been designed by *W. D. Caröe*. Cut down. – STAINED GLASS. In almost every window. – Chancel E, Crucifixion with saints, 1876. – N transept N, 1905 by *R. J. Newbery*. – N aisle W, signed by *Newbery*. – S aisle W, Christ and the centurion, 1914 by *Newbery*.

St FAGAN, Windsor Street, Trecynon. 1852–4 by *T. Talbot Bury*, reconstructed in 1856 after a fire, largely at the expense of the Baroness Windsor. Walls of snecked, rock-faced sandstone. Chancel, nave with lean-to aisles and a clerestory pierced by miniature spherical-triangle windows. S porch. All rather low and spreading. Nave extended, and stunted SW tower by *G. E. Halliday*, built in 1909–10, not helping the composition. – STAINED GLASS. N aisle NE, Suffer the Little Children, by

Heaton, Butler & Bayne. Chancel E, Christ with angels, 1952 by *Celtic Studios*.

The VICARAGE, E of the church, is also by *Talbot Bury*, 1876–7. Rendered, with an outsize Gothic porch.

ST LUKE, Queen Street, Cwmdare. 1886–7 by *E. M. Bruce Vaughan*. His usual lancet-style design, but the facing material buff-coloured brick. Bath stone dressings. – STAINED GLASS. E window of 1966–8 by *Timothy Lewis*, an impressive conception of symbols in roundels, unconventional in colour and technique. – W window of 1990, also by *Lewis*, echoing its predecessor but with much less flair.

ST MATTHEW, Windsor Terrace, Abernant. A tin tabernacle of 1891, never, like so many others, replaced by a masonry church, but still in good condition. – FONT. Dated 1827. Octagonal, classical, of coarse marble. From Holy Cross, Port Talbot, to which it was given by Bishop van Mildert of Durham.

BETHANIA CHAPEL, Wind Street. (Disused.) The siting is unusual, back from the street-line up a flight of broad steps. Built in 1853–4 by *Evan Griffiths* of Aberdare, but rebuilt in 1884. Pennant sandstone façade with a giant recessed arch rising into the pediment. Triple window within it. Tall, narrow flanking windows related to the galleries inside. Note the blazing bible carved over the door.

SCHOOL, at the back in Griffith Street, by *R. Roderick*, *c.* 1890, with its own giant recessed arch and pilasters.

CALFARIA WELSH BAPTIST CHAPEL, Monk Street. 1851–2, attributable to *Thomas Joseph* (*see* Heol-y-felin Chapel, Trecynon, below). Of finely squared, rock-faced Pennant sandstone. Overall pediment. Round-headed entrance doorway, and wheel window, in the slightly projecting centre bay. Sash windows otherwise. Very fine interior, the gallery extending round all four sides and of lavish depth. Bowed pierced ironwork forms the gallery fronts. Box pews integral with the 'big seat'. Later pulpit – see the spiky metalwork. Boarded ceiling on a deep cove. In the centre a single, deeply undercut rose. – ORGAN. 1906. Large. – VESTRY behind, dated 1871.

ENGLISH WESLEYAN METHODIST CHURCH, Green Street. Dated 1859. A temple front reduced to its simplest elements, a plain pediment on pilaster strips. Some details seem to have been lost. Internally the original galleries on cast iron columns survive. Plaster acanthus ceiling rose. Later composition of reader's desk and organ above.

HIGHLAND PLACE UNITARIAN CHURCH, Graig Isaf. 1859–60 by *H. J. Paull* of Cardiff. On a steep hill. Stone façade with sandstone ashlar dressings. Transeptal plan. Bald Dec tracery, shafted entrance doorway. Stair projection on the downhill side. Now secularized.

ST DAVID'S PRESBYTERIAN CHURCH, High Street. Geometrical Gothic, the façade flanked by the stump of a porch-steeple on one side. Blue Pennant sandstone with Bath stone dressings. By *W. D. Blessley*, 1878–9. Now secularized.

SALEM CHAPEL, Bridge Street, Robertstown. Dated 1841.

Square plan, the façade with round-headed windows in two storeys and two central doorways. Later C19 interior, galleried on three sides, the ceiling with a central plaster rose. Railed GRAVEYARD in front.

SILOA CONGREGATIONAL CHAPEL, Green Street. Dated 1855. Round-headed windows with fluted imposts, a sub-classical idiom. Inside, galleries on three sides with their original seating. Later open pews at ground level. The pulpit and 'big seat' belong to this reordering, of perhaps c. 1880. Four plaster roses in the boarded ceiling.

TRINITY PRESBYTERIAN CHURCH, Weatheral Street. A classical chapel of more than usual sophistication, built in 1867 to the design of *Evan Griffiths*, remodelled in 1894, with a hall at the W end added in 1908–9 by *J. Llewellyn Smith*. Rendered and colourwashed. The entrance front, facing E on to Weatheral Street, is crowned by an open pediment into which a bold semicircular recess is inserted. This is supported by pairs of Corinthian pilasters flanking the central Ionic arcaded windows. Projecting vestibule the full width of the façade, with central arched entrances. On the long side towards Canon Street arcaded upper windows, and the hall addition beyond echoing the Ionic order of the façade in its big Palladian window. The INTERIOR is less successful, the galleries on three sides creating a long, pinched space. Cast iron gallery supports with clustered shafts and moulded caps.

COUNCIL OFFICES, High Street. Lying back from the street and understated to a fault. This is because the building was erected as a clinic. 1938 by *Ivor Bryant*, the Council Surveyor.

CENTRAL LIBRARY, High Street. A neat, cubic, modern building. 1962–3 by *Stephen Thomas & Partners*. Two-storeyed, the upper storey projecting on pilotis in two directions.

COLLEGE OF FURTHER EDUCATION, Cwmdare Road. One of the first significant pieces of post-war modernism in the county, c. 1954–5 by *Gollins, Melvin, Ward & Partners*. A low and spreading group, ranges running out at r.-angles to one another, nowhere more than two storeys high, for fear of subsidence over worked-out mines. Reinforced concrete frames and expansive glazing. The group, intended to spread out further, with a fan-shaped assembly hall to the NW, remains incomplete. The parallel range to the SW with blue fascia panels is a later addition.

ABERDARE GIRLS' COMPREHENSIVE SCHOOL, Gadlys Road. Built as the Higher Standard Schools 1905–7, and a tour de force by the local architect, *Thomas Roderick*. Brown, coursed and squared, rock-faced Pennant sandstone lavishly dressed with red Wilderness ashlar. The architect had to cater for both boys and girls, so he laid out two identical sets of classrooms each clustered round a hall, and thrust forward between them a pompous tower, octagonal and somewhat top-heavy under its two-stage lead-covered cap, concave below, ogee above. The plan is dramatized by the shaped gables over every classroom and both halls. Huge, round-headed hall windows flanked by

bullseyes. Smaller bullseyes over the two entrances. Internally,
the glass partitions survive which allowed the head teachers in
the central halls to oversee the pupil teachers in the surrounding
classrooms.

TECHNICAL AND INTERMEDIATE SCHOOLS (now District
Council Offices), Gadlys Road. Designed by *J. H. Phillips* of
Cardiff, who won a competition in 1892, and dated 1896.
Central single-storey hall towards the road, crowned by a pair
of shaped gables, of rock-faced Pennant sandstone with grey
Forest dressings, and, behind, a row of simply gabled
classrooms with dressings of yellow brick. Master's house of
1896 to the l., also by *Phillips*. To the r. a two-storey block
carrying at the angle a whimsical clock-turret with Arts and
Crafts detail. This part is dated 1901. Presumably *Phillips*, who
tended to whimsy, was responsible.

INTERMEDIATE SCHOOL FOR GIRLS, Cwmbach Road. *c.* 1912.
Quite a distinguished Arts and Crafts composition, symmetrical, executed in coursed, squared Lias limestone with
much Bath stone ashlar. Timber mullion-and-transom
windows painted white. Interplay between the armature of
slightly tapering buttress piers, segmental arches and tellingly
placed sculpture. Not at all like the work of the County Education Architect of the day, D. Pugh Jones.

ABERDARE PARK, Gadlys Road. Public park laid out in the
1860s by *William Barron* of Sketty. (Do the boulder-strewn
rock-gardens survive?) Just inside the gates, now incongruously
surrounded by a pond, the STATUE of Lord Merthyr, 1912 by
Thomas Brock, a repetition of his earlier statue at Merthyr
Tydfil.

TRECYNON

At Trecynon the chapels stand so thick that they give a vivid
indication of the vigour of C19 Nonconformity in the Valleys. The
earliest meeting house in Trecynon is recorded in 1751, the earliest
date on a chapel is 1811, but the fabric of the buildings belongs
fairly exactly to the second half of the C19. All the chapels are
modestly classical, all are gable-ended with round-headed openings in both storeys under the gable ends.

BETHEL CHAPEL, Railway Street. (Disused.) Dated 1860. Quite
an elaborately designed façade, though rendered. Central
round-headed doorway in a channelled, concave surround. Big
semicircular window in the pedimented gable similarly treated.
Full-height channelled quoins and full-width dentilled cornice
moulding. (Elaborate interior of *c.* 1900, comparable with the
interior of Ebenezer Chapel, *see* below.)

CARMEL (BRYN SION) ENGLISH BAPTIST CHURCH, Mill
Street. Dated 1862 but rebuilt in 1899 by *Thomas Roderick*.
Plain façade of rock-faced Pennant sandstone. Interior altered.
The galleries on three sides remain, and so does the lavishly
coffered ceiling on its fluted and bracketed cove.

EBENEZER CHAPEL (Independent), Ebenezer Street. The dates
1811 and 1829 on a worn stone in the porch relate to earlier
chapels on the site. The three upper windows of the façade, with
Corinthian pilasters, belong to a building of 1852 heightened in
1874–5. Memorable porch, closed to l. and r., open in the
centre, all projecting under three equilateral gables faced with
red terracotta rosettes. This is an addition of 1902. Marbling
in the centre bay. Showpiece interior of 1902, the galleries
round all four sides, the pulpit and 'big seat' all elaborately
fretted and decorated with ebony pilasters. Splendid ceiling
plasterwork, two huge roses encircled by rosettes. The architects for the work done in 1902 were *Owen Morris Roberts &
Son* of Portmadoc, Gwynedd.*

GADLYS CHAPEL, Railway Street. (Disused.) Dated 1864.
Rendered front crowned by a pediment carried on four elegant
Ionic pilasters.

HEN-DY-CWRDD UNITARIAN CHAPEL, Alma Street. In spite
of its modest appearance, with bargeboarded gable and only
the central pair of windows arched, this is historically the
most significant of Trecynon's chapels. A meeting house was
established here in 1751. Rebuilt 1862–3 by *Evan Griffiths jun.*
(Square interior galleried on three sides, the deep gallery fronts
moulded, the cast iron columns with acanthus capitals.)

HEOL-Y-FELIN CHAPEL (Welsh Baptist), Bell Street. Structurally the earliest of the chapels: 1852 is the date on the
cast iron internal gallery supports. By *Thomas Joseph*, a local
engineer and colliery entrepreneur. Pediment carried on
stunted, baseless Tuscan pilasters. The interior has galleries on
all four sides, those at front and back very deep, with tier upon
tier of raked seating. The ceiling a boarded flat on a deep cove,
with a single handsome plaster rose, coloured in shades of
brown. – PULPIT of *c.*1900, as the Art Nouveau metalwork
indicates. – MONUMENT. Owen Harris † 1905. White marble
relief portrait.

SILOH CHAPEL, Hirwaun Road. Dated 1889 and 1902. Which
date refers to the rendered façade?

FREE LIBRARY AND PUBLIC HALL, Mill Street. 1902 by
C. H. Elford. Prominent but naive rendered frontage, a single
secular statement among all the chapels.

INDUSTRIAL REMAINS

What survives of Aberdare's early industry is of great historical
importance.

GADLYS IRONWORKS, between Elm Grove and the spur road
to the A4059, at the entrance to the Cynon Valley Transport
Depot and Works. One of the most complete remaining groups
of ironworks buildings in South Wales. The works was founded
in 1827 by Matthew Wayne, ironmaster and coal-owner of
Merthyr Tydfil, in conjunction with G. R. Morgan and

*Mrs Margaret Morris kindly found this information in the chapel archives.

E. M. Williams. Two large masonry BLAST FURNACES and a
BLOWING-ENGINE HOUSE remain intact, and there are other
ancillary buildings.

In front of the furnaces are the twin gabled ranges of the
later C19 WAGON REPAIR WORKSHOPS, seven bays long, of
Pennant sandstone rubble with red and yellow brick dressings.
Circular openings set in the gables, typical of earlier ironworking buildings. Twin arched openings, three with traceried
fanlights in the SE end. Arched small-pane windows set in the
side walls. The central spine wall is pierced by a brick-built
arcade. The brackets set between the windows may have supported travelling cranes. The steel roof structures are almost
certainly secondary, as are the yellow brick cappings to the
walls and the upper gables.

The BLOWING-ENGINE HOUSE is tall and narrow with a
hipped roof, and totally enclosed the steam engine. The beam
of the engine pivoted on the intermediate cross-wall. Three
storeys and part basement capped by a wide-eaved roof.
Snecked Pennant sandstone with bull-nosed quoins, yellow
brick dressings and stone sills. The long elevations have four
windows with long and short quoins in refractory brickwork.
Three stepped arches towards the adjacent stone-built revetment wall may have accommodated the air-blast arrangements
for the adjoining furnaces. The last two furnaces were built in
1855–6, and the engine house may be contemporary. Refurbished in 1989, retaining the then existing floor levels.

Former CALCINING FURNACES to the SW, on the NW side
of Elm Grove. These are set into a bank adjoining No. 17 and
may also date from the mid 1850s. Oval wells, now blocked, had
the calcined iron ore discharged through semicircular openings.
There are four such on the high SW side and one on the
lower SE end. The snecked Pennant rubble sandstone walls are
battered and have stock brick dressings.

ROBERTSTOWN TRAMROAD BRIDGE, Meirion Street, Trecynon. The earliest dated iron railway bridge in the world,
now used as a footbridge between Trecynon and Robertstown.
Reached by a walk N for 250 ft (76.2 metres) along the con-
creted bed of the tramroad. The bridge is dated 1811 on the
centre handrail stanchions. It has a span of 35 ft 3 in. (10.75
metres) and is carried on four main cast iron beams, each with
integral cast-in arched ribs reaching down to the lower sections
of the masonry abutments. Decking 10 ft (3.04 metres) wide of
cast iron plates, now partly renewed. Each main plate has
holes for fixing bolts to the beams below, and two raised iron
upstands, 4 ft 3 in. (1.3 metres), across its length, which, it has
been deduced, provided gripping plates for the tram-horses'
hooves. Imprints of the track-fixing chairs show that the bridge
was for single-track working. The bridge was made at the
nearby Abernant Ironworks. It has noticeably twisted towards
the N.

PERAMBULATION

The obvious place to start is by the granite WAR MEMORIAL, 1923 by *F. H. Morley* of Durham, at the foot of VICTORIA SQUARE. The square retains its early Victorian appearance, surrounded by three-storey stuccoed frontages. At the top of the slope the BLACK LION HOTEL, late Georgian in character, its cast iron porch set in front of Ionic pilasters flanking the entrance doorway. Three timber bay windows, their mullions with lotus caps. The hotel forms a backdrop to the STATUE of Griffith Rhys Jones ('Caradog'), conductor of the South Wales Choral Union, baton in hand. 1920, signed by *W. Goscombe John*.

The HIGH STREET leads off from the top end of Victoria Square over the brow of the hill, between St Elvan's church, raised up on the r., and the former St David's church, raised up on the l. Thence it descends to a newly created open space, around which stand the Council Offices, Central Library and the two chapels in Green Street. Notice beside the library the hexagonal MILESTONE dated 1860. At the far corner, where High Street joins Canon Street, the three-sided frontage of the CON-STITUTIONAL CLUB. This absurdly demonstrative building was opened in 1894. The architect was *T. C. Wakeling* of Merthyr Tydfil. Stuccoed. Classical detailing which would have looked old-fashioned even in 1864, everything over-emphatic. But its pride and joy is the precipitous pavilion roof in the centre surmounted by an enormous open ironwork crown, which is visible all over the town centre. Next door in High Street is the CYNON VALLEY BOROUGH COUNCIL DEPARTMENT OF FINANCE, a three-storey, five-bay front of *c.* 1850, with a porch on Ionic columns of cast iron.

In CANON STREET nothing except Trinity Presbyterian Church, and a r. turn at the far end down CARDIFF STREET leads back to the bottom of Victoria Square and the War Memorial. At the entrance to the square, MARKET STREET runs off to the E. Here first, on the l., the OLD COURT HOUSE (now an amusement arcade), dated 1914. By *George Kenshole*. This has an aggressive and rather ugly neo-Baroque façade. Pairs of attached Ionic columns, their capitals flaring, carry chunks of entablature. The cornice rises segmentally in the middle to crown the composition. (Handsome staircase and courtroom.) Next, on both sides of the street, the low, grey, rock-faced arcades of the MARKET. Dated 1853. That on the N belonged to the slaughterhouse, reconstructed in 1903 after a fire and recently converted to shops, that on the S to the market itself, centred on an ashlar pedimented temple front with paired Tuscan pilasters. Larger, plainer market hall to the r. Finally, back to Cardiff Street. Here only one building deserves mention, the MIDLAND BANK, 1857–8 by *William Gingell*, in the Barryesque palazzo style deemed appropriate for banks at that period. Grey Newbridge stone, rock-faced, even round the doorway and ground-floor windows. Some Bath stone ashlar.

Just beyond, the mid-C19 NATIONAL SCHOOLS, notable for
the lettering of their name. Is this the school of 1848 by *Evan
Griffiths*, promoted by the Rev. John Griffith before he turned
his attention to building St Elvan's church?

BUARTH MAEN OPEN SETTLEMENT, 2½ m. NE, on Mynydd
Aberdar (SO 0126 0530). Several small, annular house foundations associated with two enclosures *c.* 82 ft (25 metres) apart.
Low stone enclosure walls with some original facing. The original E entrance of the S sub-rectangular enclosure survives. W
side damaged. The N enclosure is less well defined, particularly
to the E. Sinuous banks to the N and small heaps of stone
suggest clearance of cultivation plots and formation of incipient
fields. Tentatively datable between *c.* 1000 B.C. and the early
centuries A.D.

On RHOS GWAWR, 1½ m. SW. Over forty small STONE CLEAR-
ANCE PILES scattered on moorland in three more-or-less
discrete groups (centred SN 9920 0090, 9947 0079 and
9957 0037). They probably result from ancient agricultural
improvement.

0090

ABERFAN

The name Aberfan has been etched into the public memory by
the dreadful coal tip slide in 1966 which overwhelmed the village
school. The COMMUNITY CENTRE in HILLSIDE CLOSE is
built on the site. 1973 by *H.M.R. Burgess & Partners*. Yellow
brick. A low, intimate group. Above it, in MOY ROAD, a small
MEMORIAL GARDEN, enclosed by a wall constructed of sandstone boulders. The tip itself, now contoured and landscaped,
can still be made out as a broad green gash down the hillside.

ST MARY, Merthyr Vale, ½ m. S. 1969–70 by *F. R. Bates, Son &
Price*. Square, with a monopitch roof on a steel frame.
Clerestory lighting above yellow brick walls. Grouped with the
VICARAGE. – STAINED GLASS. Four panels at the entrance
end, Passion subjects, designed by *John Edwards* and made by
Celtic Studios, 1970.

HAFOD-TANGLWYS-ISAF, ¼ m. SW. On the hillside. A longhouse
derivative, with a barn instead of a cowhouse. Datable to the
C17.

8090

ABERGWYNFI

ST GABRIEL. 1893–4 by *G. E. Halliday*. Alone on the hillside,
intended for a community which never arrived. Lancets. Rose
window at the ritual W end. Derelict at the time of writing.

On the main road ½ m. W, a TERRACE of mid-C19 single-storey
cottages, a rare survival.

At BLAENGWYNFI, in the valley below, the TUNNEL HOTEL
stands up conspicuously. 1891 by *G. F. Lambert* of Bridgend.

CRUG YR AFAN, 2 m. ESE. A good example of an early Bronze

Age burial CAIRN c. 65 ft (20 metres) across, on a high-level
moorland summit with wide views of surrounding ridge-tops.
Excavation in 1902 indicated that a boulder cairn enclosed by
a ring of upright stones was raised over a clay and stone mound
covering a stone cist containing a cremation and bronze dagger.
It is separated from its surrounding ditch by a broad berm, an
unusual feature of such sites in this area.

ABERPERGWM *see* GLYNNEATH

ABERTHIN   *0070*
1½ m. NE of Cowbridge

GREAT HOUSE. Little brother to St Fagans Castle (q.v.) in its
multi-gabled symmetry. Quoins of reused Sutton stone, local
sandstone for windows and doorways, now overpainted. Rendered walls. The date 1658 on a sundial formerly set on the
porch gives a *terminus ante quem*. But the porch was an addition
to the house, one-storeyed and no higher, positioned to hide the
slightly off-centre front door, the only blemish in the otherwise
scrupulous symmetry. Five-bay S front, crowned by three
gables, with three-light windows all across the ground floor,
and on the upper floor windows alternating three-light under
the gables, two-light under the spaces between the gables. Two-
light dormer windows in the gables. Square-headed lights with
sunk chamfers. Hoodmoulds. Ball finials on the gables. Chimneystacks crown the composition, in threes set lozenge-wise on
symmetrical rear stacks. The plan is single pile with a central
rear wing forming a T.
   Internally, the front door is aligned on the foot of the stair-   46
case. This rises in short flights round an open well, a typical
mid-C17 arrangement. Vertically symmetrical, turned balusters. Square newels with big acorn-shaped finials.
   Finally, the GATEHOUSE, set far forward of the house. This is
presumably also mid-C17, but reuses two segmental chamfered
medieval arches, of Sutton stone. Spy slits to l. and r. Pigeon
loft in the gable, and bakehouse attached to the l.
Though a sizeable village, Aberthin has no parish church. For
that reason, no doubt, it developed as an early centre of Nonconformity. Here, after Groeswen, Caerphilly, is the oldest site
of Methodist worship in the county. The first chapel was built
in 1749 for the Aberthin Society, with the encouragement of
Howell Harris of Trevecca, the effective founder of Calvinistic
Methodism in south-east Wales. The present VILLAGE HALL,
in Pen-y-lan Road, is the chapel which replaced it in 1780. Now
much altered. The pairs of slightly pointed windows in the two
long walls survive, but not the doorways in the gable end walls.

ABERTRIDWR

The Aber Valley remained almost entirely pastoral until the end of the C19. Once Lord Windsor decided to sink coal mines on his land here, a mushroom growth of housing appeared: long, unbroken terraces, uniformly constructed of Pennant sandstone and virulent red brick. Chapels soon appeared, too, and so did a number of hotels. A hall-and-institute was built for the benefit of the workers in the Windsor Collieries, but, surprisingly, no church.

BEULAH WELSH BAPTIST CHAPEL. 1905 by *G. A. Lundie* of Cardiff. Gabled façade of rock-faced Pennant sandstone and Forest dressings. Round-headed openings in the normal pattern. Doorway with broken pediment. Typical interior, galleried on three sides, recently intelligently modernized.

INDEPENDENT CHAPEL, above The Square. Dated 1901. Quite an arresting façade, with concentric relieving arches framing the middle window.

NAZARETH WELSH CALVINISTIC METHODIST CHAPEL (now Community Centre). Dated 1898. Also by *Lundie*. Plain Pennant sandstone façade.

WORKMEN'S LIBRARY AND INSTITUTE, The Square. 1910 by *Illtyd Thomas*. Larger and more handsomely fronted than any of the chapels. Squared and coursed Forest stone dressed with both ashlar and red brick (now painted over). Bold Diocletian window in the centre, bold battered brick buttresses at the angles.

ROYAL HOTEL, where the Pontypridd road rises steeply above the houses. Dated 1899, by *T. Thomas* of Cardiff. Flat-faced, round-arched and altogether red.

WINDSOR HOTEL, High Street. Also loftily situated. 1903–4 by *Harry Snell*, architect to the Windsor Estate. A bow on columns at the angle. Brick, stucco and three kinds of stone. Quite an expensive affair, and the first 'extensive venture' of the Glamorgan Public House Trust Company.

BAGLAN

ST CATHERINE. Built, lower down the hill than the medieval church, by *John Prichard* at the expense of his cousin, Griffith Llewellyn of Baglan Hall. 1875–82. Not large, restrained in design but exquisitely wrought. Cruciform plan, with a steeple over the crossing. Dec windows with cusped intersecting tracery. The walls are built of sandstone in two colours, khaki and mauve: the Pennant walling rough-textured khaki laid in a pattern of three exceedingly narrow courses and one wider one, the dressed Forest of Dean ashlar both colours in large bold blocks randomly disposed. Sloping plinth, sparing buttresses. Ingeniously handled steeple, the short tower square in plan, then octagonal, the spire eight-sided. Against the diagonal faces

of the tower snuggle pinnacles which start rectilinear, become
quatrefoil and carry conical caps.

Inside, the polychromy glows more sumptuously. All is
ashlar-faced, the dominant material pinkish-amber Penarth alabaster. Broad, pale green Quarella stone bands. Mosaic floors.
N passage aisle to the nave, its arches on slender round piers.
The chancel up two pink marble steps, the sanctuary up four
more. The chancel, under the tower, is simply vaulted, with
arches on short wall-shafts, stiff-leaf-capped and resting on
emblems of the four Evangelists. Other carved heads in unexpected places. Marble-banded sanctuary. Across the E wall,
full-width gabled arcading, continued round to the S to include
PISCINA and SEDILIA. (In the N wall, recess for the founder's
tomb.)

FITTINGS. A complete set by *Prichard*, the carving in wood
and stone by *Wormleighton* of Cardiff. – PULPIT and FONT of
stone and alabaster, richly carved with foliage. – STALLS,
carved with two figures of St Catherine. – REREDOS. Resurrection, inlaid in black and white marble. Designed by
H. H. Armstead. – Rich brass ALTAR RAILS, LECTERN and
HEATING GRILLES. – STAINED GLASS. By *Morris & Co.*,
1880, finely attuned to the coloration of the church. – Chancel
E, Crucifixion. Designed by *Burne-Jones*. – Transept S, St
Cecilia and angels. All by *Burne-Jones*, except two of the small
angels in roundels below, by *Morris*. – MONUMENT. Inscribed
slab, set in the vestry wall. Datable to the late C9 or early C10.
Carved with an encircled cross entirely formed of interlace.
Found in the churchyard of the medieval church.

Low WALLS enclose the churchyard and terraced burial
ground rising to the E, clearly part of Prichard's scheme.
Beyond and higher still, the roofless shell of the medieval
CHURCH (burnt out 1954). A single cell, with three-light Perp
E and square-headed Tudor SE windows. Double w bell gablet.
(PLAS BAGLAN, ½ m. E, approached from the A48 up PANT YR
ARIAN, at the S end of Baglan village. An irregular earthwork
bearing traces of a rectangular masonry tower, comparable to
C12 Norman keeps but with thinner walls. The Royal Commission suggests that it was the stronghold of the Welsh lord
of Afan *c.* 1200.)
BLAEN BAGLAN, ¾ m. NE. Derelict gentry house of *c.* 1600. The
two-and-a-half-storey porch is the only obviously eloquent
feature. Four-centred entrance arch under a hoodmould and
two-light window above with sunk chamfer moulding. The
porch originally stood against the l. bay of the five-bay front.
In the C17 the house was extended by one bay to the l. and a
kitchen wing added at the rear (masking a massive mural stair
projection).

1090   BARGOED/BARGOD

ST GWLADYS. On a steeply sloping site above the High Street.
E.E. The chancel, at the downhill end, is of 1877–9 by *Prichard*.
Nave, with N vestry, by *E.M. Bruce Vaughan*, 1893–4. The
contrasting ways in which the two architects used the local
Pennant sandstone can be well studied here. Inside, the chancel
arch is obviously Prichard's. – STAINED GLASS. E window by
R.J. Newbery, Good Shepherd above Crucifixion, flanked by
SS Peter and Paul. – Nave SE, Boer War memorial, signed
by *Newbery*.

HANBURY ROAD BAPTIST CHAPEL, High Street. Red brick
and Forest stone, with projecting porches, making an unusually
sculptural composition. Jacobean. 1906–7 by *James & Morgan*
on foundations laid a decade earlier by *D. Morgan*.

POLICE STATION, High Street. Gabled, stone, of 1904. Astonishing miniature-monumental POLICE COURT beside it, faced
with Portland stone, with a pediment carried on side piers rather
than the stout Ionic three-quarter columns which purport to
carry it. 1911 by a local architect, *George Kenshole*.

VIADUCT at the N end of the town, five arches, on strongly
splayed piers.

1060   BARRY/Y BARRI

Barry has a medieval past, as the traces of the pilgrimage chapel
on Barry Island, the ruins of the modest C14 castle in Romilly
Park, and the splendid dovecote at Cadoxton all demonstrate.
The modern town, however, owes its existence to the docks,
developed from the 1880s through the enterprise of the industrialist David Davies of Llandinam, to supplement, and if possible
divert trade from, the coal-exporting docks at Cardiff and
Penarth. An Act of Parliament establishing the Barry Dock and
Railway Company was passed in 1884. The *Builder* in 1891 commented 'about six years ago Barry was a barren beach, with a
farm-house and two or three scattered cottages in the neighbourhood, but is now in process of becoming an important seaport
town'. During the mid to late 1890s buildings of all sorts were
going up at a tremendous rate, culminating in the heroically
scaled Docks Office of 1898. Since then the town has pushed
inland to engulf the ancient churches of Cadoxton and Merthyr
Dyfan, but the earliest development survives remarkably complete. Barry Dock, the working town, is a dense network of streets
running N and S from Holton Road, the principal shopping street,
built in one campaign in 1892–3. Up on the hill to the W lies
the town's fashionable residential area, where All Saints church,
claiming the high ground, and a group of chapels scaling towards
it up Porthkerry Road, were built in the first decade of the C20
to serve the spiritual needs of the residents. Romilly Park beyond
provides for physical recreation. Barry Island S of the docks,
dominated by holiday culture, constitutes a world of its own.

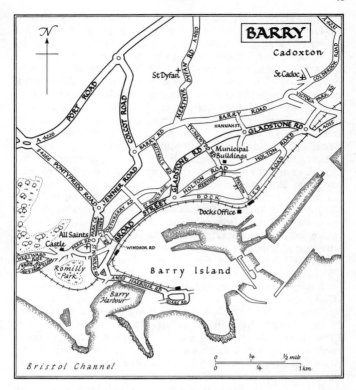

ST BARUCH'S CHAPEL, Friars Road, Barry Island. On the
headland above the harbour. Mentioned by Giraldus Cambrensis in the late C12 as containing the shrine of St Baruch,
and still noted as a place of pilgrimage by Leland in 1540.
Excavation suggested that the chapel was first built *c*.1140
in what was already a cemetery. Low walling remains of a
rectangular nave, and a narrower rectangular chancel, a rebuilding of the apsidal Norman chancel. Also evidence of a
priest's house close beside to the N.

ALL SAINTS, Park Road. By *E. M. Bruce Vaughan*, solid and
serious but without much individuality. E.E. to Dec in style.
Grey-blue Lias limestone with buff dressings of Bath stone.
Designed in 1902, and built in two stages, 1907–8 and 1914–
15. The best feature is the NE tower, making the most of its
height with sheer pilaster buttresses at the angles and a polygonal stair-turret. Spire intended. Five-bay clerestoried nave
with lean-to aisles. Slightly lower chancel. Spacious interior.
Only in the elaborate triple sedilia and piscina does the architect
allow himself an outburst of enthusiasm. – REREDOS. 1922, by
J. Wippell & Co. of Exeter. – ROOD AND SCREEN. Perp. 1934. –
STAINED GLASS. Chancel E, Crucifixion between Nativity and

Empty Tomb. 1919 by *Burlison & Grylls*. In a C15 Flemish style. – Sanctuary N. Supper at Emmaus, *c.*1971 by *Frank Roper* of Penarth. – Aisles, three N, three S, 1947–8, a set by *A. L. Wilkinson*. – S aisle W, 1949 by the same.

ST CADOC, Coldbrook Road. The parish church of Cadoxton-juxta-Barry. The small saddleback W tower, unbuttressed, shows C15 evidence in the W doorway moulded with two waves, and the trefoiled lancets at belfry level. Nave and lower chancel, oddly contrasted with one another, the former meticulously reconstructed in 1885 by *J. P. Jones* reusing old material, the latter still rendered and whitewashed. In the nave N wall one lancet, round-headed internally, of the C13. Otherwise the openings are all Perp, except the Y-traceried E window, inserted in 1828. Rood-loft stair, unusually, on the S side. Scraped interior. Late medieval wagon roof in the chancel, retaining fragments of an embattled wall-plate. – FONT. A small, low tub, with roll mouldings at top and bottom. – STOUP. Octagonal bowl. – ALTAR RAILS. Enclosing the altar on three sides, the turned balusters vertically symmetrical, the angles topped by turned finials. The handsome and unusual survival of a fitting that was standard in the C17. – STAINED GLASS. Nave S, Faith, Hope and Charity, 1887, supplied by *Morgan Bros.* of Cadoxton.

ST DYFAN, Merthyr Dyfan Road. Oddly remote in its little valley, though the high ground all around is now built over. The chancel shows its C13 date by two uneven lancets in its S wall. C15 cinquefoiled lights under hoodmoulds, chancel E and nave S and N. The nave is remarkable for its massive and irregular pink sandstone quoins. Two-stage unbuttressed W tower with single-light openings in its S wall for a mural stair, but no W doorway. Corbelled battlements. The S porch and doorway are C19, but the stoup (even if it is a reused mortar) must be medieval. And so to the interior. The tower arch, four-centred with a broad chamfer, belongs to the C15. Chancel arch similar in form and presumably similar in date. Restoration 1857 by *Prichard & Seddon*. The character of the interior, however, is due to *George Pace*, who repaired the church in 1972, lowered the floors E of the porch, and in 1974 reordered it in accordance with the tenets of the Liturgical Movement. Stone altar centrally placed in the chancel. – FONT. A tub, on a modern cruciform stem. – LIGHT FITTINGS. Black metal. By *Pace*. Typical if unusually elaborate. – TOWER SCREEN. By *Pace*, to form a vestry. – STAINED GLASS. Chancel E, Annunciation, 1933 by *J. Wippell & Co.* of Exeter. – Nave N, Christ in the Carpenter's Shop. Flat colours, picture-book style. 1975, signed by *H. W. Harvey* of York. Presumably Pace approved this.

ST MARY, Barry Dock, Holton Road. An ambitious design, by *G. E. Halliday*, exhibited by him in 1901, built 1903–5 but left palpably incomplete. Walls of squared, rock-faced Lias, Bath stone dressings. Dec chancel. Close to the street the S aisle presents an array of four huge Perp windows between buttresses. Intended SW porch and SE tower not built. Handsome six-bay arcades, the piers with four shafts and four big hollows, i.e. Perp. N aisle awaited. Handsome roofs in nave and chancel. – FONT. Grossly neo-Norman. Can it be by Halliday?

ST PAUL THE APOSTLE, St Paul's Avenue. 1891–3 by *Kempson & Fowler*. A cheap church, of red Cattybrook brick with sparing Bath stone dressings. N aisle added in 1906 by *Kempson*. SE tower not built. The mean W arrangements date from the 1960s. Battered and tapered buttresses, a typical 1890s motif. Timber arcades, octagonal piers and pierced arch spandrels. Wide chancel arch with a continuous double-wave moulding. Exposed internal brickwork painted over. – STAINED GLASS. Chancel E, Resurrected Christ with angels, 1934 by *Christopher Webb*.

BETHEL ENGLISH BAPTIST CHURCH, St Nicholas Road. 1902–3 by *G. Morgan & Son* of Carmarthen. Small tower with a busily detailed top stage of Bath stone, making the most of the hilltop site before All Saints church came and outdid it. Free-style façade, dominated by a window with strange, flattened tracery. Towering side elevation, the round-headed windows at the lowest stage for the schoolroom, paired windows at two levels for the church itself. The interior is a finely resolved design, both long and high. Galleries on three sides carried on slender iron columns and supporting a second set of columns which carry arcades and a trefoil-profile ceiling with exposed tie-beams and queenposts. Pulpit, organ and baptistery ingeniously united.

DINAM HALL, Merthyr Street. For the Presbyterian Forward Movement. Dated 1903, designed by *George Thomas*, Edwin Seward's former partner. Not like a chapel at all. On the acute angle between two roads, Tuscan columns of Portland stone carry a battlemented circular turret. Red brick and Bath stone.

HOLY TRINITY PRESBYTERIAN CHURCH OF WALES, St Paul's Avenue. 1894 by *T. G. Williams* of Liverpool. On a corner site. Large and serious. Geometrical Gothic. T-plan. Gabled façade and tower towards the corner. Pennant sandstone, snecked and rock-faced, dressed with Bath stone. Handsome, heavily timbered interior, galleried on all four sides, the ground-level seating arranged semicircularly into the transepts. Substantial hammerbeam roof with pendants. Romanesque leaf capitals for the cast iron gallery supports.

METHODIST CHURCH, Porthkerry Road. 1897–8 by *Jones, Richards & Budgen*. Lias limestone, with Bath stone dressings. Ebullient Perp façade on the model of St George's Chapel, Windsor. Buttressed sides with full-height windows and short transepts. The interior was designed for galleries but never received them, hence its barn-like air.

UNITED REFORMED CHURCH, Windsor Road. Designed in 1904 by *W. Ernest Knapman*. Fully Anglican in concept, with a clerestoried interior, and to the r. of the façade a big tower topped by gables and pinnacles. Rock-faced Pennant sandstone and Bath stone ashlar. Extensive SCHOOLS to the rear.

TABERNACLE WELSH CONGREGATIONAL CHAPEL, Holton Road. 1893–4 by *Seward & Thomas* of Cardiff. Rendered. Classical, a restrained but subtle composition, the centre bay carried up in relief across the main pediment. Painted in a way that enhances the composition.

CASTLE, Park Road. Of the castle of the de Barri family, only the fragmentary gatehouse and part of a rectangular hall abutting it survive. They can be dated to the early C14, but are of different builds. See the way the angle of the hall overlaps the battered base of the gatehouse. Entrance arch of pointed segmental profile, chamfered and with a hoodmould. Portcullis groove behind it, and evidence of a drawbridge. To l. and r. slightly bowed turrets, which can never have been impressive. Windlass room above the arch, which apparently doubled as a chapel. This intercommunicated with the upper-floor hall. Hall undercroft with slit windows, deeply splayed. Traces of another undercroft E of the gateway.

MUNICIPAL BUILDINGS, Holton Road. Barry's focal building, in an ebullient Baroque style that sustains the role, inspired, like so many civic buildings at the turn of the century, by John Belcher's Colchester Town Hall of 1898. A competition held in 1902 was won by the little-known *Charles E. Hutchinson & E. Harding Payne*, and their design was realized 1903–8, though most of the twenty-bay return front, with a large assembly hall, was never completed. Red brick and lavish Bath stone. Symmetrical plan, determined asymmetry in the façade. Stout axial clock tower, crowned by a small copper-covered dome. To the l. seven-bay public hall, its portal framed by pairs of giant Ionic columns carrying an open segmental pediment of massive projection, within which sit statues of emblematic women urgently leaning forward. To the r. seven-bay public library, the centre three bays defined by giant Ionic pilasters carrying an attic. The high, channelled ground storey gives some anchorage to the composition. Carving by *T. A. Jones* of Cardiff. The interior of the library is nothing special, the hall inaccessible at the time of writing.

CIVIC CENTRE, Holton Road. 1980 by *David Preece & Associates*. Also of red brick, also symmetrical. Windows in long bands. Full-height brick piers subdivide the façade and, where the central entrance recedes, stand free, portico-fashion.

MEMORIAL HALL, Gladstone Road. Severe cubic block in a Wren style, completed in 1932 to the designs of Major *E. R. Hinchcliffe*. Red brick and reconstituted Portland stone. The single-storey annexe which blocks the view while repeating the style is of 1966 by *Alex Gordon & Partners*.

DOCKS, off Dock View Road. The Taff Vale Railway and Cardiff Bute Docks enjoyed a virtual monopoly as the export outlet for much of the South Wales coal trade. David Davies's ambitious Barry Docks and Railway scheme of 1889–98 was created in response to the congestion that resulted from the prodigious growth in this trade during the late C19. The engineers, *Henry*

Marc Brunel and *John Wolfe Barry*, constructed two large basins with tidal entrance basin between Barry Island and the mainland. The first dock, begun in 1889, is 3,400 ft (1,036 metres) long and 1,100 ft (335 metres) at its greatest width. There is a mole 1,300 ft (396 metres) long by 200 ft (61 metres) wide within the dock, and breakwaters 2,600 ft (792 metres) long on the E side and 700 ft (213 metres) long on the W protect the entrance. The construction of a second dock was authorized in 1893, work commenced in 1894, and the new dock opened in 1898. It lies to the E of No. 1 dock and has access from it through a channel closed by a rolling caisson. This dock is 3,338 ft (1,017 metres) long and in width varies from 400 to 600 ft (122 to 183 metres). Dock walls $46\frac{1}{2}$ ft (14 metres) high, of massive limestone blocks, were built only at loading points. A multitude of railway sidings led to the towering hydraulic hoists which have now been demolished. There are two dry docks, and a new entrance lock was added in 1908. On the W breakwater is a LIGHTHOUSE 38 ft (12 metres) high, of a standard design, manufactured by *Chance Brothers* in 1890. The peak of the coal-exporting trade was reached at Barry in 1913, when over 11 million tons of coal and coke passed through the port.

The DOCKS OFFICE (now Custom House), which stands in splendid isolation on the waterfront, a monument to the immediate success of the whole enterprise, was built 1897–1900 and bears the date 1898. It cost the formidable sum of £59,000. Its architect, *Arthur E. Bell*, was the son of the resident engineer to the Dock and Railway Company. Red brick with Portland stone dressings. Wren style. The massive block, eleven bays by seven, is articulated by a giant Composite order of pilasters over a channelled ground storey. Slightly projecting three-bay centre crowned by a triangular pediment on three-quarter columns. End bays of the main front and the central bays round the sides given segmental pediments on paired pilasters. Central doorway in a concave surround as at Wren's St Mary-le-Bow. Heavy central tower, not originally envisaged, a pilastered stone clock-stage carrying a steep octagonal cupola. The interior shows the same limited imagination in its broad, low, axial hall with an imperial staircase beyond. The building has been restored in exemplary fashion after fire destroyed the roof and clock tower in 1984.

The STATUE of David Davies dominates the space in front. It is by *Alfred Gilbert* and antedates the building, having been unveiled in 1893. In a lively pose, Davies reads an unfurled plan.

CUSTOM HOUSE AND MERCANTILE MARINE OFFICE, Station Street (now Council Offices). 1903–4 by *H. M. Office of Works*. Red brick and Portland stone, but a complete contrast to the Docks Office. Arts and Crafts Baroque, wittily turning the corner and managing the hillside site.

School-building played an important part in the early develop-

ment of Barry. The town still boasts a fine set of strongly
characterized board schools.

CADOXTON BOARD SCHOOLS, Victoria Park Road. Infants'
school, single-storeyed, dated 1887. Beside it, where the ground
drops, the much higher blocks for girls and for boys, added in
1890–1 by *Seward & Thomas* and in 1895 by *George Thomas*.
Almost styleless, the main front a marvellous jumble of
windows. Coursed grey Lias limestone walls, with red brick
and Bath stone for the dressings, a vivid polychromy brought
out by the recent cleaning and restoration.

GLADSTONE COUNTY PRIMARY SCHOOL, Gladstone Road.
By *G. A. Birkenhead* of Cardiff, opened in 1906. Symmetrical,
two-storey range for boys and girls, gabled, with a central
domed lantern. One-storey range at r.-angles for infants.
Gabled, of course. Red Staffordshire brick, dressings of Forest
of Dean stone. The school was designed for 1,204 children in
all, and cost £17,850. It makes an unusually clear exposition of
board school layout.

102 JENNER PARK COUNTY SCHOOLS, built as Hannah Street
Board School, Barry Road. Dated 1899. By *Jones, Richards &
Budgen*. An enterprising design, in an early C17 Netherlandish
style, executed in red brick with Bath stone bands and voussoirs.
N-facing range of two storeys towards the road, symmetrically
disposed under a variety of shaped gables. Large tripartite
windows to fill the classrooms with light. The r.-hand bay
jumps up a storey higher, itself overtopped by an octagonal
angle turret. Round the corner in Hannah Street the symmetry
dissolves. Entrances for boys and for girls from the playground
at the back. Across the playground the single-storey infants'
school, yet more playful in design.

HOLTON ROAD BOARD SCHOOLS, Holton Road. 1890–2 by
Seward & Thomas. Red brick sparingly dressed with red sandstone. The two-storey range for boys and girls faces the major
road, the infants round the corner in Court Road. Typical
gabled main façade of rigid symmetry, the pilaster strips on the
upper storey an unusually clear reminiscence of the London
board school idiom.

ROMILLY COUNTY INFANTS' SCHOOL, Romilly Road. In
three single-storey parts. The range at the top, 1893 by
Seward & Thomas, is domestic-looking with its half-timbered
and tile-hung gables. The middle range, dated 1896, by *George
Thomas*. The lowest, built for boys, 1904–5 by *G. A. Birkenhead*.

BRYNHAFREN COMPREHENSIVE SCHOOL FOR GIRLS,
Merthyr Dyfan Road. 1969–73 by the *Percy Thomas Partnership*
(design partner *Dale Owen*). Low, rigorously ordered group
arranged round a series of courtyards. Elegantly detailed.
Curtain walling. Grey brick stair projections stepping down the
hill on the seaward side.

VALE RESOURCE CENTRE, Buttrills Road. On a splendid site
at the top of The Buttrills, overlooking the Bristol Channel.
Built as a teacher training college for women (subsequently
Polytechnic of Wales) on an expansive plan and in a swagger

Wren style with French inflections. 1913–14 by *Teather &
Wilson*. The central education block has a five-bay pedimented
centrepiece with columns, Doric below, Ionic above, framed
between channelled turret-like features. Bath stone ashlar, with
some sculpture, including a demi-angel over the doorway.
Seven-bay side ranges, of red brick. Hostel blocks, also of
red brick, lie back to l. and r. They are part of the original
composition, though now in different uses.

GARDEN SUBURB, w of Romilly Park. Laid out in 1914 by
T. Alwyn Lloyd in conjunction with *Sir Raymond Unwin* for
Barry Garden Suburb Ltd, under the aegis of the Welsh Town
Planning and Housing Trust. Roughly concentric layout.
Houses in semi-detached pairs or short rows. White walls.
Slate roofs mostly hipped. Bay windows. The earliest houses,
completed in 1917, are in PARK ROAD and WESTWARD RISE.
In 1922 a second group was built in BRON AWELON and
TAN-Y-FRON. In 1925 these roads were continued w-wards,
to house employees of the Great Western Railway. Much piece-
meal alteration since houses were individually sold off in 1969.

DOVECOTE, on a rocky outcrop above the E end of Gladstone 38
Road. Circular, of stone, with a corbelled stone dome surviving
complete. Pilaster buttresses. Pointed doorway. The Royal
Commission dates it as early as the C13. In the grounds of
Cadoxton Court, built in 1873 on the site of a by then ruined
medieval house.

COLD KNAP, 1 m. SW. Footings of a substantial Roman building
constructed of local Lias limestone and originally roofed with
ceramic tiles, on a point overlooking the Bristol Channel and
incongruously set amongst modern seaside development. Up to
nineteen rooms surrounded a central courtyard. It is unknown
whether the building was of more than one storey. An external
veranda ran the length of the SW side. Construction began
towards the end of the C3 A.D. but seems not to have been
completed. This and other evidence for Roman activity in the
vicinity of the nearby silted inlet (now a boating pool) suggests
that the building may have been intended either as a storehouse
or as an official guesthouse, as part of a maritime link between
South Wales and the south-west of England.

FLAT HOLM LIGHTHOUSE, on the island of Flat Holm, 7 m.
SE. Erected in 1737 by Bristol merchants to light the treacherous
passage up the Severn Estuary. The tapering circular tower,
68 ft (20.73 metres) high, was at that time exceeded in height
only by the tower of 1674 at Flamborough Head (North
Yorkshire). Converted from coal to oil in 1820 and to electricity
in 1969. The present internal iron staircase, and external lantern
and iron gallery, date from 1866. The island is accessible by
boat from Barry in the summer.

0080
BEDDAU

A large and sprawling village which originated with the development of the Cwm Colliery from 1912.

ST MICHAEL AND ALL ANGELS. Built by an unknown architect in 1936 at the expense of Lady Juliet Rhys-Williams and her husband of Miskin Manor. A small but whole-hearted piece of Expressionism. Rendered white. The E end steps out and up aggressively, its raison d'être to provide hidden side-lighting to the chancel. Circular end windows enclosing six-pointed stars, pentagonal side windows. Nave ceiling in five cants cut off before the higher vault of the chancel.

(At CWM COKE WORKS, Ty-nant, 1 m. NE, timber cooling towers, the sole survivors in the county of a type invented in Germany in 1894, and replaced by the familiar concrete cooling tower after 1945.)

0000
BEDLINOG

ST CADOC. Apsidal chancel with lancets. Nave with plate-traceried windows. W bellcote and porch. Overscaled buttresses. The interior dominated by the round-headed chancel arch. All this is wildly old-fashioned for 1911, the date on the foundation stone. The architect appears to have been *W. Dowdeswell*. – STAINED GLASS. In the apse, by *Celtic Studios*.

The church stands aside below the road. In the village centre SALEM WELSH BAPTIST CHAPEL, dated 1876. Rendered. Gabled façade with roughly dressed stone surrounds to all the windows. Further N, beyond the houses, the single-storey COUNTY INFANTS' SCHOOL by *D. Pugh Jones*, dated 1907, and the two-storey COUNTY JUNIOR SCHOOL, 1911, with a central pair of shaped gables. That was a piece of abnormal fantasy for *Pugh Jones*, Education Architect for the E half of Glamorgan, perhaps to celebrate the fact that this was his thirtieth school in the job.

1080
BEDWAS

ST BARRWG. Against the hillside above the village. Of local Pennant sandstone. Thick-set W tower under a saddleback roof. The W doorway apparently of Sutton stone, evidence of early date. The Y-traceried window above it, and the lancet belfry opening are both consistent with a date *c.* 1300, though the walling is much reconstructed. Nave with S porch, lower chancel, all standing up proud as the ground slopes. The consistent fenestration, lights in ones, twos and threes with pointed trefoils over trefoil heads and intersecting tracery, is presumably the contribution of *John Prichard*, whose restoration in 1875 included new windows, and the rebuilding of the N chapel. Simple pointed chancel arch and tower arch, hardly usable as

dating evidence. – FONT. Round bowl on a shallow roll. –
STAINED GLASS. Nave S window, Good Shepherd, after 1883,
signed by *W. G. Taylor*. – Chancel E, Nativity, Crucifixion and
Resurrection, after 1889, and sanctuary S, Faith, clearly by the
same maker. – Nave S lancet, First World War memorial,
signed by *Jones & Willis*.

In TRETHOMAS, ¾ m. E, lofty WORKMEN'S HALL AND INSTI-
TUTE, of red brick and cream stone with full-height Ionic
pilasters. 1923 is the date on the memorial stones.

(GWERN-Y-DOMEN, 1 m. S. A small C12 ringwork on a natural
mound rising out of the meadows S of the River Rhymni, a
site with few intrinsic defensive advantages, one would have
thought. Its S side cut away by the now disused railway line.)

BRYNGWYN ENGINE HOUSE, ½ m. W, to the N of Pandy Road.
The tall, monumental structure, formerly dated 1868, stands
in dense undergrowth. The ground-floor plinth, quoins, sills,
and keystones and imposts of the large openings to N and S
are of rusticated Pennant sandstone masonry. The two upper
storeys are largely in brick, with large round-headed E windows
on both storeys and two similar openings in the S gable. The
two other elevations were similar, but have partly collapsed.

   The structure is unique because of the mechanical operation
of its machinery. A large, inverted Cornish steam engine was
located in the upper floors, and a cranked beam connected with
a horizontal pumping line that passed through the two ground-
floor openings in the gable ends. One end led to an inclined
coal-mining tunnel, or adit, and the other probably to a balance
box, to counteract the great weight of the long line of pump
rods leading underground.

BETWS   8080

Exhilaratingly high-lying village, on a S-facing spur above Bridgend. One of the few medieval churches on the uplands to have
gathered houses round it.

ST DAVID. Memorable cubic bellcote with a pyramidal cap on
corbels and gargoyles at the angles. The church, just a small
nave with S porch and lower chancel, possesses few other old
features. The porch has a double-chamfered outer arch dying
into the imposts. In the nave two mullioned windows, one with
arched lights, the other without. In the chancel a simple priest's
door. These probably all belong to the C15 and C16. The
contemporary arch-braced roofs of nave and chancel also
survive, much repaired, the former with a collar purlin. Piscina
with a nodding arch, partly old. Everything else is Victorian,
and betrays the hand of *G. E. Halliday*, who added the N aisle
in 1893. Perp style. – FONT. Medieval. A tub-shaped bowl on
a wonderfully geometrical base.

TYLE-COCH, 1 m. NW. Lobby-entry house with a rear wing,
datable to the late C16. (Some of the fine stone internal doorways and one two-light window remain.)

Tŷ-ISAF, 1 m. w. On a s-facing hillside, its two-storey porch visible from afar. This is a C17 addition to a C16 farmhouse, which also gained a free-standing kitchen to the N and a long cowhouse range to the w.

BIRCHGROVE
                    3½ m. w of Neath

ST JOHN. 1890–1 by *J. Birch Padden* (G.R.), extended by two bays to the E in 1930. Perp. – FONT. A tiny bowl on a thick baluster stem. Dated 1829. – STAINED GLASS. E window, Christ between Mary and John, 1930, signed by *Heaton, Butler & Bayne*, long after the firm's heyday.
(GLAN BRÂN, ¾ m. NE. A late C18 villa-like farmhouse high on the hillside. Five bays, two storeys, rendered walls under a hipped roof. Single-storey porch on slender cast iron columns.)

BISHOPSTON/LLANDEILO FERWALLT

Bishopston is so called because it belonged to the bishops of Llandaff, their only extra-diocesan property in Glamorgan. Today, much belongs to the retired and to the holiday-maker. Sporadic housing extends all the way from the church to the sea.

ST TEILO. In a steep-sided, wooded valley close to a stream, built as if burrowing into the hillside. Short, thick-set w tower of indeterminate date. No buttresses, battlements on corbels, as usual. Slit-like belfry windows. The round-headed window low in the s wall cannot be taken as C12 evidence. Nor, inside, can the plain pointed arches into tower and chancel. In the chancel N wall a small lancet, probably C13, and similar windows, a lancet and a lancet pair, in the s wall. Later medieval fenestration of the nave, an ogee-headed N lancet, and to the s a two-light Perp window with a four-centred head, used in the C19 as the model for further windows in the nave. Big three-light Tudor s window. s porch added in 1851. Note the tablet naming not only the rector and churchwardens, but also the mason who erected it, *G. William*. The arch-braced roof of the nave is medieval in part. Restoration by *W. D. Caröe*, 1926–7. – FONT. Medieval. Square, on a short round stem on a square base. – FITTINGS. A set by *Caröe*, 1927–9. – STAINED GLASS. E window, war memorial, 1920.
(BISHOPSTON OLD CASTLE, ½ m. NE. Overgrown C12 ring-work. Excavation in 1898 found traces of a timber palisade, important evidence of the way these early medieval earthworks were made defensible.)
CASWELL BAY, 1½ m. SE, is overlooked by just one modest Victorian villa, CASWELL BAY HOUSE, 1877–9 by *Henry Hall* of London, and two large apartment blocks of contrasting character. To the w, REDCLIFFE APARTMENTS, *c.* 1965, is a no-nonsense and surprisingly unobtrusive five-storey slab, the

lowest storey recessed, the next enclosed, and the top three with balconies from end to end. To the E the all-too-visible CASWELL BAY COURT, 1990–2 by *The Wigley Fox Partnership*, in a clumsily simplified Victorian style.

FAIRWOOD LODGE, 2 m. N. Long, low, stuccoed house of Regency character, which would probably look less alien had more of Swansea's early villas survived. Built shortly before 1827 for John Nicholas Lucas of Stouthall, Reynoldston. Only the s front is a coherent composition, two-storeyed, of eight bays, the centre two recessed, the second and seventh brought forward as bows. Oddly, the windows in the l. bow are set within a giant relieving arch, but their twins in the r. bow are not. The house is attributed to *William Jernegan* in his old age. Later w extension.

BLAENGARW

9090

A former mining settlement (the last mine closed in 1986), at the head of the Garw Valley, where it opens out enough for a proper network of streets to develop. At the centre a triangular space, THE STRAND. Even in such an inaccessible spot, among still conspicuous coal tips, pride of place evidently continues to flourish.

ST JAMES, Church Place. 1890 by *Bruton & Williams* of Cardiff, who, for £1,085, found it 'impossible to introduce much architectural design'.

BETHANIA WELSH BAPTIST CHURCH, Herbert Street. (Disused.) 1912. Late Gothic. Clearly by *W. Beddoe Rees*, almost a twin of his Mount Calvary English Baptist Chapel, Manselton, Swansea.

MOUNT ZION ENGLISH BAPTIST CHAPEL, King Edward Street. By *W. Beddoe Rees*, dated 1905. Perp, but not especially impressive, in spite of its double flights of steps. Inside, the galleries on three sides have palmette pierced iron fronts, a speciality of the architect.

Church and chapels are, naturally, faced with the ubiquitous Pennant sandstone dressed with ashlar from Bath or the Forest of Dean. The two main secular buildings introduce a little variety.

WORKMEN'S HALL AND INSTITUTE, Katie Street. 1893–4 by *Jacob Rees* of Pentre, providing hall, library and reading room. Pennant walls enlivened by red brick outlining of the gable and round-headed windows of the admittedly chapel-like façade. In 1991 the window openings were filled in with splendidly spirited scenes in coloured tiles, by *Pioneer Arts* of Cardiff, illustrating the turbulent history of the settlement from the C18 to the late C20. Instructive inscriptions.

BLAENGARW HOTEL, The Strand. 1897 by *S. J. Williams* of Aberdare. Large. Rendered.

BLAENGWRACH

St Mary, Church Crescent. Small and simple, a rebuilding in 1830 of a chapel of 1704. Nave and lower chancel. w bell gable and w porch. Pointed-headed windows with timber Y-tracery. – STAINED GLASS. Chancel E, Good Shepherd between SS Peter and Paul. By *Joseph Bell* of Bristol.

(BLAENGWRACH FARM, $\frac{3}{4}$ m. SE. Little-altered, and now abandoned, early C17 farmhouse of one storey only. The entrance doorway, under a broad hoodmould, led directly into the hall. To the r., a large outer room. Both rooms had hearths in the end gables.)

VENALLT IRONWORKS, at the w end of Cwmgwrach, $\frac{1}{2}$ m. SW. Constructed *c.* 1839–42 to smelt iron with anthracite by means of the hot blast process then recently introduced at Ynysgedwyn. The furnaces were out of use by 1854, and the site was reused for a patent fuel works, which led to their demolition. Surviving features include the blowing-house engine, part of the cast-house, the base of the stack and the furnace walls. The office building is now a farmhouse. An interesting survival is a furnace bear with two water-cooled tuyères (air-blast nozzles) embedded in it.

CWM GWRACH BRANCH CANAL, WHARF-HOUSE AND LIME-KILN. A branch canal from the Neath Canal was built in 1817 across the valley floor to join a railway from Cwm Gwrach Collieries. At the junction, $\frac{3}{4}$ m. SW, is a derelict wharf-house of Pennant sandstone rubble. At the terminus of the branch canal, $\frac{1}{4}$ m. SE, are the remains of a limekiln in the same material.

WOOLLEN MILL. *See* Glynneath.

BLAENRHONDDA

At the head of the Rhondda Fawr, overlooked by crags on all sides. The terraced houses which extend virtually without a break through the entire length of the valley from Pontypridd, 15 m. (12 kilometres) away to the SE, here finally peter out. Mining had begun here by the later 1850s. A planned village, Bryn Wyndham, was even proposed. Blaenrhondda Colliery was sunk in 1869, followed within a decade by Fernhill Colliery. Ambitious expansion plans of the late 1950s did not materialize, and today the mines are a memory.

GARREG LWYD OPEN SETTLEMENT, 2 m. N (SN 9225 0187). Sinuous stony banks combine to form a series of small paddocks and plots associated with annular house foundations on the hillside. Excavation suggested occupation some time between the later first millennium B.C. and the early first millennium A.D. About 1 m. N is LLYN FAWR, a lake dramatically sited at the foot of the Rhigos escarpment, best viewed from the A4061. During its conversion into a reservoir in 1911 and 1913, an important hoard of bronze and iron metalwork was found dating to about 600 B.C., probably a ritual deposition at a sacred site. On CEFN GLAS just over $\frac{1}{2}$ m. NE of Garreg Lwyd, traces of a Neolithic HOUSE datable to the third millennium B.C. have been excavated.

For Tynewydd House, *see* Treherbert.

BONVILSTON/TRESIMWN 0070

ST MARY THE VIRGIN. Of the medieval church there remains the tower, a characteristic structure, unbuttressed, the battlements on a corbel table. It appears to be of late C14 or C15 date: see the W doorway with two-centred head and double-wave moulding, and the square-headed two-light window above. Tudor belfry windows. Nave and lower chancel with N transept, virtually a new building of 1863–4 by *Prichard & Seddon*, which preserved only the featureless N wall of the nave and, surprisingly, the rather crude Perp chancel arch. The Victorian work is substantially and confidently E.E. Plate tracery. Mauve coursed walling stone with mustard-coloured ashlar dressings. Successfully proportioned interior, the arch-braced roof of the nave unexpectedly high up. – PILLAR PISCINA. In the sanctuary. – FONT. An exceptionally fine piece of *c*. 1200. Circular bowl carved in relief with large, rhythmically disposed leaves. The base must be C19. – FITTINGS. Timber, in Jacobean style. A set, supplied in 1908 by *J. Wippell* of Exeter. – SCULPTURE. A fragment on the nave W wall. Small, crude figure, arms akimbo, under a round arch. Saxon, C12 or C16? – STAINED GLASS. Chancel E, Crucifixion, *c*. 1863, of fine quality. Strong colours, C13 style. Surely by *Hardman*. – Chancel SE, Noli me Tangere, *c*. 1891. All white and gold and subtle shading, in an early Renaissance style. The two windows make a fascinating contrast. – Nave S, to commemorate a drowning at sea. 1920 by *Percy Bacon*. Kempe style. – MONU-MENTS. Christopher Bassett † 1764. Gibbsian tablet. – Bassett family, *c*. 1841. Grecian tablet. Signed *Woolcott*, Bristol.

WOODLANDS LODGE, beside the A48 E of the church. Built as the lodge to Bonvilston House, to the design of *David Vaughan*, 1840. A handsome little building. Square, single-storeyed, with a high attic, not part of the original design. Pedimented porch on square piers, its composition repeated in the flat on the other three sides.

(RINGWORK, $\frac{3}{4}$ m. SE. In a marshy field, overgrown by scrub. Fortifiable earthwork, constructed by the Bonville family in the C12.)

BRIDGEND/PEN-Y-BONT AR OGWR 9080

Bridgend did not exist before the C15. It developed on the E bank of the River Ogmore as a market town serving the centre of the county. Before that there had only been the C12 castle and church of Newcastle, on the cliff-top overlooking the river from the W.

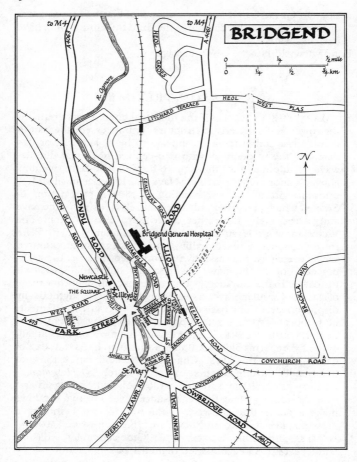

The best-known product in the post-medieval period was the fine
Rhaetic sandstone, known as Quarella, quarried close to the town
centre. Industry still failed to take root in the early C19, but the
town's municipal pretensions were satisfied with the erection of
a pompous town hall in 1843. By 1871 the population had still
not reached 4,000. In 1951 it was no more than 13,500, but since
then great expansion has taken place, as Ford carworks and other
industries have been set up around the town.

ST ILLTYD, The Square, Newcastle. Of the medieval church
only the w tower remains. This is Perp, on a moulded plinth,
its w doorway with a four-centred head and two hollow chamfers, the windows simply arched under hoodmoulds. Corbelled
battlements, small pinnacles and gargoyles. Continuous
mouldings to the tower arch. The body of the church, Dec
nave and s porch, was rebuilt with the addition of a N aisle, by

Prichard in 1849–50, before he had forged a personal style. Chancel rebuilt and N chapel added (reusing Prichard's chancel arch) in 1893–4 by *E. M. Bruce Vaughan* in a Prichardesque idiom – see the narrow-coursed Pennant sandstone walling outside and the internal ashlar facing. Cusped and crocketed rere-arches to the N windows of the chapel. – FONT. Medieval. Octagonal bowl with quatrefoils in relief. – The other fittings are of 1894 by *William Clarke* of Llandaff, a virtuoso display of wood-carving not altogether in good taste. – REREDOS. From wall to wall. (Panels fitted 1925.) – CHOIR STALLS. With fishes lying on the stall ends. – LECTERN. Supported by a sinuous angel. – Also the PULPIT. – STAINED GLASS. Chancel E, Christ between St Paul and St Illtyd. 1894. – MONUMENT. Matilda Riley †1887. An extremely late example of the Neo-classical cliché of a woman under a weeping willow mourning over an urn. Signed *Gaffin*, Regent Street, London.

ST MARY, Nolton, Merthyr Mawr Road. 1885–7 by *John Prichard*, his swan song. In a C13 style. An interior of spacious beauty is created by combining wide arches with slender piers and shafts. The aisled nave and chancel flow together, as a continuous shafted arcade runs in front of the clerestory windows, and the chancel arch on lofty detached shafts barely interrupts. Three E lancets placed very high up. Subtle colouring, the nave piers of grey Forest of Dean stone, the shafts all of a pink sandstone. A good deal of discreet foliage carving, by *William Clarke* of Llandaff. Externally the effect is more sober and straightforward. Quarella stone in the narrow courses Prichard preferred, and Bath stone ashlar dressings. The NW tower and spire, a version of Prichard's at Baglan (q.v.), was completed by *F. R. Kempson* in 1898. – FONT. Small, octagonal. Said to date to 1632. – PULPIT. A florid, over-chromatic piece by *Prichard*. – REREDOS. 1921 by *J. Coates Carter*. In C15 Netherlandish style. – FLOOR TILES. By *Godwin & Son* of Hereford. – STAINED GLASS. A full set, though probably more vivid and insistent than Prichard would have liked. – E window, Crucifixion and Christ in Majesty, by *Dixon*, *c*.1887. – W window, Te Deum, also clearly by *Dixon*. – N aisle, Christ walking on the water, and the Raising of Lazarus, by *Mayer & Co.*, *c*.1887. – S aisle, Annunciation, Nativity and Christ in the Temple, by *Heaton, Butler & Bayne*. Good Shepherd, by *Kempe & Co.*, 1921. – WAR MEMORIAL. (S aisle.) Finely lettered.

HERMON PRESBYTERIAN CHURCH OF WALES, Nolton Street. 1862 by *Robert Roberts*. Rendered. A handsome classical composition. Ionic pilasters carry a pediment broken in the middle by a large arch, to accommodate the central trio of arched windows – a distant echo of the transept ends of Wren's St Paul's Cathedral. Forecourt flanked by gable-ended caretaker's house and schoolroom, built at the same time. Well-preserved contemporary interior, galleried on three sides. Flat boarded ceiling on a plaster cove. Simple 'big seat' en suite with the pews. Later pulpit and organ.

HOPE ENGLISH BAPTIST CHURCH, Derwen Road. 1906–8 by

Philip J. Thomas of Bridgend. Gothic. On a prominent corner site, flaunting a fancifully traceried central window. T-plan, allowing a dramatic internal arrangement. The gallery describes a semicircle with countercurves into the transepts. Even more dramatic, it is cantilevered, without visible means of support. Metal gallery front of palmette design. The focal point of the chapel is the alabaster BAPTISTERY, in front of the pulpit. Full-width composition of blind pointed arches behind, canted boarded ceiling.

TABERNACLE CHAPEL, Derwen Road. Rebuilt 1988–9 by the *Burgess Partnership* (job architect *Siarlys Evans*). The façade projects in an eye-catching bow. Yellow brick.

UNITARIAN CHURCH (now New Park Street Community Church), Park Street. An important early chapel, dated 1795, the datestone the centre of a symmetrical composition. Two long windows below blank roundels, flanked by segment-headed windows in two storeys. Rendered walls, hipped roof. Entrance at the short end. The interior has unfortunately been altered, but must have had a pulpit backing on to the façade wall and galleries round the other three sides.

NEWCASTLE. First mentioned in 1106. What survives of this small but splendid Norman masonry castle, spectacularly sited on the edge of a cliff N of St Illtyd's church, gives an exceptionally clear idea of a C12 stronghold. It is datable stylistically to the later C12, and may even have been built during the short period when it was held by Henry II, 1183–9. It consists of a curtain wall, running straight along the cliff-top, but elsewhere faceted to form a roughly circular enclosure, presumably following the line of a late C11 ringwork. Strongly battered external plinth, originally ashlar-faced. To the S and W it is straddled by two mural towers, of which the former survives for a full three storeys, with inserted Elizabethan windows of sandstone in the upper two. The castle does not have a gate tower, but instead a large PORTAL beside the S tower, which constituted its only means of defence. The portal virtually intact, its significance emphasized by its rich decoration and by the stretches of Sutton stone ashlar to l. and r. The doorway itself is segment-headed, outlined by a roll which is overlapped by close-set bands decorated with rows of pellets, as if nailed on. (The motif appears in several richly decorated West Midlands parish churches, most notably on the S doorway at Quenington, Gloucestershire.)* Semicircular superarch, also with a roll, supported on side shafts, their capitals carved, one with leaves, the other with volutes and relief bands. Fine-jointed ashlar facing fills the tympanum.

Within, footings of two buildings against the E wall, that to the S with irregular outline, possibly a pre-existing structure, that to the N subsequent to the Norman wall, into which it is not bonded.

The site of OLDCASTLE, even its very existence, has been

*I owe this comparison to Dr Jeffrey West.

the subject of debate. However, the Royal Commission suggest that the TITHE BARN, on the N side of Merthyr Mawr Road opposite St Mary's Nolton, may stand on its site. The barn incorporates reused masonry, including cut stones.

OGWR BOROUGH COUNCIL OFFICES, Angel Street. Opened 1986. By the *W.C.B. Thomas Partnership*. Faced with buff reconstituted stone. Slated pitched roofs. In the centre a four-storey office block with windows in long bands, to the N the polygonal council chamber, to the S a hall, all straightforwardly expressed, without mannerisms.

MAGISTRATES' COURT, Derwen Road. (Now disused.) A late work by *John Prichard*, 1880–1. Gothic, of course, and still entirely High Victorian in character. It housed a magistrate's court, police station and superintendent's house. Grey rock-faced walling, with dressings banded in red and grey. Sheer three-storey flank towards the street, but the entrance round the corner at the foot of Brackla Street resourcefully managed. Stairs lead up l. and r. of a prettily shafted group of lancets at first-floor level. Complex flanking projections of contrasting form. The main internal space, the courtroom, has an open timber roof with cusped wind-braces and quatrefoil panels. Bridgend cannot afford to lose this building.

BRIDGEND GENERAL HOSPITAL, Quarella Road. The hospital's centre of gravity has moved stage by stage out of town. At first it occupied the former Bridgend and Cowbridge Union WORKHOUSE. Built 1836–8 by *George Wilkinson* of Witney. Two-storey, seventeen-bay range looking like an almshouse. Three central gables like pricked ears, flanked by many barge-boarded dormers. Neo-Baroque UNION OFFICES of 1911 beside the road. Single-storeyed but with presence. Beyond this the SURGICAL TREATMENT CENTRE, *c*.1898, memorable for its enormously long two-storey cast iron balconies, a medically approved feature of that moment. By *P. J. Thomas* of Bridgend. Further N again, the modern hospital of *c*.1960.

PRINCESS OF WALES HOSPITAL, Coity Road. 1981–5 by the *Alex Gordon Partnership*. Light brown brick below, dark brown cladding above. A series of pavilions under pitched roofs. An attempt to make modern institutional architecture less over-powering.

SCHOOL FOR VISUALLY HANDICAPPED CHILDREN, Ewenny Road. Built *c*.1929, in an attractive later Arts and Crafts idiom. Two-storey, broadly handled, symmetrical façade with widely spaced gables and central bell cupola. Greenish Quarella stone, rough walling and smooth ashlar nicely balanced.

SCHOOLS, Quarella Road. Designed as a board school in 1875 by *Henry C. Harris* of Cardiff. L-plan, resourcefully grouped, not yet affected by standardized ideas about board school design. Single-storeyed. Stone, with large timber mullion-and-transom windows. A little half-timbering in the gables. The influence of Norman Shaw can be felt.

BRACKLA PRIMARY SCHOOL, Brackla Way. 1974–5 by the *Welsh School of Architecture* (project architect *David Leighton*).

An attempt to escape the standard forms of prefabrication. Quirky shape to the hall roof. Many later additions by *Mid Glamorgan County Architects Department*.

PUBLIC LIBRARY, Wyndham Street. 1906–7 by *P. J. Thomas*. Narrow Baroque front with a Bath stone aedicule projecting from the red brick upper storey. (Domed entrance hall.)

WAR MEMORIAL, Dunraven Place. 1921, designed by *Walter Crook*. A helmeted female carrying a flag stands against an obelisk.

RANDALL MEMORIAL DRINKING FOUNTAIN, Nolton Street. 1860 by *J. W. Hugall* of London. Muscular Gothic typical of the date.

BRIDGE, over the Ogmore River, linking Brewery Lane and Quarella Road. Stone, of two arches. Late medieval, reconstructed in its present form after 1775. It now looks sadly incongruous spanning the concrete retaining walls of the canalized river.

STANDING STONE, by the Bowls Centre in Angel Street. In height 5 ft 11 in. (1.8 metres). Of late Neolithic or early Bronze Age date. Excavation showed it to have been erected in a substantial pit containing the partial cremation of an adult male.

RAILWAY STATION, Station Hill. Built in 1850 by *I. K. Brunel* for the South Wales Railway. The original hipped-roof pavilion survives on the W platform of the modern station. Single-storeyed, of Pennant sandstone rubble with tooled freestone dressings. Round-arched openings. Later extensions with matching paired openings. The roof projects on very wide bracket eaves over the full width of the platform and the former main entrance, and continues across a passage between the main building and a similar square, two-bay block to the NW. A similar station pavilion survives at Chepstow, Gwent.

No perambulation of Bridgend is practical. However, the area round NEWCASTLE deserves a little further exploration. By the entrance to the castle, THE SQUARE, a well-restored row of C19 cottages. Downhill from the church, in Newcastle Hill, HOSPICE (now disused), a substantial mid-C16 stone house, a most unusual survival in an urban situation. Porch towards the road with a chamfered, four-centred arch, enlarged *c.* 1600 (see the straight joint) and given a two-light window beside the doorway. The main range of the house has lost most of its external detail. Hoodmoulds to the lower windows, for a three-lighter to the l. and a two-lighter to the r., indicating where hall and service rooms lay, respectively. (Many original internal features, including three mural stairs.)

To the W of The Square, in WEST ROAD, two more houses with C16 evidence. At NEWCASTLE HOUSE the evidence is two internal stone doorways. Long, roughly symmetrical exterior of late C18 character, with a central, dentilled, pedimental gable. At NEWCASTLE COTTAGE at least the hoodmoulds can be seen of two-light stone windows above and below. They seem to relate to the early C17 remodelling of a C16 end-entry house, to make it higher and double its length towards the W. (Mural stairs beside both hearths.) From here one can work one's way back towards the river crossing and modern town centre down PARK STREET. This was the fashionable street for Victorian villa-builders. COED PARC (Mid Glamorgan County Library) on the N side, is weakly Voyseyish, of 1899. Nos. 67–69 is the house by *Henry C. Harris* 'in course of erection' in 1875. Gothic. Of the local greenish Quarella stone, like many of the other houses in the street.

In the centre of the town, further mention need only be made of NOLTON HOUSE, at the junction of Nolton Street and Brackla Street, c. 1961 by a local architect, *J. Morgan Harries*. In the Festival of Britain mood, with cantilevered concrete canopies describing many little segmental arcs. A lively contribution to the town which deserves to be cherished. Something similar in DERWEN ROAD. DUNRAVEN PLACE, the nearest thing to an urban space in the town centre, has lost its claim to being its focal point since the lamentable destruction in 1971 of the Greek Doric TOWN HALL, 1843 by *David Vaughan*.

ANGELTON BLAST FURNACE (on the N outskirts of modern Bridgend), off HEOL Y GROES. Built in 1589 by Robert Sidney of Penshurst, who had married Barbara Gamage, the heiress of the last Welsh lord of Coity. The furnace was still in use in 1600. The present heap of remains was until the 1980s still recognizable as one corner of the square stack of the masonry furnace with its lining.

BRITON FERRY/LLANSAWEL 7090

ST MARY, Church Street. In a sequestered corner of the town, almost under the legs of the A48 viaduct. Mainly of 1891–2. The earliest part is the rugged SW tower, probably post-medieval but hard to date. Strongly battered walls and peculiar duplicated battlements. Two-light Tudor belfry opening. Reset at the W end of the church an early C17 window with sunk chamfer moulding. Nave and chancel in one, with lean-to S aisle. Long, unbroken internal space, stressed by the boarded roof of trefoil section. Timber piers. The architect was *H. Francis Clarke* of Briton Ferry, working under *J. P. Seddon*'s supervision. – FONT. Medieval. Tub-shaped. – STAINED GLASS. E window, Ascension, c. 1922. Düreresque, powerfully coloured. – S aisle, Crucifixion, signed *S. Belham & Co.* and made to *Seddon*'s design. Under Morris influence.

ST CLEMENT, Neath Road. 1864–6 by *John Prichard*. E.E. The exterior is nothing special, aisled nave in one with the chancel, which confronts the road with its polygonal apse. Transepts. Stone-carving not completed. Inside, however, the piers and arcades are all of timber, ingeniously interlocking with the arch-braced roofs of nave and aisles. Stone arches to chancel and transepts. Fine tiled pavement with red marble steps in the sanctuary. – STAINED GLASS. In the apse the central lights, Crucifixion and Entombment, of 1881. Flanking lights *c*. 1902. – w window, Doubting Thomas, *c*. 1902. – N transept war memorial, by *Celtic Studios*. – Aisle windows, 1972 by the same.

OUR LADY OF THE ASSUMPTION, Neath Road. 1965 by *F. R. Bates, Son & Price* (D. Evinson). Prominent openwork campanile of reinforced concrete, forming interlocking crosses, a landmark from the A48. Cubic interior, a cylindrical hanging feature over the altar. – STAINED GLASS signed by *John Petts*, 1966. Fragmented scenes of the Passion right across the partition between vestibule and church.

WESLEYAN METHODIST CHURCH, Graig Road. 1906 by *Crouch & Butler* of Birmingham. Perp. Red brick and Bath stone. Prominent on the hillside.

PUBLIC LIBRARY AND COUNCIL OFFICES, Neath Road. Ashlar-faced pavilion with clock-turret. 1891 by *H. Alexander Clarke*.

SCHOOL, Neath Road. Three gables present big pointed windows towards the road, emphasized by red brick and buff Bath stone voussoirs. Probably *c*.1880, and not the school designed for Briton Ferry by *S. S. Teulon* in 1855.

DOCK, $\frac{1}{2}$ m. S, now split in two by the base of the new high-level M4 motorway viaduct over the River Neath. The dock was constructed to designs by *Isambard Kingdom Brunel* and opened in 1861. It consists of an inner floating dock and an outer tidal basin with an overall area of about 180 acres (73 hectares). Entry to the dock was through a single buoyant lock gate. Closed in 1959 and now largely silted up, although the Pennant sandstone dock walls are intact. The LOCK GATE, with its innovative buoyancy chambers, has been partly dismantled. On the E side of the dock, the square tower of the ENGINE HOUSE which generated hydraulic power to operate the lock.

GWALIA TINPLATE WORKS. Erected in 1892 to use steel produced by the Briton Ferry Ironworks. Acquired by the Briton Ferry Steel Co. in 1937 and closed in 1953. The building has been truncated, and only five of the stone-built bays survive. The chimneystacks have been dismantled and the building re-roofed, but brick flues in the walls mark the original hearths. A brick-built extension to the W carries a plaque dated 1898–9. On an adjacent site to the N was the VILLIERS TINPLATE WORKS (1888), of which some modern brick-built buildings remain.

IRONWORKS, $\frac{1}{2}$ m. S. An ironworks was established on the E bank of the River Neath in the 1840s. It was reconstructed in the 1890s, still as an iron-smelter, and closed in 1958. The site has been completely cleared with the exception of the blast-engine house of *c*.1910, which housed a Richardson, Westgarth quarter-crank blowing engine. It is constructed of concrete blocks in a steel frame, and has two rows of round-headed windows, now filled in.

CADOXTON-JUXTA-NEATH/ LLANGATWG NEDD

7090

ST CATWG. Of the church said to have been built by Adam of Carmarthen, Abbot of Neath, in the late C13 the unbuttressed W tower remains. Tall battered base. Two-centred W doorway arch with two continuous keeled rolls. Restored two-light Dec window above. The usual corbelled battlemented top, reduced in height in 1897. The body of the church, nave and lower chancel, is in effect of the C19. N aisle added 1843–4, but most windows, the chancel arch and probably the N arcade date from the restoration of 1871–2. E window with cusped intersecting tracery probably c. 1860. – FONT AND COVER. 1909. The cover of painted wood, carved with the River of Life. A most unusual piece, by *Arthur Grove*. – PULPIT. 1872. – STAINED GLASS. Dominating E window, Ascension between Way to Calvary and Empty Tomb, signed and dated *O'Connor*, 1860. – In the N aisle, Gethsemane, Christ in the Temple and Baptism of Christ, all by the same maker (Hardman?), datable to the early 1870s. – N aisle NW window signed by *Mayer & Co.*, Munich, after 1897. – CURIOSUM. Large relief panel of the arms of the Llewelyn family of Ynysgerwn. Polychromed lead, C18? – MONUMENTS. John Lewelyn and others, erected after 1722. Large tablet in a Corinthian frame of stone. Cabbage-like capitals. – Thomas Williams † 1802 (Chancel W wall). Coade stone tablet, signed *Coade & Seely*. – Robert Place. Neoclassical hanging wall-monument signed *Ternouth*, 1829. – George Tennant † 1833. (N aisle.) Gothic.

CADOXTON LODGE (N of the church, demolished in 1966) and YNYSGERWN (2 m. NE, demolished in 1968) were two fine examples of the classic Queen Anne type of house of the early C18, of two storeys, five bays, under a steep hipped roof with dormers and tall chimneystacks. Both had decorative plaster ceilings.

CAERAU

1070

3 m. W of Cardiff

ST MARY, Church Road. This medieval church, isolated on a hilltop above the Cardiff to Barry bypass (A432) and approached through Ely, Cardiff outer suburbia, was deconsecrated as recently as 1973. It is now a shameful ruin. The saddleback W tower stands largely intact. Blocked two-centred W doorway, with a chamfer. E doorway at an upper level. Nave largely roofless, chancel virtually levelled to the ground. The S porch, unusually, had a masonry tunnel-vault. C19 chancel arch.

HILLFORT. Triangular, 12.6 acres (5.1 hectares) in extent. Of Iron Age date. The N and SW sides are defended by three closely set banks fronted by ditches. An impressively massive bank with external ditch and counterscarp bank forms the S section of the E side, while the two parallel ramparts of the N section have been modified by the insertion of the ringwork in the NE angle (*see* below). Inturned entrance halfway along the E side, and another entrance in the SE corner with an inturned rampart to the E. Between the entrances there appears to be an internal subsidiary enclosure.

Well-preserved oval RINGWORK, constructed within the NE angle of the hillfort. Though it is unrecorded, the historical probability is that the earthwork was thrown up in the C12 for the Bishop of Llandaff.

8090

CAERAU
2 m. N of Maesteg

ST CYNFELIN. 1909–10 by *G. E. Halliday*. Quite a substantial building, half paid for by Miss Talbot of Margam. Pink rock-faced sandstone with dressings of Bath stone. Nave with lean-to S aisle and lower chancel. Cusped lancets, but in the aisle square-headed four-lighters. w façade composition, a rose window and broad, flat buttresses, one of which is carried up to form a bell gable. (Arcade on octagonal piers. – STAINED GLASS. Chancel N, 1961 by *John Petts*.)

BETHEL WELSH WESLEYAN METHODIST CHAPEL, Wesley Street. The façade of 1906, of Pennant sandstone trimmed with red brick, attempts to look novel. Semicircular central window over a strongly voussoired doorway. Gable with ball finials. Underemphasized stair projections to l. and r.

HOPE ENGLISH BAPTIST CHAPEL, Tonna Road. 1905 by *W. Beddoe Rees*. A modest essay in Arts and Crafts classicism, making an interesting contrast with his chapels in Maesteg (q.v.).

1080

CAERPHILLY/CAERFFILI

CASTLE

Caerphilly Castle is by far the largest and most impressive castle in Glamorgan; indeed, it is fully comparable with the greatest of Edward I's castles in North Wales, and, what is more, antedates them all. Its scale clearly denotes an extraordinarily wealthy and powerful lord threatened by an exceptionally menacing enemy. Such was Gilbert de Clare, its builder, who in 1263 came into his inheritance as lord of Glamorgan and one of the greatest landowners in England. In 1267, by imprisoning the Welsh lord of Senghenydd, he pushed the effective frontier of his lordship N of Caerphilly Mountain. At the same time all the Norman lords in Wales were threatened by Llywelyn the Great, who had in 1262 advanced S from his power base in North Wales almost to Abergavenny in Gwent. In 1267 Henry III was obliged to acknowledge Llywelyn as Prince of Wales, and a year later, in

September 1268, Llywelyn secured northern Senghenydd. But before this Gilbert had started to build Caerphilly Castle. Construction had begun on 11 April 1268. So his mighty new castle had a double purpose: to consolidate his own territorial gains and to act as a stronghold in the face of Llywelyn's alarming encroachments.

The site was not naturally defensible, in a triangular plain surrounded by high hills on all sides except the E, where, too, the ground rose substantially. The castle therefore had to rely on its own artificial defences, lakes to N and S, created by damming the Nant-y-Gledyr, the stream which flows down E-wards from Mynydd Meio, and to E and W by wet moats and rigorously designed masonry defences.

Though a Roman fort had existed to the NW beside the chosen site, the site itself was virgin, allowing complete freedom of design. A slight ridge from W to E across the site was cut through to form a rectangular moated area for the castle between a large, irregular outer bailey to the W and a more compact platform to the E, which would later become the central feature of a system of dams. The castle was designed on the principle of concentric fortification, here for the first time applied with complete consistency, and soon taken up by Edward I at Harlech and Beaumaris. A rectangular inner ward is surrounded by high curtain 35 walls with drum towers at the four corners and strongly fortified twin-towered gatehouses placed centrally in the E and W walls. A great hall and other residential apartments for the lord stand against the S wall of the inner ward. An outer, lower curtain wall, with curved angle bastions and a second pair of twin-towered E and W gatehouses, form a middle ward. These outer gatehouses were originally linked by drawbridges to the W outer bailey and the E central platform. The expansion of the moat to the S into a lake, by means of a monumental dam to the E, seems to have been part of the first phase of construction.

The formation of the N lake and the N dam was clearly a 36 subsequent work, though logically the defences of the castle required both lakes, not just one. The value of water defences had been borne in on Gilbert de Clare two years earlier, when he was present at the siege of Kenilworth Castle, where the almost encircling lake had enabled Simon de Montfort to hold out against the king for nine months.

Gilbert's castle was constructed of Pennant sandstone quarried in the hills to the N, probably the earliest large-scale use of a stone which later became Glamorgan's commonest building material. Four separate phases are distinguishable from one another by differences of detail, some insignificant, others immediately obvious to the eye. They can be related to the scanty facts known about the continuing struggle between Gilbert and Llywelyn as follows.*

The walls and towers of the inner and middle wards, the core

*C. N. Johns has presented the evidence in scrupulous detail in the official guide book published in 1978 (but now out of print). His conclusions are followed here.

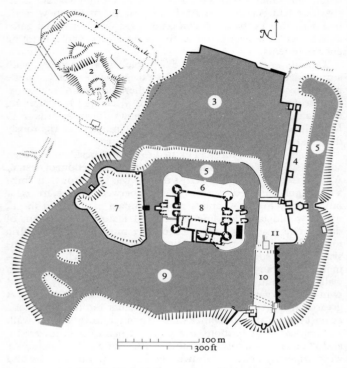

Caerphilly Castle. Plan

1	Possible Roman fort	7	Hornwork
2	Civil War earthwork	8	Inner ward
3	North lake	9	South lake
4	North dam	10	South dam
5	Moat	11	Mill
6	Middle ward		

of the castle, were built over four summer building seasons from 1268 to 1271, along with the s lake and dam. This was in spite of an attack by Llywelyn in October 1270, in which timberwork was burnt. A second attack by Llywelyn the following autumn, in response to further encroachment by Gilbert into territory traditionally held by the Welsh, led to a truce and Gilbert's agreement to desist from further fortifying the castle. Typical features of this phase are round towers and arrow slits (not loops). The second stage, which involved heightening the s and w curtain walls of the inner ward and adding a massive s kitchen tower, certainly qualified as further fortification, and so probably was not put in hand until after the truce had been overtaken by the war which broke out between Llywelyn and Edward I in 1276. The third stage, including the N lake and dam and the two distinctive gatehouses at the latter's extremities, may date from very little later, because they appear to be designed by the same master mason as work of *c*. 1272–8 at Chepstow Castle. In these works polygonal towers, cross-shaped arrow loops and continuous, rounded (bull-nosed) mouldings are typical. They must predate the second Welsh war of 1282–3, in which Llywelyn was killed. In the fourth stage the N dam was heightened and strengthened.

After the death of Gilbert de Clare in 1295 Caerphilly Castle passed to subsequent lords of Glamorgan. One of them, Hugh le Despenser, the young favourite of Edward II, sumptuously reconstructed the hall in the inner ward, employing during 1326 the king's mason, *Thomas of Battle*, and the king's carpenter, *William Hurley*. Within the year Despenser had been executed and the king deposed. The castle is known to have been maintained during the rest of the C14, and, apparently unscathed by Owain Glyndŵr's attacks on South Wales in 1404–5, continued to receive repairs at least until *c*. 1430. Little more than a century later, however, John Leland found it a ruin set in a marsh, a single tower kept up as a prison. In the mid C16 the second Earl of Pembroke kept his manorial court here, probably in the middle w gatehouse. But in 1583 he dealt the castle a severe blow in leasing it to Thomas Lewis, with express permission to remove dressed stonework for reuse at his nearby house, The Van (*see* below, p. 178). During the Civil War an earthwork redoubt was thrown up on the site of the Roman fort, to prevent what remained of the castle being put to use. Further dismantling may have taken place at this time. The leaning SE tower, which still stands 10° out of plumb, may show the effects of slighting at this time. Watercolours of the Romantic period and early photographs record the effects of decay and deliberate destruction.

By the mid C19 the state of Caerphilly Castle was no different from that of the majority of the abandoned medieval castles of England and Wales. It is the last chapter of the story which is unusual, a story of reconstruction, not for renewed use but in order to recreate its original image. The castle was part of the Welsh inheritance of the Marquesses of Bute. The third Marquess re-roofed the hall *c*. 1870, and commissioned an accurate survey of the whole castle. But it was the fourth Marquess who created the castle we see today. He had surrounding houses removed, and 1928–39 his architect *J. P. D. Grant* reconstructed many fallen sections of wall and tower. This work was scrupulously done: moulds were taken of the fallen masses of masonry, and their relationship to the standing remains was determined. The collapsed parts were rebuilt from the original stones, and many of the robbed ashlar dressings were replaced in cast concrete. So the general view of the castle from every direction is now almost miraculously convincing, but at a close look original parts can fairly readily be distinguished from the reconstructions.

Reflooding the lakes, prepared for by the fourth Marquess, was carried out after 1950, when the castle passed into the care of the state. Further, quite drastic, stone replacement in the hall. Granted the validity of the philosophy underlying the fourth Marquess's initiative, and not everyone will grant that it is valid to treat a historic ruin like this, the reinstatement could hardly have been done in a more responsible way.

Perambulation of the castle

Any building laid out on a concentric plan is difficult to explore in a logical sequence, and few visitors to Caerphilly Castle would choose such a sequence, and walk round it three times in ever-decreasing circles. The best way to appreciate the castle's qualities, both the general impact and the individual subtleties of its defensive systems, is to view it first from the S, then from the E, and thereafter to follow the normal visitor route through the outer E gate on to the central platform, from which a bridge over the inner moat leads to the middle and inner wards. The tour can end on the western outwork, with a last look back at the castle from the W, its least restored aspect.

35 The first vantage point is at the start of the FOOTPATH which leads from near the bottom of CARDIFF ROAD to the S, round to the public entrance on the E side of the castle. From here the expanse of the S LAKE distances and protects the castle, reaching almost to the foot of the WALLS of the MIDDLE WARD. The straight central stretch of wall is unrestored, part of the first great phase of construction, with two blocked arrow slits, but no surviving battlements. The only opening in the wall is a postern gate, pointed-headed but robbed of its dressings. Above it, a square-ended superstructure is built up from the wall-head, with two windows, one over the other. These lit rooms, for servants or storage, over the passage leading down to the postern (*see* p. 174). The broad, bowed walls to l. and r., enclosing the SW and SE salients of the middle ward, were reinstated in the 1930s. Behind and above, the much higher WALLS and cylindrical ANGLE TOWERS of the INNER WARD command not only the middle ward but most of the lake as well. The SW tower has been largely reconstructed, but the leaning SE tower is original. Its well-preserved details will be discussed below (pp. 173–4). Projecting from the centre of the inner ward is a broader, bowed KITCHEN TOWER, with gaping holes high up in its walls, where there once were windows. This was added in the second phase and impairs the symmetry of the original design.

To the E the public footpath skirts the S GATEWAY (Giffard's Tower). This was in peacetime the main entrance from the town, and in wartime covered the S end of the dam containing the S lake. The adjoining D-plan salient, with its projecting U-shaped turret, contains the S end of the dam platform. The gateway itself was badly damaged in a Welsh attack in 1316, and all the walls here have been substantially reconstructed in the C20. Red tile stitches indicate the dividing line between old and restored walling. The outer face of the gateway has round towers with pyramidal spurs, so was begun as part of the original programme of 1268–71. Yet there is an original arrow loop low down, and the portcullis slot is of an unusual type found in the work of c. 1280. The bull-nosed jambs are all C20, unreliable as dating evidence. C. N. Johns points out that the gate towers originally had no back wall, like those in the middle ward, and here walls were added later to provide two storeys of rooms.

From the causeway to the E, the full extent of the DAMS is revealed. The causeway itself is separated from the dams by an outer MOAT, spanned in the centre by the modern bridge which leads into the castle. The S DAM, holding back the S lake, was part of the first campaign. It is c. 240 ft (73.15 metres) long and consists of eight sheer, rectangular piers projecting between deep concave recesses, a tremendously impressive piece of medieval engineering. The fragmentary square tower (FELTON'S TOWER) at its S end stood over the, now buried, outlet of the S lake. The higher turret at its N end has a series of garderobe chutes discharging into the moat, to serve a small, vaulted guard-chamber accessible from the dam platform.

The N DAM, N of the outer E gate (*see* below, p. 172) is quite different in concept and appearance, and was added to contain the N lake as part of the improvements of c. 1280. First a straight earthen platform 370 ft (122.8 metres) long was constructed with a thick, but unbuttressed retaining wall to the E. Before completion it was decided to reinforce the wall with three massive square towers. So they butt against the lower part of the wall. Higher up, where the wall was raised subsequently, they were built integrally with it, though later settlement has pulled them jaggedly away. Gigantic angle spurs convert these towers from square to pentagonal form. Arrow loops (the side ones robbed away) serving rooms within the towers, and paired loops in the retaining wall at the level of the dam platform. Wall and towers were thus extended upwards far above the platform to provide a formidable defensive front. The N GATEWAY, at the N end of the dam platform, is of similar form, with towers rising on spurs from square bases to polygonal upper levels. No moat at this point: traditionally this was the cavalry gateway. On the N side of the N lake, a simple retaining wall, never made defensible, as the stretch of water was defence enough.

The MAIN OUTER GATEHOUSE, in the centre of the E-facing fortifications and now the visitors' entrance to the castle, was built with the dam towers and N gateway c. 1280. However, to its l. the join in the walling can be seen where it replaced the original E entrance. So the straight wall and broad, convex salient to the S belong to the first construction period, the retaining walls of a central earthen platform. Presumably the gateway takes the place of a second salient. The modern timber bridge across the moat rests on the supports for the original double drawbridge. It has been suggested that a central masonry gateway would have been required to operate the bridges, similar to the famous gateway on the Monnow Bridge at Monmouth, Gwent. The MAIN OUTER GATEHOUSE is the most elaborate design of the third stage, c. 1280, but was largely reconstructed in the 1930s, as the evenly laid Pennant walling and the concrete dressings make clear. Twin towers square in plan, but converted by pyramidal spurs to an octagonal form in all three storeys. Original arrow loops at the lowest stage. Pointed arch to the entrance passage, and reconstructed super-arch. Immediately within the arch the slot for a portcullis. The passage is further protected by arrow slits in the side walls, six 'murder-holes' in the vault, three on each side of the entrance gate. The stone frame for the gate has the bull-nosed moulding typical of the work of c. 1280. A stair-turret at the NW angle gives access to a rectangular projection which links the gateway with the N dam platform. At the foot of the projection an arched water gate. From the top of the gatehouse the inner and middle wards of Gilbert de Clare's castle can be splendidly surveyed.

The CENTRAL PLATFORM extends to the S beyond the main outer gatehouse. Its outer enclosing wall has already been noted. The straight N wall withholds the SPILLWAY which allowed water to flow from the inner moat into the outer E moat through the water gate. At the S end of the platform the substantial remains of another structure connected with the flow of water, the MILL. An outflow from the S lake powered an over-shot wheel. A rare survival of C13 technology. Entrance to the guard chamber in the wall E of the mill.

A modern bridge over the inner moat leads to the MIDDLE WARD through the E middle gatehouse. This, and the gatehouse and angle towers of the inner ward which rear up behind it, display the cylindrical forms preferred by Gilbert de Clare's first master mason, and arrow slits, not loops. From this point, too, the overbearing symmetry of his conception makes its greatest impact. From the bridge, where the walls and towers are seen at eye level, the disparity between the walls of the middle ward and the far higher walls and towers of the inner ward is again powerfully apparent. But as the walls of the middle ward descend to the moat many feet below, they also presented a formidable barrier to the would-be attacker.

The E MIDDLE GATEHOUSE consists of no more than two half-round towers, both with arrow slits to the front at bridge level. The space between them accommodated a drawbridge. Originally, the towers had no backs, so that they provided no refuge for attackers who might have penetrated into the middle ward. Later they were extended and closed at the back. The gatehouse is heavily restored, its S tower almost entirely rebuilt in the 1930s. Much-restored foundations of a large rectangular building S of the gatehouse were probably of a cistern. The CURTAIN WALLS of the middle ward were quite thin and have largely been rebuilt. Their arrow slits, aligning with those in the gatehouse towers, seem to conform to the original arrangement. The well-preserved section of wall on the S side has already been noted (*see* p. 170, above). On the N side another postern gate. The W gatehouse of the middle ward will be examined later (*see* p. 176).

And so to the INNER WARD. It is entered under the E INNER GATEHOUSE, the *pièce de résistance* of the whole castle. This is literally so, for the gatehouse was designed as a residence for the Constable of the castle, and could be sealed off and fortified in its own right should the rest of the castle be overrun by an enemy. In fact it seems to be a prototype of the keep-gatehouse, employed by Gilbert de Clare himself at Tonbridge, Kent, by Edward I at Beaumaris and Harlech, and later, for example, at Dunstanburgh in Northumberland.* The outer face of the gatehouse, two great drum towers flanking a simple double-chamfered entrance arch in a flat wall, was rebuilt from fallen masonry in the 1930s. The arrangement of arrow slits low down and lancets at two levels above is presumably authentic. Within the entry a portcullis slot and double-chamfered stone frames for gates front and back. Also arrow slits at the side and 'murder-holes' in the vault above. Doors in the side walls give access to the interior of the gatehouse. Since these are placed between the inner and outer gates, it is clear that the gatehouse could be secured by bolting both the gates. The inner (W) wall of the gatehouse is largely original. Circular stair-turrets project from its corners, lit only by arrow slits at four levels.

The flat central wall is much broader on this side. Five trefoil-headed lancets surround the entrance arch, two to light ground-floor rooms, two for rooms above, and the highest one, set over a spyhole, for the portcullis chamber. The two great twin-light windows above, reconstructed from fragments, light the Constable's great chamber. Battlements and turret-tops all conjecturally reconstructed. The interior of the gatehouse also largely reconstructed. The most significant internal feature is the little vaulted room in the thickness of the S wall communicating with the great chamber on the first floor. This has traditionally been identified as the Constable's chapel. Two-bay quadripartite vault with thick chamfered ribs. Below, a doorway opening on to the wall-walk of the curtain.

The INNER WARD is a slightly irregular rectangle *c.* 180 ft (54.9 metres) by *c.* 140 ft (42.7 metres). An elaborate set of apartments for the lord, with the Great Hall in the centre, extends along the greater part of the S side. Three-quarter-round angle towers, fitted up for further residential accommodation, define the ward. In the centre of the W wall stands a second inner gatehouse, smaller than the Constable's gatehouse, but better preserved. Of the angle towers, the SW tower is almost totally rebuilt, the NE tower a heap of fragments, but the other two deserve detailed inspection.

The SE TOWER, though leaning rakishly, survives unrestored to its full height. At ground level, above a battered base, it originally had arrow slits in three directions, of which the

*But see Richmond Castle, Yorkshire, for something similar in the C12.

central, outward-directed one is still intact. Above were rooms
at two levels, lit by trefoil-headed lancets. The hooded fireplace
of the top room is readily visible. Battlements with arrow slits,
and immediately below them, at wall-walk level, a row of closely
spaced square holes. These probably supported the beams of a
temporary overhanging timber brattice or hoard. This, the only
tower to survive to its crenellations, was taken as the model for
the battlements reinstated so extensively in the 1930s. The NW
TOWER, though heavily restored, shows the layout in full. It
has a straight wall towards the inner ward, with a plain, pointed
entrance doorway, trefoiled lancets at two higher levels, and a
spyhole immediately above it. At first-floor level doorways open
on to the wall-walk of the N and W curtain walls. Inside, three
doorways at ground level, that to the l. to the newel stair, that
to the r. into a garderobe, the central one to an unlit lower
room. Two upper rooms, both with hooded fireplaces and
window seats flanking the window embrasures.

Gilbert de Clare's GREAT HALL was sumptuously remodelled by Hugh le Despenser the Younger in the 1320s. The
present roof dates from *c*. 1870, and the restored ashlar refacing
of the exterior of the N wall and of the internal window jambs
and seats was begun in the 1950s but remains unfinished. The
hall was originally roofed in five bays – see in the S wall the
long, vertical slots and simple, polygonal corbels for the wall-
posts of the major trusses. The S, W and E walls of de Clare's
hall all survive, but there is no other original feature except a
wide, blocked arch high in the S wall, with a fragment of a
hoodmould extended as a string course to the l. The arch
originally allowed a view up into the upper-level chapel (*see*
below, p. 175). The two service doorways in the E wall are
entirely renewed, and so is the doorway in the centre of the S
wall, which opens into the vaulted passage stepping down to
the S water gate. This entrance was protected externally by
portcullises at the top and bottom of the vaulted passage. Much
more survives of Despenser's remodelling of the Great Hall.
The inside face of the N wall still makes a splendid show. Low
entrance doorway at the E end, clearly originally opening into
a screens passage, high and wide windows, two to each side of
a central fireplace. The segmental fireplace hood has virtually
all gone, but door and windows all retain their original heads.
Flattened, almost straight-sided arches, tweaked up into an
ogee at the apex. Hoodmoulds of more emphatic ogee form,
their crockets and central leaf finials largely worn away. Delicate
double shafts on the window jambs and hollow mouldings
enriched with ball-flower over the arches and originally down
the jambs too. There is nothing like this display of courtly
magnificence anywhere else in the county. But that is not all.
The six-bay roof designed by *William Hurley* has gone. But the
wall-shafts of Sutton stone survive, formed into three filleted
members and resting on corbels of buff limestone. Each corbel
is carved as three heads, crowned, as if intended as portraits of
Edward II and his Queen, and one youthful and long-haired,

as if of Despenser himself. Today the corbels are all sadly worn.

The s doorway in the E wall gives access to what remains of the upper rooms in the block of the Great Hall. (The N upper room was less high than the CHAPEL to the S. The chapel was lit by a large E window, of which only the sill survives, and by N clerestory windows, quatrefoils set in pentagonal external surrounds.) Two later additions were made to the amenities of the Great Hall, both built outside (i.e. S of) the inner curtain wall. The big kitchen tower has already been mentioned (p. 170 above). How it interlinked with the Great Hall is not clear. The other addition was a square building adjoining the Leaning Tower, with recesses, apparently fireplaces, in three of its four angles. It was presumably a kitchen or brew-house. Now demolished virtually to the ground, it can be seen only from the roof of the E inner gatehouse. The curtain wall itself was heightened during the original construction of the Great Hall, and a gallery (the Braose Gallery) created in the thickness of the wall, making it possible to pass directly from the rooms E of the Great Hall to the private apartments to the W of it. See the archway near its W end with bull-nosed moulding of c. 1280.

The PRIVATE APARTMENTS, entered from the Great Hall through a doorway remodelled c. 1280, belong to the primary build of 1268–71. The principal room was at an upper level adjoining the Great Hall. Corbels for its floor joists, the remains of a hooded fireplace in the W wall, and in the N wall a fine two-light window with fragments of its traceried head. Further W a set of narrower rooms, with hooded corner fireplaces at both levels to the NW. At the N end there seem to have been service passages. The curious junction of the external NE corner of this late C13 block with the early C14 N wall of the hall is worth examining.

So, finally, to the W side of the castle. The W INNER GATEHOUSE consists, like its counterpart to the E, of a heavily defended passage between towers with rounded outer faces and residential upper storeys. The gatehouse rises from a battered plinth, and its inner (E) face is flat, the newel stairs in the angles not in projecting turrets, but indicated externally by tiers of arrow slits. Pointed-headed doorways of two chamfered orders l. and r. of the central passage arch give access to the stairs and to vaulted ground-floor rooms. Note their drawbar slots. The vaults of the rooms have broad, chamfered ribs, and each room has an arrow slit towards the entrance passage. The s room is lit from a s trefoil-headed lancet, with a shelf on three sides of the embrasure. The N room never had a corresponding N window. The stairs give access to the wall-walk of the inner curtain wall, and at a higher level to the great chamber, which occupied the full width of the upper part of the gatehouse. The two large two-light windows facing into the inner ward have been robbed away and not restored. Between them was a hooded fireplace, and corbels surviving on the other side of the room demonstrate that it was roofed in five bays. The battlements and tower tops of the gatehouse were all reinstated in the 1930s. The entrance passage, within a triple-chamfered, segmental E arch, was protected by a portcullis at each end, by a single gate to the front, covered by the arrow slits in the N and S rooms, and by a 'murder-hole' at the W end. There are signs that, as originally planned, there was to have been a drawbridge in front of the gatehouse passage. So this was one of the earliest parts of the castle to be started, before the decision to use a concentric system of fortification all round.

Against the outer (W) face of the INNER CURTAIN WALL, immediately N of the W inner gatehouse, the remains of a gabled building, perhaps a storehouse, clearly an addition to the wall below, but integral with it higher up. This shows that the curtain wall was heightened here at an early stage, in the same way as the curtain wall on the S side of the inner ward (*see* above, p. 175).

The MIDDLE WARD is at its narrowest at this point. The round-fronted towers of the W OUTER GATEHOUSE were at first built open at the back, with forward-facing arrow slits. Its central depressed-pointed entrance arch is set in a rectangular outer recess with slots for a drawbridge. Rectangular W additions, of *c.* 1280, to form rooms l. and r. of the gateway and a habitable upper floor. The upper fireplaces, stout chimneyshaft and two square windows over the entrance arch all appear to belong to a C16 remodelling, perhaps for the Earl of Pembroke's manorial court. The gatehouse has been little restored; only the battlements are new. The flanking curtain walls, however, are largely reconstructed.

The modern bridge, on the substructure of the medieval drawbridge, gives access to the W PLATFORM or BAILEY. This is a large, irregular earthwork, within a low, stone retaining wall surrounded by water. Two curved salients, facing NW, flank the base of a gateway with pits for a drawbridge. Toothing here shows that the retaining wall was to have been carried up at least to the level of the crown of the earthwork. The W bailey's Welsh name, 'Y Weringaer' (people's fort), suggests that it was intended as a refuge for the townspeople and cattle in case of attack.

THE TOWN

The town founded by Gilbert de Clare to the S of the castle seems to have remained tiny throughout the Middle Ages. The COURT HOUSE (now a public house), though it appears C18, two-storeyed with sash windows, probably incorporates medieval walling, and began its existence as the C14 courthouse, which is known to have been repaired in 1429. No other pre-C19 building survives, after demolitions by the fourth Marquess of Bute in order to open up views of the castle from the S and E.

ST MARTIN, Cardiff Road. A large church with a complicated history but no strong personality. Designed in 1873 by *Charles Buckeridge*, who died that year, and built 1877–9 by *J. L.*

Pearson. Nave lengthened by two bays 1904–5, NW tower built 1907–10, both under *G. E. Halliday.* S aisle widened in 1938. E.E., with geometrical tracery. Rock-faced sandstone and Bath stone dressings. Nave originally with lean-to aisles, lower chancel with cross-gabled chapel and vestry. The arcades have round piers and double-chamfered arches; the clerestory has two windows per bay. All solid and serious. – FONT. Medieval. Octagonal bowl keeled down to a square base. – REREDOS. 1902. Seated figures of Christ and SS Martin and Thomas under gabled arches of pink Penarth alabaster. By *Halliday.* – LADY CHAPEL FITTINGS. 1969 by *George Pace.* – (ORGAN CASE. 1968 by the same.) – STAINED GLASS. E window, 1879, the gift of Lord Windsor. An ambitious piece, Crucifixion between Agony in the Garden and Way to Calvary. In a style derived from C13 manuscript illuminations. Presumably by *Hardman.* – S aisle, St Francis, by *Frank Roper,* overstretched on this scale.

RECTORY, W of the church. Could this also be by *Buckeridge?*
GROESWEN CHAPEL, 1½ m. W. High and isolated on the flank of Mynydd Meio, looking across to Caerphilly in the valley below. Here stood the first Methodist place of worship erected in Wales, the 'New House' built in 1742 under the inspiration of Howell Harris of Trevecca, for the 'public worship of God or a school for the education of children.' The present VESTRY alongside the road, with its mounting block and stairs to the upper room, is clearly an C18 structure. The CHAPEL itself, at r.-angles to the E, is of *c.* 1870, though the date it bears is of its predecessor's, not its own construction. Fine classical façade of dressed stone, dominated by a full-height relieving arch, enclosing the central triplet window. Tall, narrow side windows. Unaltered interior, with galleries on three sides, on cast iron columns, and a polygonal pulpit backed by an arched plasterwork frame. In this a bronze PLAQUE with a relief portrait of the Rev. William Edwards, bridge designer and for forty years minister of Groeswen Chapel. Signed by *Goscombe John* and dated 1906.

In the BURIAL GROUND an array of monuments, some of them grossly displayful. They deserve extensive examination. The Peterhead granite obelisk bearing a bronze portrait medallion, which commemorates Caledfryn, the bard and minister, was made in 1870–1, to the design of *A. H. James* of Newport.
WESLEYAN METHODIST CHURCH, Ludlow Street. Weirdly squared-up Perp. 1929–30 by *J. H. Phillips & Wride.*
UNITED REFORMED CHURCH, Van Road. 1903–4 by *W. Beddoe Rees.* Arts and Crafts Dec, with a spirelet. Newbridge sandstone with Bath stone dressings. (Inside, timber arches on columns, and provision made for galleries.)
ST ILAN LOWER COMPREHENSIVE SCHOOL, Crescent Road. With an inspiring view towards the castle. Dated 1912 and 1913. This seems to be the Higher Elementary School built to the design of *D. Pugh Jones* from 1911. Larger and a little more elaborate than usual, with arched tripartite windows and

chequered gables. Grey Pennant sandstone and red sandstone dressings.

TWYN COUNTY JUNIOR SCHOOL, East View. The red and grey gabled block to the W belongs to a school by *D. Pugh Jones* built in 1906. The handsomely monochrome U-plan ranges beyond, also by *Pugh Jones*, are dated 1922. Their height, their style, part-Wren, part-Louis XV, show unusual ambition for a post-war school.

POST OFFICE, Van Road. Late 1930s. In a Modern style.

OUTLYING MONUMENTS

CASTELL MORGRAIG, 2 m. s., close to the E of, but invisible from, the A469, accessible from the car park of the Travellers' Rest. A ridge-top castle, built on the crest of the steep escarpment, and constructed largely of quartz conglomerate quarried on site. Its plan is easily comprehended, since excavation in 1903–4 exposed walls standing 6 to 10 ft (1.8 to 3 metres) high. Entrance from the W leads into a pentagonal enclosure expanding into horseshoe-shaped bastions at four of the angles. At the fifth, towards the E and facing the entrance, the N and S walls of a rectangular keep. All this must have been constructed in a single campaign in the C13, some time before 1267, when Gilbert de Clare, lord of Glamorgan, imprisoned the native lord of Senghenydd and began the construction of Caerphilly Castle. The problem is to decide who was claiming the ridge by this construction, de Clare, before choosing a more northward-threatening site in the valley, or the Welsh themselves, before losing their grip on strategic positions in the area. In either case, the excavators concluded that the castle was never finished.

THE VAN (Y Fan), ¾ m. E. The late Elizabethan mansion of Thomas Lewis (†1594) stands on rising ground facing across to Caerphilly Castle. Well might it do so, for much of its dressed stone was robbed from the castle after the Earl of Pembroke had in 1583 granted Lewis a lease and permission to make free and unlimited use of its stonework. This provides a *terminus post quem* for the main E-facing range, the gatehouse and forecourt walls, which all belong together. These parts are characterized by straight-headed window lights and sunk chamfer mouldings. The range has a regularity almost unknown in the county in the 1580s, of two full storeys four bays wide, returning round the corner for one bay, the windows all lofty four-lighters with one transom, the lights subdivided 2 + 2 by a slight thickening of the central mullion. No hoodmoulds, but continuous string courses running over the heads of the windows. Straight-sided gables enclosing three-light attic windows crown the façade.

The house must have reached its full extent well before 1583, however, for there are windows of different, earlier, character both in the full-height porch at its N end and in the kitchen range which runs back from its S end. These all have arched lights, those in the porch under hoodmoulds with square stops, those in the NE range under normal hoodmoulds. Differences in colour in the sandstone dressings confirm these different phases, the robbed Sutton stone from the castle being of whiter hue than the rest. So the post-1583 campaign merely gave the house a show front. A later addition was the three-storey turret at the NW angle of the porch, of which part of the ashlar-faced ground storey survives. This is formed into two large four-centred recesses facing the entry into the porch, a strange arrangement.

From the mid C18 the house was abandoned, but at the time of writing a major campaign of reconstruction and re-roofing is under way. The modern stonework is easily distinguished from the old by its stronger buff colour, and, it must be admitted, by the unwarranted thinness of the mullions. Nevertheless, these works have restored the visual impact of the main range.

The GATEHOUSE has a plain four-centred entrance arch, and a heated room above it with a chimneypiece simply decorated yet richer than any which the house itself could boast. Depressed, four-centred fireplace opening, set within a rectangular surround carved with intermittent fluting and rosettes, and in the spandrels thus formed shields bearing the initials of Thomas Lewis.

To the N of the gatehouse, two early C17 blocks, without significant features. C19 BARN to the W converted misleadingly with two storeys of Tudor-style windows.

CAPEL LLANILLTERN   0070

ST ELLTEYRN. A chapel of ease to St Fagans (q.v.), rebuilt by the Windsor family in 1862–3. Just the simplest little nave and lower chancel with W bell gable. Uncoursed, roughly squared local stone and generous Bath stone dressings. The architect was *G. E. Street*. Such details as the unusual geometrical tracery of the E window, the dramatic quatrefoil W window and the hingework of the S door are typical. – FONT. A fine early C13 piece, big leaves sprouting symmetrically on the circular bowl. Rosettes too. – REREDOS. Marble. A row of bold discs. By *Street*. – STAINED GLASS. E window, Christ between SS Michael and Gabriel. Signed by *Heaton, Butler & Bayne*. The date, 1938, is amazingly late. – MONUMENTS. (Early Christian grave slab set in the nave N wall. Not shaped at all, but inscribed VENDVMAGL – HIC IACIT. Datable to the C5 or C6.) Also a series to successive occupants of the local estate of Parc. – John Williams †1651. Inscribed slab with heraldic top. – Morgan Williams †1763. Hanging monument of white and buff marble. – Catherine Price †1806. Neoclassical, with flaming urn. Signed *E. Morgan*, Canton. – John Price †1818. Neoclassical, with draped urn. Also signed by *E. Morgan*.

PENCOED HOUSE, $\frac{1}{4}$m. SW. A medieval range, orientated E–W, and converted into a two-storey, three-unit house in the C16.

Evidence of the C14 at both ends, a trefoil-headed lancet high
in the E wall, and, near the W end of the N wall, a magnificent
but inexplicable archway, two-centred, with two double-wave
mouldings front and back, the inner pair springing from a
filleted base moulding. This is so fine, and so large, that it
implies the existence of an impressive medieval house now
otherwise disappeared. Internally, three C16 stone doorways in
the N wall, two opening upstairs and downstairs into the short,
reconstructed N wing, the third perhaps originally at the head
of an external stair. Finely moulded beams and evidence of a
post-and-panel partition indicate that the ground-floor room
at the W end was an important one. Kitchen at the E end.
Later range at r.-angles to the S, perhaps originally residential,
allowing for a second household in the unit-system arrangement. The stone CHIMNEYPIECE in the hall, boldly inscribed
in Welsh, is a brought-in item, from *Sir Matthew Digby Wyatt*'s
The Ham, Llantwit Major (q.v.).

LLANFAIR-FACH, $\frac{1}{2}$ m. SE. Two-storey, two-room-plan house of
the C17 with status-giving porch. One upper two-light window
survives. The kitchen wing at the rear is an addition.

CARDIFF/CAERDYDD

Cardiff originated in a Roman fort established at the lowest crossing over the River Taff as early as *c*.A.D. 55. Stone walls enclosing a rectangle 202 by 219 yds (185 by 200 metres) were erected in the late Roman period. The present bailey walls of the castle faithfully follow their line, to the W largely medieval fabric built on the Roman foundations, to the S, E and N late C19 and early C20 reconstructions, but for long stretches visibly built on top of C4 fabric.

The history of the town begins with William the Conqueror's expedition in 1081 through South Wales to St David's. On his return he seems to have ordered the great earthen motte to be thrown up within the Roman fort, and to have established a mint. From 1093 the castle was the headquarters of the marcher lord of Glamorgan, whose successors, down to the Marquesses of Bute, controlled the town until the Municipal Corporations Act of 1835 and owned the castle until 1947, when the fifth Marquess gave it to what was by then the City of Cardiff.

The medieval borough grew up to the S of the castle, flourishing thanks to the privileges granted to those who settled there. By the later C12 it had enclosing walls and four gates. A century later it had become the largest borough in Wales. Of the town walls nothing remains. Its E and W gates were pulled down in 1781, the N gate in 1786 and the S gate in 1802. A token reconstruction of the W gate, carried out in the 1930s, stands to the W of the castle. Angel (later Castle) Street and its E-ward continuation, Duke Street, lay W–E, following the line of the castle wall, with the broad High Street striking S-wards opposite the castle S gate (Black Gate). The parish church, St Mary's, stood in St Mary Street, the S-ward extension of the High Street. St Mary's was founded *c*. 1100 and by 1147 had become a priory of Tewkesbury Abbey. Of the late C12 cruciform church and the monastic buildings, from which the monks were withdrawn as early as 1221, nothing is known. The buildings fell victim to the river, which gradually developed an oxbow, by the C16 threatening the church's foundations and leading to its abandonment in the mid C17. St John's, the town-centre chapel of ease, E of High Street, had by the C15 in effect taken over as the town's parish church. It was splendidly rebuilt in the third quarter of that century.

The Friars established houses at Cardiff, the Dominicans (Blackfriars) to the NW of the Castle by 1242, the Franciscans (Greyfriars) a little later outside the E gate of the town. Both sites were excavated for the third Marquess of Bute, the Blackfriars (excavated *c*. 1892) marked out in Coopers Fields, *see* p. 210, the Greyfriars (excavated 1892–6) now recorded only by street-names (The Friary, Greyfriars Road and Place). The splendid mansion built out of the Greyfriars buildings by Sir William Herbert *c*. 1582 partly survived until 1967, its three-storey polygonal window bays quite unlike Elizabethan architecture elsewhere in Glamorgan. Its destruction was a grievous loss.

The Act of Union of 1536–42, which created the new shire of Glamorgan out of the feudal lordships of Glamorgan and Gower, established Cardiff as its administrative centre. In 1578 Rice

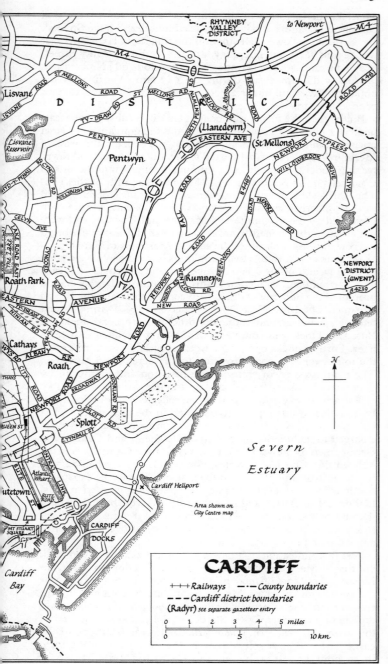

RHYMNEY
VALLEY
DISTRICT

to Newport

M4

M4

Lisvane

D   I   S   T   R   I   C   T

ST MELLONS ROAD

ST MELLONS RD

Lisvane
Reservoir

TY-DRAW RD

PENTWYN ROAD

Pentwyn

NORTH PENTWYN

(Llanedeyrn)

EASTERN AVE

BRIDGE RD

NEWPORT RD

LLANRUMNEY

BEGAN ROAD

(St Mellons)

CYPRESS

NEWPORT ROAD A48

RHYD-Y-PENAU RD

CYNCOED RD

HOLLYBUSH RD

BALL
ROAD

WILLOWBROOK

DRIVE

CELYN AVE

CYNCOED

ROAD

LAKE ROAD EAST

THE LAKE

Roath Park

Rumney

WENTLOOG RD

GREENWAY

NEWPORT

CHURCH RD

HENDRE RD

B4487

B4487

EASTERN

AVENUE

TY-DRAW RD

NINIAN RD

Cathays

ALBANY RD

PEN-Y-LAN RD

NEW ROAD

NEWPORT DISTRICT
(GWENT)

B4239

CATHAYS

Roath

CITY ROAD

NEWPORT ROAD

BROADWAY

MOORLAND RD

QUEEN ST

NEWPORT ROAD

Splott

PORTMANMOOR RD

E TYNDALL ST

N

CENTRAL LINK

Atlantic Wharf

BUTE ROAD

Severn

Estuary

Butetown

× Cardiff Heliport

Cardiff Heliport

Area shown on
City Centre map

MT STUART
SQUARE

CARDIFF
DOCKS

Cardiff
Bay

Merrick, the historian of the shire, called the town 'very well compacted beautifyed with many fair Houses and large Streets'. By that time a Town Hall stood in the middle of High Street. It was rebuilt 1847–53. The quay, at the S end of St Mary Street, enabled a modest coastal trade. But expansion and an increase in prosperity did not ensue during the C17 and C18. In 1801 the population was still under 2,000, no more than it seems to have been in the C13.

But by then the first component of Cardiff's subsequent greatness as a port was in place. In 1794 the Glamorganshire Canal opened, built to provide an outlet to the sea for the iron of Merthyr Tydfil. The canal skirted to the E of the castle and town, passing under Queen Street in a tunnel, to empty into the Bristol Channel 1 m. (1.6 kilometres) S, beside the mouth of the Taff. The Taff Vale Railway, from Merthyr to Cardiff Docks, opened in 1841, greatly increased capacity. Canal and railway were both promoted by the ironmasters of Merthyr and Dowlais, and were not conceived to benefit Cardiff. The town did not really begin to grow until the policies of the second Marquess of Bute (1793–1848) took effect. Bute's twin ambitions were to exploit the great mineral wealth of his upland properties and to provide a means of exporting them wholly under his own control. To this end he promoted the building of docks between the town and the Bristol Channel. The Bute West Dock opened in 1839. During its first ten years trade expanded one-hundredfold. A second dock, the Bute East Dock, was completed in 1855 and extended four years later. Further docks opened between 1874 and 1907, increasing the total extent of dock provision to 165 acres (66.8 hectares). The main exports, of course, were first iron and then coal. By 1913 Cardiff was the biggest coal port in the world.

The growth in Cardiff's population reflected this development. By 1841 it had just topped 10,000, and in the next twenty years trebled, to 32,954. In 1875 the boundaries of the town were enlarged to include Roath and Splott to the E, and Canton and Grangetown to the W. In 1881, by which time Cardiff was being dubbed the 'Chicago of Wales', the population reached 82,761. In the next twenty years it doubled again. Thereafter expansion continued at a less explosive rate. City status was granted in 1905. Llandaff, Whitchurch and Llanedeyrn (q.v.) were brought within the city boundaries in 1922, Rumney in 1938, and St Mellons (q.v.) in 1974. In 1961 the population was just over a quarter of a million, and in 1991 stood at 279,055.

The first indication of a new urban pride was the Town Hall, built in St Mary Street to the design of a London architect, *Sir Horace Jones*, and opened in 1853. Much more dramatic was the gesture of the third Marquess of Bute in commencing his reconstruction of Cardiff Castle, in 1869, with a clock tower dominating not only Castle Street but the whole NW quarter of the town. The style of *William Burges*'s great additions to the castle gave a special status to early French Gothic in the town throughout the rest of the century. The architect responsible for most of the public buildings of the burgeoning town during the last quarter of the century, however, was a local man, *Edwin Seward* (the 'Waterhouse of Cardiff'), now best represented by his Gothic Royal Infirmary (1882–*c.* 1908), off the Newport Road, and Elizabethan Free Library and Museum (1880–2, 1894–6), in The Hayes. Seward also designed two of the covered shopping arcades, which are one of the most enjoyable features of late Victorian Cardiff.

The major urban development of the second Marquess's time had been the construction of Bute Street, a wide, straight thoroughfare over a mile long S-wards from the town and parallel with the new dock, to a new square, Mount Stuart Square, at its S end and a grid of streets to the W. The square, built up in the mid 1850s and later rebuilt with many proud commercial premises, survives, but the rest, which as early as 1853 was being condemned as 'increasingly vile and abominable', was almost wholly redeveloped in the 1960s. Otherwise expansion in mid-century mainly took place to the E of the town. Stuccoed villas and terraces representing this period survive here and there, e.g. in Charles Street and Park Place, and, further out, N of the Newport Road.

The great period of Cardiff's suburban growth began in the mid 1870s and continued in full flood until shortly after the turn of the century. The Bute Estate still took the lead, followed by other landowners, of which the largest and most active were the Tredegar and Windsor Estates. All three pursued a policy of granting ninety-nine-year leases and retained estate architects to supply house designs to developers. Thus homogeneity and high structural standards were ensured, as much in 'artisan' areas as in those intended for the middle classes. Pennant sandstone was the normal walling material, with Bath stone for dressings, but red brick and various local sandstones were also called into play. *Alexander Roos* was the Bute Estate's architect in the mid C19 (1851–68), but his successor *E. W. M. Corbett*, son of J. S. Corbett, agent to the Estate, was responsible for the handsome Gothic style of Bute developments in the last quarter of the century. *W. G. Habershon*'s practice acted for half a century from the 1850s for the Tredegar Estate, and *H. Snell* for the Windsor Estate. At Tredegarville, Roath, from the mid 1850s the Tredegar Estate established a high standard never subsequently matched. Cathedral Road, Canton, and Ninian Road, Roath, both completed *c.* 1900, were the showpieces of the Bute Estate. Grangetown, an artisan area, is the main development in Cardiff of the Windsor Estate, their high-class housing being concentrated in Penarth (*see* p. 489).

Cardiff's architectural fame, nationally, even internationally, rests on its splendid civic centre in Cathays Park, NE of the castle. The Corporation had first tried to acquire Cathays Park from the trustees of the third Marquess of Bute in 1858. Instead, a smaller area, W of the River Taff and backing on to Cathedral Road, was transferred to the town as a public open space, its name, Sophia Gardens, honouring the widow of the second Marquess. The riverside park was greatly extended NW-wards in the 1890s, all the way to Llandaff Cathedral, making a great tree-fringed greensward up to $\frac{1}{2}$ m. (0.8 kilometre) wide and nearly 2 m. (3.2 kilometres) long. When in 1897, however, the third Marquess finally agreed to sell all 59 acres (24 hectares) of Cathays Park to the Corporation, it was earmarked not for open space but for public architecture.

The open competition held in 1897 for the new Town Hall and Law Courts in the SW section of Cathays Park was won by the brilliant London firm of *Lanchester, Stewart & Rickards*. At a stroke Cardiff entered the mainstream of British architecture. Symbolically, the opening ceremony in 1905 was made the occasion for raising Cardiff to city status. Further competitions, for the University College of South Wales (1903), Glamorgan County Hall (1908) and the National Museum of Wales (1910), produced a series of further monumental classical buildings, all, like the City Hall and Law Courts, faced with Portland stone, and governed in their height by a common cornice line. Cathays Park also became a great memorial garden, with statues in Gorsedd Gardens to the S, and also war memorials, that to the fallen in the First World War, by *Sir Ninian Comper*, in Alexandra Gardens, forming the centrepiece to the whole Park.

After 1918 Cardiff's expansion continued but with less architectural distinction. This is true of Cathays Park, where most of the inter-war buildings show a loss of confidence, and those put up after 1945 abandoned not only classicism but the coherence and monumentality appropriate to the Park. Only *John Dryburgh's* Central Police Station (1966–8) manages to be both modern and majestic. Among housing schemes, the best, and best-preserved, is Rhiwbina Garden Village, started in 1912, and carried on after the war on an enlarged scale but with diminished imagination. Glan Ely, Ely, to the W, is the major scheme of public housing of the 1920s, with semi-detached houses still in an Arts and Crafts tradition. Gabalfa, to the N, of the 1930s, is more formalized in layout, but architecturally undistinguished. The main period of public housing in Cardiff suburbs was the 1950s and '60s. The earlier schemes, such as in the S half of Ely, two-storey houses throughout, set back behind over-generous pavements and verges, are rather bleak and windswept. The later developments on the N edge of the city, at Llanedeyrn and Pentwyn, show greater variety of house types and in their road pattern of interlocking culs-de-sac feel more neighbourly.

The decline of the South Wales coal export trade after 1914 had a drastic effect on the port of Cardiff. This was not fully offset by the transfer in 1934 of Guest, Keen and Nettlefold's steelworks from Dowlais to East Moors, SE of Cardiff. By the mid 1970s steel-making there had been abandoned, and Cardiff lost its role not only as a port but also as a centre of manufacturing industry. Conversely, after the city had been designated the capital of Wales in 1956, its government functions increased and the population continued to grow. The Inland Revenue occupied mammoth tower blocks at Llanishen; Companies House was established at Heath.

All this helped in the 1980s to provide the impetus for the

redevelopment of the dock area. The Cardiff Bay Development Scheme was inaugurated in 1987, and the South Glamorgan County Council has sited its new County Hall at the s end of the Bute Docks, close to Mount Stuart Square. This is the area designated for the Cardiff Bay Opera House, a prestige project, the competition to design it being won in 1994 by *Zaha Hadid*. So far housing, some of it quite imaginative, has been concentrated at the N end of the docks, not too far distant from the city centre. How everything will be knitted together is at the time of writing hard to envisage, for the area due for regeneration is formidably extensive. In 1993 the Cardiff Bay Barrage Bill passed through Parliament, giving permission for a barrage 1,203 yds (1,100 metres) in length from Queen Alexandra Head to Penarth Head, which would create a vast non-tidal expanse, a watery playground for a post-industrial community. How far this vision will become a reality remains to be seen.

THE OLD TOWN CENTRE

CHURCHES AND CHAPELS

St John the Baptist, St John's Street. In the Middle Ages Cardiff had two churches, St Mary's, and St John's as its chapel of ease, but with the rebuilding of St Mary's in 1840 on a new site, St John's stands as the only surviving evidence of the medieval town outside the castle walls. The lofty w tower, with its crown of openwork pinnacles and battlements, makes a magnificent marker. Its connections are with Somerset and Gloucestershire, and as early as 1578 Rice Merrick recognized its similarity to the tower of St Stephen's, Bristol, attributing them both to 'Hart', a master mason identified by John Harvey as William Hart. However, only the openwork crown compares closely with the Bristol church, so it is better to see the connections with the Bristol area in more general terms. The tower stands axially to the w, and is faced with grey Lias limestone ashlar, the mouldings and buttress faces in contrasting buff Dundry stone, much restored. The ground stage is open, to form an entrance on multi-moulded arches in three directions, with a simple, low rib-vault. Above rise three tall stages, diagonal buttresses stepping in once halfway up each stage. Over the w entrance arch, large five-light w window with a transom and panel tracery, in the centre stage w, N and s one tall, slender, two-light window with pierced diapered stonework below the traceried head, and a shorter but slightly wider belfry opening. All this is very like the NW tower of Llandaff Cathedral, suggesting a date *c.*1490. At the top the prodigious crown bursts out without any architectural preparation. Angle pinnacles in the form of octagonal cages, their sides pierced with patterns in three levels, the pinnacled top surrounded by miniature pinnacles. Also a semi-independent pinnacle corbelled out on a gargoyle over each angle of the tower. Tall

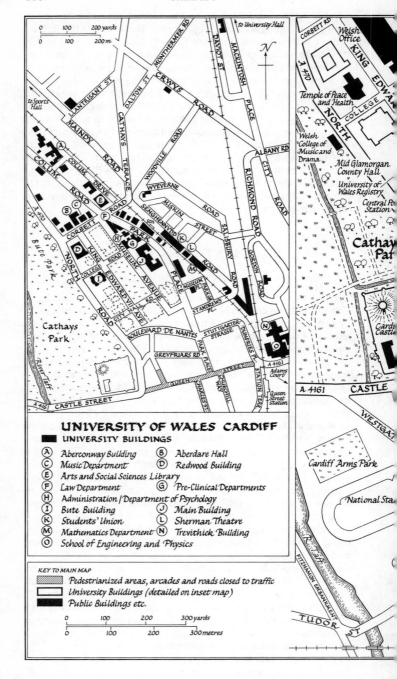

UNIVERSITY OF WALES CARDIFF

UNIVERSITY BUILDINGS

Ⓐ Aberconway Building Ⓑ Aberdare Hall
Ⓒ Music Department Ⓓ Redwood Building
Ⓔ Arts and Social Sciences Library
Ⓕ Law Department Ⓖ Pre-Clinical Departments
Ⓗ Administration / Department of Psychology
Ⓘ Bute Building Ⓙ Main Building
Ⓚ Students' Union Ⓛ Sherman Theatre
Ⓜ Mathematics Department Ⓝ Trevithick Building
Ⓞ School of Engineering and Physics

KEY TO MAIN MAP

▨ Pedestrianized areas, arcades and roads closed to traffic
▢ University Buildings (detailed on inset map)
▧ Public Buildings etc.

0 100 200 300 yards
0 100 200 300 metres

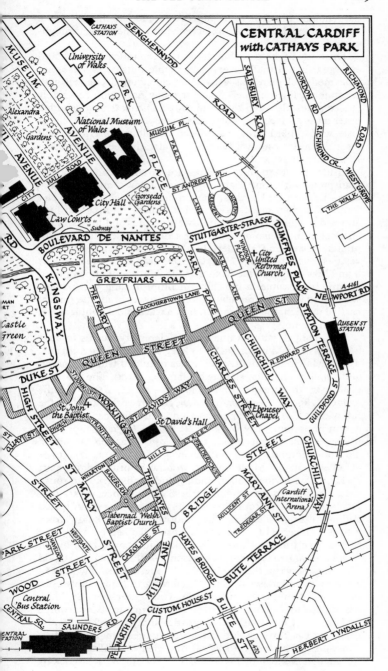

CENTRAL CARDIFF
with CATHAYS PARK

battlements pierced with panelwork and subdivided by a
normal pinnacle in the centre of each face. Crocketing throughout, of course.

The body of the C15 church has been so much renewed and
enlarged that virtually everything visible outside is Victorian.
The medieval plan was a two-bay clerestoried chancel with
separately gabled chapels and a five-bay nave with separately
gabled aisles. Between 1889 and 1891 *Kempson & Fowler* added
outer aisles, refaced all but a small area at the W end of the N
aisle with pinkish-grey, rock-faced Swelldon limestone, and
reset the aisle windows (which had already been renewed in
1852) in the new walls.

Inside, the Perp nave arcades are in command. Lozenge-
plan piers, with four shafts and four hollows, and polygonal
caps. Two-centred arches, their mouldings echoing the pier
forms. The chancel arch is similarly detailed, but rises very high
and wide. Top and bottom doorways to the rood loft, S of the
chancel arch. *Kempson & Fowler*'s outer arcades are appropriately lower and simpler. In the S outer aisle two-storey
vestries, 1975 by *George Pace*, concrete-framed, on piers to the
E and bow-ended to the W so that the light should be impeded
as little as possible: a typically uncompromising yet spatially
sensitive design. Extremely impressive tower arch, the impost
carried up high, the arch mouldings, a wave and a double wave,
dying in far up.

The chancel, with its unexpected clerestory, seems to have
been constrained by the need to keep a pre-existing S arcade.
This has a circular shaft, and arches moulded with a chamfer
and a hollow chamfer, so may be datable *c.* 1300. The N arcade
goes with the arcades of the nave. – REREDOSES. In the
chancel, 1890 by *Kempson & Fowler*, canopywork extending the
full width. The gilded figures set under the five central gables
are an important early work by *W. Goscombe John*, 1891. – In
the S chapel, of gilt wood, by *Comper*. Roundels of saints.
To commemorate Lord Kitchener †1916. – SCREENS to N
(Herbert) chapel. Made up with woodwork of two dates, part
early C16, with vinescroll moulding and profile heads in roundels, i.e. influenced by the earliest Renaissance ideas; part
Jacobean, perhaps from a pulpit. – STAINED GLASS. A varied
and interesting collection. The windows are listed below, from
E to W. – Chancel E, a beardless Christ, flanked by Mary and
St John, and beyond them SS Luke and David. 1915 by *Sir
Ninian Comper*. Typical coloration. – N chapel E, Good
Shepherd between the two St Johns. – N chapel N. Two splen-
did heraldic windows of *c.* 1855, referring to Bute family con-
nections. – In the N outer aisle, Christ between St Mary
Magdalene and donors. 1890. In the Germanic style favoured
by *Dixon*. – N inner aisle NW, apostles and patriarchs. 1869 by
Morris & Co. Strongly individualized figures, singing colours.
The apostles in the top row all designed by *William Morris*,
Abraham and Noah by *Ford Madox Brown* and Melchisedek by
Burne-Jones. – N inner aisle W, Suffer the Little Children.

1890, made by *Belham & Co.*, partly with opalescent glass
and idiosyncratic pinks, mauves and indigos, to the design of
J. P. Seddon. – MONUMENTS. Sir William († 1609) and Sir John
Herbert † 1617. Erected by the widow of the latter. Recumbent
effigies of a knight and a lawyer. Back-plate with a bracket and
head in the centre, and relief of four putti blowing bubbles (to
symbolize mortality). – Many Neoclassical tablets skied in the
tower and thus out of normal eyeshot.

EGLWYS DEWI SANT (formerly St Andrew's), St Andrew's
Crescent.* One of the few places in the network of Cardiff's
Victorian streets where a formal space was created is St Andrew's Crescent. The centrepiece of the development was laid
out E of Park Place in the 1850s by the Bute Trustees. This
oval area was from the start intended for a church, to be
dedicated to St Andrew. *Prichard & Seddon*'s original design of
1859 would have done it ample justice. This was cruciform with
a crossing steeple and various experimental features, the most
prophetic of which was the wide nave and low passage aisles,
to enhance congregational participation; taken up by G. E.
Street in 1864 at All Saints, Clifton, Bristol, it became a standard feature from Bodley's St Augustine's, Pendlebury, of ten
years later.

The rather unimpressive building which occupies the centre
of the Crescent is essentially by *Prichard & Seddon*, but drastically reduced in cost and ambition. Building began in 1860
on an eight-bay rectangular plan, but was halted at eaves level.
The upper parts were then redesigned more cheaply, and in
1862 the architect to the Bute Trustees, *Alexander Roos*, took
over. The church was consecrated in 1863. In 1956 it was
rededicated as Cardiff's church for services in the Welsh language, hence its present name.

So what of Prichard & Seddon's design survives? The polychromy of the walls was established by them, local stones laid
crazy-paving-wise (popple stone, as it was called), with ashlar
dressings of Bath stone and bands of coursed Newbridge
Pennant sandstone low down. Theirs are the low passage aisles,
and the tall clerestory above (a good feature for a town church,
as the *Ecclesiologist* noted), and so are the deep, full-height
buttresses, which the architects' original scheme with bold
transverse internal arches in the nave and a vaulted chancel
would have required. The style remains E.E., but inevitably
simpler than first envisaged. To the W a composition centred
on a two-light, plate-traceried window; E window of three lights
with bar tracery. Two-light clerestory windows. The building
has been further compromised by various additions, in particular low double-gabled transepts with vestries, by *Butterfield*,
1884–6, and NW and SW porches.

The INTERIOR adds little, spoilt as it is by recent subdivision. In the nave, stout, round piers, with shaft-rings and

---

*The former Welsh church in Howard Gardens, 1890–9 by *E. M. Bruce Vaughan*,
was destroyed by a bomb in the Second World War.

Romanesque foliage capitals, on which rest two-centred super-arches which rise to enclose the clerestory windows. Thin scissor-brace roof. Plain chancel and sanctuary. – PULPIT with tester. Timber. Perp. 1886 by *E. P. Warren*. – STAINED GLASS. Chancel E, Suffer the Little Children, by *Lavers & Barraud* *c.* 1880? – S aisle, Annunciation, *c.* 1917, and Adoration of the Kings, *c.* 1923.

ST DAVID'S CATHEDRAL (R.C.), Charles Street. By *Pugin & Pugin*, 1884–7, the interior reconstructed by *F. R. Bates, Son & Price* in the 1950s after bomb damage. Externally little altered, a dark and solemn presence in the commercial hubbub. Coursed, rock-faced Pennant sandstone dressed with red sandstone. E.E. Four-stage tower flush with the street beside the (ritual) w front. Tall five-light window with geometrical tracery. Lofty side elevations, dominated by full-height clerestory buttresses which step out boldly low down between the three confessionals and the three side chapels which flank the nave. Aisleless, two-bay choir. The INTERIOR is entered under a stone gallery on strangely modelled piers and segmental arches. Simple unbroken space of seven bays, the square, chamfered piers rising to form superarches over the clerestory windows. Multi-moulded sanctuary arch. The post-war contributions are the fussy roof structure of timber and iron, and the diapered REREDOS and circular honeycomb window over. – STAINED GLASS. Glass of *c.* 1900 in every other side window. – W window, Vision of the Immaculate Conception witnessed by Popes.

CITY UNITED REFORMED CHURCH, Windsor Place. Built in 1865–6 for a Scottish Presbyterian congregation, which explains why the architect came from Edinburgh. He was *F. T. Pilkington*, and the building is little brother to his extraordinary chapel of 1862 in Barclay Place, Edinburgh. The original plan was a Greek cross with W, N and S porches, the last carried up to form a tower and spire. Gothic. Snecked Pennant sandstone, with dressings and crisp carving in Bath stone, pink Radyr stone for tympana over windows and on the steeple: as intelligent a use of local materials as any local architect could have managed. Plate tracery and stout shafts with foliage caps of late C12 origins, but with a spikiness in the forms and an overlay of sculpture on the tracery which are Pilkington's own. Other oddities are the bowed transept ends (to accommodate galleries) and the steeply gabled top to the tower, on which the octagonal spire is seated.

But the church is not in its original state. In 1893 (see the rain-water head) the W front was rebuilt by *E. M. Bruce Vaughan* further W, its porch reconstructed on the S side in a strange two-storey form. In the process the four shafted openings low down were blocked and the four-light showpiece window above cut down. N entrance vestibule of 1980–1 by *Wyn Thomas & Partners*, overlaid on Pilkington's porch. The interior is the product of another intervention by *Bruce Vaughan*, after a fire in 1910. His is the hammerbeam roof with a construction over the crossing worthy of Pilkington. And he must have introduced the carved stone angels and foliage corbels here. – STAINED GLASS. In the S transept, 1921. Small scenes from the life of Christ exemplifying virtues.

EBENESER CHAPEL, Charles Street. Built in 1854–5 by *R. G. Thomas* of Newport for Congregationalists, and used since 1976 by Cardiff's Independent church. Cleaning has highlighted the multicoloured random stonework 'from all parts of the world and of every variety of geological epoch', i.e. stone imported as ballast by returning trading ships.* Even more notable for the mid 1850s, the plan, nave with narrow aisles and E apse, and the style, wholeheartedly Dec, make the building indistinguishable from a chapel of the Established church. W entrance under a five-light window with flowing tracery, flanked by buttresses which support big pinnacles. Two-light aisle windows, and buttresses dramatically modified *c.* 1976 to keep the wall-foot dry. Inside, the original arrangements largely survive. Thin arch-brace and hammerbeam roof on stone foliage corbels. Tall apse arch, its imposts capped by demi-angels and foliage. Gallery at the W (entrance) end only, carried on a single cast iron column with vine leaf capital. Original PEWS. The E end all reordered in 1978, and an ORGAN of that date in the apse. – STAINED GLASS. W window, 1855, early Gothic style with no figures, but tiny angels in the tracery lights. – Light of the World (after Holman Hunt) and Good Shepherd, signed *W. Davis & Son* of Cardiff. – War memorial window signed by *Daniells & Fricker*.

HALL at the back dated 1871, built as a schoolroom by *W. D. Blessley*. Also Dec.

CAPEL PEMBROKE TERRACE, Churchill Way. 1877 by *Henry C. Harris*, a rare essay for Nonconformists in High Victorian Gothic. The whole concept is highly original. Early French Gothic clearly under the influence of Burges. T-plan, the entrances l. and r. of the street front, which centres on a bold, high-gabled composition of two deep-set three-light windows with geometrical tracery over a row of four narrow arches on stout coupled shafts. This is flanked by strong buttresses, polygonal in their upper stages, with blunt pinnacles, and beyond them by dramatically bow-fronted stair-turrets with half-timbered tops. Pennant sandstone and ashlar dressings, now painted over, are the main facing materials, but the red brick outlines of the transept windows, not originally meant to be visible, give a hint of what is to be seen inside. The INTERIOR is faced throughout with polychromatic brickwork, white latticework with alternate black centres set on a red background. High and wide transverse arch to divide the galleried pulpit at the roadward end from the congregation, which was confined to a surprisingly small area, with galleries only in the transepts. The conversion to an open-plan architect's office has been well done by *The Wigley Fox Partnership*, *c.* 1982.

*John Perkins notes a considerable intermixture of local stones.

Former METHODIST FREE CHURCH, now Masonic Temple, Guildford Street. Handsome Bath stone façade of early C18 Baroque character. Paired Doric pilasters. It was built 1863–4, by *J. Hartland & Son*, and converted for its present purpose by *George Thomas* as early as 1895.

TABERNACL WELSH BAPTIST CHURCH, The Hayes. A fine classical chapel of 1865 by *J. Hartland & Son*, well-proportioned and coherent. Rendered. Four-bay recessed centre, fully occupied by four arched doorways between channelled piers, and, above, four large, round-headed windows between Corinthian pilasters. Balustraded balcony. One-bay side turrets, confirming the ground storey as a channelled support for the piano nobile above. Blank top parapet with name and dates. Handsome contemporary interior, galleried all round. Flat, coffered ceiling with a big metal rose in the centre, for ventilation. – STAINED GLASS. Of *c.* 1900. Figures of Virtues in the upper side windows. Above the entrance, Baptism of Christ, waist-deep in the River Jordan, and Last Supper.

CARDIFF CASTLE

Cardiff Castle, within its enclosing walls, has always been a world apart, for defence or for pleasure. A succession of Roman forts occupied the strategic site at the lowest crossing of the River Taff, giving its name to Cardiff, the *castrum* on the Taff. William the Conqueror, on his only visit to Wales in 1081, ordered the raising of a massive motte-and-bailey castle within the fort. Half a century later it was strengthened further when a masonry keep was erected on top of the motte, to be the stronghold of successive lords of Glamorgan. Within the bailey other buildings, now known only from early drawings or excavation, were put up in connection with the lordship, a shire hall, a chapel and houses for the knights who had to take it in turn to serve castle guard.

98   In the early C15 Richard Beauchamp, Earl of Warwick, built a new, more sumptuous, domestic range against the W enclosure wall. This was enlarged in the late C16 by Henry Herbert, second Earl of Pembroke, and further enlarged and indeed transformed twice, by the first and then by the third Marquess of Bute, whose family inherited the Cardiff Castle estate in 1776. The first Marquess's architect was *Henry Holland*, and *Capability Brown* landscaped the grounds. The third Marquess's architect was *William Burges*. Theirs were two hearts in harmony. Furthermore the third Marquess, thanks to his father's entrepreneurial genius in developing Cardiff docks, was the richest man in Britain. So Burges, between the Marquess's coming of age in 1868 and his own death in 1881, could realize his dreams. His imagination, his scholarship and his sheer high spirits combine to make Cardiff Castle, outside and in, the most successful – certainly the most enjoyable – of all the fantasy castles of the C19. After Burges's death his schemes continued to be implemented by his assistant, *William Frame*.

The last chapter in the story is an archaeological one. Between 1890 and 1923 the walls of the Roman fort were gradually exposed under the supervision first of *Frame*, then of the fourth Marquess's architects, *H. Sesom-Hiley* (1905–21) and *J. P. Grant*. Neo-Roman walls were then raised upon them, formidably high (as, e.g., at Richborough or Portchester), shutting off the castle from the outside world more firmly than ever. Only since 1947, when the fifth Marquess presented the castle to the City, has the psychological, if not the physical barrier between the two been broken down.

From the town all that is visible is the high S ENCLOSURE WALL, its neo-medieval W half by *Burges*, its neo-Roman E half by *J. P. Grant* in the 1920s, with *Burges*'s exclamatory CLOCK TOWER at the SW angle; and in the centre the medieval BLACK TOWER, through which the castle grounds are entered. Ahead stands the MOTTE and KEEP, half-l. the Beauchamp–Bute WESTERN APARTMENTS, bristling with Burges's towers. *Capability Brown*'s landscaping, though much modified, still provides a verdant barrier against the high buildings of the city which peer in over the walls from the E. Detailed description is best taken historically: fort, motte, keep, Black Tower, Western Apartments, and finally enclosure walls.

THE ROMAN FORT. The roughly rectangular fort, 9.1 acres (3.7 hectares) in area, was constructed in the last quarter of the C3 A.D., the last in a series of four forts on the site. The first and largest was a short-lived earth and timber construction datable to A.D. 55–60. A much smaller earth and timber fort was built c. A.D. 75–80 and further reduced in size early in the C2 A.D. The present structure was probably raised c. A.D. 280 and was abandoned possibly in the late C4 A.D. Following excavation, the E wall, the E section of the S wall, and the N gateway with the wall E of it, were imaginatively reconstructed between 1889 and 1923 on the instructions of the third and fourth Marquesses of Bute. Original wall facing survives up to the line of pink Radyr stone; above is reconstruction. (The core of the Roman wall remains in many places to a much greater height.) The most impressive remains are a section of the S wall, the largest surviving piece of Roman masonry in the county, which can be seen preserved in an underground gallery E of the S entrance. The walls, backed by a substantial earth bank and founded on river cobbles, stand over 16 ft (5 metres) high where best preserved, c. 11 ft (3 metres) thick at the base, tapering to c. 8 ft (2.4 metres). They probably never stood much higher, so reconstruction perhaps doubles their original height. There is no evidence for the mural gallery included in the reconstructed walls. Originally there were probably eighteen semi-octagonal towers bonded into the external wall-face, including two pairs of towers flanking the N and S gates and four corner towers. These too have been reconstructed around the E half of the fort, where all were of solid, not hollow construction, except those of the N gate, which served as guard chambers, and that midway along the E wall, which may have contained a postern gate. The N gate as reconstructed draws on excavated evidence for its two-leaved gate at the outer end of the narrow passage, but the arched superstructure is based on analogy with other sites. Nothing is visible of the S gateway midway along the S wall. Excavation has revealed traces of timber-framed buildings within the walls.

THE MOTTE-AND-BAILEY CASTLE. The castle founded by William the Conqueror on his return journey from St David's in 1081 consists of a motte 35 ft (10.67 metres) high, the largest in Wales, and as large as any erected in England. The ditch round it was filled during landscaping in the 1770s and re-excavated a century later. Inner and outer baileys were constructed within the Roman walls. The inner bailey was defined by the walls of the Roman fort, and a new cross-wall running diagonally from the motte to the Roman S gate. To enclose the outer ward massive earth banks were thrown up over the robbed core of the Roman wall, as can still be seen from within the castle enclosure, and from a display tunnel contrived beneath the S bank.

32 THE KEEP. Probably built by Robert of Gloucester (†1147) towards the end of his lordship of Glamorgan, in response to the general Welsh uprising of 1136. Regular twelve-sided shell keep, a novelty in the mid C12, comparable only to Carisbrooke Castle in the Isle of Wight. Walls primarily of Lias limestone, the angles of finely cut Sutton stone. Many putlock holes. Stumps of battlements above the internal wall-walk. The two SE facets of the curtain wall were replaced c. 1300 by a four-storey gate tower and the gable end of a hall, also of Lias limestone. The GATE TOWER has an oddly irregular faceted outline. Arrow slits at every level, and drawbar slots for doors and even for the main first-floor window (originally a doorway to the top of the now vanished fore-building). Openings largely renewed, those in the top storey dating to the late C16, for belvedere purposes. Newel stair intercommunicating with the hall at first-floor level and rising to a turret new-built in 1923. The end wall of the HALL has a C16 window high up and renewed arrow slits below. The body of the hall, inside the keep, has vanished.

The massive FOREBUILDING which extended from the keep tower down the side of the motte to the level of the bailey, was swept away by Capability Brown in the late 1770s. Its appearance is known from early views. The present flight of steps and unfinished flanking walls follow its line but give no hint of its originally formidable nature.

The cross-wall between inner and outer baileys was reinforced in stone, reusing Lias facing blocks of the Roman N and E walls. Its line is now laid out in modern stonework.

BLACK TOWER (now Museum of the Welch Regiment). In the centre of the S enclosure wall, W of the modern gateway into the castle. Its original function was as the gatekeeper's lodging, above a basement dungeon. Square in plan, probably built in

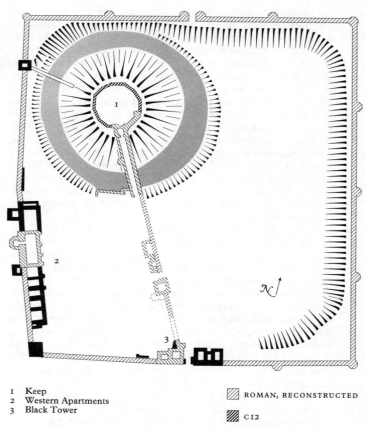

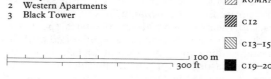

1   Keep
2   Western Apartments
3   Black Tower

ROMAN, RECONSTRUCTED

C12

C13–15

C19–20

100 m
300 ft

Cardiff Castle. Plan of site

the early C13. The dungeon has a pointed tunnel-vault 14½ ft (4.35 metres) to its apex, entered from the W, ventilated (but hardly lit) by a vent at the E apex of the vault. Three storeys of rooms above, reached by a N door at the head of the modern external steps, but originally at the level of the wall-walk of the bailey cross-wall. Rectangular W annexe for garderobes and a deep cess-pit. Polygonal NE stair-turret. Both these were early additions. Tudor windows at all three upper levels. Lias facing of the turret and renewed battlements by *John Prichard*, 1850. The simple S GATE and BARBICAN TOWER adjoining to the E were rebuilt larger by *J.P. Grant* in the 1920s. His contribution is easy to identify by the walling of glacial pebbles.

The WESTERN APARTMENTS are now the visual climax of the

castle, dominated by Burges's array of towers for the third Marquess of Bute. But these must not blind us to the interest of the incorporated earlier work. The C15 structure is traditionally ascribed to Richard Beauchamp, Earl of Warwick, who possessed Cardiff Castle 1423–39 through his marriage to Isabel Despenser. A vault boss with their arms, noted by G. T. Clark in 1862, before the Victorian work began, confirmed the tradition. Beauchamp made additions on both sides of the massive Roman and medieval W wall. To the W he added a big, polygonal defensive tower, commanding the W gate of the town. Backing on to the tower and over-riding the wall he erected an E-facing domestic block consisting of a hall and chambers over a vaulted undercroft. From its E front project four full-height turrets, the two to the S being a stair-turret and a window bay for the hall, and the two to the N the same for the chambers. Decorative machicolated battlements, and in the turrets decorative arrow loops.

In the late C16 a second, square tower was built, by Henry Herbert, Earl of Pembroke, W of the enclosure wall, at the SW corner of the C15 block. Herbert also added a N extension. *Henry Holland* after 1776 matched this with a S extension and refenestrated everything, giving the two-storey E front pointed-headed windows above and straight-headed ones under hood-moulds below. Towards the W he matched the Herbert Tower with a new projecting tower at the N angle, and added shallow intervening ranges in the re-entrants to each side of the central Beauchamp Tower. Five storeys of windows here. As Sir Richard Colt Hoare remarked in 1802, the enlarged mansion was 'so thickly beset with sash windows that little of its ancient character can be perceived'. The most splendid feature of the Holland castle must have been the now-vanished circular, cantilevered staircase in the Beauchamp Tower.

The Butes, with their vast and widespread estates, spent little time at Cardiff. The second Marquess, who inherited in 1814, although masterminding the development of Cardiff docks, did nothing to the castle, except put the finishing touches to Holland's work, suspended in 1794 at the premature death of his father, Lord Mountstuart. At his own death in 1848 the second Marquess left a six-month-old son and heir. The third Marquess grew up withdrawn and sensitive, fascinated by the Middle Ages for scholarly and for sensuous reasons. As soon as he came of age he announced his conversion to Catholicism. To someone like this the token Gothicism of Holland's castle was, of course, deplorable. Already in 1868 he was apologizing for it, 'painfully alive to the fact that [it] is very far indeed from setting anything like an example in art'. But in 1865 Bute had met William Burges. If Bute had a vision for the transformation of Cardiff Castle into something truly medieval, Burges had the skill and artistry to realize the vision. The other ingredient was money, and of that Bute had plenty. Between 1868 and Bute's death in 1900, first *Burges*, and after 1881, when Burges died, *William Frame* refashioned and enlarged the Western

Apartments with a series of new or heightened towers and a sequence of dazzling but recondite interiors.

The castle which resulted needs to be examined outside from the W, from the S and from the E in that order, and then internally. Visitors to the castle today are given partial tours of the interior, one in the winter, another in the summer, which together include almost all the decorated rooms. The account given here follows their general direction but is inclusive. It also attempts to explain how the rooms fitted together into a habitable whole.

The W FRONT. The majestic CLOCK TOWER rising sheer at the SW corner beside Castle Street was the first part which Burges conceived and built. He first suggested it in 1866, to be 'a handsome object at the present entrance of the town' – note his stress on its public role. The design was finalized in 1868, the tower built 1869–73. Sombre greenish-brown Forest of Dean ashlar, the material Burges used everywhere to distinguish his work. Over a deep, battered base the square tower rises uninterrupted to the clock-stage. Here bold arcading encloses gilt clock-faces flanked by polychromed statues of the seven planets by *Thomas Nicholls* against a star-studded background, on pedestals carved with their signs of the zodiac. Above this the wall-head projects on false machicolation, with fully tinctured shields of arms in the embrasures, and an upper stage pierced by two-light windows. The Summer Smoking Room is inside here. Clerestory windows between the two stages of the pyramidal lead-covered roof. Note the stars let into the leadwork, in imitation of the church of Notre Dame at Châlons-sur-Marne. Cylindrical NW stair-turret. So this is a bolder, blunter Big Ben, cast back into the idiom of early French Gothic.

The Clock Tower is isolated from the main residential block. 98 So to the N comes a long stretch of battlemented wall with arrow slits and timber flaps. Behind this the gable end of the low TANK TOWER. Then the much larger GUEST TOWER straddles the wall. Beyond that the three pre-Burges towers project more prominently from the enclosure wall. First the late C16 HERBERT TOWER, rectangular, of brown random stone with grey Lias quoins, rewindowed by Burges, heightened by two storeys and crowned with his deep battlements of Forest ashlar, and steep, hipped roof-end backing on to a massive chimneystack. Next the early C15 BEAUCHAMP TOWER, five sides of an octagon, rising from semi-pyramidal spurs. Coursed grey Lias walling, and C15 windows and machicolated battlements, restored by Burges. The lead-covered timber flèche, its fully octagonal crown, was conceived by Burges in 1872, and constructed 1877–9. Attached to the S side of the Beauchamp Tower, a three-storey ashlar-faced appendage, bowed at its S end. This supports and encloses the Oratory which Burges constructed on the site where the second Marquess had died, and is thus the only remaining (refaced) section of Holland's intervening additions between the towers. Otherwise Burges took these sections back to the face of the medieval enclosure

wall and restored such windows as old drawings showed had
been there. The low, angled wall which projects from the range
at this point is an attempt by *J. P. Grant* in 1921 to recreate the
town's West Gate. Burges's romantic timber bridge of 1873
was unfortunately removed for the purpose.

The NW corner is formed by the square BUTE TOWER, built
by Holland of random Lias, heightened and refenestrated by
Burges. The two-stage ashlar top and the sheer, square stair-
turret against its N wall stress uncompromisingly the closure of
the composition. Arcaded lower stage, arches on suspended
colonnettes enclosing lancets and, towards the corners, statues.
Work started here in 1873. N of the Bute Tower a long stretch
of unrestored medieval enclosure wall, and a doorway and
toothings in Burges's turret to show that he planned a wall-
head walk along it.

Starting again from the Clock Tower, one should look first
to the W down CASTLE STREET, to enjoy the ANIMAL WALL.
A vulture, a bear and other realistic animals balance on alternate
mullions of the park wall. *Burges* had the idea for the wall,
inspired by the C13 drawings of Villard de Honnecourt; *Thomas
Nicholls*, assisted by his son and *W. Antill*, modelled the
animals. The wall was first erected, in 1887–8, further E in
Castle Street between the Clock Tower and the S gate of the
castle, where it protected the moat garden from passers-by.
The sea-lion and the monkeys were set up first, then the shield-
bearing lions, retouched after the Marquess had criticized them
as 'too modest of demeanour'. The wall was moved to its
present site *c.* 1930 and supplemented with six more animals
by *A. Carrick* of Edinburgh. WEST LODGE by *Alexander Roos*,
1860–2.

The CURTAIN WALL between the Clock Tower and the
Black Tower was reconstructed and heightened by *Burges*, its
battlements equipped with timber flaps and a sloping roof for
the internal wall-walk, as he believed had been the medieval
way. This extends as far as the BLACK TOWER (*see* above).

Inside, Burges's wall supports a broad wall-walk with typical
no-nonsense timber gallery and elegant lead animal gargoyles
at intervals. It leads to the apartments in the Clock Tower
(where the public tour normally begins). Round the corner the
W range starts with a further gallery N of the Clock Tower, and
the Tank Tower, with a pitched roof to its galleried top. On
this side Burges's GUEST TOWER stands full height, replacing
Holland's S wing. Its two-stage top, arcaded below, battlemented above, echoes the Bute Tower, and on the N face where
the arcading is fully pierced, the origin of Burges's idea, in the
arcaded parapet of the Bishop's Palace at St David's, or indeed
of Swansea Castle, is obvious. Octagonal NE stair-turret.

The E front of the BEAUCHAMP RANGE is dominated by
five full-height polygonal turrets. The S-most was added in
1927, but the rest are C15, more or less altered. The windowless
stair-turret of Lias limestone served the lower end of Beauchamp's hall, a piquant contrast to the next turret, which lit

the centre of the hall. This is faced with a fine-grained oolite ashlar, the angles of its lower storey decorated with slender lozenge-plan buttresses carrying attached pinnacles. Original upper window openings, enlarged lower ones. All the tracery C19. The fourth turret, originally another stair-turret, Holland rebuilt to match its neighbour. The fifth remains little altered, ashlar-faced and unbuttressed, but with modified windows. Windows in the intervening flat walls in their medieval places. Originally all the upper windows were transomed and lit the principal rooms, with less important rooms below. The block to the N, of 3+1 bays, backed by the Bute Tower, is largely as Holland left it, with tracery added to the windows. The sole Burgesian contribution here is the deep battlementing of Forest ashlar. Underneath the full length of the Beauchamp range a tunnel-vaulted UNDERCROFT with flattened four-centred profile.

After all this minute examination one must walk well back to enjoy Burges's vision. Now the whole gallimaufry of dark and disparate towers clusters round and behind the Beauchamp block, their outlines sharp and pristine against the sky, as in a page from the *Très Riches Heures* of the Duc de Berri. Only the

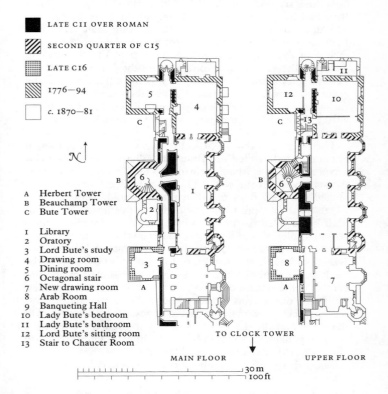

LATE C11 OVER ROMAN

SECOND QUARTER OF C15

LATE C16

1776—94

c. 1870—81

A   Herbert Tower
B   Beauchamp Tower
C   Bute Tower

1   Library
2   Oratory
3   Lord Bute's study
4   Drawing room
5   Dining room
6   Octagonal stair
7   New drawing room
8   Arab Room
9   Banqueting Hall
10 Lady Bute's bedroom
11 Lady Bute's bathroom
12 Lord Bute's sitting room
13 Stair to Chaucer Room

TO CLOCK TOWER

MAIN FLOOR   UPPER FLOOR

30 m
100 ft

Cardiff Castle, Western Apartments. Main and upper floor plans

Holland block looks alien, and one can only speculate how
Burges, had he lived longer, would have brought it into
harmony.
Now for the INTERIOR. Here Burges's imagination could run
riot. Here the arts were all called into service: painting, sculpture and wood-carving, stained glass, metalwork, inlay. Here
marbles, gilding and other surfaces which sparkled or shone
found their places. Here, above all, the arts could tell stories.
Seventeen rooms in all were decorated to Burges's designs, and
several others show his hand. Of these a dozen were all-out
showpieces. One, the grand stair, has been destroyed, in fact
so comprehensively eliminated that the received view until very
recently was that Burges's spectacular design had never been
executed. Broadly speaking, the rooms are planned in four or
even five groups. Those in the Clock Tower form the first,
segregated and self-contained. The two main state rooms were
the grand stair and the Banqueting Hall, which opened from
the head of the stair. Almost everything else fell into the category
of family rooms, linked vertically by a staircase in the Beauchamp Tower and horizontally by tortuous passages at ground-
floor and second-floor level.* Within the family area Lord
Bute had his personal rooms, mainly in the Bute Tower, but
including the library under the Banqueting Hall. Similarly,
Lady Bute had hers, most of them in the Holland block, but
including the Chaucer Room at the top of the Beauchamp
Tower. Others again were for the use of the family as a whole.
In principle, then, Cardiff Castle was no different from any
other aristocratic great house. Only in their disposition in the
various towers and in the highly specific iconography of almost
all the most elaborate rooms, was the castle idiosyncratic in
terms of its plan.
The interior of the CLOCK TOWER was designed, though
not completed, while Lord Bute was still a bachelor. Bachelor
accommodation is what is provided. The WINTER SMOKING
ROOM opens off the wall-walk, but is protected by a heavily
hinged door, by dogs inlaid in the threshold (with the date
1872) and by a devil's face leering down overhead. The room
itself has a quadripartite rib-vault, the ribs painted in Bute's
armorial colours. The decoration takes up the theme of Time. –
STAINED GLASS, in the six lancets, designed by *Frederick
Weekes* and made by *Saunders & Co. c.*1870, of the days of the
week of Norse mythology, the seventh represented by the sun
carved on the central vault boss. – PAINTING. Vault spandrels
by *Weekes* of the signs of the zodiac, walls illustrating the four
seasons, feebly overpainted in the 1970s. – SCULPTURE. On
the vault corbels, the times of day, demi-figures holding the
sun rising, high, in descent and almost hidden. On the massive
chimneyhood Diana and a relief frieze of winter pastimes.
The privacy of the rooms above is ensured by the semi-

*Ground-floor level in relation to the E side of the range. To the W the ground
level is two storeys lower, at sub-basement level.

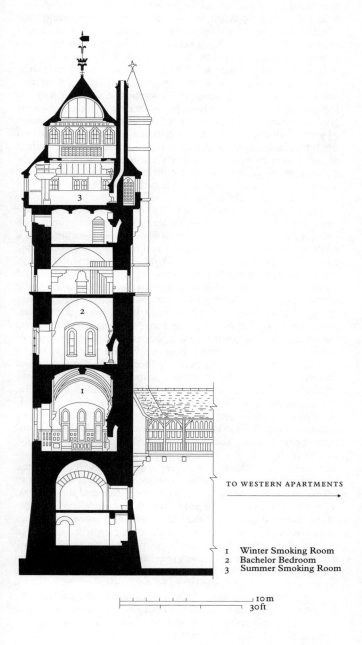

TO WESTERN APARTMENTS →

1 Winter Smoking Room
2 Bachelor Bedroom
3 Summer Smoking Room

10 m
30 ft

Cardiff Castle, Clock Tower. Section

fortified door at the foot of the newel stair. The stair leads first
to the BACHELOR BEDROOM, Lord Bute's bedroom, that is
to say. Door carved with birds among foliage. This room too is
vaulted and dimly lit by lancets. Here mineral wealth is the
theme. – STAINED GLASS. By *Saunders & Co.*, to *Weekes*'s
design. Allegories linking six jewels each to a musical instru-
ment. Sculptured vault corbels of music-making demi-figures.
Vault paintings (overpainted) illustrating classical myths of
harnessing the earth's treasures. Roundels below of famous
goldsmiths and jewellers, and a frieze inscribed with the names
of gems. Labelled berry-like specimens of minerals found on
the Bute estates inlaid in the chimneyhood, from which a shield
of arms and massive marquess's coronet project. – BATH-
ROOM, en suite. Walls lined with Penarth alabaster. Huge
marble bath brought from Rome, with added metal inserts of
sundry fish, salamanders etc.

The CLOCK CHAMBER and SERVANT'S ROOM above are
quite plain. At last the newel stair reaches its sumptuous des-
tination, the SUMMER SMOKING ROOM. At the stair-head a
relief of a dragon. Door with stiff-leaf hingework and the date
1873. The room is full of light, from paired windows at eye
level and from the galleried clerestory under the ribbed and
painted ceiling dome. Magnificent tiled floor emblematic of the
world, inspired by the C13 sanctuary pavement in Westminster
Abbey. Mainly red and yellow, with inlaid brass inscription.
The date 1871 refers to its conception. Above hangs a wonderful
chandelier, symbol of the sun, a life-size figure of Apollo balancing on a sunburst which is also a chariot wheel. Wrought
iron gallery balustrade, originally gilded. In the dome, painted
figures of the four elements, and stars with their names and
symbols. On the clerestory N wall painted tiles of Apollo,
Cupid, Venus and Jupiter, on the other three sides, roundels
by *Weekes*, representing metals and their uses. The clerestory
gallery is carried on massive corbels carved with pairs of demi-
figures representing the eight winds of classical meteorology,
modelled by *Thomas Nicholls*, 1871–2. Painted busts of as-
tronomers in roundels above. Supporting piers of gilt-jointed
Penarth alabaster and marble. On the main walls two tiers of
scenes in painted tiles, signed by *F. Smallfield* and dated 1874.
They illustrate classical legends which can be related to signs
of the zodiac, Europa and the bull (Taurus), Castor and Pollux
(Gemini) and so on. Summer on the chimneypiece, a figure of
winged Cupid over the words 'Aestate viresco'. To show how
love flourishes in the summer, relief frieze below of couples in
medieval costume dallying in a leafy wood. Foliage carving here
by *Edward Clarke* of Llandaff.

The corridor running N from the Clock Tower leads to the
GUEST TOWER, the S-most extremity of the main apartments.
The STAINED GLASS displayed here was made for the now
demolished chapel at Castell Coch. (By *Saunders & Co.* to
Burges's design.) Burges planned for the principal kitchen to be
at ground level in the Guest Tower. The upper half was the

children's quarter. NURSERY with painted tiles illustrating Aesop's fables and nursery rhymes, executed in 1879. Busts of famous storytellers over the W doors. Overmantel carved with a figure of Fame, and Aesop's fox fables on the lintel. Ceiling beams restencilled 1979. In the WALNUT ROOM above (now part of the George Thomas Suite), overmantel carved with Jack and the Beanstalk (enough to give the children nightmares).

The route N-wards from the Guest Tower at once passes a series of plain C20 arches, formed when the grand stair was removed. To the r. the NEW DRAWING ROOM (not normally shown to the public), dated 1928 on the overmantel and occupying the upper half of the grand stair-well. In its N wall double doors into the Banqueting Hall. – STAINED GLASS by *Paul Woodroffe* of Chipping Campden, 1932. Next on the l. the ARAB ROOM, constructed by *Burges* within the HERBERT TOWER. For all its small size, this was unequivocally one of the rooms of state. The Arab Room, the most exotic in the Castle, was the last Burges designed. In the inscription in the white marble panel over the fireplace Bute commemorated him and gave the date of his death, 1881. Burges derived many of the Arabisms, the jelly-mould vault, the trelliswork, the cusped arcading, from a recently published volume on Arabic art in Cairo.* Polychromatic marble floor, dove-coloured marble walls, superstructure painted and gilt by *Charles Campbell*. The mosaic armorial panel looks oddly out of place. Just one Burges witticism, the gilded parrots perched on the cornice. The room was completed in 1882 by *R. P. Pullan*, Burges's brother-in-law. *Burges* designed the Arabic stained glass.

From the Arab Room a small vaulted lobby, dated 1881, leads into the SW corner of the BANQUETING HALL, a vast room extending the full length of the Beauchamp range, but pinched for width between the precinct wall and the C15 E wall, and lit from the E by the C15 window bays. Their Perp style is developed for the major architectural features in the room. Open timber roof with hammerbeams concealed by fan-vaulting, after the roofs of Framlingham church and St Peter Mancroft, Norwich. Elaborately panelled and arcaded screen at the S end, designed by *William Frame*, the drawings for which are dated 1887. Note the twin doors to the grand stair beyond. The decoration of the room celebrates the lordship of Glamorgan. In the STAINED GLASS successive lords and their wives, figures based on cartoons by *H. W. Lonsdale* c. 1873 and made by *Saunders & Co.* The WALL-PAINTINGS and chimneypiece SCULPTURE, by *Nicholls*, concentrate on the exploits and adventures of the early C12 lord, Robert, Earl of Gloucester. Twenty-six painted subjects, conceived by *Burges* by 1875, and executed by *H. W. Lonsdale* and assistants *R. W. Maddox* and *A. Robertson*. Chimneypiece in the form of a fortress, as Burges loved, with trumpet-blowing heralds and

*A.C.T.E. Prisse d'Avennes, *L'Art arabe d'après les monuments du Kaire*, 7e–18e (1877).

ladies peeping over the battlements as Robert rides out to
battle. The face behind the barred window below is that of his
uncle Robert, Duke of Normandy. Doorways to l. and r. with
figures of monks writing in the tympana over them. These and
the dummy N doorways have lushly crocketed labels on animal
stops, some illustrating the Welsh saga, the Mabinogion. The
buffet against the N wall designed by *Burges* and dated 1879.

The doorway N of the Banqueting Hall chimneypiece leads
to the OCTAGON STAIR in the Beauchamp Tower, constructed
c.1876–81. Walls painted with foliage and roundels of Aesop
fables, 1884 by *Campbell*, recently refreshed. Heraldic lions on
the newel post have been painted out. The architecture here is
French Flamboyant. A marquess's coronet encircles the top of
the newel, and above it a thickly ribbed vault springs out.
Mouchette balustrade. Typically boyish Burges jokes in the
sculpture, at the top a crocodile about to eat a baby sliding
down the handrail, at the bottom a grey marble heraldic lion
wearing an outsize bronze visor. (Burges had seen one like it in
the Bargello in Florence.)

The foot of the Octagon Stair is a nodal point in the castle.
Three doors lead three ways. Over the r. door, to the Oratory,
a relief of an angel. Over the central door, to the library and
Lord Bute's business rooms, oddly, a lady. Over the l. door, to
the family apartments, children. Each door should be entered
in turn. The ORATORY, immediately S of the Octagon Stair,
is a tiny space, vaulted in two bays, a shrine to the memory of
Lord Bute's father, whom he never knew. Planned already
c.1869, under construction in 1873–4, dated on the door 1876.
Style early French Gothic. Black marble shafts with leaf caps
carry the vault ribs. Sculpture by *C. Fucigna*, wall-paintings by
N.H.J. Westlake, stained glass by *Lavers, Barraud & Westlake*,
1875, signed by *Westlake* as designer. Complex programme
commemorating a life cut short while celebrating faith in Resurrection. Under the altar a white marble effigy of the dead
Christ, with seated bronze soldiers asleep in front. Painting of
the Ascension above. In the apse facing the altar a white marble
bust of the second Marquess signed by *J. E. Thomas* and
inscribed at the back 'On this spot John Marquess of Bute fell
asleep and woke in eternity 1848.' In the windows, figures of
the four Evangelists. In the outer bay overpainted scenes of the
raising of Jairus's daughter and other Resurrection subjects.
The door is of bronze and bears a figure of the Virgin between
a Tree of Life and a tree severed by an axe. Grey marble dado
inlaid with shields of the Bute ancestry back to the C12. A
mosaic floor completes this dazzling and claustrophobic space.

The LIBRARY, across the passage from the Oratory, lies
under the Banqueting Hall, so is extremely large. It had to be,
to encompass all the interests of its polymath owner. On the
chimneypiece five seated figures are carved. Four represent
alphabets: Greek, Assyrian, Hebrew and Egyptian. The figure
on the r. is said to be Bute himself, as a Celtic scholar monk.
Over the pair of N doorways apes fighting over the Book of

Truth. – STAINED GLASS. Figures of prophets, apostles and kings. Cartoons prepared by *Campbell* and by *Philips,* 1874, glass made by *Saunders & Co.*, and completed after 1880 by *Worrall & Co.* – BOOKCASES. Some by *Gillow,* of walnut inset with marbles and tulipwood marquetry, some set against the walls, some standing as stalls at r.-angles to them. Two mighty DESKS, probably by *Thomas Walden,* fixed over metal heating grilles made by *Barkentin.*

A vaulted bay at the SW corner of the library leads to the bald ENTRANCE HALL, formed for the fourth Marquess *c.* 1930 (stained glass by *Paul Woodroffe*), and LORD BUTE'S STUDY, below the Arab Room in the Herbert Tower. This was designed at first for the librarian and not fitted up until *c.* 1884. Lierne rib-vault with foliage bosses and painted birds among fruiting branches. Overmantel with blind Dec tracery and painted parrots holding the initials of Bute's name in their beaks. Fussy wall-panelling probably designed by *Frame.* Best are the stained glass windows, illustrating the story of Hercules and the golden apples of the Hesperides, possibly by *Campbell, Smith & Co.* At the top of the Herbert Tower two rooms not shown to the public, the OFFICE of Lord Bute's secretary, G. E. Sneyd, with his arms and initials in a stained glass window, and the NOAH ROOM, timber-lined like a sauna and with a door opening on to the battlemented parapet.

The PRIVATE APARTMENTS are concentrated at the N end, in the Holland block and in the Bute Tower, but they include the Chaucer Room, at the top of the Beauchamp Tower. The DRAWING ROOM, N of the library, was barely touched by Burges, so that there should be somewhere, it was said, for the family to hang paintings. Just one characteristic Burges touch, the carving above the double doors into the Library, monkeys holding the 'fruits of learning'. Chimneypiece and extra plaster decoration added in the 1970s. The DINING ROOM, immediately to the W, in the Bute Tower, is a very different matter. Here is one of *Burges*'s most coherent schemes, designed in 100 1872, and illustrating the life of Abraham. The odd choice of subject is explained by the overmantel, boldly inscribed in Greek 'entertaining angels unawares'. So the theme is hospitality. On the fireplace hood three stately figures of angels and sprigs of oak leaves, for the tree under which Abraham was seated, and, on either side of the hood, Abraham, and his wife Sarah laughing behind her hand at the idea that she should bear a son in her old age (Genesis 18, vv. 1–15). The sculptor was *Thomas Nicholls.* In the windows STAINED GLASS of *c.* 1873 made by *Saunders and Co.* to *Lonsdale*'s cartoons, depicting other scenes from the life of Abraham. Oak panelling inset with glass backed with coloured tinsel. Window shutters carved and inlaid. The teenage *Goscombe John* worked on these, under his father, *Thomas John,* principal wood-carver. Massive ceiling with cylindrical beams, inspired by church roofs in Sicily. Painting here and on the chimneypiece by *Charles Campbell.*

On the floor above, Lord and Lady Bute's bedrooms. LADY

BUTE'S APARTMENT can be explored first. Her BEDROOM, above the drawing room, is quite plain, except for *Burges* panelling. Within it, her BATHROOM, with tiny stained glass roundels of noble women. Across a passage to the W, Lord Bute's Sitting Room, not his bedroom, which is one storey higher. Along the passage and up the stair, to the Chaucer Room. At the head of the STAIR, square marble pillars and four single-light windows, with glass panels, suitably coloured, of Undine, Gnome, Sylph and Salamander.

The CHAUCER ROOM, rising into the flèche at the top of the Beauchamp Tower, is one of the Castle's great set pieces. Octagonal, top-lit, its tiled floor patterned as a vine-leaf maze, it may stem from the library in the Castel S. Angelo in Rome, which Burges saw in 1877. The architecture has a Flamboyant flavour. Crocketed ogee arches span each wall-face. Above, timber vaulting on wall-shafts carries a balustraded gallery. Lantern crowned by a tiny rib-vault on slender timber piers. The Chaucerian decoration was conceived as far as possible to compliment Lady Bute, and was executed 1879–89. Walnut lower wall-panelling, with inlay of mother-of-pearl in the recessed panels. Veined marble chimneypiece, figures of ladies on the hood hanging a shield of arms on an oak tree. Under the wall-arches painted scenes from the *Legend of Good Women*, and carved arch corbels of the Good Women themselves. Under the balcony, larger fields for painting, filled with birds, lush foliage, and texts from Chaucer's *Parlement of Foules*. In the lantern, stained glass windows at two levels, the lower showing the Canterbury pilgrims convivially at table, the upper illustrating scenes from their tales. Other tiny Chaucerian subjects in the tracery heads. Stencilled timbers. The craftsmen of the Chaucer Room were *Thomas John*, joiner, *Thomas Nicholls*, carver, *Campbell & Smith*, painters, *Worrall & Co.*, stained glass makers, executing *Lonsdale*'s designs. Floor-tiles by *Simpson*, metalwork by *Hart, Son & Peard*.

LORD BUTE'S SITTING ROOM is above the dining room, the lowest of the three rooms in the Bute Tower still to be explored. Dated 1874 on the brass overmantel. Fragmented decorative programme. Legend of St Blane, patron saint of the Isle of Bute, in the frieze painted by *C. Rossiter*. On the door, said to have been painted by *Sir William Douglas*,★ the Seven Deadly Sins, outshone by Wisdom in a large roundel. Stained glass emblematic of the Four Seasons, designed by *Weekes* and made by *Saunders & Co*. On the lintel of the chimneypiece sculptured beavers.‡ The lower walls were intended for hangings. Heavily beamed ceiling as in the dining room below.

LORD BUTE'S BEDROOM, above his sitting room, 1874–6, is by contrast monumentally architectural and astonishingly

★Stylistically, Matthew Williams points out, this is indistinguishable from work by *Weekes*.

‡Why beavers? Another is in relief on the door, and yet another has been lost from the top of the fountain.

personal. First the architecture. Three trefoiled arches on each side, carried on slender piers. Ceiling of deep rectangular beams resting on massive corbels, which are themselves carried by circular shafts of green marble in front of the piers. The double-layered system absorbs windows and chimneypiece within its arcades. Now the occupant, John, Marquess of Bute. On the green marble chimneyhood, a gilt bronze statue of St John the Evangelist, his eagle poised above, gilt incised rays behind. In the stained glass, the Seven Churches of the Revelation of St John. Most insistent of all, the name John, in Greek letters, painted again and again, forwards and backwards, on the sides of the ceiling beams. The name is multiplied in reflection for anyone lying in bed below, in the mirrored underside of the ceiling panels. Plenty of heraldry too. Built-in wardrobe (dated 1877 and carved with clothes-moths) by the door to the BATH-ROOM. Segregating timber screen (dated 1875) pierced at the top *à la Turque*. Walnut panelling to the bathroom walls inset with charmingly labelled specimens of thirty-six different types of marble. Wash basin enamelled with a mermaid. The artists employed were *Fucigna* to model the figure sculpture, *Barkentin* to cast the St John, *Westlake* to design and *Lavers, Barraud & Westlake* to make the stained glass in the bedroom, and *Lonsdale* to design and *Saunders & Co.* to make the parrots in the bathroom.

A SPIRAL STAIR links all the rooms in the Bute Tower. At the top, a bronze fox on the newel. Domed vault with plants carved in the coffers and tree roots exposed below. Here is the bronze door (dated 1876) to the final paradise, the ROOF GARDEN.

The roof garden is conceived for southern Italy, not South Wales. Sunken, marble-lined, rectangular court. Surrounding mosaic-paved walks sheltered by tiled roofs carried on neo-Pompeian bronze colonnettes. Circular bronze fountain fitted with lobed basins, and carved with beavers. Bronze Virgin and Child, by *Fucigna*, at one end, Christianizing this sensuous retreat. On the walls, tile-paintings, designed by *Lonsdale* and made by *Simpson*. On the dado, animals and birds, in the fields between the sheltered windows, scenes from the Books of Kings, Elijah and the prophets of Baal etc., identified in Hebrew, a language which Lord Bute was learning in the mid 1870s. Marvellous views in all directions, Castell Coch plainly visible 7 m. (11.3 kilometres) to the N.

The archaeological investigations which led to the reconstruction of the ROMAN ENCLOSURE WALLS had begun before the death of the third Marquess. In 1899 the site of the Roman N gate was discovered. The fourth Marquess, however, decided to rebuild, with his architects, first *William Frame*, then *H. Sesom-Hiley* (1905–21), and then *J. P. Grant*. The SE, E and N walls were divested of their medieval superstructure. What was left of the grey Lias external facings of the Roman walls was exposed, outlined by a course of pink Radyr stone, and the upper parts

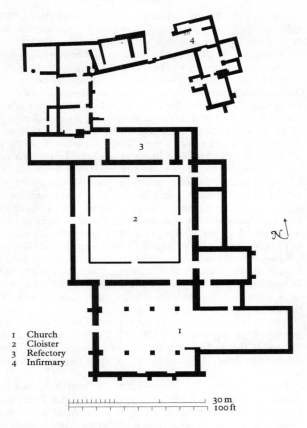

1 Church
2 Cloister
3 Refectory
4 Infirmary

30 m
100 ft

Cardiff, Blackfriars. Plan as excavated *c.* 1892

of the walls rebuilt, with their polygonal turrets, to more than
their former full height (*see* p. 195).

STABLES, ¼ m. N. Designed by *Burges* 1868–9, the N and E ranges
built 1874–5, the W and S ranges built in a simplified version
after 1928–9. The quadrangle is gabled externally, surrounded
inside by typical timber galleries. A picturesque pigeon tower
in the E range has been demolished. No evidence that the
fantastic design by Burges for the fountain in the centre of the
quadrangle was ever executed.

The site of the BLACKFRIARS, in COOPERS FIELDS, NW of the
castle, was excavated on the instructions of the third Marquess
c. 1892 by *Kempson & Fowler*. What can be seen today are the
consolidated walls, standing a few inches high and largely of
river pebbles, of the cloister and the infirmary range on its N
side. To the S a system of brick paths, as it seems, marks out
the plan of the church, which consisted of a narrow chancel,
and a four-bay aisled nave, probably curtailed from its original

six bays. Fragments of mouldings and window tracery found on site suggested that the church was built in the first half of the C14. – GRAVE SLAB commemorating John de Ecclescliffe, laid down by Lord Bute. The TILE PAVEMENT, by *Godwin* of Lugwardine, which surrounded it, reproducing tiles found in the excavation, has been almost entirely robbed away. Indeed, the whole site cries out to be properly cared for and made more explicit.

PUBLIC BUILDINGS

The buildings of the Civic Centre and the University in Cathays Park are described on pp. 222–37.

ST DAVID'S HALL, Working Street. Built 1978–82 as the National Concert Hall of Wales, by the *J. Seymour Harris Partnership* (job architect *Vernon Crofts*). Four-storey frontage angled at the S end to accommodate the entrance. The building frankly exposes its reinforced concrete skeleton, the uprights cantilevered out where the top two storeys jetty forward. Horizontal pre-cast concrete infill panels, varied in depth and coloured to imitate Bath stone. Windows, balconies and, at the top, service vents, all take their places within this grid. The entire concept is satisfyingly worked out, acknowledging in its colour and its upper overhang Edwin Seward's Free Library opposite (*see* below), without in any way imitating its forms. Unhappily oversized and ungainly roof, steep and metal-clad. The INTERIOR is prefaced by a complex full-height foyer, through which escalators and flights of stairs angle their way. Here, at level 3, the STUTTGART STAINED GLASS, 1984–5, designed by *Hans Gottfried von Stockhausen* of Stuttgart and made in Munich by the dozen craftsmen whose names are recorded in the bottom left-hand corner. This is a major work of painted rather than stained glass, an abstract design evocative of trees and mountains, loosely hung on a rectilinear armature.

The CONCERT HALL itself is an irregular octagon in plan, with thirteen blocks of seating cantilevered out at different angles and different rakes, bringing all 2,000 seats as close as possible to the action.

FREE LIBRARY (now Craft and Exhibition Centre), Trinity Street. *Edwin Seward*'s most important building and the best indication of what Cardiff architects could achieve at the end of the C19, before Londoners started to win all the competitions for the civic buildings in Cathays Park. A competition for a library and museum building held in 1880 was won by *James, Seward & Thomas*, and the first phase completed in 1882, with accommodation only for the library. From 1887 extension was under consideration, but it was not until 1893 that the design of what was to be no more than an extension to the library was settled. The extended building was opened in 1896.

The library is of two tall storeys. The first phase had elaborate Elizabethan-style façades of Bath stone to E and W, and more

utilitarian N and S frontages, faced mainly with yellow brick.
The whole building is not rectangular in plan but tapers from
N to S. The N front remains in its original condition, but all the
others have been altered or replaced by the later extension. The
widening of Working Street required a complete new E façade,
which is awkwardly planned so that it steps inwards four times
and fails to achieve the symmetry towards which it seems to
strive. The W façade consists of a N half of 1880–2 with an
inconspicuous entrance at its S end, and a S half with a strongly
emphasized entrance at its N end. Here too the problem of
enlargement was not fully resolved. The S front, entirely of
1893–6, is the shortest, but faces the open triangular space of
VICTORIA PLACE, and is the major architectural statement, a
design of real originality and weighty presence.

To go into more detail. The first phase of the W front has
low mullion-and-transom windows flanked by fluted pilaster
strips in which are inserted carved panels with boys in relief.
The upper windows are larger and more idiosyncratic, with
semicircular tops, and fanciful surrounds. The central one bows
out as an oriel. The later half of the W front continues the same
motifs, but the entrance doorway is flanked by seated female
figures representing Study and Rhetoric which carry the
massive door-hood, where there are smaller figures of a reader
and a scribe. Here and elsewhere on this and the S façades are
carved the emblems of famous early printers, Caxton, Wynkyn
de Worde, Aldine, Plantin and others. The carver was
W. Taylor of *William Clarke* of Llandaff. On the E front five
upper oriel windows, one in each section.

Now for the S front. Three broad bays. Here only are columns
employed, pseudo-Doric ones with fluted capitals, their plain
white shafts of Portland stone contrasting with the buff Bath
stone. The ground storey is articulated by fluted pilasters,
with full-width glazing between them. The over-emphasized
transoms which are an idiosyncracy of the other façades are
here used to tie the composition strongly together. Deep attic
with reliefs in panels of yellow Ham Hill stone. Central upper
relief crowned by scrolls enclosing a big bust of Minerva.

The INTERIOR consists of a series of large reading rooms at
both levels. Decoration is concentrated on the vaulted entrance
corridor constructed in 1882 across the width of the building.
This is faced with polychrome encaustic and majolica TILES
by *Maw & Co.* The pilaster panels of the Seasons and figures
of Morning and Evening were designed by *Walter Crane*. Of
the STAINED GLASS by *Frederick Weekes* installed in 1882, only
a few panels survive *ex situ*.

CENTRAL LIBRARY, Bridge Street. Opened in 1988. At the S
end of the St David's Centre and picking up the materials and
some of the idiom of St David's Hall (*see* above). Polygonal
entrance vestibule. The library occupies only the upper storeys
above two levels used for commercial purposes. Altogether a
building of compromises. The architects were *Shingler Risdon
Associates*.

CENTRAL RAILWAY STATION. Built 1932–4 by the *Great Western Railway's Architects Department*, quite an ambitious ensemble, which survives remarkably complete. Eleven-bay booking hall of Portland stone with a central clock cupola. Six single-storey platform blocks faced with cream-glazed Doulton Carrara-ware. Mullioned windows. Three island platforms in stone with canopies supported by cast iron Tuscan columns and corbels on the station buildings.

EMPIRE SWIMMING POOL, Wood Street. 1956–8, by *E. C. Roberts*, the City Engineer, with, from early 1957, *John Dryburgh*, the newly appointed City Architect. Brown brick. Glazed entrance with thin concrete verticals, an echo of a portico. Festival of Britain mood inside.

WELSH RUGBY UNION NATIONAL STADIUM, Cardiff Arms Park, Westgate Street. A huge stadium, with seating and standing room for up to 50,000 spectators, under canopies carried on angular, predatory-looking concrete supports. The architects were *Osborne V. Webb & Partners* of Cardiff (design partner *Ted Williams*), the structural engineers *G. A. Williamson & Partners* and *James & Nicholas*. The N stand was built 1968–71, the W terrace 1977–8, and the S stand 1982–3.

PERAMBULATIONS

1. The Old Town West and South of St John the Baptist church

CHURCH STREET runs W from the tower of the church into what has from the mid C19 been the principal commercial street in Cardiff. This is to the N called High Street, to the S, ST MARY STREET. Turning S, one sees at once on the r. the NATIONAL WESTMINSTER BANK, 1857 by *Thomas Lysaght*. Typical of its date. Five-bay palazzo front, the arches of the ground storey and the angle quoins given heavy vermiculation, and the arches splendid bearded heads for keystones. To the r. a new entrance in a narrow Brutalist addition, emphatic indeed, yet in its utter contrast not detracting from its neighbour. 1978 by *Holder & Mathias*. Next a real monster, HODGE HOUSE, built for the Co-operative Wholesale Society and dated 1915. Eleven bays, six storeys, Portland stone, in a classical style with French details, derived, not quite convincingly, from the Edwardian buildings of Regent Street in London. It occupies the site of the Victorian Town Hall (1847–53 by *Sir Horace Jones*). Facing it, the equally monstrous, and stylistically much looser façade of MARKET BUILDINGS, dated 1886 on the yawning entrance arch, where the name of the contractor is inscribed, *S. Andrews & Son* (i.e. Solomon Andrews, who was also the entrepreneur), but not the name of the architect, who was *J. P. Jones*. The MARKET itself, 1886–91 by *W. Harpur*, the Borough Engineer, is a period piece. Glazed roof on iron trusses sparingly decorated. Ironwork by *Andrew Handyside & Co.* of Derby. Galleries all round for lock-up shops. The floor space devoted to stalls. Next door in St Mary Street the exceedingly

tall, narrow and richly decorated frontage of the BOROUGH
ARMS public house, 1891 by *J. P. Jones*. Next again, the most
expansive commercial premises in the street, of JAMES
HOWELL & CO., drapers. The shop is in two parts, the larger
and more northerly by *W. D. Blessley*, 1895–6. Twelve bays,
four storeys. This is in a flaccid Renaissance style, chiefly
remarkable for its survival unaltered, the lower two storeys
extensively glazed between slender, decorative pilasters. The
later part is completely different, added 1928–30 by *Sir Percy
Thomas*. This is a brilliant exposition of American Beaux-Arts
classicism. Just three wide bays, but made monumental by the
Erechtheum Ionic columns and memorable by its rounded
corners with well-placed relief sculpture, designed by *Thomas*
to symbolize the drapery business. Addition at the rear towards
Wharton Street, of *c.* 1965, absorbing, bizarrely, *J. Hartland &
Son*'s Bethany Baptist Chapel of 1864–5. Its cast iron arcades
remain visible within the shop. On the w side of St Mary Street
nothing much, though the narrow, red terracotta frontage of
No. 109 is by *Alfred Waterhouse* for the Prudential Assurance
Company, 1890–1. Like a small fragment of their headquarters
building in High Holborn, London. The much larger and
equally red Nos. 102–107 were built at the same time, as the
Queen's Hotel, to *J. P. Jones*'s design.

A little way further s on the e side, the façade of MORGAN'S
ARCADE, dated 1896 and designed in a fussy Jacobean classical
style by *Edwin Seward*. The arcade itself has a curved glazed
roof and upper oriels. It starts straight, then divides and
becomes very winding, before debouching into The Hayes (*see*
below). Just beyond, Nos. 38–39, the frontage to the earliest of
the arcades, ROYAL ARCADE, by *James & Price*, 1858. In the
Nash villa style, with twin pedimental gables. On the w side,
the ROYAL HOTEL, 1864–6 by *C. E. Bernard*. The earliest
building in the street of truly Victorian scale. Nine bays
plus one. Four storeys, each differently fenestrated. Grey and
pink render, to echo Venetian marble veneers. Boldly higher s
extension, curving round the corner into WOOD STREET. 1890
by *J. P. Jones*. Channelled Bath stone. Stout columns of pink
Aberdeen granite at eye level on both frontages. Inside, the
florid staircase, rising in one flight and returning in two, was
inserted in 1901 by *R. A. Briggs*.

Facing the flank of the Royal Hotel, on the s side of WOOD
STREET, the North Italian Gothic façade of the PRINCE OF
WALES THEATRE, now an amusement arcade and somewhat
neglected, the central pair of windows boarded over. Rich stiff-
leaf in their spandrels, a whorl in the centre. Empty niches high
up l. and r. 1878 by *W. D. Blessley & T. Waring*. Utilitarian
contemporary frontage of the theatre facing St Mary Street,
interrupted by a later narrow entrance bay, surmounted by a
Grecian female between giant Doric columns. This must
belong with the internal redecoration of 1920 by *Willmott &
Smith*. The front of the PHILHARMONIC HALL (now Bingo
Hall) comes next, a tired piece of classicism dated 1876. Yellow

brick with, it seems, Caen stone dressings. Inside, the music hall refitted by *James & Morgan* in 1887 survives. The adjoining display windows of THE PHILHARMONIC, plate glass and brasswork, also deserve to survive. Gothic frontage above, and next door, No. 75, now Ristorante Il Padrino, a narrow but richly decorative Gothic affair of 1886, crowned by three diapered and crocketed gables. Unusual polychromy, with orange ironstone colonnettes. Finally, after a gap, the much more extensive Gothic showpiece, GREAT WESTERN HOTEL, curves round the corner. 1875 by *W. D. Blessley*. Clearly intended to impress the visitor arriving in Cardiff from the railway station. The walls are faced with crazy-paving stonework in which local pink Radyr stone predominates. Bath stone dressings. Three-storeyed, the windows plate-traceried at all levels, those at the bottom under straight-sided hoods, those at the top under straight-sided gables. On the corner, triple entrance flanked by corbelled-out cylindrical pinnacles (missing their caps) and crowned by an undersized pyramid-roofed clock tower. The street is closed by the bronze STATUE of the second Marquess of Bute, 1849–53 by *John Evan Thomas*.

For historical completeness, it is necessary to cross the road junction, pass under the railway and look at the former CUSTOM HOUSE in East Canal Wharf. This is the most visible reminder of the Glamorganshire Canal, constructed 1791–4 from Merthyr Tydfil to Cardiff Bay for the purpose of exporting iron. After skirting Cardiff town, the canal straightened out to continue the line of St Mary Street to the S. The Custom House stands immediately E of the canal, which has long been filled in. The present building dates from *c.* 1845, a simple classical block of five bays and two storeys, rendered, the details somewhat debased. Smoothly rusticated lower storey, even angle quoins above. Broken segmental door-hood on coupled brackets, upper window surrounds bulging up at the top with skied keystones. Rear extensions of 1865 and of 1983–5 by *Lock-Necrews, Hill & Partners*.

It is now necessary to retrace one's steps as far as Wood Street and fork l. into WESTGATE STREET. At once on the l., in HAVELOCK STREET, THOMSON HOUSE, the offices of the *Western Mail*, 1957–61, by *Ellis, Clarke & Gallanaugh*. This is a typical curtain-wall piece, three-storeyed, its long NE entrance front remodelled in 1992 but preserving at its N end an attractively coloured, full-height MOSAIC, signed by *Ray Howard-Jones* and dated 1959. Semi-abstract, but emblematic, it seems, of the coverage of the newspaper. The S end of Westgate Street itself is dominated by the former POST OFFICE, *c.* 1894–7 by the *Office of Works*, whose chief architect was *Henry Tanner*. Portland stone, the first large-scale use in Cardiff of a facing material which was soon to become *de rigueur* in Cathays Park. Classical, but unmonumental. Crowned by elaborate pedimented gables and steep roofs. Extended in Park Street in the same style in 1907. Its neighbour to the N, the former COUNTY COURT OFFICES, is another piece of official architecture, also faced with Portland stone, and dated 1904. Much smaller than its neighbour, but echoing it with its steep roof and miniature cupola. The classical idiom handled with enjoyment. Five bays, entrances in the end bays and, high above them, balconies under open segmental pediments on fancy columns. Next on the w side, the former COUNTY CLUB, *c.* 1890 by *E.W.M. Corbett* in a Queen Anne style. Then JACKSON HALL, built as a covered racquets court in 1878 by *G. E. Robinson*. A piece of High Victorian Gothic polychromy. Bright red brick dominates, laid partly in herringbone pattern. Also black brick and Bath stone. Peculiar roof like a Swiss chalet, twin timber arches under the gable end, all carried on a slender circular brick pier. Clearly under the influence of Prichard (cf. The Rest, Porthcawl). Modern glazing. Then, before the wrought iron gates to Cardiff Arms Park, GOVERNMENT OFFICES of 1950, still in a Lutyenesque Neo-Georgian. The w side of the street is terminated by CASTLE COURT, also Neo-Georgian, a range of mansion flats built *c.* 1937, red brick with Portland stone trim and an Ionic columned porch for each of its seven parts.

As one turns r. into CASTLE STREET, the great enclosure wall and Burges's soaring Clock Tower of Cardiff Castle come into view. On the s side of the street, the ANGEL HOTEL, *c.* 1890, probably by *W. Frame*, and several plain C18 houses. At the far end of the block the most impressive Neoclassical frontage in Cardiff, worthy of Henry Holland, who worked on the Castle in the 1780s. Two-storey rendered façade with, to the l., a wide end bay displaying a handsome upper Venetian window under a shallow full-height relieving arch, and a five-bay centre with paired blind arches l. and r. of a full-height arch, and square upper windows. No mouldings at all. The r. bay of the composition is unfortunately not there. In its stead, the fancifully gabled front of CASTLE ARCADE of 1887. Internally, Castle Arcade is one of the most enjoyable in Cardiff, three-storeyed for much of its length, with mid-height walkways linked by footbridges and continuous jettied top storeys under the curved glazed roof. A sharp turn halfway along brings it out into the High Street. Beyond High Street, where Castle Street changes its name to DUKE STREET, nothing except the three-arched façade of DUKE STREET ARCADE, dated 1902, and faced with grey-brown Forest of Dean ashlar. The row of colonnettes at the top stage is typical of the date. The architects were *Ware & Williams*.

HIGH STREET itself runs s and soon joins St Mary Street. No. 5, on the e side, is exceptionally early, built as the National Provincial Bank in 1835. Only the upper part survives, ashlar-faced, five bays, the centre three with an attached Ionic portico of two columns between two antae. LLOYDS BANK, No. 27, on the w side, also displays an order, of Corinthian pilasters rising through two storeys over an arcaded ground floor. This civilized piece dates from 1892 and was designed by *J. A. Chatwin* of Birmingham. Nearly opposite comes the wildly eclectic façade of HIGH STREET ARCADE, 1885 by *T. Waring*

& Son with *J. P. Jones*. The arcade itself turns through a
r.-angle and links up with the Duke Street Arcade.

With that the return to Church Street has been achieved.

2. The Old Town East of St John the Baptist church

To the S of the church lies a triangular space, with WORKING
STREET on its E side and TRINITY STREET on its W side.
QUEEN'S ARCADE, 1992–4 by the *Taylor Group*, bows back
in an extravagant concave sweep at the E end of the church.
Two flights of steps to the upper level. Ripple-pattern pavement
right across the space in front. Next to the S, ST DAVID'S
HALL (*see* p. 211). In TRINITY STREET the sober three-arched
front of *W. Harpur*'s MARKET, dated 1891. Yellow brick,
framed by pediments on Tuscan pilasters, of grey Forest of
Dean ashlar. The contrast with the market's frontage to St
Mary Street (*see* p. 213) could not be more extreme.

To the S of the former Free Library (*see* Public Buildings) the
space widens out in THE HAYES. The presiding bronze
STATUE is of the Liberal politician and industrialist John Batchelor, 'The Friend of Freedom', 1885 by *James Milo ap Griffith*.
The W side of The Hayes is fully occupied by the three parts
of DAVID MORGAN'S SHOP. The central part dated 1899
relates to Morgan's Arcade (*see* St Mary Street, p. 214) and so
is presumably by *Seward*. The addition to the l., by *James &
Morgan*, is dated 1904, that to the r., 1912. All different but all
equally fussy. Opposite, in stark contrast, the ELECTRICITY
SHOWROOMS, austere, stone-faced Neo-Georgian of 1936–7,
by *Sir Percy Thomas* (a remodelling of the Fish Market of 1901),
and the OXFORD ARCADE, a curtain-wall affair of the 1950s,
with canopies added in the 1980s by *The Wigley Fox Partnership*.

From this point one may turn E-wards into BRIDGE STREET,
and from there take the first turn l., by the Central Library,
into the St David's Centre (*see* p. 219 below); or the second
turn l. into Charles Street, to see St David's R. C. Cathedral
and the Ebeneser Chapel; or pursue the full length of the street
to the crossroads at the foot of CHURCHILL WAY to see two
impressive former chapels (for all these, *see* above, Churches
and Chapels). The W side of Churchill Way is lined with
Gothic villa pairs, of, perhaps, the 1860s. Over them looms
CHURCHILL HOUSE, a ten-storey office block by *Alex
Gordon & Partners*, completed in 1968. To the N Churchill Way
joins QUEEN STREET, now pedestrianized and the city's major
shopping street. Here, at the E end on the S side CAPITOL
SHOPPING CENTRE, a gimmicky display of 1980s polychromy
by *T. P. Bennett*. The main external accents are the polygonal
glazed projections at points of entry. Opposite, WINDSOR
PLACE runs N from Queen Street. This deserves a detour, both
for the City United Reformed Church (*see* p. 192) and for the
most complete C19 terraces to survive in Cardiff. These are still
Georgian in character, of red brick with rendered details, but
were built in the 1850s. The architect was probably *Alexander*

Roos, architect to the ground landlords, the Bute Estate. Back in Queen Street, the next block to the w, extending to the corner of Park Place, is the PARK HOTEL, completed in 1884 by *Habershon & Fawckner* at the then gigantic cost of £40,000, and originally consisting of two public halls, a hotel, ten shops and a coffee tavern. The ponderous mass is in what would have been called a Mixed Renaissance style, with the pavilion roofs approved for hotels from the 1860s. Ground storey faced with grey Forest of Dean stone ashlar, buff Bath stone ashlar above, with piers of rock-faced Pennant, an odd effect.

In PARK PLACE, on the w side, Dylan's Rock Café, built as the SOUTH WALES INSTITUTE OF ENGINEERS in 1893, to the design of *E. W. M. Corbett*, and extended in 1907 with a large library wing facing Greyfriars Road. The reddest of red brick and terracotta. Queen Anne style, with much decoration. (Burnt out 1994. This lively building surely deserves to be reconstructed.) The NEW THEATRE is the next building to the N in Park Place. 1905–6 by the London firm of *Runtz & Ford*. Arts and Crafts Baroque, telling in its interplay between plain brick walling and densely modelled forms. On the angle facing down Park Place, the curved entrance bay has an upper Ionic colonnade *in antis* between octagonal turrets, a simplified repetition of the architects' recent Gaiety Theatre, London. (The interior of the theatre, which is also dominated by Ionic columns, was restored in 1987–8 by the *Renton, Howard, Wood, Levin Partnership*, the foyer enlarged and a full-height oval stair constructed within the bow.) Across the road, Nos. 3–11 are lofty Gothic VILLAS, four pairs and a singleton, built 1875–6 by *W. D. Blessley*, and well restored 1987–9 by *The Wigley Fox Partnership*. They are five-storeyed from semi-basement to attic, and the main fenestration is gathered into full-height canted bays. Changes are rung on the details of porches and window bays from pair to pair, but all share an essentially C13 vocabulary and the materials: hammer-dressed Pennant stone from Pwllypant and Bath stone dressings. N of these, BRADLEY COURT, a crudely simplified imitation in brown brick and reconstituted stone, also by *The Wigley Fox Partnership*. Here the racetrack STUTTGARTER STRASSE cuts across, changing its name, as it swings to the s, to DUMFRIES PLACE, lined with further examples of the idiom of the 1980s. HAYWOOD HOUSE, hard up against the w side of Dumfries Place, is again by *The Wigley Fox Partnership*. Vertically parti-coloured in red and yellow brick. Three storeys of windows gathered into long, thin vertical panels with rounded tops.

PARK PLACE, N of Stuttgarter Strasse, faces Cathays Park. On this favoured stretch the earliest houses were built, Nos. 16–19 and 21–28, six stuccoed villa pairs, dating from the late 1850s or 1860s, sub-classical, sub-Italianate and one cottage orné with bargeboards. No. 20, PARK HOUSE, is completely differ-ent. 1871–5 by *William Burges*, for James McConnochie, dock engineer to the Bute Trustees. This is the house which, by its powerful early French Gothic style, its steep roofs and boldly textured walls, revolutionized Cardiff's domestic architecture. Snecked rock-faced Pennant sandstone with dressings of Bath stone and shafts of pink polished granite. Front towards the road of three bays lying back behind an arcaded loggia and two bays coming forwards under a steep gable. The distinction between the two parts maintained from basement to roof, except at first-floor level, where the solid parapet over the loggia is carried unbroken as a band across the full width of the façade, and the 3+2 windows are all identical colonnetted two-lighters under big tympana enclosing hexfoils. Mullion-and-transom ground-floor windows of three-by-three lights with trefoiled heads. The house is entered at the side up steps under a lean-to ashlar porch with arches on circular shafts. Foliage carved on the front pair of caps only. The side elevations are double-gabled, the gables crowned by three slab-like, bull-nosed chimneystacks. Stackless fourth gable, over the porch, pierced by a mighty plate-traceried window. This clearly lights the staircase, and anticipates the major peculiarity of the interior. On entering, one is immediately confronted by the underside of the staircase, and has to skirt round it in order to reach the rest of the house. Broad, straight flights, up in one and back in two. Pointed tunnel-vault high up. Mahogany balustrade of colonnettes with shaft-rings. This is the pompous route to nothing more than a modest suite of bedrooms. Downstairs, the DRAWING ROOM, behind the loggia, and the DINING ROOM with its ANTE-ROOM. Both have heavily beamed ceilings, the semi-cylindrical beams set on stone corbels, and arched, grey-and-white marble chimneypieces under mahogany overmantels with colonnettes and mirrors. The interior was not fitted up until 1880, the year when McConnochie was mayor of Cardiff. At the back, steel staircase enclosed in glass, a bluntly differentiated addition of 1990 by *Hoggett, Lock-Necrews*, who also built the block of flats behind.

Further N, three post-Burges Gothic pairs of the 1870s. Nos. 29–30 are of red brick with rubbed-brick tympana over the first-floor windows and bargeboards (an old-fashioned touch) to gables and dormers. Nos. 31–32 mix a dash of red brick with the blue-grey Pennant sandstone and buff Bath ashlar of the window bays. Columned porches open into bowed staircase bays to l. and r. Nos. 33–34, on the corner of MUSEUM PLACE, are unusually tall, and asymmetrical. Multicoloured stonework. Burges-like N porch.

Back in Queen Street there is still more to note. The four-storey double front of W.H. SMITH, facing down Charles Street, is dated 1885. It has lost many colonnettes, but not the multitude of keystones and corbels in the form of human heads. The entrance to the ST DAVID'S CENTRE comes next on the s side. 1979–82 by the *J. Seymour Harris Partnership*. Taking their cue from Cardiff's late C19 arcades, the architects retained the existing pattern of streets as top-lit walks. The entrance from Queen Street (like those from other streets) is signalled by a green-framed, triangular, glazed canopy. Plenty of internal variety in height, lighting and surfaces, terrazzo paving, marble-banded plant containers, and even the cream and acidic green superstructure more substantial than in most shopping centres. Dangling evergreens everywhere.

The most interesting remaining buildings in Queen Street are also on the s side. First comes the MIDLAND BANK, a three-bay pavilion of exceeding monumentality, 1919 by *Woolfall & Eccles* of Liverpool. Giant Ionic columns between angle piers. The expansive windows have recently been lowered. Then a complete contrast, the broad, bland, 1950s façade of BOOTS, and two of its immediate neighbours. A narrow concrete border frames a rectangle glazed by a slit window at the top, the l. two-thirds of the rest given up to a splendid Festival of Britain style design dominated by a 20-ft (6.1-metre)-high Welsh dragon rampant in red and white. Signed by *J. P.* The QUEEN'S ARCADE, 1992–4 by the *Taylor Group* (*see* p. 217), forms a broad concavity in the street frontage.

Nos. 24–26, immediately beyond this, is the oldest, most memorable and apparently incongruous façade in the whole street, *C. E. Bernard*'s Venetian Gothic apparition, built in 1878 as a block of chambers. The details – balconied windows in ones and twos, their trefoiled or ogee heads carried on spiral shafts with leaf capitals, the top cornice with pierced pinnacles – are all of scholarly accuracy. Even the white Portland stone will pass well enough, now it has been cleaned, for the Istrian stone of Venice. Doubtless the architect was under Ruskin's spell, but he had more justification than now appears, for at that time the Glamorganshire Canal passed under Queen Street near this point. Reconstructed central upper window bay of 1985 and ground storey of 1992–3. And so to the end of the street, with its STATUE of Aneurin Bevan, in an aggressive if uneasy stance. 1987, by *Robert Thomas* of Barry.

Before completing the circuit back to St John's church by way of St John's Street, one may turn to the r. into KINGSWAY, where two buildings cry out for attention. First is the egregious BANK OF WALES, dated 1989, by *Powell Dobson & Partners*, juxtaposing pilotis, full-height glazed stairwell and top pediment without regard for scale or coherence. Behind this, in GREYFRIARS ROAD, looms Cardiff's tallest building, the offices of PEARL ASSURANCE. This is by a London firm, *Sir John Burnet & Partners*, 1969–70. Twenty-five storeys high, its bulk mitigated by chamfered angles, and made almost acceptable by well-judged proportions.

CATHAYS PARK*

In Cathays Park Cardiff has the finest civic centre in the British Isles. A series of monumental buildings, some of them noble pieces of architecture, are spaciously stationed where each can be

*For map *see* pp. 188–9.

appreciated for itself, but where the coherence and splendour of the whole group adds lustre to each individual element. It is worth asking how much part planning has played in this outcome and how much good fortune.

The site, a roughly rectangular piece of ground 59 acres (24 hectares) in extent, was the s w tip of the Cathays Estate acquired by the second Marquess of Bute after 1832. It was separated from the Castle grounds by the Glamorganshire Canal, and as early as the 1850s it was suggested that the town should acquire it for a public park. Further schemes, in the 1870s, the late 1880s and early 1890s, all came to nothing. In the end it was the need to rebuild the Town Hall in St Mary Street on a larger scale which steeled the Council to find the money to acquire Cathays Park, and in 1898 it paid the third Marquess the sum of £160,000 for the entire 59 acres.

There is nothing especially imaginative about the layout of the Park, which was put in the hands of the Borough Engineer, *William Harpur*. Two broad, straight N–S roads, King Edward VII Avenue and Museum Avenue, and two narrow nameless E– W roads subdivide the w two-thirds of the site into six unequal plots. On the E third, which tapered to N and s, this grid was not imposed. The central rectangle has remained open, as ALEX-ANDRA GARDENS, but all the surrounding plots have been built on. At the N end, the pre-existing CORBETT ROAD trimmed the site off neatly, but to the s there remained an irregular area beyond the dock feeder canal, which was laid out as a public garden under the name of GORSEDD GARDENS and populated with statues. The traffic that swings across to the s of Gorsedd Gardens along the BOULEVARD DE NANTES, cutting Cathays Park off from the city centre all too effectively, enhances its precinct-like character.

The major early buildings are all the products of competitions, open to all-comers, not limited to local architects, as Cardiff's earlier architectural competitions had normally been. The success of the first competition, for the Town Hall and Law Courts, in producing a really fine winning design which could be executed without major modification, must have boosted morale. These buildings established two important precedents. The first of these was the use of Portland stone as the facing material, a stone which had been very little used in Cardiff up to that date and which more than anything else defines the unity of Cathays Park, since even the buildings of the 1960s and '70s are faced with it. Sec-ondly, all the major early buildings respected the cornice line of the Town Hall and Law Courts. In this, however, the most recent buildings have not been so deferential. Finally, there is the matter of style. The wholehearted and convincing classicism of *Lan-chester, Stewart & Rickards*'s winning design for the Town Hall and Law Courts ensured that only pure classical designs would be acceptable subsequently. The assumption held to the end of the 1930s, but the buildings which went up from 1958 onwards are all in a modern style, making in some cases slight, in others no concessions to classical preconceptions. It is a telling polarization,

which remains today in all its sharpness, since after 1972 no
further sites remained to be built on.

CITY HALL AND LAW COURTS

Lanchester, Stewart & Rickards won the double-barrelled competition in 1897 for a Town Hall (Cardiff was not raised to the
status of a city until 1905) and Law Courts to be erected in the
prime positions at the s end of Cathays Park. The adjudicator
was Alfred Waterhouse, who must have appreciated the lucidity
and panache of their plan. But it is the swaggering Baroque
style of the buildings, erected 1901–5, with slight but significant
improvements to the winning design, which has established their
reputation as setting a new standard in the emergence of the
Edwardian grand style for public buildings in Britain. No Victorian architect had hitherto demonstrated such mastery of Continental Baroque, in this case specifically the Baroque of South
Germany and Austria, combined with the neo-Baroque of Charles
Garnier's Paris Opéra. (Belcher's Colchester Town Hall design
came one year later, in 1898.) So their design had the lustre
of novelty, burnished brighter by complete self-confidence in
handling. Yet if the vocabulary is European, the composition of
the City Hall is unmistakably English, an echo of the Thames
front of the Houses of Parliament in the way a symmetrical body
is combined with a strongly off-centre tower. The tower plays an
important role in linking the two buildings, since it stands over
the side entrance to the City Hall and is aligned on the axis of the
portico of the Law Courts; though it must be admitted that this
relationship is easier to grasp from a plan than on the ground.
The other, much more obvious, way in which the buildings are
made to appear two parts of a whole is in the similarities in their
s fronts. The main features are a bulging, banded plinth, broad
areas of channelling at angles and breaks, long, round-headed
lower windows set in concave surrounds, square-headed upper
windows with aprons, and at the outer ends of each façade, three-
bay canted projections. The fenestration continues unchanged in
the projections, but they support high, rectangular attics lit by
Diocletian windows, against which expansive figural groups are
seated. What makes the façades look quite different from one
another is the contrast between the unemphasized centre of the
Law Courts and the prodigious centrepiece of the City Hall.

109 The CITY HALL must now be considered individually. The
central five bays of the s front are set strongly forward, crowned
by a square attic with chamfered corners, a ribbed lead-covered
dome and a richly modelled lantern over which rears a snarling
Welsh dragon, by *H. C. Fehr*. Large, round-headed central
window, inscribed VILLA CARDIFF. All this relates to the
domed Council Chamber which is thus given symbolic pro-
minence. Below, a small but profusely decorated porte-cochère
juts out, with military trophies and lion masks, by *Paul Montford*, over the basket-arched carriage entrances, conventional if
inappropriate symbolism for the entrance to a seat of civil

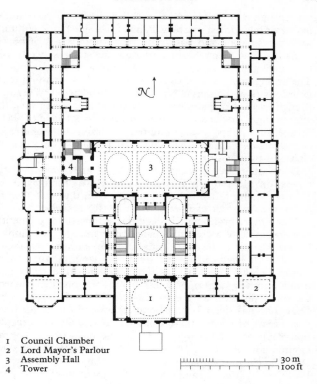

1 Council Chamber
2 Lord Mayor's Parlour
3 Assembly Hall
4 Tower

|⌐⌐⌐⌐⌐⌐⌐⌐⌐⌐⌐⌐⌐⌐⌐⌐⌐⌐⌐⌐⌐⌐⌐| 30 m
|⌐⌐⌐⌐⌐⌐⌐⌐⌐⌐⌐⌐⌐⌐⌐⌐⌐⌐⌐⌐⌐⌐⌐| 100 ft

Cardiff, City Hall.
Competition-winning plan at upper level

government. This brings us to the sculpture, so important in
the conception of the building, and, as the bold identifying
inscriptions show, meant to be registered. On the drum of the
dome, masking the windows there, maritime groups, nereids,
by *Henry Poole*, Neptune and tritons, by *F. W. Pomeroy*. The
main groups, against the attics at the ends of the façade, are,
on the SW attic Welsh Music and Poetry by *Paul Montford*,
designed as early as 1903, on the SE attic Welsh Unity and
Patriotism by *Henry Poole*. On the many-tiered heights of the
clock tower further figures, large seated ones below, smaller
standing ones above, by *Albert Hodge*. Stone pedestals in front
of the building carrying stone obelisks with bronze prows and
sterns of antique ships, i.e. rostral obelisks. Intended for lamps.

After all this the INTERIOR is yet more exhilarating, a
sequence of brilliantly managed spatial contrasts. The deep,
oblong entrance hall is opened up at the sides by square piers,
between which twin staircases with dense bronze balustrades
ascend to l. and r. Each goes up in a short straight flight, to a
broad landing, which extends N-wards to a mezzanine, but
from which a much longer flight of steps rises S-wards, leading

up through a crowd of white marble statues to a vast landing paved with coloured marbles. Pairs of massive Doric columns, with bronze caps and bases and monolithic shafts of heavily veined, yellow Siena marble, separate the staircase wells from the landing. Side lighting from tall, round-headed windows. The arrangement and its dramatic effect owe something to the grand stairs at Balthasar Neumann's Residenz at Würzburg, though instead of paintings by Tiepolo, the ceiling has, disappointingly, no decoration at all except a broad band of plaster foliage. End doorways surmounted by plaster shells and reliefs of mermaids and mermen, by *Henry Poole*. The STAINED GLASS is by *A. Garth Jones*.

On the staircases, at mezzanine level, bronze commemorative reliefs, on the E to Sir Edward James Reed, 1909 by *George Frampton*, with a fine half-length figure, on the W to Captain Scott, the Antarctic explorer, †1912, by *W. Wheatley Wagstaff*.

Much more prominent, indeed the unforgettable element of this ensemble of architecture and sculpture, are the standing, life-size figures at the stair-heads, and the dramatically isolated figure of St David in the centre of the landing, 1917 by *W. Goscombe John*. The pedestals and niches are part of the original design, but the statues, of Welsh heroes and one heroine from the C1 to the C19, were commissioned only after 1912, when D. A. Thomas (later Lord Rhondda) offered to pay for them. *James Havard Thomas* masterminded the scheme and executed the group of Boadicea, 1913–16, at the head of the W stair. Companion group of Howell the Good, by *F. W. Pomeroy*, 1916. Single figures flanking the stair, Dafydd ap Gwilym by *W. Wheatley Wagstaff* and Giraldus Cambrensis by *Henry Poole*, 1916. In the niche over the stairwell, Bishop Morgan by *T. J. Clapperton*, who had been a pupil of Goscombe John. At the head of the E stair the groups represent Llewellyn the last Prince, by *Henry Pegram*, and Henry VII, the first Tudor King of England, 1918 by *E. G. Gillick*. The single free-standing figures on this side are Owain Glydŵr by *Alfred Turner* and Sir Thomas Picton by *T. Mewburn Crook*, both dated 1916. The figure of the preacher Williams Pantycelyn is by another of Goscombe John's former pupils, *L. S. Merrifield*, 1916.

To the S a door opens directly into the circular COUNCIL CHAMBER. This is not Baroque but Bramantesque. Four broad, diagonally set piers carry spandrels pierced by bullseye windows, and a coffered dome above. Arches between the piers on three sides, their recessed heads filled in above the oddly detailed entablature, which runs right round the room and is carried within the arches by pairs of Ionic columns. The mottled marble of their shafts and bronze, swagged capitals revive the Baroque character, as do the plaster palm-fronds by *G. P. Bankart* round the spandrel windows. – STAINED GLASS in the great S window, a Michelangelesque personification of Villa Cardiff, dated 1905, by *A. Garth Jones*. – FURNITURE. The original circular scheme of seating survives intact, if overlaid with wires and video screens. – ELECTROLIERS. Wall-

brackets and a vast central pendant designed by *Rickards*.
Committee rooms along the corridor to l. and r., at the SW
angle LORD MAYOR'S PARLOUR, at the SE angle MEMBERS'
ROOM, exploiting the extra height in the attics at the angles.
Arched recesses and circular clerestory windows.

To the N of the central landing the climactic interior space,
the ASSEMBLY HALL. This has a semicircular tunnel-vault   110
subdivided into three bays by broad transverse bands. Semicircular penetrations into the vault for clerestory windows. The
side walls are low in relation to the span of the vault. Against
them stand Ionic columns set obliquely to carry the huge
diagonal scrolls which flank the windows. The bands, the
scrolls, cartouches and so on, all lavishly enriched with plaster
decoration by *Bankart*. These reinforce the architectural mem-
bering, not concealing or subverting it in the way of plasterwork
in the early C18 Austrian and South German churches which
must otherwise be the starting point for the design. Disastrous
recent painting of the black marble column shafts, in a vain
attempt to match the yellow marble on the landing. Three
bronze electroliers, identical with that in the Council Chamber.

LAW COURTS. 1901–4. The E entrance front faces the side of
the City Hall. This plays intriguing variations on the themes
established on the S fronts of the two buildings, and in the
projecting nine-bay centre unrolls a more solemn composition,
to stress the serious rather than celebratory function of the
building. Here alone is a full-scale external order used, unfluted
Doric columns carrying a simplified entablature. But there is
nothing simple about the composition to which they contribute.
The columns are arranged in pairs flanked by half-columns,
forming recessed loggias. End bays with channelled quoins and,
set back behind, large stone turrets with domical tops and
paired, diagonally projecting colonnettes, a reminiscence of
Wren. In the centre, the main doorway set forward, in line with
the columns, in a section of channelled wall with a richly carved
coat of arms above. These full nine bays are given almost the
character of a temple, or rather a church front, by the flight of
steps which rises before them. Huge flanking LAMPSTANDS,
of bronze, topped by dragons.

The S front, as already explained (*see* p. 222), although it is
the side elevation of the Law Courts, corresponds to the
entrance front of the City Hall minus the centrepiece. The attic
sculptures here, executed in 1906, represent Welsh Science
and Education, by *Donald McGill*, and Welsh Commerce and
Industry, by *Paul Montford*.

More rostral obelisks before the S façade. For the statue of
Judge Williams, *see* below, p. 229.

In the INTERIOR there is only one important space. Through
the main entrance, flights of steps divide and rise to a three-
bay HALL set transversely. This is rather beautiful, crowned by
three saucer domes on pendentives, between which lunette
windows give light front and back. Round the wall-head runs
a leafy cornice, which develops into a rich foliage capital at the

head of each wall-pier. Pretty brass electroliers, presumably designed by *Rickards*, sprout from the foliage. At the ends, screens of two widely spaced Ionic columns, beyond which lie the courts, the CROWN COURT to the N, the NISI PRIUS COURT to the S. These are square rooms, lit by lunette windows high up, with flat, enriched plaster ceilings, but have no strong architectural character.

NATIONAL MUSEUM OF WALES

Plans for a museum in Cardiff go back to the early 1880s, when it was to be combined with Edwin Seward's Free Library in The Hayes. When the library was completed without a museum, a site was earmarked in the newly laid out Cathays Park. From 1901 Seward worked on designs for a museum building for the Park, and early in 1905 the start of construction was authorized, but for some reason, whether of cost or through dissatisfaction with the design, nothing was done. Half a decade later, in 1910, after an open competition, the London firm of *Smith & Brewer* were commissioned to build what was now to be not just a museum local to Cardiff but the National Museum of Wales.

The site was the third and sole remaining of the principal S-facing positions in the Park, the best of all in that no defined N boundary hemmed it in. A grandly scaled building was called for, so something which deferred to the City Hall in the way that the Law Courts had done was impossible. Instead, Smith & Brewer designed a building which echoed the City Hall but in a different key. The City Hall was flamboyant, diverse and richly textured, the museum would be restrained, compact and severely architectural, the mood American Beaux-Arts. The original plan was for a building nearly twice as deep as broad, with principal galleries on the scale of the King's Library in the British Museum. The foundation stone was laid in 1913, but building was delayed by the First World War, so the entrance range was not opened until 1927. Lecture theatre in the E range completed in 1932. W wing largely following the original scheme, 1962–5 by *T. Alwyn Lloyd & Gordon*. A final phase to a greatly reduced design, by the *Alex Gordon Partnership*, completed in 1993, has tidied up the N end, and provides central galleries to an entirely new design. A car park now occupies the site intended for the four N-most galleries of the original scheme.

The SOUTH FRONT gathers together the major motifs of Lanchester, Stewart & Rickards's buildings with consolidated logic. So the centre, above a broad flight of steps, is occupied by a five-bay colonnade of coupled Doric columns of quasi-Greek character, behind which the entrance is recessed. To l. and r. five-bay wings project slightly, the centre three bays canted, under attics with sculptural groups, and emphasized by pairs of recessed columns identical with those in the centre. Above and behind, on a square drum with chamfered corners, a hemispherical, lead-covered dome, simply ribbed. In several of its main dimensions also the museum is correlated with the City

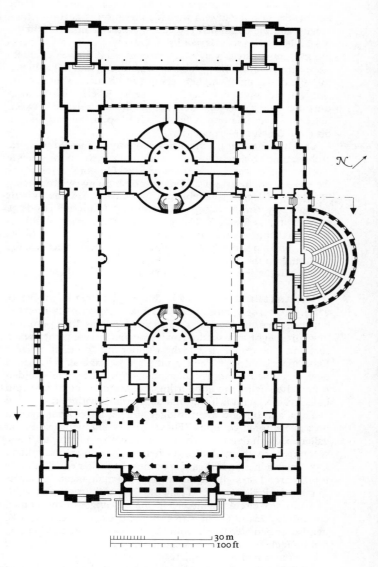

ALL STRUCTURE BELOW THE LINE WAS BUILT TO
THIS PLAN BY 1927

Cardiff, National Museum of Wales.
Plan as proposed in 1910

Hall: the rusticated courses of the basement are the same height, the cornice line of the side elevation is at a matching height, and the columned projection on the return front to the w stands on the cross-axis of its neighbour. But in two respects the museum is decisively more monumental: in being single-storeyed where the City Hall has two storeys, and in having on the w side an inner, higher stratum of cornices, those of the side galleries proper, behind the reserve galleries which form the outer face in this direction. Altogether the balance between deference and assertion is finely judged, perhaps with even a little too much cool calculation.

The SCULPTURE on the attics is tightly integrated with the architecture. Sixteen groups were envisaged in a scheme worked out in 1913, with the advice of Goscombe John. Six were executed, in 1914–15, Mining and Shipping (w attic facing w) by *T. J. Clapperton*, Prehistoric and Classic Periods (w attic facing s) by *Gilbert Bayes*, Medieval and Modern Periods (E attic facing s) by *L. R. Garbe*. Round the corner to the E, three further groups, Learning, by *Clapperton*, Music, by *David Evans*, and Art, by *Bertram Pegram*, who also executed the sculpture on the dome.

Pilastered E front, the broad bow of the lecture theatre in the centre.

The INTERIOR starts with the extraordinarily profligate ENTRANCE HALL, an endlessly fascinating space in its interplay between piers and balconies, stairs and landings, high parts and low parts, light and shade. Analysis can separate it into seven sections. The centre rises highest under the dome, lit by large Diocletian windows. Their pink glass is original. The space here is defined as an irregular octagon by sheer piers folded round the angles and supporting a continuous architrave and balcony. To l. and r. lower, darker sections, with flat, coffered ceilings, and beyond them bridges at a yet lower level, carried on austere Ionic columns. These bridges link with exhibition galleries which open into the hall in a continuous circuit. Ionic columns carry them all round where wide spans require them. Over the bridges Soanic saucer domes. At the far ends, brightly top-lit, broad, straight flights of steps, the main means of access to the principal upper-level galleries, rise and turn out of sight.

A discreet circular staircase in the SW angle of the domed central bay leads to the LIBRARY and COURT ROOM, two handsome panelled rooms with Doric pilasters and high lighting from Diocletian windows, located over the coffered sections of the entrance hall but completely hidden from it.

To the N of the domed space, where Smith & Brewer planned to site the gallery of Welsh National History, new EXHIBITION GALLERIES of neutral character by the *Alex Gordon Partnership*, opened 1993.

The LECTURE THEATRE in the E wing is the only other major room built to *Smith & Brewer*'s design. Semicircular auditorium with raked seating. Clerestory lighting round the semicircle, coming in from behind a close-set row of unfluted, baseless Doric columns. So this is a reinterpretation of an antique theatre, by way, specifically, of Ledoux's theatre at Besançon of the 1770s. The frankly C20 stage and proscenium arch break the spell. Two painted war memorial panels by *Frank Brangwyn*.

STATUES

South African War Memorial. The finest and most ambitious of the sculpture in Cathays Park, sited in a *rond-point* at the s end of King Edward VII Avenue. By *Albert Toft*, *c.*1909. It is an expression of regret and of hope. On a tall, white Portland stone plinth the winged figure of Peace is poised, brandishing before her an uprooted olive tree with a dove in its branches.* This is of dark bronze, as are the seated figures against the sides of the pedestal, a male figure representing Warfare, and a female figure of Grief.

In front of the Law Courts, Judge Gwilym Williams (†1906) by *Goscombe John*, a lively figure in wig and gown.

In Gorsedd Gardens there are four bronze statues. Isolated on the lawn s of the City Hall, the bronze equestrian statue of Lord Tredegar, by *Goscombe John*, made in 1906 and set up in 1909 to commemorate Tredegar's part in the Charge of the Light Brigade in 1854. Hence his costume, hence the reliefs of mounted battle on the pedestal. Also by *Goscombe John* are the top-coated figure of John Cory, coal-owner and philanthropist, 1906, on a fanciful neo-Greek pedestal near the sw corner of the gardens, and the statue in the centre of the gardens, of Lord Ninian Crichton Stuart M.P., killed in action in 1915. This is of 1917. Finally, facing n towards the National Museum, the much later figure of David Lloyd George, 1960 by *Rizzello*.

CATHAYS PARK NORTH OF CITY HALL ROAD

Central Police Station, immediately n of the Law Courts. Designed by *John Dryburgh*, the City Architect, and built 1966–8. Frankly modern and characteristic of its date. The contrast with the Law Courts seems appropriate, the lawyers in their traditional costume flanked by the up-to-date technology of the police. Yet its poise, regularity and sense of proportion go some way towards unifying it with its earlier neighbours. Five storeys, the short end towards the Avenue forming a pavilion-like block. The top and bottom storeys solid, the second open, the third and fourth cantilevered forward, with close-set mullions. Off-centre entrance under a trough-like concrete canopy, a Corbusian reference.

University of Wales Registry. 1903–4 by *H. W. Wills & Anderson*. One of the earliest buildings in the park, and much the smallest. Like an C18 *trianon*, of nine bays subdivided into threes, an ashlar piano nobile over a low, channelled basement,

*Vandalized in 1993.

with bullseye windows in the attic. Recessed Ionic columns
flank the entrance in a 1,2,2,1 rhythm. Posts in front topped
with Welsh dragons by *Goscombe John*. Round the corner the
walls are rock-faced, the windows in two conventional storeys,
largely an extension of 1933 by *T. Alwyn Lloyd*. Inside, the back
of the entrance hall is opened up with two Doric columns,
beyond which a corridor curves round a small courtyard. The
big block at the back, though aligned on the Registry, belongs
to the County Hall next door (*see* below).

MID GLAMORGAN COUNTY HALL. Not the largest but the
most monumental of the public buildings in Cathays Park. A
competition, held in 1908, was won by *E. V. Harris &
T. A. Moodie*, that is to say by the twenty-nine-year-old and so
far untried *Vincent Harris*. Construction went ahead smoothly,
and the building was opened in 1912. Like the best buildings
in the Beaux-Arts tradition of classicism, its basic concept is a
simple one, realized with force and consistency, so that all the
components of plan and elevations fall naturally into place.
What makes the building remain in the mind is Harris's use of
unconventionally placed, colossal figure sculpture.

The E FRONT, towards King Edward VII Avenue, is raised,
temple-like, on a flight of steps which extends the full width of
the centre five bays and is flanked by double-height steps against
the broad end bays. Here, defining the angles of this precinct,
as it were, are broad, low sculptural groups, representing
Mining (l.) and Navigation (r.). They are by *Albert Hodge*,
whose heavy neo-Greek style disguises the disparity between
the realism of the grim-faced miners in the one group and the
symbolic figure of Neptune in his seahorse-drawn carriage in
the other. The façade itself is of one monumental Corinthian
storey crowned by a continuous entablature, which breaks
forward slightly over the end bays, where pilasters flank blind
doorways. Plain, solid attics above the end bays to close the
composition. But the focus of attention is on the pairs of
columns which define the centre five bays. The front wall of
the building lies back in shadow behind them, and the central
entrance doorway is not emphasized. The way to it, however,
is marked by a pair of short, free-standing obelisks. At the
sides of the façade, single-storey arches over service entries.
Balustraded platforms over them, the balustrades decorated
with sphinxes.

The entrance front, then, makes its own, richly impressive
statement. By contrast, the INTERIOR is solemn and reserved.
Doric, but breaking out into columns only once. Steps go on
rising through the entrance vestibule, which has a flat, coffered
ceiling and stone-lined walls. At mezzanine level, an apse,
beyond which, past two Tuscan Doric columns, access is given
to a stone-lined corridor. This runs in a curve round the back
of the COUNCIL CHAMBER, the major internal space. The
Council Chamber is a noble, even a sombre room, not at all
young man's architecture. In plan a D, it has smooth ashlar
walls and a smooth plaster vault. Large lunettes penetrating the

vault provide top lighting, above a row of slot-like windows with oddly mannered imposts. At the base of the straight wall a stone-faced enclosure within the space of the room. This hides a communication corridor, and provides a base for two brooding, over-life-size stone statues, by *Hodge*. The seated, toga-clad figures represent a bard, reading a vast book, and a druid, playing a harp. The SEATING, to *Harris*'s design, suitably substantial, remains unaltered. *George Alexander* constructed it.

Behind the Council Chamber, at the back of the building, COMMITTEE ROOMS. They have stone chimneypieces and overmantels of Vanbrughian character, and large plasterwork ceiling wreaths by *Arthur Broadbent*. FURNITURE designed by *Harris* here too.

Finally, the rear of the building must be described. This is in the palazzo idiom, of nine bays, four-storeyed, the lowest storey almost hidden by the extraordinarily elaborate raking brackets supporting the balcony which serves the committee rooms. The top storey is treated as an attic above a splendidly carved cornice. Above that, a visible roof and two soaring chimneystacks. The whole ensemble has great individuality, and is effectively framed by wing walls scrolling out over service arches. (Figures on the wing walls by *Hodge*, and in the centre of the front by *Arthur Broadbent*.)

When in the early 1930s a large increase in local government business required a massive extension to the County Hall, the quality of Harris's building forced displacement of the EXTENSION BUILDING s-wards, to a site axially behind the diminutive University Registry. This works very well, so that the fact that the extension is larger than the original County Hall is not readily noticed. The architect of the extension, a finely proportioned, if conventional, three-storey classical building with a rich cornice, pitched roof and defining chimneystacks, was *Percy Thomas* of *Ivor Jones & Percy Thomas*. It was put up in 1932.

BUTE BUILDING. Now the Architecture Department of the University of Wales, but built as the Technical Institute and subsequently the University of Wales Institute of Science and Technology. *Ivor Jones & Percy Thomas* won a limited competition in 1911 and executed the E, N and S ranges 1913–16. W range, completing the quadrangle, 1927. Unexciting. E front of fifteen bays divided into three equal parts, the centre recessed behind a Doric colonnade carrying an attic. Two-storey side sections with broad, channelled angles. Neo-Grecian detailing within the colonnade. N and S elevations of fifteen unrelieved bays between projecting end bays with Doric columns and channelled angles. Square, low entrance hall, from which staircases rise to l. and r.

TEMPLE OF PEACE AND HEALTH. 1937–8 by *Sir Percy Thomas*, like a fragment of his Swansea Guildhall. The building is an oddity, built partly as a statement of faith and only partly for specific practical purposes. It was the brain-child of Lord

Davies of Llandinam to promote peace and health, in memory
of those who had fallen in the First World War. Its present users
are gratifyingly appropriate, the Welsh Centre for International
Affairs and the South Glamorgan Health Authority. They
occupy the two-storey wings, the utilitarian purpose of which
is indicated by sloping pantiled roofs. Portico-like centre: four
square piers carrying a deep slab architrave and shelf-like
cornice stand out from a white cubic block. No mouldings, just
a row of incised squares round the top of the attic. Bronze-
framed windows within the portico. Set axially behind it, a
temple-like hall, with narrow aisles demarcated by massive,
square, fluted piers of black Portoro marble, veined with gold,
from Portovenere, Liguria. Flat, coffered ceiling coloured in
emerald and gold. Large side windows light this sanctum with
inappropriate brightness. (Vaulted crypt below.)

REDWOOD BUILDING, University of Wales, Cardiff (formerly
Welsh College of Advanced Technology). 1960–1 by *Sir Percy
Thomas & Son*. By this time the firm had embraced modernism,
though without much imagination, to judge by this building.
Undifferentiated three-storey block, entered at the extreme l.
end underneath a vast relief sculpture by *Bainbridge Copnall*.
An aged man in a toga, his foot on a globe and a pile of books,
reaches out protectively over diminutive figures of a scientist
and a nurse: an awkward attempt to modernize the emblematic
tradition.

WELSH COLLEGE OF MUSIC AND DRAMA, North Road. Inexpressive, as if to be noticed as little as possible. Long, narrow
four-storey range, the top storey in an overhang. Faced with
buff brick, a material justified by the position W of the strict
confines of Cathays Park. 1976–7 by *John Dryburgh*, Cardiff
City Architect.

QUEEN ANNE SQUARE, Corbett Road, at the head of King
Edward VII Avenue. A planned layout, built in the 1930s and
1950s on a site which had been earmarked for a Welsh
Parliament House. A dainty screen of coupled Doric columns
is interrupted by two pairs of red brick entrance piers. Greensward beyond, flanked by thirty two-storey Neo-Georgian
houses, a miniature evocation of Thomas Jefferson's University of Virginia.

WELSH OFFICE. This is the massive occupant of the central
block at the N end of the park, looking across Alexandra
Gardens. The foundations of a grandiose columnar building
for Welsh Government Offices designed by *R. J. Allison* were
laid in 1914. Inevitably work soon stopped, but it was not
resumed for twenty years. The present S range is of 1934–8 by
P. K. Hanton, built for the Welsh Board of Health, still classical
in spirit, but showing the same apparent loss of nerve as Sir
Percy Thomas in the 1930s. Fifteen-bay façade, two storeys of
windows between pilaster strips under an attic. Similar three-
bay returns without the attic. Corinthian entablature right
across. Behind this a five-storey rectangle, 1972–9 by *Alex
Gordon & Partners*, massively overhanging at the top and set on

a steeply sloping plinth. The *Architects Journal* called it 'a symbol of closed inaccessible government', conveying an impression of 'bureaucracy under siege'.

WELSH NATIONAL WAR MEMORIAL, Alexandra Gardens. 115 1924–8 by *Sir Ninian Comper*, a singularly pure and beautiful classical composition by an architect normally known as a scholarly Gothicist. The architect said his inspiration came from the colonnaded remains of the 'Hadrianic cities of Tunisia'. A circle of Corinthian columns carries an entablature which in three places breaks forward rectangularly over pairs of columns flanking flights of steps. These lead down to a circular basin of water, from which rises a tall drum bearing alternately three Corinthian columns and three figures of servicemen. Crowning figure of a nude, winged youth bearing a sword, emblem of Victory. The sculpture, of bronze, was executed by *Bertram Pegram*.

Also in Alexandra Gardens, the STATUE of Lord Aberdare, 1898 by *H. Hampton*, facing the portico of the University, which he did so much to originate.

UNIVERSITY OF WALES, CARDIFF

The College of South Wales was founded in 1883. A decade later it became a college of the newly established University of Wales. In 1987 it amalgamated with the University of Wales Institute of Science and Technology under its present name. The College at first occupied the former Infirmary building in Newport Road (on the site of the present School of Engineering and Physics, *see* p. 305). Its first purpose-built building, Aberdare Hall, a residential hall for women students, was opened in 1895 (*see* below, p. 237). This stands in Corbett Road facing down the length of Cathays Park, so when the Park was acquired for the town three years later it is not surprising that the Principal, John Viriamu Jones, should have concentrated all his eloquence on persuading the Town Council to donate a site in the Park to the College. The Council duly allocated to the College the entire E third of the park N of the site for the National Museum, with an extensive frontage on to Park Place. A limited competition, held in 1903, was won by *W. D. Caröe*.

The vastly extended W range of Caröe's design of 1903 faces Alexandra Gardens. The mighty library, set centrally at r.-angles behind, went up 1905–9. The N range of the quadrangle into which the library was designed to project was built in two phases, in 1912 and 1930. The S range was built to match by *Alban Caroe* in 1954. When the great hall, which was intended to close the quadrangle to the E, was finally abandoned, *Alban Caroe* added return wings on Park Place to his own design.

Caröe senior's ambition was to evoke the colleges of the ancient universities, and in particular those parts of them which Wren and his mason-architect contemporaries had contributed in a classical style still fresh and not over-scholarly. But *Caröe*'s college was far larger and functionally more complex than any at Oxford or Cambridge, nor was there money for what he called a 'costly dominating note', such as a tower or dome. Even the cornice line had to be kept down, so as not to overtop the new municipal buildings. Inevitably, then, the building appears episodic and frittered. Only the façade of the library towards the quadrangle aspires to grandeur.

Examination should begin with the w front. This is virtually, but not quite, symmetrical and extends to no fewer than forty-seven bays in eleven sections, tied together by little more than a continuous entablature. The way to make sense of it is to learn what was intended to go on behind the façade. At ground level, a variety of study rooms and administrative offices are indicated by the variety of arcaded or arch-headed windows set in channelled walling. Above, the end pavilions have no special significance, but the intermediate accents, single bays with pairs of recessed Ionic columns and low attics, demarcate the ends of the two principal arts lecture rooms. The centre eleven bays can be grasped by the eye as a frontispiece. The three-bay Ionic temple front, with a figural frieze extended by one bay to l. and r., indicates the position of the Council Chamber, placed strategically above the main w entrance. The entrance itself is through a Gibbsian portal, but this is set in the centre of an arcaded loggia, where the arches have surprising faceted soffits, reminiscent of Rubens's house at Antwerp; the piers are faced with strangely composed niches, still waiting to be filled with statues representing the Arts, Wisdom etc., which the architect had planned. The flanking three-bay, three-storey towers do not serve identical functions, as is expressed by a slight differentiation in window forms. The main stair rises within the l. tower, whereas the tower to the r. housed the principal's office below a lecture room. Here, teasingly, four-bay arcades support mullion-and-transom windows arranged in three, not four, bays. Attic-level statues of the King, George V, and the Prince of Wales (the future Edward VIII) as Chancellor of the College. Above and behind the centre of the façade rises the gable end of the library, its sharp angle moulded as a dentilled, pedimental cornice, yet startlingly steeper than the orthodox pediment in front.

The INTERIOR maintains the same quirky air. Beyond the entrance loggia stretches a deep, low HALL, with a niche at the far end for the white marble STATUE of John Viriamu Jones, the first Principal, who had died in 1901. A finely conceived seated figure, relaxed but contemplative, 1906 by *W. Goscombe John*. The hall itself is side-lit and subdivided by piers of the form beloved by Caröe, a rectangular core with a pilaster set against each face to give either a double or a triple projection at each angle. The blurring which this creates is absolutely typical. Ionic capitals with both swags and drops. At the three-bay entrance end of the hall, long, vaulted, transverse corridors tunnel away, and a two-bay slot of space gives an awkward upwards glimpse. To the side rises the STAIRCASE. This is a delightful space, covered by twelve little saucer domes, two in the centre glazed to give some top lighting. The stairs go up in short flights round an open well, and the newels, of the same form as the hall piers, with draped Ionic caps, are carried up to support the arches and spandrels of the domes. Walls lined with pinkish-yellow Penarth alabaster. Chunky balustrades. Broad, clerestoried landing, giving access to Council Chamber and Library.

In the COUNCIL CHAMBER, a characteristic Edwardian demonstration of the crafts. Shallow segmental tunnel-vault with enriched plaster bands and central pendant, full-height wall-panelling and an overmantel carved with Gibbons-like virtuosity. Fanciful bronze electroliers.

The LIBRARY, paid for by the Drapers' Company of London, was the climax of the interior, a huge tunnel-vaulted room inspired by Thomas Burgh's great early C18 library at Trinity College, Dublin. Doorways of almost Portuguese elaboration lead into the library, or rather now into its lower third, for in 1977 it was floored over. The lower space has little character, and access to the upper library is up a cramped, utilitarian stair. But the upper space remains impressive, vaulted from end to end in six bays, the vault coffers glazed, a disconcerting effect. Large, close-set, Diocletian side windows penetrate the vault. The enormous Venetian window in the E end wall contributes further to what now inevitably seems excessive illumination. The vault is supported on an arcade with applied pilasters carrying a mighty entablature with bolection frieze. Ionic capitals of yet another form.

To complete an examination of the University it is necessary to make a new approach from Park Place. Caröe's original intention was that a great hall would stand side-on to Park Place, above the entrance into the Great Court. As the great hall was never built, the view is direct across the court to the mighty E end of the library. This is a disconcerting composition, its component parts out of scale with one another. Channelled angle turrets carry small domed cupolas. A vast intervening stretch of ashlar wall is pierced at the bottom by a Wrenian door surround and trios of small, flanking windows, and interrupted above by a grandiose aedicule. This has a broken segmental pediment on channelled imposts, within which the Venetian window of the library supports on its keystone a cartouche and a statue of St David in a niche with twisted columns. Relief sculpture here and there fails to bind these parts together. The side elevations, blind walling above two storeys of windows, are equally awkward.

The library is flanked by short bridges, arched below, colonnaded and glazed above. These lead to six-bay stretches with tall mullion-and-transom windows over arcaded loggias with applied columns. In the angles of the court, convex projections, the columns here applied at the upper level. These provided the entrances to the men's (l.) and women's (r.) cloakrooms and common rooms. Their convexity, however, is explained by the fact that free-standing circular, domed (former) LAVATORIES are placed behind them in two secondary courts. The side ranges of the Great Court gave access to the chemistry laboratories (l.) and physics laboratories (r.). Here Caröe modified his original design, closing the pediments over the central three-bay projections.

Convex angles to the SE and NE corners of the court not built, but instead the post-war return ranges by *Alban Caroe*, retaining a full classical vocabulary, even introducing new motifs, but decidedly without quirks.

When the great expansion of the University in the 1950s and '60s called for new buildings there was no question but that they should be in a contemporary idiom. They occupy a triangular site N of Caröe's building between MUSEUM AVENUE and PARK PLACE. In order to understand the history of what happened it is necessary to start at the N end. Here, wrapped round the N apex is all that was built of *Sir Percy Thomas*'s first scheme for the whole site, of 1958. Completed in 1962 for the Faculty of Arts, it is now the LAW DEPARTMENT. Four-storeyed, faced with Portland stone. Fluted panels between the bands of fenestration. Fifteen-bay façade towards Museum Avenue.

The rest of the site had to be developed under a new master plan of 1960, to a higher density, and with car parking beneath the buildings. So the height restriction which had governed everything built in Cathays Park so far was abandoned. Nor was an orderly disposition of the component parts sought for its own sake, but merely a convenient one. That was 1960s thinking. Only the use of Portland stone facing was maintained. The architects were the *Percy Thomas Partnership* (design partner *Dale Owen*). First to be built was the twelve-storey TOWER, completed 1967. Built for the Faculty of Economics and Social Studies and for the Department of Mathematics, now occupied by the Department of Psychology and by Administration. To the S, in the space remaining beyond the N end of Caröe's front, a lower and more complex group, the PRE-CLINICAL DEPARTMENTS of the School of Medicine, 1968–70. These are in themselves well proportioned and interestingly varied, set on pilotis, the windows in long bands narrowing here and there rhythmically. Towards Museum Avenue the four-storey Biochemistry block, in the centre the seven-storey Physiology block, its oversailing top storey designed for animal houses, and to the E, the four-storey Anatomy block. The pebbledashed walls of the sky-lit Dissecting Room make an enigmatic extra towards Park Place.

Beyond the confines of the Park Portland stone is seen no more. Here too a different architectural practice was employed, *Alex Gordon & Partners*. The STUDENTS' UNION, completed 1973, which faces into Caröe's Great Court from across Park Place, is of dull brown brick. Long and low, three stepped-back storeys to provide continuous balconies (and surmount the tracks of the railway which runs beneath the building). A broad flight of steps descends across a grass bank down to Park Place. Sheer reverse façade to SENGHENNYDD ROAD. Inside, the recent BARS are quite a sight, one Paris-style, one half-timbered, one heavy metal. Immediately to the S, the SHERMAN THEATRE, also of dark brown brick, virtually windowless, giving nothing away. 1970–1 by *Alex Gordon & Partners*. Recent Post-Modern embellishments. The MATHEMATICS BLOCK, by the same, 1971–2, adjoins to the S.

In CORBETT ROAD, which forms the N boundary of Cathays Park, several more buildings of the University. First, E of Colum Road, ARTS AND SOCIAL SCIENCES LIBRARY, 1972–6 by *Williamson, Faulkner Brown & Partners*. An exposition of concrete post-and-lintel construction. Entrance at the l. corner, because a building twice as wide was projected. Further N the ABER-CONWAY BUILDING. By *Burgess & Partners*, completed 1982. Red brick.

Where Corbett Road is in direct contact with Cathays Park, red brick dominates. First, past two or three Gothic VILLAS of the mid 1890s, the MUSIC DEPARTMENT. This is also by *Alex Gordon & Partners*, 1970, and, ironically, as taciturn as their theatre. In front, stark against unbroken brickwork, a big bronze SCULPTURE by *Barbara Hepworth*. Then ABERDARE HALL, women's hall of residence, the originator of the taste for red brick round here. 1893–5 by *H. W. Wills* of Swansea. By that date a style for women's colleges had been established, in particular by Basil Champneys at Newnham College, Cambridge, as Wills was clearly aware. But where Champneys had been lively, varied and fanciful, in a personal version of the Queen Anne style of the 1870s, Wills is staid, dignified and Jacobean. Red brick with red terracotta dressings. A square block of three storeys with a fourth in the prominent shaped gables. Tall, mullion-and-transom windows for the communal rooms below, mullioned windows for the study-bedrooms above. Pairs of two-storey window bays, not aligned with the gables, square on the S front flanking the col-umned entrance doorway, polygonal on the W front fused with the arcaded garden loggia. Inside, an octagonal vestibule, apparently reduced from its original height, and a dining room the full length of the W front. Behind, two later wings. That to the NE, with a library on the ground floor, of 1938–40 by *Verner O. Rees*. Mildly Neo-Georgian. That to the NW, by *Verner Rees, Laurence & Mitchell*, designed in 1963, four-storeyed, concrete-framed with red brick infill, unassumingly Modern.

For University buildings outside Cathays Park, *see* Roath, below, p. 305.

LLANDAFF/LLANDAF

It is a surprise to find a full-scale cathedral in the city suburbs. Cardiff has engulfed Llandaff, however, only in the C20, formally incorporating it within the city boundaries in 1922. Before that Llandaff was a 'cathedral village'. Much of its village atmosphere survives in The Green and the lanes leading off it.

The origins of this strange relationship lie in the early Middle Ages. The siting of Cardiff in the late C11 was governed by the site of the Roman fort, which was taken over as the bailey of the Norman castle. At some unknown period between the aban-donment of the fort and the planting of the castle, a church was founded on the W bank of the River Taff less than 2 m. (3.2 kilometres) upstream. This church must have gained considerable

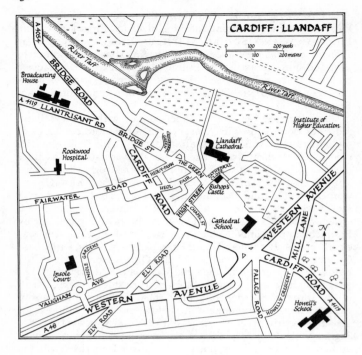

significance, because it was chosen to become the cathedral church of the new post-Conquest diocese of Glamorgan, whose first bishop, Urban, began to rebuild the little early Christian church in 1120 as Llandaff Cathedral.

The growth and prosperity of the borough of Cardiff, founded beside the castle, from the beginning stunted nearby Llandaff, which could establish only an ecclesiastical importance, not an economic one. During the C13 the cathedral was rebuilt a second time on quite a grand scale, and *c.*1300 the bishop provided himself with a stronghold overlooking it from the high ground to the SE. It seems that most of the prebendal houses, of which nothing survives, stood E of the cathedral, under the lee of the bishop's castle.

The Green, at the high level in front of the castle gate, is clearly a space of medieval origin. Only slight traces, however, of medieval houses have been noted around it.

It is only from the Georgian period that Llandaff village can show surviving houses, together with one or two gentry seats close by, as it became a fashionable retreat from Cardiff town.

During the mid C19, as the religious life of the cathedral revived, not only was the cathedral church restored, but the village was renewed and expanded, with, as it happened, a high proportion of architect-designed houses. Houses for the cathedral clergy (dean, canon and minor canons) were built by *Ewan Christian*, architect to the Ecclesiastical Commissioners, but as many as five others were designed by the talented Llandaff architect *John Prichard*, whose restoration of the cathedral was only the most important of a wide range of local commissions. In the 1890s *G. E. Halliday* built at least a further five individual houses, and a few years later Prichard's own unfinished house was incorporated into the buildings of the new diocesan theological college, *F. R. Kempson*'s St Michael's College.

A gratifyingly high proportion of Llandaff's Victorian buildings survive (*Prichard*'s school of 1860 in the High Street being the most significant casualty), so that an extensive exploration of the village centre and its environs finds plenty of reward.

LLANDAFF CATHEDRAL

INTRODUCTION

The cathedral is dedicated to S S Peter and Paul, with S S Dyfrig, Teilo and Euddogwy. After St David's, Llandaff is the most impressive medieval cathedral in Wales. On the other hand, no ancient cathedral in England or Wales has suffered a more chequered post-medieval history. Indeed, without the contributions of the C19 and C20 the building would be infinitely less impressive 91 than it is. The site, down in the water meadows beside the River Taff, overshadowed by a steep escarpment, may have suited the little Celtic church which first occupied the site (cf. Llantwit Major, Llancarfan), but leaves its successor out-of-scale with its surroundings, and standing at a lower level than the bell tower, bishop's castle, and deanery clustered round The Green.

Nothing is known of the pre-Norman monastic community, other than the dimensions of its church. This was no more than 28 ft (8.5 metres) long, 15 ft (4.6 metres) wide and 20 ft (6.1 metres) high, with narrow, low aisles and an apsidal *porticus* 12 ft (3.66 metres) in length, according to the C12 *Book of Llandaf*. In April 1120, Urban, the second Norman bishop, undertook to rebuild it larger, to provide a church appropriate to the newly organized diocese, which now came within the province of Canterbury. The scale of Urban's church, not to say its somewhat exotic character, can be judged from its surviving sanctuary arch, behind the present high altar. Its w parts were soon replaced in a second rebuilding, begun *c.* 1200 during the episcopate of Henry of Abergavenny (1193–1218), which established the scale of the present-day cathedral. Much of the early C13 choir and nave, including the w front, survives. It is a work of two periods, with 10 a clear break in design at the fourth bay from the E. It belongs to a group of churches which owe a great deal in design to Glastonbury Abbey and Wells Cathedral. The subtlety of the architecture, especially of the w front, and the quality of the sculpture suggest that leading craftsmen of this 'West Country school' were involved. In two respects the early C13 work falls short of a full-scale cathedral design. The elevation is of two storeys only, as at

Cardiff, Llandaff Cathedral.
View from the West before restoration

Rochester Cathedral and many monastic churches. And, much more exceptionally, there are no transepts, but in Scotland compare the cathedrals at Glasgow and Dunblane. The Lady Chapel belongs to the later C13, as does the remodelling of the sanctuary. The remodelling of the nave aisles is a work of the C14, and the rebuilding of the NW tower the late C15. The length of the cathedral, including the Lady Chapel, is 150 ft (45.7 metres), shorter for instance than Margam Abbey church (q.v.), its transeptless width only 64 ft (19.5 metres).

The post-Reformation story is one of unrelieved neglect for two centuries. As early as 1594 the bishop complained that the cathedral was 'more like a desolate and profane place than like a house of prayer and holy exercises'. By 1692 the main roofs were so insecure that choral service was suspended. The battlements of the NW tower were blown away in 1703, the SW tower collapsed in 1722. But soon after a first step was taken to improve matters, for in 1734 an agreement was made with *John Wood* of Bath to construct a 'neat new conventicle' incorporating the structure of the choir and the four E bays of the nave. Wood's 'temple', left incomplete in 1752, stood incongruously for over a century, while the W half of the nave continued to decay in front of it. It aroused criticism soon enough. Already in 1774 a tourist struck the note so often sounded later, calling the cathedral 'a medley of absurdities', where 'the Christian altar is raised under the portico of a Heathen temple'. By 1840 the chorus of disapproval must have been deafening. But South Wales, if not the diocese of Llandaff, was now reaping the wealth of industrial development. Fund-raising began.

Restoration of the Lady Chapel started in 1841 under the

busy English architect *T. H. Wyatt*, who was acting as honorary diocesan architect. From 1845 the dean was W. D. Conybeare, an eminent geologist determined to rescue the cathedral from dilapidation and to reveal the beauties of the medieval fabric which survived. By strange good fortune, the son of one of the vicars-choral at the cathedral, *John Prichard*, was beginning to emerge as a Puginian architect of unusual imagination. First, in 1843, the design of the E window of the Lady Chapel was put in his hands. By 1845 Prichard seems to have taken complete charge (though Wyatt continued as 'honorary architect' and did not finally sever his connection with the restoration until 1853) and by 1850 had restored the sanctuary. In 1852 he was commissioned to continue into the choir and nave, sweeping away the remainder of Wood's temple. In order to do justice to his task, Prichard then took into partnership *John Pollard Seddon*, a London architect with good connections in advanced artistic circles and a special talent for furniture design. Seddon secured the Pre-Raphaelite painter *Dante Gabriel Rossetti* and the Pre-Raphaelite sculptor *Thomas Woolner* to execute outstanding pieces for the cathedral. *Morris & Co.* regularly supplied stained glass in the 1860s. The restoration reached its climax with *Prichard*'s rebuilding of the 91 SW tower, 1867–9, to a dramatic new design. From the depths of neglect, Llandaff Cathedral had in twenty-five years been raised up as a model of good restoration practice, the surviving medieval fabric uncovered, completed where fragmentary, and where necessary boldly supplemented to Prichard's own design, with a full set of fittings by the best artists and craftsmen obtainable.

In 1941 a landmine exploded outside the S aisle, shattering its windows, bringing down the nave roof once again, and smashing most of the Victorian fittings. By then the cathedral architect was *Sir Charles Nicholson*, who seems to have envisaged two of the major post-war innovations, the flat nave roof and the removal of Rossetti's altarpiece to the N aisle. Nicholson still thought in terms of neo-Gothic, but the post-war dean, Glyn Simon, wanted the reconstruction to embody mid-c20 aspirations. In Nicholson's successor from 1949, *George Gaze Pace* of York, he found an architect who saw eye-to-eye with him. So the idea of the skied organ case was conceived, supporting *Epstein*'s Majestas, on its 117 concrete parabolic arches. The many new fittings (1956–64) are in Pace's personal style. In the St David's Chapel, added to the nave N aisle 1953–6, Gothic forms are unflinchingly but beautifully reinterpreted. Pace could never be as radical as his hero, Le Corbusier, but he was the most daring ecclesiastical architect in post-war Britain. At Llandaff he demonstrates that C20 modernism, allied to Gothic in its structural principles, can co-exist, challengingly if not comfortably, with the Gothic of the C13.

To follow the building history, detailed examination must begin at the high altar. But before entering, the visitor will want to pause and appreciate the exterior of the building, and in particular the W front. From the obliquely descending main approach Prichard's SW tower makes a magnificent show. But the Dean's Steps from the W provide a view of the W front head-on from top to bottom,

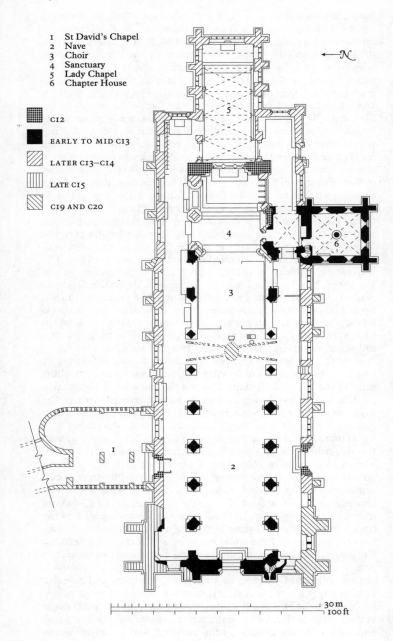

1   St David's Chapel
2   Nave
3   Choir
4   Sanctuary
5   Lady Chapel
6   Chapter House

C12

EARLY TO MID C13

LATER C13–C14

LATE C15

C19 AND C20

Cardiff, Llandaff Cathedral. Plan

the beautiful c13 nave façade between the craggy c15 Jasper Tower and Prichard's strong and soaring steeple. There is something Continental about the disparate juxtaposition, a reminder almost of Chartres. (That indeed is how contemporaries saw it in the 1860s, one complaining of 'a betrayal of Anglican traditions.') From the w door six steps lead down to the floor of the nave. From the top of the steps the full c13 elevation is excellently seen, and Epstein's Majestas confronts the viewer.

Building stones

Sutton stone, from the coast at St Brides Major, the nearest good-quality freestone, was used for the decoration of Urban's cathedral, as it was for the late c12 N doorway in the nave. The contemporary s doorway, on the other hand, is of Dundry stone, imported across the Bristol Channel from Somerset. Dundry is the stone used throughout the early c13 choir and nave. Local blue Lias was first used for walling in the mid-c13 Chapter House, where the dressings are of Sutton stone with some Dundry. Similar materials in the Lady Chapel, with Purbeck marble for the internal window shafts. Pink Radyr stone in Chapter House and Lady Chapel may indicate post-Reformation patching of the two parts of the cathedral which remained in continuous use. The Jasper Tower displays well the coarse surface and small, rectangular blocks characteristic of Lias, in contrast with the smooth c13 Dundry ashlar of the w front alongside. The c19 restoration introduced other stones, in particular limestone from Chipping Campden for Prichard's SW tower, of a warm orangey hue. For the buttresses which Prichard added to the aisles and the restored crown of the Jasper Tower, he used Bath stone. Rougher and darker stones he held at bay, so Radyr stone and Forest of Dean sandstone are restricted to the lychgate. Pace, by contrast, loved graininess. The arches for Epstein's Majestas are of bush-hammered concrete. The walls of St David's Chapel incorporate both glacial pebbles and Pennant sandstone.

The Twelfth Century

Of the church which Bishop Urban undertook to begin in 1120, the richly decorated SANCTUARY ARCH survives complete, still the focal point of the cathedral, behind the high altar. The thick walls to l. and r. which project into the aisles probably indicate the division between the c12 sanctuary E of the arch and flanking chapels which extended less far E, perhaps the same width as the present aisles. This would have made a conventional stepped E end, probably with three apses internally. Excavation in 1934 revealed what may have been the footings of a small apse. Heads of two large, round-headed windows, similarly richly decorated, set close to one another in the s wall of the sanctuary, indicate the start of the c12 choir. How far w-wards it extended is not certainly known, but it clearly had bays in a quicker rhythm than the present building. A writer in 1873 mentions the discovery of

Romanesque pier bases under the site of Prichard's sanctuary
arch. But a choir only as long as the present sanctuary would have
been unusually short. How far the nave extended w of that there
is no evidence to say. However, a nave twice the length of the
choir would fit within the E half of the C13 nave, its w end close
to the point where the C13 arcades change design.

The decoration is unusually lavish for the early C12. The sanctuary arch rests on jambs of four orders, three of them shafted
with foliage and beaded straps on the capitals. The arch itself
has five orders, two zigzag and an outer order of bold beaded
medallions enclosing eight-petal flowers. This motif recurs on the
exterior of the w-most of the two s windows, where the hood
rests on an animal head-stop. These are clues to the provenance
of Bishop Urban's masons. Decorative medallions and animal
heads both occur at Malmesbury Abbey, and medallions, more
sculptural admittedly than Llandaff's, were a feature of Old
Sarum cathedral, rebuilt by Roger of Salisbury from c. 1125.
Roger's buildings were celebrated for their lavish decoration.
Since he owned land in South Wales further w, at Kidwelly, it
may be possible to include early C12 Llandaff among the many
buildings on which Roger of Salisbury's masons worked.

11   The N and s doorways two-thirds of the way down the nave
are a puzzle. They obviously predate the start of Henry of Abergavenny's great scheme of enlargement, and stand in C13 aisle
walls remodelled if not rebuilt in the early C14. Yet they both
have scallop capitals and a multiplicity of zigzag forms, the inner
order overlapping a roll, and the hoodmould of the smaller (N)
doorway is decorated with dogtooth and rests on animal head-
stops. So they must be late C12. Where did they come from?
Perhaps from the w front of the C12 church, so recently completed
that the early C13 builders decided to reuse them, in spite of the
dramatic change in style which had meanwhile taken place. A
further puzzle is the fact that they are constructed of two different
types of stone, the N doorway of Sutton, the s of Dundry.

The Early Thirteenth Century

SANCTUARY SOUTH AISLE. Of the two bays of the s aisle s of
the sanctuary, the w one has a quadripartite rib-vault, the ribs
formed of two rolls divided by a step and carried on keeled corner
shafts with moulded bases and stiff-leaf caps (SW trumpet cap).
All this is clearly early C13 work. Thick upper walls. E wall
modified c. 1300 when a triple-chamfered arch was inserted. w
wall pared back twice, and carried on an arch with triple-shafted
imposts which are keeled and have leaf capitals. This belongs
with the early C13 work further w. The vaulted bay itself, then,
predates the w arch, but not by much. In the s wall a newel stair
against which the Chapter House was later constructed. All this
suggests that the vault was built to support a tower. No sign of a
matching N tower. But that may merely be because the comprehensive reconstruction of that side in the late C13 has left no
evidence.

The rebuilding of the CHOIR, two bays, and extension of the NAVE to six bays, fell into two equal halves. The four E bays have less substantial arcades on piers that are basically octagonal in plan; the four W bays have more substantial arcades on piers of an elaborated Greek cross plan. The W-most bay is prepared to take towers over the ends of the aisles, and the W front is correlated with the arcades. Henry of Abergavenny, the reforming bishop who first established the cathedral chapter and increased the number of its prebends, must have initiated the rebuilding, perhaps not until the second half of his episcopate. Doubtless building went on under his successor, William of Goldcliff (1219–29). It is tempting to see the change in design as a cost-cutting exercise and to relate it to the extent of the C12 cathedral. So the W bays and much of the W front were built first, while the C12 nave was left standing, and the E bays later, after it had been pulled down.

The piers of the four W bays have keeled triple shafts in the 13 cardinal directions, set on octagonal moulded bases and bearing elegant stiff-leaf capitals. This provides space on the diagonals for two continuous chamfers, between which filleted arch mouldings come down at capital level on to small, grotesque human heads 19 (one howls, another is a gagged woman). Towards the nave the shafts are carried up above the capitals to the level of the clerestory sill. In the four E bays, where the piers are smaller, keeled triple shafts are retained, but there is only one continuous chamfer, half-interrupted by a leaf sprig at capital level which carries the filleted arch moulding. The pier capitals are here given abaci, since there is no room to bring wall-shafts down on to their heads, and a single, recessed shaft rises to the clerestory sill. If the shafting in the W bays suggested the possibility of vaulting, the reduced design of the E bays closes off the possibility.

The clerestory itself is all *Prichard*'s, to a single design all through. He found evidence for what he did in a fragment against the SW tower. It is a piquant design, of five plainly chamfered arches on shafts, the arches alternately narrow and blind, and wide and glazed. This gives two lancets per clerestory bay, a system which Browne Willis's early C18 engraving, recording the cathedral before the nave roof collapsed, shows in all but the E-most bay. The E-most bay requires another look lower down. Here the main arch is under-built by a second, off-centre, arch (partly obscured on the N side by the organ), on shafts stopped well above floor level. Was this related to the medieval position of the choir stalls? The structure of the timber roof by *Nicholson & Rushton*, the flat coffered ceiling to a design by *Pace*, completed in 1955. In the aisles, stone flying buttresses in the four E bays, steeply pointed arches on triple wall-shafts in the four W bays. All by *Prichard*, responding to the difference in pier form in the two halves. N aisle roof timbered, by *Prichard*, S aisle roof plastered, a peculiar design by *Pace*.

The internal W WALL of the nave is a noble composition, 12 but one that is easy to overlook, in the dazzle of light flooding in from the great W lancets. Tall blank dado, l. and r. of the segment-headed rere-arch of the W door. The dado is defined by triple shafts with stiff-leaf capitals aligned with those of the nave piers. The three great lancets above have richly moulded rere-arches carried on multiple shafts, alternately detached shafts with shaft-rings and moulded bases and coursed-in shafts without bases (cf. Margam Abbey crossing pier). The inner detached shafts start filleted, but lose the fillet above the shaft-rings. Bunchy stiff-leaf capitals, unlike those elsewhere, carried continuously across all the shafts. The loss of the fillet and the change in foliage form are probably signs that the upper part of the W front was completed after a break in the construction programme.

10   The exterior of the W FRONT shows the sensitivity, one might even say the wit, of the C13 masons at its subtlest. The façade of the nave only has survived, together with the stair-turret of the SW tower and a fragment of its NW twin. The lowest stage, blank except for the round-headed central doorway, makes a strong, simple base for the principal stage, where the great lancets are set within shafted arcading, the narrow intervening wall surfaces under piercingly pointed arches. The W doorway deserves careful examination. Continuous chamfer outline. Inner arch on beauti-ful but overscaled shafts, recessed in deep hollows. Each shaft consists of four filleted colonnettes, juxtaposed so that they present a double-wave outer face. Polygonal bases apparently carved in situ. Elegant shaft-rings. Enormous foliage capitals, sadly battered now. Nevertheless, a lithe little man with crossed legs can still be made out sitting on the l. capital, and birds pecking the leaves of the r. capital. Tympanum with double-lobed underside, and, suspended within a vesica, a figure of a bishop, fully in the round and gratifyingly well preserved.

A peculiarity of the principal stage is the convex bow given to certain of the wall-faces. On the stair-turret the outer wall of the stairwell is bowed within a tall, narrow, pointed frame. With less justification but more elegance, the wall-faces between the lancets are also bowed, and so made visually continuous with the window reveals. Six medallion-like flowers in the spandrel area above.

In the gable a blander pattern. Regular stepping of the blind arches l. and r. of the central lancet. Trefoil-headed image niche at the apex. (For the image, see St David's Chapel, below.)

It is time to sum up and ask where Henry of Abergavenny's masons came from. The answer, once again, must be, from the West Country. Parallels with Wells Cathedral are readily apparent, in particular in the use of continuous chamfers, but in the sculpture too. The stiff-leaf capitals, tall in proportion and with prominent stalks, closely resemble capitals at Wells Cathedral and also at Glastonbury Abbey, both under con-struction from the 1180s until well into the period when work must have been in progress at Llandaff. The 'inhabited' capitals of the W doorway are particularly Wells-like. Triple shafts are a feature of the nave piers at Wells, and continuous chamfers are used there in triforium and clerestory. Compared with Wells, Llandaff's nave arcades may look modest – though not so plain as another cousin in the family, the nave of Llanthony Abbey,

Gwent, 35 m. (56 kilometres) to the NE – but their fine upright sweep gives them something of the awe-inspiring quality necessary in a cathedral.

The Late Thirteenth Century

The early C13 enlargement of the nave must have made some corresponding treatment of the C12 E end seem essential. Late in the C13 it was replaced by a five-bay Lady Chapel and reconstructed E bays of the sanctuary aisles, so that they overlapped the Lady Chapel by two bays. Externally, a plinth and a sill-level string course bind these parts together. Full-height gabled buttresses on moulded bases. The side windows of the Lady Chapel retain the original pattern, of two long, trefoil-headed lights and tracery no more than an uncusped circle. Its five-light E window is *Prichard*'s first contribution to the cathedral, *c.* 1844. Crocketed E gable and pinnacles by him, after the high gable built to *Wyatt*'s design some years earlier had been lowered. The E window of the sanctuary S aisle must also be his. Dec five-light S window, descending through the string course. In the sanctuary N aisle, Perp E window and three Dec N windows by *Prichard*, perhaps imitating windows which belonged with a rebuilding of the entire wall here in the C14 – note the change in wall-plane.

The INTERIOR of the LADY CHAPEL is an elegant but rather characterless design. Slender, filleted wall-shafts with water-holding bases and stiff-leaf capitals support a quadripartite rib-vault with transverse and ridge ribs. Foliage bosses at the intersections. The side windows rest on a filleted string course and have shafted rere-arches with moulded caps and hoods on head-stops. Original shafted rere-arch for the E window. All the window shafts are of Purbeck marble, its only use in the cathedral. Arches in the W bay open into the aisles. Here the details look earlier. Triple keeled shafts on round, water-holding bases carry stiff-leaf caps with polygonal abaci. Continuous outer chamfer. The carving on the N arch has been left unfinished.

The Later Middle Ages

The SANCTUARY, a C12 structure trapped between the C13 choir and Lady Chapel, must now have looked distressingly low and cramped. Its reconstruction and extension upwards came next. The C12 E arch was, as we know, allowed to remain. Its height had already dictated the height of the early C13 arcades. But the N and S walls were remodelled to create two bays where there had been three. Even so the new bays are slightly, though not obviously, narrower than those further W. The arcades are a tired imitation of the early C13 work, without keels or fillets and without foliage sculpture. Most interesting is the way the SW arch is arrested in mid-flight. What brings it to a halt is not the C12 window, part of which had already been removed when the decision was made to stop work. Presumably the existence in this bay of the supposed tomb of St Teilo created a dilemma which was never resolved. The upper storey on all three sides of the sanctuary is by *Prichard*, working from no medieval evidence at all. The w arch is also *Prichard*'s, modified by Pace (*see* below).

The Dec and Perp windows in the sanctuary aisles have already been mentioned. Further w, the aisle walls were rebuilt in the early C14. Three-light windows with cusped reticulated tracery and ogee tops, the s-curve emphasized externally by hoodmoulds and internally by rere-arches. The hall windows at Caerphilly Castle (q.v.), of *c.*1326, must have been their model. Small s doorway with continuous mouldings. Above it a vesica-shaped recess for an image. w bay of the s aisle reinstated by *Prichard* with a two-light window. Buttresses and top string course added by *Prichard*. Plain parapet by *Pace*.

The one major Perp piece is the NW (JASPER) TOWER. The tradition that it was paid for by Jasper Tudor, Duke of Bedford, and lord of Glamorgan 1484–95, is not documented, but suggests the right sort of date. Three stages. Set-back buttresses with many set-offs dying back to attached pinnacles just below the parapet. Windows in each stage, of two and three lights, with hexagonal tracery and in the topmost windows stone diaperwork. Octagonal sw stair-turret. The glory of the tower is its openwork crown of Somerset type, but this is virtually all a new work by *Prichard*. Browne Willis's early C18 engraving proved that such a crown had indeed existed, but could not be trusted for the details. By the mid C19 nothing remained except diagonal angle corbels. Prichard inevitably took the tower of St John's, Cardiff, as his model. Internally, the tower piers were partly remodelled in the late C15 to support the new tower. NE and SE imposts with running man corbel.

The Eighteenth Century

All trace of *John Wood*'s temple has been expunged from the fabric of the cathedral. (For the few surviving fragments *see* Prebendal House and Cathedral School, below.) It was a much more serious piece of architecture than later critics imagined, inspired by Browne Willis's theory that the first church at Llandaff had been built in Roman times, and proportioned to accord with the account of Solomon's Temple given in 1 Kings, chapter 6.

The Nineteenth Century

The great programme of restoration, or rather re-creation, began at the E end and proceeded w-wards.

T. H. Wyatt in 1841 began to restore the Lady Chapel roof. His high E gable had to be taken back again to a low pitch when *Prichard* heightened the sanctuary, and this was done some time after 1866. The parapet of the sanctuary s aisle, pierced with a Dec pattern of mouchettes, is the only remaining feature attributable to *Wyatt*.

Prichard preferred geometrical forms. His E window in the Lady Chapel, 1843–4, establishes that. Five lights, tracery of encircled

quatrefoils arranged illogically large above small, a design derived
from one of the windows in the Chapter House at York Minster.
Other new windows by Prichard in the sanctuary aisles. The
small but elaborate shafted doorway into the s sanctuary aisle is
obviously later, but was in existence by 1850. Prichard's first
major work was the reconstruction of the sanctuary. Behind
Wood's plaster, the C12 sanctuary arch and fragments of windows
reappeared, evidence which he respectfully retained, however
disjointed the s wall looked as a result. It is a notably early
example of archaeology driving out aesthetics in ecclesiastical
restoration. Recreating the C13 effect of the sanctuary, however,
depended on reconstructing the clerestory and high roof. No C13
masonry survived, so Prichard's clerestory and E gable, built
1846–50, are all his own. Three-light E window set high within
internal arcading. Quatrefoil balcony. Traceried oculus in the
gable. Two-light N and s windows, also with geometrical tracery.
Steep, simple timber roof.

The w arch marks the beginning of the next campaigns, of
1852–7 and 1857–61 by *Prichard & Seddon*, which restored choir
and nave. As explained above, the clerestory in all eight bays is a
uniform design, based on fragments of the C13 clerestory in the
SW bay of the nave. The aisle walls were also reconstructed and
given new buttresses. The Dec windows there were faithfully
restored and the C12 doorways mended. Only for the arch
between choir and sanctuary was there no evidence. On the gable
above it the seating was provided for a flèche, now removed. The
nave-choir roof-ridge was made to align with the ridge of the
sanctuary, itself conditioned by the gable height of the w front,
requiring a beetlingly high timber roof inside. In the reconstruction after bomb damage, the external effect was preserved,
but not the internal. The best-surviving element inside is the choir
s wall, where a doorway and St Teilo's tomb are bound together
into a composition by the lavish use of black polished shafting.

The lofty, uniform effect of *Prichard & Seddon*'s interior was
conceived in relation to the wonderfully coherent set of FITTINGS
executed to their design in the late 1850s. In the sanctuary,
Rossetti's altarpiece in a triple-gabled stone frame stood under the
C12 sanctuary arch, with quadruple-gabled sedilia to the s. In the
choir the E bay was occupied by the bishop's steepled throne set
well forward on the s side and on the N side a reliquary-like organ
case, now at St Mary's, Usk, Gwent. Canopied choir stalls on
each side in the next bay. w again, in the E bay of the nave, the
pulpit richly sculptured, of stone and marble, and the brass eagle
lectern. Today the Rossetti altarpiece is intact (as are six stained-
glass windows, including all those by *Morris & Co.*), removed for
safe keeping at the beginning of the Second World War, but
otherwise only scattered shreds remain (*see* under Furnishings
and Chapter House below).

For the SW TOWER, the climax of the Victorian restoration,
Prichard had virtually nothing to go on. Having reconstructed the
cathedral with a tall clerestory and steep roof, he required a
mighty vertical accent, which would also redress the effect of the

building's sunken situation. So a spire was essential, on a tower more monumental in outline than the Jasper Tower, and, of course, one in stylistic harmony with the C13 W front. Prichard made his design in 1860, and seems to have laid the foundations at once, but the bulk of the tower was not built until 1867–9. Square in plan, its angles clean and vertical, not blurred by the set-back gabled buttresses, which die away altogether halfway up. Arcaded parapet, with pinnacles set square at the angles and diagonally along the sides. Diagonally set tabernacle-like spirelets within the angles, making a rich base from which rises the octagonal spire. Impressive tautness and containment in the whole design. (The small but telling crockets up the angles of the spire were unfortunately shaved off by *Pace*.) Prichard did not wholly ignore the Jasper Tower, however: see the size and alignment of the windows at all three levels. The top, belfry, windows recessed between narrow, steeply pointed arches, an echo of the W front. Statues here and lower down, designed by *Armstead* and carved by *Edward Clarke*. Those at belfry stage are together supposed to symbolize the great Church of the World: W, negro warrior and Roman soldier; S, turbanned figure and native king; E, Chinese and Native American Indian; N, Jew and St Paul, referring to the Judaic roots of the Church. Lower down on the E face, seated figures of the four Evangelists. The standing figures on the S and W buttresses include St Peter, St Paul and Bishop Ollivant.

The Twentieth Century

The destruction wrought by the landmine which exploded outside the S aisle in January 1941 was seen after the war as a challenge and an opportunity, not for faithful reconstruction, but for a reworking in a new spirit. Between 1949 and 1957 *George Pace* made four structural contributions. Most dramatically, he introduced the concrete PARABOLIC ARCHES, on which *Epstein*'s Majestas is poised, in the place of a choir arch, now at last making a physical division between choir and nave which the Cathedral had previously lacked. It is a brilliant solution, providing a mark of separation which is not a spatial barrier. (For further comment *see* under Furnishings, below.) The NAVE ROOF was rebuilt with a nearly flat ceiling. Timber coffer pattern ignoring the bay system below. To accommodate it, *Prichard & Seddon*'s W sanctuary arch was reconstructed less steeply on shortened imposts. The S AISLE Pace faithfully reconstructed, but with a new plaster ceiling of idiosyncratic pattern. Outside the N aisle, intercommunicating with it through the Romanesque doorway, he added a complete new chapel. ST DAVID'S (Welch Regimental) CHAPEL, of 1953–6, is one of Pace's most immediately attractive works. The doorway leads into a W (ritual N) aisle spanned by a series of sharply pointed arches in cross-walls. Almost fully glazed W wall, irregularly subdivided by mullions and transoms. Arched lights. The main space lit from similar, less extensive E windows, the light reflecting off the lobed plaster vault. Full-height window beside the altar apse. – FITTINGS all designed by *Pace*, including the altar frontal. – Fine INSCRIPTIONS on the E walls, listing the Welch Regiment's battle honours. – STATUE. Weathered C13 seated figure of Christ, from the gable of the W front.

FURNISHINGS AND MONUMENTS

Lady Chapel

REREDOS. Perp. Two tiers of broad, crocketed niches, restored 1933. Elaborate image niches l. and r., Madonna and Child, by *A. G. Walker*, 1934. Posies of Welsh flowers in gilt bronze, 1964 by *Frank Roper*. – WALL-PAINTINGS. Stencil patterns in the Bodley tradition, over walls and vaults, 1909 by *Geoffrey Webb*, reinstated in 1988 with some simplification low down. – STAINED GLASS. Also by *Webb*. In the pure, legible, simply coloured style associated with Comper. – E window, Jesse Tree, 1951. – Side windows, two of 1926–8, two of 1952, completing the scheme Webb had devised in 1926. – MONUMENTS. In the NE corner, worn C13 effigy of a bishop, uncertainly identified as William de Braose †1287, though the very flat relief suggests that it is earlier than the other C13 effigies in the Cathedral. – Sir Christopher Mathew and wife, *see* under N choir aisle below. – Bishop Edward Coplestone †1849. Inscribed brass, an early example of the revival of this medieval form of monument. – Bishop Timothy Rees †1939. Life-size brass, by *A. G. Wyon*. Astonishingly late.

Choir and Sanctuary

SEDILIA. Only the seats and arm-rests of *Prichard & Seddon*'s once magnificent sedilia of 1857 remain *in situ* S of the high altar. For the surviving fragments of the canopywork, *see* under S choir aisle and Chapter House below. – BISHOP'S THRONE. By *Prichard & Seddon*. Under a lofty conical canopy. Early French Gothic. Figures of Doctors of the Church by *H. H. Armstead*, and relief panel *ex situ*. Other sculpture by him has been destroyed. – CHOIR STALLS. The seating remains of *Prichard*'s stalls, completed by 1866. Everything else is by *G. G. Pace*, 1964. – CANDLESTICKS. Gilt gesso. Continental. – DOOR, in the S wall of the sanctuary. Designed by *Seddon*. Stout carpentry, lush E.E. hingework. – STAINED GLASS. (Sanctuary E gable). By *John Piper* and *Patrick Reyntiens*, installed 1959. Two throbs of rich colour above the high altar, abstract Supper at Emmaus in the triplet, and roundel over. – MONUMENTS. C13 figure of a bishop (sanctuary S), his head surmounted by an angel-held trefoiled canopy on shafts with stiff-leaf capitals. It marks the traditional site of the tomb of St Teilo. *Prichard & Seddon* added the diapered background and shafted arch above, *Frank Roper* the miniature scenes from the saint's life below. – Bishop Alfred Ollivant †1882 (N of the high altar). On a C13-style tomb-chest, a recumbent figure signed by *H. H. Armstead*. The sculptor has made the most of the leonine head and the lawn sleeves. – Bishop Richard Lewis (sanctuary S wall). 1909 by *Goscombe John*. A dramatic Baroque conceit. The life-size bronze figure of the bishop preaching hovers against the wall, supported by putti and a scroll. – Bishop Joshua Pritchard Hughes †1938 (sanctuary s wall). Also by *Goscombe John*, a late work, 1940. Bronze portrait roundel.

North Choir Aisle

REREDOS. Dec, of stone. The most impressive medieval fitting to survive. Doubtless originally the reredos to the high altar. All-over pattern of blank, ogee, crocketed arches. Narrow side doors under similar arches. Sunk spandrel discs, robbed of their jewels. Mutilated cresting with traces of colour. – RELIEFS. Della Robbia ware. The Six Days of Creation, by *Burne-Jones*, 1893/1906. – LIGHT FITTINGS. By *G. G. Pace*, 1957. – STAINED GLASS. E window, saints, and NE window, kings, 1919. – MONUMENTS. Recumbent stone effigy of a bishop. Good quality, probably of the late C13. Emblems of the Passion behind. Loose armorial end panel. Damaged tomb-chest and arch. These various elements may not belong together. – Sir David Mathew †1461. Recumbent, bare-headed knight in armour. A handsome figure. – Bishop John Marshall †1496. Recumbent stone effigy of indifferent quality, on a tomb-chest decorated with quatrefoils and cusped end panels. Panel *ex situ* at the E end, carved with emblems of the Passion. – Sir Christopher Mathew †1526, and wife (between N choir aisle and Lady Chapel). Alabaster, under a pointed ogee arch of freestone. Elegant recumbent effigies, she with an intricately embroidered head-dress, on a high tomb-chest. Weepers, elongated figures, front and back. – Mutilated cadaver, under an arch in the N wall. Perp panelling behind. Depressed ogee crocketed arch. This too could be of the early C16. – John Nicholl †1853. Large Gothic wall-monument, erected in 1856. Pinnacled buttresses between lushly crocketed gables. Rickman-style rather than Prichard-style. Marble figures of Wisdom and Religion by *J. Evan Thomas*. Nicholl had been the most munificent contributor to the restoration of the cathedral.

South Choir Aisle

ALTAR CRUCIFIX, CANDLESTICKS and RAIL. By *G. G. Pace*, 1961. – LIGHT FITTINGS. By *Pace*, 1957. – STAINED GLASS. E window, 1866 by *Morris & Co*. Christ as king, and Zacharias, both by *William Morris*, and St Elizabeth with the boy John the Baptist, a finely characterized group by *Ford Madox Brown*. – SW window, crucified Christ between the four Evangelists. 1868 by *Morris & Co*. *Burne-Jones* designed the figures of Christ and Mark, *Madox Brown*, Matthew and John, and *Morris*, Luke. – MONUMENTS. Cross-head (under the vaulted W bay). The upper part of a composite shaft, with interlace and angle rolls, comparable to the cross-shaft at Llandough (q.v.). Late C10–C11. – Effigy of a lady (NE corner). Alabaster, recumbent under a modern arch. Called Lady Audley. – George Gaze Pace †1975. Made up from two fragments of *Prichard & Seddon*'s sedilia canopies. Two Evangelist figures, pelican and peacock among foliage, virtuoso stone-carving by *Edward Clarke*, the birds said to have been designed by *Rossetti*. Gilt bronze lettering by *Frank Roper*.

Nave and Aisles

MAJESTAS. 1957 by *Sir Jacob Epstein*, on a pair of parabolic 117 concrete arches by *Pace*. Arresting and deeply impressive, in drastic contrast but not in conflict with the building. Epstein's huge figure of Christ stares ahead impassively, but his outspread hands suggest compassion. Stylized, tubular robe. The figure is made of aluminium, attached to a concrete cylinder containing the positive organ pipes. Tiny brackets carry gilded angels and prophets rescued by Pace from the C19 organ case and choir stalls, a curious idea justified as softening what might otherwise be too stark a statement. – FONT. 1952 by *Alan Durst*. Egg-shaped, of Hopton Wood stone, with a domical wooden cover. Reliefs of Fall and Redemption, with scenes from the lives of Welsh saints on the base. Figures and inscriptions mixed up with apparent artlessness, attempting an early medieval effect. – PULPIT. 1957 by *Pace*. Wood painted black, not green as intended. More historicist than most of Pace's fittings. – ORGAN CASE. 1958 by *Pace*. – W DOOR by *Prichard & Seddon*. – S DOOR by *Pace*. The contrast between the hingework on the two doors is worth savouring. – PAINTINGS. Under the NW tower, the former ALTARPIECE, 'The Seed of David' painted by *Dante Gabriel Rossetti* 1855–64 for Prichard & Seddon's high altar. A major work of Pre-Raphaelite religious art. In the centre panel of the triptych, Adoration of Christ in the stable, by a shepherd and a king. In the side panels, David as shepherd (l.) and David as royal psalmist (r.). All the principal figures seem strangely anguished. The *Ecclesiologist* in 1861, before the l. panel had been executed, praised the composition of the r. panel as 'thoughtful, and novel without being far-fetched', but criticized the Virgin in the centre for her 'anxious expression' and 'tangled and dishevelled hair'. Gilt frame and inscription by *Donald Buttress*, 1989, reusing *Pace* cresting at the top. – SCREENS, enclosing the tower space. To the E simplified Renaissance by *Pace*, to the S simplified Gothic by *Buttress*. – PAINTED TESTER (N aisle). Executed for Bishop Marshall († 1496) and incorporated by *Pace* into the sedilia of the St Euddogwy Chapel. A great rarity, which somehow escaped the iconoclasts. Assumption of the Virgin, with the bishop kneeling in adoration. – RELIEF (S aisle). Dormition of the Virgin. Small, German, late C15. Presumably from a carved altarpiece. – STAINED GLASS. N aisle, two windows by *Morris & Co*. SS Simon, Peter and Jude, with sea miracles below, 1874, all based on designs by *Ford Madox Brown*, except St Peter, by *Burne-Jones*. The richest and most enjoyable of the Morris windows in the cathedral. – Moses between SS John the Baptist and Paul (all by *Burne-Jones*), with music-making angels below (by *Morris*), 1868. – Ruth, Anna, Dorcas, *c*. 1890 by *W. F. Dixon*. Animated

figures and elaborate draperies filling the space available, quite
different from the static Morris figures set against quarry backgrounds. – S aisle, a mixed collection. From the E, first another
window by *Morris & Co.*, dated 1869. St Stephen between David
and Samuel, with scenes involving children below. All designed
by *Burne-Jones*, except the Presentation in the Temple by *Morris*. –
Crucifixion. 1910 by *J. S. Sparrow*. Feverishly coloured. –
Towards the W end, Christ between two kings, with scenes of
Christ's sayings and parables below. This can hardly be before
*c.*1900, by *Burlison & Grylls*. – MONUMENTS. Worn C13 figure
of a bishop (S aisle), not fully in the round. Thought to represent
Bishop Henry of Abergavenny †1218. Under an arch by *Prichard*. – Worn, later C13 figure of a bishop (N aisle), with angels
holding a canopy overhead. Thought to represent Bishop William
of Radnor †1265. – Sir William Mathew †1528 (nave N). Recumbent alabaster effigies of a knight and lady on a tomb-chest with
figures on its sides of monks, ladies and shield-bearing angels.
Worth a close look. – Henry Thomas †1863 (N aisle). Double-
arched, vaulted recess on marble shafts, 1866, designed by *Prichard*. No effigy, but a polychrome marble tomb-slab, and fine
reliefs by *Armstead*. At the back, the Judgement of Solomon,
and Moses with the Tablets of the Law. Mr Thomas had been
chairman of Quarter Sessions. – Dean Charles John Vaughan (N
aisle E end). 1899–1900 by *Goscombe John*. Recumbent effigy,
imitating Armstead's Bishop Ollivant. – Archdeacon James Rice
Buckley †1924 (N aisle). Bronze wall-monument. Portrait
roundel between solemn figures of Virtues.

CHAPTER HOUSE

Attached to the S aisle of the sanctuary. Datable to the mid C13.
A small, square two-storey building, the upper storey reconstructed by *Prichard* and again by *Pace*. Its size is eloquent of the
diminutive scale of operations at Llandaff even in the cathedral's
heyday. But this is a handsome piece of architecture. Strongly
moulded plinth. Two deep-set lancets per face, with triple-
chamfered, trefoiled heads. Hoods on small head-stops. Ashlar-
faced angle buttresses. The conversion of the upper stage from
square to octagonal halfway up, by means of semi-pyramidal
spurs, was Prichard's idea. Moulded cornice and typical Prichard
gargoyles. His eight-sided roof lowered in pitch by *Pace* and
recently given a flare by *Donald Buttress*. Inside, the main room is
handsomely vaulted. The central circular shaft has a big, round,
water-holding base and a light, round cap. From it spring four
quatripartite rib-vaults. Chamfered ribs, brought down against
the walls on short shafts with moulded caps and corbels carved
as leaf sprigs or human heads. – STAINED GLASS. Seven C16
Flemish roundels, inserted by Pace.
  The upper room was reconstructed by *Pace*, with a passing
strange concrete ceiling. – FRAGMENTS of carved stonework
here, including one or two tantalizing pieces from the Victorian
fittings. – Pulpit panel with a figure of Moses cowering at the

glory of God, by *Woolner*. Another revealing example of the dark psychology of the Pre-Raphaelites. – Roundel from the central gable of the reredos. Lamb of God, carved by *Clarke*.

Among the few external MONUMENTS, three require mention. – Dean Conybeare. Memorial cross (s of the Chapter House) erected in 1867 to the design of his son, *Henry Conybeare*. Modelled on the churchyard crosses at Llangan and St Donats (qq.v.). Shaft of white Mansfield stone. Cross-head carved with reliefs of the Crucifixion and Resurrection. – John Prichard † 1886 (s of the sanctuary aisle). Restrained Gothic tomb-chest. – Garden of remembrance (s of the nave aisle). Large inscribed slab on the site where the landmine exploded. 1992, lettered by *Ieuan Rees*.

PREBENDAL HOUSE

The only building at the same level as the cathedral, NW of the Jasper Tower. The w range may date back to the C17, reconstructed *c*. 1700. Timber door hood on brackets. The range at r.-angles, 1926 by *Nicholson*, a central arch punched in it by *Pace*. This links to the curving PROCESSIONAL WAY by which *Pace* gave access to St David's Chapel and to the N door of the Cathedral. Two-storey N extension, 1985–6 by *Robert Heaton*, Pace-style. – URN, in the processional way. From the w pediment of *Wood*'s temple. Gadrooned.

THE VILLAGE

THE GREEN. Llandaff Cathedral has no close,* but it is attended at the top of the steep escarpment to the s by THE GREEN. Here, at the crest of the slope, two structures are intended to draw attention to the presence of the cathedral below. The massive C13 BELL TOWER, comparable to that at Chichester and that formerly at Salisbury, must have been impressive when complete. Now, however, there survive only part of the s wall with its angle returns, and isolated chunks at the NE and NW. These define the angles of a structure about 42 ft (12.8 metres) square. How high it stood and whether the bells were hung in a stone or a timber-framed upper stage cannot be determined. The splays of a single-light opening in the s wall. Dressed stonework only at the SE angle, a bold roll over the chamfered top of the plinth, identical to the plinth of the Chapter House.

The LYCHGATE, E of the bell tower at the head of the steep path down to the w door of the cathedral, is by *Prichard*. Small but monumental. Pink Radyr ashlar alternating with dark grey Forest of Dean stone. Coped stone roof over a shallow vault with transverse ribs.

BISHOP'S CASTLE, at the E end of The Green. Late C13, fully fortified and surviving so extensively that its impact when

---

*Speed's map of 1610, however, indicates prebendal houses to the E of the cathedral.

complete can readily be imagined. The most likely builder was
William de Braose (bishop 1266–87), a member of the great
family which held the lordship of Gower. It is a sign of the
insecurity of the cathedral community in the face of the ever-
present threat of Welsh attack that the Bishop should have
erected what is as much a fortress as a residence. The GATE-
HOUSE at the sw angle commands the length of The Green.
Square, two-storey towers with splayed angles on spurs flank a
narrow entrance arch with three chamfered orders dying into
the splays of the towers. The similarity with the E outer gatehouse at Caerphilly Castle of c. 1280 is striking. The wall above
the arch overhangs on corbels and has a central arrow loop.
Under the arch a portcullis slot and the rebate for a door. Three
further vaulted bays within, their transverse arches uncham-
fered, and an inner arch to match the outer. The N tower
has an unlit semi-basement, and arrangements above that are
unclear. In the s tower a well-appointed ground-floor room
with a hooded fireplace and arrow loops in three directions. In
the square turret behind, a spacious newel stair which must
have given access to a room above the full width of the gatehouse. Both the doorways here have a bull-nosed moulding,
another feature found in the late C13 parts of Caerphilly Castle.
The gatehouse leads into a large, rectangular walled enclosure.
Very little trace remains of the residential buildings which
originally stood within the walls. Evidence for an upper hall at
the N end of the NE wall, built where the ground drops with
impregnable steepness. Circular turret at the SE angle, the
splays of openings surviving in its front wall, the rear wall a
modern construction. Square s tower, with one small rectangular opening in its s wall. The sw enclosure wall survives
almost to full height all along, with corbel table for a battlemented wall-walk.

Today THE GREEN is quietly domestic, and can be readily
surveyed. Towards the E end, the CITY CROSS, C13 in origin.
Only the shaft is original. Big, plain cross-head, 1897. Beyond
the bell tower on the N side, THE DEANERY, a plain, rendered
house of four bays and two storeys, apparently of c. 1840, shown
on an estate map of 1776 but possibly even earlier within.
CATHEDRAL COURT, in the NW corner, was built as the
Deanery, 1861–3 by *Ewan Christian*. Planned on Puginian principles, but in a bald Tudor Gothic style with gables and excessive canted projections for the principal rooms to E and N.
Mullion-and-transom windows with spurred circles in the
upper lights. Walling of multicoloured random stone, banded
with thin courses of Pennant sandstone and lavishly dressed
with Bath stone ashlar. PENDINAS, next door, built as the
Canonry, is also by *Christian*, 1861–3, smaller, but similar in
style and materials. In front of them, WAR MEMORIAL, of
1924 by *Goscombe John*, for the Cathedral School and Llandaff
village. Three isolated bronze figures stand on granite pedestals
designed by *J. P. Grant*. The robed central female symbolizing
Llandaff is flanked by a boy cadet and a rifle-bearing workman.
The group was originally entitled 'Departure'.

The W end is closed by an attractive and appropriate group of irregularly terraced houses, 1979 by *Wyn Thomas & Partners*.

On the S side, No. 19, 1888 by *Halliday & Anderson*, introduces mock half-timbering in Norman Shaw's Old English manner. Stone below, the multicoloured crazy-paving walling being of the kind known at the time as 'split popples'. Nos. 7–13 is a larger and more ambitious essay in the same vein, a terrace of four, surely by *Halliday*, built in the late 1890s. Three stages here, stone below, tile-hanging above and half-timbering for gables and dormers. In front of this the bronze STATUE of Archdeacon James Rice Buckley, by *Goscombe John*, 1927. THE OLD HOUSE, apparently a rendered C18 building, on the corner of HEOL FAIR, has a C16 S doorway, with a four-centred head, and a mutilated two-light window over. (Further down Heol Fair on the r., BLACK HALL, incorporating the N wall of a late C13 or early C14 upper-floor hall, with two two-light windows, one filled in with reused tracery.) Opposite The Old House, ST MARY'S, a tall, narrow Gothic house of Pennant sandstone with Bath stone dressings, could well be by *Prichard*. See the handling of the porch, the corbelled chimneybreast, the shafted window. It was built soon after 1863 for Thomas Williams, Prichard's contractor for the restoration of the cathedral. After that, the HIGH STREET runs off from the SE corner of The Green. Here a row of Gothic shops, even with shafted display windows, curves round the corner. Built for Mr Seaborn the butcher *c.* 1863. In High Street itself nothing except a spacious stone pair of minor canonries, built 1859–61, ST ANDREW and ST CROSS. They are by *Ewan Christian* and match his work at the other end of The Green. The corbelled chimneystack rising from the apex of each entrance gable is an engaging detail.

CARDIFF ROAD. To see what *John Prichard* could achieve as a secular architect one need only descend to the far end of High Street and turn l. Here in CARDIFF ROAD, at once on the l., is his PROBATE REGISTRY, 1860–3. This is an excellent example of the 'true picturesque' advocated by the Ecclesiologists, in which a visually satisfying whole is created by emphasizing functional differences. E.E. T-plan, the public office in the lofty, single-storey cross-wing to the r. Two-storey main range to the l., subdivided by a complex chimneystack set end-on to the façade. Different groupings of windows to the l. and to the r. of the stack. Shafted doorway, under a steeply pointed gable, sited where it can give direct access to both halves of the building. Windows grouped in twos and threes, all shafted, the lower ones straight-headed, the upper with cusped and pointed heads, the longest also with shaft-rings. Steep roofs, elegantly varied chimneystacks. The quality of Prichard's handling of materials can be fully appreciated now the building has been cleaned. Walls of thin-coursed Pennant sandstone with bands of Bridgend stone, Bath stone dressings. Interior drastically modernized.

The OLD REGISTRY, set back from the street-line, next

door, was clearly intended as the Registrar's house, and was designed by *Prichard* as part of the whole composition. Two-storeyed. Twin two-light gabled dormers above a full-width slated veranda give an impression of symmetry. But the drawing room has a curved window bay under the veranda, and the gable-end chimneystacks do not match.

Across the road is *John Prichard*'s OFFICE, designed by him after 1863 and attached to a house left unfinished at his death in 1886 (*see* St Michael's College, below). The office is on a miniature scale. Entrance porch set lozenge-wise at the l. corner with a cylindrical turret above. Steep caps to both. Overall gable with a bargeboard. Service wing projecting low to the r. This sprightly design is further enlivened by a virtuoso mixing of materials. The two-light upper windows have shafts of green Bridgend stone with carved leaf-caps, sills and lintels of pink Radyr stone and black brick jambs. Multicoloured 'popple' walling.

ST MICHAEL'S THEOLOGICAL COLLEGE, Cardiff Road. 1905–7 by *F. R. Kempson*, incorporating the S and E walls of Prichard's unfinished house. L-plan frontage towards the road, with an inconspicuous porch in the angle. In the gable end to the r. large mullion-and-transom windows at two levels under an overall pointed relieving arch. The upper window lights the library. Three-storey range to the l. Rock-faced pink sandstone throughout. All is bland and uninspired. The rear façade, being by *Prichard*, is far more enjoyable in its use of materials and its playful sculpture, though the composition is not especially convincing, and it must have been intended to crown it with a much steeper roof.

Dormitory ranges by or imitative of *Kempson* flank the lawn behind. At the far end the blank wall of what appears to be a barn or shed built of large blocks of iron-stained Pennant rubble. This is the entrance wall of the CHAPEL, by *George Pace*, 1957–9, built in place of one of two bombed ranges. The wall is in fact in two parts canted towards one another under an asymmetrical gable, but the small metal figure of St Michael, by *Frank Roper*, over the simple doorway is the only hint that this is an ecclesiastical building, or indeed a building of any non-utilitarian significance at all. The side walls are punched through with many small rectangular windows in seemingly random patterns.

After this the interior is truly moving. White plastered walls continued up smoothly by means of a cove to the white plastered ceiling. All the light comes from the long wall on the r. Blank white altar wall against which *Harry Stammers*'s figure of Christ in Majesty hovers like a vision. The architect has created a numinous space by means of light and its reflection from smooth surfaces without introducing a single evocation of the traditional forms of church architecture. Without the inspiration of Le Corbusier's recently completed chapel at Ronchamp, he could hardly have done it. – FITTINGS by *Pace*, except the stalls at the entrance end, from the bombed chapel.

Further E on the l., No. 63. Clearly also by *Prichard*, and formerly bearing the date 1870. This has a full-width veranda, like the Old Registry (*see* above), carried across a broad, three-bay front. Three gables, the largest in the centre. All the familiar materials. Random, multicoloured walling with broad bands of Pennant sandstone. Window surrounds of Radyr stone and black brick. Round the corner, two-centred entrance arch of red and black brick, and service windows of the same. Impressive stair-hall, top-lit. Cusped timber arcading and pierced quatrefoils and discs to the stair balustrade and gallery.

CATHEDRAL SCHOOL, Cardiff Road. Set in its own grounds. The nucleus of the school is a rarity for Glamorgan, a mid-C18 mansion. This was built, as Llandaff Court, 1744–6 for Admiral Thomas Mathew, and is of exceeding plainness. The original entrance front faces SE, nine bays wide, three storeys high, of Bath stone ashlar. Thin, plain window surrounds with small keystones, those at the top level running up into the moulded stone cornice. Textbook Doric doorcase with half-columns and triangular pediment. This is surely a craftsman-designed house. The present entrance is to the NW, a repetition of the SE front except that the walls are rendered with Bath stone dressings, and the Doric pilastered doorcase fronts a porch which must be after 1850, when the house became the bishop's palace. Top parapet removed in 1915 by *W. D. Caröe* after a fire.

The effect of the double-pile interior has been spoilt by the reorientation. So the handsome full-height staircase, with three turned balusters per tread, rises immediately to the l. of the front door, but must have been intended to be seen beyond the central screen of two Doric columns.

The Gothic CHAPEL was built for the bishop to the SW of the house and linked to it by a one-storey vestibule. 1858–9 by *Ewan Christian*. E end in five gabled cants. Two-light side windows with spurred quatrefoils in the tracery. Three-light W window with fully Dec tracery. Snecked, squared masonry of local polychromatic stones, with dressings of Bath stone. Thin arch-braced roof on big stiff-leaf capitals. Ballflower on the rere-arches of the windows. So the style hovers between E.E. and Dec all through. – STAINED GLASS. In the E lancets, Christ and the four Evangelists, 1895.

The Cathedral School took over the house in 1958. Recent buildings for the school of no special interest.

There is less of note in Cardiff Road N of High Street. Mention need only be made of the self-assured little OFFICE BLOCK on the W side, built in the mid 1970s, for Office Cleaning Services (Wales) Ltd, by the *Holder & Mathias Partnership*. Grey blockwork and greenhouse-like glazing.

OUTLYING BUILDINGS

ALL SAINTS, Gabalfa Road, $\frac{3}{4}$ m. NW. Chancel by *Kempson & Fowler* 1890–1, nave 1914, by *F. R. Kempson*. Gutted 1941 and rebuilt in modified form 1953–5. Coursed Pennant sandstone, with meagre dressings of Bath stone.

East of Western Avenue

HOWELL'S SCHOOL FOR GIRLS, Cardiff Road, ½ m. SE. In 1537 Thomas Howell bequeathed money to the Drapers' Company in London to provide dowries for orphan girls. Over 300 years later, in 1852, the Company secured an Act which enabled them to direct the bequest, by then much enhanced in value, to found two schools for orphan girls, one in Denbigh, the other in Llandaff. For the school at Llandaff *Decimus Burton* was commissioned to prepare 'late Gothic' designs. When he withdrew, the Drapers put in their favoured architect, *Herbert Williams*. His L-shaped building, erected in 1858–9, survives remarkably untouched, the several additions being mostly to the rear. It is built of smoothly cut Lias limestone with dressings of Forest of Dean stone. Slate roofs, still even with their decorative bands of fish-scale pattern.

The main range lies back, its central porch flanked by buttresses and surmounted by a tall, sheer tower corbelled out at the top for a steep, pyramidal roof. Windows mostly mullion-and-transom. Over the junction of the ranges a gawky lantern with lead-covered sides and slated top. The l. wing comes forward with a one-storey, five-bay cloister-like day room towards the court. The original schoolroom lay behind. Traceried windows here. Originally the wing ended at the octagonal bell-turret. Beside the road a single-storey LODGE, enlarged behind.

Internally, the most impressive space is under the massively timbered lantern, where a broad stone stair rises in straight flights. Iron balustrade. In the wing added by *G. E. Halliday* towards the S in 1899–1900, the UPPER HALL has Perp windows and a boarded roof with tie-beams and, presumably, concealed hammerbeams. LABORATORY AND STUDIO BLOCK to the W, 1904 by *Halliday*.

WHITLEY BATCH, on the NE side of CARDIFF ROAD, N of Howell's School. 1886, an early work by *Halliday*. Quite large, gabled, of pink Radyr stone with red brick dressings, in a Home Counties style. (Inside, three medieval arches, from a cottage in Bridge Street, which Halliday persuaded his client, H. W. Thompson, to have built in.) A little further S, CHURCHILL HOTEL (formerly Llandaff Place), a pair of rather grand mid-C19 Italianate stuccoed villa pairs, not at all the normal thing in this area. Rich details, including many metal balconies. In HOWELL'S CRESCENT, NW of the school, typical twin-gabled semi-detached villas built *c*. 1896–1901. No. 13, 1979–80 by *Hird & Brooks*, low, introverted, of red brick with monopitch roofs, is in drastic contrast, and probably meant as a rebuke to its neighbours.

Fairwater Road

LLANDAFF HOUSE, on the corner of Cardiff Road, is a mid-C18 three-storey house with a plain top parapet, datable before 1776. Central first-floor window with plain side scrolls and segmental pediment. Flanking full-height canted window bays. Now deprived of the grassed forecourt which originally showed off the façade. A little way down Fairwater Road, on the l., TRENEWYDD, a large gabled house dated 1890 and bearing a welcoming inscription in Welsh. Red brick below, red tile-hanging above, red sandstone dressings. A little half-timbering in the gables. Arched doorway and stone mullioned windows, their details confirming an attribution to *G. E. Halliday*. THE HERMITAGE, next door, a miniature essay in a similar style, was put up at the same time by Halliday, strictly *Halliday & Anderson*, for himself. Here the tiling is of the fish-scale variety, and the mullion-and-transom windows are incorporated in the half-timbering of the gables, additional touches of deference to its grander neighbour.

ROOKWOOD HOSPITAL comes next on the r. The hospital has unfeelingly colonized an extraordinary High Victorian Gothic mansion. This was built shortly after 1866, the outrageous porte cochère added to the s front in 1881 together with other features to heighten the aspect from the sw. Episodic these additions may be, but they suggest the hand of *Prichard*. Rock-faced walling of pink Radyr stone throughout, with ashlar dressings and carved decoration in buff Bath stone. Two-storeyed. The E half of the main range and the service wing at the back must belong to the earlier phase. Canted bays and sash windows with shouldered tops. Rectangular chimneystacks with sloping set-offs and roofs of moderate pitch. By contrast the later parts have a more steeply pitched roof, a coped gable end and a stone parapet pierced with quatrefoils and inset with discs. Windows with mullions and transoms, the upper lights cusped. At the NW corner a circular oriel and dovecote under a candle-snuffer roof. On the s front close to the w end a full-height canted bay rises above the eaves so that its spire-like roof is fully octagonal. Between this and the porte cochère a projecting chimneybreast carries a pair of elegant octagonal stacks. Finally, the porte cochère itself. This is almost an independent building, the ridge of its saddleback roof as high as that of the house itself. It stands on arches originally open in three directions. To the s the gable end is flanked by slender octagonal turrets, between which a bowed oriel blossoms out at first-floor level. Three carved panels above the multi-moulded corbelling. Stiff-leaf and, in the concave cornice mouldings, miniature running animals. A timber-framed conservatory extends in an L from the NE angle. Inside, the main feature is the canted ceiling over the staircase, said to have been painted by *Crace*. (Also the chapel ceiling painted by *Crace*, and a richly carved chimneypiece in the dining room. Hilling.)

In the grounds NW of the house an C18 GAZEBO, built on a

hollow mound, which served as an ice-house. Octagonal, with Gothic details of Batty Langley character. It originally belonged to LLANDAFF HOUSE (*see* above), and was in position by 1776.

INSOLE (LLANDAFF) COURT, between Fairwater Road and Vaughan Avenue, ½ m. SW. Built, under the name of Ely Court, for J. H. Insole. Now a community centre, the terraced gardens a public park. Another large Victorian Gothic mansion, grey and formless. Begun in 1855 by *W. G. &E. Habershon*, extended in 1873 by 'E. J. Robinson', i.e. probably *G. E. Robinson*. Extended again *c.* 1875 by *James, Seward & Thomas*, i.e. *Edwin Seward*, who had been Robinson's assistant. £10,000 was said to have been spent on this phase. Further extensions by *Edwin Seward c.* 1895. Pennant sandstone and Bath stone dressings. The original house seems to have had plain gables and large plate glass windows, most clearly seen on the S front towards the garden. Two-storey canted window bays here and on the short E front, additions perhaps, with varied sculptured enrichment. The entrance front, facing N, is the most complex and demonstrative, with a high (originally steep-roofed) tower, richly decorated window bays, a polychromatic glazed arcade leading to a long wing reaching forward to the l. Fake half-timbered upper walls here with geometrical timber tracery. The most telling evidence that Insole was engaged in a constant process of updating his house is the single-storey porte cochère, which has early Renaissance detail, but masks a hooded Gothic doorway of Burgesian character with black marble shafts, poly-chromatic voussoirs and the stooping figures of bedesmen supporting the hood.

Inside, the influence of Burges pervades. The entrance HALL has an E.E. chimneypiece, and the stone staircase beyond used to have massive armorial animals on the newels. The room which survives most completely is the DINING ROOM, the elaborate buffet at its inner end set within an arch of Penarth alabaster. Ribbed timber ceiling on a carved cove. Painted frieze of Labours of the Months, signed by *Frederick Weekes.**

ELY RISE (now Fairwater Conservative Club), Ely Road, ½ m. SW. Yet one more Gothic house by *John Prichard*. With all his hallmarks, steep roofs, tall chimneystacks and polychromatic walling. Entrance porch with the initials of his client, W. G. David, part of a subtle composition of gables to the W. Three-bay garden front, the l. bay circular below, polygonal above, a typical Prichard veranda across the other two bays. Square entrance hall filled by a handsome timber staircase, with an alabaster chimneypiece against the N wall. On the hood a corbel carved with a pensive man seated under a tree. Original woodwork and metalwork in other rooms. Single-storey extensions of *c.* 1965 by *Burgess & Partners*.

B.B.C. BROADCASTING HOUSE, Llantrisant Road, ½ m. NW. 1963–7 by *Sir Percy Thomas & Son* (design partner *Dale Owen*). A varied group lined up beside the road, all of reinforced

*Signature found by Matthew Williams.

concrete structure, allowing characteristic sheets and bands of glazing, the dazzling white wall surfaces faced with Carrara marble aggregate. At the r. the low, fully glazed restaurant, poised over car park and services, then the four-storey admin-istration block, with the entrance from the road in its short end. The studios lie to the l., first the three sound studios, glazed only in the sides of three shallow projections, then the music studio, rising high above a glazed façade, the high part clad with sound-absorbing river pebbles below, and above with shuttered concrete at the level where the ends of the steel roof-trusses project. The l.-hand component, television studios, is characterized with less clarity.

OTHER SUBURBS

BUTETOWN AND CARDIFF BAY

The roughly 2-m. (3.2-kilometre)-square peninsula of flat marsh-land lying to the NE of Cardiff Bay provided the site for the great development of docks by the second and third Marquesses of Bute. The function of these docks was to satisfy the need for an export outlet for the ever-increasing supplies first of iron, then of coal from the Valleys, which the Glamorganshire Canal was quite unable to cope with. The second Marquess in 1827 commissioned a report from the canal engineer, *James Green*. In 1834–9 the new dock which he recommended was formed under the supervision of *William Cubitt*. This, BUTE WEST DOCK, 4,000 ft (1,219 metres) long and 200 ft (61 metres) wide, lay parallel to the E of the final, sea-lock stretch of the Glamorganshire Canal. The parallel BUTE EAST DOCK, 4,300 ft (1,309 metres) long and up to 500 ft (152 metres) wide, was opened in stages 1855–9, and enabled a huge expansion of activity. ROATH BASIN, to the SE at r.-angles to the earlier docks, was constructed 1868–74. In the 1880s work began on further expansion, in the face of the threat from the proposed docks at Barry. ROATH DOCK, E of Roath Basin, designed by *James McConnochie*, opened in 1887, and finally in 1907, ALEXANDRA DOCK, alongside Roath Basin to the S. Although the coal trade was beginning to fall off by the early C20, it was only after the Second World War that the volume of shipping sharply declined. Bute West Dock was filled in.

By the early 1980s the whole area was disused and largely derelict. In 1987 the Cardiff Bay Development Corporation was established, and at the time of writing it has already made its presence felt, primarily in new buildings at the N end of Bute East Dock. In a remarkable gesture of faith the South Glamorgan County Council has built itself a new county hall near its S end. The best Victorian buildings have also managed to survive, in particular the Pierhead Building, but also the concentration round Mount Stuart Square.

It will be interesting to see how all these scattered elements are tied together in the years to come. Much will depend on the

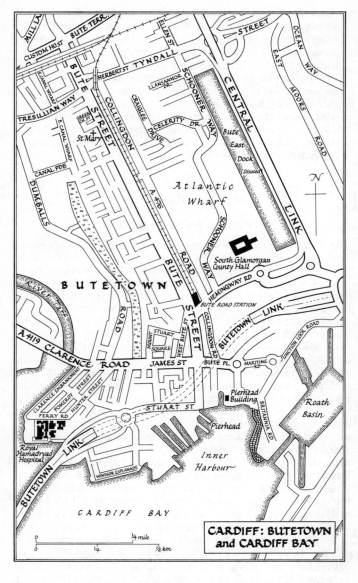

CARDIFF: BUTETOWN and CARDIFF BAY

new CARDIFF BAY OPERA HOUSE, to be sited NE of the re-excavated Dock Basin, close behind the Pierhead Building. In 1994 an international competition was won by the Iraqi architect *Zaha Hadid*. Her design enfolds the auditorium in four ranges of glazed ancillary buildings, the glass revealing blade-like concrete floor-slabs, the NE range ingeniously absorbing the fly-tower. The curved SW range, its shape echoing the oval of the Dock Basin, gives access to the auditorium courtyard. This all looks extremely promising, a building of great visual force which will do much to integrate the various structures at the head of Cardiff Bay. It is due for completion in the year 2000.

St Mary, Bute Street. 1840–5 by *Thomas Foster* of Bristol, built, for £5,700, at the expense of the second Marquess of Bute. Neo-Norman. Coursed sandstone, dressed with sandstone and Bath stone ashlar. Big and ambitious, but a foolish design. The e end towards the road is worked up into a full-scale entrance composition flanked by pyramid-roofed towers and boasting three portals decorated with zigzag. Rope-moulded rose window in the gable. Yet there is no entrance this way. For that it is necessary to traverse the flank of the building – lean-to aisles and tall clerestory – to the understated w front. Here the nave projects one bay beyond the aisles and is flanked by thin turrets. Five-bay nave. Tall, circular piers with scallop capitals. Round arches and hoodmoulds on arrestingly grotesque head-stops. Flat ceiling. w gallery, the only survivor of the galleries originally on three sides of the church. Windowless e apse, where the pulpit was originally sited. As part of the reordering by *J. D. Sedding* in 1884–5 the apse was decorated with twelve white, life-size figures of apostles by *Searle* of Exeter. Colouring of the figures intended. – ALTARPIECE. Painting of the Adoration of the Kings, 1884 by *Philip Westlake*. Early Renaissance style. – SCREEN. At the w end. Tall and wide, of wrought iron, c.1890, by *Cecil Hare* in Spanish style; it imparts an intriguingly Continental character to the interior. Brought from *Sedding*'s church of St Dyfrig, demolished in 1969. (– WAR MEMORIAL. By *J. Coates Carter*.)

St Nicholas (Greek Orthodox), Greek Church Street. 1906 by *James & Morgan*. A scholarly little essay in the Byzantine style. Centralized, with a dome and an e apse. Red brick and Bath stone. Plastered interior.

Bute West Dock. The flanking sea walls and dock entrance remain at the former entrance of the Bute West Dock. This was originally called 'The Cardiff Ship Canal' by the engineer *James Green*, whose plans were examined by Telford, Cubitt and Robert Stephenson. The resident engineer was *George Turnbull*. The sea wall is formed of massive grey-brown stone blocks with copings generally of granite. The dock basin is elliptical with granite steps descending on either side. Recesses for pairs of dock entrance gates lie at both its N and s ends, complete with iron seatings for the gate hinges.

Bute East Dock. 1852–9. The supervising engineer was *Sir John Rennie* with the resident engineers *W. S. Clarke* and *John Plews*. The lock and entrance basin partially remain, made of large blocks of brown stone, generally with granite copings. On the NW side is a former TRANSIT SHED built before 1870. Iron-framed, five bays by two with cruciform-sectioned Tuscan columns supporting an I-beam entablature clad in wood.

Two visually striking 'islands' constructed of timber piles, in the bay to the S of the Welsh Industrial and Maritime Museum. Each supports two railway-type signals, two on lattice-girder posts and two on timber posts surmounted by finials. The floating landing stage of the steam packet harbour was in the gap between the islands and the shore, connected by a pivoting bridge that ran between the wooden dolphins closer to the shore.

For Dock Warehouses, see pp. 272–3 below.

122 SOUTH GLAMORGAN COUNTY HALL, Hemingway Road. By *J.R.C. Bethell*, the County Architect, 1986–7. Late C20 civic architecture in the tradition established at the Hillingdon Civic Centre in the London suburbs, 1973–8, where Robert Matthew, Johnson-Marshall & Partners showed how to characterize a civic building without making it domineer by its bulk or formal language. At present, alone beside the Bute East Dock, such modesty may seem irrelevant, and it is important that new neighbours should not over-top it. Three main storeys only, crowned by shallow-pitched black-slated roofs, and rising under roofs of similar pitch to four storeys or even five towards the water. The sloping roof-lines echoed lower down by the continuous metal awnings over the ground storey, and even by the battered plinth all round the building. This is of purple brick, as are the walls of the Council Chamber and its flights of steps which come forward closest to the dockside. Slender rectangular piers faced with orange-brown brick rise through two storeys to support the third storey, which projects as a continuous glazed oriel, its black metal framing hard up under the roof eaves. Colours and forms all combine to give an impression of subdued repose. Perhaps all this should be seen as evidence of a late C20 loss of nerve, even a deliberate abnegation of the arrogant assertiveness of the late C19, expressed across the water and the wasteland in the Pierhead Building.

The plan of the County Hall is unexpectedly straightforward, four ranges round a large rectangular courtyard, the outer angles to the SW and the NW developed with short projections, and a longer, single-storey arm reaching out to the E for the Council Chamber.

Internally, the building impresses less. The double-height entrance hall is largely filled with a staircase rising on the diagonal from back to front. Black abstract metal sculpture here, set against a polished granite pier, 'Water, Coal and Steel' by *David Peterson*, 1988. The Council Chamber, in plan a lozenge with chamfered corners, is low-ceilinged and devoid of any special dignity.

103 PIERHEAD BUILDING. Proudly isolated at the water's edge, facing across Cardiff Bay to survey the bustling activities managed by the Bute Docks Company, whose offices it was built to house. The Trustees of the third Marquess of Bute in 1887 formed a public limited company, and the Pierhead Building was constructed a decade later, in 1896–7, to the design of *William Frame*. Frame had been assistant to William

Burges at Cardiff Castle and Castell Coch, and Burges's influence is powerful here. The architect may even have intended it
as his Castell Coch, his Red Castle. The materials are hot red
brick and hot red terracotta exactly matched. Boldly overscaled
tower over a porch with early French Renaissance detail, rising
via an oriel window to a clock stage decked with armorial
shields and crowned with arcading and deep battlements. Steep
pavilion roof. Steeply pitched roofs everywhere else, defining
the mass of the two-storey building, and an array of heavily
modelled chimneystacks. Short, symmetrical entrance front,
with mullion-and-transom windows, their top lights arched. Its
symmetry is broken by a polygonal bay at the sw angle, with
its own candle-snuffer roof. Round the corner more heraldic
decoration, and a triple chimneystack of special elaboration, all
denoting the fact that the upper room in this corner was the
manager's office. Otherwise the long sides are quieter, the large
windows in the central section lighting a hall, the rear range
accommodating offices for the company.

The stylistic eclecticism observable outside continues within,
but here the influence of Waterhouse, the doyen of late Victorian public architecture, becomes more apparent. This is true
of the glazed majolica tiling of vestibule and staircase, and even
more of the central hall, aisled in three bays with round-headed
arches on square, panelled piers, the central aisle top-lit. The
manager's office, however, reasserts romantic medievalism,
with its vaulted look-out window and its splendid hooded
chimneypiece, on coupled side shafts with fishy capitals and
turreted like a toy fort in Burges's favourite way.

WELSH INDUSTRIAL AND MARITIME MUSEUM, Bute Street.
1975–7 by *H.M.R. Burgess & Partners*. A simple rectangle,
primarily a space for some massive exhibits, yet in its very
simplicity a building with presence. Red-painted I-section steel
stanchions carry a flat space-frame roof, masked externally by
a deep, black fascia. Recessed walls of red brick set on a battered
plinth, the glazing mainly a strip at eaves level, but including
three large round-headed windows in the s wall, their iron
frames reused from a C19 engine house.

NATIONAL TECHNIQUEST, alongside in Stuart Street. Science
Exhibition Centre, 1993–5 by *Ahrends, Burton & Koralek*.
Facing the water, a fully glazed rectangular pavilion reusing an
1880s iron frame under a curved metal roof.

CARDIFF BAY VISITORS CENTRE, immediately e of the Pierhead Building. By *Alsop, Lyall & Störmer*, 1990. An extraordinary *jeu d'esprit*. A shiny white elliptical tube poised on a
series of close-set steel struts. Glazed ends and a multiplicity of
ripple-like slits on its top side light the interior without impair-
ing the tubular appearance. The structure is formed from
curved marine plywood sheeting covered in a PVC-coated
fabric, and is expected to last about five years. Will it become
such a favourite that a way will be found to extend its life-span?

NORWEGIAN CHURCH CENTRE, further e of the Pierhead
Building. The touchingly diminutive white building at the

quayside is a weatherboarded timber reconstruction, 1991–2, of the corrugated iron church put up in 1889 for the benefit of Norwegian sailors.

ROYAL HAMADRYAD HOSPITAL, Ferry Road. 1902–3 by *E. W. M. Corbett.* An ebullient performance in his favourite Queen Anne-cum-Jacobean style. Red brick, red stone and red terracotta.

CRICKHOWELL HOUSE, Welsh Health Common Services Authority Headquarters, Maritime Road. Six-storey office block, by *Holder Mathias Alcock*, completed in 1993. On a V-plan, open to the E, but the NW angle recessed and glazed from the ground up to an apex above the roof-line. Orange brick, with narrow bands of reconstituted stone low down. Such an aggressive image makes one nervous for the future. And sure enough, the NCM CREDIT INSURANCE building under construction alongside in 1994 to the designs of the same architects looks just as alarming, a glazed prow-like feature rearing over it towards the water. Walls faced with polished Brazilian granite.

PERAMBULATIONS

Both the Mount Stuart Square area, the C19 commercial heart of Butetown, and the new Cardiff Bay development centred on surviving Victorian warehouses at the N end of Bute East Dock, deserve to be explored on foot, but they require two separate explorations.

1. Butetown

Approaching from the N down BUTE STREET, one passes on the r. St Mary's church (p. 265 above) and the little Greek Orthodox church, set back beside it (p. 265 above). Thereafter there has been thorough redevelopment for $\frac{1}{2}$ m. (0.8 kilometre) on the r., and the dock enclosure wall blocks out any view to the l. Walking can begin at the junction with WEST BUTE STREET. Here on the l. BUTE ROAD RAILWAY STATION, one of the earliest locomotive railway buildings still standing. Three-storeyed, stuccoed, built *c.* 1843 as offices for the Taff Vale Railway. Extended to the S in the 1860s, two-storeyed with a canted full-height bay at the end, presumably to light the boardroom. Moulded surrounds to the windows of this part indicate the later date. The ground storey now houses the railway gallery of the Welsh Industrial and Maritime Museum. Opposite, Nos. 122–126, parts of stuccoed three-storey terraces of *c.* 1847 and 1850–1, giving a good sense of the original development of the area. At once on the l., beyond Hemingway Road, No. 54, PASCOE HOUSE, the first of the showpiece redevelopments whereby coal and shipping companies, banks and the other financial institutions on which the prosperity of the Docks depended competed with one another to present an image of dynamism and success. Pascoe House is an early example, built in 1875 by *W. D. Blessley*, as offices for the Powell

Duffryn Coal Company. Symmetrical, three-storey front extended to the N in the same style in 1907 by *E.W.M. Corbett*. In a High Victorian semi-Gothic style thought suitable for commercial buildings at that date. Massive Burgesian doorway, arcaded ground storey, segmental and straight-headed windows above, the top cornice a thick tangle of stiff-leaf. Polychromy of dark Pennant sandstone walls, with buff Bath and pink Radyr stone dressings. Next comes DOCK CHAMBERS, a three-storey, five-part terrace with a pavilion-roofed central section and pairs of shaped gables to l. and r. Red brick with Jacobean stucco trimmings. This was built as offices *c*. 1860, so it seems, for the Bute Estate (estate architect *Alexander Roos*), before the individual companies began to build for themselves. The stately Ionic frontage of the Janus-faced National Westminster Bank, next on the r., is best passed without discussion for the time being, as the main entrance is in the identical front towards West Bute Street (*see* p. 270 below). That leaves only the last two buildings on the l. No. 56, built as the CUSTOM HOUSE and dated 1898, was designed by *Henry Tanner*, chief architect to the Office of Works. Unusually handled three-bay façade of Portland stone with a separate entrance arch to the r. Three storeys under a parapet with urns and swags. In the upper two, richly detailed orders, Ionic over Doric, combined with mullion-and-transom windows. Carving by *William Clarke* of Llandaff. The street ends with the massive bulk of CORY'S BUILDINGS, dated 1889 and designed by the local firm of *Bruton & Williams*. Thirteen bays, five storeys, faced with Bath stone, and barely keeping its classical paraphernalia under control. The feature which is meant to dominate is the order of Corinthian columns with decorated leggings recessed four and four into the upper part of the façade.

Round the corner to the l., Nos. 1 and 3 BUTE PLACE, the most purely satisfying essay in classical design in Butetown. 1880–1 by *E. G. Rivers* of the Office of Works. Three storeys, ten bays, treated like a continuous terrace, though built as two offices, for the Telegraphs and Mercantile Marine departments of the Board of Trade. The architect's problem was to resolve this dualism and provide a central point of stress. This he did by carrying a Doric colonnade across the ground storey, attached in bays 1–3 and 8–10, stepped forward where the doorways occur in bays 4 and 7, and forward again in the centre two bays. Note the management of the balustrade. Round-headed ground-floor windows, triangular pediments to those on the piano nobile. The building is not just a cool design exercise, but an extraordinary colour symphony as well. Deep brownish-red sandstone ashlar for the ground storey and for the dressings above, where the walls are faced with orange-red brick. Against this warm background the Penrhyn granite colonnade stands out pale grey.

Turning back W-wards into JAMES STREET, one is confronted on the l. by another massive piece of debased classicism, the MIDLAND BANK. Built in 1874 by *F. Cutlan* for Cory

Brothers, and extended in an identical style for the bank in 1902–3 and 1914–15 by *Henry Budgen*. Like an overblown Venetian palazzo, the details a mélange such as only High Victorians could conceive. Now to the r. again, and into WEST BUTE STREET, which runs parallel to Bute Street. Here one can absorb the extraordinary magniloquence of the NATIONAL WESTMINSTER BANK. Designed by the bank's in-house architects, *F. C. R. Palmer & W. F. C. Holden*, and built in 1926–7, it was clearly intended as a *chef-d'oeuvre*. Seven bays wide, five storeys high, the lower two treated as the bank proper with a row of giant fluted Ionic columns carried across on a high plinth and paired at the end. Exquisite detailing, the column bases, for example, of the rarely used form described by Vitruvius. The upper part of the façade is treated with abrupt simplicity. The entrance doorway in the l. bay, surmounted by a bronze STATUE of Equity by *J. A. Stevenson*, leads into a transverse corridor, with a domed space at the beginning and an apse at the far end. The tripartite banking hall has a semicircular section towards West Bute Street and a top-lit central section. Greek Doric marble columns subdivide the sections, and half-columns run round the walls. Coffered ceilings everywhere, the coffers coloured orange and lavender – this too probably intended as a neo-antique effect. Also in West Bute Street, several recent pieces of intelligent infill, maintaining the street-line, UNITED KINGDOM HOUSING TRUST FLATS, 1988 by *Hoggett, Lock-Necrews*.

The short street w of the National Westminster Bank runs into the NE corner of MOUNT STUART SQUARE. On the s side of the street, ST STEPHEN'S CHURCH (now secularized and in use as a theatre and café). By *E. M. Bruce Vaughan*, the chancel built 1900–2, the nave and N aisle in 1912. Typical materials, rock-faced Pennant sandstone and dressings of Bath stone. Typical Geometrical Gothic. NE tower and spike with semi-octagonal stair-turret dying in low down. Six-bay aisle with cross-gables. (Interior all altered.) Goodhart-Rendel's comment was 'a doll's house imitation of St John's, Canton, but forty three years younger'. On the N side of the street something much more interesting, a piece of architecture by a local architect showing as much artistry as any by Londoners. This is CAMBRIAN BUILDINGS, 1907–10 by *Henry Budgen*, built as offices of the Cambrian Coal Combine. CYMRIC BUILDINGS, round the corner in West Bute Street, is an identical addition by *Budgen* of 1911. Five storeys with a sixth as an attic and low pedimental gables against the skyline. Bath stone ashlar worked into low-relief articulation so that barely a square inch of smooth surface remains, almost a Rococo effect. The surrounds of the tripartite windows can also be read as full-height pilasters with fanciful Ionic capitals. Doorways with pilasters capped by a different derivation from Ionic. Segmental windows with shallow voussoirs at ground level. Shallow full-height bows above. Everywhere the façades are enlivened by miniaturist marine sculpture.

And so to Mount Stuart Square itself, built as a spacious residential square in the mid 1850s by the Bute Estate. First one has to take in the fact that the space in the centre of the square has been completely occupied by a single huge building. This is the COAL AND SHIPPING EXCHANGE, 1884–8 by *Edwin Seward* of *Seward & Thomas*, built at a reputed cost of £60,000. Bath stone. U-plan open to the S, the side wings with complex canted projections. Three storeys over a basement, and attics in the pavilion roof. Composed façade to each point of the compass. The details of Seward's debased French Renaissance vocabulary do not require detailed analysis. As the *Builder* remarked, 'What it wants is a more decisive grouping in subordination to a leading *motif*.' Entrance spoilt by recent concrete ramps. The interior was sumptuously reworked by *Edwin Seward* in 1911–12, with sculpture by *Tom A. Jones*. Broad, low S vestibule, its plaster ceiling massively beamed and enriched. Here two mighty lions, bearing clocks which indicate the times of high water a.m. and p.m., respectively, guard the doorway into the central hall. The hall, once spectacularly lofty, is now unfortunately cropped by a false ceiling. Polished mahogany and mahogany-tinted plasterwork. Massive struts carry a balcony round all four sides, and also handsome Composite columns on which rests a swagged attic. Complex roof structure now hidden. To the N a meandering single-storey space lit by numerous mullioned windows. – STAINED GLASS. Abstract patterns reminiscent of C.R. Mackintosh. Also two galleons in full sail and the motto 'Ye olde order changeth'.

The numbering of the square itself starts in the NE corner, where examination can begin. No. 1, LLOYDS BANK, is of 1891 by *E.W.M. Corbett* in the approved Italianate style for banks. Nos. 4–5, COPTIC HOUSE, of 1910 is an early work by *Ivor Jones*, the future partner of Percy Thomas. A tentative essay in rustication. Nos. 6–9 are more significant, survivors of the original residences in the square, *c.*1858. Three-storeyed, stucco-fronted, memorable for the Venetian windows on the piano nobile, the central arched head filled in with a stucco shell. Presumably by the architect to the Bute Estate, *Alexander Roos*. When No. 9 became PERCH BUILDINGS it was given a ground-storey frontage of Bath stone in a pretty François Premier style. 1889 by *W.D. Blessley*.

On the S side of the square, Nos. 20 and 23, at the far end, are further survivors from the original development. But this side is dominated by BALTIC HOUSE, 1915 by *Teather & Wilson*. A metropolitan design. One bay plus five, as if the composition were incomplete. Arcaded ground storey with concave surrounds to the arches and fine cartouches with sea-faring emblems in the spandrels. Ionic pilasters through three storeys above. Bath stone ashlar. Fine dark red granite door surround. Now the headquarters of the Cardiff Bay Development Corporation.

The W side of the square consists at present of a few isolated survivors. At the SW corner with James Street, MOUNT

STUART HOUSE, 1898–9 by *H. Tudor Thornley*, four-storey offices of John Cory & Son. Red brick with lavish Bath stone dressings. Composite upper pilasters, and a skyline of chimneystacks and elaborate gables. Next to the N, the former BETHEL CHAPEL, a survivor from the first development of the square. 1858 by *H. J. Paull*. Thickly detailed, debased classical, the façade dominated by a Serliana motif. Brick and stone painted black and white. Nos. 33–34 are further remains of the domestic architecture of *c*.1858. ABERDARE HOUSE is a conversion of two more such houses. Bath stone front of 1920 by *Henry Budgen*. Similar to Cambrian Buildings but not so good.

And so to the N side, where EMPIRE HOUSE is dominant. 1926 by *Ivor Jones & Percy Thomas*, for Evans & Reid Coal Company, a seven-bay, seven-storey façade of Lutyenesque derivation, on a reinforced concrete skeleton. Dull red brick above Portland stone. Inside, a coffered, tunnel-vaulted passage leads to a cruciform space, defined by black and white marble pavement and high mahogany dado, with for its centrepiece a handsome Louis Quinze openwork metal lift-cage. Nos. 58–59, next door, date to *c*.1856, the first phase of the original development, and do not have elaborated piano nobile windows. Finally No. 60, BENYON HOUSE, dated 1900. The architect was *H. Tudor Thornley*. Same materials and a similar idiom to his contemporary Mount Stuart House, but somewhat more stately in effect. The two lower storeys treated as a channelled podium with a florid mid-height relief of ships in roundels. Rich Corinthian pilasters for the upper two storeys. Top attic.

As a coda one can leave Mount Stuart Square from its SW corner, and turn to the W in CLARENCE ROAD. Here, on the corner of HUNTER STREET, is another lively piece of Queen Anne by *E. W. M. Corbett*, the AVONDALE HOTEL, dated 1893. Yellow and red brick. It deserves a clean and replacement of missing bits. Hunter Street leads to Corbett's Royal Hamadryad Hospital (*see* p. 268).

2. Cardiff Bay Development

Development from 1987, under the aegis of the Cardiff Bay Development Corporation, was concentrated on the infilled N half of Bute West Dock, extending across to the water's edge of Bute East Dock. It can be approached either from the S past the South Glamorgan County Hall up SCHOONER WAY, or from the N. The latter is the more practical approach for pedestrians. At the N end of Bute Street, HERBERT STREET turns in to the l. under the railway. Here at once a group of WAREHOUSES, set back from COLLINGDON ROAD and originally on the N quayside of Bute West Dock. The earliest of these is the MARQUESS OF BUTE'S WAREHOUSE, erected before 1849. Three-storeyed. Walls of Pennant sandstone. Internal structure of cast iron for the ground storey over a

fireproof basement, the piers embossed with the name of
William Catleugh, millwright of Cardiff. Timber internal structure for the upper storeys and kingpost roof.

Herbert Street continues as TYNDALL STREET and meets
the head of SCHOONER WAY. Here at once one can begin to
savour the intermixture of C19 dock warehouses and 1980s
housing, which in materials, shapes and bulk plays all sorts of
variations on warehouse themes. First, to the E, NELSON
COURT, four-storey and five-storey terraces of brown brick
with a buff band at the top. Kite-like exposed timber trusses at
the gable ends.

Immediately S, ATLANTIC WHARF, where at the head of
Bute East Dock stands the finest of the surviving warehouses.
This was built in 1860–1 by *William Clarke* as a BONDED
WAREHOUSE, six bays by three. Open below on three rows of
cast iron Doric columns, solid red brick above, two storeys
pierced with small, sparse, round-headed windows and a pair
of hoists. Converted to offices in 1986–7 by *Holder Mathias
Alcock*, who painted the columns blue. New N entrance arrangements. (Twin rows of cast iron columns on both upper floors
preserved inside, carrying brick vaults and an iron roof
structure.)

ADMIRAL'S LANDING, the new housing complex which lines
the NW angle of Bute East Dock, exploits the warehouse idiom,
in particular the open, colonnaded ground storey, on a monumental scale. Red brick and buff reconstituted stone. Bold,
gabled stair projections, four to the W, three to the N, with
vertical glazed panels rising mushroom-shaped into the gables.
Disappointingly crude detailing, when seen close-to. The
skinny columns are particularly excruciating.

On the W side of Schooner Way, the CELTIC BAY HOTEL, a
three-storey warehouse of *c.* 1900, converted 1988–9. At its S
end BRIGANTINE PLACE leads W-wards to an attractive and
humane complex of L-plan and U-plan office blocks, WATER-
FRONT 2000, which extends to the N back to Herbert
Street. 1988–90, by *Holder Mathias Alcock*. On quite a small
scale, only three-storeyed under shallow-pitched roofs, of
brown brick with blue trim. The identifying idiosyncrasy,
the full-height angle columns with glazing behind. Further S,
SPILLERS AND BAKER'S WAREHOUSE rears up, dominant
and somewhat intimidating. It is dated 1893 and may have
been designed by *Veall & Sant.** Seven storeys. Pennant sandstone. Triangular plan, the NW side curved along the line of a
former railway. This is made the show side, the stone coursed
and a network of thick bands of red brick superimposed on it.
Segment-headed windows sunk deep in the walls with moulded
brick surrounds. Excellently converted in 1988 for housing,
by *AWT Architects*, with minimal external change. (Internal

*Can it be identified with the biscuit factory and warehouse for Messrs Spillers
Nephew Biscuit Company for which these architects received tenders of around
£20,000 in October 1894?

balconies in a glazed atrium now surround the original spiral grain-chute.)

To the S and W intricately grouped HOUSING, reached from LLANSANNOR DRIVE and MERVINION CLOSE, through which thread dock feeder canals. Planned round courtyards, mainly two-storeyed, but punctuated by four-storey pavilions with pyramid roofs. SCHOONER WAY is lined at this point by a long three-storey terrace of flats. In the centre and at the ends transparent four-storey pavilions. At its S end two more gabled WAREHOUSES of c. 1900, recently linked by an iron and glass shed to form a restaurant and bar.

CANTON AND RIVERSIDE

This is an area of diverse character. It is bounded to the E by Cathedral Road and the public parkland, Sophia Gardens and Pontcanna Fields, stretching to the River Taff. To the N it is divided from Llandaff by the B4488, and it extends S-wards to the Ely River. It is bisected N–S by Llandaff Road and E–W by Cowbridge Road. Its historic nucleus is the hamlet of Canton, at the junction of Llandaff Road and Romilly Road, where one or two pre-1850 buildings remain. The E strip, Cathedral Road and its dependent streets, is not strictly part of Canton, but is included here so that the central W suburbs can be considered together, starting at the bridge over the River Taff in Cowbridge Road East.

CHURCHES AND CHAPELS

ST CATHERINE, King's Road. The heart of this church is by *John Prichard*, who 1883–6 erected the three E bays of the nave. The cruciform plan he had intended proved over-ambitious, so in 1892–3 *Kempson & Fowler* added the chancel with S chapel and N vestry. In 1897 *G. E. Halliday* completed the building by adding the remaining two bays to the nave. Three-light E window with cusped intersecting tracery. Five-light W window with flowing tracery. Otherwise uniformity reigns. Pennant sandstone in precise courses, with dressings of Bath stone. Unexpected interior, with timber arcades such as Prichard liked. Here only the arches and their pierced spandrels are of timber, carried on extremely slender piers of quatrefoil plan with moulded caps and bases. Wide aisles, their walls of yellow brick with red and black brick bands and voussoirs. – REREDOS. Dec, richly carved. Portland stone and alabaster. Presumably by *Kempson & Fowler*. – STAINED GLASS. Much by *Daniells & Fricker*, to commemorate deaths in the First World War. In their fussy, over-detailed style. E window, Christ in Glory, with saints, 1916. Three S aisle windows, 1918, saints with architectural vignettes beneath, representative of France, England and Belgium. – Three N aisle windows, 1951, 1954 and 1957 by *Comper*. Large, simply drawn but rather inert figures of saints and a Noli me Tangere scene, in primary colours against clear glass.

St John the Evangelist, St John's Crescent. Designed by *Prichard & Seddon* in 1854, and built in stages. Nave 1854–5, aisles 1858–9, aisled chancel and crossing steeple 1868–70, the steeple a new design by *W. P. James*. Nave w bay added in 1902 by *G. E. Halliday*. There is some evidence that a saddleback tower was originally envisaged, but the executed steeple with a spire takes better advantage of the island site. The best view is from the SE, where an octagonal stair-turret dies back into the angle of the tower at belfry level. Ashlar broach spire with bracketed canopies above the broaches. Walling of multicoloured rubble, with ample Bath stone dressings. Geometrical tracery. Handsome interior, the nave arcades of doublechamfered arches with hoodmoulds on lively leaf sprigs, and circular piers with moulded caps. Cinquefoiled clerestory windows over the spandrels rather than over the heads of the arches. Transverse aisle arches of stone. The tower stands over the chancel, but its arches are kept simple, dying into the piers high up. Thus the mighty five-light E window appears unobstructed down the full length of the church. – REREDOS. Triple-gabled, like a C13 tomb canopy. 1890, designed by *Kempson & Fowler* and carved by *Clarke* of Llandaff. – STAINED GLASS. Chancel E, Ascension, with Christ in the crowning hexfoil of the tracery, an exhilarating conceit. – N aisle NE, Faith and Charity, 1919, signed by *Daniells & Fricker*. – S transept S, Christ preaching. By *G. E. R. Smith*, *c.* 1944. – S aisle SE, abstract, brilliant colours. 1981 by *Geoffrey Robinson*.

St Dyfrig's clergy house and parish hall, Fitzhamon Embankment. 1906 by *Arthur Grove*. Brick, quite simple, with Georgian details. St Dyfrig's church, 1886–93 by *J. D. Sedding*, completed by *Grove* in 1907, was demolished in 1969, and its major fittings distributed between St Mary, Butetown, and St Samson, Grangetown (which also took over the dedication).

St Luke, Cowbridge Road East. Designed by *G. E. Halliday* and built in two stages, 1909 and 1914. Red brick with minimal Bath stone dressings. Simple Dec style. Nave with separately gabled aisles, chancel with chapel and vestry, making a somewhat confused group beside the road. Plain interior. Square piers, slightly chamfered arches. Boarded roof with alternating tie-beams and hammerbeams. – CENTRAL ALTAR. By *Michael Petts*, 1987. – STATIONS OF THE CROSS. By *John Petts*, 1982–7. – STAINED GLASS. N chapel, Annunciation and Visitation distributed across five lancets. 1957 by *Comper*.

St Mary of the Angels (R.C.), King's Road. By *F. A. Walters*, 1907, the tower added in 1916. Rough-faced, squared Pennant sandstone, with Bath stone dressings. In a consistent round-arched style, the w front contrived with a bridge-like superarch, the interior of four double bays and covered by a semicircular boarded tunnel-vault. Square piers carry superarches which rise to enclose the clerestory windows. Pairs of round arcade arches on fused double columns with waterleaf

CARDIFF:
CANTON and RIVERSIDE

PONTCANNA
FIELDS

Presbyterian
Church of Wales

B U T E
P A R K

River Taff

NORTH ROAD

A 470

CATHEDRAL

PONTCANNA ST

PLASTURTON AVE

SNEYD ST

KING'S

GROVE

SEVERN

ROAD

PLASTURTON
GARDENS

PITMAN ST

RYDER

STREET

National
Recreation
Centre

SOPHIA CL.

SOPHIA
GARDENS

ROAD

TALBOT ST
St Mary of the
Angels (R.C.)

HAMILTON ST

ROAD

St David's Hospital
(site of)

A 4119

Cardiff
Bridge

ROAD EAST

COWBRIDGE ROAD

EAST A 4161

WELLINGTON STREET

LOWER CATHEDRAL RD

RIVERSIDE

River Taff

ROAD

BECKWITH RD

NINIAN

PARK

CLARE ST

FITZHAMON EMBANKMENT

NINIAN PARK
STATION

DE CROCHE
PLACE

ROAD

TUDOR ST

A 4119

capitals. So Walters had later C12 French models in mind. Dimly lit lean-to aisles extended E-wards as chapels. The tall, square tower with taller square turret enlivens the external grouping but perhaps blurs the stylistic unity.

The Nonconformist chapels of Canton are unusually numerous, most of them strung along the Cowbridge Road.

CONWAY ROAD METHODIST CHURCH, Romilly Crescent. 1869–71 by *W. G. Habershon & Pite*, soon extended by the same, and accompanied by Sunday schools for 700 children across the road, by *Habershon & Fawckner* in 1891. A handsome group, expressing the confidence of a prosperous congregation. An easy flight of steps leads up to a one-storey polygonal porch, above which rises the polychromatic Lombard-style façade. Rock-faced sandstone, the dressings of Bath stone and grey brick, with red brick alternating in the window voussoirs and corbel tables. Three-storey side elevations, for galleries to the chapel and a hall beneath. Transepts and a polygonal apse, clearly constituting the extension – see the yellow brick dressings. The interior was re-roofed after a fire in 1915. Segmental ceiling, and magnificent organ of 1920 in a matching recess. The mighty galleries, extending round to encompass the transepts, are clearly of the 1870s. Exaggeratedly bowed cast iron fronts. They are supported not on the normal posts but on gigantic cast iron brackets with E.E. foliage. Contemporary Romanesque stone pulpit. – STAINED GLASS. Five lights in the entrance front, all of 1921. In the upper triplet, Empty Tomb between scenes of Christ revealing himself to his disciples.

DAVID DAVIES MEMORIAL HALL (Presbyterian Forward Movement), Cowbridge Road. Dated 1893. Red brick and Bath stone. Fancy Jacobean and secular-looking, so that it does not seem odd that three shops complete the composition. Most conspicuous the big round-headed window to the chapel, with hoops for tracery. Expansive interior, galleried on three sides, the galleries with palmette metal fronts in a pattern largely monopolized by *W. Beddoe Rees* after 1900. Heavily beamed, flat ceiling.

GOSPEL HALL, Rectory Road. White-rendered. Round-headed windows. Built as a Methodist chapel in 1859.

NEW TRINITY UNITED REFORMED CHURCH, Cowbridge Road. Not large but conspicuous in livery of yellow and red brick. Geometrical rose window over shafted triple entrance. Designed for galleries. 1894, by *Edwin Seward* of *Seward & Thomas*. Not normally a designer of chapels, he was engaged here perhaps for family reasons (see the foundation inscription).

PRESBYTERIAN CHURCH OF WALES, Cathedral Road. (Now used as offices.) 1903 by *Edgar G. C. Down* of Cardiff. Idiosyncratic Arts and Crafts Gothic, the most conspicuous feature the serried rank of battered buttresses of rough Pontypridd stone towards the road. NW porch tower with a handsome Bath stone ashlar top. It is worth turning the corner into Gileston Street to appreciate the design of the W window. Interior now subdivided. The tremendous boarded ceiling, of trefoil profile, still survives. Bowed, wood-encased, metal tie-beams. Bright pattern in STAINED GLASS repeated in the window tracery.

ST PAUL'S CONGREGATIONAL CHURCH, Cowbridge Road. (Latterly Seventh Day Adventist church, but at the time of writing disused.) Standard Perp façade to the road. Pennant sandstone and Bath stone dressings. 1898 by *Veall & Sant*.

SALEM WELSH CALVINISTIC METHODIST CHAPEL, Market Road. Visible from Cowbridge Road and signalling its presence by its short tower with spike. 1909–11 by *Habershon, Fawckner & Co*. Fancy Perp style for both the chapel and the hall behind it. Rock-faced Pennant sandstone dressed with Bath stone. The interior survives unaltered, galleried on three sides, the organ behind the minister's rostrum.

SALVATION ARMY CITADEL, Cowbridge Road. Built for the Bible Christians by *Veall & Sant* in 1898. The usual combination of stones. Façade towards the road flanked by gallery-stair projections. Geometrical tracery.

SYNAGOGUE, Cathedral Road. (Converted to offices.) 1896–7 by *Delissa Joseph* of London, the synagogue specialist. Portly aspect towards the road, twin domed entrances flanking a semi-domed apse. The ark, set in the apse towards the E, made this arrangement necessary. Romanesque style. Snecked, rock-faced sandstone with Bath stone dressings.

PUBLIC BUILDINGS

ST DAVID'S HOSPITAL (former), Cowbridge Road. The front block, gabled and centred on a pyramid-roofed tower, is all that remains after recent demolitions. The relation to Seward's Royal Infirmary (*see* p. 307) is clear, though the materials, dominated by Pennant sandstone, show that this was a cheaper job. Built for the Union Workhouse, which *James, Seward & Thomas* had in hand 1879 and 1889.

ST WINEFRIDE'S HOSPITAL, Romilly Crescent. By *Cyril F. Bates*, 1939, with overtones of Dudok, or perhaps rather of Burnet, Tait & Lorne. Red brick on a reinforced concrete frame. Three-storeyed, symmetrical towards the road, but the entrance at the rear in strongly stepped asymmetry.

LANSDOWNE HOSPITAL, Sanatorium Road. By far the most expensive Victorian building in Canton, but devoid of architectural graces. Built 1893–5, originally in eight blocks, of yellow brick with sparse red brick dressings, as a hospital for infectious diseases, by *W. Harpur*, Cardiff Borough Engineer. The cost was £40,000.

FITZALAN HIGH SCHOOL AND COMMUNITY EDUCATION CENTRE, Lawrenny Avenue. Typical of the 1960s. The main elements are two three-storey slabs and one four-storey block. Windows in continuous bands, corrugated cladding between them, cream above, terracotta below. Vertical glazing for the stairs. The range towards Lawrenny Avenue was built 1962–3 as Leckwith Technical High School, the rest 1966–8 to create

a Comprehensive School. Both parts by *John Dryburgh*, Cardiff
City Architect.

HIGHER GRADE SCHOOL, Market Road. (Now Chapter Arts
Centre.) This was a showpiece school, designed in 1904 by
James & Morgan after a competition, built at a cost of about
£20,000 and, when it was opened in 1907, judged to have 'an
artistic and a substantial appearance'. Planned in the typical
way, two-storeyed, with classrooms grouped round a central
hall. Red Ruabon brick, with Bath stone dressings and relief
decoration in red cut brick. Classical details to the main w
front, Venetian upper windows in the wings and Ionic columns
between banded jambs to indicate the central hall. Plain blocks
behind. The original gabled roofs have largely been eliminated.

LANSDOWNE ROAD SCHOOLS, Norfolk Street. 1896–8 by
Veall & Sant. Here is a school which was designed with enjoyment and artistry and which survives unaltered. Newbridge
sandstone in thin courses, generous Bath stone dressings, and
a crown of red brick chimneystacks. Gabled, Tudor style, the
mullion-and-transom windows very large, as educational theory
demanded at the time. Two-storey N range, for 456 girls on the
ground floor, and 456 boys above; one-storey s range for 572
infants. Each range is composed with gabled end projections
and double gables in the centre linked by a straight-topped
arch bearing the name of the school in bold letters. Pretty
details, especially the trios of decorative shields in the gables.

RADNOR COUNTY PRIMARY SCHOOL, Radnor Road. Built as
a board school, *c.* 1887 by *E. M. Bruce Vaughan*, for 1,120
pupils. He used his favoured materials, Pennant sandstone with
Bath stone dressings, and his favoured style, Gothic, or as close
to Gothic as board school formulae would allow. Symmetrical
two-storey boys' and girls' range facing N towards Pembroke
Road, the one-storey infants' range (now Welsh Medium
School) to the l. Gabled ends to both, and on the larger range
gabled semi-dormers. Mullion-and-transom windows with
blind pointed arches over, the upper ones treated as giant
superarches. The school's name is spelt out in Gothic letters
across the full width of the building.

SEVERN COUNTY PRIMARY SCHOOL, Severn Road. Built in
1881–2 to the design of *John P. Jones*, under the influence of
the London board schools. This is hardly appreciable now that
the shaped gables have been removed and the main windows
modernized. Only the handling of stone and brick in the walling
can still give pleasure.

CANTON BRANCH LIBRARY, Cowbridge Road. Andrew Carnegie was unusually generous in his funding of this free library,
as a large inscription attests. 1906 by *E. M. Bruce Vaughan*,
whose ecclesiastical preoccupations are apparent. Dec. Flowing
tracery. Snecked, rock-faced Pennant stone with Bath stone
dressings. The main frontage is to the side street, where a richly
decorated entrance is flanked by lofty reading rooms of unequal
size. Internally, the original spaces survive, centred on an
arcaded vestibule.

NATIONAL RECREATION CENTRE, Sophia Gardens. 1969 by *F. D. Williamson & Associates*. Three-storey rectangle round a sports hall. An inexpressive piece of minimalism.

CARDIFF ATHLETIC STADIUM, Leckwith Road. The grandstand, *c.*1990 by *Holder Mathias Alcock*, is a colourful and memorable object, even as it turns its back to the road. Pale brick walls enclose the raked seating, and a canopy of alternately straight and segmental sections covers them. The rear of the canopy rests on groups of red-painted steel posts, alternate groups encaging stairs.

PERAMBULATIONS

The ecclesiastical and public buildings described above are widely scattered, with a string of chapels along Cowbridge Road. Three other architectural concentrations can be sought out: from the river w and then n along Cathedral Road, the remains of Canton hamlet round Romilly Crescent, and one or two items s of Cowbridge Road.

1. Cathedral Road

CARDIFF BRIDGE takes the Cowbridge Road over the River Taff. Built in 1930–1, by *George H. Whitaker*, the City Engineer, the bridge has a ceremonial character, its Portland stone balustrade punctuated by obelisks supporting bronze flambeaux. Then at once on the l., in COWBRIDGE ROAD EAST, come two contrasting office blocks. First CASTLEBRIDGE, a typical piece of Post-Modernism, of caramel and brown brick under pitched slate roofs. Tall windows, some expanding into mushroom heads. The offices are grouped round a cramped courtyard, with a central glazed pavilion over the steps up from the underground car park. Then PORTCULLIS HOUSE, 1970–3 by the *Percy Thomas Partnership* (design partner *Dale Owen*). This represents the Modernist aesthetic, a seven-storey office block behind, the five-storey range towards the road occupied by offices below, but two-storey flats above, as the row of canted oriels indicates. Syncopated bay rhythm further contrasting offices and flats. The building is faced with aggregate panels and stands on a podium of river boulders. After this the scale is sharply contracted, in two examples of inter-war Neo-Georgian, the CITY TEMPLE of 1933, and *Sir Percy Thomas*'s WESTGATE HOTEL, 1932, on the corner of LOWER CATHEDRAL ROAD.

On the diagonally opposite corner, at the foot of CATHEDRAL ROAD, another Modern intervention, TRANSPORT HOUSE, offices of the Transport and General Workers Union, by the *Alex Gordon Partnership*, opened in 1978. Canted plan to accommodate the corner. Five-storeyed, clad in pre-cast concrete aggregate panels, with close-set window mullions.

CATHEDRAL ROAD was laid out in the 1850s, broad and straight and nearly a mile (1.6 kilometres) long, on Bute land, from the walls of Cardiff Castle to the outskirts of Llandaff. The main period of residential development along it extended from the 1870s to *c.* 1900. The s section, individual villas quite soon giving way to pairs, was largely up by *c.* 1880; the N half, entirely terraced, was in the hands of the Bute Estate architect, *E. W. M. Corbett*, and was built up from 1886. Unfortunately, a number of the villas were demolished and replaced by offices in the 1970s.

The E side first demands attention. The facing materials of virtually all the C19 houses are coursed Pennant sandstone and ashlar dressings of Bath stone, now generally painted over. Nos. 2 and 4 are clearly under the spell of William Burges, the former with animals crouching on either side of the window bays, the latter with a three-bay loggia of pointed arches on slender piers clearly borrowed from McConnochie's house in Park Place. A little polychromy on No. 2. No. 6 has an undersized angle turret, and a tower-like extension at the back, concrete-faced on a reinforced concrete stem. By *Alex Gordon & Partners c.* 1970 for themselves. No. 8 is rebuilt. No. 10, however, must predate its neighbours, for it is in a cottage orné style, with big bargeboards to the gables. Nothing more until No. 18, a formulaic villa, almost opposite the former Synagogue. No. 20, by contrast, is exceptionally good, in a Tudor style close to Norman Shaw. The double-height bay window is rounded, not polygonal, and it composes with a projecting chimneybreast round the corner. Side entrance. The N end is developed into a tower under a steep slated roof from which a slab-like red brick chimneystack projects. No. 16 is High Victorian Gothic with some polychromy and gawky bargeboards.

On the w side, Nos. 15–21 are a terrace of four, uniform with the next two pairs, Nos. 23–25 and 27–29. From this point on villas die out almost entirely on both sides, terraces take over, and there is a strong sense that a single architect is in control, even when occasionally red brick takes the place of stone. The formula is of a two-storey canted bay and gabled dormer above it, with the entrance in the flat part of the façade. The doorway, rarely a porch, is normally pointed and enriched with circular shafts and elaborately carved leaf capitals. Dates are extremely rare, occurring on the E side only on Nos. 118–120, where the date is as late as 1900, and at the furthest extremity on the w side, which concludes with a terrace bearing the dates 1895 at the s end and 1900 at the N.

The slightly less grand streets immediately w were also *Corbett*'s responsibility: HAMILTON STREET, TALBOT STREET, RYDER STREET, PITMAN STREET and PLAS-TURTON GARDENS in 1886–91, PLASTURTON AVENUE and PONTCANNA STREET in a second phase, 1891 to *c.* 1900.

2. Around Romilly Crescent

ROMILLY CRESCENT lies w of the N half of Cathedral Road. Here the Conway Road Methodist Chapel makes a natural focus. To its E, No. 22 Romilly Crescent, a handsome white Grecian villa, of three bays, the lower storey brought forward as two canted bays flanking a pair of antae. Heavy roof brackets and a thick balcony balustrade suggest a date not before *c.* 1840. To the W, across LLANDAFF ROAD, a white three-storey villa, even later, so its Italianate details suggest. Canted bays and porch on Ionic columns. The metal balconies are modern replacements. Facing this, Canton Gospel Hall.

3. Riverside

Finally, there is a little more to see S of Cowbridge Road, in the district called Riverside. Those who enjoyed the Lansdowne Road schools can pursue LANSDOWNE ROAD E-wards until they reach the LANSDOWNE HOTEL, which is also by *Veall & Sant*, dated 1898, and in a Gothic style, not normally chosen by hoteliers. The chimneystacks, unfortunately, are lost.

Further E, in NINIAN PARK ROAD, at the corner of DE CROCHE PLACE, ELDON COURT, sheltered housing for the elderly, 1986–7 by the *Welsh School of Architecture* (project architect *Alwyn Jones*). Another of their exercises in pretty brickwork, here buff with red detail. Four three-storey blocks linked together by metal staircases so that the frontage to the main road is continuous, the stair bays projecting slightly under small gables, their glazed upper parts criss-crossed with diagonal timber mullions.

CATHAYS AND HEATH

The great slice of Cardiff which extends N-wards from Cathays Park to Llanishen is bounded on the E by the Rhymney Valley railway line to Caerphilly and on the W by North Road (A470) and the Caerphilly road (A469). The S half was the 500-acre (202-hectare) Cathays Estate, acquired after 1832 by the second Marquess of Bute, and released for development by his son from *c.* 1880. To the N lay The Heath, common land enclosed as early as 1801, of which Heath Park is the residue, surrounded on three sides by inter-war housing. The centre ground is straddled by Cathays Cemetery, laid out in the mid 1850s, and the University Hospital of Wales, developed in the 1960s along the N boundary of Eastern Avenue (A48), Cardiff's ring road.

ST ANDREW AND ST TEILO, Woodville Road. An ambitious Perp church, compromised externally by the stump which is all that was ever built of the SE tower. Designed by *G. E. Halliday* in 1893, the aisled nave built 1895–7, the chancel and vestries in 1901. Snecked, rock-faced Swelldon limestone of the pinkish-grey hue favoured in Cardiff *c.* 1890. Bath stone dressings. Five-bay nave arcades, the piers with four shafts and four hollows, and chancel arch, high and wide, modelled presumably on those at St John the Baptist church (*see* p. 187). Seven-light W window with a transom. Tie-beam and arch-brace roof with

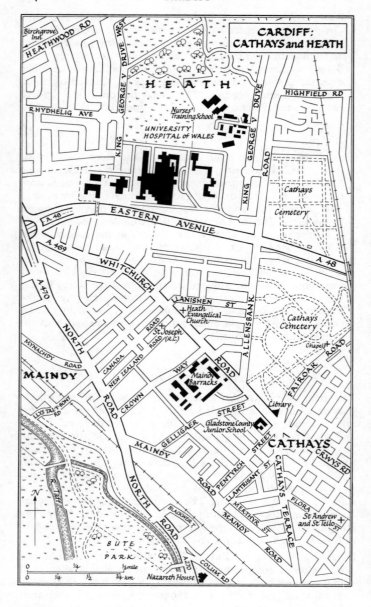

CARDIFF:
CATHAYS and HEATH

pierced spandrels. In the chancel clerestory lancets and a five-light E window. – REREDOS. Of the Netherlandish type, with shutters, 1924 by *J. Coates Carter*. – STAINED GLASS. Chancel E, Golgotha, Christ crucified between the two thieves. 1919, signed by *Kempe & Tower*, the firm's major work in the county.

ST MARK, North Road. *See* Gabalfa (p. 290).

ST JOSEPH (R.C.), New Zealand Road. 1936 by *C. F. Bates* (D. Evinson). In a round-arched style, solid but plain. Severe SE campanile. Brown brick outside, rendered within.

HEATH EVANGELICAL CHURCH, Whitchurch Road. Built as a Forward Movement Hall in 1906, the architects being *Veall & Sant*. The stout towers which flank the façade are a memorable sight. Their square domes, slated below, leaded on the curve, carry white louvred lanterns with copper-covered tips. Broad central window, five lights in an arch-headed Serliana surround. Snecked Pennant sandstone, the dressings of Bath stone, used almost without mouldings.

NAZARETH HOUSE, Colum Road. Built as almshouse and school for Catholics on a site at the further tip of Cathays Park donated by the third Marquess of Bute in 1875. *John Prichard* was responsible for the original building; *E. W. M. Corbett*, the Bute Estate architect, added the wing for an Industrial School in 1887, further large extensions in 1897–8, including the chapel, and yet more in 1908. The details of the building history are hard to work out, as Corbett maintained complete stylistic consistency at all stages. Pennant sandstone with Bath stone dressings. E.E., in deference to the Castle, no doubt.

The entrance front faces SE, of two storeys with a third in the gables. A nearly symmetrical composition around a central gable-cum-tower, with an oriel window over an arched entrance, both richly decorated with stiff-leaf. Additions on both sides: to the l. SCHOOLROOM and DORMITORIES in a range running back askew, to the r. a range running back with the lofty CHAPEL at first-floor level. This has long lancets and a complex timber roof with kingpost, tie-beam and arch-brace trusses. Access to the chapel direct from Colum Road, as the Marquess wanted his co-religionists who lived nearby to attend its services.

CEMETERY, Fairoak Road. The entrance archway and demonstrative Gothic mortuary chapels were built in 1859 by *R. G. Thomas* of Newport with *T. Waring*, Cardiff Borough Surveyor. The gable ends of the chapels form the outer elements of a five-part composition centred on an octagonal spirelet with intermediate gabled arches. E.E. to Dec style. Note the contrasted designs of the windows of the two chapels. All quite scholarly for its time, but the snecked Pennant sandstone still rather roughly laid. Dressings of Forest of Dean stone.

GLADSTONE COUNTY JUNIOR SCHOOL, Whitchurch Road. A typical board school, dated 1900. A two-storey range for boys faces the main road, and a separate single-storey block for infants stands at r.-angles to the S, entered from Pentyrch Street. The latter mimics the former, so both are of red brick with Bath stone trimmings and white-painted timber window frames in triplets. Centre-and-wings composition stressed by stepped and shaped gables. On the boys' school the main architectural motifs are the upper Venetian windows with cartouches carved in their blank arched heads, and the upper pilaster strips descending to a horizontal band of Bath stone, where they terminate in guttae.

ALLENSBANK COUNTY PRIMARY SCHOOL, Llanishen Street. Built in 1904 by *Veall & Sant* for 1,200 children. A variant of their Lansdowne Road school, Canton (*see* p. 280), but with a few more classical trimmings, raised alternating quoins and sections of bolection frieze. Pennant sandstone laid in thin courses, Bath stone dressings. Large mullion-and-transom windows and shaped gables, the central pair bridged together. Altogether an ebullient Jacobethan design. Two-storey range with the shell-headed boys' and girls' entrances both at the l. end. The r. end curtailed of one bay, it seems. One-storey infants' block entered round the side under a toy-like spirelet.

ST MONICA'S CHURCH IN WALES PRIMARY SCHOOL, Merthyr Street. Built in 1893–4 by *E. M. Bruce Vaughan* for 342 children. Single-storeyed. Perp. Snecked Pennant sandstone with Bath stone dressings. Its Gothic style and its small size both deliberately in contrast with board school norms. The building was in fact intended for use as a chapel on Sundays, thus justifying the octagonal turret on the corner, now truncated.

CATHAYS HIGH SCHOOL, New Zealand Road. 1929–30 by *G. H. Whitaker*. Red brick and Bath stone. Neo-Georgian, as one would expect by then. Long, straight frontage hard up against the road. In the centre a hall at an upper level, crowned by a broken pediment on pilaster strips, with load-bearing Ionic columns below. Five classrooms l. and r., then, beyond later infill, quoined end pavilions.

108 PUBLIC LIBRARY, on the corner between Whitchurch Road and Fairoak Road. 1906, by *Speir & Beavan*, who have exploited the site brilliantly. The style is Arts and Crafts Gothic, handled with exquisite delicacy. A pair of pavilion-like reading rooms are sited fan-wise with a low, canted entrance vestibule between them. The finely textured Pennant sandstone walls of the reading rooms are clasped by broad ashlar piers of Bath stone. Where these rise above the eaves-line, their sheer surfaces are enriched with foliage panels. Enormous four-light end windows, side windows in an alternating rhythm, all segment-headed. Sub-dividing mullions and segmental heads to some of the lights add to the intricacy of the design. Segment-headed entrance arch and more leaf sculpture over it. Note how the vestibule walls cant in a different rhythm from the sloping roof behind. An octagonal shingled turret with a tall lead spike provides a central accent.

UNIVERSITY HOSPITAL OF WALES, King George V Drive. A huge complex, in which the full range of hospital activities, teaching, research and care of the sick, were intended to be

brought together on one site. The winners of a competition in
1960 were *S. W. Milburn & Partners*, and buildings to their
design were put up over most of the next decade-and-a-half.
The MEDICAL COLLEGE, of 1966–71, is a five-storey slab set
athwart the site, with a parallel eight-storey range to the E,
consisting of three linked ward blocks. Both are constructed on
reinforced concrete frames, set on pilotis, and have continuous
bands of windows. Central canopied entrance to the Medical
College reached by a ramp. To the SW of this, the DENTAL
HOSPITAL, 1963–5, a five-storey slab on a steel frame. Black
and yellow bands between the windows make it an eye-catcher
from the A48. The other main component is the HEALTH
CARE STUDIES DEPARTMENT in the NE corner of the site,
centred on a ten-storey block. The CARDIFF MEDICAL
CENTRE, inside the main entrance at the SE corner of
the site, is much more recent, *c.* 1991–2 by *Gordon Jones* of
Powell, Alport & Partners. Long, low and shed-like, with glazed
aisles and a continuous ridge skylight. Purple brick cladding
piquantly contrasting with the exposed white metal frame.

MAINDY BARRACKS, Whitchurch Road. Headquarters of the
Welch Regiment. Castellated. Dark Pennant sandstone with
matching Forest of Dean dressings. 1881. Beside the entrance
drive, CENOTAPH, 1924 by *Lutyens*. A subtly stepped slab of
Portland stone, in principle like his much larger Cenotaph in
Whitehall.

COMPANIES HOUSE, Crown Way. Bright red brick all over. To
the l. a five-storey office block, with windows in unbroken
bands. To the r., a four-storey car park with parking decks in
unbroken bands. Designed by *Alex Gordon & Partners* and built
in 1974–5.

At MAINDY, beside the River Taff, a COTTAGE of *c.* 1875,
attributable to *William Burges*, accessible down LLYS TAL-Y-
BONT ROAD. Further N, at the junction of CAERPHILLY
ROAD with BIRCHGROVE ROAD, an unusually suavely
designed public house, the BIRCHGROVE INN, 1931–2 by *Ivor
Jones & Percy Thomas*. Slabby brick chimneystacks clasp the
central timber-framed women's room under its sweeping tiled
roof. Bars, with bedrooms over, in the gabled wings to l. and r.

ELY

The outer suburbs to the W of the city and S of the River Ely, on
both sides of COWBRIDGE ROAD WEST, were built up with
local authority housing. GLAN ELY, which extends across the
hill N of the Cowbridge Road, bisected from E to W by GRAND
AVENUE, was laid out and constructed in the late 1920s by
Cardiff City Council in the Garden City spirit. The houses, semi-
detached pairs of two designs, one with asymmetrical gables, both
with bold, round-headed porch arches, extend with remarkable
consistency the full length of the road, for well over a mile. The
housing which stretches towards Caerau, S of Cowbridge Road

West, is of the 1950s and '60s. This is much less strongly characterized and too low-density to generate a sense of neighbourhood.

ST DAVID, Cowbridge Road West. A simple church by *John
Prichard*, the nave of 1870–1, the chancel added in 1882. The
original plan was for a chapel and vestry to flank the chancel,
as the interior still demonstrates, the chancel arch flanked by
lower, narrower arches now leading nowhere. Snecked, rock-
faced Lias limestone, and Bath stone dressings. Lancets,
shafted internally. Even here Prichard had his fun with stiff-
leaf, see the chancel arch where shoots sprout over the capital
mouldings. – PULPIT. Stone. Typical *Prichard*, but brought
here from Bonvilston church. – STAINED GLASS. Chancel E,
Ascension. 1899 by *Samuel Evans* of West Smethwick.

ST FRANCIS OF ASSISI (R.C.), Cowbridge Road West. 1960.
One of the series of irrepressibly idiosyncratic post-war
churches by *F. R. Bates, Son & Price*. Here the exterior looks
particularly zany, presenting a series of lozenge-shaped
windows towards the road. Openwork concrete campanile.
(Inside, the reinforced concrete frame acts as a series of flying
buttresses to carry the gallery. (D. Evinson.) – CERAMIC
RELIEF. Way of the Cross, by *Adam Kossowski*.)

THE RESURRECTION, Glan Ely. 1934 by *Thomas Roderick* of
Aberdare. Byzantine style, based on the church of the Community of the Resurrection, Mirfield, Yorkshire, by Walter
Tapper (P. Howell). Brownish-red brick. Latin cross plan with
a short, octagonal crossing tower. The interior, though not in
any way original, is spatially impressive, dominated by the
shallow dome on squinches over the crossing. Tunnel-vaulted
nave, with penetrations for the clerestory windows. E apse.
Rendered and painted white and grey. – PULPIT. Perp, with a
tester. Inappropriate but pretty. – STAINED GLASS. Apse lights,
Annunciation, Crucifixion, Resurrection, Ascension, Pentecost. 1947 by *Francis Spear*.

ELY METHODIST CHURCH, Cowbridge Road, on the corner
of Colin Way. 1910–11 by *H. P. Sanders* of Cardiff. Perp, quite
an elaborate composition towards the road. Aisled with a
clerestory, the arcades of cast iron. W gallery with serpentine
balcony front also of iron. Pulpit end now drastically simplified.

ELY HOSPITAL, Cowbridge Road. W of St David's church.
The nucleus is the block facing the road inscribed 'Industrial
Training School 1862'. Simple Tudor Gothic.

HERBERT THOMPSON PRIMARY SCHOOL, Plymouth Wood
Road. Foundation stone laid 1925, when the Cardiff City Edu-
cation Architect was *T. Pierson Frank*. Competent Wren style.
Red brick with channelled Bath stone accents.

BRANCH LIBRARY, Grand Avenue. 1985–6 by the *Welsh School
of Architecture* (project architect *Michael Harries*). A jolly little
building, single-storeyed, of red brick, under a hipped roof with
glazed lantern. Towards the road, doorway between stout twin
columns of brick and big semicircular windows. The intention
was to reflect the materials of the Resurrection church and the

motifs of the neighbouring housing, but Soane's 'barn à la Paestum' and even the Post-Modernism of John Outram seem also to have been in mind. Inside, benches below the windows, and four more portly columns, their surfaces marbled, defining the top-lit space.

In TRELAI PARK, 1 m. E, is the site of a Roman VILLA extensively excavated in the late C19 and early C20. Built in the early C2 A.D., it went out of use in the C4.

FAIRWATER

Fairwater, and its extension, Pentrebane, form the W-ward extremity of continuously built-up Cardiff N of the valley of the River Ely. They consist almost wholly of housing estates of the late C20, replacing the prosperous industrialists' villas which from the 1890s colonized the park of Fairwater House.

FAIRWATER HOUSE, Fairwater Road, stands derelict. It was built c. 1840 by *David Vaughan*. Two-storeyed, with polygonal ends, the verandas which wrapped around them now gone.

The present-day heart of Fairwater is ¼ m. SW, where Fairwater Road meets St Fagans Road. A green, shops, the little PUBLIC LIBRARY, 1959–60 by *John Dryburgh*, Cardiff City Architect, and ST DAVID'S LUTHERAN CHURCH. This is by *Alex Gordon & Partners*, 1960–1. Dark brown brick rectangle, above which hovers the concrete roof structure. Hidden light-sources illuminate the altar wall.

CANTONIAN HIGH SCHOOL, Fairwater Road. A typical group of the 1960s, well seen from the road above. Two three-storey curtain-wall blocks, not quite linked by a lower central range. Detached hall pavilion. Buff brick for the end walls, green copper cladding for the shallow pitched roofs. Originally two separate schools, that to the W for boys, 1961–2, that to the E for girls, 1962–3. By *Cardiff City Architects Department* (City Architect *John Dryburgh*).

The few surviving original villas are widely scattered.

RADYR CHAIN, Waterhall Road, 1 m. N. Dated 1894. Red brick and Bath stone. Gothic. Some details link it with *E.W.M. Corbett*'s terrace houses in Cathedral Road. Billiard room added 1912. (Well-preserved interior.)

FAIR WOOD, Llantrisant Road. Next door to the above. A suave essay by *Sir Percy Thomas* in a Cotswold idiom. Rendered walls. 1927.

THE QUARRY, St Fagans Rise, ½ m. W. House and cottage-cum-garage, all now a public house. Also by *Sir Percy Thomas* and dated 1921 on a rainwater head. Faced with snecked, rock-faced Lias limestone quarried on the site. Bath stone dressings and Westmorland roof slates. Cotswold style with overtones of Voysey. But note the ovolo mouldings of the window mullions, a detail more historicist than Voysey employed.

TŶ BRONNA, St Fagans Road, 1 m. W. (Headquarters of the South Glamorgan Ambulance Service.) This is real *Voysey*, 107 with all his personal traits. Designed, for Hastings Watson, in 1903, with finishing touches extending to 1906.

First to catch the eye is the STABLE BLOCK of 1904, built close above the road. Clean white outline, gabled at each end, with battered angle buttresses. The house stands higher up the hillside among trees. Voysey exploited the slope by placing the entrance at the short W end, so that he could open up a five-arched veranda almost the full width of the S front, which faced the view over the valley of the River Ely. Two full storeys above that and an all-embracing hipped roof. At the angles battered buttresses from ground to eaves. The staircase immediately inside the front door is denoted by vertically proportioned windows, and one oeil-de-boeuf. The principal rooms are towards the E, the drawing room lit by a long, low window within the recessed veranda, and given a bowed E window and an oeil-de-boeuf to the S. The exterior has been spoilt by the infilling of the veranda arches and a crude balcony parapet. Inside, the typical timber STAIRCASE survives, rising immediately beyond the front door. Semicircular arch at its head, opening into a long, generously glazed vestibule with original fireplace. Floors of slate.

GABALFA

GABALFA AVENUE is the spine of a formal road layout SE of Llandaff North on what were the water meadows of the River Taff. CATHEDRAL VIEW at r.-angles indicates the orientation of the scheme in relation to the towers of Llandaff Cathedral. Unfortunately there are no interesting buildings. Most conspicuous are three eleven-storey TOWER BLOCKS off Llanidloes Road, irritatingly unrelated to the street-plan. By *John Dryburgh*, Cardiff City Architect, *c.* 1957–9. To the E, Eastern Avenue cuts Gabalfa Avenue off short. The construction of Eastern Avenue also necessitated the demolition of St Mark's church, which was rebuilt on a new site ½ m. further E, beyond the industrial estate.

ST MARK, North Road (strictly, in Cathays). 1967–8 by *Seely & Paget*. Planned for participatory worship and designed in a somewhat over-elaborate modern idiom. The church has a pentagonal plan and is constructed on ten large half-portal frames of laminated Douglas fir, reminiscent of crucks. Copper roof crowned by a lantern of fanciful shape. Equally fanciful the W tower which stands axially over the entrance. This has a concrete frame, its ground stage left open to form a porch, with brick infill above on a hexagonal plan, and open again at the bell-stage, which is gabled in all four directions. Pentagonal NW chapel, large rectangular S hall. The facing material is grey-brown Leicestershire brick, except for the entrance wall and altar wall, of reconstituted Cotswold stone blocks, a contrast which reinforces the W–E axis. – STAINED GLASS. From two war memorial windows made for the old church, the earlier of 1920 by *R. J. Newbery*.

GRANGETOWN

Grangetown grew up as an artisan and respectable working-class suburb after the Baroness Windsor had in 1857 obtained an Act enabling her to build a new town on her estate, The Grange. In 1879 it was described as 'a mass of dwelling houses' after the plans of *Robert Forrest*, agent to the Windsor Estate. The s portion, however, with Paget Street as its spine, was not developed until the 1890s.

St Dyfrig and St Samson, Pentre Gardens. 1911 by *F. J. Veall* of Cardiff. Unfinished. Inside are several fittings from *J. D. Sedding*'s church of St Dyfrig, Canton, designed in 1885 and demolished in 1969. The important one is the gesso RELIEF of the Adoration of the Kings, by *Henry Wilson*.

St Paul, Paget Street. Designed in 1888 by *J. P. Seddon & J. Coates Carter*, the nave and aisles built 1889–91, the chancel 1901–2, largely at the expense of Lord Windsor. On a spacious site, soaring above the terraces all around. Noble in its verticality – even in its present state, lacking all but the stump of the intended SE steeple – but impaired by quirks which a Pearson or a Bodley would not have admitted. Nave and chancel under a continuous ridge. Cross-gabled aisles with long, slender two-light windows. Geometrical tracery. On the w front, towards the road, the four-light window is flanked by sheer polygonal turrets with arcaded tops and pyramidal caps. The materials are highly eccentric, walling of tight-packed Pennant rubble, the generous ashlar dressings partly of pink sandstone from Penkridge in Staffordshire, and partly of Portland cement mixed with tiny pink pebbles, creating strange textural contrasts. Even an attempt at a sort of flushwork on the w front. Sculpture not executed here.

Inside, the tall and exceedingly slender piers, clustered shafts with hollow and quadrant mouldings, are faced with the same cement. Are they of concrete? In stone such etiolation would hardly be possible. They must surely be meant to outdo Bodley's newly completed St German's, Roath (*see* p. 300). Shafts for a chancel arch, but continuous boarded ceilings of trefoil section, with tie-beams and arch-braces brought down on to ugly pointed corbels. Boarded ceilings in the aisles too, in conflict with the cross-gables. – PULPIT and CHOIR STALLS. Perp. By *Coates Carter*. – STAINED GLASS. Chancel E. Crucifixion flanked by bishops. 1920. In a C15 Netherlandish style. By *Burlison & Grylls*.

St Patrick (R.C.), Pentrebane Street. 1929–30 by *Joseph Goldie*. Red brick. Basilical.

Grangetown Junior School, Holmesdale Street. The forbidding two-storey range facing the playground belongs to *E. M. Bruce Vaughan*'s board school of 1883. Grey Pennant sandstone dressed with Bath stone. Trios of trefoil-headed lancets establish the architect's preference for Gothic even for this type of commission. Many later additions.

NINIAN PARK SCHOOL, Sloper Road. The most aggressively
spectacular board school in Cardiff and the most expensive
(tender for £22,000). The architects were *Robert & Sidney
Williams* of Cardiff, the date 1899–1900. Rough-textured, grey
Pennant sandstone and thick Bath stone dressings. Elizabethan
style. Standard layout, the two-storey range for boys and girls
making a show towards the road, but their separate entrances
at the back (where Bath stone gives way to red brick). One-
storey infants' range at r.-angles facing the side street.

PUBLIC LIBRARY, Redlaver Street. 1900–1, by *E. M. Bruce
Vaughan*. Tudor Gothic, with many tall mullion-and-transom
windows, to create the brightly lit spaces the early C20 library
user expected. Harsh red brick and the minimum of Bath stone
dressings.

FERRY ROAD GASHOLDER, W of the N end of Ferry Road. Built
in 1881 for the Cardiff Gas Light and Coke Company by *J. &
W. Horton* of Smethwick. Cylindrical gasholder of plated metal
supported within by two tiers of sixteen cast iron Doric
columns. The entablature blocks crowning each tier are linked
by lattice girders with tensioning rods to the heads and feet of
adjacent columns.

LISVANE/LLYS-FAEN

Since the 1890s Lisvane has attracted middle-class residents,
prepared to commute by train to the centre of town. Cardiff's
leading late Victorian architect and its leading building contractor
were among the first to build themselves houses here (*see* below).
Most of the early houses are strung along MILL ROAD, which
snakes to the NE from Llanishen Station. Denser development
ensued only from the 1950s, and has still not stopped. The
medieval church, however, remains on the edge of farmland to
the E, and the parish N of the M4 is entirely rural.

ST DENYS. Characteristic and impressive W tower, though not
large. Saddleback roof supported on a corbel table. W belfry
opening of two lights with ogees in the tracery, suggesting a
late C14 date. No buttresses, just a slight taper to the walls all
the way up. The body of the church, narrow nave and lower
chancel with S porch and N transept, probably dates from the
early C14 – see the chancel arch and arch to the transept,
pointed but of flattened profile, of two chamfered orders dying
into the single-chamfered imposts. The porch, which stands,
most oddly, near the E end of the nave, has simple, single-
chamfered inner and outer arches. The windows all Dec or
Perp, inserted in the C19. (Restoration of 1878. Cadw.) The
well-harmonized hall and N-ward extension of the transept are
of 1979 by *Berwyn Thomas*. Inside, savagely scraped walls jar
against plastered tunnel-vaults. The church was reordered in
1979, and now the altar faces obliquely into both nave and
transept and the members of the choir sit in what was the
chancel. – SANCTUARY FITTINGS by *Frank Roper*. – FONT.

Octagonal on a circular shaft. Is this of the C15, or earlier?
BAPTIST CHURCH, Rudry Road, ¾m. NE. Built as Fairoak
Chapel and dated 1856. Small and isolated, on a bank, turning
its back to the road. Two long, round-headed windows at
each gabled end, those towards the E flanking a round-headed
doorway. Full-length, lean-to S vestry. Interior galleried on
three sides, the pulpit facing the entrance. Original open pews,
and a fireplace for the use of worshippers between services. –
BAPTISTERY. In the open air, between chapel and road. A
deep sunk rectangle, with three tiers of stone benches on three
sides and a flight of steps right down in one corner.
No. 66 MILL ROAD (formerly Lisvane House), ¼m. W. Built by
Edwin Seward for himself, the high part towards the road before
1899, the low, rambling rear part *c.*1902. In a Norman Shaw
Old English style, much compromised by the later insertion of
windows and truncation of chimneystacks. The best feature,
the fancifully detailed entrance doorway and porch under a
half-timbered gable. The interior, which has been subdivided,
was conceived by Seward as a setting for his collection of old
furniture and fittings, including a staircase dated 1688.
Also in Mill Road, THE DINGLE, *c.*1936 by *Sir Percy Thomas*,
and probably other houses by him of a similar date.
CHERRY ORCHARD, Cherry Orchard Road, ½m. NW. 1939–40
by *Sir Percy Thomas*. Voyseyesque, but with metal window
frames.
TÝ-GWYN, Lisvane Road, 300 yds SW. A small, grey mansion
in Tudor style, dated as surprisingly late as 1906. Portland
stone ashlar throughout, appropriately, since the house was
built for James E. Turner, senior partner of the great Cardiff
building firm E. Turner & Sons, constructors of the civic buildings in Cathays Park and much else.
HILL FARM HOUSE, off Capelgwilym Road, 1¼m. NW. Small,
thatched hall block of a much-altered longhouse, with its byre,
curtailed and partly rebuilt, to the W, and a later domestic
extension to the E.

LLANISHEN/LLANISIEN

The S half of Llanishen is CYNCOED, Cardiff's most opulent
inter-war suburb. Further N, on the W side of the Rhymney Valley
railway, the medieval church is accompanied by a cluster of late
Victorian streets and by sundry factories and offices, most notably
the daunting blocks of the Inland Revenue.

ST ISAN, Station Road. From the S the church presents a characteristic line-up, unbuttressed W tower, with corbelled battlements, small pinnacles, and two-light belfry openings of C15
type, nave and lower chancel. Multicoloured rubble-stone
walling unifies the three. One original lancet in the chancel,
and a Dec two-lighter with cusped ogee heads to the lights for
the sanctuary S and N. The E window, of three lights, is Perp,
with unusual diamond-shaped hoodmould stops (but cf. St

Mellons). Chancel arch of two chamfered orders dying into the chamfered imposts. The s porch is also medieval, with a remarkably small inner door, and above it a small C15 relief of the Crucifixion flanked by standing saints.

But all this is only one-third of the present building, relegated to act as s aisle and chapel when a new nave and chancel with N aisle and chapel were built in 1907–8 by *H. D. Blessley*, replacing a N aisle of 1854 by *Prichard & Seddon*. This is a parody of the old work, the walls of multicoloured stones laid like crazy-paving. Part Dec, part Perp. Prichard & Seddon's handsome arcade of short piers, quatrefoil in plan with moulded caps and bases in the form of one big roll, survives. – PISCINA. In the medieval chancel, with a shelf. – REREDOS. 1903, designed by *Halliday*, carved by *Clarke* of Llandaff. High relief stone figures, Christ between four censing angels. – STAINED GLASS. Chancel E window, Noli me Tangere, 1908. Languid figures in an idiosyncratic style. – Much else of the early C20, none of special merit. In the chancel, SS John and Chad, 1919 by *Hardman & Co.* – Nave W, war memorial, 1920 by *Morris & Co.* – Nave s, Suffer the Little Children, 1906, signed by *Jones & Willis*, and SS Anne and Elizabeth, 1925, signed by *Kempe & Tower*. – N aisle, SS George and David, 1916 by *Powell*'s; Sir Galahad at prayer, 1918 by *Clayton & Bell*; Faith and Hope, 1919 by *A. L. Moore & Son*; guardian angel and St Martin, 1923 by *Heaton, Butler & Bayne*. – MONU-MENTS. (Matthew Prichard †1623, brass, in the old chancel.) – Thomas Lewis †1764. Pedimented tablet of several coloured marbles. – John Lewis †1850. Hanging wall-monument. Still Grecian, but the figure of the seated woman, head bowed in grief, has a powerful bulk and naturalism. Signed by *John Evan Thomas*, still showing the influence of his master, Chantrey.

Former SCHOOL, in Heol Hir, W of the church. Small, Gothic, colourful. Of mauve random-laid sandstone with dressings of Bath stone and red brick. By *Kempson & Fowler*, 1894, extended in 1904 by *H. D. Blessley*.

CHRIST CHURCH, Lake Road North. 1963–4 by *H. N. Haines*. Roof with glazed gables in three directions supported internally on concrete pilotis. Low aisles faced with brown brick. A sim-plified version of Maguire & Murray's St Paul's, Bow Common, London.
    In the forecourt, CRUCIFIX by *Frank Roper*.

METHODIST CHURCH, Melbourne Road. 1900–1, by *Edwin Seward*. Fancy Perp façade of rock-faced sandstone and lavish Bath stone ashlar.

THORNHILL CREMATORIUM, Thornhill Road, 1 m. NW. Chapel of 1954 by *E. C. Roberts*. In the timid church style of the 1950s, before the architecture of crematoria was rethought in the following decade (*see* Coychurch and Llwydcoed).

CARDIFF HIGH SCHOOL, Llandennis Road. By the *Cardiff City Architects Department* (director *John Dryburgh*). The main range, centred on a four-storey curtain-wall pavilion, was built in the 1960s as Tŷ Celyn High School. The L-shaped range behind, with red brick piers, 1971–3, provided for the enlarged Cardiff High School.

COED GLAS SCHOOL, Findlas Road. Brown brick, glass and yellow glazed panels. Three-storey main block, with a series of single-storey classrooms treated as pavilions, facing Ty-Glas Avenue behind. Typical of the 1960s.

INLAND REVENUE OFFICES, Ty-Glas Avenue. Two massive slabs, one of eighteen storeys, the other of ten. Their towering presence is felt over much of north Cardiff.

In TY-GLAS AVENUE, a group of typical buildings of the 1980s. On the N side, LEISURE CENTRE, by the *Alex Gordon Partnership*, opened 1987. Of buff brick and caramel brick in broad horizontal stripes. To the E, THE ORCHARDS, by the *The Wigley Fox Partnership*, an office block mounted on pilotis but otherwise enigmatically clad overall in opaque blue-black glazing, following the fashion begun by Norman Foster's offices in Ipswich. Opposite, TŶ-GLAS public house, NORTHWAY HOUSE etc., Post-Modern offices, fenestrated with a series of forward-pointing Vs.

To the E of the church in STATION ROAD, three enjoyable late Victorian houses. The earliest is No. 90, HILL HOUSE, Gothic with a huge staircase window and some polychromy. This may be by *W. D. Blessley*, who lived in a house further w in Station Road. No. 92, THE HOLLIES, of red brick, is Italianate, but with Frenchy bullseye dormers painted white, and two broad, red, terracotta friezes, the upper one echoing the frieze of the Parthenon. No. 96, COURT SCHOOL, is less easily categorized and probably dates from *c.*1900. Chequered bands. Pilastered one-storey ballroom added to the r.

NEW HOUSE, Thornhill Road, 2 m. NW. Now a hotel. On the hillside looking down on a panorama of Cardiff. Late C18 or early C19 façade, strangely gauche. Pinched central bay with Ionic pilasters framing the doorway. Canted two-storey window bays to l. and r., and two bays of straight wall each side to close the composition. Architrave surrounds to all windows. Panels, runs of balustrading, pediments floating free of the windows they relate to, pepper the walls. Hotel extensions of 1991–2, echoing the style of the house, by *The Wigley Fox Partnership*.

RHIWBINA

The Garden Village is the special attraction of Rhiwbina.

BETHANY BAPTIST CHAPEL, Heol Llanishen Fach. 1963–4 by *J. Morgan Harries* of Bridgend. The concrete roof canopy is carried on slender piers, its zigzag profile curling up like a wave over the altar wall. The side walls take the form of mosaic-covered panels. A strip of clerestory window all round, and broad full-height glazing N and S of the altar, a typical management of the lighting.

GARDEN VILLAGE, ½ m. SW. The most extensive and the best-preserved Garden Village in Glamorgan. Plans were drawn up by *Raymond Unwin* in 1912 for the Cardiff Workers' Co-operative Garden Village Society Ltd, for an estate of 300 houses laid out N of the railway and aligned on Rhiwbina Halt. The first phase, built in 1912–13, was laid out along a straight tree-lined avenue, running s–n, LON-Y-DAIL. This was crossed by LON ISA, and of the four squarish spaces thus created, that in the SE angle was developed at the end of a short cul-de-sac, Y GROES. Houses designed by *A. H. Mottram*, semi-detached pairs of several designs: rough-cast, gabled, some with slate-hanging on the gables, some with a big sweep of roof low between the gables. Eleven pairs stand round an oblong green. On No. 7 a plaque with the date 1913 and the Society's initials.

106

The next group is at the E end of PEN-Y-DRE, beside the railway. Here some houses are of brown brick, some are in short terraces, and the windows and doorhoods consciously imitate C18 cottage precedents. These are by *H. Avray Tipping* (probably ghosted by *Eric Francis*. P. Howell). Much of the rest of this road was developed for the Garden Village Society in the period 1920–3, by *T. Alwyn Lloyd*. He built for himself the free-standing house at the W end, No. 11, HEOL WEN, which commands the length of Pen-y-dre.

The character of a Garden Village inevitably owes as much to trees and hedges as it does to buildings, and to the absence of individualistic improvements by house-owners. Rhiwbina succeeds through the control of the Society, Rhiwbina Garden Village Ltd, as it became, which employed its own maintenance team and craftsmen until it was wound up in 1976 and the houses were sold to tenants. In 1977 an enlightened City Council declared the village a Conservation Area. The only blemish is a small number of individual houses built for sale in the 1960s and early 1970s.

TWMPATH, ½ m. w. A C12 motte engulfed in suburbia, accessible up a track from BRYNTEG. This is one of the largest mottes in the county, with a flat circular top 49 ft (15 metres) in diameter. The view above the rooftops to the far distant countryside in all directions shows how a well-sited motte could command a remarkably wide area.

ROATH/Y RHATH

The ancient parish of Roath was Cardiff's immediate neighbour to the E, and in the Middle Ages the manor of Roath constituted the home farm for the lord of Glamorgan's castle there. In the C19 the lord's successors, the Marquesses of Bute, made the parish church of St Margaret the family burial place. East Moors, the part of the parish which extended as far as the coast, was marshland, built over in the later C19 by the suburbs of Adamsdown and Splott (*see* p. 311), and in the C20 by Tremorfa and also by industry and dockland under redevelopment since 1987 by the Cardiff Bay Development Corporation.

The East Moors area is not included here under Roath. Instead,

the main London to Swansea railway line is treated as the s
boundary, and the Rhymney Valley line to Caerphilly as its
boundary towards the w. St Margaret's church stands close to
the e edge of present-day Roath, while to the n it extends beyond
the A48 to include Pen-y-lan and the area around Roath Park
Lake. Thus defined, Roath is Cardiff's largest suburb. Many of
the city's finest buildings are in Roath, and its late C19 housing is
of exceptional interest.

CHURCHES AND CHAPELS

St Margaret of Antioch, Waterloo Road. There was a
medieval church here, as the grassy churchyard might indicate.
In 1800 the first Marquess of Bute added a family mausoleum
on the n side of the chancel. In 1867 the trustees of the third
Marquess decided to rebuild the church. Foundations were
laid by the Bute Estate architect, *Alexander Roos*, nave and
chancel on the pre-existing plan, with the addition of transepts
and a s aisle. The church itself, however, is by *John Prichard*,
commissioned by the third Marquess himself at his coming of
age in 1868, and built in 1869–70, one of Prichard's finest
works. *Prichard* rebuilt the mausoleum too, 1881–6, in a sumptuous, not entirely compatible, style. Both, however, are E.E.

The church is not large, and the meagre crossing tower
substituted by *J. Coates Carter* in 1926 for the steeple Prichard
had designed makes it unimpressive from a distance. Two
things hint at the glories within: the walls, laboriously constructed of split Pennant sandstone laid in courses, three
extremely shallow to one slightly less shallow, ample dressings
of Bath stone, and the chancel e window of astonishing size,
five lights and a tracery composition worthy of Lincoln
Cathedral. The w window of the n transept reuses tracery from
the w window of the old church. The mausoleum has ashlar
banded in two colours, deep buttresses with set-offs, gables
and gargoyles to complicate their form. Quatrefoil parapet.

The interior is a riot of colour, or would be were there less
stained glass. White brick for the walls, against which thin red
and black brick bands and voussoirs stand out. All the emphasis
is on the crossing arches, banded in two orders with grey-green
Bridgend stone, red Radyr stone and golden Penarth alabaster.
The crossing piers show Prichard at his most quirky. There are
three different designs: to the w the arch rests on curious
tubular corbels, to n and s there are stout cylindrical responds,
and to the e shorter responds of the same girth carry paired
colonnettes which jack the arch, here of three orders, up to a
higher level. Arch-brace roofs with cusped wind-braces. The
chancel is arcaded low down, but the entire n wall opens as a
two-bay arcade into the vaulted mausoleum. The vaulting is 94
carried on wall-shafts with big stiff-leaf capitals carved by *Clarke*
of Llandaff. Polychromy here too. Elegant ironwork enclosing
screens. Within the mausoleum, an astonishing sight, six nearly
identical sarcophagi, and a smaller seventh, of polished red

For Roath Park area see inset

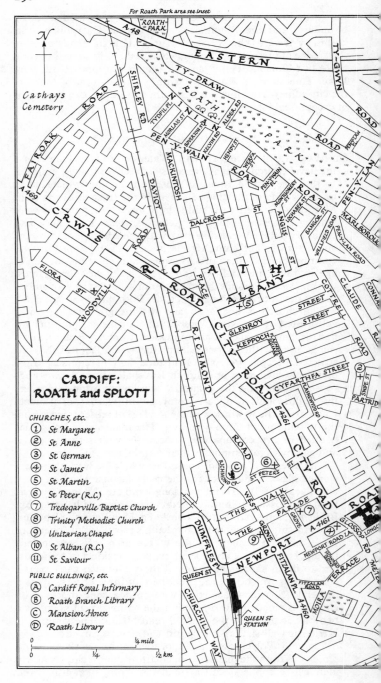

N

Cathays
Cemetery

**CARDIFF:
ROATH and SPLOTT**

CHURCHES, etc.

① St Margaret
② St Anne
③ St German
④ St James
⑤ St Martin
⑥ St Peter (R.C)
⑦ Tredegarville Baptist Church
⑧ Trinity Methodist Church
⑨ Unitarian Chapel
⑩ St Alban (R.C.)
⑪ St Saviour

PUBLIC BUILDINGS, etc.

Ⓐ Cardiff Royal Infirmary
Ⓑ Roath Branch Library
Ⓒ Mansion House
Ⓓ Roath Library

0 ¼ mile
0 ¼ ½ km

Peterhead granite, coped but otherwise absolutely plain, a dour
Scots gesture silent in the face of Prichard's Welsh rhapsodies.
(The name-plates on the sarcophagi are reused from burial
shelves of the earlier mausoleum, as the typical early C19 lettering shows.) – MOSAIC of Christ in Majesty over the entrance
arches. – REREDOS. 1925 by *Comper*. Small figures of Christ
and the twelve apostles in a row under brittle tracery. – PULPIT.
Typical *Prichard*. Alabaster. – FONT, LECTERN and PEWS also
by *Prichard*. – STAINED GLASS. The original grisaille glazing
by *Saunders & Co.* remains only in the porch and sacristy. – In
the mausoleum, 1886 by *W. F. Dixon*. – In the church an almost
complete series by *Burlison & Grylls*, 1890–1919, the earliest, N
transept NE, nave NE, to *Bodley*'s design. – Chancel E, Ascension, 1952 by *Powell*'s of Whitefriars. – S transept E, St Margaret, 1969 by *L. C. Evetts*. Good colour and use of leading.

ALL SAINTS, Kames Place, Adamsdown. (Secularized.) 1902–3
by *Seddon & Carter*. A simple rectangle set above a hall. Walling
materials, Bath, Pennant and Radyr stones, in complex interplay. Lancet style. Strange W bellcote on a slab-like buttress.

ST ANNE, Snipe Street. 1886–7 by *J. Arthur Reeve*, a former
assistant of William Burges. Tall three-bay chancel with a
flèche. N transept. N aisle and vestries, 1891–2. Rock-faced
Pennant sandstone with Bath stone dressings. Geometrical
tracery. Pearsonish interior, with four demi-angels in roundels
high on the N and S walls, carved in 1898 by *H. Gunthorp* from
models by *T. Nicholls*. The nave was never completed, a sad
come-down. S aisle of 1936 by *Caröe & Passmore*. – REREDOS.
By *Prichard*, brought here from St Margaret's, Roath, and set
up at the W end of the N aisle (now part of the hall). Alabaster
of several colours.

ST EDWARD KING AND CONFESSOR, Westville Road. Chancel
and double-gabled S transept of 1921, to a design by *Willmott
& Smith*. Red brick. Perp. Minimal nave added in 1968. –
STAINED GLASS. Chancel E, Crucifixion between Nativity and
Baptism of Christ, 1950 by *Baldwin & Lucas*.

ST GERMAN, Metal Street. By *Bodley & Garner*, 1881–4. The
church which introduced late Victorian Gothic to South Wales.
It stands on the angle of two streets, and only a flèche astride
the unbroken roof-ridge provides a vertical accent. Grey, pink-
tinged, rock-faced walling of local Swelldon stone with Bath
stone dressings. Outside, the richness of Bodley's conception
cannot be appreciated except from the NE. Here the lofty
clerestoried chancel rises high above the low E vestry and N
chancel chapel. Grandiose E window with flowing tracery,
establishing the Dec style of the whole church. Flying buttresses
span the chapel. The nave has no clerestory, but tall aisles,
their bays demarcated by ashlar-faced pilaster-buttresses with
one set-off high up, and gabled tops. Long two-light windows.
Polygonal stair-turret at the NW angle. The central windows
on the W front glazed only in the upper half.

92   The effect of the interior was justly described by Goodhart-
Rendel as 'a sort of greyhound church – strong, lithe and thin'.

Space flows almost without impediment. So that is why there is no clerestory in the nave, to enable the aisle arcades to be extremely high, on the hall-church system. Complex pier plan, of four filleted ogee-plan major shafts, with thread-like minor shafts in the angles. Chancel arch virtually the full width and height of the chancel. Nave and chancel have boarded wagon roofs of equal height decorated with stencilling, that in the chancel subdivided by stone transverse arches carried on wall-shafts (and justifying the flying buttresses outside). The E window, of three paired lights, extends the full width of the chancel, behind a free-standing traceried screen on slender shafts. Stone vaulting for the chancel chapels. – ROOD. Filling the chancel arch. Made by *Farmer & Brindley* to *Bodley*'s design, and brought from St Paul, Lorrimore Square, London. – PULPIT. By *Cecil Hare* of *Bodley & Hare*. – ORGAN CASE. This important component is also by *Bodley*, 1887. – FONT. Straightforward. By *Bodley*, 1898, the cover later, by *Hare*. – REREDOS. 1921–2 by *Hare*, with shutters added 1926–7. The late medieval Netherlandish type, with gilt statues under canopies and shutters opening the full width of the chancel. – STATIONS OF THE CROSS. 1919 by *Hare*. – STAINED GLASS. Chancel E, Crucified Christ with Annunciation below and eighteen other individual figures, 1900, by *Burlison & Grylls*, in the subdued coloration Bodley preferred, with much clear glass. – N chapel E, similar, by the same, 1905. – N chapel N, Adoration of the Kings. By *Kempe*, 1890. Small. – S chapel S, heraldic roundels. Dated 1954, by *Hugh Easton*.

In the churchyard, a CALVARY by *Frank Roper* of Penarth, 1965. Wrought iron.

CLERGY HOUSE, S of the church. 1893–4, by *Bodley*, but subdued.

Further S, at the bottom of Metal Street, ST GERMAN'S COURT, formerly school. Dated 1874. This is *Bodley*'s first contribution to the area. Advanced for its date. Gabled. Rendered walls and large timber mullion-and-transom windows. Tall red brick chimneystacks and tile-hung dormers. Had the architect been looking at St Fagans Castle (q.v.)?

ST JAMES, Newport Road. 1892–3. The masterpiece of *E. M. Bruce Vaughan*, who lived in the parish and here for once had the money to conceive an ambitious church and complete its every detail. On a conspicuous main-road site. Apsidal chancel with ambulatory, clerestoried nave and lean-to aisles. Geometrical tracery. The finest feature, the NE tower and spire, fused visually by the deft stepping of the buttresses. A good deal of sculpture, especially heads in roundels on the apse, and censing angels in the spandrels of the NW porch. The influence of Bodley's St German's is apparent, in the choice of materials, pinkish-grey Swelldon limestone for the coursed, rock-faced walling, and Bath stone dressings, and more particularly in the ashlar facing of the buttresses. They make an effective composition on the W front, two narrow between two broad, framing three long, slender windows. The interior is more routine, though the high, wide chancel arch, not interrupting the space, is another idea derived from Bodley. Piers, alternating round and octagonal, with lush stiff-leaf capitals. Archbrace nave roof with cusped wind-braces and stone wall-shafts. Oddly understated chancel, the ambulatory arches plainly moulded. – PULPIT. A sumptuous piece, of pink, green and buff stone, with small figures of famous preachers. – REREDOS. Post 1925, carved, gilt and painted, with shutters. – STAINED GLASS. Grisaille, of a simple Art Nouveau pattern. – Apse, Christ in Glory between Welsh saints. 1906, the gift of the architect. – Several windows of 1912–14 by *Burlison & Grylls*.

ST MARTIN, Albany Road. 1899–1901 by *F. R. Kempson*. Red brick with minimal dressings of Bath stone. Nave and chancel in one, lying beside the road. Lean-to N chapel. The N aisle is a passage aisle, but the S aisle is broad and gabled. Gutted in 1941 and rebuilt in 1955 by *Sir Charles Nicholson & Rushton*. So instead of the original rich polychromy, there is a typically pale post-war interior, dominated by the REREDOS, just a magnificently lettered inscription, and the STAINED GLASS in the window above, 1955 by *Hugh Easton*. This is really daring, a semi-nude, crimson-robed Christ seated on a rainbow, holding a blue globe, his head haloed by a golden sun. – N chapel E, green cross, gold chalice and Crown of Thorns. Also signed by *Easton* and dated 1956.

ST PETER (R.C.), St Peter's Street. Built in 1861 by *C. F. Hansom* of Bristol, in a Geometrical style. Pennant sandstone with bands and dressings of Bath stone and alternate voussoirs of pink Radyr stone. Cross-gabled aisles. Gabled polygonal apse. Six-bay nave with octagonal piers. Arch-brace and scissor-brace roof. The strong SW porch tower is of 1884 by *J. J. Hurley*. – STAINED GLASS. Three windows in the sanctuary by *Mayer & Co.*, 1883. – Some nave windows by *Hardman*, and others by *Sanders*.

The stocky Gothic PRESBYTERY, E of the church, is by *W. P. James*, 1872.

The CHAPELS of Roath provide a fine conspectus of Nonconformist Gothic, even despite the loss of *H. C. Harris*'s noble Brooksian Presbyterian Church of 1874–5.

ALBANY ROAD BAPTIST CHURCH, on the corner with Blenheim Road. Dated 1932. Quite large, but lacking in presence. Perp. Tower to the l. of the façade not finished. Brown brick. The SCHOOLS behind are more memorable, 1897–8 by *Habershon & Fawckner*, in what they called a Renaissance style. Strange, raised, vertical strips on the gables and upper walls. Mullion-and-transom windows. Newbridge stone with Bath stone dressings. The building incorporated a vestry hall, two schoolrooms and ten classrooms.

PLASNEWYDD PRESBYTERIAN CHURCH OF WALES, Keppoch Street. The oldest building on the site is the HALL of 1886 by *J. H. Phillips*. E.E. The CHAPEL is Perp, 1901, the earliest work of *W. Beddoe Rees*, the future chapel specialist, begun in collaboration with *J. H. James*. The façade is flanked

by stair projections, that to the r. developed upwards to form a
pretty octagonal bell-turret with gargoyles and a flared stone
spirelet. The façade itself shows the hand of an architect keen
to display his artistry. Flat ashlar pilaster buttresses frame a
subdivided four-light window under twin cusped vesicas. Thin-
coursed Pennant sandstone with Bath stone ashlar.

The interior also strives for effect. Broad for its length. Classically detailed galleries on three sides. They are carried on short,
thick iron columns with correctly detailed classical capitals;
their bowed metal fronts have an intricate pierced pattern; and
they carry tall, slender Composite columns up to support the
boarded ceiling, segmental in section over the main space, flat
over the galleries. Segmentally concave timber front to the
organ gallery, segmentally bowed pews. – STAINED GLASS.
Patterns in subdued colours in the window heads.

ROATH PARK METHODIST CHURCH, Albany Road. (Now in
use as a sale room.) 1897–8 by *Jones, Richards & Budgen*. An
ambitious essay in the Anglican manner. Cruciform plan, with
a porch tower towards Bangor Street looking as if it has strayed
from East Anglia. The Dec tracery is cuspless, however. Newbridge Pennant sandstone with Bath stone dressings. The three-
bay, aisled and clerestoried nave has clustered piers with keeled
shafts, and arches with double-wave mouldings, these too East
Anglian in feeling. But at the crossing no arches, just vertical
piers carved at the top with groups of angels. Galleries in the
transepts, but off-centre pulpit, discreetly sited organ, space
for a choir and a five-light window, with stained glass in it,
above the site of the altar. Boarded roofs of four-centred profile.

ST ANDREW'S UNITED REFORMED CHURCH, on the corner
of Marlborough Road and Wellfield Road. A showpiece indeed,
1899–1901 by *Habershon, Fawckner & Groves*, a firm not normally able to rise to such heights. The angle tower carries a
spire worthy of J. L. Pearson himself, of Bath stone ashlar
enriched with three bands of pink Radyr stone. The entrance
doorway to the church is copied from Tintern Abbey, and the
five-light window above is said to be an imitation of the transept
window at Melrose Abbey, Scotland. Another Dec window in
the transept. One-bay chancel with a rose window in the gable.
Coursed Newbridge Pennant sandstone of a dark hue. The
building was erected for the English Presbyterians of Roath
Park, cost £11,000, and seated 700 with a further 140 in the w
gallery.

TREDEGARVILLE BAPTIST CHURCH, The Parade. 1861–3 by
W. G. Habershon of London. An early example of Welsh Nonconformist Gothic, largely paid for by the coal entrepreneur
Cory family. The Latin cross plan is said to have been
demanded by Lord Tredegar, the ground landlord. Plate
tracery and bar tracery, some of it cuspless. The walls faced
with random blocks of Carboniferous limestone, pepper-and-
salt rather than truly multicoloured. The geological character
of the stone suggests that it came in, as ballast in Cory coal
ships, from Co. Galway, Ireland, rather than, as tradition has

it, from Italy. Inside, the most arresting feature is the arcaded stone baptistery, in front of the broad timber pulpit. Galleries on three sides on thin iron shafts. Large organ divided to frame the window above the entrance. Steep boarded roof, supported on arch-braces and tie-beams. – STAINED GLASS. Unusually much. Most interesting are the transept windows, c. 1880. Biblical plants, vine, lily, pomegranate, palm, with appropriate texts and heads of prophets and Evangelists. – Four large mid-C20 New Testament scenes. Suffer the Little Children, 1938 by *Powell*'s, Baptism of Christ, c. 1962, signed by *Bristow Wadley & Co.* of Cardiff, Empty Tomb and Good Samaritan.
     HALL behind in a similar style.

TRINITY METHODIST CHURCH, Four Elms Road. 1896–7 by *Ingall & Sons* of Birmingham. On a prominent site beside the Newport Road and making the most of it. Snecked Pennant sandstone with Bath stone dressings. Elaborate entrance front in a mixed E.E. and Dec style with much stiff-leaf, and moulded and shafted arches for the doorway and the rose window above. Porch tower at the most prominent corner. The transept is also part of the original build. Well-lit polygonal apse. So here we have the United Free Methodists aping the Established Church. Lush array of coupled colonnettes with stiff-leaf caps and corbels all round the apse, and singletons supporting the double hammerbeam roof. They even employed *W. Clarke* of Llandaff to carve the pulpit and rostrum furniture (now removed). – STAINED GLASS in the apse, illustrating Christ's Acts of Mercy, by *Swaine, Bourne & Co.* of Birmingham. Angels representing Virtues in the rose window. Remodelling in 1978 by *Wyn Thomas & Partners* involved adding a new vestibule to the side towards Piercefield Place, and subdividing the 'nave' horizontally.

SCHOOLROOMS (now the Elms Centre) stand alongside, almost like a second chapel with an embryonic steeple.

UNITED REFORMED CHURCH, ROATH PARK, Pen-y-wain Road. Built for Congregationalists, in 1909–10, by *Habershon, Fawckner & Co.* In an uninteresting Geometrical style. Snecked Pennant sandstone dressed with Bath stone. Spire lost.

UNITARIAN CHAPEL, West Grove. Dated 1886, the year the building was designed. Erected in 1890. The architect was *E. H. Bruton*. This is not Gothic, but it is hard to know what to call it. The two most prominent features are a shaped and pedimented gable and the oddly shapeless belfry. Red brick and eroded Ham Hill stone.

SHAH JALAL MOSQUE, Crwys Road. Built as a Calvinistic Methodist chapel in 1899 by *J. H. Phillips*. In 'no particular style', as the *Building News* correctly noted, but this hardly does justice to the ebullience of the design. Snecked Pennant sandstone and Doulting stone ashlar. Overall gable of curvaceous outline, round-headed central window with white timber-framing and a red superarch with voussoir bands. Wide, depressed arch to the entrance below, flanked by bulging stair-turrets, up which lancets step. Concave-sided turret caps with iron openwork ball finials. Contemporary iron railings. The building stands a full storey below road level, with a basement hall, which makes the chapel itself appear like a jack-in-the-box at the roadside.

PUBLIC BUILDINGS

UNIVERSITY OF WALES, CARDIFF, SCHOOL OF ENGIN-EERING AND PHYSICS, Newport Road. The centrepiece of the incongruous medley of buildings which face the road is the sensational Gothic tower, built as the entrance to the Institute of Physiology 1911–15 by *E. M. Bruce Vaughan*. Sheer polygonal turrets of Bath stone ashlar, bursting into decoration right at the top, flank a five-storey superarch, within which bands of mullion-and-transom windows alternate with bands of rich foliage. Under the arch-head, blind tracery and more lush foliage. Low, tripartite entrance on circular piers, with statues of Hippocrates and Asclepius, and busts of great C19 medical men. Crowning lantern, intended to rise to 150 ft (45.7 metres), not built. To the r. an eight-bay contemporary range with four storeys of mullion-and-transom windows and a straight top frieze. Red brick walling here. To the l. a plain rectangular completion of the original composition in an alien curtain-wall idiom, 1964 by *Sir Percy Thomas & Son*. To the r. an extension returning down WEST GROVE, 1987–93 by *Wyn Thomas & Partners*. This successfully echoes the character of Bruce Vaughan's range, especially in its materials, red brick and buff reconstituted stone. Lively fenestration pattern. Overhanging eaves, Japanese rather than Gothic.

Further N, facing THE PARADE, another four-storey range copying Bruce Vaughan's design. This is of 1921–6 by *J. B. Fletcher*, who had taken over his practice. Frieze of doctors and nurses over the doorway. Beyond this, the anonymous, five-storey SCHOOL OF NURSING, 1958–9. All this has recently been integrated into the School of Engineering and Physics. Symbol of integration is the high-level pedestrian BRIDGE across The Parade, linking to the most elaborate of the new buildings, the TREVITHICK BUILDING, for socializing and library. 1987–9 by *Wyn Thomas & Partners* (design partner *David Hamley*). T-plan. Three-storeyed towards The Parade, with the library wing running back lower towards the N. Buff brick. Broad bands of glazing low down and tucked under the eaves of the sweeping roofs. Whimsically placed porthole windows. Inside, the LIBRARY is the major space, lit by full-length glazing at the apex of the double-pitched roof.

To the s of The Parade, two further new blocks, housing classrooms and laboratories. The WEST BUILDING, *c.*1989–91, is also by *Wyn Thomas & Partners*, and exhibits the same mannerisms as the Trevithick Building. In the centre of the complex, and only visible from close-up, a four-storey block by *Holder Mathias Alcock*, 1990–2. Also with porthole windows in unexpected places, but otherwise quite grandly scaled. The double-height void at the N end, now acting as a pompous bicycle shed, may be built into in due course. At the S end, a dramatic steel-framed stair in a full-height glazed well.

COLLEGE OF ART, Howard Gardens. 1966 by *John Dryburgh*, Cardiff City Architect. Concrete-framed, faced with buff brick. Part four-storey, part six-storey. N-facing studios high up.

COLEG GLAN HAFREN, The Parade. Built as the Intermediate School for Girls, 1897–1900 by *George Thomas*. Elegant and sophisticated front to the street, three storeys of Portland stone ashlar with thin bands of red Hollington stone integrating the design. François Premier detailing, three narrow bays to the l., and a slightly projecting double entrance bay under a big shaped gable with the entrance in the r.-hand of a pair of arched entrances flanked by Ionic half-columns. The six more spacious bays to the r. are an addition. Mullion-and-transom vertical cross-windows, those at the top without the transom. In the projecting double bay a little sculpture, the date 1898 and a five-light window arched up into the gable. The original part was planned with four classrooms on each principal floor, and a lecture theatre etc. in the top storey. The ASSEMBLY HALL at the back survives, a charming, light-filled room. Canted brick piers carry segmental, voussoired rere-arches over the large, schematically traceried mullion-and-transom windows. Wainscoting below, and W gallery. Elaborate roof structure of tie-beams on brackets, kingposts and queenposts. Boarded ceiling.

No. 28, a double-fronted villa, in a Jacobean style, was incorporated into the school from the beginning. This must be by *Habershon*, who built up The Parade for the Tredegar Estate from 1857.

ALBANY PRIMARY SCHOOL, Albany Road. A typical board school, built in 1886–7 by *A. Llewellyn Batchelor*. Two-storey range towards the street for girls and boys, extended to the l. in 1897 by *S. Rooney*. One-storey infants' range behind to the r., making its mark not by architectural definition but by polychromy of unexpected subtlety. Pennant sandstone walling with buff Bath stone dressings and bands of pink Radyr stone. Pink and buff brick relieving arches over the windows.

ROATH PARK PRIMARY SCHOOL, Pen-y-wain Road. A very fine and complete Queen Anne style board school by *E.W.M. Corbett*, built 1894–5. Red pressed brick with details of red stone and red terracotta. White-painted window timberwork. Two-storey range for girls and boys. To the l., infants' range, a copy of the upper storey alongside.

STACEY ROAD PRIMARY SCHOOL, Stacey Road. Another board school, grouped in the more normal way, the one-storey infants' range lying alongside the two-storey range for boys and girls. Its tall proportions and the lancet form of its upper windows are Gothicisms which suggest an early date. *Bruton & Williams* made extensions in 1893. Roughly snecked Pennant sandstone walls, windows banded with Bath stone and black brick.

St David's Catholic Sixth Form College, Ty-Gwyn
Road. A good 1960s group. Three-storey main range, the top
one oversailing. Hall in an isolated pavilion, the clerestory
glazing revealing the lattice structure of the space-frame roof.

Ty Gwyn Court, Ty-Gwyn Road. University hall of residence. Two ten-storey towers and lower buildings, including a
dining hall. 1961–7 by *Sir Percy Thomas & Son* (partner-in-
charge *Dale Owen*). Their straightforward modernism and light
grey brickwork contrast with the redness and style-mixing of
Birchwood Grange, the suburban mansion, largely of *c.* 1920
by *J. B. Fletcher*, from which they extend.

Royal Infirmary, Glossop Road. The long rectangular site
flanking the Newport Road is stuffed with buildings erected
over a period of forty years from the first foundation of the
Glamorganshire and Monmouthshire Infirmary, as it was originally called. The site was donated in 1880, and after a competition, *James, Seward & Thomas* were appointed architects.
The Tudor Gothic style established then stamped every subsequent addition. The materials used in the earliest blocks,
however, neatly squared, snecked local stone, pink, orange and
white, with bands of pink Radyr stone and buff Bath stone
dressings, proved too expensive to sustain, so that random
rubble walling and buff brick took over.

To the w, facing Glossop Road, an elaborately symmetrical
block on a U-plan, the centre seven bays erected in 1882–3, the
wings added by *Seward & Thomas* in 1893–4. Free-standing to
the l., the chapel, erected in 1921. Attached to the r. but
independently entered from the s, outpatients department, dated 1907, by *Edwin Seward*. These were both part of
the original conception but redesigned in execution.

The central tower demonstrates most clearly the building's
pretensions, though it is less high and dominant than, say,
Waterhouse would have made it. Set back from the façade, it
rises square and then turns octagonal for two more stages under
a steep pavilion roof. Gabled projection under it, for the two-
centred entrance arch, buttressed and surmounted by a carved
panel giving dates of erection and first extension. The seven-
bay façade of which all this forms the centrepiece is two-and-
a-half storeys high and further enriched with sculpture, trios of
shields in panels between the two main storeys, and a Welsh
dragon in a sunburst within the gable. The gable itself has
kneelers and a single step each side. Similar gables in the wings,
which end, oddly, in canted projections set at r.-angles to the
façade. Mullion-and-transom windows, the upper ones with
cusped heads. All this makes for quite an idiosyncratic ensemble. At the back, half-timbered upper walls and an array of
chimneystacks, of yellow brick with vertical ribs and red bands
top and bottom.

The side ranges of the Infirmary can be examined more
cursorily. First, to the s in Longcross Street, the outpatients department of 1907. Four storeys with a flat balustrade.
Impressive double-arched entrance on octagonal shafts. Then

two three-storey ward blocks with canted s ends, the ACCI-
DENT AND EMERGENCY BLOCK dated 1918, and the
EDWARD NICHOLL WARDS of 1916. These have pierced
mouchette balustrades, maintaining the Gothic vocabulary,
now engulfed in a utilitarian top-hamper.

Along NEWPORT ROAD, first the free-standing CHAPEL,
Dec, of no special interest in spite of its prominent site. Behind
it peep out the half-timbered upper storey and double gable of
the administration block of 1893–4. The next addition to the E
lies back, as if it were an independent entity, bearing the title
KING EDWARD VII HOSPITAL WAR MEMORIAL and the
dates 1914, 1918. This is by *E. M. Bruce Vaughan*. Two wings
with canted ends and top gables, and between them a pierced
mouchette parapet. E of this, hard up against the road, the
three tall storeys of what must have been intended as a children's ward – see the inscription under the statue in the gable.
The plain, five-storey RESEARCH BUILDING behind, 1927 by
E. Stanley Hall, at last abandons medievalism. Then, after a
simple red brick insertion, more Gothic, the BRUCE VAUGHAN
WING, dated 1909. Late Perp with various carved reliefs,
including the Good Samaritan. For this, built 1907–8 and
intended as the outpatients' wing, *Seward* was still architect,
but he had to collaborate with *E. M. Bruce Vaughan*, who was
chairman of the hospital's house committee.

The INTERIOR of the Infirmary has largely been modernized.
In the SPINE CORRIDOR, several memorial tablets, two by
Goscombe John. Both are bronze relief portraits, of C. S. Vachell
†1914, and D. R. Paterson, the latter signed and exhibited at
the Royal Academy in 1927. The CHAPEL is spacious, a five-
bay nave with a low s passage aisle and three-side apse beyond a
shafted chancel arch. – STAINED GLASS. Ambitious w window,
dated 1956, depicting Christ appearing to his disciples on the
Sea of Galilee. Signed *SAFTON* in monogram.

Finally, two Gothic VILLAS of the 1870s have been incorporated into the hospital enclosure, among the all-too-few survivors of what must have been quite a grand array along
Newport Road.

ROATH BRANCH LIBRARY, Newport Road. 1900–1 by
Teather & Wilson. Red brick with Bath stone enrichment.
Gabled reading room behind a low vestibule. Semi-classical.

GAIETY THEATRE, City Road. (Formerly a cinema, now a
Bingo hall.) Much altered, but still presenting an appearance
of gay abandon. Flanking domed cylinders and central arcade
all embraced by an Ionic colonnade. Presumably built *c.* 1910.

MACKINTOSH INSTITUTE, Plasnewydd Square. A survivor
from an earlier era, the mansion of the Mackintosh family.
Rendered, battlemented, sash-windowed. s front of three bays,
linked to single-bay wings by concave pieces. Datable *c.* 1800.

THE MANSION HOUSE, Richmond Crescent. Built as The
Grove in 1891 by *Habershon & Fawckner* with typical heavy-
handedness, for James Howell the draper (*see* St Mary Street,
p. 214). Note its paired entrance doorways, one a dummy, a

precaution lest it should become necessary to split the house
into a semi-detached pair. (Rigidly symmetrical interior layout
with an imperial stair on axis at the back.) In 1913 the integrity
of the house was ensured when it became the official residence
of the Lord Mayor of Cardiff.

ROATH COURT, Newport Road. Built on the site of the medieval
manor house, 200 yds (183 metres) SW of St Margaret's church.
What one sees is an early C19 villa, enlarged in all directions and
rendered white. The stone porch with coupled Doric columns
carrying a handsome triglyph and metope frieze was brought
here in 1956, from Bowood, Wiltshire. This means it is by
Robert Adam, 1766.

HOUSING

There are four distinct areas of later C19 housing within Roath.
Though they are socially diverse from one another, the products
of differing development policies by the major ground landlords,
each is in itself architecturally homogeneous.

The earliest is TREDEGARVILLE, developed by the Tredegar
Estate over two decades from 1857. A number of villas of this
period – the earlier stuccoed, some Italianate, some domestic
Gothic, the later stone-faced – survive in the spaciously laid-
out parallel streets W of the S end of City Road, THE PARADE
and THE WALK, and EAST GROVE and WEST GROVE,
which traverse them. They were designed by the Estate architects, *W. G. & E. Habershon* (later *Habershon & Fawckner*).
RICHMOND ROAD, which runs N from here, was built up in
two parts, the sinuous S half being the later, *c.* 1876–85, with
semi-detached pairs by *Thomas Waring*; the straight N half was
developed from 1868 to the late 1870s with short terraces by
Habershon & Fawckner. RICHMOND CRESCENT is of *c.* 1888
by *Habershon & Fawckner*. All are of Pennant sandstone with
Bath stone dressings in a sub-Gothic style. For James Howell's
house, the final contribution here, *see* p. 308.

To the S of the Newport Road, artisan housing is concentrated
in a dense network of streets, bounded by GLOSSOP ROAD to
the W, the railway to the S and BROADWAY to the NE. This
area was mainly under construction in the early 1870s, and is
memorable for its street-names, taken from jewels and metals.

Further N, the Mackintosh Estate developed their property
around the family mansion, Plasnewydd, from the mid 1880s
with lower middle-class housing. Plasnewydd survives as the
MACKINTOSH INSTITUTE in Plasnewydd Square (*see* above,
p. 308). The Square is set in the centre of six parallel E–W
streets, from CYFARTHFA STREET to GLENROY STREET,
bordered to the E by COTTRELL ROAD, which were all built
up 1886–*c.* 1893 by the Estate architect, *Charles Rigg*. An area
of similar size was developed along the same lines to the N of
ALBANY ROAD. The seven parallel streets running N–S, from
MACKINTOSH PLACE to ANGUS STREET, and the three

E–W cross-streets, were built up by *Rigg* in two stages, 1884–
c. 1887 and 1891–*c*. 1898.

Immediately to the N of the Mackintosh development, ROATH
PARK intervenes. In 1887 the Marquess of Bute gave 88 acres
(35.6 hectares) at the foot of Penylan Hill for public open
space, and in 1889 the Derbyshire landscape gardeners *William
Barron & Son* were selected to lay out a larger area with a 30-
acre (12-hectare) lake and other amenities. This all exists,
ROATH PARK RECREATION GROUND s of the A48, and
ROATH PARK LAKE N of it. The long roads which bordered
them provided prime sites for high-class residential development, which the Bute Estate undertook over the ensuing
twenty-five years. The Bute Estate architect, *E. W. M. Corbett*,
was responsible for everything. Development began at the SE
corner, where BANGOR STREET and WELLFIELD ROAD were
under construction 1891–4. NINIAN ROAD, which borders the
SW edge of the Recreation Ground, was also started in 1891,
but not completed until *c*. 1910. It provides a fine display of
turn-of-the-century terrace housing, to at least six different
designs, mostly three-storeyed with a two-storey window bay
and a gable for each house, and porches treated as the opportunity for an exuberant detail or two. The first group, at the SE
end, where PEN-Y-LAN ROAD crosses over, is of brick. Then,
as far as WERFA STREET, comes a sequence in Pennant sandstone, very like Corbett's houses in the upper half of Cathedral
Road. After a two-storey section with half-timbered gables, the
Cathedral Road idiom returns, as far as KELVIN ROAD. Note
the columned porches. Down to two storeys again until the
corner of BOVERTON STREET. Beyond this the scale becomes
grander, with semi-detached pairs and interplay between red
brick and Pennant sandstone. The final run, N of TYDFIL
PLACE, returns to short terraces, but maintains the mix of
materials and introduces verandas and paired colonnettes on
the porches. At the end, round the corner to the l., SHIRLEY
ROAD, built *c*. 1905–6, uses a variant of the same design in an
array splendidly sustained for its full length. On the N side of
the Recreation Ground, development began in 1903 with PEN-
Y-LAN PLACE. TY-DRAW ROAD started from there in that
year, but was not built up for its full length until *c*. 1914.

To the N of the A48, in LAKE ROAD EAST, one showy group,
Nos. 76–90, four spacious semi-detached pairs. They are tile-
hung over red brick, and have elaborate timber balconies, now
considerably altered. At the outward angles of the outermost
houses, bold cylindrical red brick towers define the group.
Probably these too are by *Corbett*, and may constitute his swansong in Roath.

The LIGHTHOUSE at the S end of the LAKE was erected to
commemorate Scott's Antarctic expedition in 1912.

As a final comment, one can single out a remarkable change in
attitudes to office-building from the early 1970s to the early
1980s seen in FITZALAN ROAD at the W end of Newport
Road. BRUNEL HOUSE, built 1972–4 by the *J. Seymour Harris*

Partnership as an investment by the British Railways Board, is a sixteen-storey slab with concrete verticals, which makes absolutely no concession to its surroundings. At FITZALAN COURT, by *The Dale Kennedy Partnership*, opened in 1985, the offices are dispersed in six brown brick blocks of three and four storeys, their many canted projections forming interlocking courts. Intended as an advertisement for Redland Bricks.

Many other OFFICE BLOCKS along the NEWPORT ROAD, of all shapes and sizes. One of the more disciplined is LONGCROSS COURT, on the corner of CITY ROAD. 1980–3 by *W. S. Atkins & Partners*. Red brick. L-plan, four storeys and five, enclosing a raised courtyard reached by a broad flight of steps from street level.

RUMNEY/TREDELERCH

A featureless outer suburb, where the medieval church is an unexpected find. The remains of the CII and CI2 castle ½ m. (0.8 kilometre) SW, beside the River Rhymney, were excavated 1978–81 and then built over. Castle Crescent occupies its site.

ST AUGUSTINE, Church Road. The church is said to have been founded in 1108. The earliest feature, the W doorway in the tower, dates from about a century later. Transitional, its semicircular arch defined by a slightly keeled roll and supported on shafted imposts. Caen stone? The tower itself and the long, aisleless nave and lower chancel are all Perp. Windows N and S square-headed, of two and three cusped arched lights. Complex continuous mouldings on the priest's doorway, the entrance arch to the S porch, and the quite grand chancel arch, where the moulding consists of paired sunk quadrants flanking a step. Evidence of a rood loft. Unbuttressed tower, windowless except the top stage, where the two-light sound apertures are pierced with cusped diapering in the Somerset manner. Stumpy crocketed pinnacles and battlements. – FONT. CI5. Plain octagonal bowl on a spurred stem. – STAINED GLASS. Two chancel S windows recognizably by *Kempe*, one with date of death 1915. – Chancel E, *c.* 1960. – Window by the font signed and dated by *Geoffrey Robinson*, 1976. The dove descends with red and blue flames.

BLESSED SACRAMENT (R.C.), Wentloog Road. 1960 by *F. R. Bates & Son* under the influence of Sir Basil Spence. Fully glazed entrance wall, rectangular body with exposed concrete frame. Mildly Expressionist in its use of insistent pointed forms.

SPLOTT*

Splott is a homogeneous area of artisan housing, developed for the Tredegar Estate by their architects, *Habershon & Fawckner*. The grid of streets forming a wedge between RAILWAY STREET

*For map *see* pp. 298–9.

to the w and MOORLAND ROAD to the e was laid out in 1880 and steadily built up 1881–99.

ST SAVIOUR, Splott Road. Only a few streets away from St German's church and also by *Bodley & Garner*, 1887–8, s aisle 1894, but artistically a world away. The deadening stipulation in the architects' brief was that the church should be modelled on St Mary, Tenby, a C15 building. Hence the three-gabled nave and aisles, running into the three-gabled chancel and chapels. But at Tenby there is a tower with a spire, whereas the money here did not run that far. So the building remains earthbound and spreading. In its materials, St Saviour follows its neighbour: pinkish-grey, rock-faced Swelldon stone with dressings of Bath stone, and particularly in the ashlar facing of the buttresses. Early Perp tracery, the four e bays with side windows of a pretty lattice tracery pattern, the five bays of the aisles lit by ogee-headed lancets. Internally, too, one feels that Bodley is designing against the grain. Arcades the same height throughout, but the design for the chancel simpler than that for the nave. Plain chancel arch. Conventional detailing, piers with four shafts and four hollows, or continuously moulded. The boarded wagon vaults have the unfortunate effect of making the nave and chancel appear lower than the spaces which flank them. – FONT. About 1895. Octagonal, of stone. Plain but handsome. – ORGAN CASE. A fine example by *Bodley*. – LIGHT FITTINGS. 1961 by *Pace*. – HALL. Built into the w end of the nave. In a Bodley style. – STAINED GLASS. Chancel e, Christ between saints, and se, archangels. 1898, by *Burlison & Grylls* to *Bodley*'s design. – s aisle s, St German and St Margaret. The same. – N chapel e, Virgin and Child between David and Isaiah. By *Geoffrey Webb*. – N aisle N. Two windows by *Frank Roper*, 1963.

ST ALBAN'S ON THE MOORS (R.C.), Swinton Street. 1911 by *F. R. Bates* of Newport. Perp, resourcefully composed. Pennant sandstone in narrow courses with Bath stone ashlar. Cruciform plan, the low crossing tower shouldered to N and s over the transepts. Segment-headed windows with idiosyncratic tracery, but in the nave clerestory, triple lancets under relieving arches. Conspicuous ashlar-faced bay projecting from the s aisle and octagonal sw turret, also ashlar-faced. The interior is unexpectedly simple, a broad nave with passage aisles, separated from the sanctuary by two wide, segmental arches. Scissor-braced roof on carved stone corbels.

At the s end of MOORLAND ROAD, the FREE LIBRARY, 1894 by *Habershon & Fawckner*, next to the remains of their big BOARD SCHOOL of 1891. At the N end, on the corner with Carlisle Road, an enjoyable hotel by *Edwin Seward*, MOOR-LANDS, dated 1896. Netherlandish gables and other suitably fancy features. Carving by *Clarke* of Llandaff.

THE MALTINGS, East Tyndall Street. Built for the Cardiff Malting Company in 1887 by *F. Baldwin*. Extended in 1889 and again, by *Evans & Sons*, in 1901. Converted to workshops

and offices in the 1980s. Three large, red brick blocks with
pale limestone banding. Gabled, five-bay elevations to Tyndall
Street. Pairs of rectangular malting kilns far back at the rear,
retaining their distinctive pyramidal slate roofs and raised ven-
tilators.

WHITCHURCH/YR EGLWYS NEWYDD

Of pre-C19 Whitchurch there is not much to see. The medieval
church has been rebuilt on a new site. The famous Melingriffith
Tinplate Works beside the River Taff, founded in 1760 and
described in 1800 as 'not only a place of employment but the
focus of a community', went out of business a century later.
Though at the further NW extremity of continuous development,
Whitchurch remains predominantly a spacious late Victorian and
Edwardian suburb.

ST MARY, Penlline Road. A prim little church by *Prichard*,
standing in a huge churchyard. Built 1882–4. Tower of traditional Glamorgan type, tall, thin and unbuttressed, but set
over the S porch. Aisleless nave and lower chancel, Dec. Typically meticulous treatment of materials, Pennant sandstone in
thin and thinner courses and sparing Bath stone dressings.
Inside, the polychrome brick walls have been rendered over.
Big N vestry in a domestic Perp style and the abortive start
of a N aisle, 1920 by *G. E. Halliday*. – FONT and COVER.
Presumably by *Prichard*. – REREDOS. A lavish Dec piece
centred on a relief of the Supper at Emmaus. By Halliday? –
STAINED GLASS. Nave S, Nunc Dimittis, 1913 by *Jones &
Willis*. – S S John the Evangelist and Ignatius, 1914 by *Powell*'s. –
Nave W, Resurrection and Ascension, a major early window by
Celtic Studios, signed and dated 1948. – Chancel S, a brilliantly
coloured and deliberately ambiguous evocation of the Trinity.
1980 by *Alan Younger*. A welcome change from the literalism
of the earlier windows.

In ST MARY'S GARDENS, Old Church Road, ¼ m. E, the footings
of the pre-Victorian church, demolished in 1904. The outlines
of a small nave, with S porch, and a square chancel can be
made out. No sign of a chancel arch.

ST TEILO (R.C.), Old Church Road. 1964, by *F. R. Bates, Son &
Price*, and typical of their work. White outside and in, relieved
by dark red roof-trusses. Side-lit sanctuary.

METHODIST CHURCH, Penlline Road, ¼ m. NW of St Mary's.
1894 by *C. C. Jones*, enlarged and new-fronted in 1911 by *Henry
Budgen*. Gothic. An artless little aisled building, with cuspless
tracery.

ARARAT (ENGLISH) BAPTIST CHURCH, Merthyr Road, ½ m.
SE. 1914–15. Small, with an octagonal turret, and set in a walled
enclosure on the green. A textbook example of the galleried
Gothic chapel, which is not surprising, since the architect was
W. Beddoe Rees, author of a book on chapel design. The interior,
however, is disappointingly meagre, except for the galleries on

three sides, their bowed iron fronts pierced with a palmette design.

WHITCHURCH HOSPITAL, Penlline Road. Begun in 1903 to the designs of *G. H. Oatley & W. S. Skinner* of Bristol, who had won the commission in a competition of 1901. On a massive scale, with wards laid out on a herringbone plan. Red and yellow brick. To the N a Baroque entrance pavilion, of two storeys between single-storey canted wings. Channelling all across. Full-height porte cochère with paired Ionic pilasters carrying a broken pediment. Axially N of this, a large, red brick, lancet-style CHAPEL.

PUBLIC LIBRARY, Penlline Road. Set boldly across the corner with Velindre Road, small but thumpingly Jacobean. Red brick and Bath stone. 1904 by *R. & S. Williams* of Cardiff.

TŶ-MAWR, Ty-mawr Road, ½ m. WSW. The great interest of the house is its date, 1583, carved on the lintel of the hall fireplace. There is only one earlier known date on a Glamorgan house (the demolished Herbert House, Cardiff, 1582). Below the date, the initials of Howell William, whose social pretensions are expressed by the two-storey S porch. Hoodmould on square stops. Unfortunately the house has been so thoroughly altered that there are no other recognizable C16 features.

MELINGRIFFITH WATER PUMP, Ty-mawr Road, ¾ m. W. The eminent engineer *John Rennie* built this water-wheel-operated pump in 1807 so that water could be used to power the Melingriffith Tinplate Works and then feed to the adjacent Glamorganshire Canal. The undershot water wheel, 18 ft 6 in. (5.64 metres) in diameter and 12 ft 6 in. (3.8 metres) wide, operated stroke pumps encased in two cast iron cylinders via two American oak beams. Three-quarters of a mile (1.2 kilometres) of water-filled CANAL remains to the N of this point.

AMERSHAM INTERNATIONAL RADIOCHEMICAL CENTRE, Long Wood Drive, 1½ m. NW. A massive, low-lying group inconspicuously sited close beside the M4. It consists of a factory and a laboratory, and was mainly built 1974–81 by the *Percy Thomas Partnership* (design partner *Ian Pepperell*), with additions by the same completed in 1987. The group is colourful, shiny and inevitably mysterious. The main rectangular production blocks rest on a podium of purple brick, and are encased in buff glass-reinforced-plastic panels, with chocolate-coloured cladding for the service ducting above. Three clusters of slender blue and grey chimneys signal the productive purpose of the building. Cylindrical administration block at the far end, encased in mirror glass.

1080

CASTELL COCH
1 m. NW of Tongwynlais

The distant view, of unequal drum towers rising under candle-snuffer roofs from the wooded hillside, is irresistibly appealing. Here the castle of romantic dreams is given substance. The dreamer was *William Burges*, who in 1872 tempted his patron, the third Marquess of Bute, a willing accomplice, to divide his attention between Cardiff Castle and this smaller but equally delightful job.

The origins of the castle belong in sterner times, probably the late C11, during the first wave of Norman invasion. A motte of unusual size was thrown up on a strategic shelf, commanding a stretch of the River Taff where it flows between two ominously close-set hills. In the late C13, when the de Clare lords of Glamorgan were in their turn on the offensive against the native Welsh, they raised a masonry castle over the motte. This was done in two phases. During the first the motte was encased in stone towards the N and W and a curved enclosure wall erected on it, menacing the river valley below with a row of arrow slits. To the NE and SW two drum towers projected boldly, the latter rising via spurs from a square base. Next to this, on the S side of the courtyard, a rectangular hall above an undercroft. A little later the castle was further strengthened, the curtain wall heightened for a second row of arrow slits, a third drum tower set across the E end of the hall, blocking a lancet window, and, adjoining it to the N, an entrance gateway constructed with drawbridge and portcullis.

When John Leland saw Castell Coch in the late 1530s, it was 'all in ruin no big thing but high'. By the mid C19 only the SW tower and the curtain wall survived to anything approaching their full height. However, in 1850 G. T. Clark analysed the ruins, and in 1873 Burges carried out a partial excavation and published an account of his findings. So his reconstruction, drastic though it is, stands on the foundations of scholarship. Even where conjecture was inevitable Burges drew on the evidence of surviving medieval castles or illustrations of them in medieval manuscripts. He also had the newly published researches of Viollet-le-Duc to assist his visualization, the *Architecture Militaire* of 1854 and the illustrations in the *Dictionnaire* (1854–65).

The plan, then, is virtually the de Clare plan. Only the square form of the gatehouse is Burges's. The skyline, on the other hand, is entirely his creation. He decided to make the three towers, although almost equal to one another in diameter, arrestingly dissimilar in height. Ignoring Clark's suggestion that the towers originally had flat roofs, he designed sloping ones, on the authority of Swiss châteaux such as Chillon on Lake Geneva; here 'every external wall has its roof', on the grounds of practicality, to provide the maximum shelter in a rainy climate, and for the reason closest to his heart, their picturesqueness. Burges assigned distinct functions to the three towers: the NE, called by him the Well Tower, had, he suggested, housed a dungeon, the SW, adjoining the hall, the kitchen, and the SE, designated the Keep, the private rooms of the lord. Thus the different heights of the towers reflect their different functions. Construction began in 1874, and the fabric was complete in 1879, two years before Burges died, leaving sketch designs, but no more, for the decoration of the interior. This was carried out during the 1880s, under the

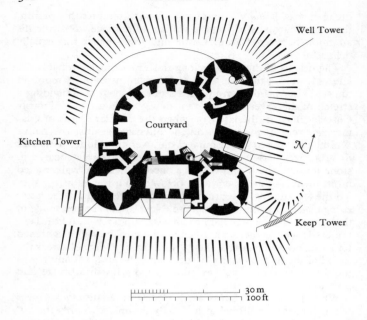

Castell Coch. Plan

direction of *William Frame*, and completed in 1891. The red-stained local limestone used for the medieval castle (hence its name, 'Red Castle') is distinguishable from the generally whiter limestone chosen by Burges, though the texture of roughly squared blocks is carefully unified. Burges's red roof tiles were replaced in 1972 by grey-green slates.

EXTERIOR. The approach is from the E. Dramatically stark geometry. To the l. the elegant cylinder of the KEEP TOWER soaring from its spurred base to the eaves of its flared, conical roof. Against it abuts the rectangular gate tower, reached by a timber drawbridge and furnished with a workable portcullis. Over the narrow, segmental entrance arch a pair of arrow slits, flanking a polychrome statue of the Virgin, the first hint of the castle's devout Victorian owner. This was modelled by *Ceccardo Fucigna* in 1878. Cross-gabled, corbelled top storey against which a boarded timber hoard projects, apparently further defensive apparatus but in reality an oriel window to Lord Bute's bedroom. To the r. the thick-set WELL TOWER, its conical roof rising from behind broad battlements. Cylindrical, separately roofed stair-turret at the back. Tall tapering chimneystacks, also cylindrical, erupt unexpectedly from roofslopes. Small windows barely break the smooth wall surfaces. It is worth scrambling round the exterior of the castle at the foot of the moat to admire the authenticity of Burges's reconstruction. Rectangular garderobe turrets project from both Keep Tower and Kitchen Tower, complete with chutes discharging into the moat. Restored arrow slits at two levels and timber shutters covering the merlons at the upper level. But the great stone apron which bellies out below the curtain wall is a C13 reinforcement of the earthen motte.

Inside the courtyard, timber balconies completely encircle the walls. Burges believed such a gallery must have existed in the C13, to make the upper level of arrow slits in the curtain wall functional. But they also give access to his principal rooms. The medieval timber galleries at Chillon are their model. At the back of the gateway a recessed timber balcony, another amenity for Lord Bute's bedroom. In the Keep Tower to the r., a three-light window for the drawing room gallery. On the Well Tower three corbel stones indicate the site of a short-lived chapel fitted up in the roof of the tower. STAINED GLASS from the chapel survives, by *Saunders and Co.*, from cartoons by *Lonsdale* based on *Burges*'s designs. Some is on display at Cardiff Castle (*see* p. 204), and a further eight lights, recently rediscovered, await display at Castell Coch.

The INTERIOR consists of no more than four decorated rooms, dining room, drawing room, and a bedroom each for Lord and Lady Bute, just enough to fulfil Burges's concept of the castle as 'a country residence for occasional occupation in the summer'.* The Marquess himself hardly ever came once work had finished, and his children stayed only when in quarantine for infectious diseases. All the same, three of the four rooms were decorated with gusto, the fourth, Lord Bute's bedroom, being left deliberately ascetic and comfortless.

At the head of the steps up from the courtyard a doorway opens straight into the BANQUETING HALL. Massive, plain, hooded chimneypiece, the hood breaking up into the canted boarded ceiling, a statue of St Lucius, by *Thomas Nicholls*, against it. Tie-beam and kingpost roof trusses. Stencilled patterns on the ceiling, painted walls, imitating masonry in the medieval way. In the gables of the end walls scenes of early Christian martyrdoms – peculiar subject, but one of interest, doubtless, to Lord Bute – designed by *H. W. Lonsdale* and executed, like the best of the painting, by *Campbell & Smith*, who seem to have supplied their estimate as early as 1878. Yet it is hard to believe that Burges himself had much of a hand in this dilute and unfocused ensemble. Furniture by his assistant, *J. S. Chapple*. The circular KITCHEN, to the w, is fitted up in a handsome, practical manner, with robust furniture by *Chapple*.

In the next room things get more exciting. This is the DRAWING ROOM, the lower of the two rooms in the Keep Tower. Octagonal, double-height, galleried and rising to a rib-vault. Satisfying integration of the vault ribs with the balcony fronts, all set on a band of stiff-leaf corbels, and of the cusped

---

*In 1876 the Marquess wrote of there being 'two halls, cellar, ground-floor room, kitchen, and great, lesser and least bedrooms with the wall-gallery'.

arches between the ribs, framing deeply splayed lancets. Tiled
fireplace splayed into the depth of the wall and surmounted by
a brattished segmental arch undercut with a row of stiff-leaf
sprigs. Above it an elegant arcade on slender columns, within
which sit figures of the three Fates, on corbels representing
youth, maturity and old age. All this Burges had designed by
1879. The overmantel is the key to the iconography of the rest
of the room, though *Nicholls* executed the carving and *Campbell*
the painting as late as 1886–7, under the direction of *William
Frame*. There are two intertwined themes: the fecundity of
nature and the fragility of life. The panelling is painted and
carved with flowers, animals and birds. The walls above painted
with La Fontaine fables, and the vault webs with birds flying
under a starlit sky. Finally, most significant of all, butterflies
are carved tier upon tier in the vault ribs, flying towards and
into the central sunburst. Furniture by *Chapple*.

The bedrooms of Lord and Lady Bute are reached up a
spiral stair which ascends from the threshold of the WINDLASS
ROOM. Note the fireplace in the Windlass Room. LORD
BUTE'S BEDROOM, fitted up in 1888, is immediately over the
Windlass Room and is heated by a stove. Stencilled walls.
Balcony towards the courtyard. LADY BUTE'S BEDROOM is
at a higher level still, at the top of the Keep Tower. It was
completed in 1891, on the basis of detailed drawings by *Burges*
for the moulded work. Here the plan is circular, the walls
arcaded on shafts with shaft-rings. Windows alternately lancets
and arrow slits, but with wooden inner glazing frames. Rectangular corbels support the lowest ring of the double dome
which gloriously covers the room. Dome coffering painted with
animals in bramble scrolls, a reference to Sleeping Beauty, and
at the very top, mirrors to throw back the light of the chandelier.
For this exotic haven *Chapple* designed suitably Burgesian
chairs, bedstead and castellar washstand.

At courtyard level a little more to see. The SERVANTS' HALL
has a pointed tunnel-vault, all *Burges*'s work. In the KITCHEN
TOWER, however, two rooms, one below the other, of the C13,
both with quadripartite rib-vaults, the ribs broad, flat bands.

A final word about the setting of Castell Coch. In the time of the
de Clares the hillside was doubtless as heavily wooded as it is
today. Lord Bute, however, planted a vineyard below the castle.
Did Burges intend the bases of the drum towers, with their
spurs, to be visible from far off, or did he envisage the castle
rising out of treetops as it does today?

0000   CEFNCOEDYCYMER

A hillside village above Merthyr Tydfil. The High Street is lined
with mid-C19 terraces, with near the top the RAILWAY ARMS,
dated 1826. A contemporary network of narrow streets to the W.

ST JOHN. Designed in 1870 by *George E. Robinson* of Cardiff.
Nave and lower chancel, S tower heavily buttressed towards

the S, with slated broach spire. Dec. All rather coarse and
artless, the battered base, and the crazy-paving walling banded
with courses of thin Pennant slabs, doubtless in heavy-handed
imitation of Prichard. Internally the walls are faced with white
brick, with thin decorative bands and alternating buff and white
voussoirs to windows and even to the chancel arch. Thin arch-
brace roofs on short, grey granite colonnettes. – STAINED
GLASS. Chancel E, Christ and the Blessed, c. 1901.

When funds for the church were being raised the curate wrote
'We here live in a nest of dissenters and each denomination has
a decent place of worship.' The streets of Cefn still demonstrate
the truth of this statement.

CARMEL BAPTIST CHAPEL, High Street. Dated 1844. A typical
example of the long-wall façade chapel, a little more elaborately
decorated than usual. The two doorways lead in either side of
the pulpit, the two long central windows light the interior
generally, the short ones to l. and r. side-light the galleries.
These survive, carried on cast iron columns and a marbled
bressumer. Circular balustraded pulpit.

EBENEZER WELSH INDEPENDENT CHAPEL, Pont-y-capel
Road. Dated 1861. Round-arched, rendered, under a pedimental gable. Disused at the time of writing.

HEN DY CWRDD, Old Chapel Road. The earliest foundation
in the village, of 1747, and set in a burial ground. The present
pedimented façade, with its unusual circular, traceried side
windows, presumably dates from 1895. Drastic restoration,
1991–3.

TABOR WELSH INDEPENDENT CHAPEL, High Street. Com-
mandingly sited at the top of the village. Dated 1904. The same
ingredients as Ebenezer, but with a porch. The interior, well
restored in 1989, remains complete, galleried on three sides,
with robustly detailed fittings.

CEFN RAILWAY VIADUCT, beyond the SW edge of the settlement, reached down Pont-y-capel Road. One of the finest
viaducts in Wales, 770 ft (235 metres) long, and 120 ft
(36.6 metres) at its highest. Designed by *H. Conybeare &
A. Sutherland*, it was built in 1866 to carry the Brecon, Newport
and Merthyr Railway over the Afon Taf Fawr. Fifteen arches
on tall, slender piers describe a gentle arc, the smooth red brick
of the arches contrasting with the vigorously rock-faced piers.

ROAD-BRIDGES. Three of 1964 by *Rendel, Palmer & Tritton*
(consultant architects *Alex Gordon & Partners*), carrying the
A465 over two rivers and a stream by means of reinforced
concrete arches of contrasting design. Those over the Taf
Fechan and the Nant Ffrwd employ twin parabolic arch ribs to
carry the roadway. The central bridge, over the Taf Fawr, has
three spans cantilevered from two piers.

TREFECHAN, ¾ m. NE. Designed in 1947 by *Arthur J. Hayes &
Gordon H. Griffiths*. A council estate, intended to function as an
independent community with its own public buildings. Quite a
formal road layout. The houses are all semi-detached pairs,
angled to the contours, and are built of a remarkable variety of

materials: brick, exposed or roughcast, pre-cast slabs, and even timber-clad. No significant public buildings.

LLWYN-ON RESERVOIR, 3 m. NW. Opened in 1926, to supply the City of Cardiff. Engineer, *Charles H. Priestley*. Castellated inspection turret at the E end of the massive, grass-faced dam.

CEFNMABLI

2 m. N of Llanedeyrn

This rambling pile was the seat of the Kemeys family until the early C20. From 1923 to *c.*1980 it was used as a hospital, but since then has stood empty. In spite of all its vicissitudes it remains eminently evocative and must be brought back into use.

Its history is puzzling, undocumented and difficult to read from the fabric. The members of the family who did most of the building were Edward Kemeys in the late C16, Sir Charles, third baronet, between 1670 and 1688, a second Sir Charles, fourth baronet, 1709–35, and Charles Kemeys-Tynte († 1860) or his son in the mid C19. The chapel was restored in 1858, and later *E. S. Hall* altered and enlarged the house.*

As viewed from the S, the enormously extended two-storey front-age appears to fall into two roughly equal halves, Tudor to the l., *c.*1700 to the r. The heart of the house, however, is in the centre, a late C16 hall with parlour wing, refaced *c.*1700. The jambs of mullion-and-transom windows are clearly visible flanking the narrower sash windows which replaced them. The lower C16 windows were larger than those above, suggesting that the hall was only one storey high. The pedimented timber porch marks the entrance into the screens passage, the two bays to its l. constituting the hall, the projection l. of that the deep hall dais bay, and the deeper two-bay projection yet further l. the parlour wing. The Tudor-style half consists of a gallery wing, with a gallery on the upper floor about 65 ft (19.8 metres) long; but the fenestration here has been much tampered with. Set forward at its W end is a one-bay block of indeterminate purpose, and beyond that a chapel of indeterminate date with C19 trimmings. The part of the house which makes the most powerful architectural impact is the seven-bay range to the r. of the porch. Walls of purplish local sandstone with a raised brick band between the storeys. Sash windows of early C18 character. The heavy hipped roof with its numerous dormers rests on bold coved eaves, and this whole superstructure is carried round over the remodelled hall and parlour wing. Hand-some brick chimneystacks with recessed arched panels. In the E wall of this range two casement windows with mullion-and-transom crosses, a C17 form used round the corner from the show front, where it was not so important to appear fashionable.

To the N a courtyard, at first sight all Victorian. But the N entrance passage is flanked by two C16 stone doorways with

*This account was written before the disastrous fire of September 1994.

four-centred heads. Within, the courtyard too was remodelled
c. 1700, and has coved eaves and a fine array of mullion-and-
transom casement windows on its w and s sides.

The INTERIOR retains one impressive room, the HALL, still
recognizably of the C16, with deep recesses flanking the dais
end. Finely moulded ceiling beams. Some late C16 small-fielded
panelling survives at the lower end, masked by panelling of
c. 1700, which continues round the whole room, a fine display.
Painted landscape overdoors have been removed for safe
keeping. A C16 doorway with four-centred head in the E wall
of the entrance vestibule E of the hall is related to the original
service arrangements.*

CHERITON   *4090*

The village, a scatter of houses dominated by the church, nestles
in the bottom of a typical Gower valley.

ST CATTWG. The only impressive work of architecture among
the churches of Gower. C13, little altered, of local limestone.
The massive tower stands between chancel and nave. s porch
and N vestry of 1874–5. Lancets in the s wall of chancel and
nave, a trefoil-headed pair in the E wall. w window inserted in
the C19, but the N wall still blank. The tower has corbelled
battlements and a gabled roof rising behind, but is devoid of
any windows except slits, so must have been designed primarily
for defence. The showpiece is the s doorway, its pointed head
enclosed by a hooded arch with three rolls, the hood on head-
stops (one original) and filleted, as is the central roll. Flanking
filleted shafts with big, boldly moulded shaft-rings and stiff-leaf
caps. The tower arches are also decorated: two chamfered
orders, the outer continuous, the inner brought down onto
octagonal caps and corbel shafts, that on the NW pier carved
with stiff-leaf. All this suggests that the church was built fairly
early in the C13 by masons who had worked at Llandaff
Cathedral. The high and broad nave retains its medieval wagon
roof, the X-shaped foliage bosses added by the incumbent, the
Rev. *J. D. Davies*, in 1874–5. – CHOIR STALLS, ALTAR RAILS,
also by *Davies* at the same date. – FONT. A broken tub, *ex
situ*. – STAINED GLASS. E window, *c*. 1971, by *Celtic Studios*. –
w window by the same.

TRINITY CALVINISTIC METHODIST CHAPEL, ¼ m. w. Of the
simplest long-wall façade pattern. Rendered white. 1817, rebuilt
1868, according to the charmingly lettered inscription panel.

GLEBE FARM. Immediately N of the churchyard. This is also
medieval, perhaps as early as the C13, but has been ruthlessly
modernized. Only the heating arrangements remain eloquent.
Full-height chimneystack to the N, and to the s a corbelled

---

*The boldly painted post-and-panel screen now in the hall at Berkeley Castle,
Gloucestershire, is said to have come from Cefnmabli.

chimneybreast serving a first-floor room, with a remarkable octagonal stack of ashlar stone.

NORTH HILL TOR, $\frac{1}{2}$m. NE. The isolated limestone outcrop overlooking the estuary was converted into a fortress by a massive earthwork bank and counterscarp thrown up to the S across the width of the promontory. Probably of the C12, when this part of Gower was held by the Turbervilles.

(LANDIMORE, 1 m. E. The ruins of a strong-house built by Sir Hugh Johnys *c.* 1500. Visible from the lane down to the marshes.)

7000   CILYBEBYLL

ST JOHN THE EVANGELIST. The short, thick W tower, with its strongly battered lower storey, probably dates from the later C16. Corbelled battlements. Nave and lower chancel rebuilt in the C19. One N and one S window with Y-tracery may belong to the campaign of 1837 for which *Philip Thomas* of Neath was architect. Kelly's Directory, however, calls the church rebuilt in 1868. – STAINED GLASS. E window, Resurrection, 1914. – MONUMENTS. Richard Herbert †1725. Marble tablet with two skulls at the top. – Councelletta Lloyd and her son, after 1817, signed *Tyley* of Bristol. Tablet with a draped urn.

  In the CHURCHYARD, the three-stepped base of a church-yard cross.

At Gellinudd, $\frac{1}{2}$m. SW, NANT LLWYD CAUSEWAY. Pennant rubble-stone tramroad causeway built by the engineer *William Brunton sen.* in 1828 for the colliery opened by George Crane in that year. At its base a small segmental arch with ashlar voussoirs bridges a stream, and a minor road now passes along its top.

6000   CLYDACH

The two churches of Clydach reflect its two stages of indus-trialization. John Miers & Co.'s Ynyspenllwch tinplate works flourished through the first half of the C19 on a site beside the river E of the present town, but had closed by the mid 1870s. In 1902 the Mond Nickel Refinery took its place, and much of this still survives in operation.

ST JOHN THE BAPTIST. Dramatically backed by factory build-ings. Erected 1845–7 at the expense of the Miers family, to the design of the County Surveyor, *William Whittington* of Neath, in an entirely pre-Ecclesiological manner. T-plan, the N transept flanked by polygonal turrets forming an entrance front. Bell gable over. Nave and short chancel. Lancets. – STAINED GLASS. Nave W, *c.* 1868. – Much of 1870, not of good quality, but an unusual attempt at a coherent scheme. S window of 1883 continuing the scheme. – NW and SW, signed by *T. F. Curtis* of

Ward & Hughes, 1902 and 1915. – MONUMENT. Richard Miers
†1855. Gothic wall-monument.

ST MARY, High Street. 1903–5 by *E. M. Bruce Vaughan* with
more money behind him than usual. The four-stage SW porch
tower makes the most of the commanding position in the centre
of the village. Nave with tall clerestory over lean-to aisles,
chancel and transeptal N chapel. Rock-faced, squared and
coursed Pennant sandstone, with Bath stone dressings. Geometrical style verging on Dec. Inside, Bruce Vaughan deploys
his normal vocabulary with minor variations. Wide nave, the
piers, alternately round and quatrefoil, banded with red Forest
of Dean sandstone, the clerestory arcaded on shafts. High and
wide chancel arch on corbel shafts with stiff-leaf. – REREDOS.
1921. An exceedingly sumptuous piece, of pink alabaster,
framing a white marble relief of the Last Supper. – STAINED
GLASS. Chancel E, Resurrection, designed in relation to the
reredos. By *T. F. Curtis* of *Ward & Hughes*, far above his normal
standard.

CALFARIA WELSH BAPTIST CHAPEL, High Street, opposite St
Mary's. A Nonconformist temple, dated 1868. Tuscan pilasters
carry entablature and pediment. The architect was the Rev.
Henry Thomas. The interior, galleried on three sides, survives
largely intact. Oddly disparate detailing.

GELLIONNEN UNITARIAN CHAPEL, 1 m. W. Alone on the
moorland brow of Mynydd Gellionnen, a poignant reminder
of the isolated spots chosen by early congregations. Founded
in 1692, but the present building dated 1801. Typical long-wall
façade design, the central pair of round-headed windows quite
broad, the two doorways and two small sash windows lighting
the ends of the galleries hard up against the angles of the façade.

HEBRON INDEPENDENT CHAPEL, Hebron Road. 1881. Pedimental façade, but the windows slightly pointed, those in the
centre with Burgundian Romanesque shafting. The interior is
provided with galleries on three sides, spacious 'big seat' and
pulpit composition, with a gigantic organ above. Ceiling on a
deep cove. – STAINED GLASS. Passion symbols, a single light
dated 1991 and signed *C.M., T.L.E.K.* – MONUMENT. Esay
Owen †1905. Greek tablet, with anchors and naturalistic
bunches of flowers.

WESLEYAN CHURCH, Clydach Road. 1902 by *Ford & Slater*
of Burslem. Perp. An elaborately traceried segment-headed
window towards the road.

MOND NICKEL WORKS (now Inco), Ynyspenllwch Road. A
series of gabled ranges of moulded red brick fenestrated with
round-headed windows fronts the S side of the Clydach to Glais
road. Most of the functional blocks built in similar style to the
S have now been replaced by more modern plant. This is the
last of the functioning non-ferrous works in the Swansea Valley.
It was established in 1902 by the Mond Nickel Co. to refine
nickel matte from Canada by the nickel carbonyl process. This
was invented by Sir Ludwig Mond (1839–1909), whose STATUE
stands opposite the works entrance.

PLAYERS FOUNDRY, ¼ m. s. A group of buildings with yellow
brick dressings alongside the present s end of the Swansea
Canal, built for John Strick's foundry established c. 1829. They
are interesting for the way in which the wooden foundry cranes
are braced by the structure. External pilasters aligned with the
ends of the heavy roof trusses which house the top pivot of the
crane have cast iron plates over their tops, and bases braced
together by wrought iron rods. The gabled WHEELHOUSE,
beside the filled-in canal lock, was built in 1829 to provide the
blast for the foundry. The by-pass water of the lock later drove
two successive turbines (now removed). Pig-iron was brought
down the Swansea Canal from Ynysgedwyn to make castings
at the foundry. The works ceased production during the Second
World War.

GARTH PIT, 1 m. s. In the fields w of the new valley road stands
the base of an ENGINE HOUSE of Pennant sandstone rubble,
now in dense undergrowth. Built to service a coal pit in 1834.
The red brick dressings go with secondary rebuilding. The
remains of a TRAMROAD can be traced w to the former Swansea
Canal.

CLYDACH UPPER FORGE, ¾ m. N. To the w of the Lower
Clydach River. Built in 1784 by the ironmaster Richard Parsons
of Ynysgedwyn, to convert pig-iron produced there. Still visible
are the large RESERVOIR, now full of colliery waste, and a
section of the DAM where the Lower Clydach River runs
through it. The dam is squat, of Pennant sandstone masonry,
some 12 ft (3.66 metres) high and as much as 9 ft (2.74 metres)
thick, similar to that at Llandyfan (Carmarthenshire).
The river now passes through the wheelpit and directly on to
the floor of the forge. A complex of anvil and hammer beds
can be seen in the shallow river bed, and also the circular tailrace culvert. The Upper Forge fell out of use at some date
after 1866.

p. 23 CARN LLECHART, 2 m. NW (SS 6973 0627). Bronze Age KERB
CIRCLE, a slightly sub-annular ring 46 ft (14 metres) wide consisting of twenty-five large, contiguous slabs set on edge and
inclining slightly outwards. They enclose a low, stony cairn, at
the centre of which is a disturbed burial cist. An atmospheric
monument. Accumulation of boulders c. 190 ft (60 metres) to
the w, which has been interpreted with varying degrees of
conviction as the remains of a Neolithic CHAMBERED TOMB.

8000   CLYNE/Y CLUN

The settlement which forms the nucleus of the parish is a hamlet
at the bend of the B4434.

YNYSBWLLOG AQUEDUCT, across the road to the N. Built to
carry the Neath Canal (1791–6) over the River Neath, by the
engineer *Thomas Dadford jun.* This was a fine and substantially
intact six-arched aqueduct until a flood in 1980 carried away
the larger part of two arches and left the present ruin.

Constructed of Pennant sandstone rubble. As with other aqueducts of the period, four longitudinal walls (including the two
outer walls) run through the structure, the inner two of which
are clearly visible as a result of the collapse. Vast quantities of
puddled clay fill the two outer chambers and the lower part of
the central one, which has a paved bed to its upper, empty half,
formerly the channel for the canal.

KERB CIRCLE on CARN CACA, $1\frac{1}{4}$ m. E (SN 8224 0079). Early
Bronze Age. Very deliberately located on the edge of a terrace
with a sharp fall beyond and good views along the Vale of
Neath. A ring of slabs up to 39 ft (12 metres) across partially
survives around the inner edge of a slight stony bank. The
hollow against the E edge of the circle is possibly a disturbed
cist. About 262 ft (80 metres) SE is a small early Bronze Age
BURIAL CAIRN with a disturbed central cist.

HILLSLOPE ENCLOSURE, $1\frac{1}{2}$ m. ESE (SN 8385 0004). Of likely   p. 27
Iron Age date, at the top of a steep slope above Melin Court
Brook. The interior, 0.2 acre (0.1 hectare) in area, enclosed by
a low rampart fronted by a ditch and wide counterscarp bank,
contains a circular drystone foundation. Rampart terminals
inturned at the W-facing entrance.

COITY/COETY   9080

ST MARY. A cruciform Dec church, quite large, and hardly
altered, though the undersized crossing tower with corbelled
top and small windows of two arched lights must belong to the
early C16. Restored with restraint by *Prichard & Seddon* in 1860.
Built of grey limestone, with a noticeable batter low down to
the walls of nave and transepts. The windows display a fine
medley of Dec tracery patterns, the stonework largely original.
Most remarkable is the five-light W window of the nave, the   26
intersecting tracery enriched with pointed trefoils and quatrefoils, and at the apex an octofoil with alternating lobes and
points. The interior is more austere, dominated by the crossing
vault and piers with their broad continuous chamfers. Notice
the battering low down here too. Squints open from the nave
into the transepts. In the transepts squints into the chancel, and
piscinas. Triple sedilia in the chancel. The other remarkable
structural feature is the long flight of steps in the N transept,
providing access to the belfry. The steps rest on continuous
double corbelling which describes two arcs across the S wall.
C15 wagon roof in the nave. – EASTER SEPULCHRE. A great
rarity, of *c.* 1500, even if heavily restored. Of timber, in the form
of a coped chest on legs. Only the gable ends and the six panels,
four carved with emblems of the Passion, two with foliage,
appear to be old. – STAINED GLASS. In the E window, part of
Prichard & Seddon's restoration, 1863, by *Morris & Co.* Patterns designed by *Webb*. Figures by *P. P. Marshall*, of Christ
rescuing Peter from the sea, curing the woman with an issue of
blood, and with Doubting Thomas. – MONUMENTS, in the

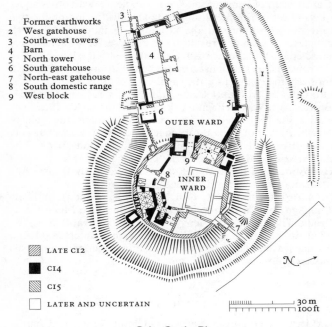

1 Former earthworks
2 West gatehouse
3 South-west towers
4 Barn
5 North tower
6 South gatehouse
7 North-east gatehouse
8 South domestic range
9 West block

OUTER WARD

INNER WARD

LATE C12

C14

C15

LATER AND UNCERTAIN

30 m
100 ft

N

Coity Castle. Plan

sanctuary. Early C14 effigies, one identified as of Sir Payne
Turbervill †1316, the other in civilian dress. Also effigy of a
child.

GILEAD WELSH INDEPENDENT CHAPEL, Heol Spencer.
Gable-end chapel rebuilt in 1890. The wrought iron gates
and overthrow to the burial ground and the caramel-coloured
render all contribute to the pleasingly old-fashioned effect.
Entrance front with plain round-arched openings and giant
relieving arch in the centre. Galleries on three sides intimately
crowding in on the pulpit and the here misnamed 'big seat'.

CASTLE. Coity Castle is, after Caerphilly (a long way after), the
most impressive ruined medieval castle in Glamorgan. The
oldest part of the masonry castle consists of a small late C12
keep integrated with a faceted curtain wall, which encloses an
inner ward about 120 ft (36.6 metres) in diameter. During the
C14 the keep was enlarged and refitted, a domestic range
erected against the opposite side of the curtain wall, and an
outer ward enclosed to the w. In the C15 the fortifications were
strengthened, mainly by means of a new gatehouse to the NE,
facing the church; and finally in the Tudor period improvements were made to the heating and lighting of the rooms, now
that the requirements of fortification were no longer para-
mount.

However, the walls of the inner ward follow the circular
form of a pre-existing castle with earth banks, taking the

characteristic form of a ringwork. This can be dated to the beginning of the C12, soon after the lordship of Coity, at that time at the w extremity of Norman penetration into Glamorgan, had been granted to the Norman family of Turberville. The building of the keep and masonry walls, and the deepening of the ditch, can be dated to the 1180s, when the Welsh became a renewed threat to the invaders. The C14 improvements cannot be closely dated, but later refortification must be the consequence of damage caused in the Welsh uprising of 1404–5. The Tudor work was done for one of the Gamages, who had inherited the castle in 1411 and remained in possession until 1584. Once again, close dating is impossible.

The visitor enters from the w through a fragmentary gatehouse in the OUTER COURT. The walls surrounding the outer court, standing to a considerable height, are part of the C14 improvements, with a s gatehouse, a sw tower apparently incorporating a mill, of which foundations survive, and a N tower. After 1405, however, the court was made more secure. This involved constructing the w gatehouse, of which the high inner arch partly survives, but not much else. The sw angle was reconstructed, eliminating the mill. At the E end of the court the Norman ditch was filled in, and the lateral enclosure walls were extended to the walls of the inner ward, that on the s armed with a series of close-set, crudely formed gun loops. A massive BARN, 95 ft (29 metres) long, was erected against the s wall. Unfortunately nothing now remains above its footings, which show that it was buttressed, had a deep central porch facing N and was of seven bays. Externally to the s three full-height buttresses survive, added against the C14 curtain wall.

The Norman KEEP was built at the NW angle of the INNER WARD, modestly projecting into the now-vanished moat, but mainly within the curtain wall. Its s and E walls are now reduced to their lower levels but they can readily be recognized among the C14 work by the blocks of local red conglomerate, with red mortar, used in their rubble core. The dressings, of both periods, are of grey Sutton stone. In the C14 the keep was incorporated with a new gatehouse set obliquely against its s flank, and was extended to the N by a narrow, full-height annexe. It was also given two vaulted lower storeys, with superimposed octagonal central piers which both survive, shorn of all but the springers of the lower vault. These are of plain square section and clearly rose to form two-centred arches. Of the upper vault, part of the springer of one rib remains, enough to show that at this level the ribs were chamfered. All that is recognizable in the two upper storeys of keep and annexe is Tudor, parts of windows and fireplaces, one virtually complete in the top storey of the annexe, immediately below its stepped gable. The top stage of keep and annexe are entirely Tudor in structure.

The main LIVING QUARTERS in the C14 were accommodated in a substantial range built against the faceted curtain wall on the opposite (s) side of the inner ward. Here the

springers of basement vaulting indicate the former arrangements. Towards the court was a dog-leg PASSAGE of four bays,
with doorways in the two E bays, the l. one leading to a broad
flight of newel stairs rising towards the E end of the hall. The
r. doorway leads into a passage at the end of which, at r.-angles,
are the springers intended for a further two bays of vaulting,
now hard up against the curtain wall. This is interpreted as
aborted vaulting for a projecting chapel, which could only have
been formed by breaching the wall. The HALL UNDERCROFT,
lying alongside the Norman curtain wall, is quite small, of three
bays by two, lit in each bay by a lancet window cut through the
thickness of the C12 wall. Dressings remain of the central lancet
only, trefoil-headed. Bases of octagonal piers and springers of
chamfered vault ribs. The wall was, however, breached in this
period by the GARDEROBE TOWER, close to the SE corner of
the hall. This is one of the best-preserved features of the castle,
prominent in most distant views. It is oval in plan, corbelled
out above cess-pit level, and had garderobes and windows at
two upper levels. A section of C15 wall-walk, corbelled out
twice, bridges across to it to the E.

The CHAPEL was built, immediately E of the aborted chapel,
in the C15. At first it was quite modest, not issuing above
principal floor level (see the crease-line of its roof), but later in
the century it was much heightened and given a lofty, probably
two-light E window, cut through the curtain wall.

In the Tudor period this range too was much remodelled.
The service area NW of the hall was refitted, and above it there
survives part of a three-light window, with segmentally arched
lights and a label with square stops. The most prominent relics
of this phase are the two massive square chimneystacks, one
still with its moulded cap of semi-classical form, which ride
high above the rest of the ruins.

Substantial stretches of the stone-slate paving of the inner
ward survive. The footings of a rectangular building occupying
much of the space belong to a demolished building of uncertain
date and purpose. Also remains of a circular kiln in the service
area.

Finally, the NE GATE TOWER. This was part of the strengthening of the fortifications in the C15. A narrow three-storey
structure projecting boldly into the ditch, it survives almost up
to corbel-table level. On its outer face it had extra-deep and
elaborate corbels for show, reminiscent of those at Raglan
Castle, Gwent. This comparison would date the gate tower to
the second half of the C15. The outer entrance arch survives,
with recessed rectangular surround and grooves for the portcullis. However, since the tower faces the churchyard, it must
have been intended as a showpiece rather than as a serious
contribution to the defences of the castle.

55 TŶ-MAWR, Byeastwood, ⅓ m. NE. An exceptionally instructive
example of a small but high-quality Glamorgan house of the
late C16. It has, facing the road, a N wall that is blank, as in so
many churches. Two rectangular projections, to the l. for a

garderobe, to the r. for a mural stair. All the windows are in the two-storey s front. They are of two and three lights, and although vertically aligned, do not achieve complete symmetry. There are also two patterns, one with arched lights under heavy hoodmoulds, and hollow chamfers, the other more advanced, not found before the last quarter of the c16, with square-headed lights and a sunk chamfer. The old-fashioned type is used for the hall and small room over it, the more up-to-date for the inner rooms, parlour below and chamber (the room which has the benefit of the garderobe) above. The entrance doorway, in the w end wall (now masked by a later addition) was protected by a drawbar – see the slot. Beside it, in the standard arrangement, the hall fireplace, and round the corner the entrance to the mural stair. All the c16 doorways have four-centred arches and plain, stopped chamfers.

COLWINSTON/TREGOLWYN 9070

St Michael and All Angels. Whitewashed. The typical grouping, of w tower, nave with s porch, and lower chancel, but here, unusually, the origin of the church in the c12 is apparent, in the round-headed chancel arch of Sutton stone. Dec image niches with cusped ogee heads flank it. Further Dec evidence in the chancel, the moulded arch to a tomb-recess in the N wall. This has a double-wave moulding keeled back into a deep hollow. The two trefoiled-headed s lancets in the chancel, rebated externally for shutters, are E.E., the two-light e window Perp. Perp, or Tudor, evidence also in nave and porch. Tudor w doorway and three-light window over in the tower. Note the corbels for the rood loft over the chancel arch. The church was restored in 1879 by *H. J. Williams* of Bristol. – wall-paintings. The image niches retain much of their original colouring, red and blue. Beside the N niche c14 figure of a bishop, identified as St Nicholas of Myra being consecrated. – (font. Octagonal.) – pulpit and lectern of 1879 by *H. J. Williams*. – stained glass. e window, martial saints. 1900 by *Clayton & Bell*. – Nave s window, by *J. Petts*, 1963. A burst of pastel-coloured light. – monuments. Worn recumbent figure, presumably of the c15, in, but not fitting, the chancel recess. – David Thomas †1769. Large white and brown marble tablet. – David Vaughan †1982. Finely lettered slate tablet.

In the churchyard a late medieval cross-head on a truncated shaft on three steps.

The village has expanded a good deal E-wards from the church. Several early cottages are caught up among recent commuters' housing. The two most interesting, both heavily modernized outside, stand s of the churchyard wall. The Old Parsonage keeps a thatched roof and white, rendered walls, but not one of the original stone windows with hollow-chamfered, arched lights remains intact. Inside, several stone doorways, mostly basket-arched, suggesting a mid-C16 date. The house was built in two units on the hearth-passage plan, both kitchen and hall having fireplaces from the start. Mural stair to the principal upper room in the hall gable, rather than in the usual way beside the hearth. The house has been extended to the W.

TŶ-MAEN, immediately to the W, is a little later, as the three-light mullioned window shows by its sunk chamfer mouldings, popular c. 1600. This window, oddly near the ground, lights a short service wing which forms the stem of a T-plan. The main, s-facing range has heated hall and kitchen with their fireplaces back-to-back, forming a lobby-entry plan.

PWLL-Y-WRACH, $\frac{3}{4}$ m. E. Nine-bay late C18 front, the centre three bays widely spaced under a pedimental feature. Probably a remodelling after 1770. Windows with rusticated surrounds flush with the rendered walls, identical in treatment to No. 3 High Street, Cowbridge (*see* p. 333).

9070   COWBRIDGE/Y BONT-FAEN

Cowbridge may be the successor to a sub-urban ROMANO-BRITISH SETTLEMENT developed around an as yet undiscovered ROMAN FORT, possibly to be identified with *Bovium*, recorded in the *Antonine Itinerary*. Cowbridge is the only example in Glamorgan of the linear country town extended along a main street. It owes this form to its position on the road from Cardiff to Swansea and to the fact that it has never developed as an industrial centre. In 1775 Francis Grose found 'the major part only thatched cottages like an Irish town', but a quarter of a century later, in 1804, Donovan, once he had passed the 'little cottages at the first entrance', decided it was 'a place of business of some respectability.' Such it remains today.

Cowbridge's origins, however, are as a planted town of the C13, rectangular in plan, walled and with three gateways. Richard de Clare established the borough in 1254. The far-extended roadside development reflects the C13 layout of burgage plots. Increased traffic on the main road doomed the lateral gates (W demolished 1754, E demolished 1768–75), and today only that to the s remains, spanning the road which led to the town's mother church at Llanblethian. The church lies alongside this road, back from the main street.

HOLY CROSS. Only a chapel of ease to Llanblethian, but built on quite a mighty scale, probably in the late C13. Of coursed local limestone, with white Sutton stone dressings. The original church consisted of a tower between chancel and wide, aisleless nave. Presumably transepts were intended. They would have given a plan very like Coity's (q.v.) of about the same date. Only the tower retains its original appearance, best seen outside from the SE. Paired trefoil-headed belfry lights. Corbelled wall-head from which angle broaches slope up to an octagonal, battlemented top stage. It is hard to see how this could have been the start of a stone spire. Yet, without arrow loops, it was surely not intended for defence either. Later NE stair-turret and NW buttressing mass. In the nave jambs of two original lancets and the mutilated N doorway. Its opposite number on the S side, moulded with a hollow chamfer, has been reset in the later S aisle.

In the C15 a S aisle was added to the nave, overlapping the tower, and a N chapel to the chancel, by, it is said on the basis of dubious documentary evidence, Lady Anne Neville in 1473. Strongly moulded plinths, buttresses, and in the chapel two original N windows with four-centred heads, now blocked. Quarella sandstone dressings. All the big Perp windows, of Bath stone, in chancel, nave and aisle belong to *John Prichard*'s restoration of 1850–2.

Inside, the E and W tower arches are late C13, the one with three continuous chamfers, the other double-chamfered, a keeled half-shaft with moulded cap applied to the inner chamfer. In the chancel the only original feature is the piscina of Sutton stone. Of the late C15 the tower S arch and the arcades to aisle and chapel. Piers with four shafts and four hollows, and four-centred arches with a keeled profile and double-wave and hollow-chamfer mouldings. This is an English West Country formula, and sounds impressive, but the details are crude and the fit between piers and arches awkward. Aisle arcade reconstructed in 1926. Nave roof also of that date. Chancel roof 1972. Low, late medieval E extension, now vestry. Two hatches in its E wall, presumably for the dispensing of alms, a most unusual feature. N porch of 1859. – FONT. Plain octagonal bowl, tapering down to a roll. Of the C14? – ALTAR RAILS. By *George Pace*, 1965. – STAINED GLASS. Chancel E, scenes from the life of Christ, before 1868 by *Baillie*. Chancel S, biblical scenes of instruction, to commemorate a headmaster of Cowbridge Grammar School, †1870. – S aisle, war memorial window, c. 1920 by *Powell*'s. – MONUMENTS. William Carne. 1616. Alabaster wall-monument with kneeling figures at a prayer desk, and miniature children below. Good of its type, familiar all over England but a rarity in these parts. – Richard Jenkins †1721, and others. Hanging wall-monument. This must be copied from a plate in James Gibbs's *Book of Architecture*, so datable after 1728. – Mary Powell †1837. Tablet with draped urn. Signed by *J. E. Thomas*. – John Bevan and wife †1841. Gothic wall-monument.

UNITED FREE CHURCH, Westgate. One of the best early 81 chapels in the county, built as Ramoth Independent Chapel and dated 1828. Though quite large for a chapel of that date, it stands modestly back beyond a grassy graveyard entered from the street through an inconspicuous archway. Rendered white, under a pyramid roof. Round-headed windows, one above and two beside the entrance doorway. The square interior retains 82 box pews and panel-fronted galleries on three sides supported by slender cast iron columns. Pulpit at the far end.

TOWN WALLS. The S GATE, at the S end of CHURCH STREET, is a simple thing, of c. 1300. Chamfered segmental arch. To the w quite a long run of WALL, as far as the small drum TOWER at the SW angle.

TOWN HALL, High Street. A four-square piece of rustic Neo-classicism, the most prominent building in the town. It incorporates part of the County Prison, reconstructed in 1806. The front block, and presumably the single-storey arcaded returns, date from 1830. The ashlar façade of Sutton stone has arched openings and bullseyes in an idiosyncratic composition, the largest windows within full-height relieving arches. Built by *Isaiah Verity* of Ystradowen, probably on the basis of plans drawn up by (or for) the Rev. *John Montgomery Traherne* in 1823. Octagonal clock-turret added in 1836. Internal restoration by *C. B. Fowler* of Cardiff, 1895.

GRAMMAR SCHOOL, Church Street (currently disused). Dated 1847 but built 1849–52, an early work by *John Prichard*. Tudor style. Squared grey limestone with Bath stone dressings. Picturesquely grouped towards the road, but with a more formal, triple-gabled S front. Octagonal stone chimneystacks.

PERAMBULATION

It is natural to start by the Town Hall. To the E, HIGH STREET and EASTGATE, as it is called beyond the line of the medieval town wall, are pleasant but devoid of buildings which require specific mention. In the HIGH STREET to the W, the three gables of Nos. 39–41, on the N side, suggest the typical development of three narrow medieval house-plots. The houses seem to have been rebuilt *c.*1600, but the only telling feature is the C18 passage doorway of No. 41, with a little Rococo carving. The taller, double-gabled house on the S side, Nos. 32–34, has concealed C16 evidence, in particular a four-light transomed window in the E wall. Corbelled chimneystack at the rear. Late C18 sash windows in the street front. This, called Great House, was the town house of the Carnes of Nash, but its two Georgian doorcases imply subdivision already in the C18. Behind Nos. 38–42 the stone walls of a large medieval WAREHOUSE. Then, after a flamboyantly gabled late Victorian interruption, the DUKE OF WELLINGTON, a simple, late medieval house set parallel to the street. Two upper chimneypieces, one with a hood on small corbels. Here CHURCH STREET comes in. In Church Street, besides the church, school and town gate, Nos. 6–7 deserve a mention. Originally one house, datable to the C16. The two-light mullioned windows, however, are not original, nor is the r.-hand doorway.

Back in the High Street, the BEAR HOTEL, on the N side, medieval in origin, Georgian in appearance. The original extent of the stone frontage is still demarcated by Sutton stone quoins. Inside, two fragments of C15 carved armorial lintels, reset and overpainted, and at the back, something impressive at last. This is the stone tunnel-vaulted undercroft of a medieval structure, originally detached and set at r.-angles to the front range. No. 58 on the S side, facing the Bear Hotel, is the handsomest

Georgian town house in Cowbridge. Three bays, three storeys, its first-floor windows with architrave surrounds. Porch on Doric columns. Next on the s side, OLD HALL, another medieval house, even more drastically reconstructed. The C19 neo-medieval stone porch, however, leads into an unexpected C20 world. In 1975 *Alex Gordon & Partners* reconstructed the C18 rear to form a one-storey screen wall with a Venetian window in it. Beyond this, a lawn, a lily-pond, and a path to the COUNTY LIBRARY and HEALTH CENTRE, a restrained 120 and understated group, white-walled with black, slated mono-pitch roofs. By students of the *Welsh School of Architecture* (project architect *John Roberts*), 1973–4. Back in the High Street, COOPERS LANE leads off on the n side, another good recent contribution, 1977–8: intricately grouped houses with white, rendered walls, stone-faced porches and black, slate-hung oriels. No. 3, just beyond, has a handsome late C18 façade of five bays and three storeys, rendered with rough and smooth textures to create an effect of quoined angles and window surrounds (cf. Pwll-y-wrach, Colwinston). EAGLE ACADEMY, on the corner of EAGLE LANE, nondescript towards the front, has at the back a fine upstairs assembly room, with a coved ceiling and balustraded balconies at one end. The OLD MASONS ARMS, opposite, is another originally medieval house, built beside the west gate and incorporating a stretch of the town wall. Blocked C14 window of two trefoiled lights and an early C17 window bay alongside, of 1 + 3 + 1 lights. In WESTGATE modest street frontages continue for some way on both sides. Nothing more requires singling out, except Ramoth Chapel (*see* United Free Church above) on the n side, and on the s two contrasting late C19 buildings, the demonstrative Nos. 24–26 (Stafford House), dated 1890, with an outrageously cusped bargeboard, and the POLICE STATION, a model of dignified restraint.

COYCHURCH/LLANGRALLO 9070

The reasons why Coychurch possesses such a grand church, or why pre-Conquest crosses stood in the churchyard, are shrouded in the mists of time. Today, the growth of modern Bridgend and its industry has almost caught up with the village.

ST CRALLO. A large and impressive cruciform church of the mid to late C13. E. A. Freeman in 1857 suggested that it would make 'an admirable model for a small colonial cathedral'. The w front is certainly a self-conscious composition. Three large lancets within a deeply chamfered arch form the central feature, with a doorway below defined by multiple mouldings, and shafts with shaft-rings. Flanking buttresses, and pointed quatre-foil windows lighting the ends of the aisles, a most unusual feature. All is bound together by the plinth with its keeled top roll. Four-bay nave, with lean-to aisles and clerestory windows only on the s side. They are cinquefoils under hoodmoulds shaped like circumflex accents. Late medieval modification of the clerestory N and S to light the rood loft. Fine S doorway, with two continuous rolls and a hood on worn heads. In the chancel, N and S, close-set, trefoil-headed lancets linked by hoodmoulds, and a three-light E window with intersecting tracery. The N transept has a three-light window with trefoiled heads. Transept and chancel have angle buttresses dying into the angles low down. In 1877 the crossing tower fell and destroyed the S transept; both were reconstructed in 1888 by *F. R. Kempson.*

17   The interior is as consistent as the exterior and powerfully austere in design. High and narrow nave. Octagonal piers with boldly moulded capitals and water-holding bases carry double-chamfered arches. Wagon roof of the C15 with shield-bearing angels and foliage bosses. A celure over the two E bays marks the position of the rood. Crossing arches of two broad chamfers which die into the walls. Hoods on angle heads. In the chancel the deeply splayed lancets are linked under a continuous, seg-mentally looping hoodmould. The E window, not included in this composition, must be a slightly later insertion. Piscina and triple sedilia under plain, straight-sided gablets. The roofs here, and in the N transept and aisles, are part of *J. Prichard*'s res-toration of 1871. – FONT. Perp. Octagonal. – PULPIT. Of timber. E.E. style, by *Prichard*, 1871. – GLASS. Engraved, in the w windows. By *Frank Roper, c.* 1963. – MONUMENTS. Early cross and shaft-head with interlace, datable to the C10 or early C11, on a later medieval shaft (N aisle). Fragment of a similar shaft with interlace (S aisle). Both used to stand in the church-yard. – The other monuments are all in the N transept. Recum-bent figure of a praying monk. Of the C14? – Thomas Ivans †1591. Crude recumbent figure of a cleric. The drop in quality is shocking. – Edward Thomas and others. Large marble tablet with Doric entablature and broken pediment. Erected 1745. – Morgan Thomas. Neoclassical marble tablet with veiled urn. Signed by *E. Morgan* of Canton and erected after 1824. – In the S aisle, Thomas Richards, Welsh–English dictionary maker, †1790. Finely lettered slate roundel, 1990.

In the CHURCHYARD, the five high octagonal steps and the shaft remain of the churchyard CROSS, in the characteristic position, opposite the S porch of the church. Beyond the S wall of the churchyard, ruined walls of the medieval RECTORY. No datable feature or comprehensible plan form.

MID GLAMORGAN CREMATORIUM, $\frac{3}{4}$m. NW, on the road to Coity. 1969–70. A major work by *Fry, Drew, Knight, Creamer,* strongly influenced by late Le Corbusier, and the most impor-tant recent display of stained glass in the county. The com-mission came to Maxwell Fry after he had lectured on the design of crematoria in 1968, giving him the chance to realize his aim 'to make people participate more closely in the cremation service through the design of the building and its approaches'.

Beside the road the square, white CARETAKER'S HOUSE and a tall primitive-looking pillar of rough stone.

The approach first passes the small, circular CHAPEL OF REMEMBRANCE. Bulging walls faced with chunks of reused stone, much of it iron-stained, interrupted by four narrow, full-height windows. Conical roof crowned by a copper flame. – STAINED GLASS. By *Timothy Lewis*, representing the four seasons. Abstract and brilliantly coloured, in the Piper way.

The main group lies lower down, between a lake and a copse. 119 The principal CHAPEL rises concrete-walled at the back, with a Ronchamp-like roof, and off-centre vertical clerestory window. The concrete, cross-enclosing 'cowl', an even more obvious borrowing from Ronchamp, was most regrettably demolished in 1993. So now the elements in the foreground of the group, the concrete entrance canopy and the stone-faced bows of the CLOISTER, dominate, and the vertical counterpoint is lost. Incinerator chimney enlarged 1993 and made all too conspicuous. – STAINED GLASS, in the cloister. Designed for the incorporation of memorial tablets, an imaginative and successful idea. Here pupils of the Swansea School of Art were given their head. Four contrasting s-facing sections, one between each bow, and to the N a continuous composition between concrete mullions. The only signature is in the monochrome windows flanking the doorway to the chapel, *A. Seleschenko*, 1983.

Inconspicuous and excluded from the main group, a second small, non-denominational CHAPEL. Square, the roof carried on a framework of slender steel rods.

COED-Y-MWSTWR, ¾ m. NE. A medium-sized country house dated 1888. Tudor style, decked with bits of strapwork. Red brick and generous dressings of greenish Bridgend stone.

CRYNANT/CREUNANT

7000

The village grew up round two anthracite mines opened in the late C19. In the centre villas and pairs similar to those at Pontardawe (q.v.).

ST MARGARET. 1909–10 by *J. Cook Rees* of Neath. E.E. Nave with s aisle and lower chancel. Bell gable. – STAINED GLASS. In all N, s and E windows, 1951–66 by *Celtic Studios*, mainly scenes of the life of Christ, a rare complete ensemble by this prolific firm. In the E window, dated 1952, credit is given to *Howard Martin*, designer, and *Hubert Thomas* and *B. T. Evans*, painters. Christ between SS Margaret and James, intended as a war memorial on the theme of sacrifice. The s and two N windows, from 1957 onwards, more coarsely drawn and coloured than the rest.

Close by to the s, the medieval CHAPEL OF EASE. Single cell, the pointed windows with timber Y-tracery of *c.* 1800.

GODRE'RHOS CHAPEL, 2 m. N. Reached across a stream in an isolated spot on Rhos Common (but note the hotel opposite). Dated 1855. A complete survival of the early, square-plan type, in which two entrances lead in on the pulpit end, and the galleries encircle the other three sides. Round-headed windows, two long between two short, reflect this disposition. The interior still in the early arrangement, the tiny space filled with five-canted gallery and box pews angled towards the pulpit, which backs on to the entrance wall. In the centre of the flat ceiling an elaborate plaster rose.

YNYSBONT BRIDGE, over the River Dulais, 1 m. N, carrying the road to Treforgan. By *William Whittington*, 1814. A single well-shaped arch.

CEFN COED COLLIERY, 1 m. SW. When it was sunk in 1926 Cefn Coed was the deepest anthracite mine in the world with two shafts over 800 yds (732 metres) deep. Two engines were installed to wind the cages up and down the shafts. The colliery itself closed in 1968, but the surface buildings and winders remained in use for the adjacent Blaenant drift until 1978. They were then acquired by West Glamorgan County Council and developed as a museum. The remains include the headframes of the Nos. 1 and 2 shafts, the engine-house range and the pumphouse, boilerhouse and chimney. Among the surviving features are a winding engine (*Worsley Mesnes*, Wigan, 1927) with an attendant suite of Lancashire boilers, and the neighbouring stack and flue of the boilerhouse. There is a secondary winder made at the Glamorgan works of *Cubitt* in the Rhondda, and the compressor house containing one of the two original compressors, by *Bellis & Morcom* of Birmingham.

CWMAMAN

A cluster of streets at the far W end of terrace development virtually unbroken for the 2-m. (1.6-kilometre) length of the valley. By the 1870s much was already built, to serve the collieries, Cwmaman and Forchaman to the W, Bedw-lwyn to the SE, Cwmneol to the NE, for this was the heartland of the Powell Duffryn Steam Coal Company.

The disposition of church and chapels is typical, the former aloof on the hillside beyond the houses, the latter slotted into the terraces which front the streets. MORIAH AMAN (now Pentecostal Church) is dated 1893. Ignorant of architectural conventions. SOAR CALVINISTIC METHODIST CHAPEL of 1895 (now disused) has a typical demonstrative, round-arched façade. SION (SEION) CHAPEL, Cwmneol Place, dated 1891, boasts a giant recessed arch breaking up into the pedimental gable. This chapel has a simple unaltered interior. Galleries on three sides.

ST JOSEPH. Built as nave and lower chancel with a W bellcote distinguished by a miniature spire. 1889–90 by *E. M. Bruce Vaughan*. The cross-gabled aisles were added in 1916–17 by *James J. Jenkins* of Porth. E.E. Rock-faced sandstone with Bath stone dressings. – STAINED GLASS. W window, *c*. 1914. Four Virtues, an unusual subject.

THEATRE, Alice Place. Built as a public hall in 1891–2 by *Thomas Roderick* of Aberdare. Like a chapel.

IRON FURNACE (ST 004 994), at the S end of the settlement. The overgrown remains of a late C16 blast furnace in the valley bottom, among the earliest evidence of industrial activity in the county. A grass-covered mound, 33 ft (10 metres) in diameter and some 8 ft (2.5 metres) high, covers the internal walls of the furnace, which are exposed on its summit.

CWMAVON/CWMAFAN

7090

ST MICHAEL AND ALL ANGELS. Only the W tower, built in 1660, and its remarkable spire of yellow brick remain from the pre-C19 church. Two-centred W doorway, and a pair of cinquefoiled lights above it. Crudely shaped belfry openings. The battlements are of yellow brick, clearly an addition of the same date as the spire. Raised bands round the spire suggest a mid-C18 date. In 1850–1 *John Prichard*, still young and inexperienced, built the nave and separately gabled N aisle, the S porch and the lower chancel. He indulged in some bizarre details, such as the Perp-style windows, especially those in the nave topped by a row of little encircled quatrefoils. Rectilinear timber construction between nave and aisle of incredible baldness. Only the tower arch and chancel arch, double-chamfered, the chamfers giving way to vertical imposts, show something of the expected Prichard refinement. – ALTAR. Supported on a late C16 tomb-chest, its sides carved with twelve doll-like, named children. Who was originally commemorated by the monument does not seem to have been established. – FONT. Tub. *Ex situ.* – STAINED GLASS. Chancel E, Christ between SS Peter and Paul. Strong, inharmonious colours, typical of *c.*1850. – N aisle E. Ascension taking place above a flowery meadow. Datable *c.*1926. – Chancel SE. Evangelist symbols. In a Celtic idiom. 1991.

The CHURCHYARD is full to bursting point with memorials. The Russell family monument in the NW corner provides the date for the Ascension window in the church.

ALL SAINTS, ½ m. up the valley, one of *Prichard & Seddon*'s first and most successful works of collaboration, 1853–5, paid for by the Governor and Company of Copper Miners in England for the men of Cwmavon Works, has been demolished.

BETHANIA WELSH INDEPENDENT CHAPEL, Salem Road. Dated 1850. Rendered. The entrance front, towards the side street, retains the characteristic early C19 arrangement of two doors flanking two long, central round-headed windows to illuminate the main space inside, with shorter windows high up to l. and r. lighting the ends of the galleries. With this layout the pulpit backs on to the entrance wall, between the doorways. The chapel also catered for the workers in the copperworks. It stood on the NW edge of a grid of close-set streets. The terraced houses, constructed *c.*1848, have now been redeveloped.

PENUEL WELSH BAPTIST CHAPEL, Jersey Terrace. Perp
façade of rock-faced Pennant sandstone, dated 1908, added to
a simple classical body of 1856. Unaltered interior of 1908.
Galleries on three sides. Coved ceiling with two roses set within
a grid pattern. Art Nouveau stained glass.

ROCK WELSH INDEPENDENT CHAPEL, Pwll-y-glaw. At the
far end of the village. Dated 1931. Echoing the traditional
classical façade formula, but with a stronger sense of architectural integration.

TABERNACLE CALVINISTIC METHODIST CHAPEL, Tabernacle Terrace. Dated 1873. A good example of the type with a
central giant arch rising into the pediment. Long, thin side
windows. Snecked Pennant sandstone, the quoins and other
dressings rusticated, of Bath stone ashlar.

YNYSAFAN RAILWAY VIADUCT, ½ m. NE. Three-arched early
C19 bridge that carried a horse-drawn railway over the River
Afan. This fairly short line took coal from collieries at Bryn
westwards to the copper- and ironworks of the English Copper
Company at Cwmavon. Squared and coursed rubble. The
segmental arches, with a single ring of voussoirs, are of 26 ft
(7.93 metres) span. The piers have full-width, triangular cutwaters, stepping in above the springing level of the arches.

CASTELL BOLAN, 1 m. W. A small motte of unusual form,
covered by ancient birchwood, on the N slope of Mynydd
Dinas. Another of the late C12 fortified sites of the Welsh lords
of Afan, suggests the Royal Commission (*see* Baglan).

CWMBACH

0000

ST MARY MAGDALENE. An early, simple church by *E. M. Bruce
Vaughan*, 1881–2, almost a twin with his church at Tylorstown
(q.v.). Arrestingly designed plate-traceried W window.

DINAS POWYS

1070

ST PETER, Mill Road. Designed by *J. Coates Carter* in 1927, and
built after his death, in 1929–30, in reduced form, omitting the
tower and N aisle. Perp. Pseudo-rustic arcade of segmental
arches on square, chamfered piers with chamfered caps. Walls
of (reused?) squared blocks. Tie-beam and queenpost roofs. –
FONT. Chubby neo-Norman. – STAINED GLASS. E window,
Nativity, 1934, signed by *Powell*'s. – W window, obviously by
Frank Roper.

CASTLE, accessible by a scramble from Lettons Way. This
masonry castle replaced the ringwork on the hilltop to the NW
as the fortified headquarters of the Somery family some time
in the C12. On the outcrop of rock at the NW angle traces of a
large thick-walled KEEP have been identified. Later in the
century the CURTAIN WALL was built, incorporating the SE
wall of the keep and enclosing a large, roughly rectangular ward

within the walls. Long stretches of walls on all sides survive to a considerable height, and even in the present overgrown state, shrouded by trees which grow on the more-or-less precipitous slopes, the ward is impressively evocative.

(RINGWORK, ½ m. NW. The original site of the Somery castle. The site, remarkable for its series of four banks and ditches successively protecting the hilltop enclosure, was excavated 1954–8 by Professor Leslie Alcock. The main period of construction was discovered to be the late C11 and early C12.)

The modern village began to grow from c. 1890, a haven of villas from workaday Barry. The best early group is in CARDIFF ROAD. Nos. 19–23 are by *W. H. Dashwood Caple*, 1891. Tudor-esque. A lively symmetrical group with canted window bays and half-timbered end gables. Hammer-dressed Lias limestone with Bath stone dressings, yellow brick quoins and thin bands of red and yellow brick. Nos. 29 and 31 are a pair also clearly by *Caple*. The design is carried on in red brick through the rest of the group. The Voyseyish VILLAGE HALL, in St Andrew's Road, is by *Teather & Wilson*, 1907. Several small but attractive, American-style housing developments of the 1960s and 1970s. In LITTLE ORCHARD, off Murch Road, a group of concrete houses by *T. G. Jones & J. R. Evans*, 1968. Exposed, ribbed concrete above, glazing and voids below. Two groups by *Hird & Brooks*. In THE MOUNT, behind the stone garden wall of a C19 villa overlooking the common, single-storeyed. Full-height glazing contrasts with strip windows above solid white walls and white chimneystacks. The later group, 1975–6, in MERE-VALE, off St Andrew's Road, are T-plan, also single-storey, yellow or red brick, with cantilevered, monopitch roofs. The only pity is that they are so secretively sited, not contributing to the general impression of the village.

(DOWNS FARM, 1 m. SE. The farmhouse started life in the later C17 as a lobby-entry house of the rare type with the hearths back-to-back in the centre and a symmetrical façade, cf. Tŷ-maen, Colwinston.)

DYFFRYN

Above Bryncoch, 2 m. NW of Neath

ST MATTHEW. 1871, by *John Norton*. An estate church, built by Howel Gwyn of Dyffryn, the benefactor of Neath, whose statue is in Victoria Park there (*see* p. 461). E.E. Snecked, rock-faced Pennant sandstone and dressings of Bath stone. Nave and lower chancel. Unbuttressed SW tower. W composition with a rose window. Shafted geometrical tracery in the E window. The interior is a period piece with its numerous stencilled texts. Canted nave roof, boarded and stencilled, on wall-shafts carved with Norton's favourite early French Gothic foliage. W vestry, to *Norton*'s design, added 1900. Wall-paintings restored 1934. – STAINED GLASS. Chancel E, Resurrection between Empty

Tomb and Noli me Tangere, 1871 (well restored in 1974). –
w, Ascension, 1900 by *Clayton & Bell*. – MONUMENTS. Two
white marble busts, of Mr and Mrs Howel Gwyn, given in
1924. They look like marriage portraits, of *c.* 1850.

CARREG BICA, Mynydd Drumau, 1 m. wsw. Standing stone
14 ft (4.3 metres) high, of later Neolithic or Bronze Age
attribution.

DYFFRYN CELLWEN

8000

A small settlement close to the northern extremity of the county.

COELBREN ROMAN AUXILIARY FORT, ¼ m. N. On a low ridge
with extensive views of surrounding hills. Almost square with
rounded corners, 5.2 acres (2.1 hectares) in extent. The rampart
fronted by ditches is best preserved w of a line between the
slight remains of entrances in the N and S sides. Entrance
causeway across the w ditches. Hardly visible continuations of
N and S ramparts beyond the line of the E defences indicate
either an annexe or, more likely, a larger early fort. Excavation
in the early C20 showed that the ramparts were constructed of
layered turves, clay, and brushwood on a raft of logs or stone.
Traces of timber corner towers were found at the SE, SW and
NW angles. A berm separated the rampart from double V-
shaped ditches. Traces of timber buildings within the rampart.
Constructed mid to late 70s A.D., abandoned *c.* A.D. 150, possibly after reduction in size in the early C2 A.D. About 650 ft
(200 metres) SE there are also traces of a MARCHING CAMP,
extending over 34.6 acres (14 hectares), which are obscured by
field banks.

ROMAN FORTLET or SIGNAL STATION on Hirfynydd ridge, 3 m.
SW. Square banked and ditched enclosure, *c.* 62 ft (19 metres)
across with the entrance in its SE bank. Sarn Helen, the ROMAN
ROAD connecting forts at Neath and Coelbren, runs past it to
the SE. Its bank can be traced to the SW and NE. Some paving
is visible.

BANWEN IRONWORKS, ¾ m. NE. The most complete example
of an ironworks to survive on the anthracite coalfield, a survival
owed to the early failure of the works. It was built by London
speculators 1845–8, during the years of the railway mania, and
may have produced only some 80 tons (81.3 tonnes) of pig-
iron. It stands as a monument to a financial scandal that
extracted money from many unsuspecting shareholders. All
the buildings are of Pennant sandstone rubble with ashlar
dressings. The cowhouse next to Tonypurddyn Farm was the
CARPENTER'S SHOP and SMITHY for the works, and a POND
to supply condensing and boiler water to the blast engine
remains to the rear. A small stone hut in a nearby field was a
RAILWAY WEIGHBRIDGE HOUSE, and the WEIGHBRIDGE
itself survives intact although buried. To the S are the foundations and ruins of TAI-GARREG, stone houses for the
workers. Between the farm and the River Pyrddin is a huge

masonry CHARGING BANK with two substantially intact FUR-
NACES and a crumbling BLAST-ENGINE HOUSE.

DYFFRYN HOUSE

0070

1½ m. s of St Nicholas

Long, low mansion in a vaguely French Second Empire style with
Barryesque reminiscences in the stunted angle towers. Various
vertical features erupt from this mass. The date, astonishingly, is
as late as 1893–4, the builder John Cory, the vastly wealthy coal
and ship owner. His architect was *E. A. Lansdowne* of Newport,
who had been runner-up to build the Cory business empire's
headquarters in Butetown, Cardiff, in 1889. The interior is unexpectedly rewarding, mainly because of the remarkable chimneypieces which Cory incorporated into the house.

Entrance from the porte cochère on the N side is direct into
the over-lofty HALL. In the enormous window above the doorway,
pictorial STAINED GLASS depicting Queen Elizabeth I at Tilbury.
In the hall is the first and most spectacular of the chimneypieces,
clearly made up, with a fine late C17 white marble cartouche of
arms in the centre, and life-size Mannerist figures of Ceres (l.)
and Prudence (r.), both carrying baskets of fruit on their heads. 47
They are of wood and must be early C17, Netherlandish or
German. Their quality is superb and one would dearly like to
know where they came from. In the OAK ROOM, W of the hall,
figures of similar character flank the chimneypiece, but these are
even more bizarre: six-winged cherubim standing in cross-legged
pose, probably made to adorn confessionals. To the E of the hall,
the BILLIARD ROOM, a late Victorian period piece, its walls lined
with early Renaissance-style panelling with built-in benches. The
DRAWING ROOM and the BOUDOIR both have Jacobean alabaster chimneypieces. They are a pair, their overmantels flanked
by male and female terms and containing reliefs, the former of
Ceres, a naive figure between two large vases of flowers, the
latter of a knight in armour riding through flames. The painted
embellishments, including the inscriptions in Old French, may
have been added in the C19. Finally, in the present BAR and in
the room beyond, formerly the BREAKFAST ROOM, a further pair
of chimneypieces. These are clearly of the late C19, of white
marble, the one grotto-like, depicting Venuses and amorini dis-
porting themselves among flowers and vines, the other with putti
holding game of various sorts and a heraldic shield. (Late C18
Coade stone chimneypiece in another room.) The house is now
a conference centre run by South Glamorgan County Council.

The GARDENS are nowadays Dyffryn's chief fame. Cory began
a 90-acre (36.4-hectare) garden, but his son in 1906 employed
Thomas H. Mawson to design the layout. A series of broad terraces
and lawns step gently away from the house to the S, with an axial
canal and lily-pond. Sub-gardens of varied character lead off to E
and W. The so-called POMPEIAN GARDEN, to the W, is entered
through a gateway dated 1909. The neo-antique effect somewhat

spoilt by the pre-cast concrete used instead of stone. At the E end of the second terrace a terracotta STATUE of an elegant palm-bearing female, signed *E. Kuhse*, 1881, and stamped with the maker's mark of *E. March & Son*, Charlottenburg, Berlin. Also a pair of hunting boys, perhaps by the same. In the centre of the longitudinal CANAL, a large bronze FOUNTAIN, in Chinese style, probably constructed *c.* 1950. Three magnificent oriental BRONZES originally set in the lily-pond, a mandarin riding a bull and a pair of demons.

To the W of the mansion, TRAHERNE RESTAURANT, by *H.M.R. Burgess & Partners*, and STAFF HOUSES, 1971 by *Sir Percy Thomas & Partners* (design partner *Dale Owen*).

EGLWYS BREWIS

0060

ST BREWIS. Small and weatherbeaten, within the confines of the Royal Air Force station. Tiny nave and lower chancel. Miniature battlemented bellcote corbelled to E and W. C13 evidence in the chancel, the crudely pointed chancel arch and the pair of cusped E lancets. Tudor S porch and nave S windows. The interior is charming, dominated by WALL-PAINTINGS, C17 texts, one dated 1654, painted on the whitewashed walls, and a gigantic arms of William and Mary. Collar-beam roofs, strengthened by splint-like ties, a device of *William Weir*, who restored the church in 1900 in accordance with S.P.A.B. principles. – ALTAR RAIL. Designed by *Philip Webb*. – PILLAR PISCINA. Medieval. Crudely shaped. – FONT. Tub-shaped, with a rope moulding at the top.

EGLWYSILAN

1080

ST ILAN. An upland church, medieval in origin, standing alone except for the predictable neighbour, a pub. Pennant sandstone walls. The sturdy, unbuttressed W tower, though perhaps as late as the C16, retains most clearly a medieval character. Moulded plinth, and a crown of battlements with stumpy angle pinnacles but no corbel table. Rectangular two-light belfry openings. The wide nave rises high above the chancel. Plain S porch. One S window in the nave with three arched lights. Otherwise all windows, and the wagon roof of the nave, belong to the restoration of 1873–5 to the designs of *Charles Buckeridge*, who had in 1871 prepared a scheme for total rebuilding. The present appearance of the interior, walls plastered and lime-washed, is owed to a further restoration, of 1980–4 by *Graham J. Hardy*. – CARVED STONE. Sandstone slab (nave N wall) incised with a rude outline figure of a warrior, dated to the C8–C10. – FONT. Cylindrical bowl, very basic. – STAINED GLASS. E window, Supper at Emmaus, and nave N window, Lilies of the Field, both dated 1899 and signed by *T. F. Curtis* of *Ward & Hughes*. – Nave S window, *c.* 1961 by *Frank Roper*.

The LYCHGATE, pyramid-roofed, presumably belongs to the campaign of the 1870s.

EWENNY/EWENNI

PRIORY. The cruciform priory church at Ewenny, dedicated to St Michael, is the most complete and impressive Norman ecclesiastical building in Glamorgan. Especially thrilling is the vaulted presbytery, the climax of the transeptal monastic part, 7 which, dim and empty of all but a few monuments, is still as evocative as when Turner painted it with sheep wandering through the screen. The nave, which serves as the parish church now as it has probably always done, is a separate space, dominated by its mighty N arcade.

William de Londres, who by 1116 had been placed by the Norman lord of Glamorgan in charge of Ogmore Castle and its lands, built a church at Ewenny and gave it to St Peter's Abbey, Gloucester. William died in 1126, and a church was consecrated, presumably before his death, in the presence of Bishop Urban of Llandaff (1107–34). This much is recorded in a letter written as early as c.1145. But in 1141, William's son, Maurice de Londres, confirmed the gift to St Peter's, Gloucester, of the churches of Ewenny and St Brides Major and of Ogmore chapel with all their possessions, 'in order that a convent of monks might be formed'. The inscription on Maurice's tombstone, carved in the early C13 and still in the church, calls him unequivocally 'the founder'. So here we have a paradox: the church was built and consecrated by 1126, yet there was no motive to build it with a long presbytery, transepts and side chapels before provision had been made for a proper complement of monks, which was not done until 1141. C.A. Ralegh Radford's solution was to suggest three stages of construction, so that the church built in the 1120s was extended and heightened after 1141 for its new monastic use. But the evidence of the building itself does not support this hypothesis, since it shows every sign of having been the product of a single campaign, as Malcolm Thurlby has recently re-emphasized. He argues that everything dates before 1126, but does not explain why a monastic church was erected over a decade and a half before the priory was founded. Stylistically, as he shows, everything at Ewenny could date to the 1120s, being heavily dependent on St Peter's, Gloucester (now Gloucester Cathedral). But could Maurice's new foundation have involved the rebuilding of William's church in the mid 1140s, imitating work at Gloucester by that time nearly half a century old?

The other remarkable feature of Ewenny Priory is the precinct fortification. N and S gateways were constructed in the C12, and enlarged c.1300, when a high stone wall was raised round the whole monastic enclosure.

After the Dissolution Ewenny was acquired by the Carnes, who formed a large house out of the conventual buildings, but left the E part of the church alone. Benign neglect enabled it to survive

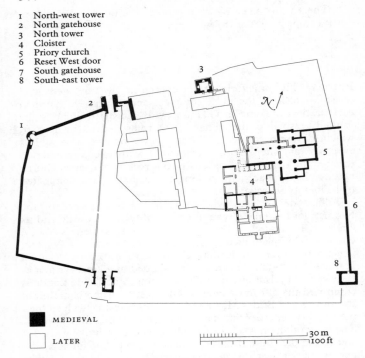

MEDIEVAL

LATER

30 m

100 ft

Ewenny Priory. Plan

until Thomas Picton Turbervill, on the advice of the antiquary
E. A. Freeman, carried out a conservative restoration 1869–86.
Today it still belongs to the Picton Turbervills, but is in the care
of Cadw: Welsh Historic Monuments, which maintains it as a
roofed monument. Meanwhile the nave is in use as the parish
church.

The visitor is naturally drawn to examine first the EXTERIOR of
the church from the N and the interior of the presbytery and
transepts, and after that the nave. The E and S sides of the
church must be viewed from the garden of the house within
the precinct enclosure wall. The following description of the
church will be divided into three parts along these lines.

The N TRANSEPT is in ruins, enabling its plan to be readily
seen. Rectangular, with a NE pilaster buttress and a NW clasping
buttress enlarged to take a newel stair. Two stepped E chapels,
the outer one small and square, little more than foundations,
but originally abutting a stretch of precinct wall to the E. More
of the inner chapel survives, showing that it had a tunnel-
vault in two bays. Entrance arch impost decorated with flat,
downward-pointing zigzag, its hoodmould given nailhead ornament and a big animal head-stop, like those over the nave
arcades at Malmesbury Abbey. Blocked arch to the crossing,

of two square orders, a C16 three-light window in the blocking. Low CROSSING TOWER with two small round-headed windows on each face. When the roofs were at their original steep pitch it can barely have appeared above them. Above a corbel table, later medieval stepped battlements with arrow loops, probably added as part of the show of defence made c. 1300 (*see* below). Underscaled pinnacles as an afterthought.

INTERIOR of the PRESBYTERY and TRANSEPTS. The illumi- 7 nation of the presbytery E bay, site of the high altar, contrasts with the dimness elsewhere. Three stepped E windows, one N and one S, accommodated by the vault, here quadripartite with moulded ribs. The other two bays are tunnel-vaulted with plain transverse ribs and subsidiary moulded ones. Short colonnettes, with scallop caps and moulded bases, are set diagonally to carry the vault of the E bay. Short pilaster strips carry the major transverse ribs. They all rest on a sill decorated with downward-pointing zigzag. Plain dado below. Similar arrangement at the crossing, where the colonnettes are coupled to carry the broad, plain inner order of the crossing arches, and pilaster strips step out between the couples to carry the equally plain outer order. All is beautifully logical, though at the crossing the floor is at a much lower level, so that the dado, of ashlar on the crossing piers, looks tall, and the colonnettes strangely puny between it and the crossing arches.

The arches into the S transept chapels are similarly detailed, but spring from much lower down, so the billet-moulded hood of the northerly arch rests on the sill of the crossing colonnettes. Note that the chapel arches are not a pair, the S arch being smaller, under a plain hood. C13 trefoil-headed aumbry in the wall between them. Transept S wall pierced by two windows below and one above, a standard arrangement. Much more unusual is the piercing of the W wall with a row of colonnettes, where a wall-passage gives access to the crossing tower. Plain doorway below into the cloister (*see* below).

Now for the NAVE. It is entered through a C16 porch into the N aisle, also of the C16, both reconstructed in 1895 by *J. T. Micklethwaite* (the aisle to a narrower plan). C12 aisle arcade, of four bays, stopping short of the W end of the nave. Stout, cylindrical piers with moulded bases and scallop caps. Family likeness to the E colonnettes, in spite of the drastic disparity in scale. Deeply splayed clerestory windows aligned not over the arches but over the piers. Plain C13 stone wall between nave and crossing, with end doorways, the S one original. Plain S doorway into the cloister (*see* below). The W bay of the nave was removed c. 1803, its doorway resited in the garden (*see* below).

The EXTERIOR from the garden has several further interesting features. The entire E wall of the presbytery, with clasping buttresses, is faced with Sutton stone ashlar, a puzzling extravagance. In the S wall of the S transept a blocked upper doorway, connecting with the internal wall-passage. The internally plain doorways in S transept and nave have finely decorated faces towards the cloister. The doorway in the E bay of the nave was the standard monks' processional entry. The second doorway, into the transept, presumably enabled them to circumvent the nave when it was in use by the lay people of the parish. The coursing of the imposts shows that the doorways were built together, though that into the nave has bold outward-pointing zigzag round the arch, that into the transept a plain roll. Outward-pointing zigzag also on the former nave W doorway, reset in a garden wall SE of the church.

FITTINGS. – FONT. Plain medieval tub, apparently recut. – SCREEN. Of timber, between crossing and presbytery. C14 upper half. Close-set mullions ballooning out at the top to enclose quatrefoils. Early C16 lower half. Linenfold panels. – TILES. Decorated with sundry patterns. Probably C14. – MONUMENTS. Ten fragments of shafts and headstones, datable C10–C12, found in the walls of the church during repairs. – Maurice de Londres. Beautiful and well-preserved tomb-slab, early C13. Foliate cross in relief, stiff-leaf on the chamfered edge and the crisply incised inscription in French: Here lies Maurice de Londres, the founder. May God reward him for his labour. – Part of a similar tomb-slab with a more elaborate cross. Possibly for Maurice's son, William, †1205. – Slab inscribed for 'W... de Lon...', presumably Maurice's grandson, who died not long after his father. The three slabs must have been made at the same time. – Fragment of an early C13 slab with a foliate staff, presumably for a prior. – Haweis de Londres †1274. Fragments of a slab incised with a figure of a lady, her feet on a stiff-leaf scroll. The inscription round the border gives the identification. – Effigy of a knight. Cross-legged. Worn. – Edward Carne †1650. Marble tomb-chest. The long poem on the S face, stressing the family's ancient lineage, is worth reading. On the black top slab inscription for John Carne †1700. – Richard Carne †1713. Oval tablet with putti and a Death's head in the surrounding drapery. Excellent quality. – Richard Turbervill †1771. Gibbsian tablet. – Richard Turbervill †1828. Doric tablet.

MONASTIC BUILDINGS. No visible remains of these, though medieval walling must be embedded in the present house SW of the church.

PRECINCT WALLS. The early C14 walls of the monastic enclosure, by contrast, have largely survived, almost to their full height, and remarkably impressive they are. They were in fact built to impress more than to afford serious protection, being weakest towards the E, where rising ground made the precinct most vulnerable, and concentrating turrets at the NW, the direction from which strangers normally approached. Why such a small and relatively poor community felt it should put on such an expensive show is hard to say. Examination can begin NW of the church and proceed anticlockwise.

The N TOWER is square and lacks only its battlements. Internal segmental vault. Arrow loops in three directions above the battered base. Trefoil-headed E lancet. Upper S door and walkway. The walls that linked this tower with the church to the E and the N gatehouse to the W have disappeared.

N GATEHOUSE. Projecting far forward from the precinct wall, its square plan converted by bold spurs into octagonal towers flanking the triple-chamfered entrance. This has the flattened arch form typical of the years *c.*1300. Behind it a portcullis slot and three vaulted bays. The innermost jambs here have nook-shafts, clear indication that the gateway originated in the C12. Footings have been excavated of a second C12 bay to the S, demolished when the gatehouse was remodelled to make it project more boldly forward of the precinct wall. Trefoiled lancet over the outer arch, lighting the portcullis chamber. Gable fitted for pigeons to nest in.

To the W of the N gatehouse a good stretch of WALL, its ragged top suggesting that it may have been equipped with battlements and cross-loops like those on the church. Next comes the semicircular-fronted SW TOWER, with extra-long arrow loops. The western enclosing wall stretches high and impenetrable right round to the S GATEHOUSE. (Here both bays of the C12 gatehouse remain, encased under later heightening. Forward-projecting tower on a spurred base added to the E, converted into a cottage by *John Prichard*, 1866.)

The S enclosure wall, which appears prominently in the foreground of the Bucks' engraving of 1741, was razed in the early C19, in order to link the house with its landscape. However, the rectangular SE TOWER stands at the far corner, converted into a dovecote. The low E wall is probably medieval in origin.

The MANSION of the Carnes shown in the Bucks' engraving of 1741 rising above the S precinct wall must have been quite grand, built probably in the late C16. In 1787 Torrington saw 'the remains of fine ceilings and painted walls al fresco', but in 1803 almost everything was pulled down. Today, to the NW is an attractive early C19 STABLE COURT. The tall, thin range S of this shows a lancet-like window high up, not acceptable as early evidence. In the SERVICE COURT to the E late C16 mullioned windows of two and three lights. The HOUSE, built 1803–5, stands immediately S of this, a plain five-bay block, of two storeys above a high basement. The bow-ended wings intended to flank it were never built. (Inside, cantilevered stone staircase rising in a bow-backed well. Trellis-pattern metal balustrade. The dining room has a little Adamesque plasterwork, a plumed centrepiece to the ceiling surrounded by thin loops and drops.)

At CORNTOWN, ½ m. SE, a large, mid-C19 GATE LODGE, taking a hint from the monastic gatehouses. Across the road, a small, Gothic SCHOOL dated 1866. Puginian under its steep roof, and bearing the hallmarks of a work by *John Prichard*. The battered base, the crisp and resourceful stonework, the windows shafted outside and in, the elegant chimneystacks: all are typical. Arms of the Turbervills.

FELINDRE

A hamlet in a deep fold in the hills, almost as if in Devon.

NEBO CHAPEL, simple, rendered, dated 1896, stands up high in its graveyard.

CORN MILL. Long range of limewashed rubble, built at two dates, the part to the E being the earlier, perhaps of the C18. It contains one of the few complete sets of corn-grinding machinery in Glamorgan. Overshot water wheel with cast iron shrouds and hub at the E end. Timber-framed windows with central mullions in the earlier part. The rear of the building is built into a bank with upper-level loading doors in a single-storey elevation.

BLAENANT-DDU DAM, $\frac{1}{2}$ m. N. One of two failed dams on the uplands N of Swansea. Built between 1860 and 1878 by *G. Couzens*, it was taken out of service in 1919 because of seepage into the mine workings below. The contemporary LOWER LLIW RESERVOIR, $\frac{3}{4}$ m. NW, by *R. Rawlinson*, was plagued by springs which erupted below its puddled dam core. The dam, with its handsome rusticated stone features, was replaced 1976–8 by a new structure by *Binnie & Partners*.

FELINDRE COLLIERY ENGINE HOUSE. Beside the road E of the Lower Lliw Reservoir. Built in 1879 as an engine house for a colliery pump. Rusticated Pennant sandstone. Now converted to a residence.

FERNDALE

A characteristic sight from the S, half-a-dozen far-extending terraces stepped down the hillside, above them a big board school and the crags of Craig Rhondda-fach. Below, on the valley floor, the light industry that has replaced the coal mines.

ST DUNSTAN, Lake Street. 1905–6 by *E. M. Bruce Vaughan*. Nave, on a slope with a hall beneath. Chancel not built. E.E. Rock-faced sandstone with red brick dressings.

PENUEL ENGLISH CALVINISTIC METHODIST CHAPEL, High Street. Simple classical façade of 1904–5 by *Lewis & Morgan*. Green sandstone, resourcefully textured, the windows outlined in red sandstone. Behind, the chapel of 1878 survives, galleried on three sides, the flat ceiling given rectilinear patterning and a big central plaster rose.

(TRERHONDDA WELSH INDEPENDENT CHAPEL, High Street. 1867, extended 1878, the oldest chapel in the Rhondda Fach. Gabled front of coursed Pennant sandstone. Handsome interior with raked ground-floor seating and galleries, and rich plaster and boarded ceiling. Cadw.)

The centre of Ferndale is dominated by the WORKMEN'S HALL of 1907 by *T. Richards* of Pontypridd, at £12,000 one of the most expensive ever erected. Built for, and doubtless largely paid for by, workmen at David Davis & Sons' collieries. Now

in poor condition, its render and its Baroque detail falling off.
In the High Street a little way w, the WESLEY HOUSE DAY
CENTRE of *c.*1980, lying back behind a pair of monkey-puzzle
trees, and the single-storey PUBLIC LIBRARY, 1989, beside
the street. Both are of red brick with monopitch roofs in several
directions, forming an intriguingly interlocked group. Both
were designed by *Wyn Thomas & Partners.*

FLEMINGSTON/TREFFLEMIN   *0070*

ST MICHAEL THE ARCHANGEL. The s transept, designed in
the early C14 as a funerary chapel for the le Fleming family, has
a three-light s window with cusped intersecting tracery, and a
cusped and ogee-headed w lancet. In 1858 the latter was taken
as the cue for the oversized Dec windows introduced throughout the nave and chancel at the drastic restoration paid for by
the Countess of Dunraven. s porch and massive w bell gable
added at that date. Inside, the transept tomb-recess in the s
wall has a richly moulded arch dominated by two filleted rolls
and resting on short colonnettes with circular moulded caps.
Roofs throughout the church of the C15, the pretty local type
with arch-braces, wind-braces and a collar purlin. That in the
chancel on short wall-posts identical with those at St Mary
Church (q.v.). – FONT. A good late C13 piece, square bowl
chamfered down to meet the round stem. – STAINED GLASS.
E window, by *Clayton & Bell.* Crucifixion and Ascension,
1907. – N windows, two more by *Clayton & Bell,* late, Nativity
dated 1921 and Christ in the Temple, 1920. – MONUMENTS.
Joan le Fleming. A fine early C14 effigy, in the s transept,   23
presumably in its original site, but reversed (see the inscription
against the wall). She wears a wimple and elegant, flowing
dress. – Edward Williams (the celebrated Iolo Morganwg,
'Stonemason bard and antiquary', and literary forger, as the
inscription forbears to mention) †1826. Large double tablet
with long inscriptions in Welsh and English. Rich Gothic frame.
Erected in 1855.
FLEMINGSTON COURT. Excellently preserved early C16 manor
house. The ivy-clad gable end abutting the s wall of the churchyard is part of a detached two-storey range N of the main house
but contemporary with it. The main house, a two-storey range,
greyly rendered, lies E–W, with on the ground floor a hall
between a parlour (w) and an unheated service room (E). Great
chamber over the hall. The early C16 windows concentrated
on the s front, with arched lights under hoodmoulds, three-
light below and two-light above, demonstrate this arrangement.
Doorways N and s into the lower end of the hall. They have
two-centred heads and continuous mouldings. Near the centre
of the s front prominent, deeply projecting chimneybreast to
serve hall and chamber. On the N side, four-light, transomed
hall window with straight-headed lights, an improvement made
later in the C16. The wing at r.-angles to the w is a later kitchen

range. The original kitchen was in the detached building outside
the courtyard to the NW.

FONMON CASTLE
1 m. SW of Penmark

Fonmon Castle is that great rarity, a medieval castle drastically
remodelled in the C18 but not subsequently Gothicized. A rambling group, unified by dark grey overall render, battlements and
sash windows everywhere. The SE tower, projecting from and
rising above the rest of the building, with a semicircular projection
towards the E, displays two arrow slits high up, to convince that
there really is medieval masonry within.

The site, falling precipitously to the E, is a typical choice for
early masonry castles (cf. Newcastle at Bridgend, Penlline). The
present approach is from the W. The history of growth seems to
be as follows. The central block to the l. of the entrance has thick
walls and can be identified as a rectangular keep of the early C12.
In the C13 this was extended a short way to the E towards the
steep scarp, with a bowed S end, and also to the N. Much larger
L-shaped S extension, with the SE tower at its angle. This includes
the present entrance hall and the three E bays of the S range.
One C16 two-light window in the E wall. Double-pile block
added to the N in the C17. Two-bay extension of the S range
c. 1800.

Internally, pre-C18 features are visible in two areas. In the SE
tower there is a mural stair, and a two-centred arched doorway
leading to an irregular room at the top of the tower irregularly
roofed with stone slabs. The lowest stage of the block N of the
C12 keep is covered by a simple stone barrel-vault.

The rationale of the remodelling of the house for Robert Jones,
carried out from 1762 by the Bristol firm of *Thomas Paty*, is not
easy to understand. An entrance was created to the S, into a
square vestibule to the l. of the SE tower. This now forms part of
the simply decorated three-bay drawing room, but it is still possible to go through from it into the S end of the present ENTRANCE
HALL.

This long, narrow room, the staircase rising in its S half, has
been formed by throwing four small rooms together. The Rococo
plaster ceilings of the 1760s, at two different levels, relate to the
two single-height upper rooms, so the amalgamation must date
to a later remodelling. This cannot have been much later, for the
staircase, with two turned balusters per tread, can be dated no
later than the late C18. Indeed, it must have represented a drastic
second thought in the 1760s, for the staircase and its gallery lead
61 to the room which is the glory of Fonmon, fitted up by *Paty* and
decorated by his plasterer, *Thomas Stocking*, in the same Rococo
style as the hall ceilings. Payments to both are recorded 1766–7.
This gallery is the upper stage of the C12 keep and its C13
extension. The room, perhaps conceived from the first as a combined drawing room and library, is tripartite, with square end

bays defined by extremely flattened segmental arches, a provincial echo of Hawksmoor's library at Blenheim, perhaps.

Stone Venetian window at the w end, sashed timber oriel to the e. Plaster flowers in the coffered undersides of the arches and bearded heads on the key-blocks. Trophies of the chase in the spandrels, and arabesques and wreaths on the flat of the ceiling, centred on an Apollo head in a sunburst. The gilt chimneypiece, flanked by lively fish-tailed herms, is copied from a plate in Thomas Johnson's *Collection of Designs*, published in 1758.

c18 STABLE, sw of the house, incorporating a late medieval barn. Its s and e walls are castellated to impress those approaching from the s. The polygonal stone chimney set on the s wall, with a trefoiled opening in each face, is a rare medieval survival, brought from East Orchard Manor, St Athan (q.v.).

Battlemented TOWER further s, of the c17 or c18, modelled on that at St Donats (q.v.).

GARTH

1½ m. SE of Maesteg

St Mary the Virgin. 1891 by *Halliday & Anderson*. A pretty little stone-faced building close beside the road. Perp. Nave and lower chancel. Half-timbered porch. Square-headed multi-cusped side windows, a rose to the w. – STAINED GLASS. Grisaille throughout, as Halliday liked. Lilies in the borders. w window centred on the Name of Jesus in a red glory.

Libanus Welsh Calvinistic Methodist Chapel. Dated 1871. Stone-faced and simply classical. Round-headed openings and rusticated surrounds. The double-length side windows are a typical device before the idea of separately expressed bays for the gallery stairs had developed. Rusticated porch with two round-headed doorways. The interior has galleries on three sides, and on the fourth, behind the pulpit, a dramatic double-depth arch on marbled columns of extreme crudity.

GELLIGAER

St Catwg. A medieval church heavily restored by *Charles Buckeridge* for the rector, the Rev. Gilbert Harries, in 1867–8. Unbuttressed w tower, lacking the normal corbel table below the battlements. Tudor w doorway and two-light belfry openings. Earlier evidence in the nave, the chamfered s doorway with two-centred arch. Only one old window remains, in the nave N wall, of two trefoiled lights. Blocked priest's door in the chancel. Blocked doorway to the rood loft. Chancel arch and wagon roof of the nave by Buckeridge. – IMMERSION FONT. Just inside the s door. Constructed as part of Buckeridge's restoration. Harries promoted the construction of immersion fonts to prevent those who demanded the total immersion of adults from having recourse to the Baptists. – CURIOSUM. The village stocks. – STAINED GLASS. Chancel E window, 1867 by *Clayton & Bell*. – Nave S window, Annunciation and Nativity, *c*. 1895 by *R. J. Newbery*. – Nave N window, SS Catwg and Gwladys, by *Frank Roper*. – MONUMENT. Rev. Gilbert Harries † 1879. Centrally placed in the sanctuary, large brass of a priest carrying the model of a church. Pontlottyn church?

OLD RECTORY, ¼ m. NW. What remains are the large additions of 1863 by *Buckeridge*. S front of Pennant stone with red brick dressings. Half-hipped gables. Fish-scale slate tympana over the windows. What a pity that this rare example of High Victorian domestic design has recently been unfeelingly modernized.

In CASTLE HILL to the E of the church, where the hill begins to descend steeply, a close-knit group of C18 and early C19 cottages, and, embedded among them, HOREB WELSH BAPTIST CHAPEL, founded 1848, itself barely bigger than a cottage. A stone façade and twin round-headed windows are the signs of its status as a religious building. The tiny interior retains its galleries on three sides, and on the far side its simple 'big seat' and railed pulpit. Behind CASTLE COTTAGES a more incongruous survivor, TWYN CASTELL, a small, tree-covered motte datable to the C12 and thought to be of indigenous Welsh construction.

LEWIS BOYS' SCHOOL, Glan-y-nant, 1 m. NE. Edward Lewis founded a charity school at Gelligaer in 1715, his will was proved in 1729, and the cairn of stones in front of the present buildings comes from the cottage which housed the school from 1760. Behind the cairn stands *John Prichard*'s prim Tudor Gothic building, of smooth snecked Pennant sandstone, which replaced the cottage in 1850–1. Thin timber hall roof. Large, rough-walled, thickly detailed extensions and master's house, 1903 by *R. S. Griffiths* of Tonypandy.

ROMAN AUXILIARY FORT. Low banks and ditches NW of the church are all that now define a square enclosure 3.5 acres (1.4 hectares) in extent. Thorough early C20 excavation uncovered a stone-faced earthen rampart with corner towers fronted by a V-shaped ditch. There was also a tower between each corner and a double gateway midway along each side. Stone-built administrative buildings, commandant's house, granaries and barracks were also identified within the standard internal road grid. Bath-house in the SE annexe. Built in the first decade of the C2 A.D. and abandoned some time after A.D. 160, possibly as late as the 190s. Reuse of uncertain character in the late C3 and early C4 A.D. Across the road, 66 yds (60 metres) NW, are traces of a rectangular enclosure which are possibly the remains of an earlier fort built *c*. A.D. 75–80.

On GELLIGAER COMMON, 1½ m. N, traces of four ROMAN PRACTICE CAMPS, which have been associated with the auxiliary forts NW of the church. All are small, between 65 ft 7 in. (20 metres) and 131 ft (40 metres) across, rectangular, and defined by banks with external ditches. That at ST 1315 9908 has entrances in the SE and NW sides with a hornwork or

1. Gower Peninsula, Pennard, Threecliff Bay

2. The Vale, Llanmihangel
3. The Valleys, Treorchy, Cwmparc looking towards Graig Fach
4. Penmaen, Parc Cwm, Neolithic chambered tomb
5. Llangennith, Hardings Down, Iron Age enclosures

2 | 4
3 | 5

6. Llantwit Major, 'Houelt' stone, disc-headed cross shaft, later ninth century
7. Ewenny, Priory, vaulted presbytery from the crossing, *c.* 1126 or 1140s
8. Margam Abbey, chapter house from the vestibule, *c.* 1200
9. Neath Abbey, dormitory undercroft, mid thirteenth century

10. Cardiff, Llandaff Cathedral, west front, early thirteenth century
11. Cardiff, Llandaff Cathedral, nave south doorway, late twelfth century
12. Cardiff, Llandaff Cathedral, west front, interior, early thirteenth century
13. Cardiff, Llandaff Cathedral, nave south arcade, early thirteenth century

| 10 | 12 |
| 11 | 13 |

14. Neath Abbey,
    church, west front,
    early fourteenth
    century
15. Cheriton, St Cattwg,
    from the north-east,
    early thirteenth
    century
16. Llantwit Major,
    St Illtyd, nave,
    thirteenth century
17. Coychurch,
    St Crallo, mid to late
    thirteenth century,
    roof fifteenth century

18. Welsh St Donats, St Donat, font, thirteenth century
19. Cardiff, Llandaff Cathedral, stiff-leaf capital of nave west pier, early thirteenth century
20. Neath Abbey, vault boss, early fourteenth century
21. Llantwit Major, St Illtyd, niche with Jesse tree, early thirteenth century
22. Ewenny, Priory, grave slab to Maurice de Londres, early thirteenth century

23. Flemingston, St Michael the Archangel, monument to Joan le Fleming, early fourteenth century
24. St Athan, St Tathan, monument to Sir Roger de Berkerolles †1351
25. St Fagans, St Mary, sedilia and piscina, early fourteenth century
26. Coity, St Mary, west window, early fourteenth century
27. Newton Nottage, St John the Baptist, pulpit, late medieval

28. Llansannor, St Senwyr, roof, late medieval
29. Llantwit Major, St Illtyd, reredos, mid to late fourteenth century
30. Cardiff, St John the Baptist, tower, late fifteenth century
31. Llangan, St Canna, churchyard cross, fifteenth century

28 | 30
29 | 31

32. Cardiff Castle, keep, *c.* 1140, gate tower added *c.* 1300
33. Bridgend, Newcastle, late twelfth century, portal
34. St Donats, St Donats Castle, from the east, outer
    gatehouse *c.* 1300

35. Caerphilly Castle, from the south-west, 1268–71
36. Caerphilly Castle, the North Dam, 1270s–80s
37. Swansea Castle, hall-parlour range, late thirteenth century, with
    arcaded parapet added *c.* 1332
38. Barry, dovecote, Cadoxton Court, thirteenth century

39. Old Beaupre, from the north-east, mainly sixteenth century
40. Oxwich Castle, east range, mid sixteenth century, from the south-east
41. St Fagans Castle, entrance front, *c.* 1590
42. Ruperra Castle, 1626, from a late eighteenth-century drawing

43. Old Beaupre, 'tower
    of the orders', 1600
44. Llanmihangel Place,
    hall, between *c.* 1528
    and 1551
45. Ruperra Castle,
    entrance porch, 1626
46. Aberthin, Great
    House, staircase,
    before 1658

47. Dyffryn House, figure of Prudence on hall chimneypiece, early
    seventeenth century, German or Netherlandish
48. Llantrithyd, St Illtyd, fragment of armorial overmantel from
    Llantrithyd Place, early seventeenth century
49. Llantrithyd, St Illtyd, monument to Sir Anthony Mansel, his wife
    and her parents, erected 1597

50. Margam, St Mary,
monuments to the
Mansel family,
c. 1611–38
51. Wenvoe, St Mary,
monument to William
Thomas †1636, detail
52. St Brides Major,
St Bridget, monument
to John Wyndham
†1697 and his
wife †1698
53. Ewenny, Priory,
monument to Richard
Carne †1713

In Memory
of Richard Carne
of Ewenney Esq:re
who Dyed the last Day
of August, in the Year of our
Lord 1713, and in the 44.
Year of his age Leaving no Issue.
He Married M:rs Mary Allen,
Eldest Daughter
of D:r James Allen;
by: M:rs Winifred Giles,
Daughter & Heiress
of Major William Gilscoo
of Gilestown
in this County

54. Pyle, Llanmihangel, *c.* 1600, from the south-east
55. Coity, Tŷ-mawr, Byeastwood, late sixteenth century, from the north
56. Radyr, Gelynis Farm, late sixteenth century, detail of south front
57. St Mary Church, Fishweir, mid sixteenth century

58. Margam, façade of Summer Banqueting House, before 1684
59. Margam, Orangery, by Anthony Keck, 1787–90, detail of centrepiece
60. Penrice Castle, from the south-west, by Anthony Keck, 1773–7

61. Fonmon Castle, library, by Thomas Paty, plasterwork by Thomas Stocking, 1760s
62. Tythegston Court, staircase, 1769–71, joiner Wishart, plasterer John Elson
63. St George-super-Ely, Coedarhydyglyn, probably by Edward Haycock, 1820, entrance hall and staircase
64. Llanharan House, staircase, after 1806

65. Wenvoe Castle, stables, probably by Henry Holland, *c.* 1780
66. St George-super-Ely, Coedarhydyglyn, probably by Edward Haycock, 1820, south front
67. Pendoylan, Hensol Castle, *c.* 1790–1815, south front
68. Margam, Abbey, by Thomas Hopper, 1830–5, from the south-west

65	67
66	68

69. Swansea, Museum, former Royal Institution of South Wales, by Frederick Long, 1839–41

70. Merthyr Tydfil, Dowlais, Guest Memorial Reading Room and Library, designed by Sir Charles Barry, opened 1863

71. Rhymney, Butetown, c. 1802–4

72. Glyntaff, Round Houses, 1838–9

73. Oystermouth, lighthouse, Mumbles Head, by William Jernegan, 1793
74. Merthyr Tydfil, Pontycafnau, by Watkin George and William Aubrey, *c.* 1793
75. Treforest, Tinplate Works, 1834–5, smithy
76. Maesteg, Llynfi Ironworks, blast-engine house, 1839

77. Pontrhydyfen, Bont Fawr aqueduct and viaduct, 1824–7
78. Neath, Neath River swing-bridge, chief engineer S.W. Yockney, 1892–4
79. Hopkinstown, Tŷmawr, Hetty engine house, 1875
80. Gelligaer, Penallta Colliery, engineer George G. Hann, 1906–9

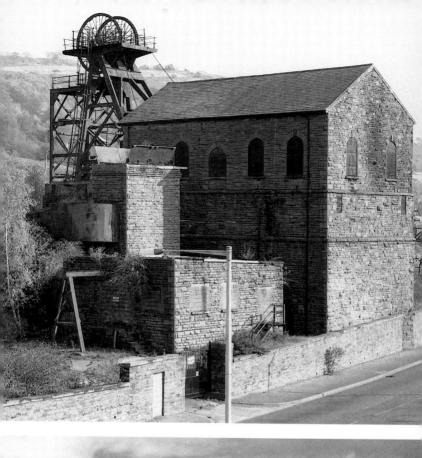

81. Cowbridge, United Free Church, former Ramoth Independent
    Chapel, 1828
82. Cowbridge, United Free Church, former Ramoth Independent
    Chapel, 1828, interior
83. Llantrisant, Penuel and Trinity Presbyterian Church of Wales, 1826,
    probably embellished 1886
84. Ystrad Mynach, Maesycwmmer, Tabor Chapel, by Rev. Thomas
    Thomas, 1876

85. Swansea, Morriston, Tabernacl Welsh Congregational Chapel, by John Humphrey, 1872–3
86. Swansea, Morriston, Tabernacl Welsh Congregational Chapel, by John Humphrey, 1872–3, interior
87. Swansea, St Andrew's United Reformed Church, by John Dickson, 1862–4
88. Maesteg, Bethania Welsh Baptist Chapel, by W. Beddoe Rees, 1908

89. Merthyr Mawr,
St Teilo, by
Benjamin Ferrey
and John Prichard,
1849–51
90. Penarth,
St Augustine, by
William Butterfield,
1865–6, interior
91. Cardiff, Llandaff
Cathedral, nave
and west towers
from the south-
east. South-west
tower by John
Prichard, 1867–9
92. Cardiff, Roath,
St German, by
Bodley & Garner,
1881–4, interior

93. Swansea, Sketty, St Paul, by Henry Woodyer, 1849–50, interior of south chapel
94. Cardiff, Roath, St Margaret of Antioch, mausoleum by John Prichard, 1881–6
95. Margam, St Mary, monument to Theodore Mansel Talbot, effigy by H.H. Armstead, 1881
96. Nicholaston, St Nicholas, pulpit by G.E. Halliday, carved by William Clarke of Llandaff, 1894

97. St Fagans, Old Rectory, by Prichard & Seddon, 1858–9
98. Cardiff Castle, remodelled by William Burges, 1868–79, from the north-west
99. Cardiff Castle, Summer Smoking Room, by William Burges, 1871–3, vault and chandelier
100. Cardiff Castle, Dining Room, by William Burges, 1872–3, chimneypiece carved by Thomas Nicholls

101. Castell Coch, reconstructed by William Burges, 1874–9, from the north-east
102. Barry, Jenner Park County Schools, former Hannah Street Board School, by Jones, Richards & Budgen, 1899
103. Cardiff, Butetown and Cardiff Bay, Pierhead Building, by William Frame, 1896–7
104. Penarth, All Saints Parish Hall, by J. Coates Carter, 1906

105. Tylorstown, Stanleytown, by T.R. Phillips, 1895
106. Cardiff, Rhiwbina Garden Village, planned by Raymond Unwin,
    Y Groes, 1912–13, by A.H. Mottram
107. Cardiff, Fairwater, Tŷ Bronna, by C.F.A. Voysey, 1903–6
108. Cardiff, Cathays Library, by Speir & Beavan, 1906

109. Cardiff, City Hall, by Lanchester, Stewart & Rickards, 1901–5
110. Cardiff, City Hall, by Lanchester, Stewart & Rickards, 1901–5, interior of Assembly Hall
111. Cardiff, South African War Memorial, by Albert Toft, *c.* 1909
112. Cardiff, National Museum of Wales, by Smith & Brewer, 1913–27, entrance hall

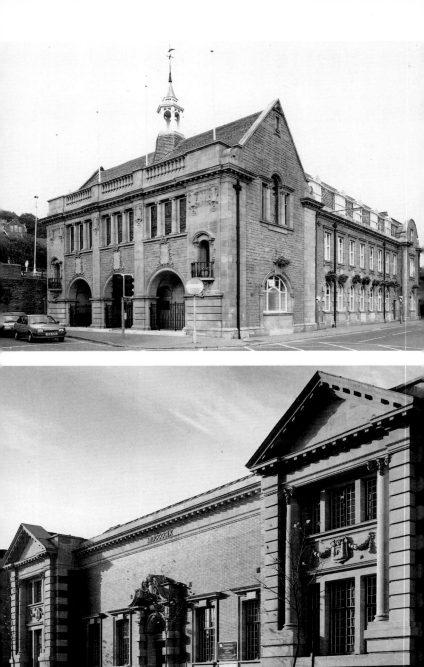

113. Pontypridd, District Council Offices, by Henry T. Hare, 1903–4
114. Swansea, Glynn Vivian Art Gallery, by Glendinning Moxham, 1909–11
115. Cardiff, Welsh National War Memorial, by Sir Ninian Comper, 1924–8
116. Swansea, Guildhall, by Sir Percy Thomas, 1932–6, Brangwyn Hall, wall-paintings by Frank Brangwyn, c. 1926–32

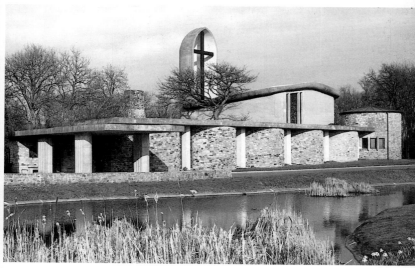

117. Cardiff, Llandaff Cathedral, Majestas by Sir Jacob Epstein, 1957
118. Cardiff, Llandaff Cathedral, St David's Chapel, by George Pace, 1953–6
119. Coychurch, Mid Glamorgan Crematorium, by Fry, Drew, Knight, Creamer, 1969–70 (photo 1992)

120. Cowbridge, County Library, by the Welsh School of Architecture, 1973–4
121. St Fagans, Welsh Folk Museum, by the Percy Thomas Partnership, 1968–74, inner courtyard
122. Cardiff, Butetown and Cardiff Bay, South Glamorgan County Hall, by J.R.C. Bethell, 1986–7

123. Swansea, Crown Court, by the Alex Gordon Partnership, 1985–8
124. Swansea, Marina, Ferrara Quay, by the Halliday Meecham
    Partnership, 1985–8, Patagonia Walk

clavicula inside the SE gap; that at ST 1315 9943 is disturbed but has indications of an entrance in the W side; that at ST 1379 9917 has entrances midway along both E and W sides, the latter with internal *clavicula*; while the largest, at ST 1386 9916, has entrances in the NE and SE sides.

LLANCAEACH-FAWR, 1½ m. W.* When so many of Glamorgan's Tudor and Jacobean mansions are either in ruins or unrecognizably transformed, it is a delight to find one so nearly perfectly preserved. The house is largely of a single period of construction, datable to the early C16. The builder was either Richard ap Lewis, a descendant of the native Welsh lords of the district, or his son David ap Richard (Prichard), who was resident here in the late 1530s. In 1981 the house was acquired by Rhymney Valley District Council, and after repair by the *Welsh School of Architecture* (project architect *Alwyn Jones*) has been opened to the public as a 'museum of living history'.

The walls are built of Pennant sandstone rubble and the angles dressed somewhat randomly with ashlar blocks, much of it Sutton stone. The walls also have a noticeable batter all the way up, which combines with the unusual height of the house, a full three storeys, to give it a sense of aloofness, even menace. Originally there was only one entrance, yet there are none of the visible trappings of defence, no sign there was ever a gatehouse, and no battlements or watch tower. The main front faces S, a flat façade, not attempting symmetry, with a two-and-a-half-storey porch near the W end, providing the only gable in this direction. Unemphasized entrance archway with a four-centred head. The principal windows, of four lights, are at first-floor level. That at the E, under a hoodmould, its arched lights moulded with a hollow chamfer, is characteristic of the early C16 work. The nearly central four-light transomed window with straight-headed lights is clearly a late Elizabethan or Jacobean improvement, as are the windows above and below it. The three-light ground-floor window at the E end is a recent replacement for a C19 doorway. In the r. half of the façade is a strange stretch of blank wall, pierced by four tiny single-light windows. The lower two illuminate stairs within the thickness of the wall, the others light small internal spaces. More such windows on the E and N fronts show that the house is full of these stairs and little rooms.

In the E end gable of the main range, the axially set windows tellingly demonstrate once more the primacy of the first floor. This front is lengthened by a full-height wing projecting to the N. The N front is completely informal. Small garderobe turret tucked into the angle of the NE wing. The main range has four-light C16 windows for the hall and the room above it, and below, at the foot of the wall, the C16 outlet for kitchen waste water. Full-height hall chimneybreast (its top recently

*This account is based on that of the Royal Commission, supplemented by the discoveries of Jeremy Lowe in 1981 and his interpretation of them (*see* Further Reading).

THIRD FLOOR

SURVIVING MASONRY

CONJECTURAL   (conj.)

C17

SECOND FLOOR

FIRST FLOOR

GROUND FLOOR

1   Porch
2   Doorkeeper
3   Household kitchen
4   Store
5   Family (or Lord's) kitchen
6   Porch room (Steward)
7   Hall
8   Lobby
9   Parlour
10 Chamber
11 Porch attic
12 Women's room
13 Men's room
14 Guard room
15 Family room (men)
16 Family room (women)
17 Women's attic
18 Attic store
19 Family attic (menservants)
20 Family attic (womenservants)

Gelligaer, Llancaeach-fawr.
Plans conjecturally restored with suggested original
room uses

reconstructed), and at the W end the only addition to the structure, a C17 staircase projection, its windows stepping up from r. to l., and with a pigeon loft fitted in under the unequal gable.

Internally it is at once clear that the house was designed to be defended. Though the porch is provided with stone benches, its inner doorway has a drawbar socket, and there is a peep-hole window immediately to the r. The main space at ground level served as the kitchen, with a large fireplace and ovens at the E end. Mural stair in the N wall, giving access to the lower end of the hall on the first floor. Beyond, to the E, a square room entered through a doorway with a drawbar socket. Here the fireplace is even larger, so the room was apparently a second kitchen. The N wing contains an unheated store room with cellar beneath, and a lobby, which is the only space in the house untouched by the restoration of the 1980s.

Now up to the principal floor. To the l. of the porch a stair, quite broad after C17 improvement, but dimly lit, ascends to a lobby across the W end of the house. Here a remodelled C16 doorway to the C17 stair-turret and a C16 doorway into the NW corner of the hall. The latter doorway retains its original door and drawbar. In the SW corner of the hall, access to the room over the porch. In the N wall of the hall, remains of a mural stair up to the second floor, and a doorway to the restored mural stair down to the kitchen. The hall chimneypiece has a flattened four-centred arched fireplace opening and a shelf on scroll brackets added in the C17. Just E of the fireplace evidence of a change of level in the hall floor, a step which was eliminated in the C17. Originally it seems to have marked a significant distinction between a lower and an upper end, not just of the hall but of the whole house. In the SE corner of the hall a doorway to the parlour, also with a drawbar socket. The parlour and the room beyond in the N wing have early C17 small-fielded panelling with a fluted frieze. The parlour fireplace opening is of the original build and could not be simpler, but the iron fireback (not *in situ*), dated 1628, may provide the date for the early C17 improvements. In the SW corner of the parlour a small C16 window, perhaps to light an internal porch, a further security measure. In the NW corner a doorway to a stair, now gone, giving access to the second floor.

At second-floor level no original fittings, but evidence of a subdivision into three parts which did not intercommunicate with one another. The C16 N mural stair to this level was replaced by the C17 staircase, which gave a well-lit ascent from the hall door. Rooms in the second storey were then, it has been deduced, linked up by a corridor. The stair balustrading here is of the C18 or later, connected with farm storage use of this storey.

In the C17 alterations the house was arranged for use in the normal way, storey by storey, the rooms on the first floor being of most importance, and all access to the second floor and attic being by the new stair. But in its original C16 form, the fear of household insecurity imposed a strict discipline of circulation on all its occupants. Only the owner, his family, and their personal servants used the rooms in the E end of the house, reached by crossing the hall dais. Other household retainers and servants, under the control of a steward or *major domo* who alone would have had access to the family, were restricted to spaces 'below the dais' to the W. His was the room over the porch, a well-lit, self-contained apartment with latrine, fireplace and secure attic storage. Doors and stairs are positioned so that he could control access to the spaces where each section of the household was probably confined every night.

For the family rooms 'above the dais' at the E end of the house, where most of the barred doors occur, personal security was evidently more important than supervision of movement. Checks included the barred door from the dais, the lobby with a possible watch room above it, and the internal porch within the parlour. If trouble arose in the parlour, the route down to the cellar, protected by a barred door, was available either for escape, through the second kitchen, or to summon help. The barred door between cellar and kitchen kept the stores in the cellar under the control of the parlour occupants, and prevented intruders coming up the escape stair. The occupants of the N wing first-floor room had a private latrine and could bar themselves in for the night. So too could those in the room above with its attic; they were probably female members of the family and female attendants. If tampering with the family's food was suspected, the connection between the kitchens could be barred, meals cooked in the second kitchen being served directly to the dais while the household was supplied from the main kitchen by the N wall service stair.

None of the security measures built into the house would have provided any real protection against a concerted assault from outside. At a time when people of note regularly wore body armour and carried personal weapons, the measures were evidently intended primarily to prevent surprise attacks, especially on senior members of the family, and to separate the sexes. Below the dais, the division and supervision of the servants' spaces, besides keeping men and women apart at night, were perhaps also intended to make conspiracy in the household more difficult. The first owner of Llancaeach-fawr had used the political situation following the Wars of the Roses to re-establish his family's ancient claim to lordship of this remote hill country. Few houses in Britain give such vivid evidence of anxiety about domestic security in times which the Duke of Buckingham (executed in 1521) is said to have described as a 'peace not much surer than war'.

TOPHILL FARM, 1 m. W. Two-storey house, much altered, but dated 1583 (on a small square of iron, perhaps from a window hood). The two-storey porch suggests its original gentry status, as does the chimneybreast in the long rear wall, to heat the hall between kitchen and parlour. Windows altered, but surviving fragments have enabled the Royal Commission to show that they originally had straight-headed lights. Puzzling plan, with barred entrance door, segregated rooms and spacious mural stair, reminiscent of Llancaeach-fawr (*see* above).

PENALLTA COLLIERY, 1 m. s. The largest remaining Edwardian 80 colliery in South Wales. Built by the great Powell Duffryn Steam Coal Company 1906–9, engineer *George G. Hann*. This was one of the last steam-powered collieries constructed, although it did also generate its own electricity. Its layout was the model for later British collieries, with one large ENGINE HALL common to both shafts, instead of the earlier arrangement with separate engine houses adjoining each shaft. This retains Art Nouveau tiling inside, although it was largely re-equipped mechanically in the 1960s. The hall is of sixteen bays, 300 ft (91.4 metres) long by 70 ft (21.3 metres) wide, with red brick pilasters and eaves courses framing a structure of Pennant sandstone rubble, largely obtained from the two shafts during sinking. Rendered panels in the four-bay w elevation, with tall segmental-headed ground-floor windows and tall upper windows in the central bays flanked by smaller ones. Casing and vent for the two VENTILATION FANS at the e end. Mansard roof originally clerestoried, as the gable profile indicates. An electric overhead crane serviced the winders, generators, compressors and fan engines, travelling along rails laid on the ledge created by the much thicker lower walls around the ground-floor windows. Round the windows elaborately moulded semicircular arcades, on panelled pilasters. Larger segmentally arched openings in the second bay from the w, and the third bay from the e, to carry the winding-cables to the shaft headframes to the s. The roof is carried on light steel trusses. The boilerhouse with its tall chimney has disappeared from the centre of the n elevation. To the s of the engine house are twin HEADFRAMES built in 1906, of steel joist construction. The easterly shaft No. 2 was the upcast shaft with an original airtight lower building made of concrete.

At r.-angles to the w, two ranges in similar style, with red brick pilasters and eaves courses, clerestory, and mansard roofs. That to the n was the five-bay COLLIERY LOCOMOTIVE SHED which spanned two railway tracks entering from the n, with the w carrying on to the workshops to the s. In line with the engine hall is the large WORKSHOPS BUILDING, 266 ft (81 metres) long and 46 ft (14 metres) wide. At the nw corner a railway entered the rope store so that the 10-ton (10.2-tonne) overhead crane could unload ropes or any machinery required the length of the building. Successively from the n the workshops housed a carpenters' shop, the electrical stores, the electrical shop, the fitting shop and the six hearths of the smiths' shop, their chimneys protruding from the roof, now mostly gone. In line to the s the smaller LAMP ROOM and OFFICES. Behind the workshops, to the w, the original OIL AND GENERAL STORES with a canopy to the e, over the adjacent railway, to cover the transfer of goods into the building. The BATHS, obliquely aligned w of the lamp room, were built in

1938 by the *Baths Welfare Committee Architects* in an early version of one of their standard Modern designs. Canteen on the ground floor with a large s w bay window.

CARN BUGAIL, 5 m. NW. Early Bronze Age burial site. A roughly circular cairn 52 ft 6 in. (16 metres) across is retained by a kerb of flat slabs with a central disturbed cist and displaced capstone. A smaller cairn with central cist lies just to the N. Traces of what was probably a ROMAN ROAD are visible as a bank on the slope to the E. At the foot of the slope, *c.* 820 ft (250 metres) SW, is a RING CAIRN, 36 ft (11 metres) wide, comprising a stony bank, open to the SE, with outer kerb of slabs which probably were originally upright.

An EARLY CHRISTIAN STONE PILLAR stands within the burial site. Roughly squared, of local Pennant sandstone, 7 ft 10 in. (2.4 metres) high. Three letters remain of an inscription in half-uncials. Datable to the C6 or C7.

0060   GILESTON/SILSTWN

A compact coastal village, church and houses nestling behind high walls. At the bottom BARN COTTAGE with a pair of four-centred doorways. West Aberthaw power station looms to the SE.

ST GILES. Nave and lower chancel of local Lias limestone, to which much of the original render still adheres. W bell-turret, corbelled to E and W, like a miniature tower. The datable features are Dec and Perp, but not necessarily indicating two different phases of work. Thus the two hoodmoulded two-light S windows in the nave, one with cusped ogee-headed lights, the other with cinquefoiled lights, look like a pair. S doorway with two plain chamfers and an image niche above. In the chancel Dec S lancets, but Perp E window of two cinquefoiled lights under a hoodmould. The chancel arch belongs to *G. E. Halliday*'s restoration in 1903. Well-preserved rood-loft arrangements, N doorway and mural stair, high-level N and S windows. The roofs, of the local type, arch-braced and wind-braced with collar purlin, virtually all renewed. – FONT. A rude tub. – SCREEN. Perp, with simple panel tracery. – SOUTH DOOR. A remarkable survival, carved with the arms of local families, which enables Mr Orrin to date it *c.* 1450–80. – ALTAR RAILS. C18. Twisted balusters. – MONUMENTS. William Giles †1724. Marble tablet with skulls on the top ledge. – Ann Willis †1760. Grey and white marble tablet decorated with applied Rococo ornament.

GILESTON MANOR. To all appearances of the early C18, a symmetrical S front of five bays and two storeys, with raised stone angle quoins and a hipped roof on big dentils. Rendered walls lined out to look like ashlar. The bracketed hood to the central door, and big flanking chimneystacks, give the façade a prim perfection. But the Royal Commission reports earlier work behind, including part of a late medieval arch-braced roof in the NW range. (Centrally placed C18 staircase

with carved tread-ends and two twisted balusters per step.)
ABERTHAW CEMENT AND LIME WORKS, I m. SE. The tall mid-
C19 ruined structures on the E foreshore of the Thaw Estuary
contain two high shaft kilns and the housing for crushing-plant,
kilns and boilers. Adjoining brick chimneystack.

GILFACH GOCH

9080

A scattered colliery development in its own short valley, the logic
behind its scatter lost now that the coal mines have vanished. The
series of parallel culs-de-sac at the S end, lined with cottage-
pairs, not terraces, formed the first GARDEN VILLAGE promoted
by the Cardiff-based Welsh Garden Cities Ltd. Built 1910–14.

ST BARNABAS. 1896–9 by *E. M. Bruce Vaughan*. On a sloping
site, the W end a self-conscious composition of plate-traceried
window and buttresses towards the road, but decapitated now
that the bellcote has been removed. Nave, with a lower chancel
added in 1933. Reconstructed in the 1950s after bomb damage.

GLYNCORRWG

8090

At the head of a minor valley tucked into the hills NE of Port
Talbot, the settlement developed after 1855 when the Glyncorrwg
Coal Company took a lease of the new railway down to a dock at
Briton Ferry. Yet there had been earlier settlement in this remote
spot, as evidence in the originally medieval church demonstrates.

ST JOHN THE BAPTIST, on the hillside above the houses. The
church's exceedingly fanciful bell gable and Perp style put one
in mind of G. E. Halliday, yet it was *E. M. Bruce Vaughan* who
rebuilt the old church in 1905. Nave and lower chancel. N
aisle and transept. Rock-faced Pennant sandstone with Forest
ashlar. Octagonal arcade piers and four-centred arches. –
FONT. Octagonal, medieval. – STAINED GLASS. Chancel E,
Good Shepherd, *c.* 1906, clearly by *Newbery*. – Nave S, women
of good works, 1909 by *Jones & Willis*. – Nave SE, Good
Samaritan, 1916 by *Newbery*, a design reused by him several
times. – Nave W, Maries. Luscious colours. Date and maker
not known. – MONUMENTS. A few tablets from the earlier
church.

Several simple CHAPELS. The most interesting was NEBO
WELSH INDEPENDENT CHAPEL, Bridge Street, 1904 by
W. Beddoe Rees, who had published the design the previous
year as a model of cheap Renaissance style. Pennant sandstone
front now denuded of all its Bath stone dressings. Interior
now subdivided but retaining the typical palmette pierced iron
gallery fronts. The Perp UNITED METHODIST CHURCH,
Bryn Road, dated 1913, was designed by *T. Gibb* of Port Talbot.

WORKMEN'S INSTITUTE AND MEMORIAL HALL, Cymmer
Road. 1925. Single-storey façade in a well-educated classical
style. Doric doorways with open pediments. Banded quoins.

Well-handled interplay between rough and smooth surfaces. The building behind has four storeys, as the ground drops precipitously.

GELLI FARM, 2 m. s. A compact group on the hillside, centred on an altered and enlarged early C17 longhouse. Across the yard to the s a contemporary free-standing kitchen, subsequently used as a second habitation, on the 'unit' system, and extended.

NANT-Y-FEDW, 2¼ m. s. Well-preserved C17 longhouse, single-storey throughout and constructed without any cut stone dressings. Doorways with slots for drawbars. The cowhouse, unusually, is sited at the uphill end.

CRUG YR AFAN. *See* Abergwynfi.

GLYNNEATH

A large and sprawling settlement. Coal-mining in the area was started before the end of the C18 by the Williams family of Aberpergwm House (½ m. w). The Neath Canal (constructed 1791–6) encouraged its expansion.

ST CADOC, Aberpergwm. Possibly of late medieval origin, but largely rebuilt 1808–9, as an estate church for the Williams family of Aberpergwm House. Remodelled for William Williams 1840–1, repaired 1883. Three-bay nave of roughly squared Pennant sandstone blocks. Octagonal w bellcote, dismantled at the time of writing. The big three-light Perp windows of red sandstone must be of 1883. The one-bay chancel, of neatly squared stonework, dates from 1840–1. The interior is largely William Williams's creation and quite a period piece, with plaster ceilings, that in the nave segmentally vaulted, that in the chancel ribbed with leaf bosses. Chancel arch decorated with plaster zigzag and imposts in the form of angel corbels. – ALTAR RAILS enclosing the altar on three sides, and chancel N and S SEATING, each seat-back with a crocketed triangular top, all clearly of 1840–1, but probably somewhat rearranged. – STAINED GLASS. E window, four panels made up of late medieval Flemish glass. – N window, Christ between SS John and Peter, 1884 by *Powell*'s. Hardman style. – MONUMENTS. Two medieval effigies, brought in, it is said from France, crudely restored and set under crocketed arches in the chancel E wall. – C18 and C19 tablets higher up on the chancel E wall, arranged as specified by Williams. – In the CHURCHYARD, an openwork Gothic monument like a shrine, intended as an eyecatcher from the drive to the House. (Signed *J. White*.)

The church stands in the former grounds of ABERPERGWM HOUSE, and is approached through a handsome pair of gatepiers. The house is now a ruin, to be seen from a respectful distance beyond a fine set of wrought iron gates. It is a remodelling of an older house, in 1876 by Morgan Stuart Williams, who later went on to restore St Donats Castle (q.v.). Can the elaborate central door surround be a C17 survival? If not, it is convincingly Jacobean-looking. Seven-bay front of two storeys, with a small part surviving of a third. Shaped l. end gable, low tower to the r. Of Pennant sandstone with Bath stone dressings. So Williams, having in 1868 rejected a High Victorian Gothic design by *John Norton*, played safe.

WOOLLEN MILL, Blaengwrach, just s of the A465. Mid-C19. Pennant sandstone rubble, partly rendered. The three tall three-storey houses at the e end of the row were a woollen mill with a block of foremen's dwellings behind. A range of ten two-storey WORKERS' HOUSES to the w connects the mill to the hipped-roofed MANAGER'S HOUSE (now a supermarket). The water wheel (now gone) was operated by lock by-pass water from the Neath Canal, which formerly ran in front of the buildings.

AQUEDUCT, $\frac{1}{4}$ m. sw of Aberpergwm church. Fine cast iron aqueduct carrying the Nant Pergwm over the Neath Canal. Cast at Neath Abbey Ironworks in 1835 with alternating faces of half-round Tuscan columns and edged panelling, to the same pattern as the Resolven aqueduct (q.v.). Flanked by turrets in Pennant sandstone ashlar with stepped pyramidal caps. Just to the sw, the substantial remains of Lock 15, GRANARY LOCK, and a lock-tail bridge.

MAESGWYN LOCK, LIMEKILN, BOATHOUSE AND MILL (SN 859 052). Around the remains of Lock 13 on the Neath Canal are a variety of interesting remains. An early C19 limekiln, of Pennant sandstone rubble, is built into the lock platform. Just downstream from the lock, at the arched, stone-built Maes Gwyn overbridge, are the remains of a pleasure boathouse, with a Gothic access doorway at first-floor level. This was built for Maes Gwyn House, a Scottish Baronial-style mansion, demolished *c.* 1970. The foundations of a mill and a millstone also survive in the outbuildings of the mansion.

GLYN-NEATH INCLINED PLANE, 1 m. e (SN 8913 0654 to SN 8992 0631). Important as one of the first powered inclined planes built on a railway. Constructed 1803–5 by *Evan Hopkin*, the Swansea Valley engineer, and worked by a Trevithick high-pressure steam engine. The formation was built 2,625 ft (800 metres) long as part of the Cefn Rhigos tramroad, to connect the ironworks at Aberdare with the Neath Canal (1791–6). The site of the engine house is clearly visible as a sunken earthwork immediately s of the track at the e end of a short level section at the top of the incline. The incline itself is in cuttings and on embankments, and is generally well preserved.

GLYNOGWR *see* LLANDYFODWG

GLYNTAFF/GLYN-TAF

0080

ST MARY. 1836–7 by *T. H. Wyatt*. A large Commissioners' church in a minimal neo-Norman style, with NW tower, now

truncated. Miniature apsed chancel. Wide barn-like interior
with a flat ceiling, but apparently designed to have aisles.* –
MONUMENTS. Ann Davis † 1852 and Elizabeth Davis † 1860,
both signed by *Jacob Morgan* of Pontypridd. Neoclassical sentimentality in little.

In the CHURCHYARD, tall obelisk, commemorating Richard
Crawshay † 1847, of the great ironmaster family.

MID GLAMORGAN CENTRE OF ART, DESIGN AND TECH-
NOLOGY, Graig-yr-helfa Road. On the hillside behind the
church. Dated 1912. Brick and terracotta, splendidly red. A
vigorous symmetrical frontage, with Arts and Crafts Baroque
details, more sumptuous than most educational buildings in
the county at that period. Was it built as the South Wales
Mining School, designed in 1912 by *Teather & Wilson*?

72 ROUND HOUSES, Graig-yr-helfa Road. Twin cylindrical towers,
three-storeyed with octagonal slated caps, stand gatehouse-like
at the inner ends of short cottage rows. Lancet windows formed
of stone slabs. Whitewashed stone walls. They were put up in
1838–9 by Dr William Price (*see* Llantrisant) in connection with
a 'Druidic museum', close to the Rocking Stone on Pontypridd
Common, where he performed his Druidical rites. The
'museum' itself, a much larger round house (four storeys of an
intended eight) on the hilltop behind, was pulled down *c.* 1950.

PONT Y DOCTOR, or MACHINE BRIDGE VIADUCT, ¼ m. W.
Large stone three-arch bridge over the River Taff built for the
entrepreneur Dr Richard Griffiths in 1809, as part of the
5-m. (8-kilometre)-long tramroad that opened up the Rhondda
Valley for colliery development. The structure is of Pennant
sandstone rubble with a central span larger than the two flanking arches. The bridge has latterly been used to carry the A4058.
Modern flanking accretions. A weighing machine for the tramroad stood at one end of the viaduct, hence its alternative name.

5090   GORSEINON

ST CATHERINE. 1911–13 by *W. D. Jenkins* of Llandeilo. Large,
in a showy Perp style, similar to his contemporary church at
Ammanford, Dyfed. SW porch tower with full-height angle
buttresses and polygonal SW stair-turret. Heavily windowed
clerestory to the nave and lean-to aisles. Chancel with S chapel.
Densely packed tracery in the E and W windows. Conventional
arcades with octagonal piers. Hammerbeam nave roof. –
CHANCEL SCREEN. Dec. Multi-gabled and pinnacled, part of
the fitting-out of the chancel by *Jones & Willis* in 1925. Designed
by *T. E. Gronow*. – STAINED GLASS. E window, 1913, Ascension between Nativity and Empty Tomb. Crowded with figures.
HALL to the N *en suite*.

BLESSED SACRAMENT (R.C.), Alexandra Road. 1968 by *Robert
Robinson*. Polygonal (fourteen-sided), with a pleated roof to

*They are shown in the plan in the Incorporated Church Building Society files.

the church and a smaller pleated roof to the lantern above.
Crowning metal feature. Walls pierced with many small cross-
shaped windows. All rather gimmicky. The interior is much
more straightforward and successful. Furnishings by *John
Petts*. – FONT. Egg-shaped, the smooth surface cut with inscriptions. – STATUES. Christ and Mary. By *John Petts*. – STAINED
GLASS. Blue, red, green, yellow, the glass in each wall all of one
colour, an idea derived from Coventry Cathedral. Naturalistic
designs of animals, birds, flowers in each window.

SEION WELSH BAPTIST CHAPEL, High Street. 1902, by
W. W. Williams of Swansea. Quite a handsome Perp façade,
behind a railed forecourt. Rock-faced sandstone and caramel-
coloured terracotta dressings. Polygonal turrets corbelled out
at the angles. Plain interior with galleries on three sides.

GORSEINON COLLEGE, Belgrave Road. By *Gollins, Melvin,
Ward & Partners*, *c*. 1955. An early example of Modernism in
the county. Far-extended, two-storey ranges with crisp concrete
frames and windows in long bands. Towards the w a range
containing a glass-walled common room above and small-
windowed staff rooms below. This is flanked by windowless
blocks faced with big, irregular pieces of local sandstone, low
to the r., high to the l., and is crowned by a curvaceous white
superstructure which makes the Corbusian derivation quite
explicit. The first stage only of what would have been a complex
layout.

HOSPITAL, Princess Street. 1932–3 by *Glendinning Moxham*.
Long and low, with a long, low Doric colonnade, white stone
against red brick.

GOWERTON/TRE-GŴYR

ST JOHN THE DIVINE, Church Street. 1880–2 by *J. Bacon
Fowler* of Brecon and Swansea. Snecked rock-faced sandstone
with green Bridgend stone dressings. Dec. Quite lofty nave and
chancel, the w front a self-conscious composition with the bell
gable carried on a relieving arch between buttresses which flank
the w window. Inside, the chancel was made more dazzling in
1900 when the walls were given a marble veneer, grey with pink
bands, the pink marble REREDOS was erected and a brilliant
and lively set of STAINED GLASS inserted. – E window, Ascension. – Sanctuary s lancet, vision of St John on Patmos. –
Chancel s, further episodes in which St John was prominent,
Last Supper, Transfiguration and Calling of the Disciples. –
Later glass in the nave. Healing of the Cripple at the Gate of
the Temple, 1928 by *J. H. Dearle*, i.e. late *Morris* glass. – Good
Samaritan theme, 1953 signed by *L. L. S.*

Church Street is signposted on the B4295 by the crazy spirelet
of the CONSERVATIVE CLUB. More serious is the COUNTY
POLICE COURT, a little further E. 1932. Small, but displaying
the robust and resourceful classicism of the County Architects'
Department in the 1930s.

CANAL LOCK, $\frac{1}{2}$ m. NE. One of four locks on the Penclawdd Canal, dug 1811–14. The lock was converted into an air-raid shelter during the Second World War. The entrance is to be found under a former lock-tail bridge. Both structures are of Pennant sandstone. The dimensions of the lock suggest that Penclawdd Canal boats were about the size of conventional narrow-boats.

9000   HIRWAUN

Hirwaun was an early centre of ironworking. From the 1830s coal-mining began on the Moor to the S. The Tower Colliery, opened by the Bute Trustees in 1878, was closed by British Coal in 1994, and in 1995 reopened as a miners' co-operative, the last working deep mine in South Wales.

IRONWORKS, $\frac{1}{4}$ m. N of the present town centre. There remain four blast furnaces standing against a high retaining wall on the N bank of the River Cynon. To the NW stood the manager's house, Tŷ-mawr, and to the NE two limekilns, with the tram-road causeway to the SE and the infilled water-storage reservoirs to the NW.

There is evidence that the present works were started by the ironmaster John Maybery in 1757, but a charcoal-fired furnace may have been in existence already by the 1660s. By 1813 there were two furnaces 40 ft (12.2 metres) high. William Crawshay, who acquired the works in 1819, made improvements, including the erection of a series of steam-powered blast (or 'blowing') engines for the furnaces (four by 1824), made at the Neath Abbey Ironworks, and the addition of large new ranges of forges and cast-houses, with typical Crawshay-style cast iron arcades and roofs (*see* Treforest). After 1880 the furnaces were heightened to 54 ft (16.5 metres) and had a 16-ft (4.9-metre) diameter, but the site soon declined to the status of a general foundry.

The four furnaces survive as large, grass-covered mounds with the rings of their internal lining of refractory brick protruding from their summits. The furnaces at the extremities of the bank retain the charging-bridge arches that enabled the furnace charge to be taken from the charging bank at the top of the high retaining wall to the furnace mouth. The N furnace stands almost to the full height of the charging-bank wall, and the bridge behind is some 13 ft (4 metres) high. The rear 'blowing'-arches to the furnace survive with characteristic cast iron lintels supporting the core of the structure.

EARLY RAILWAY CAUSEWAY. Impressive high drystone causeway, E of the ironworks, the longest such structure in South Wales. 1806–8 by *George Overton*. The stone rubble-built causeway is 13 ft 9 in. (4.2 metres) wide with a high arch over the Afon Cynon. Its deck carried a curved single line of tramroad, of which many stone sleeper blocks survive. At the N end their multiplication marks the divergence of tracks to the ironworks charging bank and to Penderyn limestone quarries. The arch

over the river has a single ring of ashlar voussoirs. Several
subsidiary openings arched in yellow brick cut through the
causeway down at road level. The ironmaster Samuel Glover
had earlier constructed a railroad across the Afon Cynon on
the site of the present road-bridge (SN 9585 0569).

In the town itself a group at the w end of the High Street contains
almost all the buildings that require mention. Two thick twelve-
storey tower blocks of the 1960s dominate its development
towards the s.

ST LLEURWG. Nave of 1858 by *Alexander Roos*, still with a
w gallery. Lancets. Chancel to match added by *E. M. Bruce
Vaughan* in 1884. s chapel. The only unusual feature, the two-
storey s porch. – Marble PULPIT and alabaster FONT of 1936
of some quality. – STAINED GLASS. Four windows in the nave
of 1887, Empty Tomb, Resurrection and Acts of Mercy. – s
chapel, 1984, watery abstract designs, by *Diane Mangold*.

ST THERESA OF LISIEUX (R.C.). 1966 by *F. R. Bates, Son &
Price*. In their usual Modern idiom, but nothing special.

WAR MEMORIAL CLOCK TOWER. Of stone, rough brown and
smooth red. Cap shaped like a coolie hat. Of Art Nouveau
derivation, though as late as *c.*1920.

High on the hillside, 1 m. sw, the remains of the three-storey
circular TOWER built by the Crawshays of Cyfarthfa. Little
more now than a heap of stones, as enigmatic as the purpose
for which it was built.

NANT HIR DAM, 2 m. NE. Visible from the Heads of the Valleys
Road as it passes over the reservoir. Designed by *J. F. La Trobe
Bateman* and built 1871–5. The contractor was A. Sutherland,
probably of Aberdare. The dam had a maximum height from
original ground level of 74 ft 9 in. (22.8 metres) and is 290 ft
(88 metres) along the crest. The puddle clay core of waterproofing was supported by clayey material with side slopes of 1
in 1, and contained by rock and gravel finished to a stone-faced
slope of 1 in 3 on the upstream face and an earthen slope of 1
in 2 on the downstream. Thus the base of the central section
of the dam is about 350 ft (106.7 metres).

CEFN RHIGOS TRAMROAD EMBANKMENT, 2 m. NW, to the N
of Rhigos. Short curved embankment with a culvert, at present
used as a footpath. Constructed *c.*1803 to link the Aberdare
Ironworks to the Neath Canal.

HOPKINSTOWN/TREHOPCYN   *0090*

ST DAVID, Gyfeillion. A typical work of *E. M. Bruce Vaughan*,
designed in 1896. Nave with lean-to s aisle built 1897–8, lower
chancel with lean-to s chapel, 1910–12. E.E. and Dec. N
windows alternating two-light and three. The w front makes the
show, with its double bell gable and handsome plate-traceried
window, rising above the narthex-like porch. Rock-faced
Pennant sandstone, as usual, with Bath stone dressings. Alternating round and quatrefoil arcade piers. – FONT. 1901 by

Bruce Vaughan, carved by *Clarke* of Llandaff. – PULPIT. A rich piece with much pink and white Penarth alabaster. 1914 by *G. E. Halliday*. – STAINED GLASS. In the E window Faith and Reason, an unusual subject. – N windows of the 1920s probably by *R. J. Newbery*.

79 HETTY ENGINE HOUSE, TÝMAWR COLLIERY, ¼ m. NW. Monumentally tall rusticated Pennant sandstone engine house beside the valley road, with attached rolled-steel I-beam head-frame to the N. The base of the engine-house podium rises one-and-a-half storeys below a projecting bull-nosed string course and is pierced by an E–W tunnel to allow communication on what was a very restricted site. Above that a recessed half-storey, set between two projecting string courses, the machinery basement of the engine house proper. The engine house is set inside a second recessed stage lit by tall semicircular arched windows with small-paned cast iron frames, five W, two S and four on the E, flanking a central high-level door under a semicircular fanlight (now blocked) and a large stone plaque bearing the date 1875. The colliery was set on a narrow terrace between river, road, railway and the steep N valley scarp, so that the diagonal legs for the headframes rose from the engine houses at a very steep angle. The winding-cables rose from small openings in the engine-house roofs near their N gables, rather than from the gable walls themselves. The fine steam winding-engine built in 1875 by *Barker & Cope* of Kidsgrove, Staffordshire, remains, sealed inside the disused engine house.

John Calvert started sinking what became Tŷmawr Colliery in 1848. The Hetty Shaft was sunk by the Great Western Colliery Company in 1875, and the colliery closed in 1983.

5090   ILSTON/LLANILLTUD FERWALLT

ST ILLTYD. Approached across a brook. A few cottages share the wooded dell. The church is a picturesque agglomeration, the tower standing slightly askew on the S side, between a porch of 1847 and a chancel chapel (now vestry). Nave, and lower chancel off axis to it towards the S. The building sequence which produced this result is hard to fathom. A blocked door in the E wall of the tower shows that it predates the S chapel. The tower itself has a corbelled parapet to E and W and a N–S saddleback roof behind the parapet, an unusual arrangement. The belfry openings, which normally assist in dating, are here mere slits. Many putlock holes. Inside, a double aumbry in the S wall at ground level. In the body of the church, only the C14 W window of the nave, of two lights, with cusped tracery under an enriched hoodmould, shows some medieval stonework. The long trefoil-headed lancets in the nave are clearly of 1847, the E window in the chancel later in the C19. Whitewashed interior, yielding no further historical information. The N tomb-recess in the chancel, the chancel arch, the blocked tower arch and the S doorway all unmoulded and plastered over. – FONT.

Octagonal bowl. – STAINED GLASS. W window, 1983 by *Paul
Lucky* of Swansea. Abstract, grisaille, with patches of bottle-
glass. – MONUMENT. James Mansel †1769. Gibbsian tablet.

The main settlement is at PARKMILL, 1 m. SW, along the main
road. At the W end, MOUNT PISGAH CHAPEL, dated as early
as 1822. This was one of the six chapels built in Gower after 1813
by Lady Diana Barham. Startlingly ambitious in its formality, a
real attempt at Palladian composition. White, rendered. Gable-
end façade towards the road with three doubly recessed
windows, round-headed between segment-headed. Flanking
porches with round arches breaking up into their pediments.
There seem never to have been galleries. The present furnishings are of the later C19. Pretty early C19 Gothic ORGAN
CASE. Recently brought in. At the E end, SCHOOL (now Girl
Guide Activity Centre), also startlingly ambitious, designed by
J.H. Baylis of Swansea, for Thomas Penrice of Kilvrough, 1876.
Tudor Gothic. Stone. Stumpy ashlar spire over the entrance
doorway.

From the school a footpath leads N-wards up the wooded
Ilston Cwm to the fragmentary remains of the medieval
CHAPEL of St Cenydd. What makes this a shrine of national
importance is the use to which it was put from 1649 to 1660 by
John Myles, vicar of Ilston, as the first Baptist chapel in Wales.
The stream runs under the very walls of the chapel.

For PARC CWM CHAMBERED TOMB, approached from
Parkmill but in Penmaen parish, *see* p. 504.

CATHOLE CAVE, 1½ m. W. Relatively easy of access halfway up
the steep, wooded NE slope of Parc Cwm. The main W-facing
entrance is fronted by a platform, where excavation produced
tools belonging almost exclusively to the later Upper Palaeolithic, *c.* 10,000 B.C., although two implements could belong to
the earlier Upper Palaeolithic, *c.* 26,000 B.C. There was also
evidence for Mesolithic activity, burial during the Bronze Age,
and some medieval activity.

KENFIG/CYNFFIG   8080

The strong castle established by Robert, Earl of Gloucester, in the
1120s and the walled borough town which grew up beside it were
gradually overwhelmed by sand from the late C14. Today all that is
visible is a particularly rumpled patch in the grassy burrows, W of
the M4 and clearly visible 1¾ m. NW from Maudlam church. Some
masonry walls exposed by the excavations of 1924–32 have not yet
entirely sanded over again. The castle consisted of a finely constructed keep of mid-C12 date, its S wall rebuilt after an attack by
the Welsh in 1295. Part of the curtain wall and gate constructed
after that date were also excavated S and W of the keep.

ST MARY MAGDALENE, Maudlam. Though today referred to
as Kenfig church, this was not the successor to the besanded
borough church (*see* Pyle). Sited on a mound, with a fine view

KENFIG · KENFIG HILL

of the wasteland of Kenfig burrows to the W. Short and broad W tower, unbuttressed, with a stair projection on the S side. Battlements corbelled only to N and S, but continued to E and W where the peak of a low saddleback roof interrupts. W porch, a most unusual arrangement, the W doorway, with two hollow chamfers, probably C15. The tower arch, of Sutton stone, is wide but not high, nearly round-headed with a plain chamfer. It may suggest a date c. 1300 for the tower. Nave with unwindowed N wall. S windows of the nave, 1878 by *Prichard*. Chancel arch and extension of the chancel to the E, 1894 by *Waller & Son* of Gloucester. – FONT. A fine C12 piece, tub-shaped, crisply carved with a scale pattern, a rope moulding at the top and a roll at the bottom. It may have been rescued from old Kenfig church. – STAINED GLASS. Chancel E, war memorial c. 1920, signed by *C. Powell*. – Nave S, clearly by *Frank Roper*.

KENFIG FARM, ⅓ m. SW of Maudlam church. An evocative farm group, facing Kenfig Pool. The farmhouse is, unusually for Glamorgan, on the classic lobby-entry plan, with the fireplaces of hall and kitchen back-to-back immediately inside the entrance doorway. The doorway itself, with four-centred arch, and the two-light kitchen window with sunk chamfer moulding, suggest an early C17 date.

8080

KENFIG HILL/MYNYDD CYNFFIG

ST THEODORE. 1889–91 by *Halliday & Anderson*. Lancets. S aisle added and nave extended in 1908–9 by *Cook & Edwards* of Bridgend. – STAINED GLASS. Chancel E, Crucifixion, 1891. In a C15 Netherlandish style. – Several post-1950 windows, e.g. aisle S, Sower and Good Shepherd, 1964 by *Celtic Studios*.

MORIAH CHAPEL. Rendered. Still in the early C19 tradition, with four simple round-headed windows. The full-width porch is an addition, but the date 1850 on it may well refer to the construction of the chapel itself.

CYNFFIG COMPREHENSIVE SCHOOL, Tytalwyn Avenue. The most complete expression of post-war Modernism in the county, designed by *Denis Clarke Hall* for 1,440 pupils and built c. 1957–61. Three far-extending ranges, mainly two-storeyed, on a gently sloping site, linked to form a rectangle open towards the S. The plan reflects the subdivision into lower, middle and upper schools. Reinforced concrete framing below, slender steel framing above, especially clearly expressed in the central range. Brick infill, pink in some places, buff in others, and some vertical boarding. Broad bands of glazing for the E- and W-facing classrooms, full-height glazing for the gymnasia at the NW and SE corners. Syncopated interplay of fixed and opening window frames. Decoration pure and simple occurs only in the rows of huge lozenges imprinted on the end walls of the SE gymnasium. This too is lifted on particularly emphatic pilotis, those at the angles tapered to echo the diagonal lines of the lozenges. Here, surely, is a building to cherish and enjoy.

CEFN CRIBBWR IRONWORKS, at SS 861 835, 1 m. E. The remains of a charcoal-fuelled furnace built by the ironworking theorist and writer *John Bedford* of Birmingham, after he had acquired the estate in 1771. The single masonry furnace has a high-level charging ramp, and the ruins of a simple casting house, at the lower level, in front of the tapping arch.

Beside the tuyère, or blast arch, is the blast-engine house (probably of the 1820s), the central wall of which originally supported the beam engine providing the blast. Three iron-ore calcining kilns remain at the high level. The site was little used: John Bedford died in 1791, and William Bryant of Merthyr Tydfil operated the site again only between 1826 and 1836. Partly as a result, the surviving ruins represent an unusually complete set of buildings of a small, later C18 ironworks.

CEFN CWSG COKE OVENS. Ten coke ovens, NW of Cefn Cribbwr Ironworks. The only structures remaining from Malins and Rawlinson's mid-C19 ironworks, which finally closed in 1900.

KNELSTON   *4080*

Nothing more than a hamlet, though both an ecclesiastical and a civil parish. The church was in ruins by 1688.

PROVIDENCE BAPTIST CHAPEL. Small, on the long-wall façade plan. Lancets and raised quoins.

STANDING STONES. One stone, N of the road at the E end of the hamlet stands *c.* 7 ft 3 in. (2.2 metres high). There are two more ¾ m. NW, in the fields SE of BURRY. Of these, one is a squarish pillar 5 ft 3 in. (1.6 metres) high, the other a wedge-shaped stone, now fallen, but originally standing *c.* 9 ft 10 in. (3 metres) high. They all probably date to the later Neolithic or Bronze Age.

LALESTON/TRELALES   *8070*

ST DAVID. Standard in plan, W tower, nave and lower chancel, but individualistic in design. The Perp tower and S porch are clearly by the same designer. Crude but vigorous. Base moulding to the tower, depressed arches to the W and S door-ways with flanking corbelled pinnacles. Gargoyles. Inside, the tower is given a low, pointed tunnel-vault. The porch retains its wagon roof, as does the nave. Rood access arrangements on the nave N side. Chancel arch with two chamfers dying into the imposts, a C14 feature. All windows replaced in the restoration of 1871. Was *Prichard* responsible? See the refined mouldings of the chancel rere-arches. – PULPIT and CHOIR STALLS. By *George Pace*, 1958. – STAINED GLASS. E window, Crucifixion. Of the time of the restoration, presumably. Clayton & Bell style. – MONUMENTS. Many rustic tablets, *c.* 1700. – Thomas Bennet † 1772. Gibbsian marble tablet.

In the CHURCHYARD the shaft of a cross on three steps.

HOREB WELSH PRESBYTERIAN CHURCH, High Street. Built in 1831. Of the long-wall façade type, the two tall windows in the centre, the two doorways flanking them. All, unusually for this early date, have pointed heads. (Inside, gallery against the entrance wall curving out at the sides. Bowed metal gallery front.)

The VILLAGE, clustered close to the church, includes several cottages and one larger house still recognizably of the C16 and C17.

GREAT HOUSE (now a hotel), on the main road N of the church. The N half of the main range, towards the road, is the earlier part, datable to the late C16. The S half was added probably in the early C17 – see one surviving original three-light mullioned window l. of the entrance doorway, with straight head and sunk chamfer moulding. This addition created a symmetrical E front, with a porch-like SE wing to balance the original NE porch. Central doorway with flattened four-centred head under a hoodmould, and two hollow chamfers on thistle stops. The massive chimneystacks, cubic with a central groove on each face to define the flues, are also part of this aggrandizement of the house. Two dummy stacks even on the main ridge. Such self-conscious composing is historically noteworthy, and one would gladly learn the exact date of enlargement. Note the pigeon loft in the SE wing. Later service range extending to the W beside the road. This has recently been heightened and enlarged to the S. Inside, the ground-floor room in the N half of the main range has a large, plain, sandstone fireplace surround and elaborately chamfered ceiling beams.

LALESTON INN, Wind Street, N of the church. A cottage of c. 1600 with a gabled two-storey window bay, unique in the county in serving two rooms at the lower level.

LAVERNOCK/LARNOG

1060

ST LAWRENCE. Sited above the cliffs of Lavernock Point, a small nave with a tiny chancel. Built of local Lias limestone. The windowless N wall is assurance that this is a medieval building. Crudely reconstructed chancel arch, perhaps reflecting a late C12 origin. All dressed stonework is of 1852, as are the roofs.

LECKWITH/LECWYDD

1070

ST JAMES. Rebuilt in 1866, and standing in forlorn disuse beside the main road. Just a nave and lower chancel. Architect unknown.

In the CHURCHYARD the usual crowd of monuments, including an obelisk on a tall plinth, erected by Charles Pearson, building contractor, to commemorate his first wife † 1855.

BRIDGE, ¾ m. N. Medieval, of three arches, the central arch rebuilt. The side arches are pointed, of two plain orders. Pointed cutwaters.

At BRYNWELL, ¾ m. W, a C12 RINGWORK and a FARMHOUSE incorporating medieval walls – see one trefoiled lancet in the N wall.

PENARTH PUMPING STATION, ½ m. N. A fine sight from the high-level stretch of the A4232. Sewage pumping station built in 1901, originally powered by burning domestic rubbish. Its red and yellow brick bulk now houses an arcade of craft and antique shops.

LLANBLETHIAN/LLANFLEIDDAN   9070

ST JOHN THE BAPTIST. The proud W tower is said to have been built at the expense of Anne Neville, Richard III's wife, in 1477. It certainly proclaims itself an exotic, with features familiar in Devon or Somerset but not in Glamorgan. Three tall stages. Slender diagonal buttresses with evenly spaced set-offs rise nearly to the top, bearing pinnacles as they die into the tower. Crowning string course with gargoyles. Battlements with small angle pinnacles. The three-light belfry windows have diapered stone sound-holes. The polygonal NE stair-turret and the moulded plinth marry with the W end of the nave in a way that shows that the tower postdates the body of the church. Nave, lower chancel and S transept (with vaulted crypt, probably for an ossuary). The broad S porch, with its handsome ashlar outer face, is also an addition, replacing an earlier smaller porch, as the position of the S door makes clear. In fact the porch does not have an E wall of its own but is boldly corbelled off the W wall of the transept.

The earliest evidence is in the short, low chancel, which is established as of the C12 by the single-light window in the N wall, its internal stonework original. Otherwise the chancel has trefoil-headed lancets in the S wall, of the C14, and the transept a two-lighter of the same period. Lofty double-chamfered tower arch, the outer chamfer continuous, the inner carried on corbels in the form of jacketed peasants. Nave roof a plain and much-restored example of the local type, with arch-braces, wind-braces and a collar purlin. Altogether the interior is over-restored, by *C. B. Fowler* of Cardiff in 1896–7. – FONT. Medieval. Tub-shaped. – PULPIT. A lavish, multicoloured piece designed by *Fowler* and carved by *W. Clarke*. Pink Penarth alabaster dominates. – STAINED GLASS. W window, 1920. First World War memorial. By *Robert J. Newbery*. – MONUMENTS. (Recumbent figure of a civilian, datable to the C13. In the S transept.) – Simple but handsome tablet, erected in 1763 to the parents of Sir Leoline Jenkins, late C17 Secretary of State, Principal of Jesus College, Oxford, and local benefactor. Signed *Kilby*, Bristol.

In the CHURCHYARD, N of the church, monument to Stanley

Philpot †1943 and his wife Annie. Gill-like. Stylized trees embrace the headstone.

ST QUINTIN'S CASTLE. On a spur across the valley from the church, ⅓m. NE. Strictly speaking, all that can be called St Quintin's Castle is the heap of stones in the middle of the site. This has been identified as the remains of a small C12 KEEP. The St Quintin family were dispossessed in 1233 by Richard Siward. On his outlawry in 1245 the castle came into the hands of Richard de Clare, lord of Glamorgan. The still impressive GATEHOUSE belongs to the newly fortified enclosure begun by his grandson, Gilbert III de Clare, presumably at his coming of age in 1312, and left unfinished after he had died on the battlefield at Bannockburn two years later. It is of the type of strongly fortified residential gatehouse conceived in the 1270s at Gilbert II de Clare's castles at Caerphilly and Tonbridge, Kent. Locally the closest comparison is with the Bishop's Castle at Llandaff (see Cardiff, p. 255). It is built of local Lias limestone blocks with dressings of Sutton stone.

The gatehouse stands well forward of the curtain wall, with which it is integrally built. Flanking towers with three-sided fronts. The depressed-pointed entrance arch has three outer chamfers, two with delicate trefoil terminations, and two more chamfers within the portcullis slot. On the inner face of the gatehouse provision for a second portcullis and less generously chamfered arches. Bull-nosed door imposts, as at Caerphilly Castle (q.v.). Large arrow loops towards the front low down, and others higher up to rake along the curtain wall. Lancet windows in the s tower relate to its conversion into a prison by the early C16. The residential upper parts have been reduced to gaping ruin by robbing of their dressed stone. They were reached by a mural stair at the back of the N tower.

The line of the CURTAIN WALL can be traced enclosing an irregular quadrilateral c. 170 ft (51.8 metres) by 160 ft (49.8 metres) at its widest points. Footings of towers at the angles l. and r. of the gatehouse. That to the NE was rectangular and must have been a substantial structure.

The VILLAGE is large and intricate, straggling across the slopes on both sides of the little River Thaw. On the w side the church holds the high ground, on the E, the castle. In the valley bottom, GREAT HOUSE. C18 front, rendered and colourwashed. Two-storeyed, of five bays with two-bay recessed ends, each part dignified with angle quoins and a pedimental gable. In the outer gables oval windows, in the central gable a round-headed window and a sundial bearing the initials T.W. (for Thomas Wilkins) and the date 1703. That is surely too early for the present appearance of the façade, and in particular for the sash windows with their narrow glazing bars. Inside, T.W. and 1710 on the hall fireplace. The hall with the room above it, the r. half of the central block, forms the oldest part of the house, with a mural stair at the back. Two-stage enlargement and subsequent remodelling. Handsome early C18 panelling in the lower room of the l. wing. What of all this should be associated with Wilkins's initials is not clear.

BREACH, 1m. SW. A small but well-preserved mid-C17 farmhouse, the entrance (S) façade almost symmetrical, the upper windows in gabled dormers. The hall window, however, is of three lights, all the others of two. A porch unfortunately hides the handsome stone entrance doorway and its emphatic hoodmould. Integral farm building to the E.

BURIAL MOUNDS, N of Breach Farm. A group of five early Bronze Age burial mounds on a slight ridge. They are low and grass-covered. Two are reasonably visible, one in the SE corner of the field on the edge of a plantation, the other in the centre of the field. SW of the latter is a much-reduced mound, clipped by road construction, which was excavated in 1937. It covered a pit containing cremated bone accompanied by grave goods.

CAER DYNNAF, on the hill above the church. HILLFORT defined by double and triple ramparts which have been obscured by traces of medieval settlement and modern field boundaries. The inner bank encloses an area of 9.4 acres (3.8 hectares). It is of Iron Age origin but there is evidence of occupation during the Roman period too.

LLANBRADACH   1090

ALL SAINTS. 1896–7 by *E. M. Bruce Vaughan*. Larger than usual for this architect, even with a substantial SE tower towards the road, an addition of 1909 not at first intended – see the W bell gable. Two-storey HALLS at the back, also by *Bruce Vaughan*. All derelict at the time of writing. Llanbradach can ill afford to lose this focal landmark.

WORKING MEN'S INSTITUTE, a short way S of the church. Dated 1912. Three-storeyed. Red brick. Wren-style. This scholarly classical essay is by *Bruce Vaughan* as well, a rare departure from his Gothic path. The building contained library and reading room, billiard room, and hall to seat 900. Now sadly unappreciated.

LLANBRADACH COLLIERY, ⅓m. N. Fine ranges of rusticated Pennant sandstone buildings remain, in secondary industrial use, from a colliery operative between 1894 and 1961. They stand on the W side of the valley with a high, rusticated stone retaining wall supporting those at higher level. The more southerly of the two upper ranges, aligned NW to SE, was a large winding-house with an arched recess on its SE gable formerly carrying winding-cables across to the shaft that stood on the valley bottom.

LLANBRADACH FAWR, 1½m. NW. Completely isolated, high on the hillside above the Rhymney Valley, yet a substantial gentry house, the seat of the rich and well-connected Thomas family. Heavily rendered exterior. No old feature is visible except the doorway of the two-storey porch, with a flattened four-centred arch under a hoodmould, and a sunk chamfer moulding, features which date it to the end of the C16. The porch is integral with the main single-pile range of the house and bears a dummy chimneystack. But the C16 composition was upset when the l. half was modernized in the late C18, with wide sash windows in both storeys and raised roof ridge. At the back, remarkable survival, a stair with solid oak treads rising in short flights up a rectangular, stone core. Added kitchen at the r. end, its hearth supplied with three ovens and flanked by mural stairs, which both, like the main stair, ascend to the roof space. So there was a third storey in the roof, inhabited both by servants and by members of the family. Simple Neoclassical plaster friezes in the two Georgianized lower rooms.

TARANYMWRTHWL, ¾ m. N, beside the A469. A close-knit farmstead group, the walls all whitewashed. Tall, compact farmhouse of c. 1600, its entrance doorway in the s gable end masked by a modern extension. Broad, two-and-a-half-storey former porch added in the C17. Sash windows. BARN built up to the NE corner of the house, and N COWHOUSE and STABLE range behind.

0070

LLANCARFAN

Llancarfan is well documented as the site of a Celtic minster. Yet no Celtic cross, as at Llantwit Major and Llandough (qq.v.), bears witness to its early importance, merely a fragment of interlace set in the nave s wall of the church. The extensive churchyard may be the successor of an early monastic enclosure.* No village centre, just a scatter of houses round the churchyard and several outlying hamlets with early buildings. Gratifying absence of later C20 housing, which has distorted so many of the more nucleated villages of the Vale.

ST CADOC. A large and airy church, the full-length s aisle and chapel almost as large as the nave and chancel. Dec and Perp windows of unusual size, limewashed walls and the complete absence of stained glass produce an impression quite unlike that of most Glamorgan churches. W tower of the usual sort, unbuttressed and crowned by battlements on a corbel table. The Saxon-looking s belfry opening must be of the drastic reconstruction in 1877. Simple C13 tower arch. The earliest reliable evidence, as so often, is the chancel arch, pointed but unmoulded and set on plain imposts crudely carved with Xs in boxes, so c. 1200. The four-bay aisle arcade is not much later, its square piers having square abaci, one corbelled out on crude heads, another on even cruder bunches of grapes. Doublechamfered, steeply pointed arches. The aisle itself has been widened and the C13 doorway reset. Its shafted imposts with schematic scalloped capitals look earlier than the badly fitting arch, moulded with a big roll and two flanking small rolls.

*No trace remains of the medieval parsonage and rectorial barn seen in the churchyard in 1871 by Sir Stephen Glynne.

The only documentary evidence comes in here: the Abbot of Gloucester (as rector of Llancarfan) ordered the rebuilding of the chancel some time between 1284 and 1307. The three E bays of the arcade must date to the C14, having double-chamfered arches on octagonal piers, and strange concave-sided capitals. They belong to the extension of the aisle the full length of the chancel. It was widened, probably at the same time. Dec windows throughout, three-light with cusped inter-secting tracery to light the chapel, two-light with cusped Y-tracery for the aisle, but no structural differentiation between the two parts. Perp improvements on the N side, two-light windows in the nave with cinquefoil cusping, further E similar windows at two levels to light the rood, and in the chancel a monster five-lighter, square-headed, enclosing a complicated arrangement of a full-width four-centred arch embracing two-light arches of similar profile. Encircled quatrefoils packed in wherever they will go. Cinquefoiled heads to the main lights. Perp also the aisle W window and the S porch. Contemporary wagon roofs, those of nave and chapel richer than the others, with moulded principals and big square bosses. – FONT. Nine-sided bowl, its lobed underside carved with crude leaves. Of the C14? – HOLY WATER STOUP, beside the S door. Tub-shaped with a triple-roll lip and a single roll at the base. – REREDOS. Perp canopywork. A highly remarkable survival though much mutilated. Canopies between openwork spires. Traces of original paint, red, blue and gold. – SCREEN to the S chapel. Perp. A lively design, the entrance arch flanked by five narrow bays to l. and r., panelled below with five different tracery patterns, the mullions faced with crocketed pinnacles. – WALL-PAINTING. The Apostles' Creed on the S wall of the nave, as ordered to be set up in churches in the C17.

GARNLLWYD, $\frac{3}{4}$ m. NE. A C15 house with a hall on the first floor. What is immediately visible, in the end gable facing SW, is a lancet high up, which lit a gallery in the hall, the base of a corbelled chimneystack, and, lower down, two single-light windows which lit a stair in the thickness of the wall. The dressings are of Sutton stone. Inside, the end truss of what must have been an exceptionally fine timber roof to an upper-floor hall, with moulded principals and vine-leaf bosses. Also a fireplace with a projecting ashlar stone hood, to heat the downstairs room. A BARN and a MILL complete an unusually evocative group.

WALTERSTON-FAWR, Walterston, $1\frac{1}{4}$ m. NE. Typical farmhouse with more surviving detail than usual. Square-headed doorway and three upper windows of two lights, all with hoodmoulds and sunk chamfer mouldings, typical of the C17. But the house is of two builds, the later, l., half, including the doorway, going with the date 1725 incised in a window sill. Rendered and colourwashed.

LLANVITHYN, $\frac{3}{4}$ m. N. Alone on a hillside, and memorable for its little E gatehouse dated 1636, white and cubic under a pitched roof. Grey-rendered, L-shaped house behind, the range facing the gatehouse dated by the Royal Commission to the early C16, extended to the r. in the C18. The main residential range comes forward two-storeyed on the S side of the court-yard. This, datable to the later C16, stands over a cellar which may be the remains of a late C12 chapel of the grange of Margam Abbey, which existed here until 1536. Virtually no readily datable feature survives. (On the E gable of the S range a stone roundel carved with three rabbits chasing each other. Their ears form a triangle, so, surprisingly, this is an emblem of the Trinity. Inside, on the W gable of this range a few plaster bosses, roses and fleurs-de-lys, typical of the late C16.)

TREGUFF, 1½ m. NW. During the C16 the house belonged to the Bassets of Beaupre. Tudor roses and the initials ER in plaster in two rooms show that it was built during their time, probably before 1573, when it was tenanted. Single-pile, two-storey range with a two-storey S porch, an irregular SW projection and a very small N wing. Rendered and limewashed walls, sandstone dressings. The S front, though regular, does not yet show a determined urge towards symmetry. Façade of four bays, the porch occupying the second. The botched sashing of the windows makes it possible to reconstruct the original pattern of fenestration. On the ground floor, four-light hall window, with a three-lighter for the parlour to the r., and, beyond the porch, a small kitchen window. Above, no such differentiation, just three three-light windows. The form of the windows was consistently square-headed under hoodmoulds, but the lower ones had hollow chamfers, the upper sunk chamfers, a differ-ence which can hardly imply any distinction in date, but reflects the change in moulding pattern which was in process in the 1570s. Perhaps the new form was felt to be more prestigious, enhancing the upper rooms.

CROSSTOWN, ½ m. SW. Much-altered late medieval house, incor-porated in a tall, plain mid-Victorian one. (In the N wall a doorway with a two-centred head, and beside it an ogee-headed trefoiled lancet with sprigs of foliage carved in the spandrels.)

MOULTON, 1½ m. E, is the site of a Romanized farm preceded by native Iron Age activity.

LLANDDEWI

In the heart of Gower. No village.

ST DAVID. Approached through the yard of CASTLE FARM. Nave with S porch, lower chancel. Saddleback top to the W tower, corbelled to E and W, pierced by a lancet to N and S. Random quoin stones, of grey Carboniferous limestone near the base, of Old Red Sandstone further up. In the body of the church there are more medieval features than usual. A small N window establishes the C12 date of the nave. Nothing earlier than the C13 in the chancel. Chamfered N lancet. The chancel arch, without dressed stonework, is slightly pointed. C13 nave S doorway and porch. C14 improvements, the chancel N window, now blocked, with Y-tracery and a keeled hood, and the ogee-headed cusped lancet in the s wall of the nave. All larger windows are modern: restorations in 1876 and 1905. – FONT. Tub-shaped, on a square base. – ALTAR RAILS. Early C18. Twisted balusters.

CASTLE FARM has a long range of stone outbuildings facing the church. The parts with brick dressings must be of the later C19. The house itelf, totally modernized outside, is in origin medieval. C16 square stair projection to the N – see one tiny original rectangular window. The overall plan of the early house, a T, with the stair tower in one angle, is not normal, and may relate to the 'palace' built here by Henry de Gower, Bishop of St David's, in the C14.

Air photography has identified a late Neolithic or early Bronze Age HENGE, 2 m. SW, visible only as a crop mark, with a bank inside a circular ditch c. 173 ft (53 metres) across.

LLANDOUGH/LLANDOCHAU   9070
1¼ m. s of Cowbridge

ST DOCHWY. A small church, none of it certainly datable before the C14 or even the C15. Heavily restored in 1869 by *Charles Buckeridge*, who of course introduced E.E. features. s porch with original C15 timber roof, the bosses carved with leaves and a central head of Christ. Nave with trefoiled lancets in the s and w walls, a double bell gable, and a N wall blank except for the rood-stair projection. The chancel effectively all of 1869, as is the shafted chancel arch. Buckeridge's most novel idea was to pierce an arcade on shafts in the chancel N wall into the vestry, pretty but not, surely, convenient. Good use of local stones, green Quarella for dressings, pink Radyr for shafts. – FONT. Medieval octagonal bowl and stem on a square base. – PULPIT. Cylindrical, of stone, clearly by *Buckeridge*. – STAINED GLASS. E window, Christ in glory, and four s lancets, of c. 1870. – BRASS. Wenllian Walshe † 1427. An elegant figure, 32 in. (81.3 centimetres) long. The earlier of the only two brasses in the county.

CASTLE, w of the church. Three fragmentary components of a semi-fortified house, probably built in the 1420s and 1430s, by John de Van, husband of the Walsh heiress, are incorporated in the walls and buildings which surround the forecourt s of the present early C19 house. At the w angle the modern mansion incorporates a large fortifiable tower, with a projecting turret which has an ogee-headed, trefoiled s lancet, the only readily datable feature. The E wall of the forecourt retains garderobe projections, and blocked apertures which must have been the windows of an upper-floor hall. In the sw corner, beside the road, an angle turret converted into a gatehouse c. 1600, when the buildings were reconstructed for the Carnes of Ewenny. (Chamfered ground-floor doorways in its E and w walls.) One- and two-light windows at two upper levels. The C19 work

consists primarily of a three-storey brick range bow-ended to
the N, built *c.* 1803.

Excavated site, s of the church, of a late Iron Age and Romanized
SETTLEMENT, with bath-house, probably a villa.

VILLAGE HALL, ½ m. S. E.E. A deft and charming little building,
converted from a barn in 1859 by *Prichard & Seddon*, and
intended for use as a school – hence the motto in the tympanum
of the principal window: Train up a child in the way he should
go. This is at the r. end, under a big gable. To the l. a group of
five trefoiled lancets framed in arcading in a 1+2+2 rhythm.
Many other characteristic details worth a careful look, including
the handling of the stonework.

LLANDOUGH/LLANDOCHAU
1070
2 m. NW of Penarth

ST DOCHDWY. 1865–6 by *S. C. Fripp* of Bristol. Elegant SE
tower, an idealized version of the local type, unbuttressed under
a steep saddleback roof. Tall, narrow belfry windows. The
tower composes with the W front when seen from the road.
Five-light W window with geometrical tracery, lean-to aisles of
awkwardly shallow roof pitch. Lower chancel, barely extending
beyond the tower, with lean-to N vestry. Inside, the shock is
the Butterfieldian brickwork of the walls. Red, with black and
white cruciform patterns in the spandrels of the nave arcades,
the chancel entirely red. Circular piers of Bath stone with heavy
square caps. Nave roof of local type, arch-braced with a collar
purlin. At the E end of the s aisle a neo-Norman arch with
much zigzag. This replicates (faithfully?) a C12 arch in the
previous church.

In the CHURCHYARD stands the so-called IRBIC CROSS,
the most impressive of all the visible remains of Glamorgan's
Celtic Christianity, a strong reinforcement of the documentary
tradition that there was a monastic establishment at Llandough
in the pre-Conquest period. The cross shaft stands 9 ft 10 in.
(3 metres) high and consists of four parts: a base, a lower shaft
of rectangular section, a massive knop, and a square-section
upper shaft, all shaped from blocks of Sutton stone. Only the
cross-head itself is missing. Every surface is carved in relief. On
the tapering faces of the base are busts of men (N and S), a
figure on horseback (W) and a row of five standing figures,
apparently ecclesiastics (E). The lower shaft has rounded angle-
shafts with strong entasis, and large patterns of interlace all
over. The name IRBICI appears here at the top of the W side.
The knop is subdivided into five horizontal bands, each with
its own interlace pattern, and forms a base for the upper shaft.
This has interlace on its four faces, and plain angle rolls. Such
decoration is typical of the late C10 and early C11.

LLANDOUGH HOSPITAL, ¼ m. SW. By *Willmott & Smith*, completed in 1934. Neo-Georgian, brick with stone dressings. Symmetrical plan, the ward blocks forming pavilions l. and r. of the

administration block. The architects had trouble encompassing within their classicism the expanses of glass required by modern hospital wards. Five-storey NURSES' HOME by the entrance. To the S of the main building various additions, 1965–76 by the *Percy Thomas Partnership* (design partner *Wallace Sweet*). To the N, ANTE-NATAL CLINIC, 1984, by the *Alex Gordon Partnership* (cf. their Princess of Wales Hospital, Bridgend).

LLANDOW/LLANDŴ

9070

HOLY TRINITY. The chancel arch is part of a peculiar and impressive composition. It is barely pointed, rests on simple imposts and is flanked by squints with chamfered segmental heads. All-embracing blind superarch, round-headed but also chamfered. Is this of the C13? Is it of more than one date? The top half of the superarch is a reconstruction of 1889. The S doorway to the nave is round-headed, perhaps of the C12. Otherwise there is late medieval evidence in the S wall of the chancel, priest's doorway and window. Small W tower on a crude battered plinth. Saddleback top. Trefoiled belfry lancets, which suggest a C13 date. Restorations of 1718 (inscription on chancel), and 1889–90 by *F. R. Kempson*. – FONT. A plain C12 tub. – STAINED GLASS. Chancel E, Crucifixion and Resurrection, 1889 by *Joseph Bell* of Bristol. – Nave S, war memorial. 1919 by *R. J. Newbery*. – Nave N, Good Shepherd, 1902 by *Lavers & Westlake*. – MONUMENT. Mary Jones †1809. Oval tablet with draped urn on a sarcophagus, signed *B. Williams*, Cowbridge.

Llandow has one of the most attractive village centres in the Vale, in spite of some recent expansion. The two best houses stand one N, one S, of the church, an accidental touch of formality.

CHURCH FARM, immediately N of the church. A small medieval house of Lias limestone, built as the parsonage. Originally it had an open hall to the W, and two service rooms below a chamber to the E, with a cross-passage between. Both entrance doorways to the cross-passage survive (that to the N masked by a later addition), as do the pair of doorways from the passage into the service rooms. All are of Sutton stone, identically stop-chamfered, with two-centred arched heads, except the N doorway, which for some reason is round-headed. Altogether a remarkable ensemble, presumably C14. The hall was subdivided horizontally in the C16 – see the three-light S window.

GREAT HOUSE, S of the church. An attractive C18 group, house and three-bay coach-house with hayloft over. The house itself has five bays, an L-plan and internal features which indicate its earlier origin, *c.* 1600.

SUTTON, ½ m. S. Sequestered and enigmatic, an unusually well-preserved gentry house of the end of the C16, built by Edward Turberville, a member of a locally widespread but at that time largely recusant family. The materials are familiar, coursed Lias limestone walls with windows and doorways of green Quarella sandstone. The idiom is characteristic of the date, doorways with four-centred heads, windows with square-headed lights, hollow-chamfered mouldings and hoodmoulds. The episodic symmetry of some fronts, nowhere amounting to a symmetrical elevation, also represents the approach to composition which seems to have been typical of Glamorgan for many Elizabethan decades. What puzzles is the plan.

The house is two-storeyed and consists of two ranges forming an L. The architecturally organized view is into the crook of the L, the w range a five-bay composition, the central bay brought forward under a gable and, as its fenestration shows, containing a staircase, the N range of two bays roughly matching the two bays r. of the stair projection. One three-light upper window l. of the stair projection, with sunk chamfer mouldings and square hoodmould stops, must be a slightly later improvement. This was the garden side of the house.

The original entrance doorway is near the N end of the outer (w) face of the long range, emphasized by no more than a hoodmould and sunk spandrels. It is closely crowded by a gabled projection to its r., which at first accommodated a broad chimneybreast with flanking mural stair and closet, but was soon deepened to provide rooms at both levels – see the straight joint at either end. The shorter, N range has a big chimneybreast with mural stair at its w end, and a gabled projection added beside it – see the straight joint to the E.

The entrance doorway leads into a square room, presumably the kitchen, with a large fireplace opening, and the mural stair beside it. This provided the only means of access to the upper rooms in the N range. Opposite the doorway is a broad opening into a passage-like room, which has a doorway at its N end. This has a four-centred head and a continuous chamfer and was originally external, masked by the addition, which has its own, much smaller doorway, the only opening in the house of Lias not sandstone. A further room to the E beyond the passage room on each floor. All this seems to suggest that the N range functioned as a semi-independent dwelling. However, there is access from this range into the HALL, which occupies the N third of the ground floor of the w range. In the w wall of the hall a wide fireplace flanked by mural stair and closet. The original fenestration to the E is unfortunately altered. From the sw corner of the hall a doorway – with original door – leads into a square lobby, from which there is access to the large PARLOUR at the s end of the range and, through a four-centred doorway with another original door, to the foot of the PRINCIPAL STAIR. The stair is of open-well form, rising in short flights, with colonnette-like balusters and acorn finials on the newel posts. It must be a mid-C17 replacement of the original stair arranged round a solid square pillar. The stairhead opens into the room over the parlour but not into the room over the hall. The latter can be reached only up the mural stair from the hall itself, which also gives access to the upper room in the w addition. So it seems that the hall range was itself subdivided, and the house may have been intended for occupation by as many as three semi-independent households.

To the s a square DOVECOTE, in what remains of the original garden wall.

Early Bronze Age BARROWS, 1⅓m. SE, including the multiphase SUTTON barrow, were excavated prior to the construction of the airfield.

LLANDYFODWG   9080

ST TYFODWG. Dramatically situated above the Little Ogmore Valley. Short W tower with corbelled battlements and bell openings of C16 form having paired arched lights. Long nave restored by *Prichard* in the 1870s, apparently from a ruinous condition. Chancel rebuilt, except for the rood-loft doorway in the N wall, by *G. E. Halliday*, 1893–4. Perp style. – FONT. Perp. Octagonal. – PULPIT. Timber. Clearly by *Prichard*. – MONUMENTS. Large slab set in the floor s of the altar, with an impressive life-size figure of a pilgrim in shallow relief, carrying staff, shell, keys. Does this date from the C14? – George Lucas †1688. Tablet signed '*Truman* fecit'.

GLYNOGWR CALVINISTIC METHODIST CHAPEL, ¼m. E. Dated 1849. Small, faced with well-laid Pennant sandstone rubble. Originally on the long-wall façade plan – see the two blocked doorways. Finely lettered date plaque above a pair of long round-headed windows.

BRYN-CHWITH, 1¼m. NE. Fine C17 farmhouse handsomely set on the hillside. Two-storey gabled porch. The two r. bays at first formed an independent house, soon extended and aggrandized for a branch of the Mathew family.

LLANEDEYRN   2080

ST EDEYRN. Norman evidence in the nave, one N and one s single-light window, the former of Radyr stone. Chancel lower than the nave, but of equal width. Dec one-light and two-light windows in both. Tunnel-vaulted s porch, probably of the C14. The illumination of the nave was dramatically improved *c.* 1500 when an enormous three-light window was inserted in each side wall. N rood-loft stair. The unbuttressed tower is an addition – see the redder tinge to its rubble walling – of the early C16. W doorway with four-centred head and double hollow chamfer. Paired arched belfry lights under hoodmoulds. Pierced stone sound panels. Chancel E wall rebuilt in 1888, when the chancel arch was probably enlarged. Lavish Perp image niche with crocketed triple canopy and flanking pinnacles, reset in the E wall. – STAINED GLASS. Chancel E, Christ as Good Shepherd, Light of the World and True Vine, 1892 by *Powell*'s.

LLANFABON

1090

ST MABON. Isolated, on a medieval upland site, but rebuilt in 1847 by *John Prichard*. At this early date in his career Prichard used the fashionable neo-Norman, and with some gusto. Just a nave, with W bellcote and S porch, and a lower chancel. Ambitious details, W doorway carved with zigzag and a simplified version of the pellet motif found on the late C12 gateway at Newcastle, Bridgend (q.v.). Chancel arch shafted with foliage caps. – FONT. A splendid piece of fake rusticity, carved with big leaves, two-headed birds and multi-pointed stars. – STAINED GLASS. *R. J. Newbery* reported inserting windows into this church. The E triplet, Crucifixion between Empty Tomb and Ascension, and the three small nave windows of 1901, could all be his.

TARANYMWRTHWL. *See* Llanbradach.

LLANFRYNACH

9070

ST BRYNACH. Completely isolated, and only lightly restored, so that it gives an unusually good idea of an un-Victorianized medieval village church. Nave with S porch, lower chancel, and a stout unbuttressed W tower crowned by a corbelled parapet. Virtually windowless N wall, like many Glamorgan churches. Windowless E wall also, though the sill and jambs inside show that a three-light window once existed. Large C19 S window in the nave, small square S and C20 N window with wooden mullions, introduced by *Alban Caroe* in 1968, in the spirit of the S.P.A.B. That leaves very little by which the medieval fabric can be dated. The nave S door has two hollow chamfers, C14 to C15. Plain pointed chancel arch on imposts of late C12 type. Rectangular window with a hollow chamfer, early C16, in the chancel, and, inside, a trefoil-headed piscina. Note the continuous stone seating along the nave walls. Nave roof of the local late medieval pattern, with arch-braces on stumpy wall-posts and three tiers of wind-braces. Renewed collar purlin. The wall-plate decorated with arcading. – WALL-PAINTINGS. Traces S of the chancel arch, interpreted as a crown of thorns above bunches of grapes. – FONT. Dated 1745. Small cup-shaped bowl, octagonal on an octagonal stem. – PEWS. C20. Highly distinctive ballooning ends. – MONUMENT. Reynold Deere †1815. Pensive females flank the inscription panel, in Flaxman fashion. Signed by *J. Wood* of Bristol.

LLANGAN

9070

ST CANNA. On its own among trees at the N end of the village. In front of the church stands the magnificent C15 CHURCHYARD

31   CROSS, all original, the four steps, the sandstone shaft and the

worn but still decipherable head, carved with the Crucifixion
(W), Pietà (E) and figures of saints (N and S).

The church itself consists of nave, lower chancel and S porch.
All looks C19. Only the doorway to the rood loft suggests its
earlier history. Called 'recently rebuilt' in 1869, using some
old walling. – FONT. Tub-shaped, with a crude pattern of
semicircles and bars on its underside. C13? – STAINED GLASS.
E window, 1932 by *William Glasby*. Ascension between St
Canna and the late vicar. – SCULPTURE. Wheel cross-head
crudely carved with the Crucifixion. Bearded Christ between
lance-bearing Longinus and sponge-bearer, comparable to
scenes on Irish stone-carving and metalwork. Small, even
cruder figure on the shaft below. Datable to the late C9 or early
C10. (In the churchyard W of the church.) – Three fragments
of an C11 cross-head. (In the porch.) – MONUMENTS. (Two
fragments of C11 or C12 headstones set into the E and S wall of
the chancel.) – John Thomas † 1764. Neoclassical tablet signed
by *Henry Wood* of Bristol.

LLANGEINOR/LLANGEINWYR
9080

ST CEIN. Alone on the hillside except for a pub. Panoramic
views. The stout W tower is late medieval, with corbelling
below the battlements and paired arched belfry openings under
hoodmoulds. Unusually wide W doorway. Virtually every
feature of the nave and lower chancel belongs to *G. E. Halliday*'s drastic restoration of 1894. Only the nave roof, arch-
braced on short wall-posts, is partly old. However, a good deal
of evidence of the rood-loft arrangement remains, the usual
doorway high in the nave N wall, two squints, and a big shelf
across the E wall of the nave, on which the rood must have
rested. Halliday's somewhat fantastic piscina and sedilia in the
chancel catch the eye. – FONT. The common tub form.

At BLACKMILL, a main-road hamlet 1¼ m. SE, PARAN BAPTIST
CHAPEL, small and rendered white. In an awkward roadside
position and awkwardly attached to a house, so not conforming
to any normal early pattern. Two plus two round-headed
windows towards the road. Of the three dates it bears, 1819,
1858, 1898, the middle one seems most likely to relate to its
present construction.

LEWISTOWN, ½ m. E, at the foot of the Ogmore Valley. A rare
case of post-war Valley development on a virtually new site. By
F. D. Williamson & Associates, c. 1967. Short terraces. Monopitch roofs. Rendered walls.

LLANGENNITH/LLANGYNYDD
4090

One of the best village groups on Gower, the church on the lower
side of a sloping green. One or two C18 farms and cottages, and
the KING'S ARMS, facing the church, complete the group.

ST CENNYDD. Dedicated to the Celtic saint who by tradition
founded a hermitage in the C6 (*see* Burry Holms below). In the
early C12 the church and land at Llangennith were granted to
the abbey of St Taurin at Evreux, which established a cell
consisting of a prior and one monk. It was suppressed in 1414
among the alien priories, and no physical evidence of it seems
to survive, except perhaps the two blocked doorways in the
nave S wall.

The church is large, essentially E.E., of unusual plan, set
into the hillside. Exceptionally long chancel. The N tower,
saddleback-roofed on corbels to N and S, and set against the E
end of the nave, is datable by the paired lancets to the C13.
Blocked round-headed arch low in its E wall. N porch. In
J. B. Fowler's restoration of 1882–4 the floor level was raised by
4 ft (1.22 metres), partly covering the two S doorways in the
nave. Nave N doorway, with an angle roll, of the C13. Chancel
E window prettily traceried, an ogee quatrefoil over three lights,
of the C14. Otherwise the windows, as also presumably the
wide, plain, pointed chancel arch, are of 1882–4. – FONT.
Square bowl with a scalloped underside, on a round shaft with
moulded base. Of Bath stone. Does this mean it is of the C19,
in spite of its appearance of authenticity? – SCULPTURE. In
the W wall, reset fragment of a C9 cross shaft, decorated with
a dense and consistent pattern of interlace. This was found in
the centre of the chancel, and is by tradition associated with
the tomb of St Cennydd. – MONUMENTS. Recumbent effigy
of a knight in chain mail with a surcoat, of the C14. He draws
his sword, and his legs, though broken, were originally crossed.
This too has been moved from the chancel, and must represent
a member of the local landowning family of de la Mare. –
Richard Portrey, 1715. Tablet under a swan-neck pediment
with side draperies.

BURRY HOLMS, 2 m. NW. On this tidal island off the NW tip of
the Gower peninsula are traces of the medieval 'hermitage
of St Kenydd-atte-Holme'. Remains of a rectangular stone
building near the E end of the island were shown by excavation
between 1965 and 1968 to belong to a C12 chapel, its apsidal
chancel later reconstructed in rectangular form. It was also
shown to stand on the site of a timber building, presumably
the church of a Celtic religious community. Traces of burial
yet earlier than that were also found. Footings of later medieval
buildings. To the S a rectangular hall and annexe with stone
bench and table: a scriptorium, it is suggested. To the NW a
rectangular building with a porch. Altogether this is eloquent
evidence for the communal life of 'hermits' over several
centuries.

PROMONTORY FORT, Burry Holms. Enclosure bank with external ditch and counterscarp bank broken by a single entrance.
The bank runs N–S across the island, isolating the W half.
Limited excavation in 1965 showed that the bank was constructed in two phases, and that the entrance was approached
across a causeway left in a rock-cut ditch. Iron Age origin likely.

Excavations also produced flintwork, evidence for Mesolithic activity.

DELFID, 1 m. N. Isolated farmhouse, no earlier than the late C18, but still retaining intact the once-typical Gower arrangement in the hall. Hearth flanked by a high-backed bench on one side and a bed in a cupboard on the other. Timber hood, fitted underneath with hooks for curing bacon, and above as a warm upstairs bed.

BURRY GREEN, 2½ m. E. Sloping, triangular green, with TILE HOUSE FARM, c. 1700 and later, at the lower end, and, among the houses facing down from above, BETHESDA PRES-BYTERIAN CHURCH, an early C19 chapel linked to its minister's house by a whitewashed stone wall and railings. Chapel and house were built at the expense of Lady Diana Barham, the dedicated evangelizer of English-speaking Gower. Long-wall façade plan, the entrance front a minimal composition, one round-headed window l. and r. of the central doorway. Hipped roof. Original wooden tracery survives in a window round the side. (The interior has the highly unusual feature of a private pew for Lady Barham, who lived at Fairy Hill nearby.)

On HARDINGS DOWN, 1 m. SE, are three settlement ENCLOS-URES of proven or probable Iron Age date. Easily seen in the winter or spring before the bracken has grown up, they are a particularly interesting group of earthworks on account of their contrasting plans. The smallest, 0.5 acre (0.2 hectare), is a simple hillslope enclosure on the steep N slope just S of a track, and consists of a sub-circular bank fronted by a ditch, on the outer edge of which is a low counterscarp bank. There is an entrance in the NW arc.

Further W, on the steep NW slope is a more complex, oval HILLSLOPE ENCLOSURE covering 1.6 acres (0.6 hectare), with outer defensive earthworks. It is defined by a rampart, which excavation suggests was a simple rubble dump, perhaps sur-mounted by a stone parapet, and an external ditch, beyond which is a counterscarp bank. Excavation in the entrance gap in the NE arc revealed a square setting of four post-holes in a cobbled passage, perhaps evidence for a double gate sur-mounted by a tower or walkway. The SE arc of the bank and ditch incorporates the hill crest, beyond which are two further parallel banks fronted by ditches. Two of the three building platforms visible within the enclosure have been excavated. Post-holes found on the platform close to the NW rampart suggested a sub-circular building c. 23 ft (7 metres) across. On the platform higher up the slope, evidence for a round house c. 33 ft (10 metres) wide, which was superseded by other timber-built structures, possibly including drying racks. Datable by pottery finds to the late Iron Age, C1 B.C.–C1 A.D.

On the hilltop is an unfinished hillfort (SS 4370 9064), an unusual survival. It was probably intended that c. 2.2 acres (0.9 hectare) should be enclosed with defences following the contours, but most of the W circuit is open, apart from a short length of bank in which the rear stone revetment is visible. Elsewhere bank and external ditch can be seen with an entrance gap in the E side. Beyond are traces of two further banks, the inner of which may be an earlier feature.

LIMEKILN, ½ m. SE. SS 4325 9075. High, stone-built kiln, 12 ft (3.6 metres) across, with two lime-raking holes, next to a small limestone quarry.

LLANGIWG
1½ m. N of Pontardawe

ST CIWG. A medieval church high up on the hillside, 'new roofed and considerably altered' in 1812, as a tablet on the S wall records. Thus the W tower now lacks the normal corbel table to support its battlements, and, more drastically, all differentiation between nave and chancel has been eliminated. Yet the N wall remains, in the medieval way, windowless. Y-traceried windows of 1812 elsewhere. – FONT. Shallow, tub-shaped. - PULPIT. Cylindrical, of stone, c. 1870. – STAINED GLASS. E window, Feed my Sheep, c. 1898.

LLANGYFELACH

ST CYFELACH. The big unbuttressed tower on the hillside is all that survives of the medieval church. Much reconstructed, it has the simplest twin belfry lights and battlements unsupported by corbels. 40 yds (36.6 metres) further down the hill stands the present church. The nave is said to have started life as a barn, the conventional Perp chancel being an addition of 1850. N chapel. The nave owes its church-like appearance to a remodelling by *W. D. Caröe* in 1913–14. Using a pink sandstone, he added the S porch and the angle buttresses with their numerous set-offs, and inserted the simple Perp windows. – SCREEN. 1916, by *Caröe*. On the model of late medieval rood screens in Gwent and Powys, complete with cove, as if for a rood loft. – STAINED GLASS. E window, Crucified Christ adored by bishops, and chancel NE, St Dubricius, 1916 by *Kempe & Tower*. – Nave NE, Good Shepherd, and Parable of the Sower in four scenes, 1947 by *Burlison & Grylls*. – Nave SE, Christ blessing and scenes, made to match, by *A. K. Nicholson*. – Nave N, 1963 by *Timothy Lewis*. By far the most impressive window in the church. To commemorate a death by drowning. Inspiration from Graham Sutherland. – SCULPTURE. Fragment of a Celtic cross shaft, set in the N wall. – MONUMENTS. Mathew Johnes and wife †1631. Brass plate, the kneeling figures little more than scratched in. – (In the N chapel.) Thomas Price †1754. Tablet in a shaped surround, signed *Palmer*. – Jane Price †1758. Simple Gibbsian tablet. – Mary Price †1782 and sister. Neoclassical wall-monument, surmounted by twin draped urns.

VELINDRE TINPLATE WORKS, ½ m. NW. A huge cold reduction
and tinning mill built, with its fellow at Trostre, Llanelli, Dyfed,
for the Steel Company of Wales. 1952–6 by *Sir Percy Thomas &
Son* (design partners *Norman Thomas* and *Howell Mendus*).
Three-storey, brick-clad OFFICES and LABORATORIES beside
the road, the MILL itself behind to the E. This consists of a
series of deep, close-set rolling mills cased in blue-grey corrugated metal sheeting, on the same pattern as the firm's steelworks at Port Talbot. Disused at the time of writing.

LLANGYNWYD

8080

ST CYNWYD. Impressive Perp w tower, unbuttressed, but not
designed along the normal lines. It has a boldly moulded plinth,
a top stage set back twice above the cinquefoiled twin bell-
openings, battlements and angle pinnacles. Sizeable w doorway
moulded with two hollow chamfers, and immediately above it
a large, four-light traceried window. This relates to the internal
arrangements, a lofty arch into the nave, with two broad plain
chamfers, and, exceptional rarity in the county, a tower-vault.
Integral with the arch, a small doorway to a mural stair, for the
use of the bellringers. The rest of the building, nave with s
porch and lower chancel, was drastically restored by *G. E. Halliday* 1891–3 at the expense of Miss Olive Talbot of Margam –
see her initials on the porch arch. Fancy Perp detailing. The
blind N wall of the nave, and in the chancel even some medieval
features were permitted to remain: a trefoiled lancet, the priest's
doorway with a keeled roll in the s wall and twin trefoiled
lancets N and s at the E end, evidence of the C14. – FONT.
Octagonal bowl chamfered neatly down to a square base. –
TILE PAVEMENT. Heraldic. 1893. – STAINED GLASS. Chancel
E, Ascension. 1893. Weak. – Tower w, angels in billowing
robes. 1893. – N and s, grisaille in Halliday's favourite design. –
MONUMENT. Hopkin Hopkin † 1742. Large plain tablet, with
additions to the inscription up to 1955.
The church stands at the centre of the compact upland village,
surrounded by high-walled lanes. Two pubs among the few
houses, and, on the N side, a terrace of rendered cottages
which incorporates BETHESDA CHAPEL, dated 1795. Two big
segment-headed windows and a central single-storey porch.
Unfortunately the chapel has been modernized.
MAESTEG COUNTY COMPREHENSIVE SCHOOL, 1 m. SE, on
the A4063. In two parts, of 1958–9 by *Glamorgan County Architects Department*, and 1989–90 by *Mid Glamorgan County Architects Department*, making a typical contrast. The former is of
neutral brown brick with large expanses of window, the latter
brighter and more restless, paired red brick buttresses and
yellow brick infill played off against vivid blue window trim.
Pitched roofs on both parts.
CASTLE, ½ m. W. The scanty remains of a castle reconstructed
by Gilbert II de Clare in the 1260s. Approached through a

farmyard and across a field, the site is shrouded in woodland which obscures its military strength. Nor do the piles of stones themselves yield much information. Only towards the w can man-made walls be clearly discerned, including part of a chamfered jamb. This belonged to a great gatehouse with twin drum towers partly excavated in 1906. The Royal Commission has demonstrated that the gatehouse in plan and defensive arrangements closely resembled the inner e gatehouse at Caerphilly Castle (q.v.), built by Gilbert de Clare from 1268. The two were no doubt raised by him contemporaneously.

RAILWAY CUTTING and EMBANKMENT, 1 m. SE. The most substantial remains of the Duffryn, Llynvi and Porthcawl Railway, constructed in 1828 by the engineer *John Hodgkinson*. The railway, of 4 ft 7 in. (1.4 metres) gauge, with edge rails, of the type which later became universal, ran for 16 m. (25.7 kilometres), linking the ironworks in the Llynfi Valley to the sea. The true depth of the cutting has been masked by considerable slippage of its sides. Deep depression of the embankment, caused by recent deterioration of the central culvert.

p. 27 CAER BLAEN-Y-CWM, 1¾ m. SW. Sub-rectangular Iron Age HILLSLOPE ENCLOSURE, 0.2 acre (0.1 hectare) in extent, defined by a bank fronted by a ditch and counterscarp bank. The gap in the N bank has been created by a later hollow-way which passes through the original entrance in the s side. N of the enclosure is a linear bank or dyke running across the slope. The linear feature to the s is probably part of a hollow-way scarped into the slope.

Y BWLWARCAU, ½ m. NE of Caer Blaen-y-cwm. A second, less accessible Iron Age HILLSLOPE ENCLOSURE. Multi-period earthworks further confused by modern boundaries. The inner enclosure of 0.7 acre (0.3 hectare), with an entrance in the E side, is defined by a prominent bank, ditch and counterscarp bank. The E side partially overlies the slighter defences of an earlier, somewhat larger enclosure which elsewhere are visible as an outer bank and ditch. This inner complex is surrounded by two or three concentric banks and ditches enclosing 17.8 acres (7.2 hectares), except on the N and NE sides where there is a steep slope. SE of the inner enclosure are a sub-rectangular yard and a medieval PLATFORM HOUSE.

0080   LLANHARAN

ST JULIAN AND ST AARON. 1856–7 by *Prichard & Seddon*. Small and inexpensive, but handled *con amore*. Nave and lower chancel, N vestry, w bellcote with an eye-catching spirelet. Typical Prichard walling, green, grey and brown Pennant stone in shallow courses contrasting with broad ashlar bands and quoins of buff Bath stone. Geometrical tracery. Wide chancel arch with a continuous sunk wave. Chancel roof on short wall-shafts which rest on foliage corbels. – FONT. Of stone, clearly by *Prichard & Seddon*. – PULPIT. Massive, of timber.

Presumably by *Prichard & Seddon*. – STAINED GLASS. E
window *c*. 1857. Ascension between Noli me Tangere and Feed
my Sheep. Strident colours. By whom?

LLANHARAN HOUSE, ½ m. E. Beautifully seen from the main
road, in its park against the wooded hillside. The house was
begun *c*. 1750 for Rees Powell, a lawyer. Very reserved S front,
of greenish sandstone ashlar, a five-bay block of three storeys
flanked by pedimented two-bay pavilions set very slightly
forward. The dome of the later staircase at the back visible
above the pitched roof. When the house was first built the
wings were single-storeyed, but a tall second storey was added
to the r. in 1870–1 and to the l. in 1897–8. Central pedimented
stone doorcase, Tuscan Doric with half-columns.

In plan the house was an L, with a kitchen wing extending N
at the E end, and, surprisingly for such a late date, a single pile.
After 1806 Richard Hoare Jenkins remodelled the interior, and
added an axial staircase, circular in plan, a real *coup de théâtre*. 64
Cantilevered stone flights rise in two easy half-turns round the
back of the well, lit from the glazed dome above. Shaped tread-
ends, but plain, wooden banisters. Elsewhere, Neoclassical
doorcases and chimneypieces with the usual swags, scrolls and
urns in low relief. The great dining room to the W, and the
room above it, given rich but conventional classical decoration
of *c*. 1898.

STABLES, E of the house. C18, quite large, of five bays, the
central bay brought forward under a gable. Pediment over the
doorway here. Two storeys of windows, rectangular below,
semicircular above.

LLANHARRY/LLANHARI   0080

ST ILLTYD. The medieval church was rebuilt in 1868 by *David
Vaughan*. Nave with W bellcote and S porch, lower chancel.
Plate tracery. The most memorable feature, the blocks of local
pink conglomerate incorporated in the walls. A few items
survive from the former church, including the surprisingly small
Perp chancel arch. – FONT. Octagonal, with simple incised or
chip-carved designs on the faces, one like a pair of elemental
trees. Probably of the C15. It says something for the austerity
of the medieval fonts of Glamorgan that this is one of the
most richly decorated of them. – STAINED GLASS. E window.
Nativity, Crucifixion and Resurrection, with Christ in Majesty
above. Of 1868 and typical of the date. By *Joseph Bell* of Bristol. –
MONUMENT. William Gibbon †1759. Cast iron slab.

LLANILID   9080

ST ILLID AND ST CURIG. An early origin for the church is
perhaps suggested by the narrow, unmoulded tower arch and
chancel arch, but both have pointed heads. Nave with S porch

and lower chancel, as usual, with a miscellany of two-light
Tudor windows inserted in their s walls. The three-light
chancel E window, square-headed with arched lights, the centre
light stepped up from the others, may be as late as the early
C17 – if a comparison with Ruperra Castle (1626) is valid (q.v.).
Tower with corbelled battlements and two-light Tudor bell-
openings, in its structure later than the rest of the church. Quite
sensitively restored in 1882–3 by *Prichard*, who 'refixed' the
chancel roof but new-roofed the nave. – FONT. Tub-shaped,
decorated with a row of linked trefoils in shallow relief. This
might date it to the C13. – PILLAR PISCINA on a circular
shaft. – AUMBRY with cusped ogee head.

The church stands alone, but in the CHURCHYARD a bristling array of Victorian tombs is a reminder that nearby Pencoed
(q.v.) did not have its own church until 1915.

CASTLE RINGWORK, immediately NE of the church. One of
the best-preserved in the county, datable to the C12. Roughly
circular, with the entrance opening to the s. In spite of the
grove of trees which covers the ringwork, the bank and ditch
are clearly visible.

4090   # LLANMADOC/LLANMADOG

ST MADOC. Drastically restored and partly rebuilt in 1865–6 by
John Prichard at the expense of the Rev. J. D. Davies. Merely
the N walls of chancel and nave are medieval. Of the tower, the
top stage was rebuilt – accurately? Its toy-like scale contrasts
oddly with its look of defensibility, with slit openings only.
Narrow chancel arch of C12 form, reconstructed and rendered
over. – FONT. Square bowl, presumably medieval. - ALTAR.
Carved by the Rev. *J. D. Davies*. Painted panels of the four
Evangelists. – STAINED GLASS. Chancel E, signed by *Celtic
Studios*. – CARVED STONES. Inscription in Roman capitals cut
in a stone now set into the sill of a nave s window. It reads
ADVECTI FILIVS/GVAN HIC IACIT (Guan, son of Advectus,
lies here), and is datable to the late C5 or early C6. – Pillar-
stone with incised cross, and the top of another incised with
crosses on two adjacent faces, datable C7 to C9 (at the W end
of the nave). Found in or near the churchyard, these stones
suggest that Llanmadoc was an important early site of Christianity in South Wales.

TRINITY PRESBYTERIAN CHAPEL. One of the simple little
Nonconformist chapels of Gower, unusual in its siting so close
to the parish church – at the E end of the village. Dated 1868.
Gable-ended on the long-wall façade plan, with just one round-
headed window each side of the porch. Iron-railed forecourt.

OLD RECTORY, s of the church. Built for the Rev. J. D. Davies
(rector 1860–1911) in the Swiss chalet style. This overbearing
building was, astonishingly, designed by *Prichard* (but cf. The
Rest, Porthcawl). In 1872 it was called a 'bare unfinished
barrack' by Kilvert, the diarist. All windows modernized.

On the summit of LLANMADOC HILL, 1 m. SW, are fourteen
mostly ruinous early Bronze Age burial cairns. The best-
preserved, topped by a pile of recent origin, is an impressive
heap of Old Red Sandstone *c.* 88 ft 6 in. (27 metres) across. At
the E end of the ridge is a well-preserved Iron Age HILLFORT
(known as THE BULWARK) which is readily viewed on the p. 29
ground. It has complicated defences which suggest that it is of
more than one phase. An inner enclosure of just under 2.5 acres
(1 hectare) is defended by a rampart fronted by a ditch, the
steep slope providing strong natural defences to the N. It is
entered from the E along a corridor defined by parallel banks
which cut across two outer lines of banks and ditches lying
across the ridge. A third bank lies beyond the entrance corridor.
Within the interior, S of the entrance, is a sub-rectangular
enclosure which may be a medieval or later modification. One
building platform can be seen in the slope W of this. The W arc
of the ditch of the inner enclosure cuts an earlier length of bank
and ditch. Beyond is another bank and ditch which crosses the
ridge N–S before swinging E, running parallel to the inner
enclosure and terminating at the entrance corridor. Finally, a
short distance further W is a bank fronted by a ditch which can
be traced N–S across the ridge for *c.* 450 ft (140 metres).

WHITEFORD POINT LIGHTHOUSE, $2\frac{1}{2}$ m. N. Unusual cast iron
tower built in 1865 to mark the S side of the channel to Llanelli
Harbour. It stands just above low-water mark and is 22 ft (6.71
metres) in diameter at a base which tapers up gracefully to the
lantern. It consists of seven courses or rings of heavy cast iron
plates bolted together by means of external flanges, unlike all
other cast iron towers, which have internal flanges and smooth
exteriors. This was possibly to facilitate erection and replacement at this mostly wave-washed site. Elegant gallery railings.
The copper glazing bars and former copper roofing reflect its
association with a copper-exporting port. This is the earliest
remaining wave-washed cast iron lighthouse.

LLANMAES/LLAN-FAES   9060

ST CATWG. W tower of the usual sort, if a rather basic example.
Unbuttressed, with corbelled battlements. Depressed-headed
W door and above it a simple two-light window with a hoodmould. Also an inscription panel giving the date of construction, 1632. The church to which the tower was added
consists of the usual nave and lower chancel. Here the evidence
is of the C13, lancets (renewed) in the S wall of the chancel,
and Sutton stone jambs of the chancel arch. Three-light Tudor
windows in the nave. Unusually complete rood-loft arrangements, the lower doorway with a moulded surround, the upper
doorway and even the timber SCREEN itself, with simple Perp
tracery. The shafted window composition in the nave N wall
was inserted in 1882 by *John Prichard*. – WALL-PAINTING.
A large scene identifiable as St George slaying the dragon. Only

the horse's trappings and the diminutive princess can be easily
made out. – FONT. Large C12 tub with a roll at top and bottom,
on its original base. – STAINED GLASS. E window, 1876. Ascen-
sion between Suffer the Little Children and Feed my Sheep.
Typical rather than good. – N windows in Prichard's setting,
Good Shepherd and King David. Signed and dated
W. F. Dixon, 1882. An early work by a firm which went on to
do more spectacular things in the county later. David, singing
with gusto and brandishing his harp, is an endearing figure.
   In the CHURCHYARD, the four-stepped base of a cross.
(BETHESDA'R FRO INDEPENDENT CHAPEL, ¾ m. SW. 1806.
   Small, gable-ended. Rendered. Three pointed-headed windows
   in the long S side. Pulpit, 'big seat' and box pews of *c.* 1820.)
GREAT HOUSE, facing the church from the E. Built in its present
   form for the Rev. Iltyd Nicholl, rector from 1699 to 1733.
   Handsome and unusual façade, behind a walled forecourt with
   big vases on the gatepiers. Symmetrical, rendered white, three-
   storeyed, of three bays, under three unequal gables, the smallest
   in the middle. The gabled frontage must have been dictated by
   the incorporation of an earlier, probably C17, range at r.-angles,
   to the S, the gable end of which contributes the r. gable. Sash
   windows, the thin glazing bars a later modification. Prominent,
   symmetrically placed, lead hopper heads and down-pipes.
   Semicircular hood to the door, on handsome carved brackets
   and with stylized plasterwork foliage on the semi-dome. Contemporary panelling in several rooms, and staircase with turned
   balusters. Also, in the first-floor and second-floor S rooms,
   plaster ceilings with rectangular borders and oak-leaf sprigs.
MALEFANT CASTLE, SE of the church, visible behind modern
   cottages. Two walls of a tower house of the C13 or later,
   standing over 20 ft (6.1 metres) high.

9070   LLANMIHANGEL/LLANFIHANGEL

2 Place and church form a romantic group, rising out of water
   meadows in a remote corner of the Vale, the one above the road,
   the other below. Both are exceptionally irregular in form, and both
   were designed with defensibility in view, the church obviously so,
   the house not so obviously. A group of big barns to the E.

ST MICHAEL AND ALL ANGELS. Fortifiable C15 W tower, with
   splendidly big arrow loops in the W and S walls, and, added to
   the N, a two-storey cross-gabled projection with another loop.
   Saddleback top to the tower corbelled in all four directions.
   The moulded plinth, returning for the W doorway, and the
   two-light window over, establish the date of the tower. Nave
   and lower chancel, with a trefoiled lancet, rebated externally
   for a shutter, in the nave N wall, probably of the early C14.
   Otherwise C15 and early C16 features. The two-light Tudor
   window in the N wall of the chancel was the E window until
   Kempson moved it in his restoration of 1888–9. C19 S porch.
   The round-headed chancel arch, rendered and featureless, may

be evidence of the earlier origin of the building. The fine nave roof is of the C15, arch-braced with wind-braces in two tiers and a collar purlin. Its two E bays are boarded, to form a celure over the rood. – FONT. Square bowl with chamfered angles. – MONUMENTS. Griffith Grant †1591. A throw-back to a C14 formula. Recumbent effigy of a civilian holding a heart, the lower part of his body hidden by the lid of the tomb-chest, which is incised with a cross and inscription. – Sir Humphrey Edwin, wife and son. Tall hanging wall-monument erected after 1722. Of London quality, and indeed Sir Humphrey had served as Lord Mayor of London. White and grey veined marble. Urn backed by knotted drapery, between fluted Corinthian pilasters. Segmental cornice, with cherubim and shield of arms above. – Charles Edwin and wife †1777. Clearly meant to match, but without the means to do so.

LLANMIHANGEL PLACE. An early C16 manor house, extended and embellished later in the century. The forecourt wall and gatehouse, and a small C17 W wing have all disappeared, but what survives is complete in itself, delightful to look at and a challenge to understand.* The original build consists of quite a long two-storey, S-facing, rectangular block. The hall, much the largest room, is at first-floor level and rises into the roof space. This was built by James Thomas, owner from c.1528 to after 1551. Later, but not much later, the appearance of the house was transformed by the addition of a short SE range with a polygonal, three-storey, gabled turret in the angle with the hall, and a NW range with a square, three-storey gabled turret over-riding the NW corner. (C19 battlements to the latter.) In both phases the windows are mullioned under hoodmoulds, with arched lights and hollow chamfers. Three-light windows bent across the angles of both turrets. Several windows, especially those of the hall and in the NW range, were renewed in the C19 in enlarged form with transoms. Doorways chamfered with four-centred heads. The two internal doorways in the rooms beneath the hall, with two-centred heads, presumably belonged to an earlier house on the site. The entrance doorway and two internal doorways at ground-floor level have drawbar sockets. So defence was a concern for James Thomas. This may also explain the siting of the hall on the upper floor. The present access to the hall at its W end up a broad, straight flight of steps cannot be original, and may be of the C19. Ceiling beams at the upper level show that at first there must have been a full-size room W of the hall. Possibly the stair replaces a narrower mural stair in the same position. The hall itself was 44 from the start a show room and is one of the all-too-rare Elizabethan interiors in the county to survive with its decorative features intact. Splendid chimneypiece, the embattled overmantel displaying six heraldic shields, which relate to James Thomas. Panelling with small fields and a carved and pierced

*I am grateful to Mr David Baer for showing me his recent discoveries in the fabric, some of which require revision of the Royal Commission's conclusions.

frieze, at the E end supporting heraldic beasts which hold a shield of arms of Elizabeth I. Steeply canted plaster ceiling enriched with thin ribs forming interlocking squares, lozenges and circles. Similar plasterwork in the window bays at the E end of the hall, that to the S in the polygonal turret, that to the N continued between the projections for hall fireplace and mural stair. The room E of the hall is lined with early C18 fielded panelling. In the SE wing an upper doorway in the S wall reveals an intention to extend the wing, never pursued.

The main, seven-bay BARN, built at the same time as the house, is one of the biggest and most completely surviving early barns in the county. A four-bay STABLE was added to the S *c.* 1600, with mullioned upper windows making a civilized show towards the house. In poor condition at the time of writing. Too important to be allowed to collapse.

4090   LLANRHIDIAN

The church stands on the hillside overlooking the marshes, to the W of the irregular village green, which is punctuated by two standing stones.

ST RHIDIAN AND ST ILLTYD. The chancel, which one sees first, shows Perp evidence: the tentatively traceried three-light E window and the two trefoil-headed S twin-lighters. Blocked N doorway. The W tower dominates by its height and by the overtopping SE stair-turret, a rarity in these parts and clearly an addition. No buttresses, of course, but a battered plinth and the usual crowning corbel table and battlements. Belfry openings to the E only, of indeterminate, probably C15, date. The tower has a vaulted ground storey, lit by three lights of similar date. The nave and S porch were rebuilt 1856–8 by *R. K. Penson* in an E.E. style. Roofs renewed 1899–1901. – STAINED GLASS. Chancel windows all of 1901 by *Jones & Willis*. Their feeble draughtsmanship is readily recognizable. – PAINTINGS. Four copies of Old Masters in the chancel. Virgin and Child of C17 Spanish type, Crucifixion attributed to '*Fiamingo*', Entombment, after Federigo Barocci, Adoration of the Shepherds, copied from a print after Raphael. – CARVED STONE (in the porch). C9 or C10. One face is carved with two exceedingly primitive and stylized figures standing between even more stylized rampant animals. The Royal Commission tentatively identifies them as St Paul and St Anthony meeting in the desert, a subject popular in contemporary Irish art. The stone seems to have been intended as a lintel, and for this too there are Irish parallels.

At OLDWALLS, a hamlet ½m. SW, EBENEZER CALVINISTIC METHODIST CHURCH. Dated 1852. Entered at the gable end, so three long, round-headed side windows face the road. Railed yard.

WEOBLEY CASTLE, 1½m. NW. One of the best-preserved fortified manor houses in Glamorgan, 'manerium batellatum', as it was described in 1440. It stands on the edge of the escarpment overlooking the marshes of the Llwchwr Estuary, and anyone who views the castle from the lower slopes can see it almost as it would have looked 500 years ago, the walls rising full-height to the corbel table, only the battlements being broken away. A branch of the de la Bere family owned Weobley Castle from 1304. The two main building phases belong to the early decades of the C14. Improvements for a new owner, Sir Rhys ap Thomas, were put in hand at the end of the C15.

The visitor approaches from the SW. The most seriously defensive feature was the rectangular tower at the SW angle with walls 7 ft (2.13 metres) thick, much thicker than those elsewhere in the building. But since this does not survive to any great height, it is the weak, indeed virtually nonexistent, defences of the entrance gateway to the W which seem of principal significance. Entrance doorway, which may originally have been covered by a low porch, and above it an ogee-headed cusped lancet. The entrance wall is continuous with the shallow addition to the W of the SW tower, where the cusped lancet has a two-centred head: the two forms of window lights seem to have been used interchangeably in both early building phases. The two-storey chamber block at the NW corner was built at the same time, completing what is in effect a new entrance range to the castle. The lower storey of this was later subdivided and vaulted to form two storage rooms. The chamber above is lit by a large two-light window looking E into the courtyard. It has Y-tracery and a transom. There was a similar window looking N, and a fireplace in the W wall. The outline of the large projecting fireplace hood can be traced in the masonry. Mural stair and passage to a latrine in the S wall. The chamber communicated with the SW angle of the hall.

The HALL, even in its roofless state, remains an impressive room. This belongs to the earlier of the two early C14 phases. External toothing reveals the intention to continue its N wall further W at full height, and it seems likely that the present entrance-and-chamber range constitutes a scaling down of over-grand ambitions. The upper end of the hall is marked by a large rectangular recess in the W wall, presumably for panelling or some other mark of distinction for the dais. The large window which was intended to illuminate the dais from the N has been completely blocked up to serve as a fireplace. The main body of the hall was lit from a well-preserved window in the E wall, with two tall ogee-headed lights with a transom. Circular stair-turret at the N angle here rising full-height and preserving its doorway on to the leads of the hall roof. Beneath the hall, the KITCHEN, with fireplaces in the N and E walls. The most remarkable feature here is the three broad rectangular windows in the N wall, with window seats, providing a comfortable view of the estuary. The PORCH to the hall and the projecting block to the E, providing rooms at two upper levels, show some early C14 evidence, but the entrance doorway and most windows are of the C16. Plain square-headed lights.

Superimposed blocked doorways suggest drastic remodelling here. The E range is also composite. Its N half, built two-storeyed, was converted to three storeys when the massive polygonal latrine tower was added at the NE corner. Main upper-floor chamber with c14 fireplaces in the N and E walls, and a third in the later S wall. The S half of the c14 E range can never have been completed, as the toothing at the upper level in the E wall shows. Immediately to the E of the building, remains of a circular limekiln, constructed in connection with this unfinished building programme.

The short central section of the S range is attributed to Sir Rhys ap Thomas. Much ruined. There may have been a first-floor chapel here (part of an enriched piscina has been excavated in this area).

CEFN BRYN. On Cefn Bryn, c. 2 m. S, a level ridge nearly 4 m. (6.44 kilometres) long, bracken-covered in summer, are a Neolithic chambered tomb, Arthur's Stone (see below), and fifteen round cairns, probably Bronze Age burial or ritual monuments. Over 200 smaller piles of stone clustering on better drained soil probably result for the most part from stone clearance associated with ancient agriculture. At least eleven 'burnt mounds', accumulations of burnt stone which may derive from ancient cooking activity, lie alongside streams. Most of the monuments are inconspicuous, but those around Arthur's Stone are easy to find and reward a visit.

ARTHUR'S STONE, a chambered tomb which is one of the best-known archaeological monuments in Wales, has not been scientifically excavated. What can be seen is a huge 40-ton (40.6-tonne) boulder capstone broken in two, underpinned by upright stones which form two low chambers. These lie in a hollow surrounded by a low stony spread 75 ft 6 in. (23 metres) across, probably the remains of a cairn. It has been suggested that the hollow was formed by mining beneath the boulder in order to insert the underpinning uprights and thus create the chambers. There is a scattered group of around seventy STONE CLEARANCE PILES on rising ground SE of Arthur's Stone.

GREAT CARN, W of Arthur's Stone. A Bronze Age burial cairn 67 ft 6 in. (c. 20 metres) across which has been rebuilt subsequent to excavation. Central grave pit datable around the mid second millennium B.C., and traces of a Neolithic settlement datable to the mid third millennium B.C.

p. 23   Two early Bronze Age RING CAIRNS downslope N of Great Carn lie 72 ft (22 metres) apart (SS 490 907). The S cairn consists of a stone bank, c. 34 ft (10.4 metres) across, around a central open area. The N entrance is flanked by two boulders, the S entrance was blocked in antiquity. Excavation found a small central pit containing charcoal and a minute amount of cremated bone. The N cairn, 35 ft 6 in. (10.8 metres) across, has an inner boulder kerb, which originally demarcated an open area approached through a S-facing entrance. A pit containing only charcoal was revealed against the inner face of the kerb. In antiquity the entrance was blocked by boulders and the interior filled with stone. In the gully w of the ring cairns is a crescent-shaped mound of BURNT STONE alongside the stream, an example of a 'cooking' mound.

CILIFOR TOP, $\frac{3}{4}$ m. E. A good example of an Iron Age HILLFORT with defences which follow natural contours. Best seen from a distance, for example either from the B4295 E of Llanrhidian, or from the top of Cefn Bryn to the s. The line of the two main banks on the NW and sw flanks of the hill is visible. The inner rampart continues around the entire hilltop. Additional outer defences to the NW and sw have been eroded by cultivation. Single entrance through the w defences. Indications of building platforms at the NW end of the enclosure, which is 7.2 acres (2.9 hectares) in extent, and a medieval RINGWORK inserted in the sw corner.

LLANSAMLET

6090

Llansamlet was for long the centre of heavy industry on the E bank of the Lower Swansea Valley. The Mansels of Margam Abbey were mining for coal here at the beginning of the C18. By c. 1840 Llansamlet collieries were producing up to 70,000 tons (71,120 tonnes) of coal per annum. Later in the C19 the smelting of copper and zinc (spelter) took over, the latter until the 1960s. Now a vast industrial estate stretching between the village and the bank of the River Tawe takes their place. Modern settlements have developed on the higher ground at Trallwn and Winsh-wen to the SE, leaving Llansamlet itself little more than a long, curving village street, with the church at a bend halfway along.

ST SAMLET. Erected c. 1878–9, a magnum opus of a local architect, *H. Francis Clarke* of Briton Ferry, with a SE tower of 1914–15 by *Glendinning Moxham*. Rock-faced sandstone with Bath stone dressings. The N view is one of enormous length, the lean-to aisle continuing unbroken to the E end. Awkwardly prominent clerestory windows. Inside, the huge naturalistic leaf capitals, on short, round piers, are equally awkward and prominent. Portrait heads on the hoodmould stops. – IMMERSION FONT of c. 1879. Of the more sophisticated sort with two flights of steps down, so that the officiating minister need not get his feet wet. – STAINED GLASS. Chancel E, Good Shepherd among heraldic grisaille, c. 1879. – Nave W, saints with scenes below. 1924. – N aisle, naive semi-abstract. 1986, signed by *Timothy Lewis*. – s aisle, entirely abstract two-lighter. 1980. Also a Joseph/Jesus typological window of 1990, signed *C.M.*

BETHEL CONGREGATIONAL CHURCH, Bethel Road. 1879–80 by *J. Thomas* of Mumbles. Pedimented façade with round-headed windows in the standard pattern for that date. Rock-faced sandstone with green ashlar dressings. Fine interior, with substantial timberwork. Galleries all round, dipping over the pulpit. Flat ceiling with two roses set in a geometrical pattern with thin Adamesque swags. Gigantic organ of 1932.

TABOR CALVINISTIC METHODIST CHAPEL, Nantyffin Road.

Dated 1878. Pennant sandstone and Bath stone ashlar. In a
Lombardic style. Long, narrow side windows and outer panels,
the façade subdivided by ashlar pilasters of exceeding thinness
which carry arches rising into the pedimental gable. Perhaps
this should be seen as an underpowered derivative of Tabernacl
Chapel at Morriston, Swansea (*see* p. 624), of half a decade
earlier.

GWERNLLWYNCHWITH ENGINE HOUSE, $\frac{3}{4}$ m. ENE, on the S
side of the M4. Tall and narrow ruined housing, of Pennant
sandstone rubble with openings dressed in red brick, shaped to
house a rotary winding-engine. It was built between 1772 and
1782, and so predates those built for colliery winding by James
Watt. For this reason the ruin is of the greatest importance to
the history of technology. It was out of use by 1786.

SCOTT'S PIT, 1 m. NE. Impressive Pennant sandstone Cornish
ENGINE HOUSE visible N of the M4. The pit was sunk 1817–
19 by a London solicitor, John Scott. It proved unremunerative,
and Scott and his partners sold it to the local coal-owner
C. H. Smith, who worked it until *c.* 1842. In 1872 the engine
house was recommissioned, but only for pumping and draining
the newly developed Cae Pridd Colliery. It remained in use for
this purpose intermittently until 1930. The engine house was
restored 1976–80 and taken into the possession of Swansea
City Council. In addition there are the foundations of a hay-
stack boiler (*c.* 1820) and of a Cornish boiler (*c.* 1872), the
foundations of a stack for furnace ventilation and the site of the
500-ft (150-metres)-deep shaft, now capped in concrete. A
tramroad ran from Scott's Pit to a shipping place at White Rock
on the River Tawe.

SMITH'S CANAL. Built by the coalowner John Smith 1783–5 to
replace the wagon-way of Chauncey Townsend as the principal
means of transporting coal raised in his Llansamlet colliery to
the river. It consisted of a single pound, 3 m. (4.83 kilometres)
long, and remained in use until the 1850s. Two sections have
survived in reasonable condition, one above the church, the
other beside the smelting works at Upper Bank, Middle Bank
and White Rock, Swansea (*see* pp. 612–14), a section which
includes an interesting cut-and-cover tunnel. The S terminus
was at Foxhole (*see* Swansea: St Thomas, p. 617).

ARCHES, 1 m. E. Four unusual hump-backed arches spanning
a cutting on *Brunel*'s South Wales Railway main line as it
runs between Neath and Swansea. They may have been intended to permit steeper sides in the cutting and so save on the
cost of excavation.

BEAUFORT TINPLATE WORKS, 1½ m. SW. Close to the E bank
of the River Tawe, on the site of the Fforest copper mills.
Established in 1860 by John Jones Jenkins (later Lord
Glantawe), a figure of major importance in the local tinplate
trade. Sold by Jenkins in 1877, and closed in 1946. Two main
blocks survive with various ancillary buildings. The annealing
house, to the E, is built of stone and is dated 1874 on the cast
copper-slag keystone of the main access arch. The tinning bays

of the w block have been rebuilt in replica form, and a water
wheel has been re-erected.

PWLL MAWR (GREAT PIT), 1½m. sw. A monumental rusticated pump-bob wall remains of a pumping-engine house of
c. 1881, on open ground E of the main railway line. This marks
the first deep shaft exploiting the Great, or Six-Foot Seam at
depth on the lower eastern valley, sunk c. 1772 by John Smith
on the site of a borehole made by Chauncey Townsend c. 1770.
The shaft, 450 ft (137 metres) deep, was worked until 1828
when a disastrous explosion led to its closure. In 1872 it was
acquired by Evan Matthew Richards and reopened in 1881,
only to close again c. 1893. The course of Townsend's wooden
RAILWAY can be seen on the hillside beside the pit.

LLANSANNOR/LLANSANWYR   9070

ST SENWYR. A small church with a diminutive w tower, crowned
by a saddleback roof gabled in both directions. Nave and
chancel of equal height and width but of two different builds.
E window of two trefoil-headed lights, perhaps late C13. Other
early openings are so small and simple as to be virtually impossible to date. The deep s porch is an addition, its entrance arch
of latest medieval form, of such a depressed profile as to be
barely pointed, set under a heavy rectangular hoodmould.
Modern square-headed Perp windows of Bath stone, part of an
unrecorded C19 restoration.

Inside, a similar C19 opening up, by means of a widely
splayed chancel arch. The best feature is the late medieval nave 28
roof, with wind-braces in three tiers and arch-braces carried
down on to short, crudely moulded wall-shafts. A collar purlin
links the undersides of the arch-braces, with carved bosses at
the intersections. A delightful design, and a speciality of this
part of the county. – FONT. Plain octagonal tub on a square
base. C14? – REREDOS. 1926 by *F. E. Howard*. – PULPIT,
CHOIR STALLS. 1910, Perp. – WALL-PAINTING. An inde-
cipherable fragment, red on white, high on the nave s wall. –
MONUMENTS. An extremely fine armoured knight, his legs
crossed, datable by the armour to c. 1400. – Edward Eustance
†1708. Rustic classical tablet. Approximation to Ionic pilasters. – A pair of tablets to members of the Truman family,
dates of death 1742 onwards, but with fine, typical early C19
lettering.

LLANSANNOR COURT. Undated, which is a pity. The house
belonged to the Gwyn family, at the peak of its local power for
the fifty years from c. 1575. During that period the main range
must have been built, its s front one of the earliest attempts at
symmetry in the county. Five bays, two storeys with a full-
height projecting central porch completely integrated with the
design. There is some subtlety in the way the windows are
arranged, four-lighters below, slightly shorter three-lighters
above, and small two-lighters in the gables. And there is a deft

designer behind details such as the delicate ball finials, and the window labels with their square stops. Four-centred porch arch, arched lights to all the windows. Cross-wing to the l. projecting deeply forward. This is identifiable as an earlier structure by its arch-braced roof. So its windows, identical with those on the main range, but arranged with no respect for symmetry, must be insertions. Grey local Lias limestone, with remains of the original white render.

The porch enters into what was the screens passage of the HALL, which opens single-storeyed to the l. Plain but handsome ceiling of moulded timber beams and moulded plaster panels. Here the chimneypiece displays knowledge of a classical idiom, with a mantelshelf in the form of an entablature on brackets. A simpler chimneypiece in the same style on the floor above. At the E end of the roof space a short fragment of a plaster frieze of prancing lions, evidence perhaps of a top-storey gallery.

In the later C19 the house was tactfully doubled in depth.

At COURT FARM, E of Llansannor Court, a contemporary eight-bay BARN, one of the largest in the Vale.

COURT DRIVE, W of Llansannor Court. A reticent but uncompromisingly modern development of eight single-storey, flat-roofed houses. White walls, strip windows under black eaves. Built in the 1970s by *Hird & Brooks* (cf. Dinas Powys).

LLANSANNOR HOUSE, 1 m. NW. Two-storeyed, rendered, with a veranda on tapering timber posts wrapped round the short entrance and long garden sides. Deep eaves on double-scroll brackets. Pedimental gables, one above the entrance, two to the garden. This suave Regency composition appears to date from after 1843. The rockface which looms over the entrance front of the house must have appealed to early Victorian romantic sensibilities.

LLANTRISANT

The village occupies a saddle between two hilltops, the most dramatic inhabited hilltop site in the county. The church is visible from the S for many miles. During the Middle Ages Llantrisant was, not surprisingly, a bone of contention between the Norman invaders and the indigenous Welsh. In 1246 Richard de Clare, lord of Glamorgan, began to build a strong castle here, and founded a borough town beside it. By the early C16 the castle was in ruins and used only as a prison. All too little of it survives today. Nor did the borough develop into a modern town. Indeed, under the Municipal Corporation Act of 1883 it eventually lost its rights and privileges as a borough. Today only the central market square, the Bull Ring, distinguishes it from any other village. But its situation, between the escarpment to the S and its great common to the N, has done more than anything else to preserve a village scale. Much recent housing scatters down to the s, and spills on to the low ground, but the new town planned in 1967 has not materialized.

St Illtyd, St Wonno and St Dyfodwg. This was originally a major Norman church. What one sees, however, is a massive C15 w tower, buttressed outer walls probably of the same period, a s porch perhaps of the C17, and a N porch, fenestration and the entire interior by *J. Prichard*, 1872–4, which most regrettably swept away the five-bay nave arcades with their cylindrical columns. Prichard's work is sympathetic to the remaining medieval fabric but wherever possible uses his favourite forms of *c.* 1300. The tower deserves analysis. It is of only two stages, on a moulded plinth and with a polygonal NE turret. Small Tudor belfry openings. The most interesting feature is the diagonal buttresses rising by four set-offs and crowned by stumpy pinnacles, imitated perhaps from the tower at Llanblethian (q.v.). Remains of gargoyles. Battlements. Tower arch of depressed four-centred outline with continuous mouldings. Responds and w doorway formed by *Seddon & Carter*, 1893–4. – FONT. An exceptional piece, octagonal, each face bearing a large disc enclosing chip-carved stars. Of the C15, like those at Llanharry and Pyle (qq.v.). (– IMMERSION FONT. 1894, under the tower.) – PULPIT. 1967 by *George Pace*. – CHANDELIER. Brass, with two tiers of branches. C18, of Bristol make. – STAINED GLASS. E window, Crucified Christ flanked by Mary and John. 1873 by *Morris & Co.*, the figures, set against a background of quarries, designed by *Burne-Jones*. The glass was commissioned by Prichard, to commemorate his ancestors, who had lived at Llantrisant. Also of the time of the restoration, both the s aisle SE window, 1872 by *G. H. Cook*, with small, charmingly Arthurian figures of SS Peter, Paul and John, and the chancel s windows, Charge to Peter and Noli me Tangere, more conventional for the date, attributable to *Clayton & Bell*. – MONUMENTS. Mid-C13 effigy of a warrior in a tunic drawing a sword, very worn. Identified as a lord of Meisgyn, one of the principal Welsh opponents of the de Clares. – Dr Richard Thomas and others. Gibbsian tablet erected before 1756. – Anne Thomas † 1843. Tablet with draped urn, signed *Porter*.

PENUEL AND TRINITY PRESBYTERIAN CHURCH OF WALES. 83 On the main road just below the village centre. 1826. Of the long-wall façade type, its characteristic pattern of openings emphasized by generous rusticated quoins and surrounds. Internally, the long central windows flank the pulpit, which backs on to the entrance wall. Galleries with canted angles line the other three sides. Plain cast iron supports. Raked seating. The pulpit and 'big seat' must belong to the improvements made in 1886. Likewise the ceiling with plaster cornice and three big rosettes.

CASTLE, on the high ground E of the church, at the crest of the hill. The 30-ft (9-metre)-high chunk of Pennant sandstone masonry was part of a cylindrical tower, the NW segment of a

circular KEEP, which was the main strength of Richard de
Clare's castle, built *c.*1246–52, probably with a gatehouse
added in 1297. Leland in the 1530s refers to the 'great and high'
tower and to other towers as well. Of these there is virtually no
trace. Three short stretches of a faceted curtain wall stand a
few feet high to the S of the keep. The Town Hall stands in the
large outer ward to the N. The Royal Commission suggests that
Llantrisant Castle began as a C12 ringwork, and that the
de Clare castle, built in more than one phase, was closely
comparable to Castell Coch (q.v.).

TOWN HALL. Built, it is said, in 1773 at the expense of Lord
Mountstuart. Just a plain four-bay block, windowless on the S
side, reached up a broad flight of steps and under the wide
segmental arch of a gabled porch. His lordship could hardly
have provided less for his pocket borough.

The focal point of Llantrisant is BULL RING, a miniature square.
It is now dominated by MODEL HOUSE, a craft and design
centre of *c.*1989 by *Graham Pryce Thomas* of Pontypridd. Three
tall storeys, the front part new, the rear a reused C19 glove
factory and workhouse, all capped by a clumsy roof with glazed
transverse gables. Miniature porch with clock. In front stands
the STATUE of Dr William Price (1800–93), Chartist and self-
styled Druid (*see* Glyntaff), in a suitably melodramatic posture.
Signed *P. W. Nicholas*, 1981, and made of glass-reinforced
plastic with stone aggregate. On the N side of Bull Ring SWAN
STREET leads to the church. Here a row of modest white
cottages, a humble CHAPEL and its graveyard right beside the
churchyard gate. On the S side of Bull Ring GEORGE STREET
runs up past the bald POLICE STATION of 1876 (where a lane
leads to the Town Hall and castle) to the PARISH OFFICES,
dated 1873, a handsome three-bay front with rusticated pointed
windows – not something Prichard can have approved of.

At the S end of HIGH STREET, halfway down the hill,
TOLL-HOUSE COTTAGE, a simple two-storey cottage dated
1785. This further evidence of the C18 borough town deserves
to survive.

CASTELLAU, 2½ m. N. Suave, white Regency villa, as seen from
the S. Six-bay façade with central doorway. Full-height bows
round the corners to E and W. Shallow slated roof on deep
cantilevered eaves. Of the cast iron veranda only the central
section remains. Remodelled from a C17 three-unit house,
probably for Edmund Traherne before 1807. Fine contemporary INTERIOR, a square entrance hall, with bow-ended
dining room to the r. To the l. bow-ended drawing room, a
handsome pair of Ionic columns with yellow scagliola shafts
across the bow. White marble chimneypiece, sleeping Cupid
on the central tablet. Beyond the entrance hall, semicircular
cantilevered staircase, a paragon of delicacy. Cast iron balustrade of Pompeian balusters alternating with vertically
symmetrical scrollwork.

CASTELLAU INDEPENDENT CHAPEL, 1 m. S of the house.
It is dated 1877. Toy-like, and naively ambitious, with its

Y-traceried, transomed lancets and angle pinnacles. Unexpectedly substantial interior, galleried on three sides, a polygonal pulpit against the fourth, backed by a decorative plaster panel, a frame for the preacher, as it were.

LLANTRISANT COLLIERY, 1¼ m. NW, to the S of Ynysmaerdy. Substantial post-1918 buildings in a unified style with large segmental openings. Impressive eleven-bay COMMON ENGINE HALL, like that at Penallta Colliery, Gelligaer (q.v.), now in agricultural use. It formerly housed two electric winding-engines and various compressors, and possibly incorporated a fan house at the S end. Services basement of rubble-stone with a railway access arch in the N gable end. Rendered brickwork above with red brick dressings. Pilasters flank each bay, externally as decoration and internally as supports for the surviving travelling-crane. Tall cast iron lights in each bay, except in the central section of the E elevation, where a five-bay arcade opens into an aisle that formerly contained electrical switchgear. Circular gable windows and roof with braced steel angle trusses and steel battens. The position of the twin mineshafts to the E is indicated by the two penultimate blind bays, which have small openings for the winding-cables up to the headstocks.

The N BUILDING is now used as a cattleshed. Eight bays long. Pennant rubble walls intended for render with red brick dressings. Cast iron windows with 'keystones' of brick, and cast iron sills. Steel roof trusses. Stores or a compressor house.

The S WINDING-HOUSE is similar in style but smaller and built on a different axis into the valley side. Three E double openings for winding-cables from a shaft 115 ft (35 metres) to the E. In the gables circular louvred openings with 'keystones', and below them central doorways flanked by large windows and openings into the basement. Four light steel angle roof trusses.

Impressive arched entrance of the former COLLIERY OFFICES SW of Ynysmaerdy farmhouse. Deep arched hood supported on corbels. Roughly plastered rubble-stone wall-panels and smooth projecting pilasters and dressings.

Much altered former COLLIERY WORKSHOP, S of the farmhouse, also with steel roof trusses.

ROYAL MINT, 1 m. N. 1967–8. Long, low blocks, largely windowless, in spite of the attentions of *Sir Frederick Gibberd & Partners*.

LLANTRITHYD/LLANTRIDDYD

0070

The glory has not altogether departed from Llantrithyd. The church and the tattered ruins of the mansion stand almost alone on the gently sloping hillside, yet inside the church more than one glorious object remains.

ST ILLTYD. The usual plan, chancel, nave with S porch, and unbuttressed W tower. The round-headed tower arch, formed without the benefit of dressed stone, is impossible to date. In the nave large lancets and two-light windows with cusped

Y-tracery, much renewed but suggesting an early C14 date. Also the sills of two other N windows, signs of thorough remodelling at some stage. Chancel arch of the C14, with continuous mouldings, a big wave and a hollow. Image niche with cusped lancet head. The chancel was largely rebuilt in 1656, the date on the E window. This, with its three arched lights under a hoodmould, the central light stepped up higher than the others, is typical of churches of that date (Berwick-on-Tweed, St Gregory by St Paul's in London). Restoration of 1897 by *G. E. Halliday*. – SCREEN. Perp. Timber, painted red, blue and gold on its w face (paintwork refreshed in 1941). – FONT. An interesting piece. Of stone, octagonal with a cartouche on each face, on an octagonal stem. The most likely date for it is the mid C17. – SCULPTURE. Two early C17 alabaster armorial cartouches with Aubrey heraldry, rescued from the house. The larger one, on the w wall, is very splendid, and slightly grotesque, apparently held in place by disembodied hands and feet. It originally formed the centrepiece of the long gallery overmantel. Smaller cartouche over the S door, surmounted by mantling. – STAINED GLASS. E window, Transfiguration. Perhaps related to the restoration and refitting of the church supervised by *Halliday* in 1897. – MONUMENTS. Recumbent C14 effigy, looking as if formed of modelling clay, in a recess in the nave N wall. Of a civilian holding his heart? Square surround with blobs. – Sir Anthony Mansel and his wife Elizabeth and her parents, John and Elizabeth Basset. Erected in 1597 by the Mansels' daughter. As the monument in all its multicoloured splendour cascades down at one's feet at the entrance to the chancel, it is hard to take in its significance. But the three generations have their places, grandparents kneeling above and behind at a prayer desk between Corinthian columns, parents recumbent on the tomb-chest, children typically miniaturized below. Big obelisks in front to l. and r. – Sir John Aubrey †1700. Hanging wall-monument, the oval inscription plate surrounded by drapery and palm branches. Of fine quality. – Sir Thomas Aubrey and wife, 1788. Neoclassical hanging wall-monument with draped urn. Of equally fine quality. The stylistic contrast between these two is instructive.

In the CHURCHYARD (S of the tower) the base of a cross, Norman, arcaded. A rarity.

LLANTRITHYD PLACE. This was one of the great C16 mansions of Glamorgan, built by John Basset (†1551) and embellished in the early C17 by Sir Thomas Aubrey. Local Lias limestone with sandstone dressings. Three two-storey ranges, each *c.* 70 ft (21.3 metres) long, set angle-to-angle with one another, forming a courtyard open towards the w. Best-preserved is the N range with windows of three and four arched lights under hood-moulds. A straight joint in the middle of the N wall shows that the house's exceptionally rationalized plan, though presumably intended from the start, was not completed in one campaign. The centre (E) range was occupied by hall and parlour with a long gallery over, hall and gallery both lit at the N end by huge

C17 six-light windows with transoms. (This wall has fallen since the Royal Commission made its survey in the 1970s.)

The gabled elevation facing the church belongs to the early C17, when the hall range was doubled in depth making provision for a spacious open-well staircase.

(GARDENS. s of the churchyard, two walled terraces, constructed probably in the late C16, largely intact though much overgrown. Below them rectangular fishponds linked by a stone-lined stream. From the SE corner of the house a raised walk led down past the ponds and up to a vantage platform on the other side of the valley.)

(CASTLE, 200 yds E. Slight traces of a ringwork datable to the beginning of the C12. The foundations of a six-bay aisled hall have been found in the NE angle of the enclosure, together with a coin hoard proving that it was in use in the early 1120s.)

CARMEL CHAPEL, ½ m. NE. Built 1834 and 'restored' 1877, since when nothing has changed, not even the gas lamps. The structure, a gable-ended rectangle two bays deep with rectangular side windows, is presumably of the earlier date, the remarkable trompe-l'oeil frontage of the latter. Below, the squared Lias limestone blocks and yellow brick dressings are real, but the rendered upper half has been skilfully coloured to imitate these materials. w gallery, pews and pulpit all of a piece.

LLANTWIT FARDRE/LLANILLTUD FAERDREF   0080

ST ILLTYD. What one sees first is the little w tower dated 1636, virtually featureless but with a saddleback roof. Nave and lower chancel, said to have been built c. 1525 – see one renewed N window in the chancel and the three-light s window, now internal. N windows in the nave with Y-tracery, probably related to a restoration in 1874, and one small blocked earlier one. Plate-traceried E window, datable 1870 by a rain-water head. The church was drastically remodelled and enlarged towards the s 1972–4. Segmental plaster ceiling in the nave. Heavily rendered walls, producing a sheltering, almost cave-like effect. Rendering of the tower also. – STAINED GLASS. Nave NW, Christ in Majesty by *Frank Roper*, 1974. – s windows 1989, a timid reaction, back to sentimental naturalism.

TOMEN-Y-CLAWDD, ¾ m. E. At Church Village, in the middle of a housing estate, NW of the A473. A tree-clad but otherwise well-preserved C12 motte, completely encircled by its ditch.

HEALTH CENTRE, Central Park, Church Village. 1986–7 by the *Welsh School of Architecture* (project architect *Helen Hollis*). Turning its single-storey back towards the road. The front block two-storeyed of five bays under a pitched roof, the centre projecting, gabled and glazed. Brick walling, grey with thin bands of yellow and red, reminiscent of late Victorian villas.

EAST GLAMORGAN GENERAL HOSPITAL, ½ m. s. A large, symmetrical group spreading across the hillside and crowned by a tall, white tower. Brown brick otherwise, long two-storey ranges terminating in glazed bows. Pitched roofs. Aware of Modernism but hesitating to embrace it. Designed by *Bradshaw, Gass & Hope* of Bolton, Lancashire, who won a competition in 1936, and largely built in 1938–9. Brought into use as a Royal Air Force hospital during the Second World War, and officially opened in 1948.

9060   # LLANTWIT MAJOR/LLANILLTUD FAWR

ST ILLTYD. The largest parish church in Glamorgan, complex in its history and puzzlingly complicated in appearance. Elderly palm trees in the churchyard add to the initial bewilderment. The origin of the present fabric belongs in the C12, as the font most obviously suggests. The remarkable group of Celtic crosses takes the history of the site back into the C9, recording royal burials in the monastic church, which by tradition was founded by St Illtyd as early as *c.* A.D. 500.

The building consists of four main parts, a chancel (formerly with S chapel), a four-bay aisled nave, with a tower rising from its W bay, a long, narrow, aisleless body, known as the 'Western church', with a two-storey S porch, and, yet further W, a ruined structure also originally two-storeyed. The 'Western church' and the lowest storey of the tower seem to have belonged to an aisleless, cruciform C12 church, remodelled in the early C13. This was relegated to the status of a sort of narthex when, late in the C13, the transepts were removed and the chancel replaced by a new aisled nave and chancel to the E. Finally, the W addition is the Ragland family chantry chapel, built in the late C15. Everything is constructed of local Carboniferous limestone; most dressings are of Sutton stone. The first restoration took place in 1888, by *G. F. Lambert* of Bridgend, and roused the ire of the S.P.A.B. In 1899 *G. E. Halliday* restored the 'Western church', and in 1905 the nave was sensitively repaired and strengthened by *Halliday* with *J. W. Rodger*, and the chancel restored by *Caröe*.

Closer examination can begin with the 'WESTERN CHURCH'. The S porch is typical of the late C13, with battered base, obtuse pointed entrance arch on vertical jambs, both of two chamfered orders, and trefoil-headed lancet above. Round-headed S doorway, so the porch must be an addition. C13 W doorway, with a filleted roll moulding and segmental head. Twin trefoiled lancets at the E end of the S wall, and another at the W end of the N wall. The 'Western church' was remodelled in the later Middle Ages: one Dec S window with a square head and reticulated tracery, and one Perp S window with a two-centred head and a hood on big, square stops, one carved with a lion's head. Handsome timber roof with major and minor arched braces, the former resting on head corbels. Collar purlin and heraldic bosses at the intersections.

The TOWER stands on four clustered piers, the major shafts keeled, the minor ones round, all rather fat, as if formed by cutting back pre-existing rectangular piers. Water-holding bases. Delicately carved capitals mixing trumpet and scroll shapes with stiff-leaf in a way characteristic of the first years of the C13 (cf. Margam Abbey chapter house, q.v.). Parts of the capitals remain *in situ* on the SW and NE piers, and further fragments are displayed S of the SW pier. The crossing arches are later, of two chamfered orders, and fit awkwardly on the piers. The trefoil-headed lancet in the S wall above suggests that this reconstruction of the tower may be contemporary with the S porch, of the late C13. The E face of the tower, within the nave, shows two crease-lines, indicating the roof-line of the early chancel at two different periods. No further evidence of the N and S transepts.

After the beauties of the crossing piers, the blunt simplicity of the later NAVE and CHANCEL comes as a surprise. The 16 rectangular piers and two-centred arches are all formed without dressed stone and plastered over. Awkwardly splayed chancel arch. The E.E. character of this part is best established by the windows, four long trefoil-headed lancets in the N wall of the chancel, and two-light plate-traceried aisle windows N and S. Three-light E windows, that of the N aisle in its original position, that of the S aisle displaced from the chancel, where a Perp window of 1905 takes its place. Dec clerestory windows. The S wall of the chancel reveals a complex history. Blocked lancet, survivor of the original fenestration, which was largely eliminated when the S aisle was extended E-wards. Two blocked arches, with a priest's door inserted, indicating that the extended S aisle had been curtailed again by *c.* 1500.

And so back to the W end. This is clearly an addition. Integral buttresses, and in the W angles remains of turning stairs to the upper level. One or two corbels for the floor timbers, and at the E end two niches, one Dec, one Perp, related to the site of the altar. At the NE corner of the chantry a two-storey square building intercommunicating with it. Fireplace at the upper level. Presumed to have been a sacristy.

The FITTINGS and MONUMENTS are numerous and of high interest. – FONT. C12. Circular bowl covered with a bold scale pattern. – IMAGE NICHE. Against the E wall of the nave S 21 arcade. An outstanding piece of early C13 sculpture. The figure of Jesse lies at the bottom, his descendants represented by heads peeping out of the deeply undercut stiff-leaf scrolls which decorate the jambs and trefoil head of the niche. Head of Christ at the apex. Moulded hood like a circumflex accent and rich foliage cross finial. What was its original site, and how did the Jesse tree theme relate to its original purpose? It has been suggested that it served as the reredos of the early C13 church. – REREDOS. Of stone. An ambitious piece, still *in situ*, built 29 integrally with the piscina in the S wall of the chancel. Mid- to late C14, Perp in conception but with many ogee arches. The reredos proper consists of a row of five image niches divided by miniature pinnacles, with an upper row of 3 + 3 niches flanking a broader central niche. Canopied double-height niches to l. and r., and in the outermost bays, doorways under triple canopied niches. Presumably the narrow space behind served as a vestry or sacristy. Top cresting largely reconstituted by *Caröe* in 1905. – SCREEN. In the W arch of the tower. Bold, of blackened iron, a typical piece by *George Pace*, 1959. Glazed in 1992. – STAIRS to upper porch. 1992 by *Graham Hardy*. – WALL-PAINTINGS. Unusually many, some of them unusually complete and enjoyable. – Chancel N wall, St Mary Magdalene, C13, and a fragmentary figure of the Virgin. – Above the chancel arch, red, white and blue perspective lozenge pattern, presumably the background to the figures of a rood, as it is now. – Nave, N wall. St Christopher, C15. Arms of James I, dated 1604. – Patches of decoration on the nave piers and elsewhere. – 'Western church', SE window splay, lozenge patterning, its function unclear. – STAINED GLASS. Chancel E, scenes from the life of Christ, 1905 by *Clayton & Bell*. – S aisle, war memorial, 1919 by the same. - MONUMENTS. The early importance of Llantwit Major is most vividly demonstrated by the group of C9 and C10 crosses now gathered together at the W end of the 'Western church'. – The 'Houelt' stone, a disc-headed cross shaft, decorated front and back with interlace, tight and well disciplined on the front, looser but still virtually symmetrical on the back. Artistically, this is the finest of all the Celtic Christian carved stones in Glamorgan, and the only one where the general similarity to Irish monuments becomes more specific, by comparison with a cross shaft at Tullylease, Co. Cork, datable 839. Inscription at the bottom explaining that Houelt had prepared the cross for the soul of Res, his father. If this is Hywel ap Rhys, King of Glywysing, †886, the stone is quite closely datable to the later C9. – Two late C9 pillar-cross shafts, both with large panels of well-controlled interlace, the taller bearing a long inscription on its main face. It records that Abbot Samson had prepared the cross for his own soul and for King 'Iuthahel', who has been identified as Ithel, King of Gwent, †848. – The 'Samson' stone. The shaft only of a cross, decorated with interlace panels in several different patterns. Several fragmentary inscriptions, and one complete one: SAMSON POSUIT HANC C[R]UCEM. Samson cannot certainly be identified with Abbot Samson (*see* above), and the shaft is datable on style to the early C10. - Cylindrical shaft decorated with bands of interlace, and crude zigzag at the bottom. Dated to the C10 or C11. – C13 coffin lid, its faceted top carved with overlapping circles, interlacing zigzag and a stylized leaf scroll. One end hollowed out to reveal the head of a priest. The inscription round the side is a warning not to tread on the tombstone. – Recumbent effigy of a priest, early C14. – Recumbent effigy of a woman, late C16. Patches of interlace on her dress, perhaps by a local craftsman under the influence of the early crosses? – Jane Seys †1747. Veined marble wall-monument with putto heads in the pediment. – John Baron Rittson Thomas †1918. Relief bust of a soldier.

In the CHURCHYARD the six steps and shaft of a CROSS,

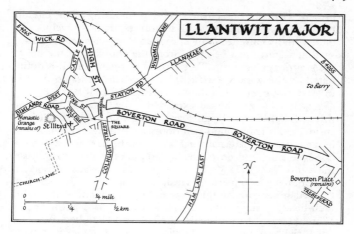

with modern head. Also, much more unusually, a CHANTRY PRIEST'S HOUSE. This stands on the s edge of the churchyard, opposite the door to the Ragland chantry where the priest officiated daily. Two-storeyed, with one heated room at each level, the upper also provided with a garderobe. The Royal Commission suspects that the windows in the N wall, though small, are too ornate to have been made for the house. Were they displaced from the church?

PERAMBULATION

Llantwit Major is a large and open-textured village, extending over a far greater area than any other in the Vale. Its growth has been conditioned in three main ways. From the mid C12 a grange of Tewkesbury Abbey established on the higher ground w of the church prevented expansion in that direction. Prosperity in the C16 and C17 produced a sustained building boom followed by two centuries of decline. In the mid C20 the Royal Air Force station at St Athan and planning policies which have encouraged the village to expand have filled in the open texture and absorbed the hamlet of Boverton ½ m. (0.8 kilometre) to the E in a built-up continuum. The remaining, somewhat fragmentary, evidence of the first two phases can be taken in by striking out in all directions from the church.

The church lies athwart a little valley, formed by a stream which flows past the w end of the churchyard. Beyond it CHURCH LANE leads up to the remains of the GRANGE of Tewkesbury Abbey. The rectangular, gabled GATEHOUSE on the r. is of the C13, with a blocked archway and doorway with two-centred heads in both the N and s walls. Trefoiled dormer window to light the upper storey. Further uphill, to the sw, the meagre remains of what must have been a splendid eleven-bay barn, also of the C13. It was unroofed as recently as 1836, so its present virtually demolished state is shocking. The circular DOVECOTE, immediately s of it, still stands up bravely, complete with its flattened conical roof and slab-covered lantern.

Now a new start must be made from the church. Up the hill to the E a triangular space, THE SQUARE, opens out. It is dominated by the WAR MEMORIAL, a disc-head cross covered in interlace, of course. On the w side, the OLD WHITE HART, a late C16 end-entry house, extended to the l. Hall window with three straight-headed lights and hollow-chamfer mouldings. Inside, the original line-up of doorway, hearth and mural stair in what was the external s gable end of the C16 house. On the opposite side, end-on to the square, another late C16 house, the OLD SWAN INN. In spite of scraped walls, this is an exceptionally complete survival, with almost all its original dressed stonework. Windows with hollow chamfers, the lights arch-headed, suggesting a slightly earlier date than for the White Hart. Most unusually, the hall and chamber above are enhanced by a double-height window bay. Entrance is into the parlour, behind the hall chimney, and the kitchen is in a wing at the back. The TOWN HALL (properly Courthouse), which faces the Old Swan Inn, is by contrast sadly over-restored. It has the same window form, with arched lights, which must date from after 1570, when the building was reported as being 'in utter ruin and decay'. Basement under the w half, a survival from the medieval courthouse. Ground floor subdivided into four units, perhaps shops. External steps at the E end up to twin doorways into the upper storey. Between them a stone sundial surrounded by crudely carved vine branches, so the roof over the steps must be modern.

From here forays can be made in several directions. To the s, in COLHUGH STREET, the best early house, some way down, is TO-HESG, of c.1600. Plastered, whitewashed – and thatched, as its name indicates. The stone surround and hood of one two-light window survives. Its main interest is that it was built as a longhouse, living quarters and byre entered through the same door. Later kitchen inserted into the byre. To the N, COMMERCIAL STREET soon leads to BETHEL BAPTIST CHURCH. Dated 1830. 'Erected for the use of the Particular Baptist'. Square plan, under a pyramid roof. The three-bay front towards the burial ground has two storeys of round-headed windows. Contemporary interior, with high-set, balustrade-fronted galleries on three sides, and the pulpit between two windows at the far end. Hat pegs. After this the street becomes HIGH STREET. Some way up, a nice pair of cottages, one each side of the road. OLD HOUSE, on the E side, is a single-unit, end-entry house of two storeys, datable c.1600, slightly extended to the l. CORNER HOUSE, on the w side, of similar plan and date, and still with its end-wall doorway, was extended when a two-unit cottage, PEAR TREE COTTAGE, was added c.1800. High Street comes to a splendid conclusion at GREAT HOUSE, a later C16 house of fine quality built curiously close to the road. Tall main block, two gables

by one, with four-square chimneystacks rising from the apex of
each gable. A four-light window for the hall, and another above
it for the great chamber. Sunk chamfers and straight-headed
lights. Three-lighters elsewhere. Lower wings to s, e and n, for
parlour, kitchen and stable, making a cruciform plan. Fine
dressed stonework here too, particularly the entrance doorway
of Sutton stone which leads into the parlour wing. This, like
many of the interior openings, has thistle stops. Altogether it is
worth pondering how a house could be so finely detailed and
yet so ineptly planned.

The return route to the village centre leads down CASTLE
STREET. The castle in question is the ruined OLD PLACE,
behind a high bramble-crowned wall on the r. It was built by
Edmund Van and his father-in-law, Griffith William, and called
'a very sumptuous newe house' in 1598. Much still stands the
full three storeys high. U-plan, but the Royal Commission
suggests that the wings, and the stair block at the back, were
additions to the original single-pile house of the 1590s. Thereafter the road continues as WEST STREET. Here WEST FARM,
a five-bay, late c18 house, with an off-centre doorway and
round-headed window over it, to demonstrate that strict symmetry still did not matter in the Vale of Glamorgan. Rough
render, with smooth rendered quoins and window surrounds,
a local speciality (cf. Pwll-y-wrach, Colwinston). PLYMOUTH
HOUSE, round the corner, facing DIMLANDS ROAD, has a
five-bay, two-storey s front, with a bargeboarded gabled dormer
over the entry bay. Timber, mullion-and-transom cross
windows. This must be an early c19 remodelling of an earlier
house. Round the corner in the w gable a two-light window
under a hoodmould demonstrates the point. (Fragments of an
arch-brace roof, suggesting an origin not later than the early
c16.) The way back to the square along WINE STREET leads
past the OLD RECTORY. Enlarged to form a school in 1878,
but retaining in the three-storey porch original early c16 mullioned windows with arched lights and hoodmoulds with square
stops.

GREAT FRAMPTON, 1 m. NE. A fine group, house and farm
buildings set in parkland. Austere mid-c18 rendered s front of
five bays and three storeys, the roof behind a plain parapet.
Central doorway under a timber pediment on brackets. This
refronts a tall c16 or c17 house, the most immediately recognizable feature of which is the NW stair projection. A long, low
service wing of the earlier period extends to the N.

BOVERTON PLACE, 1 m. E. Ruined, within what may be the
largest ivy bush in Wales. The substantial remains of a late
Elizabethan mansion, probably built by Roger Seys, Queen's
Attorney to the Council in Wales and the Marches in the 1590s.
Long hall and kitchen range, of three storeys plus gables, with
a short parlour range coming forward N-wards from the E end.
Staircase at the junction, carried up as a tower with higher
turret. (Fragments of dressed stone, many in the adjoining

Llantwit Major, Boverton Place.
Reconstruction

FARMHOUSE, show that the serried tiers of windows had straight-headed lights, sunk chamfers and small hoodmoulds.)

SW of Boverton Place, TREBEFERAD, the nucleus of what was intended to be a new village for miners resettled from the Valleys. 1936 by *T. Alwyn Lloyd* for the Welsh Land Settlement Society. Pairs of rendered, colourwashed cottages formally arranged round two culs-de-sac and a rectangular green.

THE HAM, ½ m. SE. Nothing is left of this important house of 1865 by *Sir Matthew Digby Wyatt*. (But *see* Pencoed House, Capel Llanilltern.)

DIMLANDS, ½ m. W. Only the castellated GATE LODGE of *c.* 1854 remains.

BATSLAYS, 2½ m. SE. *See* St Athan.

CASTLE DITCHES, 1 m. S. Large Iron Age coastal PROM-ONTORY FORT. Three lines of heavily overgrown banks mostly fronted by ditches define two sides of a triangular enclosure. They are most massive to the E, but continue along the N edge supplementing the natural defence provided by the steep slope. The third side is formed by sheer coastal cliffs which must have eroded the interior. The short length of bank and ditch at the W end of the enclosure appears not to be part of the main scheme. It could indicate a small earlier enclosure.

p. 29 SUMMERHOUSE CAMP, 2½ m. SE. Heavily defended coastal Iron Age PROMONTORY FORT. Three lines of closely set stony banks and ditches comprising the outer defences can be traced through woodland. Their scale is most evident on the W side, where they are crossed by a coastal path. The cliff forms the S side, which has been substantially eroded. There is an entrance through the E ramparts, beyond which is an annexe. An inner enclosure is defined by a strong bank and ditch to which no entrance is visible.

To the S of MORFA FARM, 1 m. NW, slight traces of a courtyard VILLA, possibly preceded by native structures, built in the mid C2 A.D. and finally abandoned in the second half of the C4.

LLANWONNO/LLANWYNNO   0090

St Gwynno. Extraordinarily sited in a forest clearing high on
the hills between the Rhondda and Cynon Valleys. Even more
of a surprise, the medieval walls of nave, s porch and chancel
survive. The costly restoration and remodelling of 1893 by
Halliday & Anderson is inappropriate but enjoyable. Saddleback
w bell gable carried on deep buttresses which form a porch-
like enclosure below, an ingenious arrangement. Dec windows
in chancel and nave s wall, aswirl with mouchettes, Perp nave
N windows of 1913, oversized and overcusped. Richly moulded
rere-arches to the windows inside. The rough internal stonework another Halliday mannerism. – FONT. Medieval, probably of the C14. A tub ringed by crisp mouldings. – PULPIT.
Timber, 1894. – STAINED GLASS. Throughout the building. –
E window, Christ and the Morgan family, c.1894. Nave s
windows, a set, one signed *A. Savell & Co.* – Nave N windows,
Nativity, and Resurrection between saints, also a set, unsigned
but by *R. J. Newbery*, 1913 and 1916. – MONUMENT. A small
fragment of a Celtic slab bearing an encircled cross in relief.
Set into the wall by the s door. (Another even smaller slab,
with an incised cross, forming one vertical side of a recess in
the s wall.) These remains, found in the medieval walling of
the church, though unimpressive in themselves, suggest that
Llanwonno, for all its high-lying remoteness, was an ecclesiastical site at least as early as the C9.

Gelli-wrgan, 1½m. NE. Alone on a barely accessible hillside.
A partly reconstructed longhouse, of special interest for the
datestone of 1616 associated with it.

LLWYDCOED   9000

St James, Llwydcoed Road. 1895 by *G. E. Halliday*. Hot red
brick. Domestic-looking with its large bellcote of openwork
timber structure and half-timbered s porch. Routine plan of
nave and lower chancel. Lancets, routine also. Internal walls
rendered, brick dressings including the chancel arch.

Llwydcoed Cemetery, 1½m. N. By *H.M.R. Burgess & Partners*, 1970–1. An impressive piece of modern design, if not quite
in the same class as Maxwell Fry's cemetery at Coychurch
(q.v.). Three top-lit chapels set back-to-back, their steep roofs
forming a fractured pyramid. White roughcast walls.

Scales Houses, Llwydcoed Road, E of the church. A small
development strongly influenced by Letchworth Garden City.
Rough stone walls, sweeping roofs of Westmorland slates. Sym-
metrical layout in a crescent behind two unequal terraces.
Dated 1912 on a gatepier, 1914 in the centre of the semicircle.
The architect was *E. G. Allen* of *Pepler & Allen*.

Bridge, ½m. s. Over the River Cynon, reached by a lane leading
NW from the roundabout at Gelli-isaf. A fine medium-sized
early (horse-drawn) railway bridge, dated 1834 on an E-facing

keystone. It replaces a tramroad bridge of 1804–5 on the line from Abernant Ironworks to the head of the Neath Canal. Single-span bridge of rubble sandstone with a broad semicircular arch of dressed voussoirs, set between steep wooded riverbanks. High, stepped revetment walls at both ends accommodate the 90-degree curves of the track above – see the plentifully surviving stone sleeper blocks.

LLYSWORNEY/LLYSWYRNY

9070

A compact village centred on a small green with a rectangular POUND for stray animals. The church stands at its SW corner, and, behind it up the hill, the touchingly rustic SCHOOL of 1858 and GREAT HOUSE, a sash-windowed farmhouse, on the brow.

ST TYDFIL. The usual ingredients, an unbuttressed tower, nave with S porch, lower chancel, but here the tower is central. Corbelled parapet. Tudor belfry windows. Inside, the tower arches are pointed without mouldings, differing in size and alignment. Modern squint beside the E arch, but still there are serious problems of visibility into the chancel. Though there is no datable medieval feature, these arrangements suggest an early origin for the church. So too does the crudely carved stone set in the S wall of the nave. Xs in boxes and what might be scrolled staffs. Everything else is of the insensitive restoration of 1893–4 by *Bruton & Williams* of Cardiff. – FONT. Plain, octagonal on an octagonal stem. – ALTAR RAILS. Late C17. Stout turned balusters with egg-shaped finials. – STAINED GLASS. E window, Empty Tomb. By *A. L. Moore* of London, 1908. Poor quality. – Nave N, Christ as King and as Good Shepherd. Semi-abstract, sheets of primary colours, and clear glass with thickenings like sugar lumps. 1972 by *Frank Roper*. – MONUMENT. Carne family. White and grey marble tablet, 1846.

CARNE ARMS, on the E edge of the village, beside the A4270. Drastically modernized exterior. But inside this is an excellent place to see the characteristic C16 and C17 cottage and farmhouse combination of hall fireplace and stone stairs twisting up and over it through the thickness of the wall. Similar kitchen fireplace beyond. The original entry was into the kitchen behind the hall fireplace, on the hearth-passage arrangement.

MOAT FARM, ¼m. N. The medieval moated site is now occupied by a farmhouse in origin of the late C17. The N wall characteristically windowless, with a stair projection at the W end. The original entrance was into the gable end, beside the hearth and mural stair.

NASH MANOR, ¾m. S. The seat of the Carne family. The approach from the N reveals early C19 bargeboards and sash windows given bizarre arched heads of tin. A tiny pyramid-roofed gate lodge dated 1789 leads into a tightly enclosed courtyard. Here is evidence that the origins of the house are much earlier, in the E wall a blocked three-light mullioned window at an upper level, and two more and a doorway below. Square heads and sunk chamfer mouldings. The short cross-range to the s is the earliest component, a C16 farmhouse consisting originally of two rooms below and two above. Modern entrance through a wall thickened for a mural stair. The great aggrandizement of the house in the late C16 and early C17 produced the long E range, windows of which have already been noted. A wonderful array of projecting chimneybreasts to the E. The w range, of equal length, seems to have no pre-C19 features. Inside, the interesting part of the house is at the s end of the E range. Here the large ground-floor room is wainscoted all round with small-fielded panelling. Strapwork frieze and dentilled cornice. Full-height Ionic pilasters on strapwork pedestals at the N end and flanking the chimneypiece, which has an arcaded overmantel divided by three small caryatids. This, with St Fagans Castle (q.v.), is the best display of early C17 joinery in the county, though it cannot be altogether in its original arrangement. Out of this room leads an open timber staircase, added to the s side of the cross-range. Dog gate. Turned balusters. Newels decorated with guilloche enclosing faceted ovals and rectangles. Mid-C17.

STEMBRIDGE, 1 m. w. The l. half facing the road is a mid-C17 house on a two-room plan with plain but handsome stone chimneypieces, two below, one above, subtly differentiated from one another. No original external openings. The large range to the r., incorporating a kitchen, was not added until the C18.

LOUGHOR/CASLLWCHWR

5090

Church and village (strictly, town, for borough status was granted by the lord of Gower in the early C12) under the eye of the little castle, which had been sited to command the crossing of the River Llwchwr.

ST MICHAEL, Station Road. Built on the foundations of its medieval predecessor. 1885 by *J. Buckley Wilson* of Swansea. Memorable for its outsize w bellcote. Nave with s porch, and lower chancel. Lancets. Rock-faced Pennant sandstone with Bath stone dressings. – STAINED GLASS. E window, Transfiguration. 1885, designed by the architect and made by *Heaton, Butler & Bayne*. The disposition of the design across the three lancets is certainly well managed. – MONUMENTS. Hannah Williams †1706. Slate slab, the sole survivor from the old church. – Robert Gibson †1873. Tablet, entirely Neoclassical at this late date.

CASTLE. The castle consists of a small, ruined masonry tower standing across the w scarp of a roughly rectangular mound. An outer bank wraps round it at a lower level to the w and s. The site has obvious strategic importance, on a spur overlooking the lowest fordable spot in the estuary of the River Lwchwr. So it is not surprising that excavation 1968–73 revealed a complex history. The mound was shown to be a reshaped C12 castle ringwork overlying the SE angle of the ROMAN FORT, *Leucarum*, founded in the late 70s A.D. Footings were found of a curtain wall and of a stone tower beneath the present tower.

The TOWER itself is oddly small and meagre. It is a rectangle measuring no more than 14 ft 6 in. (4.42 metres) by 11 ft (3.35 metres) internally, and is constructed entirely of Pennant sandstone slabs, without the benefit of ashlar dressings. The ground storey has in its E wall a broad doorway, with a drawbar socket. It is virtually windowless, so served as a basement. No sign of a vault. Evidence of a newel stair in the fallen chunk of masonry which was the SE angle of the tower. At first-floor level a W lancet with deep reveals and a segmental rere-arch. Similar N lancet, beside a fireplace. Garderobe in the thickness of the S wall. What remains of the top storey suggests a room at this level with similar amenities. During the C13 Loughor belonged to the de Braose lords of Gower. But the most likely builder of this modest fortified house is John Iweyn, steward of the wastrel William de Braose III, who alienated Loughor to him in 1302.

OLD TOWN HALL (No. 70 Castle Street), opposite the castle. Built in 1867 to plans made by *Henry Davies* of Llanelli. Very simple. Just a three-bay, two-storey building, of stone, entered at the upper level at the short end, where a porch on cast iron columns at the head of a flight of steps provides the stage for mayoral proclamations. Below was a police house and lock-up, above not only a courthouse but also a public reading room and library.

RAILWAY VIADUCT. Loughor Viaduct, designed by *I. K. Brunel* and *L. E. Fletcher*, carries the South Wales main line across the tidal estuary of the River Llwchwr. Constructed in 1852, and the last of Brunel's many timber viaducts to survive. It has eighteen spans each of about 40 ft (12.19 metres), supported on timber trestles and on two massive stone-faced bank seats. Originally built entirely of timber, it has since been re-decked successively by wrought iron and then steel plate girders, while an opening span of swing-bridge type at the W end was replaced by a fixed span during the C19. Parts of the substructure are original. It is not clear what reconstruction has taken place over the years. The four present longitudinal girders are supported on four timber columns which appear to emerge from water level and are presumably driven piles. They are capped at deck seating level and strapped together by horizontal members (walings) below low-water level. The walings also embrace three further vertical piles, together with raking piles at the upstream and downstream extremities, and these five members are possibly original. The similar viaduct at Barmouth, Gwynedd, is later.

MACHEN

2080

St John, Church Street. 1854–5 by *W. G. & E. Habershon*. Dec. Nave and lower chancel with the steep outline approved in the mid 1850s. Ambitiously traceried w window, but side lancets. The complicated miniature s steeple gets the architects into difficulties inside, where it is supported on a single octagonal column, against which the steps to the PULPIT also lean. Hammerbeam roof. – STAINED GLASS. e window, Charge to Peter, *c*. 1919.

PRIMARY SCHOOL, close up to the road on the s side of the A468. Built in 1908. One-storeyed, of red brick with stone dressings in unexpected places. A hamfisted effort by a local architect, *R. L. Roberts* of Abercarn.

FORGE AND TINPLATE WORKS at Ty'n-y-coedcae, 1½ m. SW. There was a forge here in the c16, and a tinplate works operated on the site 1826–86. Ruined early c19 STABLES, near the disused viaduct, are their only physical remains.

IRONWORKS. Traces of a blast furnace that was worked for a few years from 1827, in a private garden behind Waterloo Place, Ty'n-y-coedcae. The rubble-stone walls of the charging bank survive to a height of 10 ft (3 metres).

MAERDY

9090

Coal-mining started here, at the head of the Rhondda Fach, in 1875, and by 1914 four collieries had been opened. By 1941 all had closed. An ambitious development project of 1949, involving a tunnel 2½ m. (4.02 kilometres) long under the mountain to link with a colliery in the Cwmdare Valley, was intended to revive the industry for a further century. Today the pits have all gone.

The little church of ALL SAINTS, 1914 by *W. Morgan Lewis & Walters* (G.R.), and the lofty WORKMEN'S INSTITUTE of 1905 by *Edmund Williams* stand together, uneasily overlooking the approach to the cleared sites to the N, and across to the grid of late c19 terraced miners' housing on the hillside to the NW.

CASTELL NOS, 1½ m. NW. A prominent rocky outcrop, which shows signs of manmade escarpment and a ditch on the N and w sides. The Royal Commission suggests that in the late c12 it was used as a stronghold by the Welsh ruler of Meisgyn, Maredudd ap Caradog ab Iestyn.

PONT LLUEST-WEN, 2½ m. NW. Reached by a 2-m. (3.2-kilometre) walk along a gated track from the A4233 at Bryn Du. This single-arched and single-track bridge over the Afon Rhondda Fach is the oldest bridge in the Rhondda. Segmentally arched, built of snecked Pennant sandstone, probably in the early c19. The ramped roadway has stone setts between parapets that diverge widely at their ends.

MAESTEG

The major settlement in the Llynfi Valley, which grew up after
the establishment of the Llynfi Ironworks in 1837. Later on,
collieries promoted its further growth. But what makes Maesteg
remarkable is not its size, but its air of civic pride, with a triangular
central space, Talbot Street, a proud Town Hall, and handsome
council offices. Commercial Road and its continuation, Bethania
Street, form an unusually long and wide shopping street, graced
with several impressive chapels. Maesteg is, indeed, the best place
to study the work of W. Beddoe Rees, the early C 20 chapel expert,
who was a native of the town.

St David, Castle Street. A simple lancet affair of 1852–3 by
Egbert Moxham of Neath. Just a nave with N porch and W
bellcote, and a lower chancel. Pennant sandstone rubble walls
and Bath stone dressings.

St Michael and All Angels, Church Place. Built as a
memorial to Miss Olive Talbot, that bountiful benefactress to
the cause of church-building. After her death in 1894 *G. E. Halliday* immediately prepared a design for a cruciform Perp
church. Without Miss Talbot's own funding, however, this
proved unattainable. The present building, also by *Halliday*, of
1895–8, is large enough but of a drastic simplicity the architect
usually preferred to avoid. Local ashlar roughly tooled, and
dressings of green Bridgend stone ashlar, an unusual choice.
Very wide nave with passage aisles, producing sprawling proportions outside and in. Standard arcades, but a tripartite
chancel arch and also a sanctuary arch. Lancets. Encircled
quatrefoils in the clerestory. NE tower, the top stage completed
only in 1958. – (PULPIT. By *Halliday*. Green stone, pink alabaster and Irish red marble shafts.) – IMMERSION FONT. An
original fitting, at the W end of the nave. – STAINED GLASS.
Chancel E, Crucifixion above archangels, *c.* 1920, and sanctuary
S, David and Good Shepherd. Both in a florid Düreresque
style, by *R. J. Newbery*. – Nave N, Nativity, 1985 by *John Petts*.
Red. Story-book style.

St Mary and St Patrick (R.C.), Monica Street. 1906–7 by
Pugin & Pugin. Chancel and nave in one with lean-to aisles.
Perp. Rock-faced Pennant sandstone with Bath stone dressings.

88 Bethania Welsh Baptist Chapel, Bethania Street. 1908
by *W. Beddoe Rees* of Cardiff, specialist chapel designer and
author of a book on the subject, *Chapel Building*, 1903. This is
his most ambitious classical essay, in a Beaux-Arts style.
Shallow-coursed Pennant sandstone, with lavish dressings of
Portland stone. Channelled quoins overlaid with pilaster strips
define the pedimented, three-bay centre and the gallery-stair
bays to l. and r. Central Ionic columns and a Diocletian window
in the pediment impose quite a grand scale on the whole façade.
The galleried interior, to seat a thousand, is equally splendid.
The interior is reminiscent of Wren's St James Piccadilly, for
the galleries round three sides are not only carried on slender

iron shafts but in turn carry upper shafts and semicircular arches. Segmental plaster vault. Shaft caps moulded below, with swirling foliage above. Foliage corbels carry transverse arches across the vault. Exceptionally elaborate, gilt iron gallery fronts, incorporating a lyre pattern. On the fourth side the gallery continues, to support a large organ set within an Ionic arched recess. Timber pulpit below, carved with Art Nouveau details. Oak pews set on a segmental curve. At the back, handsome VESTRY, with an arched arrangement on columns fronting the stage, and Sunday school provision for 600 children.

BETHLEHEM ENGLISH PRESBYTERIAN CHURCH, Bethania Street. 1906–7 by *Arthur L. Thomas* of Pontypridd. Gothic. Pennant sandstone with red Ruabon terracotta dressings.

TABOR WELSH PRESBYTERIAN CHAPEL. 1907 by *Beddoe Rees*. Almost a twin to Bethania and nearly as grand. Ionic colonnettes rather than a full-scale order. Sadly, disused at the time of writing.

ZOAR CHAPEL, Zoar Street (now chapel of rest). 1911 by *Beddoe Rees*. Perp, and more expansive than most of his Gothic chapels. Complex seven-light central window, framed on the r. by a full-height polygonal buttress and stair projection, on the l. by a surprisingly monumental tower capped with a pyramidal spire.

WAR MEMORIAL. In front of St David's church. Sculptural group of two soldiers, one dying, the other defiant. Signed *L. F. Roslyn*, 1926.

TOWN HALL AND MARKET, Talbot Street. 1881 by *Henry C. Harris* of Cardiff. The central and dominant building of Maesteg. An arch in the channelled Bath stone podium leads to the market, and above rises the sheer Town Hall. Broad red brick pilaster strips set against grey Pennant sandstone walls. Steep roof crowned by a double-decker lantern. The moulded upper stonework has unfortunately been shaved back. Big hall added at the rear.

COUNCIL OFFICES, Talbot Street. Dated 1914, by *S. J. Harpur*. At first sight a plain two-storey, seven-bay block, of grey snecked stone, the ashlar dressings now painted pale salmon. But the broad centre bay is slightly bowed, and the three-bay portico bows in response: a whisper of Borromini. Ionic capitals with square volutes: an echo of Piranesi. Low parapet bearing the date. Inside, more miniaturized Baroque effects. Circular two-storey vestibule, with Tuscan columns below, Ionic above. A staircase rises between the columns and the bowed façade.

COLONEL NORTH MEMORIAL HALL, Talbot Street. Facing the Town Hall, and skinnily aping it. By a local architect, *E. W. Burnett*, and dated 1897.

POST OFFICE, Talbot Street. Dated 1938. Elegant Neo-Georgian.

MAESTEG GENERAL HOSPITAL, Neath Road. An eccentric design, mainly single-storey, the angles defined by three broad,

curvaceously battlemented towers. Pennant sandstone and
Portland stone dressings. 1900 and 1913 by *J. Humphreys* of
Maesteg.

76 LLYNFI IRONWORKS, W of High Street. The ironworks were
founded in 1837, and the fine steam-powered blast-engine
house with its hipped roof was built two years later. This
handsome three-storeyed ashlarwork building, later known as
the 'Cornstores', is now the entrance to the Maesteg Sports
Centre. Round-headed windows, those in the tall central storey
set in pairs under two bold segmental relieving arches, those at
the top short and close-set. On the W side of the adjacent car
park one of the four masonry BLAST FURNACES remains
visible. On the E side of High Street, four rows of workers'
houses, TALBOT TERRACE, CAVAN ROW, CHARLES ROW
and MACGREGOR ROW.

IRON BRIDGE, Llynfi Road. Locally made cast iron road-bridge
across the River Llynfi, at the lowest corner of the Llynfi Road
car park. To the W of the car park is a short length of relaid
track of the Duffryn, Llynvi and Porthcawl Railway of 1825–8.

9060 MARCROSS/MARCROES

HOLY TRINITY. In an exposed position near the cliffs, facing a
neat hemicycle of council houses. The saddleback W tower
could hardly be more basic. It is attached to a late C12 church
which, although of the usual small size and elemental plan of
nave and lower chancel, has two features of unusual elaboration. The S doorway has a billet-moulded outer arch on
grotesque heads and a roll round the arch itself on nook-shafts
with quite ambitious, if crude, foliage capitals. On the chancel
arch the motifs are different. Arch roll zigzagging like a tem-
perature chart at the apex. Plain imposts. Jambs with outlined
chamfers and tapering stops, perhaps a later embellishment,
going with the insertion of low screen walls rebated for a central
door. Trefoil-headed lancets N and S in the chancel, perhaps
of the C15. They are rebated for external shutters, and one on
the S side, most unusually, is carried down below a transom to
allow a low-level peep into the chancel. In the nave N wall a
recess for a monument, under a segmental arch decorated with
three hollow-chamfered orders and a big hoodmould. The
church was tactfully restored in 1893 by *Kempson & Fowler*. –
FONT. A tub with a roll top and bottom.

(EARTHWORKS, near Penycae Farm, ½ m. NE, are remains of a
grange of Neath Abbey. The E gable of a BARN stands up on
the W side of the road, indicating a much smaller building than
the barn at nearby Monknash Grange, q.v.)

NASH POINT, 1 m. SW. Iron Age PROMONTORY FORT, formed
by four banks set closely together across the neck of the narrow
promontory. Much of the seaward side of the enclosure and
defences has been spectacularly eroded by cliff falls. Access is
from the E, channelled through a natural hollow between the

two outer banks from which a terraced track swings s into the enclosure through an inturned entrance in the inner bank. A medieval PILLOW MOUND or rabbit warren is the only feature visible within the interior.

NASH POINT LIGHTHOUSES, $\frac{3}{4}$m. ssw. Erected in 1832 in response to an application from Thomas Protheroe of Newport and 439 other owners and masters from the Bristol Channel. The two aligning light-towers were completed on the cliff-top by the prolific lighthouse engineer *Joseph Nelson* in the year before his death. Both towers are of fine ashlar masonry painted white, the lower stage of each with weathered string courses similar to those at Bardsey and Lundy. The E or high light also has plain upper string courses. Both towers have moulded cornices at gallery level. The lower lighthouse was 67 ft (20.42 metres) high, but its lantern has now been removed. The upper light, 122 ft (37.19 metres) high, remains in use with an elegant lantern fitted in 1867. Matching single-storey KEEPER'S HOUSES attached to each, that to the w of 1832, that to the E after 1851. They are centrally planned with four heated rooms round a central chimney which rises above a large pyramidal roof. Two other pyramid-roofed dwellings flank the E lighthouse.

MARGAM

8080

Margam, sheltering below wooded slopes between the hills and the sea, has an accumulation of architecture and sculpture, both beautiful and impressive, unparalleled in Wales and extending over an entire millennium, from the c9 to the c19. An important religious site, first of early Christianity, then of Cistercian monasticism, Margam became after the Dissolution the seat of the most substantial of Glamorgan families, Mansels followed by Talbots.

The site, where the uplands come closest to the sea, has always been of strategic importance, as the remains of an Iron Age hillfort show. The collection of Early Christian crosses, now housed in the Stones Museum, demonstrates that Margam was one of the series of early ecclesiastical foundations spaced out along the course of the Roman road into West Wales. In 1147 Robert of Gloucester, lord of Glamorgan, extinguished its last traces by granting lands at Margam to St Bernard's abbey of Clairvaux, for the foundation of a new Cistercian house. The nave of the c12 abbey church survives, in use as the parish church. At the beginning of the c13 a great rebuilding programme was inaugurated, probably by Abbot Gilbert (1203–13). It began with the chapter house, which survives lacking only its vault, and continued with the entire E part of the church, presbytery, choir and transepts. This must have been a work of great sumptuousness, but all that remains above ground is a few tantalizing fragments of the s transept.

After the dissolution of the abbey in 1536, Sir Rice Mansel of

Oxwich and Old Beaupre acquired the ex-monastic buildings and most of the lands of Margam, which thereafter became the family's main seat. By the late C16 a 'faire and sumptious house' had been erected, incorporating some of the monastic buildings, mainly for service uses. Handsome late C17 stables were added to the W.

In 1768 the wheel of fortune turned again when the young Thomas Mansel Talbot inherited and soon decided to abandon and demolish the mansion at Margam in favour of Penrice Castle on Gower, close to the old family seat at Oxwich. Margam was to become a pleasure garden, dominated by a mighty Orangery, built 1787–90. The monastic remains were held in disdain, the chapter-house vault was allowed to collapse in 1799, and the remodelling of the church proposed in 1804 was on the principle that nothing should be visible above the Orangery. In the event, however, a remarkably whole-hearted restoration of the church soon took place.

To the next generation Gower once again seemed too remote, so in 1830 Thomas's son, Christopher Rice Mansel Talbot, began a huge new Tudor-style house on the high ground to the E of the pleasure garden. The C19 was the period of the family's greatest prosperity, with the development of Port Talbot from 1841. But in 1890 the male line failed, and the contents of the mansion were sold in 1942. After military use during the Second World War, the house stood empty and in 1977 was largely gutted by fire. Meanwhile, in 1973, the estate had been acquired by Glamorgan County Council. Its successor, West Glamorgan County Council, consolidated the largely roofless mansion and established Margam as a Country Park. Today Margam has become a pleasure ground again: a miniature train rumbles round past the mansion, and changing displays of sculpture dot the lawns.

It is possible to tour the grounds in a way which unfolds this history stage by stage, examining in sequence the Stones Museum, the church, the monastic remains, the Orangery, and the mansion. The historical sequence, however, begins with the hillfort.

p. 29 MYNYDD Y CASTELL, N of the C19 mansion. Iron Age HILLFORT of 6.7 acres (2.7 hectares), partly overgrown with shrubbery, on an isolated hill at the foot of the inland massif to the N, commanding the wide coastal plain. Strong natural defences, particularly to the S and SE, supplemented by a single rampart in parts fronted by a ditch and counterscarp bank. Simple entrance through the SW arc of defences with another in the NE arc. Internally, a slight bank running across the slope S of the NE entrance hints at the possibility of an earlier enclosure.

STONES MUSEUM, NW of the church. Simple early C19 single-room school, used since 1932 to house Early Christian and monastic funerary monuments and other carved stones, a few historically connected with Margam, the majority from nearby sites. The largest and most impressive stones stand free in the centre of the room, the others line the walls. It will be best to describe the free-standing stones first from E to W and then proceed round the room wall by wall. – Conbelin Stone. The tallest and most splendid of all, a late C9 or early C10 slab cross on its original base, which was first recorded standing outside the churchyard and must have had some important function in the early monastery. In the verdict of the Royal Commission it is the most impressive slab cross in the county, if not in all Wales. Disc-head carved front and back (the back very worn), interlace forming a ringed cross with square panels in the centre and at the end of each arm. On the shaft crude figures identifiable as St John (l.) and the Virgin (r.). The shaft truncated and set the wrong way round on the base, which also has pictorial carving on one face, apparently of a stag hunt. More interlace on its other faces. – Pumpeius Stone. Pillar stone with vertical inscriptions in Ogam and Latin. Mid-C6. Found at Eglwys Nunydd, near Margam. – Bodvoc Stone. Pillar stone with vertical inscription in unusually clear Roman capitals. Also dated to the C6. Found on the downs above Margam. – Ilquici Stone. C10 or C11 rectangular slab with incised wheel-cross, surrounded by interlace. Bold but worn inscription below. – Ilci Stone. Similar, but both cruder and more worn. – Effigy of a cross-legged knight, lower half only. Of the early C14. – Pillar of Thomas. Cylindrical inscribed stone, datable C8–C9. Found near Port Talbot. – Grutne Stone. Disc-head cross shaft, formerly standing S of the church. Bold inscription in crude half-uncials. Of the C10. – Shaft of a pillar-cross decorated all over with interlace (cf. the cross at Llandough, near Penarth). Late C10 or early C11. Found near Bridgend, and brought in to the museum as recently as 1969. – Fragment of a wheel-cross decorated with interlace.

Against the W wall: Slab with incomplete cross, its shaft with incised plaitwork, its disc-head in cut-out form. Dated to the C10.

Against the N wall: Tomb slab carved with a crozier and an inscription commemorating Robert, Abbot of Rievaulx (1301–7), who died at Margam. – C13 tomb slab. Stiff-leaf foliage forms a cross and decorates the chamfered edges. – Cantusus Stone. Originally a Roman milestone, bearing a C6 inscription. Found near Port Talbot. – Enniaun Stone. Mutilated disc-head cross, on a stout, tapering shaft. The cross entirely formed of interlace. On the shaft more interlace, and an inscription panel, for which compare the 'Houelt' stone at Llantwit Major (q.v.). Late C9. – Fragment carved with an interlace cross-head and a few letters. Late C9 or early C10. – Round-headed slab incised with a wheel-like cross. C7–C8 reworked in the late C9 or C10. Found near Port Talbot.

Against the E wall: Cross slab carved with a propeller-like cross and a faint inscription. Dated to the C10. Found at Eglwys Nunydd near Margam. – Two fragmentary disc-head cross shafts with interlace, C10 or C11.

Against the S wall: Two C13 grave slabs, one with a circular stiff-leaf boss on a stem between two croziers.

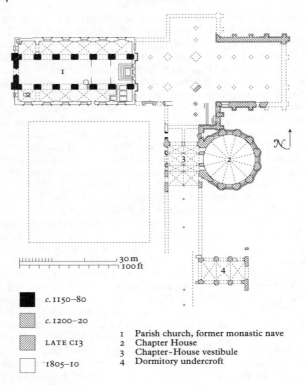

c. 1150–80

c. 1200–20

LATE C13

1805–10

1 Parish church, former monastic nave
2 Chapter House
3 Chapter-House vestibule
4 Dormitory undercroft

Margam Abbey. Plan of the monastic buildings

ST MARY. The parish church consists of the six w bays of the
nave of the C12 abbey church, erected perhaps c. 1150–70 but
remodelled and partly rebuilt c. 1805–10. So the exterior is
misleading and should be ignored for the time being. Inside,
however, the nave arcades remain in their massive simplicity,
more eloquent of the original austere Cistercian ideal than
anywhere else in Britain. Unmoulded cruciform piers on
stepped bases. Round-headed arches of two square orders
carried on chamfered imposts. Clerestory windows, now
blocked, set close over the heads of the arches. The lower part
of the spandrels ashlar-faced. No signs of supports for masonry
vaults. The w wall of the nave shows the first signs of a weak-
ening in austerity, keeled angle rolls round the three large
semicircular-headed windows.

The exterior of the nave w front is essentially of the late
C12, compromised by the early C19 neo-Norman restoration.
Pre-restoration views establish that the buttresses are old, but
that they were extended upwards at the restoration. Extraordinary arcaded, canister-like finials (possibly inspired by the
C12 lady chapel at Glastonbury Abbey). The crease-line over
the central doorway is also genuine, evidence that there was a

medieval porch. The shafting of windows and doorway,
however, with doughnut shaft-rings, must be early C19
enhancement of C12 shaft decoration. The capitals of the
doorway, scallop on the N shafts, foliage of three sorts on the
S, could well be original late C12 work. The W ends of the aisles
all early C19. The W front is uniformly faced with Sutton stone,
so that C12 and C19 work merge indistinguishably. Aisle N and
S walls with fancy neo-Norman two-light windows also of
c.1805–10, but faced with green Quarella sandstone. Plaster
groin-vaults in the aisles of c.1805–1, perhaps replicating the
medieval vault form, nave roof 1872–3. C19 E wall, of course. –
FONT. Neo-Norman. Of marble. – PULPIT. Neo-Norman. Of
stone. – CHOIR STALLS. Neo-Norman. Of mahogany, carved
by *William Clarke* of Llandaff, 1904. – HANGING LAMPS AND
ELECTROLIERS. Of brass, a handsome array. – The brass
LECTERN, iron chancel GATES, pink marble ALTAR STEPS
and blind arcade against the E wall, and the timber SCREENS
crowned with intersecting openwork arcading which enclose
the chancel to N and S, complete this remarkable late Victorian
ensemble. – STAINED GLASS. W window, Virgin and Child
flanked by SS Bernard and David. 1873, designed by *Burne-
Jones* and made by *Morris & Co.* Typical figures set against
pale, quarry backgrounds. Burne-Jones, in his account book,
called the cartoons for the figures of saints 'of colossal size and
excellence – entirely priceless – I make no charge for the genius
displayed in this work, but for the trouble of lifting the cartoon
about during the work – £15.' – E window, Christ in Majesty.
Also Burne-Jones style, colossal and rather spectacular, with
strong, deep colours and a powerful sense of pattern. Made by
Powell's, 1905. – MONUMENTS. The outstanding series of post-
medieval monuments in the county. S chapel: At the E end
three large tomb-chests bearing recumbent effigies and angle
obelisks, all made at one time. Armorial inscription tablets
fixed to nearby walls identify them as commemorating Sir Rice
Mansel † 1559, and his third wife (S), Sir Edward Mansel † 1585,
and wife (centre), and Sir Thomas Mansel and two wives (N).
Figures of kneeling children below, daughters, of stone, at the
sides, sons, of alabaster, more visible at the end. The monuments must have been set up before Sir Thomas's death in
1631, but after his baronetcy in 1611 (*see* inscription). – Sir
Rauleigh Bussye † 1623 and wife. Wall-monument with figures
kneeling at a prayer desk between Corinthian columns. –
Katherine Bussy † 1625. Wall-monument with kneeling figure
and leathery cartouche below. – Sir Lewis Mansel † 1638.
Black marble and alabaster. Recumbent figures of armoured
knight and fashionably dressed lady on an elegantly profiled
tomb-chest, decorated with emblematic reliefs flanking the
inscription panels. A distinct advance in style, if still
conservative in concept.* – N chapel: Thomas Mansel † 1705.

*Dr Adam White points out that the tomb-chest closely resembles that supporting
Maximilian Colt's effigy of Princess Mary († 1607) in Westminster Abbey.

Erected, reredos-like, against the E wall, after 1711. Three
tall panels between Doric pilasters of mottled marble. Overall
95   triangular pediment. – Theodore Mansel Talbot † 1876. Noble,
free-standing, E.E. canopy with multi-moulded arches, gables
and pinnacles, carried on four tall, slender, circular shafts of
grey marble. Hyper-realistic white marble recumbent effigy, of
a young man in a nightshirt, holding a crucifix to his chest, the
end of his sheet falling over his bald pate. Signed by
H. H. Armstead and dated 1881. – Christopher Rice Mansel
Talbot † 1890 and Olivia Emma Talbot † 1894. A pair of tablets,
one in a Jacobean, the other in an early C18 style. – Nave: W.
Bruce Knight, Dean of Llandaff, † 1845. Grecian tablet with
books and curtain. Signed by P. Rogers of Swansea.

MONASTIC BUILDINGS

The S door of the church opens on to a scene of romantic
decay. The site of the cloister garth is overshadowed by a vastly
spreading tree, the ground strewn with C13 moulded stones,
and to the E the propped façade of the chapter-house vestibule
is brushed by the tips of its branches. However delightful the
scene may be to the picturesque tourist, the historian may feel
alarm that more serious decay will soon set in.
    The form of the C12 choir is unknown. All too tantalizingly
little stands of the early C13 choir and transepts which took its
place. Foundations of the N wall of the E arm, which formed
the presbytery, show that it had four bays, giving an overall
length for the extended monastic church of 262 ft (79.85
metres). The SE crossing pier partly survives, and the bases of
two piers of the S transept, together with its E wall, enough to
show that the austerity of the first building had been thrown to
the winds. But the C12 plan left its imprint. The extreme
shortness of the transept, of just two narrow bays with E chapels,
must reflect the form of the C12 transept. Immediately to the S
stands the grandiose polygonal chapter house, built c. 1200,
and datable stylistically to shortly before the rebuilding of the
presbytery and transepts. It was the presence of the new chapter
house which necessitated the stunted plan of the rebuilt transepts, and caused the awkward junction with the SE angle of
the S transept, where a deep buttress of the sort required to
support the vaults of the new structure could be constructed to
the E but not to the S.
    Detailed examination can begin under the great tree. The
triple W DOORWAYS from the cloister walk into the chapter-
house vestibule are a classic E.E. composition. Shafts with
shaft-rings and circular moulded bases. Multiple arch mouldings keeled or filleted. A row of dogtooth on the central arch.
The capitals seem to have been prepared for leaf-carving which
was never carried out.
8   The CHAPTER-HOUSE VESTIBULE is vaulted, two bays
deep, to support the Dormitory above. Quadripartite rib-vaults
brought down to vestigial corbels to E and W and without

Margam Abbey, chapter house interior before
collapse of the vault in 1799

interruption on to central octagonal piers. Water-holding bases.
Chapter-house doorway and flanking opening very simple, with
two continuous chamfers. Keeled imposts.

The CHAPTER HOUSE is one of the earliest polygonal chapter
houses in Britain, built, it has been suggested, to outdo the
novel chapter house at Dore in Herefordshire. Both are twelve-
sided. The Margam chapter house is circular inside, and measures a full 50 ft (15.2 metres) from wall to wall. Dressed with
Sutton stone. Restrained but elegant, it is still a deeply impressive building, in spite of the collapse of the vault. Central vault
shaft surrounded by alternating polygonal and slender round
shafts, the latter with shaft-rings. Water-holding base, well-
developed stiff-leaf capital, and the snapped-off springers of
the vault. Against the walls, triple shafts for the vault ribs,

with moulded capitals. The internal walls are plain, originally
plastered below the sill-level string course, ashlar above. In each
of the nine free-standing bays a lofty pointed lancet window,
chamfered and shafted inside and out, with shaft-rings and
carved capitals, some with stiff-leaf, some with scallop variants,
all with square abaci. Remarkably well preserved and worth a
close look. E window enriched with a keeled roll. Beneath it,
an aperture within a moulded surround, circular outside, square
within. What was this for? Was the abbot's chair set directly in
front of it? External angles strengthened by broad but shallow
canted buttresses.

Further S the bases of a few more undercroft piers, indicating
a dormitory at least 190 ft (58 metres) long. Near the S end
three bays of an undercroft extending to the E with simple
quadripartite rib-vaults. Chamfered ribs on vestigial corbels.
This may have supported a bridge to a reredorter, an arrangement found at Neath (q.v.). Rebate for a door in the W bay
made when the undercroft served as an outbuilding of the post-
Reformation mansion.

In the C13 CHURCH a richer style obtained. The SE crossing
pier, though it stands only 3 ft (0.91 metre) or so high, is
evidence enough. The core of the pier is polygonal to both the
choir and the transept, with two slender coursed-in shafts in the
intervening recess. Detached shafts on circular, water-holding
bases line this complex form, alternating with the coursed-in
shafts, so that as many as nine shafts are lined up against the
SE face of the pier. The source for this design can be found in
the crossing piers at Glastonbury Abbey, and the choirs of
Worcester Cathedral and Pershore Abbey provide close parallels, so by the early C13 the Margam masons were part of a
West Country network, by no means exclusively Cistercian. In
the S transept, two lozenge-plan piers with attached shafts on
circular, non-waterholding bases. Evidence of two E chapels,
in particular piscina and aumbry in the S wall. The E wall rises
almost to full height, with two-light plate-traceried windows,
their rere-arches multi-moulded on shafts, probably renewed
in the C19. This is mostly of Quarella sandstone. The surviving
outer wall of the presbytery S aisle, of similar design, has
Sutton stone dressings and is probably original. Wall-shafts
and springing for rib-vaults. Shafted doorway further E, of
Sutton stone with Quarella shafts. The capitals everywhere are
moulded. The change of stone is puzzling, and may indicate
early C19 reconstruction.

The only evidence of improvements to the abbey buildings
after the first quarter of the C13 is in the two bays of arcading
E of the S aisle of the parish church. Here is the processional
doorway which opened from the E end of the N cloister walk
into the monks' church. Quite a simple affair with continuous
mouldings, set in a rectangular, roll-moulded frame. Trefoiled
spandrels. Blank variant of this, with formerly traceried head,
in the next bay to the W. An C18 plan shows that the entire N
wall of the cloister was decorated like this before the early C19

rebuilding of the nave S aisle destroyed it. Later C13 or C14.
CHAPEL, on the shoulder of Graig Fawr, high above the abbey
$\frac{1}{4}$ m. N. Medieval. Roofless, but the walls of the single-cell
building survive almost to full height. Two-light W window of
c. 1300, perhaps reused. Of Sutton stone, unlike the sandstone
dressings used elsewhere. The quatrefoil at the apex of the
geometrical tracery largely survives. Four-light Perp E window,
its panel tracery partly intact. Piscina with ogee trefoil head.

Of the house built by the Mansels out of the monastic buildings,
dismantled in 1792–3, nothing is left, and of its gardens and
forecourts very little. The loss of the house leaves a major gap
in Glamorgan's architectural history. Two paintings of c. 1700
show that it not only had a detached gatehouse to the S and a
tall prospect tower to the N, but that its S front was the most
serious piece of C17 classicism in the county. Regular mullion-
and-transom cross windows with architraves. To the W a grand
stable, its three-bay centrepiece pedimented on giant pilasters.
All this existed by 1684. The fine pair of late C17 GATEPIERS
standing in splendid isolation in the car park belonged to a
square enclosure containing four rectangular fishponds,
between the house and a great avenue extending almost as far
as the sea. But one spectacular piece does remain, the FAÇADE
of the Banqueting House built at the upper end of the formal
gardens on the slope E of the house. It was reconstructed c. 1800
in Thomas Mansel Talbot's pleasure grounds, and is best
described in that context.

When Thomas Mansel Talbot abandoned decaying Margam
in favour of Penrice, he decided to retain there just one part of
his inheritance, the famous collection of citrus trees, lemons
and limes as well as oranges, which already in 1727 had num-
bered over fifty. So the centrepiece of his new pleasure grounds
was an ORANGERY, longer and more capacious than any other 59
in Great Britain. Designed by *Anthony Keck* in 1780 and erected
1787–90. Its length of 327 ft (99.67 metres) considerably
exceeds that of the monastic church. Ashlar S front faced with
greenish-brown sandstone of superlative quality quarried at
Pyle, 4 m. (3.2 kilometres) SE. Palladian composition, of seventeen bays forming an almost continuous arcade emphasized
by superb vermiculated rustication of the piers and voussoirs.
The centre five bays slightly wider and stepped forward slightly
twice, the centre three under a higher attic carved with rams'
skulls and deeply looping garlands. Pedimented pavilion each
end under a triangular pediment and lit by a Venetian window
under a relieving arch. Triglyph frieze right the way across.
Small wreathed vases above. The E pavilion intended as a statue
gallery, the W pavilion fitted up as a library. No doorway
allowed to sully the façade, the statue gallery and library entered
through Venetian openings in the short returns, the fruit trees
wheeled in and out through double doors at the back of the
building. Venetian openings link the end pavilions with the
Orangery internally. Library bookshelves in an arcaded composition with Adamesque detail and plasterwork frieze. –

SCULPTURE. Deluge scene, by the Belgian sculptor *Mathieu Kessels*, c. 1830, an example of the Neoclassical sublime, brought here from Clytha House, Gwent, in 1970. – The PARTERRE and three circular ponds, in front of the Orangery, seem to belong to the mid C19. The row of Neoclassical urns are most, if not all, copies made in the 1970s.

TEMPLE OF THE FOUR SEASONS, W of the Orangery. The façade of the late C17 Summer Banqueting House, saved and erected here in 1835 at the back of a gardener's cottage. Thomas Dineley, who in 1684 saw the Summer Banqueting House, and admired sculpture, paintings and engravings in it, called it 'after ye Italian'. He might have said 'after the Roman', for this is a proper triumphal arch composition, or rather two triumphal arches, one on top of the other. Three wide bays defined by fluted columns, swagged Ionic below, swagged Composite above, both carrying richly detailed entablatures. A central arch at each level, with carved imposts which are carried as mouldings across the side bays, behind the columns, and round the backs of the niches in the side bays. Strangely elongated key-blocks to the niches, the lower ones bearing volute caps. Volute cap also to the key-block of the lower arch. Such energetic, if slightly wayward, late C17 classicism has no parallel in the county, and garden buildings of such grandeur were rare indeed at that date in the whole of Britain. The STATUES in the niches, of classical females, which seem not to personify the seasons, look of the C19. The façade is of Sutton stone.

The MANSION. On the higher ground E of the monastic site, in a dramatic relationship with the wooded hills behind and commanding distant views towards the sea. 1830–5 by *Thomas Hopper*, site architect *Edward Haycock*. There may be nothing else like it in Glamorgan, but its ancestry is clear; from James Wyatt's Ashridge, 1808–13, and William Wilkins's Dalmeny, 1814–17, Tudor Gothic mansions such as this were nothing new in the 1830s, though such scale and elaboration could only be afforded by the super-rich.

From the park gates to the W the drive ascends circuitously, skirting a lake, until it finally bursts out before the N front of the sombre, brown Pyle-ashlar mansion. Here a deep porch stands forward almost like the façade of a church. Above and behind, like a crown to the whole house, an octagonal prospect tower, a taller and more elaborately decorated version of the celebrated early C16 prospect tower at Melbury House, Dorset, Talbot's mother's family home. The N front is strongly asymmetrical. By contrast the W side has both symmetry and the prospect tower on axis behind it. Two big five-sided window bays rise into octagonal turrets crowned by crocketed stone domes. Three-sided window bays to l. and r. stopped at battlement level. From here a stately flight of steps descends to the Orangery and ruined abbey.

The long S front has a bit of everything: window bays of five sides and of three, oriel windows large and small, turrets panelled and plain, gables high and not so high, massive chimneybreasts, and decorated chimneystacks sprouting out in threes and sixes. When so much is vying for one's attention, it matters little that there are now no roofs. From the E side extends a low but spreading and complicated service wing and stable court. Thick-set tower with corbelled battlements and diapered stone louvres.

The INTERIOR retains one spectacular space, the staircase in the lower two storeys of the prospect tower. The stair rises in one straight flight and then disappears behind a ring of four-centred arches. Plaster fan-vault high up.

LODGE, 200 yds W of the church. Tudor. Gabled, with tall chimneystacks. Probably of the 1840s by *Haycock*.

The estate village at GROES, ¾m. SW, laid out by *Haycock*, was destroyed to make way for the M4 motorway.

OLD PARK, I m. S. L-plan two-storey house of the C17, with a kitchen at the outer end of each range. A fine, varied set of stone doorways, that in the E front with an entablature on brackets. The oversized late C17 staircase with turned balusters and renewed acorn finials is said to have come from the demolished abbey mansion. If so, it can only have been a minor one.

CREMATORIUM, I m. SW. Concrete chapel and incinerator chimney in isolation overlooking Eglwys Nunydd Reservoir. By *F. D. Williamson & Associates* of Porthcawl, opened 1969.

MERTHYR MAWR

8070

A village of pretty thatched cottages straggling along outside the ivy-clad park wall of Merthyr Mawr House. No modern intrusions, an indication of what many villages in the Vale must have looked like before the 1950s.

ST TEILO. Here is a Puginian vision. Since the architect was 89 *Benjamin Ferrey*, Pugin's fellow-pupil and later biographer, this is perhaps not surprising. But *John Prichard* of Llandaff was also involved, and the freshly conceived detailing, some with local precedents, suggests the latter's hand. The date is 1849–51, the style E.E.

Chancel and higher nave, both with steep, slated roofs, and a fanciful but logically designed w bellcote (inspired by the medieval bellcote at St Nicholas, Biddestone, Wiltshire) under a tall, candle-snuffer spirelet. Finely laid rubble walls of local white limestone and generous ashlar dressings of Bath stone. Admirable integration of corbel table, lancet windows, buttresses and string courses in the nave. Fine composition of the W wall, crowned by the bellcote, which is corbelled out over a long wall-shaft with stiff-leaf foliage at top and bottom. N vestry of 1963, incorporating a medieval doorway into the chancel, brought in from St Illtyd, Bridgend (q.v.).

Inside, more wall-shafts, with stiff-leaf caps and feet: a long one on the W wall (this, too, a bellcote support), medium ones supporting the nave roof, short ones in the chancel. The motif is local, found e.g. at Caerphilly Castle hall (q.v.) and Llandaff

Cathedral chapter house (*see* Cardiff, p. 254). Heavy timber roofs, with arch-braces and wind-braces. Strongly hollow-chamfered chancel arch carried on semi-octagonal responds with stiff-leaf capitals. Chancel E trio of lancets set behind slender quatrefoil shafts, with more lively stiff-leaf. – FONT. Plain octagonal medieval bowl, set on a spacious arrangement of steps of *c.* 1851. – HOLY WATER STOUP. Medieval stone, quatrefoil. Loose by the font. – PULPIT. Lavish, of stone with many black marble shafts and much stiff-leaf foliage. Not designed for its present site. – LECTERN. Brass. A handsome High Victorian piece. – FLOOR TILES. By *Minton* throughout. – STAINED GLASS. Contemporary with the church. – Chancel E, Resurrection (note the startled soldiers). – Chancel N and S, miracles of Christ. By *Wailes* (O. Jenkins). One nave N window signed by *A. J. Davies* of the *Bromsgrove Guild*, after 1918. – SUNDIAL. Dated 1720, reset on the chancel.

In the CHURCHYARD, S of the church, two medieval figural MONUMENTS, one fragmentary, both very worn. – The LAPI-DARY COLLECTION, kept under a shelter N of the church, consists of nearly a dozen small fragments of CII–CI2 head-stones and crosses, one with interlace, and one much earlier stone, bearing a fragmentary inscription in Roman capitals, dated to the C5. All were found in the churchyard or on the site of the medieval church (*see* St Roch chapel below).

The cottages in the village have undergone the usual re-windowing and other modernization, but have not been much enlarged and are still thatched, so it is worth taking in each individually. Starting E of the church, CHURCH COTTAGE, much altered, was probably built in the C17. Originally it was on a lobby-entry plan, with the entry at the r. end of the façade. Subsequently the entry was moved to the l. end. The mullioned windows are not original. Tiny DIANA COTTAGE, across the road, is that rarity, an unenlarged end-entry house which still has its entrance doorway in the end wall beside the hall fire-place. It is datable *c.* 1700, and is too small and late to have a mural stair. WELLINGTONIA, beside Church Cottage, is also on the end-entry plan, but an extension to the l., with its own doorway, masks the original one. Beyond Diana Cottage, OAK COTTAGE, larger and earlier, still with its original four-centred stone doorway, suggesting a CI6 date. It opens into an originally unheated room, with the hall to the r. Later extension to the l. Beyond is HOLLY COTTAGE, another late end-entry house, extended to the r., so that the stair projection, originally at the angle of the house, is now in the middle of the front. KEEPER'S COTTAGE, beyond again, is a lobby-entry house, enlarged into an L-plan. Finally, on the other side of the road, a COTTAGE in quite a different tradition. The hipped thatched roof with central chimneystack, and the symmetry of the miniature façade, show that this is a pattern-book estate cottage of *c.* 1800.

MERTHYR MAWR HOUSE. A severe and rational late Georgian house built 1806–8 for Sir John Nicholl, a lawyer, by *Henry Wood*, of the dynasty of Bristol masons and carvers. Five bays by three, faced with white local limestone ashlar. The windows alternate, wide tripartite ones in the infinitesimally projecting end bays, and also in the centre bay of the entrance (N) front, the others of normal shape. The lower windows extend downwards almost to the ground. Deep cantilevered eaves. Entrance porch on somewhat oversized Tuscan columns. Altogether the proportions of the house do not entirely satisfy. Veranda added to the W front in 1819.

The front door opens into a deep vestibule, with a pair of giant Doric columns at the inner end. Beside it the principal staircase rises in a narrow well. Cantilevered stone steps. Iron balustrade of a restrained Neoclassical design. Reticent Neoclassical detail in the principal rooms. Soanic marble chimneypieces. The SW room is fitted up as a library. Gothic bookcases, but giant Ionic columns with diagonal volutes, highly unusual for 1806.

The SERVICE RANGES, STABLES and walled KITCHEN GARDEN succeed one another in line to the E.

The CHAPEL of St Roch stands above the house to the N. It is a very small, roofless but otherwise complete C15 building. Four-centred S doorway, fragmentary two-light E window and W bell-gablet. Within, two outstandingly fine C11 CROSS SHAFTS, the taller of which retains much of its encircled crosshead. Both are richly decorated with interlace, and both bear an inscription within a border. Yet they did not fulfil the same function. The shorter served as a tombstone, erected by Conbelan for himself, his brother and father. The taller, which formerly stood in a field N of the village, apparently bears the terms of a charter recording a transfer of land.

The HOME FARM, NE of the church, incorporates in its N range part of the earlier hall, demolished c. 1806. This seems to have been quite an ambitious C16 house, but only a few mullioned windows of paired, arched lights survive.

Finely wooded PARK. The plan for this was drawn up in 1813 by *William Weston Young*, china painter of Swansea.

NEW INN BRIDGE, ¾ m. NE. Late medieval bridge of four arches.

CANDLESTON CASTLE, ¾ m. SW. The coastal sand dunes of MERTHYR MAWR WARREN, which have engulfed archaeological sites dating from the MESOLITHIC to the IRON AGE, rear up like breakers, threatening to crash down on the crumbling remains of the little fortified manor house of the de Cantelupes. This was built in the C14, so the few remaining details of Sutton stone and sandstone suggest. The most impressive survival, the chimneypiece of the first-floor hall, is a bit later, datable c. 1500, constructed of greenish local sandstone. The last phase of habitation dates from the early C19, when the then semi-ruin was fitted up for Sir John Nicholl, while Merthyr Mawr House was under construction. Brick dressings identify this work.

To the W a faceted, D-plan wall forms a defensive enclosure, along the lip of a low escarpment. Basically of the C14, decoratively battlemented in the early C19, when the S stretch was realigned. The C14 house consisted of two parts, a single-pile range across the E end of the enclosure, and a tower added outside the enclosure at its S end. The N half of the HALL RANGE is very ruinous, the S half largely remodelled *c.*1500 (*see* below). The early date of the range is proved by the straight joint at its SE corner, which shows that the tower, which contains undoubtedly early features, is added to the range, not the other way round.

In the TOWER a pointed, chamfered arch into a ground-floor cellar, and beside it a mural stair rising in the thickness of the W wall. This led, by means of a door of which one jamb survives, to a well-appointed first-floor chamber, with evidence of an externally corbelled fireplace in the S wall and a garderobe in the NE corner. Fragments of the parapet corbelling of the roof. Blocked W opening at the stair-head, originally opening on to the wall-walk of the enclosure wall.

The FIRST-FLOOR HALL created *c.*1500 has in its S wall a fine and substantially intact Perp chimneypiece. Filleted jamb shafts with round caps are carried up, hollow-moulded with a foliage trail, to support a shelf. Four-centred ogee arch between, decorated with a hollow moulding and square flowers. E of it a doorway into the tower chamber.

Small, ruined W extension, of indeterminate date. Early C19 STABLE added to the E wall of the tower.

NEWBRIDGE FARM, 1½m. NE, almost on the outskirts of Bridgend. An exceptional, tower-like farmhouse of *c.*1600, three-storeyed with gables in three directions, but only two rooms per storey. Mullioned windows, some hollow-chamfered, some sunk-chamfered. Fine entrance doorway with carved spandrels and a hollow-and-wave moulding. Hoodmoulds. Recent drastic restoration.

CAE SUMMERHOUSE, 1¼m. W. The form of this defended ENCLOSURE complex is unclear on account of plough damage. It originated in the Iron Age and continued to be used during the Roman occupation.

MERTHYR TYDFIL/MERTHYR TUDFUL

Merthyr Tydfil, though a medieval parish, is the child of the iron industry. The first iron furnaces and forges were erected near the head of the Taff Valley 1759–65, and by the early 1780s four ironworks were in operation, Dowlais, Plymouth, Cyfarthfa and Penydarren, stimulated by wartime need for armaments, first in the Seven Years' War, then in the American War of Independence from 1775. Already by the 1780s Dowlais, run by the Guests, and Cyfarthfa, controlled by the Crawshays, had established their dominance, not only locally but in Glamorgan as a whole. The next stage was the construction of the Glamorganshire Canal from Merthyr to Cardiff 1791–4, largely financed by the Crawshays, enabling the rapid distribution of the iron products. By the beginning of the C19 Merthyr had become the largest town in

Glamorgan, and by 1851 the population had reached 46,000, virtually twice the population of Swansea and two-and-a-half times that of Cardiff. From the mid 1830s the proliferation of railways, both in Britain, and indeed all over the world, ensured a hugely increased market for Merthyr iron until the end of the century. By c. 1870, however, the industry was under threat from two directions: the increasing expense of mining the raw material, the local ironstone, and the development from 1856 of Henry Bessemer's revolutionary steel-making process. The Penydarren works had closed in 1858, Plymouth was bought out in 1863, and only Dowlais made the transition to steel production. In the early 1880s the works at Cyfarthfa were narrowly saved from abandonment and in 1902 they were finally merged with Guest, Keen & Co.'s works at Dowlais. During the C20 the need for direct access to the coast became ever more pressing, and after the establishment of coastal works first at East Moors, Cardiff, then in the 1930s at Port Talbot, Guest, Keen & Nettlefold, as the firm had by then become, finally abandoned steel production in the Merthyr area. The results of these commercial decisions were disastrous locally. By 1930 unemployment in Merthyr Tydfil had reached 50%, and had further to rise, even though the population dropped from 80,000 in 1921 to 63,000 in 1937. Since 1945 new light industry has at last transformed the town's dependence on a single manufacture and enabled it to flourish again.

The result of this history of expansion, contraction and now renewed expansion has been to leave the town with a sprawling plan. It originally grew up around St Tydfil's church. B. H. Malkin wrote in 1803 of the early ironworkers' cottages being 'in scattered confusion, without any order or plan', but returning in 1806 was impressed by the 'great improvements', the streets 'sufficiently straight and wide' and nearly the whole of the glebe laid out in regular streets. But the ironworks at Cyfarthfa to the NW and Penydarren to the N each produced its own housing close to the works and became separated from each other by spoil-tips. The ironmasters themselves also lived on site. But while Cyfarthfa Castle and its park remain, Penydarren House has gone, and its park contains Merthyr's premier middle-class suburb. Works and tips have long been no more than a memory.

Dowlais works lay a mile or so to the NE, and always remained isolated from the main development of Merthyr. It is therefore treated separately below.

ST TYDFIL, High Street. On the site of the medieval church, and indeed the supposed site of the martyrdom of St Tydfil. Nave of 1820–1 retained but transformed by *J. L. Pearson* in what amounted to the creation of a new church, designed in 1891, approved in 1894 but not completed until 1901. Neo-Romanesque, so as to accommodate the simple classicism of the surviving nave. Iron-stained Pennant sandstone and Bath stone dressings. Sheer, semi-cylindrical apse towards the road (cf. Pearson's St Peter, Vauxhall, of thirty years earlier), short transepts, four-bay nave, and blunt, three-stage W tower. Only

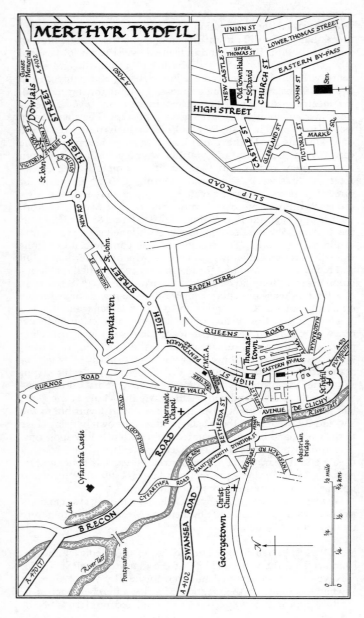

the S porch, two-storeyed and richly arrayed with shafted orders, and zigzag and billet ornament, suggests that Pearson was taking his Romanesque seriously.

The interior is another matter. Here the architect has drawn on all his scholarship to create a beautiful evocation of a Burgundian Romanesque church of the late C12, an Autun in little. Slender, square piers, faced with pilasters in all four directions, carry transverse arches, semicircular over the nave, pointed in the aisles: a Burgundian mixture, which cleverly fits between the existing walls. Flat nave ceiling, also incorporated from the late Georgian church. Groin-vaults in the aisles, on half-round responds. Chancel arch and transept arches, given paired soffit rolls, frame the vaulted apse with suitable dignity. Simple but varied foliage capitals all through. The church was closed for regular worship in 1968, restored in 1973 (with ugly pointing of the stonework) and is at present used for funerals only. – STAINED GLASS. E triplet, Crucifixion, clearly by *Kempe*. – W window, Daily Bread, with ironworks below, erected to the 'Captains of Industry' at the expense of Sir W. T. Lewis. 1896 by *R. J. Newbery*. – MONUMENTS. An C8 or C9 pillar-stone inscribed with the name ARTBEU (N aisle). – Several early C19 marble tablets, the most ambitious commemorating Rees Davies †1816. Two heavily draped females sit leaning on an urn. Signed *Edwards* of Merthyr.

CHRIST CHURCH, Aberdare Road. Completed 1857, by *James Benest*, former Borough Surveyor. Florid geometrical. Clerestoried nave with lean-to aisles, transepts and lower chancel. Wasp's-nest corbel for a W bell-turret now removed. Inside, similar corbels for the arch-braced roof. Arcade with alternate round and octagonal piers. Dec leaf capitals. – STAINED GLASS. E window, Way to Calvary, treated like a painting. *E. R. Suffling pinxit*, 1899. – S aisle SE, Good Samaritan, *c.* 1908. A much-repeated design by *R. J. Newbery*. – N aisle NE, SS Catherine and David, 1901 by *Newbery*. – N aisle centre, Suffer the Little Children, *c.* 1897, surely by *Newbery*.

ST DAVID, High Street. 1846–7 by *T. H. Wyatt & Brandon*. E.E. Large, serious and correct, but showing the strain of a tight budget. They had exhibited a design for the church back in 1842. Clerestoried nave with lean-to aisles stopping short of the W bay. Short, lower chancel. Angle buttresses. Snecked, grey Pennant sandstone with Bath stone dressings. All the display is on the W front, a shafted doorway, a shafted, two-light window treated as the centrepiece of a shafted arcade, and in the gable a trefoil under a shafted arch. Meagre bell gable on top. Lofty interior, the six-bay arcades with quatrefoil piers and double-chamfered arches. The thin tie-beam and kingpost roof seems very far away. W gallery. The climax in the chancel, three shafted lancets. – STAINED GLASS. Most remarkable is the patterned glass in the nave N windows, designed in 1922 by *J. Coates Carter*. – In the S aisle: SS David and Tydfil, 1887. Aesthetic. – Miriam and Mary, *c.* 1874. Hardmanesque. – SS Teilo and Maelog, 1922 by *Newbery*.

St John, Church Street, Penydarren. Nave 1858 to a design by
a Mr *Brigden* of Dowlais. Paired lancets. N doorway under a
stone gable. Later chancel and transept, enlivened with red
Ruabon brick dressings.

St Mary (R.C.), The Walk. 1893–4 by *J. S. Hansom*. Quite a
noble E.E. church, if entirely conventional and lacking a vertical accent. Rock-faced Pennant sandstone dressed with Bath
stone. Clerestoried nave and chancel of equal height. Lean-to
aisles and transepts. Nave arcades of alternately round and
octagonal piers and double-chamfered arches. Sanctuary
arcades with grey granite piers. Groups of five graded lancets,
mirroring each other to E and W, dominate the interior.

Bethesda Chapel, Bethesda Street (at present disused).
Classical, with the characteristic motif of the centre windows
set within a big relieving arch. Part of the chapel of 1811
and 1829 was incorporated in the reconstruction of 1880–1 by
J. Williams.

Church of Jesus Christ of Latter Day Saints, Georgetown. 1969 by *T. P. Bennett & Son*. A prominent object, with
its gold mosaic spirelet.

(Ebenezer Welsh Baptist Chapel, Plymouth Street.
1829–31. An early example of a two-storey chapel façade.
Round-headed windows, banded angle pilasters, rusticated
entrance doorway.)

High Street Baptist Church, High Street. 1841 by
T. H. Wyatt. Three-bay, stuccoed front, the centre brought
forward blank under a pediment and above a Serlian doorway.
Channelled lower walls, pedimented upper windows l. and
r. The abrupt juxtapositions even recall Ledoux. *George
Morgan & Son* of Carmarthen reconstructed the interior in
1899–1900. (Galleries on three sides and upper arcades carried
on a second tier of slender iron columns. Flat beamed ceiling.)

Hope Welsh Presbyterian Church, High Street. 1892
by *Thomas Roderick*. Cuspless Gothic. Galleried interior. HALL
behind of 1909 by *C. M. Davies*.

Shiloh Welsh Wesleyan Chapel, Church Street. Neo-
Romanesque, the fenestration incorporated in flush intersected
arcading. 1853, probably by *I. K. Brunel*. Converted into a
miners' welfare hall in 1921, when it lost an angle tower, then
into a restaurant, and burnt out in 1991, when it lost its
roof.

Synagogue, Church Street (now Olympic health centre).
1872–5. A gabled and turreted stone front in simplified Gothic,
set dramatically against trees at the head of the street. Said to
be the oldest purpose-built synagogue in Wales.

Tabernacle Welsh Baptist Chapel, Brecon Road.
By *George Morgan & Son* of Carmarthen, 1896–8. Neo-
Romanesque. Unconventional gabled façade of rock-faced
Pennant sandstone with Bath stone ashlar. Triple order to the
central doorway, stepped windows for the gallery stairs l. and
r. Triple upper window under an elaborate relieving arch.
The minimum of modelling. Fine forecourt railings, made in

Carmarthen. Substantial and unaltered interior, the curves of
the ceiling cove, the swept corners of the three-sided gallery,
the 'big seat' and pulpit all in harmony. Splendid organ a little
too large for its arched recess.

TYDFIL HALL, Penydarren Road. Built as a Presbyterian
Forward Movement Hall in 1907 by *Arthur D. Marks*. Small
but decorative front crowned by a fanciful shaped gable. The
chapel intended for the adjacent site not built.

UNITARIAN CHURCH (now S.N.U. Spiritual Centre), Lower
Thomas Street. 1901–3 by *E. A. Johnson*, in a lively Arts and
Crafts Perp style. Red brick and Bath stone. Good use of
the sloping site, the façade set back behind an arcade which
incorporates a central entrance to a basement hall and side
ones up to the chapel. Five-light window with cuspless Dec
tracery between boldly advancing buttresses. Elaborately
shaped gable. (Aisled interior with short transepts. Hammerbeam and arch-braced roof. Some stained glass.)

WESLEY METHODIST CHURCH, High Street. Now secularized
and subdivided internally. The three-bay façade remains, dated
1862, its centre bay crowned by a pediment on pilasters. Channelled lower storey.

ZION (SEION) WELSH BAPTIST CHURCH, Twynyrodyn
Road. 1841. Severe but handsome Neoclassical façade of
Pennant sandstone ashlar, a sign of remarkable sophistication.
Three broad bays, the centre bay brought slightly forward under
a pediment. Round-headed upper windows, square-headed
lower. Recessed central doorway, within a plain arch carried
on Doric columns. There is evidence that *T. H. Wyatt* was the
architect. Inside, the boarded ceiling, with big central plaster
rose, is of the 1880s, but the fittings are all of 1900–2 by *Thomas
Roderick*. Galleries round three sides, extended as choir seating
to flank the organ. The supporting iron columns spirally twisted
with well-proportioned foliage caps. Balustraded 'big seat' and
pulpit.

ZOAR-YNYSGAU WELSH CONGREGATIONAL CHAPEL, High
Street. Set back inconspicuously behind the street-line.
1841–2 to plans made by the Rev. *Benjamin Owen*. Broad façade
of rough Pennant sandstone, five bays wide, the lower storey
of the centre three opened up as a loggia by means of thick,
strangely primitive columns. The interior is remarkable and
important, the earliest really large-capacity chapel. It is galleried
on more than three sides, in seven cants, on slender fluted
columns, and lit by round-headed clerestory windows on three
(originally all four) sides. Flat ceiling on dentilled cornice. Big
central rose.

PUBLIC BUILDINGS

CIVIC CENTRE, Castle Street. 1989–90 by the *David Preece
Partnership*. Caramel-coloured brick walls with black slate roofs.
In two parts, a four-storey, w-facing office range with canted
ends, and to the E a single-storey, square pavilion of somewhat

more ceremonial character. Both have the tall, round-headed windows under gablets which signify Post-Modern allegiance.

OLD TOWN HALL, High Street. 1896–7 by *E. A. Johnson* of *Johnson & Williams* of Abergavenny and Merthyr. Large, exuberant and highly coloured. From a basement of grey Pennant sandstone spring walls of red Cattybrook brick lavishly embellished with orange terracotta. Steep roof crowned by a large clock-turret, now lacking its dome. Front block for the council offices, county courts entered separately at the back. The style is early Renaissance, in some places with Flemish overtones, in others, with French. The main entrance opens on to a handsome imperial staircase, and a great show of faience, glazed tiles and metalwork almost Art Nouveau in character. The council chamber, at the back, which doubled as a courtroom, has been altered.

CARNEGIE LIBRARY, High Street. 1935–6 by *T. Edmund Rees* of *Johnson, Richards & Rees* of Merthyr Tydfil. Hard to evaluate. Two-storeyed under a shallow, hipped roof. Constructed of smooth concrete blocks, modelled to form the central doorway and the surrounds to the timber, mullioned windows.

In front, the handsome bronze STATUE of Lord Buckland of Bwlch. A robed figure, 1931, signed by *Goscombe John*.

WAR MEMORIAL, Pontmorlais Circus. Three figures, Fate in the centre with covered head and spindle in hand, and below, a miner and a mother. Signed by Goscombe John's pupil *L. S. Merrifield*, and dated 1931.

COLLEGE OF FURTHER EDUCATION, Ynysfach Road. A straightforward modern job, 1950–2, which is to say unusually early. By *Yorke, Rosenberg & Mardall*. Five-storey concrete-framed slab, the entrance in a section glazed full-height. The intended S-ward extension including assembly hall and refectory was never built. The single-storey workshop range to the E has been demolished.

ST TYDFIL'S HOSPITAL, Upper Thomas Street. Built as the Merthyr Union Workhouse in 1853, by *Aickin & Capes* of London. Main block dated 1870, in a Dec style. Large yellow brick ranges to the N, built as the workhouse infirmary, 1896–1900 by *E. A. Johnson*. – STATUE. In the forecourt Sir W. T. Lewis (Lord Merthyr), bronze figure signed by *Thomas Brock* and dated 1898.

PRINCE CHARLES HOSPITAL, off Gurnos Road. Also straight-forwardly modern, though formally planned. Two parallel five-storey ranges with service towers, linked by a series of low cross-ranges. 1965–75 by *Sir Percy Thomas & Partners* (design partners *Norman Thomas* and *Wallace Sweet*). Additions of 1989–91 by the *Welsh Health Common Services Authority*.

Y.M.C.A., Pontmorlais West. 1909–11 by *Ivor Jones & Percy Thomas*, their first building. Confident Edwardian Baroque, red brick and yellow terracotta, four storeys, each with its own window form. Coupled Doric columns at the lowest stage. (Inside, a full-height imperial staircase, and the top storey designed for a rifle range.) Disused at the time of writing. The building crowns the top of the town impressively and must be saved.

MASONIC TEMPLE, Park Terrace. 1910 by *C. M. Davies* of Merthyr Tydfil. A jolly little building with plenty of swags. Rear façade overlooking Pontmorlais, its pediment on an odd number of pilasters.

MORLAIS CASTLE, 2 m. N. Built 1288–94 by Gilbert de Clare on a high-lying limestone ridge at the N-most extremity of his lordship of Glamorgan, with the panoramic command of many miles of upland country. Its construction caused so furious a dispute with the neighbouring lord of Brecon, Humphrey de Bohun, that Edward I confiscated the castle. In 1295 it was captured by the Welsh, who put it permanently out of action. Today, encroached on by a quarry from the w, and reached from the E across a golfcourse, the castle appears as little more than a series of heaps and screes of stones. Close examination by G. T. Clark in the 1870s and recently by the Royal Commission has established the plan, a faceted oval pointed at the N and S ends. The W side relied on the natural strength provided by the site (even before quarrying began), and defences were concentrated on protecting the E flank, where the ground falls away gently. Five circular towers punctuated the enclosure wall, those to the N and S keep-like, the other three of lesser diameter. Of the N keep the facing stonework of the circular interior wall can still be made out. Of the S keep, however, there are much more spectacular remains, nothing less in fact than the complete vaulted undercroft, reached through a small pointed doorway among the rocks. It is a magnificently coherent piece of architecture, all the more eloquent of the powers of C13 military designers for its almost miraculous survival on this wild and craggy hilltop. A twelve-sided central pier carries twelve chamfered ribs, which support a pointed vault and are brought down on to twelve wall-arches resting on twelve chamfered demi-shafts. In its way it is as impressive as anything at Gilbert's other castles, Caerphilly and Castell Coch (qq.v.), and increases one's admiration for the master masons he employed.

CYFARTHFA CASTLE, Brecon Road. The castle-style mansion of the Crawshays, built on a slope overlooking the valley of the River Taff, and, what is more to the point, overlooking the family ironworks, with the 'pierced and wounded' mountainsides behind. 1824–5 by *Robert Lugar*, under strict instructions not to exceed a budget of £30,000. The architect defended the castellated style not only as suitable for 'a bold or mountainous' country, but also because the use of rough stone quarried on site kept the cost down. His description of the view from the SW front doubtless reflected his patron's opinion: 'on the foreground, the terrace, park, and river Taff, beyond which the great iron-works become conspicuous; these, at night, offer a truly magnificent scene, resembling the fabled Pandemonium, but upon which the eye may gaze with pleasure, and the mind derive high satisfaction, knowing that several thousand persons are there constantly employed and fed by the active spirit,

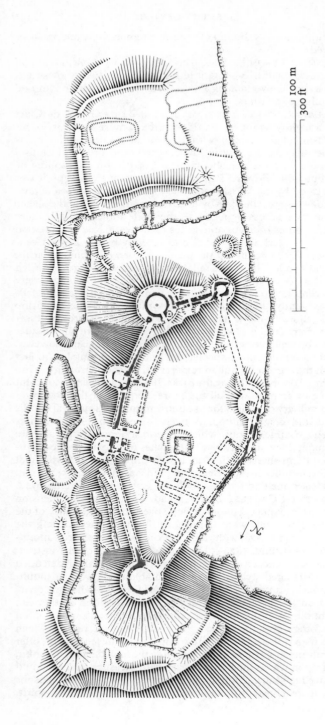

100 m

300 ft

Merthyr Tydfil, Morlais Castle. Plan

powerful enterprise, and noble feeling, of the highly respected owner.'

So this was a house to look out from or to glimpse in the distance among forests and mountains. It must be admitted that close to it gives little pleasure. Dark-hued Pennant sandstone walls virtually unrelieved by ashlar dressings. Unimaginative composition. Long sw entrance front, with stable court to the l., and the shorter se garden front both two-storeyed and battlemented, both regularly punctuated by square and canted turrets with false machicolation. The climax is the s-facing circular tower at the junction of the two fronts, with a circular turret rising higher behind. Large, regularly spaced sash windows under thin hoodmoulds. In the round tower, however, the windows are round-headed with heavy timber frames. The turreted entrance porch leads into a Gothic entrance hall with a ribbed ceiling. The staircase beyond has been demolished. The main rooms, opening to the r. of the vestibule, form an intercommunicating suite, library, drawing room and dining room, with simple classical marble chimneypieces and reticent classical plasterwork. Only the last room has a little more, an overmantel carved with double-ended cornucopias, supported by semi-nude caryatids.

In 1909 the castle and estate were acquired by the Borough Council. It then became a school, and in 1912 large additions were made at the back of the stable court. The castle is now in use as a museum, a purpose which it serves well. The GROUNDS now have much of the character of a municipal park. The PARK LAKE, below the house, however, was constructed as a reservoir, to provide a controlled supply of water for the ironworks.

By the main road, at the bottom of the drive, handsome iron GATEPIERS and RAILINGS. (The gate lodges have been demolished.) Across the road, PANDY FARM, similar in date to the castle but less formal and more endearing, supervised by a broad, low clock-turret.

CYFARTHFA IRONWORKS, which lay to the sw close to the River Taff on the far side of what is now the A470, had, to judge from early views, the most grandly architectural industrial buildings in the county. It was also the largest ironworks in the world during the first two decades of the C19, employing c. 1,500 workers. The main surviving structure is the huge masonry FURNACE BANK with six out of an original seven monumental masonry furnaces. The missing furnace in the surviving bank was replaced by a high brick arch at the end of the C19. The original furnace of 1766 stood some distance upstream.

PONTYCAFNAU, the 'bridge of troughs' (accessible to the N of 74 the Mormon Church in Georgetown). Authorized in 1793, and designed by the local engineers *Watkin George* and *William Aubrey*. The bridge deck is a decked-over trough, which carried both a water course, or leat, and a tramroad. The deck is supported by two raking members which dovetail into a king-post at mid-span. The lower end of the kingpost is connected to a horizontal member which links the two rakers. Thus at each side of the deck there is an A-frame with the addition of a central kingpost. Some later secondary bracings. Three transverse members join the two frames and each cradles the deck trough at the quarter and mid-span points. The mortice-and-tenon and dovetail jointing imitates earlier carpentry practice. The bridge carries the remains of early rails on a deck consisting of an iron box. The central upright once supported a huge upper aqueduct (hence the plural in the bridge's name) to power the famed 'Aeolus' blast water wheel, at the Cyfarthfa Ironworks, with its dual-level feeds.

YNYSFACH IRONWORKS AND ENGINE HOUSE, Ynysfach Road. Operated as part of the Crawshays' Cyfarthfa complex, 1 m. to the N. The bases remain of the four blast FURNACES, two designed by *Watkin George* in 1801 and two added in 1836. The adjoining BLAST-ENGINE HOUSE of 1836 (originally with an engine made at the famous Neath Abbey Ironworks), has been re-roofed as an iron industry museum. It displays the monumental masonry and detail that characterized all the Crawshay works: the bulk of the building is in Pennant rubble masonry, with round-headed openings and corners dressed in white ashlar from the limestone beds which outcrop *c.* 2 m. (3.22 kilometres) to the N and were accessible over Pontycafnau (*see* above).

The historically important Iron Bridge, formerly at Rhyd-y-car, dismantled *c.* 1970, has been re-erected at Chapel Row, Georgetown (*see* p. 446). It was a road-bridge, designed by the local engineering genius *Watkin George*, and shows the transition from carpentry-type mortice-and-tenon joints to the later conventional bolting of adjoining segments.

PERAMBULATION

A walk up the High Street provides a good deal more evidence of the town's architectural ambitions. Outlying survivals of early workers' housing are discussed at the end. At the bottom of the HIGH STREET, by St Tydfil's church, a splendid cast iron FOUNTAIN CANOPY. It originally stood a little further s and has lost its fountain, but it still exudes Victorian pomp and ceremony. Eight fluted columns with foliage caps carry eight semicircular arches, cusped and rope-moulded. Pierced foliage spandrels, dragon finials and a hemispherical dome of pierced foliage panels, with crowning nude classical figure. The designers were *W. Macfarlane & Co.* of Glasgow, the date of erection *c.* 1890, and the purpose to commemorate Robert and Lucy Thomas of Waunwyllt, 'the pioneers in 1828 of the South Wales Steam Coal Trade'.

Where the High Street narrows into a proper street, the first recognizable early survivor is the CROWN INN, on the E side, dated 1785. Its simple classical façade, rendered and painted, must date from half a century later. Next, opposite the Baptist Church, HOWFIELD'S BAKERY, a rendered pediment front of 1904 by *C. M. Davies*. Then, still on the same side, come two early C20 banks, both displaying a panoply of cultivated classicism to dazzle their neighbours. BARCLAYS BANK, 1901–2 by *P. J. Thomas* of Bridgend, has a black granite lower storey with blocked Tuscan columns in projecting end porches, and a white Portland stone upper storey with a rich Corinthian order and heavily pedimented windows. LLOYDS BANK, a little further up, 1922–3 by *Waller & Son* of Gloucester, is more suave, one-storeyed under an attic, nine bays by five. It is controlled by a crisply detailed Ionic order of Erechtheum derivation. Handsome banking hall with Ionic pilasters and coffered ceiling. Between the two banks, in JOHN STREET, the former POST OFFICE (now Concord Discount), facing the Railway Station. This is an enjoyable essay in Arts and Crafts Baroque by *W. T. Oldrieve* of the Office of Works, 1903–5. Red brick and green Quarella stone, the upper walls banded, and crowned by a fanciful gable. Opposite Lloyds Bank, a massive red brick block, on the corner of GLEBELAND STREET. By *E. M. Bruce Vaughan*, his only commercial job, completed in 1904. Well-scaled green dome on the corner. Terracotta decoration and some carving by *William Clarke* of Llandaff. The tall, narrow frontages of Nos. 115–117 HIGH STREET, next door, faced respectively with brown glazed tiles, red sandstone and half-timbering, make a lively group, all presumably *c.* 1900.

Here is the focal point of the town, with St David's church, the Carnegie Library and the former Town Hall ranged together. In front of the church, the cast iron WALL-FOUNTAIN should not be missed. Erected in 1863 'to commemorate the marriage of the Prince of Wales', signed by *Willis Brothers* of London as sculptors and the *Coalbrookdale Company* as casters. Relief figures of Christ and the Woman of Samaria.

CHURCH STREET, which strikes up the hill at this point, is worth pursuing, not only for the chapels and former synagogue to which it leads, but for THOMASTOWN, built *c.* 1851–6, a network of streets opening to l. and r. Two-storeyed, rendered, with a little simple classical detail, and a sense of the overall composition of terraces. At the foot of NEW CASTLE STREET a stone-faced CHAPEL (now Jehovah's Witnesses) designed uniformly with the adjacent terrace.

The upper part of the High Street has nothing further of note until in Pontmorlais the war memorial and former Y.M.C.A. building (*see* p. 440 above) come into view, the latter a real visual climax which must be saved from its current dereliction.

PENYDARREN IRONWORKS, 1 m. NE, off Baden Terrace. The bases of the blast furnaces remain built into a bank, within the confines of a fenced yard, to the S of the road up to Dowlais.

JACKSON'S BRIDGE, Georgetown. A large, early C19 masonry road-bridge over the River Taff which formerly also carried the Dowlais tramroad, one of the earliest rack railways.

At PENYDARREN, W of Penydarren Road, is the site of a ROMAN FORT built in the 70s A.D.

EARLY HOUSING

The early ironworkers' housing in Merthyr Tydfil attracted noto-
riety when it was condemned by a series of philanthropists and
sanitary inspectors in the mid C19. Not surprisingly, very little
remains of it today. Most conspicuous is the terrace off CY-
FARTHFA ROAD, Nos. 22–30 WILLIAMSTOWN. Not among the
earliest, built some time between 1836 and 1851. Two-storey
fronts of rubble-stone, of two quite wide bays with central
doorway. (Stone stairs in the thickness of the wall beside the
hearth, in the traditional Glamorgan way.) The ground rises
sharply behind to the Brecon Road skirting the park wall of
Cyfarthfa Castle.

The best-preserved terrace is Nos. 1–5 CHAPEL ROW, Georgetown, approached from Nantygwenith Street and backing on
to the River Taff. Five houses similar to those at Williamstown,
with restored sash windows. Datable c.1825. The ruined octagonal structure at the NW end was built as a CHAPEL in 1805, but
already converted to use as a storehouse by 1836. Recent executive
houses blight the setting of this evocative group.

(The only examples of what must have been the normal early
workers' houses, with one window up and one down, are Nos.
6–9 COEDCAE'R COURT, off the W end of TWYNYRODYN
ROAD. These too date from some time before 1836.)

DOWLAIS

The foundation of the Dowlais Ironworks in 1759 led to Merthyr
becoming the iron-making metropolis of the world in the first half
of the C19 and the largest town in Wales between 1800 and 1860.
From 1781 it was under the management of members of the Guest
family. Dowlais succeeded Cyfarthfa as the largest ironworks in
the decades approaching the mid C19 when it had the largest
concentration of blast furnaces – fourteen – on one site. At that
time it employed over 7,000 workers. The Dowlais Company
began steel production as early as 1856, and continued to prosper
and develop to the end of the century. In 1891, however, a partial
move was made to East Moors, Cardiff, and in 1930 steel-making
at Dowlais ceased. Much of the remains of the ironworks are now
buried under the great banks of 'reclaimed' soil with the odd
masonry revetment indicating where the great amphitheatre of
furnaces stood at the head of the Morlais Valley.

Since the 1960s Dowlais has been much redeveloped, but the
straight, narrow streets plunging down the hillside W of VIC-
TORIA STREET still evoke Victorian Dowlais. Only the buildings
listed below have survived to bear witness to the Guests and their
great ironworks.

ST JOHN, Union Street. A tablet inside the church records the
    stages by which the present building developed. Built 1827,
    chancel added 1873, transept added 1881 (to the design of
    William Lintern), nave rebuilt 1893 (to the design of *E.A.*

Johnson of Abergavenny). This final phase includes the W (ritual
N) aisle and the polygonal angle turret. Arcade, now blocked,
on round columns with moulded caps. Johnson's nave, wide
and high, is lit by extremely long lancets, mostly pairs but with
one odd triplet. Rock-faced Pennant sandstone with dressings
of Bath stone and yellow brick facing inside. – STAINED GLASS.
Chancel, Ascension, 1884, and Theological Virtues. – Transept, Resurrection between Christ as Light of the World and
as Good Shepherd, *c.*1893 signed by *Jones & Willis*. – Nave,
Creation, with vignettes below including coal-miners (not
ironworkers). 1896, a major work by *R. J. Newbery*. – MONU-
MENT. Sir Josiah John Guest †1852. Jacobean-style tablet,
erected surely a generation after Guest's death.

BETHANIA CHAPEL, South Street. Rendered four-bay front,
pedimented over the centre two. This odd arrangement reflects
a mid-C19 long-wall façade chapel, to which *E. A. Johnson* gave
its present form in 1910, with a three-bay pedimented entrance
front at the downhill end. Complete interior of 1910, galleried
on three sides, capable of seating 1,200, an impressive sight. –
STAINED GLASS. Restrained Mackintosh-style.

BEULAH CHAPEL, Victoria Street. Two-storey gabled front of
grey Pennant sandstone, dated 1856. Doorways and windows
all round-headed and emphasized by rock-faced surrounds.

IVOR ENGLISH INDEPENDENT CHAPEL, Ivor Street. Dated
1860, a rustic design for which the Merthyr builder *John Gabe*
was responsible. Two-storey rendered façade divided into three
bays by thick, crudely detailed Ionic pilasters. Double-height
windows down the sides. Deep bracketed eaves all round.
Inside, the contemporary pews and galleries on three sides
survive. Flat ceiling on a deep cove. Central plaster rose of
Neoclassical pattern. The organ, with its discordantly fancy
iron balustrade, is an addition of 1895.

GUEST MEMORIAL READING ROOM AND LIBRARY, High 70
Street. Nobly Tuscan, designed, it is said, by *Sir Charles Barry*,
although not opened until 1863, three years after his death.*
This is indeed a most unexpected building for the early 1860s,
maintaining a reserve and solemnity more to be expected half
a century earlier. Latin cross plan. High podium of massive
squared blocks of rock-faced local limestone, brought forward
to the S, as piers under the portico. This has four Tuscan
columns, their capitals unfortunately shaved back (compare
the complete capitals on the pilaster responds), a plain, slab-
like entablature, which is carried right round the building,
and a pediment. Pediments in the other three directions also,
supported on pilaster strips. Blank panels over the large rectangular windows of the principal storey. Brown Forest sandstone ashlar at this level, contrasting with the pale grey below.
The building has been converted for domestic use.

*Barry had been patronized lavishly by the Guests for many years, both at Canford
Manor, Dorset, their country seat, and at Dowlais, where he designed the spectacular, but now sadly demolished, Gothic school for Lady Charlotte in 1855.

PUBLIC LIBRARY. 1903–6 by *E. A. Johnson*. A charming building, Arts and Crafts Tudor, with runs of unmoulded mullion-
and-transom windows, and big mullioned bullseye windows in
the shaped gables. Deft touches of sculpture (by *T. A. Jones* of
Cardiff). Rock-faced local limestone amply dressed with pink
sandstone ashlar (from Alveley in Shropshire).

STABLES. The most monumental surviving building in Dowlais,
erected in 1820 by Sir John Guest for the ironworks company's
horses. The twenty-one-bay front range, two-storeyed, of
coarse sandstone, has recently been restored and converted for
domestic use. Originally a school occupied the upper storey.
Pedimented central entrance arch as high as the eaves. End
bays also pedimented, the windows here set under giant relieving arches.

BLAST-ENGINE HOUSE. Mid-C19, of red brick picked out with
yellow brick, the sole visible survivor of Dowlais Ironworks. A
rectangular block, with top parapet and windows segmental
above, round-headed below with deep sunk panels beneath
them. Massive cast iron porch on paired columns. The OP
Chocolate Factory, which now uses the building, pays the
compliment of allowing it to stand in poignant isolation.

MICHAELSTON-LE-PIT/
1070   LLANFIHANGEL-Y-PWLL

The village, surrounded by wooded hills, just eludes the stretching
tentacles of Cardiff, Penarth and Barry which encircle it. The
church is accompanied by a charming terrace in the cottage orné
idiom, Nos. 1–3 CHURCH COTTAGES, *c.* 1860, stone and red
brick with big white bargeboards, a group of COUNCIL HOUSES
of *c.* 1950, white, simple and appropriate, and an aggressive
HOUSE of *c.* 1970, with monopitch roofs.

ST MICHAEL AND ALL ANGELS. A characterful church, both
in itself and in its fittings. Cruciform plan, but the transepts so
diminutive that they are mere lean-tos. Crossing tower with a
saddleback roof pierced at belfry level by small rectangular
openings. Chancel and transepts have large, well-cut quoins of
Sutton stone, which, taken with the trefoil-headed lancet in the
N transept, suggest a date perhaps in the early C14. Nave quoins
less substantial. The S doorway in the nave, two-centred,
moulded with a step between two thin hollow mouldings, may
be later in the C14. Polygonal stoup beside it. Perp windows
inserted, chancel E and nave S. Others inserted in the C19. The
S porch must be late medieval, since it overlaps the Perp
window, but note that it has been given a plinth moulding
integrated with that of the nave S wall. Inside, the crossing
arches are disappointingly rude, two-centred but of undressed
stone. Doorway NE of the crossing to the tower stair, with a
bold stop chamfer. In the N transept an aumbry, in the S
transept a squint, showing that they were intended for side

altars. – FONT. Medieval. Octagonal on a round stem. – PULPIT. A three-decker of the C18. Quite simple. – PEWS. All arranged to face the pulpit. So those in the transepts and even those in the chancel face W. Altogether a remarkable survival from pre-ecclesiological days. – STAINED GLASS. Chancel E, Crucifixion, after 1889. Yellows and browns, reflecting the reaction towards subdued colours in the 1890s. – Chancel S, the seasons in flowers, c. 1986 by *Frank Roper*. Kitsch. – Nave NE, saints, c. 1907, signed by *Heaton, Butler & Bayne*, a routine piece. – Nave NW, St Francis, 1973, by *Roper* of course. – Nave W, the only important window in the church, dated 1955 and signed by *Sir Ninian Comper*. Four archangels, looking oddly docile.

CWRT-YR-ALA, ½m. W. Built in 1939–40 by *Sir Percy Thomas* for Sir Hubert Merritt. Ghostly Neo-Georgian, on a spectacular site.

MICHAELSTON-SUPER-ELY/ LLANFIHANGEL-AR-ELÁI

1070

ST MICHAEL. Nave and lower chancel, tiny S transept and S porch. W tower with saddleback roof. All these elements are medieval in origin, but the restoration of 1863–4 by *David Vaughan* tampered with everything. This at least makes the building visually more effective, however much it may have confused its history. The earliest feature is the course of her-ringbone masonry at the foot of the nave N wall, of the early C12. C14 S doorway. In the S wall of the nave a C14 lancet, ogee-headed and trefoiled, and a C15 cinquefoiled two-lighter under a hoodmould. The similar window in the nave N wall came from the chancel in 1864. Wide blocked arch on the N side of the chancel, for a vestry proposed in 1908. Inside, a holy water stoup on a stem by the S door, a stone bench at the W end of the N wall, and a small doorway into the tower at an upper level. The Norman character of the C19 chancel arch reflects the existence, but not the ambition of a C12 pre-decessor. – FONT. Small octagonal medieval bowl on a modern circular stem. – STAINED GLASS. Chancel E, Martha and Mary, 1864, by *Heaton, Butler & Bayne*. – MONUMENT. Small wooden tablet carved with a richly mantled shield of arms and dated 1546. It commemorates not a person but a transfer of property.

MISKIN/MEISGYN

0080

ST DAVID. At the end of an avenue of lime trees. An estate church, built largely at the expense of Emma Eleanor Williams of Miskin Manor, in 1906–7. Not, however, the work of a fashionable Londoner, but an opportunity for a well-tried local, *E. M. Bruce Vaughan*, to show his paces. The result is earnestly handsome. Over-buttressed w tower, aisleless nave and lower chancel. E.E. and Dec. Faced with green Quarella stone outside and in. Internal shafting to the windows, trickily handled in the nave, and wall-shafts to support the roof trusses. Chancel arch and sanctuary arch. – STAINED GLASS. E window, Christ between SS George and Paul. Large figures in thistly foliage. – Nave SE, SS David and Michael, 1906. By the same hand. – Three windows in the nave by *Jessie Bayes*, to members of the Rhys Williams family, *c*. 1943–64. Pastel colours but emphatic leading.

The church was built at the park gates of Miskin Manor, close to the knot of early C19 terraces which still form a compact village centre.

MISKIN MANOR, now a hotel, can be approached from the village only on foot. Car-drivers must take a circuitous route along and then over the A4119 to reach it. Victorian L-plan mansion of local stone in a Tudor style. Earlier, perhaps originally C17, service range adjoining to the N. Built in 1864, perhaps to the design of *David Vaughan* (T. Lloyd) and subsequently tinkered with. The W and S fronts both of four broad bays. Mullion-and-transom windows of Victorian expansiveness. Straight-sided gables. Jacobean-style interiors, compromised by fires in 1922 and 1952. Discreet additions for the hotel *c*. 1990 in a watered-down Tudor style.

SCHOOL, at the NE end of the village. Dated 1875, a very early board school. Single-storeyed, of stone. Two gables thrust large mullion-and-transom windows under pointed relieving arches towards the road. So the Gothic of the church school is not yet altogether abandoned. (Disused at the time of writing.)

(FELIN ISAF, 1½ m. SE. A small C12 motte and partly surviving bailey, in a flat, non-defensible position close to the River Ely. Now virtually inaccessible, since the enormous BOSCH FACTORY, 1989–90 by *A. D. Shepherd & Partners*, was built immediately to the N. It should still be possible to see it from the train.)

MONKNASH/YR AS FAWR

9070

ST MARY. High above the Bristol Channel. Of rough local limestone, nave with tiny w bell-gablet and deep s porch. Lower chancel. The first impression is of a late medieval building. N and S windows, square-headed under hoodmoulds, with one, two or three arched lights. Massive reinforcement of the N wall. Chancel E wall C19, with misleading Dec window. However, the NE one-lighter with roll moulding looks late C12. The S doorway has a plainly chamfered four-centred arch, but its rere-arch is semicircular. Matching rere-arch in the N wall (the doorway walled in). Narrow chancel arch, also semicircular, on crude massive imposts. So nave and chancel in fact constitute a complete Norman church. Arch-braced nave roof. Restoration of 1860 by *Prichard & Seddon*. – FONT. Simplest late medieval, octagonal bowl. – PULPIT. *c.* 1870. Stone. Chunky, catching the spirit of the building.

GRANGE, 200 yds NW. The only monastic grange in the county where enough remains to demonstrate the massive scale on which medieval monasteries carried on their farming. Monknash Grange belonged to Neath Abbey (q.v.). The most conspicuous element is the ruined BARN. The ivy-clad NE gable, the central porch incorporated into a modern cottage, and the SE ends of the side walls, together enable one to realize its vast size. Measuring 211 by 34 ft (64.4 by 10.4 metres) internally, it was comparable to all but the very largest monastic barns in England. Buttresses divided it into eleven bays, each with a long ventilation slit, but no datable features remain. The most likely period for its construction would be the C13.

The barn stands within the E boundary of a roughly pentagonal, 20-acre (8-hectare) ENCLOSURE defined by earth banks and ditches. Traces of other buildings in the centre of the enclosure, of which only a circular DOVECOTE, roofless and bereft of most of its nesting boxes, is readily identifiable.

The PLOUGH AND HARROW continues the group N-wards, its walls rendered white, its irregular windows of the C18. The N half was built in the early C17 on a lobby-entry plan, the s half is a later extension, as the straight joint to the l. of the entrance doorway shows.

MOUNTAIN ASH/ABERPENNAR

0090

The child of the steam coal trade. Henry Austin Bruce (later Lord Aberdare) of Dyffryn House as landowner and the entrepreneurs Thomas Powell, who was sinking pits on the estate by the 1840s, and John Nixon, whose company worked the famous Deep Duffryn mine from the 1850s, ensured its growth. By 1863 the population of Mountain Ash was already *c.* 6,000. The earliest surviving streets are the grid SE of St Margaret's church, on the E bank of the Afan Cynon. On the w bank High Street and Oxford Street were built up by the 1870s, running SE to Navigation Colliery. In the last twenty years of the C19 Miskin developed beyond it, and Penrhiwceiber Woods were felled as a further colliery and terraces set on the steeply sloping hillside took their place. By the turn of the century the present continuous 2-m. (3.22-kilometre)-long development was complete. Only the collieries have subsequently disappeared, their spoil-tips gradually giving way to light industry and to grass.

ST MARGARET. Complicated in appearance, reflecting its complex history. Coursed Pennant sandstone with Bath stone dressings. The w* half survives from *Prichard & Seddon*'s church of 1861–2. Nave and s aisle under a continuous roof, richly carved s porch and transeptal gable with bold plate-traceried end window. Matching N aisle and vestry, 1883–4 by

*Ritual w. The church is actually oriented s–N.

Prichard. 1895–8 *E. M. Bruce Vaughan* replaced the chancel with a second, larger S transept, an undersized SE tower with battlements and a short pyramidal spire, and a straight-ended chancel. Stabilizing E buttresses added in 1986–7.

Internally, the Prichard-Seddon arcades are themselves strangely complicated, the double-chamfered arches oddly related to the square caps of the circular shafts. Good foliage carving on the E piers and the chancel arch, which clearly survives from the original building. In the chancel, portrait head-stops of Queen Victoria, the Bishop of Llandaff and of benefactors. – REREDOS. 1904. Designed by *Bruce Vaughan*. Caen stone figures seated under canopies on red and green marble shafts. God flanked by Aaron and Abraham to the l., Isaiah and St Peter to the r. – FONT. 1905. – STAINED GLASS. E window, Crucifixion with St Michael, and Old and New Testament subjects, a major work by *R.J. Newbery*. 1900. It commemorates John Nixon, principal colliery owner in the Cynon Valley. – Sanctuary N and S by the same. – N transept, SS Cecilia and Margaret, by *Mary Lowndes*, 1917. – N aisle NE, 1916 by *James Clarke*, a daringly uncompromising profession of faith: a dead soldier rests his hand on the feet of the crucified Christ. – Then in the N aisle a second military subject, *c.* 1930, signed by *A. J. Davies* of the *Bromsgrove Guild*, and a pair of saints *c.* 1957, by *Celtic Studios* in their El Greco style. – S aisle. Noli me Tangere, *c.* 1924, not signed but displaying the perfervid emotionalism of *A. J. Davies* of the *Bromsgrove Guild*.

ST JOHN THE BAPTIST, Clarence Street, Miskin. The aisled nave with its showy Arts and Crafts W bellcote is of 1908–9 by *E. M. Bruce Vaughan*. Chancel 1961 in reduced form. – STAINED GLASS. S aisle window, 'Blessed are they that mourn', signed by *A. J. Davies* of the *Bromsgrove Guild*, *c.* 1932. Highly characteristic in its brilliant coloration and maudlin mood. – N aisle E window. Resurrected Christ. After 1902. Arrestingly asymmetrical, being two lights only of a three-light composition made for Mountain Ash church.

ST WINEFRED, Penrhiwceiber Road, Penrhiwceiber. 1882–3. Rock-faced local sandstone with dressings of Ombersley stone, a hint that the architect was not local. He was *Thomas Nicholson* of Hereford. Nave with W bell gable, lower chancel, managed without a chancel arch. E.E. with some fanciful touches, especially the cusped outline of the N door. S aisle squeezed in, 1911 by *Morgan & Elford* of Mountain Ash. – STAINED GLASS. E window, SS Cecilia and Winefred and Charity, signed by *Jones & Willis*, 1898. – W window, 1911, also signed by *Jones & Willis*. Christ in three guises, Old Testament scenes below.

OUR LADY OF LOURDES (R.C.), Oxford Street. Dec. 1897–9 by *Bernard Smith* of London. (– STAINED GLASS. A window by *Paul Woodroffe*, *c.* 1902.)

BETHANIA INDEPENDENT CHAPEL, Philip Street. Dated 1859. Rendered façade with good classical detail. Overall pediment on a dentilled cornice. Rusticated doorway and flanking windows, moulded surrounds to the round-headed windows above. The interior is delightfully preserved. Galleries on three sides. Flat plaster ceiling on a big cove, enriched with five plaster roses, boldly picked out in red. The VESTRY to the r. is also a period piece. Tip-up raked seating.

BETHESDA ENGLISH BAPTIST CHAPEL, Penrhiwceiber Road. 1905. An excellent Arts and Crafts façade, exploiting contrasted sandstone textures. Full-height battered buttresses frame a broad segment-headed window. Flanking upper glazed loggias under miniature hipped roofs. The architect's name remains elusive.

CAPEL FFRWD (Welsh Baptist), Duffryn Road, 1900–1 by *Morgan & Elford* of Mountain Ash. A severe façade, of dark sandstone, used for the ashlar dressings as well as the rock-faced walling. Almost as if from the Netherlands of the early C17. Mullion-and-transom windows entirely without mouldings. Roof gable banded and punctuated with kneelers. Broad porch, just an entablature carried on stocky pseudo-Tuscan columns.

HERMON WELSH CALVINISTIC METHODIST CHAPEL, Railway Terrace, Penrhiwceiber. 1896 by *D. Roderick* of Aberdare. Sandstone. Idiosyncratically classical. Bar tracery of circles in the tripartite window which breaks up into the pediment. The chapel is derelict at the time of writing.

WELSH CONGREGATIONAL CHURCH, High Street. (Now Teachers' Centre.) Dated 1904. Massive rusticated voussoirs to all the windows make the façade memorable. By *T. W. Millar* of Mountain Ash.

NAZARETH ENGLISH BAPTIST CHURCH. Prominently sited at r.-angles to the Town Hall, but baldly unenterprising. Pedimented façade of sandstone. All the openings round-headed, in pairs with a central trio. By *T. W. Millar* of Mountain Ash, 1901.

PROVIDENCE ENGLISH CONGREGATIONAL CHURCH, Union Street. 1911–12 by *T. W. Millar*. Perp. Prominent in the view of the town from the bridge, especially its polygonal tower, topless though it now is. Converted to secular use in 1994.

ELIM PENTECOSTAL CHAPEL, Knight Street. Bowed front between low side towers.

TOWN HALL, Mountain Ash. 1902–4 by *J. H. Phillips* of Cardiff, after a competition. Rock-faced Pennant sandstone generously dressed with Bath stone ashlar. Arts and Crafts Baroque, deftly enhanced with sculpture. Overall hipped roof, but the symmetry of the frontage absurdly compromised by the road curving round too close on the r. (The interior has been converted for office use.)

MOUNTAIN ASH WORKMEN'S CLUB AND INSTITUTE, Oxford Street. This four-storey monster in the palazzo style dominates the town's main shopping street.

MESSRS NIXON WORKMEN'S INSTITUTE, LIBRARY AND PUBLIC HALL, Oxford Street. One of the most splendid of all the workmen's institutes in the Valleys, and surely worth saving from its present sorry state of dereliction. Built in 1898–9 for

£8,000 to the designs of *Dan Lloyd* of Aberbeeg. In essence
Wren-style, but with many idiosyncratic variations. Yellow
brick. Doric pilasters of red brick carry a triglyph frieze across
the façade, and continue without it round the sides. Segment-
headed windows below, long round-headed ones for the piano
nobile and a bullseye window in the pedimental gable. The
central pedimented doorway is the real showpiece, enriched
with terracotta glazed and unglazed, red, yellow and even blue.
Erected at the expense of the workmen of Nixon's Navigation
Collieries, to provide for their mental and physical recreation.
It provided on the one hand a library, reading and lecture
rooms, and a theatre seating 1,500, and on the other billiards
and other games rooms and a gymnasium, with in the basement
a swimming pool 54 ft (16.45 metres) long.
(WORKMEN'S INSTITUTE AND PUBLIC HALL, Penrhiwceiber
Road. 1888 by *E. H. Bruton* of Cardiff, enlarged in 1900 by
Morgan & Elford.)

1080   NANTGARW
                    2½ m. sw of Caerphilly

NANTGARW POTTERY. The famous porcelain works were
founded by William Weston Young and William Billingsley in
1813 and ceased production in 1822. The Pardoe family reused
the site as an earthenware works from 1833 until the 1920s. Two
ranges of rubble Pennant sandstone, with the lower sections of
three 'bottle' kilns, extend along the E bank of the former
Glamorganshire Canal, w of the main valley road. Later buildings are distinguished by the use of brick dressings.

8090   NANTYFFYLLON
                    1 m. N of Maesteg

The long main street works its way steadily upwards along the w
slope of the Llynfi Valley. Two prominent chapels of the 1870s,
evidence of the comparatively early date of mining development
here.

SALEM WELSH BAPTIST CHAPEL. Dated 1872. Pedimented.
Thin Tuscan pilasters. Coupled arched windows above and
below, both on the façade and along the sides.
SILOH INDEPENDENT CHAPEL. Dated 1876. By the Rev.
Thomas Thomas of Landore, an ambitious and typical piece
which, sadly, stands derelict at the time of writing. Overall
pediment with entablature carried on Doric pilasters and
boldly broken into by a segmental arch, to provide room for
a date roundel over the triple central window. Paired entrance
doorways with spandrel carving of a dove among flowers
and leaves. Over-elongated side windows to light the gallery
stairs.

NANT-Y-MOEL   9090

At the head of the Ogmore Valley, developed as an outpost
of David Davies's great coal-mining enterprise in the Rhondda
Fawr.

ST PETER. 1887–9 by *E. M. Bruce Vaughan*. Grey-green Pennant
sandstone with red brick dressings. Lancets. (Disused.)

NEATH/CASTELL NEDD   7090

Neath originated in the early C12, when the River Neath formed
the western boundary of Norman penetration into South Wales.
Castle and borough town were established on the E bank of the
river, and the abbey was founded shortly afterwards in 1130, on
the far side of the river $1\frac{1}{4}$ m. (2 kilometres) to the W. In the later
Middle Ages town and abbey were in competition for river trade,
and in 1491 the Town Hall was reported to be in ruins. The key
to Neath's subsequent development as an industrial centre was
the availability of coal exceptionally close to the coast. Sir Humphrey Mackworth of the Gnoll, whose mansion dominated the
little town from its hilltop, pioneered both copper- and lead-
working from the 1690s, and the celebrated Neath Abbey Ironworks began operation soon after. The Vale of Neath Canal,
1794–5, and subsequent railways, opened up the hinterland. But
the town remained of very modest size, clustered around St
Thomas's church, but held back from the riverbank by a strip of
noxious industry. In 1801 there were 2,500 inhabitants, and half
a century later the population had little more than doubled. Urban
pride developed from the 1860s, aided by a local benefactor,
Howel Gwyn of Dyffryn. A spectacular church and handsome
chapels took their places along the London Road, to the S of the
town, and a network of residential streets developed to the S and
E. Today Neath has probably the pleasantest town centre in
Glamorgan, thanks to imaginative pedestrianization of the streets
round St Thomas's church, though the continued separation of
the town from the river by an inner by-pass seems a missed
opportunity.

NIDUM, W of the River Neath. Little is visible of the ROMAN
AUXILIARY FORT. Excavated foundations of the SOUTH-EAST
GATEWAY and SOUTH-EAST GUARD CHAMBER of the SW
gate are preserved in ROMAN WAY, their antiquity jarring with
the modernity of the surrounding housing estate. The double
roadway through the SE gate was flanked by towers and fronted
by a ditch, implying the former existence of a bridge. Excavations in the playing fields, across the road from the SE gate,
in which the line of the NW defence can be detected as a slight
rise, have revealed the N angle tower and evidence for timber
structures including barracks and the headquarters building.
First constructed in the mid 70s A.D., the earth and timber
defences were rebuilt in stone in the early 120s A.D., apparently

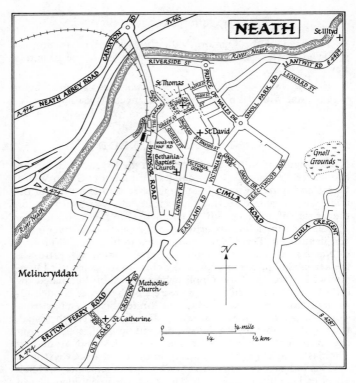

after a period of abandonment. Occupation ceased *c.*A.D. 150.
ST THOMAS, Church Place. Only the w tower survives of the
medieval church, Perp with a moulded plinth and diagonal
buttresses, which suggest a late C15 date. Of Pennant sandstone, but large upper areas are faced with blocks of squared
Sutton stone, reused presumably from the castle. The body of
the church appears all of the C18, the product of an enlargement
in 1730, when aisles were added. Cement render recently
renewed. Lower chancel with simple Venetian E window. Pedimented doorcases at the w end of the aisles – for gallery
stairs? Round-headed aisle windows given simple tracery in the
restoration of 1874. Internally, too, the C18 work is of the
simplest. Plain round arcade arches on thick square piers with
capital mouldings barely scratched in. No chancel arch. C19
boarded roof. – FONT. A handsome piece, doubtless of 1730.
Stone. Circular bowl boldly gadrooned. – ROYAL ARMS. Dated
1731. – STAINED GLASS. Plenty of it, but nothing distinguished. – w window, the four Evangelists and four major
prophets, dated 1874. – *Mayer & Co.* sign the Resurrection
window in the s aisle, and also supplied the neighbouring
window of Paul preaching at Athens, both in 1909. (– Show-
men's Guild window, 1994 by *Elizabeth Edmundson.* Under

fairground influence.) – MONUMENTS. Plenty of these, too.
The best is hidden behind the organ. Sir Robert Mackworth
†1794. Large hanging wall-monument, with an urn on a
draped, bulgy sarcophagus. Signed *Jones Dunn Drew*, Bristol. –
Henry Crane †1831. Tablet in a Gothic frame, erected after
1837. Signed by *Bedford* of Oxford Street, London. – Col.
Turner Grant †1844. Similar but unsigned.

ST DAVID, Orchard Street. Built on a site donated by Howel
Gwyn (*see* below). The town is dominated by this tremendous
statement of High Victorian confidence, *John Norton*'s masterpiece in the county. Norton, who had a good West Country
connection, had already worked in the county at Rheola,
Resolven, and this led to his commission here. 1864–6, the
tower completed *c.* 1869. This shoots up unbuttressed to its
crown, a slated pyramid with four smaller pyramids at its
base and four clockfaces. The model for this is G. E. Street's
campanile at St James the Less, London. The tower stands
between chancel and S transept, where its full height can make
maximum effect. Street is also behind the planning of the
church, with an apsidal chancel, short transepts, and nave with
low lean-to aisles and prominent plate-traceried windows in
clerestory and transept ends. A phalanx of close-set plate-
traceried windows in the apse. Lean-to W porch, with an open
arcade on short cruciform piers. Conspicuous S porch, its
shafted double-arched entrance enclosed by a superarch with
a relief sculpture of a bishop. Norton's own are the idiosyncratic
arcaded parapets and strange faceted pinnacles. Externally,
greenish-grey Pennant sandstone predominates, with Bath
stone ashlar and thin bands of pink conglomerate, stressing
lines of architectural significance and increasing in density
towards the E.

The interior of the S porch gives a foretaste of what is to
come inside the church, faced with red brick boldly patterned
in black. The spatial effect of the interior is entirely unexpected,
the nave extremely broad, the chancel arch high and wide, the
brightly lit apse broad also. Narrow aisles with stone transverse
arches. Transepts not emphasized. Shafted arcading in the
clerestory and round the apse. – PULPIT. Lavish, with marble
shafts and bosses. Presumably by Norton. – STAINED GLASS.
In the apse many small scenes. Only the three central windows
are contemporary with the church, by *Clayton & Bell*. Flanking
pair of *c.* 1900. – Nave W, large and elaborate, Welsh saints
with narrative scenes below, set in prickly late Gothic tab-
ernacles. Dated 1912. – In the N aisle two good recent windows,
both musical in theme, one by *Frank Roper*, *c.* 1981, in his
unmistakable idiom, the other signed by *John Petts*, 1984.

ST ILLTYD, Llantwit Road. Beyond the end of the town, overlooking the river. Elemental W tower, short, on a high battered
base which is tunnel-vaulted internally without dressed stone.
Crude single-light bell-openings. The usual corbelled battlements. Medieval. How can one get closer to the date? The Perp
W door and window over, which cut into the batter of the lower

walls, must be insertions. Nave and lower chancel, established
as of early date by the chancel arch, narrow, round-headed on
plain imposts. The rough-and-ready round-headed windows
belong to the drastic restoration of 1858–9 by 'Mr *Vaughan*'. –
ALTAR RAILS. Turned balusters of *c.*1700. – PULPIT. Two-
decker. Simple. Doubtless of 1859. – MONUMENTS. None to
mention inside, but the nave wall externally is inset with C18
headstones in the form of a cross and a vertical panel.

ST CATHERINE, Old Road, Melincryddan. 1888–91 by the
young *J. Coates Carter* in collaboration with *D. M. Davies* of
Neath. Rock-faced local sandstone and Bath stone dressings
and bands. An economical church, with lancets, aisled nave
and chancel differentiated only by a flèche. Yet there is a certain
dignity about its lofty proportions. w front with battered and
stepped buttresses. Timber arcades. Roof of trefoil section with
boarded ceiling. – PULPIT. Handsome and unusual. Mauve,
black and mottled grey marbles. – STAINED GLASS. e window,
Suffer the Little Children, 1911 by *Heaton, Butler & Bayne*. –
One s lancet by *Celtic Studios*, 1970.

BETHANIA WELSH BAPTIST CHURCH, London Road.
1862–3. The contractor was *J. D. Rees*. The design was
probably supplied by the Rev. *Henry Thomas* (cf. Calfaria
Chapel, Clydach). A convincing essay in the temple mode.
Tuscan pilasters carry an entablature and pediment. Projecting
porch on paired Tuscan columns of timber. Tuscan Venetian
window over. Rock-faced coursed squared Pennant sandstone,
the ashlarwork painted. Contemporary interior, galleried on
three sides, the box pews at ground level orientated to reflect
the gallery seating. Cast iron gallery fronts in a pattern of
palmettes in circles. Broad decorative cast iron pulpit enclosure.
Flat ceiling on a cove, with a single central plaster rose. Later
organ.

CHAPEL, High Street West. 1884 by *D. M. Davies*. Plain. Beside
it, MISSION HALL, dated 1903, in an advanced Arts and
Crafts style. Upper windows in a continuous run over an
expanse of red brick wall.

ENGLISH PRESBYTERIAN CHURCH OF WALES, London
Road. 1903–4 by *S. C. Jones* of Neath. Dec. Gallery stair projections flank the entrance front. Shallow transeptal projection
on the long return wall. The interior lacks its intended side
galleries. Thin hammerbeam roof.

ORCHARD PLACE ENGLISH BAPTIST CHURCH, London
Road. 1871–2 by *Lander & Bedells*. Large and ambitious, facing
across to St David's church. Rock-faced sandstone with yellow
brick dressings. Coarse, round-arched style. Elaborate arrangement of steps to the entrance doorways. Within there are galleries on all four sides. Bowed, pierced iron gallery fronts.
Plaster ceiling of complex profile and exposed roof structure of
tie-beams and queenposts. Cross-range at the rear of *c.*1905,
providing fourteen classrooms.

METHODIST CHAPEL (now Moose Hall), Castle Street. Opened
1813. Later neo-Norman frontage.

METHODIST CHURCH, Briton Ferry Road. 1913–14 by *J. Wills & Son* of Derby. Gothic. A demonstrative group with its steeple and Sunday school to the l. Brown glazed brick and yellow terracotta.

QUAKER MEETING HOUSE. Set in a walled forecourt N of the castle gatehouse. Said to have been built in 1799. Completely domestic-looking. Three bays, two storeys, sash windows with brick heads. Rubble-sandstone walls.

SOAR-MAESYRHAF INDEPENDENT CHAPEL, Maes-yr-Haf Road. Built 1864–6, influenced by Thomas Thomas of Landore. Pediment broken into by an arch over the tripartite central window. Long, thin side windows with rusticated surrounds. Fine interior, little altered. Flat boarded ceiling subdivided by plaster guilloche bands. Galleries, on fluted iron columns with leaf capitals, carried round all four sides, that behind the pulpit dipping lower than the rest. Box pews. Pulpit of *c.* 1880.

GWYN HALL, Orchard Street. 1887 by *John Norton*, on a site donated by Howel Gwyn. Gothic, but a tired performance compared to his nearby church of twenty years earlier. Rock-faced Pennant sandstone with Bath stone dressings. Central five-bay loggia with slender piers and steeply pointed arches. Large segmental hall windows above and behind, with Dec tracery. Large flanking stair towers, one pyramid-roofed, the other gabled.

CIVIC CENTRE, Prince of Wales Drive. 1962–6 by *Kenneth Hathaway*. Offices for the Borough Council and the Rural District Council in two four-storey blocks set parallel corner to corner and linked by a vestibule. Armature of slender uprights and cladding in two colours of concrete aggregate made with grey Cornish granite and white calcia flint. FOUNTAIN by the roads, jetting against a bronze sculpture by *Hathaway*, 1965. Not abstract, but 'the formation of an Aluminium Crystal magnified 25,000 times'.

PUBLIC LIBRARY, Victoria Gardens. 1904, by *D. M. Jenkins*, the Borough Engineer. Italianate. Not large. Grey Pennant sandstone with generous red sandstone dressings.

CASTLE, Castle Street. An earthwork castle was established on the bank of the River Neath by Earl Robert of Gloucester some time between 1114 and 1130. The ovoid curtain wall, of which not much more than footings are visible, must follow the line of this ringwork. Projecting from the wall on the S side the battered base of a drum tower with a spur-like projection to the E.

What impresses is the early C14 GATEHOUSE facing N, built after the castle had been razed in 1321. It was formed by placing a new tower beside an existing angle tower. Three-storeyed, rising almost to its full original height, though robbed of virtually all its dressed stone. Entrance arch of four-centred profile with multiple mouldings flanked by drum towers, linked high up by a machicolation arch. One central lancet window and one high on the r. tower. Otherwise the openings are all gaping holes, the lower ones doubtless marking the sites of arrow loops. Many putlock holes.

BRIDGE, over the River Neath, accessible from Croft Road. Built in the 1790s. Of brick. Three segmental arches. Pointed cutwaters. Its handsome design and exact craftsmanship can just be appreciated under the steel roadway now crudely clamped upon it.

PERAMBULATION

The obvious place to start is in front of St David's church. First, turning to the W, on the corner of ORCHARD STREET, CONSTITUTIONAL CLUB, of c. 1880, small but a fit companion for Norton's church and Gwyn Hall. Gothic. Red brick patterned with black brick, yellow brick and terracotta. On the angle an oriel, set on a deep, complex corbel and crowned by a polygonal candle-snuffer roof. Windows with geometrical tracery. Beyond Gwyn Hall, in GREEN STREET, the GENERAL MARKET, an aisled iron and glass structure built in 1837, enlarged 1877 and given a sober, minimally classical stone frontage towards the street in 1904, by *D. M. Jenkins*, the Borough Engineer. In QUEEN STREET, opposite the market, No. 29 is the MASONIC TEMPLE, its three-bay front dated 1848. Remarkable display of Masonic imagery, above all a large eye carved in the centre of the parapet.

The far end of Green Street meets WINDSOR ROAD. Here is a rivalrous display of early C20 stone-faced classical banks. Starting at the S, in Windsor Road itself, they are LLOYDS BANK, a Doric Trianon faced in Portland stone, and MIDLAND BANK, 1908–9 by *Glendinning Moxham* of Swansea, with an Ionic four-columned portico at an upper level, faced in Bath stone; then NATIONAL WESTMINSTER BANK, 1929 by *F.C.R. Palmer & W. F. C. Holden*, a convex façade of Portland stone. Doric half-columns. Lastly, after a gap, in THE PARADE, most ambitious of all, BARCLAYS BANK, dating from before the turn of the century. Bath stone. A regular palazzo, Ionic below and Corinthian above, the attached columns trickily spaced. Designed in 1894 for the London and Provincial Bank by *J. Buckley Wilson & Glendinning Moxham*. Steep pavilion roofs were designed for the end bays.

By following The Parade to the N or by retracing one's steps down Green Street one can reach the heart of old Neath, CHURCH PLACE and St Thomas's church and churchyard. Here at the NW corner the OLD TOWN HALL, 1820 by *Thomas Bowen* of Swansea. Neoclassical civic architecture, a rarity in Glamorgan. Single-storey, recessed centre with steps rising quite grandly behind four fluted Doric columns, which have been rendered baseless by the subsequent raising of the lowest steps. Pedimented side bays, the l. with a round-headed window under a relieving arch, the r. not matching, presumably altered. To the rear the ground drops, and here the building is two-storeyed with an arcade. Also on the N side of Church Place, the MECHANICS INSTITUTE, dated 1847, quite simple but recognizably in a Barryesque palazzo style. The architect was *Alfred Russell Wallace*, who later became celebrated as a naturalist and collaborator with Charles Darwin (see the plaque on the building).

From the SE corner of Church Place one can walk out towards the castle and to a pedestrianized terrace. Here steps lead down to the recent, well-managed SHOPPING CENTRE, *c.* 1990–1 by *Moxley Jenner*. Low Japanese-style roofs come down on to slender green metal posts and stout cylindrical stone piers. Quite a grove of trees planted to soften the effect of the car park.

Returning to St David's church, one can make a fresh start towards the E. To the S the broad green space of VICTORIA PARK, opened 1887, where there is a pretty BANDSTAND, and the bronze STATUE of Howel Gwyn of Dyffryn, the town's main Victorian benefactor (†1888). Gwyn is shown standing in a fur-lined coat and raising an admonitory finger. Signed by *M. Ricci*. To the E of the church, in ST DAVID'S STREET, ALDERMAN DAVIES CHURCH IN WALES PRIMARY SCHOOL. Stone, E.E., symmetrical. Projecting chimneybreasts now lacking their stacks. 1857 by *Egbert Moxham* of Neath. Across Gnoll Park Road, down GNOLL AVENUE, to the E, the C19 ENTRANCE GATE to Gnoll (*see* below). At the N end of Gnoll Park Road, in LEONARD STREET, the eyecatching LLEWELLYN ALMSHOUSES, 1897 by *G. E. Halliday*, built by the widow of Griffith Llewellyn of Baglan. Very red, the brick from Ruabon, the stone from Carlisle, the style smacking of Surrey. Half-timbered central gable, the rest single-storeyed with small paired gables to l. and r. Cusped, arched lights to the windows. Just beyond, in LLANTWIT ROAD, the much-altered stone building dated 1838 was erected as the WORKHOUSE, one of the first in the county. Sub-classical.

GNOLL GROUNDS, approached from Cimla Crescent. The most extensive and varied landscape garden in the county, now sadly deprived of its house, Gnoll. This took its name from the large, now entirely wooded, knoll which dominates and provides a special character to the distant view of Neath. At what date a house was first built on its brow is not known, but in 1686 the estate came into the possession of Sir Humphrey Mackworth, the pioneer of Neath's development as a centre of copper-smelting. The house, which survived until 1957, was largely built 1776–8 by his grandson, Sir Herbert, who employed as his architect *John Johnson* of Leicester. Its principal façade was three-storeyed with full-height end bows and a battlemented skyline, a fashionable formula (cf. Adam's Wenvoe Castle and Holland's remodelling of Cardiff Castle). The grounds were laid out in three stages, the first 1724–7 by *Thomas Greening* for the then elderly Sir Humphrey, featuring a bowling green, a terrace and a formal cascade. Greening's layout, a sequence of geometrical elements reaching out into the countryside to the E from the rear of the house, represents the concept of landscape gardening realized most famously in the cascade at Chatsworth, and discussed in print by Joseph Addison in 1712: 'But why may not a whole Estate be thrown into a kind of Garden by frequent Plantations?', and by Stephen Switzer, who half a decade later wrote of 'rural and extensive gardening', where may 'all the adjacent Country be laid open to view.'

The second stage in the layout of the grounds came in the 1740s for Sir Humphrey's son Herbert, for whom a much larger, informal cascade was constructed, showing the effect of William Kent's greater artifice in idealizing nature. The third was for his grandson, Sir Herbert, after 1765, mainly the building of follies, most notably the Ivy Tower of the 1790s (*see* Tonna).*

A perambulation of Gnoll grounds amounts to a 4-m. (6.4-kilometre) round trip, but is eminently worth making. The present car park is sited in the middle of Greening's layout, so it is necessary to walk first to the W, to the brow of the hill, where extensive FOUNDATIONS OF THE MACKWORTHS' HOUSE survive. The view over the town which the house commanded is now hard to appreciate through the trees. To the E, on the highest point of the knoll, Greening's circular BOWLING GREEN has been restored, and below it to the N is the long grassy TERRACE, which extends from a stone-walled bastion above the SE angle of the house in a straight line to another bastion roughly outlined by a wall at the NE angle of the enclosure wall to what were formal gardens.

Further to the E the ground descends gently to the modern car park and to a LAKE, Greening's formal pond irregularized.

A footpath along the E margin of the lake leads to Greening's CASCADE, re-formed in 1994, its series of evenly spaced ledges set within straight retaining walls. Earthworks at the head of the cascade, apparently enclosing a level platform. All this is now within a beech wood, through which a footpath ascends diagonally to the SE, to reach the start of the 1740s landscape. A raised walk contours through MOSSHOUSE WOOD, here of larches, a canalized stream flowing silently beside it. Halfway along, the HALF HOUSE, a covered seat, its polygonal stone front battlemented and opened in three segment-headed arches. Reconstructed 1993. Further NE the path rises along the side of a ravine, to reach a RESERVOIR, enlarged in 1897 from an C18 pond.

The most exciting manmade feature of the landscape, the MOSSHOUSE WOOD CASCADE, constructed in the 1740s, comes into sight at the E end of the reservoir. At its foot a simple BRIDGE (and an C18 moss house, now gone). The full height of the cascade is 180 ft (54.86 metres), the water spilling down the hillside from shelf to ledge to step in a twisting course, an artful simulation of nature fully in the spirit of William Kent

*This account is indebted to recent documentary research and landscape analysis by Elisabeth Whittle.

and on a scale of which he could only dream. At its apex a manmade cairn over which the stream is piped. In the C18 more sublime effects were achieved by damming and suddenly releasing heads of water, to create a 'descent of violent noise, and emotion'. Up here Sir Herbert constructed a GROTTO, the structure of which survives, but not the shelly or stalactitic facings, and a SEAT (now entirely remade) to enable the panoramic view back over Neath to be appreciated.

The IVY TOWER, built by *John Johnson* for Sir Herbert on the brow of the ridge ½ m. to the NW, does not belong to the woodland walk, and is described under Tonna (q.v.).

FLOATING HARBOUR, I m. SW. In 1878 the Neath Commissioners obtained an Act of Parliament to build a large floating dock in a loop of the River Neath between Neath Abbey and Briton Ferry. Uncertain trade prospects and the effect of a storm in 1885 halted the scheme but only after very substantial works had been completed. The substantial mile-long BY-PASS CANAL for the tidal river remains, together with the earthworks of extensive construction railways. W half of the large granite-built LOWER SHIP LOCK on the river near the S end of the canal. Unfortunately the hydraulic power house was dynamited in 1988 when the local authority's rubbish tip was extended.

NEATH RIVER SWING-BRIDGE, I m. SW. Constructed as part 78 of the Rhondda and Swansea Bay Railway (1892–4). The bridge has five steel-plate girder approach spans of through type supported on piers formed as paired cylindrical columns. The total length of the bridge is 388 ft (118 metres). The opening span, 180 ft (55 metres) long, is pivoted centrally on a pier consisting of six cylindrical columns, similar to those which form the piers to the approach spans, but placed in a ring. They are capped by a large cylindrical drum containing the supporting rails and the operating mechanism. The swinging span is 27 ft (8.2 metres) wide. The span itself consists of a pair of lattice girder trusses with curved (probably parabolic) upper members and Pratt truss diagonal or shear members. The whole bridge rests on steel cylinders 6 ft (1.82 metres) and 7 ft (2.13 metres) in diameter, sunk 40 ft (12.2 metres) into the bed of the river, filled with concrete and capped by massive stone caps. The central swing-span weighs nearly 300 tons (304.8 tonnes), and the weight of the complete bridge is 1,400 tons (1,422.4 tonnes). The steel girders were made by Messrs. Finch & Co. of Chepstow. The chief engineer was *S. W. Yockney* and the resident engineer *F. E. Goldwyre*; the contractor was *George Palmer*.

NEATH ABBEY/MYNACHLOG-NEDD   7090

A somewhat ignominious approach, past a carworks and under a railway line, leads to the most completely preserved monastic site in the county and the only one given the full 'guardianship' treatment, consolidated walls set in expanses of mown lawn. To the N the shattered W end of the church rises high; to the SE sprawls the gabled, post-Dissolution mansion. In the foreground, the roofless lay brothers' range encloses the site from the W, for Neath was a Cistercian house.

In 1129 Richard de Granville, a lieutenant of the Norman lord of Glamorgan, granted to the abbey of Savigny in Normandy a tract of nearly 8,000 acres (3,240 hectares) of virgin land by the 'nova villa' of Neath. In 1147, when the Savigniac order merged with that of Cîteaux, Neath Abbey came under Cistercian rule. Since it was part of the rule that monastic communities must not profit from rents but only from direct exploitation of their estate, each Cistercian community included a large body of lay brothers, who farmed both the lands round the abbey and the granges, of which Neath came to own five, in fertile parts of Gower and the Vale. The lay brothers' refectory and common room, with dormitory over, W of the cloister garth, are datable c. 1180–1200, the earliest building to survive, impressive evidence of the scale of the abbey's estate management even before the end of the C12.

What remains of the monks' quarters, S and SE of the cloister, is incorporated in the post-Dissolution mansion. The mid-C13 9 vaulted undercroft to the dormitory survives virtually complete. The church was rebuilt from c. 1280, much larger and more magnificent than before. It seems to have taken about fifty years to complete, to a unified design. It has been suggested that it was planned for twenty-four monks and forty to fifty lay brothers.

At the end of the Middle Ages the community inevitably dwindled. At the Dissolution in 1539 there were seven monks besides the abbot. But the last Abbot of Neath, Leyshon Thomas (1513–39), managed to make his abbey a centre of scholarship and ordered its finances astutely. In 1536 John Leland called Neath 'the fairest abbey in all Wales'.

The abbot's lodging was formed by Leyshon Thomas or his immediate predecessor from the S end of the monks' quarters, by then much more extensive than the few remaining monks required. After the Dissolution, in 1542, Sir Richard Williams, *alias* Cromwell, purchased the abbey site, and over the next half-century he and his son enlarged the abbot's lodging, incorporating more of the monks' quarters, to make a major mansion. Further improvements were probably made by Sir John Herbert, who bought the property at the end of the C16.

In the C18 industry invaded the abbey site. The mansion was abandoned, to be occupied by the copperworkers, who used the lay brothers' range for their furnaces. The medieval buildings were plundered for their cut stone, though the accumulation of industrial detritus did something to protect them. Not until 1924–35 was the site fully cleared. In 1944 it was placed in guardianship and in 1949 given to the nation.

Entry to the site is at the SW corner, from where one can turn to the N and examine the buildings clockwise. They are all constructed of grey-brown Pennant sandstone, against which the remaining white Sutton stone dressings contrast sharply. In the church also a buff dressed stone, used in some places in alternation with the white stone, elsewhere at random. Originally these effects

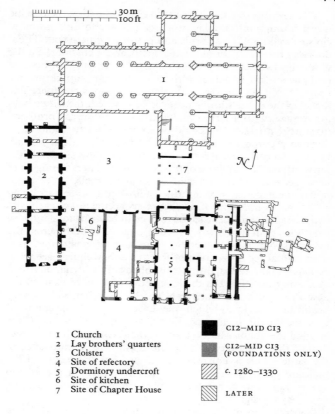

30 m
100 ft

N

	CI2–MID CI3
	CI2–MID CI3 (FOUNDATIONS ONLY)
	c. 1280–1330
	LATER

1 Church
2 Lay brothers' quarters
3 Cloister
4 Site of refectory
5 Dormitory undercroft
6 Site of kitchen
7 Site of Chapter House

Neath Abbey. Plan

would have been obscured by plaster, limewash and, in the
church, by painted decoration.

LAY BROTHERS' QUARTERS. Strongly buttressed late CI2 ten-
bay range of two storeys. The DORMITORY, lit by small lancets
on both sides, occupied the entire upper floor. One W lancet
and the complete composition of three lancets at the S end.
Below, the four S bays formed the REFECTORY, lit by large
lancets on both sides and at the S end. Cut stonework only of
interior rere-arches. In the N bay the lowest courses of a handsome E-facing doorway, with two orders of shafts which seem
to have been keeled, flanked by hollows. Evidence of vaulting,
the octagonal bases of three central columns and several corbels
in the side walls, that in the NW angle with trumpet-leaves, that
in the SE angle moulded, both on short colonnettes, from which
the vault sprang. Jambs of a fireplace in the W wall. Externally,
at the S end of the W wall, traces of a projecting latrine. The
four stacks rising from the wall-heads date from the copper-
smelting period. Traces of furnaces too.

The next bay to the N is an ENTRY, leading from the outside world through into the lay brothers' passage formed in the W cloister walk. Solid side walls and pointed tunnel-vault. The E doorway had an order of filleted shafts and a chamfer. To the W a later, two-storey PORCH, datable to the C14, not bonded into the range. Intact quadripartite rib-vault supporting the upper storey. W doorway with plain continuous chamfer. The N half of the range's lower storey is subdivided, the N two bays for storage, with inserted vaults, the S three the lay brothers' COMMON ROOM. This could be entered directly from the W, through a porch – see the outline of its gable on the W wall. Large W lancets survive in the other two bays, rebated externally for shutters. The vaulting of this room looks later. Springers of broad, chamfered ribs on plain octagonal corbels.

The CHURCH consists of an aisled four-bay E arm, a crossing with N and S transepts of two bays beyond the aisles, each with two E chapels, and an aisled nave of eight bays. Its total internal length is about 203 ft (61.9 metres), and the width across the transepts 150 ft (45.7 metres). The start of what must have been a total reconstruction of the C12 abbey church seems to be dated to the 1280s, during the abbacy of the dynamic Adam of Carmarthen. In 1284 the king, Edward I, on his tour of the new Principality of Wales, presented the abbot with 'a very beautiful baudekyn', which may have been a baldacchino, or canopy, for the high altar. Five years later Gilbert de Clare granted the abbot whatever timber was required 'for the erection of the monastery and for the reasonable maintenance of the same'. This is not much to go on. For the length of the building period there is some evidence, even in the all too sparse fragments of cut stone still *in situ*, showing at least two changes of design.

Construction of the church proceeded in the normal way from E to W, so the latest parts are seen first. The two towering fragments of the W FRONT have most to show. A narthex projected in front of the central doorway. Traces remain of blind-traceried side arches, carried on jambs with slender shafts between hollow mouldings, all very worn. The side walls of the narthex extend forward from the broad, full-height buttresses which define the width of the nave. The buttresses retain their dressed quoins, and a single, gabled set-off at clerestory sill level. More evidence inside, showing that the nave had a two-storey elevation. To N and S, slender, full-height angle shafts with moulded caps, to carry superarches over the nave W window and over the clerestory windows. Rere-arch to the SW and NW clerestory window with upright jamb and flattened arch head, with continuous hollow moulding. The form of the arcade piers is given by the SW respond, with large, half-round shafts in the cardinal directions and small rounded shafts in the angles between them. Vaulting shafts at the W end of the N and S aisles. Lower parts of triple vaulting shafts against the outer walls, with circular bases on chamfered pedestals. On the S side the cloister made large aisle windows impractical. In the N aisle the robbed sockets of long, two-light windows; in the three w bays segmental rere-arches following the vault profile (as in the clerestory); but in the two bays further E the rere-arches are carried on shafts with moulded caps. So this may indicate a break in construction and a design change.

Further E only short stretches of walling stand as high as the eaves. Most informative the N transept E wall and its return in the N choir aisle. Triple wall-shaft between the two transept chapels, irregularly banded in buff and white. Moulded cap, and the springers of a wall arch with a keel moulding and vault ribs with fillets, features not found further W. In the choir aisle the window rere-arches had complex mouldings, three rolls, the centre one filleted, and the jambs must have been shafted. The aisle vault once again sprang from triple wall-shafts, and had filleted ribs. Hollow-moulded superarch in the w bay, and in the next bay a superarch with a triple roll, the centre filleted. Uneven banding of the shafts with buff blocks among the white.

The crossing piers are very fragmentary, but show the same alternation of large and small round shafts as on the piers of the nave. Their form and scale are best indicated by the respond which survives almost to its full height against the S wall of the S transept. Against the W wall of the S transept the night stair to the monks' dormitory, with handrail sunk into the wall and a short wall-shaft resting on a smiling head-corbel wearing an abacus like a sombrero.

So much for the architecture and sculpture of the church. A word remains to be said about its liturgical arrangements, indicated with unusual clarity by the surviving bases of altars and walls. Base of the high altar one bay forward from the E wall, allowing room for a row of four minor altars against it. The MONKS' CHOIR straddled the crossing, its walls enclosing three bays E of the E crossing piers for the presbytery, and the crossing bay and the bay to its w for the monks' stalls. The site of the stalls is precisely marked by the surviving stone base which would have protected their timbers from damp. Note how the W crossing piers were cut back to make room for the stall platform. So clearly no weighty crossing tower was intended. w of the monks' stalls was a one-bay RETROCHOIR, which intercommunicated with the five remaining bays of the NAVE. This W part was for the use of the lay brothers, who entered and left the church by the small door at the W end of the S aisle. The solid walls in the W bay of the nave probably had a purely structural function. Finally, in the transepts, altar bases and traces of partition walls of the side chapels. The S transept is built askew, as the oblique corbelling of the outer face of its W wall clearly shows. This, it has been suggested, enabled the night stair to remain in use throughout the rebuilding of the church.

Sadly, little of the CLOISTER has survived. At the E end of the N walk the richly moulded jambs of the monks' processional door into the church. Complex groupings of hollows sunk back from three principal filleted rolls. Of the rooms which opened

off the E cloister walk, a few scanty foundations. Only the
BOOK ROOM and SACRISTY at the N end can show a little
more, the shafted door jamb of the former, with a filleted outer
roll. The CHAPTER HOUSE was unusually small, apparently
completely within the space under the monks' dormitory,
square and vaulted on four slender, but awkwardly close-spaced
piers, two bases of which remain. A rectangular parlour is
thought to have occupied the space beyond the S end of the E
cloister walk. The S cloister walk is defined by a sleeper wall.
The REFECTORY, entered through a doorway in the centre of
its N wall, has completely disappeared. The doorway itself must
belong to the first half of the C13, shafted in a way very similar
to the crossing piers at Margam (q.v.). Free-standing shafts
on circular water-holding bases alternate with baseless filleted
shafts coursed in with the piers. Washing places recessed l.
and r. included in the doorway composition. Compare the
contemporary arrangement at Tintern Abbey, Gwent. Continuing the dormitory range S-wards, first the ruined walls of
the SLYPE, with the base of a double-shafted doorway at its W
end. Remains of the day stair to the dormitory against the W
wall outside.

What else survives of the monastic buildings can be seen
inside the post-Dissolution mansion. Two vaulted rooms with
robbed N doorway and, in the E wall, a doorway with depressed
pointed head and chamfer, and over it a two-light window
and circular opening above. Finally, the five S bays of the
9 DORMITORY UNDERCROFT. This pure and beautiful vaulted
room must date from the mid C13. Circular piers of moderate
slenderness. Slightly projecting, circular, moulded caps and
bases. Similar half-round corbels. Quadripartite vaults of quite
sharply pointed profile, with plain chamfered ribs. The large
side lancets have been blocked or replaced by C16 windows. In
the centre of the E wall the springers for the hood of a large
fireplace. Outside, the buttressed S end wall clearly discernible. – A few of the finds made during excavation are
collected together in the dormitory undercroft. Among the
20 carved stones is a splendid early C14 VAULT BOSS. Christ in
Majesty within a pelleted quatrefoil, surrounded by leaves. This
must come from the high vault of the church. What other
sculptural glories have disappeared? – FLOOR TILES. Found
in the monks' choir. Extensive patterns, the larger requiring
sixty-four tiles to complete, the smaller sixteen. Also heraldic
tiles originally laid round the E altars beyond the presbytery. –
EFFIGY. Worn figure of an ecclesiastic holding a church, probably from the monument to Adam of Carmarthen, who began
rebuilding the abbey church.

The seven-bay REREDORTER, or latrine block, stood to the
E parallel to the S half of the dormitory, linked to it by a two-
bay BRIDGE. Reredorter and bridge, like the dormitory, do not
themselves survive, but their vaulted substructures do. The
bridge substructure is complete. Square piers, with angle shafts
and moulded imposts forming circular caps over the shafts,

support quadripartite vaults with chamfered ribs springing from short wall-shafts in the centre of each pier. Under the reredorter the springers only of the vault on circular caps on short wall-shafts. Solid E wall to the reredorter undercroft, to separate it from the full-length drain beyond.

ABBOT'S LODGING. In the years c. 1500 the abbot constructed himself a house by linking up the S ends of the dormitory and reredorter, and reusing the SE angle of the refectory, which may by that time have been partly ruinous. This formed a continuous S-facing range of two and three storeys. Work of this period is most readily recognized by the Bath stone used for window dressings. The polygonal stair-turret projecting beyond the SE angle of the dormitory belonged to the abbot's house, as its undercut string course and two two-light top windows show, and so did the garderobe turret at the W end, with single-light S windows, one for each of three storeys. Elsewhere later C16 alterations have been so drastic that the plan, and even the full extent, of the abbot's lodging cannot be grasped.

The POST-DISSOLUTION MANSION. In the half-century or more after Sir Richard Williams acquired the abbey site, the abbot's lodging and the complete undercrofts of dormitory, bridge and reredorter were incorporated into a formidable mansion, which included an entirely new block to the NE. Materials were plundered from the former monastic buildings, so all dressings are of Sutton stone. Two-storey elevations, transomed windows under hoodmoulds, with three or four straight-headed lights. Yet more expansive windows in major rooms. Straight gables, and square chimneystacks, some of them merely ornamental. Symmetrical elevations, however, were for the most part too much to expect.

The house was approached from the N, and the N half of the dormitory range with the chapter house was razed to the ground to provide a forecourt. The new NE block, though now very ruinous, is known to have had a nearly symmetrical N front, even though its lower storey was occupied by kitchens, in order to make a good first impression; but the continuous string course over window heads shows that this is later than the rest (cf. The Van, Caerphilly, of after 1583). The bridge sub-structure found a new use as a porch recessed between the unequal halves of the N front. Large mullion-and-transom windows to E and W at both levels, both in the two-bay returns N of the porch and in the small square courtyard to the S. The W-most upper window had two transoms and arched lights, an earlier form. The dormitory undercroft now became a majestic hall. Its illumination was improved by four-light transomed windows in both side walls and a pair at the S end. Also at the NW corner, a deeply recessed window, which must be examined outside from the W.

The W front is badly ruined at its N end, almost all gone above the remains of the monastic day stair. Immediately to the S of that a canted projection, with a four-light transomed

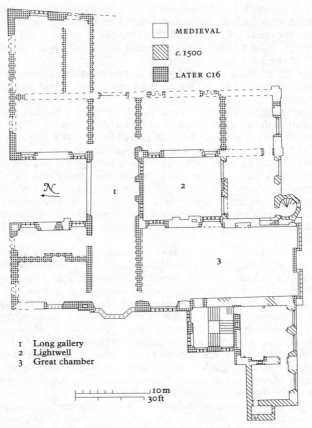

MEDIEVAL

c. 1500

LATER C16

1   Long gallery
2   Lightwell
3   Great chamber

10 m
30 ft

Neath Abbey, post-Dissolution mansion.
Upper floor plan

window in it, the outer face of the deep recess just mentioned.
It clearly supported an upper canted window, the s jamb of
which shows that it probably had as many as ten lights and two
transoms. This window probably lit the end of a long gallery.
Traces of a fireplace for it above the bridge-porch, and on the
far side of the house, among the ruins of the E front, the
substructure of a canted projection for a matching end window.
The length of the gallery must have been almost 100 ft (30.5
metres). The w front continues with mullion-and-transom
windows at both levels, the four-lighter below for the hall, a
six-lighter, arranged 2+2+2, to side-light the great chamber
above. Next comes a well-preserved stair tower, its three-light
windows without transoms. Inside, no trace of a central support
for the stairs. It abuts the N end of the abbot's lodging, but
how it linked the hall with the great chamber above, its presumed primary purpose, is not clear.

On the s front late C16 evidence consists mainly of the pair of mullion-and-transom windows for the hall, set between the buttresses supporting the end of the medieval dormitory range. Above these the outer jambs of two more lofty windows, for the room above the hall, a brilliantly illuminated great chamber. This post-Dissolution work was clearly not carried out in one campaign. Besides the differences in details already noted, there is a distinction too in the chamfering of mullions. Most windows have plain external chamfers, and sunk internal ones. But a few, in particular those on the stair tower, are plain-chamfered inside and out.

GATEHOUSE, $\frac{1}{4}$m. N. Only a fragment, hard up against the A4230. The entrance passage all but eliminated by the modern road. NE jamb of the main gate and springing of inner and outer arches. Two rooms to the N. That to the E with a C12 E doorway. That to the W the porter's lodge. The rest of what remains belongs to the C13 or C14. The distance from gatehouse to church indicates the great size of the monastic precinct.

IRONWORKS, $\frac{1}{4}$m. N. Cornish expertise in specialized casting and engineering was transferred to this site by two Quaker families, the Foxes of Falmouth, who took over the site in 1792, and Joseph Tregelles Price (who had worked with James Watt at the great Carron Ironworks at Falkirk) from 1817. The ironworks at Neath Abbey was conveniently located alongside the water-power resources of the River Clydach a short distance from its confluence with the navigable River Neath. Under Joseph Tregelles Price (1786–1854) the works gained a reputation for high-quality engineering products. The engine manufactory produced locomotives, stationary engines, cast iron roofs and floors, steamships and gasworks.* After Price's death stagnation set in, and the works finally closed in 1885.

The site is entered from the old Vale of Neath Road via the entrance immediately w of the River Clydach bridge. To the w of this is the large rendered bulk of TŷMAWR, the ironmaster's house constructed for Peter Price in 1801, used as five cottages since 1914–18. Three-storey central block with asymmetrical fenestration, flanking two-storey wings of unequal proportions. The long L-shaped and now roofless shell behind this is what remains of the great ENGINE MANUFACTORY. Two-storeyed, c. 210 ft by 44 ft (64 metres by 13.4 metres), built of Pennant sandstone rubble. The N half dates from 1800–10 and was extended in 1823. The N wing was burnt out in the 1980s, but its walls are substantially intact. Its original cast iron roof trusses had long disappeared. The projecting wing at the s provided the power for the manufactory and housed both a water wheel and a steam engine, as well as two cylinder-boring shops. The existing bracketed supports at first-floor level on the rear (w) elevation of the N block held the cast iron trough which supplied water to the wheel. A fitting shop, offices, smithy and

*A uniquely full archive of the products of the ironworks can be consulted in the West Glamorgan County Archives office in Swansea.

storehouse occupied the ground floor, with a pattern-makers' shop and pattern store above.

To the N are the two superb FURNACES of 1793, built against a rock face for ease of charging. These are two of the highest masonry blast furnaces ever constructed. The massive Pennant rubble bulk of the s furnace rises to 65 ft (19.8 metres), that of the N furnace to 53 ft (16.2 metres). The furnaces taper upwards from bases 38 ft (11.6 metres) square. Double rings of dressed voussoirs make up the semicircular arches that span the ground-floor barrel-vaults, which give access to the discharging and tuyère (blast) holes. The inner sides of these recesses are supported by large cast iron beams spanning the openings into the furnace interior. Large chambers in the rock face at the rear of the furnaces would have accommodated the blast pipes. The s furnace retains its slag notch, but the cast-houses which originally stood in front of the furnaces have been completely demolished. A road runs alongside the top of the furnaces and was originally spanned by the surviving Pennant sandstone rubble causeways that allowed railways to take charging materials to the furnace tops. The gable of the charging-house, with central semicircular doorway, stands at the end of the causeway next to the top of the s furnace. The furnaces went out of use in the mid 1840s.

Across the river opposite the furnaces is the lower structure and water-wheel housing of a forge, wrought iron bar and tin-plating mill.

To the N of the later railway viaduct is the tramroad bridge (*see* below) and weir. Yet further N, below a substantial waterfall and water-power take-off, is the former works ROLLING MILL and main FORGE, now in use as a clothing factory. Dated 1825 above the s gable door. This remarkable building still retains its original cast iron roof trusses and purlins, made at the ironworks. Characteristic circular upper openings in the s gable, blocked arcade of semicircular arches the length of its w side. All dressings are of Pennant sandstone ashlar. The water wheel powering the building stood on its E face.

Yet further N, $\frac{2}{3}$ m. above the works, the river was dammed to ensure a reserve of water and a strong steady flow to the ironworks. The present large masonry DAM (SS 7392 9877), which carries a public road, dates from *c.* 1840. It has a battered lower face of Pennant sandstone with a spillway at its w end. Original cast iron gearing controls an outlet shaft in the heavily silted former reservoir.

FORGE TRAMROAD BRIDGE. Small, early C19 stone-arched bridge with integral weir. Parapet of ogee-moulded copper slag block, prominent in the middle of the Neath Abbey Ironworks.

CLYDACH AQUEDUCT, $\frac{1}{4}$ m. sw of the abbey ruins. Twin-arched masonry aqueduct, its arches submerged in the River Clydach and thus acting as an inverted syphon. Built in 1821 by *William Kirkhouse*, engineer to the Tennant Canal. The SLUICES, with rusticated stone pillars to the SE, were built as part of the ill-fated Neath floating dock scheme. The OVERBRIDGE to the w of the aqueduct has parapets formed of cast blocks of copper slag with Roman numerals cast in.

NELSON

ST JOHN THE BAPTIST. A cheap church of 1887–9 by *E. H. Lingen Barker* of Hereford. Six-bay nave and short lower chancel. Thin W tower. E.E. with plate tracery and bar tracery. Arch-braced roof on stone corbels carved with naturalistic flowers.

NEWTON NOTTAGE/DRENEWYDD YN NOTAIS

The old village of Newton, with its medieval church, and the hamlet of Nottage, 1 m. NW, are both on the brink of absorption into Porthcawl.

ST JOHN THE BAPTIST. Overlooking the green of the old village of Newton. A church of exceptional interest which appears to be entirely of *c.* 1500, the grey walling stone contrasted with the greenish-brown sandstone of the exuberantly carved dressings, but constructionally of a piece with them. Massive W tower, supported by broad diagonal buttresses low down, and crowned by a saddleback roof. From here it was possible to walk out through a door in the E gable on to a corbelled platform, for which the corbels survive. Battlements, also corbelled, to N and S. Small rectangular belfry openings, but a trefoiled lancet lower down on the S side. Fancy W doorway composition of *c.* 1500, with benches l. and r., and short triple shafts with polygonal caps and bases. Flanking pinnacles and shield-bearing angels. The crowning hoodmould sprouts big crockets and a vigorous crocketed finial. The three-light window above, in a deep concave surround, has cusped panel tracery. The chancel shows a similar vocabulary, diagonal buttresses and a moulded plinth, windows in deep hollow surrounds (tracery renewed), the priest's door with decorated spandrels and a hoodmould on shield-bearing angels. The SW window, with cuspless four-centred lights, demonstrates the late date of all this work, which is clearly the product of a single campaign. The nave was severely restored in 1860–1 by *Prichard & Seddon*, but the outer arch of the S porch is of *c.* 1500, as is the S doorway. More late Perp evidence inside, both the high and wide tower arch on its peculiar half-round imposts, and the chancel arch, its double-chamfered imposts stopped short by a high plinth to l. and r. Doorway to the rood loft and a ledge to support the rood. – STOUP. By the S door. C13. With stiff-leaf decoration, as a corbelled shaft. – FONT. Octagonal. – PULPIT. A highly remarkable late medieval piece, of stone. It is carved with a relief of the Flagellation, crudely dramatic. Vine scroll above. An arch cut through the wall, its head also roughly carved, with angels, provides access. – WALL-PAINTING. C17

text on the N wall of the nave. – STAINED GLASS. Chancel E,
Christ between SS Peter and John. 1877 by *Morris & Co.*, the
figures designed by *Burne-Jones*. (– Tower W by *R. J. Newbery*
before 1907.) – Nave SW, the New Jerusalem and biblical
scenes, *c.* 1919 by *Henry Holiday*. Figure scenes in eastern settings. – MONUMENTS. Richard Lougher †1722. Tablet. –
Henry Knight †1825. Grecian tablet. Shrouded urn on a fluted
shaft.

In the CHURCHYARD a cross on four steps, late medieval.

TUDOR COTTAGE, Newton Nottage Road, W of the church.
Early C17 single-unit, end-entry house extended to the W.
Original mullioned windows, with straight heads and sunk
chamfer mouldings.

DAN-Y-GRAIG HOUSE, ½m. NE. A crisp, white Regency villa
built 1814–17 for the Rev. Robert Knight by *C. & D. Morgan*
of Newton. Large additions to the W before 1878 (Cadw).

NOTTAGE COURT, 1 m. NW. A compact and architecturally
coherent Jacobean house, not a common thing in Glamorgan.
Built after 1608 by Robert Lougher or his son. Five-bay front,
the first, third and fifth projecting. Two storeys with a third in
the gables over the projections. Mullioned windows with
straight heads under continuous string courses, reduced by one
light in each bay from storey to storey. One would call this a
symmetrical, E-plan composition familiar from many English
manor houses, were the l. projection not a porch coming
forward much further than the two window bays, so that the
local preference for the entrance in an end bay is preserved. The
porch has a flattened four-centred entrance under a hoodmould
and leads into the lower end of the hall. Parlour to the r. with
great chamber over and a less important room over the hall. In
a square wing behind, an C18 staircase, successor no doubt to
the original stair. Victorian rear additions. Where were the
original service rooms?

The exterior has been compromised by grey cement render,
but inside virtually all the details, of greenish Quarella stone,
survive. Windows with sunk chamfers. Four-centred doorways
chamfered down to square-cut stops like thistle-heads. Fireplace openings of flattened four-centred outline, with double
hollow chamfers and thistle stops, those in the hall and room
above provided with large jumped-up hoodmoulds, those in
parlour and great chamber with mantelshelves resting on scroll
brackets of idiosyncratic, possibly misunderstood classical
shape.

MOUNT PLEASANT, NEWTON DOWN, 1½m. N. Excavation
demonstrated that an early Bronze Age burial CAIRN overlay a
small Neolithic HOUSE of the mid to late third millennium B.C.

At DAN-Y-GRAIG, ½m. NE, excavation has revealed highly
Romanized buildings, possibly a VILLA.

NEW TREDEGAR

At the narrowest point of the Upper Rhymney Valley, long terraces fingering out along the lower slopes of the steep hillside. They are well seen from the A469 as it contours along the opposite slope. Church, chapel, hotel and war memorial cluster at the centre of the settlement.

ST DINGAT. Chancel and single-aisled nave under a continuous ridge, 1892–3 by *Seddon & Carter*. S aisle added by them in 1899, N vestry and peculiarly profiled N bell gable presumably a further addition by *Carter*. Rock-faced Pennant sandstone and yellow terracotta. E.E. Spacious interior. Five-bay arcades with circular piers and spurred capitals. Boarded roofs, that in the nave of trefoil profile, that in the chancel with concealed hammerbeams. – STAINED GLASS. E window, Ascension, *c.*1920, the backgrounds thinned. – W window, Nativity, 1960, signed by *Luxford Studios* of New Barnet.

CARMEL ENGLISH BAPTIST CHAPEL. Dated 1899. Rock-faced Pennant sandstone dressed, unusually for a chapel, with red brick. Otherwise the standard round-arched design. Galleried interior.

TREDEGAR ARMS HOTEL. Rendered, Italianate. Cast iron porch and bold relief lettering, suggesting a date not later than *c.*1870.

WAR MEMORIAL. Unusually ambitious, with a figure group. One soldier on alert, the other collapsing. Attributable to *L. F. Roslyn* (cf. Maesteg).

At ELLIOT'S TOWN, ½m. SE, ELLIOT EAST PIT. On the SW side of Elliot Street (the valley road) the former BATHS BUILDING and winding-engine house of Elliot East Pit, operated between 1883 and 1967.

The ENGINE HOUSE is two-storeyed, of rusticated Pennant sandstone, set above the E bank of the river. Both side elevations have six arched windows and blocked doors. Plaque above the E door inscribed 'East Elliot Pit 1891'. The N side faced the colliery shaft (indicated by a man-hole). Thin iron exhaust chimneys. External concrete-walled exhibition gallery, only partly completed, for the preserved twin tandem compound steam winding engine inside. The large winding-drum is sunk into the floor.

NICHOLASTON

ST NICHOLAS. A tiny jewel box, created by Miss Olive Talbot's lavish funds, the consummate craftsmanship of *William Clarke* of Llandaff, and the design of *G. E. Halliday*, luxuriating in the chance of a lifetime. Built in 1892–4, incorporating a few bits, in particular the chancel arch, from its simple predecessor. The new church is no bigger than what was there before, just a nave and lower chancel, but into it are packed so many miniaturized versions of features familiar from great churches of the mid C13 that one's head reels.

The first sight is of exaggeratedly rock-faced walls of pink conglomerate and grey millstone grit, dressings the subdued green of Quarella sandstone. The W bell gable on fancy corbelling and the NW vestry with its elaborate chimney hint at the treats to come. Figure corbels and head corbels, some minutely small. The S porch reveals the building's full ambitions, multiple shafting to both the outer arch and the inner doorway, the shafts alternately grey and pink, the multiple-moulded arches enriched with stiff-leaf.

Inside, the E.E. vocabulary becomes more intense, the windows all internally shafted, a pair on the S side vaulted too. Richly varied stiff-leaf. Marble floors throughout, the sanctuary step of red Numidian marble, the altar itself on a podium of pure white marble. Shafting of pink alabaster and green Connemara marble in the chancel. Massively timbered roofs, arch-braced with wind-braces, all the members enriched with carving, the principals carried in the nave on heads, including those of Christ and the Virgin Mary, in the chancel on demi-angels. The principal actor in this *mise-en-scène* is to be the parish priest. Hence, naturally, the REREDOS with a full array of figure carving. Hence too the PULPIT, round which stand canopied figures of the heroes of Victorian preaching: Keble, Liddon and Pusey. An enriched arch through the wall takes the preacher into it from his carved stall in the chancel. But the unexpected touch is the fantastically elaborated doorway to the vestry, its arch surrounded by tendrils forming vesica-shaped openings in which stand the Fathers of the Church, four eastern and four western, reminiscent of the prior's door at Norwich Cathedral. Splendid hingework, the architect's monogram on it, to the vestry door. – FONT. Medieval. Cylindrical. – STAINED GLASS. A full set, conceived with the architecture, exquisite but restrained. By *Burlison & Grylls*.

Above NICHOLASTON HALL, $\frac{1}{4}$ m. NW, is a site usually identified as a Neolithic CHAMBERED TOMB comprising a small stone chamber or cist within an oval cairn at the foot of the S slope of Cefn Bryn (*see* Llanrhidian). However, a surrounding cairn of burnt stone situated alongside a seepage suggests that the cist was inserted into a burnt mound, a 'cooking' site, perhaps in the Bronze Age.

OGMORE CASTLE

Beside the banks of the River Ewenny. One really impressive part survives of the C12 castle of the de Londres family, the W wall of the KEEP. Its E face retains all the original features at upper-floor level: two small round-headed windows to the l. of a partition, and to the r. a fireplace with the springers of a curved ashlar hood, and the upper parts of supporting columns with bold, simply scalloped capitals suggesting an early C12 date. This must be one

of the earliest chimneypieces to survive in Britain. N
plaster still adheres to the wall at this level. A horiz
above shows that the keep was originally only two-st
was subsequently heightened.

The keep, of local limestone with Sutton stone dress
originally a plain rectangle, with a stairway against the E
stood within and on the W side of an oval ringwork of *c*. I
the E side of the enclosure, a smaller rectangular building,
as the CELLAR, was built facing the keep. This is also of th
All that survives is part of the undercroft and a vaulted pa
sloping down into it. Slit window in the centre of each wall.
Royal Commission suggests that the superstructure may h
been half-timbered. Later additions flank the passage.

The faceted CURTAIN WALL, an early C13 strengthening
defences, follows the line of the ringwork, as at Coity Castle and
Newcastle, Bridgend (qq.v.). Integral with the curtain wall are
the large, plain rectangular HALL on the N side, a small and
extremely simple GATEHOUSE immediately SE of the keep, and
a newel stair and garderobe built on to the NW corner of the keep.
The footings of another large rectangular building beside the SE
wall of the enclosure, of uncertain date.

The OUTER WARD, to the SW, is unusually small. Within it
stands an almost intact single-storey rectangular building lacking
only its roof and dressed stonework. This has been identified as
the COURTHOUSE, rebuilt in 1454–5, when the castle belonged
to the Duchy of Lancaster, as it still does today. One of its angles
is built over a circular limekiln, itself constructed on top of a
rectangular building which must have been one of the earliest
structures in the outer ward.

OGMORE VALE

9090

ST DAVID, Wyndham. By *J. Prichard.* Nave 1876–8, chancel,
the same width and height, not completed until 1884. A cheap
church, but with many features typical of Prichard, not least
the idea to give the E end, facing the road, a splendidly big five-
light window, with geometrical tracery and delicate mouldings,
to show that even here in this remote valley there worshipped
a congregation with fine feelings.

BETHLEHEM WELSH BAPTIST CHAPEL, River Street. 1876.
Pennant sandstone and Forest ashlar. A typical two-storey
composition under a gable, the round-headed openings emphasized by rustication. Typical inside too, galleried on three sides
and with a flat, boarded ceiling centring on a large plaster rose.
(To be converted into a male voice choir centre.)

ENGLISH CONGREGATIONAL CHAPEL, on the A4061. 1902–3
by *Jacob Rees* of Pentre. Pennant sandstone with Forest ashlar
and red brick. Not in any recognizable style.

CWRT GWALIA. Sheltered housing. Brown brick with the typical
arched decorative forms of the 1980s picked out in yellow brick.
1987 by *M. Yearsley* of *Pentan Design Practice.*

OLD BEAUPRE
1 m. SW of St Hilary

Alone in the fields, approached from the W by a $\frac{1}{2}$-m.-long foot-path. Though a ruin, like almost all the other C16 mansions of Glamorgan, it is exceptional among them for two reasons. First, it has a fully developed courtyard plan, and second, it boasts the only really spectacular architectural showpiece in the county, a 'tower of the orders' which can stand comparison with any in England. Beaupre was the seat of the Basset family from at least the late C14, until 1709.

The fabric of the house is the product of three main phases of building, *c.* 1300, early C16 and late C16, the first perhaps pre-dating Basset ownership, the second put in hand by Sir Rice Mansel, whose marriage to a Basset heiress entitled him to inhabit Beaupre from 1516 until his death in 1559. Thereafter Bassets reinherited, and Sir Rice's grandson, Richard Basset, brought the development of the house to its glorious conclusion.

The house is built of local Carboniferous limestone, the dressings in the earliest ranges being of white Sutton stone, the later dressings of green Bridgend sandstone, but the porch tower of buff limestone imported from Somerset. The approach is from the N, so, since the house has grown from S to N, its history is best read backwards. Within the simple enclosure wall of the outer court one faces the GATEHOUSE. This bears the date, 1586, of Richard Basset's inheritance, and his arms within a rectangular panel flanked by baluster-like Ionic colonnettes, with the capital of a third, central colonnette appearing unexpectedly above the panel. The four-centred doorway below is flanked by fluted Ionic pilasters of an even more vestigial character. In the upper storey two three-light windows (now blocked) with square-headed lights and sunk chamfers, the typical late C16 form. These, and a four-lighter facing S, lit a large unheated chamber which must have served as a sort of summerhouse. Central gablet above with a two-light window. A dog-leg stair in the thickness of the wall gives access to the room from the W, and to the E a doorway leads out on to the wall-walk extending along the E side of the middle court. Corbelling all along, formerly surmounted by battlements. Curious windowless tower projecting far forward in the NE angle, also corbelled for battlements. Such mock fortification in the 1580s served as a status symbol, like the lofty gatehouse itself.

43   All this was as nothing to the PORCH which Richard Basset added in 1600 before the N doorway into the hall. The idea of applying coupled columns in three storeys to an entrance porch, Doric supporting Ionic, Ionic supporting Corinthian, was a French one. Perhaps the first such 'tower of the orders' was erected by Philibert de l'Orme at the Château of Anet, *c.* 1546. The idea quickly caught on in England, appearing as early as *c.* 1550 at the Protector Somerset's London palace in the Strand. Thereafter the rash spread all over the country, to Burghley,

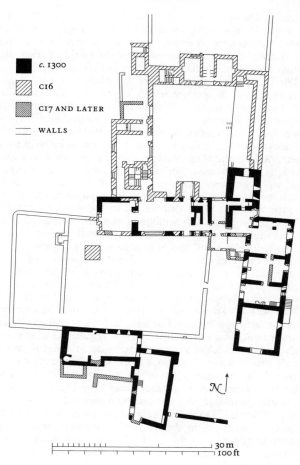

- *c.* 1300
- C16
- C17 AND LATER
- WALLS

Old Beaupre. Plan

Northamptonshire, by 1556, to Theobalds, Hertfordshire, by 1567, to Kirby and Holdenby, Northamptonshire again, by the 1570s, to Cobham, Kent, and to Stonyhurst, Lancashire, by the 1590s. Nor is Old Beaupre, at 1600, the last; the most spectacular of them all, the five-storey tower in the Schools Quadrangle at Oxford, is dated 1620.

What Richard Basset had seen to make him want such an incongruous object in the courtyard of his house it is impossible to say. But it is most unlikely that the porch was made in Glamorgan. Rather, its façade must have been shipped over in pieces from England, presumably from the Bath area via Bristol. (The side walls are faced with Sutton stone, the backing is partly of brick.) The finely proportioned columns and entablatures are in complete contrast to the inept attempts at classical detail on the gatehouse. Even the (blocked) four-light mullion-and-transom window in the top stage has mouldings, an ovolo and a wave, which bear no relation to contemporary local masonry practice. Fine strapwork surround to the shield of arms. Rusticated walling inside the porch.

The three-storey w RANGE of the main courtyard is mid-C16, extending the private rooms beyond the dais end of the hall. Spacious stair, rising in short flights round a square pillar. Rooms with four-light E windows at all three levels. At the same time the medieval open hall was floored over. The big chimneybreast projecting to the r. of the porch belongs to this phase. Within the HALL further evidence of what was done. The lofty C14 windows were blocked, the fine C15 chimneypiece with its overmantel decorated with a row of shields (cf. Llanmihangel) was removed from its position in the w wall (see the surviving flue) and resited in the N wall, within the new chimneybreast. New mullioned windows with arched lights and hoodmoulds were inserted in the s wall, one of six lights for the hall below, and two of four lights for what now became the great chamber above. The medieval gatehouse E of the hall had already been converted, its entry blocked (see the arch in the wall to the l. of the 'tower of the orders'), and a mullioned window and sharply pointed lights inserted in the blocking.

The MEDIEVAL HOUSE, in spite of the C16 modernization, remains fairly intelligible. The hall, 32 ft (9.75 metres) by 20 ft (6.09 metres) was of two main bays – see the segmental rere-arches of two blocked windows each side. It stood between a simple two-storey parlour block to the w and a complex service end to the E. Immediately E of the hall a mural stair rises in a thick wall, surrounded on three sides by vaulted passages. E again, the gatehouse, its vault and its cobbled floor both excellently preserved. Doorways in its E side wall lead to service rooms, in the block to the NE, and more particularly to the mighty KITCHEN, to the s of which further service rooms are attached (now caretaker's house). Well-preserved double kitchen hearth. Two early doorways in the E wall of this range, one with the continuously curved moulding found at Caerphilly Castle and buildings under its influence c.1300. So the main body of the medieval house forms an L.

Free-standing further s, another L-plan building. This seems to have been a self-sufficient second residence. Two-light upper window in the N wall of the E half, with cusped ogee heads and a transom, suggesting a C14 date. This appears to have lit an upper-floor hall. The w half clearly had a service function, as it has a large hearth with bread oven at the w end of its s wall.

A fine five-bay BARN of c.1500 away to the SE.

OXWICH

Oxwich Bay is wonderfully exhilarating, a broad 2-m.(1.6-kilometre) sweep of sandy beach, backed by dunes and sheltered

by irregular wooded hills. In the village, back from the sw corner
of the bay, a few picturesque thatched cottages of the c17 and
c18 peep from among recent holiday homes. The church stands
alone ½ m. se; the castle is hidden on the hillside to the s.

St Illtyd. Close to the shore surrounded by tall trees. The
approach from the w is dominated by the tower, its tapering
walls incorporating a s mural stair. Corbelled battlements. A
pair of ogee-headed lancets suggest a c14 date. The body of
the church is strangely disparate, the long nave of two distinct
builds, the short chancel lit by an unusually large two-light Dec
e window and providing in its n wall an enriched recess for a
mid-c14 monument (*see* below). Large, square-headed Tudor
windows n and s in the nave, supplemented in the c19. The
low, narrow, round-headed chancel arch gives the clue to the
building history: c12 chancel remodelled in the mid c14 as a
funerary chapel, c12 nave doubled in length and tower added,
also probably in the c14, nave remodelled c. 1500. (Chancel
ceiling decoration, 1931, by *Leslie Young*, scene-painter of Sad-
ler's Wells for Dame Lilian Baylis.) – FONT. Crudely hewn
bowl badly preserved. – STAINED GLASS. Chancel e, SS David
and Illtyd. 1893. Kempe-like. – MONUMENT. Fine c14 crocketed and cusped arch with side pinnacles. Contemporary
recumbent effigies of an armoured knight with straight legs and
a lady with crimped hair. They must represent members of the
Penrice family, who inherited Oxwich Castle from the de la
Mares in the c13.

OXWICH BAY HOTEL. Built as the rectory in 1788. Designed
by *William Jernegan*. Utterly spoilt by modern additions.

CASTLE. The only example in the county of an Elizabethan
prodigy house. For all the ruination, its vast, high-set windows
and soaring towers still convey the sense of flaunting recklessness familiar from such English houses as Hardwick, Mon-
tacute and Bramshill. Oxwich, however, is earlier than these.
Sir Edward Mansel, who inherited in 1559, had constructed
the main range by c. 1580, when the county historian, Rice
Merrick, apparently referred to it. The origins of the style
lie back in early Tudor court architecture. Huge top-storey
windows, in particular, were constructed before 1520 at Richmond Palace and Hampton Court, and can still be seen at
Thornbury Castle, Gloucestershire. Henry VIII's palaces will
have been well known to Sir Edward's father, Sir Rice, who in
1527 had married a lady-in-waiting to Princess Mary.

  Sir Rice himself built at Oxwich. The gatehouse to the w
and two-storey wing on the s side of the courtyard are his.
Presumably he abandoned his work on leasing in 1538 and
then acquiring the more conveniently situated Margam Abbey,
subsequently the family's principal seat. That his son resumed
construction at Oxwich and so much more spectacularly, suggests a folly-like quality in Sir Edward's enterprise. Yet in many
ways it looks like a completion of the earlier work. Both are
built of local grey limestone rubble, the dressings of green

Oxwich Castle.
Reconstruction

Quarella sandstone. Both employ arched heads and hollow
mouldings for all the window lights, the normal forms *c.* 1530,
but going out of fashion by *c.* 1560, let alone *c.* 1580.

It is natural to examine the earlier parts first. The GATE-
HOUSE is dominated by a magnificently mantled shield displaying Sir Rice Mansel's arms within a wreath and set in a
square frame. This is carved in Bath stone. Entrance arch
beneath it, of flattened four-centred outline, moulded with
a hollow and a wave on complex stops. Shallow projecting
segmental towers to l. and r. linked by a segmental arch to
support a wall-walk. This does not constitute more than a token
display of defensibility. The much bigger cylindrical tower at
the adjacent angle of the s (really sw) range houses the newel
stair giving access to the wall-walk. The s RANGE is two-
storeyed, the upper four-light windows largely original, with
hoods on square stops typical of the first half of the c16. The
smaller windows are restored.*

Sir Edward's E RANGE was strikingly formalized in its plan, a
single pile 115 ft (35 metres) long with three massive rectangular

---

*Mr Bernard Morris (*Gower*, vol. XLIII for 1992) has drawn attention to a straight
joint between the s and E ranges, visible during recent conversion work. This seems
to show that the s range came second, butted up against the E range, not the other
way round. But it is hard to believe that the whole castle was built by Sir Rice
Mansel before 1538, which is what that building sequence would imply.

projections at the back. Foundations only of the projecting porch towards the courtyard. The porch was not axial and the few surviving openings in the front face of the range make it obvious that symmetry was not achieved, except at the highest level, where four evenly spaced windows lit the long gallery from the side, and further gigantic windows lit it from each end. The one large window to survive intact, of 2+2+2 lights with two transoms, lit a first-floor hall. Blocked doorway into the screens passage from the porch, and at ground level a well-preserved doorway. This leads into a passage N of two vaulted rooms beneath the hall. Rubble vaults of segmental profile. The room arrangements can be much more fully read from inside the range, where the reveals of many blocked openings are apparent. Here are the reveals and sill of the dais window to the hall, showing that it had an extra tier of lights below the three that aligned with the surviving window. Above the screens passage is the only well-preserved area of dressed stone, the jambs of a fireplace flanked by two tiers of cupboards. At the N end two-light openings to the N and E show that the service rooms were in four storeys below gallery level. Staircase here, arranged presumably like the better-preserved staircase in the SW corner, rising in short flights against a square central newel. The character of the rear projections is seen vividly both from 40 the N and from the S, for almost all the windows survive, single-light below, twin-light above, making provision for rooms in six half-height storeys, which, as the Royal Commission remarks, 'could have housed a large body of retainers'.

Immediately N of the house, a ruined cylindrical DOVECOTE.

(TOWER, NE of the castle, in woodland on the hillside at a lower level. Remains of a rectangular masonry structure, presumably related to the 'castle' mentioned at Oxwich already in 1459.)

OYSTERMOUTH/YSTUMLLWYNARTH

Castle and church both originated in the C12. The charms of the area, with its views over Swansea Bay, encouraged villa-building from the late C18, from Blackpill in the N, to Langland on the high ground to the SW. The Mumbles developed a proper seafront a century later. In the C20 ever denser housing development has linked all these components together as Oystermouth has become a favourite place for retirement.

ALL SAINTS. Finds of Roman material including fragments of a mosaic pavement suggest that the church was built on the site of a VILLA. The medieval church has been relegated to forming the S aisle of what is in effect a new church, by *L. W. Barnard* of Cheltenham, 1915–16. W bay completed 1937. Only the old W tower stands free, unbuttressed, of two stages with corbelled battlements. Projecting S stair-turret corbelled back just below the top of the tower. C13 evidence in the chancel, three E lancets, broadly chamfered, and in the nave, one trefoiled lancet. Other windows of various dates and degrees of restoration. The S arcade, with clustered shafts, must belong to *R. K. Penson*'s enlargement of 1857–60. Barnard's work, nave with narrow N aisle, lower chancel, is Perp. The chancel arch hugely high and wide, like a proscenium arch. – PILLAR PISCINA, in the medieval chancel. – FONT. A good C13 piece. Square bowl with big scallops on the underside. Circular stem and moulded foot on a square base. – CHANCEL SCREEN. Perp. With rood loft and rood. By *Barnard*, 1927. – REREDOS. 1951 by *Faith Craft Works* of St Albans. Large. – STAINED GLASS. Chancel E, Christ adored, and saints. 1930 by *Powell*'s. – S aisle, four small scenes of acts of mercy. 1880 by *Joseph Bell* of Bristol. – S aisle SW, N aisle NW (lifeboat memorial) and W, all by *Timothy Lewis*, 1986, 1977 and 1989.

ST PETER, Newton. 1901–3 by *E. M. Bruce Vaughan*. Dec. Walling of Bridgend sandstone, rock-faced outside and in. Its greenish hue makes an unusual contrast with the Bath stone dressings. Quite an ambitious church, though the ambition to build a SE tower was only partly realized. Short aisled nave of three bays with a clerestory. Wide and high chancel arch. Richly appointed chancel. – STAINED GLASS. S aisle, four windows, and N aisle W window, Annunciation, Adoration of Kings and of Shepherds, St Peter and St Michael. *Kempe & Tower*, 1912. Unusually colourful for this firm. – Chancel E, 'The Holy Church'. 1921. – N aisle, two windows by *Wippell & Co.* of Exeter, 1960s. – Nave W, Christ adored. By *Celtic Studios*, c. 1966.

CLYNE CHAPEL. *See* under Clyne Castle below.

MOUNT SION CHAPEL (now Christadelphian Hall), Mumbles Road. 1850. Humble. Pointed sash windows in the gabled front.

VICTORIA METHODIST CHAPEL, Mumbles Road. 1877–8 by *A. Totten*. Ambitious, of Pennant sandstone and Bath stone, mixing Romanesque and geometrical Gothic elements. Incipient transepts. Twin towers left incomplete. Inside the same over-ambition, galleries not extended along the sides.

CASTLE. Oystermouth Castle stands compact and tidy on a broad, mown slope overlooking Swansea Bay. It was a principal castle of the lords of Gower from the C12 until 1331, when they became absentee landlords. All too little is known of its history, just a succession of destructive attacks by Welsh princes, in 1116, 1215 and 1287, and one positive event, a two-day visit by Edward I in 1284. At least four stages can be discerned in the fabric, one in the C12, two in the C13, and finally the dramatic, chapel-crowned NE block, the castle's early C14 swansong. The plan consists of a gatehouse at the lower (S) end, leading into a small, roughly triangular, inner ward, beyond and above which stands the main body of the castle, a complicated assemblage of small rectangular blocks, to which all the different stages of construction contributed. The castle is built of local limestone, probably quarried on site.

The GATEHOUSE, datable to the late C13, originally had a

pair of drum towers. Its curious appearance is due to the near removal of the fronts of the towers, so that their concave backs are fully exposed. Blocked basement doorway in each, and sockets for floor joists. The entrance passage has a portcullis groove, and segmental transverse arches, formed of voussoirs of undressed stone. Reconstructed vault. Fireplace in the room above, and one E lancet. In the inner face of the gatehouse, doorways to passages through to the drum towers, served by the blocked doors noted above. The E passage also leads to a newel stair giving access to the wall-walk. The CURTAIN WALLS survive almost to full height on both sides of the gate-house. Footings of buildings against them, that to the W with traces of two fireplaces and a garderobe in the curtain wall.

Across the INNER WARD a vaulted porch, clearly an addition to the block to which it gives access. This has been identified as the original C12 KEEP, doubled in depth towards the N in the C13 (see the straight joint in the E wall). The spine wall between the two halves is of the first build, but with fireplaces later inserted in both directions. These have segmental heads formed of untrimmed voussoirs, as in the gatehouse, but with Pennant sandstone alternating with the limestone. Traces of limestone heads. In the N half, evidence of rooms at two levels, the lower with three small barred N windows, the upper with two N lancets. Newel stair in the W wall, and a curious passage curving round it in the thickness of the wall. This links with another rectangular block, added angle-to-angle to the NW corner of the keep. Access between them at the upper level too. This NW BLOCK had a vaulted undercroft and windows at two levels above. S of it a second rectangular block, vaulted at its S end, and between them an area, clearly an infill, which provided rooms at three levels - see the fireplaces in the W wall.

That leaves the CHAPEL BLOCK, the really eloquent part of the castle. It must be examined outside the curtain wall from the E, and from within. Two sheer, buttress-like turrets frame the E end. In the gable three-light chapel window, its delicate, cusped, intersecting tracery miraculously intact. Arrow slit above it and slits in the turrets. This piquant com-bination of defence and display is something of a sham, as one turret houses a stair and the other a set of garderobes. Strong projections in the N and S walls as well, for fireplaces at the two lower levels and arched recesses for the chapel, perhaps family pews. Two-light N and S chapel windows with cusped, intersecting tracery. The tracery in all but the NW window was reconstructed in the 1840s by a local antiquary, George Grant Francis, from fragments found on site.

PIER, Mumbles Road. Ten-bay iron structure 225 ft (68.6 metres) long, designed by *W. Sutcliffe Marsh* for the Mumbles Railway and Pier Company. It was opened in 1898. Modern superstructure.

LIGHTHOUSE, Mumbles Head. A warning light built in 1793 on 73 the outer of two small tidal islands off Mumbles Head at the entrance to Swansea Bay. The Swansea architect *William*

Jernegan designed the unique double octagon tower for Swansea Harbour Trust after the first attempt at building collapsed. The inner octagon, 12 ft (3.66 metres) in diameter, contained a central shaft up which coal for the original beacon lights could be raised. The outer octagon, 23 ft (7.01 metres) broad, housed a stair winding its way around the central octagon. The outer octagon provides a platform at half-height, whilst the inner octagon, housing both an upper staircase and the winding-shaft, terminates at a summit platform 58 ft (17.68 metres) above ground level. The two fire-baskets housed on these double platforms were designed to distinguish it from the coal-light on the slender Flat Holm Lighthouse. In 1798 a lantern for a single oil-lit light and bracketed cast iron gallery were cast at the Neath Abbey Ironworks. Railings and lantern have recently been replaced, but the lighthouse remains as one of the best examples in Britain of a structure designed for the earlier widespread use of open-fire lights.

Oystermouth had its share of early C19 villas. Two survive in NORTON ROAD, ¼ m. N, both simply classical. The architecturally more convincing is NORTON HOUSE, of three bays with two Greek Doric columns *in antis* forming a one-storey portico. NORTON LODGE has a full-width veranda of cast iron. (In Newton Road is a representative of the next generation, GLYN-Y-COED, *c.* 1870, a full-blooded Gothic house by *Benjamin Bucknall*, the disciple of Viollet-le-Duc.)

The seafront S of Oystermouth Castle, dominated by the Victoria Chapel and overlooked by All Saints church, contains one building which enters into the seaside spirit, the MERMAID HOTEL, 1897–8 by *H. Tudor Thornley* of Cardiff, unfortunately derelict at the time of writing. At the far S end, BRISTOL CHANNEL YACHT CLUB, before 1926 by *Glendinning Moxham*.

CLYNE CASTLE, at BLACKPILL, 1 m. N, is approached up MILL LANE. It is a castellated mansion of 1800 and later, set on a seaward slope above the wooded Clyne Valley. Heavy planting of conifers and rhododendrons still provides an evocative setting. The first house on the site, called Woodlands, was built in 1791 to the designs of a frustratingly unidentifiable Mr *Wyatt*. Castellation came in 1800 when *George Warde*, exsoldier and mining entrepreneur, acting as his own architect, made additions which amounted to 'a new house in the Gothic style'. But what is visible today is not earlier than 1819–20, when Warde created the present S front and its E return. The S, originally the entrance, front, in spite of complete refenestration in the 1860s, is typical of the date, symmetrical, twostoreyed and battlemented with slightly projecting and slightly raised centre bays, thin polygonal turrets to l. and r. and yet thinner cylindrical turrets at the outer angles. All of randomly laid local sandstone. The only distinguishing feature is the slight convex curvature of the whole front, perhaps induced by the need to build round existing structure. The E front is in two parts, to the l. a projecting four-bay section with a blocked doorway, and to the r. a three-storey tower and a slightly lower but also three-storey continuation with two shaped gables rounding the corner. The date of the former is unclear, but the latter parts belong to the great enlargement to the w for Graham Vivian after he had acquired the house in 1860. The guiding hand of an architect appears to be lacking here too.

Inside, the planning of the house is hard to understand. The original entrance vestibule in the centre of the s front was amalgamated by Vivian with the rooms which flanked it to form an extraordinary curved DRAWING ROOM the full width of the front. The two handsome Adamesque doorcases may be of 1819, a typical contrast between external Gothic and internal classicism. The plaster ceiling, copied from the long gallery at Knole of 1608, is of course an insertion by Vivian. In the awkward space behind the drawing room is the STAIRCASE, of no special interest. At its foot, however, stand two magnificent C18 Italian doorcases of pink and white marble, brought in by Vivian. The double-height GREAT HALL, entered from the E, was created by roofing over a courtyard. What was a canted exterior wall behind the staircase juts into it. Here is another Italian importation, the massive pink marble chimneypiece, its entablature and hood carried by bold consoles on paws. Probably of the late C16. Finally, in the DINING ROOM to the NE, a doorcase and two niches of mid-C18 Rococo boiseries, said to have come from the palace of the Archbishop of Paris on the Ile St-Louis. Trophies of musical instruments over the niches.

Vivian descendants continued to live at Clyne Castle until 1952. It was then acquired for the University College of Swansea, and since 1956 has served as a student hostel.

STAFF HOUSES, w of the castle. Free-standing block, 1971 by *Sir Percy Thomas & Partners*.

In Mill Lane, castellated GATE LODGE and several picturesque COTTAGES with ornamental tiled roofs. No. 6 is the best preserved. No. 10 has been much extended to the r. They must have been put up by George Warde for his tenants, probably employing *P. F. Robinson* while he was working at Singleton Abbey nearby. At the entrance to CLYNE GARDENS, s of Mill Lane, a LODGE with fancy bargeboards in two directions, built in reverse to a published design by *Robinson*.*

The final addition to the amenities of Clyne Castle was a chapel. CLYNE CHAPEL, Mayals Road, at the SE corner of the park, was built as late as 1907 by Graham Vivian, to provide a burial place for himself and other members of the family as well as a place of worship. The old-fashioned and eccentric little building suggests that even in old age Vivian could not bring himself to employ an architect. Many strange details, not least the enormous hoodmould stops to the w window, dangling what appear to be strings of onions. Inside, the building is fascinatingly crowded with items from Vivian's collection. They can be described from E to w. – ALTAR FRONT. Italian,

*So Nigel Temple has observed.

early C18, with polychrome marble scrollwork, in the *marmi mischi* technique popular in Naples and Sicily. – RELIEF. Italian C18, of marble, representing the Transfiguration. Of quite high quality and in a style which ought to make attribution possible. – MOSAIC PANEL, set in the chancel s wall. Opus Alexandrinum, of the C13, from San Bartolommeo, Rome. – PULPIT. An enormous affair, of timber. It appears to be late C17 English. The base has clearly been cut down. Polygonal body set on a bulging, foliage-carved moulding. Circular tester not originally associated with it. – CHANDELIERS. Wrought iron brackets set in the chancel arch and Italian gesso holders hanging in the nave. – SCREEN. Of timber, in the s aisle. Did it come from an organ case? Three cusped arches under richly crocketed gables, between tall pinnacled buttresses, probably of *c.* 1840. – FONT. The oldest and most interesting object in the church. C12, Italian. Rectangular bowl carved with animals within rope borders on a stem formed of twin shafts with foliage spiralling up them. – MONUMENT. Admiral Algernon Walker-Heneage-Vivian †1952. Like an early C18 tablet, but with naturalistic fox, pheasant and flowers in high relief.

In MAYALS ROAD, opposite Clyne Chapel, BRYNAU, another cottage orné.

CLUB UNION CONVALESCENT HOME, Langland Bay Road, ¾ m. SW. Built in the 1860s as a marine villa in the meaty Gothic of the day, for a member of the Crawshay family by *John Norton*. In *c.* 1892–3 Norton extended it upwards and onwards to make the Langland Bay Hotel, a four-storey monster with a 310-ft (94.5-metre) frontage. The original part is the lower two storeys towards the E, with one square and one canted bay facing s and an E porch tower of appropriate size. Polychromy of buff Bath and red Forest ashlar against grey rock-faced limestone walls. Idiosyncratic window design, with thick chamfered mullions and imposts capped by foliage hiding birds and animals. Pointed relieving arches with alternating voussoirs and trefoils and quatrefoils punched in the tympana. On the villa scale all this will have been gaily delightful; reproduced with relentless monotony for the grand hotel, it loses much of its charm. Tall, thin, circular turret at the W end, menacingly tall rebuilding of the porch tower at the E end. The interior starkly planned with end-to-end corridors and a top-lit staircase four storeys high.

CLYNE WOOD ARSENIC- AND COPPERWORKS, Clyne Valley Country Park, ½ m. W of Blackpill. The only C18 or early C19 works in the former world centre of the non-ferrous smelting industry to preserve remains of its productive plant. The works were built between 1825 and *c.* 1840 – possibly in 1837 – for a Cornish company, but closed in 1841. Henry Kingscote reopened them in 1844, and the Jennings family had succeeded him by 1852. The site was finally abandoned for smelting purposes in 1860. Some buildings were reused as hay sheds. Large ranges of Pennant sandstone buildings, furnaces and flues survive in dense woodland. A large uphill flue terminates in the picturesque IVY TOWER further s, in reality the main

chimneystack of the works, to which have been added battlements, a Gothic window and door. A staircase leads on to the
parapet. There may originally have been a condensing chamber
in the base of the stack.

RHYDYDEFAID COLLIERY CANAL, 1 m. NW of Blackpill. A
flooded cutting at the N end of Clyne Valley Country Park is
the entrance to a colliery adit driven by Sir John Morris II
c. 1840. It was probably a colliery canal. Nearby are the bases
of early C20 engine houses and a colliery haulage engine.

PENARTH

1070

Penarth developed in the second half of the C19, first as a result
of the establishment of a dock to take the overflow traffic from
Cardiff. The Penarth Harbour and Railway Company was formed
in 1856, and the first dock opened in 1865. Under the encouragement of the Baroness Windsor, principal landowner from
1855, Penarth also established itself as a place of retirement for
sea captains, colliery owners and Cardiff businessmen. Even today
the streets throughout the centre of the town are lined with
substantial late C19 villas and semi-detached pairs. *Harry Snell*,
architect to the Windsor estate, was probably responsible for
designing them, with their lively Jacobean touches. But the buildings which stick in the mind are those of *J. Coates Carter*, idiosyncratic in their Arts and Crafts individuality and unlike anything
else in the county. The small scale of the town and the density of
notable buildings make it particularly worth exploring on foot.

ST AUGUSTINE, Church Place South. Here, upon the headland,
stood the medieval church of Penarth. Its saddleback tower
was used as a landmark by sailors. In this respect, and this
alone, the old church gave a lead to its successor. In 1865
Baroness Windsor commissioned *William Butterfield*, then at
the height of his career, to build a new church, which was
ready for consecration in 1866, having cost the remarkably
economical sum of £7,550. Yet this is one of Butterfield's most
impressive creations. Austere, grey exterior, of local rock-faced
limestone in courses of varied depth, the dressings of Bath
stone. Shafts of pink Radyr stone are also very sparingly used.
E.E. style, lancets everywhere except the plate-traceried w
window and the bar-traceried E window. The SW tower stands
almost detached, forming an entrance porch. Pilaster buttresses
at the angles stress its height, and frame the belfry lancets. A
deep band of simple arcading at the level of the nave clerestory
binds tower and church together visually. N porch as far W as
possible, so the full length of the nave, with its low lean-to
aisles and its high clerestory, stands bare. Lower chancel, not
projecting far beyond its transeptal vestry and organ chamber.

The interior, brilliantly polychromatic though it is, looks
neither wilful nor aggressive. Glowing ochre Bath stone and
Radyr stone ranging in hue from pink to deep plum dominate
below, brickwork, red patterned in cream and black, above.

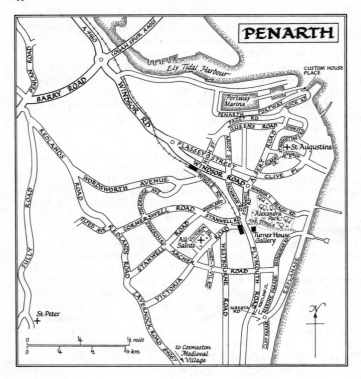

The stone is used in broad areas, pink for the shafts of the
alternately octagonal and circular piers, ochre for the extremely
broadly chamfered arches. The brick patterns, by contrast, are
small and busy, in the arcade spandrels surrounding encircled
trefoils and quatrefoils inscribed with the Beatitudes, and over
the chancel arch close-set zigzag bands. The clerestory is
shafted internally, and a walkway cuts through the thickness of
the wall. Nave roof with tie-beams and Butterfield's favourite
steeply pitched arch-braces on long, thin wall-posts. To the E
a new motif is introduced, established first in the chancel arch.
This is irregular banding of the two stones. Here Butterfield
used the darkest red sandstone, to stress the contrast and the
irregularity as much as possible. This continues in the sanctuary
arcading and the stonework round the E window. Patterning in
the brickwork, by contrast, dies away in the chancel. But the E
end is dominated by the REREDOS, patterned in marbles,
white, green, red and black, with the Name of Jesus in a huge
central lozenge. Above this, also a calculated contribution to
the whole, the STAINED GLASS of the E window, the Ascension,
by *Alexander Gibbs*, Butterfield's favourite glass-maker, using
primary colours in a bejewelled, Byzantinizing style. – FONT. A
typical piece, a square bowl of pink sandstone, bold cinquefoils

eating into its underside, set on a stem with four black marble shafts. – PULPIT. Timber. Simple. – CANDLESTICKS. Large, Islamic, of bronze. – STAINED GLASS also in the N porch, Christ carrying the cross, by *Gibbs*. – S aisle, Good Samaritan by *R. J. Newbery*, 1900. – Other N and S windows, 1900 by *W. G. Taylor*. – Nave W, Old Testament heroes, 1915 by *Clayton & Bell*.

ALL SAINTS, Victoria Square. On a spacious green, but inadequately varied in form to take advantage of its setting. For this the vicissitudes of its history are largely responsible. Built 1889–91 by *Seddon & Carter*, a nave with lofty cross-gabled aisles, full-height chancel, bell-turret and flèche. Their church at Grangetown, Cardiff (*see* p. 291), gives a clear idea of what it must have looked like. Burnt out in 1926, rebuilt by *Carter* with a N chapel. Blitzed in 1941 and rebuilt again, in 1954 by *Sir Percy Thomas & Son*, this time without the cross gables or the flèche, and with simplified E and W windows. Pennant sandstone with Bath stone dressings. The interior is still impressive, the extremely tall, lozenge-shaped piers and shallow arches enhancing the effect of uninterrupted space. Continuous boarded wagon roof painted in the Dykes Bower manner. – STAINED GLASS. Several windows by *Walker* of Wembley, 1954, reinstating pre-Blitz, even pre-fire, memorials. – Nave W, Christ in Glory, 1962 by *F. C. Spear*. Expressionist. – Also by *Spear*, 1963, Nativity in the S aisle. – N aisle, three windows by *John Petts*, St Michael expelling Satan, 1966, 'Let light break forth', 1986, and St Francis, 1978. Deliberate colouristic contrasts between the three. – S aisle, SS Francis and Clare, 1987 by *Frank Roper*, who is uncomfortable on this scale.

For the Parish Hall, E of the church, *see* p. 496.

HOLY NATIVITY, Windsor Road. 1893–4 by *Kempson & Fowler*. A cheap mission church, paid for by the Baroness Windsor. Nave and lower chancel, transepts, to serve as vestry and schoolroom. W bellcote, now truncated. Rock-faced Lias limestone with Bath stone dressings, the interior faced with meagre bands of red. – STAINED GLASS. Grisaille in most windows, with touches of yellow and red. – E window, Crucifixion. 1899.

ST LUKE, Elfed Avenue. 1959–60 by *George Pace*. Of brown brick, built to double as church and hall. Hidden lighting for the sanctuary, otherwise nothing special. – Of the fittings by *Pace*, only the wooden LECTERN is a substantial piece.

ST PETER, off Sully Road. The ancient parish church of Cogan. Nave with a deep S porch and W bellcote, lower, square-ended chancel. Early Norman, as the herringbone masonry of the nave N wall and all three walls of the chancel demonstrates. Contemporary is the plain, round-headed chancel arch on crude imposts. Trefoil-headed lancets N and S in the chancel, four-centred S doorway, of the C15. The church was rescued from dereliction in 1894 by the third Marquess of Bute, who, instead of putting a Burges-like reconstruction in hand, did the minimum to make it usable. So the interior is a touching sight, ancient plaster left adhering in patches to the walls, stone

benches against the s, w and n walls merely boxed in. –
REREDOS. 1896. Lord Bute's one extravagant gesture, in
memory of his agent, J. S. Corbett, who lived at Cogan Pill. Of
bronze. Perp. At the top a bronze group of the Transfiguration,
adapted from Fra Angelico, by *N.H.J. Westlake*. – MONU-
MENT. Big stone tablet set up externally on the s wall, a
specially good example of a local practice. It commemorates
John Davies, and his wife Mary †1800.
(ST JOSEPH, R.C., Wordsworth Avenue. 1914–15 by *F. A. Walters*, the e end completed in 1928. Italian Romanesque, on a
basilican plan. w towers not built.)
ALBERT ROAD METHODIST CHURCH. 1906 by *Henry Budgen*.
Built of snecked Pennant sandstone with Bath stone dressings.
Lofty tower. Cuspless Dec tracery in the identical six-light
windows above the entrance porch and over the site of the
pulpit. Cross-gabled side elevations. Vestry and schoolroom
behind. Altered interior. Good sculpture and boarded vault in
what was the upper part of the church.
STANWELL ROAD BAPTIST CHURCH, Stanwell Road. 1895–6
by *Jones, Richards & Budgen*. Gothic. Thin coursed Pennant
sandstone with Bath stone dressings. A five-light Perp window
is the focal point of the formulaic façade.
TABERNACLE BAPTIST CHAPEL, Plassey Street. Classical, the
façade taking its place in the street-line. 1895 by *Jones &
Thornley*. Arched upper windows. Paired Corinthian side pilasters, with the curious conceit of drapery carved across their
capitals from which birds flap. A recent Post-Modern full-
width vestibule masks the lower storey. 1989 by the *Burgess
Partnership*, who also remodelled the interior very successfully.
Galleries on three sides with bowed metal fronts now painted
red. Slender iron columns below and above, all with huge
foliage capitals. Upper arches and, what is more, an arcaded
clerestory, providing side windows at three levels. A little coloured glass in Art Nouveau patterns at the lower two levels. All
this makes for great height and brightness.
TRINITY METHODIST CHURCH, Stanwell Road. Of 1899–
1901 by *S. W. Richards & Henry Budgen*. Perp, church-like
indeed, with a tower with spire, clerestoried aisles and transepts.
Newbridge sandstone with Bath stone dressings. The
INTERIOR has four-bay arcades of East Anglian derivation.
Deeply hollowed arches, quatrefoils in the spandrels. Octagonal, red sandstone piers. Transepts awkwardly managed by
means of coupled piers. Short chancel with elaborately treated
five-light window. – REREDOS. A copy of Leonardo's Last
Supper. – PULPIT. Expensive, *c.*1911. – STAINED GLASS.
Almost a complete set, by *H. J. Salisbury* of St Albans and the
Brompton Road, culminating in an Ascension in the chancel
window, dated 1903. The SCHOOLROOM behind is also elaborately Perp. 1896 by *J. P. Jones, Budgen & Co*. Clerestoried roof
structure carried on cast iron columns inside.
ALBERT COUNTY INFANTS' SCHOOL, Albert Road. What
arrests the eye is its blue and white designs, heraldic in the

gables, friezes of fidgety schoolchildren under the eaves. These were painted by *R. Norton Nance* of St Ives, to his wife's design, and decorate the boys' and girls' classrooms added by *J. Coates Carter*, *c.*1905–10. Otherwise the classrooms are quite simple, each with a big gable to the r. and full-height windows framed by pilasters in two differing arrangements. The Gothic teacher's house lying back in the centre belongs to the original school, built by *Henry C. Harris* in 1875–6. Contrasting handling of the stonework in the two parts.

STANWELL COUNTY COMPREHENSIVE SCHOOL, Stanwell Road. The original range, facing ARCHER ROAD, is the intermediate school by *Harry Snell*, 1894–7. Lias limestone with dressings of yellow brick and bands of Bath stone. Boys' and girls' entrances l. and r. of a lofty block containing the hall.

VICTORIA COUNTY PRIMARY SCHOOL, Cornerswell Road. 1897–8. Two-storey, red brick, baldly intimidating. *J. H. Phillips* of Cardiff won a competition for it in 1896, judged by E. R. Robson, the pioneer of board school design in the 1870s.

YSGOL GYNRADD GYMRAEG (Welsh language primary school), Redlands Road. 1975–6 by the *Welsh School of Architecture* (project architect *Alwyn Jones*). Brown brick. Monopitch roofs. Open plan interior, each major space lit at a high level on one side and low down on the other.

PUBLIC LIBRARY, Stanwell Road. 1904–6 by *Harry Snell*. Jacobean. Coursed grey limestone with Bath stone dressings. An asymmetrical group towards Stanwell Road, building up from a house to a hall to the lofty two-storey library proper with a clock tower of lively outline at the corner.

DOCKS

The docks were constructed, on the S side of the estuary of the River Ely, in the early 1860s. They closed in 1963 and are partly filled in, partly in use as a marina. The approach by car is from the far W end of Windsor Road, close to the roundabout at Cogan. The former dock buildings stand at the furthest extremity to the E. There are two of them, both disused at the time of writing. They seem to have been designed by *G. E. Robinson* of Cardiff, who in 1864 called for tenders to build Dock Offices, Custom House and Dock Master's House at Penarth.

CUSTOM HOUSE. Dated 1865. Completely convincing as a building of the early C18 Baroque, except that yellow, not red brick is used, toning closely with the Bath stone dressings. The three-bay centre, crowned by a ponderous stone clock-turret with a lead cap and displaying the royal arms, is set between pedimented ends which are framed by paired Ionic pilasters. Tall rusticated ground storey. Porch on Tuscan columns.

MARINE BUILDINGS. Of the same date and materials. A fifteen-bay terrace with a French pavilion roof and over-emphatic detail, in the hotel style of that moment.

The DOCKS themselves have been transformed into Portway

Marina, with PORTWAY MARINA VILLAGE, by *Chamberlin,*
Powell, Bon & Woods, begun 1984, crowding round three sides
of the square basin to the E and along the N side of the
rectangular dock further W. Coherent yet informal, and consistent in scale and design, the most unassuming of Glamorgan's three dock redevelopments. The houses are two- and
three-storeyed, arranged in broken groups, coming together
here and there into more-or-less formal compositions. Brick
and render, varied in colour from storey to storey, and trimmed
with black brick. Black slate pitched roofs. Double-height oriels
project from the taller houses. Brick-paved walkways, also in
more than one colour. The HARBOUR MASTER'S OFFICE,
facing the basin outlet, is part of the scheme. Further development to the W, from 1993, in a more mannered idiom.

PERAMBULATION

This naturally starts at the top of the town, at the W end of St
Augustine's church. On the headland itself nothing else except
HEADLANDS SCHOOL, along ST AUGUSTINE'S ROAD to
the NE, at the corner of JOHN STREET. This was built in 1868
as the Penarth Hotel by the Taff Vale Railway Company. Sub-
classical, quite a polychromatic display in grey Lias, buff Bath
stone and red brick. Five-storey, seven-bay main block.
STABLES alongside, bearing the date. A successful attempt to
upstage the Marine Buildings down by the docks.

Downhill to the W of the church at the end of BELLE VUE
TERRACE, Albert County Infants' School. Further downhill,
the former DISTRICT COUNCIL OFFICES, 1881, distinguished by the French pavilion roofs over the end bays, and
then, on the corner of ALBERT CRESCENT, Albert Road
Methodist church. In Albert Road, just before it joins Windsor
Road, the POST OFFICE, dated 1936. Modernistic. Rounded
corner. Corrugated bands between the windows. The architect
was *A. R. Myers* of the Office of Works. Round the corner
in WINDSOR ROAD the scene becomes more urban. At the
junction *Edward Webb*'s three-storey, ashlar-faced WINDSOR
ARCADE and adjoining LLOYDS BANK of 1898. Pilasters in
three tiers, small central Dutch gable. The ambitious scale of
this scheme is not sustained further along the street.

Across the roundabout, in STANWELL ROAD, the elegant
Jacobean public library. At the end, to the l., a footpath leads
down THE DINGLE to THE ESPLANADE (as does a longer,
but more gently graded route along Plymouth Road, Holmesdale Place and Bridgeman Road – for which *see* below). In
ALEXANDRA PARK, towards the sea, CENOTAPH, 1924 by
Goscombe John. White granite stepped obelisk and against it a
seaward-facing bronze Victory, winged, standing on a prow
and bearing a laurel-wreathed sword. At its foot the Jacobean
PUBLIC BATHS, 1883–5 by *Harry Snell & Henry C. Harris*, with
a domed tower of Russian complexity of outline. Iron trussed
roof with decorative scrollwork. The PIER, opposite, was

constructed 1892–4, on a cast iron substructure designed by
H. F. Edwards. Its central section survives, but the dominant
impression is of the PIER PAVILION of 1927–8 at the landward
end, of reinforced concrete painted in pastel shades. Emerald
topee-shaped domelets and semicircular Tuscan colonnade.
Architect a certain *Somerset*, engineers *L. G. Mouchel & Partners*. The return uphill along BRIDGEMAN ROAD brings the
most substantial of Penarth's villas into sight. The Gothic TY-
LLWYD, near the beginning, is the most extravagant. HOLME
TOWER, 1901 by *Edwin Jones* of Cardiff, has been demolished.
   Bridgeman Road continues to the S as MARINE PARADE.
Here is a run of detached and semi-detached villas with Jacobean details, characteristic of the high-class housing erected in
Penarth during the 1880s and 1890s on the Windsor Estate,
most probably to the design of the estate architect, *Harry Snell*.
Local Lias limestone walling, the dressings of Bath stone and
yellow brick. Nos. 13–14 dated 1888. At the far end, on the
corner of ALBERTA ROAD, a witty 1980s reworking of the
idiom: PORTLAND CLOSE, 1983 by the *Percy Thomas Partnership* (design partner *Dale Owen*). In CLIFF PARADE, the
continuation of Marine Parade, No. 5, 1939 by *Gordon Griffiths*.
This was the height of fashion in its day, flat-roofed, white-
walled, the stair rising in a glazed curve where the wall-plane
steps out. The garden front has a semicircular full-height bow
nearly, but not quite, in the centre. Its neighbour, No. 7, half
a century on, also keeps up with the times. 1989 by *Gordon
Jones* of *Powell & Alport*. Pitched roofs resting on exposed steel
posts, purple brick walls, and much fussy detailing. Behind
these, INTERNATIONAL HOUSE, in Plymouth Road, *c.* 1965
by *Edward D. Mills & Partners*, a straightforward six-storey
slab. Reinforced concrete frame. Purplish brick end walls,
windows and grey polished panels in bands on the long sides.
Now a new start must be made in the town centre by returning
to the N end of Plymouth Road. Here is the RAILWAY HOTEL
on the W, an elephantine cottage orné of *c.* 1860, and on the E,
first an over-elaborated three-storey terrace, Nos. 2–10, dated
1886, then the idiosyncratic TURNER HOUSE GALLERY. This
was built in 1887–8 by *Edwin Seward* of *Seward & Thomas*
of Cardiff to house the art collection of Major James Pyke
Thompson, who lived at Redlands, next door. Hipped-roofed
pavilion of red brick and red Shawk stone, in a Renaissance
style. Central arched recess under a pediment, with flanking
relief candelabra, to symbolize Ruskin's Lamp of Truth. Fenestration within the arch altered, and sgraffito panels to l. and
r. eliminated. The interior was originally two-storeyed, with the
top-lit exhibition space above the caretaker's lodging. Original
staircase at the N end. The remodelling is of 1949–50 by
T. Alwyn Lloyd & Gordon. On the site of Redlands, ROXBURGH
GARDEN COURT, three-storey ranges of housing round a
quadrangle. 1975 by the *Percy Thomas Partnership* (design
partner *Dale Owen*).
   Further S in Plymouth Road the semi-detached villas typical

of middle-class Windsor estate housing *c.* 1890 establish themselves. More in HICKMAN ROAD, N of the Railway Station.
On the W side of the station a fan of roads continues the estate
housing further. WESTBOURNE ROAD and CWRT-Y-VIL
ROAD hold no special surprises, but VICTORIA ROAD, further
W, is rather different. There are red brick and half-timbered
villas and pairs, but, more important, here several buildings by
J. Coates Carter are concentrated. Starting at the N end,
opposite the Railway Station, first come the PAGET ROOMS,
built to *Coates Carter*'s design in 1906. Small and cheap, but
radical-looking stuff. Rectangular, rendered façade over a dado
of brown glazed brick. No visible roof. Wayward pattern of
apertures, small and square above, gathered under big round
arches below. Entrance arch on thin shafts with scroll capitals
set into the depth of the wall. Also two pretty little cartouches,
reassurance that this is just fun and games, not radical architecture after all. Handsomely proportioned principal room,
covered by a segmental vault with two full-length strip skylights.
At the corner of Victoria Square, in order to see everything it
is necessary first to seek out the earlier of *Coates Carter*'s church
halls, WOODLAND HALL (now Church in Wales Centre); this
is round the corner to the W in WOODLAND PLACE, facing
Stanwell Road Baptist Church. Designed in 1896, in a less
exaggerated Arts and Crafts style. Two-storey, below of red
brick dressed with Bath stone, rendered above. Two unequal
gables towards the road, that to the r. pulled forwards at the
apex to house a bell, and extravagantly downwards in its outer
slope. A big semicircular window under each gable.

104   The PARISH HALL, E of All Saints church, of 1906 is a
particularly exuberant piece of Arts and Crafts design by
J. Coates Carter. Rock-faced coursed sandstone punctuated
with boulders. Bath stone dressings. Pantiled roofs, recently
renewed. The entrance front owes a good deal to H. H. Richardson in its boldly bowed forms, both the thick-set stair-turret
to the r. and the splayed, round-headed door surround. Roof
pulled down like a hat, the ends of its brim supported by
the stair-turret and by a battered buttress. Round the sides,
semicircular windows under the gables, and long, unbroken
lines of dormers in the roof-slopes. Foundation stone with
lettering typical of the date.

Across the road from All Saints Hall, Nos. 20–22 VICTORIA
ROAD, a semi-detached pair, designed in 1892 by *Coates Carter*
(No. 20 for himself). Much more conventional, red brick and
tile-hung, but with artfully positioned fenestration. In ARCHER
ROAD, which runs across, Nos. 23–25 look like *Coates Carter*'s
work, in the deft treatment of the brickwork, especially of the
angle turret, polygonal below, cylindrical above. Then further
along on the SE side of Victoria Road a group, all probably by
Coates Carter, *c.* 1902–3, No. 60 (REDHOUSE, built for
himself), Nos. 66 (spoilt), 70 (THE WHITE HOUSE) and 76.
Though quite small, and generally square in plan, Carter's
houses are worked out with extreme ingenuity to produce

rooms contrasting in shape and size. No. 60, built in 1902, where he had only himself to please, looks much more fantastic than the others, its plunging gables interpenetrating with wild asymmetry, and an arched entrance juxtaposed to a candle-snuffer turret. The garden side is, by contrast, symmetrical, under a chalet roof (Carter's wife was Swiss). Central semi-circular window under a bowed loggia, its parapet of pierced fish-scale pattern. Red brick and tile, and large bands of render. A turret cap to the r., starting low and rising high, breaks the formality. Inside, the Arts and Crafts idiom is given further rein. Voyseyesque staircase climbing the full height of the house. Timber double doors display the architect's collection of locks and hinges. The back half of the ground floor is devoted to one complex room, divided by an arch and breaking out into various sub-spaces, one of them an inglenook.

COGAN PILL, at the N end of Windsor Road, beyond the end of the town. A substantial C16 stone house, much reconstructed in the late C19 for J. S. Corbett, the third Marquess of Bute's agent. Now the Baron's Court Restaurant and entirely sur-rounded by tarmac. Most external dressed stonework is modern. L-plan, the main range to the S, of Lias limestone rubble, entered through a two-storey porch bearing a shield of arms of Sir George Herbert and his first wife, and therefore datable to the middle decades of the C16. The porch formerly led into a passage, but now opens directly into the main internal space, the full-height HALL. Even before the recent opening out of the interior the hall was remarkably extravagant, occu-pying more than half the total volume of the original house. Five-bay collar-purlin roof, of the kind familiar from local churches, but without wind-braces. The four-light windows, one to the S and one to the E, with arched lights and hoods on square stops, though much renewed, represent the original fenestration, which must have left the hall seriously underlit. Can all this be as late as the mid C16, or is it the work of Herbert's grandfather, Sir Matthew Cradock († 1531)? The NE oriel is a C19 invention, made up from medieval stonework said to have come from St John's church, Cardiff (*see* p. 187). Also C19, of course, the lining of the walls of the hall with polychromatic brickwork.

COSMESTON MEDIEVAL VILLAGE, 1½ m. s. The deserted C13–C14 village was excavated from 1981 by the Glamorgan–Gwent Archaeological Trust, within the confines of Cosmeston Country Park. A BARN, KILNHOUSE and FARMSTEAD have been reconstructed, on the basis of the excavated stone footings. The low stone walls, deep thatched roofs and small square windows tucked under the eaves are to some extent conjectural, but must give a good idea of a peasant farmer's settlement before the Black Death.

5090 # PENCLAWDD

The village, which grew up beside the estuary of the River Llwchwr after the establishment of the copperworks, is dominated by chapels. The church stands on a medieval site $\frac{1}{4}$ m. SE, high above and beyond the houses, overlooking the Morlais Valley.

ST GWYNOUR. There was a medieval church here, but the present building is of 1850 (nave and W steeple), and 1926 (chancel, vestry and organ chamber) by the diocesan architect. No architect is known for the earlier part, though the stone broach spire (reconstructed in 1886 by *J. Buckley Wilson*) shows a certain ambition. – FONT. Octagonal medieval bowl, modelled with more variety than usual.

BETHEL INDEPENDENT CHAPEL, Bethel Road. 1910 by *W. Beddoe Rees*. A townish Beaux-Arts façade of stone, crowned by a Diocletian window within an open pediment. Ionic columns flanked by pilaster strips superimposed on channelling. The central doorway below flanked by bullseyes. Utilitarian sides. Compare Beddoe Rees's chapels at Maesteg (q.v.). The interior surpasses the façade in sophistication, finely proportioned and subtly detailed. Galleries with bowed metal fronts in a pierced palmette pattern surround it on all four sides, dipping in front of the organ in its round-headed recess. The galleries are carried on slender iron shafts and in turn carry shafts with swirling foliage capitals and semicircular arches. Above these, a segmental vault on a modillion cornice, subdivided by transverse beams on leaf corbels. Oak pews segmentally bowed towards the 'big seat' and Art Nouveauish pulpit.

TABERNACLE CALVINISTIC METHODIST CHAPEL, Main Road. 1911. Church-like. Tower with spire to the r. of the façade. Dec. Buff rock-faced walls and buff stone dressings. Also designed for galleries.

COMMUNITY CENTRE, Bankbach. Built in 1910 as a council infants' school by *W. James Nash*. Small, compact and simple, but well detailed and characteristic.

COPPERWORKS, $\frac{1}{2}$ m. E (SS 5470 9585). One wall of the smelting works used from 1788 until 1811 still stands, with a plaque dating a surviving arch to a rebuilding by Low's Patent Copper Company in 1848. The Cornishman John Vivian operated here from 1800 to 1811, before establishing his vast copperworks at Swansea. The works closed in 1868 and most of the site was used for lead- and silver-smelting, the manufacture of tinplate, and lastly for cockle-processing, from which period most of the present remains survive. The remains of the tidal dock of the works lie alongside, and a tramway, reinforced by cast copper-slag blocks, ran along the foreshore to the E, passing the tidal dock of the Penclawdd Canal (*see* below).

CANAL DOCK AND SCOURING BASIN, $\frac{3}{4}$ m. E. The Penclawdd Canal was a 4-m. (6.4-kilometre)-long waterway constructed 1811–14 to carry coal for shipping at Penclawdd. How long it

remained in use is uncertain. Much of the course of the canal
was built over by the Penclawdd branch of the Llanelly Railway
in the 1860s. The silted remains of the terminal basin are clearly
visible on the former edge of the sea, the line of which has
altered considerably since the C19. An arm of the canal ran out
alongside the dockside quay, and a culvert can still be seen that
fed water from the canal into the scouring basin. Tidal river
docks with enclosed basins or reservoirs on their landward side,
used to scour the dock periodically, by opening a connecting sluice, were a common feature of early C19 docks in South
Wales. Other examples were at Port Tennant and the Birmingham copperworks dock, both at Swansea, and at Burry Port.

PENCOED
9080

St David, Penprysg Road. 1915. Nave and lower chancel.
Salem Chapel, Coychurch Road. 1886. Rendered. Mildly
  Lombardic.
Trinity Presbyterian Church of Wales, Penybont
  Road. 1907 by *W. J. Davies* of Tondu. Arts and Crafts Jacobean, faced with Pennant and Bath stone on all sides, an
  unusually lavish approach to chapel design.
County Junior and Infants' School, Penprysg Road.
  1881 by *Henry C. Harris* of Cardiff. Local red brick and terracotta, but in its simple way aware of Shaw's and Nesfield's
  Queen Anne style. White-painted mullion-and-transom
  windows, the centre two breaking up into the roof-slope under
  white coved eaves. The teacher's house at the l., intended to
  add picturesque variety, was not built.
Sony Factory, $\frac{1}{2}$m. s. Large, low and rectangular, part black,
  part white. The American factory image.
Dyffryn, 1 m. NW. In a dell below the M4. Small late C16
  house, of two storeys, with a full-width one-and-a-half-storey
  addition on the N side. Two ground-floor heated rooms. What
  gives it special interest is the way the house was updated. The
  entrance doorway was at first in the w end wall beside the hall
  fireplace. This was later blocked and a new s doorway opened
  round the corner, to form a lobby-entry arrangement. Finally,
  a doorway was cut in the centre of the s front. Similarly the
  mural staircase curving up over the hall fireplace gave way to a
  more spacious one with a rectangular core, when the N extension was added.

PENDERYN
9000

St Cynog. Standing isolated on a spur of Moel Penderyn, yet
  in a churchyard full of pretentious Victorian monuments like a
  cemetery. The only pre-Victorian part of the church is the w
  tower, unbuttressed, with the usual battered base and corbelled
  battlements, but primitive in its detail, suggesting a late date,

possibly even in the C17. The church itself was partly rebuilt in 1843, repaired in 1876, and fully restored in 1895–6 by *E. M. Bruce Vaughan*. Perp-style windows. The chancel ceiling retains C15 foliage bosses. – STOUP. By the S door. Medieval, polygonal, chip-carved with snowflake patterns. – STAINED GLASS. Sanctuary E window, Adoration of the Magi, 1886. Designed by *Henry Holiday*, made by *Powell*'s. High Renaissance figures. Symmetrical composition. Strong colours. Altogether idiosyncratic and remarkable. Sanctuary S, Christ-child offered in the Temple, clearly by the same. – Nave NE. Saints. 1906 in the style of Burne-Jones.

0070

PENDOYLAN/PENDEULWYN

ST CADOC. Big unbuttressed W tower, apparently of *c.*1500, reconstructed in 1893 by *Bruton & Williams*. Battlements on corbels, as usual. Belfry windows of two cinquefoiled lights under a hoodmould. Similar, renewed, window, with square hood stops, over the four-centred arched W doorway. Plinth. Internally, the rough tunnel-vault and the doorway to the mural stair, moulded with a roll, may suggest an earlier origin. Nave and lower chancel, with a N rood-stair projection added at the junction of the two. The chancel E and the entire S wall and porch largely of the restoration of 1855, though the blocked priest's door in the chancel, chamfered with a two-centred head, and the S doorway, moulded with two sunk quadrants on a big stop, have survived. The chancel arch, however, is the most eloquent evidence. It must be of *c.*1500, two-centred with a roll and a hollow, and set on characteristic late Perp imposts, alternating shafts and hollows under an embattled cap. Heavy arch-braced roofs on foliage corbels, clearly of 1855. – FONT. Octagonal with quatrefoils on alternate faces. Heavily retooled, or entirely of the C19. – STAINED GLASS. Chancel E, patterned borders and tracery. Signed by *Thomas Willement* and made in 1855. Nave N, Ruth and Mary, signed *W. F. Dixon*, 1884. – MONUMENT. 1887, with a relief. Really an endowment tablet.

To the N of the church a row of COTTAGES, built in 1817 as almshouses, the larger one at the W end a replacement of 1850, to serve as the parish school. To the S of the church, unusually formal and substantial COUNCIL HOUSING of the 1950s.* The lower windows and doors even have stone frames and mullions. Well integrated with the earlier houses of the village.

HENSOL CASTLE, 1½m. NW. This enormously extended castellated mansion is quite an archaeological puzzle. The S range, not in its present form, came first. Two-storey areas of grey squared blocks represent this. In 1735 William Talbot M.P., later second Baron Talbot of Hensol, added E and W wings extending backwards from it. These survive, partly remodelled. What makes them remarkable is their Gothic character, an

*Information from Canon D.G.P. Williams.

extremely early example of the Gothic Revival in Britain, and far in advance of anything else in Glamorgan.* The date is reported by the Royal Commission to be on one of the wings. Both have five-sided central projections of four storeys with broad, pointed-headed windows sashed but given Gothic glazing bars. The original top battlements have been largely remodelled. The rendered w front gives a better idea of the 1730s work than that to the E, where the stripping of the walls has been more drastic, in order to incorporate this range into the later, far more ambitiously castle-style, remodelling.

Samuel Richardson, who bought Hensol c.1790 and died in 1815, transformed the s front. His architect, whose name seems 67 not to have been recorded, did the job with splendid panache, for it was he who brought the centre bay aggressively forward as a tower with turret shooting up higher at the back, and added the cylindrical angle turrets of random rubble-stone varied in colour. The tops of the towers strongly corbelled out. Arrow loops. In the centre a single-storey porte cochère projects yet further. Similar turrets define the rest of the façade, forming two-bay sections of three storeys, of mauve squared blocks, and beyond them three-bay sections of two storeys, of grey squared blocks, which must represent the ends of the 1730s ranges.

By the mid 1840s such a composition must have seemed far too rigidly symmetrical. Rowland Fothergill, who acquired Hensol in 1838, employed *T. H. Wyatt & David Brandon* to improve it (design exhibited 1848). They remodelled the battlements, inserted the big Perp square-headed windows, and added the tellingly off-centre window bay to the s front. They also extended the house far to the N with the elaborate service and stable courts the Victorians deemed essential.

The interior of Hensol is, unexpectedly, classical. It is of various different dates, and inadequately documented. The ENTRANCE HALL is probably of c.1910, to judge by the wreathed plaster ceiling, and the panelling incorporating doorcases over each of which is a vivid white shell hood. The STAIRCASE may be of the C18. Two twisted balusters per step. But the ceiling here and the groin-vaulted spine corridors, Doric below and Ionic above, look like work of the 1880s. Similarly unrestrained is the SE room, with its Doric columns carrying chunks of entablature.

The castle is approached from the E across a balustraded bridge and down an avenue of hornbeams. At the entrance a startled-looking mid-C19 LODGE, cruciform, with a pinnacle transfixing its front gable.

(TŶ-DU, I m. NW. The smallest motte in the county.)

CAE'RWIGAU-ISAF, ½ m. S. Late C16 single-unit house of two full storeys, extended to the N. Much of its original stone detail survives, including mullioned windows with

---

*But contemporary with the neo-Gothic castle at Clearwell in westernmost Gloucestershire, built by the Wyndhams, who were also resident in Glamorgan (*see* Southerndown, p. 574).

square-headed lights and hoodmoulds on square stops. Sunk chamfer mouldings.

6090

PENLLERGAER/PENLLE'R-GAER

St David. Rich E.E. chancel of 1886 by *J. Buckley Wilson*. Nave and transepts of 1936–7 by *Roderick & Sons* of Aberdare, replacing a chapel of ease of 1837–8 but preserving its pre-Ecclesiological E.E. style. – REREDOS. Mosaic and green marble with vine trails, of *c.*1920? – STAINED GLASS. E window, Christ in Majesty between SS John and David. 1909 by *Powell*'s. – Chancel S, Lilies of the Field and Dorcas, 1966 by *E. J. Dilworth*. – Sanctuary S, Good Shepherd, 1982 by *Celtic Studios*.

PENLLERGARE HOUSE was demolished in 1961. It was of 1835–6 by *Edward Haycock*. (One LODGE by *Haycock* survives.)
ASTRONOMICAL OBSERVATORY, $\frac{1}{4}$m. NE. In the grounds of the Lliw Valley Borough Council Offices, s of the M4 roundabout. The observatory was built by John Dillwyn-Llewelyn of Penllergare House, a pioneer of photography. The flat timber roof of the cylindrical tower has recently been restored. Adjoining is a former single-storey laboratory constructed with specially designed hollow insulating bricks (shown at the Great Exhibition of 1851).

9070

PENLLINE/PENLLYN

CHAPEL. At the castle gates. Built for John Homfray *c.*1850. Dec, with a reticulated E window. – FONT, dated 1682, and finely inscribed on the rim of the small octagonal bowl. – REREDOS. 1903. The full-height panelling to l. and r. is later. – STAINED GLASS. E window, Christ between Mary and John. 1850. – Sanctuary S, SS John and Francis, by *C. Powell*, after 1913.

Opposite the chapel, a contemporary LODGE, the end towards the drive three-sided turning square by means of monster corbels. The RUIN beside it is interpreted by the Royal Commission as being the scanty fragment of a medieval first-floor hall.

CASTLE. On the lip of a limestone cliff overlooking the valley of the River Thaw perches part of a small early C12 keep. Evidence of the early date is most obvious in the herringbone masonry low down in the N wall. In the E wall a round-headed opening at the upper level.

To the S ramble the outbuildings of a castellated mansion. Here the earliest evidence is of the late C16 or early C17, in the s face of the STABLES which back up against the keep. Three-light mullion-and-transom windows in two storeys. Two doorways with four-centred heads. They must be the relics of a large house built by the Turbervilles. The TOWER in the stable court has a doorway and window of this period low down in its s face, but was built up crazily high in the C19 as a water tower. The Tudor style E range bears the date 1875.

The s block is a symmetrical castellated villa erected between 1789 and 1804 for Miss Emilia Gwinnett. It looks like the work of an amateur. Central porch in the Batty Langley style. Pointed arch and battlemented top, but a Doric frieze and a Greek key pattern on the impost band. This is of green Bridgend stone ashlar. The house itself is pebbledashed, of five bays, with bowed projections round the corners to l. and r. Very large sash windows with stone surrounds.

Inside, the simple top-lit staircase, axially placed at the back of the house, belongs to this period. The principal rooms were decorated for the Homfray family in an idiosyncratic classical style c. 1860. Louis-Quinze-style chimneypieces of grey marble with massive over-mirrors.

FFERM GOCH, 1½m. N. Twenty-four semi-detached houses round three sides of a green, built c. 1936 by *T. Alwyn Lloyd* for unemployed miners. Their co-operative smallholdings lay across the road to the E.

MYNYDD BYCHAN, 1m. SW. A sub-oval enclosure fortified by a single bank with outer ditches. Excavation has shown that it was occupied c. 50 B.C. to A.D. 120, and again C11–C13.

PENMAEN

ST JOHN THE BAPTIST. Largely by *R. K. Penson*, 1854–5. Old walling in the nave and s porch, N chapel replacing a transeptal arrangement, chancel with bellcote entirely Penson's, as is the cut stone everywhere. E.E., with a few spirited touches, such as the shafted chancel arch on extremely low-slung head corbels. Chapel E window in the form of a spherical triangle. – PULPIT and FONT, by *Penson*, nothing special. – STAINED GLASS. Remarkable mainly for the subjects. – Nave w, Parables, c. 1873. – N chapel w, Miriam singing, c. 1876. – Nave s, David and Jonathan, 1874, to commemorate a love surpassing that of brothers. Quite powerful in design and colour.

(Ruins of the FORMER CHURCH remain in the valley ½m. SE. This was overwhelmed by sand, probably in the C14, and replaced by the present building further inland.)

(On the headland ¾m. SE, CASTLE TOWER, a C12 earthen castle of ringwork form. Excavation in 1960–1 revealed traces of a timber gatehouse and palisade, and of later drystone fortifications and a free-standing hall within the enclosure, all datable on historical grounds to before 1217.)

On PEN-MAEN BURROWS, ½m. S, the endured remains of a Neolithic CHAMBERED TOMB. Excavation in the C19 showed that the main chamber, defined by orthostats, was entered from the E via a passage. The main chamber opened to a smaller s chamber. There may have been a similar side chamber to the N. The displaced capstone partially covers the main chamber.

4 PARC CWM CHAMBERED TOMB, $\frac{3}{4}$m. NE, but approached from
p. 23   Parkmill, Ilston (q.v.). A good partial restoration of a particularly interesting Neolithic tomb, excavated in 1961–2, lies
on the floor of an attractively wooded dry valley. C19 disturbance uncovered remains of at least twenty people. A limestone rubble trapezoidal cairn 72 ft (22 metres) long lies N–S
and is retained by two closely spaced, parallel drystone walls.
The visible outer revetment is neatly constructed with an
unusual wave effect in the coursing. A passage, entered over a
sill stone, penetrates the cairn from the deeply recessed forecourt at the N end. Two chambers on each side of the passage.
Passage and chambers are constructed of upright slabs supplemented by drystone walling. The capstones are missing. The
SE corner of the cairn has been eroded, perhaps by a former
stream. (*See also* Cathole Cave, Ilston, which is in Parc Cwm.)

0060   PENMARK/PEN-MARC

The compact village centre has lost much of its charm since the
recent take-over by executive houses.

ST MARY. On a large scale, a Dec and Perp expansion from a
late Norman origin. The chancel arch is the earliest feature. It
is pointed, but has big zigzag on the clasping roll moulding and
crudely carved heads at the top of the chamfered imposts. C14
nave, see the double-chamfered S doorway, with above it a
cusped image niche flanked by little pinnacled buttresses. SW
window of two trefoiled lights under a pointed quatrefoil.
Ceiled wagon roof to the nave. The porch has a roof on wall-
plates decorated with cusped panelling. The tower, of the usual
unbuttressed type with corbelled battlements, exhibits C15 features, the moulded plinth, the W doorway with two waves and
the large three-light window over it. Most remarkable, indeed
astonishing in this part of the world, is the lofty tower arch of
positively East Anglian dimensions, moulded with two continuous double waves. The chancel was transformed in 1860
with new Perp windows, the E window an elegant piece. Well-
preserved access arrangements to the rood, in the nave N wall. –
FONT. A C13 tub on a round shaft. – ALTAR RAILS of c. 1700.
Turned balusters. – PULPIT. Octagonal, of timber. C18. –
STATUETTE. Madonna with pelican. Bronze. By *Frank Roper*,
1977. – STAINED GLASS. E window, Crucifixion. In a C15
Netherlandish style. 1898 by *R. J. Newbery*. – MONUMENTS. In
the chancel. Two rustic marble monuments, Catherine Lewis
†1682, and Thomas Lewis †1689, the latter with twisted side
columns. – The Rev. John Thomas Casberd †1844. Grecian
tablet with side and top scrolls. Signed *R. Brown*, London. –
In the nave. Robert and Mary Jones of Fonmon Castle, c. 1756.
An unusually fine wall-monument of several coloured marbles,
with a palm wreath at the top. – Oliver and Robert Jones,
c. 1834. Gothic wall-monument with military baton and a medal

dangling from the shelf. Both have been extended downwards to take later inscriptions.

In the CHURCHYARD, beside the S porch, Casberd family TOMB, a Grecian sarcophagus bearing a draped urn, set up c. 1847.

CASTLE. Extensive ivy-clad remains in the field N of the church of the castle of the Unfraville family. In origin an early C12 ringwork, thrown up on the edge of a steep escarpment to the N. In the C13 a stone curtain wall, of random Lias limestone, was erected on the line of the ringwork. Quite a long stretch survives to the W, with a strong batter on its outer face, and traces of a wall-walk at the top. Mounds show where buildings were set against its NE and SE sides. Ruins of a barn on the N side, said to have been built in 1770. There was no gate tower, just a simple gateway in the S wall, facing the church.

In the NW corner, the most substantial structure to survive, a D-plan tower, to which a rectangular garderobe block was added. This is all clearly an addition to the curtain wall, and constructed more substantially, with courses of squared lime-stone blocks. Penmark Castle was probably neglected from the early C15, when the owners of nearby Fonmon Castle (q.v.) came to possess it.

At EAST ABERTHAW, $2\frac{1}{2}$ m. SW, several early cottages, in par-ticular the BLUE ANCHOR INN, a three-unit mid-C16 house built end-on to the road. The S entrance doorway, with two-centred chamfered arch, leads into the unusually large kitchen. Well-preserved mural stair. Towards the road the original hall with a mutilated mural stair in its S wall, and a small inner room beyond. Later extension to the E. Thatched, as no doubt it was originally.

PENNARD

5080

ST MARY. Set well inland on the hilltop. This church replaces one near the castle, $1\frac{1}{2}$ m. W, which was overwhelmed by sand, probably in the C14. Various C13 pieces built in must come from this predecessor. Most memorable, though, is the peculiar W tower, corbelled battlements crowning a bell stage which is itself corbelled out. Inside, this structure is revealed as no more than a turret built over the thickness of the W wall. Two-light window with trefoiled heads lighting a W gallery, the bressumer of which shows that this is an early arrangement. Tiny C19 dormers to light the gallery. The nave is lit by large Y-traceried windows N and S, presumably introduced at the restoration of 1847. Note that they are set proud of the wall-face, which was therefore intended to be thickly plastered. In the chancel two small S lancets are perhaps reused, as are certainly the blocks carved with dogtooth which form a rough-and-ready hood-mould to one of them. E window of c. 1500, two cinquefoiled lights under a hoodmould, but flanked internally by reused E.E. shafts with moulded caps. The chancel arch is roughly pointed on plain, reused imposts. Plastered and whitewashed interior, the nave roof also plastered so that only the undersides of the elliptically profiled arch-braces show through. – FONT. Two mutilated bowls, really a stoup and a millstone, suggests Orrin, on a base intended for a shafted stem. – FONT COVER. A fine early C17 piece, still Gothic in concept, octagonal, with a band of mouchettes round the base and a big foliage finial. – PULPIT. Wood. Also of the early C17, with typical, secular-looking decoration, dragons above arcading, pairs of bearded heads at the top. (Brought in, from Shiplake, Oxfordshire.) – ALTAR RAILS. Turned balusters. C17 or early C18. – ROYAL ARMS. Small, now set over the chancel arch, but integral with panels inscribed with Creed, Decalogue and Lord's Prayer, which presumably originally formed a reredos. – STAINED GLASS. Chancel E, Virgin and Child, and Christ the Good Shepherd. 1914, signed by *T. F. Curtis* of *Ward & Hughes*. Weak.

CASTLE, 1½m. W. On the edge of the golf links, but best approached from the beach below. The roughly circular form of the curtain wall follows the line of a C12 earthen ringwork, at the brink of the precipitous drop to the N. Within this enclosure the footings of a large rectangular stone building, also of the C12, have been excavated. The masonry curtain walls and gatehouse are datable to the decades around 1300. Much pink sandstone conglomerate in the lower courses of the walls, mainly grey local limestone above, presumably indicating no more than a change in the source of building stone during construction. Some of the walls survive almost to battlement height. No corbelling. Circular turret strengthening the wall to the NW, and beyond it a later rectangular projection. The best-preserved and the most interesting part is the E-facing GATEHOUSE. Although no dressed stonework survives, the design is clear enough, a late and relatively weak imitation of the Edwardian type of gatehouse where two big drum towers flank the entrance arch. Arch of flattened pointed form, with evidence of a room over. Portcullis arrangement and long arrow slits in the towers to protect the entrance.

KILVROUGH MANOR, ½m. NW. Late C18, sash-windowed but battlemented, in the minimal castle style of Fonmon Castle (q.v.) of the early 1760s and Adam's at Wenvoe Castle (q.v.) of 1776. Kilvrough seems to have reached its present form by 1774. Three storeys, L-plan, the walls roughcast and white-washed. Five-bay N front, centrally entered through a porch of four cast iron Tuscan columns. Many blind windows, sug-gesting the incorporation of an earlier building. Nine-bay W front, the outer three bays to l. and r. in full-height polygonal projections. The ground floor here is treated as a basement, its windows small and semicircular. The plan is most eccentric, for the front door opens on to a full-height staircase which ascends to a corridor at piano nobile level, from which the three W-facing reception rooms open off. In two of these are enriched friezes, doorcases and chimneypieces, of painted wood, and plasterwork ceiling centrepieces, all Adamesque but provincial in their craftsmanship.

Beyond the present extent of the grounds, $\frac{1}{4}$ m. SE of the house, a FOLLY, drum-shaped, with lancets and battlements.

LODGE, beside the A4118. 1872 by *J.H. Baylis* of Swansea. Tudor Gothic.

GREAT KITTLE, 1 m. E. A good farm group, turning its back on bungalows to survey the wooded Bishopston Valley to the S. (The farmhouse, datable as early as the late C16, has one main storey and a second in the roof space. Projection in the centre of the S wall, to fit a bed in the hall, a typical Gower arrangement.)

PWLL-DU LIMESTONE QUARRY, $1\frac{3}{4}$ m. S. A coastal quarry serving the trade over to Devon and Cornwall via the partially extant slides down to the beach. Operative from the C17 to the C20.

VENNAWAY LIMEKILN. Small kiln visible on the A4118 $\frac{1}{4}$ m. E of Kilvrough Manor.

PENRHYS
0090

Penrhys was celebrated in the Middle Ages for its shrine to the Virgin Mary, high on the mountain ridge. (Traces of a substantial late medieval CHAPEL, a buttressed nave and a square-ended chancel of equal width. Only the N doorway of the chancel is upstanding now.) Also the restored WELL-HOUSE, and a monumental white STATUE of the Virgin, erected in 1953, more at home in Ecuador than South Wales.

Today the high ground has been overspread with an estate of nearly one thousand houses, built 1966–9 by *Alex Robertson, Peter Francis & Partners*. Short, two-storey and three-storey terraces with cement-rendered concrete walls and monopitch roofs, typical of the 1960s, but here brutally exposed to the elements.

PENRICE/PENRHYS
4080

The church and half-a-dozen whitewashed cottages stand at random round a miniature green, open to the panoramic view of Oxwich Bay and its enclosing cliffs.

ST ANDREW. The most remarkable feature of the church is its N and S transepts. They are about 26 ft (8 metres) deep, tacked on to the normal plan of nave and lower chancel. Unbuttressed W tower with the usual battlemented top on corbels, and slit windows in the S wall at four levels, corresponding to internal floors, though there are no structural stairs. The C12 origin of the body of the church is established by the chancel arch, its semicircular arch defined by an angle roll. The transepts are of the C13 or early C14, and the S one must from an early date have functioned as a porch. Its outer arch has typical mouldings of *c.* 1300, two angle rolls, one filleted. The inner arches of both transepts are quite high and wide, two-centred and given a broad chamfer. Within the s inner arch a medieval timber doorway was formed as a lower and narrower two-centred arch, constructed from three massive baulks dowelled together. This had the effect of converting a transeptal space, if necessary, into a separate room. The fenestration, E.E. in the chancel and Perp in the nave, all renewed in the restoration by *F. W. Waller* of Gloucester, 1893–4. The Perp windows, large, multi-cusped two-lighters under hoods with splendidly grotesque head-stops, must replace windows of similar size, as the side walls of the transepts are pared back to accommodate them. – MONU-MENTS. Bennet family, 1726. Stone hanging monument under an open segmental pediment, with side panels of well-carved flowers, wheat ears and peapods. – John Hancorne † 1746, aged ten weeks. Marble. A putto at full stretch holds out a napkin on which the inscription is cut. An appropriate conceit and an echo of Bernini.

MOUNTYBOROUGH. A C12 ringwork, hidden on all sides by shrubs and trees which rise above the cottages SW of the church. By at least the C13 it had been superseded by Penrice Castle, ½ m. away.

PENRICE CASTLE, ½ m. NE. The medieval castle, the C18 house below it, and the landscaped park which surrounds them both, provide a wonderfully complete impression of late C18 men-tality. Thomas Mansel Talbot, who in 1758 at the age of eleven inherited Margam Abbey and the Mansel family estates of Penrice, Oxwich and Llandough (near Cowbridge), grew up to be a man of culture who spent many years in Rome. Yet he chose to abandon the main family seat at Margam in favour of the remote fastnesses of Gower, for Penrice was 'the most romantic spot in all the county'. His first scheme was for a 'shooting box' in a Strawberry Hill Gothic style on a site above the ruins of the medieval castle. By 1773 his ideas had changed, and his new house was to be both a permanent residence, set lower down the hill below the castle, and a complete contrast to it. So urbanity and Italianate culture were to find their place, overlooked by a relic of baronial wars, and surrounded by nature tamed and idealized by the hand of the landscape gar-dener. Or, to quote an unsympathetic contemporary, Benjamin Malkin, writing in 1804: 'He has given all the elegance of Twickenham to a remote corner; has formed the artificial pieces of water in front of Oxwich Bay; and built a modern villa, scarcely large enough for his own family, under the nodding towers of the ancient castle, which is converted into an aviary'.

The main PARK GATES, of 1793, are on the A4118 at the NE corner of the park. They state Talbot's ambivalence vividly. Central stone gatepiers banded with vermiculated rustication. Iron railings with Neoclassical enrichment. Flanking them stand extravagantly ruinated walls, the porter's lodge hidden behind the W half, with a drum turret, and a single window peeping through a break in the stonework.

From here the drive drops down past the single-storey

STABLES of 1776–7, built of red brick in three ranges round a courtyard. Windows in blind arcading. A further turn brings one to the N front of the house, facing into the hill, and the medieval castle towering on its crag behind.

The MEDIEVAL CASTLE is at present in a dangerous condition and inaccessible. What is readily seen is a long stretch of curtain wall standing almost to full height. Small semicircular turret halfway along and another at the SW angle. (The curtain walls surround an unusually large enclosure, measuring 320 ft (97.5 metres) by 230 ft (70.1 metres). This is attributed to Robert de Penrice † 1283. The gatehouse is at the N corner and consists of two square turrets flanking the entrance externally and one covering it internally. Near the W extremity a round tower, known as the keep, of two storeys, with adjacent structures. Against the inner face of the E curtain wall a very long rectangular building on the steep slope.)

Thomas Mansel Talbot's HOUSE was built 1773–7 to the 60 design of the Gloucestershire architect *Anthony Keck*. It takes as its model the villa type devised by Sir Robert Taylor for London bankers and aldermen building in the Home Counties. The master mason was *William Gubbings*, the master plasterer *Thomas Keyte*. Severe block of Bath stone ashlar, five bays by three, the entrance front to the N of three storeys, its central three bays grouped under a pediment, the S front four-storeyed as the ground drops, the centre three bays in a bold full-height bow. Pedimented entrance porch on Tuscan columns. Tripartite plan, the cross-walls carrying symmetrical banks of chimneystacks. Small service wing to the E, all that remains after extensions of 1812–17 and 1893–6 were removed in 1967.

The INTERIOR of the house was fully fitted up only for Talbot's marriage in 1792. It mainly consists on the ground floor of an entrance hall with Doric details and two large, lofty reception rooms, beautifully capturing the seaward and landward views through trios of windows. Restrained Adamesque decoration. Chimneypieces of 1771 and 1773, one signed by *C. Aguatti*, Rome, another executed by *C. Albacini* and *L. Valadier*. Timber staircase of no particular pretension.

The PARK was landscaped from 1776 by *William Emes*, who formed the lakes below the house and planted the trees to screen and focus the view over Oxwich Bay.

(In the SE corner of the park an ORANGERY, erected by *Gubbings* 1791–3. Five bays with Corinthianesque pilaster strips.) GATEPIERS, with vermiculated banding as on the main gate, at the SW and NW entrances to the park.

HOME FARM, ½m. N. A quadrangular group, stone-built, of c.1800. Across the road a square GRANARY, red brick, on staddle stones, built in 1807, rebuilt 1937. An unexpected sight in Gower.

PITT FARM, ½m. S. A fine group, house and farm buildings, the boundary walls all whitewashed in the traditional Gower way. L-plan house, datable to the mid C17, of two-and-a-half storeys displaying the hoodmoulds of several blocked two-light

windows towards the road. Chimneybreast widened by corbelling near the top, to take a fireplace for an attic room.

PENTRE

Pentre and Ton Pentre originated in the 1860s. The main collieries were developed by David Davies (Maendy, 1865) and the
Cory brothers, John and Richard (Pentre and Gelli, 1870s). In
1874 Griffith Llewellyn of Baglan Hall, with William Cubitt of
the great London family of engineers, established the Rhondda
Engine Works, which became a principal supplier of colliery
equipment in South Wales.

St Peter. The most stupendous of the church benefactions
of Griffith Llewellyn. 1887–90 by *F. R. Kempson* at a cost of
£20,000. Towards the road rises a W tower of four tall stages
with a NE stair-turret, all devoid of buttresses, which emphasizes the height. Flat battlemented top, a bit of a disappointment. Stately entrance flight of steps to the SW porch.
Lofty five-bay clerestoried nave with lean-to aisles. Transepts,
with prominent stair-turrets. Elaborately planned E end; separately gabled chapel and vestry clasp and extend beyond the E
end of the chancel. The style is E.E. and surprisingly restrained.
Moulded caps for the circular nave piers, the shafted tower
arch and chancel arch, the clerestory arcades and the tiers of
arcading in the sanctuary. Plain, double-chamfered arches.
Stiff-leaf foliage is reserved for the porch arch, for the sedilia
and for the major fittings. Impressively managed steps in the
chancel.
    But the memory one takes away is of the banding of pink
and buff which outside affects all the dressed stone, and inside
affects everything, broad bands in the stonework combining
with narrow bands in the brick walling. Nave piers altogether
pink. Tie-beam roof in the nave with arch-braces and collar
purlin in the Glamorgan idiom; boarded wagon roof in the
chancel. – REREDOS. Pink veined marble wall to wall. White
marble figures under canopies, in the centre scenes of Nativity,
Crucifixion and Resurrection, with flanking prophets and Evangelists. – PULPIT. Stone, with red marble colonnettes. Scenes
from the life of St Peter. – FONT. A more architectural piece,
a pink marble cylinder on grey marble colonnettes. – STAINED
GLASS. Ascension (E) and Charge to Peter (W), clearly by
Dixon. More flamboyant than anything else in the church.
Borough Council Offices, 200 yds (183 metres) S of the
church. Plain but handsome five-bay palazzo front. Built as a
police court in 1901 by *Griffiths & Pugh Jones* of Tonypandy
and Cardiff.
At Ton Pentre, ¾ m. S, at the junction of Church Street and
Bailey Street, a church and two chapels.
St John, on the site of the medieval parish church of Ystra-
dyfodwg, 1985–7 by the Rev. *David Jenkins*, reuses the rock-
faced sandstone and red brick of its immediate predecessor,

built in 1846 and doubled in size in 1893–4 by *Bruce Vaughan*. The new church is frankly modern, low and square, under a big pyramid roof. Black glazed pantiles. Separately roofed porch. Top-lighting, as well as large side windows against which STAINED GLASS, taken from demolished local churches (St David, Pentre, and St Mark, Gelli), is suspended. The marriage of modernity and tradition continues in the CHURCHYARD, part lawn, part a thicket of Victorian monuments.

BETHESDA WELSH INDEPENDENT CHAPEL, Bailey Street. 1906–7 by *W. D. Morgan*. Large, majestically classical and with a seven-bay façade full of incident. The centre three bays under a pediment with pilasters, Doric below, Corinthian above, the capitals including heads among the foliage (a surprising archaeological quotation, from an Etruscan tomb at Vulci, Hilling notes). Arched windows above, segmental below in channelled walling. Gibbs surrounds to the upper windows in the side bays, and bullseye windows in the outer side bays. The façade even returns at the sides under small pediments. All this is further enlivened by colour, red sandstone for the central architectural framework, buff stone within it, and local dark green sandstone at the sides. The INTERIOR is equally splendid, with lily-capped cast iron columns in two storeys, to carry the galleries with their raked seating round three sides and to support the timber roof structure above. Arch-braces in the roof cove. A plaster roundel in each ceiling compartment. – PULPIT with balustraded steps, the great ORGAN above it, the 'big seat' below. – STAINED GLASS, of Art Nouveau patterns, in the windows of the entrance front.

The chapel is no longer in use for services, but is to be restored by the Rhondda Business Community. The outstanding interior must be preserved intact.

ENGLISH CONGREGATIONAL CHURCH, Church Road. 1884. Gothic.

JERUSALEM WELSH CALVINISTIC METHODIST CHAPEL, Church Road. 1881 by the Rev. *William Jones*. A large and serious classical affair, with pedimented upper windows under the three-bay pediment and one-bay side sections for the gallery stairs. Its spacious interior earned it the soubriquet, 'the Methodist cathedral of the Rhondda'. The building seems doomed.

PENTYRCH

1080

ST CADWG. 1853–7 by *Prichard & Seddon*, one of their best churches, though small and inexpensive. Exhilarating view from the E, of the steeply pitched roofs of chancel and higher nave, and the sloping fin-like buttresses almost propelling the building upwards. Charming octagonal SW turret, crowned by a transparent gabled stage and a spirelet. The architects have learnt how to take the medieval vocabulary and say something personal and vital with it. Dec style. Roughly coursed Pennant stone, with bands and voussoirs of pink sandstone in the E wall.

Bath stone ashlar. The interior is quite simple, distinguished only by the refined mouldings of the chancel arch and window rere-arches. – FONT. Medieval. Octagonal. Also a second font, of Caen stone and red Devonshire marble shafts, by *Prichard & Seddon*. – HOLY WATER STOUP. Rescued from the old church. – PULPIT. By *Prichard & Seddon*. Of Caen stone, carved with rather flattened figures, all but two of which were completed, by *Clarke* of Llandaff, as late as 1901. – STAINED GLASS. Chancel E, Good Shepherd flanked by Mary and John, with scenes below. 1906 by *R. J. Newbery*. (– MONUMENT. Medieval grave-slab with incised foliate cross, at the W end.)

BRYN CADWG, overlooking the church, was built as the vicarage in 1890 by *E. M. Bruce Vaughan*.

HOREB PRESBYTERIAN CHURCH OF WALES, Heol-y-Pentre. 1862. Gable-end façade with four round-headed windows of equal height. Galleried on three sides, the entrance at the preacher's end.

CASTELLYMYNACH, at the S end of the overgrown hamlet of Creigiau, 2 m. W, and at the time of writing about to be surrounded by new houses. Yet, within its own stone-walled garden, it retains its fascination as one of the largest late medieval houses in the county. It was built for a member of the Mathew family. Two long two-storey ranges form an L. Presumably they enclosed the S and E sides of a courtyard, for the front and rear arches of a gateway survive, now blocked, in the E range. The arch towards the supposed courtyard is the more richly moulded, with two sunk quadrants, and the heads of both are four-centred. Before 1909 the roof at this point was raised, to form a minimal gatehouse. The only other early external feature is a trefoil-headed lancet under a hoodmould near the N end of the outer face of this range. Inside, by contrast, the early evidence is in the S range, the complete arch-braced roof of a four-bay open hall. Finely moulded principals and purlins, and embattled wall-plate. Straight joints in the S wall indicate the width of what must have been a mighty chimneybreast for the hall fireplace. So the S range was the residential part. It had a cross-passage within the W bay of the hall, and two-storey ends, in the classic late medieval plan. A contemporary doorway links the range with the gatehouse, but how the rooms N of the gatehouse functioned in relation to the main part of the house is not clear. They must have been for the family's private use, for a two-storey garderobe projects from the N end wall.

In the early C17 the house was modernized, probably for Thomas Mathew, High Sheriff in 1614. The hall was halved in height. Carved and painted shields of the royal arms and the arms of Mathew, with supporters and mantling, in strapwork frames. On the staircase in the E range, a large expanse of WALL-PAINTING dated 1602. Black and white grotesque patterns in jewelled borders. It must originally have decorated the wall of a room. Still more unusual and impressive the large fragment of wall-painting in the great chamber which occupies the upper half of the medieval hall. Two muscular male nudes hold up a framed scene of ships in a gale, and from the parapet on which they recline hangs a trompe-l'oeil tapestry. Such levels of illusionism are worthy of court art of the period. The painting is technically excellent too.

PANTYGORED, 1¼ m. SW. The farmhouse has been shown by the Royal Commission to originate c. 1500 as a two-unit house of two-and-a-half storeys. Extended, rendered and sashed, it has a late C18 appearance. Lower farm buildings extend the range to the r.

CRAIG-Y-PARC, 1 m. SW. Designed by *C. E. Mallows* in 1913 and built 1914–18 for Thomas Evans, director of the Ocean Coal Company. Under the spell of Lutyens, but a beautifully resolved composition, lodge, approach, house and terraced garden fused into a complex harmony. The entrance lodge straddles the drive, with a big hipped roof and slate-hung upper walls, in a way recently demonstrated by Lutyens at The Salutation, Sandwich. Axial drive and turning circle scaled to the width of the house. This is like a gabled Tudor manor house, and even more like Lutyens's Little Thakeham. Doric columns flank the front door. Inside, the circular form is reiterated in the tiny entrance vestibule. Long access corridor to l. and r., and behind, a spacious reception room, its ends screened by Doric columns. The most original feature of the house is the way the columns continue externally on the garden side of the house, forming an atrium between the wings that come forward to l. and r. The garden drops away in a series of terraces to the S. The house is built of stone quarried on site, with dressings, including the columns, of a granitic stone from Pontypridd.

GARTH HILL, 1½ m. N. A group of five well-preserved earlier Bronze Age BURIAL MOUNDS along the ridge. The largest, second from the W and surmounted by an OS pillar, is 14 ft (4.3 metres) high and 115 ft (35 metres) across. The E-most is surrounded by a ditch.

PEN-Y-FAI

8080

ALL SAINTS. An estate church built 1900–3 at the expense of *Robert Llewellyn* beside the gates of his house, Court Colman (*see* below). The SCHOOL (now studio) to the S, of 1898–9, and the PARSONAGE to the E complete the group. According to Llewellyn, he himself 'designed the plans', but they were 'redrawn together with all details' by *John Jones*, son of the foreman who had built the church at Baglan (q.v.) to John Prichard's design for his cousin, Griffith Llewellyn. Cruciform in plan, with a lofty crossing tower. E.E. to Dec in style. The borrowings from Baglan are most obvious inside, the walls faced with green Quarella stone and banded with yellow Ham Hill stone, the handling of the crossing with shafts coming down on to heads of the four Evangelists. But of Prichard's finesse, regrettably, there is no sign. – REREDOS. Also 'roughly designed' by *Llewellyn* and executed by *William Clarke* of Llandaff. Pink Penarth alabaster and gilt and black mosaic, a cloying combination. White marble groups of Nativity, Crucifixion and Descent from the Cross by *Goscombe John*. – CHOIR STALLS. By *Clarke*. – PULPIT. Another overloaded piece, the combined effort of *Llewellyn* and *Clarke*. – FONT. Life-size kneeling angel, a copy of *Thorwaldsen*'s famous font in the Church of Our Lady, Copenhagen. – STAINED GLASS. E window, Resurrection and saints, by *Powell*'s.*

HOSPITAL, ½ m. E. A grey stone complex, with a prominent CHAPEL towards the main road. Built as the Glamorganshire Lunatic Asylum in 1861–2, to the design of *Richard Bell* of London.

COURT COLMAN, 1 m. W. Now a hotel. Built for the Llewellyn family some time after 1837. Three-storeyed, rendered, of 2+7+2 bays, the centre and ends crowned by pedimental gables. Various Palladian windows.

9090   PENYGRAIG

ST BARNABAS, Turberville Terrace. 1914–15 by *A. O. Evans, Williams & Evans*. E.E. on a high site overlooking the houses. Chancel not built. Plans by *E. M. Bruce Vaughan* of 1895 had been abandoned for lack of funds.

ST ILLTYD, Williamstown. Also high-set, beside the A4093. 1891–4 by *Bruce Vaughan*. Dec. Nave and lower chancel.

SOAR WELSH BAPTIST CHAPEL, down by the roundabout in the centre of the village. Large, of 1902 by *R. S. Griffiths & D. Pugh Jones*. Classical. Overall pediment. Upper windows treated as an arcade. Flanking stair projections. Typical contrast with the Established church in siting as well as style. The interior has been subdivided.

0070   PETERSTON-SUPER-ELY/LLANBEDR-Y-FRO

ST PETER. Quite an impressive Perp nave. The tall three-light windows with cinquefoiled arched heads and hoodmoulds are made to respond to each other N and S in an unusually orderly way. Small S doorway. W tower separately designed but also Perp. Tower arch wide and quite high, two-centred and moulded with two hollows and a wave. External moulded plinth. Four-centred W doorway, two-light window over it, and similar windows at belfry level, of cinquefoiled lights under hoodmoulds. Corbelled battlements and gargoyles. The buttresses have been added. The chancel largely reconstructed in 1890–1 by *Kempson & Fowler*, but the chancel arch is medieval and probably the earliest feature, C14, with straight jambs into

---

*Robert Llewellyn's account of his church, on which this text is based, has been printed by the parish, an enlightened gesture.

which the chamfered arch dies. Door and window for the rood loft. - FONT. Small, octagonal, of the C15. Pinnacled cover, C19. - STAINED GLASS. Nothing distinguished. Chancel E, Crucified Christ between St Peter and St Paul, 1891 by *A. Savell & Co.* - Chancel SE, Sarah and Abraham. Signed by the same. - Nave S, Christ and the woman of Samaria. Of *c.*1870, in a Hardman style, and probably by *Joseph Bell* of Bristol, who made designs for windows here. - Nave N, Christ in three roles. 1915, signed by *Jones & Willis*. - Nave S, saints, by *A. L. Wilkinson*, 1957.

CROES-Y-PARC BAPTIST CHAPEL, ½ m. SW. Dated 1843, of the long-wall façade type. Round-headed openings, two long windows between two doorways and two short outer windows to light the galleries. Inside, the (later) pulpit backs on to the entrance wall, as this fenestration pattern leads one to expect. Galleries on three sides angled in five cants. Pews of the simplest.

CASTLE. Across the road from the church is a chunk of thick stone wall in which the splays of a robbed upper window can be made out. There is nothing else to see.

PARSONAGE. *Prichard & Seddon* designed a parsonage for Peterston-super-Ely *c.*1857. This is the house 300 yds (274 metres) NW of the church, of limestone with red brick bands and window voussoirs of red brick and Bath stone, crowned by a steep roof set with steep dormers and a row of tall, elegant chimneystacks. Gabled porch in the r. bay, veranda across the rest of the front.

WYNDHAM PARK (or Glyn Cory Garden Village), ½ m. SE. John and Reginald Cory, the coal magnates, began a Garden Village here in 1909, to a plan devised by *Thomas Adams* in consultation with the garden designer *T. H. Mawson*. MAIN AVENUE runs wide and straight up the hill, with to the E of it three slightly curving roads, all that was laid out of a vast amphitheatrical scheme on the hillside. By 1914 no more than twenty-two of the projected one thousand houses had been built: two detached houses at the W end of DYFFRYN CRESCENT, five pairs halfway down the S side of CORY CRESCENT, and below them a most surprising terrace of ten flat-roofed houses, Nos. 1–10 PWLL-Y-MYN CRESCENT. Each house has a turret feature, canted window bays, and a tympanum of brightly coloured mosaic over the front door. Sadly, only one house retains its original fenestration. Who was the architect of this paradoxically early essay in the Modernistic?

PONTARDAWE

The town, indeed the whole valley, is dominated by the soaring spire of W. M. Parsons's church, 197 ft (60 metres) high, which he is said to have insisted should be higher than the chimneys of his factory. It has also proved more durable than the chimneys, which are now nowhere to be seen.

ST PETER. Built 1858–60 at the expense of W.M. Parsons,

the local ironmaster, and consecrated in 1862. A model of Ecclesiological rectitude, designed by the Swansea architect *J. H. Baylis*. The materials are conventional, snecked, rock-faced Pennant sandstone with Bath stone dressings. The plan is perfectly straightforward, a three-bay chancel with an organ chamber on its s side, clerestoried five-bay nave, w porch tower and spire. The proportions are of a proper loftiness, not only the spire, but also the clerestory and the steeply pitched roofs. The details, however, betray the recklessness of an inexperienced architect with plenty of money to spend. Dec style throughout. Huge five-light E window, in the clerestory hexfoil spherical triangles, in the aisles flowing tracery of many contorted patterns. Polygonal w buttresses to the tower bristling with gargoyles. The interior is even more overwhelming. High nave rising to a complex timber roof. Slender clustered piers with naturalistic leaf-carving imitated from the chapter house of Southwell Minster, ballflower nestling in the arch mouldings. Multi-shafted chancel arch. Chancel windows internally shafted, and roof on an enriched stone wall-plate and leaf corbels. Marble floors to chancel and sanctuary. – FONTS. The font of *c*. 1862 is unexpectedly small. There is also a marble kneeling angel holding a shell, one of the many copies of *Thorwaldsen*'s font in the Church of Our Lady, Copenhagen. – PULPIT, *c*. 1862. – LECTERN. An extraordinary three-sided stone enclosure, dated 1860. – STAINED GLASS. Chancel E, Passion subjects, *c*. 1907 by *R. J. Newbery*. – Much else, mostly of the early C20. Mention may be made of the Resurrection in the s aisle, *c*. 1868, in a Hardman manner; s aisle SE, Presentation by *Kempe & Tower*, 1921; N aisle w, saints, by the same, 1922. – Chancel N, saints, 1966 signed by *Eric Dilworth*.

ALL SAINTS. 1885–6. Built at the expense of Arthur Gilbertson of Glanrhyd, who in 1896 'enlarged and beautified' the chancel. *Gilbertson* and his builder *John Griffiths* worked out the design between them. Snecked, rock-faced Pennant sandstone with Bridgend stone dressings. Nave and lower chancel. N transept bearing a bellcote. w baptistery. Lancets, shafted internally. Rose window in the w gable. – FONT. Another shell-bearing angel. – PULPIT. Surrounded by figures of saints under canopies. Carved by *William Clarke* of Llandaff, 1900. – REREDOS. The climax of the interior. White marble seated figures of Christ and the four Evangelists under gables of pink Penarth alabaster. – STAINED GLASS. Throughout. That in the E window by *R. J. Newbery*, 1895.

ADULAM WELSH BAPTIST CHAPEL, Swansea Road. Dated 1889. Pedimented. Rock-faced sandstone with quoins of red and black brick.

WESLEYAN CHAPEL, James Street. Dated 1902. Idiosyncratic Arts and Crafts Gothic. Note the lettering.

NATIONAL SCHOOL, Brecon Road. A single-storey group, probably of *c*. 1870. Pennant rubble with Bath stone dressings. Windows with runs of arched lights.

PRIMARY SCHOOL, Upper Heathfield Road. 1914 by *W. James*

Nash. Far-extending one-storey pavilion, the hall in the centre behind a gable end. Classrooms l. and r., demarcated by red brick pilaster strips, their windows rising to the eaves of the hipped roof. A clear-cut design (which the architect had the pride to exhibit at the Royal Academy).

PUBLIC HALL AND INSTITUTE, Holly Street. Dated 1908. An unsophisticated Arts and Crafts group. Hall at the back looking like a Nonconformist chapel. The MAGISTRATES' COURT, further down the road, appears to be part of the scheme.

BRIDGE, over the River Tawe, ½ m. SE. By the famous C18 bridge-builder *William Edwards*. A single span of 80 ft (24.4 metres), constructed without voids in the haunches. Later widening.

TINPLATE WORKS, S of the town, on the NW bank of the River Tawe. Founded 1843 by William Parsons as the Primrose Forge and Tinplate Works. It was powered by water from the Pontardawe tucking mill and from the adjacent Swansea Canal. Open-hearth furnaces were added later to make it an integrated steel- and tinplate works, and under later owners, the Gilbertsons, Pontardawe became virtually a one-company town until the closure of the works in 1962. Most of the site has now been cleared, except for one large, late C19 building of Pennant sandstone with brick dressings, still in industrial use. This retains its tinning bays and a floor of iron slabs, rare survivals.

The Pontardawe HOUSING has an unusually spacious character. Instead of the long terraces built elsewhere throughout the Valleys in the late C19, here there are close-spaced, but individual three-bay houses or semi-detached pairs. Rock-faced ragstone, quoins alternately stone and red or yellow brick.

PENLLE'R CASTELL, 5 m. NW. Remote earthwork on a moorland hilltop, bearing traces of two square masonry towers. The Royal Commission suggests that this is the lord of Gower's 'New Castle of Gower' burnt by the Welsh in 1252 and subsequently reconstructed in stone.

PONTARDULAIS/PONTARDDULAIS
(LLANDEILO TALYBONT)   5000

ST TEILO, Bolgoed Road. Built in 1850–1 to the design of *William Richards* of Swansea, to replace the medieval church on the marshes.* The short chancel and boxy nave mark this as pre-Pugin Gothic, as do the big, broad lancets and thin, strip-like buttresses. Inside, w gallery and plastered nave ceiling. The contrast with such a contemporary church as St John at Skewen, not to mention Woodyer's at Sketty, Swansea, is instructive. Only the three-stage tower, with strong set-offs, and stone broach spire, acknowledges the new ideas in church design. – STAINED GLASS. Nave lancets, St Teilo dated 1905 and St

---

*The medieval church is due to be re-erected at the Welsh Folk Museum at St Fagans. The remarkable medieval wall-paintings from it have been detached and are exhibited at the museum.

David, by *A. L. Moore*. – E window, Christ between SS Teilo
and Carannog, 1952, signed by *J. Howson & C. C. Townsend*.*

ST MICHAEL, St Teilo's Street. 1900–1 by *E. M. Bruce Vaughan*.
Plan and materials in accordance with his normal practice.
Only the style, Perp, is exceptional for him. – FITTINGS.
Simple, but Perp also. – STAINED GLASS. Christ in Majesty
and St Michael, 1903.

HOPE CHAPEL, St Teilo's Street. The old chapel lies back; its
successor, dated 1872, faces the street. Gothic. Stone-fronted,
with a pair of Y-traceried windows and angle pinnacles. The
lancet windows at the sides indicate an interior without
galleries.

MECHANICS' INSTITUTE, St Teilo's Street. 1905–6 by
W. Beddoe Rees. Handsome porch on stout Ionic columns.

TALYBONT CASTLE, 1 m. SW. A motte thrown up in association
with Loughor Castle by Henry de Villers soon after 1106. Now
immediately S of the motorway, but best seen from the B4296.
The bailey to the S has been ploughed over.

TUNNEL, ¾ m. NW. The tunnel, constructed in 1839, dates from
the era of the horse-drawn tramroad, and its floor had to be
lowered to accommodate a standard-gauge railway line. The
tunnel is 236 ft (72 metres) long and about 13 ft (4 metres)
wide. Segment-headed arch on vertical side walls. In 1984 a
new concrete bed and drains were laid through the tunnel.

LLIW FORGE, Pontlliw, 1½ m. NW. Established c. 1740 in close
association with Llandyfan Forge. In the later C19 it was
developed from a simple forge into a more ambitious engineering business which supplied machinery to the local tinplate
industry. It probably closed at some date in the 1920s but
remained intact until it was stripped for scrap in the Second
World War. COTTAGES attached to the forge remain and are
still occupied.

1000   PONTLOTTYN/PONTLOTYN

ST TYFAELOG. 1862–3 by *Charles Buckeridge* for the Rev. Gilbert
Harries, rector of Gelligaer. E.E. Nave and aisles under
unbroken roofs, apsidal chancel. Here is an exercise in High
Victorian polychromy, a contrast outside between rock-faced
Pennant sandstone walls and red brick bands and dressings,
but inside now only between red brick and cream emulsion
paint. Originally the circular piers were of green Bridgend
stone, with buff Bath stone caps, the walls banded in red and
white brick. – PULPIT. Stone, cylindrical, of c. 1863.
(– IMMERSION FONT. Near the w end, similar to the font at
Gelligaer. Also a normal FONT.) – STAINED GLASS. In the
nave, c. 1907, by *R. J. Newbery*, one window signed by him. Is
the chancel E triplet, c. 1917, also his?

*I should like to thank the Rev. J.P.H. Walters for his help in identifying the
glass-makers.

Across the road from the church, the modestly classical POLICE
STATION, dated 1915, and COURT, dated 1923, are worth a
look, their rendered walls attractively colourwashed.

At FOCHRIW, $\frac{3}{4}$ m. SW, another piece of the Rev. Mr Harries's
evangelism. The polychromatic stone and brick SCHOOL-
HOUSE was built by *Buckeridge* in 1863 to serve as a school-
cum-chapel with master's house. Small for such multiple purposes, but showing its High Victorian credentials particularly
in the pointed, brick relieving arches over upper windows,
and chimneybreast with tumbled brickwork. Now entirely in
domestic use.

PONTRHYDYFEN   7090
3 m. NE of Port Talbot

A rocky outcrop, with the little church of ST JOHN, of 1917,
sheltering by it, a disused RAILWAY VIADUCT to the N, red
brick of seven arches, and the deeply impressive BONT FAWR   77
AQUEDUCT AND VIADUCT. This was built by the ironmaster
John Reynolds 1824–7 to convey water at a suitable height to
provide the water-wheel-driven blast at the Oakwood ironworks.
There is a local tradition that small boats used the structure, and
after 1841 a railway was also laid across the bridge. It is 459 ft
(140 metres) long and 75 ft (23 metres) high, built of Pennant
sandstone rubble. The four 70-ft (21-metre)-span elliptical arches
of ashlar, seated on huge stepped piers, now carry a minor
road.

AQUEDUCT TERRACE ends in an endearingly ham-fisted chapel,
BETHEL WELSH BAPTIST CHAPEL, 1903. Red sandstone
Corinthian pilasters, their parts out of scale with one another.
Top-heavy attic. Fine interior in the same spirit, the galleries
on three sides supported on thick, fluted iron columns with
lily-bearing capitals. Pierced metal fronts to galleries and
pulpit.

The little settlement even has its own PRIMARY SCHOOL. 1907
by *W. James Nash.*

PONTYCLUN   0080

A late C19 growth generated by Llantrisant Railway Station and
Llantrisant Tinplate Works.

ST PAUL. 1894–5 by *E. M. Bruce Vaughan.* The usual result
from this architect on a tight budget. Nave and lower chancel,
bellcote over the chancel arch. Snecked, rock-faced Pennant
sandstone with Bath stone dressings. Single-space interior with
arch-braced nave roof. – STAINED GLASS. E window, Ascension between SS Paul and Illtyd, after 1919. Nothing special. –
Nave N window *c.* 1962. Semi-abstract. Blue sun rising over
thorns.

PONTYCYMER

Conifer woods and bracken-covered hillsides confine the settlement to the main road close to the valley bottom almost continuously from PONTYRHYL at the s end to TYNEWYDD at the N. Long, stone terraces line the road. Where the valley widens out a little a grid of streets develops on the hillside. Quite a generous sprinkling of CHAPELS still.

BETHEL WELSH PRESBYTERIAN CHURCH, Oxford Street. Dated 1885. Rock-faced Pennant sandstone front with round-arched openings. Standard interior galleried on three sides.

TABERNACLE WELSH INDEPENDENT CHAPEL, Albany Road. Dated 1889. Domestic-looking, its square-headed windows at both levels dressed with yellow brick. Plain but substantial interior galleried on three sides, a large organ occupying the Corinthian recess behind the pulpit. Handsome VESTRY block behind, dated 1884.

TYLAGWYN BAPTIST CHAPEL, Pontyrhyl. Small. Long-wall plan with four long, round-headed windows towards the road and a central doorway now blocked. Datestone of 1831. Converted to gable-end entry in 1888.

UNITED REFORMED CHURCH, Alexandra Road. Quite a serious performance. Perp, of rock-faced Pennant sandstone with Bath stone dressings, these facing materials used not only for the façade but also for the downhill side elevation, where the two storeys of windows are linked by moulded vertical panels. Is this the Congregational Chapel designed by *P. J. Thomas* of Bridgend in 1904?

ZION ENGLISH BAPTIST CHAPEL, Main Road. With a pinched version of the giant relieving arch but pointed windows. Built in 1892 over a schoolroom started in 1887.

FFALDAU WORKING MEN'S INSTITUTE, Meadow Street. Dated 1901. Chapel-like. The low addition to the l. under a Baroque gable is the billiard room erected to *P. J. Thomas*'s design in 1906.

PRIMARY SCHOOL, Hill View. 1907 and 1908 by *D. Pugh Jones*, typical of his many council schools built after 1902. Both ranges have red brick arcading below, rendered upper storeys with red brick dressings, and rows of triangular gables.

PONTYGWAITH

ST MARY MAGDALENE, Madeline Street. 1894–6 by *G. E. Halliday*, at the expense of M. G. Llewellyn of Baglan Hall and Pentre House. The E end rears up dramatically beside the road. Pennant sandstone, rock-faced overall inside as well as out, as Halliday preferred. E.E. style. Chancel arch flanked by low, steeply pointed passage arches. Full-span sanctuary arch. Sanctuary lavishly provided with lancets, roll-moulded or shafted. So the total effect of the interior, as seen from the w, is

quite dramatic. – STAINED GLASS. A full set, clearly of 1896. Grisaille mostly, armorial in the sanctuary N, a Crucifixion scene in the E window.
(BRIDGE. Late C18. Steeply hump-backed (Cadw).)

PONTYPRIDD

0080

Pontypridd stands at the confluence of the Rivers Taff and Rhondda, and grew as communication routes developed up the valleys. The famous bridge over the Taff, completed in 1756, which still today stands at the centre of the town, remained in rural isolation for half a century. The construction 1791–5 of the canal from Cardiff to Merthyr Tydfil, followed by the turnpike road, produced the first buildings. In 1816 Brown Lenox, the famous makers of chains and anchors, established its principal works here. Foundation dates of chapels chart the settlement's growth: Baptist 1811, Calvinistic Methodist 1817, Independent 1832. In 1841 the Taff Vale Railway arrived. By the 1840s Pontypridd was the major market town for Rhondda. By c.1870 the population was 8,000; twenty-five years later it had reached 31,000, reflecting the mining boom that was taking place all along the Rhondda valleys over that period. Though ringed by mines and other industry, the town attracted a substantial middle class. Their villas still adorn the steep side of Coed-y-lan to the NW. The high point of Pontypridd's urban pride was reached in 1902 when a prestigious London architect was commissioned to design the District Council Offices. Still today, the town's architecture is predominantly late Victorian and Edwardian, in spite of several emphatic intrusions of the 1960s. Appreciation of this inheritance has very recently begun to show, particularly in the Market Square area. It deserves to spread in all directions.

ST CATHERINE, Gelli-wastad Road. By *John Norton*, 1866–70 (N aisle 1885), the immediate successor to his church in Neath (q.v.), and equally dominant in the town, but with a feminine grace the architect had previously spurned. The tower stands over the S porch rising unbuttressed in its upper stage in clear isolation from the body of the church. Elegant spire, marred only by the gabled clock-faces clamped to the corbel table at its base as part of *Kempson & Fowler*'s restoration in 1890. Lofty clerestoried nave, and lower chancel. Plate tracery in the N and S windows, bar tracery to E and W. Externally the walls are of roughly coursed Newbridge sandstone with Bath stone dressings. Inside, the same shock as at Neath, strident polychromy, red brick walls patterned with black, and also with buff stone in the banding of the arches. Cut brick outer orders to the arches and incised patterns round the chancel arch show the immediate inspiration for all this: G.E. Street's St James the Less, Vauxhall Bridge Road, London, of 1859. Piers with alternately moulded and foliage caps, the latter of the early French variety. The chancel, which should be the climax, was drastically toned down in 1919 by *Sir Giles Scott*. Whitewashed

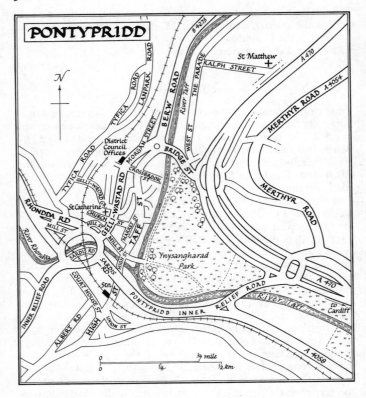

walls, black and white marble paving. – REREDOS, with a relief
of the Last Supper, and CHOIR STALLS, part of *Scott*'s scheme.
Perp. – STAINED GLASS. In the N aisle, a set *c.*1901–12,
one signed by *R. J. Newbery*. Also by him probably the two E
windows in the S aisle, 1898–1902.

ST MATTHEW, Ralph Street, Trallwn. 1907. By *Evans, Williams & Evans* (G.R.). Primarily notable for its red terracotta
arcades. Lancets. – REREDOS with copper silhouettes of Christ
and the twelve Apostles. By *Frank Roper*?

CAPEL EGLWYS BACH, Berw Road. 1899. (Now a doctor's
surgery.) A highly conspicuous object beside the river, not least
for its walls of red brick. Full-blown classical façade, a pediment
carried on two giant Corinthian half-columns, a central oeil-
de-boeuf and angle strips, all standing out in Bath stone against
the red background.

CAPEL TABERNACL (now Historical Centre), Bridge Street.
1861. Said to have been designed by the minister, Dr *E. Roberts*.
Varied texturing of the stonework. Simple but convincing
façade, two storeys of round-headed windows under a vigorously dentilled pediment. Porch of 1910 by the local firm
of *A. O. Evans, Williams & Evans*, with rusticated pilasters

inscribed with the ministers' names from 1810 until the closure of the chapel for worship in 1982. The interior, refitted in 1910 by *A. O. Evans, Williams & Evans*, retains the 'big seat', pulpit and organ, an ensemble of unusual distinction. Elaborate ceiling, with plaster swags within a boarded framework, and an octagonal central rose. Plain galleries on three sides. – STAINED GLASS. Art Nouveauish patterns.

SARDIS INDEPENDENT CHAPEL, Sardis Road. Dated 1852. Gable-end plan, treated in a simple classical way. Long arched windows l. and r. Faced with thin-coursed, snecked Pennant sandstone. The interior is probably at least twenty years later, quite large, the galleries on three sides, supported on lily-capped iron columns. Flat ceiling with moulded beams.

ST DAVID'S PRESBYTERIAN CHURCH, Gelli-wastad Road. 1883 by *Henry C. Harris* of Cardiff. Early Gothic. Bluntly grouped towards the road, the polygonal end of the hall with a big plate-traceried window played off against the gable end of the chapel with three big lancets. Rock-faced sandstone with Bath stone ashlar and some banding in pink Radyr stone. The half-timbered pavilions to l. and r. of the chapel light the gallery stairs. The broad interior is notable for its centralizing tendencies. Gallery in five cants round three sides, carried on three supports and carrying two slender shafts from which the roof structure springs.

UNITED REFORMED CHURCH, Gelli-wastad Road. Opposite St Catherine's on the downhill side of the road. Dec to Perp. Aisled, making a display of traceried windows towards the main road. Datestone 18[8]7. HALL at r.-angles to the E, with an even larger traceried window in the gable. Interior of the chapel galleried on three sides under a vertiginous roof partly supported from the gallery fronts. Built as the English Congregational Church in 1888 to the design of *Potts, Sulman & Hemmings*. The same firm added the hall in 1906.

DISTRICT COUNCIL OFFICES, on the corner of Crossbrook 113 Street and Morgan Street. 1903–4, designed by *Henry T. Hare* of London after a competition. This is far and away the most distinguished building in Pontypridd, a display of restrained Edwardian self-confidence which in its resourceful and original handling of the classical idiom can bear comparison with anything in Cathays Park, Cardiff (*see* p. 220). It takes a late C17 provincial market hall such as Windsor as its point of departure but far transcends its model. The building consists of a broad three-bay pavilion facing down Gelli-wastad Road, where the council chamber is placed above the triple-arched entrance, and offices behind in an eight-bay block of two storeys with a third in a mansard roof. Gabled bay at the far end to match the gable end of the front block. Thus the two contrasting functions of the building are visually differentiated yet combined to form two symmetrical façades at r.-angles to one another. Grey-green local sandstone is the facing material throughout, so the possibilities of colour contrasts are shunned, in favour of textural interplay between hammer-dressed walling, smooth and channelled ashlar, and relief carving, which is sparingly used on the entrance front only. To light the council chamber, three three-light windows, the lights separated by stocky Ionic half-columns, and round the corner a Palladian window, also with Ionic columns. Nowhere else are the orders used externally. Broad ashlar piers flank the entrance front, pierced by balconied arches, supported on demi-figures of Prudence and Justice, carved by *J. D. Forsyth*. Openwork flèche on the roof-ridge, less substantial than the cupola for clock and bell which Hare originally designed.

The INTERIOR is equally rational and impressive, with ribbed and groin-vaulted spine corridors at both levels, linked by a tight, vaulted staircase. Glass-domed vestibule to the Council Chamber. In the Chamber itself Ionic columns at an upper level match those outside. Segmental barrel-vault with transverse ribs. Original seating, describing a semicircle within the rectangular room. – BUSTS, in the Council Chamber, of white marble. James Roberts, signed by *Goscombe John*, 1908. Lord Pontypridd, signed by *D. Arthur Thomas*, 1902.

ARTS CENTRE, Gelli-wastad Road. Gothic. Quite scholarly Dec tracery to the windows, and, over the shafted doorway, a short steeple of extraordinary complexity. Built in 1895 as a Wesleyan chapel and school, to the design of the local architect *Arthur O. Evans*.

COED-Y-LAN LOWER COMPREHENSIVE AND INFANTS' SCHOOLS, Tyfica Road. Perched on the hillside overlooking the town, in the high-lying, healthy sort of site preferred for board schools in the 1890s. There are four parts altogether. In the centre a bare four-storey block dated 1939, by which time display in schools was shunned. The earlier parts have no such inhibitions. Their architect was *Arthur O. Evans* of Pontypridd. To the N his Intermediate Schools of 1893–4, and teacher's house of 1896. Snecked Pennant walling and yellow brick dressings. Central hall emphasized by red terracotta dressings for the big, arched windows. Shaped gables above. Buttresses with acroteria. To l. and r. entrances with Romanesque foliage imposts.

To the S a full-scale board school, in two parts. The larger and higher, dated 1897 on the foundation stones, doubtless for boys and girls, the smaller and lower for infants. Both parts are designed on the central hall principle, the halls at the back with classrooms clustered symmetrically on the other three sides. Pennant sandstone and plenty of red brick. Arcades and buttressing at ground level, segment-headed windows and gables, in a Welsh inflection of the board school style.

In YNYSANGHARAD PARK, E of the River Taff, a bronze group by *Goscombe John*, *c*. 1930, commemorating the composers of 'Land of my Fathers', the Welsh national anthem, Evan James, and his son James † 1902.

ARCHES. Slender masonry arches, designed by *Isambard Kingdom Brunel*, carrying his 1840s Taff Vale Railway over MILL STREET. The span over the Rhondda is some 110 ft

Pontypridd, bridge. Engraving of the early C19

(33.5 metres). Part of the first modern all-locomotive haulage railway in Wales.

PERAMBULATION

One can begin at the most famous and historic structure in Pontypridd, the BRIDGE over the River Taff, the Pont-y-tŷ-pridd. Constructed of roughly shaped Pennant sandstone slabs, it forms a single span of 140 ft (42.7 metres), the stepped pavement almost following the line of the semicircular arch. This produces a form of prodigious slimness, no more than twice the depth of the voussoir stones. The haunches are pierced by three circular holes, to lighten the pressure on the arch. The designer of this masterpiece was *William Edwards*, and it was completed in 1756, after three less skilfully designed bridges by him on the site had successively collapsed. The piers of the 1746 three-arched bridge were washed away, the second, of a single span, came down when the centring collapsed, and the heavy abutments of another single-span bridge of 1751 caused its collapse; but at the fourth attempt Edwards solved all the problems.

Immediately w of the bridge stands Capel Tabernacl, with Capel Eglwys Bach behind it. As the road rises SW towards the town centre, to the r. in Morgan Street, POLICE HEADQUARTERS, 1982–5 by *N. W. Megins*, a four-storey block faced with blue engineering bricks with grey panels between the windows. To the l. Morgan Street runs past the flank of the Council Offices and so into Gelli-wastad Road with its array of ecclesiastical buildings described above. TAFF STREET, which runs along parallel at a lower level, is less impressive but deserves to be pursued. At once on the l., TAFF VALE SHOPPING CENTRE, a typical development of the 1960s. Glazed shopping mall dominated by the concrete V-struts which support a central five-storey slab of offices above. This could be quite an exciting space if cared for and respected. Then, at the corner of Crossbrook Street on the r., Y.M.C.A. BUILDING, 1907–8, red brick Neo-Georgian, three storeys on an arcade now filled in for shops. Top storey a meagre curtailment. Loosely based on the competition-winning design of *Vernon Hodge & P. H. Keys*.

After this Taff Street soon widens out. Here a patriotic stone DRINKING FOUNTAIN was set up in 1895. Canopied with Celtic interlace decoration and inscriptions in Welsh on the four drinking bowls. Designed by *C. B. Fowler*. Then MARKET STREET slants up to the r. Here, where the street widens slightly to form MARKET SQUARE, a towering group, white brick with sparing red bands and Bath stone at points of emphasis. In the style which in the 1880s was called Mixed Renaissance. It consists of the MARKET TAVERN and a symmetrical group of shops, having a centrepiece with musical instruments in the pilaster capitals. This marked the entrance to the Town Hall. MARKET HALL, built as the Town Hall in 1885, in the same style facing CHURCH STREET. The whole complex was built in 1892–3 to the design of a local architect, *Thomas Rowlands*. Beyond this a second MARKET HALL with a façade in quite a different classical idiom, bold Baroque of *c*. 1910.

Then, in the continuation called High Street, at the far end on the l., the CRITERION public house, dated 1904, a stray from East Anglia with its richly pargetted gable end.

Two out-liers at the s end of the town. The first, the A.U.E.W. OFFICES, dominates the Broadway, an eight-storey tower block of *c*. 1970, which one would call Brutalist had not the concrete stair towers been clad in mustard-coloured tiles. The second is harder to find, the COURT HOUSE (now Social Services Department) behind the railway station in Court House Street. Dated 1913 and neatly imitative of H. T. Hare.

BERW ROAD-BRIDGE, Coed-pen-maen, $\frac{3}{4}$ m. NE. Early reinforced-concrete bridge, spanning the Taff. Designed by *L. G. Mouchel & Partners* in 1907 using the Hennebique system. Main span of 116 ft (35.36 metres).

4080   PORT-EYNON/PORT EINON

Church and churchyard stand in the middle of the village surrounded by white cottages. White marble figure of a lifeboatman in the SE corner of the churchyard, memorial of a local disaster in 1916.

ST CATTWG. Dominated by the big W bellcote of 1861, the little church retains few medieval features. Nave and lower chancel, small N transept, s porch. Blocked ogee-headed lancet low down in the chancel s wall (made the model for the C19 windows). The s doorway to the nave has a semicircular head, but its thin chamfer on faceted stops suggests that it is probably

of the c16. Windowless E wall, windowless W wall of 1861. The
plain, pointed chancel arch also dates from 1861. Segmental
arch to the transept, undatable. – FONT. Square bowl, on a
c13 stem, a spurred quatrefoil in plan. – STONE PANEL. Above
the pulpit, c16 heraldic shield of the Mansel family and the
initials of Rice Mansel, within a wreath of Renaissance character. – STAINED GLASS. Four windows by *Celtic Studios*, 1956
and 1973.

(At CULVER HOLE, ¾m. S, a cleft in the cliffs is blocked by a
massive wall laid to form tiers of nesting boxes inside. The
Royal Commission notes a reference to the 'dovecote in the
clyve' at Pennard as early as 1399.)

THE SALT HOUSE, ¾m. SE. The unusual ruins of c16 salt-
collecting reservoirs and boiling house, at the SW extremity of
the bay. Excavated in 1986–7 and laid out for display.

PORTH   *0090*

The town grew up at the junction of the Rhondda valleys, 1½m.
E of Dinas, where Walter Coffin in 1812 sank the first coal pit
in the area. Between 1832 and 1855 a further ten collieries for
bituminous coal were sunk in the locality. Cymmer, up the hill to
the S, was the centre of George Insole & Co.'s enterprises, and
here the chapel and early housing beside it still, at the time of
writing, remain.* Steam coal collieries were sunk at Cymmer in
1877 and Dinas in 1881. Continuous terraces of colliers' cottages
stretch for a mile along, and parallel with, the A4233 as it climbs
up the hill from the centre of Porth, through Cymmer, to Trebanog. The town centre itself is dominated by shops and modest
public buildings of the early c20, reflecting the importance of its
service industries for the Rhonddas at that period.

ST PAUL, Birchgrove Street. 1886–8 by *E. M. Bruce Vaughan*.
Perched on the hillside. Nave and slightly lower chancel, with
a short unbuttressed tower on the chancel S side, its bell stage of
timber, forming a picturesque group from the SE. Geometrical
tracery in the E window. N aisle added, apparently, in 1910.
Perp. The special feature of the interior is the elegant, Comper-
style refitting of the chancel by *H. L. North* in 1925. The transparent SCREEN, ALTAR, REREDOS and CELURE all belong,
and so does the STAINED GLASS in the E window, Crucifixion
against a clear background, designed by *F. C. Eden*. – Sanctuary
S window, 1988, signed by *Timothy Lewis*.

ST JOHN THE EVANGELIST, Maesgwyn, Cymmer. 1888–9. One
of *E. M. Bruce Vaughan*'s most successful buildings. Required
to accommodate 500 people in a church costing only £2,500,
he turned to the precedent of Lower Peover in Cheshire, and
employed a timber internal structure which incorporated nave,
aisles and chancel in one lofty space. Octagonal piers carry
transverse arches and pierced spandrels. Wide and high chancel

*The chapel is due to be rebuilt at the Rhondda Heritage Park, Trehafod.

arch. Outside everything is covered by a single, unbroken
gabled roof. Flèche over the chancel arch. Geometrical window
tracery. – STAINED GLASS. Some routine late figures by
Kempe & Tower, dates of death 1918, 1921, 1922.

CYMMER INDEPENDENT CHAPEL, Trebanog Road, Cymmer.
1834. In the characteristic early C19 arrangement whereby the
long side is treated as the façade. Four bays, round-headed
windows, two long in the middle, one higher and shorter to l.
and to r. (Interior galleried on three sides, the pulpit backing
against the entrance front.)

JERUSALEM WELSH CONGREGATIONAL CHAPEL, Cymmer.
1907–8 by *W. D. Thomas* of Porth.

LOWER RHONDDA BOROUGH COUNCIL OFFICES, Cymmer.
Built as Bronwydd House by the local architect *W. D. Thomas*
as late as 1913–14, for William Evans, founder of Thomas &
Evans's chain of grocery shops and local benefactor, who in
1922 donated Bronwydd Park to the public. Just a double-
fronted villa, but transformed by the ebullient application of
wildly inappropriate motifs in unexpected places. Semicircular
porch on coupled columns with outsize Composite capitals.
Semicircular window bay to the l. under a stone candle-snuffer
belvedere of indescribable outline. Rectangular window bay to
the r. enriched with coarse relief sculpture. Red brick and
Portland stone. Inside, the square hall remains, with black-
and-white marble floor and mahogany panelling. Cramped
staircase beyond, rising in one flight and returning in two.

PERAMBULATION

The centre of Porth lies in the valley bottom, with HANNAH
STREET as its spine. Facing down Hannah Street from the w
is the handsome five-bay front of BARCLAYS BANK, *c.*1910,
classical. The interest of the street is mainly on the N side, first
the BAPTIST TABERNACLE of 1877, enlarged in 1904 by
D. W. Jones of Porth, a rock-faced stone façade crowned by a
pediment; then the fanciful Baroque frontage of Thomas &
Evans's shop, dated 1905, four-storeyed under a shaped gable.
Big former CINEMA at the far end on the S in a vaguely Wren
style but with big Doric columns, presumably of the 1920s.
The vista is closed also at the E end by an eye-catching building,
an early C20 SHOP under a scrolly gable with red terracotta
details, most noticeably the window voussoirs creating a sunrise
effect. This is in Pontypridd Road, which forms the S boundary
of the town. Here, to the E, the EBENEZER CHAPEL, now
Elim Pentecostal, *c.*1870, with lanky Corinthian pilasters,
which faces the glowing red terracotta façade of the PUBLIC
LIBRARY, built *c.*1912 as two shops. A big Venetian window
under a Dutch gable for each shop. Turning back to the W one
passes yet another pair of high shaped gables. These belong to
the LEWIS MERTHYR COLLIERY LIBRARY AND WORK-
MEN'S INSTITUTE of 1924. Finally, at the far E end, below
St Paul's church, the CALFARIA WELSH CALVINISTIC

METHODIST CHAPEL of 1897. Dark hammer-dressed stone and ashlar dressings. Round-headed windows. Pedimental gable rather than a proper pediment. Side windows grouped, most unusually, into a symmetrical composition. Well-preserved interior, the galleries on three sides on fluted iron supports, the pews all angled to face the pulpit. Flat ceiling on a dentil frieze and decorated with a boarded rectangle and three plaster roses. 'Big seat', pulpit and organ within a plaster-surrounded recess, all of a piece.

PORTHCAWL

8070

Porthcawl owes its origin to an Act of Parliament of 1825 which authorized construction of a dock and tramway to export iron and coal, principally from Maesteg and Tondu. After 1847 the Duffryn, Llynvi and Porthcawl Railway (opened in 1828) was converted to steam. The line subsequently carried holidaying miners to what grew into Glamorgan's only seaside resort. The town has steadily expanded throughout the C20, in response to its popularity with those wanting to retire to the seaside.

ALL SAINTS, Victoria Avenue. Designed by *G. E. Halliday* in 1909 and built 1912–14. This is one of his most successful churches, even though the proposed SE tower was never built. In a Perp style. Pink sandstone and yellow Bath stone combined throughout, the exterior rock-faced with ashlar dressings, the interior ashlar-faced throughout, pink predominating. Unbroken ridge-line to chancel and nave. Lean-to chancel-chapels and aisles without a clerestory, stopped short of the W bay to provide for N and S porches. Five-light E window, W rose. The interior is a single space under a wagon roof. Arcade piers of lozenge plan. Complex arch mouldings. – REREDOS. Full-width, of stone, standing free of the E wall. Side doors to the space behind. Three figures in niches. Angels rising above the top parapet. Compare the medieval reredos at Llantwit Major. – FONT. A handsome piece, by *Halliday*. Flat cover designed for it, dated 1915. – STAINED GLASS. Chancel E, 1927–8 by *Karl Parsons*. Christ in Majesty adored by angels. Heavenly Jerusalem in the tracery. Pure and brilliant colours of exceptional intensity, for this other-worldly vision. The reredos tantalizingly prevents a close-up view. – N chapel. Virgin and Child and St David, by *L. C. Evetts*, 1964.

OUR LADY STAR OF THE SEA (R.C.), New Road. 1969 by *F. R. Bates, Son & Price*. Large mosaics designed by the architects flank the crinkled central window towards the road.

NEWTON COUNTY JUNIOR AND INFANTS' SCHOOL, New Road. 1907 by *D. Pugh Jones*. A lively single-storey council school design. Red brick with a little black brick diapering and dressings of Forest stone. Infants' range of 1915 en suite.

HARBOUR. At the pier-head, HARBOUR LIGHT of 1866, cast iron, hexagonal, painted white above black. Lantern fitted in 1911.

On the quay, JENNINGS WAREHOUSE, a rare survival of a large early C19 dockside railway warehouse, used for storing iron brought along the Duffryn, Llynvi and Porthcawl Railway. Two-storeyed, built of limestone, with a modern hipped corrugated asbestos roof. Two-light windows with brick arched heads. Fifteen bays by five. Central N entrance. The short stretch of restored early railway *in situ* on the quay to the S seems to be at the level of the intermediate openings in the N elevation.

GRAND PAVILION, The Esplanade. 1931–2 by *E. J. E. Moore*. Octagonal hall lit by segmental Diocletian windows (now blocked) and covered by a concrete dome (*L. G. Mouchel* were the consultant engineers). Galleries. Single-storey loggia in front, of coupled Tuscan columns.

POLICE STATION, John Street. (Now Information Office and Museum.) 1877 by *John Prichard*. Simple Tudor. Mullion-and-transom windows. The Police Station under a trio of gables, the superintendent's house to the r. The only feature particular to Prichard is the black brick for the polygonal chimneyshafts.

THE REST, near the Golf Course, NW of the town. Built between 1874 and 1878 as a convalescent home for miners by *John Prichard*. This unfeeling and indeed nightmarish building is hard to accept as the work of the most sensitive Victorian architect in Glamorgan – for churches, that is to say. Like a monstrous Swiss chalet, of pink, rock-faced conglomerate, with black brick used not only for chimneystacks but for the extraordinary buttress features which step outwards, not inwards, as they rise, so that they can carry balconies for the upper storey and, with the aid of timber struts, the vast overhangs of the gables. Battlemented tower at the back. Addition to the l. by *G. F. Lambert*, 1891. Tall Tudor-style range to the r., with stark chimneybreasts of black brick, added by *E. M. Bruce Vaughan* in 1909. The broad segment-headed windows and the balconies have all been altered.

ALBERT EDWARD PRINCE OF WALES COURT, Penylan Avenue. Built as an old people's home for the Royal Masonic Benevolent Institution by the *Percy Thomas Partnership* (design partner *Dale Owen*), 1970–3. Of pale grey brick, with dark grey monopitch slate roofs. To the W, hall, chapel and other communal rooms forming two courtyards, to the E a stepped series of residential ranges, with full-height window bays tucked in under the eaves. Nothing rises above two storeys, except a glazed belvedere, with its own monopitch roof. Relaxed, undemonstrative, characteristic of the date.

PORTHKERRY/PORTHCERI

0060

ST CURIG. A very small church, sunken into the ground. Nave and lower chancel present blank walls to the N. In the chancel a S lancet which may be C13, a blocked priest's door and a two-light E window of four-centred outline and trefoiled lights, i.e.

of the C15. In the nave the S doorway is the earliest feature, two-centred, chamfered. The nave windows must be early C16, square-headed with hoodmoulds on square stops. Unbuttressed W tower of squared limestone blocks, the battlements on corbelling. Two-light W window, C15. Only a slit for the bell stage. The tower arch, large, round-headed and unmoulded, is undatable. The chancel arch is a simple rebuild of 1867. – SCREEN. Perp. Simple. – STAINED GLASS. E window, SS Peter and John. By R.J. Newbery? – MONUMENT. Slab to Reynold Portreye †1629, and others. Worth examining.

In the CHURCHYARD a cross, the shaft and part of the head reconstructed after 1874, on four steps.

CHURCH FARM, 100 yds N of the church. Small, L-plan, early C16 house of two storeys, with two rooms per storey and a mural stair in the party wall between them. Several internal stone doorways with four-centred heads survive, and an upper fireplace with lintelled hood. Probably built as a priest's house. Contemporary outbuilding to the N.

VIADUCT. Of stone. Nineteen arches, their soffits of brick. Well seen from the NW against the sea as it springs out of the trees on one side of the valley and back into the trees on the other. The viaduct carried the Vale of Glamorgan Railway, constructed 1894–7 from Barry to Bridgend. It is 375 yds (343 metres) long and 110 ft (33.5 metres) at its greatest height.

CARDIFF AIRPORT, 1 m. NW. Big maintenance hangar, by the *Alex Gordon Partnership*, under construction in 1992.

THE BULWARKS, ½ m. S. An Iron Age coastal ENCLOSURE, originally more than 10.1 acres (4.1 hectares) in extent, defined by three closely spaced overgrown banks fronted by ditches and by cliffs to the S. The entrance was in the W bank. Occupation continued well into the period of Roman occupation.

PORT TALBOT   7080

The historic centre is at Aberavon, where the Afan River exits from the mountains. The name Port Talbot was at first attached to the area further SW, where tinplate works were established. The flat expanse of 'moor', more than a mile deep and extending for over 6 m. (4.8 kilometres) from Margam to the estuary of the River Neath, provided an ideal site for industry. The modern docks were constructed in 1898, and steelworks established by 1907. The Margam Works began production in 1916. Since the Second World War Port Talbot has been, with Llanwern (Gwent), one of the two major sites for a rationalized steel industry in Wales. The ABBEY WORKS were laid out and the MARGAM WORKS reconstructed 1948–52, to the design of *Sir Percy Thomas & Son*. The STEEL MILLS, far-stretching ranks of rolling mills clad in yellow corrugated steel sheeting, are a memorable sight on the approach to the town from the S.

DOCKS. The Aberavon Harbour Company was formed in 1834 to build a floating dock to serve the iron and copper industries of Cwmavon. It was opened in 1839 under the designation Port Talbot in honour of the Talbots of Margam Abbey. In form it is different from all the other docks in South Wales, being an impoundment of several meanders on an old river course and of creeks that were only partially 'improved' after being impounded. By 1890 it was almost moribund, and a new company was formed to revive it as an outlet for coal from the western central valleys. This company, the Port Talbot Railway & Dock Company, was formed in 1894 and by 1898 had built three new railways and made a start on improving the docks. Dock equipment was hydraulically operated, and to supply water for this purpose a reservoir was built in the valley above Brombil, 2 m. SE. Wharf construction of reinforced concrete, an early use of the material. Coal ceased to be shipped in 1962, but by then the import of iron ore for the steelworks had become the main item of trade. In 1972 the old docks were replaced by a new deep-water tidal harbour specifically intended for unloading large iron ore carriers.

ST MARY, Aberavon. Encircled by high-level roads and elbowed by a shopping centre in a way Osbert Lancaster would have relished. One window of the earlier church has been reset, in rearranged fashion, into the W end of the N aisle of the present building. This dates from 1858–9 and is by *Prichard & Seddon*, without much commitment. Snecked Pennant sandstone in small courses, including much stained with iron. Nave and steep-roofed chancel, S aisle and SW tower, its fortified-looking top stage of 1870. The N aisle was added in 1898 by *G. E. Halliday*. Dec style. The mid-C19 parts are marked by early Dec tracery with barbs (Chartham tracery), the S aisle arcade given anachronistic French late C12-style foliage capitals. By contrast the N arcade of 1890 has clustered shafts and moulded caps. – ALTAR TABLE. In the S aisle. Dated 1704. – REREDOS. An expensive piece, alabaster, with virulent green marble shafts, and brilliant white figures of Christ and the four Evangelists. Designed by *Kempson & Fowler* in 1890, the figures by *H. H. Armstead*. – PULPIT. En suite. – STAINED GLASS. E window 1890, Adoration of the boy Christ. By *Dixon* of London in their usual flamboyant Germanic late Gothic style. The gift, with reredos and pulpit, of Mrs Llewellyn of Baglan Hall. – S aisle E, Parable of the Talents. 1916, signed by *Daniells & Fricker*, who give their address in Fulham. – S aisle SW, Good Samaritan, 1931, signed by *Wippell & Co.* of Exeter. – W window, war memorial, 1920, also by *Daniells & Fricker*. – S aisle SE, Annunciation and Crucifixion, *Celtic Studios*, 1964.

HOLY CROSS, Tan-y-groes Street, Taibach. Below the hillside, by the motorway junction. Cruciform chapel of 1827 by *Edward Haycock*, dressed up in 1903 by *G. E. Halliday* to fit it to become a parish church. Surprisingly, he did not touch the transomed windows with their minimal Gothic tracery. – SCREEN. Three-sided. Perp. A pretty piece, designed by *Halliday*. – STAINED GLASS. Luridly lit Crucifixion between Resurrection and Ascension. After 1905.

ST AGNES, Forge Road. A large, plain church by *F. R. Kempson*, 1909–10. Lancets. The dressed stonework banded in pink and buff, as at his earlier, and infinitely more magnificent, church at Pentre (q.v.). – STAINED GLASS. E window, Christ in Majesty, 1950 by *Celtic Studios*. – W window, Nativity. In a much more agitated style, yet also signed by *Celtic Studios*. 1967.

ST PAUL, Pendarvis Terrace. Built in 1910 at the expense of Sir Arthur Vivian. Architect unknown. Cruciform with an apsidal chancel. Plate tracery. Pennant sandstone and meagre Bath stone dressings. The interior is somewhat less old-fashioned. Passage aisles and full-height arches enclosing the clerestory windows. Exposed grey brick.

ST THEODORE, Talbot Road. 1895–7 by *J. L. Pearson*, at the expense of Miss Emily Talbot of Margam Abbey, as a memorial to her brother Theodore († 1876) and sister Olive († 1894). Noble, austere, aloof and sadly lacking in colour. However, the long ridge-line, broken only by a sanctus-bellcote, is misleading, for Pearson intended to raise the generous, aisleless W bay upwards into a mighty tower – see the vault inside. Nave with low aisles and tall clerestory, transepts, straight-ended chancel with polygonally ended S chapel. Lancets throughout (except plate tracery in the S transept), some of them of prodigious size. The church is faced with Bath stone outside and in, and chancel and chapel both stone-vaulted. Shafted piers with moulded capitals, and some, apparently aimless, variation of pier forms in the nave. In the chancel Purbeck marble shafting and much dogtooth enrichment. – FITTINGS mostly by *Pearson*. – PULPIT with dark grey Purbeck marble shafts. – FONT with pale grey and dark grey fossil marble from Derbyshire and Durham. Throughout, the architect set his face against using any of the richly coloured stones of Glamorgan. – SCREENS. In the chancel, of wrought iron. – STAINED GLASS. A lively and varied collection, little of it in harmony with the church. Only the E windows of the S chapel, angels by *Clayton & Bell*, were executed under Pearson's eye. – S aisle, 1907, 1915 and 1927, also by *Clayton & Bell*. – S aisle, Christ raising the widow's son, 1914 by *Powell*'s. – N aisle, 1955 by *Powell*'s. – Aisle W windows by *L. C. Evetts*, 1974 (N), 1980 (S). – S chapel. Heavenly gifts (see Isaiah 45, v. 8). Also by *Evetts*, 1977, the most remarkable in the church, influenced by Piper and Reyntiens. – Finally, in the crucial E lancets, Christ between SS Theodore and David, by *Timothy Lewis*, 1983. Unfortunately lacking in the monumentality demanded.

ST JOSEPH (R.C.), Water Street. 1930 by *F. R. Bates & Son*. Early Christian. Brick exterior. Basilican interior.

WESLEYAN CHAPEL, Incline Row. 1891–2 by *John Wills* of Derby. Mixed style.

BEULAH CALVINISTIC METHODIST CHAPEL, Tollgate Road. Built in 1838 at Groes, rebuilt on its present site in 1976. C.R.M. Talbot of Margam Abbey paid for it, and is said to have designed it too. It is certainly wholly extraordinary, the only octagonal chapel in the county. Crown of Lombardic false machicolation. Two round-headed windows in each facet under an oculus. Droved ashlar clasping buttresses. The building is quite small. How was it originally arranged inside?

DYFFRYN WELSH PRESBYTERIAN CHAPEL, Ffrwdwyllt. (Now disused.) An ambitious but somewhat coarse classical façade, dated 1893. Pediment on upper-level Corinthian pilasters over the centre three bays, balustraded side bays. Rough-textured Pennant sandstone with Bath stone dressings. The architect's name seems not to be recorded.

DUFFRYN LOWER COMPREHENSIVE SCHOOL, Broad Street. In two parts, divided by the street. The range to the w, dated 1899, was designed by a local architect, *F. B. Smith*. The larger and more assured-looking group, with its façade towards Talcennau Road, is of 1910 by *W. James Nash*, West Glamorgan Education Architect.

EASTERN INFANTS' SCHOOL, Incline Row. 1911 by *W. James Nash*. Single-storey. An elegant classical façade of nine bays with central pediment and banded quoins. Like his school at Pontardawe (q.v.), but monochrome, using green Quarella sandstone.

TALBOT MEMORIAL PARK, Talbot Road. Gothic entrance screen of 1915, seriously behind the times. WAR MEMORIAL with bronze reliefs and crowning figure of Victory signed by *L. F. Roslyn*, 1925.

VELINDRE VIADUCT, Velindre, ⅓m. NE, at the s end of Avan Street. Early C19 horse-drawn railway bridge, widened to take two tracks of later railway. There are four arches, three over the River Afan and the most northerly over a minor road. Built of Pennant sandstone rubble with ashlar dressings.

SANDFIELDS

Three post-war churches, all committed to Modernism and all quite different, yet all by the same firm, *F. R. Bates, Son & Price* of Newport, Gwent.

HOLY TRINITY, Fairway. 1968. Boxy. Top-lit with an openwork spire.

ST THERESA OF LISIEUX (R.C.), Southdown Road. 1969. Semicircular plan. Ridge and furrow concrete roof, cantilevered over the central recessed porch.

METHODIST CHURCH. 1966. Much the most bizarre of the three. A r.-angle triangle in section, with a metal grille on the ridge. Rendered pink.

8080 # PYLE/Y PÎL

A main-road village, the church well seen beside the A48. The most evocative building, however, must have been the grand, pedimented coaching inn, built by Thomas Mansel Talbot, owner of the Margam estate, in 1788–9, but sadly demolished *c.* 1960.

ST JAMES. Built all of a piece in the C15 to replace the church of old Kenfig (q.v.) which was being overwhelmed by the sands. Largely constructed of blocks of squared grey limestone, which must be reused, most probably from Kenfig Castle. Ashlar for windows and doors of brownish local sandstone, unusually little restored. Nave and s porch, lower chancel, and unbuttressed w tower set on a moulded plinth. The tower has a s stair projection, corbelled battlements and small rectangular bell-openings. Its w door, moulded with a hollow and a quarter round is similar to the nave s door. Two-light cinquefoiled s windows under hoodmoulds in the nave, three-light traceried E window to the chancel. Internally there is a similar architectural unity, the tower arch and the chancel arch both with square imposts and double-chamfered arches dying into them, the former built integrally with the little four-centred doorway to the tower stair. Wagon roof in the nave, on wall-plates carved with shields, one on the N side dated 1471. Presumably this dates the building of the whole church. – FONT. This also must be late C15. Octagonal bowl on a square base, all unusually richly, if crudely, decorated. Circular chip-carved discs alternate on the faces of the bowl with trees such as a child might draw. By the same craftsman as the font at Llanharry (q.v.). – STAINED GLASS. Chancel E, Crucifixion between Light of the World and Good Shepherd, 1921, signed by *Charles Powell* of London. – Nave N, Samuel in the Temple and Finding of Moses, 1922, signed by *Powell*. – Nave SE, David and Jonathan. Signed by *William Glasby* of London, 1927. – Nave SW, Good Samaritan, 1931–2 by *Karl Parsons*. – MONUMENT. Edward Thomas †1693. Typical local rustic pedimented wall-tablet with side colonnettes.

In the CHURCHYARD, three-stepped base for a cross. Shaft and head renewed.

LLANMIHANGEL, ½m. NW. An exceptionally fine farmhouse of 54 *c.*1600, with an originally symmetrical s front of three bays and axial rear wing. In the main range two storeys of square rooms, the hall and parlour below with their fireplaces back-to-back, creating a lobby-entry arrangement. Chambers above reached by a mural stair behind the central stack, but with their own hearths in the gable end walls. Big kitchen in the rear wing, which was extended later to give stable, granary and dovecote each above the other. Most of the two-light windows, sunk-chamfered under hoodmoulds, survive. Original square-headed entrance doorways, one in the centre of the s front, a second in the N wall of the hall, and a third at the far NW corner of the kitchen wing. All this is extraordinarily well resolved.

In the FARM BUILDINGS to the E is embedded part of one wall of the barn of a grange of Margam Abbey. The Royal Commission has estimated that the barn was originally nearly 100 ft (30.6 metres) long.

LLANMIHANGEL MILLS AND DAM, ½m. SW, at Mill Farm, Marlas Road. Early C19 corn mill with a concealed pitchback water wheel and a nearby wheelpit at the end of a very large water course. The leat terminates at the Afon Cynffig in an impressive curved GRAVITY DAM of rubble and dressed stone some 13 ft (4 metres) high. Mills of Margam Abbey are recorded in 1291, and Llanfihangel Mill is mentioned in 1675.

MARLAS, ½ m. SW. Also in origin c. 1600, with a lobby-entry arrangement of hall-and-parlour block in the SE corner, but a plan which has developed, most unusually, into four ranges round a small central courtyard.

0090

QUAKERS YARD

The Quakers were not particularly strong in Glamorgan, yet their BURIAL GROUND beside the A470 has here given its name to a settlement. At this point the valley of the Taff is narrow and steep-sided, which has produced a remarkable series of early C19 tramroad and railway viaducts.

GREENFIELD BRIDGE, PENYDARREN TRAMROAD, ½ m. W. Impressive single semicircular arched bridge, of Pennant sandstone with ashlar dressings, carrying the former Penydarren Tramroad over the River Taff. It incorporates the abutments of the earlier wooden bridge, which had collapsed on 15 February 1815 while a train was passing over it. This and its 'sister bridge' (see below) are two of the largest early railway bridges constructed, having a span of 63 ft (19.2 metres) at a height of 27 ft 6 in. (8.4 metres) above the water. Now used as a road-bridge. The faces of the arch are recessed back in stages towards its crown, as on the Victoria Bridge to the S, and there are projecting keystones.

VICTORIA BRIDGE, PENYDARREN TRAMROAD, ¼ m. S. Built in 1815 to dimensions similar to those of the Greenfield Bridge, alongside a functioning earlier trestle rather than reusing pre-existing abutments. The abutments of the arch are stepped, and the S abutment and central pier of the earlier bridge survive immediately downstream.

VIADUCT, ½ m. W. Slender and very elegant stone-built six-arched viaduct constructed in 1840 by *Isambard Kingdom Brunel* to carry his Taff Vale Railway across the Taff. Its high chamfered arches, carried on octagonal piers with capitals, are of rusticated masonry and also spanned the earlier Penydarren Tramroad. Downstream, widening of the viaduct before 1861. This remains in use.

PONTYGWAITH BRIDGE, ¾ m. NW. Attractive stone high-arched bridge of the early C19 carrying a narrow road over the River Taff. It has a span of 55 ft (16.8 metres), a width of 13 ft 9 in. (4.2 metres) and a rise of 15 ft 9 in. (4.8 metres). Subsidence has unfortunately necessitated the rebuilding of the arch.

PONTYGWAITH OVERBRIDGE, PENYDARREN TRAMROAD, 1 m. NW. Semicircular stone-arched bridge, about 10 ft (3 metres) in span, supported partly on natural rock and partly on masonry abutments. Mid C19, crossing a secondary diversion on the tramroad.

RADYR/RADUR   1080

ST JOHN THE BAPTIST, Radyr Court Road. The polychromatic crazy-paving of the walls, a typical C19 intensification of random rubble, probably by *Prichard*, makes it hard to take the medieval origins of the church seriously. Nave with cubical W bellcote, lower chancel. Trefoiled lancets and cinquefoiled paired lights under hoodmoulds in both nave and chancel, some of them perhaps original. The chancel arch is the most convincing survival, with two chamfers dying into the imposts, probably of the C14. – FONT. Small, octagonal, on a moulded base. – STAINED GLASS. Chancel E, Resurrection. 1915, by *R.J. Newbery*. – MONUMENTS. Mabel St Maur †1888. Classical tablet of many marbles, thickly decorated. – Evan David †1926. In imitation of a rustic late C17 tablet.

CHRIST CHURCH, Heol Isaf. Designed by *G. E. Halliday* and built in two stages, the aisleless nave in 1903–4, the chancel and S tower in 1910. N vestry, now converted into a chapel. S porch. Snecked rock-faced Pennant sandstone and Bath stone ashlar. The tower is the memorable feature, unbuttressed in the Glamorgan way, but with octagonal corner turrets and Perp belfry openings in the top stage. The rest of the church is Perp, though the N and S windows are no more than cinquefoiled lancets. Wide, multi-moulded chancel arch. Boarded wagon roof in the chancel on a richly carved wall-plate. – FITTINGS. Mostly by *Halliday*. – STAINED GLASS. Chancel E, N and S, Ascension, and Christ in three roles, *c.* 1912. All by the same maker. – Nave S, dates of death 1911–24, all by another maker, marked by a florid style and monumental figures.

WHITEHALL, Drysgol Road. By *Sir Percy Thomas c.* 1927. Formal, steep-roofed, crowned with purple brick chimneystacks.

MORGANSTOWN CASTLE MOUND, 1¼ m. N. A small but well-shaped and ditch-encircled early Norman motte in the flat meadowland S of the narrow gorge of the River Taff below Garth Hill. Perhaps it was raised in conjunction with the motte underlying Castell Coch (q.v.), which is clearly visible on the opposite hillside. Its shape was sharpened *c.* 1900 and it now bears a luxuriant growth of trees and rhododendrons. Accessible only through the Garden Centre.

GELYNIS FARM, 1 m. N. Externally one of the most completely 56 preserved early vernacular houses of the county, standing in extraordinary isolation in meadows beside the River Taff, in spite of the M4 on its embankment 200 yds (183 metres) to the S. Datable to the late C16. Windows front and back, above and below, of one, two and three arched lights with hollow mouldings under hoodmoulds. The S entrance doorway, reset on a later porch, has a wave and a hollow on complex stops, and shields in the spandrels. This, and the two-storey window bay l. of it, show that the house was built for someone with pretensions, by tradition a merchant from Cardiff. The plan is of the three-unit type, hall between kitchen and inner room, all three heated.

RESOLVEN/RESOLFEN

St David. Roughcast. Lancets. 1850. – Reredos of *c.* 1930. An elaborate period piece, with riddle posts. Polychrome wood sculpture of Resurrection, Supper at Emmaus and Ascension. – stained glass. e window, Crucifixion, 1869 by *Joseph Bell* of Bristol. – In the nave nine lancets have been filled with stained glass since 1950, a remarkable achievement. None is of special merit.

Jerusalem Independent Chapel. 1875–6, rebuilt 1903. Yet this looks like a design of the 1870s, with a central circular window under a giant relieving arch, and a corbelled gable. Hammer-dressed coursed Pennant sandstone with droved quoins. A reset foundation stone of 1875 names the architect, rare accolade. He was *T. Thomas*, presumably the celebrated Rev. Thomas Thomas of Landore. The builders were *Herbert Brothers*.

Sardis English Baptist Chapel. A self-consciously advanced design of 1904, a Diocletian central window, and semi-domed stair-turrets. Snecked Pennant sandstone dressed with red brick, and red sandstone for radiating voussoirs. Unexpectedly plain interior. Galleries on three sides, supported on numerous iron columns.

Rheola, $1\frac{1}{2}$ m. ne. The estate belonged to John Edwards, business partner of John Nash, the architect, and his neighbour in the splendid double mansion which Nash built in Lower Regent Street in London. *Nash*'s office certainly produced designs for Rheola, and the se front of the present house seems to correspond with one of them. Two-storey canted bay, and two-bay range with veranda. *Nash* is also said to have enlarged the house *c.* 1812. It now forms a U in plan. The entrance range, facing sw, has a canted bay and a veranda, later strengthened with rusticated stone piers. The ne range is plainer, but this too has a canted bay. Internally the only feature attributable to Nash is the top-lit staircase. Charming wrought iron balustrade of slender reversed Ss. The carved wooden drops and swags applied to the walls of the entrance hall may be mid-C19. They are not of high quality. – lodge, on the main road. This has several Nash-like features, but a building in this position cannot have existed before the road was constructed *c.* 1860. Of the two authentic *Nash* cottages at Rheola, the Steward's House (now Brynawel), to the ne, overlooking the lake, has been drastically remodelled, and the bachelors' house is in ruins.

The private chapel by *John Norton*, 1860, seems not to have survived.

Melincwrt furnace, $\frac{3}{4}$ m. sw. The rather confused remains of an early C18 furnace at a spectacular site beside a high waterfall. The furnace was started in 1708, converted from charcoal to coke *c.* 1795, and closed in 1808. The pig which it produced was taken to the Dylais Forge at Aberdulais for conversion into wrought iron. The site is known to have had a blast furnace powered by a water wheel, an 'air furnace', a finery and foundry, and ancillary buildings. Water to power the wheel was not derived from the waterfall but conveyed from higher up the Neath Valley by a series of leats. The visible ruined structures run along the rear of the gardens of Waterfall Terrace. Those on the N, alongside Waterfall Road, are the remains of a water-wheel pit. The remains of the blast furnace itself are at the S corner of the gardens, while ruins of lower buildings and an air furnace continue further S towards the River Clydach.

LOCK AND AQUEDUCT, $\frac{1}{2}$ m. NW. Several features remain around the Neath Canal's (1791–6) Lock no. 8, Resolven Lock. They include the site of a riverside dock, the stump of a timber trestle tramroad bridge built over the River Neath 1840–3, and a lengthsman's house to the N. To the S of the road into Resolven is a cast iron aqueduct, identical in design to that at Aberpergwm, Glynneath (q.v.), carrying a stream over the canal. The next lock down, no. 7, Farmer's Lock (SN 8245 0300), has a tail-lock bridge.

RHEOLA BROOK AQUEDUCT, $1\frac{1}{4}$ m. NE. The most elaborate of the three cast iron aqueducts that carried streams over the Neath Canal (1791–6). Like those at Aberpergwm, Glynneath, and Resolven (see above), it was probably cast at Neath Abbey ironworks in the 1830s. The two side panels have eleven Tuscan columns cast into them, and the deck of the trough is formed of eight cast plates bolted together.

AQUEDUCT, VALE OF NEATH RAILWAY, in the centre of the village. Cast iron structure carrying a stream over the railway adjacent to the B4434. On the N face it carries the words 'George Hennet Bridgewater Ironworks A.D. 1849'. The Vale of Neath Railway, designed by *Isambard Kingdom Brunel*, was opened in 1851. There are six main 'fish-bellied' beams, the outer two being I-section and the inner four of inverted T-section, with a bulbed compression flange. Four floor-plates between each pair of main girders rest on the lower flanges. Four panels on each side. So, apart from the bolts, there are only four components in the structure. The aqueduct is supported on abutments of rusticated Pennant sandstone, each having three blind arches recessed into the face. The clear span is 27 ft (8.2 metres), and the overall width about 23 ft (7 metres).

TY BONT LIMEKILN, $1\frac{1}{2}$ m. SW. Reached from the A465 at Ynysarwed across an original stone-arched BRIDGE over the Neath Canal. Early C19 structure of Pennant sandstone rubble. The charging hole, at the top of the kiln, is level with the canal bank. The kiln discharged on to a lower level, on the valley side of the waterway, like nearly all Welsh canalside kilns.

4090   REYNOLDSTON

The village, quite large, lies at the heart of the Gower peninsula, loosely gathered round a sloping green.

ST GEORGE. The reset Norman window in the chancel s wall survives from the predecessor to this modest building of 1866–7. The name of the architect of the Victorian church is not recorded. Rock-faced pink local stone. E.E. Nave with ashlar w bellcote and Dec w window of 1905. s porch. N transept. Lower chancel. Over-ambitious scissor-truss roof. – FONT. Square bowl on a circular stem, all of local tufa. – PULPIT. C19. Cylindrical. Dec, with a figure of St George. – STAINED GLASS. The most interesting feature of the church. – Chancel E, Noli me Tangere and Feed my Sheep, *c.* 1867. By Hardman? – Chancel s, Annunciation by the same maker. – Transept N, Noli me Tangere and Resurrection. Also *c.* 1867, but amateurish. – Nave w, a large, impressive and exquisitely detailed window of 1905, signed by *Lavers & Westlake*, to *Westlake*'s design. Saints, with small scenes from their lives below. – MONUMENTS. Pillar-stone of C9 date. Incised cross on the front, crude interlace on the back. Found in the grounds of Stouthall (*see* below) and probably not originally associated with the church. – John Lucas † 1787. Well-lettered oval tablet on a background of yellow mottled marble. Reset under an incongruous stiff-leaf topknot.

STOUTHALL, $\frac{2}{3}$ m. SW. A severe Neoclassical villa built 1787–90 by the Swansea architect *William Jernegan* for John Lucas, of a long-established local family. Its derivation from Thomas Mansel Talbot's nearby Penrice Castle (q.v.) of the previous decade is obvious, in its three storeys with full-height bow towards the s. Stouthall cannot emulate its model in materials, render over local rubble-stone, or in scale, but Jernegan has introduced some quirks of his own. Shallow pitched roof on slender eaves brackets. The N, entrance, front, of three broad bays, comes forward slightly in the centre, where a four-column Doric porch with triglyph frieze stands under a tripartite first-floor window and a segmental Diocletian window at attic level, set within a full-height relieving arch. The flanking bays, masked by unfortunate recent additions, have never had ground-floor windows, only glazed heads to shallow relief arcading. On the w front the arcading continues, but accommodating normal sash windows. s front fenestrated in seven bays, the centre three pinched together in the bow. Architrave moulding on brackets and metal balconies for the first-floor windows. Low service court on the E side, of the early C19.

Two-storey entrance HALL, in which a simple cantilevered stair rises to a balcony on a Doric frieze to E and N, and at the inner end to a gallery open to the hall space on two Doric columns. Simple Adamesque ceiling plasterwork. The two most enriched rooms lie one above the other projecting into the s bow. Below is the oval LIBRARY, its fine bookcases *in situ*. Plaster frieze of wreaths and palmettes. Adamesque timber chimneypiece. The chimneypiece in the bow-ended SITTING ROOM above is a little richer, with plumed Ionic pilasters. Do the triple feathers in the frieze here (and in the decoration of the adjoining bedroom) suggest that a visit was anticipated from the Prince of Wales? The other ground-floor rooms are, to the E, the DINING ROOM, its function readily recognizable by the columned screen to the servery. Doric columns with palmette necking. Plasterwork oval in the main ceiling. To the W, the DRAWING ROOM, originally lit only from the W, runs the full depth of the house. White marble chimneypiece with panels of mottled marble, possibly a later insertion.

The kitchen is in the SERVICE WING to the E.

The house is now used as a field study centre, which has required the addition of the one-storey projections to the N front, and some internal disfigurements, fire doors etc.

RHOSSILI/RHOSILI

4080

The original village stood at a lower level and closer to the sea than the present church and scatter of modern houses. Excavation in 1980 on the Warren, the grass-grown dunes to the N, revealed the sites of five houses, the walls of a sixth, and the church, consisting of a nave and small chancel, their walls almost to full height, but the chancel arch robbed away. Sand overwhelmed the village, it seems, *c.* 1300. After the excavation the site was reburied.

ST MARY THE VIRGIN. This, then, is the successor to the church under the dunes. Nave and lower chancel, as usual, S porch of 1890, and a rugged little W tower, saddleback-roofed and with mere slits N and S for the bell stage. No datable feature to confirm the assumption that the fabric is of the early C14. The great surprise is within the porch, a splendid late Norman doorway. The natural, and surely correct, supposition is that this is the chancel arch removed from the church in the Warren. Keeled side shafts with delicately carved scallop capitals, outward-pointing zigzag round the arch. Hoodmould made up from runs of dogtooth and resting on worn head-stops. Such a combination suggests a date late in the C12. One seeks an explanation why such a small and remote church was treated to such finery, unparalleled in the entire Gower peninsula. Scratch dial above the l. capital, reminder that it stood as a doorway for centuries without the protection of a porch. All Dec features, except the trefoil-headed recess in the sanctuary, belong to the restorations of 1855–6 and 1890–1, the latter by *Ewan Christian*. – MONUMENT. Petty Officer Edgar Evans † 1912. Relief illustrating Scott's ill-fated expedition to the South Pole, in which Evans lost his life. – FONT. Very basic. Square bowl on the shortest of round stems.

RHOSSILI DOWN is a rugged, heather-covered moorland ridge with an interesting concentration of archaeological sites belonging to different periods, including two Neolithic chambered tombs, the Sweyne's Howes, and fourteen Bronze Age burial cairns, mostly ruinous. There is also an open settlement with adjacent cultivation plot, and a linear boundary partitioning the ridge which could date between *c.* 1000 B.C. and the early centuries A.D. They are described in the order in which they can be seen from the path running along the ridge crest N of the village.

THE BEACON. On the S summit, a disturbed but still impressive conical early Bronze Age burial cairn 59 ft (18 metres) across and edged by boulder kerb, surmounted by an OS pillar. Another distinctive Bronze Age CAIRN, of a different design but again with probable sepulchral function, lies to the N. A prominent boulder kerb edges a stony platform in which a hollow just S of its centre may indicate a disturbed burial cist. About 130 ft (40 metres) N is an ephemeral BOUNDARY WALL comprising a low, stony band which, starting close to the seaward cliff, runs ENE–SSW *c.* 1,300 ft (400 metres) across the ridge, apparently dividing it into two.

THE SWEYNE'S HOWES, two Neolithic chambered tombs, lie close together on the lower E slopes. The S tomb is ruinous, an oval cairn and large boulders and slabs which were presumably once elements of a chamber. At the NW edge of the N cairn is a dilapidated chamber, two orthostats against which leans a displaced capstone. At the foot of the ridge *c.* 720 ft (220 metres) E of Sweyne's Howes is a small OPEN SETTLEMENT, an annular bank 72 ft (22 metres) across constructed of parallel faces of slabs retaining a rubble core. It is entered via a break in the S arc and may have contained a timber building, since it seems too large to have served as a foundation itself. The annexe to the S is probably a CULTIVATION PLOT, defined to the W by a stone bank and to the E by a lynchet produced by soil moving down the slope.

p. 27 THE KNAVE, 2 m. SE. Iron Age promontory fort on a spectacular stretch of limestone cliffs. Two closely spaced parallel ramparts, each fronted by a ditch, isolate a coastal headland naturally protected by cliffs. Limited excavation in 1938 revealed that the rear of the outer bank was retained by a boulder kerb and that the outer ditch was V-shaped. Post-holes in the entrance in the NW section of the outer defence presumably supported double gates. Short length of inner bank close to the cliff, W of an inner entrance, with outer stone revetment but no ditch. No evidence for a gate across the inner entrance. The bank to the E of the inner entrance had a rear boulder revetment with an outer ditch fronted by a low counterscarp bank. Excavation produced traces of two round houses within a small enclosure, slingstones, pot boilers and pottery datable to the period CI B.C.–CI A.D.

GOAT'S HOLE CAVE, PAVILAND, 2½ m. SE. The most important cave site in the county. Halfway up the coastal cliff, the cave, 69 ft (21 metres) deep, is accessible, with care, at low tide. Although material of Mesolithic, Neolithic and Roman date has been found, it is best known for a rich assemblage of finds of the Upper Palaeolithic period, including the burial of the 'Red Lady', discovered by Dean William Buckland in 1823. This is in fact the skeleton of a man in his mid twenties impregnated with iron ochre, perhaps as part of a funeral ritual or possibly to decorate or preserve clothing. It dates to *c.* 25,000 B.C. and is the most complete skeleton of the period known from Britain.

Perched precariously on the cliff-top above the cave is an Iron Age PROMONTORY FORT consisting of four parallel ramparts across the narrow headland, protected on three sides by steep or sheer cliffs. An outer bank fronted by a ditch runs across the neck of the promontory, with an entrance perhaps beyond the W end. Quarrying has disturbed the bank and the area to the rear. A second rampart, *c.* 65 ft (20 metres) behind the first, consists of a bank fronted by a rock-cut ditch and crossed by a causeway coinciding with a break towards the E end of the bank. Only *c.* 20 ft (6 metres) behind is another rock-cut ditch broken by a causeway, while 75 ft (23 metres) to the seaward is the inner and most substantial defence, just behind the narrowest point of the promontory. What may have been building platforms are visible in the rocky surface behind this bank.

RHYMNEY/RHYMNI

1000

Rhymney was an iron town. Its wide, straight main street, extending for over ½ m., still retains many rendered mid-C19 terraces. Its religious buildings are also notably early. The 1960s and '70s saw much rebuilding of early housing, so the present impression of modern expansion on all sides is rather misleading.

ST DAVID. A strong, severe and minimally classical church erected 1840–3 by the Rhymney Iron Company to the design of a London architect, *Philip Hardwick*. Rock-faced Pennant sandstone in large, squared blocks, with hammer-dressed quoins of the same sombre hue. Two-stage entrance tower, with round-headed belfry windows and a pyramidal cap, in axis with the pedimented nave. Shallow pedimented chancel. The pair of low W (ritual E) vestries clearly an addition. Large, round-headed side windows, disregarding the fact that there are galleries inside. Inside, unfluted Greek Doric columns support the galleries. – STAINED GLASS. E window, Ascension, *c.* 1856. Strong colours. Romanesque foliage borders.

BEULAH CHAPEL, Brynteg Crescent. Dated 1866. Gable-end façade. Tall round-headed windows flank a circular one. Rendered and picked out in bright blue.

EBENEZER WELSH CALVINISTIC METHODIST CHAPEL, Glan Elyrch. Stone façade dated 1906, perhaps remodelling one of 1846.

PENUEL WELSH BAPTIST CHURCH, Coronation Terrace. Built in 1839, repaired in 1859, the date on the façade. A grandly scaled and remarkable example of chapel design of the period. The exterior is drably rendered, but the pyramid roof and pattern of the round-headed windows of the entrance front, the outer two coming down further than the inner two, suggest an internal arrangement in the early C19 tradition. The central doorway leads into an internal lobby, against which the balustraded pulpit backs. Balustraded gallery over the lobby. Extra spacious 'big seat'. Galleries on thin iron posts round the other three sides, canted at the angles. The box pews below follow the same canted layout, so that the entire seating is angled towards the pulpit. Clerestory windows on all four sides. Later boarded ceiling with plaster rose.

71 BUTETOWN, $\frac{3}{4}$ m. NW. All that was built of a proposed model village for the workers of the Union Iron Company, on the initiative of the works manager, R. Johnson, c. 1802–4. Three parallel rows, each composed in a Palladian way, with a three-storey centre, and the ends of the two-storey ranges projecting slightly. Jeremy Lowe has suggested that the central sections were 'barracks', for single men. The foundations of a fourth row, completing the pattern, were laid to the S. Squared and coursed stone walls, deep eaves. Simple classical details, reminiscent of James Adam's Lowther Village, Westmorland, of the 1770s. The name Butetown dates from after the second Marquess of Bute bought into the ironworks in the mid 1820s. No sign now of the Bute Works built in 1828, 'adapted from the most striking parts of the ruins of Dandyra in Upper Egypt'.

UPPER FURNACE IRONWORKS, 1 m. N, to the E of Butetown. Remains of functional structures of the ironworks at Old Furnace Farm, Llechryd. They belonged to what is said to have been the first Rhymney furnace, of 1801. The farmhouse range is continued to the S by two derelict rubble-stone buildings, identified as stables. The upper floor, entered from the higher ground to the E, is said to have been used as living quarters. The N structure is dated 1802, on the keystone of a ground-floor window. Ashlar dressings here, brick dressings elsewhere.

Further S, a two-storey white-rendered building with a hipped roof, now a club but once probably the ironworks manager's house. Its roof is one of the few surviving cast iron arched roofs prefabricated in the local ironworks. In the field to the S again, the circular hearth and bowl of a blast furnace standing to a height of 7 ft (2.13 metres). This consists of vitrified refractory brick with, inside, a massive 'bear', or lump of solidified slag that has eaten into the furnace base. Lower part of the furnace lining formed by corbelling out the courses of brickwork. To the E, the high furnace charging bank and traces of the earthworks of the large pond, which supplied water to drive the blast water wheel.

RUDRY/RHYDRI

ST JAMES. Small W tower with saddleback roof and minimal bell-openings. W doorway with continuous rounded moulding, early C14. Nave and lower chancel. Their walling is old. Traces of a priest's door on the S side of the chancel, and perhaps of a rood-loft entrance in the nave N wall. Otherwise everything is of the restoration of 1885 by *J. Prichard*. E window with geometrical tracery. Lancets elsewhere with uncarved label stops. Another unsympathetic restoration in 1961. – FONT. Plain square bowl. Is this medieval under the emulsion paint? – STAINED GLASS. E window, 1934 by *W. Maile & Son*. Kempe-style.

CHAPEL, ½m. NE. 1834, rebuilt 1902, but retaining the pedimentally pitched roof and large, round-headed windows typical of the earlier period.

GWAUN-Y-BARA, I m. NW. Interesting as an early example, datable between 1689 and *c.*1701, of a three-unit house designed from the outset to present a symmetrical frontage, with a central entrance. Two storeys, five unequal bays, the centre three relating to the hall, the outer ones to parlour and kitchen. The builder, Roger Williams, was an early ironmaster.

RUPERRA CASTLE/RHIW'RPERRAI

2080

This splendidly direct and uncompromising building is an out- 42 standing example of the nostalgia for the chivalric past felt in the early C17, even as Inigo Jones was rooting classicism in Britain. The house was built, apparently in 1626, by Sir Thomas Morgan, who had served as steward of the household to the second Earl of Pembroke and was knighted at Wilton. This connection with an English courtier must have familiarized him with the idea of a house as a rectangular block with cylindrical angle towers, an idea which underlay Robert Smythson's concept of Wollaton Hall, Nottinghamshire, of 1580, and was realized by Lord Howard of Bindon at Lulworth Castle, Dorset, *c.*1608. Ruperra was burnt in 1785, remodelled by *Thomas Hardwick*, abandoned in the early C20 and now stands as a shell, desperately in need of consolidation.

The body of the house is three-storeyed and nearly square, arranged not in an up-to-date way as a double pile but as four ranges round a tiny light-well. The hall in the SE corner, but no other room can be firmly identified. It is a pity that it is not possible to establish more about how the house was originally used, for its external appearance, for all its regularity, is subtly varied to suggest the different status of each side.

The entrance front faces S. Here is a tall, narrow two-storey 45 porch faced with Bath stone. Semicircular entrance arch flanked by shell-headed niches and surmounted by the royal arms (of Charles I) in an Ionic aedicule with the arms of the Earls of Pembroke (l.) and of the Morgans (r.), a neat display of family allegiance. Entablature at this level, and another, with a fluted frieze, at the top. Five-bay façade, the windows all of three lights, the central light rising a little higher than the others, an idiosyncrasy stressed by the hoodmoulds, which follow this outline. This form of three-light window recurs on the other façades, but in alternation with two-lighters. To E and W this gives a rhythm 3,2,3,2,3 and to the N, 2,2,3,2,2. Two-light windows in the towers.

Originally only the towers were battlemented, and the top storey was an attic, the windows set in straight-sided gables, three per façade. The present heightened walls and battlements are a remodelling post 1785. The depressingly dark grey render is also not original. Inside, the building is now a chaos of crumbling walls and tilted timbers; but it is apparent that much of the internal structure is of brick, the earliest known use of brick on a large scale in Glamorgan.

STABLES N of the house, a standard Neoclassical range with projecting end bays where the windows are set in large relieving arches. They could well be by *Hardwick*. A further STABLE COURT N of that, of *c.*1900, distinguished by a clock-turret of Voyseyesque outline.

1070   ST ANDREWS MAJOR/SAINT ANDRAS

ST ANDREW. The unbuttressed W tower has the usual corbelled battlements, and belfry openings little more than rectangular slits. Battered reinforcement of the W wall, so the doorway is to the S, late medieval with a four-centred arch. Also late medieval the body of the church, nave with S porch, and lower chancel, both showing much Old Red Sandstone in their walls. Perp S windows. N aisle clearly an addition, see the junction in the W wall. Tudor N windows. N chapel rebuilt in 1921 by *Teather & Wilson*, retaining the medieval W arch to the aisle. The S doorway, two-centred with a broad chamfer, might suggest an earlier origin for the building, but in this part of the world may easily belong to the C15. Handsome late C15 aisle arcade of four bays, octagonal piers carrying two-centred arches, with a continuous broad chamfer and no capitals. The N wall provides evidence of a different pattern of windows before the Tudor insertions. In the chancel N wall the lower part of the jamb of an arch. It is clear that the rood extended across both nave and aisle. The chancel arch and the E windows belong to a restoration of 1875–9. Wagon roof in the chancel, boarded and painted in 1889. – FONT. Norman. Tub-shaped, with a roll round the top. – STAINED GLASS. Chancel SE, Good Samaritan, 1922 signed by *Horace Wilkinson*. – Chancel SW, St Curig, *c.*1911, signed by *Kempe & Tower*. – MONUMENT. William Hurst †1803. Small oval tablet with an urn and symbols of mortality. – WAR MEMORIAL. For the 1914–18 war. White marble relief, a girlish Victory upper right, a putto below left.

In the CHURCHYARD, cross shaft on five steps.

RECTORY (former), E of the church. Simple late Georgian, built 1827–33. Behind it, serving as a garage, a two-storey stone building with two large C15 transomed windows at ground-floor level, each of two cinquefoiled lights under a square hood. This must have been the medieval rectory.

DOWNS FARM, *see* Dinas Powys, p. 339.

At BIGLIS, 1¼ m. S, is the excavated site of a SETTLEMENT which began with unenclosed occupation in the C2 B.C. Subsequently it was enclosed by palisades and later by a stony boundary bank, activity continuing until the C4 A.D.

ST ATHAN/SAIN TATHAN   0060

ST TATHAN. Exceptional in its cruciform plan with crossing tower, and in the elaboration of the S transept, the burial chapel of the de Berkerolles family. The earliest evidence is of *c.* 1300. In the chancel four lancets under segmental rere-arches in the S wall, all renewed (the E window an invention of 1890). Simple tomb-recess, under a segmental arch, hollow-chamfered and plain-chamfered, under a filleted hoodmould. Similarly restrained vocabulary for the crossing arches, though those to E and W have later been widened. In the nave the W and S doorways are simply chamfered under filleted hoodmoulds, the latter a sophisticated composition of three chamfered orders of different steepnesses, the innermost dying into the imposts.

Later in the C14 the church was transformed. Three-light W window with intersecting tracery enclosing trefoils and a pointed quatrefoil. The S transept was given special attention, brightly illuminated from a square-headed E window of three lights with cusped reticulated tracery, and a sumptuous arch-headed, reticulated S window, its external hoodmould crocketed with head-stops and even a head at the apex. Internally the transept is fitted as a chapel, with a squint to allow the priest to see into the chancel, a crocketed piscina and an enriched image niche, as well as the canopied recess for the primary monument (*see* below). C15 nave S porch, its roof of the pretty local pattern, with arched braces and a collar purlin, carved with the de Berkerolles arms. Wagon roofs of the C15 in the church. The tower, diagonally buttressed, may also be a C15 structure, though it was clearly intended from the start to build a crossing tower. The restoration of 1888 contributed the W window of the S transept, all those in the N transept, as well as the Y-traceried windows in the nave. – FONT. Goblet-shaped. Quite large. Of what medieval date? It is of Sutton stone, so probably C12. – STAINED GLASS. Chancel E window, Resurrection 1905, by *A. L. Moore.* Too much like a painting. – Nave SE, David and Suffer the Little Children, 1918, also by *Moore.* – Nave NW, SS Anna and Simeon, 1929 by *R. J. New-bery.* – MONUMENTS. Sir Roger de Berkerolles †1351. In the 24 position of honour in the S wall, under a fine ogee-arched canopy with big leaf finials. Boldly cusped sub-arches springing from the crouched figure of a winged and bearded man, pre-

sumably intended to represent God. Recumbent effigies of an
armoured knight with crossed legs and a fashionably dressed
lady turning slightly towards him. Arcaded tomb-chest with
small, highly unusual, figures of monks and laymen kneeling,
interpreted by Geoffrey Orrin as representing the various orders
of society. – Sir William de Berkerolles † 1327, and wife. Parents
of Sir Roger. Not such fine quality, nor so well preserved.
Recumbent knight, his crossed legs now broken. Against the
sides of the tomb-chest, small, naively carved children under
crocketed arcading. Surely erected retrospectively, later even
than Sir Roger's monument.

CASTLETON, ½ m. NE. No castle survives here, though the site is
fortifiable, above steep slopes to E and S. The two-storey farmhouse retains various four-centred-headed internal doorways,
and the head of a window of three arched lights under a
hoodmould with square stops. These point to an early C16
date. Three-unit plan, hall between parlour end (E) and service
end (W). There must have been a detached kitchen. The walls
of the parlour end, extra thick to N and E, are carried up higher
than the rest, so perhaps there was a fortifiable tower here. (A
few pieces of internal decoration, plaster ceiling in the room
over the parlour, dotted with fleurs-de-lys, and crude carving
on the parlour fireplace lintel, recumbent animals and patches
of interlace – cf. the C16 monument in Llantwit Major church.)
Among the farm buildings to the N, a BARN with opposed
entrances which the Royal Commission suggests may have been
converted from a gatehouse.

St Athan, East Orchard Manor.
Conjectural reconstruction

EAST ORCHARD MANOR, ¾ m. E. One of the most romantic
ruins in the county, all the more intriguing for being so hard to
get at. Seven ruined medieval buildings are scattered seemingly
without rhyme or reason on the wooded hillside above the

valley of the River Thaw. This was the seat of the de Berkerolles, who presumably built the hall block, the largest building in the group, with its detached kitchen or bakehouse to the N, and to the S the detached chapel (see the traces of a piscina). The Stradlings of St Donats, who inherited as early as 1411, no doubt added the barn and other farm buildings. The Joneses of Fonmon Castle, who bought East Orchard in 1756, abandoned the buildings and robbed their dressed stonework (see the fine chimney reused on the stables at Fonmon, p. 351). So it is remarkable that so many high walls still survive, but impossible to date them with any accuracy.

BATSLAYS, 1 m. W. One of the best-preserved small farmhouses in Glamorgan, in that the stone walls have not been rendered, and several two-light upper windows remain. They have sunk chamfer mouldings and small hoodmoulds, suggesting an early C17 date. A C19 porch covers the original doorway, which leads into one corner of the hall, at the side of the hearth, in the lobby-entry arrangement. Mural stair on the far side of the hearth. Unheated inner room. The room above this, unusually, has a window, now blocked, in the E gable-end wall. Small extension to the W.

ST BRIDES MAJOR/SAINT-Y-BRID   8070

St BRIDGET. An interesting church, housing a fine series of monuments. Its C12 origin is established by the chancel arch, plain, round-headed, on imposts with groove-like mouldings. This is reminiscent of Ewenny Priory, so it is worth noting that the churches of both St Brides and Ewenny were granted to St Peter's Abbey, Gloucester, before 1138. The chancel was rebuilt in the C14, as is demonstrated by the two-light E window with ogee forms in the tracery, and the N and S lancets given ogee heads (one N lancet visible in the vestry). The origins of the nave are hard to date, as the only early feature is the N door, straight-headed on shoulders. Large plain squints cut through the wall l. and r. of the chancel arch. Tower arch with continuous mouldings, two hollow chamfers and a wave. The stout tower on its bold plinth is Perp, with diagonal buttresses, not a normal feature round here, and, more startlingly, arrow loops in the stair projection facing S towards the rising ground (but cf. Llanmihangel). Belfry openings of paired cinquefoiled lights under a square hoodmould. Top pinnacles corbelled out on grotesque heads.

The building was seriously compromised by *Egbert Moxham*'s obtrusive restoration in 1851, when many large windows were inserted. One feature which escaped was the highly unusual plaster vault in the chancel. Segmental profile. No mouldings. Of what date can this be? – FONT. Plain. Perp. Octagonal on an octagonal stem. – PULPIT. Stone. C19. Another of Moxham's excessive contributions? – SCULPTURE. Small figure of a martyred saint, identified as St Bridget. Early C16. – Fragment of a canopied niche (beside the font). – STAINED GLASS. E window, Christ and the heavy laden. Strong colours, limp gestures. Signed by *William Glasby*, 1926. – MONUMENTS. John le Botiler. An incised slab hidden under the altar, but see the rubbing on the chancel N wall. Life-size figure of an armoured man holding an armorial shield. Identified as John le Botiler of Llantwit, a retainer of the Berkeleys and Despensers, who died soon after 1335. – John Butler † 1540 and wife. Elaborate Perp tomb-chest, set against the chancel N wall, with kneeling children under double canopies. Life-size recumbent figures on it, he in armour and with crossed legs, an extraordinary feature for the mid C16. Depressed ogee-arched canopy bearing an armorial display. This sumptuous piece is made all the more enjoyable by the illumination from the four-light mullioned window which replaces the back wall. – John Wyndham † 1697 and wife † 1698. A charming conceit, half-length busts turned intimately towards one another, in a bow-backed recess under a bow-fronted canopy, with curtains looped back to Composite side columns. The idea goes back to Nicholas Stone and his contemporaries *c.* 1620. – Several late C17 rustic tablets of the sort found hereabouts. – Thomas Wyndham † 1814. Neoclassical wall-monument. A semi-naked man on a Grecian couch is summoned to heaven by two angels, or rather the two sons who had predeceased him. Signed by *Sebastian Gahagan*. – Rev. Charles Gally † 1821. Chaste Neoclassical tablet, signed *Lancaster & Walker*, Bristol. Willow branch and urn.

In the CHURCHYARD, N of the chancel, cross shaft on five steps.

BRYN SION PRESBYTERIAN CHAPEL. On the hillside opposite the church. 1859. Simplest Gothic. Original fittings.

On the Wick road (B4265) beyond the village, several substantial farms, the last, PENUCHA'R-DRE FARM, enhanced by a two-storey porch with four-centred doorway and two-light mullioned window above. This is a C17 addition to a late C16 single-unit end-entry house later extended to l. and r.

SUTTON FARM, 2 m. w. Close to the sea, close to the famous Sutton stone quarries, and sadly hemmed in by bungalows. Built in the early C17 with just a hall below and a chamber above. Originally entered through the seaward gable end, and later extended in that direction. Several original mullion-and-transom windows with hoodmoulds, the lower three-lighter for the hall.

OLD CASTLE-UPON-ALUN, 1¼ m. E. Two ranges datable *c.* 1600, set oddly close to one another at an oblique angle. That to the N a longhouse in origin, that to the s originally part domestic, part barn. Both have been drastically modernized.

TÝ-MAEN, 1½ m. N. A well-preserved farmhouse, with a barn close to the road. Two-light and three-light straight-headed windows with sunk chamfers suggest a C17 date. But the plan remains the traditional one with the entry into one end of the kitchen. Hall with fireplace backing on to the passage. Parlour in the wing that projects to the N.

For Dunraven Castle and Promontory Fort, *see* Southerndown.

ST BRIDES MINOR/
LLANSANFFRAID-AR-OGWR   8080

ST BRIDE. The church is at the W end of Sarn, inconspicuous enough and now barred off from the A4063. Just a nave with a S porch, and a lower chancel. The latter retains medieval features, paired cinquefoiled lancets at the E end of the S wall and a priest's door with a continuous hollow chamfer. The chancel arch has a double chamfer dying into the imposts. All this one would call Dec, but in this part of the world a C15 date may be indicated. In the nave only an image niche with a crocketed quatrefoil head, S of the chancel arch. (Arch-braced roof to the S porch.) *G. E. Halliday* restored the church in 1896, and added the N aisle. – FONT. Tub-shaped bowl on a modern base. – SIDE ALTAR and FLOWER STAND, recently made up from lengths of medieval mullion.

MAENDY, I m. NE. A substantial and well-preserved farmhouse of the lobby-entry type, of rare interest in bearing a date, 1607, on the bressumer of the hall fireplace. Two-storey porch, giving access to the r. to the hall and to the l. to the kitchen. Many original window openings under hoodmoulds, but their sunk-chamfered mullions and frames have been cut away.

ST BRIDES-SUPER-ELY/
LLANSANFFRAID-AR-ELÁI   0070

ST BRIDE. Small, overshadowed by a yew tree. At first sight all looks normal enough. Chancel with a three-light Perp E window and S doorway for a small-scale priest. Nave with two square-headed Perp windows, of two cinquefoiled lights under a hood-mould. Saddleback W tower, without either corbel table or buttresses, but with trefoil-headed belfry windows and broadly chamfered W doorway, probably of the late C13. In 1849, however, the church was restored and several alien pieces installed. The first and most incongruous is the Norman outer arch of the S porch, found in 1840 reused in an almshouse at Margam Abbey and brought here by Mrs Charlotte Traherne, the rector's wife, sister of C.R.M. Talbot of Margam. Much renewed, but doubtless authentic in design. Shafted arch with two-way zigzag, and shafted outer arch, the shafts with enriched trumpet capitals, the arch with a shuttlecock motif. Is the S doorway also an importation? It is Norman, tall and narrow, under a gable with a scale pattern in the spandrels. The chancel arch is also Norman, but even more a replica rather than an original. Rows of Xs on the imposts and thin angle shafts with scallop caps. Finally, a late C15 image niche was inserted to fill the centre light of the E window. It is vaulted and has three ogee crocketed arches. The entire window came from the demolished chapel of St Mary at Sant-y-Nyll, ⅓ m. N. – FONT. Bowl irregularly octagonal, on matching stem and foot. – STAINED GLASS. Ten Swiss or German roundels and a C15 fragment of an angel, set in the E window in 1957. – STATU-ETTE. In the E niche, Virgin and Child, gilt wood, C16 Venetian. Sansovinesque. Introduced in 1950.

SANT-Y-NYLL, ⅓ m. N. Neo-Georgian, dated 1920 on the rain-water heads.

9060   ST DONATS/SAIN DUNWYD

ST DONATS CASTLE (Atlantic College). St Donats is, apart from Cardiff and Fonmon, the only castle in Glamorgan which has remained continuously occupied. Its position, on the spur of a combe running down to the Bristol Channel, has a drama unlike that of any other castle in the county. In the C12 it belonged to the de Hawey family, who built the earliest parts of the surviving fabric, as the Royal Commission demonstrated in 1993. With the marriage in 1298 of Peter de Stradling to the de Hawey heiress, St Donats came to a family which remained powerful in the Vale until the mid C18. Most of the primary fabric, dating from the C14 and C15, is Stradling work. After 1738 the castle was tenanted, and by 1803 was only partly habitable. Repairs were first taken in hand in the 1870s, by Dr John Nicholl Carne. From 1901 Morgan Stuart Williams, an industrialist from Aberpergwm, modernized and embellished it, but his work was completely eclipsed after the American newspaper tycoon William Randolph Hearst bought the castle in 1925 and proceeded, with the help of *Sir Charles Allom*, to equip it with two new rooms for entertaining on a massive scale, and to stuff it with imported medieval structures from various parts of England and France. It is these imports which, for all their incongruity, make St Donats unforgettable today.*
Since 1962 the castle has been occupied by Atlantic College, the first of the United World Colleges, the aim of which is 'to use education as a practical force for world peace and understanding.'

Approaching from the N, where the higher ground made it necessary to concentrate the castle's defences, the visitor is first confronted with a modern battlemented wall. Beyond this rises the Stradlings' castle. Well provided it may be with moat, portcullis and arrow loops, but no-one can call it daunting.

---

*Hearst's attitude was well expressed in the telegram he sent to his London agent: 'Want buy castle in England please find which ones available St Donats perhaps satisfactory at proper price'.

There is no particularly dominating keep, just two concentric curtain walls, the inner one with a plain, rectangular tower beside the gateway, the outer one with a low, square-fronted gatehouse, of *c.* 1300. The castle is built of local Lias limestone with white Sutton stone and buff sandstone dressings.

The N-facing OUTER GATEHOUSE stands forward of the outer curtain wall, approached by a later stone-walled bridge replacing the original drawbridge over the moat. It lacks the expected outer angle towers, but small turrets rise above the inner (S) angles. Battlements projecting on corbel tables crown the gatehouse and curtain wall. Simple pointed entrance arch with a single chamfer, above which rises a blind arch of two chamfered orders enclosing a later armorial shield. Portcullis groove behind. Two widely spaced, double-chamfered lancets light the portcullis room above. Pointed tunnel-vaulted entrance divided into two bays in front of the door frame and one bay beyond it. The PORTCULLIS ROOM is handsomely fitted up. Reached by a newel stair in the SW turret which also provides access to the roof, it is lit on three sides by trefoil-headed lancets, that to the W perhaps inserted later. The N lancets have internal hollow chamfers brought down on to unusual palmette stops. But the most remarkable feature is the hooded stone chimneypiece in the E wall. The sloping hood rests on a keeled roll, below which is a deep, straight lintel supported on slender circular shafts with moulded caps and bases, also circular. All this agrees well with a date *c.* 1300 or a little later. Adjoining the gatehouse to the W a large crow-stepped gable end of buff-coloured stone breaches the curtain wall, though it reinstates the defences with three arrow loops in the gable.

The so-called OUTER COURT is no more than a narrow space between the two curtain walls. To the r. it is cut off by the side elevation of the range whose crow-stepped gable end has just been noted. Fairly regularly arranged three-light windows with hollow-chamfered arched heads and hoodmoulds suggest that this range belongs to the early C16. The INNER GATEHOUSE was inserted to incorporate an original plain C12 gate opening in the wall. The roll-moulded imposts of this are closely comparable with those of the C12 chancel arch in the church (*see* below) and are clear evidence that the first masonry defences of the castle were constructed in the C12. The plain chamfered arch, however, belongs with the gatehouse, suggesting a date *c.* 1300 for it.

The deep, rectangular MANSELL TOWER s of the gateway also shows C12 evidence, in particular a blocked round-headed window in its N wall, and the Sutton stone quoin of its NW angle. NW of the gateway the Sutton stone quoin of an obtuse angle in the curtain wall. All this is enough to demonstrate that the de Hawey castle consisted of a faceted curtain wall (further traces of it have been spotted elsewhere in the castle) entered through a simple 'hole in the wall' with a defensive tower beside it. So its plan resembled that of Newcastle, Bridgend (q.v.),

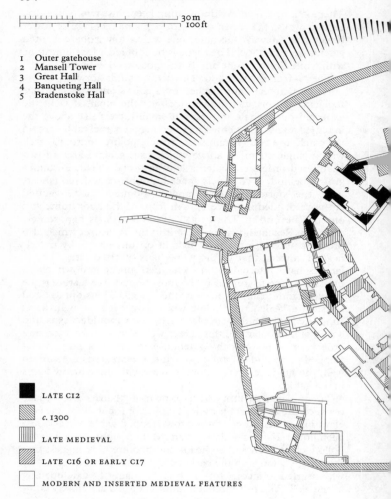

St Donats Castle. Plan

Key:
1 Outer gatehouse
2 Mansell Tower
3 Great Hall
4 Banqueting Hall
5 Bradenstoke Hall

LATE C12
c. 1300
LATE MEDIEVAL
LATE C16 OR EARLY C17
MODERN AND INSERTED MEDIEVAL FEATURES

datable to the 1180s, and of the first masonry phase at Coity
Castle (q.v.). The remodelling of c. 1300 included building a
corbelled wall-head over the gateway and extending the Mansell
Tower forwards (but reusing its C12 quoin stones).

Within the INNER COURT a miscellany of buildings confronts the eye. Attached to them at various points, terracotta
busts in enriched relief roundels with early Renaissance motifs,
reminiscent of the celebrated busts of emperors at Hampton
Court of before 1529. They were already in place in 1804, and
it seems that some may have been at St Donats since the C16.
However, they are not all of equal quality, and the Caligula

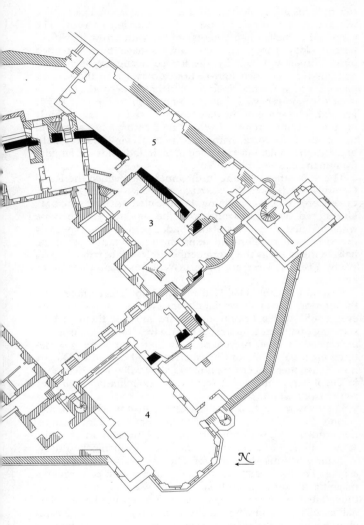

high on the Mansell Tower is a copy of one at Hampton
Court. All are seriously eroded. They deserve to be investigated
further.

The GREAT HALL, on the s side of the inner court, is a fine
late C15 piece, dressed with buff Quarella stone. Powerfully
projecting porch to the l., with a three-sided oriel over the
deeply hollow-moulded entrance arch. Inner arch also with
continuous mouldings, alternating waves and hollows, coming
down on to stops of prodigious size. Even farther-projecting
dais bay to the r. with a handsome square-headed three-light
window with panel tracery and a heavy hoodmould. The top

row of lights are shield-shaped, for armorial stained glass. The window in the recessed centre is an insertion of 1901. The oversized corbelled battlements, armed with arrow loops and fierce-looking gargoyles, must always have been intended purely for show. Internally, the service arrangements at the E end survive well: two four-centred doorways in the screens passage and a further doorway and hatch beyond. The hall itself is much renewed, but the inner arch to the dais bay is original. The space of the dais bay is evocative, a tall, brightly lit room within a room. The hall roof perhaps has some old timber in it. Its form, with three tiers of wind-braces, arch-braces, and a collar purlin pinned to their undersides, is familiar from many churches in the Vale.

The only other building in the inner court which the Royal Commission dates to the late C15 is in the NE corner, a narrow three-storey block, containing the so-called PRIEST'S ROOM. Unrestored two-light windows in the top storey. Otherwise what evidence remains is of the Tudor period – see especially the three-light mullion-and-transom upper window W of the hall. In the W range the prominent double-height window bays are by *Thomas Garner* for Morgan Williams. Rainwater heads here dated 1901.

Beyond the Great Hall William Randolph Hearst takes over the interior. The medieval chimneypieces, windows, doorways, even roofs, which he introduced are most of them of out-standing quality and interest in themselves, but so many are so overscaled for their present surroundings that there is some-thing nightmarish about the experience of being in St Donats now. Since these pieces are imports, they will not be described in detail here, but they deserve close examination as if they were in a museum.

In the SW range, first the BREAKFAST ROOM. Here a timber ceiling from St Botolph's church, Boston, Lincolnshire, tierceron-ribbed, with much original colour, and an exquisite stone chimneypiece and overmantel from Bradenstoke Priory, Wiltshire, bearing the name of Thomas Walshe, abbot there *c*.1514. The BANQUETING HALL beyond is entered through a magnificent stone screen from a major West Country church, though its precise provenance is unfortunately not known. The hall is ceiled by a much larger section of roof from the Boston church with equally well-preserved colour. French C16 hooded chimneypiece bearing the Valois arms. The LIBRARY above has another Perp stone chimneypiece and a timber door flanked by standing figures under canopies, and the INNER LIBRARY a simpler chimneypiece of the same period.

The GUN ROOM, W of the Great Hall, has a chimneypiece made up of a mélange of ill-fitting pieces of French provenance. This leads into the BRADENSTOKE HALL, constructed for Hearst between the two curtain walls. The seven-bay roof is from the refectory at Bradenstoke Priory, of arch-brace and collar-brace construction, datable to *c*.1320. Three exquisite contemporary two-light windows from the same source.* Two more French C16 chimneypieces, one mightier than the other. In the NW wall an important indigenous survivor, a rich C14 doorway leading to the screens passage of the Great Hall. Two continuous hollow chamfers and a keeled hood.

The terraced GARDENS probably date back to an early period, though in their present form they are the creation of Morgan Williams – see the second level, a Tudor-style garden with banner-bearing heraldic beasts rampant on pedestals – and Hearst. At the bottom, CAVALRY BARRACKS, dated to the C17, a long, low stone range with crow-stepped gables at the ends.

For Atlantic College *Alex Gordon & Partners* of Cardiff, in the mid 1960s, provided some well-designed and -sited new buildings. Beside the approach road, STUDENT HOUSING, and below to the l., quadrangular ADMINISTRATION BLOCK. Black brick, black weatherboarding, white trim. Flat roofs. Uncompromising modernity throughout. Nothing, that is to say, to detract from the historic castle, and very little that impinges on its setting.

ST DONAT. The church lies below to the W of the castle in a little wooded combe. The five stages of its growth can be well understood. The chancel arch is of the C12, plain round-headed, on jambs that have angle shafts with primitive caps. The double-chamfered tower arch probably dates that part to the early C14. Late C14 N chancel chapel – see the square-headed three-light E window with cusped reticulated tracery. The chancel itself was reconstructed in the C15, with Perp windows in deeply hollow-moulded external reveals. Piscina with cusped ogee hood. The nave, with N porch, is late Perp – see the two square-headed S windows with cinquefoiled lights, and doorway and window for the rood loft. The building is visually unified by the corbelled parapets with gargoyles to the nave and corbelled tower battlements, with small pinnacles. Compare the treatment of the late C15 hall of the castle. The body of the church was restored in 1878, and the tower in 1907 by *Halliday*. – FONT. Circular bowl with a roll top and bottom and scale-patterned sides, as if encircled by two rows of shields. Circular stem. – LECTERN. Medieval, wood. Two-sided head. Base carved with elaborate, pinnacled openwork panels. Brought in in 1913. – STAINED GLASS. E window, St Donat, *c.*1862. Is this the window executed by *Clayton & Bell*? – MONUMENTS. (Sir Edward Stradling, his wife and forebears. Three couples on three painted panels. Dated 1590, and said to have been executed by a painter called *Byrd*. A great rarity. Stolen in 1991, subsequently recovered, but not at present displayed in the church.) – Sir Edward Stradling †1609 (N

*The secret demolition of large parts of Bradenstoke Priory by Hearst's workmen in 1929 became a *cause célèbre*. The Society for the Protection of Ancient Buildings put up posters in London Underground stations showing before and after photographs.

chapel). Hanging wall-monument with figures of a man in armour and a woman facing each other across a prayer desk. Compare the Carne monument at Holy Cross, Cowbridge. – Sir Edward Stradling † 1726, and Sir Thomas Stradling † 1738, the last of the line (N chapel). White veined marble tomb-chest with armorial end panels in relief.

In the CHURCHYARD, a C15 cross on three steps, the tall shaft and cross-head carved with the Crucifixion surviving complete.

In the undergrowth N of the church, the ruins of the substantial late medieval RECTORY. S half largely intact. Square sandstone fireplace surrounds for hall and parlour.

WATCH TOWER, on the crest of the ridge W of the church. Battlemented. Thought to date to the C18.

1070 ST FAGANS/SAIN FFAGAN

ST MARY. What matters is the early C14 work of the chancel and nave, unmatched for its decorative finesse in the churches of Glamorgan. The church was restored and enlarged by *G. E. Street* in 1859–60, at the expense of the Baroness Windsor. Interior and exterior must be considered together. Best of all 25 are the triple sedilia and piscina, cinquefoiled arches on trefoil shafts with round caps and bases, hoods on lively heads and leaf spandrels squaring off the composition. Steeply pointed chancel arch on triple shafts. Hollow chamfer filled in immediately above the shaft caps. The tracery of the chancel windows, repaired by *Street*, is firmly geometrical, the three-light E window a composition of three hexfoiled spherical triangles in a circle. Internal moulded arch and hood and jamb shafts. Two-light windows N and S, with quatrefoils and trefoils in the tracery. All have hoodmoulds on dragon stops or lively heads. Note the colour contrast between the darker stone of the tracery and hoods, and the lighter stone of the mullions and jambs. In the nave a three-light window of more advanced character, with many ogee forms in the tracery. It has an internally shafted E jamb with a truncated projection, a support, it is suggested, for the rood beam. To the W of the S porch a lancet which is given a tracery trefoil over its trefoiled head. To the E of the porch the lancet is copied by *Street*. Street also added the wide N aisle in a matching, but less idiosyncratic style, the gabled N vestry and the diagonal buttresses at the E angles of the chancel. Simple tower arch, part of the C14 build, with two chamfered orders dying into the vertical imposts.

But it is clear that the nave at least had earlier origins. Arches and jambs of two C12 windows visible internally in the S wall. In the C15 the S porch was added, and the chancel given a fine wagon roof. The unbuttressed tower itself is a late rebuilding. Its squared masonry, crude two-light bell-openings and uncorbelled battlements all suggest that. In fact it bears a shield of arms datable after 1616, but the date 1730 high up on the W face is surely too late to apply to the whole tower. *Street*'s restoration included new roofs and new encaustic tile floors. – FONT. Perp. Octagonal, with a big quatrefoil on each face and a panelled stem. – PULPIT and CHOIR STALLS by *Street*. Timber. – TOWER SCREEN. 1860 by *Street*. – STAINED GLASS. A fine series by *Hardman*, inserted by members of the Windsor family. In date order they are: Nave SE, 1859, Christ raising the widow's son. – Chancel SE, 1864, Presentation in the Temple and Mary with Elizabeth and Zacharias, and NE, Raising of Lazarus story. – Chancel SW and NW, 1870, the four Evangelists. – Lady Chapel E, 1871, Entombment and Empty Tomb. – Nave SW, 1874, Baptism of Christ.

TABERNACLE PRESBYTERIAN CHAPEL, Crofft-y-genau Road. Dated 1837. On the early type of plan where entry is in the long wall. A pair of tall round-headed windows near the centre, circular ones over the doorways and short outer windows relating to the galleries. Porches part of a remodelling of 1900. Derelict at the time of writing.

OLD RECTORY, Greenwood Lane. 1858–9 by *Prichard & Seddon*. 97 Quite a spectacular display of French late medieval features, precipitous roof-slopes, double-height stone dormers rising almost to the roof-ridge, and elegant rectangular chimneystacks. The full-width veranda on the garden front is part of the original design.

The village centre, though on a main road, retains its countrified character. To the E, in Cardiff Road, the NATIONAL SCHOOL of 1851. Grey stone. Tudor. Matching master's house dated 1851 alongside. To the N, in Crofft-y-genau Road, the jolly Jacobean PLYMOUTH ARMS, remodelled by *Edwin Seward*, is dated 1895. The most picturesque scene is on CASTLE HILL to the W, where the service buildings of the castle appear above a row of thatched cottages as the road drops steeply. Among the undergrowth here the line of the medieval CURTAIN WALL of the castle has been traced. At the foot of the group, SILVER STREAM COTTAGE shows a medieval trefoiled lancet in its gable end.

ST FAGANS CASTLE. The most important Elizabethan house in the county, since 1946 at the heart of the Welsh Folk Museum. The approach is from the bottom of Castle Hill, through the Museum's GALLERY AND ADMINISTRATION BLOCK, a long, low, externally uncommunicative modern building by the *Percy Thomas Partnership* (design partner *Dale Owen*), 1968–74. Detached white canopy tethered over the entry. Grey brick walling, white-painted fascia board at eaves level. The administration block lies to the r., with behind it a red brick cube, all that was built of an earlier scheme by *Sir Percy Thomas*. The three main galleries are laid out in a rising sequence round a 121 courtyard. Satisfying structure of reinforced concrete beams, giving clerestory windows at two levels, and support for metal-framed display screens.

Inside the museum grounds stand about twenty reconstructed buildings, from all over Wales. Buildings indigenous

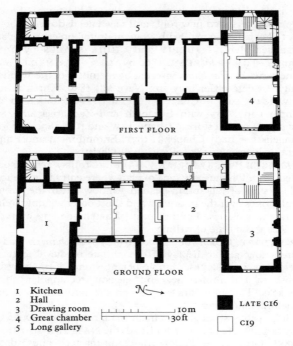

1 Kitchen
2 Hall
3 Drawing room
4 Great chamber
5 Long gallery

10 m
30 ft

LATE C16
C19

St Fagans Castle. Plans

to Glamorgan which deserve mention are, in the order encountered, KENNIXTON FARMHOUSE, a typical C17 Gower farmhouse with later fenestration; the circular corbelled PIGSTY from Hendre'fan Prosser, Glyntaff; and the early industrial TERRACE of six cottages from Rhyd-y-car, Merthyr Tydfil, built by Richard Crawshay for his iron ore miners. The LONGHOUSE, though not of Glamorgan provenance, is also instructive, its interior surprisingly spacious. The medieval church of St Teilo, Llandeilo Talybont (*see* Pontardulais), still awaits re-erection here.

The Elizabethan St Fagans Castle was built not long before 1596, probably by Nicholas Herbert, who bought the property in 1586. The mansion is approached nowadays through the garden from the N, but its E-facing entrance front must be addressed first here. It is seen beyond a FORECOURT, which is enclosed by a high embattled stone wall, running straight in front of the house, and turning in a faceted curve round its S side. Wall-walk, but no sign of a serious concern for defence. Yet the curve represents the line of the curtain wall of the medieval castle. In the centre of the forecourt, a magnificent lead CISTERN with embossed decoration and the date 1620.

41   The HOUSE itself demonstrates a complete break with medieval assumptions. It has a fully symmetrical entrance (E) front, and N and S ends which are nearly so. Straight-sided gables

arranged to enforce symmetry in all four directions, but on the entrance front in a rhythm 1+3+1 in counterpoint to the 1+2+1+2+1 of the fenestration pattern. Two storeys with a third in the gables. E-plan, with short wings and two-storey central porch, and a broad corridor at the back of the house, forming an embryonic double-pile arrangement, very advanced for *c*.1590. Large, four-light mullioned windows, those on the entrance front with a transom. No hoodmoulds, but continuous string courses across the heads of the windows at both levels. Three-light, transomed windows on the other three fronts. Three-light windows in the gables. Straight heads to the lights and sunk chamfer mouldings, as one would expect at this date. Rendered and colourwashed walls. That is all. Decoration is resolutely banished; order and regularity must suffice to impress. Even in England such coherence would be impressive at that date. Indeed, influence from England must be suspected, perhaps in the form of 'plats', i.e. plans and elevations, drawn up by a London surveyor. The chimneystacks, of red brick, vertically ribbed, are all of 1852–60.

The INTERIOR was fitted up in the early C17 by Sir Edward Lewis of The Van, Caerphilly (q.v.), who bought St Fagans in 1616. But there are C19 importations too, after 1850, when the Windsor family took up residence. This description follows the present-day visitors' route.

The porch leads into a SCREENS PASSAGE. Simple screen with one doorway, opening into the HALL. This is panelled with an enriched frieze. The elaborate timber overmantel bears the Windsor arms, and must be a C19 confection of old components. The DRAWING ROOM (originally parlour) in the NE wing is also panelled and has a wooden chimneypiece with the Lewis arms. Short but handsome Corinthian columns below flanking the fireplace and above, with enriched shafts, flanking the mantled shield of arms. Satyrs cavort in strapwork at the side. Post-1945 plaster ceiling. The main STAIRCASE belongs to the modernization of 1852–60. Its predecessor probably rose in short flights round a solid core. On the upper floor, the broad CORRIDOR to the W must have doubled as a communication passage and a long gallery.

In the NE wing the huge room which presumably formed the original GREAT CHAMBER has been subdivided. Chimneypiece brought in from Tŷ-Mawr, Whitchurch, Cardiff (*see* p. 314). The centre range at first-floor level was originally subdivided into three rooms. Of these, that to the N is panelled with a decorated frieze incorporating on the W side the initials of Sir Edward Lewis and the date 1624. Overmantel with small caryatids. The S room of the three was originally the largest, and the upper room in the porch formed a closet off it, but it has been subdivided. Chimneypiece with an overmantel dated 1635. Elaborate strapwork crown. Finally, back to the ground floor to the KITCHEN in the SE wing. This retains its two mighty fireplaces, each with a broad segmentally arched opening. The floor level here is lower than in the rest of the house, to enable the windows to be set high in the walls for proper ventilation without interrupting external symmetry – a telling detail.

The GARDENS are much as they would originally have been, walled enclosures to the N of the house, and a sequence of roughly formalized rectangular ponds below the steep slope to the S. The series of terraces descending from the level of house down to the ponds was created for the Windsors in 1865–6 and extended in the early C20.

(PENTREBANE FARM, 1 m. N. Mid-C19 model farm, built as the Home Farm to St Fagans Castle. Large barn with two pairs of porches.)

0070   ## ST GEORGE-SUPER-ELY/SAIN SIORYS

The church stands apart from the village centre, flanked to the E by a white cottage with a flight of steps from the upper storey down into the churchyard, and to the W by a cottage orné of *c.* 1860.

ST GEORGE. A handsome church, cruciform in plan with a crossing tower. Transepts lower than nave and chancel. S porch. The nave, with its windowless N wall, is probably the earliest part, the rest being an enlargement of the late C14. Tower and N transept reconstructed in 1838, the four-gabled tower top with oversized finials, a new invention. Chancel and S transept are clearly of a single build – see the walling as well as the windows, single or paired trefoil-headed lancets under hoodmoulds. The geometrical E window is of the C19. The interior, rendered and whitewashed, owes its character to the reconstruction of 1838. Plain, steeply pointed crossing arches, and thin-ribbed plaster vault. The nave roof is medieval, of wagon type with square bosses, and so is the roof of the S transept, with arch-braces. In the chancel two contrasting tomb-recesses. That to the E, presumably associated with the C14 rebuilding, has a segmental arch with two rolls and a hood on heads wearing chain mail helmets. The other is bigger and perhaps a little later, boldly cusped and hoodmoulded. – FONT. Probably C15. Octagonal. An encircled quatrefoil on each face. – STAINED GLASS. S transept, SS Teilo and Margaret of Scotland, *c.* 1957 by *Hubert Thomas* of *Celtic Studios*. – MONUMENTS. John Llewellin †1786. Small black and white tablet with urn. – Mary Llewellin. 1838. Gothic wall-monument. The inscription explains that the rebuilding of the church in that year was paid for by John Montgomery Traherne of Coedriglan, the antiquary.

In the CHURCHYARD, cross on three steps.

CASTLE FARM, ½ m. W, in the centre of the modern village. The glory of Castle Farm is the C15 first-floor hall, its roof open on arch-brace trusses. But originally the five-bay space was subdivided, to give a three-bay hall and a two-bay chamber beyond, both open to the roof. The present hammerbeam truss is a C19 antiquarian substitution for the partition wall between them. The hall has its original stone chimneypiece in the W wall, the jambs and corbelled hood enriched by a continuous double roll. The exterior has also received the attentions of the antiquary, so that the lancet in the S wall and traceried window in the N wall are neither to be taken as medieval evidence. The great thickness of the N and W walls, however, and the steep slope beyond the former, suggest that these parts of the fabric belonged to an earlier, fortifiable structure, which must have been ruined before its reuse in the present non-defensive building in the C15.

COEDARHYDYGLYN (formerly Coedriglan), 1 m. S. Beautifully sited on the slope of a wooded valley. Completed in 1820 for the Rev. John Montgomery Traherne. His architect is unrecorded. An exquisite Regency villa, white, with a single-storey, three-bay portico of green sandstone. Unfluted Greek Doric columns carry an entablature and big acroteria. Two-storey, seven-bay entrance front facing S, the second and sixth bays brought slightly forward under small pedimental gables. Deep Tuscan eaves. N front with a similarly projecting central bay. The W end, where the ground slopes steeply, is of five bays, the centre three canted to take advantage of the view. Timber veranda following the cant. Inside, the principal rooms on the ground floor, library between SW drawing room and NW dining room, all have reticent but subtly varied Greek detailing in the plaster cornices and marble chimneypieces. The outstanding feature is the axially sited, top-lit staircase (originally covered by a five-sided dome). The stair rises in a square well, a straight flight dividing into two and returning to reach an L-shaped landing with an arcaded loggia on the W side. Delicate balustrade, palmettes alternating with balusters. The whole stair is almost identical to that at Clytha House, Gwent, by Edward Haycock. So *Haycock* was probably Traherne's architect too.

ST HILARY/SAINT HILARI

0070

A compact village in the heart of the Vale, the church at its centre. Several quite large houses in walled grounds.

ST HILARY. W tower of the early C16, with a moulded plinth, angle buttresses, a four-centred head to the W doorway and arched lights and hoodmoulds to the W window and the belfry openings. It has been carefully joined on to the nave, with quoin stones cut to shape. The chancel arch is the earliest feature of the church, late C12, just pointed, on plain imposts. Otherwise the medieval evidence is of the C14. The chancel has an ogee-headed N lancet, and the separately gabled S aisle was added at this period. Aisle arcade of four bays with two-centred arches and two big continuous hollow chamfers carried down into the piers without interruption. Dec, too, the tower arch, two-centred with a wave and two hollows, so the present tower had a predecessor.

In 1861–2 the church was given an ambitious and coherent restoration. This was at the expense of Mrs Charlotte Traherne of Coedriglan, St George-super-Ely (q.v.), as a memorial to her husband, the Rev. J. M. Traherne, who had prepared designs before his death in 1860. *Sir Gilbert Scott* was the chosen architect. He inserted large windows throughout, renewed the roofs and added the S porch. All are thoughtfully, and in many respects unconventionally, designed. Five-light Dec chancel E window, four-light Perp S aisle window. Elsewhere all windows but one are square-headed three-lighters with cusped ogee heads to the lights and are surmounted by a row of tiny blind encircled quatrefoils, which Geoffrey Orrin suggests may reproduce a series of medieval consecration crosses. The nave N window is especially elaborate, set under a hoodmould on leaf stops and within a deep frame with ballflower. This must reflect the memorial function of the stained glass here (*see* below). The S porch is flanked by ashlar buttresses with scalloped offsets. The interpenetration of impost and arch mouldings here is a virtuoso detail out-designing Prichard. Roofs of tie-beam and kingpost pattern, more at home in the South of England than in South Wales. – Timber PULPIT, READING DESK and elaborately carved PEWS by *Scott*. – REREDOS. c. 1872. Relief of the Last Supper in a shafted marble frame related to the E window above, so presumably by Scott. – CHANDELIER. Of the corona type. In a pivoted position, between S door and font, and clearly by *Scott*. – STAINED GLASS. Nave N. Commemorating the Rev. George Traherne †1853. Christ carrying the Cross, and adoring angels. Apparently by *Cox & Sons*, to the design of *Charlotte Traherne*. – S aisle SE window, Ascension between Noli me Tangere and Pentecost, 1862 by *Clayton & Bell*. – Chancel E window, scenes from the life of Christ, also by *Clayton & Bell*, 1872, under *Scott*'s direction. – MONUMENTS. Recumbent effigy of a civilian, probably of the C14, originally of good quality, set under a crudely moulded segmental arch in the nave N wall, not the site it was intended for. – Thomas Basset †1423. Armoured knight with straight legs, the figure defaced, the inscription intact. – Daniel Jones †1841. Signed by *John Evan Thomas*. With a profile medallion portrait, encircled by a snake biting its tail, a traditional symbol of eternity. – William West James Basset †1871. Also with a relief profile portrait, of a bewhiskered man. In a laurel wreath.

In the CHURCHYARD, the four medieval steps for a shafted cross.

The village clusters round the churchyard. VILLAGE FARM, to the E, turning its back on the road, is a substantial mid-C16 house, with hall between parlour and kitchen. Doorways protected by drawbars gave entry both N and S into a passage within the kitchen, behind the hall hearth. Several S windows with paired arched lights and hoodmoulds, heavily restored. On the edge of the village to the SE, THE COTTAGE, not a cottage but a Regency villa, of three bays plus a broad canted bay at the r. end, imitated presumably from John Nash's Rheola, Resolven (q.v.).

THE MANOR HOUSE, on the edge of the village to the S, looks mid-C19. Five-bay, two-storey S front, parapeted, the centre bay canted forward under a strapwork balustrade. Irregular W front, with a stone porch carried on a pair of Ionic columns, brought in the 1980s from the demolished Verlands House, Cowbridge.

CHURCH COTTAGE, NW of the church. Of interest not for itself, but for the C18 circular stone PIGSTY in the garden. Conical stone roof. The Royal Commission notes the existence of eighteen others elsewhere in the county.

ST LYTHANS/LLWYNELIDDON 1070

ST BLEIDDIAN. Unbuttressed W tower, the saddleback top of extremely steep pitch and the Dec belfry openings all by *Prichard & Seddon*, who restored the church *c.* 1861. Nave and lower chancel, displaying local Old Red Sandstone in their quoins. Chancel E window with reticulated tracery by *Prichard & Seddon*. Tudor S chapel, with its own W doorway, renewed, but preserving its flattened four-centred head. Square hood and initials RB (for Robert Button of Dyffryn House) in the spandrels. In the nave S wall original Perp windows, and a small doorway with a broad hollow moulding on stops. Stoup beside it. S porch of *c.* 1861. Inside only one thing is notable, the bizarre arcade to the S chapel. One is tempted to assume that it is a bold stroke of the 1960s, but its 'crudity' was remarked upon in the late C19. A short, stout oval pier and two similar responds carry two flattened segmental arches, the expedient of the C16 mason, who was forced to cut through the thick chancel wall into the new Button chapel. – FONT, C12. A mighty tub encircled with six rows of zigzag. – PULPIT and ALTAR RAILS, of timber, by *Prichard & Seddon* (also the inlaid ALTAR TABLE).

NEOLITHIC CHAMBERED TOMB, ¾ m. SW. The chamber, 6 ft 7 in. (2 metres) high, is at the E end of a low mound 88 ft (27 metres) long. It is trapezoidal in plan, open to the E, and formed by slabs which support the single capstone.

WHITTON LODGE, 2½ m. SW, is the site of a late Iron Age enclosed settlement which developed into a Romanized farm.

ST MARY CHURCH/LLAN-FAIR 0070

A perfectly compact village. Church, rectory and a grove of sycamore trees stand in the middle, encircled by a lane and the houses of the village.

ST MARY. Only one memorable feature of the original building survived the sweeping restoration by *Prichard & Seddon* in 1862: the late medieval roofs of nave and chancel. They both conform to the pretty local pattern, arch-braced, the arches resting on short moulded wall-shafts. Wind-braces in three tiers. Collar purlin pinned to the underside of the arch-braces. In the chancel E bay a CELURE, painted dark blue with gilt stars and other gilding to highlight the sanctuary. Knots carved on the wall-post capitals here. What do they signify? Simple unbuttressed W tower with a crudely moulded base and corbelled battlements. N wall of chancel and nave with one trefoil-headed lancet and a projection for the rood stair.

With so little left to guide them, *Prichard & Seddon* chose an E.E. style and proceeded to enjoy themselves. S porch with carved panel of the Annunciation. Chancel arch with keeled rolls dying into vertical jambs. Shafted rere-arches to the E lancets, SEDILIA and charming N PISCINA. – PULPIT. Large and integral with the chancel arch, of lobed form, resting on a deep leaf corbel copied from the famous refectory lectern at Beaulieu Abbey, Hampshire. – The timber ALTAR with typical butterfly dowels, and the PEWS are also clearly by *Prichard & Seddon*. – STAINED GLASS in the E window, part of the scheme. Nativity, Presentation, Flight into Egypt, i.e. continuing the Marian story. By *William Miller*, it seems. – Medieval fittings are the PILLAR PISCINA with twisted stem, and the plain tub FONT.

THE OLD RECTORY, immediately N of the church, is at first sight a typical two-unit house of the C16. Yet it is of special interest for two reasons. First, there is documentary evidence that it was built by the rector Thomas Wilkins † 1623. Second, it reuses two medieval two-light windows, one Perp with cinquefoiled lights and a straight head under a hood, the other perhaps *c.* 1300, with two chamfered lancets sharing a colonnette. If these came from the church, this may have implications for the date at which the church was rebuilt in the C16.

57 FISHWEIR, 1 m. SE. Impressive two-storey, mid-C16 house facing SE, now a farmhouse, but built for gentry and used as the residence of the elder sons of the Bassets of Old Beaupre (q.v.). Two-unit plan, kitchen to the l., hall to the r., with a great chamber above the former. (Plaster frieze of roses, fleurs-de-lys and other devices in the great chamber.) Windows with hollow chamfers, arched lights and hoodmoulds, the upper windows four-lighters, which emphasizes the importance of the upper storey. Mural stair in the N wall.

BARN of C16 date to the NE, of eight bays, the tallest surviving barn in Glamorgan. Now unroofed but conserved.

ST MARY HILL

ST MARY. Alone, in a large circular walled churchyard, with a panoramic view. W tower with corbelled-out battlements, rebuilt 1879–81 by *Prichard*. Nave and S porch heavily restored, and new chancel arch, 1884–5 by *Prichard*. The chancel had been much reconstructed in 1803 (see the tablet in the E wall), but the E window typical of *Prichard*. Norman chancel arch reset in the nave N wall. AUMBRY in the E wall of the chancel with a medieval head, perhaps of the C14, an ogee trefoil-headed arch flanked by latticework in relief. Fleur-de-lys tufts. – FONT. Bulbous tub on a moulded foot. Of the C12? – MONU-MENTS. Several rustic tablets of the C17 and C18, particularly. Watkin Hopkin, father and son, †1699, 1702. The verses refer to the son. – Anne Bassett †1841. Slab with plaster reliefs of a cherub in clouds and drops of flowers. – Archdeacon John Griffiths †1897. Plaster bust, one of those donated to the parishes where he had been incumbent.

The CHURCHYARD CROSS is a reconstruction of 1887, incorporating the worn medieval head, which is carved with Crucifixion scenes front and back, and with saints to the sides (cf. Llangan).

ST MELLONS/LLANEIRWG

2080

Now officially part of Cardiff, and lapped on all sides by housing estates, yet preserving its village character at the centre, where the WHITE HART and the BLUEBELL INN stand together beside the Newport Road, as a lane slants up to the church.

ST MELLON. The church stands proudly on a knoll among pine trees looking S beyond the encroachments of suburbia to the Severn, and N direct to the wooded hills E of Caerphilly. Perhaps this commanding position explains the peculiar siting of the tower, halfway down the S side of the nave, for maximum effect as a seamark. The tower, unbuttressed, is of purplish rubble-stone, is not bonded into the nave, and is clearly earlier than the S chapel, which is adapted to its E wall. Battlements, and small Perp twin sound-openings. Beside it to the W, grey stone porch. *G. G. Scott* restored the church in 1858–9, at the expense of E. A. Freeman, the antiquary, who lived locally. (Other restorations, 1868–9 by *Charles Buckeridge*, and by *Ewan Christian* – chancel.)

The church itself is unusually large and complex. Dec nave, lower chancel, and lofty S aisle reaching nearly to the E end as a chancel chapel. The E windows in chancel and chapel and the (oddly skied) nave W window are all of three lights with cusped reticulated tracery. Walling of mixed grey, mauve and caramel stone. Small S window in the chancel of two ogee-headed lights. A Perp refenestration transformed the church. Very large three-light windows were inserted in the nave, three N and one S, and in the S chapel, three S. They have panel tracery and four-centred heads under heavy hoodmoulds with fancy square stops. Their stonework is weathered white. The chapel may have been extended W-wards at the same time. Deep N chapel which may be as late as the C17, see the rectangular, mullioned E window.

Inside there is further evidence of remodelling and addition, especially round the chancel arch. This is of the primary build,

Dec, with two double waves separated by a step, carried on short, moulded imposts. Linked to it the arch into the s chancel chapel, which yet has continuous mouldings on its E side. Two unequal arches from chapel to nave. Awkward arrangement of arches into the N chapel too. Wagon roofs throughout. – IMAGE NICHE. Perp, in the E wall of the s chapel. On an elaborate foliage corbel. The most exquisite object in the church, but sadly deprived of its canopy when the window above was lengthened. – FONT. Is this Perp? Panelled stem, shallow bowl like a capital. – BENCHES. A full set in the nave. Late medieval with simplified poppy heads. – PULPIT. Stone. Cylindrical. This must be by *Scott.* – STAINED GLASS. E window, of Nativity, Crucifixion and Resurrection. By *Clayton & Bell*? It dates from 1882. – MONUMENT. David Richards † 1825 (N chapel). Made up. Mid-C19 canopywork jammed on to the inscription panel.

In the CHURCHYARD, opposite the s porch, a MONUMENT which consists of a broken column set on a high pedestal. The inscription explains this design: it commemorates Joseph Benjamin Hemingway, † 1856, 'contractor' of Quarry Hill House.

BETHANIA EVANGELICAL CHURCH, Oldhill. Built in 1869–70 for Calvinistic Methodists. Gothic, with a handsome geometrical window over the entrance. Designed by the eighteen-year-old *H. C. Harris.*

ST ILLTYD'S R.C. HIGH SCHOOL, Newport Road. Three-storey main block, flat-roofed with windows in continuous bands. Typical of its date, 1964. By *Lewis E. Trevers* (D. Evinson). At the far end of the playing fields to the s, PEN-Y-PIL (Cae'r Castell), an undocumented ringwork where pottery of the C12 has been found.

WILLIAM NICHOLLS CONVALESCENT HOME, ¼m. NE, between Newport Road and Tyr Winch Road. Built as Tŷ-to-maen for Richard Allen, a magnum opus of *E. M. Bruce Vaughan,* the prolific church architect. 1885 is the date on the rainwater heads, and the house was reported in 1889 to be nearly complete at a cost of almost £15,000. Purple rubble walling with Bath stone dressings. For this money Bruce Vaughan pulled out all the stops, employing a Tudor Gothic style, with much decorative carving; but the mullion-and-transom windows go oddly with the Frenchy pinnacled dormers and the outbreak of red brick and stone chequering on the tower. Most of the incident is concentrated on the s front facing the garden, where the arcaded entrance stands between the windows of the principal reception rooms. Inside eclecticism continues. From the ENTRANCE HALL rises a Jacobean-style open timber staircase beyond an E.E. arcade of slender marble columns with leaf capitals. In the DINING ROOM, a massive canopied chimneypiece *à la* Burges (and another in the NE room). What makes the house delightful is the stone-carving by *William Clarke* of Llandaff – see especially the roundel over the front door, with an angel bearing a scroll inscribed:

Ingredientibus pax et exeuntibus – and the STAINED GLASS in the hall, stairwell and principal rooms, ultra-naturalistic birds and flowers, probably by *Joseph Bell* of Bristol.

To the NW, STABLE COURT with half-timbered gables.

SWALEC (South Wales Electricity Board Headquarter Offices), ½m. NE, Wern Fawr Lane. 1968 by *Gollins, Melvin & Ward*. An uncompromising rectangle, of three storeys, the lowest partly recessed. Continuous bands of windows between white mosaic-faced strips express the structure. Feebly revisionist extension at the back, *c.* 1990 by the *Powell Dobson Partnership*. Pitched roofs and gablets.

ST MELLONS BUSINESS PARK, 1 m. E, to the E of Cypress Drive. Here are juxtaposed two contrasting approaches to aestheticizing industrial buildings. The more westerly group, completed in 1986, consists of three low, irregularly placed steel-framed sheds, with ridge-and-furrow roofs and slender pilotis, up which plants climb. The easterly group, by *The Wigley Fox Partnership*, is ruthlessly formalistic, five square pavilions, with jutting roofs carried on massive pilotis which develop a rhythm as insistent as the columns of an antique temple.

ST NICHOLAS

0070

ST NICHOLAS. Quite a large church, w tower, nave with s porch and lower chancel with a separately gabled s chapel extending w almost to the porch. The historical evidence has been confused by the restoration of 1859–60 by *Prichard & Seddon*, who inserted many new windows, mixing Dec and Perp motifs. Early C14 tower unbuttressed and with corbelled battlements, the belfry openings in the form of paired trefoiled lancets. Tower arch, with two broad chamfers dying high up into single-chamfered imposts. Contemporary doorway to a stair in the thickness of the tower s wall. In the nave Perp windows. Two transomed three-lighters on the N side, their hoods on fancy square stops (cf. St Mellons), one three-lighter to the s of a different design, in a deep hollow surround, the tracery forming a row of shields. s doorway two-centred with two hollow chamfers. In the E wall of the porch a row of three-light mullioned openings now blocked. They appear to have been windows, rendered useless when the s chapel was built. The s chapel itself has been much reconstructed, the s wall rebuilt in 1803, the windows all of 1859–60. However, the crudely detailed arch from the nave into the chapel, two-centred with a double-wave moulding on polygonal imposts and fused jamb shafts, looks C16. That leaves the chancel. The chancel arch matches the tower arch, i.e. is of the early C14. Otherwise all features are of 1859–60. – FONT. Perp. Octagonal on an octagonal stem. – PULPIT. 1880. Showy. – STAINED GLASS. Chancel E, Crucifixion. By *Clayton & Bell*, 1860. – MONUMENTS. In the E wall of the chapel a large, late C18 Ionic half-column, to which a small wreathed marble disc is pinned. Presumably this had a commemorative function. – Several white marble tablets, the best to Sir Charles Tyler † 1835, signed by *J. E. Thomas*. Draped urn at the top, armorial display at the foot.

TREHILL PRESBYTERIAN CHURCH OF WALES. Up a lane beyond the w end of the village. Simple Gothic.

St Nicholas church lies inconspicuously back to the N of the A48. On the main road two buildings catch the eye. On the s side the gawky VILLAGE HALL, built in 1896 by *Lansdowne & Griggs* of Newport. On the N, BLACKSMITHS' ROW, thatched and buttressed to prevent it collapsing into the road. The E part of the row was built in the early C17 as a two-unit hearth-passage house, modernized into a lobby-entry plan by moving the entrance doorway slightly to the r. The central section was originally, it seems, the smithy. The w part is a separate cottage, added in the C18.

LLANEWYDD, the house which concludes the village to the w, is by *Sir Percy Thomas*, 1939–40, in his characteristic sub-Voysey domestic style.

DYFFRYN HOUSE. *See* p. 341.

The parish has a remarkable concentration of C12 earthworks. Y GAER, $\frac{1}{2}$m. NW, is a large, well-preserved ringwork, approached by means of a lane running N from Trehill. COTTRELL'S CASTLE, a motte $\frac{3}{4}$m. W, stands in parkland N of the A48. COED-Y-CWM, $\frac{3}{4}$m. SW, is another ringwork. Excavation 1963–5 found C12 potsherds and evidence of serious fortification in timber and stone.

(WORLETON MOAT, at Dyffryn, $1\frac{1}{4}$m. S, is the best-preserved moated site in the county.)

TINKINSWOOD, 1 m. S. Neolithic CHAMBERED TOMB exca-
p. 23 vated in 1914. Remains of about fifty individuals were found. The trapezoidal cairn 131 ft (40 metres) long is aligned NE–SW and retained by drystone walling. Restoration for public display is not entirely satisfactory, but the monument remains impressive. The rectangularity of the corners has been over-emphasized, and an over-elaborate and distracting herringbone pattern distinguishes restored walling from original.

The cairn was divided into compartments by transverse lines of slabs on edge, perhaps to facilitate construction. At the E end is a recessed forecourt leading to a chamber 6 ft 7 in. (2 metres) high built of upright slabs covered by a massive *c.* 40-ton (40.6-tonne) capstone. There is a drystone bank against the E side of the chamber and the entrance is in the NE corner through a short, slab-lined and roughly paved passage. The stone-lined pit towards the NW edge of the cairn is a later intrusion.

8000   SEVEN SISTERS/BLAENDULAIS

ST MARY. 1910–11 by *J. Cook Rees* of Neath. Quite large. Clere-storied nave with aisles and lower chancel. E.E., with some Perp-style sculpture. Otherwise fairly predictable, and, of course, seriously behind the times. – STAINED GLASS. E window.

Adoration of the Shepherds and Magi, and angelic choir above. 1921 by *Clayton & Bell*. In a brilliantly coloured, early C16 style. It redeems the church. – In the S aisle several by *Celtic Studios*, 1959–81.

SEION CALVINISTIC METHODIST CHAPEL. 1905. Idiosyncratic façade, the centre rising high under a gable with ball finials. Disused at the time of writing.

SOAR INDEPENDENT CHAPEL. 1900–1. Also with ball finials. Modernized.

CLAYPONS TRAMROAD EXTENSION, extending from 2 m. W to 1½ m. NE. One of the finest surviving examples in Wales of an early C19 'hybrid' railway, intermediate between the horse-worked railway used from the C17 and the modern locomotive-hauled railway that spread in the C19 from Britain to the rest of the world. The line was constructed from Ystradgynlais to Onllwyn, to take limestone to Ynysgedwyn Ironworks (*see* Ynysmeudwy) from the hills to the N. Heavily engineered and impressive, it includes as its major monuments an engine house and two bridges. It was constructed 1832–4 by the nationally known engineers *John* and *William Brunton*. Under threat from the further expansion of open-cast coal-mining.

SKER HOUSE/Y SGÊR

7070

2½ m. NW of Porthcawl

Isolated on the edge of the sand burrows, and accessible only down a long farm track. This must always have been a remote situation for a major house. Did the dogged adherence to the Roman faith of the Turbervilles, who built the house in the C16, provide the motive for the choice of such a site? Tenanted from the late C17 until as recently as 1977, the house has now started to collapse, the whole S end having fallen since the Royal Commission published its survey in 1981. Plans in 1994 for a building preservation trust to restore the house to habitable condition.

Before the Reformation Sker was a grange of Neath Abbey (q.v.). Both the main house and the range of BARNS to the NE are mainly medieval in their walling. The HOUSE consisted until the recent collapse of a long, narrow, two-storey medieval building lying roughly N–S, which was completely transformed in the late C16 by Jenkin Turberville, who came into the property in 1561, or his brother James, resident by 1590. Mullion-and-transom windows with sunk chamfers and hoodmoulds, and doorways and fireplaces of flattened four-centred outline, all of local sandstone, typical for Glamorgan in the late C16. Gabled projections, for staircases or closets, were added to front and back, most of them crowned, originally or subsequently, by thick, square chimneystacks. Massive composition of chimneystacks at the N end.

The two important architectural characteristics of the Turberville mansion, one forward-looking, one backward-looking, were, respectively, the symmetry imposed on the E front, and the siting of the hall at an upper level, in the castle tradition, above a low, unvaulted ground storey. The two transomed, four-light windows to the E, then, lit the hall, the gabled projection to the r. had its fellow to the l., and the three-storey N end was matched by a three-storey S end. Original windows only at the top level in the surviving N third of the house. More problematically, the original entrance doorway, which must have been on the E front, i.e. the show front of the house, has completely disappeared, and the original means of access to the upper-floor hall is not clear. A stair survives in the NW projection, rising in short flights round a rectangular newel, and the present (modern) entrance porch on the W side leads to a mural stair. Above the porch a four-light transomed window, which lit the dais end of the hall from the W. (In the hall a plaster frieze round all four walls, with dragons, birds and bunches of grapes, and the roof structure for a canted plaster ceiling.)

7090   SKEWEN/SGIWEN

Skewen is a main-road settlement, its growth generated by the Crown Copperworks to the S. Its streets are dominated by its chapels, some on the NEW ROAD, others of equal interest and pretension on the roads which run parallel to it to N and S. The churches are inconspicuous on hillside sites at the edges of the village.

BETHANIA INDEPENDENT CHAPEL, Evelyn Road. Built in 1906–7, by *Lloyd & Martyn* of Swansea. To a standard round-arched design, enlivened by the red sandstone of the dressings. Unaltered interior. Galleries on three sides.

CALFARIA WELSH BAPTIST CHAPEL, Stanley Road. Dated 1893, though the memorial stones were laid in 1895. A modest affair with a timid version of the favourite full-height recessed arch.

ENGLISH CALVINISTIC METHODIST CHAPEL, New Road. Also of 1893, but a good deal grander on this main-road site. By *Benjamin Williams* of Swansea. Pennant sandstone and Forest dressings. Entablature and pediment carried on upper-level pilasters, their pedestals merging into the rock-faced surface of the façade. All openings arched, the outer ones full-height windows, a very old-fashioned idea.

HERMON WELSH CALVINISTIC METHODIST CHAPEL, Winifred Road. Dated 1897. A plain rock-faced, pedimented façade with arched openings.

HOREB WELSH BAPTIST CHAPEL, New Road. Dated 1868, when the vocabulary of Victorian chapels was more newly minted. Central full-height recessed arch. Long, thin flanking windows on the front and along the sides of the building. Snecked Pennant sandstone with Forest smoothly rusticated quoins for emphasis. Simple interior. Galleries on three sides, and, above the pulpit, a full-width semicircular recess filled with a movable screen. What dramatic appearance was this provided for?

NEW ROAD UNITED METHODIST CHAPEL, New Road. Something quite different, of 1909 by *J. Cook Rees*. Baldly Gothic. Rock-faced Pennant and white Portland dressings. The central section, rising high, is framed by buttresses, octagonal in their top half. Simple interior. Gallery at the entrance end with rich metal front. Behind the pulpit raked seating in a deep recess, with the organ high up at the back.

ST JOHN THE BAPTIST, St John's Terrace, New Road. A Puginian piece designed in 1848 by *R. C. Saunders*, executed in 1849–50 to a modified design by *Egbert Moxham*. Steep-gabled, nave with lean-to aisles and cusped spherical-triangle windows in the clerestory. Lower chancel. The interior is as one would expect, with piers of alternating form, steep chamfered arches and a spindly exposed timber roof. – STAINED GLASS. Chancel E, scenes from the life of Christ, perhaps by Clayton & Bell, contemporary with the S aisle SE window, Empty Tomb, date of death 1863. – Sanctuary N and S, Woman of Samaria and Parables, *c.*1881. – Five aisle windows of the 1960s by *Celtic Studios*.

ALL SAINTS, Woodland Road. 1904–5 by *J. Cook Rees* of Neath. Nave and lower chancel. Of yellow Morriston brick and yellow terracotta, in a lancet style with classically regular angle quoins.

COEDFRANC JUNIOR SCHOOL, Stanley Road. Dated 1903. How much does this date refer to? *J. Cook Rees* was about to erect a school at Coedfranc in 1897. In the standard gabled vocabulary for board schools and council schools at the turn of the century.

CARNEGIE COMMUNITY CENTRE, Evelyn Road. This too is by *J. Cook Rees*, built in 1904 as a public library. Semi-Baroque, in tomato-coloured brick and mustard-coloured terracotta.

At JERSEY MARINE, 2½m. S, behind the Tower Hotel, two unusual reminders of Victorian recreations. The more conspicuous is the four-storey, octagonal TOWER, built before 1867 to support a camera obscura. Windows in every face at every stage. Brick with cast stone quoins. Lanky battlements. The cupola and lantern for the camera obscura itself have gone.

HANDBALL COURT. 1864. High rubble-stone wall in three cants, patterned in red and yellow brick.

CROWN COPPERWORKS, ½m. SE. The roofless buildings of the former works survive sandwiched between the Tennant Canal and the River Neath, visible to the E from the main dual-carriageway of the A465. The gable end of one large building, constructed of cast copper-slag blocks with multi-flues encased in the structure. Tall brick chimney alongside. These ruins are one of the few survivals of this former world centre of copper-smelting. The Rose Copper Company of Birmingham founded the works before 1797, and production of copper continued until the works were converted for zinc-smelting *c.*1866. Use as a patent fuel works ceased after the 1920s, and the site is now a scrapyard. The water-supply reservoir, linked to the works by an aqueduct over the Tennant Canal, remains on the W side of the A465.

TENNANT CANAL, RED JACKET PILL LOCK, 2 m. s. The canal was built 1820–4 by George Tennant to open up the estate around Neath which he had purchased in 1816. The engineer was *William Kirkhouse*. The canal started at a junction with the Neath Canal at Aberdulais and ended at Port Tennant on the E side of the River Tawe at Swansea. It carried traffic until the 1930s, but is now used only to supply water to local industries. The barge lock at Red Jacket Pill was built by *William Kirkhouse* in 1817–18 to allow vessels of up to 50 or 60 tons (51 or 61 tonnes) to lock out of the Neath River and reach Swansea by means of an earlier canal constructed in the 1780s. The stub of this canal can be seen passing under a bridge beside the barge lock. The canal junction bridge and overflow nearby belonged to the later line of the Tennant Canal.

CUTTING, ½ m. SE. A deep cutting on the Tennant Canal created by *William Kirkhouse* in 1821. During construction enormous problems were encountered with quicksand, and part of the canal bed is laid in an inverted arch with vertical walls to seal off the troublesome layer on either side. A high stone causeway carried the Mines Royal Copperworks tramroad over the centre of the cutting. At the SW end (SS 731 969), stone-arched bridge for a tramroad over the Tennant Canal, also by *William Kirkhouse*, 1821.

RIVER DOCK AND LOCK, ½ m. SE. One of three river locks on the Tennant Canal. The fine rusticated masonry indicates that it was built as part of the unfinished Neath harbour scheme. Large rectangular DOCK BASIN at canal level and the remains of timber loading stages projecting into the river.

SOUTHERNDOWN

SUNSHINE HOME. Built as a hotel. 1852 by *J. P. Seddon*, his first work in the county. An important early attempt to capture a new building type for Puginian Gothic, even if small fry compared with Seddon's later hotel at Aberystwyth. E.E. Entrance at the short, double-gabled end, where the porch hood, of Bath stone ashlar, has a big pointed trefoiled arch under a bold gable. The building itself is faced with local limestone, hammer-dressed, the upper windows segment-headed under trefoiled relieving arches. Recent unsympathetic alterations.

Seddon's designs of 1856–8 for a group of houses nearby were not realized.

DUNRAVEN CASTLE, ¾ m. SE. (Now a country park.) Here, virtually on the cliff-top, stood the mighty castellated seat of the Wyndhams and later of the Earls of Dunraven, one of the major landowning families in South Glamorgan. The house was built 1802–6, remodelled in 1858 by *Egbert Moxham*, and extended with a tower and wing on the seaward side by *George Devey*, 1886–8. All that survives is the remarkable rectangular WALLED GARDEN in the sheltered fold behind. Castellated. At

the highest point, to the NE, the angle in the wall is marked by
a tall circular turret with a castellated parapet on corbels and
three big trefoil-headed openings, almost like arrow loops. It is
built over an icehouse. What is the date? Could it be a C17
mock-fortified banqueting house?

DUNRAVEN Iron Age PROMONTORY FORT is defined by two
parallel banks fronted by ditches which combine with high,
sheer coastal cliffs to isolate the headland. The entrance was
probably at the W edge but has been eroded by cliff-falls, as
have the fringes of the interior. Remains of an outer NW annexe.
The E sweep of the banks was disturbed in the C19 by the
construction of Dunraven Castle. Slight hollows within the
enclosure may be house platforms. Medieval PILLOW
MOUNDS, i.e. rabbit warrens, are best seen at the far end of
the promontory.

SULLY/SILI

1060

ST JOHN THE BAPTIST. Much altered in a piecemeal way.
A C12 chancel arch is reported to have existed until c.1830.
Unbuttressed W tower of Old Red Sandstone rubble with corbelled battlements, slit windows and a lancet low down that
looks modern. Is the entrance through the S wall of the tower,
a most unusual arrangement, pre-C19? Rendered nave, with
two late C15 three-light windows in the S wall, with ogee-
headed lights set under a square hood and sunk in a hollow
surround, and two N windows of 1927. The chancel, of Old
Red Sandstone rubble, also shows medieval openings in the S
wall, a two-light Perp window and a priest's door, two-centred,
with a chamfer and hood on worn heads. Inside, the C13 date
of the chancel is established by the typical trefoil-headed piscina
outlined with a roll. Roofs, 1895 by *Seddon & Carter*. – FONTS.
The large one, of Caen stone, designed and executed by
J. Castle of Oxford, was in the Great Exhibition of 1851. Goblet-
shaped. Angels prepare to swoop out from it. Top wreath of
Dec foliage. The little one, of wood, shaped like a capstan, with
a lid to match, is obscure in origin. The smallness of the bowl
suggests an C18 date. – STAINED GLASS. Chancel E, Christ as
Saviour of the World between SS John the Baptist and Paul.
Signed by *A. L. Wilkinson* and dated 1949. – Nave SW, Holy
Family and saints. 1933, signed by *Abbott & Co.* of Lancaster,
but designed by the donor, *Isaac John Williams*, Keeper of Art
at the National Museum of Wales.

HOSPITAL, ¾ m. SW. An outstanding example of inter-war Functional architecture, which has survived almost unaltered. Built
for tubercular patients, whose cure required the maximum of
light and air. Designed by *W. A. Pite, Son & Fairweather*, who
won a competition in 1931, revised their design to eliminate
Neo-Georgianisms, and erected the building 1932–6. The long,
four-storey entrance range facing N accommodated the nurses.
In five parts, canted back in the centre, with typical cylindrical

stair towers lit by full-height windows. Behind this a large
administration and service court, and axially at the back,
beyond a stair tower over the patients' entrance, the s-facing
wards. These are the most impressive part, also canted, to form
two Vs towards the sea, with faceted glazing along the oblique
façades. Dazzling white-rendered walls everywhere. Brick construction, except the ward ranges, which are steel-framed to
facilitate the expansive glazing.

COG FARM, ¾ m. E. Model farm probably of *c.* 1816–17, built on
an E-plan but later enlarged. The rear barn and stable range
have arch-brace roofs of cast iron, evidence of a connection
with the Guests of Dowlais, Merthyr Tydfil.

6090   SWANSEA/ABERTAWE

Swansea is roughly triangular in shape, defined to the E by the
River Tawe and to the s by the curving sweep of Swansea Bay.
The natural barrier to the N is the serpentine escarpment of
Townhill, which still provides a sheltering backdrop to the town
centre, though it was outflanked by industrial development in the
C19 and its crown colonized by housing in the early C20. Only
towards the w, reaching out to the rural delights of Oystermouth
and the Mumbles headland, was growth physically unrestricted.
The successive stages of Swansea's formation, as it redefined its
ambitions from century to century, can still be traced area by area.

The medieval town grew from the castle and borough established after 1106 by Henry de Newburgh, Earl of Warwick and
first Norman marcher lord of Gower. The spectacular surviving
fragment of the castle is an early C14 extension, called the 'new
castle', added to the s of the C12 structure. Also in the early C14
town walls were constructed, now all gone, and the Bishop of St
David's founded the Hospital of the Blessed St David, the only
other medieval building of which anything survives. This stands
close to St Mary's church, s w of the castle. A second medieval
church, St John's, stood in the continuation of the High Street

beyond the town wall, $\frac{1}{3}$ m. N of the castle. Both churches have been entirely rebuilt in the C19 and C20.

By the Act of Union of 1536–43 the lordships of Gower and Glamorgan were merged into a single shire, its county town not Swansea, but Cardiff. Yet the successors of the Gower lords, the Dukes of Beaufort, kept a feudal hold on the town, cramping its development until almost the end of the C18. Nevertheless, the town's industrial beginnings date from this period, as the coal measures which lay uniquely near the surface began to be exploited. By the Elizabethan period there was a flourishing trade in the export of coal, which between the 1590s and the 1630s increased four-fold. Loading bays or quays were built along the banks of the River Tawe. The town's spine during this period remained the High Street, extending SE of the castle into Wind Street. The Strand, curving round parallel with them to the E, indicates the original waterfront, before the New Cut (completed in 1845) gave the river a straighter course. The first dock appears to have been the 'towne dock' of 1624, and by the beginning of the C18 warehouses were in existence along The Strand. Also by this date the main coal-producers had all acquired their own 'coale places' on the banks of the river.

By 1800 the population had passed 6,000, and Swansea was the largest town in Wales. From the 1780s to the 1830s the town expanded on to The Burrows, the flat reclaimed sandbanks W of the river mouth, in response to a new ambition for the town: that it should become a fashionable seaside resort. The elegant terraces of Gloucester Place, of Somerset Place and of Cambrian Place, with its former Assembly Rooms, indicate this ambition clearly enough. The handsomely Greek headquarters of the Royal Institution of South Wales, begun in 1839, and the Guildhall, monumentally reconstructed in the following decade, established the shift in the town's centre of gravity.

Eventually, however, Swansea's industrial growth blighted its pretensions to becoming the 'Brighton of Wales'. Easily mined coal was available in such quantities close to the River Tawe that by the early C18 it was not only being exported, but used to fire copper-smelting works along the riverbanks. First, in 1717, came Dr John Lane's Llangyfelach works at Landore, 2 m. (1.6 kilometres) inland. By the end of the C18 seven copper-smelting works were in operation, and in 1800 the Cornishman John Vivian arrived, following the copper ore from Cornwall to profit from its smelting. The Vivian family's Hafod works, on the W bank S of Landore, became the most celebrated of all these enterprises, while the Morfa works of Williams, Foster & Co. became the biggest. Lead had also been smelted from the beginning, zinc followed, and tinplating boomed in the later C19. The sulphurous fumes given off by the smelting processes polluted the environs of the works, so, although the Morrises of Morriston or the Vivians of Hafod might provide housing for their workers close by, they themselves led a migration westwards. Even the centre of the town, downriver from the source of pollution, lost its attraction, in particular for holiday-makers.

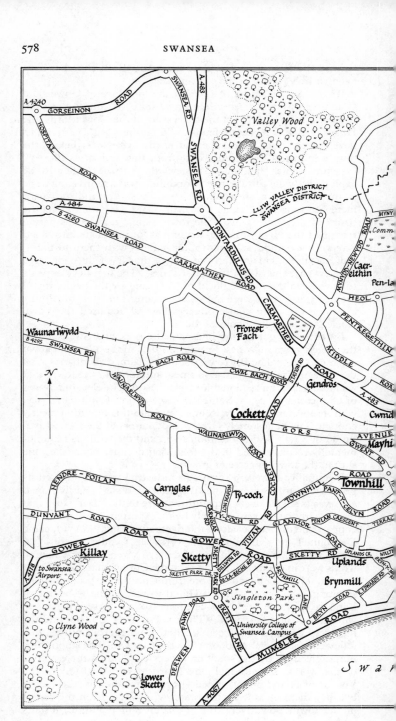

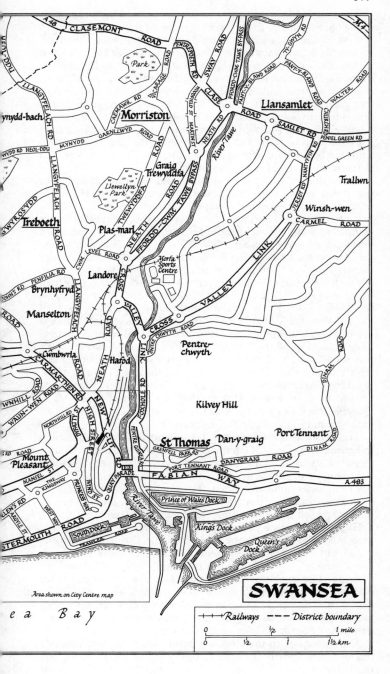

SWANSEA

The villas of Oystermouth and Sketty, planted from the 1780s in the countryside to the w, were segregated from Swansea's C19 growth by the Vivians' Singleton Abbey estate. During the half-century from the 1840s the intervening area, with St Helen's Road as its main artery, from St Mary's church in the E to Brynmill to the w and from the sea to Townhill, the natural barrier to the N, was built up with middle-class houses and terraces. Much of this, particularly in Uplands, remains today largely homogeneous and unspoilt, testimony to Victorian Swansea's middle-class pride. Through the C19 the population of Swansea rose steadily, and in 1891 stood at 90,349. The significance of the drastic westward shift was belatedly underlined when the new Guildhall was built at the w end of St Helen's Road 1932–6.

Throughout the C19 the industrial and maritime character of the E end of the town was being reinforced. The first serious attempt at improving the facilities was made in 1768, and the first of a series of Harbour Acts was passed in 1791. Piers were completed and the river channel deepened in 1810. An important development was the creation, in 1824, of Port Tennant, a tidal harbour on the E side of the river, as the terminus of the Tennant Canal. The first floating dock, the North Dock, was opened in 1852, after the present straight course of the river had been formed by digging the New Cut 1842–5. The river's old course became the Dock. The South Dock, cut through The Burrows s of the old Guildhall, followed in 1859, hugely increasing the port capacity, with an eye to the export trade in coal from Aberdare. The expansion of the Valleys coalfields required further dock provision to the E of the river, the Prince of Wales Dock, 1881, largely on the site of Port Tennant, and the King's Dock, 1909. Working-class suburbs, St Thomas and Port Tennant, developed on the flank of Kilvey Hill overlooking the new docks. The Queen's Dock, of 1920, serviced the new oil refinery at Llandarcy, at the mouth of the River Neath further E.

The docks were the target of three nights of German bombing in February 1941, which left the High Street devastated, St Mary's church a shell, and laid waste the streets in between. Post-war redevelopment, here as in so many English bomb-damaged cities, has been sadly undistinguished. The High Street today, and the new streets radiating out from Kingsway Circus, immediately to the sw, do not contain a single memorable new building.

Happily, the same cannot be said of Swansea's most recent piece of self-renewal. In the mid 1970s the City Council – city status had been granted in 1969 – decided to make the South Dock, which had been closed in 1969 and partly infilled, into an amenity. The dock was re-excavated and used as moorings for pleasure boats and historic vessels associated with a Maritime Museum. The new housing in the Maritime Quarter, intricately grouped and imaginatively designed, now covers the whole area between the South Dock and the shoreline.

This successor to the Regency development of The Burrows has prospered partly because of the death of the smelting and tinplating industries in the Swansea area. By 1960 the Lower

Swansea Valley was totally devastated and deserted, officially recognized as 'the most extensive contiguous area of industrial dereliction to be found anywhere in the United Kingdom'. Since 1967 the mountains of polluted waste have been cleared, and new industrial estates established. Morfa has given its name to an athletics stadium, and the slopes across the Tawe from Landore are heather-clad once again.

CENTRAL SWANSEA

CHURCHES AND CHAPELS

St Mary. The nave of the medieval church was rebuilt in 1739 by *Thomas Woodward* of Worcester, and the whole church 1894–8 by *Sir Arthur Blomfield*. This in its turn was gutted in 1941 and rebuilt with modifications by *Leslie T. Moore* and *Sir Percy Thomas*, 1954–9. Moore withdrew before rebuilding actually began (P. Howell). Almost on a cathedral scale, but a routine design. E.E. Rock-faced snecked sandstone, the dressings of Bath stone. Lofty s tower, almost detached. sw porch. Wide six-bay nave with wide aisles. Transepts opening inconspicuously off the chancel, the chancel arch not breaking the space. Chancel E wall pierced by three arches into the Lady Chapel beyond. This replaces the medieval Herbert chapel which was spared by Blomfield but not by the Blitz. The nave arcades are of the familiar type of circular piers and double-chamfered arches, but in the post-war rebuilding the aisles were heightened and transverse arches introduced, and the aisle windows doubled in size. – FONT CANOPY. Massive iron superstructure by *G. G. Pace*, 1972. A modernist reworking of Bishop Cosin's font canopy in Durham Cathedral. The cover also by *Pace*. – PAINTING. Deposition, by *Ceri Richards*, 1958. Movingly stark. – STAINED GLASS. An interesting collection, much of it experimental, from which the building will increasingly benefit if it is continued with the enterprise shown so far. – Lady Chapel E, a pair, entirely abstract, designed by *John Piper* and made by *Patrick Reyntiens*, 1965–6. Shadowed blue, punctured by vivid spots, particularly red. Piper designed a painted wall-hanging for the space between these windows, but it is not at the time of writing *in situ*. – Chancel E, Christ between the four Evangelists. Also N and s lancets. Designed by *E. Liddell Armitage*, made by *Powell*'s, 1958–60. Expressionist. Too heavily leaded. – The rest are by teachers and students at Swansea School of Art. N aisle NE. Welsh Guards Falklands memorial, 1985 by *Rodney Bender*. Apparently abstract, but with a detailed programme, based on Dylan Thomas's poem 'And death shall have no dominion'. – N aisle NW, a pair by the font, 1981 by *Kuni Kajiwara*. Near monochrome. Inspired by the destruction and rebuilding of Swansea after the Second World War. – Nave W. Two lancets, to commemorate the wedding of the Prince and Princess of Wales. 1982 by *Catrin*

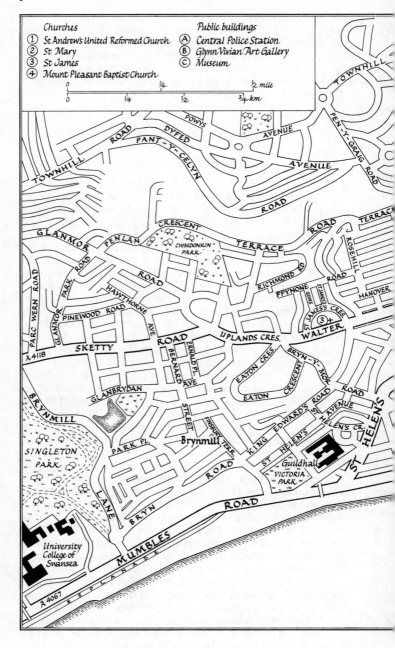

Churches
1 St Andrew's United Reformed Church
2 St Mary
3 St James
4 Mount Pleasant Baptist Church

Public buildings
A Central Police Station
B Glynn Vivian Art Gallery
C Museum

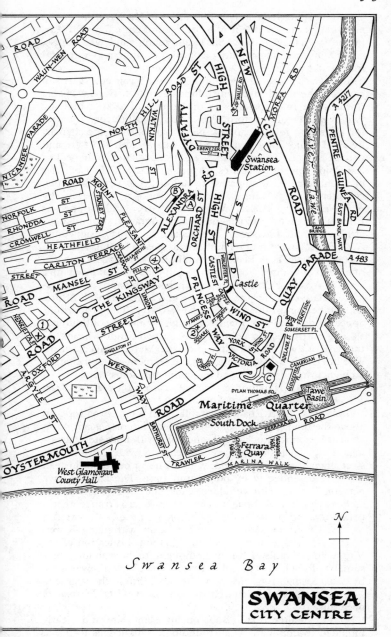

Swansea Station

Castle

Maritime Quarter

South Dock

Dylan Thomas Sq.

Tawe Basin

Ferrara Quay

MARINA WALK

West Glamorgan County Hall

Swansea Bay

SWANSEA
CITY CENTRE

Jones. Clasping hands, as a Pop artist might have done it. – MONUMENTS. Fragment of a C14 recumbent effigy of a lady, in the N chancel aisle. – Sir Hugh Iohnys and wife. Brass, *c.* 1500, of a man in armour, 32 in. (81.3 centimetres) long, and fragmentary figure of his wife. In the sanctuary.

CHRIST CHURCH, Oystermouth Road. Swansea's garrison church. The aisled nave, which forms a triple S (ritual W) gable towards the road, belongs to the church of 1871–2 built by *J. T. Nicholson* of Hereford. E.E. Geometrical tracery. Quatrefoil piers with foliage capitals. New chancel with side chapels, by *E. M. Bruce Vaughan,* 1912–13. – CHANCEL SCREEN and CHOIR STALLS, Perp, 1914. – STAINED GLASS. Chancel E, Ascension and other scenes, 1879, signed by *W. H. Constable* of Cambridge. Unimpressive technique. – N (ritual) chapel, commemorating young deaths, *c.* 1900–1, probably by *R. J. Newbery.* – Aisles. Magnificat, 1919, and Supper at Emmaus, signed by *Kempe & Tower.* Adoration of the Kings, attributable to the same. Annunciation, *c.* 1937, signed by *C. C. Powell,* and Empty Tomb, 1938, clearly by the same.

ST AUGUSTINE, Park Place, Brynmill. Built in 1904 as a chapel of ease to St Gabriel (*see* below). A full-blooded but insensitive essay in Arts and Crafts Perp. Red brick with bands and dressings of Bath stone for the long nave and lower chancel. A little half-timbering on the S porch and N vestry. The proportions appear broad and low, mainly through the use of continuously sloping buttresses. Straight, crudely cusped window heads. At the base of the E and W gable ends kneel large winged angels. The interior is a disappointment, the segment-headed chancel arch enclosing a timber rood being the only idiosyncrasy.

ST BARNABAS, Hawthorne Avenue. 1913–14 by *E. M. Bruce Vaughan.* Elaborate Dec E front.

ST GABRIEL, Bryn Road, Brynmill. Well sited, broadside-on above the road. Built in 1888–9 to the design of *Thomas Nicholson* of Hereford. Rock-faced sandstone with Bath stone dressings. Perp. Clerestoried nave and chancel with lean-to aisles sweeping almost to the E end. W tower never built, but instead the nave extended W by one bay in 1931. The arcades have octagonal piers with moulded caps and double-chamfered arches dying in well above the caps, an awkward arrangement. – CHANCEL SCREEN. 1914 by *Geoffrey Lucas.* – STAINED GLASS. Chancel E, Adoration of the Lamb, with many figures, *c.* 1923. – S chapel windows, Annunciation, Education of the Virgin and Expulsion of Eve, thought to be suitable, presumably, for a Lady Chapel, *c.* 1930. – Nave W window, saints, by *Celtic Studios,* 1960. More by the same firm in the N aisle.

VICARAGE, E of the church, dated 1892. By *H. C. Portsmouth* of Swansea.

ST JAMES, Walter Road. Built on an island site and clearly intended to dominate its surroundings. This it fails to do, as the proposed SW tower and spire were never built. 1863–7 by *Thomas Nicholson* of Hereford. Rock-faced walls and Bath stone dressings. Nave and lean-to aisles, not providing enough room for a clerestory. Transepts in the E bay of the nave, chancel nearly as high as the nave. Altogether an uneloquent group. Elaborate Dec tracery. Inside, the aisle arcades carry on across the transepts. – STAINED GLASS. Chancel E, Christ in Glory, 1953–4 by *Gerald Smith* of *A. K. Nicholson*'s firm. Complex iconography diagrammatically presented. – Nave W, the Church as a ship, or rather as a galleon in full sail. Later 1950s, also by *Smith*.

ST JUDE, Mount Pleasant. A lively group for the sloping site. Designed by *E. M. Bruce Vaughan* in 1904. Hall 1905–6, church built on top 1913–15. Rock-faced sandstone and Bath stone dressings. E.E. Clerestoried nave and chancel in one, their ridge riding above the rest of the church, which consists of lean-to N aisle and gabled S aisle and chapel, N transept and lean-to N chapel, which pinch between them a slim, octagonal bell-turret. Unified interior space. Conventional arcades, of circular piers and double-chamfered arches. – STAINED GLASS. Chancel E, Christ in Majesty with Moses, Elijah and saints. 1919. – S chapel, war memorial, *c.*1920, signed by *C. Powell*. – Nave W, war memorial by *Celtic Studios*, 1949.

ST MATTHEW, High Street. On the site of the medieval church of St John. Of *William Jernegan*'s simple, rectangular church of 1823–4 only walling of squared sandstone blocks survives. Its lancets disappeared in 1885–6, when *Bucknall & Jennings* extended it W-wards and replaced all the windows in a sub-classical style. Short chancel formed internally by a similarly sub-classical, triple-arch arrangement. The Low Church persuasion is apparent in the W gallery, a rarity in the 1880s, and in the Decalogue, Creed and Lord's Prayer flanking the altar.

ST DAVID'S PRIORY CHURCH (R.C.), St David's Place. 1847 by *Charles Hansom*, the nave lengthened in 1864 by his former pupil, *Benjamin Bucknall*, perhaps merely completing Hansom's original design. Conventional. Geometrical style. Coursed, squared sandstone with Bath stone dressings. Nave and chancel in one with lean-to aisles all along. Bell-turret over the chancel arch. No clerestory, but timber dormers, added by *Bucknall*. The four-bay nave has arcades with round piers and double-chamfered arches. – STAINED GLASS. Chancel E, Crucifixion and saints, *c.*1900 by *Hardman*. Exceedingly elaborate canopywork. – Two N windows, 1985–6 by *Catrin Jones*, Blessed Philip Powel on his way to Tyburn.

The Tudor-style PRESBYTERY at the SW corner is also by *Bucknall*. Polygonal stair-turret.

ARGYLE PRESBYTERIAN CHURCH OF WALES, St Helen's Road. 1873, by *Alfred Bucknall* of Sketty, Benjamin Bucknall's brother. A large temple-style building, presenting towards the street a recessed giant Composite portico with two free-standing columns, but managing only Doric pilasters round the side. Rendered over brickwork. Now disused, the interior stripped out.

BETHESDA BAPTIST CHAPEL, Prince of Wales Road. Classical, of *c.*1870. Doric pilasters. Three-sided pedimented porch with

Corinthian pilasters. The memorable feature, the miniature domed turrets at the four angles of the building. Disused at the time of writing.

BRUNSWICK METHODIST CHURCH, St Helen's Road. 1872–3 by *Habershon, Pite & Fawckner*. In a Romanesque style. Rock-faced Pennant sandstone with Bath stone dressings.

EBENEZER ENGLISH BAPTIST CHURCH (formerly Welsh Independent), Ebenezer Street. 1862–3 by the Rev. *Thomas Thomas* of Landore, who also preached at the opening ceremony. Rock-faced sandstone with Bath stone dressings. Pedimented façade. The trio of central arched windows accommodated by the characteristic device of turning a big arch up through the underside of the pediment. The motif goes back through Hawksmoor, Wren and Alberti to antiquity. How far was the architect aware of that pedigree? (Interior galleried all round, the gallery dipping under the organ. Cast iron columns with foliage caps. Box pews. Two plaster ceiling roses.)

EBENEZER NEWYDD (formerly SION) WELSH CONGREG-ATIONAL CHAPEL, Henrietta Street. 1896 by *W. W. Williams*. Cuspless semi-Gothic. Small, on a square plan. The semicircular gallery creates an unusually attractive space. Central plaster ceiling rose, ringed with jostling cherubim, a surprising conceit.

MOUNT PLEASANT BAPTIST CHURCH, The Kingsway. 1874–6 by *George Morgan* of Carmarthen, virtually rebuilding a chapel of 1825–6. Nonconformist architecture at its most nobly classical, made yet more characteristic by certain impurities. Corinthian four-column portico, the pediment a trifle too steep. Balustraded staircase bays l. and r. with paired Corinthian pilasters to the front and round the sides. Five round-headed doorways below, five round-headed windows with balustrading above. The entire façade is executed in Bath stone ashlar, a rare and impressive achievement. In fact Mount Pleasant is the only chapel with a free-standing portico to survive in the county. Rendered sides with pilasters and full-height arched windows. INTERIOR with galleries on Doric entablatures and plain, cast iron columns on three sides, and on the fourth, behind the small pulpit, a grandly scaled organ recess in the shape of a Venetian window subdivided by Doric columns.

Lying back to the r., CLASSROOMS dated 1884, a pedimented block, with two storeys of arcaded windows on both the façade and the six-bay return. This too is all faced with Bath stone. Is it by Morgan? Lying back to the l., the pedimented LECTURE HALL. This has Corinthian pilasters, but is rendered. 1904–5 (Cadw).

PANTYGWYDR ENGLISH BAPTIST CHURCH, on the corner of Glanbrydan Avenue and Ernald Place, Brynmill. 1906–7 by *C. T. Ruthen*. Gothic. Rock-faced Pennant sandstone and Bath stone ashlar. Arresting angle tower, the bell-stage corbelled out on polygonal shafts at the angles and in the centre of each face too. Shingled flèche with lead-covered tip. The body of the church juggles Dec and Perp, with some original variations of the architect's own. Huge transeptal windows, the centre of two-storey side elevations which demonstrate the galleried internal arrangement intended. Since only the deep gallery at the entrance end was constructed, the transept windows remain unimpeded inside. Contemporary organ gallery above the pulpit. Organ added *c*.1920.

RHYDDINGS UNITED REFORMED CHURCH, Finsbury Terrace, Brynmill. 1913–14 by *W. Beddoe Rees*. Typical of his trim style. Pennant sandstone with Bath stone dressings. Perp. The corner site acknowledged by a neat octagonal bell-turret.

ST ANDREW'S UNITED REFORMED CHURCH, St Helen's 87 Road. Formerly Scottish Presbyterian. 1862–4 by *John Dickson*. Quite out of the ordinary run, with its landmark façade. Tall flanking towers, square in plan but turning octagonal at the top. Pinnacles. Hawksmoor's towers at All Souls College, Oxford, come to mind. Hawksmoor's sculptural quality, however, is lacking. In the centre, a large five-light geometrical window. Six-bay side elevations with long, transomed windows between shallow buttresses. Rock-faced sandstone and Bath stone dressings. (Interior remodelled after a fire in 1964.)

UNITARIAN CHURCH, High Street. Set back from the street-line. 1845–6, replacing a Baptist chapel of 1698. Entrance front dominated by a large Perp window, which must be late C19. (Aisled interior.)

YORK PLACE ENGLISH BAPTIST CHAPEL, York Street. Nearly square, rendered, under a pyramidal roof. Against the full-width entrance lobby, clearly an addition, the original pedimented doorcase on Ionic columns has been reset. The date 1830 on the doorcase dates the chapel, but its interior fittings must be a generation later. Galleries on three sides, supported on iron columns with Spalato capitals. – STAINED GLASS. Green, red and blue patterns, reminiscent of C.R. Mackintosh. – MONUMENTS. Two mighty Grecian headstones in the porch, dates of death 1839 and 1851.

THE CASTLE

The lord of Gower had his principal castle at Swansea. What survives of it in Castle Square is truly impressive, yet its history is tantalizingly obscure. The castle is first mentioned in 1116, ten years after Henry I had granted Henry Beaumont, Earl of Warwick, the right to conquer Gower. Traces of a motte-and-bailey castle, which must have been Beaumont's, have been recorded approximately 100 yds (91.4 metres) N of the surviving range, on the site of Worcester Place. Excavated footings of walls indicate that the stone castle which succeeded the motte-and-bailey formed a large rectangle, extending from the line of Welcome Lane a further 100 yds (91.4 metres) towards the N to the surviving range in the S. It stood on the edge of the escarpment to the E down to the River Tawe (now The Strand, since the course of the river has been diverted further to the E).

The surviving fragment is of three unequal parts: a roughly

L-shaped range which contains a first-floor hall and parlour, a short, much-ruined section of curtain wall extending between the NW corner of this range, and a square tower, which owes its survival to subsequent use as a prison. This all appears to be work of the late C13, and may belong to a major reconstruction and improvement of the castle after Rhys ap Maredudd had ravaged Swansea in 1287. The splendid arcaded parapet along the outer wall-head of the hall–parlour range is clearly an addition, and can be closely dated because of its similarity to the parapet added by Henry de Gower, Bishop of St David's 1328–47, to his episcopal palaces at St David's and Lamphey. Henry de Gower is known to have turned his attention to Swansea, for he founded the Hospital of the Blessed St David there in 1332 (*see* below, p. 601); but the tradition, first recorded by Leland, that he built the castle cannot be correct. The most likely explanation for the occurrence of the de Gower parapet at Swansea Castle must be, as Mr C. J. Spurgeon has suggested, that his masons working on the Hospital were called in by the lord of Gower to improve the castle. Yet a puzzle remains. From 1331 the lord of Gower was John Mowbray, the first of a sequence of absentee lords. He is known to have paid no more than a few brief visits to Wales. So what motive did he have to finish off his Gower stronghold with such a flourish?

The castle is built of coursed and roughly squared Pennant sandstone blocks, with dressed Sutton stone, showing white against the dark, greenish-brown walls. The earliest recognizable fabric is reported to be in the SE corner, where the walling up to first-floor level is more roughly laid than elsewhere, but it is masked by the shallow garderobe tower built against it.

37   The HALL–PARLOUR RANGE is otherwise all of one build, except for the parapet. Its outer S and E walls survive to virtually their full height. Semicircular W garderobe turret combined with a mural stair, rising higher than everything else. Broad, rectangular SE garderobe tower. Between them a three-bay hall range, its lower storey pierced by three magnificent arrow loops. Large, voussoired hall windows robbed of dressed stone, but in the W bay small windows at two levels, the upper with two ogee trefoiled lights. The arcaded parapet cuts the voussoirs of the hall window heads, and the arcade shafts also impinge on them as they descend below the line of the wall-head, clear evidence that the parapet is an addition. The arcading itself cuts back above a sloping sill through the full depth of the wall and is expressed on the external wall-face as a series of chamfered two-centred arches on polygonal shafts with caps. Where the arcading crosses a gable end, as on the garderobe tower, the arches are solid. The function of the arcading is to support a raised wall-walk; fragments survive of the corbelled battlements furnished with arrow slits which provided protection for the wall-walk. Doorway from the mural stair-turret at the W end on to the wall-walk.

Round the corner to the E the range is much shorter, but carries arcading on its E side and across its N gable. Two small lancets, instead of arrow loops, below, a larger lancet above, and the socket of a second. Since the ground drops here, a sub-basement underpins this range, with, in the E wall towards the river, two arrow loops and an arched doorway giving direct access to the river.

The inner, N side of the hall–parlour range is less impressive and does not survive to full height. Added round-ended stair-turret N of the hall. From this side there is access to the interior. Five basement rooms with pointed tunnel-vaults, three in the hall range, a wedge-shaped one at the angle, and a square one under the N end of the parlour. Hall and parlour both have internal window seats. At the W end of the hall a rectangular service room roofed N–S and lit by the two storeys of small windows. It is linked to the hall by three close-set doorways, and to a now-vanished kitchen by a doorway in the W wall. N lancet window at gable level.

The NE TOWER is much altered, and its interior arrangements are unclear. Arrow loops in the N and E walls, similar to those under the hall. (Reminders inside of its later use as a prison, cell doors, stencilled numbers etc.)

PUBLIC BUILDINGS

GUILDHALL, St Helen's Crescent. *Percy Thomas* of the Cardiff firm of *Ivor Jones & Percy Thomas* won an open competition in 1930 with a design that displayed porticoes in three directions. Second thoughts forced by cost limitations stripped away the porticoes, leaving an austere, white, Portland stone group virtually devoid of mouldings. Professor Reilly saw it as 'a classical approach to modernism'. By this he meant a classicist's reaction to modernism. These sheer white surfaces and these juxtapositions of blocky forms cannot disguise the fact that the Guildhall is in its rigidity, its axiality and in the decisive distinction between exterior and interior a classical building through and through. Its similarity to contemporary buildings being erected by totalitarian regimes is presumably merely coincidental.

It was built 1932–6, in four blocks round a central courtyard. Each block is functionally distinct, the Council's ceremonial rooms being in the E block, an assembly hall in the S, the Law Courts in the W, and the municipal offices in the N. The first three function virtually independently of the others, approached by central flights of steps which enter the building under tall arches with coffered soffits. The entrance pavilions are windowless, and rise higher than the main body of the building. This consists of a piano nobile in which the windows have architrave surrounds, and an irregularly channelled podium, through which the ground-floor windows are cut. To the E the entrance pavilion forms a base for the thin clock tower. This soars 160 ft (48.8 metres) high, and is more subtle than may at first appear, for the angles are recessed, and the tower itself tapers slightly and has even a slight entasis. Open

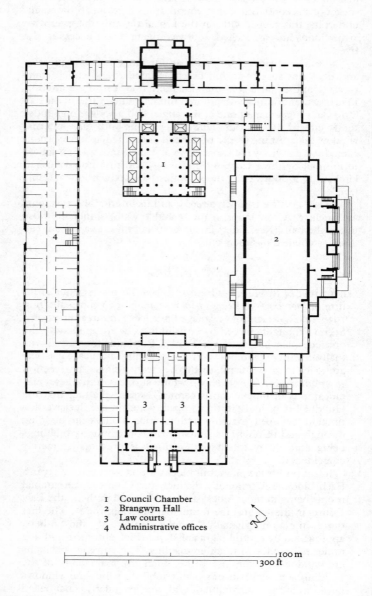

1 Council Chamber
2 Brangwyn Hall
3 Law courts
4 Administrative offices

100 m
300 ft

Swansea, Guildhall.
Plan of principal floor

belfry stage with Adamesque columned screens, acroteria and the prows of Roman ships.

The INTERIOR is a complete contrast, almost overpowering in its neo-antique panoply.* Within the E entrance, beyond the vestibule, steps rise between walls of polished Bath stone under a coffered tunnel-vault coloured bronze and green. This leads to a similarly vaulted ANTE-HALL with in the centre of each wall a pair of Doric columns carrying an entablature across a semicircular arch, in imitation of Roman baths. Travertine floor patterned in gold and green. Beyond to the W lies the COUNCIL CHAMBER, a heady environment for councillors, like the interior of a temple. It is top-lit from the centre of the elaborately coffered ceiling, and fluted Ionic columns stand close-set on all sides. The Ionic order is imitated from the Temple of Apollo at Bassae, an antique temple famous for the survival of internal columns, a touch of scholarship that reinforces the temple connotation. The column shafts are veneered with Australian walnut. Seating for councillors within this sanctum. Outside the colonnades, a narrow access passage and walnut-veneered walls, with a tapestry frieze by *Warner Brothers* of Braintree, illustrating the Gorsedd Procession.

From the ante-hall, rooms open to the S. First comes one with pairs of fluted Greek Doric columns and a flat ceiling coffered in purple and pink. Then the gilt and white REFRESH-MENT ROOM (now George Hall), a little less pompous. Fluted pilaster strips crowned by relief ovals, and rectangular frieze panels in between, carved in relief with scenes of entertainment through the ages. A groin-vaulted corridor beyond, giving access to the Brangwyn Hall.

The three-bay S VESTIBULE, behind the triple-arched S entrance, is the principal approach to the Brangwyn Hall. Plaster groin-vault. The BRANGWYN HALL is an assembly 116 and concert hall, seating over 1,300, and with a stage backed by an organ behind an elaborate metal grille. Prominent, rectilinear, pendant light fittings of Art Deco character. But what gives the Hall its name and interest are the WALL-PAINTINGS by *Frank Brangwyn*. The seventeen tempera panels, close-up views into a luxuriant and brilliantly coloured jungle, are, surprisingly, a war memorial, and are known as the British Empire Panels. They were painted not for Swansea but for the House of Lords in the Palace of Westminster. In 1924 it was proposed that the series of paintings in the Royal Gallery there should be completed to commemorate peers who had died in the 1914–18 war. The Earl of Iveagh undertook to pay for them and chose the artist. During 1925–6 Brangwyn worked on war scenes, but he and his patron wanted something more

---

*Thomas, in his autobiography, explains how he and the Labour councillors who were employing him took advantage of the Slump: 'Owing to the fall in prices which took place after the contract was started, there was money available to carry out improvements in the design and decorations which were not included in the original estimates.'

optimistic, so these were set aside,* and Brangwyn started again on a 'synthetic panorama of the beauty of Greater Britain ... [to show] what the Forces of the Empire fought *for.*' The whole scheme symbolizes the flora, fauna and ethnography of the British Empire, stressing its unity rather than illustrating its constituent parts. When in 1930 the first five panels were set in place in the House of Lords, however, the peers rejected them. Undeterred, Brangwyn completed the set, and after they had been exhibited at the Ideal Home Exhibition in 1933, the artist's Welsh parentage helped to recommend them to Swansea.

The LAW COURTS are entered independently from the w. The giant entrance arch opens into the ASSIZE HALL, lined with polished Perrycot stone, and crossed by two bridges carried on monolithic Doric columns. The twin COURT-ROOMS, Civil and Criminal, lie beyond, walnut-panelled and lit by lunette windows high up.

The OFFICES in the N range are, of course, utilitarian by contrast with all this. Handsomely detailed spine corridors, nevertheless, at both levels.

123 CROWN COURT, St Helen's Road. 1985–8 by the *Alex Gordon Partnership*. A temple of justice. The site opposite the Guildhall dictated the facing material, Portland stone ashlar, and doubtless encouraged symmetry and formalism too. Two storeys crowned by a deep horizontal eaves band supported on slender rectangular piers, and broken only in the centre by the two V-plan projections which flank the broad, canted window bay above the cavernous entrance. So there is strong central emphasis, reinforced by the broad flight of entrance steps. The translation into classical terms is easy to make, even though classical forms are studiously avoided. But the building is also an essay in mannerist wit. Faceted shapes throughout, used in many places to confound expectations. Thus the angles of the building are chamfered back, and the oriel windows of the courtrooms at first-floor level are blind where they project but glazed where they recede.

WEST GLAMORGAN COUNTY HALL, Oystermouth Road. 1979–84 by the *West Glamorgan County Architects Department*, Director *J. Webb*. The job architect was *C. W. Quick*. Large, low and white, its arms angling out spider-like in all directions. Concrete-framed structure, faced with white aggregate panels. Four and five storeys, the lowest recessed, the others with windows in unbroken bands. Civic significance is indicated at the entrance, by the straight, tree-lined steps and ramp of purple brick that lead towards it and by the Council Chamber projecting polygonally above it. Full-height ENTRANCE HALL of irregular shape, traversed by concrete balconies and bridges. Various works of art and craft are mounted on the walls, including part of *Ceri Richards*'s 'Norwegian Mural', commissioned in 1944 by the Norwegian Government in Exile

*The war scenes are in the National Museum of Wales, Cardiff.

and executed in the British Council offices in Cardiff, now demolished.

H.M. PRISON, Oystermouth Road. 1861. Front of dark local sandstone, rock-faced and ashlar. The entrance arch is rusticated, but otherwise this is a half-hearted attempt at the architecture of menace.

CENTRAL POLICE STATION, in the angle between Alexandra Road and Orchard Street. 1912–13 by *Ernest E. Morgan*, Borough Architect of Swansea from 1913. Red brick and Portland stone. A powerful Baroque composition, striking evidence of how confident even a relatively inexperienced local architect could be at this time in handling the classical vocabulary on a large scale. The principal façade to Alexandra Road, of fifteen bays and two storeys plus attic, has a stone-faced centre framing the main entrance with a pair of giant Ionic columns and supporting an emphasized section of attic, and channelled ends. Similar, more subdued, frontage to Orchard Street. On the angle between them a convex porch in a concave bay, and, above and behind, a square, brick clock tower with an octagonal, stone-faced top stage.

MUSEUM, Cambrian Place. Built as the Royal Institution of 69 South Wales, a splendid Greek Revival building now more isolated than originally intended. 1839–41 by *Frederick Long* of Liverpool. As befits a 'Philosophical Institution' devoted to 'the advancement of Science, Literature and the Arts', Long's design is both rational and scholarly. The building is faced with Bath stone ashlar, single-storeyed with a blind attic. Three-bay portico supported by correct Greek Ionic columns. Three bays to the l. and three to the r., demarcated by antae and lit by Vitruvian windows, i.e. with slightly tapering sides. The central doorway leads to a handsome imperial staircase with a cast iron balustrade of idiosyncratic design. Library to the r., lecture room (altered) to the l. The one-storey laboratory, shaped outside like a sarcophagus, does not survive.

GLYNN VIVIAN ART GALLERY, Alexandra Road. *Glendinning* 114 *Moxham*'s masterpiece, 1909–11. Red brick and Bath stone. The façade, not large, is monumental. The centre five bays are single-storeyed, with a high blank area of walling below the crowning entablature, and a grandly scaled central doorway. This has blocked Doric columns, which carry an open swan-neck pediment, and winged cherub heads and an armorial shield within it. Wider end bays brought forward slightly, and further emphasized by pediments, channelled quoins and giant Frenchy Ionic columns flanking tripartite windows at two levels. The INTERIOR is also full-blooded. Top-lit hall surrounded by a stoutly balustraded balcony on double-strength consoles. Similar, smaller brackets support the segmental glazed roof. At the w end a flight of stairs rises through an arch, and returns to reach the balcony and a series of intimate galleries, some side-lit, some top-lit.

EXTENSION of 1973–4 by *Swansea City Architects Department*. A windowless concrete box hovers over a recessed, glazed

ground storey. Battered plinth of red brick. Visually arresting
in its own right, this nevertheless does nothing to impair Moxham's façade.

CENTRAL LIBRARY AND COLLEGE OF ART, Alexandra Road.
1886–7 by *Henry Holtom* of Dewsbury. Pale red brick and Bath
stone. Thirteen-bay Italianate façade, rather weakly articulated
and given an undersized central tower. Three storeys, with
enriched Doric pilasters below, pedimented windows on the
piano nobile, and a blind attic decorated with swagged discs in
square panels. Inside, the entrance vestibule has a coffered
vault, the corridors are vaulted, and at the back there is an
impressive circular reading room with a dome carried on
cast iron columns forming aisles and provision for radiating
bookcases.

GRAND THEATRE, Singleton Street. Designed by *William Hope*
and opened in 1897. Remodelled and aggrandized 1982–7 for
Swansea City Council. The original frontage, now painted pink
and grey, has its name emblazoned in mannered lettering across
the centre, and slightly projecting ends with steep French pavilion roofs. In front of this an arcade has been added, supporting
a central loggia with curved glazing, and to l. and r. monumental
two-storey pedimented foyers with paired, unfluted, Greek
Doric columns below and, above, Tuscan Doric columns
forming Venetian windows, their arched central lights breaking
up into the pediments. Such confident and cultured classicism
is quite a rarity nowadays. The architects were *McColl Associates*. At the back, bold abstract shapes, a completely different
aesthetic, and the responsibility of a different architect, *John
Colgate* of *Swansea City Architects Department*. The fly tower is
a big, black, glistening box, and the S front builds up to it in
an abstract assemblage of cream walls and red roofs interlocking
apparently at random. The late Victorian INTERIOR of the
theatre has been well restored. Rollicking high relief plasterwork
on the balcony fronts.

PALACE THEATRE (disused), High Street. On a wedge-shaped
site at the corner with Prince of Wales Road. 1888 by *Alfred
Bucknall & E. W. Jennings*. An early attempt at Baroque revival.
The circular entrance tower has lost its dome. Built at the
expense of the Swansea Tramway Company.

WORKING MEN'S CLUB AND INSTITUTE, Alexandra Road.
Dated 1885, an early example of a type of building which would
soon become familiar in the Valleys. Red brick and Bath stone.
Three storeys plus an attic with flamboyant dormer windows.
Second Empire style. By an obscure local architect, *Benjamin
Williams*.

BRITISH BROADCASTING COMPANY HEADQUARTERS, Alexandra Road. Jacobean style. A post-bombing reconstruction of
H. W. Wills's Poor Law Union Offices of 1898–9. A good deal
of pretty sculpture survives.

TELEPHONE EXCHANGE, The Strand. 1970 by *Alex Gordon &
Partners*. Twelve-storey block with full-height, concrete-faced
service tower. The recladding of 1991–2 does not make it loom

any less ominously over the High Street and Castle Square.
TECHNICAL COLLEGE (now part of Swansea Institute of Higher
Education), Mount Pleasant. In several parts, mid- to late C19
and mid- to late C20. What dominates is of 1897–8,
H. W. Wills's entrance tower and back-to-back ranges filling
the angle between Mount Pleasant and Bryn-Syfi Terrace. Red
brick and Portland stone. Tudor style, the five-storey tower
with a four-centred entrance arch and angle buttresses. Arched
lights to the mullion-and-transom windows. In the ranges
behind, similar windows with straight-headed lights. Good
ironwork. The building is unfinished at its N end. A bridge
across Bryn-Syfi Terrace links to a lower range faced with
Pennant sandstone. Pretty cupola. This must be the block
added in 1907–8 by *G.E.T. Laurence*.

Further down the hill, within the complex, parts of the former
GRAMMAR SCHOOL, now disused and at the time of writing
in disrepair. The Grammar School, first established in 1682,
was refounded with a new set of buildings on Mount Pleasant,
erected 1851–3. They were in a Tudor style, designed by *Thomas
Taylor*. The surviving early Gothic three-storey range on the
downhill side is an addition of 1869 by *Benjamin Bucknall*.
Snecked Pennant sandstone with Bath stone dressings. The
tall, plate-traceried and double-transomed windows of the main
storey lit a dining hall and library, spanned internally by dia-
phragm arches. This bold expression of a structural feature is
a reminder that Bucknall was an admirer of Viollet-le-Duc.
(Hooded fireplaces and stencilled walls in the main rooms.)

The many recent additions are of no special interest. Uphill
from Wills's building, a curtain-wall block of four and five
storeys massed in a way that echoes it.

In STANLEY TERRACE, on a precipitous site W of Mount
Pleasant, the former CAMBRIAN DEAF AND DUMB
ASYLUM. Pennant sandstone with Bath stone dressings.
Tudor style. Centre three bays by *J. H. Baylis*, *c.*1855. Two-
storey flanking wings presumably also by him, soon after 1860.
The six-bay Victoria Wing added to the l. is dated 1899.

DYNEVOR COMPREHENSIVE SCHOOL, between Pell Street
and De-la-Beche Street. Built from 1891 in more than one
phase, left incomplete, and after war damage, shorn of its top
storey and gables and given a glazed, flat-roofed third storey.
The original elevations are of Pennant sandstone with meagre
Bath stone dressings. Mullion-and-transom windows. The first
part was built as the Higher Grade school for 480 boys, 1891
by *T. P. Martin* of Swansea. In 1909 *G.E.T. Laurence* made an
addition. Reconstruction completed 1958, HALL added 1960,
by *H. T. Wykes*, Swansea Borough Architect.

PRIMARY SCHOOL, St Alban's Road, Brynmill. Built as a board
school by *G. E. T. Laurence*, opened 1896. Red brick.

MOUNT PLEASANT HOSPITAL, Mount Pleasant. This was the
Swansea Union Workhouse. Its first buildings on this site,
1860–1 by *W. Richards*, partly survive. The handsome if sombrely
coloured Baroque range towards the road was built 1902–4 as

the Infirmary, to the designs of *W. H. Wills* of *Wills & Williams* of London. Snecked Pennant sandstone and Forest of Dean ashlar. Central three-bay pavilion of three storeys under an open segmental pediment carried on bulgy Doric pilasters. At the ends of the range, front and back, one-bay wings come forward, crowned by miniature domes. Unfortunate recent additions in all directions obscure the lines of this composition.

VICTORIA PARK, St Helen's Avenue. Laid out as a public park in 1887, and quite small, though originally it included the site of the Guildhall. The seaward angle is dominated by the PATTI PAVILION, with its memorable boat-shaped, corrugated-iron-clad roof. Cast iron structure, now largely concealed. Built probably in 1891, as a winter garden at the country house of the singer Dame Adelina Patti, Craig y Nos Castle, Ystradgyn-lais, just over the border in Breconshire. Re-erected here in 1920, after Patti had bequeathed it to the citizens of Swansea.

UNIVERSITY COLLEGE OF SWANSEA
(Singleton Park)

In 1919 Swansea Technical College was admitted as a constituent part of the University of Wales. Coincidentally, in the same year the second Lord Swansea sold Singleton Abbey, his family home and estate, to the Corporation of Swansea. In 1920 the Corporation rented and in 1923 sold the house and the nucleus of the estate to the University College, which made the Abbey its administrative headquarters. The first permanent college building, the Library, was opened in 1937, SW of the Abbey. From 1957 a new start was made, further to the SW, with buildings grouped in relation to an axial approach from the Mumbles Road below. This has created a compact group of buildings across the lower slopes of the park, leaving to the N and NW tracts of undulating green dotted with forest trees. In the park and round its edges several estate buildings survive, so that it still makes sense to explore Singleton Abbey and its park separately from the university campus.

SINGLETON ABBEY. The nucleus, far from anything monastic, is a Neoclassical villa, octagonal in plan, erected in 1784 under the name of Marino by Edward King, a customs official. In 1817 this was bought by someone far more significant in Swansea's history, John Henry Vivian, son of the founder, and himself for many years the manager, of the copper-smelting works at Hafod, which became the principal source of Swansea's C19 prosperity. In 1818 King's curious edifice was absorbed as the canted three-bay centre of a standard Regency box by the addition of rectangular one-bay extensions to either side. But Vivian did not want to appear merely as a recently arrived industrialist: his roots in the Cornish gentry mattered to him too. So in 1823 he began to plan a much more radical trans-formation and extension to the design of a leading Neo-medieval exponent, *P. F. Robinson*. Work started in 1827, and a decade later Robinson published *Domestic Architecture in the Tudor Style*, a monograph in all but name on Singleton Abbey. The house survives, with limited losses, much as it appears in the engraved plates of the book.

The house is approached from the E where its pretensions are at once apparent. The drive turns towards it between the high parapets of a pseudo-bridge and a pair of heraldic mastiffs, and opens into the forecourt, which is dominated by a tall, octagonal lamp standard surrounded by four mounting blocks. On the forecourt walls stand font-like flower vases. The house itself continued this exclamatory style, until, in 1987, the 63-ft (19.2-metre)-high tower at the r. of the entrance front was pulled down. The two-storey body of the house is crowned by small, steep-sided gable up and down which crocket-shaped animals scramble, the bulbous tops of polygonal buttresses, and an array of variously patterned chimneystacks. Mullion-and-transom windows. The E front has a one-storey porch in its l. bay, and a single-storey dining room projecting to the r. This is what it appears, an afterthought, run up early in 1837 when Princess Victoria was expected to visit. Deliberately chapel-like, three bays by one, with Dec traceried windows under ogee, crocketed hoodmoulds and full-height buttresses bearing empty image niches. The S front is the least altered, its canted central three bays and its symmetry clearly indicating that Marino and its wings survive in Tudor disguise. This explains why the walls are rendered throughout, not faced with stone. Even the curious fenestration pattern, three-storeyed in the cant, two-storeyed in the side bays, was imposed by the pre-existing house. The W front is more irregular and has been altered. In particular Robinson's large L-shaped conservatory has gone. Terrace walls and steps of Robinson's formal garden here. The service ranges stood to the N and NW, but were badly damaged by fire in 1896. Simple STABLE BLOCK free-standing to the N, built between 1837 and 1851.

The INTERIOR retains much original work, and still demonstrates the planning problems produced by the need to wrap the new house round the old one. No major S-facing room was possible. Instead, Robinson provided a lavishly spacious stair-hall beyond the entrance hall. Ceilings with thin beams and bosses at the intersections throughout, and wide, four-centred arches below and above on three sides of the (originally) cantilevered timber stair. Heraldic glass in the staircase window, by *Willement*, before 1840. The entrance hall and the room N of it both have made-up timber overmantels (not shown in Robinson's plates), the former with a C16 standing figure surrounded by heraldic panels in a profusion of thistly Düreresque mantling, the latter incorporating a Nativity scene. Flanking the fireplace, what appear to be C16 pew-ends, with relief figures of St Jerome and the Woman of Samaria. N of this, an anteroom, its overmantel centred on the arms of the French dauphin. In the dining room, a chimneypiece with twisted columns and carved window pelmets, as shown in Robinson's

engraving. Later heraldic frieze. The w-facing drawing room was remodelled later in the C19 and given a classical plaster cornice and a pair of marble chimneypieces. The back stairs, on the axis of the s front, and the ground-floor room in the centre of the s front, with a bowed inner end, survive from the original house of 1784.

To the NE of the Abbey the SCHOOL OF SOCIAL STUDIES, a crisp three-storey block of grey brick, 1961–2 by *Sir Percy Thomas & Son* (design partner *Dale Owen*). The ground floor open on square pilotis which carry shallow pointed arches,

SINGLETON PARK

ABBEY MEADOW

Swansea, University College. Isometric plan

substituted for the segmental arches originally intended. Windows in continuous bands, narrowing sharply at intervals.

Of J. H. Vivian's park buildings, the most conspicuous is BRYNMILL LODGE, at the SE corner, a landmark on the Mumbles road. This is clearly by *Henry Woodyer*, the architect to whom Vivian transferred his allegiance in his later years (*see* Sketty, p. 617). Gothic, three-storeyed and gabled in all four directions, built integrally with the entrance arch. Triangular peep window for the porter. Finely squared and snecked local stone with Bath stone dressings. Its date is not known, though it is as emphatically post-Pugin as the house is pre-Pugin. But *Robinson* did provide some LODGES, single-storeyed in the cottage orné tradition, of randomly laid stone with roof-slopes coming low down and big lozenge-plan chimneystacks. One survives, somewhat enlarged, at the SW corner of the park, at the foot of Sketty Lane. A second, THATCHED LODGE, within the NW segment of the park, on the road to the Home Farm, remains thatched, a charmingly unaltered specimen. Robinson published the design for this in 1833.

The HOME FARM itself was a well-appointed complex, though now partly derelict, the barn roofless, the pretty octagonal well-head falling apart.* *P. F. Robinson* seems to have laid it out. The Bailiff's House incorporates a set of early C16 windows from New Place, Swansea, the town mansion of Sir Matthew Cradock (†1531), demolished in 1840. Three-lighters below, two-lighters above, slightly too big for the gablets they are set in. Arched lights and hollow-chamfered mullions. The lower windows have hoodmoulds with extravagant lozenge-shaped stops.

In the EDUCATIONAL GARDEN at the N end of the park-like campus, gaily painted, timber SWISS CHALET, dated 1826 and bearing inscriptions in French and German. Also published by *P. F. Robinson*. In the gardeners' compound, VERANDAH, a small Gothic house of stone, dated 1853. Attributed to Woodyer.

The UNIVERSITY COLLEGE campus is, as explained above, approached from MUMBLES ROAD. The tightly knit group of buildings which cluster round the axial main drive are mostly by *Sir Percy Thomas & Son*, 1957–63, in the undemonstrative modern idiom of that period. Earliest is the NATURAL SCIENCE BUILDING, W of the main drive. Spreading two-storey block on an H-plan. Brown brick. Windows in rectangular panels, showing in their proportions that the firm had not entirely shaken off its pre-war classicism. FULTON HOUSE, the axial building at the head of the drive, is a more confident statement. 1958–62, design partner *Norman Thomas*. Still symmetrical, still on an H-plan, and faced with brown brick, but the centre range glazed from top to bottom and virtually from side to side. Behind the glass are four dining halls, one at first-floor level for the entire student body, and three at the level above. Reinforced concrete structure with slender internal pilotis. Severe decorative scheme in the main hall by *Misha Black*. On the W wall, Rape of Europa by *Ceri Richards*, 1970. Three HALLS OF RESIDENCE, thirteen-storeyed, set *en échelon* at the back of the site, 1960–8, design partner *Dale Owen*.

To the E of the main drive, ENGINEERING DEPARTMENT, *c.* 1967–73. In a freer arrangement, an eight-storey slab between, with, on the downhill side, a large, four-storey double court-yard, and, set at r.-angles on the uphill side, a slab of only two

*In the opinion of Nigel Temple.

tall storeys. They form a courtyard to the E, the fourth side of which is closed by the most distinguished building on the Campus, the LIBRARY EXTENSION of 1963–4, design partner *Dale Owen*. Two tall storeys, the upper fully glazed, with an exposed structure of steel portal frames, black, slender and close-set. Double-height interior with a broad bridge across the space and seating at both levels. The MAIN LIBRARY, set to the NE, on the croquet lawn of Singleton Abbey, is all that was executed of a pre-war master plan. In 1934 *Verner O. Rees* won the competition for the whole layout, and built the library 1935–7. Brown brick with Portland stone dressings. Sub-classical. Clerestory windows subdivided by close-set imposts. Internally, exposed reinforced concrete trusses carry a coffered concrete ceiling.

The Engineering Department and library stand on the S side of THE MALL, the access road which links the main drive to Singleton Abbey. On the N side of The Mall, TALIESIN, theatre and art gallery, opened in 1984. By the *Peter Moro Partnership*. Moro had made his name as a theatre designer twenty years earlier with the Nottingham Playhouse. Here he presents the more sculptural, non-rectilinear image popular by the end of the 1970s. Brown brick. The plan is an irregular polygon, the entrance slanting into the depths of the building. Oblique angles in the foyer too, with balconies at several levels. Auditorium with two boldly canted balconies.

PERAMBULATIONS

1. The town centre, starting from St Mary's Square

ST MARY'S SQUARE lies by the civic church. Modern shopping parades on most sides. To the W QUADRANT SHOPPING CENTRE, 1976–80 by the *Building Design Partnership*. On the S side, ST DAVID'S SHOPPING CENTRE, opened in 1982. This has created a series of intricately interlinked spaces between St Mary's church and St David's Priory. STATUE of Sir H. Hussey Vivian, first Lord Swansea of Singleton, resited here on its tall pedestal of Aberdeen granite. Originally set up in Castle Square in 1886. The bronze statue, of a substantial figure in frock coat and gown, standing by a pile of books, is signed by *M. Raggi*, 1884. To the E, in St Mary's Square, SWANSEA COUNTY COURT AND OFFICES, dated 1908. Red brick and Bath stone. Arts and Crafts Tudor. Chimneybreast with a cartouche pinned to it, turning the corner into PRINCESS WAY. Across the road, the CROSS KEYS INN, of stone, showing towards ST MARY'S STREET a reconstructed C17 front (1950 by *Victor Ward*), but at the back a much earlier structure. This belonged to the Hospital of the Blessed St David, founded by Henry de Gower, Bishop of St David's, in 1332. Trefoiled lancets of Sutton stone, boldly chamfered. The window at mid-height, a two-lighter, lit a room which lay behind a first-floor hall in the range facing St Mary's Street.

CAER STREET, to the W of the hospital, soon leads into Castle
Square, but not before breaking out into a rash of half-
timbering: BEAU NASH HOUSE, dating amazingly to the
1950s. At the corner one should turn r. into WIND STREET.
Here at once on the S side, MIDLAND BANK, the showiest of
the classical banks which form the leitmotif of the street. 1908–
10 by *F. Adams Smith*, enlarged 1914. Portland stone and just
a little yellow brick walling. The main front exhibits the usual
motifs, a channelled arcaded ground storey in a 1+3+1 rhythm,
and above, side bays with channelled quoins and open top
pediments. But all this is overshadowed by the columned
entrance turret on the corner, rising concave above convex to
a balcony and dome. A little way down on the other side,
No. 6, a stone-faced frontage with superimposed pilasters and
mullion-and-transom window bays, is of 1897. No. 7, tall and
narrow, banded in buff Bath stone and local pink sandstone,
and crowned by a scroll-framed gable, must be of a similar
date. Next to note on the S side, BARCLAY'S BANK, the
channelled lower storey of black marble, the centre three bays
demarcated by Ionic half-columns with garlanded capitals, the
side bays set slightly forward with channelled quoins. The
architect of this urbane performance was *Glendinning Moxham*,
1915. A short way further on, past Nos. 53–55, survivors from
the original street-line of *c.* 1800, the NATIONAL WESTMIN-
STER BANK, 1927–9, presumably by the in-house architects of
the National Provincial Bank, *F. C. R. Palmer & W. F. C.
Holden*. This is a significant time lapse, for Baroque flam-
boyance has given way to a precise classicism, though the
narrow-wide-narrow rhythm persists. In fact the central one-
bay banking hall flanked by the two entrances is more explicitly
expressed than ever, by means of giant Ionic columns. Portland
stone. Thereafter interest crosses back to the N side, and first
to No. 10, built as the GENERAL POST OFFICE 1898–1901,
the centrally dominant building in the whole street. Conceived
like a late medieval Flemish town hall, it is faced with Bath
stone and generous areas of green Bridgend stone. Recessed
centre and ends, three-bay projections under big shaped gables.
Steeply pitched roof and central openwork cupola. The
'government architect' who designed this showpiece does not
deserve his anonymity. *W. T. Oldrieve* was architect to the Post
Office at the time. The final building to note is LLOYDS BANK,
1910–12 by *Waller & Son* of Gloucester. A five-bay Portland
stone palazzo, in the usual rhythm, with rich Ionic half-columns
in the central bays above.

After this the inner bypass cuts across, but by taking the underpass
it is possible to reach one of the architecturally most impressive
corners of the town. First a fragment of Regency Swansea, Nos.
1–6 PROSPECT PLACE, which demonstrate three different
ways of using relieving arches, small or giant, to enliven a
terrace front. Presumably all were originally of exposed red
brick, as No. 6 still is. Round to the l. on the corner of FERRY
SIDE and BATH LANE, another early C19 survivor, rendered,

with flat rusticated window surrounds and etiolated, giant Ionic angle pilasters. Much more important are the public buildings. The OLD GUILDHALL fronting on to SOMERSET PLACE is the noblest classical building in Swansea. *Thomas Bowen*'s Guildhall of 1825–9 was swallowed up in the grandiose Corinthian palazzo built 1848–52 by the little-known *Thomas Taylor* of London. Bath stone. Nine bays by six. Two storeys with arched windows at both levels, those below absorbed in channelling, those above moulded and given imposts which interlink them as an arcade. The most remarkable feature is the handling of the Corinthian columns of the upper storey. In the end bays of each façade they stand proudly forward, and the entablature breaks forward over them. The centre bays, two on the short end, three on the long front, have attached columns of distinctly lesser projection. Reconstructed in 1993–4 by *The Wigley Fox Partnership*, retaining only the three columned external walls, for the National Centre for Literature. SOMERSET PLACE, opposite, is a lively newcomer, dated 1987, really part of the Marina development. Four-storey terrace of red brick punctuated by five-storey gabled projections faced with buff reconstituted stone. Arch-topped vertical strips of windows the full height of these, a hackneyed reference to the hoists of C19 warehouses.

The OFFICES OF THE ASSOCIATED BRITISH PORTS, on the corner, facing ADELAIDE STREET, were built for Swansea Harbour Trust in 1902–3 by *Edwin Seward* of Cardiff. Red brick and Portland stone counterpointed with endless resource. Arts and Crafts Baroque. A good deal of sculpture, in particular seated figures over the entrance doorway and on the tower, high up against the octagonal stage which supports the domical copper cap. In its composition – a long symmetrical front, and a tower over the short return – the building surely echoes the City Hall in Cardiff (*see* p. 222), then still under construction. (Domed stair-hall, and first-floor boardroom with segmental coffered ceiling.) Continuing in Adelaide Street, the EVENING POST building, a straightforward 1960s block, makes an abrupt contrast. Built 1964–7. *Mercer & Howells* and *Ellis, Clarke & Gallanaugh* were involved in its design. Then comes the EXCHANGE BUILDINGS, 1913–14 by *Charles T. Ruthen*. Portland stone. Classical. On the façade to Adelaide Street the building adopts the façade formula of contemporary banks, in spite of the extra storey to fit in. Large arched windows, to light a ground-floor restaurant, in channelled surrounds. Above, paired Ionic columns with square volutes. Fully channelled end bays under complex attics. Mullion-and-transom windows in the two main storeys. The curved principal front, round in CAMBRIAN PLACE, unrolls yet more elaborately. It is in five sections, channelled in the centre, where there are giant, recessed, Ionic columns, an attic and a scroll-framed clock, and also at the ends, to match the Adelaide Street façade. The exchange hall, originally under a stained-glass dome, is entered from Cambrian Place. Offices in the upper storeys. Further E

in Cambrian Place, first another piece of early C20 classicism,
PEMBROKE BUILDINGS, *c.* 1913 by *H. C. Portsmouth.* Handsome five-bay palazzo of three storeys, Portland stone below,
red brick and Bath stone above.

The ASSEMBLY ROOMS next door, part of the street-line, is one
of the most important survivals of Regency Swansea, designed
(after a design of 1804 by *S. P. Cockerell* had been rejected) by
William Jernegan in 1810, and opened in 1821. The five-bay
façade is curious, almost Soanic in its use of incised lines.
Dark grey stone below, rendered above. A colonnade of widely
spaced Doric columns carrying a slab-like architrave is set
against channelled walling, while in the upper storey the end
bays are channelled and flanked by pilaster strips. Incised voussoirs over the windows and door in the channelled walling.
Incised rectangular panels above and below the windows where
the walls are smooth. Soanic touches in the adjacent terrace,
Nos. 6–37 – a terrace of eight in spite of the numbering. Three-
storeyed, faced with red brick. Highly eccentric and rather
lovable, with metal canopies tucked into the relieving arches
over the outsize piano nobile windows, and an oddly syncopated fenestration pattern. Retracing one's steps one can
admire the Museum (p. 593), standing in splendid isolation at
the entrance to Cambrian Place. From here it is a short walk
down Gloucester Place to the former South Dock, now the
Maritime Quarter.

In GLOUCESTER PLACE, an early C19 stucco terrace on the r.
with rusticated stone door surrounds. Further along on the l.
Benjamin Bucknall's little neo-Norman ST NICHOLAS
CHURCH for seamen, of 1868. Now converted into an arts'
workshop.

MARITIME QUARTER. Of the three dock redevelopments in the
county, at Cardiff, Penarth and Swansea, this is the only one
so far completed. The acknowledged prototype is Honfleur in
Normandy. The quarter's watery spine consists of the long,
narrow SOUTH DOCK and the square TAWE BASIN to the E,
close to the outlet into the River Tawe. The dock had been
closed in 1969 and partly infilled. A few buildings associated
with its original function have been retained; but otherwise
everything on this wedge-shaped tract between the Oystermouth Road and the shoreline of Swansea Bay postdates 1975.
The project was masterminded by the City Council, which
acquired every site as it came on the market, re-excavated the
dock and let the water back in. Further funding came from the
Welsh Development Agency and the European Community.
Most of the housing development has been undertaken by
housing associations. Closeness to the city centre is a major
reason why the development has succeeded. The pedestrian
approach, from the NE down Gloucester Place, has been
described above. Vehicles driving into the Maritime Quarter,
however, must make for its W tip, turning S off OYS-
TERMOUTH ROAD (A4067) into BATHURST STREET, and so
into TRAWLER ROAD, which skirts the S side of the South

Dock and runs through to the wharf on the riverbank at the far
SE corner.

Gloucester Place leads into DYLAN THOMAS SQUARE. The
bronze STATUE, 1984, of the seated, tousle-haired poet is
signed by *John Doubleday*. Beyond is the narrow sluice between
the South Dock and Tawe Basin, and beside it the PUMP-
HOUSE, dated 1900, a piece of genuine maritime architecture
at the outset. Red brick, with black brick outlines to the blind
arches. Now converted into a restaurant. The MARITIME AND
INDUSTRIAL MUSEUM to the W is also housed in an early
C20 building. This is the formidable twenty-one-bay banana
warehouse on the N quay of the South Dock, built in 1901.
Dark red brick. Lombardic gable ends. Cast iron colonnade on
the landward side. In the water at this point a fine collection of
historic transport vessels. Further on, VICTORIA QUAY and
ARETHUSA QUAY, recent four- and five-storey terraces raised
on arcades beside the waterfront. Deliberate imitation of Victorian warehouses in the vertical balcony strips under gablets.
Red and yellow brick and buff blockwork. MARRIOTS HOTEL,
across the W end of the dock, is a variant on the same theme.
1986–7 by *Cobban & Lironi* of Glasgow.

The heart of the Maritime Quarter lies S of the water. From
Dylan Thomas Square it is a short step across the bridge W of
the Tawe Basin to the MARITIME VILLAGE, four loosely
interlocked squares SE of the South Dock, 1984–7 by the *Burgess
Partnership*. Two-, three- and four-storey terraces of flats, with
emphasized gable ends. Metal balconies coloured bright red
and blue. FERRARA SQUARE, the most formal space, is at the
W end. Here a Victorian statue has been resited. Bronze figure
of J. H. Vivian by *J. Evan Thomas*, dated 1857, on a tall plinth
of polished Cornish granite. (It originally stood in the courtyard
of the Old Guildhall.)

Across Trawler Road to the SE, FERRARA QUAY, the most
ambitious part of the entire scheme. 1985–8 by the *Halliday
Meecham Partnership* of Alderley Edge, in collaboration with
Robin Campbell, the City Council's special projects officer.
Their efforts have created a thorough-going Post-Modern
environment, where echoes of vernacular architecture jangle
against classical quotations, where celebration of the city's
industrial and maritime past is juxtaposed to parody and joke,
where every corner seems to spring a new surprise. Buildings,
sculpture and inscriptions conspire to make the visitor smile.

Facing South Dock across TRAWLER ROAD, four- and five-
storey terraces of red and yellow brick, with gabled end
pavilions and green and blue metal balconies. The Victorian
warehouse reminiscences are meant to be recognized. At the W
end SEA GATE creates a climax. Curved range with a polygonal
end and, to the N, a clock tower incorporating flying figures of
winds copied from the Athenian Tower of the Winds of the C4
B.C. Below it a lock gate has been built into the wall, from
which cascades marble water, transformed as it touches the
ground into Ionic volutes to provide a series of seats. Sundry

inscriptions and armorial panels, carved by *Philip Chatfield*, some referring to Ferrara (the Italian city twinned with Swansea, and its famous Palazzo Schifanoia).

124 The centre of Ferrara Quay is pedestrianized. PATAGONIA WALK leads in under a giant four-storey arch and through a pergola-like open triangular pediment on posts. Further w CHELHYDRA WALK does the same under an open segmental pediment. Here three-storey gabled pavilions with prominent porthole windows stand among lavish landscaping. Ingeniously concealed underground garaging.

Finally to the s, MARINA WALK, a complete seafront promenade. Here the terraces are three-storeyed and rendered, and have shiny round canopies to the first-floor balconies, in parodic reference to Regency seaside architecture. In two places the terraces curve back, to form ST VINCENT CRESCENT and OCEAN CRESCENT. In the centre of the circular space created by the former, GLOBE SUNDIAL by *Wendy Taylor*. In the similar site in the latter, LIGHTHOUSE TOWER, with a crazy metal sculpture on top by *Robert Conybear*. Shops in the Crescents also. At the far E end of Marine Walk, TOWER OF THE ECLIPTIC, 1989 by *Robin Campbell*. At first sight this appears a Heath Robinson assemblage, but it is in fact an Observatory, run by the Swansea Astronomical Society. Rectangular observatory block of white painted brick, cylindrical stair-turret of beige brick glazed at the top and crowned by a figurehead representing Charles Darwin. Well-lettered inscription panels on three sides, referring to light and the cosmos.

2. The hillside N of the town centre

During the second half of the C19 the town expanded westwards, and the hillside behind gradually became covered with terraces and villas of the middle classes, who continued to favour Swansea as a seaside resort and focus of cultural activities in the county.

The route to the W and N from ST MARY'S SQUARE can take in many chapels and public buildings along the way (*see* pp. 586–96). Immediately to the W lies the QUADRANT CENTRE, 1976–80 by the *Building Design Partnership* (partner-in-charge *Kit Evans*), which provides covered shopping close to the site of the celebrated Oxford Street Market of 1889 (destroyed by bombing), by *J. Buckley Wilson & Glendinning Moxham*. The present covered MARKET, N of the Quadrant Centre, is much smaller and dates from 1959–61 by *Sir Percy Thomas & Partners* (design partners *Norman Thomas* and *Howell Mendus*). Roof in four bays on curved steel braces painted blue. OXFORD STREET itself has little to offer. The only eye-catcher is *C. T. Ruthen*'s CARLTON CINEMA, just beyond the corner with Union Street. Built in 1913–14 for the Swansea Electric Cinema Company, closed in 1977 and still forlornly derelict. But this is of real historical importance as one of the earliest showpiece cinemas, and a splendidly swaggering piece of Baroque design. The memorable feature is the convex glazing of the central arch, lighting a monumental oval staircase. Giant Ionic flanking columns, drastically out of scale with the three tiers of colonnettes on the domed stair-towers which round out the façade. The front is faced with Doulton's white Carrara ware, above a bronzed ground storey. Reliefs of playing putti on the towers.

In UNION STREET, round the corner to the N, MOND BUILD-INGS, another piece of *Ruthen*'s Baroque, dated 1911 in the central pediment. Sir Alfred Mond paid for it, to be the local headquarters of the National League of Young Liberals. Of Portland stone and in the hybrid style of Ruthen's Exchange Buildings (*see* above). Over the (altered) ground-floor shops, two storeys linked by part-fluted giant Ionic columns. Swagged capitals, some with boys sitting on the swags. Mullion-and-transom windows in broad bows. Over the chamfered entrance corner, an open attic belvedere decorated with dragons. Door-ways at the outer ends of the building, with pediments and blocked columns.

Union Street runs into THE KINGSWAY, where the Y.M.C.A. BUILDING stands opposite, a busily detailed classical block in thin-coursed red brick and Portland stone, by *Glendinning Moxham*, 1912–13. MOUNT PLEASANT BAPTIST CHURCH is a short way to the E. To the W the road-name changes to ST HELEN'S ROAD, where further mighty chapels appear at intervals. Otherwise nothing special here. Evidence on the N side of the original development of the road in the mid C19. First PAGEFIELD HOUSE (Quaker Meeting House) of 1858, red brick, Tudor, with fancy bargeboards. Then, some way further on, Nos. 137–148, an ambitious stuccoed composition of the 1840s. Four villa pairs decorated with Corinthian pil-asters and linked by single-storey screens of Ionic columns. After that, on the corner of BRYN-Y-MOR ROAD, the sur-viving pavilion of *Alexander Graham*'s INFIRMARY, 1867–9. Pennant sandstone. Three storeys under a steep roof and spirelet.

To gain a more coherent picture of Swansea's mid-Victorian domestic architecture, it is necessary to start again in The Kingsway and cross into CRADOCK STREET as it runs N to join the next E–W road contouring round the base of the hillside. At this point called DE-LA-BECHE STREET, to the E it soon becomes ALEXANDRA ROAD, where the handsomest group of public buildings in Swansea is clustered, all of red brick with stone dressings (*see* pp. 593–4). Continuous terraces of houses begin to the W, where the road changes name twice more, first to MANSEL STREET, then WALTER ROAD. Characteristic close-set gables and single-storey window bays. Stuccoed frontages.

ST JAMES'S CRESCENT, enclosing St James's church on the N side, is the centrepiece of the only street layout that breaks the grid-iron pattern on the hillside. Here and in ST JAMES'S GARDENS, climbing up the hill behind, more stuccoed terraced housing, sub-classical rather than gabled. A few stone-built

houses, just a few years later, inserted here and there. In
FFYNONE ROAD, the broad, straight road which runs across
at r.-angles, several more impressive houses. At the W end it is
lined on both sides with stuccoed houses of the 1850s. Above
is a terrace of five, making a symmetrical composition by means
of pilasters and slight projections and recessions. Below, RICH-
MOND VILLAS, semi-detached pairs in the same style. HILL-
SIDE, which looks directly down the W half of St James's
Gardens, is an Italianate villa, faced with Bath stone ashlar.
Tower at one angle, arcaded at the top. Strapwork embellishments. The house which looks down the E half of the
Gardens, also ashlar-faced, is, on the other hand, symmetrical.
Full-height canted window bays, the lower windows with tri-
angular pediments.

Further E, on the corner of FFYNONE DRIVE, a one-storey
LODGE dated 1901. A characteristic little classical essay of the
turn of the century. Doric columns at the angles, and a mansard
roof with tall dormers. Is this by Glendinning Moxham? Finally,
lying back in its own grounds up the hill, the MANSION
HOUSE, official residence of the Lord Mayor of Swansea.
This substantial and irregularly composed Tudor Gothic villa,
formerly known as Brooklands House, was built 1859–63 by the
local architect *William Richards*, for his brother. Dark walling of
snecked Pennant stone with dark ashlar dressings.

Back in Walter Road, a detour to the S down Bryn-y-Mor Road
into EATON CRESCENT leads to another villa once in its own
spacious grounds, BRYN-Y-MÔR, now Stella Maris Ursuline
Convent. This belongs to an earlier phase of Swansea's development as a marine resort, and is a late work by *William Jernegan*,
c. 1820. Neoclassical, of course, just three bays and two storeys.
Entrance front with broad pilaster strips, to the rear, windows
under relieving arches. No original interiors, as the house was
burnt out in 1867. Large later additions.

To the N of Walter Road, in MIRADOR CRESCENT, neo-Wren
JEHOVAH'S WITNESSES' HALL, built c. 1914 by *Glendinning
Moxham* for Christian Scientists. The very ambitious Wren
pastiche church he designed to go with it was never built. At this
point there is another name change, as Walter Road becomes
UPLANDS CRESCENT. Here both sides are lined with stuccoed terraces of two-and-a-half-storeyed houses, the insistently
close-set gables retaining their bargeboards. Single-storey
canted bay windows. More in the roads to the N, in particular
RICHMOND TERRACE, with a fine array of cut-out bargeboards. At the E end of RICHMOND ROAD, the house called
RICHMOND is probably by *G. Moxham*, 1903, in a Norman
Shaw style.

Finally, after Uplands Crescent has become SKETTY ROAD, the
best group of all, lying back on the N side of the road. BECK
HALL (University College hall of residence) consists of four
linked pairs of classical villas, faced with Bath stone. The
slightly overblown detail suggests a date c. 1860. On either side,
long, continuous terraces, three-storeyed, with double-height

canted bays, and serried bargeboarded gables. Of red brick.
Similar terraces in the side-roads here, presumably all part of
the great expansion to the w which took place in the 1850s.
No. 50 Sketty Road, beyond HAWTHORNE ROAD, is a classical
villa of *c.* 1860 faced with Bath stone ashlar.

An out-lier, high above everything else, CWMDONKIN NURSING
HOME, reached from Uplands Crescent, via Glanmor Road
and PENLAN CRESCENT. 1902–3 by *Glendinning Moxham*.
Tile-hung gables over a Doric colonnade.

NORTHERN COMMUNITIES

The smelting and tinplating industry on which Swansea's prosperity and growth during the C19 so greatly depended was largely
concentrated on the banks of the River Tawe immediately NE of
the town. The White Rock, Hafod, Morfa, Upper and Middle
Bank and Landore copperworks were the most important, with
the major tinplate works further N at Morriston (*see* below, p.
623). On the rising ground to the w, upwind of the poisonous
fumes, close-set streets of terraced houses were laid out, separated
from Swansea itself by the Town Hill. These form a series of
communities, barely differentiated from one another, but each
with its own identity and name. To the N of the Carmarthen
Road, from E to w, lie Hafod, Cwmbwrla and Cwmdu, and N of
these, w of the Neath road, Manselton, Brynhyfryd, Landore and
Plas-marl extend in loose sequence. Everything of architectural
interest in these communities is listed together in this section. At
the end accounts will be found of the scanty industrial remains,
arranged from s to N.

CHURCHES, CHAPELS AND PUBLIC BUILDINGS

ST JOHN THE BAPTIST, Odo Street, Hafod. 1878–80, an unexpected date for this essay in full-blown Perp.* By *Henry
Woodyer*, not an architect who otherwise favoured such a style.
The explanation is that the church was a Vivian benefaction.
J. H. Vivian, as early as 1849, had conceived the notion of
building a church here on the model of the late medieval St
Mary's, Truro, in Cornwall, but much wider. Thirty years later
his son realized the idea. Only the E front displays the full
splendour of the design. Gabled chancel and full-length gabled
s aisle share a boldly moulded plinth. The one has a seven-
light, the other a six-light E window, opening up the wall-space
between slender flanking buttresses. The design continues for
three bays on the s side, with four-light windows, but thereafter
the design is drastically reduced, to two-lighters with enriched
Y-tracery. To the w, evidence that a tower was intended at the
end of the aisle. The complete design for the s front, with the
tower, is engraved on a brass plate set in the N wall inside.

*This account is based on notes compiled by Peter Howell.

The INTERIOR must have looked extremely strange before the recent E–W subdivision, two equal seven-bay spaces separated by an arcade of octagonal piers carrying pronouncedly four-centred arches. Vestigial chancel arch. Handsome roof, of arch-brace and collar-beam type, the trusses twice as closely spaced over the chancel as over the nave. Horizontal metal ties as well, part of the original design. – FONT and PULPIT. Of stone, designed by *Woodyer*. – CHOIR STALLS. Arm-rests carved with figures and dragons. Brought in? – STAINED GLASS. Chancel N, Christ preaching. 1928 by *A. K. Nicholson*.

ST LUKE, Stepney Street, Cwmdu. 1889–90 by *E. M. Bruce Vaughan*. Rock-faced Pennant sandstone and Bath stone. Nave with cross-gabled aisles, lower chancel. There was even money for an economical SW tower. Twin-shafted belfry openings, pyramidal spire rising behind an ashlar parapet. Arcades with round piers. – STAINED GLASS. Chancel E, Crucified Christ between St Luke and St Peter, 1921 by *Wippell & Co.* of Exeter. – Nave W, Luke and Paul at Troas. 1968 by *Celtic Studios*. – N aisle, three windows by the same. – NW window, a delayed war memorial. Poppies. 1988 by *Wendy Gee*.

ST MARK, Park Terrace, Cwmbwrla. 1887, by *Habershon & Fawckner*. A minimal design.
VICARAGE by *J. Buckley Wilson* and SCHOOL alongside.

ST MICHAEL AND ALL ANGELS, Manor Road, Manselton. 1904–6 by *E. M. Bruce Vaughan*. Perp, not this architect's normal style. Otherwise no surprises. Uncoursed Pennant sandstone with Bath stone dressings. Nave with S aisle, porch and transept. Lower chancel as the ground drops. Double W bell gable. The interior space is almost continuous between nave and chancel. Octagonal aisle piers. – FONT. Octagonal, the cardinal faces enlarged and decorated with ogee quatrefoils. An unhackneyed design. – STAINED GLASS. Chancel E, Christ in Majesty with St Michael and Virtues triumphing over Vices. A major early window by *Celtic Studios*, 1947. Designed by *Howard Martin*, who set up the Studios on the strength of this commission. In the aisles, five later windows by the firm, 1973–85.

ST PAUL, Neath Road, Landore. J. T. Micklethwaite's abandoned design of 1899 may have influenced the church built by *E. M. Bruce Vaughan* in 1902–3. Quite large and ambitious. Dec, with flowing tracery. The usual rock-faced, coursed brown sandstone, but red sandstone for the dressings. As seen on the slope from below, a complex composition, chancel with cross-gabled S vestry and polygonal S tower with battlements and spike. Higher nave behind, the aisles lean-to, the clerestory unusually lofty with large three-light windows. The interior changes to Bath stone, with rock-faced sandstone walls. Octagonal piers, double-chamfered arches. The chancel arch wide and high.

ST JOSEPH'S CATHEDRAL AND CONVENT (R.C.), Bryn-Melyn Street, Cwmbwrla. Raised to cathedral status in 1987, for the new diocese of Menevia. 1886–8 by *Pugin & Pugin*. Impressively lofty outside and in, despite the meagreness of the timber NW belfry. Geometrical style. Coursed, rock-faced sandstone and Bath stone dressings. The treatment of the arcade is remarkable: short, thick octagonal piers of pink sandstone set on tall plinths and crowned by deep, plain capitals of Bath stone. Music-playing angels in the spandrels of the arches, and, far above, an arch-braced roof supported on long wall-posts. High and wide chancel arch elaborately shafted above statue niches. Five-sided chancel. – STAINED GLASS. S aisle SW, *c.* 1988 by *Catrin Jones*, symposium-like Last Supper. Pure colours, white outlines.

Two-storey PRESBYTERY E of the church and linked to it by a cloister. Also by *Pugin & Pugin*.

BRYNHYFRYD WELSH BAPTIST CHAPEL, Llangyfelach Road, Landore. Not dated, but presumably of the 1890s. Gothic. Only a four-bay body, but a hefty landmark façade. Symmetrical below, with a gabled entrance on exaggerated leaf caps, and a conspicuous Geometrical window between side towers. But these, as they break free of the roof, diverge dramatically, the l. one with a steep pavilion roof on machicolations, the r. one corbelled out as a belfry and crowned with pierced battlements and fat, truncated pinnacles. Gothic interior, galleried on three sides on clustered timber shafts. Tall, blind-traceried recess behind the pulpit.

DINAS NODDFA BAPTIST CHAPEL, Dinas Street, Plas-marl. 1884 by *George Morgan* of Carmarthen. Dramatic Italian Romanesque façade overlooking the valley, with a big wheel window in the centre over paired shafted doorways decorated with zigzag and dogtooth. Shafted windows at two levels to l. and r. Inside, bowed gallery fronts of pierced metalwork in a refined Neoclassical design. The gallery was extended round the fourth side in 1928; the organ on it dates from 1951. Before that there was a tremendous marble pulpit in a clerestoried apse.

MOUNT CALVARY ENGLISH BAPTIST CHAPEL, Elgin Street, Manselton. 1909 by *W. Beddoe Rees*. Perp, typical of the architect, except that neither stair projection is extended up as a tower. Interior in a mixed style, the palmette-pattern metal gallery fronts being a Beddoe Rees speciality. Galleries on all four sides, providing just enough room for the organ above the pulpit. Thin, arch-braced roof on hammerbeams. – STAINED GLASS. Charming design incorporating inverted red hearts and green leaves.

SILOH CONGREGATIONAL CHAPEL, Siloh Road, Landore. 1876–7 by *Thomas Freeman* of Brynhyfryd and the Rev. *Thomas Thomas*. In the temple style. Enriched Doric pilasters and entablature support the pediment and return round the sides. Three gabled doorways and a huge window above subdivided by colonnettes, its arched head with spoke-like tracery rising into the pediment. Long narrow side windows. These and the arcaded outcrops behind the ends of the pediment relate to the gallery stairwells. The usual materials, rock-faced Pennant sandstone and Bath stone ashlar, enlivened by pink Mansfield stone for arch heads and colonnettes.

BRYNHYFRYD INFANT AND JUNIOR SCHOOLS, Brynhyfryd Street, Brynhyfryd. By *G.E.T. Laurence*, architect to Swansea School Board, *c.* 1904. Two single-storey, gabled ranges, of Pennant sandstone trimmed with yellow and black brick. Windows pointed and segment-headed.

MANSELTON PRIMARY SCHOOL, Manor Road, Manselton. 1900–2 by *G.E.T. Laurence*, quite unlike his normal phlegmatic performances, inspired by the need to pile halls and classrooms for infants, girls and boys one above the other on the tightly confined site. A three-storey gabled range with five-storey canted ends crowned by broken segmental pediments and flanked by polygonal stair towers with decorative caps. An ingenious and dramatic composition worthy of an Elizabethan prodigy house. Pretty detailing somewhat lost in the stretches of rough Pennant sandstone walling.

MORRIS CASTLE, off Salem Road, Landore. The ruins of a courtyard building with three-storey battlemented angle turrets. The two surviving turrets are visible against the skyline on the top of a rocky outcrop of Craig Trewyddfa. This, extraordinarily, was not merely an eyecatcher, but workers' housing constructed for Sir John Morris in 1774 (*see* Morriston, below, p. 623). It is estimated that twenty families could have been accommodated in it. Walls of Pennant sandstone with string courses of black copper slag.

At HAFOD, in the grid of streets between NEATH ROAD and St John's church, TERRACED HOUSING provided in the mid C19 by J.H. Vivian for his employees in the Hafod Copperworks. The earliest is at the bottom, facing Neath Road, two terraces erected *c.* 1840. Much use of moulded blocks of copper slag in the houses and front garden walls. In ODO STREET, at the top of the hill, the COMMUNITY CENTRE was built as an infants' school 1845–6. Copper-slag blocks used here, too, as quoins.

MORFA ATHLETICS STADIUM, E of the River Tawe. The GRANDSTAND is a splendid object, *c.* 1987 by the *Director of Development Swansea City Council*, brightly coloured and memorably shaped. Sheer brick end walls, golden with red outlining to stress the tapering profile. Cantilevered concrete canopy. The stand houses a sports hall, changing rooms for 500, bars and restaurants, recalling the prodigality of Victorian public halls.

INDUSTRIAL REMAINS

WHITE ROCK COPPERWORKS (SS 6627 9476). Now an area of open land on the E bank of the lower River Tawe, designated the White Rock Industrial Archaeology Park because of the surviving structural remains of early industrial activity. A partnership from the brass-making centre of Bristol set up in 1736 what was then the third Swansea copperworks. A cut-and-cover CANAL TUNNEL of 1783–5 remains on the site, with on its W side the remnants of the much-altered GREAT WORKHOUSE of 1736, built of Pennant rubble sandstone with brick dressings. Also on the site is a re-excavated C17 RIVER DOCK flanked on the N by a series of rubble sandstone quays built in the C19. The stone ARCH in the middle of the site both carried flues to a discharge chimney and supported an inclined railway carrying vast quantities of waste on to Kilvey Hill, after the introduction of lead- and silver-smelting to the site in 1870–1. The works closed in 1924. To the E, the remains of two CONDENSING FLUES ascending the hillside.

HAFOD COPPERWORKS (SS 6627 9511). The Hafod works, founded in 1810 by the Cornishman John Vivian, became the largest copperworks in Swansea and continued rolling copper until its closure in 1980. The City Council has retained certain buildings on site. The two ENGINE HOUSES and their chimneys, built successively to drive the rolling mills 1860–2 and in 1910, remain with adjacent rolling machinery, no longer protected by its rolling shed. A Musgrove uniflow engine of 1910 remains *in situ*. At the entrance to the works is a very large battered WALL that once formed the abutment to bridges giving access to the works over the Swansea Canal. Built of cast copper-slag blocks, the largest surviving example of its use for constructional purposes. Also a late C19 white-rendered OFFICE BLOCK (now used as a social club). The LOCO-MOTIVE SHED by the river (built for the first standard-gauge articulated locomotive in Britain) bears the name 'Vivians' spelt out in polychrome brickwork on its river façade.

LIMEKILN, immediately to the S. Rectangular kiln of Pennant sandstone rubble, at the entrance to the Hafod works. This is one of the last intact examples of the fifty-four limekilns that once stood alongside the Swansea Canal. Copper slag was used to form the charging ramp (now removed). Limestone was brought from Mumbles via the Oystermouth Railway and the Swansea Canal.

HAFOD MORFA COPPERWORKS (SS 6607 9517). Four principal buildings survive. The large stone shed was probably originally built in 1828 as the Morfa copper-rolling mill of the Cornish firm of Williams, Foster & Co. The building with a (former clock) turret was built in the late C19 as an electrical power house. It is due for reuse as an exhibition centre on the lower Swansea valley. Also a mid-C19 stone-built laboratory building and a red brick office block of *c.* 1900, near the works entrance. Latterly the Morfa works were united with the adjacent Hafod Copperworks, and closed in 1980.

MORFA QUAY (SS 6644 9535). River quay of Pennant sandstone rubble with deck rails for a broad-gauge crane, situated on the riverside of the former Morfa works site. The quay was built in 1835 and is one of the few left of the almost continuous wharves that once lined 3 m. (4.8 kilometres) of navigable river.

MORFA BRIDGE. Adjacent to Morfa Quay. A survivor of the many lifting and swivelling bridges that once allowed the passage of considerable sailing ships up the tidal river. This is

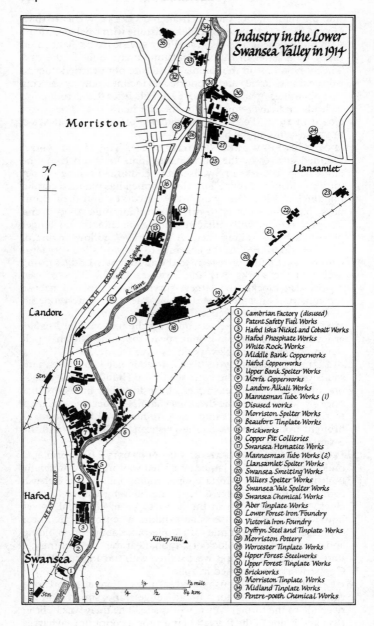

Industry in the Lower
Swansea Valley in 1914

Morriston

Llansamlet

Landore

Stn

Hafod

Swansea

Stn

Kilvey Hill ▲

Swansea Canal

R. Tawe

NEATH ROAD

HIGH ST.

N

① Cambrian Factory (disused)
② Patent Safety Fuel Works
③ Hafod Isha Nickel and Cobalt Works
④ Hafod Phosphate Works
⑤ White Rock Works
⑥ Middle Bank Copperworks
⑦ Hafod Copperworks
⑧ Upper Bank Spelter Works
⑨ Morfa Copperworks
⑩ Landore Alkali Works
⑪ Mannesman Tube Works (1)
⑫ Disused works
⑬ Morriston Spelter Works
⑭ Beaufort Tinplate Works
⑮ Brickworks
⑯ Copper Pit Collieries
⑰ Swansea Hematite Works
⑱ Mannesman Tube Works (2)
⑲ Llansamlet Spelter Works
⑳ Swansea Smelting Works
㉑ Villiers Spelter Works
㉒ Swansea Vale Spelter Works
㉓ Swansea Chemical Works
㉔ Aber Tinplate Works
㉕ Lower Forest Iron Foundry
㉖ Victoria Iron Foundry
㉗ Dyffryn Steel and Tinplate Works
㉘ Morriston Pottery
㉙ Worcester Tinplate Works
㉚ Upper Forest Steelworks
㉛ Upper Forest Tinplate Works
㉜ Brickworks
㉝ Morriston Tinplate Works
㉞ Midland Tinplate Works
㉟ Pentre-poeth Chemical Works

½ mile
0   ¼   ½   ¾ km

an iron bascule bridge of 1909, supported on timber abutments and piles, and has a water tank under its W end, which when filled caused the main deck of the bridge to lift clear of its timber supports. It was built for Williams, Foster and Co. to take the huge amounts of waste from the Morfa works to new tips on the E side of the river.

UPPER BANK COPPERWORKS (SS 6656 9530). The Addis Plastics Factory on the E bank of the River Tawe occupies the re-roofed rubble Pennant sandstone sheds built as part of the Upper Bank Works, possibly 1838–42, when the important zinc-copper alloy of Muntz's Yellow Metal was first made here for the sheaving of ships' bottoms. Note the gable ends pierced with large circular openings and the quay walls on the river frontage. The works had been founded c. 1757 by the London merchant Chauncey Townsend and were supplied with coal by his wooden-track railway. Initially, lead and zinc were smelted here, but conversion to copper-smelting took place in 1777. The works closed in 1928.

LANDORE RIVER QUAY (SS 6627 9588). Sea-going vessels engaged in the ore and coal trades used the River Tawe intensively. By the beginning of the C19 the 3-m. (4.8-kilometre) dredged and navigable length of the river was almost continuously lined with stone-built quays and tidal dock basins. Good examples survive at Morfa, White Rock and Upper Bank. The oldest, Landore Quay, was built 1772–4 as the 'new quay' for the coal and copper magnate John Morris I by the famous Glamorgan engineer *William Edwards*, who carried out several commissions in the valley. Morris regarded the quay as a major innovation in constructional technique, possibly because it was the first masonry quay built locally using hydraulic mortar from Aberavon, instead of timber-revetted earth.

LANDORE VIADUCT, ½ m. E (SS 663 959). Constructed for the South Wales Railway 1847–50 by their chief engineers *I. K. Brunel* and *L. E. Fletcher*. It originally consisted of a timber viaduct 1,760 ft (536 metres) long, rising straight to the E of the river crossing, and on a gentle curve to the W. Abutments and five piers of masonry, with further timber trestles. Four of the piers survive. The largest span, that across the river, was 110 ft (33.5 metres). The viaduct had a clear width of 28 ft (8.5 metres) between parapets and was built to carry the broad-gauge tracks of the South Wales line. Reconstructed 1886–9 with a wrought iron superstructure, and again 1978–89, using steel fabricated beams for the deck, and retaining the river span truss of 1886–9 by *Finch & Co.* of Chepstow and *Palmer* of Neath.

PONT-Y-SHOOT, CWM GELLI (SS 6598 9640). Tramroad causeway, built before 1825. Constructed of a mixture of Pennant sandstone rubble and copper-slag blocks. Later heightenings and rebuildings. The line served colliery levels further up the Nant Gelli Valley.

ST THOMAS

St Thomas and its extension to the E, Dan-y-graig, developed from 1824, after the creation of Port Tennant. It has always been overwhelmingly a working-class area. Grid-like, close-set streets climb steeply up the lower slopes of Kilvey Hill. Today, the traffic tearing along the A483 cuts it off from the docks and gives it even more the character of a world apart, though it is readily visible from the city centre across the river. Maesteg House, the residence of the Grenfell family, which stood above St Thomas's church on the SW slope of Kilvey Hill, has been demolished. The Grenfells' copperworks, Upper Bank and Middle Bank, were on the E bank of the River Tawe, $\frac{3}{4}$ m. N (*see* p. 615).

ALL SAINTS, Kilvey Road. Largely paid for by the Grenfell family. Nave of 1842–4, with Y-tracery. Chancel and S aisle of 1858–9 by *R. K. Penson*. The three-sided apse with gables in all directions and Dec split-cusped tracery is something of a surprise. – STAINED GLASS. A colourful array of 1868 and other dates. No makers' names known.

ST STEPHEN, Gelli Street, Port Tennant. 1905–7 by *E. M. Bruce Vaughan*. Chancel not built. (– IMMERSION FONT, at the W end of the N aisle.)

ST THOMAS, Lewis Street. Built in 1886–7 by *Thomas Nicholson* of Hereford at the expense of the Grenfell family. E.E. Snecked Pennant sandstone with Bath stone dressings. Nave and aisles, lower chancel with side chapels. NE tower and stone broach spire. The interior shows unusual colouristic ambition. Chancel arch on triple black marble shafts. Chancel chapel arcades given piers, caps and hoods of red sandstone, but Bath stone arches. E window of five graded lancets, their rere-arches carried on black marble shafts. Red sandstone arcading, on black shafts, below. – PULPIT. Expensive. – STAINED GLASS. N aisle, Faith, Hope and Charity, 1894 by *Jones & Willis*. – S aisle, two windows by *Celtic Studios*, 1972, 1978.

The VICARAGE, across the road, is by *J. Buckley Wilson & Glendinning Moxham*, 1892.

NORWEGIAN CHURCH, King's Road. A mission church for seamen. Corrugated iron rendered and whitened. Dumpy tower. Pointed windows. Moved here in 1910 from its original site at Newport, Gwent, to serve the Norwegians among the dock community. One can imagine it standing diminutively at the far end of a fjord.

MOUNT CALVARY BAPTIST CHAPEL, Ysgol Street. 1904, a handsome example of *W. Beddoe Rees*'s chapel architecture in Gothic dress. Galleried chapel above a hall, with schoolroom at r.-angles beyond. Rock-faced Pennant sandstone and Bath stone dressings. Diversified façade, a square, buttressed porch tower to the l., a richly traceried Dec window of five lights under the main gable, and, to close the composition at the r., a polygonal gallery-stair-turret with an ashlar top.

DAN-Y-GRAIG CEMETERY, Danygraig Road. 1856 by *William*

Richards of Swansea. The complete set of buildings survives, though now neglected. At the gate a Gothic LODGE, and behind it, set axially to the entrance drive, a rectangular RECEIVING HOUSE. The two Greek-cross-plan CHAPELS lie back further, that to the W in a round-arched style (and at present roofless), built for Dissenters, that to the E, in a Geometrical Gothic style, for members of the Established church. WAR MEMORIAL in front of the latter, to *Sir Reginald Blomfield*'s standard pattern, a sword set against a large cross.

ST THOMAS PRIMARY SCHOOL, Windmill Street. Red brick, four storeys high, the most prominent object in the view of St Thomas from the centre of Swansea. 1897 by *G.E.T. Laurence*, built for 1,200 children, infants, girls and boys stacked above one another over a basement, an unusual arrangement but the only practicable one on this steeply sloping site. Arranged on each level with classrooms round a central hall, the standard plan at that date. Understated embellishments of Board School Queen Anne derivation.

(At PENTRE CHWYTH, $\frac{3}{4}$m. NE, much-altered terraces of housing for the Grenfells' copper-workers in TAPLOW TERRACE and RIFLEMAN'S ROW.)

At FOXHOLE, $\frac{1}{2}$m. N., the remains of stone-built coaling stages, at the S terminus of the canal built by John Smith 1783–5 to serve his colliery at Llansamlet.

SKETTY

Sketty was the domain of the copper magnate Vivian family of Sketty Hall and Singleton Abbey (*see* p. 596). In the mid C19 the head of the family was John Henry Vivian, who favoured as his architect not a local man, but Henry Woodyer. In 1847 Woodyer (a pupil of Butterfield) showed his colours as a disciple of Pugin and the Ecclesiologists with his church at Highnam, Gloucestershire, begun that year. Vivian quickly got on to him after that, and three Woodyer buildings still survive at Sketty, though two of them have subsequently been much enlarged.

ST PAUL. 1849–50 by *Woodyer*, added to in 1907 and again in 1928–9 by *Glendinning Moxham*. As first built, the church had the piquant plan of tower, nave and chancel in line, the nave developed to the N with an aisle and porch, the chancel developed to the S with the Vivian family burial chapel. Moxham's additions, a S aisle of 1907 and N vestry and organ chamber of 1928–9, have neutralized this effect, however earnestly they imitate Woodyer's idiom. Snecked, hammer-dressed local stone with Bath stone ashlar. Geometrical, Dec and Perp features, in imitation of an accretive medieval church. W tower, ashlar-faced in its bell-stage and with multi-cusped bell-openings and a shingled broach spire. Pretty timber N porch. Arcade with double-chamfered arches on octagonal piers, enlivened with ballflower on the capitals. S chapel E window a traceried spherical triangle. Cusped arch-braced nave roof, scissor-braced roof in the chancel. The chancel, lengthened in 1929, is dominated by the extraordinary stone canopy over the sedilia. So Woodyer was full of ideas, all imported from England. Chancel arch enlarged by Moxham. – REREDOS. 1878. Relief of the Last Supper. – STAINED GLASS. Chancel N, Good Samaritan. 1856, by *Hardman*. In a C13 style, as one would expect. – S aisle, Faith and Charity, *c.* 1877. Overtones of the Aesthetic Movement. Also scenes from the life of St Paul, *c.* 1885, in an excessively painterly style. – Chancel E, Ascension, *c.* 1923, signed by *Kempe & Tower*. – Four windows in the sanctuary, 1939 in a similar style. – The VIVIAN CHAPEL must be treated on its own. It is dominated by the standing, white marble figure of Jessie Vivian † 1848. By *Pietro Tenerani*, and oddly out of place in this Gothic shrine. – The tiled PAVEMENT with initials and armorial GLASS may be by *Willement*, who in 1850 made designs for wall-paintings in the church, apparently not executed. – The other MONUMENTS consist of a scatter of brass inscription plates, many of them concentrated in the two wall-tombs against the E wall. Dec, with big gabled canopies sheltering tomb-chests with carved and tinctured heraldic shields.

Opposite the church, in Gower Road, *Woodyer*'s little SCHOOL (now Stewart Hall) of 1853. Gothic. Late C13 details. Symmetrical, to reflect the fact that it is designed for boys and for girls. The gabled schoolrooms with big pointed-headed, transomed windows flank a two-storey centre where the entrance doorways are set behind a timber loggia of plain, sharply pointed arches.

The third building by *Woodyer* stands 100 yds E of the church, on the corner of Brynmill Lane. This, PARC BECK NURSES' HOME, incorporates a square, late C18 villa named Parc Wern, made much larger, irregular and Gothic by Woodyer 1851–3, for J. H. Vivian's son, Henry Hussey Vivian and his wife. Woodyer's designs* were executed with only slight modifications, but have been drastically compromised by later C19 heightening and elaboration. L-plan, with the entrance to the E and the main front looking S down the hill to the sea. Extensive service range extending from the NW corner. Stone-faced throughout, in a C13 style, i.e. with lancets in groups, and on the front, where the windows are larger and transomed, lancet heads to the lights. From the N and E Woodyer intended the irregular group of buildings, from which steep gables and tall chimneystacks rose irregularly, to evoke a medieval manor house. Loftier and more formal S front, with the two full-height window bays of the late C18 villa. This façade was later given a third storey, with a triple gable for every one of Woodyer's and a SE tower rising higher, and presumably intended to go on higher still. Elaborated E entrance and, to the N, Woodyer's drum-turret heightened and enlarged.

*Which survive in the British Architectural Library Drawings Collection.

ST BENEDICT (R.C.), Llythrid Avenue. 1961 by *F. R. Bates, Son & Price*. The firm's attempt to emulate Le Corbusier's Ronchamp, in its blank bowed entrance front and its side wall pierced with many small windows. V-plan concrete campanile. Simple hall interior, reached at the end of a curving corridor.

NEW BETHEL WELSH CONGREGATIONAL CHURCH, Carnglas Road. 1869–70. Pennant sandstone and vermiculated Bath stone dressings. An odd Italianate front, a central two-bay projection under a pedimental gable, with pedimented Tuscan doorways in the recessed side sections. Original galleried interior dominated by a vast plaster ceiling rose of ostrich feathers. – In the large BURIAL GROUND, a prominent MONUMENT to the local chapel designer Thomas Freeman † 1902.

SKETTY JUNIOR SCHOOL, Tycoch. 1909 by *W. James Nash*. Two single-storey blocks of centre-and-wings plan, set at an acute angle to each other, face-outwards, one to Carnglas Road, the other to Tŷ-coch Road. Morriston red brick and Bath stone dressings. The front to Carnglas Road is subtly detailed and deserves study.

SINGLETON HOSPITAL, Sketty Lane. Two ten-storey blocks. The first stage was completed in 1961. By *O. Garbutt Walton*, architect to the Welsh Region Hospital Board. Many later additions.

SKETTY HALL, Sketty Lane, ½ m. SW. Two-storeyed, rendered white. The S front, seen from Singleton Park, consists of three parts: a three-bay bow, a flat three-bay section, and a five-bay section slightly set back. The first two of these appear in Thomas Rothwell's engraving of 1792. The third was added in the early C19 and may go with the date 1802 over the main doorway on the entrance side; it may be the addition made by *William Jernegan*, which replaced the original building on the site, Mansel Mansel's marine villa of 1758. Single-storey S porch on coupled Doric columns, probably an addition by *E. Haycock* in 1832. This was rebuilt and a good deal of balustrading added for Glynn Vivian after 1888.

HENDREFOELAN, Hendre-foilan Road, 1 m. NW. (Now University College, Swansea, Department of Adult Education.) A severe grey stone mansion built *c.*1860 for Lewis Llewellyn Dillwyn M.P., by *William B. Colling*. Tudor style. Asymmetrical entrance (N) front of typical Puginian pattern, the gabled porch set between a big chimneybreast and the mullion-and-transom staircase window. The E front, however, is symmetrical, with two square, single-storey window bays; so is the S front, its two outer bays with double-height canted window bays under gables, the inner two crowned by gabled semi-dormers. Both these fronts, then, suggest allegiance to early C19 formulae. Nothing special inside.

COEDSAESON (now No. 11 Parc Wern Road). Dated 1893 in the stained-glass window of Flora on the staircase. Not large, but a reckless mixture of red brick, Bath stone and half-timbering. Three-storey half-timbered bay rising to become a snuffer-topped turret. Attributable to *J. Buckley Wilson & Glendinning Moxham*, who published designs in 1894 for a group of such houses.

(HILL HOUSE, Cockett Road, ½ m. N. Now part of Hill House Hospital. Plain, seven-bay, three-storey house, built by Illtyd Thomas between 1768 and 1786. The end bays are distinguished by pilaster strips above, and below by tile-hung projecting bays added in the 1920s. Cast iron veranda between them.)

The leafy suburban streets of Sketty may conceal further gems of domestic architecture. All that can be certainly reported here are groups of houses by *C. T. Ruthen*. Nos. 29–47 DILLWYN ROAD are five semi-detached pairs of 1905, and Nos. 1–11 DE-LA-BECHE ROAD form two terraces of 1906. In GOWER ROAD a number of large individual houses and pairs in Norman Shaw Old English style as deployed in Swansea *c.*1900 by *Glendinning Moxham*.

LOWER SKETTY, 1 m. SW. The spread of mid-C20 housing estates has obliterated all but a few traces of the villas which industrialists and successful professional men erected overlooking Swansea Bay and the Mumbles. The most significant of these was Sketty Park House, built *c.*1810 for the Morris family from the materials of Clasemont, Sir John Morris of Morriston's seat, erected in 1775 by *John Johnson* but evacuated by the family a generation later when the fumes from their tinplate works became unbearable. Sketty Park House was itself demolished *c.*1973, but one remarkable feature of its ornamental grounds still remains, on a tree-covered mound in SAUNDERS WAY. This is a large, Gothic BELVEDERE, built of stone, presumably at the same time as the house, on an octagonal plan, with angle buttresses, Y-tracery and a stair-turret for access to the roof. The real surprise is inside, for it is vaulted in stone on a central pier, like a chapter house. Simply chamfered shafts run up unbroken to form the ribs of the vault.

Further S, in DERWEN FAWR ROAD, three white Regency villas can still be seen: BIBLE COLLEGE, much heightened and enlarged, EMANUEL SCHOOL on the E side, and on the W side the best-preserved of the three, GWERN EYNON.

In SKETTY LANE, University Sports Fields, and SPORTS PAVILION, a late work by *Glendinning Moxham*, designed 1930, built 1932.

TOWNHILL

The Town Hill, above the escarpment of Mount Pleasant and sloping back steadily N-wards towards the Carmarthen road, remained undeveloped until after the turn of the C20. The Town Council, once the decision had been made in 1908 to lay it out for housing, took the enlightened step of inviting architects to erect prototype houses to a set of fixed prices. This produced the

South Wales Cottage Exhibition, judged in 1910, the nucleus of what is now the MAYHILL ESTATE. Houses were judged in four classes by cost, from up to £202 per house, the equivalent of a terraced house in the Valleys, to £350 per house. Medal-winners were mostly London-based practices. *E.C.P. Monson* won the gold medal in the cheapest class, *P. Morley Horder* that in the most expensive. In the two mid-price classes (£231 and £260) five medals were shared by *Pepler & Allen* and the Swansea architect *C. T. Ruthen*, the latter gaining more medals than anyone else (and subsequently going on to become Director-General of Housing to the Ministry of Health).

The layout of the Mayhill Estate, by *James Crossland*, centres on two circuses, LLEWELYN CIRCLE and CADWALADR CIRCLE, linked by ISLWYN ROAD. The exhibition cottages are Nos. 1–7, 12–13 (by *Morley Horder*), and 18–22 LLEWELYN CIRCLE, Nos. 1–5 (odd) TAN-Y-MARIAN ROAD, and Nos. 1–8 and 11–14 NICANDER PARADE. They are mainly in pairs and terraces of four. Quite a diversity of facing materials, Pennant sandstone, slate-hanging, a little half-timbering, but inevitably render dominates. Medals were awarded on the understanding that winners were prepared to build twelve more cottages to the same design and specification for the same price, if called on by the Town Council to do so. Unfortunately, it seems that no call was made to medal-winners to rise to this challenge. Sadly, too, unaltered cottages are virtually impossible to find. Nos. 11–25 (odd) TAN-Y-MARIAN ROAD were built also in 1909–10, as prototypes, by *Swansea Borough Council*, in a similar, if less artful, garden suburb style. Nos. 2–12 (even) ISLWYN ROAD form a terrace of six, but designed to disguise their terraced character, *à la* Letchworth. 1914 by *H. C. Portsmouth*.

The TOWNHILL ESTATE, laid out in 1914 by *Ernest E. Morgan*, the Borough Architect, in consultation with *Sir Raymond Unwin*, was developed 1920–9 further to the W. Here the house designs are standardized and of no special interest. The switchback ascent of CEIRIOG ROAD is positively Alpine.

OUR LADY OF LOURDES (R.C.), Pen-y-graig Road. 1968 by *F. R. Bates, Son & Price*. A cubical body, partly outlined by a concrete frame, behind which the side wall curves back. Brown brick, the frame outlined by thin green strips. Skeletal concrete campanile.

TRAINING COLLEGE (now part of Swansea Institute of Higher Education), Pant-y-Celyn Road. On a splendid site, looking S across the town to the sea. The original three-storey range, 1911 by *G.E.T. Laurence*, stands forward to catch all the view it can. Its length is broken into five sections canted back from one another so that it cannot be seen in its entirety. Elizabethan-style, with central and intermediate towers, shaped gables and tall, thin buttresses. Small cupolas over the ends. It sounds livelier than it is.

MAYHILL JUNIOR SCHOOL, Creidiol Road. 1932 by *E. E. Morgan*. Spectacularly sited, with a panoramic view of Swansea and its bay. In acknowledgement of the view, the school is a D in plan, the classrooms ranged round the curve. Single-storeyed.

OUTER SWANSEA

COCKETT

ST PETER, Cockett Road. 1856–7 by *R. K. Penson*, nave and chancel in one. Overhanging w bell gable. Gabled s aisle of 1882 by *J. Bacon Fowler*. Roughly coursed Pennant sandstone with Bath stone dressings. Geometrical tracery. Arcade cut through the wall, and supported on circular piers of pink sandstone conglomerate. – CRUCIFIX. Mosaic. By *John Petts*. – STAINED GLASS. Chancel E, Good Shepherd. 1879. Hardman style. – Chancel s, Raising of Tabitha. Signed by *Jones & Willis*.

ST TEILO, Cheriton Crescent, Caereithin. 1961–3 by *George Pace*, an important demonstration of his gruff, highly personal idiom, just before its apotheosis in the William Temple Memorial church at Wythenshawe, Manchester. Hangar-like exterior, the walls faced with purple engineering bricks. Precipitous N roof-slope, slated and interrupted at its E end by a glazed projection to light the altar. In the w wall random slot windows and an abrupt square doorway at one corner. Round on the s side, serried ranks of tall, thin lights, glazed now only at clerestory level. Had a tower been built as planned, all this might have looked less baffling. As it is, one must go inside.

Spacious, airy interior, divided into six bays, nave and chancel one uninterrupted space with a full-length s aisle. The cruck-like trusses of laminated timber are dramatically asymmetrical. The blocking of the s aisle windows has dimmed what must have been intended as brilliant cross-lighting. The brickwork of the E wall painted white and reflecting the light from the NE window, the window itself masked by the N leg of the E-most truss. Black metal cross and square Crown of Thorns against the wall. The altar itself set well forward, in accordance with the tenets of the Liturgical Movement of that period. – LECTERN, ALTAR RAILS, slatted ORGAN CASE in the NW corner, all by *Pace*.

CEFN COED HOSPITAL, Waunarlwydd Road. 1912–29 by *George T. Hine*. A mighty complex on the rigidly formal plan favoured for hospitals in the early C20. Red brick and Bath stone trim. The huge WATER TOWER, with its idiosyncratic Baroque crown, is a landmark for miles around. The CHAPEL imitates Norman Shaw's church at Bedford Park, London.

At Fforest-fach, ¾ m. N, a GARDEN VILLAGE was begun in 1910 to designs by *Pepler & Allen*. LLWYN DERW encloses a segmental area s of CARMARTHEN ROAD, into which a series of short, spoke-like roads penetrate. All the housing in twos, threes and fours, now much altered.

KILLAY

St Hilary. 1925–6 by *Glendinning Moxham*. Brick. Nave and chancel in one. A greatly simplified version of the late C19 type (e.g. Caröe's St David's, Exeter), where the side windows are set between buttresses under segmental relieving arches. The intended aisles never built. Dec style. – STAINED GLASS. A series of windows by *Shrigley & Hunt* of Lancaster. E window, Last Supper, presumably *c.* 1926, nave SE and NE and war memorial, 1947, all according to the conventions of *c.* 1900. Then, on the N side, the luridly modernistic Noli me Tangere window of *c.* 1954, astonishingly signed by the same firm. – The parish has subsequently patronized *Celtic Studios*, 1963, 1985.

MORRISTON

Morriston is now incorporated in the N suburbs of Swansea, but anyone who looks up and down WOODFIELD STREET, its short, straight high street, immediately senses self-containment and deliberation in its layout. It originates from Sir John Morris's decision in 1768 to build a planned village for the workers at his copperworks. The grid-iron plan, devised by *William Edwards*, was nothing unusual in that first era of town planning, except for the island siting of the church, still today a telling feature. The plan was not built up until the period *c.* 1790–1815, but no early building has survived. In 1873 the centre of gravity lurched lopsidedly when a spectacular chapel was constructed on the E side of Woodfield Street. This, Capel Tabernacl, is still the dominant feature of Morriston. Tin-plating, the principal local industry, is now no more than a memory. Daniel Edwards's great Dyffryn Works, built in 1873, was closed in 1961 and razed to the ground.

St John. The decision to rebuild the chapel of ease erected in 1789 was taken in 1854, but *R. K. Penson*'s design was not carried out until 1859–62 and remains incomplete, a blemish all the more apparent in its situation, isolated in the middle of the road. The two steep gables of the chancel and the much higher nave behind face N down Woodfield Street, for the church is not orientated. Oddly, this axial plan is disrupted by the tower, with polygonal stair-turret rising higher, on the E (ritual S) side. Aisles intended, but the W (ritual N) aisle not built. Inconspicuous clerestory. Walls of uncoursed Pennant sandstone. Dec. Unadventurous interior, piers alternately round and octagonal, double-chamfered chancel arch on triple-shafted corbels. – STAINED GLASS. Chancel E, Crucifixion, 1960–1 by *Celtic Studios*. Other windows by the same.

St David, Woodfield Street. 1889–91 by *E. M. Bruce Vaughan*. E.E. Snecked rock-faced sandstone, the dressed stone painted over. Chancel and higher nave. Strong buttressing towards the road. E window above, a trio of lancets under an ashlar spandrel area with a hoodmould. The motif is repeated on a smaller scale in the cross-gabled bays of the aisles. Bell-gablet over the chancel arch. The interior holds no surprises. Wide five-bay nave, the arcade piers all cylindrical. Shafted chancel arch. – REREDOS and PULPIT by *Bruce Vaughan*. (– IMMERSION FONT, at the W end of the nave.) – STAINED GLASS. Some attributable to *Celtic Studios*.

BETHANIA CALVINISTIC METHODIST CHAPEL, Woodfield Street. 1878. Pedimental front with Corinthianesque foliage bands resting on quoins. Galleries on three sides supported by spiral cast iron columns. Five ceiling rosettes, the central one large and handsome. – STAINED GLASS. In two windows at the pulpit end.

LIBANUS CHAPEL, Libanus Street. A sub-classical rendered front painted red and white, the details suggesting an early C20 date. A datestone, *ex situ*, in the form of an open book, records its foundation and rebuildings, 1782, 1796, 1831, but no further. This seems to be because the present structure is essentially *John Humphrey*'s of 1857. The original Libanus was by *William Edwards*, so part of the original layout of Morriston.

SEION WELSH BAPTIST CHAPEL, Clase Road, Tirpenry. Dated 1869–70, by the Rev. *H. Thomas* of Ystradgynlais. A proper temple, on an open site surrounded by its graveyard. Strongly tapered Tuscan pilasters carry an entablature all the way round. Long, thin, round-headed side windows. Rock-faced sandstone dressed with ashlar of the same colour. Inside fine fittings survive almost in their entirety in an interior made magnificent by a colour scheme of red, white, blue and buff. Galleries round three sides rest on slender, fluted cast iron columns with bulbous leaf capitals, their sinuous, pierced fronts also of cast iron. Cast iron also the curved pulpit balustrades and the 'big seat', below. Plaster arch on Corinthian pilasters backing the pulpit and two fine ceiling rosettes. The organ is not original.

SOAR BAPTIST CHAPEL, Pentrepoeth Road. 1907 by *Henry A. Ellis*. Gothic.

85 TABERNACL WELSH CONGREGATIONAL CHAPEL. Built largely on the initiative of Daniel Edwards, the local tinplate entrepreneur. 1872–3 by *John Humphrey* of Morriston. Huge and abundantly embellished, a temple in conception, but round-arched in style and given a wonderfully incongruous steeple to the r. of the façade. Rock-faced sandstone for the walls and lavish Bath stone dressings. The façade is dominated by paired Corinthian columns in three bays, carrying not an entablature but arches with prominent discs in the spandrels. Richly detailed pediment. Flanking bays which establish the rhythm of the side elevation, with two storeys of round-headed windows. Massive top balustrade. Four doorways in the façade, two more in each side. The chapel has a seating capacity of 1,450, and was reported at the time to have cost £8,000–10,000. A goodly part of the cost must have been accounted for by the steeple, a square tower, with a pilastered belfry and above that an octagonal clock-stage and finally a short spire.

86 Nor is the INTERIOR lacking in any way. The effect of the

gallery with its steeply raked seating carried round all four sides is sensational, especially where it swoops downwards above the pulpit, apparently under the weight of the gigantic tripartite ORGAN. Gothic detailing of the organ case. Segmental ceiling subdivided by emphatic transverse beams.

POLICE STATION (former), Martin Street. 1875, Tudor-style, with five equal gables towards the road, and tall chimneystacks.

TREBOETH

ST ALBAN, Llangyfelach Road. 1927–8 by *J. B. Fletcher*. Still E.E. at this late date. – STAINED GLASS. E window, Te Deum, *c.* 1927 by *A. K. Nicholson*.

MYNYDDBACH CONGREGATIONAL CHURCH, Llangyfelach Road. Mynydd-bach was a focal point of Welsh Independent worship from the late C17. A chapel was built in 1762. The present one is a rebuilding of 1865–6 by *John Humphrey* of Morriston. Exceptionally scholarly version of a typical classical chapel façade. Rendered, yet crisply detailed. Giant pilasters, with capitals of the type discovered by Robert Adam in Diocletian's palace at Split, demarcate three bays. In the outer ones, windows with architrave surrounds, in the centre a Venetian window, also with Diocletian pilasters. To make room for it, a semicircular arch breaks up into the pediment. Porch added 1930. Spacious interior, galleried all round. Coved plaster ceiling criss-crossed by guilloche bands.

CAERSALEM NEWYDD WELSH BAPTIST CHAPEL, Llangyfelach Road. Tuscan façade of 1873, pedimented with four full-height pilasters. Long, round-headed windows in the outer bays. Rock-faced Pennant sandstone, the ashlar dressings painted over. Compare the slightly earlier Welsh Baptist chapels at Clydach and Neath, and in particular Morriston.

MYNYDDBACH GIRLS' COMPREHENSIVE SCHOOL, Heol Ddu. 1950s by *H. T. Wykes*, Swansea Borough Architect. Flat-roofed ranges of two storeys and of three, grouped in two three-sided courts open to the E. Windows in long bands. The brickwork is all load-bearing.

PENLAN BOYS' COMPREHENSIVE SCHOOL, Heol Gwyrosydd. 1950s by *H. T. Wykes*. The five-storey range at the back of the site is straight and formidably long. Ground storey recessed behind pilotis, top storey cantilevered out, but the structure is conventional, of load-bearing brick. Large addition of 1994 in front.

TALYGARN

The dominant figure at Talygarn is G. T. Clark (1809–98), the remarkable industrialist and antiquary who combined being manager of the Dowlais Ironworks for forty-five years with writing his classic *Medieval Military Architecture in England* (1884) and publishing much material on the history of Glamorgan. He turned his hand to architectural design also, as church and mansion demonstrate.

St Anne. The church was designed and paid for by *Clark* in 1887. Quite large, generally Perp in style, but with a Dec E window. Nave, chancel and four-square s tower. The overall effect, it must be admitted, is inartistic. – STAINED GLASS. E window, Virgin and Child between SS Elizabeth and Anne, a memorial, like the whole church, to Clark's wife, who died in 1885. In style the glass is dependent on Burne-Jones.

The former CHAPEL stands roofless in the churchyard. Largely rebuilt, it is said, in 1687 by Sir Leoline Jenkins. Large segment-headed s windows with vestigial keystones.

Talygarn House, ½ m. E. G. T. Clark's mansion is on an astonishing scale and its internal decoration takes the breath away. He acquired the estate in 1865 and was engaged in enlarging and decorating the house until his death in 1898. Most of the additions were made 1879–82: the SE tower is dated 1880, the s tower 1881. Inside, he went on with improvements nearly to the end of his life, the panelling in the billiard room bearing the date 1895. In 1922 the house and grounds were sold by his grandson and became a miners' rehabilitation centre.

The exterior is Gothic, the entrance (N) front stone-faced and ecclesiastical-looking with large Dec and Perp traceried windows. The four-bay, single-storey room r. of the porch was Clark's library, lit by big Perp four-light windows. Then, to the r. lying back, the gabled staircase bay, lit by a window with reticulated tracery. The chapel-like projection which comes next is the great hall, its N window modelled on the chancel window of the C14 church at Claybrooke, Leicestershire. Billiard room of 1894 beyond. The whole front must have looked completely episodic in Clark's day, for the four-bay dining room which gives some coherence to it, by balancing the library to the l. of the porch, is an addition of 1926.

The s front towards the garden is quite different. Harled walls, steep roofs with semi-dormers, and three towers of contrasting height and form, the central one with a corbelled and crow-stepped top stage, evoke the residually fortified residence of a C16 Scottish laird. The original, pre-Clark house is the projecting E third, to which Clark added three contrasting towers.

The INTERIOR, in yet another contrast, is frankly Continental. Clark turned to various Italian virtuoso decorators. The inlaid and relief-carved wainscot is in an early Renaissance style, part Florentine, part François Premier. Portrait heads (Sir Henry Layard etc.) and heraldry show that they were working to Clark's specification. Marble chimneypieces in similar style. The ceiling paintings in gesso borders, heavily derivative from early C16 Venetian models, are of lesser quality. The entrance vestibule leads through an arch to a big, square open-well staircase. To the r. a heavily wainscoted E–W corridor, the panelling signed by *G. Biraghi*, gives access to the principal rooms. First, on the N side, the LIBRARY, denuded of all fittings except two marble chimneypieces, supplied by *Terrazzi* of Verona. Beyond that a second, principal STAIRCASE, lofty and pompous, under a coved vault embellished with emblems and Clark's much-repeated initials. Heraldic lions on the newel posts, inlaid stair risers. Grisaille glass in the traceried window. The corridor widens out thereafter, in Clark's day a boudoir and a lobby now thrown together, and gives room for a fireplace with a massive overmantel carried on herms. At its w end a glazed and traceried wall, entry into the now demolished conservatory. To the S the DRAWING ROOM, one of the earliest rooms to be fitted up, *c.* 1873 largely by *Biraghi*, and perhaps the most fantastic. The coved ceiling painted by *P. Santi*, after Veronese, the doors inlaid with satyrs and satyresses, by *Cortellazzo* of Vicenza, and the gigantic overmantel mirror with bristling border are only the most obvious decorative components. To the N, the GREAT HALL, of five bays open to an arch-braced timber roof, with a stone-vaulted oriel at the dais end and a massive columned and colonnetted overmantel, by *Howard* of Berners Street based on Clark's drawing of a tomb at Assisi. To the l. of this a stained glass window commemorating John Jones of Dowlais, clerk of works at Talygarn 1865–1907. Heraldic N window, 1903 by *Powell*'s. Finally, the BILLIARD ROOM, in the NW corner, suffocatingly enclosed in its full-height panelling, signed by *Biraghi* and dated 1895.

TONDU

The development of the area began after the foundation of the Tondu Ironworks (*see* below).

ST JOHN, Aberkenfig. Designed as a cruciform church by *John Prichard* in 1868, but built without its transepts. S transept 1933 by *Harry Teather*, to a slightly modified design. Geometrical tracery as usual. Bath stone in courses of different depths. The interior is one of Prichard's attempts at Butterfieldian polychromy. Red brick patterns against grey brick and greenish-grey Bridgend stone, timid and unconvincing compared with what Butterfield himself would have done. Sanctuary steps of white marble with green lozenges and rectangles. Some typical fittings by *Prichard*. – FONT. Octagonal bowl chamfered down to a circular stem. – PULPIT. Of stone. Trilobed on a square base, with runs of stiff-leaf at strategic points. A handsome piece. – S DOOR. Instructive in its carpentry. – STAINED GLASS. A set, delicate grisaille, by *Clayton & Bell*, doubtless to Prichard's instructions.

WESLEYAN CHAPEL, ¼ m. N on the A4063. 1867 by *Wilson & Willcox*. Ambitious, of rock-faced limestone and Bath stone ashlar, with a short spire and geometrical tracery. T-plan. Former SCHOOL en suite (now environmental centre).

BETHARRAN INDEPENDENT CHAPEL, Brynmenin, ¾ m. NE.

Founded in 1809 in what must have been a lonely roadside spot. The present smartly painted building, if the date tablet is correctly interpreted, was built in 1859 and given lean-to additions in 1904. Gable-end façade, the central doorway under a relieving arch, with a pair of square windows above and a flanking pair of round-headed ones.

COYTRAHEN HOUSE, ¾ m. N. All that remains of the elegant five-bay villa with side pavilions, c. 1776, is the arcaded ground storey of the central block, converted into a bungalow. And pebbledash has blurred the details even of that.

IRONWORKS, ¼ m. NW. The ironworks were established in the 1820s by Sir Robert Price, a Herefordshire landowner, but only properly developed by John Brogden & Sons after 1853–4. Two furnaces, a small forge and one hundred coke ovens were then in production, and the last furnace remained in blast until 1895 or soon after. A tall, stone-faced blast-furnace CHARGING BANK remains, with a stone-built, brick-lined lift shaft, 23 ft (7 metres) by 16 ft 6 in. (5 metres), alongside, formerly used for raising raw materials on to the furnace charging bank. The BLAST-ENGINE HOUSE, possibly dating from the 1830s, stands at the SW end of the furnace bank. This roofless masonry structure had three floors and a basement. Later two-storey structure.

A range of seven stone-built iron ore CALCINING KILNS, 62 ft by c. 36 ft (19 by 11 metres) overall, stand back about 20 ft (6 metres) from the edge of the charging bank. A rare survival. Huge banks of perhaps a hundred beehive-shaped COKING KILNS lie behind the calcining kilns and to the SW. These have top openings for charging and bottom openings for discharging in front of the continuous ranges of kilns. Very few of the thousands of such kilns built in Britain survive, and these form one of the most extensive series remaining in Britain.

In DERLLWYN ROAD several foremen's houses of iron-stained Pennant sandstone date back to the mid C19, as also FOXTROY RESIDENTIAL HOME. This is of two storeys, the seven-bay centre recessed between gabled end bays in which the windows, the upper ones arched, are set under giant round-headed relieving arches. Bargeboards. It is said to have been the ironworks company's shop. At the W end of the road PARK TERRACE, fifty cottages in two terraces face-to-face, almost as isolated now as when first built.

ABERKENFIG HORSE-DRAWN-RAILWAY BRIDGE, 1 m. S. Built in the 1820s as part of the Duffryn, Llynvi and Porthcawl Railway, a horse-drawn tramroad. This concern, taken over by the Llynfi Railway Company in 1854, had been abandoned by 1864. The bridge is constructed of coursed rubble-stone and flanked by slightly swept-out abutments. Fine arch-ring of hammer-dressed voussoirs. The rubble abutment built against its upper side is later. On the bridge deck the lowest courses of parapet walls remain.

GLAN-RHYD RAILWAY VIADUCT, 1 m. SE. Over the River Ogmore, and now situated under the M4 viaduct. Bridge of three stone-built arches, designed in 1829 by the engineer *John Hodgkinson*, one of the last structures remaining from the Bridgend Railway, which was one of the few early horse-drawn railways designed for general goods traffic. It connected with the Duffryn, Llynvi and Porthcawl Railway, which led to the harbour at Porthcawl. Inscription on the w side 'THIS BRIDGE WAS ERECTED IN THE YEAR 1829 BY MORGAN THOMAS, LALESTON, MASON'. Coursed and squared rubble with a single ring of ashlar voussoirs and projecting keystones. Elaborate stepped and moulded cutwaters on each side of the two river piers. Projecting string course at deck level, and a capped parapet wall above. The bridge is 12 ft 2 in. (3.7 metres) wide between parapet walls, and the viaduct deck is *c.*146 ft 8 in. (44.7 metres) long.

TONGWYNLAIS
1080

ST MICHAEL AND ALL ANGELS, 1875–7 by *John Prichard*. Cheap and simple, just a nave with w bellcote, and lower chancel. Snecked, squared, local limestone. Bath stone dressings. Geometrical tracery. The architect's hand can be recognized in the details, especially the chubby quadrant mouldings on the mullions and tracery. – FONT and PULPIT of stone, both cylindrical and typical of *Prichard*.

TAFFS WELL VIADUCT, ¾ m. NW. In 1901 the Barry Railway Company opened a branch from St Fagans on the Barry–Rhondda line which crossed the Taff Valley on the Walnut Tree Viaduct and ran to Penrhos, w of Caerphilly. Its four brick arches and seven steel Pratt truss spans have gone, but one blue brick pier still dominates the dual-carriageway of the A470 below Castell Coch.

TONMAWR
8090
6 m. NE of Port Talbot

A remote valley-bottom hamlet.

FFORCHDWM VIADUCT, ¾ m. NE. The piers survive of a fine three-span viaduct, of Pennant sandstone rubble, built in 1842 for the Glyncorrwg Mineral Railway. The arches were demolished in 1979. The road from Tonmawr to this point is built on the railway formation.

TONNA
7090

ST ANNE. 1891–2 by *E. H. Lingen Barker* of Hereford, at the expense of the Rev. David Griffiths. A varied composition dominated by the s porch tower with its spire. Rock-faced local sandstone, with generous Bath stone dressings. The octagonal bell-stage with its clasping pinnacles, reminiscent of Prichard's church at Baglan (q.v.), is all ashlar-faced like the spire. Otherwise the plan is cruciform with an apse. Geometrical tracery. The whole concept, then, is retardataire for its date. Disappointing interior. – STAINED GLASS. Apse windows, scenes from the life of the Virgin, 1891 by *Joseph Bell* of Bristol. – S transept, Ascension, flanked by Baptism of Christ and Empty Tomb, *c.*1900, signed by *Mayer & Co.* – W window, by the same?

Long terraces of rock-faced Pennant sandstone extend on both sides of the road to NE and SW of the church. Further SW, where the main road to Neath is called HENFAES ROAD, TYN-YR-HEOL, a handsome five-bay, two-storey house of *c.*1700, under a hipped roof with dormers. In fact it has a T-plan with the hall in a range at the back. The central revolving doors are a relic of its use as a ladies' seminary in the early C20.

BLAEN-CWM BACH ROMAN MARCHING CAMP, 2 m. E, on the hilltop. It covers *c.*66 acres (27 hectares), its elongated axis following the ridge. Best preserved are the W side and NE section of low rampart fronted by a ditch. The entrance midway along the W rampart was protected by an outwork.

IVY TOWER, ¾m. S, off Fairyland Road. A large, stone, castellated summerhouse, of two storeys on an octagonal plan. Now partly ruined. It was built *c.*1780 by *John Johnson* on the ridge-top 1 m. NE of Gnoll, the mansion of the Mackworths (*see* Neath, p. 461).

ABERDULAIS FALLS TINPLATE WORKS, ½m. NW. The waterfall here probably powered the first copperworks in south-west Wales, but the reconstructed water wheel sits in the wheelpit of a later tinplate works, founded in 1830. There are an impressive masonry header tank (the 'bastion'), the foundations of the adjoining rolling mills, various walls and a 60-ft (18-metre)-high chimney. The early copperworks may have lain S of the river where a leat leads from the waterfall towards the rear of the C17 Dulais Rock Public House.

ABERDULAIS AQUEDUCT AND BASIN, ¼m. NW. Constructed in 1823 by the engineer *William Kirkhouse* to complete the Tennant Canal. Aqueduct 340 ft (104 metres) long, carried on ten masonry arches, and continued to the NW by a cast iron trough over an earlier navigable cut. In the basin, remains of sunken boats and at the N end a buried dry dock by a slip-way. At the junction of the Tennant and Neath Canals a roving bridge, PONT GAM ('crooked bridge'), its flanking walls carried on a corbelled series of masonry courses. The only LOCK on the canal's main line is S of the aqueduct, with OFFICE and LOCK-KEEPER'S HOUSE.

NEATH CANAL DEPOT, ⅓m. W. The most completely surviving depot of the South Wales valley canals. The Pennant sandstone rubble buildings stand on either side of the Neath Canal (1791–6) at Lock no. 1. They consist of the canal manager's house and stables on the E side, and on the W side a long timber storage shed with a sawpit inside, and an open shed with block and tackle hoisting gear where lock gates were made. Attached to this is a store and a smithy.

GLYNCORRWG MINERAL RAILWAY, 1½–2 m. SE. The last of the large horse-worked railways to be built in South Wales, 7 m. (12 kilometres) long and completed on a monumental scale by the notable South Wales engineer *William Kirkhouse* 1839–42. The section from Aberdulais to Tonmawr includes two INCLINES (*see also* Cefn Morfydd Incline below), the foundations of an ENGINE HOUSE, massive rock-cut excavations and a fine OVERBRIDGE.

CEFN MORFYDD EARLY RAILWAY INCLINE, ¾ m. SE. A causeway supporting the head of an inclined plane on the Glyncorrwg Mineral Railway. Still very impressive, although a large part was blown up to prevent its use as a navigation marker by German bombers during the Second World War.

PENLAN-FACH EARLY RAILWAY BRIDGE, ⅓ m. E. Squared Pennant sandstone arch, 19 ft 4 in. (5.9 metres) in span, carrying a track over both the former Glyncorrwg Mineral Railway incline up Cefn Morfydd and a stream. Single row of arch voussoirs. Stepped abutments, stone pilasters flanking the N side of the arch.

TONYPANDY

9090

The major settlement in the lower Rhondda Fawr. Continuous terraced housing links Tonypandy, Llwynypia and Clydach Vale into one. Development began in earnest after Archibald Hood opened a shaft to the steam coal seam at Llwynypia in 1862. A further seven collieries were opened in the area over the following decade, and two more by 1891. By the turn of the century the coking coal from these mines had become world-famous.

ST ANDREW, Church Street. 1876–7, by *W. D. Blessley*, chancel added 1886–7 by *E. M. Bruce Vaughan*. S aisle, 1904. Largely paid for by Archibald Hood, owner of Llwynypia Colliery. Cruciform, but no tower. Rock-faced local sandstone, as usual, but a touch of polychromy in the window voussoirs. E.E. in style, with geometrical tracery. – STAINED GLASS. Chancel E, Christ between SS Andrew and Peter, 1904 by *R. J. Newbery*.

ST THOMAS, Clydach Vale, 1 m. W. 1894–6 by *E. M. Bruce Vaughan*. Nave with N aisle and lower chancel, raised above a hall on the S side. Small N porch tower. A larger NE tower has been demolished. S transept added 1912. – ALTAR. Painted front depicting the Lamentation. From a demolished church in Cardiff. – STAINED GLASS. Chancel E, Resurrection, 1920 by *Jones & Willis* of Birmingham.

BETHANIA CALVINISTIC METHODIST CHAPEL, in Church Street just beyond the viaduct. 1908–9 by *R. S. Griffiths*. A broad façade, of Pennant sandstone with ashlar dressings now painted over. A somewhat disjointed attempt to classicize the standard composition. The central triplet enclosed between stumpy Ionic pilasters and under a floating pediment. Note the open bible on a cartouche here. Double-width entrance doorway. The interior is finely preserved and coloured with exceptional subtlety. Adamesque decoration on the ceiling cove. Corinthian pilasters between the upper windows. Deep floral capitals to the fluted cast iron columns which carry the gallery round all four sides. The substantial ORGAN was brought in, in 1983, from Moriah Chapel, Ynyshir (q.v.).

EBENESER INDEPENDENT CHAPEL, Dunraven Street. 1867–8. Semi-classical. Arcaded loggia between projecting turrets. Alternating large and small arched windows to the main façade. Railings at two levels, and iron finials on every apex, a happy survival. Magnificent interior, galleried on four sides. Pulpit and gallery fronts lavishly decorated with fretwork panels and ebony colonnettes. Flat ceiling richly patterned and centred on two enormous complex ventilator roses. Subtle colouring in browns and buffs.

To the visitor approaching from the S, DUNRAVEN STREET, the main street of Tonypandy, presents a gamut of characteristic buildings. First, on the l., at the corner of TRINITY ROAD, the big, dark Gothic group of the TRINITY CALVINISTIC METHODIST CHAPEL, 1886, with its Sunday school behind, and above, the much more demonstrative HALL of 1893. Lancets. Red brick and Bath stone trimmings. Next, on the same side, the impressively three-dimensional frontage of Ebeneser Chapel. As the road rises, the first of the signs of prosperity in the early C20, a row of shops with Baroque details dated 1914 (boarded up at the time of writing); and at a higher level to the r. MORIAH CHAPEL, dated 1905. Perp. Then, on the r., the simple pedimented front of BETHEL BAPTIST CHAPEL, facing a terrace of shops with enriched terracotta bands, and, up a side street, the Art Deco POST OFFICE of 1938. On the l. further terraces of shops, with dates of 1915 (Baroque terracotta details) and 1905. Thereafter terraced housing to recall the mid-C19 beginnings of the town, especially Nos. 137–145 Dunraven Street, and a group in Gilfach Road. Finally, on the l. just before the viaduct, the broad, pedimented front of the TOWN HALL, grey sandstone with red and yellow brick dressings. Dated 1892 and looking rather like a chapel of that date. Now converted to commercial uses, a blow to civic pride! At the N end of the main street, LLWYNYPIA COL-LIERY ENGINE HOUSE. A large eight-bay, two-storey engine house in red and yellow brick with stepped buttresses, set below the old Llwynypia road near its junction with the new. The S gable has a round window with blocked tracery, over a date-stone of 1905. The building is three bays wide, with round-headed windows on two storeys. Its substantial width is spanned by a steel-trussed roof. Longitudinal steel tracks sup-ported on intermittent internal buttresses carry the bow-trussed travelling crane which bears the name 'J Booth & Bros. Ltd Engineers Rodney nr. Leeds'.

Also a GASOMETER painted in 1993–4 by *Andrew Cooper* with mosaic-like camouflage, and STATUES of a miner family, 1993.

On the hillside which overlooks them, LLWYNYPIA TER-
RACES, built from 1865 to house the miners working at the
colliery. They are one of the few surviving examples of terrace
layout in the Valleys before the Sanitary Controls of the 1870s.
Pedestrian access only to the terraces. Each cottage faces the
valley with three windows up and three down, but towards the
hill there is only the doorway, one small window beside it and
one full-size above.

At LLWYNYPIA, 1 m. N, RHONDDA COLLEGE, 1954–5 and
1958–9 by *Sir Percy Thomas & Son*. In the mildly modern
style adopted after the Second World War by firms which
had previously practised in Neo-Georgian. Central entrance
pavilion flanked by long two-storey, not quite symmetrical
ranges with windows in long bands. Flat roofs everywhere.
Brown brick.

TONYREFAIL   0080

ST DAVID, High Street. By *E. M. Bruce Vaughan*, 1902–3. Nave
with N aisle and W bell-turret. Transeptal vestries and lower
chancel. Rock-faced Pennant sandstone with Forest dressings.
E.E. Plate-traceried windows. Circular arcade piers. –
STAINED GLASS. E window, St Francis against a grisaille back-
ground with naturalistically treated animals in roundels. Not
consistent in style, perhaps, but attractive. 1984, signed *J.M.V.*
METHODIST CHAPEL, High Street. Large, in a minimal classical
idiom. Dated 1905.
In SCHOOL STREET, a typical gabled group of early COUNCIL
SCHOOLS, 1909–10 by *D. Pugh Jones*. Behind them, COM-
MUNITY RESOURCE CENTRE (Day Centre for the Elderly),
by the *Welsh School of Architecture* (project architect *Norman
Robson-Smith*), completed in 1993. A charming building, low,
on a lightweight steel frame painted white. Red brick cladding
low down. Monopitch roofs rise towards each other, that
towards the view largely glazed. Clerestory glazing above a
high-level trough which carries the service ducting the length
of the building.
TONYREFAIL SCHOOL, Gilfach Road, Bryngolan, $\frac{3}{4}$ m. w.
Designed as a grammar school by *D. Pugh Jones* and opened in
1933. Red brick. Long, two-storey façade, formed into a centre-
and-ends composition and with returns extending far back.
Windows of Georgian proportions but also battered buttresses.
Behind, a free-standing group of 1970–3 by *J. Morgan Harries*
of Bridgend, a complete contrast in its lack of stylistic reference.

TREBANOS   7000

ST MICHAEL AND ALL ANGELS. 1912 by *G. T. Bassett* of Aberystwyth. Small. Lancets. – STAINED GLASS. Chancel E, Crucifixion, 1912 by *T. F. Curtis* of *Ward & Hughes*. – In the nave,
one N and four S windows by *Celtic Studios*, 1951–5.

TREFOREST
1½ m. SE of Pontypridd

TINPLATE WORKS. One of the most important surviving sets of industrial buildings in Wales, dated 1834–5. They were built by the Crawshays of Cyfarthfa, operators, at Merthyr Tydfil, of the largest ironworks in the world. Whereas at Cyfarthfa there is now little to see, Treforest remains as the most extensive series of buildings associated with the South Wales iron industry. Here alone, furthermore, is it possible to examine the structural evidence for the tinplating industry, which has almost completely disappeared elsewhere. The structurally most important parts of the buildings are the roofs, of wrought iron and cast iron trusses, almost the only survivors of a type once common in the large South Wales ironworks and pioneers of the modern large-span industrial roof.

The site extends along the W bank of the River Taff, and can be reached from the A473 either from the S or from the N. It will be most convenient to describe the buildings from S to N. They are all of Pennant sandstone rubble, now painted white, with quite elaborate ashlar dressings towards the river, but brick dressings at the sides and rear, which were less readily visible.

The place to start is by the large ashlar slab inscribed 'WC [for William Crawshay] 1835 PERSEVERANCE'. This is set above the stone retaining wall of a very large leat which ran behind the rolling mill at the SW end of the site. From the leat seven iron launders ran into the rolling mill with its large forge.

The ROLLING MILL is a range 500 ft (150 metres) long, dated 1835 on the SE gable. This was where the iron was rolled into thin sheets. The monumental NE elevation has twenty high, round-headed doorways, giving railway and other access to the interior. Circular ventilation windows above. Gable ends with three round-headed openings, wide between narrow, and oculi in the gables, small between large. Raised keystones and impost blocks to all openings. The walls have been raised in brick and the roof renewed. The interior, a vast open space, gives little indication now of the high-level iron channels that entered from the rear to drive a series of water-balance hammers and water wheels, which activated massive shears and rolling mills.

In front of the rolling mill was the tailrace pond for the works, now filled in. The small SMITHY, to the E of this space, brick below, clad with corrugated asbestos above, has an internal cast iron frame. This is the last surviving example of a structure typical of the vast ranges of open ironworking forges once common in many South Wales ironworks, with wall-plates supported on cast iron arches. Here there are only four bays, each framed with an iron arch-brace, cast in two halves, springing from a pair of iron posts. Six circular tension braces are set between wall-plate and arch-brace, decreasing in size upwards to the crown. Three wooden roof trusses span each bay. The

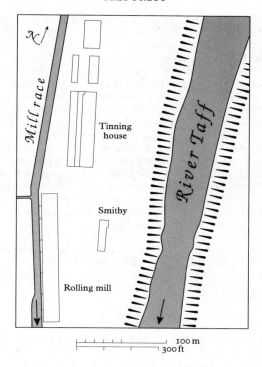

Treforest, tinplate works. Plan

iron castings appear to be prefabricated components standard to all the Crawshay works.

Next to the N is the former TINNING HOUSE, where the iron sheets were covered in molten tin. The main, gabled range, where the tinning took place, lies to the E, towards the river. Smaller parallel range to the W. A railway ran between the two. The E front of the main range is opened up with alternating round-headed doorways and windows, nineteen in all. Raised keystones and impost blocks. In the N gable, three bold circular ventilation holes. Functionally, the W wall is the most interesting. The long series of projecting brick stacks, now truncated, originally rose above the tinning bays and their hearths. Internally, the furnaces have gone, but huge 'fish-bellied' cast iron beams under brick relieving arches span the inner sides of the former working areas under the stacks. Trios of windows in the lower outer wall of each stack lit the working areas. Doorways alternated with the tinning bays, with large tilt-opening windows above them, to ventilate what was a very hot and noxious working environment. Two of these survive at the S end. A spine wall divides the interior lengthways. It is punctuated by a series of round-headed doorways, now blocked, and high-set apertures. In front of these are the remains of 'desks', where groups of women in threes sorted and scoured the plates that had been tinned in the bays opposite. The doorways related to transport ways, some on rails, which ran into the building to the W. The E and the S half of the W range retain their original iron roofs. Though they are constructed of wrought iron, their design is based on the kingpost truss, characteristic of early C19 timber roofs, with additional struts. The main members of each truss are flat standard strips, the subsidiary struts are circular in section, and the purlins L-section and designed to provide fixing for the roof covering.

The two buildings at the N end of the site, now linked together, are similar in design to the rolling mill and tinning house but considerably smaller. Subsidiary range to the W. The N-most building is dated 1834 and bears William Crawshay's initials. This may have been a cold rolling mill. The original functions of the other buildings in this group are not clear. Annealing, descaling and pickling were the other processes which had to be provided for in a tinplate works. The southerly building, with high-set openings and internal evidence of an upper floor, is said to have had a secondary use as a foundry and moulding loft.

TREHAFOD

0090

COLLIERY VENTILATION FURNACE, Darren y Pistyll Terrace. The last surviving colliery ventilation chimney in Glamorgan, situated at the foot of a cliff on the N bank of the Rhondda. Of the C19, precise date unknown. Square tapering brick stack with a vaulted tunnel running back into the hillside.

LEWIS MERTHYR COLLIERY, Coedcae Road. Now the Rhondda Heritage Park. Three pits, the Bertie, Trefor and Hafod shafts, were sunk in the late 1870s, by W.T. Lewis (later Lord Merthyr). The colliery, into which they had been consolidated in 1900, closed in 1983. The main element to survive of what became one of the most productive and profitable collieries in the Rhondda is the two winding houses, with their large engines (one steam, one electric), and their adjoining headgear.

Both WINDING HOUSES are long, low, two-storey structures built of rusticated ('bull-nosed') Pennant sandstone, the E one (for the Trefor shaft) dated 1878, the W one (Bertie shaft) 1890. The contemporary HEADGEAR of lattice steelwork, also quite low, stands on the N side of each winding house, connected to it by shallow diagonal struts. Both winding houses have three-bay S gables towards the road and brick infilled N gables replacing the original timber framing and cladding. Five-bay side elevations. Round-headed windows with prominent voussoirs and fixed metal frames. Central double doors under arched fanlights.

Between the two shafts, the LAMP ROOM AND FAN ROOM, of rubble Pennant sandstone, two-storey to the S, three-storey to the N. Red brick quoins and dressings. Round-headed windows, with fixed metal glazing. The building is probably late C19 and, like many colliery structures, has a corrugated iron roof.

The OLD LAMP ROOM is a one-storey building, E of the Bertie headgear, built of coursed Pennant sandstone rubble with a raised slatted ventilator and round-headed windows with fixed metal frames.

To the E of the engine houses is the tall, tapering yellow brick CHIMNEY, on a square rusticated masonry plinth. Its top section has two groups of projecting cornices but has been slightly shortened.

TREHARRIS
0090

ST MATTHIAS. 1895–6 by no less an architect than *J. L. Pearson*. This is however a modest performance, impaired by a reduction in the design, involving the omission of the S aisle, after building had started. Snecked, hammer-dressed Pennant sandstone with Bath stone dressings. Nave and chancel in one and full-length N aisle, separately gabled. E.E., the lancets widely spaced in pairs or threes with encircled quatrefoils in the spandrels between their heads. Nave and chancel defined internally only by a timber screen, and by a change in the arcade design. To the W of it an octagonal and a circular pier carrying oddly depressed double-chamfered arches; to the E two arches of better proportions on a quatrefoil pier. – STAINED GLASS. Clearly by three different designers, of whom one only is identifiable. – Chancel E, Christ between St Paul and St John the Evangelist, with scenes below. About 1920. Nave SW, Empty Tomb and Noli me Tangere, *c.* 1929. Nave W, Ascension. 1920. N aisle E, Annunciation, *c.* 1929. All these appear to be by *R. J. Newbery*. – Chancel S, Good Shepherd and Light of the World. 1940. Nave SE and S, saints, *c.* 1938 and 1943. N aisle W, Peace and Victory, after 1945. All very retardataire. – N aisle, two N windows *c.* 1950.

PARISH HALL, N of the church, of 1907. Red brick on a deep battered basement of rock-faced sandstone.

FREE LIBRARY. Designed by a local architect, *W. Dowdeswell*, and opened in 1909. An enjoyably reckless little piece of Edwardian Baroque. Single-storey front of three bays. The outer ones project slightly, framed by channelled angle quoins and lit by yawningly wide Venetian windows with stumpy Ionic colonnettes. Central doorway flanked by colonnettes of the same stumpy order carrying brackets on which perches an open segmental pediment.

CEFNFFOREST, 1 m. NW. Longhouse of *c.* 1600, the hall end expanded in the C17 to form a three-unit T-plan house. Cowhouse and shared entry largely intact.

9090

TREHERBERT

The streets of Treherbert are notably straight and broad: BUTE STREET along the valley bottom, DUMFRIES STREET, its parallel on the hillside, and the series of cross-streets too. This must be an imposed layout, for the houses of colliers of the pits sunk on the estate of the Marquess of Bute from 1855. The present terraces reflect the success of mining here from the 1870s.

BETHANY ENGLISH BAPTIST CHAPEL, Bute Street. Dated 1873. Handsome classical façade of an unusual pattern. Three bays under a pediment. The windows, round-headed above, square-headed below, set within giant relieving arches. Elsewhere the wall surface is channelled.

BLAEN y CWM WELSH BAPTIST CHAPEL, Wyndham Street. 1870. Geometrical Gothic.

LIBANUS WELSH BAPTIST CHURCH, Bute Street. 1858, largely remodelled in 1908–9 by *R. S. Griffiths* of Tonypandy. Palladian.

WORKMEN'S INSTITUTE, Wyndham Street. (Disused.) 1908–9 by *W. D. Morgan* of Pentre. Arts and Crafts Baroque. Bulgy porch columns. Local green sandstone.

At TYNEWYDD, the original settlement, to the NW, a looser pattern of housing.

ST ALBAN, St Alban's Road. 1890–1 by *E. M. Bruce Vaughan*. Broad nave and chancel in one. Geometrical tracery. Archbraced roof. Curious timber chancel arch. Flèche demolished 1991.

TYNEWYDD HOUSE. Substantial and well-preserved three-unit farmhouse dated 1652 by the Royal Commission. (16[–]2 is cut on the porch sundial.) The two-storey porch leads into the kitchen. Hall to the r. and parlour beyond, in a gabled but non-projecting wing. Stair behind the hall and narrow service rooms behind the parlour. The windows, which were of timber, are mostly altered. (Much original timberwork inside.) It must have seemed the product of an alien civilization when first built in the empty fastnesses of the Upper Rhondda.

1090

TRELEWIS

ST MARY. 1886 by *E. M. Bruce Vaughan*. Snecked rock-faced sandstone with dressings of red moulded brickwork. Nave and chancel in one, lower sanctuary, but two arches inside, to the chancel as well as to the sanctuary. Lancets.

(TAFF MERTHYR GARDEN VILLAGE, ½ m. N. Built by the Taff Merthyr Colliery.)

TAFF MERTHYR COLLIERY. Closed in 1993, and the extensive colliery structures all immediately demolished.

TREORCHY/TREORCI   9090

The Abergorky Colliery, sunk in 1865 to the steam coal seam, was the principal cause of Treorchy's growth. The long terraces of two-storey cottages which line both sides of HIGH STREET were mostly erected by 1878.

ST MATTHEW. Built as a dual-purpose church-and-school, to the design of *George E. Robinson* of Cardiff, 1871. Patterned stonework of the walls, making stones of every shape usable. The apse is an addition. – STAINED GLASS. 1984. Three abstract crosses.

ST GEORGE, Tallis Street, Cwmparc. 1895–6 by *G. E. Halliday*. Paid for by M. G. Llewellyn of Baglan Hall and Pentre House. Nave and separately gabled s aisle, chancel with s tower against it. Arts and Crafts Perp. Squared-up forms everywhere, e.g. the tower top, windows, roof trusses. Only the w composition, reminiscent of Prichard, is less up-to-date. Rock-faced Pennant sandstone, even for the quoins. Internal dressings of Doulting stone. s aisle arcade arches with wave mouldings which die into lozenge-shaped piers. – PISCINA and AUMBRY contrived in a window splay. – REREDOS. Pink alabaster, designed by *Halliday*, carved by *Clarke* of Llandaff. – IMMERSION FONT at the w end, strictly non-architectural.

AINON WELSH BAPTIST CHAPEL, Ynyswen. 1899 by *Roderick* of Blaencwm.* Rock-faced stone front in a simple classical style. Interior galleried on three sides. Three large plaster roses in the ceiling. Behind the pulpit a decorative arch, and flanking doorways brought into use during baptisms.

BETHLEHEM PRESBYTERIAN CHAPEL, High Street. 1881. Rock-faced walls and round-headed windows. Pediment on giant pilaster strips. Long, thin windows l. and r. to light the gallery stairs. The interior is distinguished only for its pews in a semicircular layout, echoed in the shape of the galleries, which extend round three sides.

CROWN HOTEL, High Street. Arts and Crafts Baroque of *c.* 1910. A positively apoplectic display of red terracotta.

Cwmparc, extending up the valley to the SW, served David Davies's Parc & Dare Collieries (opened 1865, 1870). Its streets tunnel relentlessly across the valley slope above the colliery sites. The dominant building, near the railway station, is the PARC & DARE WORKMEN'S HALL. The earlier part of 1895 by *Jacob Rees* of Pentre, facing STATION ROAD, is Tudor and nothing special. Behind, in DYFODWG STREET, rises, sensationally, a four-storey classical composition of 1913. Pale Doric pilasters in three tiers carry a central pediment. Dark ashlar ground storey. The connection with chapel architecture is obvious.

MAENDY CAMP, 1 m. s. Iron Age HILLTOP ENCLOSURE clearly defined by two widely spaced stone banks fronted by slight

*The name was kindly supplied from the chapel records by Mr E. M. Lewis.

ditches, on a spur overlooking Afon Rhondda Fawr, midway
between the valley floor and the high hills to the s. The central
enclosure of ½ acre (0.2 hectare) is entered from the s through
a wide gap. The more substantial outer bank is roughly concentric with the inner enclosure except to the NE, where it is
interrupted by a rocky scarp. Slightly inturned entrance to the
s. Various lesser stony banks visible in a wide area between the
two main banks may have formed internal annexes and pens.
Early Bronze Age BURIAL CAIRN SW of the inner enclosure.

TROEDYRHIW

0000

ST JOHN THE BAPTIST. 1850–1 by *John Prichard*, partly at the
expense of Anthony Hill, owner of the Plymouth Ironworks
(*see* Abercanaid). Well sited, the ground dropping towards the
E. Nave and chancel under a continuous ridge. Provision made
for lower transepts, but only the s one built. Snecked sandstone
with Bath stone dressings, the transept rock-faced. Lancets
throughout in various combinations. Lively w composition, a
development of the w end of Merthyr Mawr church (q.v.).
Here there are six trefoil-headed lancets, graded and paired.
The centre pair are linked by a plate-traceried head and clasped
by slender shafts which rise to support the buttresses of the
double bell gable. Internal shafting at the w end, in a less
felicitous arrangement. Handsome roofs, of arch-brace and
wind-brace construction, in the chancel brought down on to
stone wall-shafts and stiff-leaf corbels. Similar shafting into
the transepts. – ORGAN CASE. A fine mid-Victorian piece. –
STAINED GLASS. Chancel E, Crucifixion and fifteen small
Passion scenes. 1863. Typical of the early phase of medi-
evalizing stained glass revival. Clearly by *William Wailes*.
The main part of the settlement extends across the valley bottom
with a network of close-set streets. Several chapels, of course,
the showiest MOUNT ZION UNITED REFORMED CHURCH,
Cardiff Road, undated. In YEW STREET, TABERNACLE
ENGLISH BAPTIST CHAPEL, dated 1895, faced with red and
yellow brick, and NAZARETH CALVINISTIC METHODIST
CHAPEL, dated 1897, faced with Pennant sandstone.
AFON TÂF HIGH SCHOOL, off Yew Street. Designed by
K. W. Craven and *T. B. Donne*, Merthyr Tydfil Borough Architects, and opened in 1968. Flat-roofed, concrete-framed blocks
of two and three storeys loosely arranged on three sides of a
tree-filled quadrangle. Windows in continuous bands.

TYLORSTOWN

0090

HOLY TRINITY. On a mound above the main road. By
E. M. Bruce Vaughan, 1882–3. Cheap and simple. Three-sided
E apse. Five-light plate-traceried w window. – STAINED
GLASS. w window, Christ in Majesty. Made by the monks of

Prinknash Abbey, c.1980. – MONUMENT. Rev. John Rees
†1913. Brass plate in a Baroque alabaster surround.

WELFARE HALL. 1933. Red brick and stone. In a French Baroque
style which had been a favourite twenty years before.

CONSERVATIVE CLUB. Greenish grey stone. Also Baroque, but
not dated. Conspicuous radiating voussoirs to the principal
windows.

CEMETERY, ½ m. SW, halfway up the hill to Penrhys. Quite an
ambitious CHAPEL of 1884 by *W. H. Jenkins* and *T. R. Phillips.*

STANLEYTOWN, ½ m. SE, isolated on the steep hillside below 105
Pen-yr-heol. The Stanley Building Club erected this group of
eighty terraced houses in 1895, for a tender price of £166 each,
the unusually large number doubtless helping to keep the price
down. *T. R. Phillips* of Pontypridd was the architect.

TYTHEGSTON/LLANDUDWG

8070

ST TYDWG. Just a nave with S porch and a lower chancel, all
heavily restored by *Prichard* in 1876. The only eloquent feature
now is the chancel arch, of four-centred outline and with continuous mouldings, a hollow chamfer flanked by two sunk
quadrants. However, the window rere-arches are original and
suggest that Prichard's restoration may have been faithful. So
the whole building may be Perp in origin. Rood-stair projection,
abnormally for Glamorgan, on the S side. – FONT. Round bowl
on a moulded stem. – PULPIT. Cylindrical, of stone. Clearly
Prichard's. – S DOOR. Typical *Prichard* too. – MONUMENT.
Lucy Lord †1856. Neoclassical tablet with a willow branch
weeping over an urn. Signed by *T. Gaffin* of London.

To the E of the church the short VILLAGE STREET, with cottages,
some of the C16 and C17, set endways on to it, an unusual
layout. All the early houses started on a single-unit end-entry
plan. CWRTISAF, at the far end, of C16 origin, was replanned
when a two-storey porch was added in the C17, and the house
was extended to the W c.1741.

TYTHEGSTON COURT, W of the church on the far side of the
A4106. The estate belonged to the Turbervilles from the C12,
passed by descent to the Loughers, and in 1732 to Robert
Knight. The medieval origins of the house are suggested by the
three-storey tower at its SW corner, but the transformation into
the prim Georgian building seen today was effected by Robert
Knight's son Henry, between 1765 and 1771, and grandson,
another Henry, from the mid 1790s. Drawings of the house
made by both Henrys before and after the remodelling help to
explain a certain awkwardness, external and internal. Pebbledashed render, intended to hide the history in the walls.

Two two-light Tudor windows to the W, but no early feature
visible in the tower, which was partly taken down and reconstructed in 1769. S front of one bay (the tower) plus six plus
one, which the elder Henry built up to match. Lower windows
segment-headed with rusticated surrounds. Massive Doric

porch, two pairs of columns carrying an entablature, of timber painted white. This is an addition of the 1790s. The present drastic asymmetry of this façade results from the younger Henry's decision to create a taller, two-storey E front. The E front is of six bays, the windows of the lower storey set under shallow arcading with thin imposts and paterae in the spandrels. Plain sash windows. To the N, lower ranges of various dates enclosing a service court.

Internally the constraints of pre-C18 fabric make themselves felt, but have been more successfully overcome, in what is one of the most important C18 decorative schemes in the county. The porch leads into a square entrance HALL, appropriately but insistently Doric, with triglyph and metope friezes supporting the mantelshelf, over the doorcases and running right round the room. Remarkably wide fireplace opening, perhaps reflecting the width of a predecessor. From the E side of the hall the staircase rises with elegant turned balusters, two per tread, slightly constrained for space, but brightly lit at the upper level, where there is a delightful outburst of decorative plasterwork. The principal joiner's name was *Wishart*, the principal plasterer's *Johnson*, but the stair-head seems to have been entrusted to a certain *John Elson*, whose only other known work, at Powderham Castle, Devon, is no longer extant. Stylistically it mixes naturalistic swags and drops of flowers on the walls, with a Gothick cornice, and a ceiling which is a handsome imitation of the Adam style. Vine scrolls, however, are included, a motif which Adam himself would have confined to the dining room. The decoration is dated to 1769–71 by the shield of arms, Knight impaling a blank, indicating the period between the elder Henry's separation from his wife and his death. So plagiarism of the Adam style reached Glamorgan almost as soon as anywhere in the country, it seems.

Adamesque plasterwork also in the pretty groin-vaulted lobby cut through the thickness of the original end wall of the house, from the hall into the SE room. This leads into the younger Henry's main contribution, the DRAWING ROOM in the E range, fitted up originally as a library, but with two pairs of large niches and matching doors to balance the windows, so little wall-space is left for books. Neoclassical detail, frieze with griffins and candelabra, top-heavy chimneypiece on short Corinthian pilasters.

(STORMY CASTLE, 2 m. NW. The remains of a motte of the Sturmi family, thrown up some time before 1154. Top flattened in modern times for a summerhouse. Traces of buildings to the s, which may relate to Sturmieston, a settlement largely cleared away after the Sturmi estate came into the possession of Margam Abbey *c.* 1166.)

VAYNOR/Y FAENOR   *0010*

A minimal rural group, church and tavern, but, unusually, on the side of a valley rather than on high ground. The craggy shoulder of Morlais Hill looms over it to the s.

ST GWYNNO. 1870, by *G. E. Robinson* of Cardiff, at the expense of Robert Thompson Crawshay, the Merthyr ironmaster. A crude performance, chancel, higher nave and sw porch tower, the s stonework multicoloured crazy-paving. Ill-proportioned trefoiled lancets, w window with cusped intersecting tracery, all flat-faced. Heavy buttressing on the s side, and on the tower almost to full height, framing two-light shafted openings at belfry level. A gabled cap by *George Pace* has unceremoniously replaced the spire, and red pantiles cover the roofs, an innovation of 1987. Simple interior with thin arch-braced roof. – STAINED GLASS. Chancel E, Crucifixion between Nativity and Ascension, *c.* 1872, possibly by Joseph Bell of Bristol. – Nave w, Christ between SS Peter and Paul. 1908, a typically florid piece. – Nave N, Virgin and Child. Signed by *A. L. Wilkinson*, 1934. – MONUMENTS. Many tablets. – William Williams. White marble hanging monument, signed by *Joseph Edwards*, the Merthyr Tydfil sculptor, and dated 1874. A vision of a palm-bearing angel. – Richard Frederick Crawshay † 1903. An unusual Italian Gothic wall-monument, with much crinkly foliage. An arch on colonnettes frames a coped casket. Gilt mosaic background. Was it made in Italy? – William Henry Harris † 1956. Relief of a pilgrim, in the style of Eric Gill.

The large CHURCHYARD is terraced down the hillside. At the far w end the overgrown remains of the simple medieval CHURCH. Squat tower-like w bellcote. Among the many monuments, one takes pride of place, the massive red conglomerate slab E of the church commemorating its founder, Robert Thompson Crawshay † 1879. The curt inscription ends with the words: God forgive me.

HY BRASAIL, ¼ m. w. An ordinary farm group expanded in 1912 into the strangest Italianate villa. Two belvedere towers, one higher than the other, the belvederes enclosed by Tuscan colonnettes. Bath stone ashlar throughout. Said to have been built to lure an Italian contessa to cool, misty South Wales.

PONTSARN VIADUCT, ½ m. SW. Built to carry the Brecon, Newport and Merthyr Railway over the Taf Fechan. It has eight segmental arches. 1866 by *Henry Conybeare & Alexander Sutherland.*

TAFF RESERVOIRS. Seven large Victorian and Edwardian reservoirs were constructed in the valleys N of Merthyr Tydfil, although only parts of three of them are in Glamorgan. Cardiff Corporation obtained powers to build reservoirs on the upper Taff in 1884, and the middle one, CANTREF, was completed in 1892. Engineer, *J.A.B. Williams*. With the substantial increase in Cardiff's population, the lower LLWYN-ON reservoir was due to be finished in 1915, but the outbreak of the

First World War delayed its completion until 1926. Engineer, *Charles H. Priestley*. The village of YNYS-Y-FELIN was destroyed by the construction of the new dam, and Cardiff Corporation built the new CAPEL BETHEL on the E side of the valley, opposite the dam. The third reservoir in Glamorgan is on the tributary of the lesser Taff, the Taf Fechan, to the E. The TAF FECHAN RESERVOIR was planned in 1913, but was also delayed by the outbreak of war and only completed in 1927. The reservoirs all have castellated VALVE TOWERS and DAMS with details formed of rusticated masonry.

0070 ## WELSH ST DONATS/LLANDDUNWYD

ST DONAT. A simple late medieval church, nave and much lower chancel, massive W tower. Square-headed two-light windows with arched heads and hoodmoulds, of the C16, in all three parts. Little uniformity, however, among them, so the origins of the fabric may be earlier than appears. The chancel arch is plain, crudely pointed, and of indeterminate age. Late medieval roofs, arched brace in the chancel, in the nave of the attractive local pattern with arched braces on short wall-posts with moulded caps and bases, and a moulded collar purlin. Unbuttressed tower with corbelled battlements, as usual, and a round-headed W doorway with double-wave moulding, perhaps of the early C16. Victorian restoration (1891 by *Kempson & Fowler*) was less obtrusive than usual, the three-light S window in the nave its only obvious trace. – HOLY WATER STOUP. By the S
18   door. – FONT. Small but handsome, and for once fairly closely datable. The water-holding moulding of the circular base demonstrates its C13 date. Circular bowl strongly scalloped on its underside.

The church stands at the N end of a knot of houses, most of them recent. W of it a good farm group, and in the middle of the knot GREAT HOUSE, a modest, two-storey C18 house of three three-bay units, the centre higher than the sides. Off-centre entrance doorway, apparently not to be taken as evidence of earlier structure inside.

PRISK FARM, 1 m. W. The elaborately modelled C17 or C18 plaster ceiling which made this unique among the farmhouses of Glamorgan collapsed *c.* 1989.

1070 ## WENVOE/GWENFÔ

ST MARY. The present standard plan, of nave with lower chancel and W tower, is misleading. The tower originally stood N of the chancel and was rebuilt in its present position in 1699 (see the inscription over the W door). The battlements at a level above the corbel table hint at post-medieval interference. The drastic restoration of 1876 has left no datable earlier feature in nave or chancel. N vestry 1930, N transept 1989–91, by *James Carter* of

Alan Barker Partnership. – REREDOS. By *Comper*. Virgin and
saints in a row under arches. – SCREEN. By *E. P. Warren.* –
STAINED GLASS. Chancel E, Crucifixion, and SE, Agony in
the Garden, the latter dated 1867. Hardman style. – Nave S,
Ascension and Good Shepherd, signed by *Lavers & Westlake*,
dated 1896. Good examples of their miniaturist technique.
Baptism of Christ, not signed. – Tower arch, Jesse Tree, *c.* 1982
by *Frank Roper*. – N transept, Risen Christ in priestly robes,
1992 by *Celtic Studios*. – MONUMENTS. These are what make
the church worth visiting, three fine hanging wall-monuments,
outstanding in the county. – William Thomas †1636. Black-   51
shafted Corinthian columns flank the oval inscription panel
and its broad alabaster surround, in which are seated figures in
shallow relief, trumpet-blowing angels of Fame and Victory
(above), and Prudence and Temperance (below). Crowning
figures of Faith, Hope and Charity in the round. Almost of
metropolitan quality and strongly influenced by Nicholas
Stone. – Sir John Thomas †1704, and wife. Grey and white
marble double monument with broken segmental pediment
and putto heads, with successive inscriptions in contrasting
lettering. – Peter Birt †1791. White marble. Adamesque.
Wreaths and cornucopias in the side panels, a fancy wreathed
urn on top.

WENVOE CASTLE. Of the extremely large but uninspired castellated mansion designed by *Robert Adam* for Peter Birt, and
executed with some modification in 1776–7, all that survives is
the E flanking pavilion. This is a plain, sashed, four-bay block
faced with green Quarella stone ashlar. Two storeys, with an
attic above a block cornice, and the remains of battlements. At
a lower level, to the NE, the fine STABLE COURT, attributed
not to Adam but to *Holland*, who was working at Cardiff Castle
in the late 1770s. The stables are classical, forming three sides   65
of a rectangular courtyard, the entrance range of five three-bay
sections in a centre-and-ends composition. Windows in blind
arcading. Large central arch under an attic and clock-turret.
The lower side ranges are one-storeyed with central three-bay
pediments (one surviving). Quarella ashlar here too, but Bath
stone for the impost moulding which runs right across.

COED Y CYMDDA, 1 m. NE. A small ENCLOSURE defended by   p. 27
a single bank and ditch, datable to the early first millennium
B.C. It has been excavated prior to destruction by quarrying.

WICK/Y WIG   9070

ST JAMES. The Norman origin of the church is established by
one round-headed light in the S wall of the chancel, and by the
chancel arch, turned in cut stones, but unmoulded and resting
on plain imposts. Later squints to l. and r. to improve visibility
of the altar. The other medieval features inside are the two
image niches in the E wall of the chancel, the l. one tall and
narrow with an enriched gable over a cusped head and small

fleurs-de-lys and roses on the jambs. Of the C15? Medieval w
tower, unbuttressed, with a saddleback roof. Nave rebuilt in
1871 by *Prichard* – see such details as the design of the s door.
– FONT. C12. Tub-shaped. Rope moulding round the lip. –
MONUMENTS. Elizabeth Lloyd †1723. An example of the
rustic local style of the period. – Frances Hewett † 1828. Draped
female grieving over an urn. Genteel taste of its period.

In the churchyard, stump of a CHURCHYARD CROSS, on
three steps.

GENERAL BAPTIST AND UNITARIAN CHURCH, Chapel Road.
'Established' in 1792, but the two pointed windows with yellow
brick surrounds indicate a late C19 remodelling. Central
doorway into the tiny interior. Galleries on three sides on timber
posts. Pulpit against the far wall, between two windows.

In WEST STREET several cottages set end-on to the road (cf.
Tythegston). WEST COTTAGE is the only one with visible early
features. Two-centred doorway with hollow chamfer, suggesting a C16 date. Two-storeyed, lobby-entry plan, the w half
originally built as a barn.

BROUGHTON MALTINGS, $\frac{3}{4}$ m. s. Three-storey rural maltings
with a four-storey barley kiln at its E end, surmounted by a
hipped pyramidal roof. Six-bay block of local limestone rubble
with a sill projecting over an adjacent stream next to the road
on its s elevation. The openings have been considerably altered,
through conversion into a 'Welfare Hotel' in 1905, to allow the
families of miners to have holidays, and in the 1960s into flats.
Some original openings, dressed with black brick, visible at the
E end and elsewhere. Remains of the lower part of two taking-
in doors high in the s wall.

LOWER MONKTON, $\frac{3}{4}$ m. SE. A handsomely grouped farmstead.
The T-plan farmhouse, white rendered and regularized, is in
origin of the C16. (Two stone chimneypieces of that date, one
exceptionally ambitious, with spandrels providing for heraldic
display, elaborate fleur-de-lys stops, and a top-heavy hoodmould.) Three-bay barn between cowhouse and stable, all in
one range, datable *c*. 1800.

0090   YNYSHIR

ST ANNE, Church Terrace. 1885–6 by *E. M. Bruce Vaughan*.
Aisled nave and lower chancel. The five-bay aisles cross-gabled,
which gives a curiously spreading w front towards the road,
since there is no clerestory. E.E. Rock-faced Pennant sandstone
with generous Bath stone dressings. Arcades on short round
piers. – PULPIT. With standing figures of famous preachers. –
STAINED GLASS, dominating the interior. – E window, Martha
and Mary, 1885 by *Joseph Bell* of Bristol. – w window, Charge
to Peter, 1905 by *R. J. Newbery*.

BETHANY BAPTIST CHURCH, Ynyshir Road. An early chapel
of the long-wall façade type. Two long, round-headed windows
towards the road.

MORIAH CALVINISTIC METHODIST CHAPEL, Ynyshir Road.
1909–10 by *R. S. Griffiths*. Central Palladian window with
Baroque scrolls over. Rock-faced Pennant sandstone, with
Forest ashlar dressings.

YNYSHIR MINERS' HALL, Ynyshir Road. 1905–6 by *E. Williams* of Cardiff, remodelled *c.* 1930. Stone façade towards the
road, nearly in the Modern style.

YNYSMEUDWY   7000
2 m. NE of Pontardawe

ST MARY. 1911–12 by *J. Cook Rees* of Neath. Nave with N aisle,
lower chancel with bellcote over the chancel arch. Snecked,
rock-faced walls. Geometrical tracery. Octagonal piers. –
STAINED GLASS. Chancel E, Crucifixion. Figures and foliage
in a German late Gothic style, set against clear glass.

YNYSMEUDWY CANAL DOCKS AND TRAMROADS (SN 7377
0500). Until 1837 Ynysgedwyn Ironworks depended on bituminous coal brought in from lower down the Swansea Valley.
In 1828 the owner of the works, George Crane, opened a
colliery at Cwm Nant Llwyd, 1½ m. S, as a source of supply,
and connected it to the Swansea Canal by a tramroad and
branch canal. At the head of the incline (SN 7374 0459) which
took the tramroad down to the valley floor are the stone supporting walls of a winding drum. This was designed by *William
Brunton Senior* and used the weight of loaded wagons descending the incline to haul wagons along the level section from the
colliery to the incline head. This section includes a fine stone-
revetted causeway over the Nant Llwyd. At the foot of the
incline, which is carried on a stone retaining wall, the portal of
another coal level, refronted in the 1860s, is visible. The tramroad was carried across the River Tawe on a timber trestle, of
which the abutments and base remain. On the W bank of the
river the coal was trans-shipped to barges on the branch canal.
The loading dock and dry dock survive.

YNYSYBWL   0090

CHRIST CHURCH. A cheap church of 1884–7 by *E. M. Bruce
Vaughan*. Rock-faced Pennant sandstone with Bath stone dressings. Three-sided apsidal chancel. Nave with W bell gable.
Shafted arch to the S porch. That is all. – STAINED GLASS. E
window, Christ surrounded by a Crown of Thorns, an effective
piece, by *Frank Roper*.

YSTALYFERA   7000

ST DAVID. 1889–90 by *J. Buckley Wilson* with *Glendinning
Moxham*. An awkward, cruciform design. Cigarette-shaped NE

bell-turret crowned by a spirelet, tucked into the angle of one of the transepts. Geometrical tracery in the E window, and, outmodedly, Y-tracery elsewhere. Broad, low interior, the surfaces rock-faced, the windows deeply splayed, the chancel arch almost semicircular. Arch-braced roofs. – STAINED GLASS. E window, Ascension, 1940, signed by *Horace Wilkinson*. – S transept E window, saints, by the same. 1938.

AQUEDUCT AND WEIR, $\frac{1}{4}$ m. N. The largest aqueduct on the Swansea Canal, built by *Thomas Sheasby* 1794–8, using hydraulic mortar from Aberavon. The Swansea Canal aqueducts were probably the first in Britain to use such mortar as the waterproofing agent instead of puddling clay. This one consists of three segmental arches built on top of a feeder weir, the crest of the weir being paved to prevent any scouring of the foundations. A large circular culvert through the N end of the aqueduct carried the tailrace water from a fulling mill at Gurnos.

YNYSGEINON TRAMROAD VIADUCT, $1\frac{1}{2}$ m. SW. The E abutment, of Pennant sandstone, and the most easterly of the piers survive of a five-arch viaduct across the River Tawe, on a line 1,312 ft (400 metres) long leading from Ynysygeinon Colliery to the Swansea Canal. In 1824 the Rev. Edward Thomas of Ynysygeinon had applied to the Swansea Canal Company to build a railway to carry 'coal, culm and other goods, wares and merchandise to and from the said canal'.

IRON AND TINPLATE WORKS, $\frac{1}{2}$ m. SW. The high Pennant sandstone wall revetting the W side of the valley, behind single-storey factory units to the S of Ystalyfera, belonged to the charging bank of the Ystalyfera Ironworks blast furnaces. Built in 1838, Ystalyfera was claimed by the 1850s to be the largest tinplate works in the world. Its bank of eleven blast furnaces was second only to that at Dowlais, Merthyr Tydfil (q.v.). From the 1860s, however, all anthracite ironworks went into decline, and by 1864 Ystalyfera had only six furnaces in blast. The owner, James Palmer Budd, struggled to keep the works going, both for the sake of the workforce and out of personal pride, but the few remaining furnaces were blown out in 1885. There was a sixteen-mill tinplate works, where production continued until after the Second World War. The buildings were demolished in 1946. Much of the works site was reclaimed from the flood-prone valley of the Tawe, and impressive iron-slag embankments contain its course to the S of the site.

Nearly all the rows of HOUSES which line the hillside between Godre'r-graig and Ystalyfera were built for workers in this business.

CRIMEA COLLIERY, GODRE'R-GRAIG, $1\frac{1}{2}$ m. SW. One of the most intact sets of mid-C19 colliery buildings, located in undergrowth W of the main Swansea Valley road. Beam-engine house and adjacent winding support, of Pennant sandstone rubble, built in 1854, remain, together with the embankment of a tramroad down to a tipping stage on the Swansea Canal.

GODRE'R GRAIG LOCK AND DRY DOCK, $1\frac{1}{2}$ m. SW. The

substantial remains of Lock 17 on the Swansea Canal (1794–8) and of others in what was an extensive flight of locks. Visible on the w side of the new valley road. Dry dock, with stepped walls of Pennant sandstone, added to the platform of Lock 17 after 1875. The bases of the brick pillars for a former roof remain. The lock by-pass was used to drain the dock when required for the maintenance of boats. There are also remains of a pitch-boiling hearth and of the timber uprights which supported cross-pieces to carry boats under repair.

YSTRAD

9090

St Stephen, Penrhys Road. 1896 by *E. M. Bruce Vaughan.* Larger than most of his Valleys churches, and showing many of his idiosyncracies. Snecked local sandstone, Bath stone dressings, red brick string course low down. Five-bay nave with N aisle, lower chancel. E.E. Geometrical tracery. Side windows alternating one- and two-light. Arcade with circular piers. Stiff-leaf foliage here and there.

The Star Hotel of 1913, on the main road, makes an odd bedfellow for the church. Baroque. Plenty of red brick.

Tyntyle, ⅓m. NE. Isolated on the steep mountainside. A little-altered longhouse, probably of the early C17. The original doorway into the raised passage between hall and cowhouse survives, but a new entrance, sheltered by a porch, has been made directly into the hall.

Hen Dre'r Gelli, house circles, ¾m. SW. These were excavated in the early C20, producing Roman-British pottery, but are now indicated merely by undiagnostic accumulations of stones.

YSTRAD MYNACH

1090

Holy Trinity. Paid for by the Rev. George Thomas, who became the first vicar, and built 1855–7 by *John Norton,* his earliest appearance in the county. Well crafted, the Pennant sandstone walls and ashlar dressings of a uniform warm brown hue. No buttresses. Lancets, mainly in pairs, but w and e triplets. Nave with a sheer w wall, s porch and stocky N tower. Double-gabled transepts and chancel projecting only slightly beyond them. This is a somewhat eccentric plan, and the blunt detailing, especially at the top of the tower, is equally personal. Close inspection suggests that the church is not all of one build, though it is difficult to imagine that the apparently blocked arches between tower and transepts indicate an intended aisle. Inside, the roofs suggest that the e half of each transept must be an addition. – FONT. Presumably by Norton. Square on angle shafts. – PULPIT. Brass openwork on a stone base, an attractive piece, given in 1888. – STAINED GLASS. Worth a close look. The w window looks *c.* 1860, with nine small Old

Testament scenes. – Probably by the same maker, the Raising of Jairus's daughter, nave N, and, perhaps, St Katherine, nave s. – The NE pair of lancets has further small scenes of an even more miniaturist character, c. 1873. – Three s lancets, in transept and chancel, attributable to *Lavers & Barraud*. – E window, the latest and finest, 1888 by *Henry Holiday*, made by *Powell*'s. Empty Tomb and ascended Christ, with scenes from the life of Christ below. In a classicizing style like that of such contemporary painters as Lord Leighton and Albert Moore.

COUNCIL OFFICES, ½ m. SE. Ystrad Fawr House, a simple and not altogether regular Italianate mansion built by the Rev. George Thomas, c. 1852–7. Five-bay, stone-faced E front, s-facing conservatory with stout stone Tuscan columns. Spoilt by recent additions.

COLLEGE OF FURTHER EDUCATION, Twyn Road. 1960 by *T. Alwyn Lloyd & Gordon*, an early example of concrete-framing and curtain-walling in the county. Four-storey and two-storey blocks not clearly distinguished from one another.

PENALLTA WORKMEN'S HALL AND INSTITUTE, High Street. 1923 by *H. Gabe Jones*. A simple, classical three-storey front.

At HENGOED, up on the hilltop 1 m. N, among much mid-C20 housing, WELSH BAPTIST CHAPEL, founded in 1710, one of the earliest in the uplands, and rebuilt in 1829, in what must then still have been an isolated position, typical for early chapels. Large for its date. Gable-end plan, the interior with galleries on three sides producing a two-storey façade of three bays, with doorways in the outer bays. Inside, the 'big seat' and pulpit against the far wall are clearly of 1829, characteristic late Georgian joinery. Box pews. Fireplace and surrounding benches l. of the pulpit steps. Even the rows of hatpegs on the side walls partly survive. The galleries, most unusually, rest on timber posts. Late C19 boarded ceiling.

84 At MAESYCWMMER, ¾ m. NE, TABOR CHAPEL, Tabor Road. Dated 1876. A particularly fine example of a classical chapel of that period, designed by the Rev. *Thomas Thomas* of Landore. Stone façade of thin-coursed Pennant sandstone and buff ashlar dressings. Ionic pilasters carry an entablature and pediment into which breaks a traceried oculus under a relieving arch. Twin arched entrance doorways under an arched tripartite central window. Long, narrow side windows, also arched, of course.

MAESYCWMMER VIADUCT. Stone viaduct of fifteen arches, 850 ft (260 metres) long, built to the design of *Charles Liddell* in 1857 to carry the Newport, Abergavenny and Hereford Railway across the Rhymney Valley. A C19 FLANNEL MILL stands beneath it.

YSTRADOWEN

ST OWAIN. Effectively sited at a bend in the road. 1865–8 by *John Prichard*. A perfected replication of the former church,

perfected in its steep roofs, perfected in the tidy coursing of its
Lias limestone walls, perfected in its late C13 style and in its
stylistic consistency. Slender w tower with saddleback roof and
ridge cross. Ingenious management of the tower stairs. The
interior was originally stronger meat, with polychromatic patterning in the brick walls, but this has been painted out. s
doorway with aggressive floriated knobs. Arch-braced roofs. –
FONT. Octagonal on a square base, with a well-matched
steeple-like COVER brought from Llanbradach. – PULPIT. Cylindrical. Typical of *Prichard*. – CHOIR STALLS. Also part of the
original fittings. – STAINED GLASS. One of the most attractive
features of the church, grisaille, but with a blood-red disc
in each light. The intention must have been to pick up the
polychromy in the walls.

MOTTE. Immediately w of the churchyard, from where it is
dramatically seen. Early C12. Unfinished towards the NW. In
size second only to Cardiff among Glamorgan mottes.

TALYFAN CASTLE, $\frac{3}{4}$m. SE. The puzzling remains of a castle of
the powerful St Quintin family. On a low hilltop, having far-
seeing views over the Vale of Glamorgan in all directions. Very
fragmentary walls. Part of a curved curtain wall to the E; in
the centre several walls rising to about 10 ft (3.05 metres)
high, including a curved section with a r.-angled outer face
to the NW.

ARCHITECTURAL GLOSSARY

Numbers and letters refer to the illustrations (by John Sambrook)
on pp. 662–9.

ABACUS: flat slab forming the top of a capital (3a).

ACANTHUS: classical formalized leaf ornament (3b).

ACCUMULATOR TOWER: see Hydraulic power.

ACHIEVEMENT: a complete display of armorial bearings.

ACROTERION: plinth for a statue or ornament on the apex or ends of a pediment; more usually, both the plinth and what stands on it (4a).

AEDICULE (lit. little building): architectural surround, consisting usually of two columns or pilasters supporting a pediment.

AGGREGATE: see Concrete.

AISLE: subsidiary space alongside the body of a building, separated from it by columns, piers, or posts.

AMBULATORY (lit. walkway): aisle around the sanctuary (q.v.).

ANGLE ROLL: roll moulding in the angle between two planes (1a).

ANSE DE PANIER: see Arch.

ANTAE: simplified pilasters (4a), usually applied to the ends of the enclosing walls of a portico in antis (q.v.).

ANTEFIXAE: ornaments projecting at regular intervals above a Greek cornice, originally to conceal the ends of roof tiles (4a).

ANTHEMION: classical ornament like a honeysuckle flower (4b).

APRON: raised panel below a window or wall monument or tablet.

APSE: semicircular or polygonal end of an apartment, especially of a chancel or chapel. In classical architecture sometimes called an exedra.

ARABESQUE: non-figurative surface decoration consisting of flowing lines, foliage scrolls etc., based on geometrical patterns. Cf. Grotesque.

ARCADE: series of arches supported by piers or columns. Blind arcade or arcading: the same applied to the wall surface. Wall arcade: in medieval churches, a blind arcade forming a dado below windows. Also a covered shopping street.

ARCH: Shapes see 5c. Basket arch or anse de panier (basket handle): three-centred and depressed, or with a flat centre. Nodding: ogee arch curving forward from the wall face. Parabolic: shaped like a chain suspended from two level points, but inverted. Special purposes. Chancel: dividing chancel from nave or crossing. Crossing: spanning piers at a crossing (q.v.). Relieving or discharging: incorporated in a wall to relieve superimposed weight (5c). Skew: spanning responds not diametrically opposed. Strainer: inserted in an opening to resist inward pressure. Transverse: spanning a main axis (e.g. of a vaulted space). See also Jack arch, Triumphal arch.

ARCHITRAVE: formalized lintel, the lowest member of the classical entablature (3a). Also the moulded frame of a door or window (often borrowing the profile of a classical architrave). For lugged and shouldered architraves see 4b.

ARCUATED: dependent structurally on the arch principle. Cf. Trabeated.

ARK: chest or cupboard housing the

tables of Jewish law in a synagogue.

ARRIS: sharp edge where two surfaces meet at an angle (3a).

ASHLAR: masonry of large blocks wrought to even faces and square edges (6d).

ASTRAGAL: classical moulding of semicircular section (3f).

ASTYLAR: with no columns or similar vertical features.

ATLANTES: *see* Caryatids.

ATRIUM (plural: atria): inner court of a Roman or C20 house; in a multi-storey building, a toplit covered court rising through all storeys. Also an open court in front of a church.

ATTACHED COLUMN: *see* Engaged column.

ATTIC: small top storey within a roof. Also the storey above the main entablature of a classical façade.

AUMBRY: recess or cupboard to hold sacred vessels for the Mass.

BAILEY: *see* Motte-and-bailey.

BALANCE BEAM: *see* Canals.

BALDACCHINO: free-standing canopy, originally fabric, over an altar. Cf. Ciborium.

BALLFLOWER: globular flower of three petals enclosing a ball (1a). Typical of the Decorated style.

BALUSTER: pillar or pedestal of bellied form. *Balusters*: vertical supports of this or any other form, for a handrail or coping, the whole being called a *balustrade* (6c). *Blind balustrade*: the same applied to the wall surface.

BARBICAN: outwork defending the entrance to a castle.

BARGEBOARDS (corruption of 'vergeboards'): boards, often carved or fretted, fixed beneath the eaves of a gable to cover and protect the rafters.

BAROQUE: style originating in Rome *c.*1600 and current in England *c.*1680–1720, characterized by dramatic massing and silhouette and the use of the giant order.

BARROW: burial mound.

BARTIZAN: corbelled turret, square or round, frequently at an angle.

BASCULE: hinged part of a lifting (or bascule) bridge.

BASE: moulded foot of a column or pilaster . For *Attic* base *see* 3b.

BASEMENT: lowest, subordinate storey; hence the lowest part of a classical elevation, below the piano nobile (q.v.).

BASILICA: a Roman public hall; hence an aisled building with a clerestory.

BASTION: one of a series of defensive semicircular or polygonal projections from the main wall of a fortress or city.

BATTER: intentional inward inclination of a wall face.

BATTLEMENT: defensive parapet, composed of *merlons* (solid) and *crenels* (embrasures) through which archers could shoot; sometimes called *crenellation*. Also used decoratively.

BAY LEAF: classical ornament of overlapping bay leaves (3f).

BAY: division of an elevation or interior space as defined by regular vertical features such as arches, columns, windows, etc.

BAY WINDOW: window of one or more storeys projecting from the face of a building. *Canted*: with a straight front and angled sides. *Bow window*: curved. *Oriel*: rests on corbels or brackets and starts above ground level; also the bay window at the dais end of a medieval great hall.

BEAD-AND-REEL: *see* Enrichments.

BEAKHEAD: Norman ornament with a row of beaked bird or beast heads usually biting into a roll moulding (1a).

BELFRY: chamber or stage in a tower where bells are hung.

BELL CAPITAL: *see* 1b.

BELLCOTE: small gabled or roofed housing for the bell(s).

BERM: level area separating a ditch from a bank on a hill-fort or barrow.

BILLET: Norman ornament of small half-cyclindrical or rectangular blocks (1a).

BLIND: *see* Arcade, Baluster, Portico.

BLOCK CAPITAL: *see* 1a.

BLOCKED: columns, etc. interrupted by regular projecting blocks (*blocking*), as on a Gibbs surround (4b).

BLOCKING COURSE: course of stones, or equivalent, on top of a cornice and crowning the wall.

BOLECTION MOULDING: covering the joint between two different planes (6b).

BOND: the pattern of long sides (*stretchers*) and short ends (*headers*) produced on the face of a wall by laying bricks in a particular way (6e).

BOSS: knob or projection, e.g. at the intersection of ribs in a vault (2c).

BOW WINDOW: *see* Bay window.

BOX FRAME: timber-framed construction in which vertical and horizontal wall members support the roof (7). Also concrete construction where the loads are taken on cross walls; also called *cross-wall construction*.

BRACE: subsidiary member of a structural frame, curved or straight. *Bracing* is often arranged decoratively e.g. quatrefoil, herringbone (7). *See also* Roofs.

BRATTISHING: ornamental crest, usually formed of leaves, Tudor flowers or miniature battlements.

BRESSUMER (*lit.* breast-beam): big horizontal beam supporting the wall above, especially in a jettied building (7).

BRICK: *see* Bond, Cogging, Engineering, Gauged, Tumbling.

BRIDGE: *Bowstring*: with arches rising above the roadway which is suspended from them. *Clapper*: one long stone forms the roadway. *Roving*: *see* Canal. *Suspension*: roadway suspended from cables or chains slung between towers or pylons. *Stay-suspension* or *stay-cantilever*: supported by diagonal stays from towers or pylons. *See also* Bascule.

BRISES-SOLEIL: projecting fins or canopies which deflect direct sunlight from windows.

BROACH: *see* Spire and IC.

BUCRANIUM: ox skull used decoratively in classical friezes.

BULLSEYE WINDOW: small oval window, set horizontally (cf. Oculus). Also called *oeil de boeuf*.

BUTTRESS: vertical member projecting from a wall to stabilize it or to resist the lateral thrust of an arch, roof, or vault (IC, 2c). A *flying buttress* transmits the thrust to a heavy abutment by means of an arch or half-arch (IC).

CABLE or ROPE MOULDING: originally Norman, like twisted strands of a rope.

CAMES: *see* Quarries.

CAMPANILE: free-standing bell tower.

CANALS: *Flash lock*: removable weir or similar device through which boats pass on a flush of water. Predecessor of the *pound lock*: chamber with gates at each end allowing boats to float from one level to another. *Tidal gates*: single pair of lock gates allowing vessels to pass when the tide makes a level. *Balance beam*: beam projecting horizontally for opening and closing lock gates. *Roving bridge*: carrying a towing path from one bank to the other.

CANTILEVER: horizontal projection (e.g. step, canopy) supported by a downward force behind the fulcrum.

CAPITAL: head or crowning feature of a column or pilaster; for classical types *see* 3a; for medieval types *see* IB.

CARREL: compartment designed for individual work or study.

CARTOUCHE: classical tablet with ornate frame (4b).

CARYATIDS: female figures supporting an entablature; their male counterparts are *Atlantes* (*lit*: Atlas figures).

CASEMATE: vaulted chamber, with embrasures for defence, within a castle wall or projecting from it.

CASEMENT: side-hinged window.

CASTELLATED: with battlements (q.v.).

CAST IRON: hard and brittle, cast in a mould to the required shape. *Wrought iron* is ductile, strong in tension, forged into decorative patterns or forged and rolled into e.g. bars, joists, boiler plates; *mild steel* is its modern equivalent, similar but stronger.

CATSLIDE: *See* 8a.

CAVETTO: concave classical moulding of quarter-round section (3f).

CELURE or CEILURE: enriched area of roof above rood or altar.

CEMENT: *see* Concrete.

CENOTAPH (*lit.* empty tomb): funerary monument which is not a burying place.

CENTRING: wooden support for the building of an arch or vault, removed after completion.

CHAMFER (*lit.* corner-break): surface formed by cutting off a square edge or corner. For types of chamfers and *chamfer stops see* 6a. *See also* Double chamfer.

CHANCEL: part of the E end of a church set apart for the use of the officiating clergy.

CHANTRY CHAPEL: often attached to or within a church, endowed for the celebration of Masses principally for the soul of the founder.

CHEVET (*lit.* head): French term for chancel with ambulatory and radiating chapels.

CHEVRON: V-shape used in series or double series (later) on a Norman moulding (1a). Also (especially when on a single plane) called *zigzag*.

CHOIR: the part of a cathedral, monastic or collegiate church where services are sung.

CIBORIUM: a fixed canopy over an altar, usually vaulted and supported on four columns; cf. Baldacchino. Also a canopied shrine for the reserved sacrament.

CINQUEFOIL: *see* Foil.

CIST: stone-lined or slab-built grave.

CLADDING: external covering or skin applied to a structure, especially a framed one.

CLERESTORY: uppermost storey of the nave of a church, pierced by windows. Also high-level windows in secular buildings.

CLOSER: a brick cut to complete a bond (6e).

CLUSTER BLOCK: *see* Multi-storey.

COADE STONE: ceramic artificial stone made in Lambeth 1769–c.1840 by Eleanor Coade (†1821) and her associates.

COB: walling material of clay mixed with straw. Also called *pisé*.

COFFERING: arrangement of sunken panels (coffers), square or polygonal, decorating a ceiling, vault, or arch.

COGGING: a decorative course of bricks laid diagonally (6e). Cf. Dentilation.

COLLAR: *see* Roofs and 7.

COLLEGIATE CHURCH: endowed for the support of a college of priests.

COLONNADE: range of columns supporting an entablature. Cf. Arcade.

COLONNETTE: small medieval column or shaft.

COLOSSAL ORDER: *see* Giant order.

COLUMBARIUM: shelved, niched structure to house multiple burials.

COLUMN: a classical, upright structural member of round section with a shaft, a capital, and usually a base (3a, 4a).

COLUMN FIGURE: carved figure attached to a medieval column or shaft, usually flanking a doorway.

COMMUNION TABLE: unconsecrated table used in Protestant churches for the celebration of Holy Communion.

COMPOSITE: *see* Orders.

COMPOUND PIER: grouped shafts (q.v.), or a solid core surrounded by shafts.

CONCRETE: composition of *cement* (calcined lime and clay), *aggregate* (small stones or rock chippings), sand and water. It can be poured into *formwork* or *shuttering* (temporary frame of timber or metal) on site (*in-situ* concrete), or *pre-cast* as components before construction. *Reinforced*: incorporating steel rods to take the tensile force. *Pre-stressed*: with tensioned steel rods. Finishes include the impression of boards left by formwork (*board-marked* or *shuttered*), and texturing with steel brushes (*brushed*) or hammers (*hammer-dressed*). *See also* Shell.

CONSOLE: bracket of curved outline (4b).

COPING: protective course of masonry or brickwork capping a wall (6d).

CORBEL: projecting block supporting something above. *Corbel course*: continuous course of projecting stones or bricks fulfilling the same function. *Corbel table*: series of corbels to carry a parapet or a wall-plate or wall-post (7). *Corbelling*: brick or masonry courses built out beyond one another to support a chimney-stack, window, etc.

CORINTHIAN: *see* Orders and 3d.

CORNICE: flat-topped ledge with moulded underside, projecting along the top of a building or feature, especially as the highest member of the classical entablature (3a). Also the decorative moulding in the angle between wall and ceiling.

CORPS-DE-LOGIS: the main building(s) as distinct from the wings or pavilions.

COTTAGE ORNÉ: an artfully rustic small house associated with the Picturesque movement.

COUNTERCHANGING: of joists on a ceiling divided by beams into compartments, when placed in opposite directions in alternate squares.

COUR D'HONNEUR: formal entrance court before a house in the French manner, usually with flanking wings and a screen wall or gates.

COURSE: continuous layer of stones, etc. in a wall (6e).

COVE: a broad concave moulding, e.g. to mask the eaves of a roof. *Coved ceiling*: with a pronounced cove joining the walls to a flat central panel smaller than the whole area of the ceiling.

CRADLE ROOF: *see* Wagon roof.

CREDENCE: a shelf within or beside a piscina (q.v.), or a table for the sacramental elements and vessels.

CRENELLATION: parapet with crenels (*see* Battlement).

CRINKLE-CRANKLE WALL: garden wall undulating in a series of serpentine curves.

CROCKETS: leafy hooks. *Crocket-ing* decorates the edges of Gothic features, such as pinnacles, canopies, etc. *Crocket capital*: *see* 1b.

CROSSING: central space at the junction of the nave, chancel, and transepts. *Crossing tower*: above a crossing.

CROSS-WINDOW: with one mullion and one transom (qq.v.).

CROWN-POST: *see* Roofs and 7.

CROWSTEPS: squared stones set like steps, e.g. on a gable (8a).

CRUCKS (*lit.* crooked): pairs of inclined timbers (*blades*), usually curved, set at bay-lengths; they support the roof timbers and, in timber buildings, also support the walls (8b). *Base*: blades rise from ground level to a tie- or collar-beam which supports the roof timbers. *Full*: blades rise from ground level to the apex of the roof, serving as the main members of a roof truss. *Jointed*: blades formed from more than one timber; the lower member may act as a wall-post; it is usually elbowed at wall-plate level and jointed just above. *Middle*: blades rise from halfway up the walls to a tie- or collar-beam. *Raised*: blades rise from halfway up the walls to the apex. *Upper*: blades supported on a tie-beam and rising to the apex.

CRYPT: underground or half-underground area, usually below the E end of a church. *Ring crypt*: corridor crypt surrounding the apse of an early medieval church, often associated with chambers for relics. Cf. Undercroft.

CUPOLA (*lit.* dome): especially a small dome on a circular or polygonal base crowning a larger dome, roof, or turret.

CURSUS: a long avenue defined by two parallel earthen banks with ditches outside.

CURTAIN WALL: a connecting wall between the towers of a castle. Also a non-load-bearing external wall applied to a C20 framed structure.

CUSP: *see* Tracery and 2b.

CYCLOPEAN MASONRY: large irregular polygonal stones, smooth and finely jointed.

CYMA RECTA and CYMA REVERSA: classical mouldings with double curves (3f). Cf. Ogee.

DADO: the finishing (often with panelling) of the lower part of a wall in a classical interior; in origin a formalized continuous pedestal. *Dado rail*: the moulding along the top of the dado.

DAGGER: *see* Tracery and 2b.

DEC (DECORATED): English Gothic architecture *c.* 1290 to *c.* 1350. The name is derived from the type of window Tracery (q.v.) used during the period.

DEMI- or HALF-COLUMNS: engaged columns (q.v.) half of whose circumference projects from the wall.

DENTIL: small square block used in series in classical cornices (3c). *Dentilation* is produced by the projection of alternating headers along cornices or string courses.

DIAPER: repetitive surface decoration of lozenges or squares flat or in relief. Achieved in brickwork with bricks of two colours.

DIOCLETIAN or THERMAL WINDOW: semicircular with two mullions, as used in the Baths of Diocletian, Rome (4b).

DISTYLE: having two columns (4a).

DOGTOOTH: E.E. ornament, consisting of a series of small pyramids formed by four stylized canine teeth meeting at a point (1a).

DORIC: *see* Orders and 3a, 3b.

DORMER: window projecting from the slope of a roof (8a).

DOUBLE CHAMFER: a chamfer applied to each of two recessed arches (1a).

DOUBLE PILE: *see* Pile.

DRAGON BEAM: *see* Jetty.

DRESSINGS: the stone or brickwork worked to a finished face about an angle, opening, or other feature.

DRIPSTONE: moulded stone projecting from a wall to protect the lower parts from water. Cf. Hoodmould, Weathering.

DRUM: circular or polygonal stage supporting a dome or cupola. Also

one of the stones forming the shaft of a column (3a).

DUTCH or FLEMISH GABLE: *see* 8a.

EASTER SEPULCHRE: tomb-chest used for Easter ceremonial, within or against the N wall of a chancel.

EAVES: overhanging edge of a roof; hence *eaves cornice* in this position.

ECHINUS: ovolo moulding (q.v.) below the abacus of a Greek Doric capital (3a).

EDGE RAIL: *see* Railways.

E. E. (EARLY ENGLISH): English Gothic architecture *c.* 1190–1250.

EGG-AND-DART: *see* Enrichments and 3f.

ELEVATION: any face of a building or side of a room. In a drawing, the same or any part of it, represented in two dimensions.

EMBATTLED: with battlements.

EMBRASURE: small splayed opening in a wall or battlement (q.v.).

ENCAUSTIC TILES: earthenware tiles fired with a pattern and glaze.

EN DELIT: stone cut against the bed.

ENFILADE: reception rooms in a formal series, usually with all doorways on axis.

ENGAGED or ATTACHED COLUMN: one that partly merges into a wall or pier.

ENGINEERING BRICKS: dense bricks, originally used mostly for railway viaducts etc.

ENRICHMENTS: the carved decoration of certain classical mouldings, e.g. the ovolo (qq.v.) with *egg-and-dart*, the cyma reversa with *waterleaf*, the astragal with *bead-and-reel* (3f).

ENTABLATURE: in classical architecture, collective name for the three horizontal members (architrave, frieze, and cornice) carried by a wall or a column (3a).

ENTASIS: very slight convex deviation from a straight line, used to prevent an optical illusion of concavity.

EPITAPH: inscription on a tomb.

EXEDRA: *see* Apse.

EXTRADOS: outer curved face of an arch or vault.

EYECATCHER: decorative building terminating a vista.

FASCIA: plain horizontal band, e.g. in an architrave (3c, 3d) or on a shopfront.

FENESTRATION: the arrangement of windows in a façade.

FERETORY: site of the chief shrine of a church, behind the high altar.

FESTOON: ornamental garland, suspended from both ends. Cf. Swag.

FIBREGLASS, or glass-reinforced polyester (GRP): synthetic resin reinforced with glass fibre. GRC: glass-reinforced concrete.

FIELD: see Panelling and 6b.

FILLET: a narrow flat band running down a medieval shaft or along a roll moulding (1a). It separates larger curved mouldings in classical cornices, fluting or bases (3c).

FLAMBOYANT: the latest phase of French Gothic architecture, with flowing tracery.

FLASH LOCK: see Canals.

FLÈCHE or SPIRELET (lit. arrow): slender spire on the centre of a roof.

FLEURON: medieval carved flower or leaf, often rectilinear (1a).

FLUSHWORK: knapped flint used with dressed stone to form patterns.

FLUTING: series of concave grooves (flutes), their common edges sharp (arris) or blunt (fillet) (3).

FOIL (lit. leaf): lobe formed by the cusping of a circular or other shape in tracery (2b). Trefoil (three), quatrefoil (four), cinquefoil (five), and multifoil express the number of lobes in a shape.

FOLIATE: decorated with leaves.

FORMWORK: see Concrete.

FRAMED BUILDING: where the structure is carried by a framework – e.g. of steel, reinforced concrete, timber – instead of by load-bearing walls.

FREESTONE: stone that is cut, or can be cut, in all directions.

FRESCO: al fresco: painting on wet plaster. Fresco secco: painting on dry plaster.

FRIEZE: the middle member of the classical entablature, sometimes ornamented (3a). Pulvinated frieze (lit. cushioned): of bold convex profile (3c). Also a horizontal band of ornament.

FRONTISPIECE: in C16 and C17 buildings the central feature of doorway and windows above linked in one composition.

GABLE: For types see 8a. Gablet: small gable. Pedimental gable: treated like a pediment.

GADROONING: classical ribbed ornament like inverted fluting that flows into a lobed edge.

GALILEE: chapel or vestibule usually at the W end of a church enclosing the main portal(s).

GALLERY: a long room or passage; an upper storey above the aisle of a church, looking through arches to the nave; a balcony or mezzanine overlooking the main interior space of a building; or an external walkway.

GALLETING: small stones set in a mortar course.

GAMBREL ROOF: see 8a.

GARDEROBE: medieval privy.

GARGOYLE: projecting water spout often carved into human or animal shape.

GAUGED or RUBBED BRICKWORK: soft brick sawn roughly, then rubbed to a precise (gauged) surface. Mostly used for door or window openings (5c).

GAZEBO (jocular Latin, 'I shall gaze'): ornamental lookout tower or raised summer house.

GEOMETRIC: English Gothic architecture c. 1250–1310. See also Tracery. For another meaning, see Stairs.

GIANT or COLOSSAL ORDER: classical order (q.v.) whose height is that of two or more storeys of the building to which it is applied.

GIBBS SURROUND: C18 treatment of an opening (4b), seen particularly in the work of James Gibbs (1682–1754).

GIRDER: a large beam. Box: of hollow-box section. Bowed: with its top rising in a curve. Plate: of I-section, made from iron or steel plates. Lattice: with braced framework.

GLAZING BARS: wooden or sometimes metal bars separating and supporting window panes.

GORSEDD CIRCLE: modern stone circle; one is erected annually at different Welsh sites in connection with the national Eisteddfod.

GRAFFITI: *see* Sgraffito.

GRANGE: farm owned and run by a religious order.

GRC: *see* Fibreglass.

GRISAILLE: monochrome painting on walls or glass.

GROIN: sharp edge at the meeting of two cells of a cross-vault; *see* Vault and 2b.

GROTESQUE (*lit.* grotto-esque): wall decoration adopted from Roman examples in the Renaissance. Its foliage scrolls incorporate figurative elements. Cf. Arabesque.

GROTTO: artificial cavern.

GRP: *see* Fibreglass.

GUILLOCHE: classical ornament of interlaced bands (4b).

GUNLOOP: opening for a firearm.

GUTTAE: stylized drops (3b).

HALF-TIMBERING: archaic term for timber-framing (q.v.). Sometimes used for non-structural decorative timberwork.

HALL CHURCH: medieval church with nave and aisles of approximately equal height.

HAMMERBEAM: *see* Roofs and 7.

HEADER: *see* Bond and 6e.

HEADSTOP: stop (q.v.) carved with a head (5b).

HELM ROOF: *see* IC.

HENGE: ritual earthwork.

HERM (*lit.* the god Hermes): male head or bust on a pedestal.

HERRINGBONE WORK: *see* 6e (for brick bond). Cf. Pitched masonry.

HEXASTYLE: *see* Portico.

HILL-FORT: Iron Age earthwork enclosed by a ditch and bank system.

HIPPED ROOF: *see* 8a.

HOODMOULD: projecting moulding above an arch or lintel to throw off water (2b, 5b). When horizontal often called a *label*. For label stop *see* Stop.

HUSK GARLAND: festoon of stylized nutshells (4b).

HYDRAULIC POWER: use of water under high pressure to work machinery. *Accumulator tower*: houses a hydraulic accumulator which accommodates fluctuations in the flow through hydraulic mains.

HYPOCAUST (*lit.* underburning): Roman underfloor heating system.

IMPOST: horizontal moulding at the springing of an arch (5c).

IMPOST BLOCK: block between abacus and capital (1b).

IN ANTIS: *see* Antae, Portico and 4a.

INDENT: shape chiselled out of a stone to receive a brass.

INDUSTRIALIZED or SYSTEM BUILDING: system of manufactured units assembled on site.

INGLENOOK (*lit.* fire-corner): recess for a hearth with provision for seating.

INTERCOLUMNATION: interval between columns.

INTERLACE: decoration in relief simulating woven or entwined stems or bands.

INTRADOS: *see* Soffit.

IONIC: *see* Orders and 3c.

JACK ARCH: shallow segmental vault springing from beams, used for fireproof floors, bridge decks, etc.

JAMB (*lit.* leg): one of the vertical sides of an opening.

JETTY: in a timber-framed building, the projection of an upper storey beyond the storey below, made by the beams and joists of the lower storey oversailing the wall; on their outer ends is placed the sill of the walling for the storey above (7). Buildings can be jettied on several sides, in which case a *dragon beam* is set diagonally at the corner to carry the joists to either side.

JOGGLE: the joining of two stones to prevent them slipping by a notch in one and a projection in the other.

KEEL MOULDING: moulding used from the late C12, in section like the keel of a ship (1a).

KEEP: principal tower of a castle.

KENTISH CUSP: *see* Tracery and 2b.

KEY PATTERN: *see* 4b.

KEYSTONE: central stone in an arch or vault (4b, 5c).

KINGPOST: *see* Roofs and 7.

KNEELER: horizontal projecting stone at the base of each side of a gable to support the inclined coping stones (8a).

KNOTWORK: *see* Interlace. Used on early Christian monuments.

LABEL: *see* Hoodmould and 5b.

LABEL STOP: *see* Stop and 5b.

LACED BRICKWORK: vertical strips of brickwork, often in a contrasting colour, linking openings on different floors.

LACING COURSE: horizontal reinforcement in timber or brick to walls of flint, cobble, etc.

LADY CHAPEL: dedicated to the Virgin Mary (Our Lady).

LANCET: slender single-light, pointed-arched window (2a).

LANTERN: circular or polygonal windowed turret crowning a roof or a dome. Also the windowed stage of a crossing tower lighting the church interior.

LANTERN CROSS: churchyard cross with lantern-shaped top.

LAVATORIUM: in a religous house, a washing place adjacent to the refectory.

LEAN-TO: *see* Roofs.

LESENE (*lit.* a mean thing): pilaster without base or capital. Also called *pilaster strip*.

LIERNE: *see* Vault and 2c.

LIGHT: compartment of a window defined by the mullions.

LINENFOLD: Tudor panelling carved with simulations of folded linen. *See also* Parchemin.

LINTEL: horizontal beam or stone bridging an opening.

LOGGIA: gallery, usually arcaded or colonnaded; sometimes freestanding.

LONG-AND-SHORT WORK: quoins consisting of stones placed with the long side alternately upright and horizontal, especially in Saxon building.

LONGHOUSE: house and byre in the same range with internal access between them.

LOUVRE: roof opening, often protected by a raised timber structure, to allow the smoke from a central hearth to escape.

LOWSIDE WINDOW: set lower than the others in a chancel side wall, usually towards its W end.

LUCARNE (*lit.* dormer): small gabled opening in a roof or spire.

LUGGED ARCHITRAVE: *see* 4b.

LUNETTE: semicircular window or blind panel.

LYCHGATE (*lit.* corpse-gate): roofed gateway entrance to a churchyard for the reception of a coffin.

LYNCHET: long terraced strip of soil on the downward side of prehistoric and medieval fields, accumulated because of continual ploughing along the contours.

MACHICOLATIONS (*lit.* mashing devices): series of openings between the corbels that support a projecting parapet through which missiles can be dropped. Used decoratively in post-medieval buildings.

MANOMETER or STANDPIPE TOWER: containing a column of water to regulate pressure in water mains.

MANSARD: *see* 8a.

MATHEMATICAL TILES: facing tiles with the appearance of brick, most often applied to timber-framed walls.

MAUSOLEUM: monumental building or chamber usually intended for the burial of members of one family.

MEGALITHIC TOMB: massive stonebuilt Neolithic burial chamber covered by an earth or stone mound.

MERLON: *see* Battlement.

METOPES: spaces between the triglyphs in a Doric frieze (3b).

MEZZANINE: low storey between two higher ones.

MILD STEEL: *see* Cast iron.

MISERICORD (*lit.* mercy): shelf on a carved bracket placed on the underside of a hinged choir stall seat to support an occupant when standing.

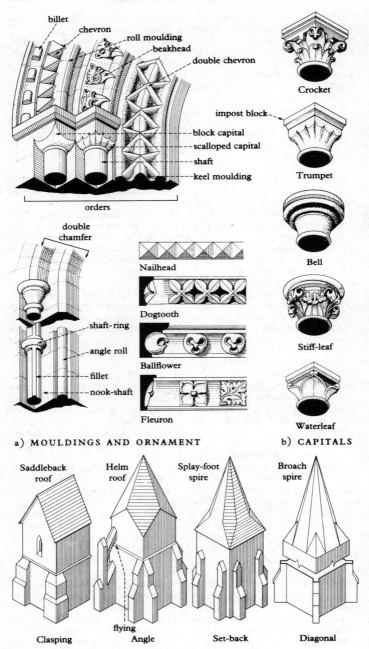

a) MOULDINGS AND ORNAMENT

b) CAPITALS

c) BUTTRESSES, ROOFS AND SPIRES

FIGURE 1: MEDIEVAL

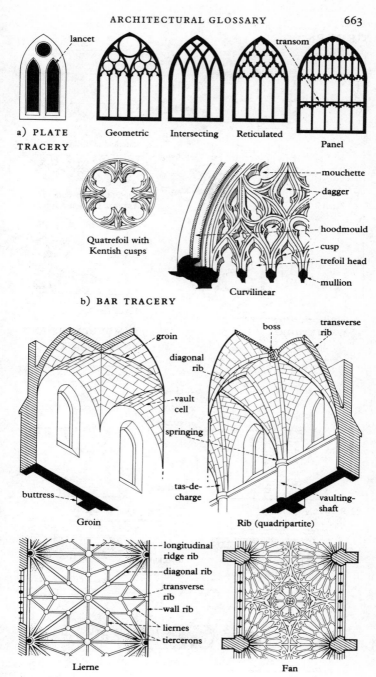

a) PLATE TRACERY

Geometric Intersecting Reticulated Panel

lancet

transom

Quatrefoil with Kentish cusps

mouchette
dagger
hoodmould
cusp
trefoil head
mullion

Curvilinear

b) BAR TRACERY

groin
diagonal rib
vault cell
springing
buttress
tas-de-charge

Groin

boss
transverse rib
vaulting-shaft

Rib (quadripartite)

longitudinal ridge rib
diagonal rib
transverse rib
wall rib
liernes
tiercerons

Lierne

Fan

c) VAULTS

FIGURE 2: MEDIEVAL

ORDERS

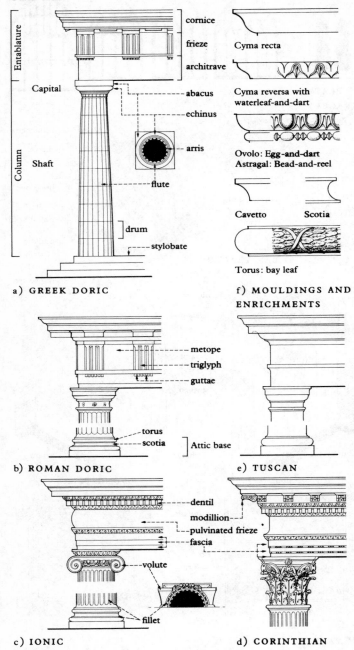

a) GREEK DORIC

b) ROMAN DORIC

c) IONIC

d) CORINTHIAN

e) TUSCAN

f) MOULDINGS AND ENRICHMENTS

FIGURE 3: CLASSICAL

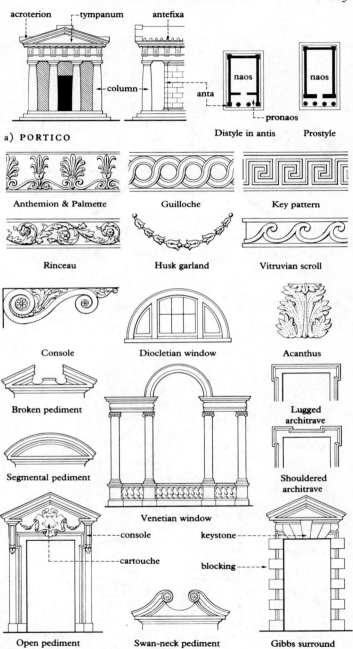

a) PORTICO

Distyle in antis　　Prostyle

Anthemion & Palmette　　Guilloche　　Key pattern

Rinceau　　Husk garland　　Vitruvian scroll

Console　　Diocletian window　　Acanthus

Broken pediment　　Lugged architrave

Segmental pediment　　Shouldered architrave

Venetian window

Open pediment　　Swan-neck pediment　　Gibbs surround

b) ORNAMENTS AND FEATURES

FIGURE 4: CLASSICAL

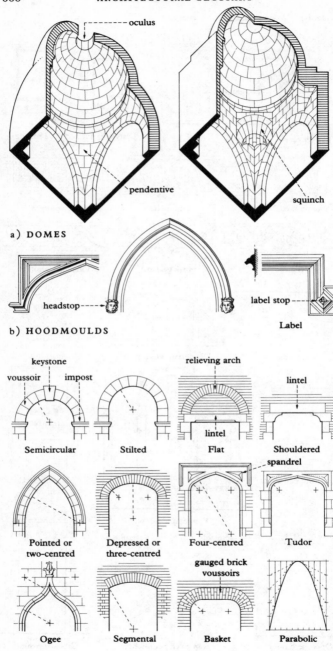

a) DOMES

b) HOODMOULDS

c) ARCHES

FIGURE 5: CONSTRUCTION

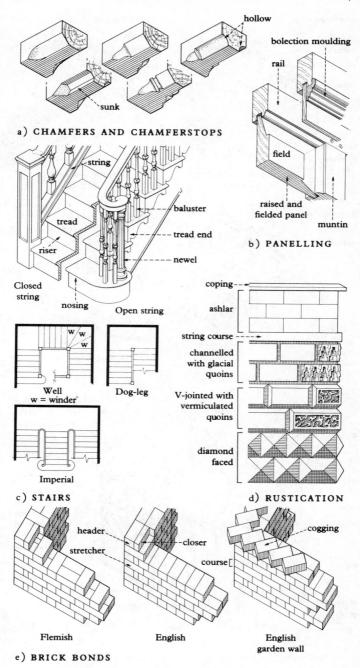

a) CHAMFERS AND CHAMFERSTOPS

b) PANELLING

c) STAIRS

d) RUSTICATION

e) BRICK BONDS

FIGURE 6: CONSTRUCTION

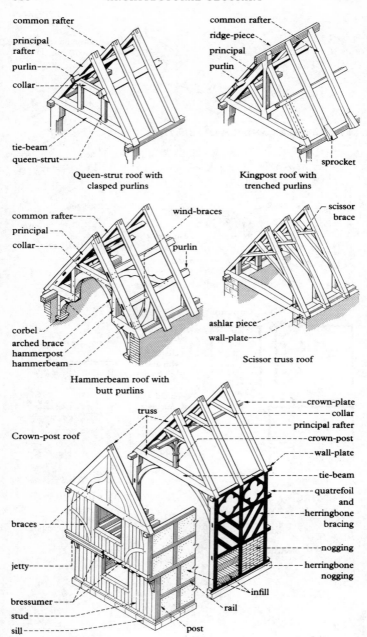

Queen-strut roof with
clasped purlins

Kingpost roof with
trenched purlins

Hammerbeam roof with
butt purlins

Scissor truss roof

Crown-post roof

Box frame: i) Close studding   ii) Square panel

FIGURE 7: ROOFS AND TIMBER-FRAMING

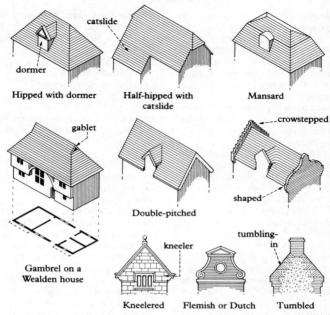

a) ROOF FORMS AND GABLES

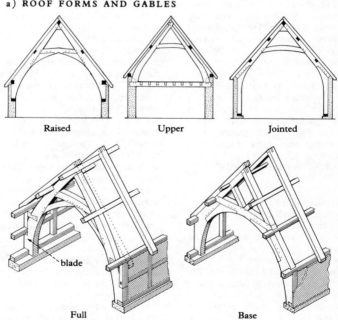

b) CRUCK FRAMES

FIGURE 8: ROOFS AND TIMBER-FRAMING

MIXER-COURTS: forecourts to groups of houses shared by vehicles and pedestrians.

MODILLIONS: small consoles (q.v.) along the underside of a Corinthian or Composite cornice (3d). Often used along an eaves cornice.

MODULE: a predetermined standard size for co-ordinating the dimensions of components of a building.

MOTTE-AND-BAILEY: post-Roman and Norman defence consisting of an earthen mound (motte) topped by a wooden tower within a bailey, an enclosure defended by a ditch and palisade, and also, sometimes, by an internal bank.

MOUCHETTE: see Tracery and 2b.

MOULDING: shaped ornamental strip of continuous section; see Cavetto, Cyma, Ovolo, Roll.

MULLION: vertical member between window lights (2b).

MULTI-STOREY: five or more storeys. Multi-storey flats may form a *cluster block*, with individual blocks of flats grouped round a service core; a *point block:* with flats fanning out from a service core; or a *slab block*, with flats approached by corridors or galleries from service cores at intervals or towers at the ends (plan also used for offices, hotels etc.). *Tower block* is a generic term for any very high multi-storey building.

MUNTIN: see Panelling and 6b.

NAILHEAD: E.E. ornament consisting of small pyramids regularly repeated (1a).

NARTHEX: enclosed vestibule or covered porch at the main entrance to a church.

NAVE: the body of a church w of the crossing or chancel often flanked by aisles (q.v.).

NEWEL: central or corner post of a staircase (6c). Newel stair *see* Stairs.

NIGHT STAIR: stair by which religious entered the transept of their church from their dormitory to celebrate night services.

NOGGING: see Timber-framing (7).

NOOK-SHAFT: shaft set in the angle of a wall or opening (1a).

NORMAN: see Romanesque.

NOSING: projection of the tread of a step (6c).

NUTMEG: medieval ornament with a chain of tiny triangles placed obliquely.

OCULUS: circular opening.

OEIL DE BOEUF: see Bullseye window.

OGEE: double curve, bending first one way and then the other, as in an *ogee* or *ogival arch* (5c). Cf. Cyma recta and Cyma reversa.

OPUS SECTILE: decorative mosaic-like facing.

OPUS SIGNINUM: composition flooring of Roman origin.

ORATORY: a private chapel in a church or a house. Also a church of the Oratorian Order.

ORDER: one of a series of recessed arches and jambs forming a splayed medieval opening, e.g. a doorway or arcade arch (1a).

ORDERS: the formalized versions of the post-and-lintel system in classical architecture. The main orders are *Doric, Ionic,* and *Corinthian.* They are Greek in origin but occur in Roman versions. *Tuscan* is a simple version of Roman Doric. Though each order has its own conventions (3), there are many minor variations. The *Composite* capital combines Ionic volutes with Corinthian foliage. *Superimposed orders*: orders on successive levels, usually in the upward sequence of Tuscan, Doric, Ionic, Corinthian, Composite.

ORIEL: see Bay window.

OVERDOOR: painting or relief above an internal door. Also called a *sopraporta.*

OVERTHROW: decorative fixed arch between two gatepiers or above a wrought-iron gate.

OVOLO: wide convex moulding (3f).

PALIMPSEST: of a brass: where a metal plate has been reused by turning over the engraving on the back; of a wall-painting: where one overlaps and partly obscures an earlier one.

PALLADIAN: following the examples and principles of Andrea Palladio (1508–80).

PALMETTE: classical ornament like a palm shoot (4b).

PANELLING: wooden lining to interior walls, made up of vertical members (*muntins*) and horizontals (*rails*) framing panels: also called *wainscot*. *Raised-and-fielded*: with the central area of the panel (*field*) raised up (6b).

PANTILE: roof tile of S section.

PARAPET: wall for protection at any sudden drop, e.g. at the wall-head of a castle where it protects the *parapet walk* or wall-walk. Also used to conceal a roof.

PARCHEMIN PANEL: with a vertical central rib or moulding branching in ogee curves to meet the four corners of the panel; sometimes used with linenfold (q.v.).

PARCLOSE: *see* Screen.

PARGETTING (*lit.* plastering): exterior plaster decoration, either in relief or incised.

PARLOUR: in a religious house, a room where the religious could talk to visitors; in a medieval house, the semi-private living room below the solar (q.v.).

PARTERRE: level space in a garden laid out with low, formal beds.

PATERA (*lit.* plate): round or oval ornament in shallow relief.

PAVILION: ornamental building for occasional use; or projecting subdivision of a larger building, often at an angle or terminating a wing.

PEBBLEDASHING: *see* Rendering.

PEDESTAL: a tall block carrying a classical order, statue, vase, etc.

PEDIMENT: a formalized gable derived from that of a classical temple; also used over doors, windows, etc. For variations *see* 4b.

PENDENTIVE: spandrel between adjacent arches, supporting a drum, dome or vault and consequently formed as part of a hemisphere (5a).

PENTHOUSE: subsidiary structure with a lean-to roof. Also a separately roofed structure on top of a C20 multi-storey block.

PERIPTERAL: *see* Peristyle.

PERISTYLE: a colonnade all round the exterior of a classical building, as in a temple which is then said to be *peripteral*.

PERP (PERPENDICULAR): English Gothic architecture *c.* 1335–50 to *c.* 1530. The name is derived from the upright tracery panels then used (*see* Tracery and 2a).

PERRON: external stair to a doorway, usually of double-curved plan.

PEW: loosely, seating for the laity outside the chancel; strictly, an enclosed seat. *Box pew*: with equal high sides and a door.

PIANO NOBILE: principal floor of a classical building above a ground floor or basement and with a lesser storey overhead.

PIAZZA: formal urban open space surrounded by buildings.

PIER: large masonry or brick support, often for an arch. *See also* Compound pier.

PILASTER: flat representation of a classical column in shallow relief. *Pilaster strip: see* Lesene.

PILE: row of rooms. *Double pile*: two rows thick.

PILLAR: free-standing upright member of any section, not conforming to one of the orders (q.v.).

PILLAR PISCINA: *see* Piscina.

PILOTIS: C20 French term for pillars or stilts that support a building above an open ground floor.

PISCINA: basin for washing Mass vessels, provided with a drain; set in or against the wall to the S of an altar or free-standing (*pillar piscina*).

PISÉ: *see* Cob.

PITCHED MASONRY: laid on the diagonal, often alternately with opposing courses (*pitched and counterpitched* or herringbone).

PLATE RAIL: *see* Railways.

PLATEWAY: *see* Railways.

PLINTH: projecting courses at the

foot of a wall or column, generally chamfered or moulded at the top.

PODIUM: a continuous raised platform supporting a building; or a large block of two or three storeys beneath a multi-storey block of smaller area.

POINT BLOCK: *see* Multi-storey.

POINTING: exposed mortar jointing of masonry or brickwork. Types include *flush*, *recessed* and *tuck* (with a narrow channel filled with finer, whiter mortar).

POPPYHEAD: carved ornament of leaves and flowers as a finial for a bench end or stall.

PORTAL FRAME: C20 frame comprising two uprights rigidly connected to a beam or pair of rafters.

PORTCULLIS: gate constructed to rise and fall in vertical gooves at the entry to a castle.

PORTICO: a porch with the roof and frequently a pediment supported by a row of columns (4a). A portico *in antis* has columns on the same plane as the front of the building. A *prostyle* porch has columns standing free. Porticoes are described by the number of front columns, e.g. tetrastyle (four), hexastyle (six). The space within the temple is the *naos*, that within the portico the *pronaos*. *Blind portico:* the front features of a portico applied to a wall.

PORTICUS (plural: porticūs): subsidiary cell opening from the main body of a pre-Conquest church.

POST: upright support in a structure (7).

POSTERN: small gateway at the back of a building or to the side of a larger entrance door or gate.

POUND LOCK: *see* Canals.

PRESBYTERY: the part of a church lying E of the choir where the main altar is placed; or a priest's residence.

PRINCIPAL: *see* Roofs and 7.

PRONAOS: *see* Portico and 4a.

PROSTYLE: *see* Portico and 4a.

PULPIT: raised and enclosed platform for the preaching of sermons. *Three-decker:* with reading desk below and clerk's desk below that.

Two-decker: as above, minus the clerk's desk.

PULPITUM: stone screen in a major church dividing choir from nave.

PULVINATED: *see* Frieze and 3c.

PURLIN: *see* Roofs and 7.

PUTHOLES or PUTLOG HOLES: in the wall to receive putlogs, the horizontal timbers which support scaffolding boards; sometimes not filled after construction is complete.

PUTTO (plural: putti): small naked boy.

QUARRIES: square (or diamond) panes of glass supported by lead strips (*cames*); square floor-slabs or tiles.

QUATREFOIL: *see* Foil and 2b.

QUEENSTRUT: *see* Roofs and 7.

QUIRK: sharp groove to one side of a convex medieval moulding.

QUOINS: dressed stones at the angles of a building (6d).

RADBURN SYSTEM: vehicle and pedestrian segregation in residential developments, based on that used at Radburn, New Jersey, U.S.A., by Wright and Stein, 1928–30.

RADIATING CHAPELS: projecting radially from an ambulatory or an apse (*see* Chevet).

RAFTER: *see* Roofs and 7.

RAGGLE: groove cut in masonry, especially to receive the edge of a roof-covering.

RAGULY: ragged (in heraldry). Also applied to funerary sculpture, e.g. *cross raguly:* with a notched outline.

RAIL: *see* Panelling and 6b; also 7.

RAILWAYS: *Edge rail:* on which flanged wheels can run. *Plate rail:* L-section rail for plain unflanged wheels. *Plateway:* early railway using plate rails.

RAISED-AND-FIELDED: *see* Panelling and 6b.

RAKE: slope or pitch.

RAMPART: defensive outer wall of stone or earth. *Rampart walk:* path along the inner face.

REBATE: rectangular section cut out of a masonry edge to receive a shutter, door, window, etc.

REBUS: a heraldic pun, e.g. a fiery cock for Cockburn.

REEDING: series of convex mouldings, the reverse of fluting (q.v.). Cf. Gadrooning.

RENDERING: the covering of outside walls with a uniform surface or skin for protection from the weather. *Lime-washing:* thin layer of lime plaster. *Pebble-dashing:* where aggregate is thrown at the wet plastered wall for a textured effect. *Roughcast:* plaster mixed with a coarse aggregate such as gravel. *Stucco:* fine lime plaster worked to a smooth surface. *Cement rendering:* a cheaper substitute for stucco, usually with a grainy texture.

REPOUSSÉ: relief designs in metalwork, formed by beating it from the back.

REREDORTER (*lit.* behind the dormitory): latrines in a medieval religious house.

REREDOS: painted and/or sculptured screen behind and above an altar. Cf. Retable.

RESPOND: half-pier or half-column bonded into a wall and carrying one end of an arch. It usually terminates an arcade.

RETABLE: painted or carved panel standing on or at the back of an altar, usually attached to it.

RETROCHOIR: in a major church, the area between the high altar and E chapel.

REVEAL: the plane of a jamb, between the wall and the frame of a door or window.

RIB-VAULT: see Vault and 2c.

RINCEAU: classical ornament of leafy scrolls (4b).

RISER: vertical face of a step (6c).

ROCK-FACED: masonry cleft to produce a rugged appearance.

ROCOCO: style current *c.* 1720 and *c.* 1760, characterized by a serpentine line and playful, scrolled decoration.

ROLL MOULDING: medieval moulding of part-circular section (1a).

ROMANESQUE: style current in the C11 and C12. In England often called Norman. *See also* Saxo-Norman.

ROOD: crucifix flanked by the Virgin and St John, usually over the entry into the chancel, on a beam (*rood beam*) or painted on the wall. The *rood screen* below often had a walkway (*rood loft*) along the top, reached by a *rood stair* in the side wall.

ROOFS: Shape. For the main external shapes (hipped, mansard etc.) see 8a. *Helm* and *Saddleback*: *see* 1c. *Lean-to:* single sloping roof built against a vertical wall; lean-to is also applied to the part of the building beneath. Construction. *See* 7. *Single-framed* roof: with no main trusses. The rafters may be fixed to the wall-plate or ridge, or longitudinal timber may be absent altogether. *Double-framed* roof: with longitudinal members, such as purlins, and usually divided into bays by principals and principal rafters. Other types are named after their main structural components, e.g. *hammerbeam, crown-post* (*see* Elements below and 7). Elements. *See* 7. *Ashlar piece:* a short vertical timber connecting inner wall-plate or timber pad to a rafter. *Braces:* subsidiary timbers set diagonally to strengthen the frame. *Arched braces:* curved pair forming an arch, connecting wall or post below with tie- or collar-beam above. *Passing braces:* long straight braces passing across other members of the truss. *Scissor braces:* pair crossing diagonally between pairs of rafters or principals. *Wind-braces:* short, usually curved braces connecting side purlins with principals; sometimes decorated with cusping. *Collar* or *collar-beam:* horizontal transverse timber connecting a pair of rafter or cruck blades (q.v.), set between apex and the wall-plate. *Crown-post:* a vertical timber set centrally on a tie-beam and supporting a collar purlin braced to it longitudinally. In an open truss lateral braces may rise to the collar-beam; in a closed truss they may descend to the tie-beam.

Hammerbeams: horizontal brackets projecting at wall-plate level like an interrupted tie-beam; the inner ends carry *hammerposts,* vertical timbers which support a purlin and are braced to a collar-beam above.

Kingpost: vertical timber set centrally on a tie- or collar-beam, rising to the apex of the roof to support a ridge-piece (cf. Strut).

Plate: longitudinal timber set square to the ground. *Wall-plate:* plate along the top of a wall which receives the ends of the rafters; cf. Purlin.

Principals: pair of inclined lateral timbers of a truss. Usually they support side purlins and mark the main bay divisions.

Purlin: horizontal longitudinal timber. *Collar purlin* or *crown plate:* central timber which carries collar-beams and is supported by crown-posts. *Side purlins:* pairs of timbers placed some way up the slope of the roof, which carry common rafters. *Butt* or *tenoned purlins* are tenoned into either side of the principals. *Through purlins* pass through or past the principal; they include *clasped purlins,* which rest on queenposts or are carried in the angle between principals and collar, and *trenched purlins* trenched into the backs of principals.

Queen-strut: paired vertical, or near-vertical, timbers placed symmetrically on a tie-beam to support side purlins.

Rafters: inclined lateral timbers supporting the roof covering. *Common rafters:* regularly spaced uniform rafters placed along the length of a roof or between principals. *Principal rafters:* rafters which also act as principals.

Ridge, ridge-piece: horizontal longitudinal timber at the apex of the roof supporting the ends of the rafters.

Sprocket: short timber placed on the back and at the foot of a rafter to form projecting eaves.

Strut: vertical or oblique timber between two members of a truss, not directly supporting longitudinal timbers.

Tie-beam: main horizontal transverse timber which carries the feet of the principals at wall level.

Truss: rigid framework of timbers at bay intervals, carrying the longitudinal roof timbers which support the common rafters. *Closed truss:* with the spaces between the timbers filled, to form an internal partition.

See also Cruck, Wagon roof.

ROPE MOULDING: *see* Cable moulding.

ROSE WINDOW: circular window with tracery radiating from the centre. Cf. Wheel window.

ROTUNDA: building or room circular in plan.

ROUGHCAST: *see* Rendering.

ROVING BRIDGE: *see* Canals.

RUBBED BRICKWORK: *see* Gauged brickwork.

RUBBLE: masonry whose stones are wholly or partly in a rough state. *Coursed:* coursed stones with rough faces. *Random:* uncoursed stones in a random pattern. *Snecked:* with courses broken by smaller stones (snecks).

RUSTICATION: *see* 6d. Exaggerated treatment of masonry to give an effect of strength. The joints are usually recessed by V-section chamfering or square-section channelling (*channelled rustication*). *Banded rustication* has only the horizontal joints emphasized. The faces may be flat, but can be *diamond-faced,* like shallow pyramids, *vermiculated,* with a stylized texture like worm-casts, and *glacial* (frost-work), like icicles or stalactites.

SACRISTY: room in a church for sacred vessels and vestments.

SADDLEBACK ROOF: *see* IC.

SALTIRE CROSS: with diagonal limbs.

SANCTUARY: area around the main altar of a church. Cf. Presbytery.

SANGHA: residence of Buddhist monks or nuns.

SARCOPHAGUS: coffin of stone or other durable material.

SAXO-NORMAN: transitional Romanesque style combining Anglo-Saxon and Norman features, current *c.* 1060–1100.

SCAGLIOLA: composition imitating marble.

SCALLOPED CAPITAL: *see* 1a.

SCOTIA: a hollow classical moulding, especially between tori (q.v.) on a column base (3b, 3f).

SCREEN: in a medieval church, usually at the entry to the chancel; *see* Rood (screen) and Pulpitum. A *parclose screen* separates a chapel from the rest of the church.

SCREENS or SCREENS PASSAGE: screened-off entrance passage between great hall and service rooms.

SECTION: two-dimensional representation of a building, moulding, etc., revealed by cutting across it.

SEDILIA (singular: sedile): seats for the priests (usually three) on the s side of the chancel.

SET-OFF: *see* Weathering.

SGRAFFITO: decoration scratched, often in plaster, to reveal a pattern in another colour beneath. *Graffiti*: scratched drawing or writing.

SHAFT: vertical member of round or polygonal section (1a, 3a). *Shaft-ring:* at the junction of shafts set *en delit* (q.v.) or attached to a pier or wall (1a).

SHEILA-NA-GIG: female fertility figure, usually with legs apart.

SHELL: thin, self-supporting roofing membrane of timber or concrete.

SHOULDERED ARCHITRAVE: *see* 4b.

SHUTTERING: *see* Concrete.

SILL: horizontal member at the bottom of a window or door frame; or at the base of a timber-framed wall into which posts and studs are tenoned (7).

SLAB BLOCK: *see* Multi-storey.

SLATE-HANGING: covering of overlapping slates on a wall. *Tile-hanging* is similar.

SLYPE: covered way or passage leading E from the cloisters between transept and chapter house.

SNECKED: *see* Rubble.

SOFFIT (*lit.* ceiling): underside of an arch (also called *intrados*), lintel, etc. *Soffit roll:* medieval roll moulding on a soffit.

SOLAR: private upper chamber in a medieval house, accessible from the high end of the great hall.

SOPRAPORTA: *see* Overdoor.

SOUNDING-BOARD: *see* Tester.

SPANDRELS: roughly triangular spaces between an arch and its containing rectangle, or between adjacent arches (5c). Also non-structural panels under the windows in a curtain-walled building.

SPERE: a fixed structure screening the lower end of the great hall from the screens passage. *Spere-truss*: roof truss incorporated in the spere.

SPIRE: tall pyramidal or conical feature crowning a tower or turret. *Broach:* starting from a square base, then carried into an octagonal section by means of triangular faces; and *splayed-foot:* variation of the broach form, found principally in the south-east, in which the four cardinal faces are splayed out near their base, to cover the corners, while oblique (or intermediate) faces taper away to a point (1c). *Needle spire:* thin spire rising from the centre of a tower roof, well inside the parapet: when of timber and lead often called a *spike.*

SPIRELET: *see* Flèche.

SPLAY: of an opening when it is wider on one face of a wall than the other.

SPRING OR SPRINGING: level at which an arch or vault rises from its supports. *Springers:* the first stones of an arch or vaulting rib above the spring (2c).

SQUINCH: arch or series of arches thrown across an interior angle of a square or rectangular structure to support a circular or polygonal superstructure, especially a dome or spire (5a).

SQUINT: an aperture in a wall or through a pier usually to allow a view of an altar.

STAIRS: *see* 6c. *Dog-leg stair:* parallel flights rising alternately in opposite directions, without an open well. *Flying stair:* cantilevered from the walls of a stairwell, without newels; sometimes called a *Geometric* stair when the inner edge describes a curve. *Newel stair:* ascending round a central supporting newel (q.v.); called a *spiral stair* or *vice* when in a circular shaft, a *winder* when in a rectangular compartment. (Winder also applies to the steps on the turn). *Well stair:* with flights round a square open well framed by newel posts. *See also* Perron.

STALL: fixed seat in the choir or chancel for the clergy or choir (cf. Pew). Usually with arm rests, and often framed together.

STANCHION: upright structural member, of iron, steel or reinforced concrete.

STANDPIPE TOWER: *see* Manometer.

STEAM ENGINES: *Atmospheric:* worked by the vacuum created when low-pressure steam is condensed in the cylinder, as developed by Thomas Newcomen. *Beam engine:* with a large pivoted beam moved in an oscillating fashion by the piston. It may drive a flywheel or be *non-rotative. Watt* and *Cornish:* single-cylinder; *compound:* two cylinders; *triple expansion:* three cylinders.

STEEPLE: tower together with a spire, lantern, or belfry.

STIFF-LEAF: type of E.E. foliage decoration. *Stiff-leaf capital see* 1b.

STOP: plain or decorated terminal to mouldings or chamfers, or at the end of hoodmoulds and labels (*label stop*), or string courses (5b, 6a); *see also* headstop.

STOUP: vessel for holy water, usually near a door.

STRAINER: *see* Arch.

STRAPWORK: late C16 and C17 decoration, like interlaced leather straps.

STRETCHER: *see* Bond and 6e.

STRING COURSE: horizontal course or moulding projecting from the surface of a wall (6d).

STRING: *see* 6c. Sloping member holding the ends of the treads and risers of a staircase. *Closed string:* a broad string covering the ends

of the treads and risers. *Open string:* cut into the shape of the treads and risers.

STUCCO: *see* Rendering.

STUDS: subsidiary vertical timbers of a timber-framed wall or partition (7).

STUPA: Buddhist shrine, circular in plan.

STYLOBATE: top of the solid platform on which a colonnade stands (3a).

SUSPENSION BRIDGE: *see* Bridge.

SWAG: like a festoon (q.v.), but representing cloth.

SYSTEM BUILDING: *see* Industrialized building.

TABERNACLE: canopied structure to contain the reserved sacrament or a relic; or architectural frame for an image or statue.

TABLE TOMB: memorial slab raised on free-standing legs.

TAS-DE-CHARGE: the lower courses of a vault or arch which are laid horizontally (2c).

TERM: pedestal or pilaster tapering downward, usually with the upper part of a human figure growing out of it.

TERRACOTTA: moulded and fired clay ornament or cladding.

TESSELLATED PAVEMENT: mosaic flooring, particularly Roman, made of *tesserae*, i.e. cubes of glass, stone, or brick.

TESTER: flat canopy over a tomb or pulpit, where it is also called a *sounding-board.*

TESTER TOMB: tomb-chest with effigies beneath a tester, either free-standing (tester with four or more columns), or attached to a wall (*half-tester*) with columns on one side only.

TETRASTYLE: *see* Portico.

THERMAL WINDOW: *see* Diocletian window.

THREE-DECKER PULPIT: *see* Pulpit.

TIDAL GATES: *see* Canals.

TIE-BEAM: *see* Roofs and 7.

TIERCERON: *see* Vault and 2c.

TILE-HANGING: *see* Slate-hanging.

TIMBER-FRAMING: *see* 7. Method of construction where the structural frame is built of interlocking timbers. The spaces are filled with non-structural material, e.g. *infill* of wattle and daub, lath and plaster, brickwork (known as *nogging*), etc. and may be covered by plaster, weatherboarding (q.v.), or tiles.

TOMB-CHEST: chest-shaped tomb, usually of stone. Cf. Table tomb, Tester tomb.

TORUS (plural: tori): large convex moulding usually used on a column base (3b, 3f).

TOUCH: soft black marble quarried near Tournai.

TOURELLE: turret corbelled out from the wall.

TOWER BLOCK: *see* Multi-storey.

TRABEATED: depends structurally on the use of the post and lintel. Cf. Arcuated.

TRACERY: openwork pattern of masonry or timber in the upper part of an opening. *Blind tracery* is tracery applied to a solid wall. *Plate tracery*, introduced c. 1200, is the earliest form, in which shapes are cut through solid masonry (2a).
Bar tracery was introduced into England c. 1250. The pattern is formed by intersecting moulded ribwork continued from the mullions. It was especially elaborate during the Decorated period (q.v.). Tracery shapes can include circles, *daggers* (elongated ogee-ended lozenges), *mouchettes* (like daggers but with curved sides) and upright rectangular *panels*. They often have *cusps*, projecting points defining lobes or *foils* (q.v.) within the main shape: *Kentish* or *split-cusps* are forked (2b).
Types of bar tracery (*see* 2b) include *geometric(al)*: c. 1250–1310, chiefly circles, often foiled; *Y-tracery*: c. 1300, with mullions branching into a Y-shape; *intersecting*: c. 1300, formed by interlocking mullions; *reticulated*: early C14, net-like pattern of ogee-ended lozenges; *curvilinear*: C14, with uninterrupted flowing curves; *panel*: Perp, with straight-sided panels, often cusped at the top and bottom.

TRANSEPT: transverse portion of a church.

TRANSITIONAL: generally used for the phase between Romanesque and Early English (c. 1175–c. 1200).

TRANSOM: horizontal member separating window lights (2b).

TREAD: horizontal part of a step. The *tread end* may be carved on a staircase (6c).

TREFOIL: *see* Foil.

TRIFORIUM: middle storey of a church treated as an arcaded wall passage or blind arcade, its height corresponding to that of the aisle roof.

TRIGLYPHS (*lit.* three-grooved tablets): stylized beam-ends in the Doric frieze, with metopes between (3b).

TRIUMPHAL ARCH: influential type of Imperial Roman monument.

TROPHY: sculptured or painted group of arms or armour.

TRUMEAU: central stone mullion supporting the tympanum of a wide doorway. *Trumeau figure:* carved figure attached to it (cf. Column figure).

TRUMPET CAPITAL: *see* 1b.

TRUSS: braced framework, spanning between supports. *See also* Roofs and 7.

TUMBLING or TUMBLING-IN: courses of brickwork laid at right-angles to a slope, e.g. of a gable, forming triangles by tapering into horizontal courses (8a).

TUSCAN: *see* Orders and 3e.

TWO-DECKER PULPIT: *see* Pulpit.

TYMPANUM: the surface between a lintel and the arch above it or within a pediment (4a).

UNDERCROFT: usually describes the vaulted room(s), beneath the main room(s) of a medieval house. Cf. Crypt.

VAULT: arched stone roof (sometimes imitated in timber or plaster). For types *see* 2c.
Tunnel or *barrel vault:* continuous semicircular or pointed arch, often of rubble masonry.

Groin-vault: tunnel vaults intersecting at right angles. *Groins* are the curved lines of the intersections.

Rib-vault: masonry framework of intersecting arches (ribs) supporting *vault cells,* used in Gothic architecture. *Wall rib* or *wall arch:* between wall and vault cell. *Transverse rib:* spans between two walls to divide a vault into bays. *Quadripartite* rib-vault: each bay has two pairs of diagonal ribs dividing the vault into four triangular cells. *Sexpartite* rib-vault: most often used over paired bays, has an extra pair of ribs springing from between the bays. More elaborate vaults may include *ridge ribs* along the crown of a vault or bisecting the bays; *tiercerons:* extra decorative ribs springing from the corners of a bay; and *liernes:* short decorative ribs in the crown of a vault, not linked to any springing point. A *stellar* or *star* vault has liernes in star formation.

Fan-vault: form of barrel vault used in the Perp period, made up of halved concave masonry cones decorated with blind tracery.

VAULTING SHAFT: shaft leading up to the spring or springing (q.v.) of a vault (2c).

VENETIAN or SERLIAN WINDOW: derived from Serlio (4b). The motif is used for other openings.

VERMICULATION: *see* Rustication and 6d.

VESICA: oval with pointed ends.

VICE: *see* Stair.

VILLA: originally a Roman country house or farm. The term was revived in England in the C18 under the influence of Palladio and used especially for smaller, compact country houses. In the later C19 it was debased to describe any suburban house.

VITRIFIED: bricks or tiles fired to a darkened glassy surface.

VITRUVIAN SCROLL: classical running ornament of curly waves (4b).

VOLUTES: spiral scrolls. They occur on Ionic capitals (3c). *Angle volute:* pair of volutes, turned outwards to meet at the corner of a capital.

VOUSSOIRS: wedge-shaped stones forming an arch (5c).

WAGON ROOF: with the appearance of the inside of a wagon tilt; often ceiled. Also called *cradle roof.*

WAINSCOT: *see* Panelling.

WALL MONUMENT: attached to the wall and often standing on the floor. *Wall tablets* are smaller with the inscription as the major element.

WALL-PLATE: *see* Roofs and 7.

WALL-WALK: *see* Parapet.

WARMING ROOM: room in a religious house where a fire burned for comfort.

WATERHOLDING BASE: early Gothic base with upper and lower mouldings separated by a deep hollow.

WATERLEAF: *see* Enrichments and 3f.

WATERLEAF CAPITAL: Late Romanesque and Transitional type of capital (1b).

WATER WHEELS: described by the way water is fed on to the wheel. *Breastshot:* mid-height, falling and passing beneath. *Overshot:* over the top. *Pitchback:* on the top but falling backwards. *Undershot:* turned by the momentum of the water passing beneath. In a *water turbine,* water is fed under pressure through a vaned wheel within a casing.

WEALDEN HOUSE: type of medieval timber-framed house with a central open hall flanked by bays of two storeys, roofed in line; the end bays are jettied to the front, but the eaves are continuous (8a).

WEATHERBOARDING wall cladding of overlapping horizontal boards.

WEATHERING or SET-OFF: inclined, projecting surface to keep water away from the wall below.

WEEPERS: figures in niches along the sides of some medieval tombs. Also called *mourners.*

WHEEL WINDOW: circular, with radiating shafts like spokes. Cf. Rose window.

WROUGHT IRON: *see* Cast iron.

LANGUAGE GLOSSARY

Adapted, with omissions and a few augmentations, with the permission of the Director General of the Ordnance Survey, from the OS publication *Place Names on Maps of Scotland and Wales*. Crown copyright reserved.

a = adjective
ad = adverb
f = feminine
n = noun masculine

nf = noun feminine
np = noun plural
pl = plural
pr = preposition

abad, *n* abbot
abaty, *n* abbey
aber, *n & nf* estuary, confluence, stream
adeiladu, *verb* to build
aderyn, *pl* adar, *n* bird
ael, *nf* brow, edge
aelwyd, *nf* hearth
aethnen, *nf* aspen, poplar
afallen, *nf* apple tree
afon, *nf* river
ailadeiladu, *verb* to rebuild
allt, *pl* elltydd, alltau, *nf* hillside, cliff, wood
Annibynnol, *a* Independent
ar, *pr* on, upon, over
ardd, *n* hill, height
argoed, *nf* wood, grove

bach, *a* small, little, lesser
bach, *pl* bachau, *nf* nook, corner
bala, *n* outlet of a lake
banc, *pl* bencydd, *n* bank, slope
bangor, *nf* monastery originally constructed of wattle rods
banhadlog, *nf* broom patch
banw, *n* young pig
bar, *n* top, summit
bechan, *a* see bychan
bedd, *pl* beddau, *n* grave
Bedyddwyr, *a* Baptist
beidr, *nf* lane, path
beili, *pl* beiliau, *n* bailey, court before a house bailiff
bellaf, *a* far
bendigaid, *a* blessed
betws, *n* oratory, chapel

beudy, *n* cow-house
blaen, *pl* blaenau, *n* end, edge; source of river or stream; highland
bod, *n & nf* abode, dwelling
bôn, *n* stock, stump
bont, *nf* see pont
braich, *n & nf* ridge, arm
brân, *pl* brain, *nf* crow
bre, *nf* hill
brith, *f* braith, *a* speckled; coarse
bro, *nf* region; vale, lowland
bron, *pl* bronnydd, *nf* hillbreast (breast)
bryn, *pl* bryniau, *n* hill
bugail, *pl* bugelydd, bugeiliaid, *n* shepherd
bwla, *n* bull
bwlch, *pl* bylchau, *n* gap, pass
bwth, bwthyn, *n* cottage, booth
bychan, *f* bechan, *pl* bychain, *a* little, tiny

caban, *n* cottage, cabin
cader, cadair, *nf* seat, stronghold
cadlas, *nf* close, court of a house
cae, *pl* caeau, *n* field, enclosure
caer, *pl* caerau, *nf* stronghold, fort
cafn, *n* ferry-boat, trough
canol, *n* middle
cantref, *n* hundred (territorial division)
capel, *n* meeting house, chapel
carn, *pl* carnau, *nf* heap of stones, tumulus
carnedd, *pl* carneddau, carneddi, *nf* heap of stones, tumulus

carreg, *pl* cerrig, *nf* stone, rock

carrog, *nf* brook

carw, *n* stag

cas (in Casnewydd etc.), *n* castle

castell, *pl* cestyll, *n* castle; small stronghold; fortified residence; imposing natural position

cath, *nf* cat. (In some names it may be the Irish word cath meaning 'battle'.)

cau, *a* hollow; enclosed

cawr, *pl* ceiri, cewri, *n* giant

cefn, *pl* cefnydd, *n* ridge

cegin, *nf* kitchen

ceiliog, *n* cock

ceiri, *np see* cawr

celli, *nf* grove

celynen, *pl* celyn, *nf* holly tree

celynog, clynnog, *nf* holly grove

cemais, *n from np* shallow bend in river, or coastline

cennin, *np* leeks

cerrig, *np see* carreg

cesail, *nf* hollow (arm-pit)

ceunant, *n* ravine, gorge

cewri, *np see* cawr

chwilog, *nf* land infested with beetles

cil, *pl* ciliau, *n* retreat, recess, corner

cilfach, *nf* nook

clas, *n* quasi-monastic system of the Celtic Church, existing in Wales, Cornwall and Ireland from the Dark Ages to *c.* 1200. *Clasau* comprised a body of secular canons

clawdd, *pl* cloddiau, *n* ditch, hedge

cloch, *nf* bell

clochydd, *n* sexton, parish clerk

cloddiau, *np see* clawdd

clog, *nf* crag, precipice

clogwyn, *n* precipice, steep rock hanging on one side

clwyd, *pl* clwydydd, *nf* hurdle, gate

clynnog, *nf see* celynog

coch, *a* red

coeden, *pl* coed, *nf* tree

collen, *pl* cyll, coll, *nf* hazel

colwyn, *n* whelp

comin, *pl* comins, *n* common

congl, *nf* corner

cornel, *nf* corner

cors, *pl* corsydd, *nf* bog

craf, *n* garlic

craig, *pl* creigiau, *nf* rock

crib, *n* crest, ridge, summit

crochan, *n* cauldron

croes, *nf* cross

croesffordd, croesheol, croeslon, *nf* cross-roads

crofft, *pl* crofftau, *nf* croft

croglofft, *nf* garret, low cottage with loft under the roof

crug, *pl* crugiau, *n* heap, tump

cwm, *pl* cymau, cymoedd, *n* valley, dale

cwmwd, *n* commote (territorial division)

cwrt, *n* court, yard

cyffin, *n* boundary, frontier

cyll, *np see* collen

cymer, *pl* cymerau, *n* confluence

Cynulleidfaol, *a* Congregational

cywarch, *n* hemp

dan, *pr* under, below

derwen, *pl* derw, *nf* oak

diffwys, *n* precipice, abyss

dinas, *n & nf* hill-fortress (city)

diserth, *n* hermitage

disgwylfa, *nf* place of observation, look-out point

dôl, *pl* dolau, dolydd, *nf* meadow

draw, *ad* yonder

du, *a* black, dark

dwfr, dŵr, *n* water

dyffryn, *n* valley

eglwys, *nf* church

(ei)singrug, *n* heap of bran or corn husks

eisteddfa, *nf* seat, resting place

eithinog, *nf* furze patch

elltyd, *np see* allt

ellyll, *n* elf, goblin

eos, *nf* nightingale

erw, *pl* erwau, *nf* acre

esgair, *nf* long ridge (leg)

esgob, *n* bishop

ewig, *nf* hind

-fa, *nf see* ma-

fach, *a see* bach

faenor, *nf* Vaynor. cf. maenor

fawr, *a see* mawr

felin, *nf see* melin

ffald, *pl* ffaldau, *nf* sheep-fold, pound, pen, run

ffawydden, *pl* ffawydd, *nf* beech tree

fferm, *nf* farm

ffin, *nf* boundary

ffordd, *nf*   way, road
fforest, *nf*   forest, park
ffridd, ffrith, *pl* ffriddoedd,
    nf   wood; mountain enclosure,
    sheep walk
ffrwd, *nf*   stream, torrent
ffynnon, *pl* ffynhonnau, *nf*   spring,
    well
fron, *nf*   *see* bron
fry, *ad*   above

gaer, *nf*   *see* caer
ganol, *n*   *see* canol
gardd, *pl* gerddi, garddau,
    nf   garden; enclosure or fold into
    which calves were turned for first
    time
garreg, *nf*   *see* carreg
garth, *n*   promontory, hill
    enclosure
garw, *a*   coarse, rough
gefail, *nf*   smithy
(g)eirw, *np*   rush of waters
gelli, *nf*   *see* celli
glan, *nf*   river bank, hillock
glas, *a*   green
glas, glais (as in dulas, dulais), *n &*
    nf   brook
glo, *n*   charcoal, coal
glyn, *n*   deep valley, glen
gof, *n*   smith
gogof, *pl* gogofau, *nf*   cave
gorffwysfa, *nf*   resting place
gris, *pl* grisiau, *n*   step
grug, *n*   heath, heather
gwaelod, *n*   foot of hill (bottom)
gwastad, *n*   plain
gwaun, *pl* gweunydd, *nf*   moor,
    mountain meadow, moorland
    field
gwely, *n*   bed, resting place, family
    land
gwen, *a*   *see* gwyn
gwerdd, *a*   *see* gwyrdd
gwernen, *pl* gwern, *nf*   alder tree
gwersyll, *n*   encampment
gwrych, *n*   hedge, quickset hedge
gwryd, *n*   fathom
gwyddel, *pl* gwyddyl, gwyddelod,
    n   Irishman
gwyddrug, *nf*   mound, wooded
    knoll
gwyn, *f* gwen, *a*   white
gwynt, *n*   wind
gwyrdd, *f* gwerdd, *a*   green

hafn, *nf*   gorge, ravine

hafod, *nf*   shieling, upland summer
    dwelling
hafoty, *n*   summer dwelling
helygen, *pl* helyg, *nf*   willow
hen, *a*   old
hendref, *nf*   winter dwelling, old
    home, permanent abode
heol, hewl, *nf*   street, road
hir, *a*   long

is, *pr*   below, under
isaf, *a*   lower (lowest)
isel, *a*   low
iwrch, *pl* iyrchod, *n*   roebuck

lawnd, lawnt, *nf*   open space in
    woodland, glade
llaethdy, *n*   milkhouse, dairy
llan, *nf*   church, monastery;
    enclosure
Llanbedr   St Peter's church
Llanddewi   St David's church
Llanfair   St Mary's church
Llanfihangel   St Michael's church
llannerch, *nf*   clearing, glade
lle, *n*   place, position
llech, *pl* llechau, *nf*   slab, stone,
    rock
llechwedd, *nf*   hillside
llethr, *nf*   slope
llety, *n*   small abode, quarters
llidiard, llidiart, *pl* llidiardau,
    llidiartau, *n*   gate
llom, *a*   *see* llwm
lluest, *n*   shieling, cottage, hut
llumon, *n*   stack (chimney)
llwch, *n*   dust
llwch, *pl* llychau, *n*   lake
llwm, *f* llom, *a*   bare, exposed
llwyd, *a*   grey, brown
llwyn, *pl* llwyni, llwynau, *n*   grove,
    bush
llyn, *n & nf*   lake
llys, *n & nf*   court, hall
lôn, *nf*   lane, road

ma-, -fa, *nf*   plain, place
maen, *pl* meini, main, *n*   stone
maenol, maenor, *nf*   stone-built
    residence of chieftain of district,
    rich low-lying land surrounding
    same, vale
maerdref, *nf*   hamlet attached to
    chieftain's court, lord's demesne
    (maer, steward + tref, hamlet)
maerdy, *n*   steward's house, dairy

maes, *pl* meysydd, *n*   open field, plain

march, *pl* meirch, *n*   horse, stallion

marchog, *n*   knight, horseman

marian, *n*   holm, gravel, gravelly ground, rock debris

mawnog, *nf*   peat-bog

mawr, *a*   great, big

meillionen, *pl* meillion, *nf*   clover

meini, *np*   *see* maen

meirch, *np*   *see* march

melin, *nf*   mill

melyn, *f* melen, *a*   yellow

menych, *np*   *see* mynach

merthyr, *n*   burial place, church

Methodistaidd, *a*   Methodist

meysydd, *np*   *see* maes

mochyn, *pl* moch, *n*   pig

moel, *nf*   bare hill

moel, *a*   bare, bald

môr, *n*   sea

morfa, *n*   marsh, fen

mur, *pl* muriau, *n*   wall

mwyalch, mwyalchen, *nf*   blackbird

mynach, *pl* mynych, menych, myneich, *n*   monk

mynachdy, *n*   monastic grange

mynwent, *nf*   churchyard

mynydd, *n*   mountain, moorland

nant, *pl* nentydd, naint, nannau, *nf*   brook

nant, *pl* nentydd, naint, nannau, *n*   dingle, glen, ravine

neuadd, *nf*   hall

newydd, *a*   new

noddfa, *nf*   hospice

nyth, *n & nf*   nest, inaccessible position

oen, *pl* ŵyn, *n*   lamb

offeiriad, *n*   priest

onnen, *pl* onn, ynn, *nf*   ash tree

pandy, *n*   fulling mill

pant, *n*   hollow, valley

parc, *pl* parciau, parcau, *n*   park, field, enclosure

pen, *pl* pennau, *n*   head, top; end, edge

penrhyn, *n*   promontory

pensaer, *n*   architect

pentref, *n*   homestead, appendix to the real 'tref', village

person, *n*   parson

pistyll, *n*   spout, waterfall

plas, *n*   gentleman's seat, hall, mansion

plwyf, *n*   parish

poeth, *a*   burnt (hot)

pont, *nf*   bridge

porth, *n*   gate, gateway

porth, *nf*   ferry, harbour

pwll, *pl* pyllau, *n*   pit, pool

rhaeadr, *nf*   waterfall

rhandir, *n*   allotment, fixed measure of land

rhiw, *nf & n*   hill, slope

rhos, *pl* rhosydd, *nf*   moor, promontory

rhyd, *nf & n*   ford

saeth, *pl* saethau, *nf*   arrow

sant, san, *pl* saint, *n*   saint, monk

sarn, *pl* sarnau, *nf*   causeway

simnai, simdde, *nf*   chimney

siop, *nf*   shop

sticil, sticill, *nf*   stile

swydd, *nf*   seat, lordship, office

sych, *a*   dry

tafarn, *pl* tafarnau, *n & nf*   tavern

tai, *np*   *see* tŷ

tâl, *n*   end (forehead)

talwrn, *pl* talyrni, tylyrni, *n*   bare exposed hillside, open space, threshing floor, cockpit

tan, dan, *nf*   under, beneath

teg, *a*   fair

tir, *n*   land, territory

tom, tomen, *nf*   mound

ton, *pl* tonnau, *nf*   wave

ton, tonnen, *pl* tonnau, *n & nf*   grassland, lea

torglwyd, *nf*   door-hurdle, gate

towyn, *n*   *see* tywyn

traean, traen, *n*   third part

traeth, *n*   strand, shore

trallwng, trallwm, *n*   wet bottom land

traws, *a & n*   cross, transverse

tref, *nf*   homestead, hamlet, town

tros, *pr*   over

trwyn, *n*   point, cape (nose)

tŵr, *n*   tower

twyn, *pl* twyni, *n*   hillock, knoll

tŷ, *pl* tai, *n*   house

tyddyn, ty'n, *n*   small farm, holding

tylyrni, *np*   *see* talwrn

tywyn, towyn, *n*   sea-shore, strand

uchaf, *a*   higher, highest

uchel, *a*   high

uwch, *pr* above, over

ŵyn, *np* *see* oen

y, yr, 'r (definite article) the
yn, *pr* in
ynn, *np* *see* onnen
ynys, *pl* ynysoedd, *nf* island; holm, river-meadow

ysbyty, *n* hospital, hospice
ysgol, *pl* ysgolion, *nf* school
ysgubor, *pl* ysguboriau, *nf* barn
ystafell, *nf* chamber, hiding place
ystrad, *n* valley, holm, river-meadow
ystum, *nf & n* bend shape

INDEX OF PLATES

INDEX OF ARTISTS

INDEX OF PLACES

Principal references are in **bold** type; demolished buildings are shown in *italic*. For central Cardiff and its inner suburbs, see the Index of Streets and Buildings in Cardiff (below); Llanedeyrn, Radyr, St Fagans, St Mellons and Tongwynlais are included in this index.

INDEX OF STREETS AND BUILDINGS
IN CARDIFF

This index covers central Cardiff and its inner suburbs, but does not include Llanedeyrn, Radyr, St Fagans, St Mellons or Tongwynlais, which have their own entries in the gazetteer and are included in the Index of Places above. Principal references are in **bold** type; demolished buildings are shown in *italic*. Portrait statues are listed under 'statues'.